Baseball Prospectus
2001

Jeff Bower
Clay Davenport
Jeff Hildebrand
Gary Huckabay
Rany Jazayerli
Chris Kahrl
Keith Law
Mat Olkin
Dave Pease
Joseph S. Sheehan
Michael Wolverton
Keith Woolner
Derek Zumsteg

Brassey's Sports

Brassey's

WASHINGTON, D.C.

Copyright © 2001 by Brassey's, Inc.

Published in the United States by Brassey's. All rights reserved. No part of this book may be reproduced in any manner whatsoever without written permission from the publisher, except in the case of brief quotations embodied in critical articles and reviews.

ISBN 1-57488-323-2

Printed in the United States of America on acid-free paper that meets the American National Standards Institute Z39-48 Standard.

Brassey's, Inc.
22841 Quicksilver Drive
Dulles, Virginia 20166

Designed by Pen & Palette Unlimited

First Edition

10 9 8 7 6 5 4 3 2 1

Contents

Welcome v
Chris Kahrl

Baseball Prospectus Online vii
Joseph S. Sheehan

Tools

Davenport Translations 1
Clay Davenport

Support-Neutral Statistics 6
Michael Wolverton

Reliever Evaluation Tools 10
Michael Wolverton

National League

Arizona Diamondbacks 15
Atlanta Braves 31
Chicago Cubs 46
Cincinnati Reds 63
Colorado Rockies 77
Florida Marlins 93
Houston Astros 109
Los Angeles Dodgers 125
Milwaukee Brewers 139
Montreal Expos 157
New York Mets 173
Philadelphia Phillies 187
Pittsburgh Pirates 201
St. Louis Cardinals 218
San Diego Padres 231
San Francisco Giants 246

American League

Anaheim Angels 261
Baltimore Orioles 276
Boston Red Sox 294

Chicago White Sox	311
Cleveland Indians	328
Detroit Tigers	345
Kansas City Royals	360
Minnesota Twins	377
New York Yankees	394
Oakland Athletics	409
Seattle Mariners	427
Tampa Bay Devil Rays	443
Texas Rangers	459
Toronto Blue Jays	475

Fungoes

Re-Thinking Pitcher Abuse *Rany Jazayerli*	491
Analyzing PAP *Keith Woolner with Rany Jazayerli*	505
Park Factors *Clay Davenport*	517
Top 40 Prospects *Rany Jazayerli*	519
Equivalent Average Leader Boards *Clay Davenport*	529
Prospectus Fielding Runs Leader Boards *Clay Davenport*	536
Parks and Park Factors	542
Biographies	544
Dedications	545
Index	546

Welcome

by Chris Kahrl

It is my great pleasure to invite you in to read the *Baseball Prospectus 2001*. If you are one of the old-timers who has every edition of the Prospectus stretching back to BP 1996, it would appear we haven't managed to run you off with our blend of hardcore analysis, insights, and jokes Henny Youngman wouldn't tell. If you're new to the *Prospectus*, either because a friend showed you a previous edition or you read some of the things we've had to say on our site or on ESPN.com, you're just as welcome. What's important to remember is that there isn't an inequality between you or us as readers versus the "experts": we're fans, like you. While we spend more time than the surgeon general recommends researching, reading, or writing about the game, we're basically a bunch of guys with day jobs who just happen to love baseball, and love learning and talking about it almost as much. Rather than golf or watch football or go mountain-climbing or follow the futures market, we've found a much more creative way to ignore friends and family.

Because there are more of you who don't know our roots, the *Baseball Prospectus* started off as a quest for wish fulfillment by five guys and somehow continues to be a lot of fun to this day. Gary Huckabay, Clay Davenport, Joseph S. Sheehan, Rany Jazayerli, and myself shared and dared to pursue the crazy idea that maybe we ought to stop waiting for somebody else to write the book that we wanted to read.

In a sense, we were brats of the '80s, because we were spoiled rotten by Bill James' *Baseball Abstracts,* right up until he stopped writing them. Drawing on the lessons offered by James and Craig Wright on the analysis side, and the published thoughts of managers such as Earl Weaver from within the game, we were predisposed to study and question the basis of commonly held assumptions about the game. Our early ideas were forged in Usenet discussion groups—generally tough crowds where baloney doesn't go very far unless it's served with plenty of mustard.

We basically only knew each other from the content of our arguments, our research, and our jokes. When we started bandying about the idea of doing a book, I had never met any of the men involved. Because of a set of shared beliefs and a sense of fun, we didn't need to. We were united by a faith in the value of shedding light through research and convinced we had something of value to say on the subject of baseball.

We also weren't the only thoughtful thinkers from these public forums. Great researchers and analysts such as Sherri Nichols, Dale Stephenson, Harold Brooks, David Grabiner, and a host of others taught us and perhaps learned from us in the give-and-take of ideas freely discussed or evaluated, championed, or discarded. The ideas of BP are in many ways the product of ideas developed on virtual barstools everywhere, by hundreds of people.

However, most of them had lives and a well-adjusted set of priorities, or maybe they had to go golfing. You know how the story goes from here on out. From the little acorn in fertile soil, you get a big tree, the squirrels and birds move in, and now we're at the forefront of the burgeoning business of baseball outsiders, the people outside of the game commenting on what's going on in the inside. We've been at the forefront of the development of online news sources, and thanks to the unstinting efforts of Joe Sheehan and Dave Pease, we now crank out analysis and content on a daily basis. What began as a hobby has virtually become a second job.

As I've sort of hinted, none of this would be possible without the contributions of what seems to be growing into hundreds of people. I know we're going to forget some of you, but that oversight is more a matter of our annual scramble to crank out the book. First off, I'd like to thank Don Rodgers and his wife, Jan, for their work as our layout team, Pen & Palette. There isn't a tandem in the world as fast on their toes, and this project would be virtually impossible without them. At Brassey's, I'm extremely grateful to the efforts past and present of Will Allison, Jeanne Hickman, Julie Kuzneski, and Don McKeon.

I owe a debt that we can't repay to the first people to go to bat for the *Prospectus* in television and radio in Chicago: Rob Goldman and the rest of the gang at CLTV, and Mike Murphy of WSCR. Experience has taught us that we're extremely fortunate to be writing at a time when other analysts who share some of our ideals have done great work for all of us to enjoy, and for that reason alone we should grateful for Rob Neyer, David Schoenfield, and John Sickels of ESPN.com, and Mat Olkin and Paul White of *Baseball Weekly.* We're also especially grateful to Peter Gammons of ESPN's *Baseball Tonight* for his willingness to sing our praises when we least expected it.

As much as we're outside the industry, we shouldn't pretend that we aren't heavily dependent on so many good people within it. I'm grateful to all of the personnel of the teams that were willing to discuss their players and their teams frankly, but especially Billy Beane and Grady Fuson of the Athletics and Jim Hendry of the Cubs. I'm always going to be glad for the largesse of the Chicago White Sox, especially Scott Reifert and his public relations staff. Monique Giroux of les Expos has always been helpful, as well as Sharon Pannozzo of the Chicago Cubs. Warren Miller and especially Desta Kimmel of the Houston Astros were last-minute heroes when we were struggling with our decision of whom to honor on this year's cover. I'm also grateful to Rob Antony and announcer John Gordon of the Twins for past good deeds.

I'm a lucky dog indeed that Keith Woolner, Clay Davenport, and Tom Fontaine patiently took the time to answer my nagging requests for more information, Larry Moffi for a couple of great beer sessions to talk about the game, and to so many readers for taking the time to make me think or laugh or both.

Jeff Bower would like to thank the player development folks, media relations departments, and announcers for the teams that he covered, for their patience, as well as their insights into the players on the respective ballclubs, but will single out Amy Randall, Rick Williams, Greg Hunter, Bryan Price, Jim Slaton, and Tim Hevly in particular for their efforts.

Jeff Hildebrand would like to thank Mike Drago of the *Reading Eagle/Times* and Sue Leopold.

Gary Huckabay would like to say thanks to Reid Nichols, Jamey Newberg, Scott Chiamparino, Scott Boras, Tyler Pope, Mark Murphy, Lou Walts, Brian Sabean, Rick Ankiel, Brian Jones, Chad Hutchinson, Steven Rubio, Lee Ott, Greg Spira, Steven Carter, Jeff Pease, Joel Zuhars, Leo Chang, Sherrett Walker, Julie Wonus, Ray Krouse, David Herschman, Virginia Gray, Erik Brent, Bryce Lynn, Billy Beane, Peter Gammons, Bil Burke, Sherri Nichols, John Sickels, Mark Wolfson, Ray Fosse, Jeff Barton, Dave Henderson, David Koppett, and everyone else who made this effort possible.

Rany Jazayerli is grateful to Rob Neyer for keeping his optimism about the Royals in check, Greg Hall for his support and encouragement, and Brent Strom for his willingness to listen to criticism.

Keith Law says thanks to all the folks in baseball who took the time to help him research the players he covered, especially including Rob Egan, Doug Scopel, Matt Provence, Canio Costanzo, Josh Whetzel, and especially Chuck Valenches of the Pirates organization, as well as the members of the media who have helped beat the drum for us over the last six years.

Mat Olkin is grateful to Jim Callis, Jeff Wilpon, Rob Neyer, Jayson Stark, Paul Siebel, Bob Schaefer, Dan Duquette, Ron Shandler, John Hunt, Pat Quinn, Don Zminda, Steve Byrd, Bill James, and Craig Wright.

Dave Pease would like to thank Theo Epstein of the San Diego Padres.

Michael Wolverton would like to thank the amazing folks at Retrosheet (www.retrosheet.org), who provided the play-by-play data necessary to calculate the pre-1991 SNWL numbers referenced in the SNWL team comments.

Keith Woolner would like to say thanks to Gary Gillette.

Lastly, Derek Zumsteg wants to thank the BP crew, the couple of genuinely helpful people in the Angels organization, Jeff Bower and Jason Barker for being good sports, the regulars hanging out at alt.sports.baseball.sea-mariners, and the King County sheriff's deputy at the Kingdome who famously let him off once for no good reason.

That's a lot of people we're grateful to, and as I said before, we've undoubtedly forgotten literally hundreds of people who have helped to bring you this book and the ideas in it. The *Baseball Prospectus* isn't a product of one man or one organization. It is a labor of love crafted by fans as much as it is written by us for you. Enjoy it, engage or embrace or reject the ideas, and feel free to write in to us on-line. If there's one thing this project will demonstrate over and over again, it's that there's always something new to learn about baseball.

Chris Kahrl
Bethesda, Maryland

Baseball Prospectus Online

by Joseph S. Sheehan

The book you're reading is the product of three very hectic months of work, or at least it's supposed to be. In reality, it always takes a little bit longer than planned to get a *Baseball Prospectus* annual out the door, as we fine-tune projections, change player comments, and rewrite essays to make sure the information in these pages is the freshest of any book or magazine on the market.

So if the book takes about a quarter of the year to produce, what does the BP staff do the rest of the time? Well, after reintroducing ourselves to wives and girlfriends and children and pets, we turn our attention to our website, Baseball Prospectus Online, at www.baseballprospectus.com.

Every day, BP's staff of writers and analysts publish some of the best baseball content on the Web. Our site, live since 1996 and in its current form for about two years, is the place to go on the Internet for the kind of thoughtful, intelligent baseball analysis that readers of our six books have come to expect. We'll be continuing that tradition in 2001 with the features and columns that baseball fans worldwide visit us to read:

The Daily Prospectus, a Monday-through-Friday take on any and all things baseball. Part op-ed page, part feedback forum, part analysis, the Daily Prospectus is the first place to point your browser each and every day.

Chris Kahrl's Transaction Analysis, his bi-weekly look at what every team did, why they did it, and what the impact will be. Kahrl's column is the site's most popular feature and our longest-running section.

Rany Jazayerli's Doctoring the Numbers. Jazayerli, the inventor of Pitcher Abuse Points, crunches player performance to provide an interesting analysis of a different topic each week. New to the site in 2000, it immediately became one of BP.com's most popular columns.

Keith Law's The Imbalance Sheet. Not the place to turn if you're looking for the same old coverage, Law's column analyzes the business of baseball and tells you the real story behind the headlines.

The Week in Quotes. Derek Zumsteg scours the globe for the pithy, the witty, and the downright inexplicable things baseball people say.

Clay Davenport's Equivalent Average reports and Michael Wolverton's Support-Neutral statistics and Reliever Evaluation Tools updated five times a week.

That's not all. The BP staff kicks around baseball topics over the Prospectus Roundtable. Each month, we publish interviews with people in and around the game, people like Ryan Anderson, Billy McMillon, Mark Wolfson and others who have more to contribute than cliches and platitudes. Staff writers like Keith Woolner, Jeff Bower, Dave Pease, and Derek Zumsteg provide thoughtful analysis and no-holds-barred commentary throughout the season. The BP Mailbag allows you to see what our readers have to say about the content, and lets us answer some of your questions.

Not enough? Check out Clay Davenport's Equivalent Average Player Cards on every hitter in major-league history, with their full statistical lines as well as Equivalent Average and Equivalent Runs. Davenport Translations for all the players who don't appear in this book—believe us, there are a few—are also available at the site beginning in March.

In the fall, BP.com is the proud home of the Internet Baseball Awards. Tired of the award voting being restricted to beat writers? Come make your voice heard, then watch as the winners are announced after the World Series.

Whether you've devoured the entirety of BP2K1, or you're just a bit tired from carrying the biggest book on the market, take a few minutes to check out Baseball Prospectus Online. You'll agree: it's the place to browse for baseball fans on the Web.

The Davenport Translations

by Clay Davenport

Welcome to Baseball Prospectus 2001. In this book, we try to give you a comprehensive look at every significant player in baseball today, whether he's a 20-year veteran like Cal Ripken or a touted prospect who hasn't spent a day in Double-A like Josh Hamilton. We let you in on how good he is and maybe even how good he can be. We tell you whether the guy who hit .318 for your team last September is a keeper or just a kid who had the best month of his life; we tell you whether your team is ready to win now, is laying the groundwork for a run at the pennant in 2003, or is just blundering around in the dark.

To do all this, we've had to make choices, some of which you will find confusing, at least initially. Be patient: it's worth it.

The first choice we made is to put no "real" statistics in this book. If you want to know exactly how many home runs Dernell Stenson hit for Pawtucket last year, then you need to look for *The Sporting News Baseball Guide*, the *Baseball America Almanac*, or the various STATS, Inc. handbooks. The question our numbers address is not "What did he do?" but rather "How good was he?" You can't answer that by looking at the basic numbers, because a 29-year-old hitting .325 with 20 doubles at Albuquerque isn't nearly the same thing as a .325, 20-double, 19-year-old at Akron. Context—the league, the park, the age of the player—matters.

Instead of serving up "real" stats, we've applied statistical tests to every player in order to strip out as much of the context as we could and measure the real value of the performance. It's similar to what is done in disaster studies, where damage from different countries and different times is statistically converted to "1999 United States dollars" in order to make them directly comparable. In *Baseball Prospectus 2001*, all player statistics have been converted into a new statistical line, one with the same intrinsic value as the player's original statistics, one which preserves as much as possible the relative importance of various offensive components, but which can be compared against a single, global standard.

We call these new statistical lines Translations, or sometimes Davenport Translations (DTs). In some ways, these DTs are similar to the Major League Equivalencies (MLEs) developed by Bill James and published in the STATS Minor League Handbook, but there are significant differences:

1. The MLEs are conversions of minor-league statistics to the context of the environment of the parent club, meaning you still have 30 different standards to adjust for. The DTs convert everybody, including major leaguers, to the same unified scale.
2. MLEs are produced for Double-A and Triple-A players. The DTs exist for everybody, from the major leagues to the rookie leagues, and even Mexican, Japanese, and independent leagues.
3. The books with MLEs will show you only last season's MLEs. The DTs will always show you the last three seasons, so you can tell whether last year's performance was an improvement, a decline, or more of the same.

Building Them

The first rule of DTs is that performance is all that counts. Potential, athleticism, size, good looks, brains, bank account... the DTs neither know nor care, unless and until the player uses those attributes on the baseball field.

For hitters, the first thing we do is assess the player's intrinsic value within his own league in both hitting and fielding. Hitting is measured with a statistic called Equivalent Average (EqA) and fielding is measured with what we'll call Prospectus Fielding Runs (PFR).

Equivalent Average combines the player's abilities to hit for average, hit for power, draw walks, and steal bases into one number. In that respect, it is similar to several measures you'll find in other publications this spring, such as Linear Weights, Runs Created, Extrapolated Runs, Total Average, and OPS.

How is EqA different from the others? One way is that the Equivalent Average system has two distinct parts. Equivalent Runs (EqR) measures the total number of runs that result from this player's performance. EqA is its complementary rate statistic, in the same way that hits and batting average are complementary total and rate statistics. However, EqA is measured per out, not per at-bat.

Secondly, we find that the ratings you get from EqA and EqR are easier to understand than the ratings you get from any of the other measures, in terms of visceral feel and historical perspective. Why? Because they are expressed in terms that any fan already understands. EqR is expressed in runs and reads the way run or RBI totals do. The number "100," as the mark of a very good season (in terms of runs scored), is especially well known, but "191," the single-season RBI record, is also very well known. Your appreciation of those numbers applies to EqR.

Look at the league-leading figures: in 2000, the RBI titles went to Todd Helton (147) and Edgar Martinez (145), while the runs-scored titles belonged to Jeff Bagwell (152) and Johnny Damon (136). The EqR titles belonged to Carlos Delgado and Barry Bonds, with 149 and 133. All-time? You know about Hack Wilson and his 191 RBI in 1930, and you know about Babe Ruth's 177 runs scored in 1921 to set the 20th-century mark in that category. The EqR record for a season belongs to Ruth, with 183 in 1923.

For careers, the spread grows a little bit: Hank Aaron had 2,297 RBI and Ty Cobb had 2,246 runs scored, but Aaron had the most EqR with 2,605.

EqA tracks the scale of batting average very closely. You know in your gut how good a .300 batting average is supposed to be, and that is how good a .300 EqA actually is. Again, peaks are similar. 2000's batting-average leaders were Todd Helton and Nomar Garciaparra, at .372 apiece; the EqA leaders were Jason Giambi's .372 and Barry Bonds's .363. Among single-season records, Nap Lajoie's 20th-century BA record of .426 in 1901 compares to Ruth's 1920 record EqA of .419. As with EqR, the career EqA record outdistances the career BA record, as Ruth's .375 EqA eclipses Cobb's .366 BA.

(For a complete explanation of the calculation of Equivalent Runs and Equivalent Average, please see sidebar.)

What these tools do is place a player's absolute run contribution into an explicit team context, then make certain that the effect on the team's winning percentage is the same before and after the adjustments; this makes an implicit adjustment for the league's offensive level.

The park factor we've used is based on runs only and accounts for a five-year period whenever possible. This is a change from earlier editions, and is explained in the article "Park Factors" on page 517. For batter lines, we've used AB-H+CS as a measure for outs. A perfectly average player will emerge with an EqA of .260.

Fielding

The Prospectus Fielding Runs have been completely reworked since last season and we are even happier about the results than before. PFR depends primarily on a player's range: how many plays he makes, rather than how many he screws up. Factors that influence how many real chances he gets—how many balls the team's opponents put into play, how much of a groundball/flyball ratio the pitching staff has, whether they allow more balls to be hit to the left or right side than normal, how many opponents they allow to reach first base—are analyzed to predict the number of plays—putouts, assists, errors, double plays—that an average player at the position would make. The final rating is then figured by looking at how many plays above or below average the player is in each category.

Here's how the adjusted EqA is calculated, in gory detail:

First, calculate the basic equivalent average (beqa) for the player (eqa1) and league (eqa2), using the formula:

$$beqa = [h+tb+1.5*(bb+hbp)+sb]/(ab+bb+hbp+cs+sb/3)$$

Then the basic equivalent runs:

$$beqr = (2*eqa1/eqa2 - 1)*(ab+bb+hbp)*rppa$$

(rppa is runs per plate appearance for the entire league $[r/(ab+bb+hbp)]$.

To adjust for league and park effects, define the number of runs for an average team in a season:

$$avgtm = (lg\ runs\ per\ out)*(lg\ outs\ per\ game)*pf*dh*162$$

Replace an average player with the player we are testing:

$$tmplus = avgtm + beqr - (player\ outs)*dh*pf*(lg\ runs\ per\ out)$$

Calculate the pythagorean exponent:

$$pyth = .45 + 1.5*log[(tmplus+avgtm)/162]$$

Calculate the winning percentage of the team-plus-player versus an average team:

$$winpct = (tmplus/avgtm)*pyth/[1+(tmplus/avgtm)*pyth]$$

In the standard universe we are creating for our adjusted statistics, we can say that the proper pythagorean exponent will always be exactly 2.00, that league runs per out will be exactly .17235, and there will be exactly 27 outs per game. So we run the pythagorean equation backwards:

$$newtmplus = [winpct/(1-winpct)]**0.5$$

And run the tmplus and avgtm formulae backwards to get adjusted EqR:

$$eqr = .17235*[(newtmplus-1)*27*162 + (player\ outs)]$$

Which converts into EqA via the following:

if (eqr.ge.0) then
$$eqa = [eqr/5.0/(player\ outs)]**0.4$$

else
$$eqa = -[-eqr/5.0/(player\ outs)]**0.4$$

Last year, the PFR were expressed as a rating based around 100. This caused a fair amount of confusion, so this year it's much simpler; they are expressed the same way that Pete Palmer would express Fielding Runs, as a number of runs better or worse than an average fielder at the position with the same playing time.

Once you have the player's rating, offensive and defensive, within his league, you must have some way of equalizing the leagues. Each league has been assigned a difficulty rating based upon how well players from that league have performed when moving to other leagues over the past five years.

Here is another change from previous editions of *Baseball Prospectus*. Before, we used error rates in leagues to estimate the qualitative differences among them; it worked well in the early 1990s, but in recent years a decline in errors throughout organized baseball (better parks? more lenient official scorers?) has blurred the differences. The new ratings are tougher than the old ones, and some players have lost as much as 30 points of EqA as a result.

The rating shown is a multiplier that is applied to the player's adjusted EqA, although it is also used (in different ways) to adjust the pitching and fielding statistics. The ratings conform to the established minor league levels, with the Japanese leagues rating about equal to North America's Triple-A leagues, and the Mexican League (2000 data not available) comparable to the middle-A leagues. See Table 1 for how the professional leagues ranked in terms of difficulty, and a variety of statistical measures, in 2000.

Pitching

The pitching DTs have been totally revised this year, in light of some excellent research done by Voros McCracken and published on the rec.sport.baseball Usenet newsgroup last year. McCracken found that to a large extent, the number of hits allowed per ball in play varied little from pitcher to pitcher, and that the variance appeared to be largely due to team effects and chance. Moreover, ratings built using only strikeouts, walks and home runs, plus a team-average number of hits per ball in play, correlated better with statistics in future years than ratings that use the pitcher's actual hits allowed.

The pattern has not held up throughout history; Jim Palmer, in particular, allowed far fewer hits, year after year, than the K/W/HR process would suggest. Despite such exceptions, though, we found the results of our tests on the concept sufficiently compelling to alter our procedures. We modified McCracken's method to use the average of actual hits allowed and the team-average rate of hits per ball in play.

Unlike the batter translations, pitcher translations are made by components, not by the total ranking. Normalized strikeout rates, walk rates, and home-run rates are modified by the difficulty factor separately from all other considerations. These numbers allow us to set the translated number of outs in play per nine innings pitched. The translated hit rate depends upon this, the league-average ratio of hits to outs in play and the degree to which the pitcher was above or below the team average in the minors. We use only the square root of the latter figure; if, for instance, a pitcher allowed 25% more hits than he "should have" allowed in the minors, his translation will reflect a rate only 11.8% higher. Translated runs are built up from these statistics and modified by how much the pitcher had over- or under-performed his projected run rates in the actual stats.

Table 1

League	EqA	RPPA	ERA	BA	OBA	SLG	Rtg
American	.801	.1378	4.92	.276	.346	.443	1.000
National	.783	.1318	4.64	.266	.338	.432	.961
International	.766	.1288	4.38	.266	.335	.416	.864
Japanese Pacific	.768	.1282	4.40	.264	.341	.406	.849
Japanese Central	.741	.1153	3.91	.262	.321	.402	.849
Pacific Coast	.796	.1427	4.84	.277	.348	.435	.846
Eastern	.742	.1278	4.18	.262	.332	.392	.794
Southern	.718	.1170	3.72	.250	.324	.373	.787
Texas	.774	.1356	4.43	.271	.344	.413	.784
Carolina	.722	.1224	3.86	.252	.324	.372	.751
California	.760	.1397	4.43	.264	.343	.392	.745
Florida State	.727	.1258	3.91	.260	.328	.377	.745
Midwest	.719	.1256	3.84	.250	.327	.365	.726
Mexican	—	—	—	—	—	—	.716
South Atlantic	.720	.1255	3.81	.254	.323	.369	.707
Northwestern	.708	.1254	3.84	.248	.327	.351	.698
New York-Penn	.698	.1241	3.66	.247	.322	.342	.692
Pioneer	.786	.1596	4.99	.275	.357	.405	.668
Appalachian	.739	.1388	4.18	.257	.331	.379	.639

Wilton Forecasts

The Wilton forecasting system used here is a blend of two very different types of forecasts, analogue and regression. The primary base for the Wilton forecast is the player's average performance over the last three years. To that, we add a series of adjustments based on multiple regression analysis. Most of these are age-based; players over 30 have their stolen bases reduced by 10% per year, for instance. There are also a few other adjustments, based on the player's overall trend or performance in certain categories.

A second series of adjustments is made by looking for players who have had similar statistical profiles over a three-year period and then by seeing how their performance changed in the fourth year. We've developed a database that includes most minor-league players in the 1990s as well as every major-league player since 1920, and for all of these players their statistics have been translated to the same standard as the DTs here. The similarity search is thus based on fully normalized data, so that players from 1968 and 2000 whose "real" statistics are identical will not be regarded as similar.

For example, the system identified Babe Ruth's 1928–31 seasons as the best match for Mark McGwire's 1998–2001, with Willie McCovey's 1972–75, Reggie Jackson's 1980–83, Harmon Killebrew's 1970–73, and Mike Schmidt's 1983–86 also ranking among the top comps. For Nomar Garciaparra's 1997–2000, you get a very different set of comps: Don Mattingly's 1985–88, Joe Jackson's 1914–17, Harry Heilmann's 1919–22, Fred Lindstrom's 1930–33, and Robin Yount's 1980–83 were the best. How each of these players did in his fourth year, compared to his preceding three-year average, represents a completely separate adjustment.

All of this is done in the realm of translated statistics. The final step for the Wilton projections is to retranslate the numbers back to the "real world." We've made two assumptions in doing this: that the two major leagues, and all of their parks, will have the same adjustments in 2001 as they had in 2000. What appears on the 2001 line for a player is a projection of the player's actual 2001 statistics, not his translated statistics. (See Figure 1.)

All player statistics through 2000 are translated. A perfectly average player would have the statistics shown in Figure 2 for 650 plate appearances:

Again, the 2001 statistics—the Wilton forecast—are not translated; they are a projection of actual 2001 performance. (They do not, however, represent a forecast of 2001 playing time.)

Positions are listed as: C=catcher, 1B=first base, 2B=second base, 3B=third base, SS=shortstop, LF=left field, CF=center field, RF=right field, OF=outfield (less than 50% of outfield appearances at any one outfield spot), DH=designated hitter, UT=utility player, and IF=multi-position infielder.

Players bat R (right-handed), L (left-handed) or B (switch-hits).

Age is the player's calendar age on July 1, 2001. It may not be fair to list a player born June 30, 1970 as being 31 and a player born July 1, 1970 as 30, but that is the standard.

Among the categories, Year and Team should be self-explanatory. Lge=League, AB=at-bats, H=hits, DB=doubles, TP=triples, HR=home runs, BB=walks, SO=strikeouts, R=runs, RBI=runs batted in, SB=stolen bases, CS=caught stealing, Out=AB−H+CS. BA=batting average (H/AB), OBP=on-base percentage [(H+BB+HBP)/(AB+BB+HBP)], SLG=slugging average [(H+DB+2TP+3HR)/AB], EQA=Equivalent Average (see page 1), and EQR=Equivalent Runs (see page 1).

Defensive ratings are given by Games-Position PFR. "151-3B 3" means "estimated 151 full games at third base, three runs better than average."

Figure 1

Troy Glaus   3B   Bats R   Age 24

YEAR	TEAM	LGE	AB	H	DB	TP	HR	BB	SO	R	RBI	SB	CS	OUT	BA	OBP	SLG	EQA	EQR	DEFENSE	
1998	Midland	Tex	185	43	8	1	11	29	45	32	29	2	1	143	.232	.340	.465	.266	26	48 3B	1
1998	Vancouvr	PCL	221	62	10	0	14	17	54	26	34	2	2	161	.281	.337	.516	.275	32	57 3B	3
1998	Anaheim	AL	165	38	6	0	2	14	45	19	24	1	0	127	.230	.291	.303	.199	11	45 3B	2
1999	Anaheim	AL	548	134	24	0	32	65	130	83	78	5	1	415	.245	.330	.464	.263	73	150 3B	8
2000	Anaheim	AL	555	158	32	1	49	105	148	113	96	14	13	410	.285	.400	.611	.316	115	151 3B	3
2001	Anaheim	AL	550	151	25	1	38	81	152	102	124	5	3	402	.275	.368	.531	.296	96		

Figure 2: The Average Hitter

AB	H	DB	TP	HR	BB	SO	R	RBI	SB	CS	OUT	BA	OBP	SLG	EQA	EQR
588	159	31	3	21	57	100	85	80	10	5	434	.270	.340	.440	.260	75

The Davenport Translations

Tools

For pitchers, all statistics are translated; there are no projections for 2001. (See Figure 3.) A perfectly average pitcher would have the statistics shown in Figure 4.

As with hitters, ages are set as of July 1, 2001.

Categories are: IP=innings pitched, H=hits, ER=earned runs, BB=walks, K=strikeouts, ERA=earned run average (9ER/IP), W=wins, L=losses, H/9=hits per nine innings, HR/9=home runs per nine innings, BB/9=walks per nine innings, K/9=strikeouts per nine innings, KW=(see below), and PERA=peripheral ERA.

Wins and losses are assigned by using the number of innings, divided by nine, to assign decisions. Wins are set by using the pythagorean theorem with average run support and unearned runs: w=[25/(25+(era/.9)^2]*decisions.

KW and PERA are indices for performance that are independent of runs. KW is based on the normalized strikeout and walk rates per nine innings, essentially (K/BB/2). An average major-league pitcher has a KW score of 1.00. Generally speaking, pitchers with higher KW rates will retain more value from one year to the next than pitchers of equal ERAs but poor KWs.

PERA is Peripheral ERA—what you would have expected the pitcher's ERA to be from looking at the strikeout, walk, hit, and home-run rates. It is a modified version of the batter's EqA statistic: EqA=(2*H+3*HR+1.5*BB)/(3*IP+H+BB), followed by PER=[2*(EqA/.6538)−1]*(3*IP+BB+H)*.1154. PERA is 9*PER/IP.

Figure 3

Tim Hudson — Throws R — Age 25

YEAR	TEAM	LGE	IP	H	ER	HR	BB	K	ERA	W	L	H/9	HR/9	BB/9	K/9	KW	PERA
1998	Modesto	Cal	34.0	22	15	2	22	24	3.97	2	2	5.82	0.53	5.82	6.35	0.55	3.38
1998	Huntsvil	Sou	127.0	137	89	21	68	67	6.31	5	9	9.71	1.49	4.82	4.75	0.49	6.19
1999	Midland	Tex	17.0	9	1	0	3	11	0.53	2	0	4.76	0.00	1.59	5.82	1.83	1.14
1999	Vancouvr	PCL	45.7	37	18	3	25	42	3.55	3	2	7.29	0.59	4.93	8.28	0.84	3.88
1999	Oakland	AL	135.3	114	49	7	50	126	3.26	10	5	7.58	0.47	3.33	8.38	1.26	3.30
2000	Oakland	AL	200.0	158	86	21	67	161	3.87	13	9	7.11	0.94	3.02	7.24	1.20	3.39

Figure 4: The Average Pitcher

IP	H	ER	HR	BB	K	ERA	W	L	H/9	HR/9	BB/9	K/9	KW	PERA
180.0	180	90	20	60	120	4.50	10	10	9.00	1.00	3.00	6.00	1.00	4.50

Support-Neutral Records

by Michael Wolverton

Support-Neutral pitching statistics measure the performance of a starting pitcher in terms of how much he adds to or subtracts from his team's chance of winning a game. Using situational scoring tables and some basic laws of probability, we calculate the probabilities that a pitcher's start will lead to a W or an L for him, as well as a win or a loss for his team. When totaled over all of a pitcher's starts, that gives us the SN measures:

- Support-Neutral Wins and Losses (SNW/SNL): a starter's expected W/L record, given the way he pitched in each game and assuming that he had league-average support from his offense and his bullpen.
- Support-Neutral Value Added (SNVA): the number of games the starter is worth to an average team in the standings above or below what a league-average starter is worth.

Each of these numbers is calculated separately for each individual start, then summed to arrive at seasonal totals. Looking at a starter's performance game-by-game removes distortions that can be introduced by looking at cumulative run prevention (e.g., ERA or John Thorn and Pete Palmer's Adjusted Pitching Wins). In particular, the SN stats recognize that a pitcher can cost his team only a single game in a single start, so it puts a limit on how much a single bad outing (e.g., 11 runs allowed in two innings) can hurt his season or career value.

We'll provide a brief summary of the SN stats here; for more detail on the benefits of measuring pitching performance this way, along with the math behind the stats, visit www.baseballprospectus.com and click on the link for the Starting Pitching Report.

The basic idea behind the calculation of the SN stats is pretty simple. For example, a starter's SNW total is calculated by determining, for each start he makes, the probability that he would get the win given the way he pitched in that game, then summing the individual probabilities of his starts. The sum gives you the number of wins a pitcher could expect to get for an average team given his performances.

A "performance" here consists only of the number of innings pitched, the number of runs (not earned runs) given up while the starter was in the game, the number of outs and locations of any baserunners when the starter left the game, the park in which the game was played and whether the pitcher was at home or on the road. SN stats assume that these are the only things that influence whether the pitcher wins or loses.

Calculating these probabilities is a little complicated. The starter gets a W when two things happen: he leaves the game with the lead and his team never gives it up. To figure the probability of a pitcher getting a W for an average team, we look at all the different possible sequences of innings that could lead to a W. For example, consider a game in which the home-team starter is pulled after finishing the eighth inning having given up one run. Such a start would result in a W for the starter if...

- his team scored two runs in the first eight innings and his relievers gave up none in the ninth, or
- his team scored three runs in the first eight innings and his relievers gave up none in the ninth, or
- his team scored three runs in the first eight innings and his relievers gave up one run in the ninth, or
- etc., etc., etc.

We figure out each of the individual probabilities above, substituting "league average" for "his," and then we combine them using the simplest laws of probability, i.e., multiplying whenever it says "and" and adding whenever it says "or." The individual-inning probabilities (e.g., the probability of "average relievers gave up one run in the ninth inning") come from the league single-inning scoring distribution for that year. For example, in 2000, major-league teams scored no runs in about 70% of the innings, one run in 16% of the innings, two runs in 8% of the innings, etc. Park effects are factored in by changing the definition of "average team." For example, an average team will score more runs at Coors Field and fewer at Dodger Stadium, and the run-scoring distribution is altered to reflect that.

The end results are three probabilities: the start resulting in a W for the pitcher (SNW), the start resulting in an L for the pitcher (SNL), and the start resulting in a win for an average team (SNVA). If the start mentioned above—eight innings, one run allowed at home—had occurred at Dodger Stadium, it would calculates to a 0.72 SNW and a 0.07 SNL. This start will result in a team win 82% of the time; since SNVA is concerned with comparing a starter to a league-average pitcher, and since an average pitcher's starts will presumably result in 50% wins, this start gets an SNVA rating of 0.82 – 0.50 = 0.32 wins above average.

The only major aspect of the SN stats left to explain is how they remove bullpen support from a starter's numbers. The input used to calculate SNW, SNL, and SNVA includes the state of the bases when the starter leaves the game. So, for example, if a starter gets yanked with two outs and runners on first and third in the seventh after three runs have scored, and his reliever allows both runners to score, the SN stats will be calculated based on:

- six full innings, three runs in, runners on first and third with two outs

rather than, for example, what that game's box score would tell you:

- six full innings, two outs, five runs allowed.

This method provides results which are more "support-neutral," in that a starter's numbers will not be skewed by really good or really poor bullpen support.

Quick Guide to the SN Numbers

The tables and discussions of Support-Neutral stats in this book deal with the following measures:

- a pitcher's Support-Neutral W/L record (SNW, SNL)
- his Support-Neutral Winning Percentage (SNPct): SNW/(SNW+SNL). This is the Support-Neutral rate statistic, analogous to RA
- his actual W/L record (W, L)
- his runs allowed per nine innings (RA, or ERA without the "E")
- his Adjusted Pitching Wins (APW), a measure of the number of wins a pitcher is worth, computed from the number of runs he prevented that a league average pitcher would have allowed. This is a modified version of the *Total Baseball* measure using runs rather than earned runs. It is included in the tables for comparison with SNVA
- his Support-Neutral Value Added (SNVA)
- his Support-Neutral Wins Above Replacement (SNWAR), the number of SNWs a pitcher has above what a .425 pitcher would get in the same number of Support-Neutral decisions.

The park-effect numbers appearing with the Support-Neutral team sections are two-year averages of one-year park factors from 1999 and 2000. The exceptions, for which one-year factors were used, are the ballparks that were new in 2000—in Seattle (Safeco debuted in 1999, but 2000 was its first full season), Detroit, Houston, and San Francisco. The DH is accounted for by treating it as a "ground rule" of the park and incorporating it into the park effect. We combine the effect of the park itself with the effect of the rules played in that park (DH or no DH). As a result, the park effects used for the calculation of the SN numbers are adjusted so that the difference between AL and NL scoring in 2000 was added to or subtracted from each park, depending on which league it came from: each AL park inflated run scoring by an additional 3% over the raw park factor, and each NL park deflated run scoring by an additional 3%.

2000 Support-Neutral Leader Boards

Top 20 Major League Starters (ranked by SNWs over a .425 pitcher):

Pitcher	Team	SNW	SNL	SNPct	W	L	RA	APW	SNVA	SNWAR
Pedro Martinez	BOS	19.9	3.1	.867	18	6	1.82	8.1	8.1	10.2
Randy Johnson	ARI	19.1	7.8	.709	19	7	3.22	4.8	5.4	7.6
Kevin Brown	LAD	17.3	7.1	.710	13	6	2.97	4.5	4.8	7.0
Greg Maddux	ATL	17.9	8.9	.667	19	9	3.28	4.5	4.2	6.5
Mike Mussina	BAL	16.3	9.4	.634	11	15	3.98	3.0	3.3	5.4
Tom Glavine	ATL	15.7	9.5	.623	21	9	3.77	3.1	2.9	5.0
Chan Ho Park	LAD	15.2	9.3	.621	18	10	3.66	2.7	2.7	4.8
David Wells	TOR	16.1	10.9	.597	20	8	4.51	2.1	2.5	4.6
Jeff D'Amico	MIL	12.0	5.6	.682	12	7	3.05	3.3	3.1	4.5
Bartolo Colon	CLE	13.3	7.5	.640	15	8	4.12	2.5	2.7	4.5
Curt Schilling	P/A	13.9	8.6	.616	11	12	3.85	2.8	2.5	4.3
Chuck Finley	CLE	14.2	9.3	.605	16	11	4.46	2.2	2.4	4.2
Mike Hampton	NYM	14.1	9.2	.606	15	10	3.68	2.6	2.3	4.2
Brad Radke	MIN	14.7	10.1	.593	12	16	4.73	2.0	2.1	4.1
Al Leiter	NYM	13.5	8.8	.606	16	8	3.63	2.6	2.2	4.0
Darryl Kile	STL	14.9	10.7	.582	19	9	4.22	2.0	2.0	4.0
Mike Sirotka	CHW	13.6	9.1	.597	15	10	4.61	1.6	2.1	3.9
Roger Clemens	NYY	13.7	9.4	.592	13	8	4.23	2.0	2.0	3.8
Kris Benson	PIT	14.1	10.3	.577	10	12	4.30	1.7	1.7	3.7
Frank Castillo	TOR	10.2	5.1	.665	10	5	3.81	2.2	2.4	3.7

We at *Baseball Prospectus* often point out that the only thing predictable about pitching is that it's unpredictable. That may be true in general, but the top major-league starters in 2000 were as predictable as the jokes in an Adam Sandler movie. The top seven cumulative SNWAR totals since 1992 are owned by Greg Maddux, Randy Johnson, Pedro Martinez, Roger Clemens, Kevin Brown, Mike Mussina, and Tom Glavine. As you can see in the table above, the top six starters in 2000 were all members of that old guard. Only Clemens prevented a perfect seven-for-seven, and his #18 ranking in 2000 was nothing to complain about.

Martinez had the third-best season since 1979 by SNWAR, finishing behind only Clemens's 1997 and Dwight Gooden's 1985. Even more impressive was that he had by far the best single-season Support-Neutral Winning Percentage (SNPct) during that same period, blowing away Greg Maddux's mark of .836 in 1995.

Bottom 10 Major League Starters (ranked by SNWs over a .425 pitcher):

Pitcher	Team	SNW	SNL	SNPct	W	L	RA	APW	SNVA	SNWAR
Roy Halladay	TOR	1.6	7.3	.183	4	6	11.13	-3.5	-2.6	-2.2
Vladimir Nunez	FLA	1.7	7.1	.189	0	6	8.80	-2.7	-2.7	-2.1
Sean Bergman	MIN	2.4	7.3	.249	4	5	9.62	-2.7	-2.2	-1.7
Jaime Navarro	M/C	0.5	4.5	.092	0	6	13.50	-2.3	-1.9	-1.7
Scott Erickson	BAL	3.5	8.4	.295	5	8	7.87	-2.6	-2.5	-1.6
Chad Durbin	KCR	3.2	7.7	.293	2	5	8.83	-2.5	-2.1	-1.4
C.J. Nitkowski	DET	1.8	5.5	.250	2	7	9.00	-2.1	-1.8	-1.3
Jay Witasick	K/S	6.0	11.2	.351	6	9	6.53	-2.0	-2.5	-1.3
Omar Daal	A/P	7.2	12.4	.365	4	18	6.61	-2.5	-2.6	-1.2
Ryan Rupe	TAM	4.0	8.0	.333	5	6	7.42	-2.0	-2.1	-1.1

Roy Halladay edged Vladimir Nunez for the prestigious Mike Kekich Trophy in 2000. Nunez looked like a sure bet to win the award, but Halladay was called on to make a late September start, got bombed, and claimed the title.

The most interesting name on this list, though, is Jaime Navarro at number four. Navarro had his worst season in 2000, which is saying something, because his recent career has been nothing but awful. By SNWAR, Navarro was the fifth-worst starter in the majors in 1994, 21st-worst in 1997, sixth-worst in 1998, and 12th-worst in 1999. Despite that record, there were *still* two teams willing to trot him out for seven disastrous starts in 2000. It's amazing how many chances you get if you have a couple of good years under your belt, no matter how long ago they were.

The next two tables compare starters' expected records (E(W)/E(L)) with their actual records. E(W) is equal to SNW for those games where the starter goes five or more innings, and zero otherwise. E(L) is identical to SNL.

Luckiest 10 Magor League Starters [ranked by (W − E(W)) + (E(L) − L)]:

Pitcher	Team	E(W)	E(L)	W	L	Diff.
Tim Hudson	OAK	13.7	10.2	20	6	10.5
John Halama	SEA	7.2	12.0	14	9	9.8
Scott Elarton	HOU	11.6	10.3	17	7	8.6
Andy Pettitte	NYY	13.1	10.8	19	9	7.7
Cal Eldred	CHW	6.7	6.1	10	2	7.4
Willie Blair	DET	4.2	6.3	8	3	7.2
Shawn Estes	SFG	11.7	9.7	15	6	7.0
Dave Burba	CLE	12.2	9.2	16	6	6.9
David Wells	TOR	16.0	10.9	20	8	6.9
Garrett Stephenson	STL	11.2	11.0	16	9	6.8

The 2000 Lew Burdette Award, given to the luckiest pitcher in the majors, goes to Tim Hudson. Hudson is an exciting young pitcher who had a fine year, but his 20 wins and runner-up finish in the AL Cy Young Award voting had as much to do with the support he received from the A's offense as they did with his pitching.

A couple of familiar faces appeared on the Luckiest list in 2000—Andy Pettitte at number four and David Wells at number nine. Wells has the 20th-luckiest career record for the seasons we have the Support-Neutral numbers (1979-present, except 1991), while Pettitte is number 22 on the same list. (In case you're wondering, Dwight Gooden is number one.) Pettitte has been on the lucky side of the ledger in each of his six seasons, and ranked as high the tenth-luckiest pitcher in the majors in 1996. Wells hasn't been as consistent with his good luck throughout his career, but his good fortune the past three seasons has been amazing: he finished fifth, 14th, and ninth among major-league starters in luck in 1998, 1999, and 2000.

Unluckiest 10 Major League Starters {ranked by [W − E(W)] + [E(L) − L]}:

Pitcher	Team	E(W)	E(L)	W	L	Diff.
Mike Mussina	BAL	16.1	9.4	11	15	-10.7
Masato Yoshii	COL	9.9	9.2	6	15	-9.7
Omar Daal	A/P	7.0	12.4	4	18	-8.6
Brad Radke	MIN	14.6	10.1	12	16	-8.6
Joe Mays	MIN	8.9	9.9	7	15	-7.0
Jeff Weaver	DET	12.6	9.6	11	15	-6.9
Pete Schourek	BOS	6.2	6.3	3	10	-6.9
Chris Holt	HOU	11.4	12.1	8	15	-6.3
Curt Schilling	P/A	13.9	8.6	11	12	-6.2
David Cone	NYY	7.5	11.8	4	14	-5.7

Mike Mussina is the unfortunate recipient of 2000's Bob Friend Award, given to the hard-luck starter of the year. Mussina was actually among baseball's luckiest pitchers over the first nine years of his career, with an actual W/L record of 136-66 compared to an expected record of 121–70. The run support dried up in a big way last year as Mussina's record provided yet another counterexample to the myth that pitchers have a special "ability to win" beyond their ability to prevent runs.

If Brad Radke doesn't get away from the Twins' anemic offense soon, he may go down as one of the game's all-time hard-luck pitchers. 2000 marked the third time in his six-year career that Radke has finished among the majors' five unluckiest starters. In the years for which we have data, Radke already has the fifth-unluckiest career record, a mediocre 78–84 (.481) compared to his fine 81–64 (.559) expected record. Radke ranks fifth behind Mike Morgan, Jose DeLeon, Jim Beattie and Danny Darwin. Another of 2000's unluckiest pitchers, Curt Schilling, ranks ninth on the career list, with a 104–86 (.547) actual record that falls well below his 113–75 (.602) expected record.

Reliever Evaluation Tools

by Michael Wolverton

The biggest problem with using ERA to evaluate relievers is that much of a reliever's job occurs in the context of other pitchers' work. A reliever's ability to prevent runs is based not just on how many of his own runners he keeps from crossing the plate, but also the context in which he enters the game (inherited runners) and the context in which he leaves the game (runners he turns over to successors). By ignoring a reliever's ability to handle inherited runners, ERA fails to measure a big part of what that reliever did. And by including a reliever's runners allowed in by his successors, ERA measures things that reliever didn't do.

For the past couple of years, we have been using a set of reliever evaluation tools that incorporate the role that context plays in a reliever's performance. We'll give a brief summary of those tools here; there's a lot more detail, including formulas and a longer discussion of the benefits of the tools, at www.baseballprospectus.com. Just click on the Reliever Report link.

The basic measure of a reliever's contribution is Adjusted Runs Prevented (ARP). ARP evaluates each reliever's appearance in terms of how it changed run expectation. We use a situational scoring table to map each of the 24 possible base/out states into the expected number of runs that would score in the remainder of the inning starting from that state. For example, in 2000, an average team with one out and runners at second and third would expect to score 1.50 runs in the remainder of the inning; with two outs and a runner on second, a team would expect to score 0.33 runs.

We then calculate the value of an appearance as the difference between the expected runs when the appearance started and the expected runs when the appearance ended, plus the number of runs that scored during the appearance itself. For example, if a reliever entered a game with one out and runners on second and third, and was pulled after getting a strikeout and surrendering a double that scored both runners, the value of that appearance would be 1.50 – 0.33 – 2 = –0.83 runs.

The idea of measuring performance according to effect on run expectation is not new and it's not ours. Gary Skoog proposed this approach, which he called Value Added, to evaluate all players in the 1987 Bill James Baseball Abstract. Steve Schulman has been using the same basic approach—he calls it Runs Prevented—to evaluate relievers in the past few editions of the STATS Baseball Scoreboard. We have made a few extensions to their methods; the most important is that ARP is adjusted for the park in which the reliever's appearance takes place, along with the league scoring level for the appropriate year.

ARP represents a reliever's cumulative run prevention above average over the course of a season. We would also like to have a measure of a reliever's rate of run prevention using the same basic approach. Runs Responsible Average (RRA) is a rate stat indicating how well the reliever prevented runs per inning. It is directly comparable to park-adjusted Run Average (ARA), except it incorporates the context in which the reliever entered and exited each game.

2000 Leaders

The tables below show relievers rated by the two metrics mentioned above, ARP and RRA. For comparison, the tables also show metrics that evaluate relievers based on the conventional methods of charging runs to pitchers, i.e., metrics that do not consider inherited runners, etc.: Park-Adjusted Runs Allowed Average (ARA) is the rate stat comparable to RRA, and Adjusted Pitching Runs (APR—a modified version of Pete Palmer's/Total Baseball's stat) is the cumulative stat comparable to ARP.

Table 1 presents the top 20 relievers in the majors in 2000, ranked by Adjusted Runs Prevented.

Gabe White had no problems adjusting to his new high-altitude home in Coors Field, overtaking his former teammate Scott Sullivan and others down the stretch to finish with the best ARP in the majors. Derek Lowe had the best ARP in the AL, a feat he accomplished despite being a little below average in handling inherited runners.

Because relievers pitch so few innings, you'd expect there to be a lot of variability among the top relievers from year to year. And in fact there are several new and surprising names on the 2000 list. But there are also a fair number of relievers who have been consistently excellent. Three of the top ten relievers in the majors last year were holdovers from 1999's top ten: Sullivan (seventh in 1999), Lowe (sixth in 1999), and Keith Foulke (first in 1999). Two others in last year's top ten were bouncing back from a subpar 1999 after finishing in 1998's top ten: Jim Mecir (fifth in 1998) and Robb Nen (fourth in 1998).

At the other extreme, Table 2 shows the worst 10 relievers from 2000, ranked by ARP.

It's bad enough that Darren Holmes was charged with 28 runs in 20 1/3 innings, but when you add to that the fact that

Table 1: Top 20 Relievers in the Majors in 2000 by Adjusted Runs Prevented

Pitcher	Team	IP	R	ARA	APR	RRA	ARP
Gabe White	C/C	84.0	23	1.97	30.2	2.15	28.5
Scott Sullivan	CIN	105.7	41	3.45	20.6	2.96	26.3
Derek Lowe	BOS	91.3	27	2.49	27.5	2.71	25.2
Jim Mecir	T/O	85.0	31	3.25	18.4	2.71	23.5
Curtis Leskanic	MIL	77.3	23	2.82	20.4	2.47	23.4
Keith Foulke	CHW	88.0	31	3.04	21.1	2.81	23.3
Jeff Tam	OAK	85.7	30	3.15	19.5	2.79	22.9
Robb Nen	SFG	66.0	15	2.26	21.5	2.20	22.0
Rich Garces	BOS	74.7	28	3.16	16.9	2.78	20.1
Mike Myers	COL	45.3	10	1.55	18.4	1.32	19.5
Danny Graves	CIN	91.3	31	3.01	22.1	3.27	19.5
Bob Wells	MIN	86.3	39	3.76	13.8	3.17	19.4
Jose Jimenez	COL	70.7	27	2.68	19.8	2.95	17.6
LaTroy Hawkins	MIN	87.7	34	3.23	19.2	3.39	17.6
Bobby Howry	CHW	71.0	26	3.16	16.1	2.97	17.5
Matt Herges	LAD	87.7	28	3.12	20.2	3.40	17.5
Al Levine	ANA	77.0	31	3.51	14.4	3.16	17.4
Rick White	T/N	99.7	44	4.02	13.0	3.68	16.8
Turk Wendell	NYM	82.7	36	4.24	8.8	3.40	16.5
Billy Koch	TOR	78.7	28	3.07	18.6	3.31	16.5

Table 2: Worst 10 Relievers in the Majors in 2000 by Adjusted Runs Prevented

Pitcher	Team	IP	R	ARA	APR	RRA	ARP
Darren Holmes	A/S	20.3	28	12.60	-16.7	15.49	-23.3
Rich Rodriguez	NYM	37.0	40	10.53	-21.9	10.69	-22.6
Pat Mahomes	NYM	67.0	44	6.40	-9.0	8.01	-21.0
Miguel Batista	M/K	17.3	29	14.83	-18.5	15.42	-19.7
Jeff Wallace	PIT	35.7	32	8.32	-12.4	9.89	-18.6
Allen Watson	NYY	22.0	25	10.23	-12.3	12.44	-17.7
Darwin Cubillan	T/T	33.3	36	9.17	-14.7	9.88	-17.3
Brad Rigby	K/M	13.7	21	13.43	-12.5	16.61	-17.3
Pedro Borbon	TOR	41.7	37	7.65	-11.4	8.73	-16.4
Jose Mesa	SEA	80.7	48	5.74	-4.9	6.94	-15.6

he was among the worst pitchers in the majors at handling inherited runners (see Table), you have a truly horrific year. Holmes's ARP total was the second-worst in the three years we've been tracking the numbers; only Vic Darensbourg's -28.7 ARP for the Marlins in 1999 "bottoms" Holmes's 2000.

The Mets' 2000 bullpen numbers were spoiled by having two of the worst three relievers in the majors. The Mets' team ARP of -9.7 ranked them 18th in the major leagues, but if you take away the cumulative -33.6 ARP put up by Rich Rodriguez and Pat Mahomes, the Mets would have ranked sixth.

Table 3 presents the team numbers from 2000, with bullpens ranked best to worst by ARP.

The Rockies had the best bullpen in the majors last year, their second team relief title in the past three years. They had three of the top 13 individual ARP totals in the majors and four relievers with ARP totals better than 10.0. The Red Sox had the best bullpen in the AL and in fact were close enough to the Rockies that they were effectively tied for best in the majors. As with the Rockies, the key for the Red Sox was having multiple top-flight performances: Lowe, Rich Garces, and Hipolito Pichardo were all among the majors' top 25 relievers, and even Rod Beck showed that he still has something left.

Table 3: Team Numbers in 2000 by Adjusted Runs Prevented

Team	IP	R	ARA	APR	RRA	ARP
COL	506.7	285	3.95	70.3	3.94	70.9
BOS	566.3	273	4.06	71.6	4.08	70.4
ANA	552.0	280	4.42	47.6	4.52	41.6
CIN	502.3	253	4.47	40.4	4.46	41.0
CLE	532.7	273	4.39	47.5	4.58	36.6
TAM	529.3	279	4.65	32.2	4.66	31.6
MIN	512.3	268	4.35	48.0	4.64	31.5
LAD	479.0	218	4.45	39.7	4.62	30.7
CHW	535.3	281	4.53	39.7	4.72	28.3
MIL	502.0	236	4.45	41.5	4.79	22.9
DET	478.7	247	4.67	27.9	4.81	20.4
OAK	464.0	258	5.00	10.1	4.84	18.2
SFG	430.3	213	4.92	13.3	4.84	17.1
ARI	437.3	230	4.85	17.0	4.97	11.3
ATL	400.0	207	4.87	14.7	4.95	11.2
NYY	459.7	253	4.96	12.3	5.25	-2.6
SEA	485.0	254	5.05	7.8	5.28	-4.6
NYM	446.7	243	5.30	-5.2	5.39	-9.7
SDP	481.3	255	5.28	-4.4	5.41	-11.2
FLA	457.7	252	5.46	-13.2	5.58	-19.3
PIT	521.7	307	5.46	-15.2	5.55	-20.3
STL	433.0	266	5.70	-24.1	5.62	-20.5
HOU	449.7	282	5.39	-9.9	5.62	-21.3
KCR	495.7	325	5.65	-24.9	5.75	-30.5
MON	516.7	325	5.74	-31.1	5.79	-34.1
TEX	485.0	331	5.74	-29.4	5.85	-35.0
TOR	479.7	309	5.55	-18.9	6.02	-43.7
CHC	476.7	295	5.84	-34.0	6.04	-44.4
BAL	437.0	291	6.01	-39.5	6.28	-52.6
PHI	434.3	299	6.28	-52.1	6.42	-59.0
ML	14488.0	8088	5.02	279.8	5.15	74.5

Despite not quite having the same run-prevention numbers as the Rockies or Red Sox, the Reds' story is arguably even more impressive. They moved the NL's sixth-best reliever in 1999 (Scott Williamson) into the rotation midway through the season and got a lousy season from their lefty specialist (Dennys Reyes). Yet they still managed, once again, to have one of the league's best bullpens thanks to the devastating one-two punch of Danny Graves and Scott Sullivan.

Another tool we use to evaluate relievers is Inherited Runs Prevented (IRP), which isolates the reliever's performance in handling inherited runners. Tables 4 and 5 show the best and worst relievers at handling inherited runners in 2000.

The columns in these tables are easy to understand through an example. Take Bob Wells's line. Wells inherited 70 runners in 2000 (IRnr). Based on the bases those runners occupied and how many outs there were when Wells entered the game, 29.2 of them would be expected to score (Expected Inherited Runs start, or EIRs). Only 20 of them actually did score (Inherited Runs, or IR) and none were still left on base when Wells left the game (Expected Inherited Runs finish, or EIRf). Combine those numbers and park-adjust, and you find that Wells prevented 8.5 inherited runners from scoring that would have scored with league-average pitching (IRP).

The other effect we want to isolate is how much help the reliever got from his successors he turned runners over to them. For this we use a measure called Bequeathed Runs Saved (BRS). Tables 6 and 7 present the relievers who received the most and least assistance from their successors:

Again we'll use an example to explain what these numbers mean. Take Mike Holtz's line. Holtz turned over 32 runners that were his responsibility to his successors (Own Bequeathed Runners, or OBRnr). Given where those runners were and how many outs there were when Holtz was removed, 9.0 of them would have been expected to score (Expected Bequeathed Runs, or EBR). In fact, his successors allowed 15 of them to score (Bequeathed Runs, or BR), meaning (after a park adjustment step) that Holtz's successors

Table 4: Best Relievers in 2000 by Inherited Runs Prevented (IRP)

Pitcher	Team	IRnr	EIRs	IR	EIRf	IRP
Bob Wells	MIN	70	29.2	20	0.0	8.5
Rick White	T/N	44	15.6	8	0.0	7.6
Curtis Leskanic	MIL	31	9.5	3	0.0	7.0
Jeff Zimmerman	TEX	66	25.5	17	1.5	6.9
Jim Mecir	T/O	46	17.3	11	0.0	6.5
Scott Kamieniecki	C/A	26	8.6	2	0.5	6.1
Scott Sullivan	CIN	50	19.8	13	0.4	5.9
Turk Wendell	NYM	40	12.8	6	1.5	5.8
Kerry Ligtenberg	ATL	39	15.6	9	0.5	5.7
Buddy Groom	BAL	59	19.2	13	0.7	5.5

Table 5: Worst Relievers in 2000 by Inherited Runs Prevented (IRP)

Pitcher	Team	IRnr	EIRs	IR	EIRf	IRP
Jose Mesa	SEA	36	10.4	20	0.3	-10.8
Pat Mahomes	NYM	35	12.7	20	0.0	-7.7
Jose Santiago	KCR	33	14.4	21	0.3	-6.7
Carlos Almanzar	SDP	44	16.1	22	0.0	-6.4
Darren Holmes	A/S	16	6.7	12	0.6	-6.3
Pedro Borbon	TOR	41	16.0	20	2.2	-6.2
Nelson Cruz	DET	27	8.1	14	0.0	-5.9
Jose Paniagua	SEA	62	17.9	22	1.1	-5.8
Steve Kline	MON	40	13.0	17	1.5	-5.7
Brian Williams	C/C	28	10.9	16	0.0	-5.6

Table 6: Relievers in 2000 by Best Bequeathed Runs Saved (BRS)

Pitcher	Team	OBRnr	EBR	BR	BRS
Rob Ramsay	SEA	32	9.9	4	6.6
Kelly Wunsch	CHW	41	14.3	8	6.2
Mike Venafro	TEX	42	16.0	10	5.6
Tim Worrell	B/C	16	6.3	1	5.3
LaTroy Hawkins	MIN	27	9.5	4	5.1
Jeff Brantley	PHI	13	5.3	0	5.0
Justin Speier	CLE	28	12.1	7	4.8
Mike Magnante	OAK	40	12.9	9	4.3
Terry Adams	LAD	21	6.9	3	4.3
Bill Simas	CHW	28	10.5	6	4.2

Table 7: Relievers in 2000 by Worst Bequeathed Runs Saved (BRS)

Pitcher	Team	OBRnr	EBR	BR	BRS
Mike Holtz	ANA	32	9.0	15	-5.8
Arthur Rhodes	SEA	27	7.5	12	-5.6
Danny Patterson	DET	25	8.8	13	-4.3
Willie Blair	DET	14	5.8	10	-4.3
Kevin Beirne	CHW	17	9.6	14	-4.2
Jeff Zimmerman	TEX	30	10.6	15	-4.2
Tim Crabtree	TEX	30	10.6	15	-4.1
Daniel Garibay	CHC	13	5.3	9	-4.1
Mike James	STL	11	4.1	8	-3.9
Guillermo Mota	MON	12	4.1	8	-3.9

caused Holtz to be charged with 5.8 more runs than he would have been charged with if he'd gotten league-average relief.

The previous four tables isolate some interesting components of relief performance not measured by traditional run assignment. But what about putting those components all together to find out how badly traditional run assignment can underrate or overrate a reliever's contribution?

Measuring this is easy. As we mentioned above, ARP and Palmer's Adjusted Pitching Runs are each attempting to measure the same thing—runs prevented as compared to an average pitcher. APR represents the traditional run assignment approach, comparing the league-average run scoring to the number of runs charged to the pitcher. ARP represents the run-expectation approach that, for the reasons we've argued in this article, should give a more accurate picture of a reliever's performance. The amount that traditional run assignment overrates or underrates a reliever, then, is the difference between those two measures. Tables 8 and 9 present the lists for 2000.

There are lots of names here that we've already seen in the tables that deal with inherited and bequeathed runners. What these tables give you is an idea of how traditional run assignment can distort the picture of a reliever's effectiveness. Since relievers pitch relatively few innings, and since a high percentage of those innings involve inherited and bequeathed runners, the distortion can be pretty significant.

Consider Mike Holtz again. His 5.53 park-adjusted RA makes him appear to be a below-average reliever. However, when you take into account his excellent handling of inherited runners and the fact that he got league-worst support from his successors, you find that his overall contribution to the Angels run prevention efforts was that of a 3.30-RA pitcher—more than two full runs per nine innings better!

In no way would I claim that the tools presented here are the final word in reliever evaluation. There are some shortcomings of these measures that are easy to see now, and perhaps others that will come to light as more results become available. For example, an argument could be made that, by limiting our notion of "context" to just those aspects that affect run prevention, we are ignoring other things that are crucial to a reliever's performance. For instance, what about the score of the game?

There are plenty of interesting issues here, but we'll have to leave a detailed discussion of the advantages and disadvantages of competing definitions of "context" for another time. While there may be no way to combine all aspects of a reliever's performance into a single number, we think these stats are an important part of the puzzle.

Table 8: Relievers in 2000 Most Underrated by APR versus ARP

Pitcher	Team	IRP	BRS	ARA	RRA	APR	ARP	Diff.
Mike Holtz	ANA	4.6	-5.8	5.53	3.30	-1.5	8.6	10.1
Jeff Zimmerman	TEX	6.9	-4.2	5.44	4.29	-1.8	7.0	8.9
Turk Wendell	NYM	5.8	-1.9	4.24	3.40	8.8	16.5	7.8
Arthur Rhodes	SEA	3.6	-5.6	4.73	3.75	3.6	11.2	7.6
Anthony Telford	MON	3.4	-3.3	4.43	3.59	6.7	14.0	7.3
Steve Reed	CLE	4.9	-2.9	4.59	3.57	3.8	10.1	6.4
Kerry Ligtenberg	ATL	5.7	-1.6	3.77	2.71	8.3	14.4	6.2
Scott Sullivan	CIN	5.9	-1.4	3.45	2.96	20.6	26.3	5.7
Aaron Fultz	SFG	-1.8	-3.3	5.45	4.71	-1.9	3.8	5.7
Bob Wells	MIN	8.5	1.2	3.76	3.17	13.8	19.4	5.7

Table 9: Relievers in 2000 Most Overrated by APR versus ARP

Pitcher	Team	IRP	BRS	ARA	RRA	APR	ARP	Diff.
Pat Mahomes	NYM	-7.7	3.7	6.40	8.01	-9.0	-21.0	-12.0
Jose Santiago	KCR	-6.7	4.0	4.12	5.57	8.2	-2.9	-11.1
Jose Mesa	SEA	-10.8	-1.1	5.74	6.94	-4.9	-15.6	-10.7
Carlos Almanzar	SDP	-6.4	3.1	5.01	6.38	1.5	-9.2	-10.7
Steve Kline	MON	-5.7	3.9	3.99	5.04	11.1	1.4	-9.6
Mike Timlin	B/S	-4.4	3.7	4.65	5.92	3.9	-5.2	-9.1
Hector Carrasco	M/B	-5.5	1.5	5.00	6.01	1.6	-6.9	-8.6
Dennys Reyes	CIN	-4.2	3.4	6.31	7.85	-5.4	-12.9	-7.5
Braden Looper	FLA	-4.9	-0.3	6.03	6.99	-6.3	-13.4	-7.1
Nelson Cruz	DET	-5.9	0.5	3.09	4.66	9.6	2.4	-7.1

Arizona Diamondbacks

We said that the Diamondbacks would slip by at least a dozen games in 2000, based on the assumption that they'd stick with the same crew that accomplished an unlikely 100-win season in 1999. The Snakes settled for a 15-game decline.

You already know the basic issue: there isn't a whole team here. There are a couple of old aces, a couple of old hitters, some old guys in the bullpen, and some old guys on the bench. There isn't a single good young position player in the organization. Now, there's no law in professional sports against exclusively employing the elderly, but if you want to sustain any success, relying too heavily on players over 30 is a serious problem.

Revolutions eat their young. In this case, the meal was Buck Showalter, the victim of a failure to remain true to the team's original vision. The Diamondbacks were established on the principle that no Jerry Colangelo operation was going to suffer through the normal growing pains of an expansion franchise. If the Rockies could go to the playoffs in their third year of existence and the Marlins could win the World Series in their fifth year, was there any reason to build a franchise through player development alone? Why force the good people of Phoenix to watch the modern versions of Marv Throneberry or Doug Ault when the Diamondbacks could buy instant respectability by signing recognizable veteran talent?

To be as charitable as possible to the Diamondbacks, let's consider whether or not the Rockies and Marlins are good role models for an expansion franchise on the make. The Rockies lucked into a playoff slot in 1995 courtesy of Dusty Baker's odd decision to tank the last game of the season. That enabled the Rockies to avoid a one-game playoff with the Astros. Colorado's biggest asset that season was the league's best bullpen (featuring Steve Reed, Bruce Ruffin, Curtis Leskanic, and Darren Holmes) and a decent, if fragile, rotation that included Billy Swift, Kevin Ritz, Bret Saberhagen, and Armando Reynoso. Bob Gebhard had imported one of the best hitters available (Larry Walker), so they had the Blake Street Bombers and Walt Weiss's 98 walks. Mostly, they were a pitching team good enough to overcome a weak offense—a fact masked by a great offensive environment—and post a modest .535 winning percentage. Five years later, it's pretty obvious that it was not a team destined for better things.

The 1997 Marlins were a brilliant exposition on what a good GM can do with an open checkbook and a one-year deadline to build a team to beat the Braves. The Fish were already armed with the products of an outstanding player-development program (notably Edgar Renteria and Charles Johnson) and had nabbed Gary Sheffield, Robb Nen, and Jay Powell in trades. They had already signed Kevin Brown, Al Leiter, Livan Hernandez, and Devon White as free agents before the 1996 season. Ordered to win in '97, Dave Dombrowski signed one of the best hitters available (Moises Alou) and one of the best starters available (Alex Fernandez), plus Bobby Bonilla and Dennis Cook. He traded for Cliff Floyd and Darren Daulton and Craig Counsell, building a team to do the one thing it had to do: go toe-to-toe with the Braves in a short series. It was a risk that succeeded.

In the Rockies and Marlins, you have two teams that assembled good pitching staffs through the expansion draft, free agency, and trades. Both teams added top-tier free-agent outfielders. While the Rockies weren't old enough as a franchise to have any homegrown talent, the Marlins had developed a couple of future stars of their own and had benefited from laying out the money to assemble a top-notch player-evaluation staff.

So, working with those examples of expansion teams being successful relatively quickly, what did the Snakes do? Like both the '95 Rockies and the '97 Marlins, the D'backs have assembled a good rotation. Unfortunately, Randy Johnson started to feel his age and first-half workload in the second half of 2000, and getting Curt Schilling cost the team just about the last dregs of talent in a farm system drained by getting Matt Mantei and Dan Plesac the previous year. Todd

---

Diamondbacks Prospectus

2000 record: 85–77; Third place, NL West
Pythagenport W/L: 85–77
Runs Scored: 792 (10th in NL)
Runs Allowed: 754 (5th in NL)
Team EqA: .246 (tied for 13th in NL)
2000 Batters' Age: 30.8 (2nd oldest in NL)
2000 Pitchers' Age: 31.8 (oldest in NL)
Ballpark: Bank One Ballpark; neutral park; Park Factor of .999
2000: An easy schedule helped them start well, but they eventually reached their level.
2001: They're not getting any younger; the team OBP will be brutal.

Stottlemyre was an expensive mediocrity before he became an expensive injured mediocrity. Armando Reynoso is a healthier version of Todd Stottlemyre. Brian Anderson is the team's one relatively young starting pitcher.

Despite the amount of money and prospects expended in assembling the D'backs' bullpen, it's not nearly as good as those of the Marlins or Rockies. It's handicapped by an almost pathological distrust of Byung-Hyun Kim and a neurotic faith in relics like Dan Plesac and Mike Morgan.

The offense is the oldest in the league, now that the Cubs have started rebuilding, and it's closer to becoming the league's worst than suddenly becoming adequate. It's also where the priorities of Buck Showalter, Jerry Colangelo, and, theoretically, Joe Garagiola Jr. have had the greatest impact. Good citizenship abounds. Luis Gonzalez, Matt Williams, Jay Bell, and Steve Finley are all well-regarded as teammates and professionals. They're also all on the wrong side of 33. While the Rockies added Larry Walker and the Marlins added Moises Alou, the Snakes picked up Tony Womack.

This situation isn't all that unfamiliar to Buck Showalter. Looking back on his swan song with the Yankees in 1995, Showalter made it to the playoffs with an ancient, unproductive Don Mattingly and a flaccid Ruben Sierra in the heart of the order. The lineup had only one talented player within a typical career's peak range, Bernie Williams. Showalter might have learned then that older talent is risky; instead, he only seems to have grasped that a combustible bullpen can blow a two-game lead in a best-of-five series.

Still, the Diamondbacks were in first place for most of the season, so they had to be doing something right, didn't they? They were 33–19 at the end of May, four games up on the Rockies and seven ahead of the Giants. They'd also had the benefit of two series apiece against the Phillies, Pirates, and Brewers, and three series against the last-place Padres. Playing more than half of your games against last-place clubs is an easy way to make your team look good over a short stretch, and the Snakes ran up a 21–7 record against the league's lightweights in the first two months. The quick start against crummy teams created extra drama when the Snakes played .500 ball in June, July, and August while the Giants were posting a blistering 59–27 record over the last three months.

The Snakes had a critical pair of problems: the pitching and the hitting. First, Showalter ran his pitching staff in the early months as if there were no tomorrows. By the end of May, the Big Unit had tossed nearly 100 innings. You might argue that the only way the Snakes were going to win was by putting Randy Johnson on a pace for a career high for starts and innings pitched in the early going, but with four months to go and the schedule only getting tougher, it was a miscalculation.

Less explicable was Omar Daal. Daal went from being one of the league's best starters in 1999 to a 5.30 ERA during the first two months of 2000. Then he plunged into an abyss only Micah Bowie might appreciate before being consigned to the depths of professional hell: Philadelphia. The attempt to get value out of Todd Stottlemyre's "damaged desperado" routine was a season-long problem that only put a heavier burden on a bullpen already saddled with unrealistic expectations for Matt Mantei and an inclination to overreact whenever Byung-Hyun Kim gave up a run.

The offense was the bigger problem. The Snakes never had a month in which they posted a significantly better-than-league OBP. They failed to get good offensive contributions from the positions usually stocked with a team's best hitters, first base and right field.

Those twin weaknesses were the product of the organization's $10 million gamble on Travis Lee. If Lee had flopped from the outset of his big-league career, the Snakes would at least have been able to go shopping. Instead, the worst thing happened: Lee started well enough for a player with very little experience above A ball, only to lose ground in each of the next two seasons. In this, Lee was similar to other hitters who shot up to the majors without enough Double-A or Triple-A experience, people like Jon Nunnally and Mike Caruso.

Already hampered by Erubiel Durazo's bum wrist, the Snakes ended up undercompensating at first base and right field with temps like Greg Colbrunn and Danny Bautista. So while players like Steve Finley and Luis Gonzalez and even Jay Bell had solid seasons by their own standards, the Snakes spent the entire year coming to terms with the failure of the Travis Lee experiment, leaving them weak at two lineup positions.

All of these disappointments after the success of 1999 had the Colangelistas in the front office smelling blood. Because Showalter had a tremendous amount of authority within the organization, there was a rush among the front office staffers who have helped to foster the Colangelo management myth to single out Showalter for the team's problems. The distance between expectations and reality were highlighted by Colangelo's claim that he considered firing Showalter in July, when the Diamondbacks were in first place.

Certainly Showalter deserves blame for being the architect of a team that was not going to sustain the limited success of 1999. But the trouble is that the people who believe in that vision, the vision of the Snakes spending big money and winning big, are still in the organization after spending the last four months of the season undermining and excommunicating their fearless leader.

They're already cranking up a propaganda campaign that tries to suck you into the idea that everything will be fine now that Buck the Evil One has been banned from the magic kingdom. You're supposed to believe that unheralded genius Joe Garagiola Jr. is going to rock the house. Then Joe G. Jr. opens his mouth and out comes "Tony Womack is going to be like Rickey Henderson." If you're a Snakes fan, pray it's just propaganda and not a heartfelt belief. Bob Brenly might be an affable guy, but the self-appointed acolytes of the Colangelo myth will betray the next man who fails to live up to their unrealistic expectations.

Addiction to your own publicity is an adaptive dead end—baseball as a big-budget mishmash of pre-packaged pizzazz lacking organizational substance. Think "Lethal Weapon 4" in doubleknits. Bud Selig is currently griping to Congress that the difference between the Yankee dynasties of yesteryear and the Yankee dynasty of the present is the difference between quality management and big money. According to the czar, the objective of rationalizing the game's economics is to make quality management the critical difference between winners and losers.

For teams like the Diamondbacks, who can go only as far as the money they blow (or borrow against future television revenues) can take them, that presents a very grim future. This organization can't survive on its wits alone. The Diamondbacks are what you get when you let a bunch of advertising executives take over a team. They sign players they've heard of. Rather than come to terms with the organizational problem, the Snakes are trying to solve their offensive problems by signing a hitter old enough to make the other old men feel young: Mark Grace. On being named manager, Bob Brenly announced his faith that the Snakes' roster matched up with that of any playoff team. He's angling to be the perfect spokesman of a shared delusion that this team is going to be bigger and better than ever.

Having promised winning now and winning often, the Snakes have fallen on their collective forked tongues. Even assuming they recognize the problem in 2001, they can just rebuild, right? Yes, but only in the same way the Orioles are rebuilding, which is by shopping for other people's talent if they want to help themselves inside of five years.

Right now, they aren't developing any talent of their own. The Diamondbacks' minor-league rosters read like a strange shopping list of randomly identified skills. They've got a pile of pitchers who have just had Tommy John surgery and a pile of big third basemen who throw hard and strike out a ton. They've got shortstops who don't hit while committing tons of errors. They've got two kinds of outfielders: guys who can run and guys who can throw, but none of them hit unless you consider born-DH Jack Cust an outfielder. Effectively, there is no homegrown talent, and there has been no effort to acquire or develop other people's talent. Considering the casual stupidity reflected in the decision to discard Jackie Rexrode, there is no sign that the organization can even identify minor-league talent.

HITTERS (BA: .270, OBP: .340, SLG: .440, EqA: .260)

Rod Barajas — C — Bats R — Age 25

YEAR	TEAM	LGE	AB	H	DB	TP	HR	BB	SO	R	RBI	SB	CS	OUT	BA	OBP	SLG	EQA	EQR	DEFENSE		
1998	High Des	Cal	436	104	14	0	16	15	83	44	51	0	0	332	.239	.270	.381	.212	34	93-C	-6		
1999	El Paso	Tex	499	127	28	1	10	16	79	54	64	1	0	372	.255	.285	.375	.217	41	107-C	-4		
2000	Tucson	PCL	412	83	15	0	12	7	66	32	58	3	2	331	.201	.221	.325	.168	19	84-C	2	12-1B	-1
2001	Arizona	NL	405	99	14	0	15	22	71	38	51	2	1	307	.244	.283	.390	.223	36				

There's a difference between feeling good that an undrafted free agent got this far and thinking he's a prospect. If the Snakes had a great catcher, or if Brad Cresse turns into one, Rod Barajas would be an adequate backup. Right now, the Snakes have an adequate catching tandem. Stinnett is now a Red, so Barajas gets first crack at backing up Miller.

Danny Bautista — OF — Bats R — Age 29

YEAR	TEAM	LGE	AB	H	DB	TP	HR	BB	SO	R	RBI	SB	CS	OUT	BA	OBP	SLG	EQA	EQR	DEFENSE	
1998	Atlanta	NL	145	37	8	0	4	7	20	17	18	1	0	108	.255	.289	.393	.226	13	30-LF	-5
1999	Calgary	PCL	131	33	4	1	5	8	18	16	18	2	2	100	.252	.298	.412	.232	13	36-CF	2
1999	Florida	NL	207	60	10	1	5	1	28	31	23	2	0	147	.290	.297	.420	.236	20	53-OF	5
2000	Florida	NL	90	18	3	0	4	4	19	9	11	1	0	72	.200	.234	.367	.193	6	21-LF	1
2000	Arizona	NL	263	81	16	6	7	16	28	42	44	4	2	184	.308	.354	.494	.278	38	66-RF	-1
2001	Arizona	NL	261	75	13	2	9	16	37	36	42	4	1	187	.287	.329	.456	.262	33		

(Danny Bautista *continued*)

After coming over in exchange for Andy Fox, it was almost as if a switch was flipped and Danny Bautista finally sorted out how to lay off of the low outside pitch once in a while, which led to good things. But even an improved Bautista is just a better version of what he's been: a nice platoon partner and defensive replacement for somebody like Ryan Klesko and now maybe Jack Cust.

Jay Bell — 2B — Bats R — Age 35

YEAR	TEAM	LGE	AB	H	DB	TP	HR	BB	SO	R	RBI	SB	CS	OUT	BA	OBP	SLG	EQA	EQR	DEFENSE			
1998	Arizona	NL	556	138	27	5	21	78	121	80	66	3	5	423	.248	.347	.428	.259	72	133-SS	2	14-2B	0
1999	Arizona	NL	589	163	32	5	36	73	125	124	101	5	4	430	.277	.360	.531	.288	96	148-2B	-13		
2000	Arizona	NL	569	149	30	5	17	61	82	82	63	6	3	423	.262	.336	.422	.254	69	141-2B	-4		
2001	Arizona	NL	490	128	25	2	21	72	91	79	85	4	2	364	.261	.356	.449	.272	70				

How many incarnations does Jay Bell get? A first-round pick by the Twins in 1984, he was traded to the Tribe for Bert Blyleven and debuted at 20 as one of the lesser lights in the failed Indians rebuilding effort that featured Cory Snyder and Joey (not yet Albert) Belle. Traded to the Pirates for Felix Fermin, he became the bunting fiend of the Bonds/Bonilla/Van Slyke Pirates. Finally left alone, he plugged along as a power-hitting shortstop, until he had his tremendous 1997 season with the Royals, then topped that with an even better 1999. His defensive reputation has gone from excellent to awful to good to second base. That projection looks high, but Bell has routinely surprised us.

Jeff Brooks — 3B/1B — Bats R — Age 21

YEAR	TEAM	LGE	AB	H	DB	TP	HR	BB	SO	R	RBI	SB	CS	OUT	BA	OBP	SLG	EQA	EQR	DEFENSE			
1998	Lethbrid	Pio	241	49	9	0	1	11	61	19	21	0	0	192	.203	.244	.253	.148	8	64-3B	-9		
1999	Missoula	Pio	288	71	12	1	7	8	89	25	30	2	1	218	.247	.271	.368	.208	22	68-3B	-19		
2000	High Des	Cal	504	105	24	2	7	9	122	43	51	2	1	401	.208	.227	.306	.162	21	83-3B	-25	19-1B	0
2001	Arizona	NL	366	87	20	1	6	13	100	29	34	1	1	280	.238	.264	.347	.199	25				

A third-round pick in 1997, Jeff Brooks is typical of a system that doesn't convert tools into skills. He's big, strong, and throws hard, and if you wanted only somebody who looked like he could play, Brooks would be your All-Star. After three years as a professional, Brooks has no idea what he's doing at the plate or in the field, and that strong arm only intimidates the folks sitting along the first-base line. Jeff Brooks makes Josh Booty look like a Hall of Famer.

Alex Cabrera — 1B — Bats R — Age 29

YEAR	TEAM	LGE	AB	H	DB	TP	HR	BB	SO	R	RBI	SB	CS	OUT	BA	OBP	SLG	EQA	EQR	DEFENSE	
2000	El Paso	Tex	205	57	13	1	17	16	59	31	40	1	1	149	.278	.333	.600	.292	34	52-1B	3
2000	Tucson	PCL	77	18	4	1	2	3	21	12	7	0	0	59	.234	.275	.390	.217	6		
2000	Arizona	NL	81	21	2	1	5	2	20	10	13	0	0	60	.259	.285	.494	.250	9	12-1B	1
2001	Arizona	NL	183	52	8	1	19	15	75	29	49	0	0	131	.284	.338	.650	.308	34		

Cut by the Cubs in 1996, Alex Cabrera spent the next two years in Mexico and 1999 in Taiwan. He's another rabbit pulled out of scout Junior Noboa's hat. Cabrera was signed as roster filler and surprised everybody by smacking 39 taters in 74 games in the minors. He swings from a Julio Franco stance in which he keeps the bat wrapped around his head, but without Franco's tremendous bat speed he merely kills junk. I'm not sold on his being more than a part-timer and platoon partner. Sold to Japan.

Alex Cintron — SS — Bats B — Age 22

YEAR	TEAM	LGE	AB	H	DB	TP	HR	BB	SO	R	RBI	SB	CS	OUT	BA	OBP	SLG	EQA	EQR	DEFENSE	
1998	Lethbrid	Pio	256	53	8	2	2	7	38	22	18	3	2	205	.207	.230	.277	.152	9	64-SS	-2
1999	High Des	Cal	484	116	18	2	2	9	68	49	40	6	3	371	.240	.256	.298	.175	24	120-SS	-12
2000	El Paso	Tex	513	126	25	3	3	16	59	59	40	4	4	391	.246	.270	.324	.191	31	124-SS	-20
2001	Arizona	NL	401	102	19	1	2	16	53	34	34	4	3	302	.254	.283	.322	.200	27		

Alex Cintron has yet to hit well enough to deserve a prospect label, despite being hailed as the organization's shortstop of the future. He's a contact hitter with no speed and little power. Although credited as having good defensive tools, he's been accused of spacing out in the field. At best, he was able to hold his own (at least by his standards) as a very young player making the jump to Double-A.

J.D. Closser — C — Bats B — Age 21

YEAR	TEAM	LGE	AB	H	DB	TP	HR	BB	SO	R	RBI	SB	CS	OUT	BA	OBP	SLG	EQA	EQR	DEFENSE	
1999	Sth Bend	Mid	179	36	3	0	3	24	40	21	19	0	0	143	.201	.297	.268	.192	12	30-C	-8
1999	Missoula	Pio	276	61	10	0	6	45	66	36	26	2	1	216	.221	.332	.322	.228	27	62-C	-6
2000	Sth Bend	Mid	346	68	14	1	7	42	67	41	28	2	1	279	.197	.286	.303	.198	24	71-C	-10
2001	Arizona	NL	340	78	11	0	10	54	76	46	43	3	1	263	.229	.335	.350	.239	37		

J.D. Closser's receiving skills need to improve to compensate for his weak arm, but he's young enough to learn in plenty of time for his hitting to gel. He's already a patient hitter with good power. While he struggled this year, he was young for the Midwest League. The selection of Brad Cresse in the 2000 draft means that Closser will get plenty of time to develop. If he makes the improvements he needs, he'll be one of the best catching prospects in baseball in two years.

Greg Colbrunn — 1B/PH — Bats R — Age 31

YEAR	TEAM	LGE	AB	H	DB	TP	HR	BB	SO	R	RBI	SB	CS	OUT	BA	OBP	SLG	EQA	EQR	DEFENSE	
1998	Colorado	NL	120	33	7	2	2	7	22	11	11	2	3	90	.275	.320	.417	.239	13	25-1B	1
1998	Atlanta	NL	45	14	3	0	1	1	10	6	10	1	0	31	.311	.365	.444	.275	6		
1999	Arizona	NL	135	42	4	3	5	10	22	19	22	1	1	94	.311	.375	.496	.287	21	27-1B	0
2000	Arizona	NL	331	101	22	1	14	37	42	46	53	0	1	231	.305	.389	.505	.295	55	82-1B	-1
2001	Arizona	NL	274	85	15	2	11	32	40	47	55	2	2	191	.310	.382	.500	.293	44		

Handed the starter's job in August out of desperation, Greg Colbrunn had a tremendous month (.425/.466/.688), only to revert to a more typical .245/.331/.425 in September. Colbrunn will man third base or an outfield corner or even catch in an emergency, so as pinch-hitters go, he's handy. When Bob Brenly played, he was asked to play both infield corners when he wasn't catching, so I wouldn't be surprised if Brenly used Colbrunn a little more aggressively.

Jason Conti — OF — Bats L — Age 26

YEAR	TEAM	LGE	AB	H	DB	TP	HR	BB	SO	R	RBI	SB	CS	OUT	BA	OBP	SLG	EQA	EQR	DEFENSE	
1998	Tulsa	Tex	527	135	24	6	11	46	106	86	45	10	7	399	.256	.322	.387	.238	55	110-LF	8
1999	Tucson	PCL	509	123	18	5	7	45	86	73	42	14	5	391	.242	.307	.338	.221	45	126-CF	2
2000	Tucson	PCL	375	97	15	3	9	15	58	53	41	6	2	280	.259	.294	.387	.226	34	90-CF	-11
2000	Arizona	NL	92	21	4	3	1	5	28	11	14	3	0	71	.228	.274	.370	.218	8	24-RF	2
2001	Arizona	NL	379	95	17	3	7	30	73	47	42	11	3	287	.251	.306	.367	.231	37		

Jason Conti is cast from the Mike Kingery mold. He has a strong, accurate arm, isn't really cut out for center field, but doesn't seem to hit well enough to be a regular in one of the corners. What you don't see is that he played a good chunk of 1999 with a hamate bone injury, then rushed back after having it operated on in March 2000. Conti is a good bet to outhit that projection, and with the defense, he should be the team's best option as a reserve outfielder.

Craig Counsell — 2B/3B — Bats L — Age 30

YEAR	TEAM	LGE	AB	H	DB	TP	HR	BB	SO	R	RBI	SB	CS	OUT	BA	OBP	SLG	EQA	EQR	DEFENSE			
1998	Florida	NL	342	88	19	5	5	50	44	45	42	3	0	254	.257	.358	.386	.257	43	100-2B	9		
1999	Florida	NL	67	11	1	0	0	4	9	4	2	0	0	56	.164	.211	.179	.044	0	10-2B	-1		
1999	LosAngls	NL	109	28	7	0	0	8	13	21	9	1	0	81	.257	.308	.321	.213	8	27-2B	1		
2000	Tucson	PCL	192	52	8	2	2	16	22	29	17	2	1	141	.271	.329	.365	.235	19	18-3B	0	18-2B	-1
2000	Arizona	NL	153	47	7	1	2	17	17	22	10	3	3	109	.307	.383	.405	.267	20	17-2B	0	13-3B	4
2001	Arizona	NL	300	81	14	1	3	38	37	46	35	6	2	221	.270	.352	.353	.248	34				

Here is a good example of the kind of useful player you can get on waivers. If not for the beaning that ended his 1998, Craig Counsell would have had reasonable expectations of making Mickey Morandini money, which is as indicative of Morandini's good luck as it is of Counsell's bad break. He needs only to play for the Devil Rays to complete his circuit of baseball's teal-and-purple '90s expansion set.

Brad Cresse — C — Bats R — Age 22

YEAR	TEAM	LGE	AB	H	DB	TP	HR	BB	SO	R	RBI	SB	CS	OUT	BA	OBP	SLG	EQA	EQR	DEFENSE	
2000	High Des	Cal	170	42	3	0	11	10	52	22	31	0	0	128	.247	.302	.459	.248	20	36-C	-9
2000	El Paso	Tex	42	9	0	0	1	4	13	6	7	0	0	33	.214	.308	.286	.203	3		
2001	Arizona	NL	108	27	3	0	8	9	48	13	21	0	0	81	.250	.308	.500	.263	14		

He led the NCAA in home runs and RBI at LSU before getting picked in the fifth round in June. Brad Cresse is being hailed as the new Mike Piazza by a franchise desperate for a minor-league hero. Skip Bertman didn't let Cresse call games in college, but Ron Hassey has been working with him on his game-calling and his throwing. At the plate, Cresse uppercuts everything while still hacking at outside breaking stuff. He struggled in the Arizona Fall League, which puts a crimp in his shot at arriving by the end of 2001.

Jack Cust — DH — Bats L — Age 22

YEAR	TEAM	LGE	AB	H	DB	TP	HR	BB	SO	R	RBI	SB	CS	OUT	BA	OBP	SLG	EQA	EQR	DEFENSE	
1998	Lethbrid	Pio	218	48	11	1	5	53	84	34	23	5	4	174	.220	.376	.349	.255	29	51-LF	0
1998	Sth Bend	Mid	63	14	2	0	0	4	21	4	3	0	0	49	.222	.269	.254	.164	3	15-1B	-1
1999	High Des	Cal	442	104	23	1	19	66	151	62	59	0	1	340	.235	.336	.421	.253	55	97-LF	-16
2000	El Paso	Tex	443	98	23	3	13	87	158	68	46	6	4	349	.221	.350	.375	.250	54	123-LF	-16
2001	Arizona	NL	400	98	19	1	15	73	150	67	63	3	2	304	.245	.362	.410	.265	55		

Jack Cust is almost the only prospect in the Snakes' organization who isn't some leftover from the set of *Baywatch*. Other than his awful defense, comparisons to Ryan Klesko don't work: Cust doesn't have Klesko's power and he's significantly more patient. Like Klesko, he'll probably end up platooning; at El Paso, his OPS pushed 1100 against right-handed pitchers while being below 700 against left-handers. He slumped terribly in the second half, fueling organizational complaints that he's too passive at the plate.

David Dellucci — OF — Bats L — Age 27

YEAR	TEAM	LGE	AB	H	DB	TP	HR	BB	SO	R	RBI	SB	CS	OUT	BA	OBP	SLG	EQA	EQR	DEFENSE	
1998	Arizona	NL	420	108	19	11	6	31	96	44	50	3	5	317	.257	.312	.398	.234	42	103-LF	4
1999	Arizona	NL	108	41	6	1	1	10	23	26	14	2	0	67	.380	.446	.481	.319	19	22-RF	-1
2000	Tucson	PCL	121	24	6	2	2	9	16	11	12	2	0	97	.198	.254	.331	.193	8	27-RF	-2
2000	Arizona	NL	50	14	3	0	0	4	8	2	2	0	2	38	.280	.333	.340	.216	4		
2001	Arizona	NL	211	55	10	3	4	21	39	28	28	3	2	158	.261	.328	.393	.244	23		

After surgery on his left wrist to correct a rare condition ended his 1999 season, David Dellucci struggled with a broken finger and tendinitis in his hand in 2000. Almost anything that gets written about him is going to be prefaced by some sort of discussion of the tragedy that a guy hitting almost .400 went down with an injury. Not to kick a guy while he's down, but Dellucci's track record makes it pretty clear that 1999 was a fluke. He will have to fight for a bench job.

Erubiel Durazo — 1B — Bats L — Age 27

YEAR	TEAM	LGE	AB	H	DB	TP	HR	BB	SO	R	RBI	SB	CS	OUT	BA	OBP	SLG	EQA	EQR	DEFENSE	
1998	MNT	Mex	410	103	16	1	14	62	0	0	0	3	2	309	.251	.350	.398	.256	51		
1999	El Paso	Tex	220	64	12	1	8	31	42	34	31	1	0	156	.291	.381	.464	.284	34	60-1B	-7
1999	Tucson	PCL	113	38	5	0	7	12	17	20	19	1	0	75	.336	.403	.566	.316	21	29-1B	0
1999	Arizona	NL	155	49	4	2	10	23	41	29	27	1	1	107	.316	.408	.561	.314	30	41-1B	2
2000	Arizona	NL	197	51	9	0	8	31	40	33	31	1	0	146	.259	.362	.426	.268	27	52-1B	-3
2001	Arizona	NL	279	83	9	0	16	46	50	51	61	1	0	196	.297	.397	.502	.302	49		

Unfortunately, being good enough to run off Travis Lee has not cemented a job for Erubiel Durazo as much as it created a sense that first base is up for grabs. He really should be this team's regular at first base if he's 100% in the spring, but injuries have become an issue: he hurt his back during the winter of 1999, then made three trips to the DL because of wrist problems before undergoing season-ending surgery in August. The signing of Mark Grace cuts off his path to a job.

National League

Steve Finley — CF — Bats L — Age 36

YEAR	TEAM	LGE	AB	H	DB	TP	HR	BB	SO	R	RBI	SB	CS	OUT	BA	OBP	SLG	EQA	EQR	DEFENSE	
1998	San Dieg	NL	631	163	41	6	16	43	96	98	70	12	3	471	.258	.309	.418	.242	68	157-CF	3
1999	Arizona	NL	591	150	31	8	33	55	89	94	93	6	4	445	.254	.320	.501	.265	81	155-CF	6
2000	Arizona	NL	542	147	27	4	33	57	81	94	88	11	6	401	.271	.348	.518	.281	84	144-CF	-1
2001	Arizona	NL	522	134	25	3	26	58	84	79	89	10	3	391	.257	.331	.466	.266	71		

Steve Finley managed to top his impressive 1999 season, but his attempt to play through back pain in September only aggravated a team-wide offensive collapse. It isn't really fair to single out Finley: Jay Bell was worthless in June and July, when the Snakes let the Giants catch them, while Tony Womack was Tony Womack all year. Finley isn't running as much as he used to, but between his commitment to conditioning and the fact that he's still able to play center field, it isn't hard to apply the old Bill James observation that a player with "young players'" skills can retain his value a lot longer than, say, Kevin Maas.

Hanley Frias — IF — Bats B — Age 27

YEAR	TEAM	LGE	AB	H	DB	TP	HR	BB	SO	R	RBI	SB	CS	OUT	BA	OBP	SLG	EQA	EQR	DEFENSE	
1998	Tucson	PCL	249	61	7	3	1	20	40	24	16	11	5	193	.245	.301	.309	.209	19	54-SS	-5
1999	Tucson	PCL	78	20	2	0	0	6	15	11	5	2	1	59	.256	.310	.282	.201	5	14-3B	-3
1999	Arizona	NL	150	39	3	2	1	26	17	25	15	3	3	114	.260	.369	.327	.244	17	35-SS	-1
2000	Arizona	NL	113	23	4	0	2	15	17	17	6	2	2	92	.204	.297	.292	.199	8	15-SS	0
2001	Arizona	NL	145	35	4	1	2	19	23	20	15	5	2	112	.241	.329	.324	.230	14		

The man has problems beyond his control. Danny Klassen can hit and handle all three infield positions. Craig Counsell bats left-handed and can play second base or third base. Hanley Frias doesn't do nearly as much, but benefits by meeting lower expectations. With Tony Womack's ability to cover almost any position in a pinch, the Snakes should be assembling a bench with some offensive punch. That would cost Frias his job.

Luis Gonzalez — LF — Bats L — Age 33

YEAR	TEAM	LGE	AB	H	DB	TP	HR	BB	SO	R	RBI	SB	CS	OUT	BA	OBP	SLG	EQA	EQR	DEFENSE	
1998	Detroit	AL	545	148	34	5	25	56	55	84	71	10	6	403	.272	.347	.490	.274	79	111-LF	8
1999	Arizona	NL	613	197	44	3	25	57	59	105	101	6	4	420	.321	.385	.525	.298	102	141-LF	2
2000	Arizona	NL	621	187	42	2	30	68	80	100	105	2	4	438	.301	.379	.520	.293	102	152-LF	-3
2001	Arizona	NL	543	163	34	2	21	60	67	91	102	4	2	382	.300	.370	.486	.286	83		

Last year, we said we wouldn't want to rely on Luis Gonzalez hitting .320 with power again. While the small-minded among us would point out that he didn't hit .320, what he did do was have his first 30-homer season. Although the Snakes make all sorts of mistakes as far as assessing player worth, there is value to being able to identify players who will age well. Like Finley, Gonzalez was pretty fast when he was young and is a good athlete who takes care of himself. Unlike Finley, Gonzo is a good offensive player when he isn't hitting 30 bombs.

Brian Gordon — LF — Bats L — Age 22

YEAR	TEAM	LGE	AB	H	DB	TP	HR	BB	SO	R	RBI	SB	CS	OUT	BA	OBP	SLG	EQA	EQR	DEFENSE	
1998	Sth Bend	Mid	473	114	20	3	7	9	107	36	44	2	2	361	.241	.258	.340	.191	29	99-RF	-6
1999	Sth Bend	Mid	186	37	9	2	0	4	38	15	13	3	2	151	.199	.218	.269	.140	6	38-LF	-3
2000	High Des	Cal	470	112	21	6	9	26	111	61	39	5	5	363	.238	.280	.366	.211	37	114-LF	-9
2001	Arizona	NL	387	96	19	3	8	27	94	44	44	8	3	294	.248	.297	.375	.227	36		

A high-school hitter picked in 1997 who missed most of 1999 with a wrist injury, Brian Gordon finally pushed his walk rate up to a barely-acceptable once every 10 at-bats. Sometimes, high-school hitters figure things out even when they're not in an organization that works on developing patience. Gordon doesn't look like a great bet; he still strikes out a ton and hasn't started hitting yet despite the benefit of playing in great hitters' parks.

Victor Hall — CF — Bats L — Age 20

YEAR	TEAM	LGE	AB	H	DB	TP	HR	BB	SO	R	RBI	SB	CS	OUT	BA	OBP	SLG	EQA	EQR	DEFENSE	
1999	Missoula	Pio	146	32	2	0	0	9	35	12	6	5	3	117	.219	.271	.233	.163	6	34-LF	-1
2000	Sth Bend	Mid	168	35	5	3	2	8	45	14	12	5	3	136	.208	.248	.310	.180	9	39-CF	-7
2000	Missoula	Pio	243	52	6	4	2	49	44	30	13	14	7	198	.214	.350	.296	.233	26	70-CF	-3
2001	Arizona	NL	255	64	5	3	1	36	74	43	22	18	7	198	.251	.344	.306	.235	27		

Among the Diamondbacks' tools goofs, Victor Hall is the one you think just might turn into a ballplayer. He didn't start playing baseball until he was a junior in high school. He's blazing fast, nabbing 47 bags at Missoula, and despite only four years of baseball (not pro baseball, but baseball) experience, he seems to have figured out that walks are good. He could grow up to be Tom Goodwin, which makes him about the third-best Snakes hitting prospect.

Danny Klassen — IF — Bats R — Age 25

YEAR	TEAM	LGE	AB	H	DB	TP	HR	BB	SO	R	RBI	SB	CS	OUT	BA	OBP	SLG	EQA	EQR	DEFENSE			
1998	Tucson	PCL	277	69	19	1	8	15	53	35	35	4	1	209	.249	.297	.412	.235	28	47-SS	-3	21-2B	5
1998	Arizona	NL	109	22	2	1	3	8	31	12	8	1	1	88	.202	.262	.321	.189	7	29-2B	-3		
1999	Tucson	PCL	240	54	14	2	4	17	49	28	24	3	2	188	.225	.278	.350	.207	18	58-SS	3		
2000	Arizona	NL	77	18	2	0	2	7	22	12	7	1	1	60	.234	.305	.338	.215	6	19-3B	2		
2000	Tucson	PCL	100	26	5	1	2	16	23	19	10	1	1	75	.260	.366	.390	.259	13	25-SS	6		
2001	Arizona	NL	218	55	12	1	6	21	53	29	29	4	2	165	.252	.318	.399	.242	24				

Danny Klassen got a shot at platooning with Lenny Harris at third base to open the season, but got hurt in July. Klassen's problem is that the organization already has two good utility infielders in Frias and Counsell. He was all thumbs in the Brewers' organization, but to his credit, a combination of hard work and coaching has turned him into a good infielder.

Damian Miller — C — Bats R — Age 31

YEAR	TEAM	LGE	AB	H	DB	TP	HR	BB	SO	R	RBI	SB	CS	OUT	BA	OBP	SLG	EQA	EQR	DEFENSE	
1998	Arizona	NL	170	48	15	2	3	10	40	18	14	1	0	122	.282	.329	.447	.258	21	44-C	0
1999	Arizona	NL	297	78	14	0	12	15	74	33	44	0	0	219	.263	.302	.431	.241	31	86-C	1
2000	Arizona	NL	326	87	16	0	12	31	69	40	43	2	2	241	.267	.332	.426	.252	38	89-C	5
2001	Arizona	NL	303	83	14	0	11	29	72	41	48	2	1	221	.274	.337	.429	.258	37		

What does Damian Miller have to do to get respect? He threw out 40% of basestealers, has made big strides as a receiver, and can hit enough to be an asset at the bottom of the order. Yet more ink gets shed on guys like Henry Blanco or Joe Girardi, who can't hit and who get granted defensive reputations. Miller isn't an All-Star or even a latter-day Don Slaught; he's just a good catcher, especially for a team spending lots of money in other places.

Lyle Overbay — 1B — Bats L — Age 24

YEAR	TEAM	LGE	AB	H	DB	TP	HR	BB	SO	R	RBI	SB	CS	OUT	BA	OBP	SLG	EQA	EQR	DEFENSE	
1999	Missoula	Pio	302	73	16	2	7	23	61	33	48	3	1	230	.242	.297	.377	.225	28	68-1B	1
2000	Sth Bend	Mid	267	72	13	2	5	17	40	34	32	4	1	196	.270	.316	.390	.237	27	64-1B	-3
2000	El Paso	Tex	238	65	13	1	5	19	41	29	31	1	1	174	.273	.330	.399	.244	26	60-1B	-5
2001	Arizona	NL	313	86	15	1	9	26	58	41	46	3	1	228	.275	.330	.415	.252	36		

The first player to drive in 100 runs in a short-season league, Lyle Overbay moved up to El Paso to replace Alex Cabrera with less than a full professional year under his belt. He's a line-drive hitter and another Snake draftee out of the Big West Conference (Nevada). Overbay looks more like the next Rico Brogna than a prospect.

Ryan Owens — 3B — Bats R — Age 23

YEAR	TEAM	LGE	AB	H	DB	TP	HR	BB	SO	R	RBI	SB	CS	OUT	BA	OBP	SLG	EQA	EQR	DEFENSE			
1999	High Des	Cal	98	28	4	1	3	5	31	11	16	0	1	71	.286	.323	.439	.248	11	21-3B	-6		
1999	El Paso	Tex	111	28	5	0	1	5	39	8	13	0	1	84	.252	.292	.324	.201	8	27-3B	-4		
2000	El Paso	Tex	208	39	6	2	4	14	63	22	17	3	2	171	.188	.243	.293	.170	10	54-3B	-10		
2000	Sth Bend	Mid	282	59	12	0	8	33	84	36	31	6	2	225	.209	.296	.337	.216	24	48-3B	-5	15-2B	-4
2001	Arizona	NL	280	63	9	1	7	28	93	30	29	4	2	219	.225	.295	.339	.216	24				

National League

Ryan Owens was the team's seventh-round pick in 1999 out of Cal State Fullerton. He was rushed to Double-A just as Jeff Brooks was being rushed to High Desert despite never having played above the Pioneer League. Owens played his way down to the Midwest League and continued to struggle while Brooks was terrible all year. How could the organization blow the assignments? Now neither player has even mastered the Cal League, and the organization either needs to sign a minor-league free agent or start one of them at El Paso in 2001. Guess what? Owens has a strong arm.

Mike Rose — C — Bats B — Age 24

YEAR	TEAM	LGE	AB	H	DB	TP	HR	BB	SO	R	RBI	SB	CS	OUT	BA	OBP	SLG	EQA	EQR	DEFENSE
1998	Quad Cit	Mid	280	68	9	1	6	39	60	35	28	4	4	216	.243	.336	.346	.233	28	71-C -7
1999	Kissimme	Fla	313	71	12	1	9	44	74	44	23	5	3	245	.227	.325	.358	.233	32	83-C -6
2000	El Paso	Tex	349	76	14	1	7	49	74	40	40	4	5	278	.218	.315	.324	.217	30	93-C -5
2001	Arizona	NL	359	87	15	1	11	56	85	55	49	7	3	275	.242	.345	.382	.252	44	

Cut loose from the Astros for breaking organization rules repeatedly, Mike Rose isn't considered a top prospect. He's closer to where Kelly Stinnett and Damian Miller were five or six years ago: power and patience, merely adequate defensively. Catchers who can hit a little aren't that rare, except to the teams that have eyes only for the Mike Mathenys of the world. Rose could slip on to the Diamondbacks this year before Cresse arrives.

Rob Ryan — OF — Bats L — Age 28

YEAR	TEAM	LGE	AB	H	DB	TP	HR	BB	SO	R	RBI	SB	CS	OUT	BA	OBP	SLG	EQA	EQR	DEFENSE
1998	Tucson	PCL	388	102	14	1	13	52	60	53	48	6	2	288	.263	.359	.405	.261	50	102-OF -1
1999	Tucson	PCL	406	96	21	3	13	45	69	51	60	3	2	312	.236	.324	.399	.243	45	99-RF -6
2000	Tucson	PCL	326	80	14	1	5	32	38	39	36	1	1	247	.245	.327	.340	.228	31	84-LF -2
2000	Arizona	NL	27	8	0	1	0	4	7	4	2	0	0	19	.296	.403	.370	.273	4	
2001	Arizona	NL	341	88	15	1	8	43	54	47	46	3	1	254	.258	.341	.378	.248	39	

Rob Ryan's window of opportunity outside of Tucson is almost shut. He's no longer young and he's lost ground offensively. If he hits like he could a couple of years ago, he might be able to claim a share of the job in right field, but Jack Cust is almost ready and Luis Gonzalez has two more years on his contract.

Kelly Stinnett — C — Bats R — Age 31

YEAR	TEAM	LGE	AB	H	DB	TP	HR	BB	SO	R	RBI	SB	CS	OUT	BA	OBP	SLG	EQA	EQR	DEFENSE
1998	Arizona	NL	277	71	14	1	11	34	69	36	33	0	1	207	.256	.349	.433	.262	36	79-C 3
1999	Arizona	NL	285	65	10	0	14	20	78	34	35	2	1	221	.228	.290	.411	.231	28	78-C -1
2000	Arizona	NL	242	52	7	0	8	15	52	21	32	0	1	191	.215	.275	.343	.202	17	70-C -1
2001	Cincnnti	NL	270	65	7	0	13	26	70	32	43	0	1	206	.241	.307	.411	.237	28	

Kelly Stinnett's career as a regular is dead, but considering that Jeff Reed is still around, Stinnett should be able to play as long as he wants. He had his best chance at stardom and big money taken from him when the Brewers wasted two years of his career so that they could play Mike Matheny. The Snakes were smart enough to take him on and use what was left of the best years of his career.

Carlos Urquiola — OF — Bats L — Age 21

YEAR	TEAM	LGE	AB	H	DB	TP	HR	BB	SO	R	RBI	SB	CS	OUT	BA	OBP	SLG	EQA	EQR	DEFENSE	
1998	Sth Bend	Mid	169	44	9	2	0	7	16	20	11	3	3	128	.260	.292	.337	.206	12	35-2B -16	
1999	Sth Bend	Mid	383	111	8	1	1	12	35	42	23	8	7	278	.290	.316	.324	.213	29	36-2B -1	28-LF -2
2000	High Des	Cal	161	46	4	1	0	8	17	17	7	7	2	117	.286	.325	.323	.225	14	27-CF -3	
2000	El Paso	Tex	221	54	6	1	0	13	18	22	13	6	4	171	.244	.291	.281	.190	13	39-CF -6	
2001	Arizona	NL	306	89	8	1	0	19	30	38	29	11	7	224	.291	.332	.324	.226	27		

Carlos Urquiola is a poor man's shorter, slower Tony Womack. He's fast enough to leg out choppers for base hits against minor-league shortstops. He should never have been moved off of second base. As an outfielder, he'll never be more than a bit player, while as a second baseman he could have a career. Can nobody in the organization teach a 20-year-old with speed and experience how to improve at second base?

Matt Williams 3B Bats R Age 35

YEAR	TEAM	LGE	AB	H	DB	TP	HR	BB	SO	R	RBI	SB	CS	OUT	BA	OBP	SLG	EQA	EQR	DEFENSE	
1998	Arizona	NL	515	136	21	1	22	41	96	73	71	5	1	380	.264	.322	.437	.252	61	127-3B	10
1999	Arizona	NL	628	184	34	1	34	32	88	93	129	2	0	444	.293	.329	.513	.273	86	153-3B	13
2000	Arizona	NL	374	101	19	2	11	14	48	41	44	1	2	275	.270	.301	.420	.235	37	94-3B	2
2001	Arizona	NL	442	120	21	1	19	30	66	54	72	1	1	323	.271	.318	.452	.255	53		

A broken foot cost Matt Williams the first 43 games of the season, he missed two weeks with a strained quad that never did heal entirely, and he might have surgery on his heel. The accumulated injuries aren't bad luck, they're a reflection of what happens to older players as their careers wind down. What's amazing is that with everything that went wrong, he was still a treat to watch in the field.

Tony Womack SS Bats L Age 31

YEAR	TEAM	LGE	AB	H	DB	TP	HR	BB	SO	R	RBI	SB	CS	OUT	BA	OBP	SLG	EQA	EQR	DEFENSE			
1998	Pittsbrg	NL	661	186	28	7	3	36	88	85	44	54	8	483	.281	.319	.359	.241	69	145-2B	12		
1999	Arizona	NL	615	167	26	9	4	44	64	99	38	55	12	460	.272	.322	.363	.243	67	111-RF	5	15-2B	-2
2000	Arizona	NL	621	164	23	12	7	22	69	89	53	40	11	468	.264	.294	.374	.229	59	143-SS	-12		
2001	Arizona	NL	579	158	19	8	4	42	70	95	55	50	11	432	.273	.322	.354	.242	62				

As a child, I might have believed that Tony Womack was a great leadoff man, but I learned to be skeptical at an early age. It was probably because I noticed that Cookie Monster never eats the cookies, despite making a lot of noise and carrying on.

Tony Womack doesn't eat the cookies. He's as fun to watch as any Muppet; base-path commandos usually are. But the real world isn't *Sesame Street* and Tony Womack's core skill is the ability to flirt with 500 outs. When the Snakes figure that out, they'll be on the road to adulthood. Then they can wonder what it means that Ernie and Bert have been living together for 30 years, and Ernie just lays around the house all day, taking baths and worrying about making the place nice for Bert.

PITCHERS (ERA: 4.50, H/9: 9.00, HR/9: 1.00, BB/9: 3.00, K/9: 6.00, KW: 1.00, PERA: 4.50)

Brian Anderson Throws L Age 29

YEAR	TEAM	LGE	IP	H	ER	HR	BB	K	ERA	W	L	H/9	HR/9	BB/9	K/9	KW	PERA
1998	Arizona	NL	198.0	210	103	38	21	77	4.68	9	13	9.55	1.73	0.95	3.50	1.83	4.74
1999	Arizona	NL	126.0	136	62	16	23	63	4.43	6	8	9.71	1.14	1.64	4.50	1.37	4.52
2000	Arizona	NL	205.7	213	91	34	32	87	3.98	12	11	9.32	1.49	1.40	3.81	1.36	4.54

Brian Anderson is an example of how a pitcher who's hittable and homer prone can do everything else well enough to make himself a fine third starter. In addition to the outstanding control, he's got a great pickoff move and can handle the bat well enough to help himself. His career isn't about to reach critical mass and turn him into a star; he's just a guy who locates pitches and changes speeds so well that he'll be a very good third starter.

Nick Bierbrodt Throws L Age 23

YEAR	TEAM	LGE	IP	H	ER	HR	BB	K	ERA	W	L	H/9	HR/9	BB/9	K/9	KW	PERA
1998	High Des	Cal	123.3	117	62	11	66	46	4.52	6	8	8.54	0.80	4.82	3.36	0.35	4.76
1999	El Paso	Tex	73.0	75	42	3	37	35	5.18	3	5	9.25	0.37	4.56	4.32	0.47	4.63
1999	Tucson	PCL	42.0	54	39	9	30	29	8.36	1	4	11.57	1.93	6.43	6.21	0.48	8.43
2000	El Paso	Tex	33.7	37	28	1	22	22	7.49	1	3	9.89	0.27	5.88	5.88	0.50	5.42
2000	Tucson	PCL	18.0	12	9	3	13	8	4.50	1	1	6.00	1.50	6.50	4.00	0.31	4.69

The question of whether Nick Bierbrodt will develop into a prospect has been put off again. He missed a good part of 1999 with elbow problems, a strained back cost him almost three months during 2000, and he went down with a tender elbow during winter ball. Assuming he can pitch, he would be in the mix for the fifth spot in the rotation. He's got a good sinker he can get into the mid-90s, with a good curve and change-up.

National League

Chris Capuano — Throws L — Age 22

YEAR	TEAM	LGE	IP	H	ER	HR	BB	K	ERA	W	L	H/9	HR/9	BB/9	K/9	KW	PERA
2000	Sth Bend	Mid	92.7	74	42	5	51	56	4.08	5	5	7.19	0.49	4.95	5.44	0.55	3.73

An eighth-round pick out of Duke in 1999, Chris Capuano waited until he finished up his B.A. to make his pro debut. His velocity flirts with the low 90s, a slight improvement from college, and Capuano supports that with a good curve and change-up. His best weapon is his delivery, as he hides the ball well. If his strikeout rate improves as he advances, he's an A-ball pitcher worth remembering.

Chris Cervantes — Throws L — Age 22

YEAR	TEAM	LGE	IP	H	ER	HR	BB	K	ERA	W	L	H/9	HR/9	BB/9	K/9	KW	PERA
1998	Sth Bend	Mid	31.3	30	8	0	8	19	2.30	2	1	8.62	0.00	2.30	5.46	1.19	3.06
1999	Sth Bend	Mid	106.0	113	59	20	39	47	5.01	5	7	9.59	1.70	3.31	3.99	0.60	5.72
2000	Sth Bend	Mid	54.0	67	36	7	13	29	6.00	2	4	11.17	1.17	2.17	4.83	1.12	5.61
2000	El Paso	Tex	90.0	106	50	16	19	45	5.00	4	6	10.60	1.60	1.90	4.50	1.18	5.62

He gets compared to Brian Anderson because his out pitch is his change-up and he doesn't walk anybody. Left-handed minor-league control fiends aren't extremely successful as a group; Chris Cervantes is young enough to avoid becoming Terry Burrows. He was supposed to strut his stuff in the Arizona Fall League, but was hampered by a bad knee.

Geraldo Guzman — Throws R — Age 28

YEAR	TEAM	LGE	IP	H	ER	HR	BB	K	ERA	W	L	H/9	HR/9	BB/9	K/9	KW	PERA
2000	El Paso	Tex	47.0	48	25	3	23	30	4.79	2	3	9.19	0.57	4.40	5.74	0.65	4.76
2000	Tucson	PCL	36.0	24	7	3	10	30	1.75	3	1	6.00	0.75	2.50	7.50	1.50	2.48
2000	Arizona	NL	58.7	64	33	7	18	43	5.06	3	4	9.82	1.07	2.76	6.60	1.19	4.95

Cut from the Expos organization in 1991, Geraldo Guzman spent seven years as a carpenter before Junior Noboa rediscovered him. A shortage of work visas forced the Snakes to put him in Taiwan in 1999, but once he reappeared stateside we all got to see a guy who throws in the high 90s with a sweet slider. Guzman was unfairly compared to Jim Morris of the D-Rays. He isn't a publicity stunt and should be given every opportunity to win the open fifth slot in the rotation.

Darren Holmes — Throws R — Age 35

YEAR	TEAM	LGE	IP	H	ER	HR	BB	K	ERA	W	L	H/9	HR/9	BB/9	K/9	KW	PERA
1998	NY Yanks	AL	50.0	49	17	4	12	29	3.06	4	2	8.82	0.72	2.16	5.22	1.21	3.76
1999	Arizona	NL	47.7	48	19	3	20	29	3.59	3	2	9.06	0.57	3.78	5.48	0.73	4.38
2000	Arizona	NL	6.3	12	6	1	1	4	8.53	0	1	17.05	1.42	1.42	5.68	2.00	9.25
2000	Memphis	PCL	14.0	9	3	0	3	5	1.93	2	0	5.79	0.00	1.93	3.21	0.83	1.62
2000	St Louis	NL	8.0	11	8	2	2	4	9.00	0	1	12.38	2.25	2.25	4.50	1.00	7.34
2000	Baltimor	AL	5.0	12	11	3	4	6	19.80	0	1	21.60	5.40	7.20	10.80	0.75	18.24

His best shot at coming back from last season's waive-a-whirl is to somehow convince the Devil Rays that he's about to set the saves record. Or that he's unique because he can do that Dr. McCoy thing with his eyebrows. Or maybe just that he can juggle. Darren Holmes will not have to pitch for food.

Randy Johnson — Throws L — Age 37

YEAR	TEAM	LGE	IP	H	ER	HR	BB	K	ERA	W	L	H/9	HR/9	BB/9	K/9	KW	PERA
1998	Seattle	AL	158.0	140	82	17	52	197	4.67	8	10	7.97	0.97	2.96	11.22	1.89	3.86
1998	Houston	NL	80.3	59	13	4	25	94	1.46	8	1	6.61	0.45	2.80	10.53	1.88	2.61
1999	Arizona	NL	263.3	207	83	27	57	306	2.84	19	10	7.07	0.92	1.95	10.46	2.68	2.95
2000	Arizona	NL	241.0	207	88	20	62	289	3.29	16	11	7.73	0.75	2.32	10.79	2.33	3.27

Because he tossed 95⅔ innings in the first two months of the season, it wasn't a surprise when Randy Johnson started complaining that he wasn't bouncing back physically between starts. The Big Unit was downright mortal over the last three months, giving up 61 runs in 117 innings, but don't expect him to mail his Cy Young Award to Kevin Brown. Towards season's end, rumors were circulating that Johnson was tipping his pitches. Because he wasn't himself in the second half, we might be able to write off that talk as just another bit of Bobby Valentine bluster.

Byung-Hyun Kim — Throws R — Age 22

YEAR	TEAM	LGE	IP	H	ER	HR	BB	K	ERA	W	L	H/9	HR/9	BB/9	K/9	KW	PERA
1999	El Paso	Tex	20.0	8	8	1	9	21	3.60	1	1	3.60	0.45	4.05	9.45	1.17	1.68
1999	Tucson	PCL	28.7	21	9	2	15	27	2.83	2	1	6.59	0.63	4.71	8.48	0.90	3.46
1999	Arizona	NL	27.0	20	13	2	16	26	4.33	1	2	6.67	0.67	5.33	8.67	0.81	3.74
2000	Arizona	NL	69.7	56	38	8	38	92	4.91	3	5	7.23	1.03	4.91	11.89	1.21	4.30

Byung-Hyun Kim seems to have a strange relationship with the organization; they lose confidence in him anytime he has a bad week. One sign of a bad organization is when they project their lack of confidence onto a pitcher and use it as a reason to demote him; Kim felt he was fine, but the Snakes were busy panicking at the end of July and sent him to Tucson. What makes Kim effective isn't his good heat, it's the slider coming out of his sidearm motion. Left alone, he should become even more dominant.

Mike Koplove — Throws R — Age 24

YEAR	TEAM	LGE	IP	H	ER	HR	BB	K	ERA	W	L	H/9	HR/9	BB/9	K/9	KW	PERA
1998	Lethbrid	Pio	22.7	24	15	5	3	11	5.96	1	2	9.53	1.99	1.19	4.37	1.83	5.10
1999	Sth Bend	Mid	76.3	77	30	11	34	51	3.54	4	4	9.08	1.30	4.01	6.01	0.75	5.28
2000	High Des	Cal	23.7	15	4	0	10	15	1.52	3	0	5.70	0.00	3.80	5.70	0.75	2.16
2000	El Paso	Tex	43.7	39	30	3	18	28	6.18	1	4	8.04	0.62	3.71	5.77	0.78	3.85

If there's one neat thing about the Snakes' organization, it's that they love sidearmers. Mike Koplove rarely tops 90 mph and has a slider, so throwing sidearm is a sensible adaptive choice. I don't know if you could build a good major-league bullpen with too many sidearmers; it has long been assumed that one of their assets is the difference between them and almost everyone else. Koplove had a very good AFL campaign, so he might get fast-tracked.

Matt Mantei — Throws R — Age 27

YEAR	TEAM	LGE	IP	H	ER	HR	BB	K	ERA	W	L	H/9	HR/9	BB/9	K/9	KW	PERA
1998	Florida	NL	52.3	38	19	1	22	51	3.27	4	2	6.54	0.17	3.78	8.77	1.16	2.68
1999	Florida	NL	35.7	25	11	4	22	42	2.78	3	1	6.31	1.01	5.55	10.60	0.95	4.01
1999	Arizona	NL	28.7	22	10	1	16	41	3.14	2	1	6.91	0.31	5.02	12.87	1.28	3.48
2000	Arizona	NL	45.0	32	23	4	29	44	4.60	2	3	6.40	0.80	5.80	8.80	0.76	3.95

Because of his awful first half, Matt Mantei spent much of the season being second-guessed and accused of overthinking on the mound. By August, he had junked his curve and was bumping a slider from the project stage to his second pitch. He's still pumping gas up around 98 mph but is too wild to be the kind of closer the Snakes pretended he was when they gave up three top prospects to get him.

Jason Martines — Throws R — Age 25

YEAR	TEAM	LGE	IP	H	ER	HR	BB	K	ERA	W	L	H/9	HR/9	BB/9	K/9	KW	PERA
1998	Sth Bend	Mid	30.0	34	19	3	20	15	5.70	1	2	10.20	0.90	6.00	4.50	0.38	6.38
1999	High Des	Cal	67.3	68	34	7	30	37	4.54	3	4	9.09	0.94	4.01	4.95	0.62	4.90
2000	El Paso	Tex	81.0	72	33	4	27	44	3.67	5	4	8.00	0.44	3.00	4.89	0.81	3.38

Another of the organization's sidearmers. Like most of the type, Jason Martines doesn't throw hard, relying on a sinker/slider combo. He doesn't get hit hard very often, and unlike a lot of right-handed sidearmers, he was tough on left-handed hitters, limiting them to a .221 average. He may know his limitations: he walked twice as many lefties as righties in half as many plate appearances. An 11th pitcher in the making.

Mike McCutcheon — Throws L — Age 23

YEAR	TEAM	LGE	IP	H	ER	HR	BB	K	ERA	W	L	H/9	HR/9	BB/9	K/9	KW	PERA
1998	Lethbrid	Pio	52.3	63	43	9	37	20	7.39	1	5	10.83	1.55	6.36	3.44	0.27	7.55
1998	Sth Bend	Mid	45.0	52	32	5	28	16	6.40	1	4	10.40	1.00	5.60	3.20	0.29	6.41
1999	Sth Bend	Mid	81.0	88	54	11	42	39	6.00	3	6	9.78	1.22	4.67	4.33	0.46	5.89
2000	Sth Bend	Mid	53.3	62	35	3	23	19	5.91	2	4	10.46	0.51	3.88	3.21	0.41	5.20
2000	El Paso	Tex	38.7	39	19	2	12	20	4.42	2	2	9.08	0.47	2.79	4.66	0.83	3.91

National League

Mike McCutcheon keeps getting moved back and forth between starting and relieving; even with that uncertainty, he allowed only three home runs all year. Because he's left-handed, he won't have to worry about the standard reluctance to take a small pitcher seriously. McCutcheon might slip into a big-league relief role at some point this year.

Mike Morgan — Throws R — Age 41

YEAR	TEAM	LGE	IP	H	ER	HR	BB	K	ERA	W	L	H/9	HR/9	BB/9	K/9	KW	PERA
1998	Minnesot	AL	96.3	99	35	11	20	46	3.27	7	4	9.25	1.03	1.87	4.30	1.15	4.21
1998	ChiCubs	NL	22.0	29	20	8	13	8	8.18	0	2	11.86	3.27	5.32	3.27	0.31	9.54
1999	Texas	AL	140.0	169	88	19	37	58	5.66	5	11	10.86	1.22	2.38	3.73	0.78	5.59
2000	Arizona	NL	99.3	118	50	9	33	47	4.53	5	6	10.69	0.82	2.99	4.26	0.71	5.31

How long has Mike Morgan been pitching? He's been traded in three different decades. He's been traded for Chicken Stanley and Kenny Landreaux and Tom Dodd and Kenny Dixon and Scott Downs and Todd Zeile. He's been traded with Dave Collins (now a coach) and Fred McGriff (now a Devil Ray, which is sort of the same thing). He's been traded for Brian Doyle and Dale Murray, but not Brian Doyle Murray. Of the 12 teams he's played for, he's outlasted ten ownership groups. At this rate, our kids will be writing about Mike Morgan.

Ben Norris — Throws L — Age 23

YEAR	TEAM	LGE	IP	H	ER	HR	BB	K	ERA	W	L	H/9	HR/9	BB/9	K/9	KW	PERA
1998	Sth Bend	Mid	81.3	100	53	16	34	27	5.86	3	6	11.07	1.77	3.76	2.99	0.40	6.86
1998	High Des	Cal	38.3	47	28	11	19	9	6.57	1	3	11.03	2.58	4.46	2.11	0.24	7.99
1999	High Des	Cal	38.7	40	28	6	24	24	6.52	1	3	9.31	1.40	5.59	5.59	0.50	6.20
1999	El Paso	Tex	113.7	128	58	15	53	55	4.59	6	7	10.13	1.19	4.20	4.35	0.52	5.86
2000	Tucson	PCL	54.7	81	47	7	26	20	7.74	1	5	13.34	1.15	4.28	3.29	0.38	7.74
2000	El Paso	Tex	43.0	38	12	1	17	15	2.51	4	1	7.95	0.21	3.56	3.14	0.44	3.34

Ben Norris struggled terribly at Tucson to open the year, earning a demotion to El Paso. When he's going good, he fools you with a mix of cutters, sinkers, and a plus change-up. He completely owned left-handed hitters last year, allowing them to hit .193 with no home runs. He's already been given the "bulldog" halo granted to thespians who have mastered body language. Norris may yet grow up to be Doug Johns, or he might slip onto the roster as a situational reliever now that the Snakes have lost Dan Plesac.

John Patterson — Throws R — Age 23

YEAR	TEAM	LGE	IP	H	ER	HR	BB	K	ERA	W	L	H/9	HR/9	BB/9	K/9	KW	PERA
1998	High Des	Cal	118.0	111	63	19	43	77	4.81	5	8	8.47	1.45	3.28	5.87	0.90	4.77
1999	El Paso	Tex	94.3	102	64	18	42	75	6.11	3	7	9.73	1.72	4.01	7.16	0.89	6.11
1999	Tucson	PCL	30.0	40	24	3	18	20	7.20	1	2	12.00	0.90	5.40	6.00	0.56	7.16
2000	Tucson	PCL	14.7	19	11	1	8	7	6.75	1	1	11.66	0.61	4.91	4.30	0.44	6.37

John Patterson has a great throwing motion, but he started complaining about a sore elbow in camp, and by May had to have Tommy John surgery on his elbow. Even with an accelerated rehab schedule, we shouldn't see him in the majors until September, if he gets called up at all. The surgery shouldn't impact his long-term outlook. When he comes back, he should still be throwing in the high 90s; he'll just have to take his time bringing back his power curve.

Dan Plesac — Throws L — Age 39

YEAR	TEAM	LGE	IP	H	ER	HR	BB	K	ERA	W	L	H/9	HR/9	BB/9	K/9	KW	PERA
1998	Toronto	AL	49.0	39	20	3	14	51	3.67	3	2	7.16	0.55	2.57	9.37	1.82	2.89
1999	Toronto	AL	22.7	26	17	3	7	25	6.75	1	2	10.32	1.19	2.78	9.93	1.79	5.35
1999	Arizona	NL	21.3	22	9	3	7	23	3.80	1	1	9.28	1.27	2.95	9.70	1.64	4.98
2000	Arizona	NL	39.3	35	20	4	21	37	4.58	2	2	8.01	0.92	4.81	8.47	0.88	4.57

A career ruined by the save rule? Dan Plesac was a good starting-pitcher prospect when George Bamberger decided to keep him as a middle reliever for the 1986 Brewers. He threw in the high 90s back then with a pretty good slider and change-up. Instead of making the classic long-relief-to-starter move that Bambi was familiar with, Plesac got a couple of saves in a co-closer role and by 1988 had been turned into a one-inning closer. It was as much a waste of talent back then as it is now.

Bret Prinz — Throws R — Age 24

YEAR	TEAM	LGE	IP	H	ER	HR	BB	K	ERA	W	L	H/9	HR/9	BB/9	K/9	KW	PERA
1998	Lethbrid	Pio	38.3	46	24	5	14	15	5.63	1	3	10.80	1.17	3.29	3.52	0.54	5.85
1999	Sth Bend	Mid	125.0	138	110	36	62	51	7.92	3	11	9.94	2.59	4.46	3.67	0.41	7.35
2000	El Paso	Tex	57.0	73	26	8	15	42	4.11	3	3	11.53	1.26	2.37	6.63	1.40	6.00

Not even the people who know something about pitching can know everything about pitching. Bret Prinz changed from being a "normal" starter to being a sidearming reliever and picked up velocity and movement in the process. He now throws in the low 90s, with a slider and change-up for show. Prinz was the organization's Pitcher of the Year, but then struggled in the AFL.

Armando Reynoso — Throws R — Age 35

YEAR	TEAM	LGE	IP	H	ER	HR	BB	K	ERA	W	L	H/9	HR/9	BB/9	K/9	KW	PERA
1998	NY Mets	NL	65.0	62	31	5	30	32	4.29	3	4	8.58	0.69	4.15	4.43	0.53	4.40
1999	Arizona	NL	162.7	168	80	18	55	66	4.43	8	10	9.30	1.00	3.04	3.65	0.60	4.68
2000	Arizona	NL	165.3	170	91	19	43	74	4.95	7	11	9.25	1.03	2.34	4.03	0.86	4.41

Armando Reynoso throws a half-dozen kinds of junk for strikes and owns one of the best pickoff moves you'll see from a right-handed pitcher. He's a classic example of a starter who just isn't going to give you more than 30 starts or 170 innings; if you can live with that, you've got yourself a decent fourth or fifth starter. The Snakes declined to pick up Reynoso's option for 2001, then signed him to a cheaper two-year deal.

Johnny Ruffin — Throws R — Age 29

YEAR	TEAM	LGE	IP	H	ER	HR	BB	K	ERA	W	L	H/9	HR/9	BB/9	K/9	KW	PERA
1998	Louisvil	Int	56.3	41	29	5	48	38	4.63	3	3	6.55	0.80	7.67	6.07	0.40	4.77
1998	Norfolk	Int	36.7	32	17	2	21	27	4.17	2	2	7.85	0.49	5.15	6.63	0.64	4.21
1999	Albuquer	PCL	51.0	41	22	7	27	42	3.88	3	3	7.24	1.24	4.76	7.41	0.78	4.44
2000	Tucson	PCL	54.3	48	20	4	24	44	3.31	4	2	7.95	0.66	3.98	7.29	0.92	3.93

Johnny Ruffin throws in the high 80s... with his slider. His fastball is well into the 90s. I suppose if he had a neck like Todd Worrell's or a silly mustache or six fingers, he'd be taken more seriously. A strained hip in August cost him a shot at replacing Vicente Padilla as the Diamondbacks' primary right-handed setup man.

Curt Schilling — Throws R — Age 34

YEAR	TEAM	LGE	IP	H	ER	HR	BB	K	ERA	W	L	H/9	HR/9	BB/9	K/9	KW	PERA
1998	Philadel	NL	257.0	236	103	23	55	244	3.61	16	13	8.26	0.81	1.93	8.54	2.22	3.46
1999	Philadel	NL	174.7	152	67	22	36	128	3.45	11	8	7.83	1.13	1.85	6.60	1.78	3.51
2000	Philadel	NL	109.7	106	43	14	25	80	3.53	7	5	8.70	1.15	2.05	6.57	1.60	4.08
2000	Arizona	NL	94.0	90	38	9	11	60	3.64	5	5	8.62	0.86	1.05	5.74	2.73	3.38

This is your basic problem player for any organization. My own half-baked theory is that watching Mitch Williams as he cost Curt Schilling his shot at a World Series ring has left Schilling unwilling to sit still when he thinks there's an injustice that can be righted by him opening his mouth. He'll almost never come off the mound if he can avoid it, fearful that those damned relievers are just going to blow the game, and he'd rather take the hit himself than get left with another might-have-been.

Only a manager with a lot of self-assurance is going to keep Schilling pitching effectively into his late thirties by making him learn to love those guys in the pen. Terry Francona was never going to stand up to Schilling, and I doubt Bob Brenly will, either. Schilling is smart (hey, he's the world's most famous "Squad Leader" player, which is like passing the bar exam, only harder) and outspoken, which makes him a natural target for beat writers hungry for quotes or controversy. When things go sour, he'll be the first to complain; on an old, bad team, that's going to be a problem. At his best, Roger Clemens Lite; just not a good bet to age well.

National League

Russ Springer — Throws R — Age 32

YEAR	TEAM	LGE	IP	H	ER	HR	BB	K	ERA	W	L	H/9	HR/9	BB/9	K/9	KW	PERA
1998	Arizona	NL	31.3	29	16	4	12	30	4.60	1	2	8.33	1.15	3.45	8.62	1.25	4.41
1998	Atlanta	NL	19.3	23	11	1	15	16	5.12	1	1	10.71	0.47	6.98	7.45	0.53	6.66
1999	Atlanta	NL	46.0	31	19	5	19	41	3.72	3	2	6.07	0.98	3.72	8.02	1.08	3.14
2000	Arizona	NL	61.0	62	33	10	28	49	4.87	3	4	9.15	1.48	4.13	7.23	0.88	5.56

He's entering the second year of a two-year, $4 million contract. Spending that kind of money on a middle reliever is an even better example than Travis Lee's $10 million bonus of why the entire organization would be fired if baseball clubs had real boards of directors. Even if Russ Springer had been a lock to repeat his 1999 performance, the value of that performance is not worth spending ten times as much what it costs to scout and sign the next Jeff Tam.

Todd Stottlemyre — Throws R — Age 36

YEAR	TEAM	LGE	IP	H	ER	HR	BB	K	ERA	W	L	H/9	HR/9	BB/9	K/9	KW	PERA
1998	St Louis	NL	154.3	145	75	21	46	119	4.37	8	9	8.46	1.22	2.68	6.94	1.29	4.29
1998	Texas	AL	60.3	65	29	4	24	53	4.33	3	4	9.70	0.60	3.58	7.91	1.10	4.73
1999	Arizona	NL	99.0	102	47	11	33	62	4.27	5	6	9.27	1.00	3.00	5.64	0.94	4.67
2000	Arizona	NL	93.0	95	50	16	30	63	4.84	4	6	9.19	1.55	2.90	6.10	1.05	5.16

Todd Stottlemyre refused to have surgery on his torn labrum and rotator cuff after 1999, instead attempting to work his way back through conditioning alone. He pitched while the muscles in his elbow frayed, through a hamstring injury, even after a hernia operation, and still he didn't quit. Now he's talking about retiring if he isn't healthy next spring, and his being healthy is about as likely as a Dave Pease swimsuit calendar. He's not a role model, because nobody should try this at home. It's more like Ronnie Lott cutting off his fingertip: it doesn't tell us that he's a hero. It tells us he likes to play, he's tough, and he's probably crazy.

Greg Swindell — Throws L — Age 36

YEAR	TEAM	LGE	IP	H	ER	HR	BB	K	ERA	W	L	H/9	HR/9	BB/9	K/9	KW	PERA
1998	Minnesot	AL	65.3	62	23	8	15	42	3.17	4	3	8.54	1.10	2.07	5.79	1.40	3.97
1998	Boston	AL	24.0	24	12	3	11	17	4.50	1	2	9.00	1.13	4.13	6.38	0.77	5.14
1999	Arizona	NL	62.7	52	17	7	17	43	2.44	5	2	7.47	1.01	2.44	6.18	1.26	3.41
2000	Arizona	NL	73.3	69	27	6	16	53	3.31	5	3	8.47	0.74	1.96	6.50	1.66	3.51

Tom Kelly gets a lot of crap for the things he's done over the years, and he deserves some of it. But TK is also the guy who saved Flounder's career after he seemed doomed to join Doug Drabek in the dustbin as part of Drayton McLane's Excellent Checkbook Adventure. Greg Swindell is one of the few well-used left-handed setup men in the game.

Jeremy Ward — Throws R — Age 23

YEAR	TEAM	LGE	IP	H	ER	HR	BB	K	ERA	W	L	H/9	HR/9	BB/9	K/9	KW	PERA
1999	El Paso	Tex	24.3	18	7	1	9	17	2.59	2	1	6.66	0.37	3.33	6.29	0.94	2.74

The organization's second-round pick in 1999 out of Long Beach State, Jeremy Ward was converted to closer after pitching a full season in the Big West Conference, then pitched at two professional levels and went to the AFL. He impressed everybody with a mid-90s fastball and a tight slider and was supposed to have a shot at the majors in 2000. Then came the elbow trouble and Tommy John surgery late enough in the season that 2001 is probably lost.

Support-Neutral Statistics			ARIZONA DIAMONDBACKS							Park Effect: -2.3%	
PITCHER	GS	IP	R	SNW	SNL	SNPCT	W	L	RA	APW	SNVA	SNWAR
Brian Anderson	32	209.3	100	13.1	10.0	.568	11	7	4.30	1.7	1.6	3.3
Omar Daal	16	88.3	77	3.2	8.5	.275	2	9	7.85	-2.6	-2.5	-1.8
Nelson Figueroa	3	15.7	13	0.6	1.3	.308	0	1	7.47	-0.4	-0.4	-0.2
Geraldo Guzman	10	57.0	32	3.6	3.3	.524	5	3	5.05	0.0	0.2	0.7
Randy Johnson	35	248.7	89	19.1	7.8	.709	19	7	3.22	4.8	5.4	7.6
Byung-Hyun Kim	1	2.3	4	0.1	0.3	.200	0	0	15.43	-0.3	-0.1	-0.1
Mike Morgan	4	19.3	13	0.8	1.5	.350	0	2	6.05	-0.2	-0.4	-0.2
Armando Reynoso	30	169.7	100	11.4	10.2	.528	11	12	5.30	-0.4	0.6	2.2
Curt Schilling	13	97.7	41	6.5	3.7	.634	5	6	3.78	1.3	1.3	2.1
Todd Stottlemyre	18	95.3	55	5.3	6.2	.463	9	6	5.19	-0.1	-0.4	0.4
TOTALS	162	1003.3	524	63.7	52.9	.546	62	53	4.70	3.9	5.3	14.2

2000 was a good news/bad news year for Randy Johnson. The good news was the best first half by any starting pitcher of the past 20 years according to Support-Neutral Value Added (SNVA). Through the end of June, SNVA showed Johnson as being worth a whopping 4.4 wins more than an average pitcher. His Support-Neutral W/L record at that time was around 11–2. Considering all the outstanding seasons by starters over the past 20 years, it's saying a lot that Johnson's 2000 first half was the best.

The bad news is relative: Johnson's second half was a far cry from his first. He was still above average, but his SNVA of 0.9 during the last three months was only good enough to rank him 40th among major-league starters over that period. Does the drop-off bode ill for Johnson's future? Not necessarily. The most comparable recent seasons—off-the-charts first halves followed by so-so second halves—are Maddux's 1998, Bret Saberhagen's 1987, and Bartolo Colon's 1998. All three of those pitchers had plenty left after their Jekyll-and-Hyde seasons.

For a quick explanation of SN stats, see page 7.

Reliever Evaluation Tools											
PITCHER	G	IP	R	ARA	APR	IRNR/G	EIRS/G	IRP	BRS	RRA	ARP
Brian Anderson	1	4.0	1	2.30	1.3	2.00	1.32	-0.7	0.0	3.88	0.6
Omar Daal	4	7.7	11	13.22	-6.8	1.00	0.44	0.7	0.1	8.59	-2.9
Geraldo Guzman	3	3.3	4	11.06	-2.2	0.00	0.00	0.0	-0.2	10.34	-1.9
Darren Holmes	5	3.3	6	16.59	-4.2	1.80	0.85	-2.7	-0.5	23.28	-6.7
Byung-Hyun Kim	60	68.3	35	4.72	3.6	0.43	0.13	4.2	1.2	4.47	5.5
Matt Mantei	47	45.3	24	4.88	1.6	0.13	0.03	0.4	0.9	4.63	2.9
Mike Morgan	56	82.3	42	4.70	4.5	0.68	0.26	-1.7	0.9	5.17	0.2
Vicente Padilla	27	35.0	10	2.63	10.0	0.52	0.19	0.9	-1.0	2.21	11.6
Dan Plesac	62	40.0	21	4.84	1.6	0.89	0.29	-1.4	0.7	5.12	0.4
Armando Reynoso	1	1.0	2	18.43	-1.5	2.00	0.93	1.0	-0.6	4.19	0.1
Johnny Ruffin	5	9.0	9	9.22	-4.0	1.00	0.30	-0.5	0.3	10.20	-5.0
Russ Springer	52	62.0	36	5.35	-1.1	0.75	0.26	-1.8	1.5	6.15	-6.6
Greg Swindell	64	76.0	29	3.52	14.2	0.41	0.12	3.8	3.8	3.65	13.0
TOTALS	387	437.3	230	4.85	17.0	0.58	0.20			4.97	11.3

For a quick guide to RET, see page 10.

Atlanta Braves

In 2000, the Braves missed the NLCS for the first time since 1990, their vaunted rotation suffered its biggest injury ever, and the team started replacement-level players at three positions for much of the season. So this seems an appropriate time to pop the question: how much longer can the team's run continue?

Despite the untimely end to their season, the Braves still have the best core talent in the National League. Chipper Jones and Andruw Jones are two of the top seven or eight players in the league. Javy Lopez is a good catcher who is overshadowed by the Mike Piazzas and Jason Kendalls with whom he shares an era. Rafael Furcal was the NL Rookie of the Year while playing both second base and shortstop and has tremendous upside, regardless of his real age.

That's just the offense. Even with the loss of John Smoltz for the entire season after Tommy John surgery, the Braves had the best rotation in baseball. Greg Maddux and Tom Glavine reversed declines to pitch at their established level. The underrated bullpen again suffered losses due to injury, but by the end of the year, its core of Kerry Ligtenberg, John Rocker, and Mike Remlinger was again among baseball's best.

So even after the embarrassing sweep at the hands of the Cardinals, the Braves are in excellent shape. Because of the distribution of their core talent—excellent players at catcher, shortstop, third base, and center field—the problem they need to address, first base, is among the easiest to rectify. They could use a left-handed bat there, preferably an inexpensive one. The December signing of Rico Brogna fills the latter requirement, anyway.

(At this writing, there's a lot of uncertainty stemming from Chipper Jones's expressed desire to move to the outfield and the team's efforts to trade Brian Jordan. How these issues play out will impact whether the team has one or more holes to fill, and which young players like Wes Helms and George Lombard will get an opportunity in the spring.)

> **Braves Prospectus**
>
> **2000 record:** 95–67; First place, NL East; Lost to Cardinals in Division Series, 3-0
> **Pythagenport W/L:** 91–71
> **Runs Scored:** 810 (6th in NL)
> **Runs Allowed:** 714 (1st in NL)
> **Team EqA:** .264 (6th in NL)
> **2000 Batters' Age:** 30.5 (3rd oldest in NL)
> **2000 Pitchers' Age:** 31.6 (2nd oldest in NL)
> **Ballpark:** Turner Field; slight pitchers' park; Park Factor of .979
> **2000:** Easily their roughest season, both in process and results, since 1990.
> **2001:** Still the best team in the division, but there are reasons to be concerned.

The key to optimism about the Braves' future is that even though they have appeared in every postseason since 1991, they're a fairly young team. Other than Brian Jordan and B.J. Surhoff, no player in their lineup is older than 30. Their up-the-middle players are 30 (Lopez), 30 (Quilvio Veras), 24 (Andruw Jones), and 20 (Furcal). Not only do the Braves have a decade of success behind them, but they have upside in their starting lineup.

The chink in the armor is an aging rotation. Then again, this isn't the Angels trying to get by with Tim Belcher and Ken Hill. Glavine and Maddux have room to decline and still help the team. The Braves failed to sign Mike Hampton, but getting Smoltz back will be a big boost to a team that plugged Andy Ashby into his spot last season. We've seen a significant improvement in the ability of pitchers to pitch well after the increasingly-common elbow surgery; at worst, Smoltz should match the performance the Braves got from Ashby in 2000.

Looking forward, the Braves have a tremendous crop of pitchers coming through the system. Even with the trades of Bruce Chen, Jimmy Osting, and Luis Rivera and the elbow injuries that have plagued the organization, the sheer number of live arms with major-league ability and quality performance histories is staggering.

The Braves' high-A affiliate, the Myrtle Beach Pelicans, led the Carolina League with an astounding 2.51 ERA, a mark more than a run better than their closest competitor. That team was led by right-handers Nathan Kent and Christian Parra and left-hander Horacio Ramirez. Matt Belisle, who may be the organization's top pitching prospect, also pitched in the Carolina League for a couple of months after 15 great starts at Macon in the South Atlantic League.

It should be noted that Myrtle Beach was an excellent environment for pitchers in 2000, reducing run-scoring by nearly 20% as compared to other Carolina League parks. (It was an even better pitchers' park in 1999.) The translations you'll see in this chapter take that into account, so you can read lines from Myrtle Beach—and there were some Playstation numbers put up there—the same way you would any DT lines.

From a development standpoint, having such an extreme pitchers' park in the system raises interesting questions. Is it easier to develop pitchers, especially young ones, in a forgiving park? It certainly seems like a pitchers' park should reduce the wear on young arms by allowing a pitcher to throw fewer pitches in the same number of innings. Fewer baserunners should also mean fewer pitches thrown from the stretch.

It also seems like a pitchers' park would minimize the riskiness of in-game experimentation: it's easier to work on that four-seam fastball if a mistake ends up a flyout or a long single as opposed to a 450-foot bomb off the words "Hit Sign, Win Steak."

At the upper levels, we've seen the problems teams like the Twins and Rockies have had in bringing pitching prospects through hitters' havens like Salt Lake and Colorado Springs. You can tell a man that his 6.00 ERA is acceptable, even good, considering his environment, but do the other impacts—more pitches, more negative reinforcement, more nibbling to avoid well-hit balls—destroy otherwise good pitchers?

One possible way of looking at this question is a matched-set study of pitchers of comparable age, performance, and workload, but playing in different environments. If there's a benefit to pitchers' parks, maybe it would show in better development of those pitchers. And even if it does, would an organization filled with pitchers' parks damage the development of hitters coming through the system?

What we can say is that the Braves have quality pitching talent at more than just Myrtle Beach. Matt McClendon and Derrick Lewis were effective at Double-A Greenville. In addition to Belisle, Dan Curtis split time between Macon and Myrtle Beach and was effective at both levels. The Braves' #2 pick in 1999, Matt Butler, had a good year at Macon and gets high marks for his knowledge on the mound.

What can we expect from this group? Is the next Glavine/Smoltz/Maddux trio going to emerge from the Classes of 2000 in Macon and Myrtle Beach? Probably not. Just three years ago, in *Baseball Prospectus 1998,* we raved about the pitchers the Braves had coming through the system, people like Damian Moss, Derrin Ebert, and Bruce Chen. But of that collection, only Chen has since established himself as a major-league starter. The rest, a group that includes the above pitchers plus prospects like Kevin McGlinchy and Jason Marquis, have encountered injuries and ineffectiveness. Save for some good pen work by McGlinchy in 1999 and Chen in 2000, none of the top prospects in the system in 1997 have helped the Braves.

Even though not all of these pitchers will go on to great careers, the likelihood is that at least one will. There's an old joke about investing: "How do you make a small fortune in the stock market? Start with a large one." It applies to pitcher development as well: How do you develop one or two major-league pitchers? Start out with eight or nine who have the potential to make it. The attrition rate of pitchers coming through the minors is high, so the best defense is quantity.

The Braves have that right now, so when the current contracts of the big three are up, they should have one or two in-house options available to replace them. By that time, they'll have added Andruw Jones to their list of big-ticket items, so cheap replacements for the expensive starting pitchers will be essential.

If you're the Marlins or Expos, on the way up but still trying to close a talent gap, the thought of chasing a Braves team that doesn't appear to be coming back to the pack anytime soon has to be daunting. The Braves, like the Yankees, are combining a significant advantage in available cash with solid player development and quality management to build what may be a perpetual winning machine.

For all the success the Braves have had, you wonder if they might be better if they never brought players in from outside the organization. Yes, they made one of the two best free-agent signings ever in Greg Maddux, but they've also spent a lot of money and playing time on guys who never made much of a contribution. Meanwhile, the players that they have developed and given jobs to are not only good, they're almost always the best players on the team.

Table 1 shows the regulars the Braves brought to the majors and the ones they imported from other teams, as well as the approximate number of wins they were responsible for over an average player at that position in 2000, using the tools developed by Clay Davenport and Michael Wolverton and an estimate of 11 runs per win.

Players the Braves developed were collectively responsible for the majority of the Braves' positive performance in 2000. Greg Maddux was the only import who was worth more than a single win last year. (Quilvio Veras would have been worth at least a win had he not been injured.) The imported outfielders, Brian Jordan and Reggie Sanders, were a disaster, and the veteran arms brought in, Andy Ashby, John Burkett, and Terry Mulholland, provided innings but no real quality.

In the 1990s, the Braves developed talent like no other organization. In addition to the players listed above, Brave

National League

Table 1

All-Brave	Wins	Part-Brave	Wins
Andruw Jones	4.4	Greg Maddux	4.2
Chipper Jones	3.4	Mike Remlinger	0.8
Tom Glavine	2.9	Quilvio Veras	0.5
Kerry Ligtenberg	1.3	Andy Ashby	0.3
Bruce Chen	0.5	John Burkett	-0.6
Rafael Furcal	0.3	Andres Galarraga	-0.8
Javy Lopez	0.3	Terry Mulholland	-0.9
John Rocker	0.2	Brian Jordan	-1.2
Kevin Millwood	0.1	Reggie Sanders	-1.7
Total	+13.4	Total	+0.6

exports like Ryan Klesko, David Justice, and Jermaine Dye played well for other teams in 2000. Other than Maddux, though, no Brave free-agent signing of note has given the team more than a season's worth of good play. And the team's trades have been a mixed bag, particularly when acquiring position players.

The above chart reflects just one season, but even if you look back, you don't see newcomers helping the Braves the same way their own players have. They've gotten some good seasons from imports (Andres Galarraga's 1998 and Denny Neagle's 1997 and '98 among them) but the Braves are, and have been, a homegrown team that has had much more success with internal solutions than external ones.

Now if they would just act that way. The bad moves the team has made lately all involve bringing in older players from outside the organization—trading away Rob Bell as part of the deal for Bret Boone; trading Chen for Ashby; signing Brian Jordan, a contract the team is now desperately trying to get out from under.

Developing players is only part of the equation. The organization has to have the confidence in its player-development program to take its fruits and give them jobs. The Braves, more than just about any other team, should know this. Implementing that knowledge over the next couple of years will be essential to keeping the team competitive and affordable.

HITTERS (BA: .270, OBP: .340, SLG: .440, EqA: .260)

Paul Bako — C — Bats L — Age 29

YEAR	TEAM	LGE	AB	H	DB	TP	HR	BB	SO	R	RBI	SB	CS	OUT	BA	OBP	SLG	EQA	EQR	DEFENSE	
1998	Detroit	AL	304	85	13	1	3	23	73	24	29	1	1	220	.280	.330	.359	.233	29	84-C	1
1999	Houston	NL	217	55	14	1	2	23	54	16	16	1	1	163	.253	.325	.355	.230	21	62-C	2
2000	Florida	NL	163	40	6	1	0	20	45	10	14	0	0	123	.245	.331	.294	.217	13	48-C	0
2000	Atlanta	NL	59	11	5	0	2	4	14	8	6	0	0	48	.186	.238	.373	.195	4	17-C	0
2001	Atlanta	NL	205	53	10	1	3	21	56	25	25	0	0	152	.259	.327	.361	.238	21		

The season-ending injury to Eddie Perez left the Braves with only Fernando Lunar behind Javy Lopez, so claiming Paul Bako off waivers was a good idea. Bako, a left-handed, low-power, average defensive backstop, is a near-perfect complement to Lopez. He'll be around for a while and have a lot of years like 1998.

Wilson Betemit — SS — Bats B — Age 19

YEAR	TEAM	LGE	AB	H	DB	TP	HR	BB	SO	R	RBI	SB	CS	OUT	BA	OBP	SLG	EQA	EQR	DEFENSE
1999	Danville	App	260	60	10	1	3	14	69	21	28	2	1	201	.231	.271	.312	.190	16	66-SS -9
2000	Jamestwn	NYP	276	71	11	1	4	19	41	39	24	1	2	207	.257	.306	.348	.217	23	68-SS -18
2001	Atlanta	NL	218	60	8	1	3	16	54	25	26	1	1	159	.275	.325	.362	.235	21	

Like Adrian Beltre, Wilson Betemit signed prior to turning 16 and then made a play for free agency. The Braves paid a fine, gave Betemit some money, and were suspended from scouting in the Dominican Republic for six months, but kept the player. The shortstop didn't play until the case was settled, then tore up the New York-Penn League. The Braves' top long-term prospect could be in Double-A by August.

Bobby Bonilla — OF — Bats B — Age 38

YEAR	TEAM	LGE	AB	H	DB	TP	HR	BB	SO	R	RBI	SB	CS	OUT	BA	OBP	SLG	EQA	EQR	DEFENSE	
1998	Florida	NL	99	28	3	0	5	12	21	11	16	0	1	72	.283	.360	.465	.271	14	23-3B	-3
1998	LosAngls	NL	241	60	5	1	8	28	35	30	32	1	1	182	.249	.327	.378	.238	25	56-3B	-15
1999	NY Mets	NL	120	19	5	0	4	18	15	12	17	0	1	102	.158	.273	.300	.189	8	22-RF	-3
2000	Atlanta	NL	241	61	11	3	5	33	48	22	26	0	0	180	.253	.345	.386	.249	28	43-LF	-13
2001	StLouis	NL	154	33	5	1	3	26	30	21	19	0	0	121	.214	.328	.318	.226	15		

Bobby Bonilla played a bit more than expected due to the injuries and ineffectiveness that plagued Reggie Sanders and Brian Jordan. Never a good defensive outfielder, he's a disaster now and needs to be restricted to a pinch-hitting or spot DH role. There are a few AL teams he could help that way, a pair of Sox among them. Signed by the Cardinals.

Junior Brignac — CF — Bats R — Age 23

YEAR	TEAM	LGE	AB	H	DB	TP	HR	BB	SO	R	RBI	SB	CS	OUT	BA	OBP	SLG	EQA	EQR	DEFENSE	
1998	Eugene	Nwn	273	55	10	1	2	12	84	21	19	5	4	222	.201	.242	.267	.156	11	67-SS	-21
1999	Macon	SAL	271	66	12	2	5	8	72	23	26	6	3	207	.244	.268	.358	.205	20	67-CF	-1
1999	Myrtle B	Car	263	56	7	1	6	17	86	25	27	5	5	212	.213	.266	.316	.188	16	64-CF	-1
2000	Myrtle B	Car	493	104	13	2	8	29	151	47	38	12	5	394	.211	.260	.294	.182	28	128-CF	9
2001	Atlanta	NL	407	93	12	1	8	34	131	45	37	16	4	318	.229	.288	.322	.214	34		

Looking for a quick and dirty way to eliminate players from prospect status? If a guy has more strikeouts than total bases, it's a good sign that he doesn't have what it takes. Junior Brignac turned that trick at Myrtle Beach in 2000, after almost doing so in a half-season in 1999. The Braves have way too many guys like this.

Troy Cameron — 3B — Bats B — Age 22

YEAR	TEAM	LGE	AB	H	DB	TP	HR	BB	SO	R	RBI	SB	CS	OUT	BA	OBP	SLG	EQA	EQR	DEFENSE			
1998	Macon	SAL	484	89	15	2	14	47	171	49	43	1	1	396	.184	.260	.310	.186	29	64-SS	-29	56-3B	-12
1999	Macon	SAL	479	93	18	1	15	51	170	51	51	3	4	390	.194	.275	.330	.200	35	115-3B	-14		
2000	Myrtle B	Car	421	84	16	2	14	44	136	46	41	0	1	338	.200	.281	.347	.208	33	120-3B	-1		
2001	Atlanta	NL	414	84	15	1	15	52	149	43	48	1	1	331	.203	.292	.353	.220	38				

Troy Cameron's glove-work got better in his second year at third base, and he made more contact at the plate. If he continues to improve at this pace, he could reach the majors by the end of the Bush administration. The Jeb Bush administration. As a former #1 pick, he'll get all kinds of chances.

Mark DeRosa — SS — Bats R — Age 26

YEAR	TEAM	LGE	AB	H	DB	TP	HR	BB	SO	R	RBI	SB	CS	OUT	BA	OBP	SLG	EQA	EQR	DEFENSE	
1998	Greenvil	Sou	459	100	19	1	6	38	61	47	32	4	6	365	.218	.282	.303	.192	29	125-SS	-5
1999	Richmond	Int	362	89	14	1	1	16	49	33	32	4	4	277	.246	.285	.298	.190	22	93-SS	-6
2000	Richmond	Int	371	99	18	2	3	31	37	53	29	9	3	275	.267	.327	.350	.233	36	88-SS	2
2000	Atlanta	NL	13	4	1	0	0	2	1	3	2	0	0	9	.308	.400	.385	.274	2		
2001	Atlanta	NL	345	83	15	1	2	35	42	42	29	9	3	265	.241	.311	.307	.217	29		

At this point, Mark DeRosa needs to get some work in at the other infield spots. He's not going to hold a starting shortstop job at the major-league level. On the other hand, he's not an offensive disaster and can definitely play shortstop, so he makes a useful fifth infielder. The Kurt Abbott signing may block him.

Rafael Furcal — SS/2B — Bats B — Age 20

YEAR	TEAM	LGE	AB	H	DB	TP	HR	BB	SO	R	RBI	SB	CS	OUT	BA	OBP	SLG	EQA	EQR	DEFENSE			
1998	Danville	App	269	62	10	2	0	21	34	23	13	16	7	214	.230	.289	.283	.197	19	65-2B	0		
1999	Macon	SAL	346	90	9	1	1	30	38	39	21	25	10	267	.260	.323	.301	.220	30	74-SS	-10		
1999	Myrtle B	Car	190	50	9	2	0	10	43	22	9	10	5	145	.263	.300	.332	.214	15	38-SS	5		
2000	Atlanta	NL	459	131	20	3	4	65	75	81	34	36	14	342	.285	.377	.368	.263	61	97-SS	-11	25-2B	0
2001	Atlanta	NL	464	134	20	3	2	57	78	93	46	41	13	343	.289	.367	.358	.263	61				
2001	Atlanta	NL	416	121	20	2	2	50	69	86	42	40	12	307	.291	.367	.363	.265	55				

National League

Give Bobby Cox a lot of credit for this one. Even the most generous assessments had Rafael Furcal starting the season in the minors; Cox evaluated the player, not the age, and was amply rewarded. By observation, he's a better shortstop than the numbers above indicate, and better there than at second base. We've listed his age as 20 because all sources, including the team, are sticking to that. The midseason *Real Sports* report that claimed Furcal is three years older hasn't been substantiated elsewhere. That said, we've provided two Wiltons for him. The first is based on a baseball age of 20, the second on an age of 23.

Andres Galarraga — 1B — Bats R — Age 40

YEAR	TEAM	LGE	AB	H	DB	TP	HR	BB	SO	R	RBI	SB	CS	OUT	BA	OBP	SLG	EQA	EQR	DEFENSE
1998	Atlanta	NL	564	170	21	1	46	61	137	103	119	6	6	400	.301	.392	.587	.312	109	149-1B -9
2000	Atlanta	NL	498	147	21	1	28	29	118	63	94	2	5	356	.295	.352	.510	.278	73	121-1B -11
2001	Texas	AL	284	77	10	0	15	27	73	40	53	1	1	208	.271	.334	.465	.260	36	

It was as if he'd never left. Andres Galarraga's 2000 season was perfectly in line with his 1998 performance, showing about the decline you'd expect from a 39-year-old. Galarraga tired in the second half, so the Rangers would be well-served to have a left-handed bat around to play about 60 games. With Ken Caminiti and Mike Lamb, they should be covered.

Marcus Giles — 2B — Bats R — Age 23

YEAR	TEAM	LGE	AB	H	DB	TP	HR	BB	SO	R	RBI	SB	CS	OUT	BA	OBP	SLG	EQA	EQR	DEFENSE
1998	Macon	SAL	517	127	24	2	22	62	108	70	63	4	2	392	.246	.332	.427	.254	64	124-2B -12
1999	Myrtle B	Car	519	146	33	4	11	38	92	64	54	4	3	376	.281	.333	.424	.252	60	121-2B -7
2000	Greenvil	Sou	470	115	22	1	14	54	74	57	48	12	3	358	.245	.324	.385	.242	52	123-2B -3
2001	Atlanta	NL	430	122	25	2	14	50	78	73	70	10	2	310	.284	.358	.449	.277	62	

As quickly as the Braves moved Furcal though the system, you'd think they'd show that same aggressiveness with Marcus Giles. Giles's secondary skills are great for a middle infielder, and while he doesn't look like he'd be a great fielder, he actually plays the position well. A Giles/Furcal double-play combination would be excellent as well as cheap; with Andruw Jones approaching free agency, that's important.

Wes Helms — 3B — Bats R — Age 25

YEAR	TEAM	LGE	AB	H	DB	TP	HR	BB	SO	R	RBI	SB	CS	OUT	BA	OBP	SLG	EQA	EQR	DEFENSE
1998	Richmond	Int	451	113	21	1	11	27	102	47	62	4	1	339	.251	.307	.375	.229	42	121-3B -5
1999	Greenvil	Sou	112	28	3	0	6	4	36	10	18	0	0	84	.250	.279	.438	.232	11	27-1B -1
2000	Richmond	Int	539	141	21	5	18	19	96	64	73	0	4	402	.262	.293	.419	.230	51	125-3B -12
2001	Atlanta	NL	340	90	14	1	13	21	72	38	50	1	1	251	.265	.307	.426	.246	38	

Wes Helms came back from shoulder problems that wiped out his 1999 to post the best EqA of his career. If Chipper Jones does move off of third base, Helms is the only real option the Braves have to step in there; that's a really good reason to not move Jones.

Andruw Jones — CF — Bats R — Age 24

YEAR	TEAM	LGE	AB	H	DB	TP	HR	BB	SO	R	RBI	SB	CS	OUT	BA	OBP	SLG	EQA	EQR	DEFENSE
1998	Atlanta	NL	589	160	33	7	32	38	121	90	89	25	4	433	.272	.320	.514	.274	85	159-CF 27
1999	Atlanta	NL	595	159	35	4	25	68	97	91	77	18	11	447	.267	.351	.466	.270	84	162-CF 30
2000	Atlanta	NL	662	197	37	5	34	49	94	116	96	19	6	471	.298	.353	.523	.286	103	161-CF 19
2001	Atlanta	NL	604	190	35	3	37	66	101	121	133	24	6	420	.315	.382	.566	.313	115	

Because of the way he plays defense, there's a reasonable argument that Andruw Jones is the best player in baseball. He's certainly the best defensive player in the game, and his offense gets better each year. He'll take a big step forward in 2001 on his way to chasing Alex Rodriguez's $21 million salary after 2002.

Chipper Jones — 3B — Bats B — Age 29

YEAR	TEAM	LGE	AB	H	DB	TP	HR	BB	SO	R	RBI	SB	CS	OUT	BA	OBP	SLG	EQA	EQR	DEFENSE
1998	Atlanta	NL	613	189	28	4	36	93	87	125	106	15	6	430	.308	.400	.543	.309	114	158-3B 9
1999	Atlanta	NL	569	177	34	1	45	116	89	109	102	20	3	395	.311	.429	.612	.337	130	152-3B -12
2000	Atlanta	NL	584	177	33	1	35	85	60	111	103	13	7	414	.303	.393	.543	.305	106	147-3B -7
2001	Atlanta	NL	542	168	25	1	38	116	71	130	134	17	6	380	.310	.432	.570	.332	121	

(Chipper Jones *continued*)

That was one of the quieter .305 EqA seasons you'll see. Chipper Jones played the 2000 season with a bone spur in his right elbow. It affected him at the plate and in the field for the first couple of weeks and held down his numbers. His bat can carry first base, and he has experience in the outfield, so the threat of a position change is serious.

Brian Jordan — RF — Bats R — Age 34

YEAR	TEAM	LGE	AB	H	DB	TP	HR	BB	SO	R	RBI	SB	CS	OUT	BA	OBP	SLG	EQA	EQR	DEFENSE	
1998	St Louis	NL	572	179	34	6	26	38	62	101	89	16	5	398	.313	.365	.530	.292	92	133-RF	-1
1999	Atlanta	NL	579	160	28	4	22	43	76	94	106	9	7	426	.276	.336	.453	.259	73	140-RF	-1
2000	Atlanta	NL	494	129	20	1	18	30	75	67	75	9	2	367	.261	.309	.415	.242	53	130-RF	4
2001	Atlanta	NL	487	133	20	2	19	39	72	67	76	10	3	357	.273	.327	.439	.260	61		

When you sign a 32-year-old player with an injury history who is coming off his career year, you don't get to complain when he gets hurt and his performance slips. Brian Jordan's rib cage and shoulder problems limited his time and made him a replacement-level right fielder when he played. Healthy, he's an average right fielder thanks to his glove; at $7 million per year, he's a problem the Braves need to solve.

Wally Joyner — 1B — Bats L — Age 39

YEAR	TEAM	LGE	AB	H	DB	TP	HR	BB	SO	R	RBI	SB	CS	OUT	BA	OBP	SLG	EQA	EQR	DEFENSE	
1998	San Dieg	NL	450	138	28	1	14	50	41	61	83	1	2	314	.307	.377	.467	.281	66	115-1B	-2
1999	San Dieg	NL	328	83	15	2	5	53	51	34	42	0	1	246	.253	.360	.357	.248	38	87-1B	4
2000	Atlanta	NL	226	63	8	0	6	27	29	23	31	0	0	163	.279	.358	.394	.256	27	42-1B	-2
2001	Atlanta	NL	242	61	6	0	7	41	33	36	34	0	0	181	.252	.360	.364	.256	30		

His performance improved when he got more playing time in the second half. Last season was the first in Wally Joyner's career in which his primary role was coming off the bench, and it showed. He got more spot starts and even a stretch as a semi-regular in August while Galarraga nursed a sore thumb. If he wants to, he can hang around and get 200 at-bats a year for a while.

Ryan Langerhans — RF — Bats L — Age 21

YEAR	TEAM	LGE	AB	H	DB	TP	HR	BB	SO	R	RBI	SB	CS	OUT	BA	OBP	SLG	EQA	EQR	DEFENSE	
1999	Macon	SAL	461	100	19	1	7	39	105	46	35	7	5	366	.217	.282	.308	.196	31	101-RF	0
2000	Myrtle B	Car	406	85	11	5	7	21	108	44	32	11	7	327	.209	.256	.313	.185	24	85-RF	-7
2001	Atlanta	NL	289	64	10	2	5	21	89	28	25	10	4	229	.221	.274	.322	.204	22		

He's a better story than prospect. Ryan Langerhans took a fastball in his face at the end of the 1999 season, then rebounded to have a passable season at a higher level in 2000. Like many of the outfielders in the Braves' system (Junior Brignac, Tyrone Pendergrass, George Lombard), he's more tools than talent.

Keith Lockhart — 2B — Bats L — Age 36

YEAR	TEAM	LGE	AB	H	DB	TP	HR	BB	SO	R	RBI	SB	CS	OUT	BA	OBP	SLG	EQA	EQR	DEFENSE			
1998	Atlanta	NL	371	97	17	0	11	27	35	51	38	2	2	276	.261	.313	.396	.235	37	83-2B	5		
1999	Atlanta	NL	162	42	3	1	1	17	20	19	20	2	1	121	.259	.333	.309	.222	14	19-2B	1		
2000	Atlanta	NL	278	73	12	3	2	24	29	31	31	4	1	206	.263	.321	.349	.229	26	58-2B	-1	13-3B	0
2001	Atlanta	NL	169	41	7	1	3	19	19	20	19	1	1	129	.243	.319	.349	.230	16				

Keith Lockhart hurts you if he has to play too much. After Quilvio Veras's knee blew up, Lockhart had to become the semi-regular second baseman; the difference between him and Veras cost the Braves a couple of games during the season. He's been a .230 EqA hitter for about 700 at-bats now, so it may be time to declare him done.

George Lombard — LF — Bats L — Age 25

YEAR	TEAM	LGE	AB	H	DB	TP	HR	BB	SO	R	RBI	SB	CS	OUT	BA	OBP	SLG	EQA	EQR	DEFENSE	
1998	Greenvil	Sou	417	101	16	2	16	48	149	53	40	17	3	319	.242	.325	.405	.250	50	107-LF	-15
1999	Richmond	Int	234	44	9	2	6	29	97	19	23	14	5	195	.188	.284	.321	.210	20	58-LF	-3
2000	Richmond	Int	426	106	22	5	9	45	135	59	40	21	7	327	.249	.327	.387	.245	49	106-LF	-8
2000	Atlanta	NL	39	4	0	0	0	1	13	8	2	4	0	35	.103	.143	.103	—	-1		
2001	Atlanta	NL	394	92	16	2	13	48	143	63	47	27	8	310	.234	.317	.383	.247	47		

National League

The power George Lombard showed in the 1999 Arizona Fall League disappeared over the winter. The trade for Reggie Sanders had doomed him to Richmond in 2000, anyway. The signing of Dave Martinez does not bode well for him.

Javy Lopez — C — Bats R — Age 30

YEAR	TEAM	LGE	AB	H	DB	TP	HR	BB	SO	R	RBI	SB	CS	OUT	BA	OBP	SLG	EQA	EQR	DEFENSE	
1998	Atlanta	NL	495	140	19	1	35	29	80	75	104	5	3	358	.283	.330	.537	.278	73	128-C	1
1999	Atlanta	NL	247	76	15	1	11	17	39	32	41	0	2	173	.308	.359	.510	.282	36	57-C	-4
2000	Atlanta	NL	485	137	18	1	24	28	75	57	84	0	0	348	.282	.326	.472	.261	61	122-C	-6
2001	Atlanta	NL	366	103	13	0	18	29	61	47	65	1	1	264	.281	.334	.464	.267	49		

It's hard to shake the feeling that Javy Lopez came along just a few years too late. A catcher who plays passable defense and hits a consistent .280 with 25 home runs would have been a god in the 1980s. Unfortunately, this is the age of Piazza and Pudge, so Lopez gets lost in the shuffle. (Greg Maddux not liking the way he catches doesn't help his image.) He still has a few good years, and probably one great one, left in him. That projection is very low.

Asdrubal Oropeza — 3B — Bats R — Age 20

YEAR	TEAM	LGE	AB	H	DB	TP	HR	BB	SO	R	RBI	SB	CS	OUT	BA	OBP	SLG	EQA	EQR	DEFENSE	
1998	Eugene	Nwn	109	24	4	0	4	6	35	13	14	0	0	85	.220	.261	.367	.203	8	28-3B	3
1999	Jamestwn	NYP	274	63	7	0	10	21	64	37	29	3	1	212	.230	.290	.365	.219	24	72-3B	5
2000	Macon	SAL	409	78	17	1	9	33	98	41	31	2	3	334	.191	.256	.303	.180	23	112-3B	-3
2001	Atlanta	NL	308	68	8	0	11	29	79	29	35	1	1	241	.221	.288	.354	.217	26		

After two good years in short-season leagues, Asdrubal Oropeza struggled a bit in his first year of full-season ball. Nevertheless, he's still a solid prospect, with a mix of offensive skills and a good glove. By the time he's ready for Atlanta, Chipper Jones will be a left fielder, so he'll get an opportunity.

Eddie Perez — C — Bats R — Age 33

YEAR	TEAM	LGE	AB	H	DB	TP	HR	BB	SO	R	RBI	SB	CS	OUT	BA	OBP	SLG	EQA	EQR	DEFENSE	
1998	Atlanta	NL	152	51	9	0	7	14	26	18	32	1	1	102	.336	.398	.533	.305	26	38-C	-1
1999	Atlanta	NL	311	77	13	0	8	13	38	29	29	0	1	235	.248	.290	.367	.216	25	83-C	1
2000	Atlanta	NL	22	4	1	0	0	0	2	1	2	0	0	18	.182	.182	.227	.042	0		
2001	Atlanta	NL	110	28	4	0	3	8	15	12	15	0	0	82	.255	.305	.373	.230	10		

A nice guy catches a bad break: Eddie Perez tore his right rotator cuff in May, ending his season. He's nothing special offensively or defensively, Greg Maddux's blessing notwithstanding. Perez played winter ball and will be back as the Braves' back-up catcher this year.

Reggie Sanders — LF — Bats R — Age 33

YEAR	TEAM	LGE	AB	H	DB	TP	HR	BB	SO	R	RBI	SB	CS	OUT	BA	OBP	SLG	EQA	EQR	DEFENSE	
1998	Cincnnti	NL	486	128	18	5	15	49	128	83	58	18	9	367	.263	.339	.414	.254	59	118-CF	-4
1999	San Dieg	NL	485	137	24	7	26	58	102	87	69	28	12	360	.282	.366	.522	.289	81	118-LF	-4
2000	Atlanta	NL	343	79	21	1	11	27	73	41	35	19	4	268	.230	.290	.394	.233	35	83-LF	-4
2001	Arizona	NL	341	86	15	3	12	41	80	57	48	18	7	262	.252	.332	.419	.257	44		

Reggie Sanders was injured early and often, which was no big surprise. He was the worst left fielder in the league for four months, though, which was a surprise. Sanders is the kind of player who can disappear in his mid-thirties, so his days as a regular... OK, whatever it is he's been... could easily be over. Signed by the Diamondbacks.

B.J. Surhoff — LF — Bats L — Age 36

YEAR	TEAM	LGE	AB	H	DB	TP	HR	BB	SO	R	RBI	SB	CS	OUT	BA	OBP	SLG	EQA	EQR	DEFENSE	
1998	Baltimor	AL	574	167	31	1	26	48	72	81	96	7	7	414	.291	.347	.484	.271	79	147-LF	0
1999	Baltimor	AL	671	212	33	2	31	37	71	103	106	5	1	460	.316	.353	.510	.283	98	148-LF	13
2000	Baltimor	AL	410	123	22	0	16	24	42	55	57	8	2	289	.300	.342	.471	.269	54	102-LF	4
2000	Atlanta	NL	129	37	8	2	1	10	11	12	10	3	0	92	.287	.342	.403	.255	15	28-LF	-1
2001	Atlanta	NL	526	153	23	1	22	44	58	76	92	7	2	375	.291	.346	.464	.273	73		

(B.J. Surhoff *continued*)

B.J. Surhoff walks a thin line. In a good year, he plays a quality defensive left field for 160 games, runs a .280 EqA, and is a bit above average. In an off year, he cashes checks and uses up 420 outs without moving you closer to a title. The difference between the two is fairly small, and he was on the wrong side of it in 2000. Signed through 2002, he's a problem for the Braves in left field and a disaster if he is moved to first base.

Quilvio Veras — 2B — Bats B — Age 30

YEAR	TEAM	LGE	AB	H	DB	TP	HR	BB	SO	R	RBI	SB	CS	OUT	BA	OBP	SLG	EQA	EQR	DEFENSE	
1998	San Dieg	NL	531	148	26	2	7	83	73	84	48	23	10	392	.279	.382	.375	.265	71	128-2B	11
1999	San Dieg	NL	482	135	25	2	6	58	83	89	39	23	16	363	.280	.360	.378	.251	57	117-2B	4
2000	Atlanta	NL	300	89	8	0	7	46	47	51	36	23	13	223	.297	.398	.393	.274	44	79-2B	-7
2001	Atlanta	NL	354	99	14	1	7	62	59	74	45	24	13	268	.280	.387	.384	.272	52		

Through July 14, the day Quilvio Veras blew out his right ACL, the Braves scored 5.08 runs per game and were 54-36. After losing Veras, they scored 4.88 runs per game and went 41-31.

If Veras doesn't get hurt, the Braves could have an easier road in September. Does that change the Division Series? Probably not, but you have to wonder just how big an impact losing the team's first real leadoff hitter since Otis Nixon had.

Veras has been a fragile player for six years, but he's also been one of the best leadoff hitters in the game when healthy. He'll be a good signing for some team as long as that team accepts that he's going to miss 30 or so games.

Walt Weiss — SS — Bats B — Age 37

YEAR	TEAM	LGE	AB	H	DB	TP	HR	BB	SO	R	RBI	SB	CS	OUT	BA	OBP	SLG	EQA	EQR	DEFENSE	
1998	Atlanta	NL	353	100	14	3	1	58	50	66	28	7	1	254	.283	.389	.348	.263	45	91-SS	1
1999	Atlanta	NL	281	63	13	4	2	31	45	36	28	5	3	221	.224	.308	.320	.214	23	79-SS	-6
2000	Atlanta	NL	194	50	6	2	0	23	30	28	17	1	1	145	.258	.344	.309	.227	18	58-SS	3
2001	Atlanta	NL	199	46	7	2	1	32	33	28	19	3	1	154	.231	.338	.302	.230	19		

The end of a career. Unlike Veras, Walt Weiss isn't worth the trouble of working around his frequent absences. He doesn't do enough things to justify a utility infield slot, so he's got to find someone who both likes him and is utterly desperate at shortstop. Of course, the same could have been said of Ozzie Guillen in April 1998. Retired.

A.J. Zapp — 1B — Bats L — Age 23

YEAR	TEAM	LGE	AB	H	DB	TP	HR	BB	SO	R	RBI	SB	CS	OUT	BA	OBP	SLG	EQA	EQR	DEFENSE	
1998	Macon	SAL	74	15	4	1	2	6	19	6	8	0	0	59	.203	.272	.365	.209	6	16-1B	-3
1999	Macon	SAL	438	85	16	1	15	30	172	44	44	2	1	354	.194	.251	.338	.190	28	113-1B	-5
2000	Myrtle B	Car	406	98	20	1	8	42	110	50	40	1	1	309	.241	.320	.355	.228	39	96-1B	-3
2001	Atlanta	NL	344	80	17	1	10	36	114	40	42	1	1	265	.233	.305	.375	.232	34		

The Braves' #1 pick in 1996 took more than a year to get his swing back following a broken hand in 1998. His 2000 season looks like a natural progression from his 1997 EqA of .228. His shot at a career depends on him hitting well at Greenville in 2001, but even if he does, the upside here is more Orlando Merced than Fred McGriff.

National League

PITCHERS (ERA: 4.50, H/9: 9.00, HR/9: 1.00, BB/9: 3.00, K/9: 6.00, KW: 1.00, PERA: 4.50)

Andy Ashby — Throws R — Age 33

YEAR	TEAM	LGE	IP	H	ER	HR	BB	K	ERA	W	L	H/9	HR/9	BB/9	K/9	KW	PERA
1998	San Dieg	NL	214.7	217	93	27	56	123	3.90	12	12	9.10	1.13	2.35	5.16	1.10	4.42
1999	San Dieg	NL	197.3	196	95	28	49	111	4.33	10	12	8.94	1.28	2.23	5.06	1.13	4.44
2000	Philadel	NL	99.0	107	65	14	30	42	5.91	3	8	9.73	1.27	2.73	3.82	0.70	5.10
2000	Atlanta	NL	94.3	98	45	11	19	46	4.29	5	5	9.35	1.05	1.81	4.39	1.21	4.26

Bobby Cox and Leo Mazzone have done a phenomenal job for ten years, but their refusal to give Bruce Chen a deserved rotation job cost the team wins, money, and four years of a talented pitcher. The trade made no sense at the time; it looked worse when Andy Ashby pitched at his established level after the trade, while Chen was one of the best pitchers in the NL during the second half.

Ashby signed with Dodgers for three years and $22.5 million. The park will mask his decline and make him look better than the #4 starter he is.

Steve Avery — Throws L — Age 31

YEAR	TEAM	LGE	IP	H	ER	HR	BB	K	ERA	W	L	H/9	HR/9	BB/9	K/9	KW	PERA
1998	Boston	AL	122.3	119	62	12	53	53	4.56	6	8	8.75	0.88	3.90	3.90	0.50	4.60
1999	Cincnnti	NL	95.3	73	53	10	63	43	5.00	4	7	6.89	0.94	5.95	4.06	0.34	4.42
2000	Greenvil	Sou	26.0	45	38	10	23	9	13.15	0	3	15.58	3.46	7.96	3.12	0.20	13.03
2000	Myrtle B	Car	40.3	41	15	6	36	15	3.35	2	2	9.15	1.34	8.03	3.35	0.21	7.04
2000	Richmond	Int	19.7	22	26	4	17	6	11.90	0	2	10.07	1.83	7.78	2.75	0.18	7.95

It's a sad story: Steve Avery hasn't struck out more batters than he's walked at any level above the Carolina League since 1997. Last year was simply disastrous; he had neither location nor stuff and was bludgeoned at both Double-A and Triple-A.

Stan Belinda — Throws R — Age 34

YEAR	TEAM	LGE	IP	H	ER	HR	BB	K	ERA	W	L	H/9	HR/9	BB/9	K/9	KW	PERA
1998	Cincnnti	NL	59.0	46	23	7	25	46	3.51	4	3	7.02	1.07	3.81	7.02	0.92	3.77
1999	Cincnnti	NL	42.0	41	24	10	15	34	5.14	2	3	8.79	2.14	3.21	7.29	1.13	5.70
2000	Colorado	NL	36.7	37	22	5	11	33	5.40	1	3	9.08	1.23	2.70	8.10	1.50	4.67
2000	Atlanta	NL	10.7	16	12	4	4	9	10.13	0	1	13.50	3.38	3.38	7.59	1.13	9.80

One of the more amusing stories in 2000 was Stan Belinda's scorching review of Coors Field after his release by the Rockies. Belinda had actually pitched better in Colorado than elsewhere during his time in purple and black, with ERAs of 5.66 at home and 9.00 on the road. He'll be an NRI somewhere this spring and is good enough to end up as the closer for a bad team.

Matt Belisle — Throws R — Age 21

YEAR	TEAM	LGE	IP	H	ER	HR	BB	K	ERA	W	L	H/9	HR/9	BB/9	K/9	KW	PERA
1999	Danville	App	67.3	83	47	7	30	23	6.28	2	5	11.09	0.94	4.01	3.07	0.38	6.09
2000	Macon	SAL	92.7	88	54	17	23	46	5.24	4	6	8.55	1.65	2.23	4.47	1.00	4.60
2000	Myrtle B	Car	71.0	80	47	14	14	38	5.96	2	6	10.14	1.77	1.77	4.82	1.36	5.50

Matt Belisle may have the best command in the low minors, and he carved up the Sally League for three months before jumping to Myrtle Beach. Command pitchers without dominant stuff often go through an adjustment period at Double-A. The Braves have a lot of talented A-ball arms; Belisle has had the most success and the least DL time to date, making him the Braves' second-best pitching prospect behind Matt McClendon.

John Burkett — Throws R — Age 36

YEAR	TEAM	LGE	IP	H	ER	HR	BB	K	ERA	W	L	H/9	HR/9	BB/9	K/9	KW	PERA
1998	Texas	AL	192.3	213	111	15	37	121	5.19	8	13	9.97	0.70	1.73	5.66	1.64	4.23
1999	Texas	AL	147.0	170	79	14	35	91	4.84	6	10	10.41	0.86	2.14	5.57	1.30	4.83
2000	Atlanta	NL	130.7	158	75	12	43	91	5.17	6	9	10.88	0.83	2.96	6.27	1.06	5.42

He wasn't good enough to make the Devil Rays' rotation in the spring, so naturally he went to Pitcher Heaven and held his own for most of the season. He did his best work as part of the regular rotation: six good starts, averaging six innings with an ERA of 2.27 and a 3-to-1 strikeout-to-walk ratio. No fantasy value, though.

Matt Butler — Throws R — Age 21

YEAR	TEAM	LGE	IP	H	ER	HR	BB	K	ERA	W	L	H/9	HR/9	BB/9	K/9	KW	PERA
2000	Macon	SAL	139.3	142	102	31	83	58	6.59	4	11	9.17	2.00	5.36	3.75	0.35	6.64

The Braves' #2 pick in 1999, Matt Butler was another of the quality arms at Macon. His big year—trust me, the DTs hammer A-ball pitching lines—was credited in part to an improved change-up, and he also gets praise for his adaptability on the mound.

Derrin Ebert — Throws L — Age 24

YEAR	TEAM	LGE	IP	H	ER	HR	BB	K	ERA	W	L	H/9	HR/9	BB/9	K/9	KW	PERA
1998	Richmond	Int	157.3	185	89	16	46	64	5.09	6	11	10.58	0.92	2.63	3.66	0.70	5.19
1999	Richmond	Int	145.3	162	70	13	41	60	4.33	7	9	10.03	0.81	2.54	3.72	0.73	4.70
2000	Richmond	Int	144.0	186	93	24	42	70	5.81	5	11	11.63	1.50	2.63	4.38	0.83	6.42

As you can see, Derrin Ebert's career has hit a bit of a stall. He's all set to write a book on the best restaurants in Richmond, Va., though. If he was right-handed, he would have had a job in Atlanta last year (Don Wengert?). Ebert is as qualified as a dozen other guys and gets a new life this spring with the Devil Rays.

Tom Glavine — Throws L — Age 35

YEAR	TEAM	LGE	IP	H	ER	HR	BB	K	ERA	W	L	H/9	HR/9	BB/9	K/9	KW	PERA
1998	Atlanta	NL	219.0	196	66	14	68	127	2.71	16	8	8.05	0.58	2.79	5.22	0.93	3.46
1999	Atlanta	NL	227.3	246	105	17	70	116	4.16	12	13	9.74	0.67	2.77	4.59	0.83	4.50
2000	Atlanta	NL	232.3	213	93	22	54	126	3.60	14	12	8.25	0.85	2.09	4.88	1.17	3.56

Tom Glavine's 1999 looks more like a blip than a trend now, as most of his peripheral numbers reverted to normal. Analyst Voros McCracken has a theory that pitchers really control only their walks, strikeouts, and home runs allowed, and that hits allowed on balls in play can vary wildly without reflecting a change in the pitcher's ability. Glavine's last three years are an interesting data point in that case.

Scott Kamieniecki — Throws R — Age 37

YEAR	TEAM	LGE	IP	H	ER	HR	BB	K	ERA	W	L	H/9	HR/9	BB/9	K/9	KW	PERA
1998	Baltimor	AL	53.7	62	37	7	23	23	6.20	2	4	10.40	1.17	3.86	3.86	0.50	5.85
1999	Rochestr	Int	21.3	23	14	6	6	9	5.91	1	1	9.70	2.53	2.53	3.80	0.75	6.31
1999	Baltimor	AL	55.7	49	29	4	24	37	4.69	3	3	7.92	0.65	3.88	5.98	0.77	3.88
2000	Clevelnd	AL	34.0	39	18	5	15	28	4.76	2	2	10.32	1.32	3.97	7.41	0.93	6.01
2000	Atlanta	NL	24.3	22	16	3	18	14	5.92	1	2	8.14	1.11	6.66	5.18	0.39	5.60

The Indians' decision to give Scott Kamieniecki a two-year, $3.8 million contract was strange enough, given his level of ability and health record. Odder still was releasing him after two months of league-average pitching. The Braves, who were auditioning striking SAG members for bullpen jobs (Don Wengert?), signed Kamieniecki, and he was the main right-handed setup guy for about two weeks. He'll have a job somewhere.

Derrick Lewis — Throws R — Age 25

YEAR	TEAM	LGE	IP	H	ER	HR	BB	K	ERA	W	L	H/9	HR/9	BB/9	K/9	KW	PERA
1998	Macon	SAL	101.7	109	74	13	72	46	6.55	3	8	9.65	1.15	6.37	4.07	0.32	6.45
1999	Myrtle B	Car	111.7	108	66	25	109	50	5.32	4	8	8.70	2.01	8.79	4.03	0.23	7.79
2000	Greenvil	Sou	150.3	155	80	8	86	79	4.79	7	10	9.28	0.48	5.15	4.73	0.46	5.00

Derrick Lewis took a nice step forward in 2000, with significantly improved command of three pitches, including a low-90s fastball. He's always kept the ball in the park (just 27 home runs allowed as a pro), and taking the big step forward at Double-A bodes well for him. He's not young, so continuous improvement is a must.

Kerry Ligtenberg — Throws R — Age 30

YEAR	TEAM	LGE	IP	H	ER	HR	BB	K	ERA	W	L	H/9	HR/9	BB/9	K/9	KW	PERA
1998	Atlanta	NL	69.7	51	24	6	22	64	3.10	5	3	6.59	0.78	2.84	8.27	1.45	2.89
2000	Atlanta	NL	51.0	43	20	6	20	43	3.53	3	3	7.59	1.06	3.53	7.59	1.08	3.97

After missing all of 1999 to Tommy John surgery, Kerry Ligtenberg may have come back a bit too quickly. A trip to the DL and some careful handling had him pitching at his 1998 level. He's a better bet than John Rocker to lead the Braves in saves in 2001.

National League

Greg Maddux — Throws R — Age 35

YEAR	TEAM	LGE	IP	H	ER	HR	BB	K	ERA	W	L	H/9	HR/9	BB/9	K/9	KW	PERA
1998	Atlanta	NL	239.0	196	75	14	41	166	2.82	18	9	7.38	0.53	1.54	6.25	2.02	2.61
1999	Atlanta	NL	212.0	243	95	15	31	114	4.03	12	12	10.32	0.64	1.32	4.84	1.84	4.20
2000	Atlanta	NL	239.3	217	87	18	35	158	3.27	16	11	8.16	0.68	1.32	5.94	2.26	3.06

Like Glavine, Greg Maddux bounced back from a subpar 1999. Like Glavine, the big difference was in his number of hits allowed, lending some credibility to the idea that that number isn't so reflective of performance or of much predictive value. Maddux is going to win 300 games; he's actually got a chance to move close to 350, mostly depending upon how long he wants to pitch.

Jason Marquis — Throws R — Age 22

YEAR	TEAM	LGE	IP	H	ER	HR	BB	K	ERA	W	L	H/9	HR/9	BB/9	K/9	KW	PERA
1998	DanvillC	Car	102.0	127	77	6	54	69	6.79	3	8	11.21	0.53	4.76	6.09	0.64	6.03
1999	Myrtle B	Car	28.7	24	2	0	21	22	0.63	3	0	7.53	0.00	6.59	6.91	0.52	4.09
1999	Greenvil	Sou	52.3	52	34	9	28	22	5.85	2	4	8.94	1.55	4.82	3.78	0.39	5.82
2000	Greenvil	Sou	62.3	73	42	15	22	29	6.06	2	5	10.54	2.17	3.18	4.19	0.66	6.71
2000	Atlanta	NL	22.7	22	15	4	10	14	5.96	1	2	8.74	1.59	3.97	5.56	0.70	5.34
2000	Richmond	Int	19.3	26	20	2	12	14	9.31	0	2	12.10	0.93	5.59	6.52	0.58	7.34

An injury-plagued 1999 didn't slow Jason Marquis down; he pitched well at Greenville and ended up in Atlanta when the rest of the bullpen went down. A two-level jump and simultaneous role change (from starting to middle relief) had the anticipated effect, and Marquis was back in the minors in August. He's been rushed a little but is a good long-term bet.

Matt McClendon — Throws R — Age 23

YEAR	TEAM	LGE	IP	H	ER	HR	BB	K	ERA	W	L	H/9	HR/9	BB/9	K/9	KW	PERA
1999	Jamestwn	NYP	20.0	21	16	5	14	11	7.20	0	2	9.45	2.25	6.30	4.95	0.39	7.46
2000	Myrtle B	Car	36.0	27	10	3	10	22	2.50	3	1	6.75	0.75	2.50	5.50	1.10	2.83
2000	Greenvil	Sou	122.3	128	63	9	52	54	4.63	6	8	9.42	0.66	3.83	3.97	0.52	4.73

This looks like a nice steal for the Braves. Matt McClendon slipped into the fifth round in the 1999 draft, signed for first-round money, then pitched like he was worth it. His performance at Greenville wasn't all that impressive, with an ERA of 3.78 and a strikeout-to-walk ratio of less than 2-to-1. The danger is that he's being rushed, so tread lightly for the next year or so.

Kevin McGlinchy — Throws R — Age 24

YEAR	TEAM	LGE	IP	H	ER	HR	BB	K	ERA	W	L	H/9	HR/9	BB/9	K/9	KW	PERA
1998	DanvillC	Car	128.3	129	68	14	38	66	4.77	6	8	9.05	0.98	2.66	4.63	0.87	4.37
1998	Greenvil	Sou	31.7	35	19	7	13	13	5.40	1	3	9.95	1.99	3.69	3.69	0.50	6.41
1999	Atlanta	NL	68.3	64	23	6	25	56	3.03	5	3	8.43	0.79	3.29	7.38	1.12	4.06
2000	Atlanta	NL	8.3	11	4	1	5	8	4.32	0	1	11.88	1.08	5.40	8.64	0.80	7.33

Kevin McGlinchy missed almost all of 2000 with shoulder tendinitis; that sounds bad, but with Braves' pitchers getting group discounts on Tommy John surgeries, it could have been worse. He's expected to return in 2000, probably to a middle-relief role. Long term, I think he can grow into a #3 starter.

Kevin Millwood — Throws R — Age 26

YEAR	TEAM	LGE	IP	H	ER	HR	BB	K	ERA	W	L	H/9	HR/9	BB/9	K/9	KW	PERA
1998	Atlanta	NL	167.0	173	87	19	51	132	4.69	8	11	9.32	1.02	2.75	7.11	1.29	4.61
1999	Atlanta	NL	219.7	163	76	23	50	173	3.11	15	9	6.68	0.94	2.05	7.09	1.73	2.80
2000	Atlanta	NL	205.7	207	109	24	52	140	4.77	9	14	9.06	1.05	2.28	6.13	1.35	4.29

As expected, Kevin Millwood declined from his 1999 peak. But look at the ratios: Millwood's strikeout, walk, and home-run rates haven't changed all that much over the three seasons. The difference each season is in his hits allowed.

Think of it in these terms: if a hitter's batting average runs from .260 to .320 to .275 while the rest of his offensive profile remains unchanged, it's conceded that he hit in "good luck" the second year. Why wouldn't that concept also apply to pitchers? Batting average, for or against, is volatile.

(Kevin Millwood *continued*)

Put differently, we allow that a pitcher's offensive support can vary to a great degree. Why wouldn't his defensive support be subject to a similar effect, one that would cause his hits allowed and/or slugging percentage allowed to fluctuate? As McCracken puts it, hits allowed on balls in play is comparable to how we regard clutch hitting for batters: "... the level of control, if it exists, is very small and not very significant in the evaluation of players."

For more on these concepts, please check out Voros McCracken's work at http://www.baseballstuff.com/mccracken/pitching.html. Our thanks to Mr. McCracken for his effort and allowing us to discuss his theories in *Baseball Prospectus 2001*.

Gabe Molina — Throws R — Age 26

YEAR	TEAM	LGE	IP	H	ER	HR	BB	K	ERA	W	L	H/9	HR/9	BB/9	K/9	KW	PERA
1998	Bowie	Eas	56.0	53	33	8	31	44	5.30	2	4	8.52	1.29	4.98	7.07	0.71	5.35
1999	Rochestr	Int	54.3	45	23	4	24	41	3.81	3	3	7.45	0.66	3.98	6.79	0.85	3.68
1999	Baltimor	AL	23.0	21	17	4	13	13	6.65	1	2	8.22	1.57	5.09	5.09	0.50	5.51
2000	Rochestr	Int	25.3	31	19	4	11	18	6.75	1	2	11.01	1.42	3.91	6.39	0.82	6.53
2000	Baltimor	AL	13.3	23	12	2	7	8	8.10	0	1	15.53	1.35	4.73	5.40	0.57	9.39

In the fine tradition of Gus Gandarillas and Ryan Brannan, Future Closers of America presents ... Gabe Molina! Molina was thrown into the B.J. Surhoff deal and was one of the few ambulatory people in the Braves' organization not given a real chance in the Atlanta pen. Great relievers aren't made or born, folks; they just happen.

Damian Moss — Throws L — Age 24

YEAR	TEAM	LGE	IP	H	ER	HR	BB	K	ERA	W	L	H/9	HR/9	BB/9	K/9	KW	PERA
1999	Macon	SAL	35.7	41	33	16	20	22	8.33	1	3	10.35	4.04	5.05	5.55	0.55	9.35
1999	Greenvil	Sou	31.3	49	31	7	20	14	8.90	1	2	14.07	2.01	5.74	4.02	0.35	9.70
2000	Richmond	Int	153.7	130	67	16	100	94	3.92	9	8	7.61	0.94	5.86	5.51	0.47	4.80

He's a good story, having made a reasonably successful comeback from Tommy John surgery in 1998. His command is still a problem; Damian Moss led Triple-A with 106 walks, and it's not like he's Ryan Anderson.

Terry Mulholland — Throws L — Age 38

YEAR	TEAM	LGE	IP	H	ER	HR	BB	K	ERA	W	L	H/9	HR/9	BB/9	K/9	KW	PERA
1998	ChiCubs	NL	107.3	97	47	7	35	58	3.94	6	6	8.13	0.59	2.93	4.86	0.83	3.57
1999	ChiCubs	NL	107.0	128	62	14	26	37	5.21	4	8	10.77	1.18	2.19	3.11	0.71	5.39
1999	Atlanta	NL	58.3	61	23	5	11	33	3.55	3	3	9.41	0.77	1.70	5.09	1.50	3.98
2000	Atlanta	NL	151.7	188	88	22	34	65	5.22	6	11	11.16	1.31	2.02	3.86	0.96	5.68

Unlike Burkett, with whom he shared roles, Terry Mulholland pitched better as a reliever. As a ground-ball pitcher who eliminates the running game and can pitch often, he helps a team that uses him properly. That's not as a rotation starter. Like Burkett, little to no fantasy value. His role with the Pirates is unclear at this writing.

Christian Parra — Throws R — Age 23

YEAR	TEAM	LGE	IP	H	ER	HR	BB	K	ERA	W	L	H/9	HR/9	BB/9	K/9	KW	PERA
1999	Jamestwn	NYP	44.0	52	27	5	24	28	5.52	2	3	10.64	1.02	4.91	5.73	0.58	6.30
1999	Macon	SAL	29.0	36	19	6	16	17	5.90	1	2	11.17	1.86	4.97	5.28	0.53	7.51
2000	Myrtle B	Car	140.0	111	70	17	72	85	4.50	7	9	7.14	1.09	4.63	5.46	0.59	4.18

Christian Parra was the best pitcher in the Carolina League, the top performer on that awesome Myrtle Beach staff. He, like teammate Nathan Kent, doesn't project as well as McClendon or Belisle in the long term, despite better numbers in 2000.

Odalis Perez — Throws L — Age 23

YEAR	TEAM	LGE	IP	H	ER	HR	BB	K	ERA	W	L	H/9	HR/9	BB/9	K/9	KW	PERA
1997	Macon	SAL	80.7	84	49	9	38	48	5.47	4	5	9.37	1.00	4.24	5.36	0.63	5.25
1998	Greenvil	Sou	131.3	140	78	23	52	94	5.35	6	9	9.59	1.58	3.56	6.44	0.90	5.69
1998	Richmond	Int	24.7	27	11	5	7	17	4.01	2	1	9.85	1.82	2.55	6.20	1.21	5.56
1998	Atlanta	NL	10.7	11	5	1	4	4	4.22	1	0	9.28	0.84	3.38	3.38	0.50	4.56
1999	Atlanta	NL	98.0	98	59	12	47	73	5.42	4	7	9.00	1.10	4.32	6.70	0.78	5.10

He didn't pitch anywhere in 2000 following Tommy John surgery. Reports out of instructional league in Florida were very positive. Look for 2001 to be a recovery year and 2002 to be the next beginning of what will be a good career.

Horacio Ramirez — Throws L — Age 21

YEAR	TEAM	LGE	IP	H	ER	HR	BB	K	ERA	W	L	H/9	HR/9	BB/9	K/9	KW	PERA
1998	Eugene	Nwn	53.3	82	49	9	19	20	8.27	1	5	13.84	1.52	3.21	3.38	0.53	7.99
1998	Macon	SAL	50.3	71	55	14	20	18	9.83	1	5	12.70	2.50	3.58	3.22	0.45	8.50
1999	Macon	SAL	70.7	70	35	11	33	20	4.46	4	4	8.92	1.40	4.20	2.55	0.30	5.36
2000	Myrtle B	Car	130.3	154	90	39	53	67	6.21	4	10	10.63	2.69	3.66	4.63	0.63	7.53

Like Parra and Kent, Horacio Ramirez isn't the prospect you might expect from his numbers. His best pitch is a slider, and a left-hander with a good slider can chew up a high-A league.

All five of the Myrtle Beach starters are good prospects. If you're looking for a ranking, use McClendon, Belisle, Ramirez, Parra, and Kent. Matt Butler would be somewhere between Belisle and Parra.

Mike Remlinger — Throws L — Age 35

YEAR	TEAM	LGE	IP	H	ER	HR	BB	K	ERA	W	L	H/9	HR/9	BB/9	K/9	KW	PERA
1998	Cincnnti	NL	158.7	162	93	23	77	117	5.28	7	11	9.19	1.30	4.37	6.64	0.76	5.50
1999	Atlanta	NL	81.3	65	23	9	30	68	2.55	6	3	7.19	1.00	3.32	7.52	1.13	3.60
2000	Atlanta	NL	70.7	55	28	6	31	60	3.57	4	4	7.00	0.76	3.95	7.64	0.97	3.51

Overworked early during John Rocker's stay on Elba, Mike Remlinger fought through summer fatigue and ended the year as a big part of the Braves' pen. He throws hard, keeps the ball in the park, has no platoon split, and makes good money. He can marry my daughter anytime, especially now that the goofy beard is history.

John Rocker — Throws L — Age 26

YEAR	TEAM	LGE	IP	H	ER	HR	BB	K	ERA	W	L	H/9	HR/9	BB/9	K/9	KW	PERA
1998	Richmond	Int	18.0	13	4	1	9	16	2.00	2	0	6.50	0.50	4.50	8.00	0.89	3.16
1998	Atlanta	NL	36.3	22	10	4	20	34	2.48	3	1	5.45	0.99	4.95	8.42	0.85	3.25
1999	Atlanta	NL	70.7	49	24	5	31	88	3.06	5	3	6.24	0.64	3.95	11.21	1.42	3.00
2000	Atlanta	NL	52.3	45	25	5	40	64	4.30	3	3	7.74	0.86	6.88	11.01	0.80	5.20

His protestations aside, it's clear that the aftermath of John Rocker's discourse on urban diversity in the late 20th century had a negative impact on his performance. After his demotion and recall, his performance was right in line with what he did in 1999, maybe better. He's prone to MillitelloMoments(tm); the rest of the time he's nasty.

Rudy Seanez — Throws R — Age 32

YEAR	TEAM	LGE	IP	H	ER	HR	BB	K	ERA	W	L	H/9	HR/9	BB/9	K/9	KW	PERA
1998	Richmond	Int	19.7	15	11	1	7	22	5.03	1	1	6.86	0.46	3.20	10.07	1.57	2.90
1998	Atlanta	NL	34.7	26	14	2	15	41	3.63	2	2	6.75	0.52	3.89	10.64	1.37	3.15
1999	Atlanta	NL	52.0	45	20	3	18	34	3.46	3	3	7.79	0.52	3.12	5.88	0.94	3.38
2000	Atlanta	NL	20.3	15	10	3	7	17	4.43	1	1	6.64	1.33	3.10	7.52	1.21	3.50

Tough break for "Traction Action," whose back remained healthy long enough for his elbow to blow. Coming off midseason Tommy John surgery, he'll be hard-pressed to have any value in 2001.

Jacob Shumate — Throws R — Age 25

YEAR	TEAM	LGE	IP	H	ER	HR	BB	K	ERA	W	L	H/9	HR/9	BB/9	K/9	KW	PERA
1998	Macon	SAL	40.7	45	66	9	98	30	14.61	0	5	9.96	1.99	21.69	6.64	0.15	13.86
1999	Myrtle B	Car	18.0	14	24	0	44	15	12.00	0	2	7.00	0.00	22.00	7.50	0.17	10.05
1999	Greenvil	Sou	54.0	44	31	8	60	30	5.17	2	4	7.33	1.33	10.00	5.00	0.25	6.78
2000	Greenvil	Sou	41.7	35	28	5	43	23	6.05	2	3	7.56	1.08	9.29	4.97	0.27	6.35

Through 1998, Jacob Shumate looked like the second coming of Bill Bene, a #1 pick with all the control of Sam Kinison on a coke bender. Slow, steady improvement in his control—he finally struck out as many as he walked in 2000—has him on the brink of prospect status again. He closed for Greenville in the second half. Shumate is a long shot, but one with a huge upside.

John Smoltz — Throws R — Age 34

YEAR	TEAM	LGE	IP	H	ER	HR	BB	K	ERA	W	L	H/9	HR/9	BB/9	K/9	KW	PERA
1997	Atlanta	NL	259.0	242	102	23	59	203	3.54	18	11	8.41	0.80	2.05	7.05	1.72	3.55
1998	Atlanta	NL	169.7	150	61	11	42	148	3.24	13	6	7.96	0.58	2.23	7.85	1.76	3.10
1999	Atlanta	NL	190.0	173	71	14	35	137	3.36	13	8	8.19	0.66	1.66	6.49	1.96	3.09

After leading the league in innings pitched in 1996 and 1997, John Smoltz battled his elbow for the next two seasons before finally succumbing to Tommy John surgery last spring. He's expected back for the 2001 season; don't expect the peak John Smoltz, but 150 innings of a 4.00 ERA seems like a reasonable expectation.

Tim Spooneybarger — Throws R — Age 21

YEAR	TEAM	LGE	IP	H	ER	HR	BB	K	ERA	W	L	H/9	HR/9	BB/9	K/9	KW	PERA
1999	Danville	App	21.7	17	13	0	18	14	5.40	1	1	7.06	0.00	7.48	5.82	0.39	4.17
2000	Myrtle B	Car	44.3	22	12	3	24	30	2.44	4	1	4.47	0.61	4.87	6.09	0.63	2.43

In addition to the ridiculous starting staff, the Pelicans featured a dominant bullpen. Unlike the starters, none of these guys, who all put up 1968-style stat lines, are serious prospects. Tim Spooneybarger is the youngest of the bunch and has the best name, so he makes the book.

Billy Sylvester and Bradley Voyles, both 24, split the closer duties for Myrtle Beach (Sylvester broke his thumb in July). If you add their ERAs together, you don't get to 2.00, so you understand the kind of seasons they had. Sylvester was hammered in the AFL and Voyles wasn't invited.

Adam Wainwright — Throws R — Age 19

YEAR	TEAM	LGE	IP	H	ER	HR	BB	K	ERA	W	L	H/9	HR/9	BB/9	K/9	KW	PERA
2000	Danville	App	25.7	35	22	8	3	16	7.71	1	2	12.27	2.81	1.05	5.61	2.67	7.56

The Braves draft two kinds of players: high-school pitchers and toolsy outfielders. It's a high-risk strategy. Adam Wainwright was their #1 last year, a tall, thin, high-school right-hander. He adds to the organizational depth on the mound and is at least two years behind the Myrtle Beach class.

Support-Neutral Statistics — ATLANTA BRAVES — Park Effect: -6.2%

PITCHER	GS	IP	R	SNW	SNL	SNPCT	W	L	RA	APW	SNVA	SNWAR
Andy Ashby	15	98.0	49	5.8	5.2	.531	8	6	4.50	0.5	0.3	1.2
John Burkett	22	119.7	68	6.8	7.3	.484	9	4	5.11	-0.2	-0.3	0.8
Tom Glavine	35	241.0	101	15.7	9.5	.623	21	9	3.77	3.1	2.9	5.0
Greg Maddux	35	249.3	91	17.9	8.9	.667	19	9	3.28	4.5	4.2	6.5
Kevin Millwood	35	210.3	115	12.8	12.4	.508	10	13	4.92	0.1	0.1	2.1
Terry Mulholland	20	122.0	83	6.6	8.5	.437	9	8	6.12	-1.5	-1.0	0.2
TOTALS	162	1040.3	507	65.6	51.7	.559	76	49	4.39	6.5	6.3	15.7

Here's an amazing fact. Despite being effectively tied with Boston for the best starting rotation in the major leagues, the 2000 Braves were the worst Atlanta rotation in almost a decade. If that isn't a testament to the greatness of the recent Braves' starting rotations, I don't know what is. The Braves' 2000 league-leading Support-Neutral Value Added (SNVA) of 6.3 wins above average ranks it well behind every other Atlanta rotation since 1992 (and possibly even 1991 as well; I don't have the numbers for that year). Since 1992, Braves rotations have a cumulative SNVA of 98 wins above average. The second-best team over that span, the Red Sox, has an SNVA of 32 wins, or about a third of the Braves' total.

Has there ever been a decade-long domination of the league by one team's starters comparable to the current Braves' run? Surprisingly, the answer may be yes. It's impossible to separate starter performance from reliever performance prior to 1980 or so, but if you look at overall run prevention, the current Braves have strong competition from the Cardinals of the 1940s, led by Harry Brecheen, and the Cubs of the aughts, led by Mordecai (Three-Finger) Brown. Regardless of whether the current Braves are the very best or merely among the best, we should enjoy their historic run while it lasts.

For a quick explanation of SN stats, see page 7.

Reliever Evaluation Tools

PITCHER	G	IP	R	ARA	APR	IRNR/G	EIRS/G	IRP	BRS	RRA	ARP
Stan Belinda	10	11.0	12	10.26	-6.2	0.60	0.39	0.3	0.4	11.00	-7.1
John Burkett	9	14.7	11	7.05	-3.0	0.33	0.07	0.7	0.7	7.19	-3.2
Bruce Chen	22	39.7	15	3.56	7.2	0.36	0.15	-1.6	-0.5	3.96	5.5
Scott Kamieniecki	26	24.7	18	6.86	-4.6	0.62	0.21	4.1	-1.4	5.26	-0.2
Kerry Ligtenberg	59	52.3	21	3.77	8.3	0.66	0.26	5.7	-1.6	2.71	14.4
Jason Marquis	15	23.3	16	6.45	-3.2	0.40	0.15	-0.8	0.7	7.07	-4.9
Kevin McGlinchy	10	8.3	4	4.51	0.6	0.80	0.32	-1.5	-0.5	5.63	-0.4
Greg McMichael	15	16.3	8	4.61	1.1	0.60	0.21	1.4	-2.2	2.89	4.2
Kevin Millwood	1	2.3	0	0.00	1.3	2.00	0.35	0.4	0.0	-1.12	1.6
Gabe Molina	2	2.0	4	18.80	-3.0	0.00	0.00	0.0	0.0	19.20	-3.1
Terry Mulholland	34	34.7	13	3.53	6.4	0.88	0.27	-1.8	2.8	4.98	0.8
Mike Remlinger	71	72.7	29	3.75	11.7	0.54	0.17	-0.1	3.2	4.15	8.4
Luis Rivera	5	6.7	1	1.41	2.8	0.60	0.22	0.1	0.5	1.98	2.4
John Rocker	59	53.0	25	4.43	4.5	0.29	0.06	0.2	2.4	4.81	2.3
Rudy Seanez	23	21.0	11	4.92	0.6	0.26	0.10	0.5	-0.2	4.36	2.0
Chris Seelbach	2	1.7	2	11.28	-1.1	0.50	0.15	0.3	0.0	10.34	-1.0
Dave Stevens	2	3.0	4	12.54	-2.4	0.00	0.00	0.0	0.0	12.80	-2.5
Ismael Villegas	1	2.7	4	14.10	-2.6	2.00	0.67	-1.4	0.0	19.45	-4.2
Don Wengert	10	10.0	9	8.46	-3.6	0.40	0.16	-0.4	-0.8	8.62	-3.8
TOTALS	376	400.0	207	4.87	14.7	0.53	0.18			4.95	11.2

For a quick guide to RET, see page 10.

Chicago Cubs

Another year, another debacle, another chapter in the timeless, sudsy, sunny story of Wrigley Field, right? It just isn't Chicago if a Daley isn't mayor, a third airport isn't in the works, and the Cubs aren't creating some new hopeless master plan. So is that all there is?

For the first time since the Dallas Green/Jim Frey master plan flopped during the laughably termed "Renewal Era," the answer is almost an outright "no." There's a great rebuilding project going on here, but it is at risk because of the absence of a shared vision at the management level.

While the White Sox get—and deserve—attention for a player-development effort that has born fruit at the same time that a window of opportunity to dominate the AL Central for several years has opened, the Cubs are mounting an outstanding player-development program of their own. It won't win now. It won't win in 2002. But it is the kind of effort that can duplicate the success seen on the South Side.

The rebuilding of the Cubs' farm system is comprehensive. Jim Hendry's player-development staff has had at least three good drafts in a row. They're especially strong scouting the Midwest and upper Midwest regions. Internationally, the Cubs have an established presence in the Dominican Republic, are moving into Venezuela, and, thanks to Pacific Rim Coordinator Leon Lee, trail only the Red Sox in opening up Korea.

What's already in the minors? In addition to blue-chip prospects Corey Patterson and Hee Seop Choi, the organization boasts a good group of shortstops. Luis Montanez and Bobby Hill were picked in 2000, while Nate Frese is already making good progress. Jim Deschaine hit well in the Midwest League, but he's expected to move off of shortstop. Hill probably will as well, but that's the nice thing about concentrating on talent at the more difficult positions: if they can hit, you can always move them to an easier position.

The organization's real strength is pitching. Beyond the touted trio of Ben Christensen, Carlos Zambrano, and Juan Cruz, the Cubs have a number of guys with a chance to survive long enough to become prospects. However, the Cubs have rushed just about all of their top pitching prospects. Whether it's Zambrano or Chistensen or Kyle Farnsworth or Ruben Quevedo, they push their young pitchers up the chain as fast as possible. While no one's career has been derailed yet, it's something to worry about.

Andy MacPhail commands a lot of respect in the industry, stemming from his days with the Twins; this despite his use of jargon that even Montgomery Burns would consider too preppy. (Is there another grown man saying things like "even-steven" or using "ballyhoo" as a verb?) He's also the last remaining member of the management troika of MacPhail, general manager Ed Lynch, and manager Jim Riggleman that rode into town in 1995, claiming they'd turn around the franchise. After three years and no progress, the Cubs' brief appearance in the playoffs in 1998 gave all three of them new leases on life. To the extent that their preservation allowed the farm system and player-development program to continue its rebuilding effort at its own pace without the interference that could have come from bringing in a new management team, it was a good thing.

Firing Jim Riggleman after 1999 was a bit of scapegoating, but it wasn't as if the Cubs were firing Casey Stengel. This year, while it obviously pained MacPhail to accept Ed Lynch's resignation, it's appropriate to identify Lynch as the architect of the bad things that came out of 1998. First, in the desperate drive for that playoff spot, Lynch asked his minor-league staffers about Jon Garland and Todd Noel. He rejected their advice to keep both no matter what the cost to the team's playoff chances; both were given up to bring in adequate relievers Matt Karchner and Felix Heredia—not the players who were going to put the Cubs over the top. Second, Lynch's subsequent decision to leave the roster almost unchanged for 1999 ruined any opportunity for the organization to use 1998 as a first step towards bigger and better things. Instead, 1999 was a preview of the ten-year reunion of the '98 team.

So now Jim Hendry is MacPhail's right-hand man. Everything isn't perfect. The Cubs still aren't doing a great job of

---

Cubs Prospectus

2000 record: 65–97; Sixth place, NL Central
Pythagenport W/L: 68–94
Runs Scored: 764 (11th in NL)
Runs Allowed: 904 (15th in NL)
Team EqA: .253 (12th in NL)
2000 Batters' Age: 31.2 (oldest in NL)
2000 Pitchers' Age: 28.0 (7th youngest in NL)
Ballpark: Wrigley Field; neutral park; Park Factor of .997
2000: The sun was hot, the beer was cold and the team was lousy.
2001: The sun will be hot, the beer will be cold and the team will be better.

evaluating players outside the organization. The absence of knowledge about the Yankees' organization led the Cubs to ask for time when the Yankees wanted an answer last summer, leaving Sammy Sosa twisting in the wind. Now they'll have to retain Sosa for the start of the season to avoid the public-relations hit the organization would take with advertisers and season-ticket holders if they were to lose both Sosa and Mark Grace.

While Hendry's player-development program cranks out players, the Cubs will face the basic problem of any franchise that's gearing up for a good run through player development: what do you do with the major-league team in the meantime? For years, the Cubs have played at being contenders, usually cobbling together a collection of adequate or marginally famous players to support the Sosa/Grace tandem. Paying top dollar for players has not really been the problem as much as the particular players getting paid. Whether it's Mickey Morandini, Gary Gaetti, Joe Girardi, Scott Servais, Lance Johnson, or Matt Karchner, the Cubs have made a nasty habit of spending good money on replacement-level players. So the first order of business is going to be acquiring good taste. Nabbing Rondell White and Bill Mueller for two mediocre pitchers is a good start.

There are still major obstacles to progress. The Cubs have been handicapped by two prima donnas, one of whom is now in the proud purple and teal of the Diamondbacks. The other one isn't Sammy Sosa. Sosa has turned out to be worth every penny paid out to him by TribCorp despite initial expectations that the enormous contract he signed in 1997 would be a millstone that would keep the Cubs from ever making the playoffs. He is the kind of player you can build a good offense around, and having both Eric Young and Rickey Gutierrez to get on base in front of him is good planning. Having Girardi and Damon Buford in the lineup is not.

No, the guy who needs to get with the program is manager Don Baylor. If there was one thing written in *Baseball Prospectus 2000* that deserved greater thought, it was the off-the-cuff comment that Baylor is a "pretty good manager." That was based on the theory that having managed in Coors, he'd be able to adapt to a high-offense environment like Wrigley Field. Instead, the Cubs led the National League in just two offensive categories: sacrifice bunts and men left on base. That doesn't seem like a coincidence, since Baylor's Rockies almost achieved the same dubious feat in his last year managing them. In each of his last two years as a manager, Baylor's shortstop led the league in sacrifice hits. Normally, it's a pitcher who does that.

One of Baylor's first acts as manager was to start firing on Sammy Sosa, publicly criticizing his defense and baserunning. If Baylor wanted to be an adult instead of adulated, he would have brought up the subject of Sosa's defense and baserunning with the person it concerned, Sosa. A good manager should note a player's weaknesses and try to see what can be done about them. Showing up the team's best player for public consumption was unprofessional, a sign of how things work under Don Baylor.

One of Baylor's other public fronts was to jabber about how the Cubs would become a better fundamental team. "Fundamental" is usually synonymous with "tactical indiscretions," like bunting a lot or making Joe Girardi and Damon Buford regulars. It was either winter bravado or ignorance of the players at hand. A lineup with Henry Rodriguez, Sammy Sosa, Damon Buford, and either Shane Andrews and Willie Greene isn't a contact-hitting team or one with which you should try to scrap out runs.

Baylor now spends his time airing his opinions on how the Cubs would be better if they just got as many of his old Rockie players as possible, or how they won't contend without a veteran closer. Setting aside the tremendous historic legacy of the Rockies dynasty, Baylor already had a veteran closer in Rick Aguilera. Baylor labors under the impression that he needs to win the World Series this year, or at least that working Jon Lieber and Ruben Quevedo hard for that elusive goal of 70 wins is worthwhile. The longer Baylor is left unsupervised, the more damage he'll do, costing his team runs due to roster makeup, lineup assembly, bullpen mismanagement, and starting pitcher abuse.

Does anyone else think of Mark Grace when they hear The Who's "Behind Blue Eyes"?

The Cubs' 2000 season needs to be remembered as the end of an era. Mark Grace's career has been symbolic of the fortunes of the Cubs franchise. Just as the Cubs are never as good as they think they are, Grace is not as great a player as WGN would have you believe. But Grace as the player who epitomizes baseball's gloriously bad franchise hardly touches on the extent to which he represents something deeper and fundamentally wrong about the relationship between baseball and the media.

Courtesy of local news, Grace has been a Chicago fixture, the guy who regurgitates "we need to take it one game at a time" or "we didn't play as well as we're capable of" or, by June, "we're beating ourselves" on a nightly basis. Don't think that most local sports anchors aren't grateful for that kind of consistency. They eagerly portray Grace as a star or as the team's leader, which conveniently keeps them in Grace's good graces so that they can fill those crucial ten seconds with another pre-packaged observation for local audiences.

More than just sound bites are required to maintain this kind of popularity. Grace has been more than happy to trash teammates off the record, wooing and titillating local writers with unquotable gossip that he swears (wink) he can't be quoted on. Off-the-record character assassination might be stock in trade for journalists, but that doesn't make it acceptable or true. What it does is twist the integrity of the media so that even in the putative act of providing news, they're picking favorites and distorting the way people perceive players.

In a perfect world, people wouldn't pretend that those ten seconds tell them anything about a player as a person, but because of his televised omnipresence, Grace is held up as a good guy. The guy sitting on the next barstool will probably claim he knows that Albert Belle or Barry Bonds are bad guys, and considering either player's thorny relationship with the media, are we surprised? We still have a black and white problem in the age of color television.

Grace has been so spoiled by a worshipful local media that he's taken seriously when he compares how he's being treated to what happened to Rick Sutcliffe, Greg Maddux, and Andre Dawson, while taking another petty jab at Sosa by pretending Sammy is the exception to this "rule." Cub apologists would remember that Ryne Sandberg was given just about everything he ever asked for, while an analyst would note that Sutcliffe and Dawson were both jettisoned for good reason: they wanted too much for what anyone expected them to contribute. But Grace is too busy playing victim and nailing himself up on a cross of corporate gold to notice that if it wasn't for the public-relations disaster of the Larry Himes years, the Cubs could have shown him the door before he became a 10-and-5 nuisance.

With a lineup already stocked with decent on-base guys like Eric Young, Ricky Gutierrez, and Bill Mueller, what the Cubs need is power. If Grace can't recognize that, television producers need to re-think using him as a color analyst. So Gracie heads out with parting shots: "We'll see if Andy [MacPhail] wants [Hee Seop] Choi hitting behind Sosa 300 times. Good luck. Sosa will walk 300 times." America loves to listen to people feel sorry for themselves, from Bill Clinton to Britney Spears, and now Mark Grace.

HITTERS (BA: .270, OBP: .340, SLG: .440, EqA: .260)

Shane Andrews — 3B — Bats R — Age 29

YEAR	TEAM	LGE	AB	H	DB	TP	HR	BB	SO	R	RBI	SB	CS	OUT	BA	OBP	SLG	EQA	EQR	DEFENSE	
1998	Montreal	NL	498	118	25	1	27	56	128	49	69	1	6	386	.237	.314	.454	.249	60	139-3B 11	
1999	Montreal	NL	283	51	7	0	11	39	83	27	35	1	0	232	.180	.280	.322	.202	21	64-3B -2	15-1B -1
1999	ChiCubs	NL	67	16	3	0	5	6	20	12	13	0	1	52	.239	.310	.507	.259	9	16-3B 1	
2000	ChiCubs	NL	194	44	5	0	13	23	55	24	36	1	1	151	.227	.314	.454	.252	24	44-3B 0	
2001	StLouis	NL	317	69	8	0	19	44	95	41	53	1	1	249	.218	.313	.423	.245	37		

Shane Andrews lost more than three months to a back injury, which basically blew his great opportunity to hit 30 home runs and become wealthy. Even after the Matt Stairs and Bill Mueller acquisitions, Andrews would still have value as the right-handed thumper to back them up and play on those hot days when the wind is blowing out at Wrigley. He's Scott McClain's lucky twin. "What did you boys get for Christmas?" "A major-league job!" "A Post-It® with directions to Colorado Springs."

Brant Brown — OF — Bats L — Age 30

YEAR	TEAM	LGE	AB	H	DB	TP	HR	BB	SO	R	RBI	SB	CS	OUT	BA	OBP	SLG	EQA	EQR	DEFENSE
1998	ChiCubs	NL	351	100	17	6	15	28	89	56	47	3	5	256	.285	.339	.496	.269	48	80-CF -4
1999	Pittsbrg	NL	343	77	20	3	15	17	108	46	53	2	3	270	.224	.269	.431	.225	32	74-RF -1
2000	Florida	NL	74	14	7	0	2	2	31	4	6	1	0	60	.189	.211	.365	.181	4	
2000	ChiCubs	NL	90	14	1	0	3	9	27	7	10	2	1	77	.156	.239	.267	.162	4	17-LF 0
2001	Milwauke	NL	236	54	13	1	9	19	81	29	33	3	2	184	.229	.286	.407	.230	23	

A romantic will tell you the story that Brown hasn't been the same since the dropped fly ball on a sunny September day in Milwaukee, but he just had his age-27 season. Try to remember what he originally was: an athletic first baseman who didn't hit enough to play first base, was moved to the outfield, and had one good year. Ed Lynch deserved a lot of the flak he took over the years, but he had the good sense to deal Brown when his value was highest. Now the Cubs have both Brown and Jon Lieber, and Cam Bonifay has... his self-respect. Brown has been signed by the Brewers as a minor-league free agent.

National League

Roosevelt Brown — OF — Bats L — Age 25

YEAR	TEAM	LGE	AB	H	DB	TP	HR	BB	SO	R	RBI	SB	CS	OUT	BA	OBP	SLG	EQA	EQR	DEFENSE	
1998	Daytona	Fla	242	64	11	3	6	17	52	34	27	1	1	179	.264	.316	.409	.240	25	58-LF	0
1998	WestTenn	Sou	161	37	7	0	5	7	32	14	17	2	1	125	.230	.268	.366	.207	12	35-RF	-3
1999	WestTenn	Sou	126	32	7	0	3	10	31	9	9	3	1	95	.254	.315	.381	.235	13	30-RF	-1
1999	Iowa	PCL	263	82	21	1	16	16	52	38	57	2	2	183	.312	.356	.582	.297	44	64-LF	-2
1999	ChiCubs	NL	64	13	6	1	1	2	13	6	9	1	0	51	.203	.227	.375	.193	4	12-LF	-3
2000	Iowa	PCL	362	99	18	0	12	28	61	50	43	6	2	265	.273	.334	.423	.254	43	89-RF	-10
2000	ChiCubs	NL	91	31	4	0	4	3	21	10	14	0	1	61	.341	.367	.516	.285	13	19-LF	0
2001	ChiCubs	NL	396	119	20	1	19	38	82	63	78	4	1	278	.301	.362	.500	.286	61		

Maybe we're stubborn, but Rosie Brown looks to us like a better hitting prospect than Henry Rodriguez was when the Expos took a chance on him. Although he's not a good defensive outfielder, you'd think a team that's accepted the shortcomings of Rodriguez, Glenallen Hill, and Brant Brown would cut him some slack. He would make a great fourth outfielder to spot start during Rondell White's inevitable aches and pains, but he may get lost in the shuffle.

Damon Buford — CF — Bats R — Age 31

YEAR	TEAM	LGE	AB	H	DB	TP	HR	BB	SO	R	RBI	SB	CS	OUT	BA	OBP	SLG	EQA	EQR	DEFENSE	
1998	Boston	AL	215	61	12	4	11	21	38	36	41	4	5	159	.284	.350	.530	.280	33	54-CF	2
1999	Boston	AL	296	73	16	2	6	18	67	38	36	8	2	225	.247	.294	.375	.225	27	82-CF	0
2000	ChiCubs	NL	499	123	18	3	14	39	110	60	45	3	6	382	.246	.310	.379	.228	47	136-CF	-1
2001	ChiCubs	NL	343	84	15	2	11	34	79	43	46	6	3	262	.245	.313	.397	.240	37		

If Brown makes a good fourth outfielder, Damon Buford makes a great fifth outfielder and right-handed-hitting caddy for Corey Patterson. He can hurt left-handed pitchers and hold his own in center field. On the Cubs, he gets miscast as a regular. Buford's counting stats look adequate because of the regular playing time, but nobody is an asset as a regular when he doesn't post a .300 OBP or slug .350 against right-handed pitching.

Hee Seop Choi — 1B — Bats L — Age 22

YEAR	TEAM	LGE	AB	H	DB	TP	HR	BB	SO	R	RBI	SB	CS	OUT	BA	OBP	SLG	EQA	EQR	DEFENSE	
1999	Lansing	Mid	291	70	12	3	11	33	74	45	39	1	0	221	.241	.320	.416	.246	33	76-1B	-6
2000	Daytona	Fla	349	84	16	3	12	27	89	43	47	2	1	266	.241	.301	.407	.234	35	84-1B	1
2000	WestTenn	Sou	128	34	7	0	8	20	39	21	19	2	1	95	.266	.365	.508	.286	21	35-1B	1
2001	ChiCubs	NL	326	90	14	2	19	40	97	52	66	3	1	237	.276	.355	.506	.285	51		

The organization's symbol of progress, Hee Seop Choi has made big strides defensively, and he can hit. I'm not saying he'll hit like Reggie Jackson, but like Reggie his longest drives go to left-center field. Concerns about his conditioning have been overstated. He's not Kent Hrbek, and he moves around the bases well. If the Cubs make him wait, he's a great candidate for the NL Rookie of the Year award in 2002, but after this season and a great Arizona Fall League run, he should force his way up sooner than that.

Nate Frese — SS — Bats R — Age 23

YEAR	TEAM	LGE	AB	H	DB	TP	HR	BB	SO	R	RBI	SB	CS	OUT	BA	OBP	SLG	EQA	EQR	DEFENSE	
1998	Willmspt	NYP	179	36	5	0	2	11	41	20	14	2	1	144	.201	.251	.263	.160	7	50-SS	9
1999	Lansing	Mid	377	79	20	2	3	38	73	45	31	4	2	300	.210	.286	.297	.196	25	99-SS	27
2000	Daytona	Fla	434	105	18	3	6	47	95	51	37	4	3	332	.242	.320	.339	.224	40	108-SS	14
2001	ChiCubs	NL	392	98	16	1	6	46	89	52	43	7	3	297	.250	.329	.342	.233	39		

A ballplayer. Nate Frese is one of scout Mark Servais's finds in the Midwest. He came out of Iowa as a college pitcher, but the Cubs saw something and made him a shortstop. He's big and rangy and goes to the hole well. He knows how to take a walk and keeps improving as a hitter. I don't know how they saw it, but this is a very good piece of scouting. While a lot of the other shortstop prospects in the organization will probably get moved to other positions (although not 2000 top pick Luis Montanez), Frese could stake a claim on the job by 2002 if he survives the jump to Double-A.

Joe Girardi — C — Bats R — Age 36

YEAR	TEAM	LGE	AB	H	DB	TP	HR	BB	SO	R	RBI	SB	CS	OUT	BA	OBP	SLG	EQA	EQR	DEFENSE	
1998	NY Yanks	AL	254	73	12	4	3	14	34	32	31	1	4	185	.287	.329	.402	.240	26	78-C	-2
1999	NY Yanks	AL	209	52	17	1	2	8	24	23	26	3	1	158	.249	.276	.368	.212	16	62-C	-4
2000	ChiCubs	NL	365	100	13	1	6	27	57	45	38	1	0	265	.274	.328	.364	.235	35	96-C	5
2001	*ChiCubs*	*NL*	*284*	*72*	*11*	*1*	*5*	*25*	*43*	*30*	*33*	*1*	*1*	*213*	*.254*	*.314*	*.352*	*.226*	*26*		

He's the team's resident grumpmeister, right down to whining about the Marlins for exulting over a sweep of the Cubs. Joltless Joe Girardi needs to accept that however many rings the Yankees put on his fingers, nobody will cut him any slack. He's still one of the worst plate-blockers in the majors. Unlike Mike Piazza, he positions himself properly but drops just about every ball thrown at him.

Ross Gload — 1B/LF — Bats L — Age 25

YEAR	TEAM	LGE	AB	H	DB	TP	HR	BB	SO	R	RBI	SB	CS	OUT	BA	OBP	SLG	EQA	EQR	DEFENSE			
1998	KaneCnty	Mid	515	130	28	1	11	41	90	57	65	2	3	388	.252	.309	.375	.228	48	125-1B	-3		
1999	Brevard	Fla	499	125	22	2	8	39	88	62	54	1	1	375	.251	.308	.351	.221	43	129-1B	2		
2000	Portland	Eas	403	97	20	2	13	20	59	45	46	2	1	307	.241	.278	.397	.221	35	49-LF	-4	47-1B	-3
2000	Iowa	PCL	102	36	7	1	11	7	13	18	27	1	1	67	.353	.398	.765	.349	24	25-LF	-4		
2000	ChiCubs	NL	31	6	0	1	1	3	9	4	3	0	0	25	.194	.265	.355	.203	2				
2001	*ChiCubs*	*NL*	*513*	*141*	*24*	*1*	*22*	*45*	*88*	*68*	*87*	*1*	*1*	*373*	*.275*	*.333*	*.454*	*.262*	*66*				

Ross Gload was acquired with left-hander David Noyce for Henry Rodriguez. He uppercuts everything, which paid off this year. His chances took a big hit when the Cubs got Matt Stairs in exchange for doing the Athletics the favor of claiming Eric Ireland on waivers. Before the trade, Gload probably had a two-month window to stake a claim on a semi-regular job. Now, he'll have to have a huge camp just to beat out Rosie Brown.

Jeff Goldbach — C — Bats R — Age 21

YEAR	TEAM	LGE	AB	H	DB	TP	HR	BB	SO	R	RBI	SB	CS	OUT	BA	OBP	SLG	EQA	EQR	DEFENSE	
1999	Lansing	Mid	403	84	18	1	12	43	72	53	42	0	2	321	.208	.290	.347	.212	33	79-C	-12
2000	Daytona	Fla	425	79	11	1	9	22	86	40	47	3	3	349	.186	.233	.280	.157	17	99-C	-22
2001	*ChiCubs*	*NL*	*327*	*72*	*8*	*0*	*11*	*29*	*81*	*29*	*36*	*1*	*1*	*256*	*.220*	*.284*	*.346*	*.211*	*26*		

The organization feels Jeff Goldbach's Y2K glitch was the product of pressure. Goldbach was touted as one of the best of the 1999 Lansing Lugnuts, but he was also the youngest guy on the team. Trying to keep up with Patterson or Choi or Tydus Meadows or even Dave Kelton wouldn't be easy, considering Goldbach's inexperience while attempting to jump to the Florida State League. His hitting suffered, and the feeling is that he took those struggles with him behind the plate: he dropped from throwing out 27% of base-stealers in 1999 to 21% in 2000 and needs to improve his footwork. Goldbach is no longer the Cubs' only catching prospect now that they have Yoon-Min Kweon. He's too young for us to say that this year is critical, but everyone wants to see improvement.

Mark Grace — 1B — Bats L — Age 37

YEAR	TEAM	LGE	AB	H	DB	TP	HR	BB	SO	R	RBI	SB	CS	OUT	BA	OBP	SLG	EQA	EQR	DEFENSE	
1998	ChiCubs	NL	604	183	37	3	18	90	52	92	87	3	7	428	.303	.396	.464	.287	94	156-1B	9
1999	ChiCubs	NL	592	175	44	4	15	74	42	101	82	2	4	420	.296	.376	.459	.279	86	155-1B	5
2000	ChiCubs	NL	513	140	35	2	11	86	26	71	77	1	2	375	.273	.383	.413	.272	73	137-1B	4
2001	*Arizona*	*NL*	*410*	*111*	*22*	*1*	*7*	*68*	*28*	*68*	*57*	*2*	*2*	*301*	*.271*	*.374*	*.380*	*.263*	*54*		

For all of the attention paid to his leading baseball in hits in the 1990s, consider the other decade leaders, in order: Honus Wagner, Ty Cobb, Rogers Hornsby, Paul Waner, Lou Boudreau, Richie Ashburn, Roberto Clemente, Pete Rose, and Robin Yount. Grace is the only guy on the list who doesn't deserve any support for the Hall of Fame (Pete Rose's issues aside). Count Grace out unless somebody puts Ryne Sandberg on the Veterans Committee in 20 years, and Ryno takes a page from Frankie Frisch's book and starts inducting teammates willy-nilly.

National League

Willie Greene — 3B — Bats L — Age 29

YEAR	TEAM	LGE	AB	H	DB	TP	HR	BB	SO	R	RBI	SB	CS	OUT	BA	OBP	SLG	EQA	EQR	DEFENSE			
1998	Cincnnti	NL	360	95	15	1	15	55	75	57	48	6	3	268	.264	.366	.436	.271	51	69-3B	1	22-RF	0
1999	Toronto	AL	225	46	6	0	13	18	51	22	40	0	0	179	.204	.263	.404	.217	20				
2000	ChiCubs	NL	302	60	14	2	10	31	65	33	35	4	0	242	.199	.277	.358	.213	25	75-3B	10		
2001	ChiCubs	NL	311	72	14	1	15	46	74	47	49	4	0	239	.232	.331	.428	.258	40				

There was once a time when Willie Greene was legitimately one of the best prospects in baseball, but as Steven Geswein points out, he might have been the victim of one of those subtle injuries that can wreck a career. In 1995 at Indianapolis, he ripped up some hand ligaments and hasn't had the same bat speed since. It isn't hard to envision the nightmare of being an injured minor leaguer in the Reds organization in the Marge Schott days, relying on an underfunded medical staff in the primitive conditions of old Bush Stadium. Greene is nothing more than a utility man now, and I'm coming around to believing he needs to be compared to Justin Thompson, a guy with so much talent that even being damaged goods wasn't going to keep him out of the majors.

Ryan Gripp — 3B — Bats R — Age 23

YEAR	TEAM	LGE	AB	H	DB	TP	HR	BB	SO	R	RBI	SB	CS	OUT	BA	OBP	SLG	EQA	EQR	DEFENSE	
1999	Eugene	Nwn	265	62	10	1	8	14	73	23	26	1	0	203	.234	.282	.370	.215	22	66-3B	3
2000	Lansing	Mid	507	131	17	0	17	45	95	61	61	2	0	376	.258	.322	.393	.240	53	122-3B	0
2001	ChiCubs	NL	309	84	7	0	13	28	78	37	50	1	0	225	.272	.332	.421	.254	37		

The Midwest League batting champ, he's compared to Jeff Bagwell for his quick, diving stroke. Ryan Gripp kills off-speed stuff and can get around on good heat. He does not get a lot of credit for his glove, but he has a good arm and decent hands. Gripp is the best third-base prospect in the system, but he'll have to race to pass Dave Kelton on the field as well as in the hearts and minds of the organization.

Ricky Gutierrez — SS — Bats R — Age 31

YEAR	TEAM	LGE	AB	H	DB	TP	HR	BB	SO	R	RBI	SB	CS	OUT	BA	OBP	SLG	EQA	EQR	DEFENSE	
1998	Houston	NL	500	134	27	3	2	53	79	58	47	12	7	373	.268	.345	.346	.238	52	134-SS	4
1999	Houston	NL	270	69	7	5	1	33	42	32	23	1	4	206	.256	.341	.330	.227	25	71-SS	-6
2000	ChiCubs	NL	452	122	20	2	10	58	54	69	52	7	2	332	.270	.360	.389	.258	56	116-SS	-7
2001	ChiCubs	NL	399	104	18	2	6	60	58	62	50	7	5	300	.261	.357	.361	.250	47		

Dislocating his shoulder when he fell down with a strained hamstring cost him a month of the best season of his career. Ricky Gutierrez has some pretty severe defensive limitations. Like Jeff Blauser before him, he's not going to give you that great stop in the hole, and he isn't a wiz on the deuce. He is going to give you a solid offensive contribution; if the Cubs had a good line-up core, he'd be a quality support player.

Bobby Hill — SS — Bats B — Age 22

YEAR	TEAM	LGE	AB	H	DB	TP	HR	BB	SO	R	RBI	SB	CS	OUT	BA	OBP	SLG	EQA	EQR	DEFENSE
2000	NWK	ATL	399	85	13	3	5	58	67	44	32	21	7	321	.213	.315	.298	.218	36	

Bobby Hill is the University of Miami shortstop and Scott Boras client drafted by the White Sox in '99 who rejected their offers and signed instead with Newark in the Atlantic League. After leading the league in OBP, he was re-drafted by the Cubs. He's young enough that he probably didn't put as big a dent in his future as Jason Varitek did following Boras's orders. The Cubs expect him to start in Double-A, probably at second base after a 38-error season for Newark. With only an independent-league season on his resume, we have no projection for him.

Eric Hinske — 3B/1B — Bats L — Age 23

YEAR	TEAM	LGE	AB	H	DB	TP	HR	BB	SO	R	RBI	SB	CS	OUT	BA	OBP	SLG	EQA	EQR	DEFENSE			
1998	Willmspt	NYP	258	61	9	0	8	24	65	28	37	7	2	199	.236	.304	.364	.227	24	61-1B	12		
1999	Daytona	Fla	449	105	20	3	14	46	104	52	51	7	5	349	.234	.308	.385	.232	45	51-1B	3	51-3B	-7
2000	WestTenn	Sou	457	106	17	6	18	60	138	65	60	7	3	354	.232	.323	.414	.247	54	113-3B	-6		
2001	ChiCubs	NL	450	118	18	4	19	53	132	69	74	10	3	335	.262	.340	.447	.266	61				

(Eric Hinske *continued*)

He's a big, blocky guy who can man any of the corners, infield or outfield. At third base, Eric Hinske lacks the arm strength or the range to ever be more than a temp. Now that Bill Mueller has been acquired, Hinske won't have to be a regular, so he'll now be evaluated as a bench player. He could have a good Denny Walling career, but seems doomed to go down the same road Dave Hansen paved.

Jeff Huson   IF   Bats L   Age 36

YEAR	TEAM	LGE	AB	H	DB	TP	HR	BB	SO	R	RBI	SB	CS	OUT	BA	OBP	SLG	EQA	EQR	DEFENSE			
1998	Tucson	PCL	80	19	2	1	1	4	15	5	9	0	1	62	.237	.279	.325	.193	5	12-SS	-6		
1999	Anaheim	AL	224	60	5	2	0	14	25	20	17	10	1	165	.268	.311	.308	.217	18	28-2B	5	12-SS	-2
2000	ChiCubs	NL	131	28	7	1	0	11	8	18	11	2	1	104	.214	.275	.282	.184	8	13-SS	0	12-3B	-1

Jeff Huson is just one of Don Baylor's coterie of veteran lackeys. It isn't that he is a bad player to have around, it's that in the National League, your bench players have to double as pinch-hitters. Between Huson and Jose Nieves, the Cubs were stuck with two offensive zeroes who make even those throwaway pinch-hitting situations, when you're down by a bunch and just getting the pitcher out of the game, easy outs for the opposition. That makes a bad team worse. Retired, and now coaching.

Dave Kelton   3B   Bats R   Age 21

YEAR	TEAM	LGE	AB	H	DB	TP	HR	BB	SO	R	RBI	SB	CS	OUT	BA	OBP	SLG	EQA	EQR	DEFENSE	
1999	Lansing	Mid	509	112	12	2	10	22	132	48	44	9	5	401	.220	.254	.310	.182	28	113-3B	-20
2000	Daytona	Fla	527	117	21	4	15	27	136	56	59	3	4	414	.222	.261	.362	.201	38	97-3B	-17
2001	*ChiCubs*	*NL*	*370*	*90*	*12*	*2*	*11*	*23*	*117*	*38*	*43*	*6*	*3*	*283*	*.243*	*.288*	*.376*	*.222*	*33*		

Here's an example of a player on whom scouts and statheads can't see eye to eye. Dave Kelton is touted for his athleticism and reflexes at third base, his quick bat, and the power he's shown. But he's also error-prone, strikes out a lot, and hears "Ball four!" only about once a week. There is talent here, but the shortcomings are just as obvious. Kelton is young enough to improve with some good instruction, but he needs to start making progress instead of merely adapting his skill set to his league.

Cole Liniak   3B   Bats R   Age 24

YEAR	TEAM	LGE	AB	H	DB	TP	HR	BB	SO	R	RBI	SB	CS	OUT	BA	OBP	SLG	EQA	EQR	DEFENSE	
1998	Pawtuckt	Int	429	101	23	1	15	30	70	54	49	2	3	331	.235	.291	.399	.226	40	104-3B	-3
1999	Pawtuckt	Int	348	82	16	0	11	32	57	44	33	0	4	270	.236	.301	.376	.222	31	88-3B	0
2000	Iowa	PCL	412	89	17	1	16	30	79	49	45	3	2	325	.216	.273	.379	.213	34	110-3B	-15
2001	*Toronto*	*AL*	*386*	*96*	*15*	*0*	*17*	*38*	*74*	*51*	*63*	*1*	*2*	*292*	*.249*	*.316*	*.420*	*.245*	*43*		

Cole Liniak serves as a cautionary tale for Kelton believers. He is still very young, but how many guys put in more than 300 games in Triple-A before their 24th birthday? He should have been up once Shane Andrews went down in May. The Cubs weren't contending, and they can't spare the space on the 40-man roster to keep him around just to help Iowa. They should have evaluated him in the majors when they had the chance. Traded to the Blue Jays in a minor deal.

Gary Matthews Jr.   OF   Bats B   Age 26

YEAR	TEAM	LGE	AB	H	DB	TP	HR	BB	SO	R	RBI	SB	CS	OUT	BA	OBP	SLG	EQA	EQR	DEFENSE	
1998	Mobile	Sou	256	65	14	2	5	39	53	43	34	5	1	192	.254	.354	.383	.255	32	68-CF	12
1999	LasVegas	PCL	416	89	17	3	6	48	101	42	38	11	4	331	.214	.302	.313	.212	34	119-CF	-4
2000	Iowa	PCL	211	47	10	2	4	14	42	21	17	4	1	165	.223	.271	.346	.205	16	57-CF	-2
2000	ChiCubs	NL	159	30	1	2	4	13	26	23	13	3	0	129	.189	.254	.296	.182	9	39-LF	1
2001	*ChiCubs*	*NL*	*326*	*75*	*12*	*2*	*6*	*38*	*71*	*42*	*33*	*10*	*2*	*253*	*.230*	*.310*	*.334*	*.226*	*31*		

One of the organization's "story" players, in that he's "Little Sarge" and some people still haven't let go of 1984. That good year at Mobile is starting to look like a fluke. His future with the organization depends on whether or not the team keeps Corey Patterson out of spring training. If they don't, Matthews will probably be Buford's token left-handed-hitting caddy.

National League

Tydus Meadows — LF — Bats R — Age 23

YEAR	TEAM	LGE	AB	H	DB	TP	HR	BB	SO	R	RBI	SB	CS	OUT	BA	OBP	SLG	EQA	EQR	DEFENSE	
1998	Rockford	Mid	138	33	2	0	6	11	34	24	17	2	1	106	.239	.304	.384	.230	13	33-LF	0
1999	Lansing	Mid	451	104	22	3	11	43	93	49	44	7	5	352	.231	.305	.366	.225	42	103-LF	-8
2000	Daytona	Fla	169	43	7	1	5	12	41	20	17	5	2	128	.254	.312	.396	.238	18	43-LF	-4
2000	WestTenn	Sou	256	62	11	3	5	14	75	29	27	2	1	195	.242	.287	.367	.216	21	64-LF	-3
2001	*ChiCubs*	*NL*	*408*	*107*	*19*	*2*	*11*	*36*	*108*	*54*	*55*	*8*	*2*	*303*	*.262*	*.322*	*.400*	*.246*	*45*		

Tydus Meadows is not as patient as you'd like, and he doesn't have as much power as he will in a couple of years. He needs at least a full season at Double-A so he can learn what pitches he can drive. In four or five years, Meadows might be a new Geronimo Berroa, a bargain regular for a savvy shopper.

Chad Meyers — 2B/OF — Bats R — Age 25

YEAR	TEAM	LGE	AB	H	DB	TP	HR	BB	SO	R	RBI	SB	CS	OUT	BA	OBP	SLG	EQA	EQR	DEFENSE		DEFENSE	
1998	Daytona	Fla	187	45	6	2	2	25	33	23	16	8	3	145	.241	.339	.326	.235	19	45-2B	-14		
1998	WestTenn	Sou	296	69	9	0	1	41	46	41	20	19	6	233	.233	.332	.274	.220	27	73-2B	-14		
1999	WestTenn	Sou	240	60	16	1	2	18	43	31	21	10	4	184	.250	.317	.350	.229	23	57-2B	-4		
1999	Iowa	PCL	173	52	10	2	0	24	19	29	12	11	5	126	.301	.392	.382	.271	24	39-2B	-2		
1999	ChiCubs	NL	143	33	8	0	0	7	25	15	5	3	2	112	.231	.281	.287	.187	8	24-2B	0	11-CF	0
2000	Iowa	PCL	302	73	4	0	3	34	42	38	21	21	10	239	.242	.326	.285	.217	26	62-2B	-15	15-OF	-3
2000	ChiCubs	NL	53	9	3	0	0	2	10	8	5	1	0	44	.170	.212	.226	.119	1				
2001	*ChiCubs*	*NL*	*379*	*98*	*14*	*1*	*3*	*50*	*61*	*62*	*36*	*21*	*9*	*290*	*.259*	*.345*	*.325*	*.239*	*40*				

Everyone has kidded themselves about Chad Meyers, us included. He cannot play an adequate second base and he is never going to hit the way an outfielder needs to. That doesn't make him useless. He still has his core skills: he can run, and he can get on base. For a pinch-hitter and utility man you'd keep around to lead off innings, you could do a lot worse.

Jose Nieves — SS — Bats R — Age 26

YEAR	TEAM	LGE	AB	H	DB	TP	HR	BB	SO	R	RBI	SB	CS	OUT	BA	OBP	SLG	EQA	EQR	DEFENSE		DEFENSE	
1998	WestTenn	Sou	314	78	21	3	6	8	58	29	26	9	6	242	.248	.269	.392	.214	26	81-SS	-16		
1998	Iowa	PCL	74	17	3	0	0	2	11	6	3	1	1	58	.230	.250	.270	.158	3	19-SS	2		
1999	Iowa	PCL	388	91	22	2	8	20	63	43	45	8	5	302	.235	.277	.363	.211	31	96-SS	-8		
1999	ChiCubs	NL	182	45	8	1	2	5	24	15	17	0	2	139	.247	.282	.335	.198	12	50-SS	1		
2000	ChiCubs	NL	200	42	6	3	5	8	40	16	23	1	1	159	.210	.240	.345	.185	12	28-3B	2	15-SS	-3
2001	*ChiCubs*	*NL*	*317*	*73*	*15*	*2*	*8*	*18*	*57*	*29*	*33*	*3*	*2*	*246*	*.230*	*.272*	*.366*	*.211*	*25*				

The new Manny Alexander. Like His Mannyness, Jose Nieves's skills are summed up by the monomaniacal drive to do everything harder, whether it's getting into a hole (swing harder) or trying to make a play in the field (throw harder). He hasn't been on base often enough to know if he can run harder. Nieves isn't going to survive the organization's wave of shortstops coming through the system.

Augie Ojeda — SS — Bats B — Age 26

YEAR	TEAM	LGE	AB	H	DB	TP	HR	BB	SO	R	RBI	SB	CS	OUT	BA	OBP	SLG	EQA	EQR	DEFENSE	
1998	Bowie	Eas	260	60	9	1	1	28	31	31	16	0	2	202	.231	.310	.285	.200	18	68-SS	-1
1999	Bowie	Eas	468	108	16	2	8	41	51	58	46	3	1	361	.231	.301	.325	.211	37	133-SS	6
2000	Iowa	PCL	395	100	19	1	7	25	28	43	33	10	4	299	.253	.306	.359	.225	36	101-SS	0
2000	ChiCubs	NL	78	17	3	1	2	8	8	10	8	0	1	62	.218	.291	.359	.212	6	19-SS	4
2001	*ChiCubs*	*NL*	*429*	*106*	*19*	*1*	*7*	*43*	*41*	*53*	*46*	*8*	*3*	*326*	*.247*	*.316*	*.345*	*.228*	*40*		

Augie Ojeda is a good shortstop, a switch-hitter with a little power, and a great bunter. No, this isn't a collection of skills you find in one player very often, but with two right-handed-hitting starters without a lot of range in the middle infield, Ojeda was and continues to be the best choice for the utility job. Plus, anybody named Augie is an instant cult hero.

Corey Patterson   CF   Bats L   Age 21

YEAR	TEAM	LGE	AB	H	DB	TP	HR	BB	SO	R	RBI	SB	CS	OUT	BA	OBP	SLG	EQA	EQR	DEFENSE	
1999	Lansing	Mid	470	116	24	7	14	13	93	55	45	13	5	359	.247	.271	.417	.225	43	102-CF	-3
2000	WestTenn	Sou	459	109	21	4	18	32	119	59	65	13	7	357	.237	.295	.418	.235	48	118-CF	5
2000	ChiCubs	NL	42	7	0	0	2	3	13	8	2	1	1	36	.167	.237	.310	.172	2	11-CF	-1
2001	ChiCubs	NL	373	102	18	5	17	25	101	54	63	12	5	276	.273	.319	.485	.265	50		

Corey Patterson is still one of the best prospects in the game, but not a lock to win the job in center field this spring. He has the arm and range for the position and will be one of the best in the league when he improves his routes to the ball. In 2000, he started spreading his stance, but not quite to a Von Hayes stretch. The Cubs spent a lot of time working on his bunting for base hits and apparently almost none on his selectivity. He kills off-speed stuff, struggles with heat, and adjusts well within at-bats. Without improvement, he'll be a mix of Garret Anderson's and Devon White's better skills. But he's going to improve.

Jorge Piedra   CF   Bats L   Age 22

YEAR	TEAM	LGE	AB	H	DB	TP	HR	BB	SO	R	RBI	SB	CS	OUT	BA	OBP	SLG	EQA	EQR	DEFENSE	
1998	GreatFls	Pio	273	73	14	3	1	19	34	34	15	5	3	203	.267	.316	.352	.225	24	70-CF	-2
1999	Vero Bch	Fla	59	13	3	0	1	6	10	9	4	1	1	47	.220	.292	.322	.204	4	14-CF	-4
2000	Vero Bch	Fla	362	85	9	3	6	21	65	41	38	9	3	280	.235	.282	.326	.204	26	91-CF	-2
2000	Daytona	Fla	139	39	7	1	1	4	17	17	12	4	2	102	.281	.301	.367	.222	12	34-CF	2
2001	ChiCubs	NL	347	95	13	2	6	27	58	47	41	12	5	256	.274	.326	.375	.241	37		

The real prize in the second Ismael Valdes deal was an undrafted high-school find by the Dodgers. Jorge Piedra has shown pretty good range in center field. He may merely hold his own at Double-A, but he's young enough to afford a year or two of learning pitch identification against advanced competition.

Jeff Reed   C   Bats L   Age 38

YEAR	TEAM	LGE	AB	H	DB	TP	HR	BB	SO	R	RBI	SB	CS	OUT	BA	OBP	SLG	EQA	EQR	DEFENSE	
1998	Colorado	NL	254	65	14	1	8	35	53	39	33	0	0	189	.256	.348	.413	.257	32	75-C	1
1999	Colorado	NL	103	22	1	0	3	15	23	9	10	0	1	82	.214	.319	.311	.214	9	26-C	-3
1999	ChiCubs	NL	150	37	10	2	1	26	32	17	15	1	1	114	.247	.365	.360	.252	18	45-C	-3
2000	ChiCubs	NL	231	49	6	0	5	40	64	24	25	0	1	183	.212	.331	.303	.220	21	64-C	1
2001	ChiCubs	NL	153	30	2	0	4	30	40	18	16	0	0	123	.196	.328	.288	.219	14		

Jeff Reed is a good caddy for a team that has a right-handed-hitting catcher with power and a great arm, but instead of Charles Johnson, the Cubs have Joe Girardi. Reed would have problems beating Mike Ditka in a footrace, and not just because you'd have to surgically remove the golf cart from Da Coach's keister.

Jason Smith   SS   Bats L   Age 23

YEAR	TEAM	LGE	AB	H	DB	TP	HR	BB	SO	R	RBI	SB	CS	OUT	BA	OBP	SLG	EQA	EQR	DEFENSE	
1998	Rockford	Mid	473	101	14	5	7	21	131	49	46	9	3	375	.214	.248	.309	.179	26	107-SS	11
1999	Daytona	Fla	143	31	5	1	4	8	34	15	18	4	2	114	.217	.265	.350	.203	11	37-SS	-13
2000	WestTenn	Sou	492	111	20	5	11	13	135	48	52	8	5	386	.226	.247	.354	.193	31	114-SS	-18
2001	ChiCubs	NL	367	87	15	3	10	20	106	37	41	8	3	283	.237	.276	.376	.218	31		

He was a Double-A All-Star this year after missing most of 1999 with hamstring problems. Jason Smith came out with a hot start only to struggle terribly in the second half. Although he has a strong arm and a little bit of power, he doesn't really have the range to stick at short. He's the left-handed version of Jose Nieves.

Sammy Sosa   RF   Bats R   Age 32

YEAR	TEAM	LGE	AB	H	DB	TP	HR	BB	SO	R	RBI	SB	CS	OUT	BA	OBP	SLG	EQA	EQR	DEFENSE	
1998	ChiCubs	NL	651	195	21	1	64	70	160	134	151	16	9	465	.300	.368	.630	.311	126	155-RF	3
1999	ChiCubs	NL	625	172	23	2	58	69	161	106	125	5	7	460	.275	.350	.597	.296	110	160-RF	6
2000	ChiCubs	NL	607	188	32	1	48	81	157	99	127	6	4	423	.310	.392	.603	.317	119	150-RF	-10
2001	ChiCubs	NL	579	180	23	1	52	96	158	119	160	6	5	404	.311	.409	.623	.329	125		

National League

That's right, we're projecting Sammy Sosa to improve. Why? Not counting intentional passes, he's drawn 70 and 72 walks in the last two seasons, despite never having drawn 60 in a season before (no, not even in 1998). He's led the NL in road home runs each of the last two years.

One of the effects of the new schedule is that Sosa will get more games against division rivals. If the Cubs don't trade him, that would mean more games against the Brewers and Pirates and more games at Enron Field. Sosa should win another home-run title.

Rondell White — OF — Bats R — Age 29

YEAR	TEAM	LGE	AB	H	DB	TP	HR	BB	SO	R	RBI	SB	CS	OUT	BA	OBP	SLG	EQA	EQR	DEFENSE	
1998	Montreal	NL	362	107	19	2	18	28	53	54	57	15	7	262	.296	.357	.508	.283	56	96-CF	13
1999	Montreal	NL	541	164	24	5	22	25	80	78	59	7	5	382	.303	.346	.488	.273	74	130-LF	-6
2000	Montreal	NL	293	88	17	0	13	23	63	49	53	5	1	206	.300	.355	.491	.280	43	74-LF	4
2000	ChiCubs	NL	67	21	2	0	2	4	11	7	7	0	2	48	.313	.367	.433	.259	8	18-LF	2
2001	ChiCubs	NL	375	112	16	1	17	33	70	59	69	9	4	266	.299	.355	.483	.280	55		

Acquiring him is a calculated risk, but if Rondell White is ever going to resemble the player he was before the knee problems, it will be at Wrigley. A free agent after 2001, it would be smart if he were used the same way Dusty Baker used Ellis Burks, given regular rest to avoid injury. It would be good for the Cubs, good for White, and bad for the Expos, who would look like schmucks for getting only Scott Downs after so many juicy Rondell rumors over the years.

Eric Young — 2B — Bats R — Age 34

YEAR	TEAM	LGE	AB	H	DB	TP	HR	BB	SO	R	RBI	SB	CS	OUT	BA	OBP	SLG	EQA	EQR	DEFENSE
1998	LosAngls	NL	463	136	24	1	9	43	30	80	44	40	14	341	.294	.360	.408	.265	62	113-2B -16
1999	LosAngls	NL	461	129	23	2	2	57	25	66	39	39	21	352	.280	.365	.351	.250	55	110-2B -7
2000	ChiCubs	NL	611	177	38	2	6	53	37	92	44	49	7	441	.290	.353	.388	.263	78	147-2B -2
2001	ChiCubs	NL	476	134	25	1	5	60	31	95	51	39	12	354	.282	.362	.370	.261	62	

Eric Young came in boasting that he'd steal 80 bases, which was like Don Baylor's preseason claim that Sosa should steal 30: off by about 30 steals. He was placed in the awkward position of being Baylor's translator thanks to Baylor's tendency to fire on his players through the media. Young would explain that it wasn't an unprofessional way of doing things, but the motivational ploy of a great leader.

Julio Zuleta — 1B/LF — Bats R — Age 26

YEAR	TEAM	LGE	AB	H	DB	TP	HR	BB	SO	R	RBI	SB	CS	OUT	BA	OBP	SLG	EQA	EQR	DEFENSE	
1998	Daytona	Fla	364	97	16	1	11	25	67	47	55	2	1	268	.266	.328	.407	.246	40	74-1B -1	
1998	WestTenn	Sou	139	36	5	0	2	5	32	13	15	0	1	104	.259	.294	.338	.206	10	26-1B -1	
1999	WestTenn	Sou	484	120	27	3	15	22	133	55	67	2	2	366	.248	.296	.409	.232	47	116-1B -2	
2000	Iowa	PCL	390	108	18	1	21	23	79	58	70	3	3	285	.277	.328	.490	.265	52	82-1B -10	18-LF -1
2000	ChiCubs	NL	68	19	7	0	3	2	18	12	11	0	1	50	.279	.325	.515	.266	9	10-1B -2	
2001	ChiCubs	NL	385	104	18	1	16	25	93	47	61	3	2	283	.270	.315	.447	.252	45		

Even with all the first-base candidates the Cubs have brought in, Julio Zuleta's chances of getting 200 at-bats as a platoon player are fairly good. He slugged .640 against left-handers last year in the PCL despite some problems with breaking stuff. He's not quite good enough to play regularly, but he'll be useful as a Mark Carreon for the aughts.

PITCHERS (ERA: 4.50, H/9: 9.00, HR/9: 1.00, BB/9: 3.00, K/9: 6.00, KW: 1.00, PERA: 4.50)

Rick Aguilera — Throws R — Age 39

YEAR	TEAM	LGE	IP	H	ER	HR	BB	K	ERA	W	L	H/9	HR/9	BB/9	K/9	KW	PERA
1998	Minnesot	AL	73.0	70	29	6	12	53	3.58	4	4	8.63	0.74	1.48	6.53	2.21	3.43
1999	Minnesot	AL	20.3	9	3	2	2	12	1.33	2	0	3.98	0.89	0.89	5.31	3.00	1.21
1999	ChiCubs	NL	44.7	42	20	5	8	27	4.03	2	3	8.46	1.01	1.61	5.44	1.69	3.64
2000	ChiCubs	NL	46.3	45	25	10	15	32	4.86	2	3	8.74	1.94	2.91	6.22	1.07	5.29

Rick Aguilera's season ended early when he took a line drive off of his thumb at the end of August, cutting short his bid for his seventh 30-save season. After passing Bruce Sutter, Goose Gossage, and Tom Henke on the all-time saves leader board in 2000, Aggie is now eighth on the list, which won't get him any Hall of Fame consideration. He's wearing a couple of World Series rings and has had a hell of a career, so nobody should weep for him.

Micah Bowie — Throws L — Age 26

YEAR	TEAM	LGE	IP	H	ER	HR	BB	K	ERA	W	L	H/9	HR/9	BB/9	K/9	KW	PERA
1998	Greenvil	Sou	154.7	137	75	16	57	100	4.36	8	9	7.97	0.93	3.32	5.82	0.88	3.96
1999	Richmond	Int	69.7	66	25	4	14	59	3.23	5	3	8.53	0.52	1.81	7.62	2.11	3.30
1999	ChiCubs	NL	46.7	71	49	7	25	33	9.45	1	4	13.69	1.35	4.82	6.36	0.66	8.40
2000	Iowa	PCL	41.7	58	47	13	34	24	10.15	1	4	12.53	2.81	7.34	5.18	0.35	10.28
2000	WestTenn	Sou	104.7	100	66	13	57	57	5.68	4	8	8.60	1.12	4.90	4.90	0.50	5.17

He was touted as a key player in the Terry Mulholland/Jose Hernandez trade, but Micah Bowie was the third-best pitcher in the package, after the 2001 contenders for the fifth starter's job (Joey Nation and Ruben Quevedo). He's a nibbler who throws in the high 80s, with a curve that merely tumbles and an adequate change-up. Bowie was cut loose and signed with Oakland.

Ben Christensen — Throws R — Age 23

YEAR	TEAM	LGE	IP	H	ER	HR	BB	K	ERA	W	L	H/9	HR/9	BB/9	K/9	KW	PERA
1999	Eugene	Nwn	19.3	22	16	4	16	11	7.45	0	2	10.24	1.86	7.45	5.12	0.34	7.99
1999	Daytona	Fla	20.3	27	21	8	13	11	9.30	0	2	11.95	3.54	5.75	4.87	0.42	10.11
2000	Daytona	Fla	57.7	50	30	14	18	36	4.68	3	3	7.80	2.18	2.81	5.62	1.00	4.97
2000	WestTenn	Sou	38.7	39	23	4	16	25	5.35	1	3	9.08	0.93	3.72	5.82	0.78	4.77

The Cubs' exercise in moral relativism, Ben Christensen throws a great two-seam fastball into the mid-90s and a slider in the mid-80s. He rattled off ten straight quality starts this year before being shut down with shoulder problems that don't appear to require surgery. Anyone who wants to pretend they know what Roger Clemens intended to do with that bat fragment in the World Series should first make it their business to get Christensen indicted for what he did with intent and malice aforethought to Anthony Molina. Otherwise, they should just keep their peace.

Juan Cruz — Throws R — Age 20

YEAR	TEAM	LGE	IP	H	ER	HR	BB	K	ERA	W	L	H/9	HR/9	BB/9	K/9	KW	PERA
1999	Eugene	Nwn	74.0	99	65	22	37	33	7.91	2	6	12.04	2.68	4.50	4.01	0.45	8.68
2000	Lansing	Mid	87.3	86	61	12	62	56	6.29	3	7	8.86	1.24	6.39	5.77	0.45	6.08
2000	Daytona	Fla	39.3	36	35	11	21	32	8.01	1	3	8.24	2.52	4.81	7.32	0.76	6.40

The organization's breakout pitcher last year, Juan Cruz throws regularly in the low 90s, topping out at 96. His slider buckles knees and he's perfecting a change. Cruz throws out of a low three-quarters delivery and works inside. He's included here just for reference: everyone who's seen him swears by his stuff, but he's young enough for all sorts of good or bad things to happen to him.

Courtney Duncan — Throws R — Age 26

YEAR	TEAM	LGE	IP	H	ER	HR	BB	K	ERA	W	L	H/9	HR/9	BB/9	K/9	KW	PERA
1998	WestTenn	Sou	153.0	144	93	12	107	98	5.47	6	11	8.47	0.71	6.29	5.76	0.46	5.24
1999	WestTenn	Sou	37.3	44	47	5	48	25	11.33	0	4	10.61	1.21	11.57	6.03	0.26	9.20
1999	Daytona	Fla	57.0	71	75	13	45	25	11.84	1	5	11.21	2.05	7.11	3.95	0.28	8.61
2000	WestTenn	Sou	65.7	62	42	4	39	39	5.76	2	5	8.50	0.55	5.35	5.35	0.50	4.70

National League

The Cubs claim that they don't talk up their prospects, but Courtney Duncan was hyped early in his career, then quickly looked like a complete washout after it became apparent his mechanics were a mess. The Cubs restarted his career by making him a closer. Duncan teamed with Jay Yennaco and Will Ohman to give West Tenn a great bullpen trio, and he dominated right-handed hitters. It's better for a team to look at a guy like Duncan than to give Brian Williams guaranteed money.

Kyle Farnsworth — Throws R — Age 25

YEAR	TEAM	LGE	IP	H	ER	HR	BB	K	ERA	W	L	H/9	HR/9	BB/9	K/9	KW	PERA
1998	WestTenn	Sou	76.3	72	36	10	20	47	4.24	4	4	8.49	1.18	2.36	5.54	1.17	4.13
1998	Iowa	PCL	97.7	123	89	22	39	55	8.20	2	9	11.33	2.03	3.59	5.07	0.71	7.22
1999	Iowa	PCL	37.3	36	16	6	10	20	3.86	2	2	8.68	1.45	2.41	4.82	1.00	4.55
1999	ChiCubs	NL	127.0	133	71	25	43	59	5.03	5	9	9.43	1.77	3.05	4.18	0.69	5.60
2000	Iowa	PCL	24.0	23	10	1	19	16	3.75	2	1	8.63	0.38	7.13	6.00	0.42	5.35
2000	ChiCubs	NL	76.0	89	53	12	41	62	6.28	2	6	10.54	1.42	4.86	7.34	0.76	6.62

Kyle Farnsworth does not yet have a reliable breaking pitch or a change-up. His fastball deserves comparison to Dave Stewart's for its speed, lack of movement, and the sound it makes as it goes whistling into the alleys. To hear pitching coach Oscar Acosta talk, though, Farnsworth doesn't need to throw anything else. Like Stewart, if Farnsworth shows anything approaching consistency with his slider or forkball, he'll be an outstanding reliever. It would be nice to see if the Cubs have a plan for him to get there, instead of brave talk.

Daniel Garibay — Throws L — Age 28

YEAR	TEAM	LGE	IP	H	ER	HR	BB	K	ERA	W	L	H/9	HR/9	BB/9	K/9	KW	PERA
1998	MxCyTigr	Mex	139.7	142	90	24	97	93	5.80	6	10	9.15	1.55	6.25	5.99	0.48	6.51
1999	MxCyTigr	Mex	79.0	93	87	21	62	48	9.91	2	7	10.59	2.39	7.06	5.47	0.39	8.59
2000	ChiCubs	NL	73.3	85	49	8	32	38	6.01	2	6	10.43	0.98	3.93	4.66	0.59	5.71

A Mexican League junk-balling mystery in camp, Daniel Garibay turned out to be a nifty situational reliever, as left-handed hitters posted a .284 OBP against him with no home runs. He was hung out to dry in the rotation after the trades of Ismael Valdes and Scott Downs. The Cubs lost all eight of his starts, even the three quality ones. Garibay is better off as a spot lefty.

Jeremi Gonzalez — Throws R — Age 26

YEAR	TEAM	LGE	IP	H	ER	HR	BB	K	ERA	W	L	H/9	HR/9	BB/9	K/9	KW	PERA
1998	ChiCubs	NL	106.0	120	69	13	37	57	5.86	4	8	10.19	1.10	3.14	4.84	0.77	5.38

He's been gone for more than two years because of elbow problems that initially weren't taken seriously enough. Jeremi Gonzalez has been pitching in the winter leagues, and he's still on the 40-man roster. He almost didn't make our cut, but Cal Eldred made it back, so anything is possible. He's a dark horse for the fifth spot in the rotation.

Felix Heredia — Throws L — Age 25

YEAR	TEAM	LGE	IP	H	ER	HR	BB	K	ERA	W	L	H/9	HR/9	BB/9	K/9	KW	PERA
1998	Florida	NL	39.3	38	30	1	30	31	6.86	1	3	8.69	0.23	6.86	7.09	0.52	5.10
1998	ChiCubs	NL	17.0	19	9	1	5	13	4.76	1	1	10.06	0.53	2.65	6.88	1.30	4.48
1999	ChiCubs	NL	51.0	55	32	6	20	42	5.65	2	4	9.71	1.06	3.53	7.41	1.05	5.19
2000	ChiCubs	NL	57.3	46	28	5	27	43	4.40	3	3	7.22	0.78	4.24	6.75	0.80	3.76

Any left-hander with a fastball in the mid-90s is going to get the benefit of the doubt. Baylor fell lock-step into the habit of using Felix Heredia as a situational reliever, even when he already had a good situational lefty in Garibay. Heredia may have to go elsewhere to be really turned loose, but it's going to be more cost-effective for another team to trade for him now than to sign him when he's the new Arthur Lee Rhodes.

Jon Lieber — Throws R — Age 31

YEAR	TEAM	LGE	IP	H	ER	HR	BB	K	ERA	W	L	H/9	HR/9	BB/9	K/9	KW	PERA
1998	Pittsbrg	NL	163.7	177	91	23	36	112	5.00	7	11	9.73	1.26	1.98	6.16	1.56	4.79
1999	ChiCubs	NL	197.7	217	99	25	38	157	4.51	10	12	9.88	1.14	1.73	7.15	2.07	4.64
2000	ChiCubs	NL	242.3	239	120	32	44	160	4.46	12	15	8.88	1.19	1.63	5.94	1.82	4.06

(Jon Lieber *continued*)

Jon Lieber threw a career-high number of innings by September 1. It showed, as he allowed a third of the 36 home runs hit off of him all year in the last month. While the results of Keith Woolner's essay on pitcher abuse are compelling (see page 491), Lieber is an example of the kind of pitcher who is especially tough to evaluate. He's exceptionally economical with his pitches, topping 120 pitches just twice during the entire season. Yet just as obviously, he was worn out. Lieber illustrates that we're only just beginning to map the road to better pitcher usage. Because of Baylor, I'm less enthusiastic about Lieber's chance of blossoming into one of the game's great starters, or even just staying healthy. The ability is there.

Oswaldo Mairena — Throws L — Age 25

YEAR	TEAM	LGE	IP	H	ER	HR	BB	K	ERA	W	L	H/9	HR/9	BB/9	K/9	KW	PERA
1998	Tampa	Fla	48.3	55	31	11	29	29	5.77	2	3	10.24	2.05	5.40	5.40	0.50	7.31
1999	Norwich	Eas	52.7	49	28	5	30	29	4.78	2	4	8.37	0.85	5.13	4.96	0.48	4.86
2000	Norwich	Eas	29.3	30	20	2	13	18	6.14	1	2	9.20	0.61	3.99	5.52	0.69	4.59
2000	Iowa	PCL	14.0	12	8	1	2	3	5.14	1	1	7.71	0.64	1.29	1.93	0.75	2.80

Twenty years ago, you would have just about given up on seeing young Nicaraguans in the major leagues. It will be kind of fun to see which teams start ramping up Nicaraguan academies in the years to come. Oswaldo Mairena isn't going to make anyone forget El Presidente or the Cold War, but he's a perfectly serviceable left-handed spot reliever with a big-bending curve.

Mike Meyers — Throws R — Age 23

YEAR	TEAM	LGE	IP	H	ER	HR	BB	K	ERA	W	L	H/9	HR/9	BB/9	K/9	KW	PERA
1998	Rockford	Mid	77.7	79	45	8	40	44	5.21	3	6	9.15	0.93	4.64	5.10	0.55	5.19
1999	Daytona	Fla	97.0	77	44	18	47	73	4.08	5	6	7.14	1.67	4.36	6.77	0.78	4.68
1999	WestTenn	Sou	30.7	24	7	2	11	32	2.05	2	1	7.04	0.59	3.23	9.39	1.45	3.12
2000	WestTenn	Sou	53.7	45	24	8	28	31	4.02	3	3	7.55	1.34	4.70	5.20	0.55	4.71
2000	Iowa	PCL	56.3	71	51	12	31	32	8.15	1	5	11.34	1.92	4.95	5.11	0.52	7.67

Mike Meyers had one of those years you have to cringe through: he pitched with tendinitis and had started leaving his pitches up by the time he reached Iowa. He throws in the high 80s and occasionally gets over 90 mph, with a great curve and a quality change-up; he knows how to set people up with them. When Kevin Tapani breaks down in August, Meyers should be first in line for his job.

Joey Nation — Throws L — Age 22

YEAR	TEAM	LGE	IP	H	ER	HR	BB	K	ERA	W	L	H/9	HR/9	BB/9	K/9	KW	PERA
1998	Macon	SAL	130.0	186	115	27	50	66	7.96	3	11	12.88	1.87	3.46	4.57	0.66	7.90
1999	Macon	SAL	24.7	29	12	2	12	14	4.38	1	2	10.58	0.73	4.38	5.11	0.58	5.74
1999	Myrtle B	Car	85.7	96	71	18	46	46	7.46	2	8	10.09	1.89	4.83	4.83	0.50	6.85
2000	WestTenn	Sou	149.0	156	104	33	70	99	6.28	5	12	9.42	1.99	4.23	5.98	0.71	6.31
2000	ChiCubs	NL	11.7	12	9	2	7	7	6.94	0	1	9.26	1.54	5.40	5.40	0.50	6.32

That's an unimpressive translation, but 476 strikeouts in 472 career minor-league innings is impressive. I'm not quite ready to call Joey Nation the next Sid Fernandez, but there are things to like here. He doesn't throw especially hard, but he has good control, a very good curve, and knows how to pitch. He'll have to fight Quevedo for the fifth starter job. A point in his favor is that Nation is left-handed and the set four starters are all right-handers.

Phil Norton — Throws L — Age 25

YEAR	TEAM	LGE	IP	H	ER	HR	BB	K	ERA	W	L	H/9	HR/9	BB/9	K/9	KW	PERA
1998	Daytona	Fla	61.0	57	34	7	31	31	5.02	3	4	8.41	1.03	4.57	4.57	0.50	4.84
1998	WestTenn	Sou	112.7	122	67	18	48	76	5.35	5	8	9.75	1.44	3.83	6.07	0.79	5.74
1999	WestTenn	Sou	80.3	74	37	8	46	50	4.15	4	5	8.29	0.90	5.15	5.60	0.54	4.87
1999	Iowa	PCL	75.3	93	64	24	37	42	7.65	2	6	11.11	2.87	4.42	5.02	0.57	8.32
2000	Iowa	PCL	150.3	159	102	22	110	89	6.11	5	12	9.52	1.32	6.59	5.33	0.40	6.63
2000	ChiCubs	NL	8.7	13	8	4	6	5	8.31	0	1	13.50	4.15	6.23	5.19	0.42	11.77

Phil Norton's 2000 season was a real disappointment, though he still has a great curve and can reach the low 90s. The Cubs are considering converting him to relief. He isn't really cut out for situational work. If he was used as a long reliever, the way Gabe White has been or Felix Heredia or Valerio de los Santos should be, he could be an asset.

National League

Will Ohman — Throws L — Age 23

YEAR	TEAM	LGE	IP	H	ER	HR	BB	K	ERA	W	L	H/9	HR/9	BB/9	K/9	KW	PERA
1998	Willmspt	NYP	33.3	47	52	18	17	16	14.04	0	4	12.69	4.86	4.59	4.32	0.47	11.42
1998	Rockford	Mid	21.3	28	19	8	9	11	8.02	0	2	11.81	3.38	3.80	4.64	0.61	9.00
1999	Daytona	Fla	96.7	108	75	22	48	58	6.98	3	8	10.06	2.05	4.47	5.40	0.60	6.84
2000	WestTenn	Sou	64.7	60	27	6	39	51	3.76	4	3	8.35	0.84	5.43	7.10	0.65	4.96

The left-hander in the three-headed bullpen monster that deserved MVP honors for West Tenn's championship run in the Southern League. Will Ohman throws a sinker into the low 90s, with a good curve and change-up. Left-handed hitters have problems getting the ball out of the infield against him. Having him and Mairena gives the team a lot of flexibility in entertaining offers for Felix Heredia.

Ruben Quevedo — Throws R — Age 22

YEAR	TEAM	LGE	IP	H	ER	HR	BB	K	ERA	W	L	H/9	HR/9	BB/9	K/9	KW	PERA
1998	Macon	SAL	100.7	123	62	24	39	55	5.54	4	7	11.00	2.15	3.49	4.92	0.71	7.08
1998	DanvillC	Car	28.7	30	29	4	17	18	9.10	0	3	9.42	1.26	5.34	5.65	0.53	5.96
1999	Richmond	Int	101.3	111	63	27	32	72	5.60	4	7	9.86	2.40	2.84	6.39	1.13	6.43
1999	Iowa	PCL	41.7	32	18	1	23	34	3.89	3	2	6.91	0.22	4.97	7.34	0.74	3.32
2000	Iowa	PCL	70.7	67	40	10	32	56	5.09	3	5	8.53	1.27	4.08	7.13	0.88	4.96
2000	ChiCubs	NL	86.7	93	72	19	44	54	7.48	2	8	9.66	1.97	4.57	5.61	0.61	6.56

After a couple of short and ugly stints, Ruben Quevedo was called up to enter the rotation at the end of July. He rattled off four straight quality starts, the third of which was a 133-pitch complete game against the Dodgers. He then had seven straight bad starts. Quevedo throws in the low 90s with a good slider and splitter and an adequate curve and change-up. If the Cubs would be patient, he would be a good one. He's being worked hard in winter ball, so his chances of getting hurt are increasing.

Steve Rain — Throws R — Age 26

YEAR	TEAM	LGE	IP	H	ER	HR	BB	K	ERA	W	L	H/9	HR/9	BB/9	K/9	KW	PERA
1998	Iowa	PCL	97.7	111	83	17	70	57	7.65	2	9	10.23	1.57	6.45	5.25	0.41	7.25
1999	WestTenn	Sou	41.3	35	12	5	18	32	2.61	4	1	7.62	1.09	3.92	6.97	0.89	4.15
2000	Iowa	PCL	29.3	32	17	6	7	23	5.22	1	2	9.82	1.84	2.15	7.06	1.64	5.56
2000	ChiCubs	NL	48.7	46	23	9	22	45	4.25	2	3	8.51	1.66	4.07	8.32	1.02	5.34

Steve Rain is somebody you should love to watch pitch in the same way that you can't get enough of Charlie Kerfeld. He's one of the biggest guys on the mound today, he throws hard, owns a good slider, and there are times when his splitter is unhittable. Rain puts on weight almost as easily as our own Joe Sheehan, so conditioning is always a bit of an issue. Teams can do a lot worse for a tenth or 11th pitcher.

Steve Smyth — Throws L — Age 23

YEAR	TEAM	LGE	IP	H	ER	HR	BB	K	ERA	W	L	H/9	HR/9	BB/9	K/9	KW	PERA
1999	Eugene	Nwn	23.3	28	17	4	8	7	6.56	1	2	10.80	1.54	3.09	2.70	0.44	6.17
1999	Lansing	Mid	47.3	69	41	9	32	24	7.80	1	4	13.12	1.71	6.08	4.56	0.38	8.97
2000	Daytona	Fla	125.7	137	74	20	68	57	5.30	5	9	9.81	1.43	4.87	4.08	0.42	6.21

A 1999 fourth-rounder out of USC, Steve Smyth is already an organizational favorite. He's got the "fiery competitor" label and throws four pitches for strikes. He might end up getting bumped into relief, because while the Cubs like him, they're also realistic about a left-hander who doesn't throw hard.

Jerry Spradlin — Throws R — Age 34

YEAR	TEAM	LGE	IP	H	ER	HR	BB	K	ERA	W	L	H/9	HR/9	BB/9	K/9	KW	PERA
1998	Philadel	NL	78.0	62	34	9	18	62	3.92	5	4	7.15	1.04	2.08	7.15	1.72	3.14
1999	San Fran	NL	56.3	57	30	4	26	44	4.79	2	4	9.11	0.64	4.15	7.03	0.85	4.66
2000	KansasCy	AL	75.0	75	40	7	20	52	4.80	3	5	9.00	0.84	2.40	6.24	1.30	4.09
2000	ChiCubs	NL	14.7	19	14	2	4	11	8.59	0	2	11.66	1.23	2.45	6.75	1.38	6.05

(Jerry Spradlin *continued*)

Jerry Spradlin belongs to a religious group that expects its members to constantly proselytize for new recruits. I have no idea if that has created issues in some clubhouses, but it might help explain why he's been with five teams in less than three years. Being outspoken on issues of faith is a way to make yourself a marked man in any line of work, not just baseball. He's a good last man in a major-league pen.

Kevin Tapani — Throws R — Age 37

YEAR	TEAM	LGE	IP	H	ER	HR	BB	K	ERA	W	L	H/9	HR/9	BB/9	K/9	KW	PERA
1998	ChiCubs	NL	210.0	235	115	30	55	110	4.93	9	14	10.07	1.29	2.36	4.71	1.00	5.17
1999	ChiCubs	NL	132.0	142	73	11	27	61	4.98	6	9	9.68	0.75	1.84	4.16	1.13	4.17
2000	ChiCubs	NL	189.3	200	104	31	39	125	4.94	8	13	9.51	1.47	1.85	5.94	1.60	4.83

He suffered a knee injury that shut him down early, but once again, the Cubs shut him down too late: his last five starts were awful. It looks like Kevin Tapani finally started getting his forkball back to where it once was after what seemed like a two-year hiatus following surgery on his index finger in 1997. So far, he's managed to survive serious injuries to everything but his arm. If he had a manager who could sort out when he needs an extra day off, Tapani might avoid these season-ending meltdowns and have a good year.

Nathan Teut — Throws L — Age 25

YEAR	TEAM	LGE	IP	H	ER	HR	BB	K	ERA	W	L	H/9	HR/9	BB/9	K/9	KW	PERA
1998	Rockford	Mid	93.0	106	67	24	29	33	6.48	3	7	10.26	2.32	2.81	3.19	0.57	6.56
1998	Daytona	Fla	61.0	88	51	12	22	31	7.52	2	5	12.98	1.77	3.25	4.57	0.70	7.75
1999	Daytona	Fla	120.3	182	134	34	52	51	10.02	2	11	13.61	2.54	3.89	3.81	0.49	9.22
2000	WestTenn	Sou	123.7	145	74	27	51	59	5.39	5	9	10.55	1.96	3.71	4.29	0.58	6.73

You'll almost never see somebody move up after having a season as bad as Nathan Teut did in the Florida State League in 1999. He's one of those big soft-tossers that organizations take a chance on in the hope that he fills out and adds velocity. As Joey Nation's peer within the organization, he hasn't pitched as well despite the advantage of age. Teut had a good AFL season after being added to the Cubs' 40-man roster.

Todd Van Poppel — Throws R — Age 29

YEAR	TEAM	LGE	IP	H	ER	HR	BB	K	ERA	W	L	H/9	HR/9	BB/9	K/9	KW	PERA
1998	Oklahoma	PCL	81.7	85	47	14	28	44	5.18	3	6	9.37	1.54	3.09	4.85	0.79	5.32
1998	Pittsbrg	NL	45.3	51	30	4	16	26	5.96	2	3	10.13	0.79	3.18	5.16	0.81	5.02
1999	Nashvill	PCL	153.0	167	103	29	72	99	6.06	5	12	9.82	1.71	4.24	5.82	0.69	6.24
2000	Iowa	PCL	38.0	38	20	3	11	35	4.74	2	2	9.00	0.71	2.61	8.29	1.59	4.03
2000	ChiCubs	NL	84.7	79	35	9	39	64	3.72	5	4	8.40	0.96	4.15	6.80	0.82	4.57

Todd Van Poppel finally got a break and was allowed to do what he'll continue to do effectively, which is pitch in relief. His only stretches of major-league success were in Oakland's bullpen in the first half of 1995 and a brief stint in the Pirates' pen in 1998. Every attempt to use him as a rotation regular has been a disappointment. The A's, Tigers, Angels, Royals, Rangers, and Pirates all saw his talent and all let themselves get frustrated that he wasn't the next Nolan Ryan. That didn't stop the Cubs from starting him twice in September.

Kerry Wood — Throws R — Age 24

YEAR	TEAM	LGE	IP	H	ER	HR	BB	K	ERA	W	L	H/9	HR/9	BB/9	K/9	KW	PERA
1998	ChiCubs	NL	160.7	123	72	14	76	189	4.03	9	9	6.89	0.78	4.26	10.59	1.24	3.59
2000	ChiCubs	NL	134.7	112	70	15	71	110	4.68	6	9	7.49	1.00	4.75	7.35	0.77	4.33

If you had told me that Kerry Wood would throw only around 130 innings this year, my first instinct would have been to credit the Cubs with a lot of good sense. Instead, they rushed him back to get him on the mound by May, keeping his recovery time closer to 12 than 18 months. He wound up at 130 innings because he missed three weeks in August. Wood is still relying on his curve far too often for somebody coming back from Tommy John surgery. He's not out of the woods yet.

Tim Worrell — Throws R — Age 33

YEAR	TEAM	LGE	IP	H	ER	HR	BB	K	ERA	W	L	H/9	HR/9	BB/9	K/9	KW	PERA
1998	Detroit	AL	60.7	61	35	9	16	43	5.19	3	4	9.05	1.34	2.37	6.38	1.34	4.61
1998	Oakland	AL	35.3	32	16	5	7	31	4.08	2	2	8.15	1.27	1.78	7.90	2.21	3.81
1999	Oakland	AL	69.0	65	33	5	28	59	4.30	4	4	8.48	0.65	3.65	7.70	1.05	4.11
2000	ChiCubs	NL	60.3	59	19	6	20	43	2.83	5	2	8.80	0.90	2.98	6.41	1.08	4.28

He signed what looked like a worrisome two-year deal for almost $3 million, but was then quickly traded for Bill Mueller. The Cubs sang Tim Worrell's praises during the year, talking about his nifty slider and his tough attitude. It was a nice piece of salesmanship, and a reminder that some trading partners obsess over cost certainty when savvy waiver-wire and minor-league shopping would make more sense.

Michael Wuertz — Throws R — Age 22

YEAR	TEAM	LGE	IP	H	ER	HR	BB	K	ERA	W	L	H/9	HR/9	BB/9	K/9	KW	PERA
1998	Willmspt	NYP	79.3	81	42	12	25	26	4.76	4	5	9.19	1.36	2.84	2.95	0.52	4.91
1999	Lansing	Mid	152.3	191	105	20	46	67	6.20	5	12	11.28	1.18	2.72	3.96	0.73	5.93
2000	Daytona	Fla	155.3	176	101	33	75	83	5.85	5	12	10.20	1.91	4.35	4.81	0.55	6.74

Michael Wuertz is somebody about whom the organization is getting more and more enthusiastic. The big three of Christensen, Cruz, and Carlos Zambrano are getting more attention, but after those guys, Wuertz and John Webb are the starters the Cubs seem to like the best. Wuertz throws a sinker in the low 90s and complements it with a good slider. He's a long way off from Wrigley.

Jay Yennaco — Throws R — Age 25

YEAR	TEAM	LGE	IP	H	ER	HR	BB	K	ERA	W	L	H/9	HR/9	BB/9	K/9	KW	PERA
1998	Trenton	Eas	49.0	51	38	13	22	14	6.98	1	4	9.37	2.39	4.04	2.57	0.32	6.64
1998	Pawtuckt	Int	58.0	73	40	6	15	25	6.21	2	4	11.33	0.93	2.33	3.88	0.83	5.52
1998	Syracuse	Int	37.3	52	25	4	9	20	6.03	1	3	12.54	0.96	2.17	4.82	1.11	6.18
1999	Knoxvill	Sou	40.7	52	36	12	17	18	7.97	1	4	11.51	2.66	3.76	3.98	0.53	8.02
1999	Syracuse	Int	77.7	101	60	11	39	33	6.95	2	7	11.70	1.27	4.52	3.82	0.42	7.00
2000	WestTenn	Sou	62.7	61	37	10	36	44	5.31	3	4	8.76	1.44	5.17	6.32	0.61	5.71

He's a minor-league Rule 5 pick and likely to more than repay the investment. Jay Yennaco struggled as a starter in the Red Sox and Blue Jays organizations, but he throws into the mid-90s with a pretty good slider. Unlike Courtney Duncan, he doesn't have a major platoon split, so of West Tenn's co-closers, Yennaco is a little more likely to become a solid major-league reliever.

Carlos Zambrano — Throws R — Age 20

YEAR	TEAM	LGE	IP	H	ER	HR	BB	K	ERA	W	L	H/9	HR/9	BB/9	K/9	KW	PERA
1999	Lansing	Mid	144.7	148	87	16	65	52	5.41	6	10	9.21	1.00	4.04	3.24	0.40	5.05
2000	WestTenn	Sou	55.3	41	17	4	23	26	2.77	4	2	6.67	0.65	3.74	4.23	0.57	3.15
2000	Iowa	PCL	54.0	51	29	4	41	34	4.83	2	4	8.50	0.67	6.83	5.67	0.41	5.44

Carlos Zambrano owns a mid-90s fastball that runs in on right-handers, plus a slider that flirts with being unhittable and a functional curve. He moved from starting at Double-A to closing at Iowa. The Cubs are saying they'll make a determination which direction they want to go with him before the end of camp.

Support-Neutral Statistics						CHICAGO CUBS					Park Effect: -6.9%	
PITCHER	GS	IP	R	SNW	SNL	SNPCT	W	L	RA	APW	SNVA	SNWAR
Jamie Arnold	4	15.3	19	0.3	2.1	.131	0	3	11.15	-1.0	-0.9	-0.7
Scott Downs	18	94.0	59	4.9	6.9	.414	4	3	5.65	-0.7	-0.9	-0.1
Kyle Farnsworth	5	27.3	25	0.9	2.7	.242	1	3	8.23	-0.9	-0.9	-0.7
Dan Garibay	8	43.3	30	2.3	3.2	.421	0	5	6.23	-0.6	-0.5	-0.0
Jon Lieber	35	251.0	130	15.3	12.3	.555	12	11	4.66	0.8	1.3	3.6
Andrew Lorraine	5	28.0	19	1.3	1.8	.428	1	2	6.11	-0.3	-0.2	0.0
Joey Nation	2	11.7	9	0.3	1.0	.252	0	2	6.94	-0.2	-0.3	-0.2
Phil Norton	2	8.7	10	0.2	1.3	.116	0	1	10.38	-0.5	-0.6	-0.4
Ruben Quevedo	15	84.3	68	3.7	7.5	.332	3	8	7.26	-2.1	-1.9	-1.1
Jerry Spradlin	1	3.0	4	0.1	0.5	.122	0	0	12.00	-0.2	-0.2	-0.2
Kevin Tapani	30	195.7	113	10.8	11.3	.490	8	12	5.20	-0.5	-0.2	1.4
Ismael Valdes	12	67.0	40	4.5	3.4	.572	2	4	5.37	-0.3	0.5	1.2
Todd Van Poppel	2	11.7	6	0.6	0.7	.469	1	1	4.63	0.0	-0.0	0.1
Kerry Wood	23	137.0	77	8.8	7.5	.541	8	7	5.06	-0.1	0.5	1.9
TOTALS	162	978.0	609	54.1	62.1	.465	40	62	5.60	-6.7	-4.1	4.7

Rather than play like the strong hitters' park it has traditionally been, Wrigley Field looked like the most extreme pitchers' park in the majors in 2000. There were 20% fewer runs scored per inning in Cubs home games than in Cubs road games last year. (The –6.9% park effect listed above is an average of the 1999 and 2000 single-year park effects.)

I wonder if one contributing factor was that most of the 2000 Cubs starting rotation, for whatever reason, completely lost the ability to pitch on the road. At home, the Cubs had the ninth-best rotation in the majors, worth 2.2 wins above average according to Support-Neutral Value Added (SNVA). But they were by far the majors' worst rotation on the road, with an SNVA of 6.3 wins below average. The five worst offenders—Kevin Tapani, Daniel Garibay, Jon Lieber, Ruben Quevedo, and Ismael Valdes—had an outstanding combined Support-Neutral W/L record of 22-15 (.584) at Wrigley, but a terrible 15-22 (.404) on the road. Remember, those SNWL home records are park-adjusted with that –6.9% effect; the splits in the raw numbers are even greater.

It's hard to separate cause and effect here—it's certainly possible that the Cubs had a comparatively hard time on the road partly because Wrigley Field was a pitchers' park last year. But the home/road split among the starters was so extreme that it can't be explained by the park alone. It's also possible that the Cubs starters struggled on the road for some other reason, and those struggles contributed to the surprising Wrigley Field park factor in 2000.

For a quick explanation of SN stats, see page 7.

Reliever Evaluation Tools											
PITCHER	G	IP	R	ARA	APR	IRNR/G	EIRS/G	IRP	BRS	RRA	ARP
Rick Aguilera	54	47.7	28	5.54	-1.8	0.39	0.11	-5.1	-2.7	5.92	-3.8
Jamie Arnold	8	17.3	9	4.90	0.6	0.88	0.34	0.7	-1.8	4.04	2.2
Kyle Farnsworth	40	46.0	33	6.77	-8.0	0.65	0.26	-2.1	1.2	6.99	-9.2
Daniel Garibay	22	31.3	24	7.23	-7.1	0.55	0.24	-4.5	-4.1	7.07	-6.5
Mark Guthrie	19	18.7	11	5.56	-0.8	1.05	0.36	-4.5	-3.2	6.16	-2.0
Felix Heredia	74	58.7	31	4.98	1.4	0.84	0.25	-2.7	-3.2	5.24	-0.3
Matt Karchner	13	14.7	11	7.08	-3.1	1.08	0.35	-1.7	1.7	9.08	-6.3
Andrew Lorraine	3	4.0	6	14.15	-4.0	1.00	0.27	-0.2	-0.1	14.78	-4.3
Oswaldo Mairena	2	2.0	4	18.87	-3.0	0.00	0.00	0.0	0.0	13.25	-1.8
Will Ohman	6	3.3	3	8.49	-1.2	0.83	0.42	-0.6	-0.6	8.39	-1.2
Ruben Quevedo	6	3.7	13	33.45	-11.5	0.50	0.20	-2.0	-3.2	32.18	-11.0
Steve Rain	37	49.7	25	4.75	2.5	0.68	0.28	1.1	-2.0	4.06	6.3
Jerry Spradlin	7	12.0	11	8.65	-4.6	0.57	0.18	0.2	0.0	8.79	-4.8
Todd Van Poppel	50	78.3	32	3.85	11.7	0.40	0.15	-1.3	2.1	4.19	8.8
Brian Williams	22	24.3	27	10.47	-14.3	0.73	0.26	-6.8	-3.2	11.41	-16.8
Tim Worrell	54	62.0	20	3.04	14.8	0.44	0.14	-0.5	3.2	3.70	10.3
Danny Young	4	3.0	7	22.01	-5.6	0.00	0.00	0.0	-1.3	17.74	-4.2
TOTALS	421	476.7	295	5.84	-34.0	0.62	0.22			6.04	-44.4

For a quick guide to RET, see page 10.

Cincinnati Reds

The last 13 months in the life of the Cincinnati Reds have been quite exciting. Set aside their surprising run to a playoff game in 1999, one that left them just a win shy of the postseason. It's the events since then that show that the Reds may have come upon a formula for success in their market; the execution hasn't been perfect, but the decisions they've made show a heightened awareness of how to build a team in the early 21st century.

One of the key elements is the recognition that top-tier talent is an investment, not a cost, and that the very best players in the game are unique and have to be paid accordingly. The salaries of the top 0.5% of players in baseball seem excessive, but the return those players provide often justifies the cost. Put simply, a $15 million player is generally a better investment than an $8 million player.

The centerpiece transaction for the Reds was the acquisition and signing of Ken Griffey Jr. Griffey is exactly the kind of player that is worth a large investment, a Hall of Fame talent who plays a key defensive position and can be expected to play well for the length of his contract. An additional benefit is that Griffey is one of the most popular, and therefore most marketable, players in the game.

Taking advantage of twin facts—Griffey's 10-and-5 rights and his desire to play in Cincinnati—the Reds were able to acquire Griffey for a moderate cost in talent and a significant "hometown discount." This gave them a franchise-caliber talent worth between five and seven wins a season, something around which to build the rest of the team. And thanks to the miracle of deferred money, that franchise talent is costing the Reds a mere $9 million a year in current funds.

A second tenet is that there is a large class of players whose compensation is inflated beyond what they contribute. Baseball's "middle class," as it were, is populated by players who cost from $5 to $10 million per year without returning that kind of performance. Most of the game's worst free-agent signings and most overpaid players are in this group. Many are in decline, having gotten contracts on the heels of their best seasons. Many are older and have a higher risk of injury.

A key mistake the Reds made was re-signing shortstop Barry Larkin to a three-year deal for $9 million per year ($6 million per year in present value, the rest in deferred money). Larkin is a Hall of Fame talent who has been a Red his entire career, one of the best players in franchise history. Unfortunately, he is also 37 and in decline, particularly on defense. He's not going to be an asset at shortstop for much longer, and if he moves to third base, he is unlikely to be any better than an average player at that position.

Larkin, for all his achievements, is now a monkey wrench in the Reds' plan. He'll be the team's second-highest-paid player, consuming 15–20% of the payroll, without playing at a championship level. It's a mistake, but one the Reds can overcome by executing the rest of the plan.

One way to make up the money the Reds are paying Larkin is by refusing to overpay for replaceable talent. The Reds were very aggressive in this regard in the 2000–01 offseason. They dumped a slew of players who were arbitration-eligible and due to make $2 million to $4 million by virtue of their service time and performance, but who carry little upside and could not be expected to add a lot of value on the field.

Ron Villone, Chris Stynes, and Steve Parris are three 2000 Reds regulars who are playing elsewhere now. Combined, they will make about $7 million in 2001. Together, they were worth less than two wins for the Reds over replacement-level talent in 2000; even if you expected the same level of performance from them in 2001—as a group, unlikely—they would be a poor investment at half that $7 million.

Finding these guys and letting them perform for your team before they become arbitration-eligible is an essential part of a success plan. Trading them or letting them go elsewhere when they start to become expensive is another. The Reds weren't dumping salary when they traded Villone, Stynes, and Parris; they were dumping replaceable talent.

Reds Prospectus

2000 record: 85–77; Second place, NL Central
Pythagenport W/L: 87–75
Runs Scored: 825 (5th in NL)
Runs Allowed: 765 (6th in NL)
Team EqA: .262 (7th in NL)
2000 Batters' Age: 29.3 (8th oldest in NL)
2000 Pitchers' Age: 28.4 (tied for 7th oldest in NL)
Ballpark: Cinergy Field; slight hitters' park; Park Factor of 1.022
2000: Only a disappointment when compared to the accident of 1999.
2001: They took some heat for dumping salary, but they didn't lose anyone important and should be over .500 again.

How will the Reds replace them? By using minor-league free agents, NRIs, and the Rule 5 draft to advantage. While the best players, even the top two-thirds of players, in the major leagues are uniquely talented as compared to their peers, the rest of the player pool isn't that much different from the top of the pool at Triple-A. And many of these Triple-A players are available for a small cost through trades or low-risk signings.

Every year we see a handful of players emerge from anonymity to have a significant impact on the season. A quality organization that invests not only in player development but in player acquisition will always have a number of candidates in camp who can provide league-average or better performance for a low salary if given the opportunity. Matt Stairs. Jeff Zimmerman. Brian Daubach. Jim Mecir. None of these players were heralded when they finally established themselves, but all were able to make significant contributions for the minimum salary or a little more.

If you find one of these players each year, just one guy who costs $500,000 for two years and adds a couple of wins to your total, you've gone a long way towards being able to afford the truly great players who are essential to a championship.

We've focused on the on-field and expenditures part of the plan, but that's not all there is to it. Maximizing the revenue that a successful team generates is also important. It's not because revenue is the sole, or even the primary, factor in assembling a winning team; the success of the White Sox in 2000 and the Reds in 1999 make that point clear.

Making money, though, does increase a team's margin of error. It adds to the team's ability to invest in its good young talent, buying out years of arbitration and free agency. It gives the team payroll flexibility, so that it can add talent during the season. So maximizing revenue is an important part of the success plan.

The Reds have been a mixed bag in this area. They play in a small market, which limits the amount of revenue they can get by selling their local broadcast rights. And like many small-market/low-revenue teams, they spend a lot of their time complaining about their lot in life and playing up their disadvantages as compared to teams in large cities. This kind of anti-marketing simply encourages fans to stay home and care less about the team.

Last July, in the wake of the Barry Larkin signing, the team went so far as to guarantee that ticket prices would rise in 2001 and left open the possibility that they would rise for the remainder of 2000. They got the backlash they richly deserved and, more importantly, squandered any goodwill that signing the popular veteran had generated. The team's eagerness to blame rising player salaries for increased ticket prices—a myth perpetuated by sports-team ownership for decades—cost them a chunk of the primary benefit of the $27 million they were investing in Larkin.

On the other hand, the Reds did get a big boost in picking up Griffey, and he helped their attendance jump from 2.06 million to 2.58 million, a 25% increase. The team will soon move into a new stadium, which will increase the revenue that's available to the Reds as ticket demand increases and they can charge more for a better customer experience. The added revenue will enable the team to improve the on-field product, and a better on-field product could lead to postseason appearances, which are highly profitable.

Of the steps to success outlined here, the only one over which teams don't have full control is that of a new ballpark. Yet by 2004, more teams will be playing in parks built since the first Bush administration than before it. Of the others, many play in large markets that provide ample media revenue, or have deep-pockets ownership that can afford to invest in the team in an effort to improve the product.

The Reds, and specifically Jim Bowden, are doing pretty much what they need to do to win without having a large payroll. They're committing to one or two eight-figure players and being careful about the allocation of resources everywhere else. No amount of teeth-gnashing over the departures of people like Steve Parris should change their course.

Despite seasons of 96 and 85 wins and coming within a hairbreadth of the playoffs in 1999, the Reds dumped manager Jack McKeon after the 2000 season. It's hard to find enough fault with McKeon to justify the decision; his biggest on-field impact was in his use of the bullpen, and that was an unqualified success. He didn't play or not play anyone of note; frankly, he did a really good job with the talent he was given.

McKeon's biggest fault appears to be one of timing. In 1999, he benefited from career years by Pokey Reese and Sean Casey, among others, and did such a good job with the pitching staff that the Reds jumped from 77 to 96 wins and almost made the playoffs.

In the offseason, the Reds went out and acquired the nominal best player in the game, Ken Griffey Jr., and the expectation was that they would build on their success. But baseball teams don't work that way: the Reds had overachieved in 1999, and they regressed in 2000 as Reese and Casey performed closer to their levels of ability. Key players, like Larkin and Pete Harnisch, suffered injuries that they had avoided in 1999. The sainted Griffey did not play up to expectations either, having his worst full season since his rookie campaign. With all that, the Reds still won 85 games.

Had McKeon moved the Reds from 77 to 96 wins over two seasons, he would have been hailed as a genius. Heck, had he moved them to 85 wins he would have kept his job. But because the team played above its head in 1999, the

National League

inevitable return to form in 2000 was perceived as a step backward and cause for McKeon's dismissal.

Firing McKeon was disappointing, although consistent with baseball tradition. The hire with whom they replaced him could set the team back a year or two.

Bob Boone was a heck of a defensive catcher in the 1970s and 1980s, and he even learned to hit a little towards the end of his career. He was regarded as an intelligent player and a potential manager, and he got his chance to run a team in 1995 with the Royals. Boone's tenure in Kansas City can only be described as one of tumultuous change. When he chose to go in a certain direction, he did so at full speed—at least until he decided to change directions again, which usually happened quickly.

He wasn't afraid to be radical: in his first season as manager, he immediately installed a four-man rotation in Kansas City, becoming the last manager to try it on a long-term basis. That lasted for a half-season, until Kevin Appier broke down under the repeated assault of 120-pitch outings on three days' rest.

On August 11 that year, the Royals made 12 transactions in one day, trading Vince Coleman and releasing several others to make room for Johnny Damon, Michael Tucker, and others. By the following April, Damon was batting third and Tucker was behind him at cleanup... until the late innings, when both would be pinch-hit for against any left-handed reliever.

It was that sort of knee-jerk overmanaging that doomed Boone after a promising 70–74 record in his first season. He made Damon the fourth outfielder, demoted Mike Sweeney to the minors, and put on so many double steals of second and home with two outs that opponents simply stopped throwing to second, knowing that the Royals were unlikely to drive in the runner from third anyway.

Even when a team does most things right in acquiring and developing players, even when a team spends money wisely, it can still muck things up with a poor decision at the wrong time. If you're a Reds fan, hope that Boone has learned from his first, disastrous tenure in the hot seat. Failing that, you hope he's gone before the Austin Kearns Era begins.

HITTERS (BA: .270, OBP: .340, SLG: .440, EqA: .260)

Kimera Bartee — CF — Bats R — Age 28

YEAR	TEAM	LGE	AB	H	DB	TP	HR	BB	SO	R	RBI	SB	CS	OUT	BA	OBP	SLG	EQA	EQR	DEFENSE	
1998	Toledo	Int	216	50	5	0	3	12	42	20	12	4	2	168	.231	.277	.296	.189	13	47-CF	6
1998	Detroit	AL	98	20	5	1	3	6	31	19	15	8	5	82	.204	.250	.367	.204	8	22-CF	1
1999	Toledo	Int	417	106	11	7	9	29	77	49	33	13	7	318	.254	.303	.379	.228	39	102-CF	0
1999	Detroit	AL	77	15	1	3	0	8	18	11	3	3	3	65	.195	.271	.286	.181	5	25-CF	1
2000	Louisvil	Int	454	117	17	3	6	37	70	54	38	17	8	345	.258	.316	.348	.226	42	110-CF	-4
2001	Anaheim	AL	461	117	15	5	9	39	86	69	57	19	9	353	.254	.312	.367	.234	47		

The weird thing is that Jim Bowden actually traded a player and used a 40-man roster spot to grab Brian R. Hunter after the Rockies placed him on waivers in July. Kimera Bartee was already in the organization and is a nearly identical player to Hunter, maybe better defensively. Bartee was released by the Reds and has been invited to the Angels' camp.

Mike Bell — 3B — Bats R — Age 26

YEAR	TEAM	LGE	AB	H	DB	TP	HR	BB	SO	R	RBI	SB	CS	OUT	BA	OBP	SLG	EQA	EQR	DEFENSE			
1998	Binghmtn	Eas	278	62	11	1	10	27	51	37	41	2	3	219	.223	.295	.378	.222	25	48-2B	-13	14-3B	-3
1999	Norfolk	Int	135	33	9	1	1	7	23	9	20	3	2	104	.244	.289	.348	.211	11	20-2B	-6	11-1B	0
2000	Louisvil	Int	431	105	24	1	19	36	79	60	64	0	0	326	.244	.310	.436	.246	49	111-3B	-8		
2000	Cincnnti	NL	27	6	0	0	2	4	7	5	4	0	0	21	.222	.323	.444	.254	3				
2001	Colorado	NL	331	95	21	1	16	34	64	54	66	1	0	236	.287	.353	.502	.255	39				

When did the Reds corner the market on scions? They have father-and-son Boones, father-and-son Griffeys, and the third generation of Bells to make the major leagues. With the youngest Boone at third base for Cincinnati, Mike Bell's next chance at a job will come at altitude, but he's behind an excellent player in Jeff Cirillo.

Aaron Boone — 3B — Bats R — Age 28

YEAR	TEAM	LGE	AB	H	DB	TP	HR	BB	SO	R	RBI	SB	CS	OUT	BA	OBP	SLG	EQA	EQR	DEFENSE			
1998	Indianap	Int	334	76	16	1	6	24	70	46	33	10	4	262	.228	.291	.335	.212	27	77-3B	6		
1998	Cincnnti	NL	183	51	14	2	2	14	34	24	28	5	1	133	.279	.345	.410	.258	22	51-3B	2		
1999	Cincnnti	NL	472	127	27	4	13	24	75	51	65	12	5	350	.269	.315	.426	.246	53	129-3B	13		
2000	Cincnnti	NL	292	80	13	1	12	20	49	41	40	6	1	213	.274	.339	.449	.264	38	81-3B	7		
2001	Cincnnti	NL	354	94	18	1	11	30	64	50	49	10	2	262	.266	.323	.415	.249	41				

What you see is what you get. Aaron Boone is a league-averge hitter and a good defensive third baseman. Well, he was, anyway, before tearing his ACL in July. Chris Stynes played well in his absence, but it wasn't Stynes's dad who became the boss in November. Aaron Boone had no speed to lose, so he should be back at his level in 2001.

Ben Broussard — LF/1B — Bats L — Age 24

YEAR	TEAM	LGE	AB	H	DB	TP	HR	BB	SO	R	RBI	SB	CS	OUT	BA	OBP	SLG	EQA	EQR	DEFENSE			
1999	Billings	Pio	141	39	7	0	7	21	35	19	21	0	0	102	.277	.376	.475	.284	22	29-LF	-1		
1999	Chattang	Sou	128	24	4	0	6	8	44	19	15	0	0	104	.188	.245	.359	.194	9	16-LF	-1	12-1B	1
2000	Chattang	Sou	301	68	6	3	12	57	81	52	41	7	1	234	.226	.355	.385	.258	40	65-LF	-10	14-1B	-4
2001	Cincnnti	NL	220	56	8	1	10	37	75	39	37	5	0	164	.255	.362	.436	.273	32				

It's not as bad as it looks. Ben Broussard was hitting .353/.471/.565 when he broke his hand in May. After he came back he was terrible, hitting .214/.378/.413. That's not a hitter who's lost; it's one who's not swinging the bat properly. He's the reason Sean Casey is available and could be elsewhere by the trade deadline.

Wilmy Caceres — SS/2B — Bats B — Age 22

YEAR	TEAM	LGE	AB	H	DB	TP	HR	BB	SO	R	RBI	SB	CS	OUT	BA	OBP	SLG	EQA	EQR	DEFENSE			
1998	Burlingt	Mid	150	37	2	0	2	3	26	16	11	3	2	115	.247	.268	.300	.183	8	31-SS	-3		
1998	Charl-WV	SAL	398	90	9	4	1	12	65	32	21	9	7	315	.226	.257	.276	.168	18	101-SS	-12		
1999	Clinton	Mid	479	108	18	2	1	17	71	47	21	21	11	382	.225	.253	.278	.172	24	107-SS	-5		
2000	Chattang	Sou	546	135	21	3	2	25	74	57	28	18	10	421	.247	.283	.308	.196	36	78-SS	4	56-2B	-3
2001	Anaheim	AL	472	118	15	3	1	28	72	63	43	21	9	363	.250	.292	.301	.205	34				

He's Travis Dawkins without the hype or the hot month at Double-A. Wilmy Caceres is an old-style, defense-first shortstop who doesn't hit well enough to be taken seriously. He's fast enough to make his way as a utility player. His strong AFL season raised his profile and got him traded to the Angels, who are just desperate enough to make him the starter.

Sean Casey — 1B — Bats L — Age 26

YEAR	TEAM	LGE	AB	H	DB	TP	HR	BB	SO	R	RBI	SB	CS	OUT	BA	OBP	SLG	EQA	EQR	DEFENSE
1998	Cincnnti	NL	306	82	19	1	8	41	42	44	52	1	1	225	.268	.360	.415	.262	40	78-1B -3
1999	Cincnnti	NL	592	188	38	3	24	52	83	97	89	0	2	406	.318	.381	.514	.293	95	145-1B -6
2000	Cincnnti	NL	481	146	29	2	19	44	75	64	78	1	0	335	.304	.369	.491	.285	72	122-1B -3
2001	Cincnnti	NL	485	164	33	2	24	55	76	93	114	2	1	322	.338	.406	.563	.315	90	

Sean Casey suffered a hairline fracture of his left thumb about 15 minutes into the season and didn't start hitting until deep into June. He's a good player who will end up overrated—and probably overpaid—thanks to high batting averages. Trading him is a good idea.

Juan Castro — IF — Bats R — Age 29

YEAR	TEAM	LGE	AB	H	DB	TP	HR	BB	SO	R	RBI	SB	CS	OUT	BA	OBP	SLG	EQA	EQR	DEFENSE			
1998	LosAngls	NL	223	47	5	0	3	15	35	27	15	0	0	176	.211	.261	.274	.169	10	31-SS	4	24-2B	2
1999	Albuquer	PCL	414	92	19	3	4	26	71	37	35	1	2	324	.222	.268	.312	.187	25	50-SS	0	39-3B	-1
2000	Louisvil	Int	61	16	5	1	1	9	13	7	7	0	1	46	.262	.357	.426	.259	8	13-SS	0		
2000	Cincnnti	NL	225	53	10	2	4	11	31	19	21	0	2	174	.236	.271	.351	.199	15	38-SS	6	17-2B	2
2001	Cincnnti	NL	310	73	16	1	4	25	53	29	30	0	2	239	.235	.293	.332	.206	23				

If baseball really was all about pitching and defense, guys like Juan Castro would get more playing time and money. It's not, so Castro spends a lot of time in Motel 6s. He's an excellent defender who hits like an excellent defender.

National League

Gookie Dawkins — SS — Bats R — Age 22

YEAR	TEAM	LGE	AB	H	DB	TP	HR	BB	SO	R	RBI	SB	CS	OUT	BA	OBP	SLG	EQA	EQR	DEFENSE		
1998	Burlingt	Mid	374	85	7	4	1	26	64	33	22	13	5	294	.227	.278	.275	.186	22	100-SS -17		
1999	Rockford	Mid	309	69	9	3	6	23	41	33	21	15	7	247	.223	.277	.330	.205	23	75-SS -13		
1999	Chattang	Sou	128	39	3	0	2	10	18	15	9	7	3	92	.305	.355	.375	.252	15	31-SS -2		
2000	Chattang	Sou	379	81	18	4	6	29	74	45	26	11	5	303	.214	.272	.330	.201	27	54-SS -4	39-2B	-3
2000	Cincnnti	NL	41	9	1	0	0	2	7	4	3	0	0	32	.220	.256	.244	.149	1	13-SS 1		
2001	Cincnnti	NL	402	101	14	3	6	40	74	51	43	11	5	306	.251	.319	.346	.227	38			

He apparently wants to be known by his nickname, "Gookie." That's from a lost Egyptian dialect and means "vastly overrated." Travis Dawkins will eventually work his way up to a .250 EqA or so, but his chance to be a real player depends entirely on his learning to walk 70 times a year. He's got time and a great guy to learn from in Barry Larkin.

Alejandro Diaz — CF — Bats R — Age 22

YEAR	TEAM	LGE	AB	H	DB	TP	HR	BB	SO	R	RBI	SB	CS	OUT	BA	OBP	SLG	EQA	EQR	DEFENSE
1999	Clinton	Mid	222	52	10	1	5	6	38	23	27	11	6	176	.234	.258	.356	.201	16	55-CF -1
1999	Chattang	Sou	220	50	8	6	5	4	33	20	25	3	1	171	.227	.247	.386	.204	16	55-CF 6
2000	Chattang	Sou	499	120	16	5	12	6	80	58	54	9	10	389	.240	.253	.365	.196	33	122-CF 8
2001	Cincnnti	NL	358	93	15	3	9	9	70	37	41	11	6	271	.260	.278	.394	.220	31	

Most tools goofs don't have much value on the baseball field. Alejandro Diaz can't hit worth a darn, but if he played 150 games in a major-league outfield (or, say, 50 for the Texas Rangers), he'd be a Gold Glove candidate. He projects as a right fielder defensively; unfortunately, he projects as a small businessman offensively.

Adam Dunn — LF — Bats L — Age 21

YEAR	TEAM	LGE	AB	H	DB	TP	HR	BB	SO	R	RBI	SB	CS	OUT	BA	OBP	SLG	EQA	EQR	DEFENSE
1998	Billings	Pio	124	26	1	0	3	12	27	13	7	1	1	99	.210	.285	.290	.191	8	29-RF -7
1999	Rockford	Mid	318	77	12	1	8	30	70	39	28	8	5	246	.242	.317	.362	.230	31	63-LF -10
2000	Dayton	Mid	438	97	16	1	13	71	112	67	53	9	3	344	.221	.337	.352	.240	48	115-LF -6
2001	Cincnnti	NL	364	97	12	1	13	54	94	62	56	12	3	270	.266	.361	.412	.266	49	

The Reds' lack of a high-A affiliate has forced them to choose between forcing prospects to Double-A or risking them stagnating in middle-A. Diaz was pushed, while Adam Dunn was left in the Midwest League to have a big year. Of the Reds' pool of outfield prospects, only Austin Kearns is a better bet than Dunn.

David Espinosa — SS — Bats B — Age 19

He's the Reds' 2000 first-round pick who signed a major-league contract in one of the more interesting draft deals in recent memory. David Espinosa will go right on the 40-man roster, which forces the Reds to push him to the majors quickly; he'll have to stay up for good or risk being lost on waivers by 2005.

Ken Griffey Jr. — CF — Bats L — Age 31

YEAR	TEAM	LGE	AB	H	DB	TP	HR	BB	SO	R	RBI	SB	CS	OUT	BA	OBP	SLG	EQA	EQR	DEFENSE
1998	Seattle	AL	632	186	30	3	61	75	108	122	148	17	5	451	.294	.375	.641	.318	129	158-CF 8
1999	Seattle	AL	601	174	26	3	49	85	98	119	128	22	7	434	.290	.383	.587	.311	117	148-CF 4
2000	Cincnnti	NL	521	135	21	3	37	85	110	93	106	5	4	390	.259	.371	.524	.291	89	141-CF 8
2001	Cincnnti	NL	563	163	25	2	48	102	113	120	145	13	6	406	.290	.398	.597	.317	115	

It would be something if Ken Griffey Jr. spent the second half of his career underrated. His defense is now very good, yet he did not win a Gold Glove for the first time since 1989. His performance slip in 2000 was overstated because of his batting average. There are two MVP awards left in his career, one of which he'll earn in 2001.

Drew Henson   3B   Bats R   Age 21

YEAR	TEAM	LGE	AB	H	DB	TP	HR	BB	SO	R	RBI	SB	CS	OUT	BA	OBP	SLG	EQA	EQR	DEFENSE
1999	Tampa	Fla	258	60	8	0	10	19	82	27	26	1	1	199	.233	.286	.380	.219	22	48-3B -15
2000	Tampa	Fla	21	5	1	0	1	1	8	3	1	0	0	16	.238	.273	.429	.227	2	
2000	Norwich	Eas	227	57	9	1	6	14	81	33	30	0	3	173	.251	.296	.379	.219	19	45-3B -5
2000	Chattang	Sou	65	11	4	0	2	3	26	6	9	1	0	54	.169	.206	.323	.164	3	16-3B -3
2001	*Cincnnti*	*NL*	*224*	*59*	*7*	*0*	*11*	*21*	*101*	*27*	*38*	*0*	*1*	*166*	*.263*	*.327*	*.442*	*.253*	*27*	

Drew Henson can be a top-tier third baseman, but he needs at-bats to develop, and he's not getting them. With at least another season of college football ahead of him, it's unlikely that he'll play baseball full-time until 2002 at the absolute earliest. He's only a mid-level baseball prospect as long as he's playing football half the year. The Reds can help themselves by trading him back to the Yankees.

Brian L. Hunter   OF   Bats R   Age 30

YEAR	TEAM	LGE	AB	H	DB	TP	HR	BB	SO	R	RBI	SB	CS	OUT	BA	OBP	SLG	EQA	EQR	DEFENSE
1998	Detroit	AL	594	155	29	3	5	35	84	65	36	35	11	450	.261	.304	.345	.224	54	139-CF 18
1999	Detroit	AL	55	13	2	1	0	4	10	7	2	0	3	45	.236	.299	.309	.186	3	18-CF 2
1999	Seattle	AL	483	114	13	5	4	28	73	69	33	42	5	374	.236	.279	.308	.212	38	119-LF 7
2000	Colorado	NL	195	46	3	1	1	17	29	30	11	12	3	152	.236	.300	.277	.205	14	49-OF 0
2000	Cincnnti	NL	40	8	1	0	0	6	8	11	1	5	0	32	.200	.304	.225	.214	3	12-CF 2
2001	*Philadel*	*NL*	*334*	*81*	*10*	*3*	*2*	*28*	*55*	*54*	*29*	*27*	*6*	*258*	*.243*	*.301*	*.308*	*.218*	*29*	

This Brian Hunter was baseball's luckiest man for about eight months. First, the Mariners offered him arbitration after he'd been the worst regular in baseball in 1999. Then he won the case when the assigned arbitrators were mysteriously replaced by two Magic 8-Balls and a Quiz Wiz. The Mariners later released Hunter... who signed a week later to play in beautiful downtown Denver. He was eventually dumped on the Reds, but he had a lot of money and an inflated batting average to show for his time.

    Contrast that karma with the other Brian Hunter. The Braves tried to sneak him through waivers in May so he could go to Richmond during a roster crunch, but the Phillies claimed him. Hunter didn't gain any playing time in the deal and dropped about a million games in the standings; the move cost him a playoff share as well. Signed by Philly to create maximum confusion.

Austin Kearns   RF   Bats R   Age 21

YEAR	TEAM	LGE	AB	H	DB	TP	HR	BB	SO	R	RBI	SB	CS	OUT	BA	OBP	SLG	EQA	EQR	DEFENSE
1998	Billings	Pio	107	24	4	0	1	12	26	8	7	0	0	83	.224	.305	.290	.201	8	27-RF -4
1999	Rockford	Mid	433	92	26	2	10	32	131	46	31	8	4	345	.212	.274	.351	.207	34	108-RF -8
2000	Dayton	Mid	500	120	21	1	20	62	103	74	66	7	3	383	.240	.328	.406	.247	58	129-RF -6
2001	*Cincnnti*	*NL*	*450*	*118*	*21*	*1*	*19*	*53*	*112*	*68*	*73*	*7*	*1*	*333*	*.262*	*.340*	*.440*	*.262*	*58*	

Austin Kearns is the Reds' best prospect, bar none. Scouts love him for his tools while people like us get excited about the power and plate discipline he's shown at age 20. His 2000 performance is inflated by the level—a real comer doesn't usually get 900-odd ABs in the Midwest League—so he may look like a relative disappointment this year. Ignore it: Kearns will be a star.

Barry Larkin   SS   Bats R   Age 37

YEAR	TEAM	LGE	AB	H	DB	TP	HR	BB	SO	R	RBI	SB	CS	OUT	BA	OBP	SLG	EQA	EQR	DEFENSE
1998	Cincnnti	NL	545	165	33	9	18	76	65	93	70	24	3	383	.303	.390	.495	.299	94	140-SS -2
1999	Cincnnti	NL	582	164	28	3	12	83	54	99	68	23	7	425	.282	.373	.402	.269	79	153-SS 5
2000	Cincnnti	NL	397	119	27	4	10	41	29	66	37	12	6	284	.300	.367	.463	.277	57	97-SS -11
2001	*Cincnnti*	*NL*	*375*	*102*	*19*	*2*	*7*	*61*	*35*	*70*	*51*	*13*	*5*	*278*	*.272*	*.374*	*.389*	*.265*	*50*	

There are no surprises here: when shortstops get to be 36, they lose range and get hurt. Barry Larkin was due, anyway: he'd played 145 games in three of the last four seasons. There's a case for the three-year, $27 million contract he signed, beginning with the fact that a third of it is deferred money. Still, the trend here is bad, and Larkin could be a Tony Gwynn-sized problem for the Reds by early 2002.

National League

Brandon Larson — 3B — Bats R — Age 25

YEAR	TEAM	LGE	AB	H	DB	TP	HR	BB	SO	R	RBI	SB	CS	OUT	BA	OBP	SLG	EQA	EQR	DEFENSE	
1998	Burlingt	Mid	69	14	1	0	2	2	17	4	7	1	1	56	.203	.225	.304	.160	3	18-3B	6
1999	Rockford	Mid	252	60	11	1	9	16	73	24	32	5	1	193	.238	.287	.397	.228	24	63-3B	-1
1999	Chattang	Sou	172	41	6	0	9	6	54	20	29	2	3	134	.238	.271	.430	.224	16	42-3B	-4
2000	Louisvil	Int	63	16	5	1	2	3	17	9	4	0	0	47	.254	.288	.460	.242	7	16-3B	3
2000	Chattang	Sou	437	105	17	0	17	20	130	49	50	7	3	335	.240	.280	.396	.222	39	104-3B	-22
2001	*Cincnnti*	*NL*	*347*	*89*	*12*	*0*	*16*	*24*	*109*	*41*	*52*	*7*	*2*	*260*	*.256*	*.305*	*.429*	*.243*	*38*		

Brandon Larson is a former #1 pick and a converted shortstop trying to make the majors on his power. Other than the pedigree—and the injury history of *South Park*'s Kenny McCormick—there's nothing to separate him from a dozen other moderate-power, not-much-else prospects.

Jason LaRue — C — Bats R — Age 27

YEAR	TEAM	LGE	AB	H	DB	TP	HR	BB	SO	R	RBI	SB	CS	OUT	BA	OBP	SLG	EQA	EQR	DEFENSE	
1998	Chattang	Sou	381	111	27	4	10	23	65	47	51	2	2	272	.291	.342	.462	.265	49	89-C	-9
1998	Indianap	Int	51	11	4	0	0	3	8	5	4	0	1	41	.216	.259	.294	.169	2	13-C	1
1999	Indianap	Int	263	61	10	1	10	11	52	34	29	0	2	204	.232	.271	.392	.213	21	65-C	2
1999	Cincnnti	NL	90	18	7	0	3	10	30	11	9	3	1	73	.200	.294	.378	.227	9	27-C	2
2000	Louisvil	Int	308	70	16	1	12	16	55	45	39	2	1	239	.227	.279	.403	.223	28	73-C	-7
2000	Cincnnti	NL	99	23	2	0	5	3	18	11	11	0	0	76	.232	.279	.404	.223	9	29-C	0
2001	*Cincnnti*	*NL*	*351*	*89*	*21*	*1*	*14*	*25*	*71*	*42*	*52*	*2*	*1*	*263*	*.254*	*.303*	*.439*	*.243*	*38*		

Jason LaRue got jobbed out of playing time when the Reds brought in Benito Santiago. Eddie Taubensee's big September in 1999 had buried LaRue as a starter, anyway. He'll be around for a while; think Brook Fordyce's career path.

Jackson Melian — OF — Bats R — Age 21

YEAR	TEAM	LGE	AB	H	DB	TP	HR	BB	SO	R	RBI	SB	CS	OUT	BA	OBP	SLG	EQA	EQR	DEFENSE	
1998	Greensbr	SAL	476	102	15	1	6	30	126	47	32	5	5	379	.214	.266	.288	.178	25	128-RF	-6
1999	Tampa	Fla	474	112	16	7	6	36	113	48	44	5	4	366	.236	.297	.338	.212	38	123-CF	-10
2000	Norwich	Eas	294	68	6	2	9	12	75	26	31	10	1	227	.231	.266	.357	.209	23	78-CF	-4
2001	*Cincnnti*	*NL*	*375*	*93*	*12*	*2*	*10*	*31*	*99*	*46*	*44*	*10*	*2*	*284*	*.248*	*.305*	*.371*	*.230*	*36*		

Most analysts, including the BP staff, thought the Reds had made out like bandits in the Denny Neagle trade. Less than a year later, though, it doesn't look nearly as good: Jackson Melian has a long way to go, and he isn't the outfield prospect that Austin Kearns or Adam Dunn or even Ben Broussard is. Drew Henson is sacrificing his baseball development to play football and Ed Yarnall didn't even sniff Cincinnati despite the team's need for pitching. There's a lot of upside to the deal, but one of these three guys is going to have to take a big step forward to fulfill it.

Alex Ochoa — OF — Bats R — Age 29

YEAR	TEAM	LGE	AB	H	DB	TP	HR	BB	SO	R	RBI	SB	CS	OUT	BA	OBP	SLG	EQA	EQR	DEFENSE	
1998	Minnesot	AL	248	65	14	2	2	9	31	34	24	5	3	186	.262	.290	.359	.214	20	57-RF	-3
1999	Milwauke	NL	277	80	13	3	8	41	41	43	37	4	4	201	.289	.390	.444	.281	42	67-LF	-2
2000	Cincnnti	NL	244	73	20	3	12	21	25	46	52	7	4	175	.299	.361	.553	.293	41	59-LF	1
2001	*Cincnnti*	*NL*	*289*	*86*	*18*	*2*	*10*	*30*	*36*	*49*	*51*	*7*	*5*	*208*	*.298*	*.364*	*.478*	*.277*	*42*		

He's a tremendous fourth outfielder. Some good fourth outfielders stay that way and have careers as good players on winning teams, making money and generating good memories. Others end up as marginal starters on bad teams, making more money and playing more without ever having to worry about not being free on Columbus Day. I have a sneaking suspicion that Gerald Williams... er, Alex Ochoa will fall among the latter.

Pokey Reese — 2B — Bats R — Age 28

YEAR	TEAM	LGE	AB	H	DB	TP	HR	BB	SO	R	RBI	SB	CS	OUT	BA	OBP	SLG	EQA	EQR	DEFENSE			
1998	Cincnnti	NL	134	34	2	2	1	14	26	20	16	3	2	102	.254	.324	.321	.221	12	25-3B	3	14-SS	-8
1999	Cincnnti	NL	585	162	36	4	10	27	76	77	48	29	6	429	.277	.315	.403	.245	64	144-2B	27		
2000	Cincnnti	NL	520	128	19	5	12	38	81	71	43	26	3	395	.246	.304	.371	.234	52	129-2B	14		
2001	*Cincnnti*	*NL*	*484*	*129*	*22*	*5*	*11*	*39*	*76*	*77*	*60*	*28*	*4*	*359*	*.267*	*.321*	*.401*	*.249*	*56*				

(Pokey Reese *continued*)

All things considered, Pokey Reese is an average second baseman, above average in his best years. The problem is that he's going to cost a lot more than he's worth very soon, and the Reds think he's right behind Ken Griffey as a building block. Like Sean Casey, an excellent trade chip: the perceived value is much greater than the actual value.

Benito Santiago — C — Bats R — Age 36

YEAR	TEAM	LGE	AB	H	DB	TP	HR	BB	SO	R	RBI	SB	CS	OUT	BA	OBP	SLG	EQA	EQR	DEFENSE	
1998	Toronto	AL	29	9	6	0	0	1	5	3	4	0	0	20	.310	.333	.517	.275	4		
1999	ChiCubs	NL	351	85	16	3	7	27	67	27	33	1	1	267	.242	.300	.365	.221	31	92-C	3
2000	Cincnnti	NL	253	64	13	1	7	15	42	21	41	2	2	191	.253	.297	.395	.228	24	67-C	2
2001	Cincnnti	NL	200	47	9	1	4	17	38	21	21	1	1	154	.235	.295	.350	.214	16		

At this point, Benito Santiago is the poster child for the selection of known mediocrity over potential quality. He's neither going to kill you nor push you towards a championship. Guys like Creighton Gubanich and Tom Wilson deserve better than to watch him on television from their rooms at Red Roof Inn.

Chris Stynes — UT — Bats R — Age 28

YEAR	TEAM	LGE	AB	H	DB	TP	HR	BB	SO	R	RBI	SB	CS	OUT	BA	OBP	SLG	EQA	EQR	DEFENSE			
1998	Cincnnti	NL	350	89	10	1	6	31	34	52	26	14	1	262	.254	.322	.340	.232	34	60-LF	4	14-3B	0
1999	Cincnnti	NL	113	26	1	0	2	11	12	17	13	4	2	89	.230	.298	.292	.202	8	23-2B	0		
2000	Cincnnti	NL	380	122	23	1	11	27	51	66	36	4	2	260	.321	.369	.474	.280	54	69-3B	2		
2001	Boston	AL	293	89	16	1	8	27	38	49	47	6	1	205	.304	.363	.447	.275	41				

Don't get too excited. Chris Stynes is a serviceable bench player who had a year at the top of his range. The increased playing time had more to do with Aaron Boone's injury than Stynes's performance. He can help a good team or play too much for a bad one. Traded to the Red Sox, he could end up as the regular third baseman.

Eddie Taubensee — C — Bats L — Age 32

YEAR	TEAM	LGE	AB	H	DB	TP	HR	BB	SO	R	RBI	SB	CS	OUT	BA	OBP	SLG	EQA	EQR	DEFENSE	
1998	Cincnnti	NL	436	120	20	0	14	50	87	61	74	1	0	316	.275	.350	.417	.259	54	113-C	-8
1999	Cincnnti	NL	423	126	20	2	20	25	63	55	79	0	2	299	.298	.338	.496	.271	57	110-C	-12
2000	Cincnnti	NL	267	69	8	0	7	17	41	27	23	0	0	198	.258	.307	.367	.225	24	67-C	-6
2001	Clevelnd	AL	222	63	5	0	8	19	37	30	37	0	0	159	.284	.340	.414	.252	25		

Bad timing: Eddie Taubensee's first bad year since 1997 coincided with the initial year of his new contract. He missed the last couple of months after surgery for a ruptured disk, so there's a case to be made that he'll rebound. He's a relative bargain at $2.2 million; even his 1998 level of performance would be worth the money. The Indians got a steal.

Michael Tucker — OF — Bats L — Age 30

YEAR	TEAM	LGE	AB	H	DB	TP	HR	BB	SO	R	RBI	SB	CS	OUT	BA	OBP	SLG	EQA	EQR	DEFENSE	
1998	Atlanta	NL	420	103	27	3	14	47	105	55	46	7	3	320	.245	.325	.424	.250	50	106-RF	-4
1999	Cincnnti	NL	296	72	7	4	11	33	76	50	40	8	4	228	.243	.325	.405	.246	34	80-RF	5
2000	Cincnnti	NL	271	69	13	3	14	39	60	50	32	11	6	208	.255	.361	.480	.277	42	70-OF	-1
2001	Cincnnti	NL	262	66	11	3	10	37	66	45	40	10	3	199	.252	.344	.431	.263	35		

Other than Ken Griffey, the Reds have a distinct lack of outfielders who are fully qualified to start every day. Michael Tucker is a decent bench player who would be more valuable if he took some ground balls at second base and tried to be Terry Shumpert.

Ron Wright — 1B — Bats R — Age 25

YEAR	TEAM	LGE	AB	H	DB	TP	HR	BB	SO	R	RBI	SB	CS	OUT	BA	OBP	SLG	EQA	EQR	DEFENSE	
1998	Nashvill	PCL	56	11	2	0	0	8	18	5	6	0	0	45	.196	.304	.232	.183	3	14-1B	0
1999	Altoona	Eas	82	17	6	0	0	6	28	4	4	0	0	65	.207	.266	.280	.176	4	11-1B	2
2000	Louisvil	Int	61	12	3	0	2	6	19	8	11	0	0	49	.197	.269	.344	.201	4	13-1B	-1
2000	Chattang	Sou	246	56	12	0	10	27	74	30	39	1	1	191	.228	.307	.398	.234	25	53-1B	-8
2001	Cincnnti	NL	196	47	9	0	9	25	65	26	31	0	0	149	.240	.326	.423	.250	23		

The good news is that he played more than he had since his big 1997 in the Pirates' system. He also hit reasonably well at Chattanooga after a failed Triple-A trial. The back problems are never going away though, and unlike Jose Canseco or Mark McGwire, Ron Wright doesn't have a track record that encourages teams to work around his absences.

Dmitri Young — LF — Bats B — Age 27

YEAR	TEAM	LGE	AB	H	DB	TP	HR	BB	SO	R	RBI	SB	CS	OUT	BA	OBP	SLG	EQA	EQR	DEFENSE			
1998	Cincnnti	NL	541	164	40	2	16	46	88	81	82	2	4	381	.303	.360	.473	.274	75	86-LF	-8	37-1B	0
1999	Cincnnti	NL	373	108	26	2	14	24	67	59	51	2	1	266	.290	.336	.483	.268	49	78-RF	-2		
2000	Cincnnti	NL	550	161	37	5	17	27	75	64	81	0	3	392	.293	.329	.471	.260	68	90-LF	-3	28-1B	-2
2001	Cincnnti	NL	453	143	34	2	16	36	72	74	87	2	1	311	.316	.366	.506	.286	68				

He's becoming a tweener, which probably could have been predicted once he moved off of third base in the mid-1990s. Dmitri Young doesn't hit enough to play first base or left field, and he doesn't field well enough to be an asset in either corner outfield spot. That projection is within reach, and would still only make him worth a win or so.

PITCHERS (ERA: 4.50, H/9: 9.00, HR/9: 1.00, BB/9: 3.00, K/9: 6.00, KW: 1.00, PERA: 4.50)

Justin Atchley — Throws L — Age 27

YEAR	TEAM	LGE	IP	H	ER	HR	BB	K	ERA	W	L	H/9	HR/9	BB/9	K/9	KW	PERA
1999	Chattang	Sou	90.7	114	53	14	25	40	5.26	4	6	11.32	1.39	2.48	3.97	0.80	6.07
1999	Indianap	Int	22.3	36	13	6	2	4	5.24	1	1	14.51	2.42	0.81	1.61	1.00	8.30
2000	Louisvil	Int	115.7	164	85	24	26	49	6.61	3	10	12.76	1.87	2.02	3.81	0.94	7.22

He's a marginal prospect whose appearance in the Arizona Fall League should tell you a lot about the state of pitching in this organization. Justin Atchley didn't do anything in the AFL (4.70 ERA) to change his outlook: cloudy.

Rob Bell — Throws R — Age 24

YEAR	TEAM	LGE	IP	H	ER	HR	BB	K	ERA	W	L	H/9	HR/9	BB/9	K/9	KW	PERA
1998	DanvillC	Car	159.3	182	99	16	60	101	5.59	6	12	10.28	0.90	3.39	5.71	0.84	5.31
1999	Chattang	Sou	67.3	76	33	10	17	43	4.41	3	4	10.16	1.34	2.27	5.75	1.26	5.22
2000	Louisvil	Int	39.0	36	20	7	12	36	4.62	2	2	8.31	1.62	2.77	8.31	1.50	4.64
2000	Cincnnti	NL	138.3	126	72	27	58	93	4.68	6	9	8.20	1.76	3.77	6.05	0.80	5.15

Despite a monthlong trip to Triple-A and a nasty bout with the long ball, Rob Bell had a very productive rookie season. He made every start without being overworked, stayed healthy, and, other than the home runs, actually pitched pretty well. His balky elbow is sound, so look for a step forward in 2001.

Lance Davis — Throws L — Age 24

YEAR	TEAM	LGE	IP	H	ER	HR	BB	K	ERA	W	L	H/9	HR/9	BB/9	K/9	KW	PERA
1998	Burlingt	Mid	49.0	37	22	7	34	19	4.04	2	3	6.80	1.29	6.24	3.49	0.28	4.85
1999	Rockford	Mid	117.3	136	70	20	57	49	5.37	5	8	10.43	1.53	4.37	3.76	0.43	6.47
2000	Chattang	Sou	106.0	101	47	7	55	57	3.99	6	6	8.58	0.59	4.67	4.84	0.52	4.50
2000	Louisvil	Int	30.3	31	20	5	8	11	5.93	1	2	9.20	1.48	2.37	3.26	0.69	4.88

Lance Davis's first good pro year was enough to get him a spot in the Arizona Fall League, but there's a lot of evidence that the season was a fluke. His peripheral numbers were way out of line with his ERA, and there was no great leap forward in his stuff or mechanics. He won't be a factor until 2002, if ever.

Elmer Dessens — Throws R — Age 29

YEAR	TEAM	LGE	IP	H	ER	HR	BB	K	ERA	W	L	H/9	HR/9	BB/9	K/9	KW	PERA
1998	Nashvill	PCL	28.7	29	12	3	7	8	3.77	2	1	9.10	0.94	2.20	2.51	0.57	4.18
1998	Pittsbrg	NL	72.0	87	48	10	22	35	6.00	2	6	10.88	1.25	2.75	4.38	0.80	5.78
2000	Louisvil	Int	21.7	23	10	1	7	10	4.15	1	1	9.55	0.42	2.91	4.15	0.71	4.18
2000	Cincnnti	NL	143.0	162	65	8	34	71	4.09	8	8	10.20	0.50	2.14	4.47	1.04	4.32

He became the glue of the Reds' rotation during their August funk. Elmer Dessens is a strong ground-ball pitcher, so he can get away with peripherals that would scare you off of other guys. As a cheap arm to swing between the #5 slot and the pen, he's an asset to the Reds.

Osvaldo Fernandez — Throws R — Age 32

YEAR	TEAM	LGE	IP	H	ER	HR	BB	K	ERA	W	L	H/9	HR/9	BB/9	K/9	KW	PERA
1998	Binghmtn	Eas	12.0	11	9	1	7	9	6.75	0	1	8.25	0.75	5.25	6.75	0.64	4.73
2000	Louisvil	Int	53.7	56	28	4	19	31	4.70	3	3	9.39	0.67	3.19	5.20	0.82	4.45
2000	Cincnnti	NL	77.3	66	29	5	25	30	3.38	5	4	7.68	0.58	2.91	3.49	0.60	3.31

Osvaldo Fernandez's performance was comparable to that of Dessens, right down to getting lots of groundball outs. He's come a long way back from blowing out his elbow, so it's hard to not be glad for him. Remember when he was the Cuban defector of the month?

Keith Glauber — Throws R — Age 29

YEAR	TEAM	LGE	IP	H	ER	HR	BB	K	ERA	W	L	H/9	HR/9	BB/9	K/9	KW	PERA
1998	Burlingt	Mid	12.3	14	13	3	8	6	9.49	0	1	10.22	2.19	5.84	4.38	0.38	7.66
1998	Indianap	Int	15.0	20	18	1	15	10	10.80	0	2	12.00	0.60	9.00	6.00	0.33	8.37
1999	Chattang	Sou	46.7	41	13	2	9	15	2.51	4	1	7.91	0.39	1.74	2.89	0.83	2.82
1999	Indianap	Int	64.7	82	50	10	21	35	6.96	2	5	11.41	1.39	2.92	4.87	0.83	6.32
2000	Chattang	Sou	37.3	43	23	4	14	15	5.54	1	3	10.37	0.96	3.38	3.62	0.54	5.42
2000	Louisvil	Int	28.0	25	5	1	6	11	1.61	3	0	8.04	0.32	1.93	3.54	0.92	2.89

He may be the master of the Two Good Weeks. Keith Glauber has been a prospect, a suspect, a sleeper, and a rehab case, and a big reason is that he seems to have a couple of weeks a year in which he can't be hit. He has more upside than his competition, so he makes the book.

Danny Graves — Throws R — Age 27

YEAR	TEAM	LGE	IP	H	ER	HR	BB	K	ERA	W	L	H/9	HR/9	BB/9	K/9	KW	PERA
1998	Cincnnti	NL	78.0	73	29	6	25	36	3.35	5	4	8.42	0.69	2.88	4.15	0.72	3.81
1999	Cincnnti	NL	108.3	86	37	9	40	58	3.07	8	4	7.14	0.75	3.32	4.82	0.73	3.34
2000	Cincnnti	NL	89.0	78	28	7	34	44	2.83	7	3	7.89	0.71	3.44	4.45	0.65	3.74

Jack McKeon finally pulled back on the reins late in 2000. Prior to August 27, Danny Graves had just one stretch in which he threw an inning or less in three straight appearances. From that point on, he had ten straight one-inning appearances and then a final one of two-thirds of an inning. It's an open question how Bob Boone will use him, but I'd guess he'll be the primary closer—70 games, 85 innings—in 2001.

Pete Harnisch — Throws R — Age 34

YEAR	TEAM	LGE	IP	H	ER	HR	BB	K	ERA	W	L	H/9	HR/9	BB/9	K/9	KW	PERA
1998	Cincnnti	NL	200.3	172	77	24	57	128	3.46	13	9	7.73	1.08	2.56	5.75	1.12	3.68
1999	Cincnnti	NL	192.3	180	76	22	46	101	3.56	12	9	8.42	1.03	2.15	4.73	1.10	3.85
2000	Cincnnti	NL	127.7	126	66	19	37	59	4.65	6	8	8.88	1.34	2.61	4.16	0.80	4.63

He shouldn't have opened the season on the active roster, and after six starts out of the Jeff Bower Catalogue, even he agreed. Pete Harnisch had a 9.95 ERA when he went on the DL with shoulder weakness. He returned just before the All-Star break to post a 3.49 ERA in 16 starts. Not a good bet for 2001.

National League

Ty Howington — Throws L — Age 20

YEAR	TEAM	LGE	IP	H	ER	HR	BB	K	ERA	W	L	H/9	HR/9	BB/9	K/9	KW	PERA
2000	Dayton	Mid	129.7	158	100	15	92	63	6.94	3	11	10.97	1.04	6.39	4.37	0.34	7.11

The team's #1 pick in 1999 wasn't impressive in his first season, struggling with the strike zone. Even with the so-so performance, the organization is happy with his development. Ty Howington is at least three years, and probably a minor surgery, away from being relevant.

Larry Luebbers — Throws R — Age 31

YEAR	TEAM	LGE	IP	H	ER	HR	BB	K	ERA	W	L	H/9	HR/9	BB/9	K/9	KW	PERA
1998	Memphis	PCL	162.7	174	96	30	55	71	5.31	7	11	9.63	1.66	3.04	3.93	0.65	5.59
1999	Memphis	PCL	122.3	124	62	19	39	53	4.56	6	8	9.12	1.40	2.87	3.90	0.68	4.93
1999	St Louis	NL	44.3	43	23	7	13	13	4.67	2	3	8.73	1.42	2.64	2.64	0.50	4.63
2000	Louisvil	Int	108.0	95	52	11	41	49	4.33	6	6	7.92	0.92	3.42	4.08	0.60	3.96
2000	Cincnnti	NL	20.0	26	14	1	10	7	6.30	1	1	11.70	0.45	4.50	3.15	0.35	6.15

Jim Bowden's ability to collect guys like Larry Luebbers gives the Reds a cushion when things go wrong during the season. If the Blue Jays had guys like Luebbers, Dessens, and Fernandez in their organization, they might have changed last October's storylines. Luebbers is a useful 11th or 12th pitcher who could surprise people if he were to get a job.

Hector Mercado — Throws L — Age 27

YEAR	TEAM	LGE	IP	H	ER	HR	BB	K	ERA	W	L	H/9	HR/9	BB/9	K/9	KW	PERA
2000	Louisvil	Int	72.7	69	27	2	49	48	3.34	5	3	8.55	0.25	6.07	5.94	0.49	4.71
2000	Cincnnti	NL	13.7	12	6	2	6	11	3.95	1	1	7.90	1.32	3.95	7.24	0.92	4.53

March 2000: rotoheads everywhere bid themselves into a frenzy for an unknown Mexican League player who might—might—get saves for the Reds. April 2000: Hector Mercado sent to Triple-A. Mercado is left-handed and throws hard; he'll be around for a while.

Steve Parris — Throws R — Age 33

YEAR	TEAM	LGE	IP	H	ER	HR	BB	K	ERA	W	L	H/9	HR/9	BB/9	K/9	KW	PERA
1998	Indianap	Int	78.7	78	45	10	27	69	5.15	3	6	8.92	1.14	3.09	7.89	1.28	4.64
1998	Cincnnti	NL	95.0	87	43	9	28	63	4.07	5	6	8.24	0.85	2.65	5.97	1.13	3.77
1999	Indianap	Int	33.7	39	17	6	10	21	4.54	2	2	10.43	1.60	2.67	5.61	1.05	5.87
1999	Cincnnti	NL	125.7	118	52	14	42	72	3.72	7	7	8.45	1.00	3.01	5.16	0.86	4.18
2000	Cincnnti	NL	188.3	217	96	25	57	97	4.59	9	12	10.37	1.19	2.72	4.64	0.85	5.40

Steve Parris was the only Red to make it through the year in the rotation. He's become an innings sponge, someone who can make 30 starts and keep you in most of them. He may be better as a swingman, somebody to spot against heavily right-handed teams and use out of the bullpen against other ones. He'll be the Blue Jays' #4 starter.

Eddie Priest — Throws L — Age 27

YEAR	TEAM	LGE	IP	H	ER	HR	BB	K	ERA	W	L	H/9	HR/9	BB/9	K/9	KW	PERA
1998	Buffalo	Int	83.7	98	55	12	28	31	5.92	3	6	10.54	1.29	3.01	3.33	0.55	5.72
1998	Chattang	Sou	24.3	16	7	2	10	17	2.59	2	1	5.92	0.74	3.70	6.29	0.85	2.83
1998	Indianap	Int	32.0	35	20	7	7	15	5.63	1	3	9.84	1.97	1.97	4.22	1.07	5.58
1999	Chattang	Sou	72.0	98	45	10	16	34	5.63	3	5	12.25	1.25	2.00	4.25	1.06	6.26
1999	Indianap	Int	65.7	82	40	12	21	24	5.48	2	5	11.24	1.64	2.88	3.29	0.57	6.46
2000	Chattang	Sou	164.0	191	92	10	67	81	5.05	7	11	10.48	0.55	3.68	4.45	0.60	5.18

Yeah, that Eddie Priest. After bouncing between the Reds and Indians for a while, he's back in the Reds organization, providing depth and helping Chattanooga win games. He's wildly overqualified for the Southern League and could toss 150 good innings in the right major-league situation.

Brian Reith — Throws R — Age 23

YEAR	TEAM	LGE	IP	H	ER	HR	BB	K	ERA	W	L	H/9	HR/9	BB/9	K/9	KW	PERA
1998	Greensbr	SAL	106.7	92	55	14	43	54	4.64	5	7	7.76	1.18	3.63	4.56	0.63	4.22
1999	Tampa	Fla	128.0	175	102	27	44	61	7.17	3	11	12.30	1.90	3.09	4.29	0.69	7.44
2000	Tampa	Fla	109.3	104	47	10	42	57	3.87	6	6	8.56	0.82	3.46	4.69	0.68	4.25
2000	Dayton	Mid	31.3	36	15	4	9	16	4.31	1	2	10.34	1.15	2.59	4.60	0.89	5.29
2000	Chattang	Sou	27.3	34	17	5	11	17	5.60	1	2	11.20	1.65	3.62	5.60	0.77	6.74

Brian Reith was "the other guy" acquired in the Denny Neagle trade, a 6'5" right-hander with good command. He immediately became the second-best pitching prospect in the Reds' system. Long term, he's a fantastic prospect due to his control; in the short term, he'll have to adjust to better hitters.

Chris Reitsma — Throws R — Age 23

YEAR	TEAM	LGE	IP	H	ER	HR	BB	K	ERA	W	L	H/9	HR/9	BB/9	K/9	KW	PERA
1998	Sarasota	Fla	12.0	11	5	0	6	5	3.75	1	0	8.25	0.00	4.50	3.75	0.42	3.67
1999	Sarasota	Fla	87.3	120	86	23	37	48	8.86	2	8	12.37	2.37	3.81	4.95	0.65	8.27
2000	Sarasota	Fla	58.7	58	35	7	21	27	5.37	2	5	8.90	1.07	3.22	4.14	0.64	4.61
2000	Trenton	Eas	84.0	80	34	13	23	38	3.64	5	4	8.57	1.39	2.46	4.07	0.83	4.44

After nursing him back to health and effectiveness, the Red Sox traded Chris Reitsma to the Reds for a month of Dante Bichette. Reitsma broke his elbow in 1997 and had never thrown 100 innings in a pro season before 2000. He's healthy now, with a good fastball and a change-up, and is working on a curve. He chewed up the Arizona Fall League and has to be considered a sleeper candidate for the Reds' rotation. 2002 looks like a real good year for him.

Dennys Reyes — Throws L — Age 24

YEAR	TEAM	LGE	IP	H	ER	HR	BB	K	ERA	W	L	H/9	HR/9	BB/9	K/9	KW	PERA
1998	Albuquer	PCL	41.7	31	13	5	17	40	2.81	3	2	6.70	1.08	3.67	8.64	1.18	3.52
1998	LosAngls	NL	27.3	27	17	1	19	27	5.60	1	2	8.89	0.33	6.26	8.89	0.71	5.04
1998	Indianap	Int	23.0	20	10	1	14	20	3.91	2	1	7.83	0.39	5.48	7.83	0.71	4.22
1998	Cincnnti	NL	37.7	36	19	2	24	36	4.54	2	2	8.60	0.48	5.73	8.60	0.75	4.86
1999	Cincnnti	NL	61.0	54	28	4	32	61	4.13	3	4	7.97	0.59	4.72	9.00	0.95	4.20
2000	Cincnnti	NL	43.3	43	28	4	23	30	5.82	2	3	8.93	0.83	4.78	6.23	0.65	5.03

Last year, the Reds dredged up Osvaldo Fernandez, Elmer Dessens, and Larry Luebbers, but stubbornly refused to put Dennys Reyes in the rotation. Even worse, they're using him in a spot-lefty role (63 appearances, 43⅔ innings) that fits him like a Speedo. He still has significant upside, and not just on a scale. The pickup of Jeff Wallace and open spots in the rotation have created an opportunity for him to start. Tremendous potential, both for the Reds and your fantasy team.

John Riedling — Throws R — Age 25

YEAR	TEAM	LGE	IP	H	ER	HR	BB	K	ERA	W	L	H/9	HR/9	BB/9	K/9	KW	PERA
1998	Chattang	Sou	97.3	113	72	16	57	55	6.66	3	8	10.45	1.48	5.27	5.09	0.48	6.80
1999	Chattang	Sou	39.3	41	24	3	21	23	5.49	1	3	9.38	0.69	4.81	5.26	0.55	5.14
1999	Indianap	Int	33.3	18	8	1	18	19	2.16	3	1	4.86	0.27	4.86	5.13	0.53	2.34
2000	Louisvil	Int	71.0	64	25	8	29	56	3.17	5	3	8.11	1.01	3.68	7.10	0.97	4.27
2000	Cincnnti	NL	15.0	11	6	1	6	15	3.60	1	1	6.60	0.60	3.60	9.00	1.25	2.99

John Riedling is a hard thrower who, converted to relief, had the first extended success of his career. If Scott Williamson ends up in the rotation—or Oakland—Riedling would be in line to get his innings. A name to remember.

Scott Sullivan — Throws R — Age 30

YEAR	TEAM	LGE	IP	H	ER	HR	BB	K	ERA	W	L	H/9	HR/9	BB/9	K/9	KW	PERA
1998	Cincnnti	NL	98.0	96	61	14	32	70	5.60	4	7	8.82	1.29	2.94	6.43	1.09	4.67
1999	Cincnnti	NL	110.7	84	36	9	38	66	2.93	8	4	6.83	0.73	3.09	5.37	0.87	3.07
2000	Cincnnti	NL	103.7	85	39	12	30	80	3.39	7	5	7.38	1.04	2.60	6.95	1.33	3.46

He reversed his pattern last year. In 1998 and 1999, Scott Sullivan was worked hard and lost his effectiveness in September. Last year, he never got settled in the first half, but pitched very well after the All-Star break (although he did seem to tire again in September). There aren't many sidearm fly-ball pitchers, but he's one of them.

National League

Travis Thompson — Throws R — Age 23

YEAR	TEAM	LGE	IP	H	ER	HR	BB	K	ERA	W	L	H/9	HR/9	BB/9	K/9	KW	PERA
1999	Billings	Pio	19.3	15	1	0	4	13	0.47	2	0	6.98	0.00	1.86	6.05	1.63	2.12
2000	Clinton	Mid	36.3	26	13	7	15	22	3.22	2	2	6.44	1.73	3.72	5.45	0.73	4.06
2000	Dayton	Mid	125.0	141	60	13	43	59	4.32	6	8	10.15	0.94	3.10	4.25	0.69	5.15

His total line over two years looks like a season out of Rick Reed's career. The real test comes at Double-A this year, and Travis Thompson is not the kind of pitcher who does well initially at higher levels. Like Reith, his long-term outlook is pretty good.

Ron Villone — Throws L — Age 31

YEAR	TEAM	LGE	IP	H	ER	HR	BB	K	ERA	W	L	H/9	HR/9	BB/9	K/9	KW	PERA
1998	Buffalo	Int	20.7	21	14	3	12	19	6.10	1	1	9.15	1.31	5.23	8.27	0.79	5.84
1998	Clevelnd	AL	27.0	28	15	3	18	14	5.00	1	2	9.33	1.00	6.00	4.67	0.39	5.90
1999	Cincnnti	NL	139.7	110	62	7	59	82	4.00	8	8	7.09	0.45	3.80	5.28	0.69	3.21
2000	Cincnnti	NL	139.0	148	83	19	62	64	5.37	5	10	9.58	1.23	4.01	4.14	0.52	5.51

Doomed. Well, maybe. At this writing, Ron Villone is property of the Rockies. There's still a chance he ends up somewhere else, even back with the Reds, by Opening Day. Someone with his stuff should have a much better strikeout rate, and if left alone as a reliever, he would. Simply flipping him and Reyes might have been worth a couple of games.

Scott Williamson — Throws R — Age 25

YEAR	TEAM	LGE	IP	H	ER	HR	BB	K	ERA	W	L	H/9	HR/9	BB/9	K/9	KW	PERA
1998	Chattang	Sou	94.7	87	50	6	43	67	4.75	5	6	8.27	0.57	4.09	6.37	0.78	4.07
1998	Indianap	Int	19.7	20	9	2	9	12	4.12	1	1	9.15	0.92	4.12	5.49	0.67	4.99
1999	Cincnnti	NL	91.3	54	26	7	35	90	2.56	7	3	5.32	0.69	3.45	8.87	1.29	2.42
2000	Cincnnti	NL	110.7	95	42	6	60	113	3.42	7	5	7.73	0.49	4.88	9.19	0.94	4.00

What made Scott Williamson's return to starting a success was that he was more economical with his pitches. His strikeout and walk ratios both dropped precipitously as he did a better job of getting ahead of hitters and getting outs early in the count. The injury that shut him down in September wasn't serious; he'll be a valuable pitcher in 2001.

Mark Wohlers — Throws R — Age 31

YEAR	TEAM	LGE	IP	H	ER	HR	BB	K	ERA	W	L	H/9	HR/9	BB/9	K/9	KW	PERA
1998	Richmond	Int	11.3	22	29	6	37	11	23.03	0	1	17.47	4.76	29.38	8.74	0.15	24.48
1998	Atlanta	NL	20.0	19	23	2	30	18	10.35	0	2	8.55	0.90	13.50	8.10	0.30	8.49
2000	Louisvil	Int	19.7	30	22	5	9	11	10.07	0	2	13.73	2.29	4.12	5.03	0.61	9.14
2000	Cincnnti	NL	27.7	19	13	3	14	17	4.23	1	2	6.18	0.98	4.55	5.53	0.61	3.53

His comeback was one of the year's best stories, but while he showed flashes, he's just a shadow of his 1995–96 self. Long outings simply aren't going to happen, and with Danny Graves getting saves, it's hard to see what Mark Wohlers's role with the Reds will be.

Ed Yarnall — Throws L — Age 25

YEAR	TEAM	LGE	IP	H	ER	HR	BB	K	ERA	W	L	H/9	HR/9	BB/9	K/9	KW	PERA
1998	Binghmtn	Eas	43.3	22	6	1	18	31	1.25	5	0	4.57	0.21	3.74	6.44	0.86	1.81
1998	Portland	Eas	14.3	10	7	3	4	9	4.40	1	1	6.28	1.88	2.51	5.65	1.13	3.68
1998	Charlott	Int	67.7	76	55	11	34	34	7.32	2	6	10.11	1.46	4.52	4.52	0.50	6.25
1999	Columbus	Int	139.0	134	59	5	55	107	3.82	8	7	8.68	0.32	3.56	6.93	0.97	3.85
1999	NY Yanks	AL	17.0	16	7	1	8	12	3.71	1	1	8.47	0.53	4.24	6.35	0.75	4.20
2000	Columbus	Int	46.7	43	29	5	26	26	5.59	2	3	8.29	0.96	5.01	5.01	0.50	4.90
2000	Louisvil	Int	64.3	72	33	8	33	44	4.62	3	4	10.07	1.12	4.62	6.16	0.67	5.93

He's a good pitcher who never recovered from a terrible spring. At 25, Ed Yarnall is past the point of being a prospect. He needs to get a rotation job in March and make 32 starts or risk falling into the Land of the Perisho. Step one is strike one.

Support-Neutral Statistics — CINCINNATI REDS — Park Effect: +5.2%

PITCHER	GS	IP	R	SNW	SNL	SNPCT	W	L	RA	APW	SNVA	SNWAR
Rob Bell	26	140.3	84	7.6	9.4	.447	7	8	5.39	-0.2	-0.8	0.4
Elmer Dessens	16	104.7	51	6.5	4.4	.596	10	5	4.39	0.9	1.0	1.9
Osvaldo Fernandez	14	79.0	33	5.8	3.4	.633	4	3	3.76	1.2	1.2	1.9
Pete Harnisch	22	131.0	76	8.2	7.1	.537	8	6	5.22	0.1	0.5	1.7
Larry Luebbers	1	6.7	3	0.4	0.3	.573	0	1	4.05	0.1	0.0	0.1
Denny Neagle	18	117.7	48	8.2	4.6	.641	8	2	3.67	1.9	1.7	2.8
Steve Parris	33	192.7	109	11.1	10.9	.505	12	17	5.09	0.3	0.0	1.8
Ron Villone	23	126.7	87	7.2	9.1	.441	10	9	6.18	-1.2	-0.8	0.3
Scott Williamson	10	55.3	21	4.5	1.9	.701	3	3	3.42	1.1	1.2	1.8
TOTALS	163	954.0	512	59.6	51.1	.538	62	54	4.83	4.3	4.2	12.6

Quick, name the team that had the major leagues' best starting rotation during the second half of 2000. Yes, it was the Reds, with a Support-Neutral Value Added (SNVA) of 4.8 wins above average over the last three months of the season. Cincinnati starters were only so-so in the first half, but their 4.2 SNVA for the year ranked them fifth in the majors.

Despite the strong showing by the rotation as a whole, the Reds didn't have a single starter among the majors' top 30 in Support-Neutral Wins Above Replacement (SNWAR). Denny Neagle's overall SNWAR got him into the top 30, but his numbers with the Reds alone would have ranked him 37th. Even in the second half, when they were by far the best staff in the league, the Reds' best pitcher, Pete Harnisch, ranked only 25th in the NL.

The key to the Reds' rotation was depth. If you remove the performance of the best three starters and rank rotations according to the performance of the remaining pitchers, Cincinnati had easily the best bottom of a rotation in the majors. (See the Los Angeles Dodgers chapter for the other side of this coin.) It was an amazing year for a rotation full of relative no-names. In fact, the Reds have generally had good rotations over the past few years with virtually no stars, to go with excellent bullpens. Don Gullett may be the most underappreciated pitching coach in the game.

For a quick explanation of SN stats, see page 7.

Reliever Evaluation Tools

PITCHER	G	IP	R	ARA	APR	IRNR/G	EIRS/G	IRP	BRS	RRA	ARP
Manny Aybar	32	50.3	31	5.47	-1.5	0.41	0.10	1.3	-0.1	5.23	-0.2
Norm Charlton	2	3.0	9	26.65	-7.1	0.00	0.00	0.0	0.0	25.66	-6.8
Elmer Dessens	24	42.7	22	4.58	2.9	0.46	0.20	2.7	2.6	4.58	2.9
Osvaldo Fernandez	1	0.7	0	0.00	0.4	2.00	0.75	-0.2	0.0	4.24	0.1
Keith Glauber	4	7.3	3	3.63	1.3	0.50	0.10	0.4	0.0	3.45	1.4
Danny Graves	66	91.3	31	3.01	22.1	0.71	0.26	-0.6	0.5	3.27	19.5
Andy Larkin	3	6.7	4	5.33	-0.1	0.33	0.07	-0.8	0.3	7.10	-1.4
Larry Luebbers	13	13.7	12	7.80	-4.0	0.62	0.32	-0.2	-2.4	6.82	-2.5
Hector Mercado	12	14.0	7	4.44	1.2	0.58	0.27	0.8	-0.3	3.63	2.4
Chris Reitsma	1	1.0	0	0.00	0.6	0.00	0.00	0.0	0.0	0.00	0.6
Dennys Reyes	62	43.7	31	6.31	-5.4	0.85	0.30	-4.2	3.4	7.85	-12.9
John Riedling	12	14.3	7	4.34	1.4	0.00	0.00	0.0	-1.1	3.90	2.1
Scott Sullivan	78	105.7	41	3.45	20.6	0.64	0.25	5.9	-1.4	2.96	26.3
Ron Villone	12	14.3	8	4.96	0.4	0.75	0.25	-0.4	0.4	5.55	-0.6
Gabe White	1	1.0	2	17.76	-1.4	0.00	0.00	0.0	0.0	17.11	-1.3
Scott Williamson	39	57.3	27	4.18	6.5	0.56	0.24	0.7	-0.6	3.95	8.0
Scott Winchester	5	7.3	4	4.84	0.3	0.40	0.08	0.4	0.0	4.24	0.8
Mark Wohlers	20	28.0	14	4.44	2.4	0.15	0.03	0.6	-0.1	4.38	2.5
TOTALS	387	502.3	253	4.47	40.4	0.59	0.22			4.46	41.0

For a quick guide to RET, see page 10.

Colorado Rockies

When the Age of Reason comes to a strange and faraway place, you start off wanting to tip your cap to the missionaries carrying the good word to where previously there was only false hope. But out on the fringe of the Great Plains, you can't help but wonder whether the longer the missionary lives in this violently different world of too many runs, the more that world changes him at the same time that he tries to change it.

We've always been ones to stress organizational patience, but Bob Gebhard had seven years to play with a major-league team. At the end of that stretch he had one accidental playoff appearance, some futzing around .500, and a basic failure to come to terms with the uniqueness of playing baseball in Denver. There had been good moves, ones that reflected modest ambition as well as the ability to identify talent: signing Larry Walker in the free-for-all after the last labor war and acquiring Pedro Astacio for Eric Young in 1997. The Rockies had also made a point of making room for homegrown hitters: Neifi Perez inherited shortstop from Walt Weiss, and Todd Helton inherited first base from the Big Cat.

From the very start, Gebhard tried to adapt to his environment. The Rockies even had a physicist study how much farther hit baseballs would fly. In the end, though, the Gebhard era must be termed a failure. Beyond his conservative nature and dubious taste in managers, Gebhard never addressed two persistent problems.

The first problem was how he assessed the value of his players. The poster children for park effects are Dante Bichette and Vinny Castilla. Setting aside Fonzie's defensive problems, the biggest shortcomings of the remaining original Blake Street Bombers was not that they depended on the environment to make them famous sluggers, but that they didn't walk enough. In his seven years as a Rockie, Bichette drew 206 walks. Castilla drew 185 in almost as much time. Talking about raw totals gives both men the benefit of the doubt: Coors inflates offense, which inflates the number of plate appearances, which inflates all counting stats, walks included.

Rather than look past the altitude-inflated batting and slugging averages and see that neither player was helping the Rockies much, Gebhard built his lineup around them, signing both to expensive contract extensions. That blind spot hurt the team on the field and in the wallet.

The second problem was that the Rockies would talk themselves into acquiring or using curveball pitchers, when any appreciation for what the park does to breaking stuff would hint that those hurlers weren't cut out for pitching at 5,280 feet. Darryl Kile is the most spectacular example, but Greg W. Harris, Mike Harkey, and a young Juan Acevedo deserve to be remembered.

Gebhard wasn't going to be the GM who came to terms with the limitations of some of his stars or who scrapped the team that was spinning its wheels. To be fair, he was dealing with an owner convinced he knew what he was doing. Jerry McMorris may be the man who saved Denver from the indignity of losing its franchise because the original majority owners were destroyed by their shady business practices, but like many owners, he's better off watching his team than managing it.

After finally showing Gebhard the door, the Rockies did something smart. They hired a baseball guy who—strangely enough—had spent a year on an involuntary sabbatical, studying baseball. During his time outside of the industry, Dan O'Dowd had taken the time to study park effects and seems to have given some thought to modeling player performance in different ballparks. Considering that's one of our basic points in assessing player value, it isn't surprising that we think Dan O'Dowd is one of the sharper tacks in the drawer.

Empowered by ownership's disgust with the previous regime's failures, O'Dowd was allowed to do as he pleased. He responded by managing the roster with a ruthlessness that would have made the winner of Survivor blush. The Blake Street Bombers were out. By the end of his first year, O'Dowd had turned over 40 players in 14 different trades. By Opening Day 2000, there were only six players left from Opening Day 1999. By the end of 2000, only 12 players were left from that season's opener.

Rockies Prospectus

2000 record: 82–80; Fourth place, NL West
Pythagenport W/L: 87–75
Runs Scored: 968 (1st in NL)
Runs Allowed: 897 (13th in NL)
Team EqA: .246 (tied for 13th in NL)
2000 Batters' Age: 28.9 (6th youngest in NL)
2000 Pitchers' Age: 29.6 (4th oldest in NL)
Ballpark: Coors Field; obscene hitters' park; Park Factor of 1.288
2000: They tried, and discarded, a number of ideas under Dan O'Dowd.
2001: The Great Changeup Experiment, Year One.

Following Gebhard's failures, O'Dowd had the freedom to keep testing and trying different combinations and to try an almost evolutionary strategy of finding what worked and discarding what did not. O'Dowd was operating with a lot of latitude because expectations were virtually nonexistent. This helped the Rockies avoid letting part of one season—their 45–33 start—change what was going to have to be a multi-year project. While nobody could anticipate the Giants' tremendous second-half run, the Rockies didn't waste time, as Arizona did, trying to keep up.

When the team hit the skids after its July 3 peak by losing seven consecutive series, O'Dowd wasn't stunned. It was a lesson and an opportunity to keep trying new combinations. The adaptive pressure was to keep changing instead of sinking, Bill Bavasi-style, into shock that the initial plan had not survived contact with reality.

While some of the roster shuffling was a successful attempt to clear away players with multi-year contracts for whom he had no use, O'Dowd was also exploring how different types of hitters might perform at altitude. Jeffrey Hammonds and Tom Goodwin and Jeff Cirillo can all contribute to a team, but in distinctly different ways. All of them thrived at Coors Field to different extents. In Coors, Hammonds's strikeouts went from a career rate of more than 17% of his plate appearances to about 11% while he did maximum damage. Goodwin hit .342 in four months and Cirillo hit .403 with 36 doubles.

Even in the face of apparently good performances, O'Dowd didn't stand pat. Having tested how much value a player like Tom Goodwin might have at Coors, O'Dowd flipped him four months into his three-year contract to make room for a somewhat similar player in Juan Pierre.

On an organizational level, O'Dowd has a significant problem. The Rockies will be at a permanent competitive disadvantage if they want to try to develop and use talent the same way other baseball teams do. Coors Field does more than just turn fly balls into home runs or inflate run scoring or help players hit for higher averages with more extra-base hits. It does more than flatten out breaking stuff. On an annual basis, Coors Field cuts strikeouts by 15 to 20%. That's the result of pitchers having fewer weapons they can use effectively and it means more balls in play and runs by the bushel.

For a hitter with less than outstanding strike-zone judgment, that can be 20 extra plate appearances that don't end in nearly automatic outs. As the Rockies seem to have learned, there are offensive players who will get even more out of Coors than they will elsewhere for that reason, with Jeffrey Hammonds being the latest example. That's something the Rockies can accept and take advantage of, but it also means adjusting their expectations about what any pitcher can do for them.

O'Dowd has tried to figure out what kind of pitchers succeed in Coors. He didn't have a good answer on his own, so he got one of the best consultants in the business, Craig Wright, to study the issue. Wright's report made the observation that the one thing that pitchers with any kind of success in Coors seemed to have in common was a good change-up.

O'Dowd took that observation and applied it. Consider the pitchers he brought in during his first year who then pitched more than 30 innings with the Rockies: Gabe White, Masato Yoshii, Rolando Arrojo, Jose Jimenez, Mike Myers, Julian Tavarez, John Wasdin, Scott Karl, Stan Belinda, and Kevin Jarvis. Myers and Belinda throw sidearm. Some of them have good change-ups; Tavarez, Jimenez, Karl, and Arrojo do not, but Tavarez and Jimenez both have sinkers that are hard to drive. Is there any pattern? Yes. All of them walk fewer than three guys per nine innings (you could argue about Jimenez after his year with the Cardinals, but he had good control in the minors). After a couple of months, Belinda and Karl were cut, and Arrojo was traded. Everyone else pitched well.

Based on the decisions to sign Denny Neagle and Mike Hampton, each the owner of a quality change-up, it looks like O'Dowd is committing to Craig Wright's observation. In management circles, that's courage, but the Neagle contract brings up another major problem. Because of the cumulative effect of what happens in Coors to breaking stuff—strikeout rates and balls in play going farther and faster—the Rockies have to throw more pitches at home than anybody else. They averaged 17 more pitches per game at home than the NL in 1999, and almost 11 more per game in 2000. More runners on base—because it's Coors—means more pitches from the stretch, making a tough workload even tougher. While the move to bring in control pitchers like Gabe White or Masato Yoshii or even Kevin Jarvis seems to have helped mitigate the effect to some extent, it's something that needs to be taken under consideration in assembling and managing the pitching staff.

Why, then, invest nearly $180 million in two starting pitchers? Coming to terms with the limitations the ballpark puts on the way you can use people isn't easy. While that great change-up might give Neagle an advantage over a pitcher of similar age (pretend Arrojo is his printed age for the sake of argument), you have to worry whether he is worth this kind of commitment.

Because of the environment, a starting pitcher is going to have less impact in Denver than elsewhere. The Rockies have to learn from what Gabe White did for them and give their relievers balanced workloads. One of the triumphs of

2000 was building the league's best bullpen. The Rockies can't afford to carry two situational left-handers and a one-inning closer among 11 pitchers.

By signing Neagle and Hampton, the Rockies may be hazarding a guess that change-ups work better in Coors, but they're also being terribly conventional in an environment where they can't afford to be. Rather than trying to build a normal team, one that features identifiable top starters and an identifiable closer, they should instead adapt to their environment, learn from the great bullpens of their 1995 and 2000 teams, and build a staff on the notion that pitching at Coors Field requires a team effort, rather than traditional usage patterns.

O'Dowd could make a major and lasting impact by creating a player-development program that reflects an appreciation of Coors Field. The Triple-A affiliate at Colorado Springs gives Rockie minor leaguers experience at altitude before they reach the majors, but it isn't enough. The organization should dump traditional pitcher-development models all together and concentrate on team pitching efforts through balanced workloads. It might be a good idea to shift the team's Double-A affiliation to one of the Texas League's great hitters' parks and move the high-A affiliate from the Carolina League to one of the tougher California League parks. Such moves would cause some confusion, but Denver has a base of fans who already accept the idea that their teams in other sports win because they have a home-field advantage on which they capitalize. O'Dowd has the opportunity to help create a new brand of baseball.

As it is, the Rockies could win the division in 2001, but with a little more creativity, they could become the favorite for the next several years.

HITTERS (BA: .270, OBP: .340, SLG: .440, EqA: .260)

Kevin Burford — LF — Bats L — Age 23

YEAR	TEAM	LGE	AB	H	DB	TP	HR	BB	SO	R	RBI	SB	CS	OUT	BA	OBP	SLG	EQA	EQR	DEFENSE	
1998	Clinton	Mid	461	101	21	2	6	45	134	50	41	5	2	362	.219	.295	.312	.206	35	104-LF -10	
1999	Portland	Nwn	219	49	15	1	4	34	50	31	17	3	2	172	.224	.333	.356	.237	23		
2000	Salem VA	Car	478	117	29	2	13	41	82	56	57	4	2	363	.245	.311	.395	.236	49	62-LF -10	16-1B -5
2001	Colorado	NL	452	144	32	2	14	51	93	87	86	8	3	311	.319	.388	.491	.267	57		

Acquired for John VanderWal, Kevin Burford is turning into a pretty good prospect despite not really being favored by the Rockies. He wasn't a Rockies draftee, so it's not surprising that he isn't a tools guy or a good defensive player, just somebody who can hit. He still needs to make the jump to Double-A, but after belting 60 extra-base hits in 2000, he looks like a good risk.

Brent Butler — IF — Bats R — Age 23

YEAR	TEAM	LGE	AB	H	DB	TP	HR	BB	SO	R	RBI	SB	CS	OUT	BA	OBP	SLG	EQA	EQR	DEFENSE	
1998	Pr Willm	Car	490	122	19	1	10	32	76	54	61	1	2	370	.249	.301	.353	.217	41	110-SS -6	
1999	Arkansas	Tex	527	123	13	1	11	19	51	54	41	0	2	406	.233	.265	.324	.189	31	51-SS 1	42-3B 3
2000	ColSprin	PCL	429	104	23	1	7	32	47	53	39	1	2	327	.242	.299	.350	.216	35	94-2B -14	25-SS -1
2001	Colorado	NL	496	154	26	1	12	37	57	70	82	0	1	343	.310	.358	.440	.241	49		

While Brent Butler hasn't made much progress in the last three years, he's also been one of the youngest players in his leagues, so he hasn't had a lot of time to consolidate any gains. Since a career-high 63 walks in 1997 in the Midwest League, he's been much less selective. Drawing walks as often as Andre Dawson is acceptable as long as you hit like Andre Dawson. Butler could make an adequate utility infielder and platoon partner for Todd Walker.

Jeff Cirillo — 3B — Bats R — Age 31

YEAR	TEAM	LGE	AB	H	DB	TP	HR	BB	SO	R	RBI	SB	CS	OUT	BA	OBP	SLG	EQA	EQR	DEFENSE
1998	Milwauke	NL	614	196	26	1	16	76	82	98	68	9	4	422	.319	.397	.443	.286	92	145-3B 12
1999	Milwauke	NL	607	192	28	1	16	66	78	92	82	5	4	419	.316	.388	.445	.281	88	150-3B 12
2000	Colorado	NL	578	163	42	2	9	56	67	91	91	2	4	419	.282	.350	.408	.255	69	151-3B -1
2001	Colorado	NL	617	231	39	2	18	80	77	140	143	8	4	390	.374	.446	.532	.300	96	

(Jeff Cirillo *continued*)

Jeff Cirillo signed a four-year extension with an option for 2006, so he'll be in purple and black for the rest of his useful career and then some. As much as I like Cirillo, this is not a good move. Locking up a useful player for his entire decline phase is a waste of resources. Disregard the jarring projection: it is based on his playing at Coors while the past performance is translated to a neutral park. It's easy to get confused by the difference, which is the same problem the Rockies have to deal with in evaluating themselves.

John Cotton — UT — Bats L — Age 30

YEAR	TEAM	LGE	AB	H	DB	TP	HR	BB	SO	R	RBI	SB	CS	OUT	BA	OBP	SLG	EQA	EQR	DEFENSE			
1998	WestTenn	Sou	318	76	9	2	9	8	78	30	34	5	2	244	.239	.263	.365	.205	23	25-3B	-3	25-RF	-4
1999	Carolina	Sou	163	37	4	0	7	6	55	18	13	0	0	126	.227	.257	.380	.205	12	35-3B	-14		
1999	ColSprin	PCL	227	55	11	1	9	11	67	32	30	2	1	173	.242	.281	.419	.228	22	26-3B	2	14-LF	-3
2000	ColSprin	PCL	305	77	15	3	10	20	107	37	38	7	0	228	.252	.300	.420	.241	33	51-LF	-11		
2001	Pittsbrg	NL	323	76	11	1	11	21	112	37	43	5	1	248	.235	.282	.378	.221	28				

John Cotton was drafted in 1989 by a young Indians' director of player development named Dan O'Dowd. He was a second baseman, but like all minor-league second basemen with limited career prospects and healthy doses of ambition, he took up the utility job. He parlayed 12 years in the minors into a spot on the Olympic team. A left-handed version of Terry Shumpert, he should have a fine future as a coach.

Chone Figgins — 2B — Bats B — Age 23

YEAR	TEAM	LGE	AB	H	DB	TP	HR	BB	SO	R	RBI	SB	CS	OUT	BA	OBP	SLG	EQA	EQR	DEFENSE	
1998	Portland	Nwn	272	64	9	1	1	13	64	23	17	9	3	211	.235	.272	.287	.186	16	65-SS	-1
1999	Salem VA	Car	454	101	8	2	1	27	88	47	18	12	7	360	.222	.269	.256	.170	21	120-SS	-17
2000	Salem VA	Car	537	126	24	9	3	48	111	68	36	14	10	421	.235	.298	.330	.211	43	134-2B	-32
2001	Colorado	NL	418	118	19	4	1	39	89	61	44	16	8	308	.282	.344	.354	.215	33		

Definitely a scouty sort of player, Chone Figgins might have a nifty name, but he's a ham-handed infielder. How many guys move off of shortstop and do even worse at second base? Not many, though Wil Cordero and Shawon Dunston come to mind. Figgins doesn't throw as hard as either of them and still committed 38 errors. Although he made progress as a hitter, he was repeating a level, so wait and see what he does at Double-A before getting excited.

Choo Freeman — CF — Bats R — Age 21

YEAR	TEAM	LGE	AB	H	DB	TP	HR	BB	SO	R	RBI	SB	CS	OUT	BA	OBP	SLG	EQA	EQR	DEFENSE	
1999	Ashevlle	SAL	491	108	18	2	9	29	140	57	44	6	2	385	.220	.268	.320	.193	32	127-CF	-7
2000	Salem VA	Car	438	102	15	4	5	25	108	57	41	6	4	340	.233	.277	.320	.196	29	125-CF	-11
2001	Colorado	NL	312	92	11	3	6	21	92	41	44	6	3	223	.295	.339	.407	.225	27		

Choo Freeman was a three-sport star in high school who was signed away from being a wide receiver at Texas A&M. The Rockies are trying to portray Freeman as a victim of expectations, and I'd agree: their initial expectations were far too high. He's still learning to keep his hands back and wait on pitches and hasn't started drawing walks or hitting for power. He has not improved in the field with experience. Nevertheless, Freeman is young enough to merit the organization's confidence that he isn't the next Derrick Gibson.

Jeff Frye — 2B — Bats R — Age 34

YEAR	TEAM	LGE	AB	H	DB	TP	HR	BB	SO	R	RBI	SB	CS	OUT	BA	OBP	SLG	EQA	EQR	DEFENSE			
1999	Boston	AL	113	32	0	0	2	13	10	13	12	2	2	83	.283	.362	.336	.241	12	21-2B	-1		
2000	Boston	AL	236	68	7	0	3	25	35	31	13	1	4	172	.288	.359	.356	.242	25	45-2B	-4	11-RF	-1
2000	Colorado	NL	84	26	5	0	0	6	15	11	4	3	0	58	.310	.361	.369	.257	10	20-2B	-1		
2001	Toronto	AL	190	53	3	0	4	22	44	27	27	1	1	138	.279	.354	.358	.246	21				

Jeff Frye became a free agent after finishing a multi-year deal that only Dan Duquette would make the mistake of giving him. Outside of Fenway, he won't hit 30 doubles again, but he's a decent OBP-oriented temp for a team lacking a good second baseman. The Blue Jays have signed him to replace Craig Grebeck.

National League

Jody Gerut — OF — Bats L — Age 23

YEAR	TEAM	LGE	AB	H	DB	TP	HR	BB	SO	R	RBI	SB	CS	OUT	BA	OBP	SLG	EQA	EQR	DEFENSE	
1999	Salem VA	Car	512	123	28	6	9	43	67	58	44	10	6	395	.240	.301	.371	.225	47	125-OF	-10
2000	Carolina	Sou	378	92	27	2	3	60	56	40	46	9	6	292	.243	.349	.349	.242	42	89-LF	-3
2001	Colorado	NL	326	107	24	3	5	51	55	75	58	10	5	224	.328	.419	.466	.274	44		

The organization's on-base machine, Jody Gerut had a good year despite a bad knee that was finally operated on this winter. He lost power to the injury and to Carolina's Five County Stadium, which isn't a good place for left-handed power hitters. Before the injury, Gerut could play all three outfield slots. If his power improves, he's a lot closer to Rusty Greer than Darren Bragg.

Jeffrey Hammonds — OF — Bats R — Age 30

YEAR	TEAM	LGE	AB	H	DB	TP	HR	BB	SO	R	RBI	SB	CS	OUT	BA	OBP	SLG	EQA	EQR	DEFENSE	
1998	Baltimor	AL	171	48	12	1	7	26	34	37	29	6	2	125	.281	.384	.485	.291	29	43-OF	1
1998	Cincnnti	NL	87	26	3	1	0	13	17	14	10	1	1	62	.299	.390	.356	.261	11	25-CF	3
1999	Cincnnti	NL	262	69	12	0	16	23	60	40	37	2	5	198	.263	.325	.492	.261	34	67-OF	7
2000	Colorado	NL	439	127	22	1	16	35	78	77	83	11	6	318	.289	.347	.453	.266	58	106-RF	-2
2001	Milwauke	NL	383	114	20	1	16	46	78	61	67	6	3	272	.298	.373	.480	.286	59		

The Brewers are going to be disappointed by his performance and handicapped by the contract. Jeffrey Hammonds slugged .415 outside of Coors Field, and that's normal. His knees are permanently damaged, one so badly that it has no cartilage left. There's pretty much no way he can hold up as an everyday center fielder, which is what he's supposed to be until Jeromy Burnitz is traded. Hammonds has a clean shot at being the most reviled outfielder in Brewer history.

Todd Helton — 1B — Bats L — Age 27

YEAR	TEAM	LGE	AB	H	DB	TP	HR	BB	SO	R	RBI	SB	CS	OUT	BA	OBP	SLG	EQA	EQR	DEFENSE	
1998	Colorado	NL	519	145	25	1	24	49	51	68	85	2	3	377	.279	.348	.470	.269	71	135-1B	12
1999	Colorado	NL	559	155	33	4	29	58	73	95	89	4	5	409	.277	.351	.506	.278	83	149-1B	-4
2000	Colorado	NL	552	176	43	2	34	88	57	111	113	4	3	379	.319	.415	.589	.324	113	152-1B	21
2001	Colorado	NL	579	221	40	2	48	97	65	156	196	7	3	361	.382	.470	.706	.342	123		

The debate over how much Todd Helton owes to Coors Field in what will be an annual pursuit of .400 should not be taken as slander. Sure, the man has an advantage, but it's the same one Neifi Perez has and he isn't flirting with .400. Helton is a great hitter in the prime of his career, a first in Rockies history. Plus, there aren't many great players nicknamed "Fatboy."

Phil Hiatt — 1B/OF — Bats R — Age 32

YEAR	TEAM	LGE	AB	H	DB	TP	HR	BB	SO	R	RBI	SB	CS	OUT	BA	OBP	SLG	EQA	EQR	DEFENSE			
1998	Buffalo	Int	457	100	14	0	23	29	156	63	55	2	1	358	.219	.270	.400	.218	40	73-1B	-2		
1999	Indianap	Int	313	65	9	0	13	22	110	35	39	0	0	248	.208	.263	.361	.203	23	35-1B	3	16-LF	1
2000	ColSprin	PCL	495	118	21	1	23	44	164	67	66	8	2	379	.238	.305	.424	.242	55	117-1B	-3		
2001	LosAngls	NL	415	92	12	0	18	40	152	48	57	5	1	324	.222	.290	.381	.233	42				

Phil Hiatt's days of playing third base are long past. The nicest thing to be said is that he could still have had value as a platoon mate for Todd Hollandsworth in left field before the Rockies signed Ron Gant for that role. After playing in more than a thousand minor-league games, he really ought to team with Scott McClain to get a Minor League Players Association up and running.

Todd Hollandsworth — OF — Bats L — Age 28

YEAR	TEAM	LGE	AB	H	DB	TP	HR	BB	SO	R	RBI	SB	CS	OUT	BA	OBP	SLG	EQA	EQR	DEFENSE			
1998	LosAngls	NL	178	49	8	4	3	9	39	25	20	4	3	132	.275	.314	.416	.240	19	45-LF	-1		
1999	LosAngls	NL	264	75	11	2	9	21	58	38	30	4	2	191	.284	.339	.443	.260	33	56-OF	0	10-1B	0
2000	LosAngls	NL	265	63	8	0	9	26	57	41	24	11	4	206	.238	.308	.370	.231	26	67-CF	-1		
2000	Colorado	NL	162	45	6	0	9	9	36	32	18	6	3	120	.278	.316	.481	.260	21	39-LF	2		
2001	Colorado	NL	324	107	15	1	15	32	73	70	65	21	5	222	.330	.390	.522	.277	45				

Winner of the game that's had a great run since 1993, "Who Wants to Be a Power Hitter." Unlike so many eager participants, Hollandsworth didn't even have to mail in an entry card. He's is a useful fourth outfielder. Playing as part of a platoon in Coors, he'll do a convincing John Lowenstein act for a couple of years.

Matt Holliday   LF/3B   **Bats R**   **Age 21**

YEAR	TEAM	LGE	AB	H	DB	TP	HR	BB	SO	R	RBI	SB	CS	OUT	BA	OBP	SLG	EQA	EQR	DEFENSE	
1999	Asheville	SAL	454	95	16	0	12	39	123	53	44	4	1	361	.209	.278	.324	.200	32	105-3B	-30
2000	Salem VA	Car	470	111	20	1	7	30	77	51	55	4	3	362	.236	.283	.328	.201	33	104-3B	-15
2001	Colorado	NL	372	113	14	0	11	32	82	56	60	6	1	260	.304	.359	.430	.242	37		

As an organization, the Rockies love big, strapping ath-a-letes. Like Choo Freeman, Matt Holliday is another ex-high school football player burdened with high expectations. Like Freeman, he failed to make much progress in his second full season, but he did an improved job of going with the pitch and hitting to right field. Coaching tips from Buddy Bell couldn't prevent the inevitable: the Rockies are moving Holliday to left field.

Butch Huskey   OF   **Bats R**   **Age 29**

YEAR	TEAM	LGE	AB	H	DB	TP	HR	BB	SO	R	RBI	SB	CS	OUT	BA	OBP	SLG	EQA	EQR	DEFENSE	
1998	NY Mets	NL	375	97	15	0	15	25	62	45	61	7	6	284	.259	.307	.419	.238	39	92-RF	-3
1999	Seattle	AL	260	77	7	0	16	25	41	43	48	3	1	184	.296	.358	.508	.284	39	50-LF	-1
1999	Boston	AL	123	33	6	0	7	6	18	17	26	0	0	90	.268	.302	.488	.255	15		
2000	Minnesot	AL	213	47	9	0	6	22	45	20	26	0	2	168	.221	.300	.347	.214	18	15-RF	1
2000	Colorado	NL	88	26	4	0	4	14	13	14	15	1	1	63	.295	.392	.477	.289	14	18-LF	1
2001	Colorado	NL	353	119	15	0	21	44	64	69	88	3	3	237	.337	.411	.558	.288	53		

The man, the myth, the legend. Once in a while Butch Huskey crushes pitches so convincingly that he can dislocate his shoulder (it happened once) and maybe even top Joey Meyer's famed 600-foot-plus shot. A Totch Huskeysworth platoon would be a great way for the Rockies to put some runs on the board in any ballpark without spending an insane amount of cash. Ron Gant is essentially the same player as Huskey, and expected to play the same role.

Aaron Ledesma   IF   **Bats R**   **Age 30**

YEAR	TEAM	LGE	AB	H	DB	TP	HR	BB	SO	R	RBI	SB	CS	OUT	BA	OBP	SLG	EQA	EQR	DEFENSE			
1998	TampaBay	AL	298	98	14	3	1	9	45	29	29	7	6	206	.329	.350	.406	.252	33	56-SS	3	18-2B	0
1999	TampaBay	AL	293	79	13	0	1	11	32	31	30	1	1	215	.270	.302	.324	.208	21	45-SS	0	17-2B	3
2000	Colorado	NL	39	8	1	0	0	2	8	3	2	0	0	31	.205	.259	.231	.148	1				
2000	ColSprin	PCL	217	59	5	1	0	11	33	20	25	5	1	159	.272	.309	.304	.209	16	20-3B	-2	12-2B	-2
2001	LosAngls	NL	234	61	8	2	0	13	36	28	23	5	1	174	.261	.300	.312	.216	19				

After getting most of his playing time on the road, Aaron Ledesma barely got a chance to save himself with some home cooking before he was demoted to Colorado Springs. Throw that projection out the window: he's got as much of a chance at getting 300 plate appearances for the Rockies as Ralph Wiggum does. "I can't hit my way off the Rockies, that's unpossible!"

Brent Mayne   C   **Bats L**   **Age 33**

YEAR	TEAM	LGE	AB	H	DB	TP	HR	BB	SO	R	RBI	SB	CS	OUT	BA	OBP	SLG	EQA	EQR	DEFENSE	
1998	San Fran	NL	281	79	11	0	5	36	44	27	35	2	2	204	.281	.365	.374	.254	33	76-C	-6
1999	San Fran	NL	325	97	19	0	6	39	61	37	40	2	2	230	.298	.382	.412	.271	44	90-C	3
2000	Colorado	NL	324	83	11	0	7	40	45	29	53	1	3	244	.256	.339	.355	.236	33	91-C	-4
2001	Colorado	NL	274	87	9	0	9	44	43	53	53	2	1	188	.318	.412	.449	.268	35		

Brent Mayne is in the best possible spot for a backup catcher. Because the Rockies are going to get more plate appearances as a team and endure longer games than other teams, a good backup catcher can log 50 starts and a couple hundred plate appearances. The only problem is that neither he nor Ben Petrick throws well.

Scott McClain   3B   **Bats R**   **Age 29**

YEAR	TEAM	LGE	AB	H	DB	TP	HR	BB	SO	R	RBI	SB	CS	OUT	BA	OBP	SLG	EQA	EQR	DEFENSE			
1998	Durham	Int	473	123	24	0	27	52	115	72	83	4	1	351	.260	.335	.482	.269	66	121-3B	2		
1999	Durham	Int	536	117	23	1	21	57	163	80	76	3	2	421	.218	.296	.382	.226	51	79-3B	-6	12-1B	-3
2000	ColSprin	PCL	431	92	18	2	15	44	98	49	52	4	5	344	.213	.292	.369	.219	39	111-3B	-6		
2001	Colorado	NL	449	126	22	1	26	57	119	75	93	3	3	326	.281	.362	.508	.258	55				

Scott McClain is already on the downside of his career, having spent his best years starring in Rochester, Durham, and Colorado Springs. He shouldn't give up; Ron Coomer didn't get his big break until after he was 28. McClain never would have been a star, but he would have had a career like Steve Buechele's if he'd gotten the opportunity. A smart agent could have put him on the right team at the right time, but even then, his chances would have hinged on whether the manager took a shine to him. A good union wouldn't make its membership dependent on random management choices.

Adam Melhuse — DH — Bats B — Age 29

YEAR	TEAM	LGE	AB	H	DB	TP	HR	BB	SO	R	RBI	SB	CS	OUT	BA	OBP	SLG	EQA	EQR	DEFENSE			
1998	Knoxvill	Sou	239	50	10	0	9	48	45	33	23	2	2	191	.209	.341	.364	.243	28	49-C	-6	13-1B	2
1999	Knoxvill	Sou	380	81	14	0	12	77	87	52	41	2	3	302	.213	.349	.345	.241	43	42-LF	-3	25-1B	-1
1999	Syracuse	Int	71	17	1	0	2	8	21	11	12	1	1	55	.239	.316	.338	.221	6	17-C	-1		
2000	SanAnton	Tex	59	18	3	0	2	7	10	11	6	1	0	41	.305	.389	.458	.288	9				
2000	Albuquer	PCL	106	27	5	0	1	16	23	14	12	2	1	80	.255	.352	.330	.239	11	15-C	-1	10-1B	0
2000	ColSprin	PCL	138	30	3	1	2	15	39	16	12	1	2	110	.217	.294	.297	.196	9	22-LF	0		
2000	Colorado	NL	23	4	1	0	0	2	5	2	2	0	0	19	.174	.240	.217	.129	1				
2001	Colorado	NL	330	97	12	0	11	53	78	59	59	2	1	234	.294	.392	.430	.255	38				

One of the player types we've seen very little of in the last ten years is the professional pinch-hitter. Nowadays, guys who ought to be playing regularly get stuck in the role, like John Vander Wal or Dave Hansen. Adam Melhuse is a throwback to the older Greg Gross model. He doesn't have a primary defensive position, but in the best offensive environment of a high-offense era, there's a lot of value to a guy who can hit, catch, and play first base or left field.

Carlos Mendoza — OF — Bats L — Age 26

YEAR	TEAM	LGE	AB	H	DB	TP	HR	BB	SO	R	RBI	SB	CS	OUT	BA	OBP	SLG	EQA	EQR	DEFENSE	
1998	Orlando	Sou	139	40	2	2	1	12	19	17	13	8	1	100	.288	.355	.353	.253	16	25-LF	0
1998	Durham	Int	201	50	6	0	0	12	29	25	9	5	6	157	.249	.294	.279	.186	12	47-CF	-3
1999	Durham	Int	266	70	6	2	1	26	38	45	20	6	6	202	.263	.340	.312	.224	24	62-LF	-3
2000	ColSprin	PCL	347	100	14	7	1	46	51	54	29	15	8	255	.288	.375	.378	.260	44	88-OF	-8
2001	Colorado	NL	267	93	12	4	1	38	40	62	42	13	8	182	.348	.430	.434	.269	34		

Carlos Mendoza had spent most of the last two years hurt before signing with the Rockies as a minor-league free agent. He's an interesting player for a bench role, because how many guys have both speed and patience? Jason Tyner freaks should keep in mind two key words in that sentence: "bench" and "patience." A fifth outfielder.

Elvis Pena — SS/2B — Bats B — Age 24

YEAR	TEAM	LGE	AB	H	DB	TP	HR	BB	SO	R	RBI	SB	CS	OUT	BA	OBP	SLG	EQA	EQR	DEFENSE			
1998	Ashevlle	SAL	435	96	18	2	4	51	89	54	31	13	6	345	.221	.313	.299	.212	36	109-2B	-20		
1999	Carolina	Sou	358	91	18	4	2	35	68	40	23	10	4	270	.254	.326	.344	.231	35	76-2B	-14	23-SS	1
2000	Carolina	Sou	494	133	16	5	3	52	79	72	31	23	7	368	.269	.345	.340	.241	53	115-SS	-17	10-2B	-2
2001	Colorado	NL	467	150	21	4	4	61	83	103	64	32	10	327	.321	.400	.409	.257	55				

A spray hitter, Elvis Pena led the Southern League in stolen bases and runs while batting second behind Juan Pierre most of the year. Among the Rockies' shortstop prospects, Pena has the least chance of staying at the position but the best chance of having a career. His arm is only adequate and he's weak going to his right. Still, a switch-hitting utility man who can walk and run has value on a team that already has a great defensive shortstop, assuming the Rockies keep Neifi Perez.

Neifi Perez — SS — Bats B — Age 26

YEAR	TEAM	LGE	AB	H	DB	TP	HR	BB	SO	R	RBI	SB	CS	OUT	BA	OBP	SLG	EQA	EQR	DEFENSE	
1998	Colorado	NL	637	157	22	7	9	35	66	73	51	4	5	485	.246	.287	.345	.207	48	157-SS	24
1999	Colorado	NL	677	168	23	9	11	18	51	91	58	9	4	513	.248	.269	.357	.204	48	152-SS	17
2000	Colorado	NL	637	159	34	9	8	21	59	76	57	2	5	483	.250	.274	.369	.207	47	158-SS	25
2001	Colorado	NL	621	192	31	11	14	33	57	88	102	8	7	435	.309	.344	.462	.239	61		

Neifi Perez is everything Rey Ordonez is supposed to be, with even better defense and a little bit of power. While 42 of his 60 extra-base hits came at Coors, those 18 on the road are more than guys like Ordonez or Rey Sanchez hit in a year. He's seeking a contract similar to Edgar Renteria's four-year, $22 million deal. The Rockies would be wiser to take a one-year hit in arbitration than to sign Perez long-term.

Ben Petrick — C — Bats R — Age 24

YEAR	TEAM	LGE	AB	H	DB	TP	HR	BB	SO	R	RBI	SB	CS	OUT	BA	OBP	SLG	EQA	EQR	DEFENSE
1998	New Havn	Eas	357	74	16	2	14	44	91	42	38	4	4	287	.207	.298	.381	.226	35	77-C -15
1999	Carolina	Sou	68	17	2	1	3	7	16	13	15	2	1	52	.250	.325	.441	.254	8	15-C -5
1999	ColSprin	PCL	274	69	11	3	13	35	56	39	43	6	4	209	.252	.341	.456	.263	37	61-C -10
1999	Colorado	NL	60	17	3	0	3	8	12	11	9	1	0	43	.283	.368	.483	.285	9	16-C -4
2000	ColSprin	PCL	242	62	15	2	7	24	41	27	32	4	1	181	.256	.323	.421	.250	28	57-C -7
2000	Colorado	NL	141	39	8	1	2	17	31	26	15	1	2	104	.277	.361	.390	.254	17	40-C -4
2001	Colorado	NL	372	125	26	3	15	50	77	80	85	5	3	250	.336	.415	.543	.287	55	

Ben Petrick is not a good catcher, but he has the physical talent to become one. He's got the arm strength and the agility, but he needs to perfect his footwork. If Terry Steinbach could do it, then Petrick can too if he works at it and the organization is patient. At the plate, he's still prone to chasing outside breaking stuff, but if there's a park which makes that less of a problem, it's Coors. Petrick will give us another example of what a good player can do while spending the prime of his career in Coors.

Juan Pierre — CF — Bats L — Age 23

YEAR	TEAM	LGE	AB	H	DB	TP	HR	BB	SO	R	RBI	SB	CS	OUT	BA	OBP	SLG	EQA	EQR	DEFENSE
1998	Portland	Nwn	264	74	7	1	0	9	12	27	19	12	5	195	.280	.306	.314	.211	20	57-LF -3
1999	Asheville	SAL	589	148	20	3	1	28	39	55	39	23	9	450	.251	.289	.301	.200	40	132-LF -2
2000	Carolina	Sou	450	133	12	3	1	22	27	48	28	23	7	324	.296	.332	.342	.234	43	103-CF 3
2000	Colorado	NL	195	52	2	0	0	10	14	21	16	5	5	148	.267	.305	.277	.192	12	49-CF -2
2001	Colorado	NL	606	207	17	3	1	37	39	96	80	21	9	408	.342	.379	.384	.238	56	

An acolyte from the Ozzie Guillen school of patience, where you're taught that you'll start drawing walks as soon as you get some respect instead of seeing so many pitches you can hit, Juan Pierre will be more annoying than John Leguizamo. He could win a batting title in Coors without coming close to a .400 OBP, and part of me wants to see if he will. There was some concern about his arm, but he's picked up the Rickey Henderson trick of unloading the ball quickly and accurately, and he can fly to the gaps.

Terry Shumpert — UT — Bats R — Age 34

YEAR	TEAM	LGE	AB	H	DB	TP	HR	BB	SO	R	RBI	SB	CS	OUT	BA	OBP	SLG	EQA	EQR	DEFENSE	
1998	ColSprin	PCL	367	86	20	5	7	26	63	44	32	7	7	288	.234	.289	.373	.217	32	41-2B -9	27-OF -5
1999	ColSprin	PCL	75	22	6	1	3	3	9	10	10	2	1	54	.293	.321	.520	.270	10		
1999	Colorado	NL	252	76	23	2	8	26	39	48	29	10	0	176	.302	.371	.504	.294	41	45-2B 7	11-OF -2
2000	Colorado	NL	257	57	9	6	7	23	37	42	31	6	4	204	.222	.298	.385	.227	25	29-LF 0	16-2B -2
2001	Colorado	NL	270	74	16	4	9	29	42	45	44	7	4	200	.274	.344	.463	.241	28		

Seeing Terry Shumpert get a major-league job is nice, because you'd hate for anybody to lose his shot at a career because he came up with the Royals in their most clueless decade. Shumpert was supposed to be the Royals' second baseman of the future before they got silly and brought in Chico Lind and Keith Lockhart. Now he's a utility man who can play anywhere in a pinch and give you some power.

Juan Sosa — SS — Bats R — Age 25

YEAR	TEAM	LGE	AB	H	DB	TP	HR	BB	SO	R	RBI	SB	CS	OUT	BA	OBP	SLG	EQA	EQR	DEFENSE
1998	Salem VA	Car	543	130	17	7	8	35	85	61	38	25	8	421	.239	.288	.341	.214	45	116-SS -15
1999	Carolina	Sou	491	118	18	4	5	19	69	49	31	19	8	381	.240	.270	.324	.198	33	111-SS 0
2000	ColSprin	PCL	441	102	22	5	7	21	55	47	49	13	6	345	.231	.270	.351	.205	33	107-SS -6
2001	Colorado	NL	441	131	20	5	10	34	61	72	65	18	5	315	.297	.347	.433	.239	44	

Juan Sosa came back relatively quickly from a broken wrist at season's start. His basic problem is that he's being squeezed out of the organization before he even gets a chance. Perez is locked in ahead of him, Pena is a better choice for the big-league utility role, and Juan Uribe is on the way. If the Rockies don't do something smart, Sosa will end up an add-on in a package deal because he's a year away from getting bumped off the 40-man roster.

Juan Uribe — SS — Bats R — Age 21

YEAR	TEAM	LGE	AB	H	DB	TP	HR	BB	SO	R	RBI	SB	CS	OUT	BA	OBP	SLG	EQA	EQR	DEFENSE	
1999	Asheville	SAL	432	94	23	1	6	15	84	41	31	4	3	341	.218	.248	.317	.179	23	122-SS	-8
2000	Salem VA	Car	495	111	15	4	12	25	104	48	49	9	3	387	.224	.264	.343	.200	35	131-SS	-8
2001	Colorado	NL	383	114	18	3	10	22	89	55	58	11	3	272	.298	.336	.439	.234	36		

Juan Uribe flashes an outstanding throwing arm, especially from deep in the hole. Neifi Perez claims Uribe is the guy who will make him move to second base, but it's more like he's the guy who could end Perez's career as a Rockie. In another year, the projection will show you 20-homer power in Coors, which will be good for an All-Star appearance or two as long as the real shortstops all stay in the AL.

Larry Walker — RF — Bats L — Age 34

YEAR	TEAM	LGE	AB	H	DB	TP	HR	BB	SO	R	RBI	SB	CS	OUT	BA	OBP	SLG	EQA	EQR	DEFENSE	
1998	Colorado	NL	442	144	37	2	22	59	57	101	58	12	4	302	.326	.409	.568	.318	86	110-RF	3
1999	Colorado	NL	419	137	23	3	30	48	49	89	89	7	3	285	.327	.410	.611	.326	87	102-RF	1
2000	Colorado	NL	304	80	19	5	7	39	37	53	40	4	4	228	.263	.361	.428	.264	41	82-RF	4
2001	Colorado	NL	301	107	21	3	18	49	37	76	84	7	4	198	.355	.446	.625	.315	55		

It doesn't look like keeping Larry Walker healthy for a full season is in the cards. He doesn't hurt himself doing stupid things on the field; he's just fragile, and accepting that isn't easy. His elbow was a problem all year, but Walker was desperate to avoid being shut down. He's under contract for five more years, which ought to get him well over 400 home runs if he doesn't burn out. Will he be the first guy to suffer in Hall of Fame voting because of Coors Field?

Todd Walker — 2B — Bats L — Age 28

YEAR	TEAM	LGE	AB	H	DB	TP	HR	BB	SO	R	RBI	SB	CS	OUT	BA	OBP	SLG	EQA	EQR	DEFENSE	
1998	Minnesot	AL	523	166	41	3	13	46	58	83	60	15	6	363	.317	.375	.482	.285	79	130-2B	0
1999	Minnesot	AL	525	145	37	4	6	47	76	58	43	16	10	390	.276	.337	.396	.247	59	94-2B	-5
2000	Minnesot	AL	76	18	0	0	2	6	9	13	7	3	0	58	.237	.293	.316	.212	6	19-2B	-7
2000	SaltLake	PCL	243	62	11	1	1	23	34	35	25	4	2	183	.255	.320	.321	.219	21	59-2B	-6
2000	Colorado	NL	166	45	8	3	6	16	18	23	29	3	1	122	.271	.338	.464	.266	22	42-2B	-6
2001	Colorado	NL	489	170	37	3	11	49	65	101	96	11	4	323	.348	.407	.503	.278	66		

While the Twins gave up on him too soon, keep in mind some of the factors aside from Tom Kelly's taste in players. Todd Walker is arbitration-eligible, and you neither want to tear him down over his defense nor pay through the nose to keep him. Defensive statistics are murky enough, but can you imagine trying to explain them to arbitrators who sometimes know less about baseball than your average Eskimo? Sending Walker to the Rockies was the nicest thing the Twins could have done for him. Even with park adjustments built in, he's going to outslug that projection.

Jeff Winchester — C — Bats R — Age 21

YEAR	TEAM	LGE	AB	H	DB	TP	HR	BB	SO	R	RBI	SB	CS	OUT	BA	OBP	SLG	EQA	EQR	DEFENSE	
1999	Asheville	SAL	315	60	11	1	12	20	97	32	31	0	0	255	.190	.248	.346	.191	20	65-C	-27
2000	Asheville	SAL	401	84	16	0	13	21	116	42	48	3	3	320	.209	.263	.347	.198	28	88-C	-15
2001	Colorado	NL	291	77	11	0	15	23	89	36	49	2	1	215	.265	.318	.457	.229	27		

Jeff Winchester is clumsy in the field, but he's young enough to grow out of it. Like Choo Freeman and Matt Holliday, he did not improve as much in his second full season as you'd want to see. He's here in the book because he's a catcher with power in the organization that has Coors Field as its end destination. If he continues to avoid walks, he'll give us an idea of what Mark Parent could have done in Coors.

PITCHERS (ERA: 4.50, H/9: 9.00, HR/9: 1.00, BB/9: 3.00, K/9: 6.00, KW: 1.00, PERA: 4.50)

Pedro Astacio — Throws R — Age 31

YEAR	TEAM	LGE	IP	H	ER	HR	BB	K	ERA	W	L	H/9	HR/9	BB/9	K/9	KW	PERA
1998	Colorado	NL	207.7	234	128	25	53	138	5.55	8	15	10.14	1.08	2.30	5.98	1.30	4.97
1999	Colorado	NL	232.0	244	107	22	50	177	4.15	13	13	9.47	0.85	1.94	6.87	1.77	4.19
2000	Colorado	NL	197.3	210	90	17	49	160	4.10	11	11	9.58	0.78	2.23	7.30	1.63	4.29

Pedro Astacio is a workhorse and an ace waiting to get out of the thin air and remind everyone that this was one career Tommy Lasorda couldn't cripple. He throws four good pitches for strikes and will make an All-Star team if he gets traded over the winter. He's been dangled to the White Sox, Reds, and Athletics at various times. He's likely to be dealt before the season begins now that it's clear he won't be tossed out of the country for hitting his wife.

Robert Averette — Throws R — Age 24

YEAR	TEAM	LGE	IP	H	ER	HR	BB	K	ERA	W	L	H/9	HR/9	BB/9	K/9	KW	PERA
1998	Charl-WV	SAL	77.0	82	39	4	35	32	4.56	4	5	9.58	0.47	4.09	3.74	0.46	4.73
1998	Chattang	Sou	77.7	92	47	9	34	21	5.45	3	6	10.66	1.04	3.94	2.43	0.31	5.92
1999	Rockford	Mid	117.7	114	52	4	47	51	3.98	7	6	8.72	0.31	3.59	3.90	0.54	3.87
1999	Chattang	Sou	34.7	39	19	1	19	9	4.93	2	2	10.13	0.26	4.93	2.34	0.24	5.16
2000	Chattang	Sou	125.7	130	59	11	30	51	4.23	7	7	9.31	0.79	2.15	3.65	0.85	4.11
2000	Carolina	Sou	28.0	28	16	5	11	17	5.14	1	2	9.00	1.61	3.54	5.46	0.77	5.37

Robert Averette was nabbed for Brian L. Hunter, which not only made room for an upgrade in center field on the big-league team but garnered the Rockies a decent pitching prospect. His slider was named the best breaking pitch in the Southern League in *Baseball America*'s Tools Poll. Averette lives and dies by his command, but throws harder than you'd expect, in part because of a big leg kick. He'll show up in the rotation at some point this year.

Brian Bohanon — Throws L — Age 32

YEAR	TEAM	LGE	IP	H	ER	HR	BB	K	ERA	W	L	H/9	HR/9	BB/9	K/9	KW	PERA
1998	NY Mets	NL	51.7	46	22	5	20	32	3.83	3	3	8.01	0.87	3.48	5.57	0.80	4.00
1998	LosAngls	NL	92.0	73	37	11	35	58	3.62	5	5	7.14	1.08	3.42	5.67	0.83	3.68
1999	Colorado	NL	199.3	223	111	18	61	101	5.01	9	13	10.07	0.81	2.75	4.56	0.83	4.83
2000	Colorado	NL	178.3	171	73	13	50	82	3.68	11	9	8.63	0.66	2.52	4.14	0.82	3.74

As tough as a pitcher can be without frightening people, Brian Bohanon pitched hurt all through 1999 before going under the knife for a fifth time. Although he was pulled from the rotation early in the year, he managed to lead the NL in road ERA. He's a good example of the kind of guy who ought to be mixed and matched by opponent and the schedule.

Giovanni Carrara — Throws R — Age 33

YEAR	TEAM	LGE	IP	H	ER	HR	BB	K	ERA	W	L	H/9	HR/9	BB/9	K/9	KW	PERA
1999	Indianap	Int	148.3	141	71	24	61	77	4.31	7	9	8.56	1.46	3.70	4.67	0.63	5.00
2000	ColSprin	PCL	92.3	87	37	9	28	60	3.61	6	4	8.48	0.88	2.73	5.85	1.07	3.96
2000	Colorado	NL	14.0	21	15	3	7	12	9.64	0	2	13.50	1.93	4.50	7.71	0.86	8.77

Giovanni Carrara is a hefty Venezuelan soft-tosser who can throw strikes. He spent 1998 in Japan pitching for Seibu. Sort of like Larry Luebbers, he's the kind of journeyman to have around if you're a major-league team with five relatively durable big-league starters. Carrara can be your sixth starter in case somebody has to miss a month. Signed by the Dodgers.

Shawn Chacon — Throws R — Age 23

YEAR	TEAM	LGE	IP	H	ER	HR	BB	K	ERA	W	L	H/9	HR/9	BB/9	K/9	KW	PERA
1998	Salem VA	Car	48.7	56	45	10	40	28	8.32	1	4	10.36	1.85	7.40	5.18	0.35	8.01
1999	Salem VA	Car	66.3	72	49	6	37	35	6.65	2	5	9.77	0.81	5.02	4.75	0.47	5.60
2000	Carolina	Sou	158.7	165	88	18	88	103	4.99	7	11	9.36	1.02	4.99	5.84	0.59	5.56

Shawn Chacon struggled with elbow woes in 1998, then was suspended for marijuana use in 1999. Finally pitching an entire season, he got off to a slow start before blazing through the Southern League. He possesses a great fastball that stays in the mid 90s late into the game, and he complements it with a hard curve and change-up. It's very tough to hit him hard, so he gave up few extra-base hits. Chacon could be the first Rockies pitching prospect to pan out; despite this, they're not high on him.

Bobby Chouinard — Throws R — Age 29

YEAR	TEAM	LGE	IP	H	ER	HR	BB	K	ERA	W	L	H/9	HR/9	BB/9	K/9	KW	PERA
1998	Louisvil	Int	40.0	51	32	6	15	22	7.20	1	3	11.48	1.35	3.38	4.95	0.73	6.50
1998	Arizona	NL	36.7	40	23	5	10	21	5.65	1	3	9.82	1.23	2.45	5.15	1.05	5.01
1999	Tucson	PCL	59.0	67	33	9	14	40	5.03	3	4	10.22	1.37	2.14	6.10	1.43	5.24
1999	Arizona	NL	39.0	29	14	3	10	19	3.23	2	2	6.69	0.69	2.31	4.38	0.95	2.69
2000	ColSprin	PCL	16.7	17	9	3	3	8	4.86	1	1	9.18	1.62	1.62	4.32	1.33	4.72
2000	Colorado	NL	32.3	33	13	2	6	19	3.62	2	2	9.19	0.56	1.67	5.29	1.58	3.62

As part of the settlement of his domestic-violence case, Bobby Chouinard worked out over the winter on a prison work-release program so that he would be able to pitch during the regular season. To the organization's credit, the Rockies have been very involved in helping Chouinard and his family put together a workable solution. Chouinard is only a good middle reliever, so it isn't as if the Rockies were helping him just to keep a great player; they did it because it was the right thing to do.

Tim Christman — Throws L — Age 26

YEAR	TEAM	LGE	IP	H	ER	HR	BB	K	ERA	W	L	H/9	HR/9	BB/9	K/9	KW	PERA
1999	Salem VA	Car	43.0	45	26	2	15	30	5.44	2	3	9.42	0.42	3.14	6.28	1.00	4.20

He's missed two of the last three years with elbow problems but has shown good velocity and is still on the 40-man roster. It isn't likely that the Rockies will carry a third left-handed reliever behind Mike Myers and Gabe White, but Tim Christman could move up quickly if he's healthy.

Aaron Cook — Throws R — Age 22

YEAR	TEAM	LGE	IP	H	ER	HR	BB	K	ERA	W	L	H/9	HR/9	BB/9	K/9	KW	PERA
1998	Portland	Nwn	73.0	88	58	20	47	19	7.15	2	6	10.85	2.47	5.79	2.34	0.20	8.31
1999	Asheville	SAL	111.7	158	107	28	52	34	8.62	2	10	12.73	2.26	4.19	2.74	0.33	8.53
2000	Asheville	SAL	131.7	138	65	20	27	56	4.44	7	8	9.43	1.37	1.85	3.83	1.04	4.67
2000	Salem VA	Car	39.3	55	39	8	13	20	8.92	1	3	12.58	1.83	2.97	4.58	0.77	7.49

High-school pitchers are risks. From an organizational point of view, it's tough to hang your hat on them because they take longer than any other kind of player to develop. Brian Bohanon was a first-round pick in 1987 and didn't really make it until ten years and three surgeries later. Aaron Cook was a second-round pick in 1997 and had his first good season by repeating Asheville. A hard thrower, he showed improved command of his fastball and slider, but needs to work on changing speeds. The Rockies should not be in any rush to get him to Double-A.

Chuck Crowder — Throws L — Age 24

YEAR	TEAM	LGE	IP	H	ER	HR	BB	K	ERA	W	L	H/9	HR/9	BB/9	K/9	KW	PERA
1999	Portland	Nwn	24.0	27	18	5	19	19	6.75	1	2	10.13	1.88	7.13	7.13	0.50	7.79
2000	Salem VA	Car	151.7	132	97	14	101	76	5.76	6	11	7.83	0.83	5.99	4.51	0.38	4.87

A fourth-rounder out of Georgia Tech in 1999, Chuck Crowder has already impressed by racking up 16 strikeouts in a single game. He throws hard for a left-hander, in the low 90s, but his mechanics are a mess. He's not a great bet to survive his throwing motion for any length of time. The Rockies may be able to iron out his mechanics without compromising his ability to fool hitters. He's on the fast track.

Mike DeJean — Throws R — Age 30

YEAR	TEAM	LGE	IP	H	ER	HR	BB	K	ERA	W	L	H/9	HR/9	BB/9	K/9	KW	PERA
1998	Colorado	NL	72.7	74	24	3	17	22	2.97	5	3	9.17	0.37	2.11	2.72	0.65	3.60
1999	Colorado	NL	62.3	77	45	8	21	26	6.50	2	5	11.12	1.16	3.03	3.75	0.62	5.92
2000	Colorado	NL	54.3	51	22	5	19	28	3.64	3	3	8.45	0.83	3.15	4.64	0.74	4.05

Considering he was bouncing back from a 1999 season derailed by bone chips in his elbow (they were removed over the winter), Mike DeJean had a decent season as a mop-up man. He was once touted as a closer of the future, but now he's got to hope that he lucks into the kinds of contracts that have been handed out to Russ Springer and Doug Henry.

Mark DiFelice — Throws R — Age 24

YEAR	TEAM	LGE	IP	H	ER	HR	BB	K	ERA	W	L	H/9	HR/9	BB/9	K/9	KW	PERA
1998	Portland	Nwn	76.7	87	55	15	13	32	6.46	2	7	10.21	1.76	1.53	3.76	1.23	5.42
1999	Salem VA	Car	140.7	161	101	40	40	73	6.46	4	12	10.30	2.56	2.56	4.67	0.91	6.74
2000	Carolina	Sou	121.0	163	74	27	20	57	5.50	4	9	12.12	2.01	1.49	4.24	1.42	6.79

Mike DiFelice is in the wrong organization. He's got a four-pitch assortment and throws nothing but strikes, but he doesn't fool left-handed hitters very often and gives up a ton of fly balls. The Rockies need somebody like this about as much as they need a team break-dancer. His best hope is escaping the organization so he can mimic Anthony Telford's career.

Jerry DiPoto — Throws R — Age 33

YEAR	TEAM	LGE	IP	H	ER	HR	BB	K	ERA	W	L	H/9	HR/9	BB/9	K/9	KW	PERA
1998	Colorado	NL	70.0	58	24	5	18	40	3.09	5	3	7.46	0.64	2.31	5.14	1.11	3.02
1999	Colorado	NL	87.3	88	34	6	29	58	3.50	6	4	9.07	0.62	2.99	5.98	1.00	4.13
2000	Colorado	NL	13.7	15	5	1	3	8	3.29	1	1	9.88	0.66	1.98	5.27	1.33	4.20

It was considered highly unlikely that Jerry DiPoto would pitch at all in 2000 after having neck surgery in April. Now he's looking good for 2001 and will probably chair a bullpen by committee. Considering DiPoto has stretches of Reardon-style jack-o-matic action against left-handed hitters, Buddy Bell will be wise to mix and match his relievers by situation.

Randey Dorame — Throws L — Age 22

YEAR	TEAM	LGE	IP	H	ER	HR	BB	K	ERA	W	L	H/9	HR/9	BB/9	K/9	KW	PERA
1999	San Bern	Cal	144.0	131	59	17	42	86	3.69	9	7	8.19	1.06	2.63	5.38	1.02	3.94
2000	Vero Bch	Fla	52.7	52	18	6	15	29	3.08	4	2	8.89	1.03	2.56	4.96	0.97	4.28
2000	SanAnton	Tex	53.7	52	35	9	21	17	5.87	2	4	8.72	1.51	3.52	2.85	0.40	5.10

Randey Dorame was the prospect packaged with Todd Hollandsworth in the Tom Goodwin deal. That's right, Tom Goodwin fetched a better hitter *and* a pitching prospect. Dorame was signed by the Dodgers out of Mexico, which you'd think would have given him a Fernando halo. As with Dennys Reyes before him, the Dodgers decided they liked their gringos better. He has the usual lefty assortment (high-80s fastball, curve, and change-up) and he knows how to change speeds and move his pitches around.

Craig House — Throws R — Age 23

YEAR	TEAM	LGE	IP	H	ER	HR	BB	K	ERA	W	L	H/9	HR/9	BB/9	K/9	KW	PERA
1999	Portland	Nwn	31.0	34	20	2	17	29	5.81	1	2	9.87	0.58	4.94	8.42	0.85	5.41
2000	Salem VA	Car	14.3	8	5	0	11	12	3.14	1	1	5.02	0.00	6.91	7.53	0.55	2.84
2000	Carolina	Sou	19.7	16	13	0	16	17	5.95	1	1	7.32	0.00	7.32	7.78	0.53	4.30
2000	Colorado	NL	15.0	13	8	2	11	7	4.80	1	1	7.80	1.20	6.60	4.20	0.32	5.53

Craig House was a 1999 12th-round pick, and anyone who throws over 100 mph with a good slider moves up quickly. As you may have heard, House's delivery is insane. He basically doesn't plant his front foot, almost leaping out of his shoes as he slings the ball to the plate. It should surprise nobody that his shoulder was hurting in September and in the Arizona Fall League. Attempts to make his delivery normal cut the velocity and movement on his fastball.

Kevin Jarvis — Throws R — Age 31

YEAR	TEAM	LGE	IP	H	ER	HR	BB	K	ERA	W	L	H/9	HR/9	BB/9	K/9	KW	PERA
1999	Vancouvr	PCL	95.7	104	53	21	33	40	4.99	4	7	9.78	1.98	3.10	3.76	0.61	6.03
2000	ColSprin	PCL	37.0	17	5	1	12	12	1.22	4	0	4.14	0.24	2.92	2.92	0.50	1.42
2000	Colorado	NL	115.3	126	58	14	21	50	4.53	6	7	9.83	1.09	1.64	3.90	1.19	4.52

I don't have an explanation, but the Rockies were 13–6 when Kevin Jarvis started and 9–3 when Julian Tavarez started. Both work quickly and both are ground-ball pitchers. Jarvis can throw just about any pitch for a strike, although none of them move especially well. Signed by the Padres, where he'll get a shot at the rotation.

National League

Jason Jennings — Throws R — Age 22

YEAR	TEAM	LGE	IP	H	ER	HR	BB	K	ERA	W	L	H/9	HR/9	BB/9	K/9	KW	PERA
1999	Asheville	SAL	53.3	61	33	5	10	32	5.57	2	4	10.29	0.84	1.69	5.40	1.60	4.56
2000	Salem VA	Car	138.3	143	76	13	46	71	4.94	6	9	9.30	0.85	2.99	4.62	0.77	4.51
2000	Carolina	Sou	33.3	36	26	7	11	20	7.02	1	3	9.72	1.89	2.97	5.40	0.91	5.86

Jason Jennings was the club's top pick from 1999 out of Baylor, where he was the NCAA Player of the Year. His sinking fastball isn't high-octane so much as high-movement; that and his knack for using his change-up make him extremely tough to hit. Jennings was a two-way star in college, DHing when he wasn't pitching. That experience should have particular value on the Rockies, where any easy out is a bad thing, and where having a pitcher who could pinch-hit would make it a lot easier to carry 12 pitchers. Jennings is likely to come up in September and could stick in 2002.

Jose Jimenez — Throws R — Age 27

YEAR	TEAM	LGE	IP	H	ER	HR	BB	K	ERA	W	L	H/9	HR/9	BB/9	K/9	KW	PERA
1998	Arkansas	Tex	167.0	145	74	14	82	54	3.99	10	9	7.81	0.75	4.42	2.91	0.33	4.14
1998	St Louis	NL	20.3	22	9	1	7	10	3.98	1	1	9.74	0.44	3.10	4.43	0.71	4.40
1999	Memphis	PCL	25.3	28	11	1	11	11	3.91	2	1	9.95	0.36	3.91	3.91	0.50	4.80
1999	St Louis	NL	159.0	166	104	15	59	95	5.89	6	12	9.40	0.85	3.34	5.38	0.81	4.71
2000	Colorado	NL	70.3	61	21	2	18	37	2.69	6	2	7.81	0.26	2.30	4.73	1.03	2.86

Jose Jimenez has started to develop a decent slider and forkball to complement his outstanding sinking fastball. Pitching as a closer, he rarely gets the work he needs to maintain his feel for anything but the sinker. He'll continue to thrive in the closer's role, although he's cut out for a heavier workload than it provides.

Josh Kalinowski — Throws L — Age 24

YEAR	TEAM	LGE	IP	H	ER	HR	BB	K	ERA	W	L	H/9	HR/9	BB/9	K/9	KW	PERA
1998	Asheville	SAL	155.0	176	113	24	78	100	6.56	5	12	10.22	1.39	4.53	5.81	0.64	6.27
1999	Salem VA	Car	148.7	128	54	6	80	91	3.27	10	7	7.75	0.36	4.84	5.51	0.57	3.88
2000	Carolina	Sou	23.3	33	29	2	13	16	11.19	0	3	12.73	0.77	5.01	6.17	0.62	7.30

Before elbow problems shut him down last year, Josh Kalinowski had a devastating curve he could throw at different speeds and an adequate sinker that he located well. Maintaining a consistent delivery has been difficult for him, hence the elbow problem, but the Rockies say he'll be fine in 2001. He'll probably repeat in Carolina unless the Salem rotation makes it to Double-A en masse out of camp.

David Lee — Throws R — Age 28

YEAR	TEAM	LGE	IP	H	ER	HR	BB	K	ERA	W	L	H/9	HR/9	BB/9	K/9	KW	PERA
1998	Salem VA	Car	50.7	59	33	5	22	24	5.86	2	4	10.48	0.89	3.91	4.26	0.55	5.61
1999	Colorado	NL	49.7	42	16	2	19	32	2.90	4	2	7.61	0.36	3.44	5.80	0.84	3.27
2000	ColSprin	PCL	46.3	49	36	10	26	30	6.99	1	4	9.52	1.94	5.05	5.83	0.58	6.64

The Rockies consistently burn fantasy leaguers with their closer situation. Where else do you find people agonizing over the fate of David Lee or Jim Stoops? They added Travis Thompson to the 40-man roster because he was supposed to be a closer of the future, only to take him off again. Remember that the Gregg Olsons of the world—the guys who come through a system as closers and succeed in the majors in that role—are very rare. Traded to the Yankees.

David Moraga — Throws L — Age 25

YEAR	TEAM	LGE	IP	H	ER	HR	BB	K	ERA	W	L	H/9	HR/9	BB/9	K/9	KW	PERA
1998	Jupiter	Fla	41.7	38	19	4	12	22	4.10	2	3	8.21	0.86	2.59	4.75	0.92	3.76
1998	Harrisbg	Eas	37.3	41	28	4	23	14	6.75	1	3	9.88	0.96	5.54	3.38	0.30	6.03
1999	Jupiter	Fla	123.3	126	83	20	61	51	6.06	4	10	9.19	1.46	4.45	3.72	0.42	5.71
2000	Harrisbg	Eas	66.7	65	29	4	27	23	3.92	4	3	8.78	0.54	3.65	3.11	0.43	4.16
2000	Carolina	Sou	54.0	56	23	6	12	29	3.83	3	3	9.33	1.00	2.00	4.83	1.21	4.27
2000	ColSprin	PCL	30.7	45	22	6	6	4	6.46	1	2	13.21	1.76	1.76	1.17	0.33	7.25

(David Moraga *continued*)

He's one of a zillion left-handers who doesn't throw 90. When David Moraga was picked up by the Rockies on waivers, they taught him how to throw a slider. That ought to send up all sorts of warning signals about the Expos organization: a soft-tossing left-hander reached the majors without being taught how to properly throw a slider? It isn't like he was a reliever and didn't have the time to work on it.

Mike Myers — Throws L — Age 32

YEAR	TEAM	LGE	IP	H	ER	HR	BB	K	ERA	W	L	H/9	HR/9	BB/9	K/9	KW	PERA
1998	Milwauke	NL	48.0	43	18	5	20	32	3.38	3	2	8.06	0.94	3.75	6.00	0.80	4.19
1999	Milwauke	NL	40.3	44	22	6	11	30	4.91	2	2	9.82	1.34	2.45	6.69	1.36	5.13
2000	Colorado	NL	45.7	24	7	1	15	34	1.38	4	1	4.73	0.20	2.96	6.70	1.13	1.63

Life as a situational lefty has its moments. What other kind of pitcher can approach three months without allowing a run, as Mike Myers did? Ryan Klesko ended that streak on July 1 with a home run. Myers has an especially funky sidearm delivery and is one of the best situational relievers in baseball. In a division with Barry Bonds, that's going to be important.

Brian Rose — Throws R — Age 25

YEAR	TEAM	LGE	IP	H	ER	HR	BB	K	ERA	W	L	H/9	HR/9	BB/9	K/9	KW	PERA
1998	Boston	AL	37.3	40	28	8	12	17	6.75	1	3	9.64	1.93	2.89	4.10	0.71	5.85
1999	Pawtuckt	Int	26.7	28	10	6	8	22	3.38	2	1	9.45	2.03	2.70	7.43	1.38	5.73
1999	Boston	AL	97.0	103	49	15	23	49	4.55	5	6	9.56	1.39	2.13	4.55	1.07	4.89
2000	Pawtuckt	Int	29.3	27	14	3	13	15	4.30	1	2	8.28	0.92	3.99	4.60	0.58	4.39
2000	Boston	AL	53.0	53	30	9	16	23	5.09	2	4	9.00	1.53	2.72	3.91	0.72	4.95
2000	Colorado	NL	64.3	68	29	5	19	33	4.06	3	4	9.51	0.70	2.66	4.62	0.87	4.33

Dan Duquette is a man on a mission. The Red Sox draft a lot of New England players, and the Duke demonstrates an uncanny knack for trading them. Brian Rose, Jeff Taglienti, Matt Kinney... you'd think they'd all be Red Sox fans and natural Red Sox players. Maybe it's one man's way of making an entire region less nostalgic about its also-ran franchise.

Rose should be at the bottom of the big-league rotation in 2001. It will be interesting to see how well he adapts to Coors Field. He's always been given good marks for his learning curve, his ability to throw four pitches for strikes, and his ability to change speeds.

Jeff Taglienti — Throws R — Age 25

YEAR	TEAM	LGE	IP	H	ER	HR	BB	K	ERA	W	L	H/9	HR/9	BB/9	K/9	KW	PERA
1998	Michigan	Mid	68.3	64	27	3	22	55	3.56	4	4	8.43	0.40	2.90	7.24	1.25	3.53
1999	Sarasota	Fla	27.0	26	14	2	16	15	4.67	1	2	8.67	0.67	5.33	5.00	0.47	4.91
1999	Trenton	Eas	17.7	10	9	3	6	11	4.58	1	1	5.09	1.53	3.06	5.60	0.92	2.89
2000	Trenton	Eas	47.7	59	29	6	8	20	5.48	2	3	11.14	1.13	1.51	3.78	1.25	5.28
2000	Carolina	Sou	11.0	10	6	2	3	4	4.91	0	1	8.18	1.64	2.45	3.27	0.67	4.42

Jeff Taglienti was a throw-in in the deal that sent Rolando Arrojo and Mike Lansing to the Red Sox. He throws in the low 90s and has good control, but his first extended dance with Double-A was less than a complete success. In camp, he should have a couple of beers with Jim Stoops and David Lee to get a lecture on the subject of expectations. Traded to the Reds.

Julian Tavarez — Throws R — Age 28

YEAR	TEAM	LGE	IP	H	ER	HR	BB	K	ERA	W	L	H/9	HR/9	BB/9	K/9	KW	PERA
1998	San Fran	NL	81.7	92	40	6	34	42	4.41	4	5	10.14	0.66	3.75	4.63	0.62	5.12
1999	San Fran	NL	53.0	62	36	7	22	28	6.11	2	4	10.53	1.19	3.74	4.75	0.64	5.90
2000	Colorado	NL	120.3	119	52	6	34	52	3.89	7	6	8.90	0.45	2.54	3.89	0.76	3.71

Courtesy of his outstanding sinker, Julian Tavarez gets a ton of ground-ball outs. In small parks like Coors or Wrigley Field (now that he's signed with the Cubs), that's handy. But don't expect great things. Although he's physically mature and entering a good age range to build on last year's success as a starter, his peripheral numbers aren't so hot, and the Cubs are a significantly worse defensive team than the Rockies. Given his headhunter reputation, maybe he's being brought in as a mentor for Ben Christensen.

John Thomson — Throws R — Age 27

YEAR	TEAM	LGE	IP	H	ER	HR	BB	K	ERA	W	L	H/9	HR/9	BB/9	K/9	KW	PERA
1998	Colorado	NL	158.3	165	68	13	35	86	3.87	9	9	9.38	0.74	1.99	4.89	1.23	4.04
1999	ColSprin	PCL	19.7	33	22	3	8	12	10.07	0	2	15.10	1.37	3.66	5.49	0.75	8.74
1999	Colorado	NL	64.0	80	46	6	24	29	6.47	2	5	11.25	0.84	3.38	4.08	0.60	5.81

John Thomson worked slowly through rehab on a torn labrum and might be ready to go in camp. Still, there's little chance that he's going to get back to where he was in 1998. He's the last of Jim Leyland's victims, although who knows what damage Leyland might do through consultation. Dallas Green is busy wreaking havoc with the Phillies, after all.

Chin-Hui Tsao — Throws R — Age 20

YEAR	TEAM	LGE	IP	H	ER	HR	BB	K	ERA	W	L	H/9	HR/9	BB/9	K/9	KW	PERA
2000	Ashevlle	SAL	131.0	137	72	16	47	89	4.95	6	9	9.41	1.10	3.23	6.11	0.95	4.95

Pacific Rim coordinator Tim Ireland's first big addition to the organization, Chin-Hui Tsao had a great debut, earning Most Valuable Pitcher honors in the Sally League. He throws in the mid 90s with a slider, splitter, and change-up and has outstanding mechanics. He's almost certain to skip a level and move up to Double-A but shouldn't be in the majors until 2002. If you're a fantasy leaguer, you don't care, but if you're a Rockies fan or you like talented pitching in any environment, get excited. Not surprisingly, Tsao says he misses good Chinese food. Those of us who don't live in California can feel his pain.

John Wasdin — Throws R — Age 28

YEAR	TEAM	LGE	IP	H	ER	HR	BB	K	ERA	W	L	H/9	HR/9	BB/9	K/9	KW	PERA
1998	Boston	AL	94.7	103	49	12	23	55	4.66	5	6	9.79	1.14	2.19	5.23	1.20	4.79
1999	Boston	AL	73.3	60	30	11	14	54	3.68	4	4	7.36	1.35	1.72	6.63	1.93	3.41
1999	Pawtuckt	Int	28.0	19	9	1	7	19	2.89	2	1	6.11	0.32	2.25	6.11	1.36	2.08
2000	Boston	AL	44.7	44	20	6	12	34	4.03	2	3	8.87	1.21	2.42	6.85	1.42	4.41
2000	Colorado	NL	35.7	40	18	3	6	29	4.54	2	2	10.09	0.76	1.51	7.32	2.42	4.29

John Wasdin has been on that fence between fifth starter and long reliever for five years, struggling whenever he inherits runners. He's got outstanding control, a breaking pitch that works, and a good change-up. His numbers won't be pretty, but as a spot starter and long reliever, Wasdin could be extremely effective sparing starters from going too long into games and sparing the core of the bullpen from coming in too soon.

Gabe White — Throws L — Age 29

YEAR	TEAM	LGE	IP	H	ER	HR	BB	K	ERA	W	L	H/9	HR/9	BB/9	K/9	KW	PERA
1998	Cincnnti	NL	94.3	84	45	17	24	67	4.29	5	5	8.01	1.62	2.29	6.39	1.40	4.27
1999	Cincnnti	NL	59.3	65	28	11	11	51	4.25	3	4	9.86	1.67	1.67	7.74	2.32	5.15
2000	Colorado	NL	81.0	60	18	3	9	68	2.00	7	2	6.67	0.33	1.00	7.56	3.78	1.95

Unstoppable force, meet immovable object. Gabe White came into Coors as one of the most homer-prone but effective pitchers in baseball. Send him to the most homer-prone park in baseball and something's got to give. Who guessed the ballpark? White is the linchpin around which the rest of the pen revolves. Maybe he'll get saves, and maybe he won't, but he'll be extremely valuable however Bell chooses to use him.

Masato Yoshii — Throws R — Age 36

YEAR	TEAM	LGE	IP	H	ER	HR	BB	K	ERA	W	L	H/9	HR/9	BB/9	K/9	KW	PERA
1998	NY Mets	NL	163.0	163	82	25	50	95	4.53	8	10	9.00	1.38	2.76	5.25	0.95	4.80
1999	NY Mets	NL	167.7	161	82	25	50	88	4.40	9	10	8.64	1.34	2.68	4.72	0.88	4.52
2000	Colorado	NL	167.7	186	81	17	34	73	4.35	9	10	9.98	0.91	1.83	3.92	1.07	4.50

Did Masato Yoshii adapt to pitching at Coors? 18 of his 29 starts were on the road; his ERA was 5.85 in Coors, 5.87 on the road. He gave up more home runs per inning on the road. He did lose about two strikeouts per game at Coors. Overall, he seemed to adapt his forkball/fastball assortment pretty well. Yoshii had minor elbow surgery over the winter, but he's expected to be 100% in camp and be the fourth or fifth starter.

Support-Neutral Statistics — COLORADO ROCKIES — Park Effect: +60.4%

PITCHER	GS	IP	R	SNW	SNL	SNPCT	W	L	RA	APW	SNVA	SNWAR
Rolando Arrojo	19	101.3	77	5.1	7.3	.409	5	9	6.84	-0.2	-1.1	-0.2
Pedro Astacio	32	196.3	119	12.9	9.5	.575	12	9	5.46	2.2	1.8	3.4
Rigo Beltran	1	1.3	6	0.0	0.7	.002	0	0	40.50	-0.4	-0.3	-0.3
Brian Bohanon	26	157.3	98	10.1	7.2	.583	10	10	5.61	1.5	1.6	2.7
Kevin Jarvis	19	104.7	78	6.2	6.0	.509	3	4	6.71	-0.0	0.2	1.0
Scott Karl	9	45.0	37	1.9	3.5	.354	1	3	7.40	-0.3	-0.7	-0.4
Brian Rose	12	63.7	41	4.4	3.3	.570	4	5	5.80	0.5	0.5	1.1
Julian Tavarez	12	68.7	35	5.4	2.9	.649	5	3	4.59	1.3	1.2	1.9
John Wasdin	3	17.7	9	1.3	0.6	.684	0	2	4.58	0.3	0.4	0.5
Masato Yoshii	29	167.3	112	10.2	9.2	.526	6	15	6.02	1.0	0.5	2.0
TOTALS	162	923.3	612	57.5	50.3	.533	46	60	5.97	5.9	4.1	11.7

The 2000 Rockies rotation was by far the team's best ever. The only other above-average Colorado starting rotation was the wild-card-winning group of 1995. That one had a Support-Neutral Value Added (SNVA) of 1.3 wins above average, compared to the 4.1 of the 2000 version.

You might speculate that the secret to success is finding pitchers who can pitch in Coors; you'd be right, at least based on 2000. The Rockies' rotation was actually below average on the road with a –0.7 SNVA, but they were the second-best rotation in the majors at home, just behind the Red Sox, with a 4.8 SNVA. None of the Rockies' regular starters had an especially hard time at Coors and several—including Julian Tavarez (3.6-0.6 SNWL record at Coors), Masato Yoshii (4.6-2.2), and Pedro Astacio (6.0-4.8)—were outstanding.

Astacio now has posted the two best seasons by a Rockies' starter. His Support-Neutral Wins Above Replacement (SNWAR) last year, 3.4, fell just short of his total from 1999, 3.5. After six years of looking, the Rockies have finally found a legitimate ace.

For a quick explanation of SN stats, see page 7.

Reliever Evaluation Tools

PITCHER	G	IP	R	ARA	APR	IRNR/G	EIRS/G	IRP	BRS	RRA	ARP
Manny Aybar	1	1.7	3	12.63	-1.4	1.00	0.42	0.4	0.1	15.53	-1.9
Stan Belinda	47	35.7	32	6.30	-4.4	0.68	0.35	1.6	0.3	7.16	-7.8
Brian Bohanon	8	19.7	3	1.07	9.0	1.25	0.70	2.7	1.4	0.66	9.9
Giovanni Carrara	8	13.3	19	10.00	-7.1	0.12	0.02	0.1	0.8	9.47	-6.3
Bobby Chouinard	31	32.7	17	3.65	5.6	0.42	0.21	2.5	-0.1	2.92	8.3
Rich Croushore	6	11.3	11	6.81	-2.0	1.33	0.92	0.1	0.9	6.92	-2.2
Mike DeJean	54	53.3	31	4.08	6.6	0.37	0.16	4.4	3.0	3.47	10.2
Jerry Dipoto	17	13.7	6	3.08	3.2	0.76	0.26	-1.1	0.3	4.71	0.7
Craig House	16	13.7	11	5.65	-0.7	0.56	0.32	-0.1	-0.2	7.30	-3.2
Kevin Jarvis	5	10.3	5	3.40	2.1	0.40	0.23	0.7	-0.6	3.41	2.1
Jose Jimenez	72	70.7	27	2.68	19.8	0.36	0.15	-0.4	1.7	2.95	17.6
Scott Karl	8	20.7	19	6.45	-2.9	1.38	0.83	-1.4	0.7	7.02	-4.2
David Lee	7	5.7	9	11.15	-3.7	0.29	0.22	0.3	0.1	11.20	-3.8
Brent Mayne	1	1.0	0	0.00	0.6	0.00	0.00	0.0	0.0	0.00	0.6
David Moraga	1	1.0	5	35.09	-3.3	0.00	0.00	0.0	0.0	28.06	-2.5
Mike Myers	78	45.3	10	1.55	18.4	0.82	0.35	3.3	1.1	1.32	19.5
Julian Tavarez	39	51.3	33	4.51	3.9	0.64	0.26	1.7	-1.6	3.83	7.8
Pete Walker	3	4.7	9	13.53	-4.3	0.00	0.00	0.0	0.0	10.70	-2.9
John Wasdin	11	18.0	14	5.46	-0.5	0.82	0.38	2.3	0.7	5.63	-0.9
Gabe White	67	83.0	21	1.78	31.6	0.73	0.34	1.1	1.8	1.97	29.8
TOTALS	480	506.7	285	3.95	70.3	0.61	0.29			3.94	70.9

For a quick guide to RET, see page 10.

Florida Marlins

The razing and rebuilding job that General Manager Dave Dombrowski embarked on immediately after the Marlins' 1997 world championship boat parade was as thorough a remodeling job as a team can undergo. The "out with the old, in with the new" approach produced an extremely young, inexperienced team—an ideal environment in which to observe the effects of normal player growth on team performance.

Those effects were clearly evident last year when the Marlins surprised nearly everyone by hovering around .500 for most of the season, eventually finishing with a 79–82 record. This on the heels of the 1999 campaign when Manager John Boles saw the club go 64–98 with essentially the same players. In fact, the final edition of the 1998 squad that inattentive skipper Jim Leyland ran aground at 54–108 wasn't a dramatically different group than the 2000 team.

Last year's performance didn't set off any raucous celebrations along the Fort Lauderdale River, but it did allow the Marlins to join a unique group. Since World War II, only two other National League teams have improved by at least ten games in consecutive seasons: the 1948–50 Philadelphia Phillies and the 1967–69 New York Mets. The South Florida media quickly promoted this fact as offering hope that the club might be on the brink of emerging as the 1950 Whiz Kids or 1969 Miracle Mets. However, those two teams played in the Fall Classic while the 2000 Marlins finished 15 games back in the wild-card race, so the occurrence is more of a statistical novelty than a predictive tool, not unlike when Mark Whiten hit four home runs in a game.

A better approach to forecast what the future may hold for the Fish is to compare them with similar ballclubs. To do that, we'll use the 1999 Marlins as the baseline. While most of the player movement that shaped the 1999 team occurred between the 1997 World Series and the end of the 1998 season, Leyland's crew still had some remnants from 1997 on its roster. Edgar Renteria, Craig Counsell, and Gregg Zaun each led the team in games played at their respective positions. The final piece of the 1999 team was obtained early that year when Mike Lowell came over in a trade with the Yankees.

At the beginning of 1999 the Marlins were one of the greenest teams in recent memory, with Mike Redmond, 28 years old, the oldest everyday player. At all other positions the Marlins starters were 26 or younger. Since World War II, only about 1% of all teams have fielded a lineup in which at least seven of the eight regular position players were 26 or younger. The 14 teams are listed in Table 1.

As should be expected given their youth, only three of these clubs were even average offensively. However, with the exception of the 1979 Twins, they all improved over the next three years as their inexperienced players blossomed. The 1999 Marlins' hitters fall in the middle of this group. Of the six teams below them, only the 1961 Phillies' and 1967 Athletics' offenses matured into anything out of the ordinary, and both teams had special circumstances. Richie Allen exploded onto the scene as a rookie with the Phillies in 1964 and posted a .340 EqA; the Athletics took Reggie Jackson with the second selection of the 1967 amateur draft, and, two years later, he smoked the Junior Circuit to the tune of a .354 EqA.

The Marlins don't currently have anybody on the roster or in the farm system who is going to emerge as an Allen or Jackson in the next year or two. First baseman Derrek Lee is probably their best hope, but despite a breakout 2000 season, there is still skepticism about whether he can become a very good, if not great, player. Other than Abraham Nunez, there's nobody in the minors who is likely to turn into anything more than a useful bench player. It's not that there aren't talented athletes in organization, but the Marlins have a poor track record of turning tools into on-field results. They also have been quick to move players from positions where they could help the team and have as a result become a breeding ground for utility men.

Assuming they follow the typical growth curve, the Marlins should peak at an EqA of around .260 with the players that they have right now. It's difficult for a team to consistently

---

Marlins Prospectus

2000 record: 79–82; Third place, NL East
Pythagenport W/L: 74–87
Runs Scored: 731 (15th in NL)
Runs Allowed: 797 (8th in NL)
Team EqA: .256 (tied for 9th in NL)
2000 Batters' Age: 26.0 (youngest in NL)
2000 Pitchers' Age: 26.4 (2nd youngest in NL)
Ballpark: Pro Player Stadium; moderate pitchers' park; Park Factor of .955
2000: Many of the kids took a nice step forward after two years of misery.
2001: They should be around .500 again as they sort through who will and who won't be around in 2002.

Table 1

		EqA	Next 3 Yrs Peak EqA
1955	Pittsburgh Pirates	.239	.258
1961	Philadelphia Phillies	.240	.267
1966	Kansas City Athletics	.247	.269
1967	Boston Red Sox	.269	.270
1968	New York Mets	.245	.260
1972	San Diego Padres	.243	.250
1973	Cleveland Indians	.257	.268
1975	Montreal Expos	.237	.258
1977	Atlanta Braves	.241	.247
1979	Minnesota Twins	.263	.254
1981	San Diego Padres	.256	.262
1985	Minnesota Twins	.255	.268
1993	Montreal Expos	.260	.269
1999	Florida Marlins	.248	?

challenge for the playoffs with a league-average offense unless it has tremendous pitching.

In *Baseball Prospectus 2000,* we argued that the time had come for Dombrowski to stop collecting prospects and use some of the surfeit to put the final touches on a first-rate rebuilding effort. While he did the former, he neglected the latter. Although the only significant trades he made did bring in veterans, acquiring Manny Aybar and Henry Rodriguez at the trading deadline was merely window dressing to sell a wild-card dream, not a real attempt at a long-term solution.

Twelve months later, what Dombrowski needs to do hasn't changed; however, the situation is more urgent since the team's core is a year older and a year closer to free agency. Dombrowski's task also may be trickier to pull off following disappointing campaigns for many of the organization's better prospects. Previously hot commodities like Julio Ramirez, Amaury Garcia, Jose Santos, Nate Bump, Jason Grilli, Scott Comer, and Mike Tejera either regressed or were injured last year and won't fetch nearly as much in return today as they would have before the 2000 season.

While procrastination limits the solutions a business can pursue, waiting does enable that business to more clearly identify its needs. Heading into last season, first base and second base were eyed with skepticism. Now most observers consider Lee and Luis Castillo to be among the team's building blocks. The two scars on the Fish that apparently aren't going to heal with time are at shortstop and catcher. Alex Gonzalez confirmed that his All-Star first half of 1999 was a fluke, and the team is steadfast in its belief that Pablo Ozuna can't handle the defensive chores at shortstop. Ramon Castro has been considered the eventual solution behind the plate ever since he arrived from Houston, but 200 lousy at-bats at the big-league level have soured the Marlins on him. Shortstop and catcher are probably the two hardest positions to fill on the diamond, but the off-season presented the Marlins with a unique opportunity.

Two of the most attractive players on the free-agent market, shortstop Alex Rodriguez and catcher Charles Johnson, call Miami home. With salary escalation reaching the point where players are willing to sacrifice a few acres of waterfront property to shorten their commute, Dombrowski should have aggressively pursued one or both. He made noise about his intent to improve the offense over the winter, via trades and free-agent signings, but the club's self-imposed payroll cap of $32 million appeared to restrict the search to players who won't have the impact the team needs to reach the next level.

In December two things changed the direction of the Marlins' 2001 season. The team reached an agreement with the city of Miami to build a new baseball-only stadium. With that in the works, owner John Henry loosened the purse strings and let Dombrowski sign Johnson to a five-year, $35 million contract.

Johnson improves the product on the field: he should be worth about three wins over Ramon Castro's expected 2001 performance. He may even pay his way in terms of greater attendance at the turnstiles and increased revenues from advertising and sales of team merchandise. Perhaps most important, the signing shows a good-faith commitment to winning for a community with which it has had a shaky relationship.

Even with Johnson aboard, the team is pinning its hopes squarely on the shoulders of the pitching staff. In Ryan Dempster, A.J. Burnett, Brad Penny, and Chuck Smith, Florida has the makings of a potentially dominant rotation, and the anticipated arrivals of Josh Beckett, Wes Anderson, Geoff Goetz, and Claudio Vargas aren't far off. Not many clubs in recent memory have assembled a better collection of strong, raw arms than the Marlins.

Of the teams listed in Table 1, the 1968 New York Mets, stands out as having the same caliber of young pitching as the Marlins. Manager Gil Hodges's staff included Tom Seaver, Jerry Koosman, and Nolan Ryan, who were joined a year later by Gary Gentry and Tug McGraw. The 1969 team stunned the nation by playing David to Earl Weaver's Goliath, slaying the Orioles in the World Series four games to one.

Given the similarity between the Marlins and the pre-Watergate Mets, should the Pro Player faithful keep their social calendars open for October baseball in the near future? Probably not. The Mets were a one-season wonder that parlayed extraordinary pitching and good luck (their 100–62 record exceeded their Pythagorean mark by eight games) into postseason hardware. Following their miracle campaign, they managed only back-to-back 83-win seasons in 1970 and 1971, despite having the best team ERA in the National League both years.

Then again, almost anything is possible in one season. If two members of the Marlins' rotation step forward with career years like Tom Seaver and Jerry Koosman had in 1969, John Boles's squad would probably make the playoffs. More realistically, the team will be better than last year but not even improve its won-loss record; last year's club won so many close games that it outperformed its projected record by five wins. Until the Marlins shore up their offense, playoff appearances will be as rare as presidential elections that hinge on Palm Beach County.

HITTERS (BA: .270, OBP: .340, SLG: .440, EqA: .260)

Chip Ambres — OF — Bats R — Age 21

YEAR	TEAM	LGE	AB	H	DB	TP	HR	BB	SO	R	RBI	SB	CS	OUT	BA	OBP	SLG	EQA	EQR	DEFENSE	
1999	Utica	NYP	110	23	2	2	4	15	27	14	9	3	2	89	.209	.306	.373	.228	11	26-CF	-2
2000	KaneCnty	Mid	333	68	12	2	6	35	80	31	21	10	5	270	.204	.283	.306	.199	24	81-CF	2
2001	Florida	NL	269	61	9	2	7	36	70	38	30	10	4	212	.227	.318	.353	.238	29		

Like many of the Marlins' position prospects, Chip Ambres made little progress last year. A strained hamstring early in the campaign robbed him of his blinding speed and helped produce some ugly numbers. Though things improved when he returned from the disabled list in late June, he never got comfortable. Despite the problems, Ambres retained the plate discipline absent in nearly all of the organization's other tools players, and he projects to be an exciting player in the majors, possibly as soon as 2003.

Jeff Bailey — C/1B — Bats R — Age 22

YEAR	TEAM	LGE	AB	H	DB	TP	HR	BB	SO	R	RBI	SB	CS	OUT	BA	OBP	SLG	EQA	EQR	DEFENSE			
1999	KaneCnty	Mid	281	63	12	1	7	22	84	33	34	0	0	218	.224	.287	.349	.211	22	21-C	-4		
2000	Brevard	Fla	469	101	14	1	13	37	132	45	50	1	1	369	.215	.278	.333	.201	34	38-1B	-3	14-C	-4
2001	Florida	NL	439	99	13	1	13	43	135	43	50	0	0	340	.226	.295	.349	.222	39				

Jeff Bailey's receiving skills were ahead of his offense when he was selected in the second round of the 1997 draft. Since then, shoulder and bicep surgery has limited him to primarily first base and DH. While the Marlins were pleased with his development as a hitter over the second half of last year (13 of his 14 home runs came after July 1), his bat will be an asset only if he can catch on a full-time basis.

Dave Berg — IF — Bats R — Age 30

YEAR	TEAM	LGE	AB	H	DB	TP	HR	BB	SO	R	RBI	SB	CS	OUT	BA	OBP	SLG	EQA	EQR	DEFENSE			
1998	Florida	NL	186	59	6	0	4	26	43	18	23	3	0	127	.317	.401	.414	.284	27	21-3B	0	20-2B	-2
1999	Florida	NL	307	88	17	1	3	22	56	40	24	1	2	221	.287	.338	.378	.241	31	28-SS	3	25-2B	5
2000	Florida	NL	213	54	15	1	1	21	43	23	21	3	0	159	.254	.333	.347	.236	21	37-SS	-3		
2001	Florida	NL	185	50	5	0	3	22	40	24	23	1	0	135	.270	.348	.346	.247	21				

Despite Alex Gonzalez's pathetic 2000 season, Dave Berg wasn't moved into a starting role because his ability to play six positions makes him so valuable off the bench, plus he was playing with a partially torn rotator cuff. A bench player's numbers can fluctuate wildly from year to year due to limited at bats, so don't let last year fool you—Berg is one of the best utility men in the game.

Todd Betts — 3B/1B — Bats L — Age 28

YEAR	TEAM	LGE	AB	H	DB	TP	HR	BB	SO	R	RBI	SB	CS	OUT	BA	OBP	SLG	EQA	EQR	DEFENSE			
1998	Akron	Eas	328	72	13	2	12	48	76	42	33	1	0	256	.220	.324	.381	.239	36	58-3B	-3		
1999	Akron	Eas	383	86	14	1	13	43	74	43	45	1	1	298	.225	.309	.368	.228	37	73-3B	-3	16-1B	0
2000	Portland	Eas	427	107	18	1	7	45	66	53	48	2	2	322	.251	.328	.347	.230	41	55-1B	-8	53-3B	-6
2001	Florida	NL	363	87	13	1	8	53	68	48	44	1	1	277	.240	.337	.347	.242	40				

(Todd Betts *continued*)

Hopefully, last year's .321 batting average will gain him exile from a five-year sentence in the Eastern League. Todd Betts could be a cheap stopgap for a team that needs on-base skills at the hot corner, but his lack of power will likely keep that from happening. At least he can take solace in the fact that four years in Akron helped him to set scads of team records and become as revered in the Rubber City as bowling legend Earl Anthony.

Luis Castillo   2B   Bats B   Age 25

YEAR	TEAM	LGE	AB	H	DB	TP	HR	BB	SO	R	RBI	SB	CS	OUT	BA	OBP	SLG	EQA	EQR	DEFENSE	
1998	Charlott	Int	379	94	9	2	0	62	67	55	13	23	10	295	.248	.354	.282	.231	38	98-2B	-14
1998	Florida	NL	156	34	4	2	1	21	31	23	11	3	0	122	.218	.314	.288	.212	13	44-2B	-3
1999	Florida	NL	491	147	19	4	1	60	80	68	27	39	16	360	.299	.376	.360	.260	62	120-2B	-4
2000	Florida	NL	545	177	15	3	2	70	81	94	26	57	23	391	.325	.402	.374	.275	77	134-2B	-11
2001	Florida	NL	488	143	15	3	1	72	83	106	47	45	14	359	.293	.384	.342	.270	68		

Luis Castillo spent most of the season trying to top Enzo Hernandez's anti-record of 12 RBI in a full season. He eventually did (finishing with 17) but not before establishing a new mark for most hits per RBI with 10.6, obliterating the old standard of 8.3 posted by Lloyd "Little Poison" Waner. However, RBI are not what Castillo is about; getting on base is, and he does it very well, pacing all major-league leadoff hitters with a .419 on-base percentage. Although I have concerns about his durability, Castillo is one of the cornerstones of the Marlins' future and someone Dave Dombrowski needs to lock up with a multi-year deal.

Ramon Castro   C   Bats R   Age 25

YEAR	TEAM	LGE	AB	H	DB	TP	HR	BB	SO	R	RBI	SB	CS	OUT	BA	OBP	SLG	EQA	EQR	DEFENSE	
1998	Jackson	Tex	168	37	4	0	6	9	34	20	18	0	1	132	.220	.270	.351	.201	12	46-C	1
1998	Portland	Eas	89	20	3	0	2	6	21	8	8	0	0	69	.225	.274	.326	.196	6	11-C	-2
1999	Calgary	PCL	341	73	13	0	12	19	62	31	44	0	0	268	.214	.258	.358	.199	24	81-C	0
1999	Florida	NL	68	12	5	0	2	9	13	4	4	0	0	56	.176	.273	.338	.203	5	19-C	2
2000	Calgary	PCL	212	59	13	0	11	11	39	31	31	0	0	153	.278	.314	.495	.262	27	55-C	-2
2000	Florida	NL	140	34	4	0	2	14	34	10	14	0	0	106	.243	.316	.314	.214	11	42-C	0
2001	Florida	NL	288	71	8	0	12	27	61	32	41	0	0	217	.247	.311	.399	.243	32		

Ramon Castro was handed a starting job in spring training but was overmatched offensively and sent to Calgary. There, Cannons' hitting coach Sal Rende improved Castro's balance by opening up his stance. However, when he was recalled in late July, he reverted to lunging at pitches. Castro is a strong catch-and-throw receiver whose over-aggressiveness at bat won't allow him to be as good as he could be. The Charles Johnson signing makes Castro trade bait.

Cesar Crespo   2B/OF   Bats B   Age 22

YEAR	TEAM	LGE	AB	H	DB	TP	HR	BB	SO	R	RBI	SB	CS	OUT	BA	OBP	SLG	EQA	EQR	DEFENSE			
1998	Columbia	SAL	436	93	17	2	4	32	120	37	34	17	7	350	.213	.269	.289	.188	27	105-2B	-18		
1999	Brevard	Fla	438	106	15	1	5	46	99	46	30	10	4	336	.242	.315	.315	.217	37	97-2B	-14		
2000	Portland	Eas	490	108	19	3	8	60	127	71	45	23	10	392	.220	.307	.320	.218	43	114-CF	-7	16-2B	-2
2001	Florida	NL	469	112	17	1	7	56	127	65	45	21	8	365	.239	.320	.324	.232	47				

The PTBNL in the Al Leiter deal spent last year learning to play center field, his third position in three years. The latest switch was made not because Cesar Crespo can't handle a middle infield spot, but because the Marlins want to improve his versatility. That's patently absurd considering that the organization is awash in quality utility men. With his on-base skills, Crespo could be an asset around the keystone, while in the outfield his upside is Gary Pettis with more pop and minus the Gold Glove defense.

Matt Erickson   IF   Bats L   Age 25

YEAR	TEAM	LGE	AB	H	DB	TP	HR	BB	SO	R	RBI	SB	CS	OUT	BA	OBP	SLG	EQA	EQR	DEFENSE			
1998	KaneCnty	Mid	457	119	22	1	4	53	67	58	45	6	3	341	.260	.348	.339	.239	47	99-3B	-6		
1999	Portland	Eas	365	85	12	2	1	37	68	30	28	1	2	282	.233	.306	.285	.199	25	100-2B	-2		
2000	Portland	Eas	341	86	19	2	2	44	69	42	30	4	2	257	.252	.346	.337	.238	35	50-SS	-2	35-3B	9
2001	Florida	NL	331	80	14	1	2	46	67	45	31	5	2	253	.242	.334	.308	.231	33				

Matt Erickson is another guy Florida has converted into a utility player, as they gave him 50 starts at shortstop in his repeat season at Portland. In Erickson's case, though, the transformation was justifiable given his age and his failure to develop the power you want in a third baseman. Erickson plays great defense at third and could be another Bill Mueller, if there's a team like the Giants that is willing to accept his limitations.

Cliff Floyd — LF — Bats L — Age 28

YEAR	TEAM	LGE	AB	H	DB	TP	HR	BB	SO	R	RBI	SB	CS	OUT	BA	OBP	SLG	EQA	EQR	DEFENSE	
1998	Florida	NL	599	170	44	3	24	45	105	87	91	25	14	443	.284	.337	.487	.269	83	134-LF	-4
1999	Florida	NL	253	74	18	1	11	27	44	35	46	3	5	184	.292	.365	.502	.280	38	57-LF	-3
2000	Florida	NL	425	126	24	0	23	44	77	72	87	23	3	302	.296	.372	.515	.296	72	92-LF	-5
2001	Florida	NL	400	116	25	1	21	53	77	81	76	20	6	290	.290	.373	.515	.301	72		

A strenuous off-season regimen designed to shake the injury jinx failed when Cliff Floyd tore knee cartilage in late July, shelving him for the fifth time in four years. The Marlins don't have many offensive players with star potential, so to continue their climb in the NL East they need positive contributions from every position. That means either Floyd has to stay healthy or Dombrowski needs to find a productive fourth outfielder. Despite the team's financial constraints, the latter is more likely.

Andy Fox — UT — Bats L — Age 30

YEAR	TEAM	LGE	AB	H	DB	TP	HR	BB	SO	R	RBI	SB	CS	OUT	BA	OBP	SLG	EQA	EQR	DEFENSE			
1998	Arizona	NL	507	139	20	5	10	41	91	67	43	13	7	375	.274	.348	.393	.252	60	49-2B	-6	39-RF	-2
1999	Arizona	NL	275	68	11	2	6	29	58	32	31	3	1	208	.247	.338	.367	.242	30	71-SS	-8		
2000	Arizona	NL	87	18	1	0	2	3	15	9	11	2	1	70	.207	.233	.287	.161	4	16-3B	0		
2000	Florida	NL	166	41	3	2	3	16	35	18	10	8	3	128	.247	.323	.343	.231	16	27-SS	-2		
2001	Florida	NL	284	69	10	2	6	31	58	37	32	7	3	218	.243	.317	.356	.237	30				

He was acquired from the Diamondbacks in early June, apparently on orders from the Department of Redundancy Department, since the Fish were steadfast in their commitment to Alex Gonzalez and already had Dave Berg on the roster. Andy Fox would form a reliable platoon with Berg at shortstop, but if the team sticks with Gonzalez, Fox is excess baggage.

Amaury Garcia — 2B/LF — Bats R — Age 26

YEAR	TEAM	LGE	AB	H	DB	TP	HR	BB	SO	R	RBI	SB	CS	OUT	BA	OBP	SLG	EQA	EQR	DEFENSE			
1998	Portland	Eas	546	126	16	4	10	34	129	61	48	13	9	429	.231	.278	.330	.200	39	130-2B	-15		
1999	Calgary	PCL	464	119	26	6	12	35	76	66	36	11	7	352	.256	.314	.416	.242	51	110-2B	-10		
2000	Calgary	PCL	469	114	19	2	10	29	81	57	33	20	9	364	.243	.291	.356	.218	40	91-2B	-9	25-LF	-2
2001	ChiSox	AL	458	112	18	4	10	38	89	67	56	19	11	356	.245	.302	.367	.227	44				

Amaury Garcia's performance slipped in his second season at Calgary, and his raw numbers are worse than they look since Burns Stadium's 3,500-foot elevation inflates offense. For the second straight season, Garcia took unusual advantage of the elevation: his OPS at home was 253 points higher than on the road. He isn't going to hit enough to be an everyday second baseman, and his inability to play shortstop limits him as a reserve. He's been traded to the White Sox, who could use a utility man with sock.

Alex Gonzalez — SS — Bats R — Age 24

YEAR	TEAM	LGE	AB	H	DB	TP	HR	BB	SO	R	RBI	SB	CS	OUT	BA	OBP	SLG	EQA	EQR	DEFENSE	
1998	Charlott	Int	419	102	19	7	8	20	79	59	40	2	4	321	.243	.285	.379	.216	35	102-SS	-13
1998	Florida	NL	87	14	3	0	3	9	28	12	7	0	0	73	.161	.247	.299	.175	5	21-SS	0
1999	Florida	NL	565	155	29	7	14	8	107	79	56	2	4	414	.274	.299	.425	.235	56	132-SS	-11
2000	Florida	NL	390	80	18	4	7	7	72	34	41	6	1	311	.205	.223	.326	.172	19	97-SS	-6
2001	Florida	NL	451	114	21	4	14	18	92	46	58	5	2	339	.253	.281	.410	.233	45		

Alex Gonzalez was the worst shortstop in baseball last season. In an effort to regain his superficially impressive 1999 form, the club employed a host of hitting and psychological specialists, to no effect. Perhaps more effective would be a copy of *The Rey Quinones Story*, the tale of an undisciplined middle infielder with an attitude problem and an erratic glove who was out of baseball by age 25, free to pursue his dream of opening a cantina.

Mike Gulan — 3B/OF — Bats R — Age 30

YEAR	TEAM	LGE	AB	H	DB	TP	HR	BB	SO	R	RBI	SB	CS	OUT	BA	OBP	SLG	EQA	EQR	DEFENSE			
1998	Portland	Eas	160	39	12	1	3	6	44	17	15	2	1	122	.244	.274	.387	.216	13	24-3B	-6		
1999	Calgary	PCL	278	61	16	1	8	7	86	27	33	1	1	218	.219	.245	.371	.196	19	51-3B	3		
2000	Calgary	PCL	414	103	26	1	11	17	104	43	46	3	1	312	.249	.287	.396	.225	37	51-3B	-6	41-LF	-4
2001	Florida	NL	316	75	19	1	8	17	90	31	35	3	1	242	.237	.276	.380	.222	28				

He took advantage of the thin air of Calgary to post the best stat line of his nine-year minor-league odyssey. At this point in his career, a more relevant question than whether Mike Gulan will get another cup of coffee in the majors is what organization will hire him as a coach to spread his infectious attitude and knowledge of the game.

Mark Kotsay — RF — Bats L — Age 25

YEAR	TEAM	LGE	AB	H	DB	TP	HR	BB	SO	R	RBI	SB	CS	OUT	BA	OBP	SLG	EQA	EQR	DEFENSE			
1998	Florida	NL	587	167	27	7	12	33	57	76	69	9	5	425	.284	.324	.416	.246	64	143-RF	14		
1999	Florida	NL	499	134	24	8	8	23	47	55	47	5	5	370	.269	.301	.397	.229	46	107-RF	8	13-1B	0
2000	Florida	NL	536	158	33	4	11	35	43	83	53	17	9	387	.295	.338	.433	.257	65	130-RF	6		
2001	Florida	NL	484	137	24	6	10	35	45	69	67	15	7	354	.283	.331	.419	.258	60				

To drive home the point that Mark Kotsay needed to improve his production, Boles goofed off by rotating him with Brant Brown and Danny Bautista for the first month of the season. When moved into the second spot in the batting order, Kotsay recognized that he needed to become more patient at the plate, a virtue not stressed in the organization. His strong defense and rifle arm combine to make him an above-average right fielder who has room to grow offensively. Look for him to take another step forward in 2001.

Derrek Lee — 1B — Bats R — Age 25

YEAR	TEAM	LGE	AB	H	DB	TP	HR	BB	SO	R	RBI	SB	CS	OUT	BA	OBP	SLG	EQA	EQR	DEFENSE	
1998	Florida	NL	462	112	25	1	20	45	112	65	78	5	2	352	.242	.322	.431	.251	55	118-1B	4
1999	Florida	NL	220	46	9	1	5	14	66	21	19	2	1	175	.209	.256	.327	.189	14	56-1B	3
1999	Calgary	PCL	330	76	15	1	13	24	87	43	50	2	3	257	.230	.288	.400	.225	31	84-1B	0
2000	Florida	NL	483	134	19	3	27	56	115	68	66	0	3	352	.277	.357	.497	.278	72	126-1B	6
2001	Florida	NL	445	113	19	1	21	52	120	62	73	3	2	334	.254	.332	.443	.264	60		

Credit John Boles for not giving up on Derrek Lee after a disastrous 1999 campaign. The son of Japanese baseball legend Leon Lee spent the winter working with Greg Vaughn to reestablish the plate discipline that had vanished since he joined the Marlins' organization. As you can see, the results of his improved strike-zone recognition were dramatic. Lee is a future Gold Glover at first base, and his continued climb into the upper echelon of sluggers is crucial to the future success of the franchise.

Mike Lowell — 3B — Bats R — Age 27

YEAR	TEAM	LGE	AB	H	DB	TP	HR	BB	SO	R	RBI	SB	CS	OUT	BA	OBP	SLG	EQA	EQR	DEFENSE	
1998	Columbus	Int	509	139	30	2	21	28	84	66	79	2	0	370	.273	.317	.464	.256	61	115-3B	-2
1999	Calgary	PCL	80	20	1	0	2	7	18	8	7	0	0	60	.250	.310	.338	.218	7	21-3B	2
1999	Florida	NL	311	78	12	0	13	22	65	31	45	0	0	233	.251	.310	.415	.240	33	76-3B	5
2000	Florida	NL	514	138	31	0	24	47	70	70	89	4	0	376	.268	.339	.469	.268	70	134-3B	1
2001	Florida	NL	429	119	20	1	20	51	72	65	78	1	0	310	.277	.354	.469	.280	65		

Mike Lowell played the final four months of 1999 at less than 100% after beating testicular cancer. His strength returned last year and he emerged as the third sacker the team envisioned when they acquired him from the Yankees. Lowell is rock solid in all facets of the game, and though he'll never be mistaken for Troy Glaus, he will be a valuable contributor to the next good Marlins' club. Since last year's Wilton was dead-on, I'm not going to disagree with this year's projection.

Kevin Millar — 1B/3B/LF — Bats R — Age 29

YEAR	TEAM	LGE	AB	H	DB	TP	HR	BB	SO	R	RBI	SB	CS	OUT	BA	OBP	SLG	EQA	EQR	DEFENSE			
1999	Calgary	PCL	139	33	8	1	4	8	19	16	17	1	0	106	.237	.279	.396	.222	12	20-LF	0		
1999	Florida	NL	354	100	16	4	9	35	60	47	63	1	0	254	.282	.358	.427	.265	46	87-1B	-4		
2000	Florida	NL	262	68	14	2	14	32	44	35	40	0	0	194	.260	.355	.489	.278	39	29-1B	1	14-LF	-1
2001	Florida	NL	284	77	14	1	13	42	50	47	52	1	0	207	.271	.365	.465	.285	45				

National League

After hearing that the team wanted more power at first base, Kevin Millar went on the Shane McMahon Suspiciously Accelerated Beefing Up Program, adding 15 pounds of muscle and 65 points of slugging average. He's an outstanding guy to have on the bench as a pinch-hitter and emergency corner infielder, albeit with the range of Popeye Zimmer circa 1998. If Millar wants to make the big money, he needs to find his way into the American League. Or the WWF.

Abraham Nunez — OF — Bats B — Age 21

YEAR	TEAM	LGE	AB	H	DB	TP	HR	BB	SO	R	RBI	SB	CS	OUT	BA	OBP	SLG	EQA	EQR	DEFENSE	
1998	Sth Bend	Mid	381	80	10	1	8	50	87	33	34	4	6	307	.210	.304	.304	.205	29	109-CF	-3
1999	High Des	Cal	481	95	19	2	14	59	127	59	52	15	6	392	.198	.286	.333	.211	40	130-RF	0
2000	Brevard	Fla	109	20	3	0	1	21	39	12	8	5	2	91	.183	.321	.239	.204	9		
2000	Portland	Eas	225	51	13	2	5	35	69	30	30	5	4	178	.227	.331	.369	.238	25		
2001	Florida	NL	317	70	11	1	9	47	97	44	36	10	4	251	.221	.321	.347	.238	35		

Abraham Nunez is the best position prospect on the Fish Farm, and, like nearly all the others, is the product of a trade. Dombrowski selected him as the PNTBL from the list Arizona submitted in the Matt Mantei trade after the Marlins' original choice, Steve Randolph, was determined to be damaged goods. Talk about dumb luck. Nunez is a John Sickels "Seven Skills" player, though a torn shoulder muscle limited him to DH for all but the final week of last season and caused him to be shuttled between Portland and Brevard County depending on which team was playing an AL affiliate. He'll probably start the year in the Eastern League but should get a September look-see in Miami.

Pablo Ozuna — 2B/SS — Bats R — Age 22

YEAR	TEAM	LGE	AB	H	DB	TP	HR	BB	SO	R	RBI	SB	CS	OUT	BA	OBP	SLG	EQA	EQR	DEFENSE	
1998	Peoria	Mid	547	159	23	5	8	19	60	78	43	22	12	400	.291	.321	.395	.239	56	121-SS	-13
1999	Portland	Eas	501	123	23	5	5	5	53	45	35	14	8	386	.246	.263	.341	.197	33	114-SS	-17
2000	Portland	Eas	466	120	21	3	6	30	59	53	42	19	14	360	.258	.308	.354	.221	41	113-2B	-2
2001	Florida	NL	457	130	19	4	8	23	57	65	54	28	12	339	.284	.319	.396	.249	52		

He dropped off many prospect lists with a mediocre 1999 campaign after being aggressively pushed to Double-A. He should find his way back onto those lists following an encouraging repeat season with Portland. Pablo Ozuna is a line-drive contact hitter whose biggest improvement was a dramatic surge in walks. Prior to the season, he was moved from shortstop to second base, ostensibly because of a weak throwing arm, but probably because the Marlins had more doubts about Castillo than Gonzalez. Implausibly, there is now some thought of trying Ozuna in the outfield. Given Alex Gonzalez's murky future, the club should swallow hard, put Ozuna back at shortstop, and tolerate his defensive limitations.

Julio Ramirez — CF — Bats R — Age 23

YEAR	TEAM	LGE	AB	H	DB	TP	HR	BB	SO	R	RBI	SB	CS	OUT	BA	OBP	SLG	EQA	EQR	DEFENSE	
1998	Brevard	Fla	565	134	17	7	11	33	166	57	42	27	14	445	.237	.282	.350	.212	46	135-CF	12
1999	Portland	Eas	570	131	27	7	10	25	158	61	49	31	9	448	.230	.264	.354	.209	45	137-CF	4
2000	Calgary	PCL	344	77	15	2	5	14	88	31	37	11	9	275	.224	.259	.323	.188	21	90-CF	-4
2001	ChiSox	AL	412	97	18	4	7	29	118	60	45	21	10	326	.235	.286	.350	.216	35		

It was an extremely disappointing season for Julio Ramirez, but one the organization should have seen coming like a freight train since the cause has been evident for years: Ramirez has no idea of the strike zone. Batters with both low-walk and high-strikeout totals almost inevitably wash out when they reach the highest levels of the game. Instead of gushing over his speed and how he can beat the snot out of hanging curveballs, the Marlins should have been drilling Ramirez in the skills necessary to be an effective major-league hitter. Traded to the White Sox, where he might platoon.

Mike Redmond — C — Bats R — Age 30

YEAR	TEAM	LGE	AB	H	DB	TP	HR	BB	SO	R	RBI	SB	CS	OUT	BA	OBP	SLG	EQA	EQR	DEFENSE	
1998	Florida	NL	120	40	7	0	3	5	15	10	13	0	0	80	.333	.369	.467	.279	16	34-C	3
1999	Florida	NL	244	73	3	0	3	23	32	21	27	0	0	171	.299	.371	.348	.250	27	74-C	5
2000	Florida	NL	213	55	6	2	0	10	18	16	15	0	0	158	.258	.313	.305	.208	16	66-C	1
2001	Florida	NL	181	48	2	0	3	15	20	18	20	0	0	133	.265	.321	.326	.226	16		

(Mike Redmond *continued*)

The coaches and managers in the Florida farm system loved his defense and the way he handled pitchers, saving him from a career as a minor-league nomad. Mike Redmond repaid the parent club with two offensive seasons out of line with his true ability level, which is closer to what he did last year. He'll carve out a few more years as a good-field, no-hit backup signal caller, then embark on a managerial career.

Henry Rodriguez — LF — Bats L — Age 33

YEAR	TEAM	LGE	AB	H	DB	TP	HR	BB	SO	R	RBI	SB	CS	OUT	BA	OBP	SLG	EQA	EQR	DEFENSE	
1998	ChiCubs	NL	420	104	17	1	32	52	106	56	83	1	3	319	.248	.331	.521	.273	62	97-LF	11
1999	ChiCubs	NL	447	130	24	0	26	49	107	67	80	1	4	321	.291	.361	.519	.284	69	103-LF	3
2000	ChiCubs	NL	261	64	14	1	17	18	71	35	47	1	2	199	.245	.300	.502	.256	33	57-LF	0
2000	Florida	NL	109	29	3	0	3	13	22	10	10	0	0	80	.266	.349	.376	.248	12	23-LF	-1
2001	*Florida*	*NL*	*364*	*92*	*13*	*0*	*23*	*49*	*96*	*53*	*69*	*2*	*2*	*274*	*.253*	*.341*	*.478*	*.276*	*55*		

Picking up Henry Rodriguez from the Cubs at the trade deadline to fill in for Cliff Floyd was a seemingly noteworthy event in the rebuilding of the Marlins. It marked the first time since hauling in Darren Daulton for the 1997 stretch drive that they had traded prospects for an established big leaguer, instead of vice versa. It was never intended to be more than a symbolic gesture, though—Dombrowski made Andy MacPhail include a suitcase full of greenbacks to buy out Rodriguez's 2001 option, making him a free agent.

Nate Rolison — 1B — Bats L — Age 24

YEAR	TEAM	LGE	AB	H	DB	TP	HR	BB	SO	R	RBI	SB	CS	OUT	BA	OBP	SLG	EQA	EQR	DEFENSE	
1998	Portland	Eas	489	114	29	1	12	49	153	64	63	3	0	375	.233	.309	.370	.229	47	129-1B	-7
1999	Portland	Eas	442	110	13	1	13	50	118	55	50	0	0	332	.249	.330	.371	.238	46	105-1B	1
2000	Calgary	PCL	430	115	25	2	17	54	120	62	59	2	1	316	.267	.352	.453	.269	59	112-1B	-5
2001	*Florida*	*NL*	*426*	*111*	*19*	*1*	*16*	*54*	*128*	*60*	*68*	*1*	*0*	*315*	*.261*	*.344*	*.423*	*.265*	*57*		

The Marlins' second-round pick in 1995 has improved incrementally at each rung of the minor-league ladder, but not fast enough to beat Derrek Lee to the first-base bag. Nate Rolison finally started hitting for power commensurate with his size last year and was named the best power prospect in the Pacific Coast League. He dismantles right-handed pitching (.353/.446/.630 with Calgary) and could be a solid contributor as the good half of a platoon split with a different club.

Brett Roneberg — OF/1B — Bats L — Age 22

YEAR	TEAM	LGE	AB	H	DB	TP	HR	BB	SO	R	RBI	SB	CS	OUT	BA	OBP	SLG	EQA	EQR	DEFENSE	
1998	KaneCnty	Mid	246	57	3	0	3	18	54	28	26	1	2	191	.232	.285	.280	.184	14	62-RF	-5
1999	KaneCnty	Mid	519	119	24	2	6	53	90	61	44	1	1	401	.229	.303	.318	.209	40	119-RF	-1
2000	Brevard	Fla	462	105	16	1	2	58	68	42	35	2	1	358	.227	.314	.279	.204	34	115-RF	-5
2001	*Florida*	*NL*	*452*	*112*	*15*	*1*	*3*	*58*	*78*	*54*	*45*	*1*	*1*	*341*	*.248*	*.333*	*.305*	*.228*	*42*		

Though just 22 years old, Brett Roneberg is entering his sixth year on the Fish Farm. The man from Down Under hasn't received much attention, but he's got an interesting mix of skills: he has a camera eye, makes contact, hits for a fair average, and plays solid defense in the outfield corners and at first base. Roneberg is young enough and big enough to add a bit of sock to his game, which would make him a valuable chess piece off the bench.

Jose Santos — 3B/OF — Bats R — Age 23

YEAR	TEAM	LGE	AB	H	DB	TP	HR	BB	SO	R	RBI	SB	CS	OUT	BA	OBP	SLG	EQA	EQR	DEFENSE			
1998	Savannah	SAL	394	95	14	3	14	37	125	49	49	9	4	303	.241	.313	.398	.239	42	101-3B	-4		
1998	KaneCnty	Mid	122	21	8	1	2	15	53	13	9	2	1	102	.172	.270	.303	.192	8	27-3B	2		
1999	KaneCnty	Mid	469	101	22	2	13	57	142	59	64	7	2	370	.215	.311	.354	.227	46	125-3B	-14		
2000	Brevard	Fla	457	92	13	1	7	40	142	44	44	3	1	366	.201	.276	.280	.185	27	75-3B	-8	41-LF	-3
2001	*Florida*	*NL*	*460*	*98*	*17*	*1*	*11*	*53*	*156*	*49*	*46*	*5*	*1*	*363*	*.213*	*.294*	*.326*	*.217*	*40*				

The Florida State League is a difficult environment for hitters, but this is ridiculous—Jose Santos was considered the best power prospect in the organization before falling apart last year. There is no obvious reason for his precipitous drop, which makes me wonder if he was hiding an injury. He needs to rebound in a big way this season if he is to have any kind of a career.

Mark Smith   LF/RF   Bats R   Age 31

YEAR	TEAM	LGE	AB	H	DB	TP	HR	BB	SO	R	RBI	SB	CS	OUT	BA	OBP	SLG	EQA	EQR	DEFENSE
1998	Nashvill	PCL	92	26	7	1	5	8	21	12	20	2	1	67	.283	.352	.543	.288	15	
1998	Pittsbrg	NL	129	26	3	0	3	10	24	18	14	7	0	103	.202	.274	.295	.201	9	23-LF -1
1999	YKL	JpC	287	68	11	1	16	20	0	20	22	3	0	219	.237	.287	.449	.241	31	
2000	Florida	NL	194	48	7	1	5	15	51	21	26	2	0	146	.247	.307	.371	.229	18	38-LF -2
2001	Montreal	NL	218	50	8	1	7	21	38	27	29	3	0	168	.229	.297	.372	.230	21	

Mark Smith returned to the States and crashed the Marlins' Spring Fling, earning the last spot on the bench with a monster March. Although Smith claimed to have learned how to hit a curveball in Japan, the highlight of his summer happened off the field when he saved a man's life by pulling him from the wreckage of a burning car. He was outrighted to Calgary after the season because roster space is limited and Dombrowski understands that Smith's species is abundant.

Derek Wathan   SS   Bats B   Age 24

YEAR	TEAM	LGE	AB	H	DB	TP	HR	BB	SO	R	RBI	SB	CS	OUT	BA	OBP	SLG	EQA	EQR	DEFENSE
1998	Utica	NYP	229	52	7	1	0	14	37	21	16	3	4	181	.227	.275	.266	.173	11	52-SS -2
1999	KaneCnty	Mid	476	103	16	2	1	33	59	45	35	13	6	379	.216	.271	.265	.177	25	122-SS 6
2000	Brevard	Fla	374	83	16	3	6	33	61	39	37	8	6	297	.222	.287	.329	.205	28	90-SS 3
2000	Portland	Eas	143	30	5	1	0	9	22	11	14	2	1	114	.210	.259	.259	.164	6	41-SS -3
2001	Florida	NL	383	86	15	1	4	37	61	42	30	12	7	304	.225	.293	.300	.208	30	

The younger of Duke's two sons who are playing in the minor leagues is more athletic than his pear-shaped sibling, Dusty, but the scouting report is the same: fundamentally sound, good defensively, can't hit. Derek Wathan is more suited to be a utility man than any of the other prospects the Marlins are shuttling around the diamond, but thus far he hasn't played anywhere but shortstop.

Preston Wilson   CF   Bats R   Age 26

YEAR	TEAM	LGE	AB	H	DB	TP	HR	BB	SO	R	RBI	SB	CS	OUT	BA	OBP	SLG	EQA	EQR	DEFENSE
1998	Charlott	Int	354	86	21	2	19	26	120	55	58	8	4	272	.243	.297	.475	.251	43	88-CF -2
1999	Florida	NL	486	134	20	4	26	40	147	64	67	8	4	356	.276	.342	.494	.273	69	128-CF 1
2000	Florida	NL	613	160	35	3	30	46	175	89	114	32	14	467	.261	.320	.475	.261	81	156-CF 3
2001	Florida	NL	531	137	29	2	26	47	168	82	84	23	7	401	.258	.318	.467	.267	74	

Preston Wilson put up some big counting numbers last year: 187 strikeouts, 31 home runs, 36 stolen bases, and 121 RBI. Frankly, too much attention was paid to all of them. More significant are his rate stats, which show him to be a scarcely above-average center fielder. This really isn't a bad thing, since a quality team doesn't need stars at every position. It becomes problematic only after this season, when Wilson is eligible for salary arbitration and the Marlins may be tempted to sign him to a long-term contract. They need to recognize what they have and decide if they want to overpay for it.

PITCHERS (ERA: 4.50, H/9: 9.00, HR/9: 1.00, BB/9: 3.00, K/9: 6.00, KW: 1.00, PERA: 4.50)

Antonio Alfonseca — Throws R — Age 29

YEAR	TEAM	LGE	IP	H	ER	HR	BB	K	ERA	W	L	H/9	HR/9	BB/9	K/9	KW	PERA
1998	Florida	NL	67.3	73	36	11	31	37	4.81	3	4	9.76	1.47	4.14	4.95	0.60	5.91
1999	Florida	NL	75.3	75	26	4	25	39	3.11	5	3	8.96	0.48	2.99	4.66	0.78	3.94
2000	Florida	NL	67.7	79	34	7	21	39	4.52	4	4	10.51	0.93	2.79	5.19	0.93	5.23

A decent reliever, Antonio Alfonseca poses as a closer, but when he enters the game, he doesn't exactly slam the door. Rather, he turns on the porch light, chats for a while, occasionally coughs up a donation, and celebrates wildly when the solicitor leaves. Arbitration-eligible with the Rolaids Relief Award in tow, he will be seeking a ten-fold raise. It wouldn't be the worst idea to deal "Pulpo" for some much-needed position-player prospects and have one of the Marlins' other power arms handle ninth-inning duties.

Armando Almanza — Throws L — Age 28

YEAR	TEAM	LGE	IP	H	ER	HR	BB	K	ERA	W	L	H/9	HR/9	BB/9	K/9	KW	PERA
1998	Arkansas	Tex	29.3	29	17	3	22	27	5.22	1	2	8.90	0.92	6.75	8.28	0.61	5.91
1998	Memphis	PCL	33.0	34	19	1	22	29	5.18	1	3	9.27	0.27	6.00	7.91	0.66	5.10
1999	Calgary	PCL	16.7	27	24	3	18	13	12.96	0	2	14.58	1.62	9.72	7.02	0.36	11.16
1999	Florida	NL	15.3	8	4	1	8	17	2.35	1	1	4.70	0.59	4.70	9.98	1.06	2.46
2000	Florida	NL	45.7	39	26	3	37	38	5.12	2	3	7.69	0.59	7.29	7.49	0.51	5.08

Armando Almanza's collapse coincided precisely with the late-season meltdown of the Marlins' bullpen. He had a 1.86 ERA on August 11, then allowed 17 runs in just 7⅔ innings the rest of the season. Almanza has electric stuff that can be nearly untouchable, both for the batter and the catcher. He might yet develop into a real weapon, but it's going to take more than three minutes of game situations twice a week to tame the wildness he's shown ever since the Cardinals moved him to the bullpen.

Wes Anderson — Throws R — Age 21

YEAR	TEAM	LGE	IP	H	ER	HR	BB	K	ERA	W	L	H/9	HR/9	BB/9	K/9	KW	PERA
1999	KaneCnty	Mid	126.3	118	66	17	57	71	4.70	6	8	8.41	1.21	4.06	5.06	0.62	4.81
2000	Brevard	Fla	103.7	108	66	13	83	53	5.73	4	8	9.38	1.13	7.21	4.60	0.32	6.60

Wes Anderson is a premium talent who fell to the Marlins in the 14th round of the 1997 draft because everybody was convinced he was going to play for the University of Arkansas. He has suffered bouts of shoulder tendinitis in each of the last two seasons, which isn't surprising since he is still maturing physically. When his textbook mechanics aren't affected by injury, the ball explodes out of his hand, generating heat and movement rivaling any pitcher's in the system. To their credit, the Marlins have tried to be careful with him, including holding him out of the Arizona Fall League.

Manny Aybar — Throws R — Age 26

YEAR	TEAM	LGE	IP	H	ER	HR	BB	K	ERA	W	L	H/9	HR/9	BB/9	K/9	KW	PERA
1998	Memphis	PCL	78.3	59	24	8	18	44	2.76	6	3	6.78	0.92	2.07	5.06	1.22	2.83
1998	St Louis	NL	78.3	87	55	6	38	46	6.32	3	6	10.00	0.69	4.37	5.29	0.61	5.31
1999	St Louis	NL	94.3	100	62	12	30	62	5.92	3	7	9.54	1.14	2.86	5.92	1.03	4.91
2000	Cincnnti	NL	49.3	49	28	6	18	26	5.11	2	3	8.94	1.09	3.28	4.74	0.72	4.70
2000	Florida	NL	26.3	17	7	3	11	12	2.39	2	1	5.81	1.03	3.76	4.10	0.55	3.04

Acquiring Manny Aybar before the trading deadline when the Fish were flirting with .500 was aimed more at improving public relations than bettering the team. His ERA halved upon arriving in Miami, but Aybar's peripheral numbers indicate that was more a result of good fortune than real improvement on his part. He still throws a low-90s fastball with good sink, but inconsistent command of his slider and a non-existent third pitch limit his upside to palatable middle relief.

Josh Beckett — Throws R — Age 21

YEAR	TEAM	LGE	IP	H	ER	HR	BB	K	ERA	W	L	H/9	HR/9	BB/9	K/9	KW	PERA
2000	KaneCnty	Mid	53.7	52	26	9	17	32	4.36	3	3	8.72	1.51	2.85	5.37	0.94	4.82

Josh Beckett began what, contractually, has to be a rapid rise to the big leagues. He showed the ability and poise that caused some scouts to call him the best pitching prospect of his generation, throwing a 95-mph fastball, a big breaking curveball, and a change-up so improved that it became his number-two pitch. He made just 12 starts, twice being shut down with shoulder tendinitis that he says resulted from pumping too much iron. Injury is the only thing that can derail him from assuming a permanent role in The Show by 2004.

Ricky Bones — Throws R — Age 32

YEAR	TEAM	LGE	IP	H	ER	HR	BB	K	ERA	W	L	H/9	HR/9	BB/9	K/9	KW	PERA
1998	SaltLake	PCL	44.7	39	19	5	20	26	3.83	3	2	7.86	1.01	4.03	5.24	0.65	4.25
1998	KansasCy	AL	52.7	46	15	3	20	35	2.56	4	2	7.86	0.51	3.42	5.98	0.88	3.54
1999	Baltimor	AL	43.7	55	25	6	16	25	5.15	2	3	11.34	1.24	3.30	5.15	0.78	6.28
2000	Florida	NL	75.0	91	41	6	23	49	4.92	3	5	10.92	0.72	2.76	5.88	1.07	5.24

He made the club out of spring training and was a major surprise in helping the Marlins fashion the best bullpen in the majors during the first half of the season. Unfortunately, he misplaced his charm bracelet over the All-Star break, posting an ERA of 10.00 the remainder of the season. Bones's stuff and random stretches of effectiveness got him a one-year deal to stay in Miami.

Nate Bump — Throws R — Age 24

YEAR	TEAM	LGE	IP	H	ER	HR	BB	K	ERA	W	L	H/9	HR/9	BB/9	K/9	KW	PERA
1998	San Jose	Cal	56.3	38	16	5	30	32	2.56	4	2	6.07	0.80	4.79	5.11	0.53	3.36
1999	Shrevprt	Tex	85.3	84	47	15	38	38	4.96	4	5	8.86	1.58	4.01	4.01	0.50	5.45
1999	Portland	Eas	40.7	56	38	4	12	21	8.41	1	4	12.39	0.89	2.66	4.65	0.88	6.23
2000	Portland	Eas	139.3	170	94	27	52	62	6.07	5	10	10.98	1.74	3.36	4.00	0.60	6.60

He was a mechanical mess the first few months of his repeat season at Double-A, resulting in erratic control and a loss of five mph from his low-90s heat. Things came together for Nate Bump when he started relying more heavily on his sinking fastball and less on his knuckle-curve and change-up. While his season numbers are disappointing, he posted a 2.39 ERA in his final 11 starts, allowing just 59 hits in 68 innings. Bump will need better command of his secondary pitches to succeed in the majors, or even in the high altitude of Calgary, which is where he'll begin 2001. Bump left the Arizona Fall League early after developing shoulder tendinitis.

A.J. Burnett — Throws R — Age 24

YEAR	TEAM	LGE	IP	H	ER	HR	BB	K	ERA	W	L	H/9	HR/9	BB/9	K/9	KW	PERA
1998	KaneCnty	Mid	105.7	91	39	7	55	94	3.32	7	5	7.75	0.60	4.68	8.01	0.85	4.04
1999	Portland	Eas	112.7	138	99	20	70	77	7.91	3	10	11.02	1.60	5.59	6.15	0.55	7.40
1999	Florida	NL	40.3	36	22	3	22	28	4.91	2	2	8.03	0.67	4.91	6.25	0.64	4.39
2000	Florida	NL	80.3	78	44	8	38	47	4.93	4	5	8.74	0.90	4.26	5.27	0.62	4.76

There was some concern that A.J. Burnett would miss the entire season after he ruptured a ligament in his pitching thumb in spring training. Much to management's delight, he busted his tail in rehab and returned in late July, stronger than he was before the injury. Not surprisingly, he struggled to find a consistent rhythm after returning. The only thing nastier than Burnett's repertoire (95-octane gas and a Mussina-like spike curve) is his mound personality. I expect him to strike fear in the league in 2001.

Scott Comer — Throws R — Age 24

YEAR	TEAM	LGE	IP	H	ER	HR	BB	K	ERA	W	L	H/9	HR/9	BB/9	K/9	KW	PERA
1998	KaneCnty	Mid	86.7	106	68	32	11	43	7.06	2	8	11.01	3.32	1.14	4.47	1.95	7.38
1999	Brevard	Fla	122.3	118	39	7	7	50	2.87	9	5	8.68	0.51	0.51	3.68	3.57	2.89
2000	Portland	Eas	120.0	184	131	47	34	38	9.82	2	11	13.80	3.53	2.55	2.85	0.56	9.82

(Scott Comer *continued*)

Sometimes we at *Baseball Prospectus* don't heed our own advice. Scott Comer earned an honorable mention in our Top 40 Prospects list last year despite being a change-up pitcher in high-A ball—albeit one with control that was off the charts. Comer got absolutely throttled in Double-A, bathing bleacher patrons with horsehide by serving up an all-time Eastern League record total of 28 home runs. He won't be on this year's list.

Reid Cornelius   Throws R   Age 31

YEAR	TEAM	LGE	IP	H	ER	HR	BB	K	ERA	W	L	H/9	HR/9	BB/9	K/9	KW	PERA
1998	Tucson	PCL	89.3	102	68	18	28	42	6.85	3	7	10.28	1.81	2.82	4.23	0.75	6.04
1998	Charlott	Int	47.0	48	24	5	12	21	4.60	2	3	9.19	0.96	2.30	4.02	0.88	4.26
1999	Calgary	PCL	166.0	170	88	9	70	85	4.77	7	11	9.22	0.49	3.80	4.61	0.61	4.42
2000	Calgary	PCL	41.7	42	20	5	17	15	4.32	2	3	9.07	1.08	3.67	3.24	0.44	4.91
2000	Florida	NL	120.7	129	69	18	43	42	5.15	5	8	9.62	1.34	3.21	3.13	0.49	5.32

Reid Cornelius's right arm was a flamethrower when he was originally drafted by the Expos. Twelve years later, after multiple trips to the disabled list and an elbow surgery, it's more like a Zippo in need of new flint. He took Alex Fernandez's rotation spot in May and supplied 125 innings of replacement-level pitching. Given the Marlins' rising young arms, he can look forward to the late spring foliage in Calgary.

Vic Darensbourg   Throws L   Age 30

YEAR	TEAM	LGE	IP	H	ER	HR	BB	K	ERA	W	L	H/9	HR/9	BB/9	K/9	KW	PERA
1998	Florida	NL	67.7	52	30	6	28	60	3.99	4	4	6.92	0.80	3.72	7.98	1.07	3.40
1999	Florida	NL	34.0	47	33	3	18	13	8.74	1	3	12.44	0.79	4.76	3.44	0.36	7.02
2000	Florida	NL	60.0	60	31	7	24	49	4.65	3	4	9.00	1.05	3.60	7.35	1.02	4.79

Vic Darensbourg is similar to Billy Wagner in that he's a short, hard-throwing left-handed reliever. The similarities end there. We typically don't endorse the LaRussa School of Bullpen Management and its strict late-game platoon matchups, but that's the only way Darensbourg is effective—his career OPS is 223 points lower against left-handed hitters than righties. Since he was able to keep his roster spot after his wretched 1999 season, I suspect that he'll be able to do the same next year, too.

Ryan Dempster   Throws R   Age 24

YEAR	TEAM	LGE	IP	H	ER	HR	BB	K	ERA	W	L	H/9	HR/9	BB/9	K/9	KW	PERA
1998	Portland	Eas	41.3	36	25	11	15	20	5.44	2	3	7.84	2.40	3.27	4.35	0.67	5.40
1998	Florida	NL	52.7	70	47	7	36	28	8.03	1	5	11.96	1.20	6.15	4.78	0.39	7.77
1998	Charlott	Int	32.0	32	13	4	11	18	3.66	2	2	9.00	1.13	3.09	5.06	0.82	4.70
1999	Calgary	PCL	29.7	28	14	5	9	20	4.25	1	2	8.49	1.52	2.73	6.07	1.11	4.61
1999	Florida	NL	143.3	143	73	21	81	106	4.58	7	9	8.98	1.32	5.09	6.66	0.65	5.69
2000	Florida	NL	219.3	208	99	29	83	174	4.06	12	12	8.53	1.19	3.41	7.14	1.05	4.60

The youngest survivor of the 1998 Leyland Massacre, Ryan Dempster has been able to put the atrocities he witnessed and suffered behind him and is climbing into the upper echelon of major-league starters. A strenuous off-season regimen added a few mph to Dempster's low-90s four-seam fastball, along with the strength and stamina to maintain his stuff deeper into games. He also improved his command of his fastball and vicious slider, slicing his walk rate by nearly two a game. While Felipe Alou likens Dempster to Curt Schilling, let's hope that we won't be seeing any similarities between his workloads and those meted out by Terry Francona.

Alex Fernandez   Throws R   Age 31

YEAR	TEAM	LGE	IP	H	ER	HR	BB	K	ERA	W	L	H/9	HR/9	BB/9	K/9	KW	PERA
1999	Florida	NL	136.0	129	57	10	36	77	3.77	8	7	8.54	0.66	2.38	5.10	1.07	3.65
2000	Florida	NL	50.3	56	24	7	14	22	4.29	3	3	10.01	1.25	2.50	3.93	0.79	5.15

After being handled with kid gloves in 1999, it appeared that Alex Fernandez might make it all the way back, especially after his velocity returned to its pre-injury level in April 2000. However, during a shortsighted 121-pitch outing, he strained a ligament in his elbow trying to compensate for his still-painful shoulder. Arthroscopic surgery to tighten his shoulder capsule followed and he missed the rest of the season. Fernandez hopes to be ready to pitch again by May or June, but there are smarter bets than wagering he will regain his old form. Like, oh, Traci Lords winning an Oscar.

Geoff Goetz — Throws L — Age 22

YEAR	TEAM	LGE	IP	H	ER	HR	BB	K	ERA	W	L	H/9	HR/9	BB/9	K/9	KW	PERA
1998	Columbia	SAL	69.7	68	51	6	48	32	6.59	2	6	8.78	0.78	6.20	4.13	0.33	5.46
1998	KaneCnty	Mid	37.7	47	28	10	30	18	6.69	1	3	11.23	2.39	7.17	4.30	0.30	9.03
1999	KaneCnty	Mid	46.7	54	32	8	27	23	6.17	1	4	10.41	1.54	5.21	4.44	0.43	6.84
2000	Brevard	Fla	60.3	43	23	3	45	36	3.43	4	3	6.41	0.45	6.71	5.37	0.40	3.95
2000	Portland	Eas	21.0	28	17	5	11	14	7.29	0	2	12.00	2.14	4.71	6.00	0.64	8.16

Thanks to the Marlins' willingness to think outside the box, Geoff Goetz is back on the prospect map. He had been plagued by shoulder tendinitis since being the first high-school pitcher selected in the June 1997 draft, so instead of starting, the Marlins limited him to 55 pitches in relief every third day. Goetz stayed pain-free and led the Florida State League in ERA before being promoted to Portland. The plan is to move him back into the rotation; with his injury history and somewhat violent delivery, I think he'll eventually settle in the bullpen.

Jason Grilli — Throws R — Age 24

YEAR	TEAM	LGE	IP	H	ER	HR	BB	K	ERA	W	L	H/9	HR/9	BB/9	K/9	KW	PERA
1998	Shrevprt	Tex	115.0	111	67	17	43	66	5.24	5	8	8.69	1.33	3.37	5.17	0.77	4.82
1998	Fresno	PCL	40.3	47	28	7	18	26	6.25	1	3	10.49	1.56	4.02	5.80	0.72	6.40
1999	Fresno	PCL	97.3	115	64	23	40	52	5.92	3	8	10.63	2.13	3.70	4.81	0.65	6.95
1999	Calgary	PCL	40.3	50	40	6	22	18	8.93	1	3	11.16	1.34	4.91	4.02	0.41	6.90
2000	Calgary	PCL	41.0	54	31	4	20	15	6.80	1	4	11.85	0.88	4.39	3.29	0.38	6.65

The definition of a lost season. Jason Grilli blew an opportunity to win a job in spring training and pitched poorly at Calgary before being shut down in late May with a bone spur in his elbow. While his raw stuff is major-league caliber, he still has a tendency to overthrow and lacks command of his off-speed pitches. Grilli has never had extended stretches of dominance in the minors (or even at Seton Hall, for that matter), and it's reaching the point where results may be a better indicator than potential.

Gary Knotts — Throws R — Age 24

YEAR	TEAM	LGE	IP	H	ER	HR	BB	K	ERA	W	L	H/9	HR/9	BB/9	K/9	KW	PERA
1998	KaneCnty	Mid	141.3	155	109	27	81	75	6.94	4	12	9.87	1.72	5.16	4.78	0.46	6.66
1999	Brevard	Fla	85.0	102	65	17	38	38	6.88	2	7	10.80	1.80	4.02	4.02	0.50	6.83
1999	Portland	Eas	76.3	81	43	16	33	40	5.07	3	5	9.55	1.89	3.89	4.72	0.61	6.14
2000	Portland	Eas	145.3	164	114	25	67	72	7.06	4	12	10.16	1.55	4.15	4.46	0.54	6.24

He put the "any publicity is good publicity" adage to the test in spring training when, after walking seven batters in two innings, he announced that he wasn't concerned since it was only March. Too bad that Boles had ripped into the team for ignoring results just a few days earlier. Knotts was soon spotted heading out of camp towards the local Greyhound station. A durable hurler with average stuff, he has probably already had his 15 minutes of fame in the Marlins' organization.

Brandon Leese — Throws R — Age 25

YEAR	TEAM	LGE	IP	H	ER	HR	BB	K	ERA	W	L	H/9	HR/9	BB/9	K/9	KW	PERA
1998	Brevard	Fla	44.3	61	38	7	9	17	7.71	1	4	12.38	1.42	1.83	3.45	0.94	6.43
1998	Portland	Eas	118.0	137	76	21	38	57	5.80	4	9	10.45	1.60	2.90	4.35	0.75	5.94
1999	Portland	Eas	77.0	108	67	11	20	32	7.83	2	7	12.62	1.29	2.34	3.74	0.80	6.66
2000	Portland	Eas	160.7	181	96	32	53	58	5.38	6	12	10.14	1.79	2.97	3.25	0.55	6.00

Brandon Leese figured out how to retire Eastern League batters in his third go'round with the Sea Dogs. He's a grinder with average to below-average stuff but can succeed when he has command of all four of his pitches. That's really just a long-winded way of saying that once he dons a Calgary uniform this year, he can officially be referred to as a "Triple-A pitcher."

Braden Looper — Throws R — Age 26

YEAR	TEAM	LGE	IP	H	ER	HR	BB	K	ERA	W	L	H/9	HR/9	BB/9	K/9	KW	PERA
1998	Memphis	PCL	38.7	41	16	4	14	30	3.72	2	2	9.54	0.93	3.26	6.98	1.07	4.84
1999	Florida	NL	80.7	91	40	7	27	42	4.46	4	5	10.15	0.78	3.01	4.69	0.78	4.96
2000	Florida	NL	65.3	68	38	3	31	24	5.23	3	4	9.37	0.41	4.27	3.31	0.39	4.62

(Braden Looper *continued*)

Questions about his durability have been replaced by worries about his inability to get hitters out—particularly left-handed hitters, who hammered him at a .359/.469/.538 clip. Looper's lack of an effective secondary pitch enables batters to sit on his hard sinking two-seamer and led to a precipitous drop in his strikeout rate. Unless Looper can develop a consistent breaking pitch, his name will be added to the growing list of college closers who flopped in the majors.

Dan Miceli — Throws R — Age 30

YEAR	TEAM	LGE	IP	H	ER	HR	BB	K	ERA	W	L	H/9	HR/9	BB/9	K/9	KW	PERA
1998	San Dieg	NL	69.0	64	30	7	26	57	3.91	4	4	8.35	0.91	3.39	7.43	1.10	4.19
1999	San Dieg	NL	66.3	65	39	8	32	50	5.29	3	4	8.82	1.09	4.34	6.78	0.78	5.02
2000	Florida	NL	47.0	44	22	4	15	33	4.21	2	3	8.43	0.77	2.87	6.32	1.10	3.87

Dan Miceli's numbers were skewed by a few poor outings before he gave in to forearm inflammation and missed two months of the campaign. "The Godfather" is armed with a full complement of airborne weaponry and is a handy guy to have around, capable of filling any bullpen role, including closing. He's also ultra-intense and an expert in Muay Thai fighting; it would be scary to see somebody charge the mound with Miceli atop it.

Vladimir Nunez — Throws R — Age 26

YEAR	TEAM	LGE	IP	H	ER	HR	BB	K	ERA	W	L	H/9	HR/9	BB/9	K/9	KW	PERA
1998	Tucson	PCL	91.7	97	55	13	37	54	5.40	4	6	9.52	1.28	3.63	5.30	0.73	5.36
1999	Arizona	NL	33.3	28	13	2	16	24	3.51	2	2	7.56	0.54	4.32	6.48	0.75	3.72
1999	Florida	NL	72.3	64	45	9	29	49	5.60	3	5	7.96	1.12	3.61	6.10	0.84	4.26
2000	Florida	NL	66.7	85	59	12	29	37	7.97	1	6	11.48	1.62	3.92	5.00	0.64	6.99
2000	Calgary	PCL	86.0	91	42	10	36	64	4.40	5	5	9.52	1.05	3.77	6.70	0.89	5.18

It's high time to make a decision. While Vladimir Nunez's only major-league success has been in relief, he desperately wants to start. He likes to vary his arm angles and to pitch backwards like his idol, Orlando Hernandez, but the Marlins feel he doesn't need to rely on deception and would improve his command if he threw from a consistent arm slot. Nunez will be given another audition for the rotation in spring training, but I expect him to wind up in the bullpen, where he can junk his inconsistent soft stuff and better maintain his focus.

Brad Penny — Throws R — Age 23

YEAR	TEAM	LGE	IP	H	ER	HR	BB	K	ERA	W	L	H/9	HR/9	BB/9	K/9	KW	PERA
1998	High Des	Cal	152.3	152	79	24	36	108	4.67	7	10	8.98	1.42	2.13	6.38	1.50	4.57
1999	El Paso	Tex	85.7	110	56	10	25	64	5.88	3	7	11.56	1.05	2.63	6.72	1.28	5.91
1999	Portland	Eas	30.0	30	17	4	14	22	5.10	1	2	9.00	1.20	4.20	6.60	0.79	5.21
2000	Florida	NL	116.3	117	66	13	51	67	5.11	5	8	9.05	1.01	3.95	5.18	0.66	4.93

Brad Penny surprised the Marlins by dominating the Grapefruit League, earning a spot in the rotation a year earlier than anticipated. He pitched well before a strained shoulder turned down his heat and ultimately landed him on the disabled list. When he returned, he had a new grip on his fastball that improved his control and helped him post a 3.04 ERA the remainder of the season. Penny has the complete package to become a #1 starter if he can negotiate the injury gauntlet while his body matures.

Bobby Rodgers — Throws R — Age 26

YEAR	TEAM	LGE	IP	H	ER	HR	BB	K	ERA	W	L	H/9	HR/9	BB/9	K/9	KW	PERA
1998	Brevard	Fla	32.3	36	23	5	10	19	6.40	1	3	10.02	1.39	2.78	5.29	0.95	5.46
1998	Portland	Eas	76.0	70	43	11	30	42	5.09	3	5	8.29	1.30	3.55	4.97	0.70	4.63
1999	Portland	Eas	113.0	150	93	19	74	64	7.41	3	10	11.95	1.51	5.89	5.10	0.43	7.97
2000	Portland	Eas	50.0	41	29	5	36	34	5.22	2	4	7.38	0.90	6.48	6.12	0.47	4.88

Like most of the Marlins' mound prospects, Bobby Rodgers is a hard thrower with command problems. An advantage that such a pitcher enjoys is that if he bombs as a starter, he is more likely than a soft-tosser to blossom in a relief role. With his high strikeout rate and ability to keep the ball in the yard, Rodgers was a prime candidate to make the transition. His breakout season in relief at Portland means he should be part of a fairly wide-open spring competition for bullpen jobs.

Jesus Sanchez — Throws L — Age 26

YEAR	TEAM	LGE	IP	H	ER	HR	BB	K	ERA	W	L	H/9	HR/9	BB/9	K/9	KW	PERA
1998	Florida	NL	165.3	175	99	20	86	111	5.39	6	12	9.53	1.09	4.68	6.04	0.65	5.60
1999	Florida	NL	75.0	83	50	16	52	52	6.00	2	6	9.96	1.92	6.24	6.24	0.50	7.39
2000	Florida	NL	176.3	191	112	31	65	102	5.72	7	13	9.75	1.58	3.32	5.21	0.78	5.69

As in real estate, location is everything for Jesus Sanchez. He's blessed with a live fastball and an excellent change-up, but even Pro Player Stadium can't hold the mortar shots launched when he leaves pitches up and over the plate. Since Sanchez is the lone southpaw on the starting staff and a nifty pinch-runner, Boles is hoping that he can iron out his control problems. Although there is little reason for such optimism, I think he'll eventually succeed. Of course, I had the same hunch about New Coke.

Chuck Smith — Throws R — Age 31

YEAR	TEAM	LGE	IP	H	ER	HR	BB	K	ERA	W	L	H/9	HR/9	BB/9	K/9	KW	PERA
1999	Oklahoma	PCL	79.7	70	34	9	33	48	3.84	5	4	7.91	1.02	3.73	5.42	0.73	4.19
2000	Oklahoma	PCL	62.3	71	32	4	42	49	4.62	3	4	10.25	0.58	6.06	7.07	0.58	6.05
2000	Florida	NL	119.0	110	51	6	46	98	3.86	7	6	8.32	0.45	3.48	7.41	1.07	3.75

Smith was stolen from the Rangers in a three-way deal in early June. He pitches with a chip on his shoulder because he feels he labored nearly ten years in the bushes because of his height and skin color. That may be true, but he also never consistently threw his wide array of pitches for strikes until 1999. Smith enters the season penciled into the Marlins' rotation; if he keeps his stuff in the strike zone, there's no reason he can't continue to be effective.

Joe Strong — Throws R — Age 38

YEAR	TEAM	LGE	IP	H	ER	HR	BB	K	ERA	W	L	H/9	HR/9	BB/9	K/9	KW	PERA
1999	Orlando	Sou	34.0	42	30	10	21	19	7.94	1	3	11.12	2.65	5.56	5.03	0.45	8.53
2000	Calgary	PCL	43.0	41	18	1	19	22	3.77	3	2	8.58	0.21	3.98	4.60	0.58	3.84
2000	Florida	NL	19.3	26	15	3	10	15	6.98	0	2	12.10	1.40	4.66	6.98	0.75	7.45

Mighty Joe's 16-year trek to the majors makes Smith's route look positively direct. Joe Strong isn't listed here because of his performance and certainly not for his potential now that he's been outrighted to Calgary. Anybody who perseveres as long as he did to reach his dream deserves a tip of the cap. Way to go, Joe.

Claudio Vargas — Throws R — Age 22

YEAR	TEAM	LGE	IP	H	ER	HR	BB	K	ERA	W	L	H/9	HR/9	BB/9	K/9	KW	PERA
1999	KaneCnty	Mid	91.7	101	55	17	46	47	5.40	4	6	9.92	1.67	4.52	4.61	0.51	6.37
2000	Brevard	Fla	130.3	137	91	26	55	84	6.28	4	10	9.46	1.80	3.80	5.80	0.76	5.94

The Marlins thought so highly of Claudio Vargas's physical abilities that they added him to their 40-man roster after the 1999 season despite his having thrown only ten innings above low-A ball. Vargas repaid that confidence with a strong season at Brevard County, improving his mental approach to pitching and his numbers across the board. Vargas hasn't been hyped as much as the other arms in the farm system, but only Beckett and Anderson have higher ceilings.

Support-Neutral Statistics — FLORIDA MARLINS — Park Effect: -16.3%

PITCHER	GS	IP	R	SNW	SNL	SNPCT	W	L	RA	APW	SNVA	SNWAR
A.J. Burnett	13	82.7	46	4.4	4.5	.492	3	7	5.01	-0.3	-0.1	0.6
Reid Cornelius	21	121.0	71	6.4	7.8	.449	3	10	5.28	-0.7	-0.7	0.3
Ryan Dempster	33	226.3	102	13.4	10.7	.556	14	10	4.06	1.6	1.3	3.2
Alex Fernandez	8	52.3	25	2.4	3.0	.446	4	4	4.30	0.2	-0.2	0.1
Jason Grilli	1	6.7	4	0.2	0.5	.246	1	0	5.40	-0.0	-0.1	-0.1
Vladimir Nunez	12	60.3	59	1.7	7.1	.189	0	6	8.80	-2.7	-2.7	-2.1
Brad Penny	22	118.0	67	6.9	7.2	.491	8	7	5.11	-0.5	-0.2	0.9
Jesus Sanchez	32	182.0	118	8.9	13.3	.400	9	12	5.84	-2.2	-2.1	-0.6
Chuck Smith	19	122.7	53	8.0	5.1	.611	6	6	3.89	1.1	1.3	2.4
TOTALS	161	972.0	545	52.3	59.4	.468	48	62	5.05	-3.4	-3.5	4.8

Despite being only the 22nd-best rotation in the majors, the 2000 Marlins' starters turned in a performance about which there is much to like. Ryan Dempster had a terrific, if unsung, sophomore season, and Chuck Smith had a terrific, if unsung, rookie season. (I'll spare Rangers GM Doug Melvin embarrassment by not mentioning where *both* of those pitchers started.) The other two important youngsters, A.J. Burnett and Brad Penny, had solid seasons and can be expected to improve.

If it weren't for Vladimir Nunez's dismal year—he was the second-worst starter in the majors—the Marlins' rotation would have been close to average. It seems reasonable to expect that a rotation featuring a horrible individual performance would improve the next year, the theory being that the horrible starter would be gone, or at least unlikely to repeat his putrid year. A check of the numbers from past seasons confirms this hypothesis. There have been 17 pitchers who were two or more wins below replacement level in a season since 1979. Their teams' rotations improved the next season by an average of 2.8 wins according to Support-Neutral Value Added, going from an average SNVA of –5.6 to –2.8.

For a quick explanation of SN stats, see page 7.

Reliever Evaluation Tools

PITCHER	G	IP	R	ARA	APR	IRNR/G	EIRS/G	IRP	BRS	RRA	ARP
Antonio Alfonseca	66	69.0	31	4.45	5.7	0.08	0.02	0.2	1.1	4.61	4.5
Armando Almanza	69	47.3	31	6.49	-6.8	0.93	0.34	-3.6	-3.0	6.58	-7.3
Manny Aybar	21	27.3	8	2.90	7.0	0.38	0.23	0.8	0.7	2.58	7.9
Ricky Bones	56	77.3	43	5.51	-2.7	0.73	0.22	-3.6	-3.4	5.11	0.8
Reid Cornelius	1	4.0	3	7.43	-1.0	0.00	0.00	0.0	0.0	8.07	-1.3
Vic Darensbourg	56	62.0	32	5.12	0.6	0.73	0.25	2.2	-0.9	5.07	0.9
Braden Looper	73	67.3	41	6.03	-6.3	0.77	0.23	-4.9	-0.3	6.99	-13.4
Ron Mahay	18	25.3	17	6.65	-4.1	0.44	0.19	0.3	0.4	6.83	-4.6
Dan Miceli	45	48.7	23	4.68	2.8	0.31	0.08	2.9	1.6	4.37	4.5
Vladimir Nunez	5	8.0	4	4.96	0.2	0.00	0.00	0.0	-0.9	3.66	1.4
Brad Penny	1	1.7	3	17.84	-2.3	0.00	0.00	0.0	0.2	20.15	-2.8
Joe Strong	18	19.7	16	8.06	-6.3	1.06	0.31	-2.5	-0.1	9.72	-9.9
TOTALS	429	457.7	252	5.46	-13.2	0.60	0.20			5.58	-19.3

For a quick guide to RET, see page 10.

Houston Astros

How much difference can a ballpark make? That's what the Houston Astros had to be asking themselves all winter. Well on their way to establishing a mini-dynasty atop the NL Central after three straight division titles, the Astros' greatest concern a year ago was figuring out how to dispel their awful run of luck in the playoffs. There were no thoughts of a 90-loss season, no time spent contemplating how to finish ahead of the Brewers for third place. On the contrary, the Astros had reason to be more optimistic than ever, with the opening of Enron Field heralding an era of increased revenues and increased payroll for a team that had already established itself as one of baseball's elite despite a payroll only marginally above average.

A year later, Astros fans can be forgiven for pining for the Astrodome, exploding scoreboards, and rainbow-colored uniforms. For more than 30 years, the Astrodome provided one of the most underappreciated home-field advantages in sports. With its spacious dimensions and tough hitting background, it offered pitchers of all stripes the opportunity to hone their craft in confidence, knowing that the ballpark would forgive the occasional 380-foot mistake. The Astros would not have won the NL West in 1986 without Mike Scott, and Mike Scott would never have been Mike Scott without the Astrodome. Darryl Kile was nurtured by the Astrodome for seven years, then plunged into the abyss the moment he left. Jose Lima couldn't stick with the Tigers—this after they had given up 1,100 runs in 1996—but became a 20-game winner inside the Astrodome.

Without their security blanket, the Astros gave up 944 runs last season, a 269-run jump from their 1999 total. The last team to see such a huge increase from one (non-strike) season to the next was the 1915 Athletics, who struggled when Connie Mack sold off all the stars from his 1914 World Series team.

After earning a deserved reputation as one of the best-run organizations in baseball, it seems a cruel twist of fate that the Astros would be hobbled by a single decision as seemingly minor and noncontroversial as establishing the dimensions of their new ballpark. Yet that is exactly the conventional wisdom on why the Astros collapsed.

Is that fair? Table 1 breaks down the Astros' scoring.

The Astros' pitchers were certainly affected by Enron Field, but no more than their opponents were. The team as a whole had a +5 run differential at home, compared to –11 on the road; the Astros' overall home-field advantage was six games, an average number.

What really stands out, though, is that despite finishing 72–90, the Astros were outscored by just six runs all season, in part due to their major-league-worst 15–31 record in one-run games. The Pythagorean method projects that the Astros should have won 80.5 games; no NL team has underperformed so badly since the 1997 Astros missed by 10.1 wins (and still won the division). The Astros were really a .500 team in sheep's clothing, and their failure to reach 81 wins had nothing to do with the ballpark. Rather, it was due to bad luck and a god-awful bullpen, felled by an injury to Billy Wagner, the best closer in baseball.

That isn't to say that Enron Field can be held entirely blameless for the implosion of what was one of the best pitching staffs in baseball. But the impact of Enron Field could have been dampened if the Astros had used some foresight in designing their pitching staff for 2000.

Not all pitchers are created alike, and some pitchers are going to be less affected by ballparks than others. In particular, fly-ball pitchers are more likely to surrender drives that would have been warning-track blasts in the Astrodome but that became home runs at Enron Field. A pitching staff that keeps the ball down is therefore particularly suited for Enron and its hitters' park brethren.

In 1999, the Astros actually had the most ground-ball-oriented staff in the NL (their 1.55 G/F ratio was the highest in the league). This was a staff ideally suited for the new stadium... until the Astros started to tinker.

Faced with Mike Hampton's impending free agency, the Astros elected to ship him to the Mets, receiving Octavio Dotel in return, while re-upping Jose Lima to a 3-year contract.

Astros Prospectus

2000 record: 72–90; Fourth place, NL Central
Pythagenport W/L: 81–81
Runs Scored: 938 (2nd in NL)
Runs Allowed: 944 (16th in NL)
Team EqA: .271 (2nd in NL)
2000 Batters' Age: 29.2 (8th youngest in NL)
2000 Pitchers' Age: 27.5 (6th youngest in NL)
Ballpark: Enron Field; excellent hitters' park; Park Factor of 1.072
2000: They were probably the biggest disappointment in baseball, as the pitching collapsed, even accounting for the new park.
2001: Despite their offseason moves, they'll move back into the NL Central race.

Table 1: Astros Home-Road Split—2001

	Home	Rank	Away	Rank	Total	Rank
Runs Scored	505	2nd	433	4th	938	2nd
Runs Allowed	500	15th	444	12th	944	16th

Hampton is the second-most ground-ball-oriented pitcher in baseball while Dotel is the exact opposite: his 0.51 G/F ratio was the lowest in the major leagues in 2000 (minimum: 100 innings). Had the Astros made more of an effort to keep Hampton (who, in the Astros' defense, had already indicated he wanted to test free agency) and instead traded the fly-ball-chucking Lima, they might not have had the second-lowest G/F ratio in the NL in 2000, and they certainly would have avoided Lima's record-setting pyrotechnics.

That's all water under the bridge now. The Astros may not have had Hampton—or Carl Everett—for the 2000 season, but they still wouldn't have made a dent in the playoff race even if they had kept both of them. Hampton was 2.3 wins above average according to SNVA, and Lima was his mirror image (-2.3 SNVA). If they had kept Hampton and traded Lima, they would have picked up 4.6 wins; figuring Everett to be worth, at most, four to five wins over the guys who replaced him (Lance Berkman and Daryle Ward, no slouches), that means the Astros would have won maybe nine more games. Even if you replace Hampton on the Mets with a replacement-level pitcher, there's no way you can work the math to give the Astros a shot at the playoffs.

This winter, the Astros expressed interest in re-signing Hampton before he signed with the Rockies. Hampton does not seem to hold a grudge against the team for moving him. What does appear to have hurt the Astros' chances is that Hampton wants nothing to do with manager Larry Dierker. Indeed, only slightly less compelling a story than the Astros' collapse on the field was the sudden bickering in the clubhouse and the general disenchantment that many of the Astros' veterans, notably Jeff Bagwell, had with their manager.

On the surface, this represents an astonishing change in attitude toward a man who had won almost universal praise since coming down from the broadcast booth to lead the Astros to three straight division crowns. (If imitation is the sincerest form of flattery, the hirings of Buck Martinez and Bob Brenly tell you what the rest of baseball thinks of Larry Dierker.) In 2000, the Astros were pointing fingers at the manager they had rallied behind after he underwent brain surgery just a year before. Larry Dierker isn't a hard-ass who rubbed his players the wrong way—if anything, he may be too nice for his own good. What in the name of Chuck Tanner is going on here?

Bill James has explored the subject of managers in a lot more depth than we can here, and one of the principles he presented is that all managers appear to lose their effectiveness the longer they stay on the job with the same team. James's explanation for this tendency was that "if a manager is successful, he changes the needs of the organization. By so doing, he often makes himself obsolete." When Larry Dierker was hired, the Astros needed a calming hand, a laid-back attitude after several years of Terry Collins's boot camp. But what has happened since Dierker took the job is that the pendulum has swung the other way: players not faced with firm expectations will cease to expect maximum effort from themselves, and a clubhouse without firm rules from above will tend to rule itself. It appears that veterans like Bagwell, seeing little inclination from their manager to establish order and discipline on the team, have been forced to take that duty upon themselves.

When Mitch Meluskey, a rookie, popped Matt Mieske in the face over a squabble during batting practice in June and wasn't seriously disciplined, Dierker's control over his team became that much more tenuous. He's been brought back for another year but hardly given a vote of confidence, and the possibility remains that he could become a lame-duck manager, making tactical decisions on the field but having no influence on his players once the game is over.

We've been big supporters of Dierker throughout his tenure, making these developments more than a little disturbing for us. Just as disturbing, though, is that Dierker's golden touch with his pitching staff left him last year, and it wasn't just because of Enron Field. In his first three seasons as manager, Dierker was able to get more innings from his starting pitchers than almost any manager in baseball, while still keeping their pitch counts among baseball's lowest. According to the PAP data used in the last two editions of *Baseball Prospectus,* the Astros' starters' pitch counts ranked just sixth and eighth in the NL in 1998 and 1999, despite their ranking second in the league in innings thrown.

In 2000, Dierker continued to get a lot of innings from his starters...but he was also forcing them to work harder than ever, as the Astros ranked 2nd in the NL in PAP^3. (For more on PAP^3, see page 491.) For years, we had wondered how to apportion the success of the Astros pitchers between Dierker and pitching coach Vern Ruhle, and a look at the PAP data from before and after Ruhle got the axe on June 23 gives us an answer in Table 2.

The Astros' rotation was worked more than twice as hard after Ruhle's firing, which is a bad, bad sign for fans hoping that Dierker's magic touch might return this season: it looks like the magic touch wasn't his after all. In particular, the handling of Scott Elarton, the Astros' best young starter, borders on the criminal; see Table 3.

Extrapolated over a full season, Elarton's second-half workload would have ranked third in all of baseball, behind only Livan Hernandez and Randy Johnson. So the Astros have a manager who isn't respected by his players and whose greatest accomplishment appears to be the work of his

Table 2: Astros Pitchers Before and After Ruhle's Firing

	GS	PAP	PAP/S	PAP³/S	I	II	III	IV	V
Through 6/22	71	556	7.8	2047	35	20	12	3	1
6/23 onward	91	1285	14.1	4470	39	16	25	9	2

Table 3: Scott Elarton Before and After Ruhle's Firing

	GS	PAP	PAP/S	PAP³/S	I	II	III	IV	V
Through 6/22	12	52	4.3	830	8	2	2	0	0
6/23 onward	18	487	27.1	9907	3	3	7	3	2

pitching coach—who now works for the Phillies. Is there any reason for optimism here?

Actually, there is. The Astros still have Gerry Hunsicker, the most underrated GM in the game, and they are deeper, position for position, than any team in baseball. Even after giving away Roger Cedeno in an abysmal trade for some middle-relief help, they have four starting outfielders (Moises Alou, Richard Hidalgo, Lance Berkman, and Daryle Ward). They have two future Hall of Famers on the right side of their infield (Jeff Bagwell and Craig Biggio) and five reasonable options for the left side (Bill Spiers, Julio Lugo, Adam Everett, Keith Ginter, and Morgan Ensberg).

But you can't field 12 men, so the Astros need to whittle that lineup down and convert the excess into the pitching depth that they really need, an idea they applied badly by trading Cedeno and Meluskey for a couple of relievers. Not only was that a terrible decision for the team on the field, but it ran counter to the Astros' need, as a middle-market team, to hold on to as many players with less than four years' service time as possible.

There are no easy choices when you're a mid-market team trying to survive in a large-market world. But while every choice may be difficult, some are more sensible than others. The Astros deserve a better fate than to be remembered as the perennial also-ran of the National League, and here's hoping they make the right decisions and that their new collection of stars forges a better destiny than the previous one did.

HITTERS (BA: .270, OBP: .340, SLG: .440, EqA: .260)

Moises Alou   OF   Bats R   Age 34

YEAR	TEAM	LGE	AB	H	DB	TP	HR	BB	SO	R	RBI	SB	CS	OUT	BA	OBP	SLG	EQA	EQR	DEFENSE
1998	Houston	NL	598	189	34	4	41	82	81	108	126	10	3	412	.316	.403	.592	.320	120	140-LF -3
2000	Houston	NL	450	151	25	2	27	44	42	75	100	3	3	302	.336	.397	.580	.314	83	97-RF -8
2001	Houston	NL	317	109	19	1	20	42	53	67	83	3	1	209	.344	.421	.599	.324	62	

Is he the Comeback Player of the Decade? After missing all of 1999 with a torn ACL, Moises Alou not only came back strong at age 34, he set career highs in all three major averages. This after a first comeback from breaking his foot so badly in 1993 that the video is still used by anorexics and hospital personnel to induce vomiting. Durability may always be an issue for him, and the repeated injuries have reduced his range to a fraction of what it once was. Regardless of whether the Astros trade him to make room for the young'uns, Alou should be on an AL team by 2002 and a full-time DH until Bud Selig takes his job away.

Jeff Bagwell   1B   Bats R   Age 33

YEAR	TEAM	LGE	AB	H	DB	TP	HR	BB	SO	R	RBI	SB	CS	OUT	BA	OBP	SLG	EQA	EQR	DEFENSE
1998	Houston	NL	555	170	27	1	38	107	84	128	114	18	7	392	.306	.424	.564	.323	116	147-1B 5
1999	Houston	NL	566	167	29	0	42	139	120	134	117	23	10	409	.295	.442	.569	.331	129	156-1B 2
2000	Houston	NL	585	170	30	1	43	96	109	137	116	8	6	421	.291	.402	.566	.312	114	153-1B 7
2001	Houston	NL	539	171	25	0	43	115	106	133	147	13	5	373	.317	.437	.603	.330	117	

Jeff Bagwell is one of the few players in baseball who could have an MVP season without having a year any better than his established norm. As his DTs show, he actually had a bit of an off year, a fact hidden by Enron Field. Bagwell should bounce back this year. That said, I still think the Astros have to move him, because he's getting to the overpaid portion of his career, and the Astros have so many options to replace him. Only two players since 1960 have scored at least 500 runs over a four-year span: Bagwell (1997–2000) and Craig Biggio (1995–98).

Glen Barker — CF — Bats B — Age 30

YEAR	TEAM	LGE	AB	H	DB	TP	HR	BB	SO	R	RBI	SB	CS	OUT	BA	OBP	SLG	EQA	EQR	DEFENSE	
1998	Jacksnvl	Sou	457	105	24	3	4	33	138	60	35	14	4	356	.230	.285	.322	.206	34	109-CF	18
1999	Houston	NL	74	21	0	0	2	9	18	19	12	13	6	59	.284	.369	.365	.258	10	23-CF	1
2000	New Orln	PCL	108	26	2	0	2	7	13	10	8	7	2	84	.241	.287	.315	.209	8	25-CF	1
2000	Houston	NL	67	14	1	1	2	6	22	16	5	8	6	59	.209	.282	.343	.208	6	23-CF	2
2001	Houston	NL	158	39	5	1	3	16	40	24	15	13	6	125	.247	.316	.348	.225	15		

He's got a tough enough role as the fifth outfielder/pinch runner/desperation pinch hitter, and it's made worse by backing up the deepest outfield in baseball. Glen Barker's value has less to do with his skills than the overall needs of his team, which means he's going to start bouncing around the majors, hoping to parlay his fresh legs and reliable glove into a few more days at the major-league minimum. We should all be so lucky.

Lance Berkman — OF — Bats B — Age 25

YEAR	TEAM	LGE	AB	H	DB	TP	HR	BB	SO	R	RBI	SB	CS	OUT	BA	OBP	SLG	EQA	EQR	DEFENSE	
1998	Jackson	Tex	428	106	19	1	17	65	90	57	60	3	2	324	.248	.350	.416	.259	55	114-LF	0
1999	New Orln	PCL	227	65	11	0	8	32	45	32	40	5	1	163	.286	.375	.441	.278	33	53-LF	1
1999	Houston	NL	94	22	2	0	4	11	20	9	14	4	1	73	.234	.314	.383	.239	10	23-LF	-1
2000	New Orln	PCL	114	33	2	1	6	25	20	14	21	3	3	84	.289	.420	.482	.300	21	25-LF	1
2000	Houston	NL	351	98	23	1	20	49	68	69	60	5	2	255	.279	.369	.521	.291	58	83-RF	-3
2001	Houston	NL	407	127	22	2	23	67	84	89	93	10	2	282	.312	.409	.545	.309	75		

It's hard to say where Lance Berkman would have figured into the Rookie of the Year voting if he hadn't been overqualified by a few days of service time, but consider that he had more homers and more total bases than Pat Burrell in 55 fewer at-bats. (Also consider that one overeager voter gave him a third-place vote even though he wasn't eligible.) A phenomenal hitting talent, Berkman has passed Daryle Ward on the Astros' depth chart for the moment. He's as good a bet as anyone to go Hidalgo on the league and hit 40 home runs.

Craig Biggio — 2B — Bats R — Age 35

YEAR	TEAM	LGE	AB	H	DB	TP	HR	BB	SO	R	RBI	SB	CS	OUT	BA	OBP	SLG	EQA	EQR	DEFENSE	
1998	Houston	NL	660	216	48	2	23	62	106	126	90	48	9	453	.327	.403	.511	.309	120	153-2B	-10
1999	Houston	NL	644	185	38	0	21	79	101	113	71	22	13	472	.287	.374	.444	.275	93	148-2B	6
2000	Houston	NL	376	95	13	4	7	54	68	61	31	11	2	283	.253	.366	.364	.258	48	96-2B	3
2001	Houston	NL	422	121	23	1	12	66	74	83	67	17	7	308	.287	.383	.431	.273	60		

Craig Biggio's 1999 season looked, at the time, like a small dip in a career that had reached impressive heights, but as the curtain opened on the 2000 season, that dip looked more and more like the precipice of a dizzying descent. Biggio has made a career out of accomplishing things no one thought he could do, but now, at age 35 and coming off his worst season in 10 years—*before* he tore up his knee—we'll find out if Biggio saved his greatest trick for last. I believe he'll rebound some, and so docs Wilton; expect him to return to his 1999 levels and stay there for two or three years.

Tim Bogar — SS — Bats R — Age 34

YEAR	TEAM	LGE	AB	H	DB	TP	HR	BB	SO	R	RBI	SB	CS	OUT	BA	OBP	SLG	EQA	EQR	DEFENSE	
1998	Houston	NL	158	27	5	1	1	8	34	13	9	2	1	132	.171	.220	.234	.126	4	34-SS	10
1999	Houston	NL	312	74	16	2	4	33	49	43	29	2	4	242	.237	.318	.340	.221	28	83-SS	5
2000	Houston	NL	304	60	9	2	6	31	52	30	29	1	1	245	.197	.277	.299	.191	19	79-SS	7
2001	Houston	NL	239	52	9	1	4	33	43	27	23	1	1	188	.218	.313	.314	.209	19		

When you let your incumbent shortstop go, make a blockbuster trade to pick up a grade-A shortstop prospect, then find out that said prospect isn't ready, Tim Bogar is what happens. With Julio Lugo now having proven he can hit, if not field, like a major-league shortstop, you would think Bogar's career in Houston was over. But he had a worse season than this in 1998 and was rewarded with a two-year contract, so who knows?

National League

John Buck — C — Bats R — Age 20

YEAR	TEAM	LGE	AB	H	DB	TP	HR	BB	SO	R	RBI	SB	CS	OUT	BA	OBP	SLG	EQA	EQR	DEFENSE	
1999	Auburn	NYP	239	49	8	0	4	17	51	25	22	2	1	191	.205	.263	.289	.179	13	63-C	-4
2000	Michigan	Mid	401	92	16	0	10	37	90	41	50	1	2	311	.229	.298	.344	.214	33	100-C	0
2001	Houston	NL	257	67	6	0	8	32	65	34	36	2	1	191	.261	.343	.377	.240	27		

A seventh-rounder in 1998, John Buck has developed into one of the best catching prospects in the low minors. At age 19, he showed the secondary skills (55 walks, 43 extra-base hits) of a veteran, and many observers think his defense has more potential than his offense. As with most of their hitting prospects, the Astros have the luxury of time. In an ideal world, Buck will be ready in about three years, giving the Astros all the leverage they need when Mitch Meluskey starts clamoring for a big contract.

Kevin Burns — 1B — Bats L — Age 25

YEAR	TEAM	LGE	AB	H	DB	TP	HR	BB	SO	R	RBI	SB	CS	OUT	BA	OBP	SLG	EQA	EQR	DEFENSE	
1998	Kissimme	Fla	481	108	18	2	15	52	140	50	57	4	2	375	.225	.304	.364	.225	45	124-1B	-1
1999	Jackson	Tex	356	86	16	1	9	32	80	42	42	3	2	272	.242	.309	.368	.227	33	90-1B	-6
2000	Round Ro	Tex	256	67	13	1	6	19	63	36	32	1	1	190	.262	.317	.391	.236	26	31-1B	-2
2001	Houston	NL	290	76	11	1	9	31	75	38	42	3	1	215	.262	.333	.400	.242	31		

He's a middling first-base prospect who's two years older than Aaron McNeal and not a demonstrably better player today. Burns is left-handed and will take a walk, so he can aspire to be a graduate of the Mark Sweeney school of pinch-hitting. He ought to be counting the days until he's granted minor-league free agency next winter, because he has no future in this organization.

Ken Caminiti — 3B — Bats B — Age 38

YEAR	TEAM	LGE	AB	H	DB	TP	HR	BB	SO	R	RBI	SB	CS	OUT	BA	OBP	SLG	EQA	EQR	DEFENSE	
1998	San Dieg	NL	464	121	24	0	33	69	101	91	86	6	2	345	.261	.361	.526	.289	77	116-3B	-12
1999	Houston	NL	275	77	10	1	13	42	55	43	53	5	2	200	.280	.381	.465	.284	43	71-3B	-6
2000	Houston	NL	206	58	10	0	14	38	35	38	40	3	0	148	.282	.396	.534	.307	39	49-3B	-7
2001	Texas	AL	223	58	9	0	12	41	43	40	42	2	1	166	.260	.375	.462	.278	34		

Addiction is not something to be trifled with, and addicts are not people to be held in contempt—certainly not addicts of the one mind-altering drug that our society not only legalizes, but glorifies. The thinking of much of the medical establishment today is that alcoholism is as much a genetically determined biochemical alteration of the brain as it is a behavioral defect. In short, don't look down on Ken Caminiti for falling off the wagon, because there but for the grace of God goes you. Here's hoping Caminiti conquers his demons once again. He stays in-state for 2001 after signing a deal with the Rangers to play both corners and DH. He plays well when he's able.

Roger Cedeno — OF — Bats B — Age 26

YEAR	TEAM	LGE	AB	H	DB	TP	HR	BB	SO	R	RBI	SB	CS	OUT	BA	OBP	SLG	EQA	EQR	DEFENSE	
1998	LosAngls	NL	245	63	13	1	2	26	53	36	18	8	2	184	.257	.328	.343	.233	24	54-LF	-4
1999	NY Mets	NL	456	141	22	4	4	54	94	81	34	52	16	331	.309	.386	.401	.278	67	124-RF	4
2000	Houston	NL	258	67	1	4	6	38	44	48	23	22	11	202	.260	.355	.364	.250	32	61-OF	-4
2001	Detroit	AL	356	96	11	4	7	49	73	75	41	35	12	272	.270	.358	.382	.267	50		

It was a terribly disappointing, injury-marred season for Roger Cedeno—just two doubles in 74 games?—but he still managed a .383 OBP, and the ability to get on base is still baseball's seminal skill. Cedeno is best suited for a team that has enough power from non-traditional spots to get away with a corner outfielder swatting only five home runs a year. The Tigers don't really fit that description, but they made a great deal anyway.

Raul Chavez — C — Bats R — Age 27

YEAR	TEAM	LGE	AB	H	DB	TP	HR	BB	SO	R	RBI	SB	CS	OUT	BA	OBP	SLG	EQA	EQR	DEFENSE	
1998	Tacoma	PCL	234	49	3	0	4	18	40	23	29	1	1	186	.209	.273	.274	.178	12	72-C	13
1999	Tacoma	PCL	352	84	18	1	2	23	61	32	32	1	2	270	.239	.293	.313	.200	24	91-C	4
2000	New Orln	PCL	306	69	5	0	4	26	46	25	32	2	0	237	.225	.292	.281	.193	19	84-C	-1
2000	Houston	NL	43	11	1	0	1	2	6	3	5	0	0	32	.256	.289	.349	.210	3	10-C	-1
2001	Houston	NL	312	77	6	0	5	31	52	31	32	1	0	235	.247	.315	.314	.209	23		

(Raul Chavez *continued*)

That Raul Chavez has gotten cups of coffee with three different teams in the last four years despite a complete lack of offense in the minors is testament to his formidable defensive reputation. That he has yet to play in more than 14 major-league games in a season suggests that there's only room for one Mike Matheny in baseball. Chavez is a reasonable insurance policy as a Triple-A catcher, nothing more.

Eric Cole — LF — Bats R — Age 25

YEAR	TEAM	LGE	AB	H	DB	TP	HR	BB	SO	R	RBI	SB	CS	OUT	BA	OBP	SLG	EQA	EQR	DEFENSE	
1998	Quad Cit	Mid	508	122	22	3	10	16	112	51	60	12	7	393	.240	.267	.354	.203	36	125-RF -3	
1999	Kissimme	Fla	466	104	23	3	10	28	139	44	47	10	6	368	.223	.272	.350	.205	35	83-RF -5	14-2B 1
2000	Round Ro	Tex	545	133	28	0	18	27	106	63	66	11	6	418	.244	.286	.394	.224	50	128-LF -7	
2001	Houston	NL	486	127	23	1	16	32	115	59	66	10	5	364	.261	.307	.412	.233	48		

Eric Cole was a nondescript outfielder until 2000, when his average tools across the board all improved a notch, and, more importantly, he got to play in the new bandbox at Round Rock. The Astros love his makeup, but when you take the park effects out of the equation, he projects as nothing more than a spare outfielder for a team that really doesn't need one.

Morgan Ensberg — 3B — Bats R — Age 25

YEAR	TEAM	LGE	AB	H	DB	TP	HR	BB	SO	R	RBI	SB	CS	OUT	BA	OBP	SLG	EQA	EQR	DEFENSE
1998	Auburn	NYP	206	38	8	0	4	33	55	24	20	5	2	170	.184	.305	.282	.205	16	56-3B -3
1999	Kissimme	Fla	439	89	19	1	12	51	104	52	49	8	3	353	.203	.292	.333	.212	37	114-3B -13
2000	Round Ro	Tex	490	118	19	0	21	66	116	67	60	5	6	378	.241	.336	.408	.249	58	136-3B 4
2001	Houston	NL	424	106	14	0	19	61	106	65	67	9	4	322	.250	.344	.417	.252	51	

Along with Keith Ginter, Morgan Ensberg was the first Astros hitter to be promoted directly from Double-A to the majors under Gerry Hunsicker's watch. That's a hell of an accomplishment for a guy who hit .230 and .239 in his first two pro seasons. Ensberg is just another example of how it's easier for a prospect with secondary skills to learn how to hit for average than the other way around. He's not young, and he's going to have to fight Ginter for a starting job, because the utility spot already belongs to Bill Spiers. Still, Ensberg deserves a future.

Tony Eusebio — C — Bats R — Age 34

YEAR	TEAM	LGE	AB	H	DB	TP	HR	BB	SO	R	RBI	SB	CS	OUT	BA	OBP	SLG	EQA	EQR	DEFENSE
1998	Houston	NL	185	48	7	1	1	18	29	14	32	1	0	137	.259	.328	.324	.224	16	49-C 1
1999	Houston	NL	326	89	8	0	6	35	63	29	33	0	0	237	.273	.343	.353	.239	33	88-C 3
2000	Houston	NL	217	57	12	0	8	22	42	22	31	0	0	160	.263	.340	.429	.257	27	59-C -4
2001	Houston	NL	225	61	6	0	6	33	45	32	34	0	0	164	.271	.364	.378	.251	26	

All the noise about his 24-game hitting streak only underscores how fluky hitting streaks are, how little they correlate with talent (remember, Ted Williams had a higher batting average than DiMaggio *during* the 56-game streak), and how overemphasized they are in current baseball culture. We know batting average is overrated, so why not batting streaks? We really should be glorifying consecutive on-base streaks, but I'm not sure anyone even knows what the longest on-base streak in history is.

None of this has anything to do with Tony Eusebio, who had his best season and has yet to have a bad one in an eight-year career as a second-stringer.

Adam Everett — SS — Bats R — Age 24

YEAR	TEAM	LGE	AB	H	DB	TP	HR	BB	SO	R	RBI	SB	CS	OUT	BA	OBP	SLG	EQA	EQR	DEFENSE
1998	Lowell	NYP	74	17	5	1	0	8	14	7	6	1	0	57	.230	.316	.324	.221	7	21-SS -3
1999	Trenton	Eas	345	82	6	0	9	30	67	42	35	10	3	266	.238	.309	.333	.221	31	98-SS -5
2000	New Orln	PCL	459	105	24	1	4	61	102	66	30	8	3	357	.229	.330	.312	.224	42	123-SS -4
2001	Houston	NL	352	95	18	1	5	44	79	60	42	15	3	260	.270	.351	.369	.247	40	

Everyone agrees that Adam Everett is a fabulous defensive player, even if his defensive numbers are just ordinary. Many opposing managers thought that major-league pitchers would blow the bat right out of his hands. He did post a .414 OBP the last two months of the season, but then went 1-for-23 in the Olympics against hurlers from the Netherlands and South Africa. While it would be nice if he could get the ball out of the infield now and then, it's hard for a shortstop with a fantastic glove and a .350 OBP to not have value. I think he projects as a better version of Dick Schofield, and I mean that as a compliment.

Keith Ginter — 2B — Bats R — Age 25

YEAR	TEAM	LGE	AB	H	DB	TP	HR	BB	SO	R	RBI	SB	CS	OUT	BA	OBP	SLG	EQA	EQR	DEFENSE	
1998	Auburn	NYP	253	59	11	1	6	43	73	34	25	3	3	197	.233	.351	.356	.244	29	68-2B	-4
1999	Kissimme	Fla	386	84	13	2	10	46	104	48	32	4	5	307	.218	.310	.339	.219	34	102-2B	-10
2000	Round Ro	Tex	466	126	21	2	18	59	137	73	60	11	6	346	.270	.368	.440	.272	67	122-2B	-11
2001	Houston	NL	393	108	16	2	17	60	119	68	71	7	4	289	.275	.371	.455	.271	55		

Ensberg and Keith Ginter were selected back to back in the middle rounds in 1998, which is a great example of how the Astros have found success drafting college seniors. Ginter's tools don't impress anyone, but he was the runaway MVP of the Texas League, and the Astros love his desire to improve. He should get along famously with Craig Biggio—Ginter was plunked by 24 pitches last year. He didn't play a single game at third base all year, then primarily played third base in the Arizona Fall League. He has a good chance to break camp with the Astros as the starter, with Spiers filling in against tough right-handers. He should have a good season, enough to pick up a few Rookie of the Year votes.

Richard Hidalgo — CF — Bats R — Age 25

YEAR	TEAM	LGE	AB	H	DB	TP	HR	BB	SO	R	RBI	SB	CS	OUT	BA	OBP	SLG	EQA	EQR	DEFENSE	
1998	Houston	NL	215	66	11	0	9	16	35	32	37	3	3	152	.307	.360	.484	.276	30	58-CF	1
1999	Houston	NL	386	87	23	2	15	51	69	47	53	6	5	304	.225	.322	.412	.244	45	108-LF	10
2000	Houston	NL	555	164	39	3	39	47	103	106	106	11	6	397	.295	.369	.587	.304	101	150-CF	19
2001	Houston	NL	460	146	30	2	34	55	88	95	116	12	5	319	.317	.390	.613	.313	87		

Last season, we wrote that Richard Hidalgo was "as good a candidate for a breakout season as anyone in the game," but we never thought he would hit 44 home runs. Richard Hidalgo is no Enron Field illusion, as he hit 28 bombs and slugged .654 on the road. If you believe the numbers above, he's one hell of a center fielder. At age 25 and still years from free agency, Hidalgo is dollar-for-dollar one of the ten most valuable commodities in baseball.

Royce Huffman — 3B/2B — Bats R — Age 24

YEAR	TEAM	LGE	AB	H	DB	TP	HR	BB	SO	R	RBI	SB	CS	OUT	BA	OBP	SLG	EQA	EQR	DEFENSE			
1999	Martnsvl	App	201	44	13	3	1	18	32	20	19	5	1	158	.219	.287	.328	.209	16	25-3B	0	15-LF	-3
2000	Kissimme	Fla	466	115	25	2	5	64	56	58	41	13	3	354	.247	.342	.341	.240	50	64-3B	-2	47-2B	-6
2001	Houston	NL	291	85	18	2	3	46	43	62	39	14	2	208	.292	.389	.399	.273	40				

Royce Huffman may be Bill Spiers's heir apparent. Huffman, another college senior who also played football at TCU, started more than 50 games at both second base and third base. He hit an even .300 on the year, with 33 doubles, 84 walks, and 32 steals, but just five home runs. That's Spiers. But Huffman, like Ginter and Ensberg ahead of him, bats right-handed, and Spiers's left-handed bat is a big part of his value. It's tough to be slotted as a utility prospect after just one full season in the minors, but Huffman is already 24 and needs to start hitting for power if he wants more than just a bench job.

Julio Lugo — SS/2B — Bats R — Age 25

YEAR	TEAM	LGE	AB	H	DB	TP	HR	BB	SO	R	RBI	SB	CS	OUT	BA	OBP	SLG	EQA	EQR	DEFENSE			
1998	Kissimme	Fla	515	130	18	9	6	36	81	53	44	19	9	394	.252	.304	.357	.224	47	98-SS	-4		
1999	Jackson	Tex	447	120	20	3	7	34	57	56	30	13	6	333	.268	.323	.374	.236	45	111-SS	-10		
2000	New Orln	PCL	101	29	4	1	2	9	20	16	9	7	5	77	.287	.345	.406	.250	12	17-2B	5		
2000	Houston	NL	419	112	21	4	9	30	87	70	35	19	9	316	.267	.321	.401	.243	46	57-SS	-8	43-2B	-5
2001	Houston	NL	476	146	24	6	15	46	89	93	79	29	11	340	.307	.368	.477	.277	69				

The trade for Adam Everett was a fairly explicit vote-of-no-confidence in Julio Lugo's defensive ability, since he is clearly a better hitter than Everett. But when Everett showed up in March swinging a wet newspaper, the Astros had little choice but to give Lugo a chance. He did exactly what he needed to do: hit well enough to overshadow his problems in the field. He's never going to be a great shortstop, but teams need to stop acting like they play on Lake Wobegon and that every shortstop is capable of above-average defense. With Lugo, Everett, Ensberg, Ginter, Spiers, Biggio, and Chris Truby stuffed into three positions, the Astros may be deeper on the infield than they are in the outfield.

Carlos Maldonado   C   Bats R   Age 22

YEAR	TEAM	LGE	AB	H	DB	TP	HR	BB	SO	R	RBI	SB	CS	OUT	BA	OBP	SLG	EQA	EQR	DEFENSE	
1998	Everett	Nwn	149	33	5	0	4	5	19	11	14	0	0	116	.221	.251	.336	.186	9	38-C	-1
1999	Wisconsn	Mid	307	77	6	0	1	28	35	24	23	2	3	233	.251	.313	.280	.200	21	83-C	-3
2000	Round Ro	Tex	426	101	21	1	4	22	75	36	39	3	2	327	.237	.279	.319	.196	28	116-C	-10
2001	Houston	NL	346	89	9	0	6	28	57	34	38	2	1	258	.257	.313	.335	.213	27		

The Astros, with their excess of middle-infield prospects, wisely traded Carlos Hernandez to Seattle last March and got pretty good value in return. While Hernandez will likely never contribute in the majors, Carlos Maldonado is a young catcher with modest but developing offensive skills, and he will probably be ready to back up Brad Ausmus in 2002 after Eusebio's contract expires. Gerry Hunsicker doesn't get nearly enough credit for working with details like these.

Aaron McNeal   1B   Bats R   Age 23

YEAR	TEAM	LGE	AB	H	DB	TP	HR	BB	SO	R	RBI	SB	CS	OUT	BA	OBP	SLG	EQA	EQR	DEFENSE	
1998	Quad Cit	Mid	379	90	10	0	12	22	120	42	44	1	1	290	.237	.284	.359	.211	30	89-1B	8
1999	Michigan	Mid	536	131	20	1	25	23	132	61	77	3	1	406	.244	.277	.425	.228	51	126-1B	5
2000	Round Ro	Tex	361	95	18	1	8	15	96	31	49	0	2	268	.263	.294	.385	.221	31	86-1B	-1
2001	Houston	NL	397	112	14	0	18	28	111	50	68	2	1	286	.282	.329	.453	.253	46		

Aaron McNeal has tremendous raw power, but his home-run total dropped from 38 to 11 last year; he is not the dead-pull hitter you would expect a young right-handed slugger to be. Scouts say his strength comes from his hands, allowing him to wait until the last moment before committing and helping him hit to all fields. That's a pretty mature approach at the plate, and I'm impressed that he didn't struggle at Double-A after jumping from the Midwest League. It's prospects like McNeal that give the Astros the most underrated minor-league system in baseball.

Mitch Meluskey   C   Bats B   Age 27

YEAR	TEAM	LGE	AB	H	DB	TP	HR	BB	SO	R	RBI	SB	CS	OUT	BA	OBP	SLG	EQA	EQR	DEFENSE	
1998	New Orln	PCL	399	124	25	0	16	72	58	60	57	1	0	275	.311	.419	.494	.307	72	102-C	-7
1999	Houston	NL	33	7	0	0	1	5	6	4	3	1	0	26	.212	.316	.303	.220	3		
2000	Houston	NL	335	94	15	0	14	49	69	42	62	1	0	241	.281	.378	.451	.280	50	91-C	-7
2001	Detroit	AL	229	67	8	0	10	40	47	40	41	1	0	162	.293	.398	.459	.298	39		

Mitch Meluskey avoided the serious shoulder problems that have plagued him throughout his career and was one of the best catchers in the league. But he also got into a fight with a teammate and came to symbolize the friction in the Astros' clubhouse as they continued to underachieve. He threw out just 22% of base-stealers. For being a bad guy with a bad arm, he was traded to Detroit. He's one of the top three catchers in the AL.

Jhonny Perez   OF   Bats R   Age 24

YEAR	TEAM	LGE	AB	H	DB	TP	HR	BB	SO	R	RBI	SB	CS	OUT	BA	OBP	SLG	EQA	EQR	DEFENSE			
1998	Jackson	Tex	439	105	9	0	9	33	79	45	29	12	6	340	.239	.293	.321	.207	33	63-2B	-11	53-SS	-15
1999	Jackson	Tex	277	61	14	2	3	14	48	29	19	4	4	220	.220	.259	.318	.185	16	57-2B	-2		
2000	Round Ro	Tex	274	71	8	1	5	9	42	32	23	7	2	205	.259	.284	.350	.212	21	56-LF	-3		
2001	Houston	NL	270	72	10	1	5	19	47	36	30	11	3	201	.267	.315	.367	.228	25				

Two years ago, Julio Lugo was considered the defensive shortstop in the Astros' system because his competition was Jhonny Perez, which explains why Perez is now an outfielder. He would have value as an outfielder who can play the middle infield in a pinch, but he still hits like a middle infielder who can play the outfield in a pinch, so his outlook has dimmed considerably.

Bill Spiers   All   Bats L   Age 35

YEAR	TEAM	LGE	AB	H	DB	TP	HR	BB	SO	R	RBI	SB	CS	OUT	BA	OBP	SLG	EQA	EQR	DEFENSE			
1998	Houston	NL	392	111	27	4	5	43	58	69	45	11	2	283	.283	.361	.411	.265	51	83-3B	-1		
1999	Houston	NL	396	113	17	5	4	42	42	54	37	8	5	288	.285	.354	.384	.251	46	60-3B	6	26-LF	-5
2000	Houston	NL	353	100	16	2	3	43	36	37	38	6	4	257	.283	.362	.365	.251	40	43-3B	3	23-SS	0
2001	Houston	NL	346	97	17	4	3	46	40	57	45	7	5	254	.280	.365	.379	.250	40				

National League

Since arriving in Houston five years ago, Bill Spiers has become the flag-bearer for his mold of player: the left-handed hitter who can man every infield position and get on base. Spiers has played between 122 and 132 games every year as an Astro, posting an OBP under .350 just once; you can bet that the Astros appreciate the difference between him and, say, Lenny Harris. The Astros' enormous flexibility in the infield and outfield means that Spiers may play any non-battery position at any time.

Chris Truby — 3B — Bats R — Age 27

YEAR	TEAM	LGE	AB	H	DB	TP	HR	BB	SO	R	RBI	SB	CS	OUT	BA	OBP	SLG	EQA	EQR	DEFENSE	
1998	Kissimme	Fla	214	53	9	1	10	14	35	24	31	2	1	162	.248	.299	.439	.242	23	51-3B	10
1998	Jackson	Tex	306	73	15	2	11	14	57	31	41	4	2	235	.239	.277	.408	.224	28	70-3B	2
1999	Jackson	Tex	467	109	16	2	18	25	100	53	58	10	5	362	.233	.275	.392	.219	41	116-3B	12
2000	New Orln	PCL	269	69	9	2	2	12	34	25	24	4	1	201	.257	.288	.327	.205	19	62-3B	3
2000	Houston	NL	258	64	16	3	10	6	52	26	53	2	1	195	.248	.277	.450	.235	26	66-3B	-2
2001	Houston	NL	462	129	22	2	19	31	87	62	76	6	2	335	.279	.325	.459	.253	54		

On rare occasion, an organizational soldier gets a chance. Chris Truby climbed the ladder slowly and had to repeat Double-A at age 25 when Carlos Villalobos was acquired from the Tigers in the first Brad Ausmus trade. When Villalobos was released last year, Truby did just enough in Triple-A to get a chance when Ken Caminiti went down. Eleven homers in 78 games (nine of them at home) impressed a lot of people; even so, he couldn't muster a .300 OBP, and the Astros have plenty of options at third base should he falter. Long-term, Truby isn't a starter. He could settle into the Craig Paquette role as a power-hitting hacker from the right side.

Daryle Ward — LF/1B — Bats L — Age 26

YEAR	TEAM	LGE	AB	H	DB	TP	HR	BB	SO	R	RBI	SB	CS	OUT	BA	OBP	SLG	EQA	EQR	DEFENSE			
1998	New Orln	PCL	463	126	24	1	19	33	77	63	76	1	0	337	.272	.322	.451	.255	55	53-LF	1	46-1B	0
1999	New Orln	PCL	240	76	12	1	21	19	42	43	48	1	1	165	.317	.372	.637	.315	46	58-1B	1		
1999	Houston	NL	151	41	5	0	8	7	29	11	28	0	0	110	.272	.304	.464	.250	17	23-LF	-4		
2000	Houston	NL	264	65	9	2	18	11	57	33	42	0	0	199	.246	.276	.500	.248	30	36-LF	-1		
2001	Houston	NL	330	100	16	1	25	26	68	53	79	1	0	230	.303	.354	.585	.293	54				

Daryle Ward is proof that you really can have too many players at the bottom of the defensive spectrum. He doesn't have Berkman's patience, and he's unlikely to ever be a decent outfielder unless he loses weight. On the other hand, he would make a fine first baseman and he did hit .324/.349/.648 after the All-Star break. Ward's primary value to Houston is as an insurance policy should Bagwell be traded or leave town; if Bagwell re-ups on a long-term deal, Ward needs to be moved immediately.

PITCHERS (ERA: 4.50, H/9: 9.00, HR/9: 1.00, BB/9: 3.00, K/9: 6.00, KW: 1.00, PERA: 4.50)

Jose Cabrera — Throws R — Age 29

YEAR	TEAM	LGE	IP	H	ER	HR	BB	K	ERA	W	L	H/9	HR/9	BB/9	K/9	KW	PERA
1999	New Orln	PCL	47.3	33	20	4	15	26	3.80	3	2	6.27	0.76	2.85	4.94	0.87	2.73
1999	Houston	NL	28.3	21	7	3	8	24	2.22	2	1	6.67	0.95	2.54	7.62	1.50	3.01
2000	Houston	NL	58.3	71	35	8	13	34	5.40	2	4	10.95	1.23	2.01	5.25	1.31	5.51

Of all the problems the Astros had in their bullpen last year, Jose Cabrera's complete inability to build on his 1999 performance was the knockout blow. There was nothing wrong with Cabrera's arm; he simply couldn't finish off hitters. All eyes this spring will be on the status of Billy Wagner, but which Cabrera shows up this year could have just as much impact on the Astros' hopes.

Octavio Dotel — Throws R — Age 25

YEAR	TEAM	LGE	IP	H	ER	HR	BB	K	ERA	W	L	H/9	HR/9	BB/9	K/9	KW	PERA
1998	Binghmtn	Eas	64.0	45	23	5	25	50	3.23	4	3	6.33	0.70	3.52	7.03	1.00	2.95
1998	Norfolk	Int	94.0	84	50	10	41	86	4.79	4	6	8.04	0.96	3.93	8.23	1.05	4.27
1999	Norfolk	Int	67.0	54	35	10	33	66	4.70	3	4	7.25	1.34	4.43	8.87	1.00	4.43
1999	NY Mets	NL	83.0	68	50	12	42	71	5.42	3	6	7.37	1.30	4.55	7.70	0.85	4.49
2000	Houston	NL	124.0	126	69	20	47	118	5.01	5	9	9.15	1.45	3.41	8.56	1.26	5.24

Give the Astros credit for trying to turn lemons into lemonade: they badly needed a closer, and Octavio Dotel had trouble with stamina (opponents hit .388/.458/.767 after the 75-pitch mark). The experiment worked fairly well: Dotel struck out 49 batters in 34 innings of relief and is a nice backup closer if Wagner isn't able to return strong. The Astros may be tempted to bring him back to the rotation when a starter inevitably comes up lame. They concede Dotel is more ready to contribute as a reliever but would have more value in the rotation.

Scott Elarton — Throws R — Age 25

YEAR	TEAM	LGE	IP	H	ER	HR	BB	K	ERA	W	L	H/9	HR/9	BB/9	K/9	KW	PERA
1998	New Orln	PCL	86.0	70	48	8	47	69	5.02	4	6	7.33	0.84	4.92	7.22	0.73	4.16
1998	Houston	NL	54.3	40	23	6	19	46	3.81	3	3	6.63	0.99	3.15	7.62	1.21	3.23
1999	Houston	NL	120.0	108	53	8	37	102	3.97	7	6	8.10	0.60	2.78	7.65	1.38	3.50
2000	Houston	NL	190.0	190	98	22	64	109	4.64	9	12	9.00	1.04	3.03	5.16	0.85	4.56

From August 1 to September 17, Scott Elarton threw 110 or more pitches in 10 straight starts, clearing 125 pitches four times in that span. I dare anyone to defend this usage pattern for a 24-year-old pitcher coming off rotator-cuff surgery on a team going nowhere. While the Astros proudly proclaim that Elarton has developed into the ace everyone said he would be, his numbers look less like those of an ace and more like the ones of an overworked young pitcher.

Wayne Franklin — Throws L — Age 27

YEAR	TEAM	LGE	IP	H	ER	HR	BB	K	ERA	W	L	H/9	HR/9	BB/9	K/9	KW	PERA
1998	Vero Bch	Fla	78.3	85	56	14	35	40	6.43	3	6	9.77	1.61	4.02	4.60	0.57	6.03
1999	Jackson	Tex	45.7	32	15	5	21	23	2.96	3	2	6.31	0.99	4.14	4.53	0.55	3.42
2000	New Orln	PCL	41.3	49	32	7	22	25	6.97	1	4	10.67	1.52	4.79	5.44	0.57	6.75
2000	Houston	NL	21.0	24	13	2	9	17	5.57	1	1	10.29	0.86	3.86	7.29	0.94	5.44

The Astros have an acute need for left-handed relief, and Wayne Franklin is probably their best in-house option. He was not terribly effective last season, but he had a big 1999, and his ability to retire left-handed hitters makes him a weapon. He'll be up and down in 2001, pitching fairly well but always just a couple bad pitches from New Orleans.

Jason Green — Throws L — Age 26

YEAR	TEAM	LGE	IP	H	ER	HR	BB	K	ERA	W	L	H/9	HR/9	BB/9	K/9	KW	PERA
1998	Kissimme	Fla	59.7	66	44	9	44	36	6.64	2	5	9.96	1.36	6.64	5.43	0.41	6.96
1999	Jackson	Tex	38.3	42	24	3	26	30	5.63	1	3	9.86	0.70	6.10	7.04	0.58	6.00
2000	Round Ro	Tex	37.3	41	13	2	13	30	3.13	2	2	9.88	0.48	3.13	7.23	1.15	4.53
2000	Houston	NL	18.3	16	13	2	15	16	6.38	1	1	7.85	0.98	7.36	7.85	0.53	5.65

National League

The rare four-pitch reliever, Green benefited more than almost anyone from the chaos in the Astros bullpen, getting a call-up in August despite not overpowering hitters in the minors. He has to throw strikes to be effective, and he didn't, allowing more walks (20) in 18 innings than he did in 54 innings in the minor leagues. As punishment, the Astros let him be claimed on waivers by the Rockies, a sign that we really are headed for a Texas-style penal code in this country.

Carlos Hernandez Throws L Age 21

YEAR	TEAM	LGE	IP	H	ER	HR	BB	K	ERA	W	L	H/9	HR/9	BB/9	K/9	KW	PERA
1999	Martnsvl	App	48.7	43	31	5	32	32	5.73	2	3	7.95	0.92	5.92	5.92	0.50	5.02
2000	Michigan	Mid	99.7	104	73	18	68	61	6.59	3	8	9.39	1.63	6.14	5.51	0.45	6.69

Like Wilfredo Rodriguez, Carlos Hernandez is a left-hander out of Venezuela and a sign that the pipeline that started with Bobby Abreu hasn't dried up yet. Hernandez did not develop major-league velocity until recently, which gives him an advantage in that he's already learned to hit his spots. He's still several years away, and that still may not be enough time for the Astros to figure out what to do with the 15 pitchers ahead of him.

Fernando Hernandez Throws R Age 30

YEAR	TEAM	LGE	IP	H	ER	HR	BB	K	ERA	W	L	H/9	HR/9	BB/9	K/9	KW	PERA
1999	Tucson	PCL	15.3	21	15	3	4	9	8.80	0	2	12.33	1.76	2.35	5.28	1.13	6.99
2000	Round Ro	Tex	27.0	21	17	2	18	24	5.67	1	2	7.00	0.67	6.00	8.00	0.67	4.22
2000	New Orln	PCL	55.0	45	38	8	39	59	6.22	2	4	7.36	1.31	6.38	9.65	0.76	5.27

In his fifth organization, approaching 30, Fernando Hernandez has a slight chance to be the next Billy Taylor, a late-blooming reliever who could give a smart organization a couple of effective years at a warehouse price. Hernandez was just beginning to find himself in relief when he missed most of 1998 and 1999, but last year he struck out 131 batters in 91 innings, allowing just 60 hits, between Double-A and Triple-A. He's a six-year minor-league free agent.

Chris Holt Throws R Age 29

YEAR	TEAM	LGE	IP	H	ER	HR	BB	K	ERA	W	L	H/9	HR/9	BB/9	K/9	KW	PERA
1999	Houston	NL	159.3	184	86	12	49	97	4.86	7	11	10.39	0.68	2.77	5.48	0.99	4.88
2000	Houston	NL	203.3	237	114	17	57	113	5.05	9	14	10.49	0.75	2.52	5.00	0.99	4.92

The Astros keep waiting for Chris Holt to turn the corner with his sinker and start dominating hitters, but he's regressed each season since coming back from a rotator-cuff tear. He isn't keeping the ball down as much as he used to (his G/F ratio dropped from 2.02 to 1.82), and in all honesty there's little in his record to suggest that he's ever going to be better than he is now. His 21–42 lifetime mark is the worst of any active pitcher (minimum: 60 decisions). Sent to Detroit in the Brad Ausmus trade, he'll be a decent #5 starter whose stats will look good thanks to Comerica Park.

Rick Huisman Throws R Age 32

YEAR	TEAM	LGE	IP	H	ER	HR	BB	K	ERA	W	L	H/9	HR/9	BB/9	K/9	KW	PERA
1998	Fresno	PCL	66.7	66	48	21	37	51	6.48	2	5	8.91	2.84	5.00	6.89	0.69	7.20
1999	New Orln	PCL	47.7	44	31	9	20	42	5.85	2	3	8.31	1.70	3.78	7.93	1.05	5.14
2000	New Orln	PCL	49.7	38	35	8	24	43	6.34	2	4	6.89	1.45	4.35	7.79	0.90	4.29

I admit to having a weakness for Rick Huisman, going back to the days when he and Salomon Torres were the best pair of pitching prospects in baseball. That was nine years ago, enough time for Huisman to blow out his arm, take the long road back, and spend the last six years as a middle reliever in Triple-A. He's getting better in his thirties, allowing barely one base runner an inning in each of the last two years. Like Hernandez, he's a minor-league free agent who could make an immediate contribution to any team daring enough to give him a shot.

Eric Ireland Throws R Age 24

YEAR	TEAM	LGE	IP	H	ER	HR	BB	K	ERA	W	L	H/9	HR/9	BB/9	K/9	KW	PERA
1998	Quad Cit	Mid	183.0	191	115	40	90	97	5.66	7	13	9.39	1.97	4.43	4.77	0.54	6.35
1999	Kissimme	Fla	155.0	153	81	28	39	78	4.70	7	10	8.88	1.63	2.26	4.53	1.00	4.79
2000	Round Ro	Tex	166.3	169	97	25	71	75	5.25	7	11	9.14	1.35	3.84	4.06	0.53	5.31

(Eric Ireland *continued*)

For the third straight year, the Astros let Eric Ireland pitch beyond the boundaries of common sense; for the third straight year, he thrived on the abuse. Last year was his most impressive performance; his success at Double-A and his dramatic improvement in the second half mean we can finally take him seriously as a prospect despite his lack of an overpowering fastball. I remain unconvinced that he will stay healthy. Over the last three years, Ireland has thrown 571 innings without making 30 appearances in any season. The last major-league pitcher to do that was Ed Lopat, from 1944-46; Lopat was 26 when his streak started. Ireland was waived, claimed by the Cubs, and traded to the A's.

Brad Lidge — Throws R — Age 24

YEAR	TEAM	LGE	IP	H	ER	HR	BB	K	ERA	W	L	H/9	HR/9	BB/9	K/9	KW	PERA
1998	Quad Cit	Mid	10.0	9	4	0	6	3	3.60	1	0	8.10	0.00	5.40	2.70	0.25	3.85
1999	Kissimme	Fla	19.3	12	8	0	14	11	3.72	1	1	5.59	0.00	6.52	5.12	0.39	3.01
2000	Kissimme	Fla	36.3	33	24	8	20	25	5.94	1	3	8.17	1.98	4.95	6.19	0.63	5.86

Unlike Ireland, Brad Lidge has no problem keeping his innings down. That's because the former #1 pick has suffered a number of injuries. What makes his health record so frustrating to the Astros is how well he's pitched when he's able to take the mound (just 14 times the last two seasons). He was healthy enough to pitch in the AFL briefly and handled himself well for someone who has yet to pitch above A-ball. He definitely knows how to pitch and could be the Jeff D'Amico of 2003. Of course, that would mean he missed most of 2001 and 2002.

Jose Lima — Throws R — Age 28

YEAR	TEAM	LGE	IP	H	ER	HR	BB	K	ERA	W	L	H/9	HR/9	BB/9	K/9	KW	PERA
1998	Houston	NL	221.0	224	104	38	30	137	4.24	12	13	9.12	1.55	1.22	5.58	2.28	4.41
1999	Houston	NL	237.0	245	104	30	38	157	3.95	13	13	9.30	1.14	1.44	5.96	2.07	4.18
2000	Houston	NL	194.0	237	127	37	52	103	5.89	7	15	10.99	1.72	2.41	4.78	0.99	6.19

When he was going 37–18 in 1998 and 1999, Jose Lima's antics on the mound and the salsa music loud enough to wake the dead could be forgiven. Last year was the other side of the coin, and it's only too easy to blame his execrable season on a lack of focus. One thing is clear: it wasn't the park. Lima had a 6.32 ERA and gave up 21 home runs in 88 innings on the road. To his credit, he made no excuses for his season, and his talent edges his stubbornness; he'll probably bounce back about 70%, making him a useful #3 starter at best.

Tony McKnight — Throws R — Age 24

YEAR	TEAM	LGE	IP	H	ER	HR	BB	K	ERA	W	L	H/9	HR/9	BB/9	K/9	KW	PERA
1998	Kissimme	Fla	142.7	188	112	25	63	61	7.07	4	12	11.86	1.58	3.97	3.85	0.48	7.21
1999	Jackson	Tex	148.7	134	71	24	52	75	4.30	8	9	8.11	1.45	3.15	4.54	0.72	4.51
2000	Round Ro	Tex	29.7	39	22	7	11	15	6.67	1	2	11.83	2.12	3.34	4.55	0.68	7.51
2000	New Orln	PCL	112.0	121	67	15	39	46	5.38	4	8	9.72	1.21	3.13	3.70	0.59	5.20
2000	Houston	NL	34.0	33	16	3	7	19	4.24	2	2	8.74	0.79	1.85	5.03	1.36	3.67

Known for his curveball, Tony McKnight suffered some nagging injuries earlier in his career, and some scouts thought his curveball had lost some bite. He still had a decent season on the strength of an improved change-up, and he did his best pitching when he was called up to Houston late in the year. He's been healthy for the past three years and his late-season performance gives him a leg up on a rotation spot in spring training. I would be surprised if he weren't at least a league-average pitcher this year.

Greg Miller — Throws L — Age 21

YEAR	TEAM	LGE	IP	H	ER	HR	BB	K	ERA	W	L	H/9	HR/9	BB/9	K/9	KW	PERA
1999	Augusta	SAL	119.7	119	76	18	80	68	5.72	4	9	8.95	1.35	6.02	5.11	0.43	6.10
2000	Kissimme	Fla	130.7	141	89	32	57	64	6.13	4	11	9.71	2.20	3.93	4.41	0.56	6.58

The forgotten part of the Carl Everett trade, Greg Miller will be remembered very soon if he continues to improve at his current pace. The classic finesse left-hander, Miller was outstanding in the Florida State League at age 20 and even managed to avoid the organization's edict to overwork their best pitching prospects. The Astros' deliberate one-level-at-a-time style will probably work to Miller's advantage, as he has time to spare and will probably need a year or two to adjust to the fact that hitters in the high minors don't swing at everything with a bend in it.

Wade Miller — Throws R — Age 24

YEAR	TEAM	LGE	IP	H	ER	HR	BB	K	ERA	W	L	H/9	HR/9	BB/9	K/9	KW	PERA
1998	Jackson	Tex	57.0	49	27	10	31	32	4.26	3	3	7.74	1.58	4.89	5.05	0.52	5.15
1999	New Orln	PCL	152.0	147	93	22	76	92	5.51	6	11	8.70	1.30	4.50	5.45	0.61	5.28
2000	New Orln	PCL	99.3	90	47	9	42	59	4.26	5	6	8.15	0.82	3.81	5.35	0.70	4.15
2000	Houston	NL	103.3	101	57	11	32	74	4.96	4	7	8.80	0.96	2.79	6.45	1.16	4.25

While the Astros have better pitching prospects, Wade Miller already has a half-season in the Astros' rotation under his belt and is the one pitcher most likely to make an impact this year. Miller has a repertoire that's as varied as it is nasty; he also has the makings of a ground-ball pitcher, with a G/F ratio greater than 2.00 in Triple-A last year. He projects as a #2 starter; the Astros' rotation is in such disarray that he could end up the #2 starter this year by default.

Mike Nannini — Throws R — Age 20

YEAR	TEAM	LGE	IP	H	ER	HR	BB	K	ERA	W	L	H/9	HR/9	BB/9	K/9	KW	PERA
1999	Auburn	NYP	69.0	61	23	5	21	38	3.00	5	3	7.96	0.65	2.74	4.96	0.90	3.45
1999	Michigan	Mid	81.3	108	60	16	34	36	6.64	2	7	11.95	1.77	3.76	3.98	0.53	7.37
2000	Michigan	Mid	93.3	91	52	9	35	46	5.01	4	6	8.78	0.87	3.38	4.44	0.66	4.38
2000	Kissimme	Fla	72.7	83	38	8	17	33	4.71	3	5	10.28	0.99	2.11	4.09	0.97	4.87

The Astros, who are usually more conservative than Rush Limbaugh when it comes to promoting young pitchers, started Mike Nannini in the Midwest League at age 18 in 1999. He wasn't up to the challenge then, but with a refined change-up, he had no trouble with the league in 2000 and didn't miss a beat when he was promoted to Kissimmee. He's 95% the pitcher that Josh Beckett is with just half the hype. Nannini probably won't surface this year, but his upside is higher than anyone else's in the organization, majors or minors. One note of caution: he threw exactly as many innings last year as Eric Ireland did.

Roy Oswalt — Throws R — Age 23

YEAR	TEAM	LGE	IP	H	ER	HR	BB	K	ERA	W	L	H/9	HR/9	BB/9	K/9	KW	PERA
1998	Auburn	NYP	63.7	53	30	8	38	30	4.24	3	4	7.49	1.13	5.37	4.24	0.39	4.72
1999	Michigan	Mid	140.7	149	87	16	60	76	5.57	5	11	9.53	1.02	3.84	4.86	0.63	5.19
2000	Kissimme	Fla	41.7	53	17	3	14	27	3.67	3	2	11.45	0.65	3.02	5.83	0.96	5.58
2000	Round Ro	Tex	121.0	109	43	9	24	88	3.20	8	5	8.11	0.67	1.79	6.55	1.83	3.20

The Astros thought highly of Roy Oswalt after a promising 1999, but no one expected this. Oswalt started last season pitching for Kissimmee, and by the end of the year he was an Olympic star after posting the first ERA under 2.00 in the Texas League in ten years. While the Astros claim he still needs to work on things like fielding and holding runners, they say that about all their pitchers. Talent like this won't stay on the farm beyond about midseason.

Brian Powell — Throws R — Age 27

YEAR	TEAM	LGE	IP	H	ER	HR	BB	K	ERA	W	L	H/9	HR/9	BB/9	K/9	KW	PERA
1998	Jacksnvl	Sou	87.7	82	39	9	25	30	4.00	5	5	8.42	0.92	2.57	3.08	0.60	3.91
1998	Detroit	AL	83.0	94	58	15	31	43	6.29	3	6	10.19	1.63	3.36	4.66	0.69	6.03
1999	New Orln	PCL	44.3	50	42	7	27	23	8.53	1	4	10.15	1.42	5.48	4.67	0.43	6.65
2000	New Orln	PCL	96.0	98	70	15	48	38	6.56	3	8	9.19	1.41	4.50	3.56	0.40	5.66
2000	Houston	NL	31.0	32	17	6	10	12	4.94	1	2	9.29	1.74	2.90	3.48	0.60	5.43

Brian Powell is one of the "jewels" of the Brad Ausmus/C.J. Nitkowski trade, in which Gerry Hunsicker somehow surrendered an everyday catcher and valuable left-handed swingman for five non-prospects. To Randy Smith, if you can believe it. Brian Powell is a finesse right-hander who doesn't have enough guile to get out Triple-A hitters; he's here because the Astros were desperate enough to give him five starts last year. Don't expect them to make that mistake again.

Jay Powell — Throws R — Age 29

YEAR	TEAM	LGE	IP	H	ER	HR	BB	K	ERA	W	L	H/9	HR/9	BB/9	K/9	KW	PERA
1998	Florida	NL	34.7	35	20	6	21	20	5.19	1	3	9.09	1.56	5.45	5.19	0.48	6.16
1998	Houston	NL	32.3	22	9	1	14	31	2.51	3	1	6.12	0.28	3.90	8.63	1.11	2.60
1999	Houston	NL	73.3	81	37	3	35	65	4.54	3	5	9.94	0.37	4.30	7.98	0.93	4.94
2000	Houston	NL	27.0	29	17	1	15	13	5.67	1	2	9.67	0.33	5.00	4.33	0.43	5.06

(Jay Powell *continued*)

Having done next to nothing since being a great midseason pickup for the Astros in 1998, Jay Powell may be looking at the beginning of the end of his career in Houston. When a reliever starts losing the strike zone and then develops arm problems, the two are usually related. There's no reason to believe Powell's strained shoulder is going to suddenly heal, and there's no reason to think he's going to bounce back with a great year any time soon.

Tim Redding   Throws R   Age 23

YEAR	TEAM	LGE	IP	H	ER	HR	BB	K	ERA	W	L	H/9	HR/9	BB/9	K/9	KW	PERA
1998	Auburn	NYP	65.0	56	55	5	62	44	7.62	2	5	7.75	0.69	8.58	6.09	0.35	5.75
1999	Michigan	Mid	95.3	93	81	8	84	75	7.65	2	9	8.78	0.76	7.93	7.08	0.45	6.15
2000	Kissimme	Fla	139.7	133	80	13	72	97	5.16	6	10	8.57	0.84	4.64	6.25	0.67	4.75
2000	Round Ro	Tex	23.0	16	17	7	24	14	6.65	1	2	6.26	2.74	9.39	5.48	0.29	7.36

Tim Redding was a draft-and-follow in 1997, a year after the Astros picked up Oswalt the same way. The Astros draft-and-follow as good as anyone in the business, which is important because most of their top draft picks are either projects or signability picks. Redding vaulted into prospect status after he was moved to the bullpen in mid-1999, though the Astros made the unconventional move of putting him back in the rotation in 2000. He was phenomenal, finishing third in the minors with 192 strikeouts. His control needs work, and he probably needs another year in the minors, which the Astros will happily give him. He should be on all the prospect lists for 2002.

Shane Reynolds   Throws R   Age 33

YEAR	TEAM	LGE	IP	H	ER	HR	BB	K	ERA	W	L	H/9	HR/9	BB/9	K/9	KW	PERA
1998	Houston	NL	222.3	253	102	28	50	170	4.13	12	13	10.24	1.13	2.02	6.88	1.70	4.97
1999	Houston	NL	223.3	240	105	23	32	166	4.23	12	13	9.67	0.93	1.29	6.69	2.59	4.12
2000	Houston	NL	128.7	144	74	15	34	77	5.18	5	9	10.07	1.05	2.38	5.39	1.13	4.93

Shane Reynolds suffered only a minor decline before his back acted up. After three months of 3.99 ball, he posted an ERA of more than 11.00 in July and then missed the final two months of the season. He's rehabilitated the injury without surgery. While back injuries can cripple hitters (think Don Mattingly), they rarely create lingering problems for pitchers. Reynolds should be at full health and in typical form again this year—once he recuperates from a jogging injury to his knee.

Wilfredo Rodriguez   Throws L   Age 22

YEAR	TEAM	LGE	IP	H	ER	HR	BB	K	ERA	W	L	H/9	HR/9	BB/9	K/9	KW	PERA
1998	Quad Cit	Mid	147.7	133	95	19	79	86	5.79	5	11	8.11	1.16	4.81	5.24	0.54	4.89
1999	Kissimme	Fla	137.7	114	74	18	78	89	4.84	6	9	7.45	1.18	5.10	5.82	0.57	4.64
2000	Kissimme	Fla	46.3	48	43	13	37	31	8.35	1	4	9.32	2.53	7.19	6.02	0.42	8.04
2000	Round Ro	Tex	51.7	58	52	17	57	34	9.06	1	5	10.10	2.96	9.93	5.92	0.30	10.12

Shoulder tendinitis that refused to calm down, followed by a hamstring pull, held up Wilfredo Rodriguez's season; he struggled with his release point when he returned. Left-handers who throw 93 to 95 mph can afford an off year. His control was much improved in the Texas League playoffs, and he is still rightfully considered among the Astros' best pitching prospects. This is one deep organization.

Doug Sessions   Throws R   Age 24

YEAR	TEAM	LGE	IP	H	ER	HR	BB	K	ERA	W	L	H/9	HR/9	BB/9	K/9	KW	PERA
1998	Auburn	NYP	28.0	27	15	5	12	18	4.82	1	2	8.68	1.61	3.86	5.79	0.75	5.32
1999	Kissimme	Fla	41.7	37	13	2	18	32	2.81	3	2	7.99	0.43	3.89	6.91	0.89	3.71
2000	Round Ro	Tex	75.3	80	42	12	41	48	5.02	3	5	9.56	1.43	4.90	5.73	0.59	6.07

He's not a very well-known prospect, but we gave Doug Sessions a mention last year after he blew through the low minors. Last year came the real test, and he survived the Double-A experience, if barely. Like most everyone else in this organization, he's a fly-ball pitcher and may struggle to establish himself in Enron Field for a few years.

Tom Shearn   Throws R   Age 23

YEAR	TEAM	LGE	IP	H	ER	HR	BB	K	ERA	W	L	H/9	HR/9	BB/9	K/9	KW	PERA
1998	Quad Cit	Mid	106.3	96	54	21	66	47	4.57	5	7	8.13	1.78	5.59	3.98	0.36	5.88
1999	Kissimme	Fla	131.3	147	94	25	67	64	6.44	4	11	10.07	1.71	4.59	4.39	0.48	6.55
2000	Round Ro	Tex	125.7	134	92	24	73	63	6.59	4	10	9.60	1.72	5.23	4.51	0.43	6.54

National League

This is not the organization in which to be a grade-C pitching prospect. Tom Shearn has a 35–27 career record and was one of the starters for the Texas League champions last season. If he's smart, he's writing all this into his résumé, because in two years he's going to have to mail out 29 copies, and he won't have a team of Scott Boras's finest to write up a 70-page tome with the title *Tom Shearn: Historical Performance*.

Joe Slusarski   Throws R   Age 34

YEAR	TEAM	LGE	IP	H	ER	HR	BB	K	ERA	W	L	H/9	HR/9	BB/9	K/9	KW	PERA
1998	New Orln	PCL	46.3	51	35	9	11	21	6.80	1	4	9.91	1.75	2.14	4.08	0.95	5.48
1999	New Orln	PCL	60.7	65	32	7	17	25	4.75	3	4	9.64	1.04	2.52	3.71	0.74	4.72
2000	New Orln	PCL	18.3	15	12	3	8	14	5.89	1	1	7.36	1.47	3.93	6.87	0.88	4.43
2000	Houston	NL	75.0	77	32	6	17	45	3.84	4	4	9.24	0.72	2.04	5.40	1.32	3.96

Desperation, thy name is Slusarski. If Dierker's Midas touch from 1997 to 1999 left one glimmer of gold behind, it was with Juicy Joe. At age 34, after spending all but a few weeks in the minors since 1992, he had a 4.21 ERA and a +5.1 ARP, second-best on the team, behind the departed Doug Henry. For those of you who think he can do it again, have I got a bridge to sell you!

Marc Valdes   Throws R   Age 29

YEAR	TEAM	LGE	IP	H	ER	HR	BB	K	ERA	W	L	H/9	HR/9	BB/9	K/9	KW	PERA
1998	Montreal	NL	35.0	40	33	6	19	23	8.49	1	3	10.29	1.54	4.89	5.91	0.61	6.60
1999	Durham	Int	38.0	37	25	4	13	16	5.92	1	3	8.76	0.95	3.08	3.79	0.62	4.35
2000	Durham	Int	45.0	50	26	3	18	18	5.20	2	3	10.00	0.60	3.60	3.60	0.50	4.91
2000	Houston	NL	55.7	67	36	2	19	29	5.82	2	4	10.83	0.32	3.07	4.69	0.76	4.89

Russ Johnson is not going to be a superstar, but you'd think a guy who can play shortstop and get on base would be worth more than Marc Valdes, whom the Devil Rays were using to fill out their Triple-A rotation. This is exactly what the Astros can not afford to do: convert their excess position players into staff filler. The Roger Cedeno trade was another example of this kind of waste. If they can't get full value for Daryle Ward or Julio Lugo, they need to have the courage to trade Moises Alou or Jeff Bagwell instead, knowing that their role players can produce in starting roles if they get the chance.

Travis Wade   Throws R   Age 25

YEAR	TEAM	LGE	IP	H	ER	HR	BB	K	ERA	W	L	H/9	HR/9	BB/9	K/9	KW	PERA
1999	Auburn	NYP	33.7	29	13	0	18	22	3.48	2	2	7.75	0.00	4.81	5.88	0.61	3.54
2000	Kissimme	Fla	43.7	40	14	6	14	26	2.89	3	2	8.24	1.24	2.89	5.36	0.93	4.26
2000	Round Ro	Tex	29.3	33	21	4	8	15	6.44	1	2	10.13	1.23	2.45	4.60	0.94	5.17

I am convinced the independent leagues have a lot more talent than anyone realizes. Travis Wade was signed out of the Texas–Louisiana League following the 1998 season, after a career in which he had given up 58 hits and 29 walks in 39 innings, with a 10.62 ERA. Two years later, he was closing games for Kissimmee with an ERA under one, which is a compliment to both the independent leagues and the Astros' scouting department. Like most independent-league finds, Wade has to pitch twice as well for half the opportunity. Root for him; just don't sink your 401(k) into his baseball cards.

Billy Wagner   Throws L   Age 29

YEAR	TEAM	LGE	IP	H	ER	HR	BB	K	ERA	W	L	H/9	HR/9	BB/9	K/9	KW	PERA
1998	Houston	NL	57.0	49	22	7	24	79	3.47	3	3	7.74	1.11	3.79	12.47	1.65	4.19
1999	Houston	NL	72.3	37	15	5	20	104	1.87	7	1	4.60	0.62	2.49	12.94	2.60	1.74
2000	Houston	NL	27.7	28	17	5	14	23	5.53	1	2	9.11	1.63	4.55	7.48	0.82	5.88

Why do pitchers do this? Why does baseball encourage it? When your arm hurts, tell someone! The culture of sport dictates that a player should hurt his team by trying to play when he's physically incapable, and any player that pulls himself from competition because he feels he is doing his team a disservice is selfish. Not only does this place players at risk of permanent injury, it doesn't do anyone any good. The Astros were not helped because Wagner denied for two months that his arm hurt. The 1978 Red Sox lost the division because Butch Hobson refused to go on the DL with a bum arm and made 43 errors at third base. Grow up, guys. In the Marines, they say that pain is weakness leaving the body, but in sport, it's weakness *entering* the body.

Support-Neutral Statistics — HOUSTON ASTROS — Park Effect: +12.0%

PITCHER	GS	IP	R	SNW	SNL	SNPCT	W	L	RA	APW	SNVA	SNWAR
Octavio Dotel	16	91.0	63	4.9	5.8	.461	1	5	6.23	-0.7	-0.5	0.4
Scott Elarton	30	192.7	117	12.0	10.3	.539	17	7	5.47	-0.1	0.8	2.5
Dwight Gooden	1	4.0	4	0.1	0.5	.171	0	0	9.00	-0.1	-0.1	-0.1
Kip Gross	1	4.0	6	0.0	0.7	.054	0	1	13.50	-0.3	-0.3	-0.3
Chris Holt	32	203.7	130	11.5	12.1	.488	8	15	5.74	-0.6	-0.3	1.5
Jose Lima	33	196.3	152	9.4	14.1	.399	7	16	6.97	-3.0	-2.3	-0.6
Tony McKnight	6	35.0	19	2.2	2.0	.523	4	1	4.89	0.2	0.1	0.4
Wade Miller	16	105.0	66	5.7	5.6	.506	6	6	5.66	-0.2	-0.0	0.9
Brian Powell	5	25.3	19	1.3	2.2	.374	1	1	6.75	-0.3	-0.4	-0.2
Shane Reynolds	22	131.0	86	7.4	8.2	.474	7	8	5.91	-0.6	-0.5	0.8
TOTALS	162	988.0	662	54.5	61.3	.470	51	60	6.03	-5.9	-3.5	5.3

One of the main reasons cited by the media, and even by the Astros themselves, for the team's Y2K collapse is the impact of Enron Field on the pitching staff. The theory is that Astros pitchers under Larry Dierker had learned to take advantage of the spacious dimensions of the Astrodome but were poorly suited to the cozier Enron Field.

We can measure the effect of the new park on Astros starters by looking at the Home Field Advantage (HFA) that a rotation got from a park, defined here as the difference between Support-Neutral Value Added (SNVA) at home and SNVA on the road. During the Dierker/Astrodome years, 1997 through 1999, the Astros had an average HFA of 3.6 wins per year. The average for all teams was 2.0 wins, so the Astrodome arguably provided the rotation with a benefit of only 1.6 wins per year. In 2000, the Astros' HFA was 2.1 wins, or almost exactly league average, meaning the Astros' HFA dropped by about 1.5 wins from their 1997–99 average. Jose Lima accounted for nearly all of that by himself.

The "pitchers can't handle the park" theory just doesn't hold water when applied to the 2000 Astros. Even if you accept that the 1.5-win drop in Home Field Advantage is real and not just noise, those 1.5 wins represent an insignificant fraction of the 22 wins the Astros dropped in the standings from their 1997–99 average to their 2000 total.

For a quick explanation of SN stats, see page 7.

Reliever Evaluation Tools

PITCHER	G	IP	R	ARA	APR	IRNR/G	EIRS/G	IRP	BRS	RRA	ARP
Tim Bogar	2	2.0	1	4.30	0.2	0.00	0.00	0.0	0.0	4.02	0.3
Jose Cabrera	52	59.3	40	5.80	-4.0	0.40	0.18	0.3	1.8	6.17	-6.4
Octavio Dotel	34	34.0	17	4.30	3.4	0.74	0.30	1.1	1.6	4.55	2.5
Wayne Franklin	25	21.3	14	5.64	-1.1	0.64	0.25	0.5	0.0	5.47	-0.6
Jason Green	14	17.7	16	7.79	-5.1	0.50	0.25	2.3	1.2	7.19	3.9
Kip Gross	1	0.3	2	51.61	-1.7	0.00	0.00	0.0	-0.5	17.18	-0.4
Doug Henry	45	53.0	26	4.22	5.8	0.49	0.23	1.6	-0.4	4.17	6.0
Chris Holt	2	3.3	1	2.58	1.0	0.00	0.00	0.0	0.7	4.64	0.2
Scott Linebrink	8	9.7	5	4.45	0.8	0.38	0.17	1.2	1.7	4.73	0.5
Mike Maddux	21	27.3	20	6.29	-3.3	0.33	0.14	2.7	0.5	5.43	-0.7
Rusty Meacham	5	4.7	6	11.06	-3.0	0.60	0.26	0.3	0.0	10.55	-2.8
Yorkis Perez	33	22.7	18	6.83	-4.1	0.76	0.37	3.3	1.4	6.14	-2.4
Brian Powell	4	6.0	2	2.87	1.6	0.00	0.00	0.0	0.0	3.11	1.4
Jay Powell	29	27.0	18	5.73	-1.6	0.34	0.12	0.2	0.5	5.62	-1.3
Joe Slusarski	54	77.0	36	4.02	10.1	0.85	0.36	-3.0	1.0	4.60	5.1
Marc Valdes	53	56.7	41	6.22	-6.5	0.66	0.28	-3.0	3.9	7.29	-13.2
Billy Wagner	28	27.7	19	5.91	-2.2	0.54	0.14	-2.1	1.3	6.99	-5.5
TOTALS	410	449.7	282	5.39	-9.9	0.57	0.24			5.62	-21.3

For a quick guide to RET, see page 10.

Los Angeles Dodgers

If *L.A. Baseball* had been a staple of the Fox network's Wednesday-night lineup, it would have been cancelled a year ago and replaced by something less gory, like *When Good Staplers Go Bad* or *Donut Talk with Gary Huckabay*.

News Corporation's dalliance with the grand old game has been less than successful, if not an outright failure. The Fox Dodgers have spent more and gotten less in return than the people who bought Amazon at 200. The team hasn't made the postseason on Fox's watch, and the Dodgers haven't won a postseason game since Michael Dukakis had a chance. That's a long time for an organization that used to be one of the crown jewels of the game.

With each season under Fox, the Dodgers move further and further away from their storied history. Their player development has become a joke. Their international efforts are earning them suspensions and fines. The managers rent, they don't buy. Since Tommy Lasorda's health forced him out of the dugout in 1995, the Dodgers have had four skippers, with Jim Tracy the latest. The instability stretched into the front office as well, where there's a near-constant shuffling of bodies through the lower-profile jobs in player development and acquisition.

And the one person with job security is the one who brought you:

  Alan Mills for three years, $6.5 million

  Devon White for three years, $12.4 million

  Carlos Perez for three years, $15 million

  Mark Grudzielanek for four years, $18 million

  Eric Karros for three (more) years, $24 million

  Randy Dorame, Todd Hollandsworth, and Kevin Gibbs for Tom Goodwin

Kevin Malone has been throwing Fox's money away like the people behind *Titus*, but when it came time to toss a body overboard, it was Davey Johnson who got wet and Malone who kept his nameplate and expense account.

> **Dodgers Prospectus**
>
> **2000 record:** 86–76; Second place, NL West
> **Pythagenport W/L:** 88–74
> **Runs Scored:** 798 (8th in NL)
> **Runs Allowed:** 729 (2nd in NL)
> **Team EqA:** .266 (tied for 4th in NL)
> **2000 Batters' Age:** 29.5 (7th oldest in NL)
> **2000 Pitchers' Age:** 29.2 (5th oldest in NL)
> **Ballpark:** Dodger Stadium; good pitchers' park; Park Factor of .940
> **2000:** It's not just about payroll: the lack of top-of-the-order OBP hurt them, as did poor #4 and #5 starters.
> **2001:** They've spent even more money without addressing the OBP problem. They could still win by default.

This isn't a defense of Johnson. He didn't do his best work in Los Angeles, although his performance in 2000 was much better than it was in 1999. He adjusted nicely to the lack of a left-handed reliever; other than a minor flare-up with Adrian Beltre at midseason, he avoided the animosity with players that had marked his first Dodger campaign.

But how do you evaluate Kevin Malone's performance and conclude that he's an asset? He's spent millions of dollars on players without great track records and with low upsides, none of whom have justified the investment. He's yet to make a trade that has had a positive impact on the team. He allowed Johnson to take much of the blame for the Dodgers' struggles, fostering the impression that the flawed team Johnson had been given was championship caliber.

That's an ungenerous appraisal, to be sure. Let's look at it differently. What has Malone done that could be viewed positively?

Well, his pursuit and signing of Kevin Brown certainly garnered a lot of attention for the Dodgers. Brown was the big free-agent prize after the 1998 season, and acquiring him certainly generated some excitement and media attention for the Dodgers.

Malone hasn't been afraid to make a deal. While his trades for Shawn Green, Terry Adams, Ismael Valdes, and Tom Goodwin have been a mixed bag on the field, they have created the impression that the team is working hard to build a winner and, again, have kept the Dodgers in the spotlight.

Malone is an entertaining general manager to cover. He's quotable and accessible. These things make him good for the media corps and contribute to some positive coverage. Malone's "new sheriff in town" quote that spiced the Dodger-Padre rivalry may have made him look silly, but it certainly got attention.

Kevin Malone serves as an example of what corporate ownership values. There's no doubt that Fox would like the Dodgers to be a winning team, and the same can be said of Disney in Anaheim or the Tribune Company in Chicago. But what these entities really want is to be liked, to be popular. An entertainment company measures success by how many people see and spend money on its product, regardless of quality.

Viewed in that light, Kevin Malone is an excellent general manager for the Fox Dodgers. He's kept the team reasonably competitive (in part because of the vast Fox coffers), and, more importantly, he's kept them from being ignored. His baseball decision-making hasn't been particularly good, but he hasn't stood aside: he's signed people and made trades and done things that require press conferences and 36-point headlines. He looks particularly good when compared to Davey Johnson, who isn't as good with the media and whose positives are much harder to convey to management and the public.

The problems are that the things that make headlines don't always contribute to on-field success, and a good relationship with the local media doesn't help you win baseball games. Until Fox makes winning a greater priority than image, Malone will keep his job, and the team will hover between mediocrity and contention.

Another problem we're seeing with media-company ownership is that a long-term outlook is anathema to organizations whose performance is measured by last night's Nielsen ratings and weekend box-office estimates. Baseball teams aren't football teams. The best ones take a few years to get really good, and they sustain that success by constantly making good choices. The best teams of the last decade didn't make a lot of splashy free-agent signings. They developed their own talent and then let it play or used the fruits of the system to acquire players in trades—the best players, not the most popular ones.

Almost every decision the Dodgers have made since Malone arrived has had a significant public-relations element. After the 1998 season, they had to extend Jeff Shaw's contract at an outrageous cost or risk him demanding a trade. Given the cost of acquiring Shaw, the organization had little choice; the Pastaman's last supper, as it were.

The same can be said of the decision to sign Carlos Perez, after a strong September 1998. Perez, along with Mark Grudzielanek, had come over from the Expos at a steep cost. Signing him avoided arbitration and reinforced the notion that he'd been a good pickup. The Pastaman's last, uh, dessert.

The biggest moves of the Malone era—the Kevin Brown signing and the Shawn Green acquisition and signing—were expensive statements. The two players are among the best, but not *the* best, in the game, and were coming off peak or near-peak seasons. Each signing carried considerable risk, and each generated a media frenzy. You can guess which was more important to the parent company.

This kind of decision-making won't last forever. Unlike television and movies, success in baseball isn't measured just by eyeballs. Eventually, the team on the field has to win. Otherwise, people will eventually realize they're being taken. (Offer not valid on the north side of Chicago.) A team that spends lots of money on big signings and makes high-profile trades and never reaches the postseason will deal with a frustrated, dwindling fan base. No amount of bread and circuses can hold the attention of a populace that never sees a payoff.

The Dodgers two biggest moves at the winter meetings represented more of the same. They were the first team to sign a significant free agent, picking up a declining Andy Ashby for three years and $22.5 million. Then, after the two big free-agent pitchers had signed elsewhere, they gave Darren Dreifort—who has never thrown 200 innings in a season nor posted an ERA under 4.00 as a starter—a five-year contract worth $55 million. As a result, the Dodgers will pay their top four starters $45 million in 2001.

Not everything the Dodgers did in the offseason can be criticized. After a courtship with Kevin Kennedy, the Dodgers hired from within, making bench coach Jim Tracy the manager. Kennedy would have been the media-friendly choice; Tracy is pretty much an unknown, with some minor-league managing experience and a coaching background. The move is a first step towards putting baseball ahead of beat writers.

More to the point is that Fox wants to be successful in baseball. They don't want to be another Tribune Company, racking up 70-win seasons before crowds of 38,000 drunk and happy people. Despite all the backward steps they've taken along the way, this management group is not accustomed to failure. Having done it wrong for a few years, it seems that they are intent on getting it right and will move in that direction, most likely without Kevin Malone, over the next few years.

And that, friends, is baseball's nightmare. It's not the Yankees with $150 million in local media revenues and an owner completely committed to winning. It's a multinational corporation headed by one very rich man who is willing to operate the team at a significant loss until he eventually stumbles upon the right management personnel to make a winner. If Fox, or Carl Pohlad, decides to spend $200 million on payroll, they can do it without blinking an eye. Hell, Fox spends that much to promote, if not feed, *Ally McBeal*.

That's the real danger of corporate ownership. Not mediocre, poorly run teams more concerned with profit and image than success. The real danger is the reverse: an obsession with winning without any concern for cost or any fear of consequence. Right now, there exists some relationship between revenue and payroll, and that relationship does keep the teams—with the growing exceptions of the Yankees and Expos—within a certain expenditure range. Severing that

Los Angeles Dodgers

relationship to support a payroll that the baseball operation alone could never hope to cover would actually create the imbalance that so many people wrongfully believe already exists.

If the Dodgers lose $50 million on a $175 million payroll, so what? News Corporation folds that into their bottom line and writes it off. Fox, Disney, Time Warner, Tribune—these organizations can support payrolls that would make the 2000 Yankees look like the staff of *Baseball Prospectus*.

Dodger fans may be unhappy with what they've seen so far, but baseball fans can only hope it continues.

HITTERS (BA: .270, OBP: .340, SLG: .440, EqA: .260)

Luke Allen — 3B — Bats L — Age 22

YEAR	TEAM	LGE	AB	H	DB	TP	HR	BB	SO	R	RBI	SB	CS	OUT	BA	OBP	SLG	EQA	EQR	DEFENSE	
1998	San Bern	Cal	401	99	21	3	3	20	95	35	32	8	5	307	.247	.286	.337	.206	30	101-RF	-1
1998	SanAnton	Tex	78	21	2	0	3	4	18	7	7	1	1	58	.269	.305	.410	.234	8	21-RF	-1
1999	SanAnton	Tex	539	132	14	7	12	33	111	69	62	7	4	411	.245	.289	.364	.216	45	130-3B	-36
2000	SanAnton	Tex	345	81	14	3	6	28	75	42	46	7	3	267	.235	.293	.345	.214	28	86-3B	-9
2001	LosAngls	NL	440	113	14	3	10	37	102	54	53	11	4	331	.257	.314	.370	.241	47		

Luke Allen is a non-prospect. He'd be a non-prospect if the Dodgers had Adrian Zmed at third base, let alone Adrian Beltre. He doesn't hit, field, or run, and regresses a bit with each year he spends in San Antonio. In spite of all this, the Dodgers used an Arizona Fall League spot on him. This speaks badly for the organization.

Bruce Aven — OF — Bats R — Age 29

YEAR	TEAM	LGE	AB	H	DB	TP	HR	BB	SO	R	RBI	SB	CS	OUT	BA	OBP	SLG	EQA	EQR	DEFENSE	
1999	Florida	NL	384	110	18	2	12	39	77	55	66	2	0	274	.286	.365	.438	.271	53	86-LF	-2
2000	Pittsbrg	NL	149	37	9	0	5	3	29	17	23	2	3	115	.248	.263	.409	.213	12	29-OF	-7
2000	LosAngls	NL	20	5	0	0	2	3	7	2	4	0	0	15	.250	.348	.550	.288	3		
2001	LosAngls	NL	213	57	7	0	7	21	48	26	31	1	1	157	.268	.333	.399	.254	26		

The Pirates lost Bruce Aven in a roster crunch, and the Dodgers were the beneficiaries. Aven wasn't, as the Dodgers have about $27 million tied up in corner outfielders, severely curtailing his opportunities. He can hit well enough to be a fifth outfielder and pinch-hitter.

Adrian Beltre — 3B — Bats R — Age 22

YEAR	TEAM	LGE	AB	H	DB	TP	HR	BB	SO	R	RBI	SB	CS	OUT	BA	OBP	SLG	EQA	EQR	DEFENSE	
1998	SanAnton	Tex	248	66	16	1	9	30	41	33	38	10	3	185	.266	.348	.448	.268	34	57-3B	-7
1998	LosAngls	NL	198	45	8	0	8	14	35	19	23	3	1	154	.227	.288	.389	.225	18	59-3B	0
1999	LosAngls	NL	544	149	28	5	15	54	99	81	64	14	6	402	.274	.346	.426	.260	69	151-3B	-5
2000	LosAngls	NL	517	149	29	2	20	49	75	69	81	11	5	373	.288	.352	.468	.272	72	135-3B	4
2001	LosAngls	NL	483	147	26	2	19	54	83	91	86	21	5	341	.304	.374	.484	.297	82		

Continuous improvement is one of the things you most like to see in a young player. Adrian Beltre improved from 1999 to 2000, and he also improved within 2000, having a very good second half. The early-signing issue is already a fading memory; what remains is the talent.

Hiram Bocachica — 2B — Bats R — Age 25

YEAR	TEAM	LGE	AB	H	DB	TP	HR	BB	SO	R	RBI	SB	CS	OUT	BA	OBP	SLG	EQA	EQR	DEFENSE	
1998	Harrisbg	Eas	298	69	15	3	3	15	62	30	21	11	5	234	.232	.285	.332	.208	23	72-CF	-3
1998	Ottawa	Int	41	8	2	1	0	5	14	4	4	1	0	33	.195	.294	.293	.205	3	11-CF	0
1998	Albuquer	PCL	100	20	4	1	3	10	24	11	12	3	2	82	.200	.297	.350	.218	9	25-CF	7
1999	SanAnton	Tex	485	121	19	7	8	47	77	61	44	15	8	372	.249	.326	.367	.236	50	120-2B	-18
2000	Albuquer	PCL	471	125	29	2	17	29	102	71	57	6	8	354	.265	.322	.444	.250	55	115-2B	-11
2001	LosAngls	NL	444	113	23	2	13	40	95	58	59	10	6	337	.255	.316	.403	.248	52		

(Hiram Bocachica *continued*)

Mark Grudzielanek's contract means that Hiram Bocachica won't be playing second base for the Dodgers. Given how he plays it, that's not the end of the world. Bocachica should be a good, cheap bench player who can contribute in a lot of ways. He can play four positions, hit a little, and pinch-run. He makes an interesting test case for Jim Tracy.

Chin-Feng Chen   LF   Bats R   Age 23

YEAR	TEAM	LGE	AB	H	DB	TP	HR	BB	SO	R	RBI	SB	CS	OUT	BA	OBP	SLG	EQA	EQR	DEFENSE	
1999	San Bern	Cal	507	124	16	4	21	52	134	59	73	12	4	387	.245	.318	.416	.246	58	112-LF	-3
2000	SanAnton	Tex	524	127	23	2	5	43	138	50	51	12	8	405	.242	.302	.323	.210	41	127-LF	1
2001	LosAngls	NL	374	90	12	1	8	39	109	46	40	11	4	288	.241	.312	.342	.233	38		

The DT looks bad, but keep in mind that Chin-Feng Chen was in just his second year as a professional and his second year in the United States. The disappearance of his power was an extreme example of a player adjusting to older competition. This is a critical season for Chen; look for him to bounce back, hit well at both San Antonio and Las Vegas, and reach Chavez Ravine in September.

Alex Cora   SS   Bats L   Age 25

YEAR	TEAM	LGE	AB	H	DB	TP	HR	BB	SO	R	RBI	SB	CS	OUT	BA	OBP	SLG	EQA	EQR	DEFENSE	
1998	Albuquer	PCL	293	65	12	4	4	12	38	31	33	7	5	233	.222	.257	.331	.190	18	80-SS	-5
1999	Albuquer	PCL	293	75	7	5	3	10	36	37	27	6	3	221	.256	.293	.345	.212	23	76-SS	-2
2000	Albuquer	PCL	107	34	6	2	0	4	10	13	14	3	2	75	.318	.351	.411	.255	12	30-SS	0
2000	LosAngls	NL	358	87	21	5	4	21	50	39	31	4	1	272	.243	.296	.363	.221	31	97-SS	-8
2001	LosAngls	NL	371	94	18	6	4	24	51	44	39	9	4	281	.253	.299	.367	.231	36		

Left-handed-hitting everyday shortstops are fairly rare. Mike Caruso was the regular for about two seasons with the White Sox, who also employed Ozzie Guillen for ten years. Bill Spiers had one year with the Brewers, and you have to go back to Ernest Riles and Craig Reynolds. Cora is a passable stopgap; the Dodgers need something more to win.

Bubba Crosby   LF   Bats L   Age 24

YEAR	TEAM	LGE	AB	H	DB	TP	HR	BB	SO	R	RBI	SB	CS	OUT	BA	OBP	SLG	EQA	EQR	DEFENSE	
1998	San Bern	Cal	201	40	8	1	0	12	39	20	11	2	3	164	.199	.244	.249	.146	7	49-CF	1
1999	San Bern	Cal	369	89	16	1	1	28	74	33	25	7	4	284	.241	.300	.298	.202	26	87-CF	-3
2000	Vero Bch	Fla	278	61	10	4	7	22	47	33	35	12	5	222	.219	.285	.360	.218	25	68-LF	-6
2001	LosAngls	NL	320	73	9	2	4	31	64	37	27	13	4	251	.228	.296	.306	.217	27		

Here's a test of the Arizona Fall League's power to save a career. Bubba Crosby hadn't hit worth spit since being drafted in the first round in 1998. In the AFL, he hit .340 with some power, so he's back on the prospect track. Still, he's one-dimensional; there's not much chance of him ever contributing to the Dodgers.

Kevin Elster   SS   Bats R   Age 36

YEAR	TEAM	LGE	AB	H	DB	TP	HR	BB	SO	R	RBI	SB	CS	OUT	BA	OBP	SLG	EQA	EQR	DEFENSE	
1998	Texas	AL	295	69	10	1	8	32	59	33	35	0	2	228	.234	.313	.356	.224	27	80-SS	6
2000	LosAngls	NL	223	51	7	0	14	35	49	28	31	0	0	172	.229	.333	.448	.260	30	48-SS	-12
2001	LosAngls	NL	157	34	4	0	7	27	38	20	23	0	0	123	.217	.332	.376	.250	19		

They shoot shortstops, don't they? The Dodgers moved Mark Grudzielanek to second base to make room for Alex Cora, then let Kevin Elster—who played with John McGraw in the minors—win the job in spring training. In Davey We Rust. Elster might have retired again, but check back in 2010.

Geronimo Gil   C   Bats R   Age 25

YEAR	TEAM	LGE	AB	H	DB	TP	HR	BB	SO	R	RBI	SB	CS	OUT	BA	OBP	SLG	EQA	EQR	DEFENSE			
1998	SanAnton	Tex	241	60	17	1	4	11	47	21	21	1	1	182	.249	.282	.378	.215	20	25-C	-4	20-LF	-3
1999	SanAnton	Tex	350	85	18	1	12	38	63	36	44	1	0	265	.243	.319	.403	.242	38	71-C	-3	20-RF	0
2000	SanAnton	Tex	356	87	16	1	8	22	70	32	42	1	1	270	.244	.295	.362	.218	30	75-C	1	12-RF	-1
2000	Albuquer	PCL	48	15	2	0	2	4	8	6	14	0	1	34	.313	.365	.479	.273	7				
2001	LosAngls	NL	339	89	17	1	11	35	69	45	50	1	1	251	.263	.332	.416	.258	43				

Taking advantage of Angel Pena's problems, Geronimo Gil now has a chance at a career. He'll go to camp trying to outplay Pena and Paul LoDuca, and squeeze in as a backup to Chad Kreuter. Gil can play and will spend a few years as a quality backup starting in 2002.

Tom Goodwin — CF — Bats L — Age 32

YEAR	TEAM	LGE	AB	H	DB	TP	HR	BB	SO	R	RBI	SB	CS	OUT	BA	OBP	SLG	EQA	EQR	DEFENSE	
1998	Texas	AL	514	148	13	3	2	72	80	95	31	30	18	384	.288	.377	.337	.251	60	138-CF	4
1999	Texas	AL	401	103	11	6	3	36	56	58	31	36	11	309	.257	.318	.337	.232	40	106-CF	0
2000	Colorado	NL	308	70	8	6	4	43	71	53	37	31	6	245	.227	.324	.331	.239	34	85-CF	1
2000	LosAngls	NL	214	54	4	1	1	15	38	28	11	15	3	163	.252	.301	.294	.212	17	55-CF	6
2001	LosAngls	NL	434	102	8	5	4	60	87	71	36	36	12	344	.235	.328	.304	.237	47		

There are worse ideas than trading for Tom Goodwin. The butterfly ballot. *Judge Judy*. Letting Bobcat Goldthwait do your LASIK surgery. Goodwin is worth the roster spot as a defensive replacement and pinch-runner. He just doesn't deserve millions of dollars, job security, and 500 at-bats a year. This is the most recent of Kevin Malone's bad ideas.

Shawn Green — RF — Bats L — Age 28

YEAR	TEAM	LGE	AB	H	DB	TP	HR	BB	SO	R	RBI	SB	CS	OUT	BA	OBP	SLG	EQA	EQR	DEFENSE	
1998	Toronto	AL	628	178	32	4	37	49	127	104	99	29	11	461	.283	.340	.524	.280	96	142-RF	2
1999	Toronto	AL	608	190	38	0	45	60	107	129	119	19	7	425	.313	.383	.597	.313	116		
2000	LosAngls	NL	619	166	46	4	23	81	113	95	94	22	5	458	.268	.359	.467	.278	93	151-RF	-7
2001	LosAngls	NL	557	158	30	1	33	79	109	113	109	30	7	406	.284	.373	.519	.304	104		

It's a perfectly nice season by a perfectly nice player. The problem is the Dodgers paid Shawn Green with the expectation that he'd keep having 1999. That, more or less, is the problem with most free-agent signings: unrealistic expectations based on one season's performance. Green will be a .290-.300 EqA player for the next few years. Here's hoping he doesn't get labeled a disappointment.

Mark Grudzielanek — 2B — Bats R — Age 31

YEAR	TEAM	LGE	AB	H	DB	TP	HR	BB	SO	R	RBI	SB	CS	OUT	BA	OBP	SLG	EQA	EQR	DEFENSE
1998	Montreal	NL	400	110	14	1	9	20	47	52	41	10	5	295	.275	.323	.382	.238	41	105-SS -18
1998	LosAngls	NL	196	54	4	0	3	5	22	12	22	7	0	142	.276	.300	.342	.221	16	51-SS 8
1999	LosAngls	NL	493	159	23	5	7	25	61	70	44	4	5	339	.323	.367	.432	.267	62	115-SS -5
2000	LosAngls	NL	626	176	38	5	7	36	76	99	48	11	3	453	.281	.328	.391	.243	66	146-2B -12
2001	LosAngls	NL	520	143	21	2	7	35	67	65	59	12	3	380	.275	.321	.363	.242	55	

In fairness to Mark Gruzdzielanek, he was having a decent season when he picked up a virus in July. From that point forward, he was in and out of the lineup and not much good when he played. He's still overpaid and overrated, just not as much as it looks here. The contracts given to him and Carlos Perez are damaging this team.

Dave Hansen — PH — Bats L — Age 32

YEAR	TEAM	LGE	AB	H	DB	TP	HR	BB	SO	R	RBI	SB	CS	OUT	BA	OBP	SLG	EQA	EQR	DEFENSE
1998	HAN	JpC	408	99	12	1	11	35	0	0	0	0	0	309	.243	.302	.358	.223	36	
1999	LosAngls	NL	108	27	8	1	2	25	19	14	16	0	0	81	.250	.400	.398	.279	17	
2000	LosAngls	NL	123	35	6	2	8	24	30	18	25	0	1	89	.285	.401	.561	.309	24	
2001	LosAngls	NL	158	41	6	1	6	27	24	25	27	0	0	117	.259	.368	.424	.278	24	

Take that projection with a grain of salt, because projecting even the best pinch-hitters is a crapshoot. In 150 at-bats, just about anything can happen. Dave Hansen deserves a chunk of Eric Karros's at-bats but won't get them.

Todd Hundley — C — Bats B — Age 32

YEAR	TEAM	LGE	AB	H	DB	TP	HR	BB	SO	R	RBI	SB	CS	OUT	BA	OBP	SLG	EQA	EQR	DEFENSE	
1998	NY Mets	NL	126	22	3	0	4	15	51	9	14	1	1	105	.175	.267	.294	.185	8	27-LF	-4
1999	LosAngls	NL	381	80	12	0	25	39	107	48	54	2	0	301	.210	.290	.438	.239	42	103-C	-11
2000	LosAngls	NL	303	86	14	0	24	41	65	48	67	0	1	218	.284	.372	.568	.301	54	79-C	-9
2001	ChiCubs	NL	311	79	12	0	20	46	83	45	59	0	0	232	.254	.350	.486	.278	47		

(Todd Hundley *continued*)

It was good to see Todd Hundley get back to his established level of performance at the plate, if not the field. In 2001, the Cubs are saying they will use him to catch about half the time, and have him play another 60 games at first base. Wilton can't really work with his career path, so the projection is off; he's at least a .280 EqA player.

Eric Karros — 1B — Bats R — Age 33

YEAR	TEAM	LGE	AB	H	DB	TP	HR	BB	SO	R	RBI	SB	CS	OUT	BA	OBP	SLG	EQA	EQR	DEFENSE	
1998	LosAngls	NL	519	157	17	1	26	46	87	62	90	7	2	364	.303	.362	.489	.282	77	133-1B	4
1999	LosAngls	NL	585	177	33	0	36	45	112	72	108	6	5	413	.303	.354	.544	.288	92	147-1B	11
2000	LosAngls	NL	592	149	25	0	32	55	114	82	103	4	3	446	.252	.319	.456	.254	73	149-1B	16
2001	*LosAngls*	*NL*	*548*	*152*	*20*	*0*	*32*	*64*	*111*	*82*	*107*	*4*	*2*	*398*	*.277*	*.353*	*.489*	*.286*	*87*		

That projection is high, though not so high as the Dodgers were when they gave Eric Karros a three-year, $24-million contract extension. Even at his best, he was overrated because he had only a decent OBP and power that didn't stand out for a first baseman. He's a name to keep in mind when people talk about how players don't stay with one team anymore.

Chad Kreuter — C — Bats B — Age 36

YEAR	TEAM	LGE	AB	H	DB	TP	HR	BB	SO	R	RBI	SB	CS	OUT	BA	OBP	SLG	EQA	EQR	DEFENSE	
1998	ChiSox	AL	245	65	10	1	2	32	40	27	33	1	0	180	.265	.357	.339	.243	26	75-C	1
1999	KansasCy	AL	321	72	10	0	7	31	59	29	35	0	0	249	.224	.303	.321	.211	25	87-C	2
2000	LosAngls	NL	215	57	9	0	7	51	45	31	28	1	0	158	.265	.410	.405	.286	34	67-C	4
2001	*LosAngls*	*NL*	*239*	*55*	*5*	*0*	*6*	*44*	*50*	*33*	*29*	*0*	*0*	*184*	*.230*	*.350*	*.326*	*.246*	*28*		

In a charming repeat of 1992, Chad Kreuter has parlayed 250 good plate appearances into a nice contract and a semi-regular job. He's a fair backup who can play the position and whose main offensive skill is walks. As long as his playing time doesn't increase, he's an asset.

Jim Leyritz — UT — Bats R — Age 37

YEAR	TEAM	LGE	AB	H	DB	TP	HR	BB	SO	R	RBI	SB	CS	OUT	BA	OBP	SLG	EQA	EQR	DEFENSE			
1998	Boston	AL	128	37	5	0	9	21	30	17	24	0	0	91	.289	.397	.539	.306	24				
1998	San Dieg	NL	147	41	8	0	5	20	37	18	19	0	0	106	.279	.390	.435	.281	22	19-C	-1	16-1B	-1
1999	San Dieg	NL	136	33	5	0	8	13	35	17	20	0	0	103	.243	.326	.456	.258	17	22-C	-4	14-1B	-1
1999	NY Yanks	AL	66	16	4	1	0	12	15	8	5	0	0	50	.242	.359	.333	.243	7				
2000	NY Yanks	AL	55	12	1	0	1	6	13	3	4	0	0	43	.218	.307	.291	.204	4				
2000	LosAngls	NL	61	13	1	0	1	6	11	3	8	0	0	48	.213	.293	.279	.191	4				
2001	*LosAngls*	*NL*	*123*	*26*	*3*	*0*	*4*	*20*	*31*	*14*	*15*	*0*	*0*	*97*	*.211*	*.322*	*.333*	*.234*	*13*				

This is the sixth edition of *Baseball Prospectus*, and every year there are one or two players who make the book for no reason other than had too many at-bats to be ignored. Jim Leyritz, who is still a serviceable bench player, falls into that category this year. Nevertheless, he played so little in 2000 that it's hard to know if his skills are still intact.

Paul LoDuca — C — Bats R — Age 29

YEAR	TEAM	LGE	AB	H	DB	TP	HR	BB	SO	R	RBI	SB	CS	OUT	BA	OBP	SLG	EQA	EQR	DEFENSE			
1998	Albuquer	PCL	440	113	23	2	5	47	41	49	40	12	5	332	.257	.333	.352	.236	45	80-C	-1	17-1B	1
1999	Albuquer	PCL	73	21	4	0	1	8	1	11	5	1	1	53	.288	.386	.384	.266	10	17-C	-4		
1999	LosAngls	NL	96	22	1	0	3	9	8	11	10	1	2	76	.229	.308	.333	.213	8	27-C	1		
2000	Albuquer	PCL	271	74	20	2	2	23	15	31	34	4	3	200	.273	.333	.384	.241	29	46-C	-2		
2000	LosAngls	NL	66	16	3	0	2	5	7	6	8	0	2	52	.242	.296	.379	.214	5	15-C	3		
2001	*LosAngls*	*NL*	*246*	*62*	*13*	*1*	*3*	*28*	*18*	*33*	*27*	*4*	*3*	*187*	*.252*	*.328*	*.350*	*.239*	*26*				

Along with Kreuter, Paul LoDuca gives the Dodgers a couple of good #2 catchers. If Angel Pena doesn't get over his weight problems, the Dodgers can get by in 2001. Beyond that, they'll have to find a more permanent solution.

National League

Lamont Matthews — OF — Bats L — Age 23

YEAR	TEAM	LGE	AB	H	DB	TP	HR	BB	SO	R	RBI	SB	CS	OUT	BA	OBP	SLG	EQA	EQR	DEFENSE			
1999	Yakima	Nwn	253	46	9	0	11	20	97	27	28	1	2	209	.182	.244	.348	.189	16	66-CF	4		
2000	San Bern	Cal	485	98	20	4	18	59	177	54	55	4	5	392	.202	.293	.371	.220	45	128-OF	8		
2001	LosAngls	NL	279	55	11	0	12	35	115	30	33	2	2	226	.197	.287	.366	.225	27				

Lamont Matthews doesn't have much future in this organization because of Gary Sheffield's presence. That said, he's hit well since the Dodgers made him their 10th-round pick in 1999 and stands out in this organization for his walks and power. He could have a huge year at San Antonio.

Tony Mota — RF — Bats B — Age 23

YEAR	TEAM	LGE	AB	H	DB	TP	HR	BB	SO	R	RBI	SB	CS	OUT	BA	OBP	SLG	EQA	EQR	DEFENSE	
1998	Vero Bch	Fla	253	64	13	3	5	13	31	30	23	5	4	193	.253	.292	.387	.223	23	54-CF	-1
1998	SanAnton	Tex	223	49	9	3	2	8	40	14	17	9	5	179	.220	.247	.314	.181	13	49-CF	-2
1999	SanAnton	Tex	350	97	21	1	12	32	61	48	55	7	3	256	.277	.338	.446	.261	44	59-RF	-2
2000	Albuquer	PCL	367	85	11	2	5	19	62	43	35	5	4	286	.232	.269	.313	.189	22	81-RF	-2
2001	LosAngls	NL	349	90	12	1	10	25	63	42	43	9	4	263	.258	.307	.384	.240	37		

One of the frustrations in the performance-analysis field is determining which performance changes are development and which are just flukes. Tony Mota was one of those tough calls a year ago; he was young enough for the uptick to be real, and the gains were across the board—average, power, patience. Now, it looks like a mirage. Mota will eventually have a career as a fourth outfielder.

Jorge Nunez — SS — Bats R — Age 23

YEAR	TEAM	LGE	AB	H	DB	TP	HR	BB	SO	R	RBI	SB	CS	OUT	BA	OBP	SLG	EQA	EQR	DEFENSE			
1998	Med Hat	Pio	311	73	7	6	4	10	53	33	27	10	2	240	.235	.259	.334	.197	21	65-SS	-8		
1999	Hagerstn	SAL	572	125	21	6	10	30	109	73	42	19	5	452	.219	.259	.329	.196	38	122-2B	-13	15-SS	-3
2000	Vero Bch	Fla	536	130	16	4	4	27	118	57	28	23	12	417	.243	.280	.310	.198	36	124-SS	-24		
2001	LosAngls	NL	479	111	13	3	7	35	105	53	40	25	9	377	.232	.284	.315	.214	40				

Jorge Nunez looked like a steal when the Dodgers got him thrown into the Shawn Green deal. He hit .288 and stole a lot of bases in the Florida State League; however, nothing else was good, particularly defensively, so despite lots of tools—including great speed—his prospect status is tenuous.

Angel Pena — C — Bats R — Age 26

YEAR	TEAM	LGE	AB	H	DB	TP	HR	BB	SO	R	RBI	SB	CS	OUT	BA	OBP	SLG	EQA	EQR	DEFENSE			
1998	SanAnton	Tex	484	135	24	1	16	35	88	58	73	5	3	352	.279	.332	.432	.254	57	112-C	-8		
1999	Albuquer	PCL	124	30	6	1	1	8	23	11	18	2	1	95	.242	.288	.331	.206	9	28-C	0		
1999	LosAngls	NL	121	25	4	0	5	11	23	14	21	0	1	97	.207	.273	.364	.206	9	35-C	0		
2000	Albuquer	PCL	309	80	9	2	13	20	77	38	43	2	1	230	.259	.304	.427	.241	33	60-C	0	14-1B	-1
2001	LosAngls	NL	277	71	10	0	11	27	66	35	41	3	1	207	.256	.322	.412	.254	34				

He's eating himself out of millions of dollars. Angel Pena again reported to spring training overweight, killing any chance he had of beating out Kreuter for the backup catcher job. He needs a new organization and an appetite suppressant, not necessarily in that order.

F.P. Santangelo — UT — Bats B — Age 33

YEAR	TEAM	LGE	AB	H	DB	TP	HR	BB	SO	R	RBI	SB	CS	OUT	BA	OBP	SLG	EQA	EQR	DEFENSE			
1998	Montreal	NL	387	85	13	0	6	43	67	54	24	7	3	305	.220	.331	.300	.222	35	75-LF	3	26-2B	-3
1999	San Fran	NL	257	67	16	3	3	49	51	46	25	9	4	194	.261	.400	.381	.276	39	59-CF	0		
2000	LosAngls	NL	144	29	2	0	2	19	31	19	10	3	2	117	.201	.316	.257	.201	11	30-OF	-2		
2001	LosAngls	NL	192	41	7	1	2	29	40	25	16	4	2	153	.214	.317	.292	.221	17				

One of the game's best bench players had one of the game's worst years. F.P. Santangelo has been brutal in two of the last three seasons, but a torn ligament in his left hand ended his 2000 season early. He'll be a valuable part of the 2001 Dodgers, albeit with minimal fantasy value.

Gary Sheffield — LF — Bats R — Age 32

YEAR	TEAM	LGE	AB	H	DB	TP	HR	BB	SO	R	RBI	SB	CS	OUT	BA	OBP	SLG	EQA	EQR	DEFENSE	
1998	Florida	NL	139	38	9	1	7	26	15	22	29	4	2	103	.273	.395	.504	.297	25	34-RF	-1
1998	LosAngls	NL	312	101	16	1	18	68	28	55	60	17	5	216	.324	.453	.554	.335	70	83-RF	-2
1999	LosAngls	NL	556	166	16	0	35	93	60	100	97	9	5	395	.299	.403	.516	.304	100	132-LF	-4
2000	LosAngls	NL	509	163	23	3	42	93	66	101	103	3	6	352	.320	.429	.625	.333	113	119-LF	-8
2001	LosAngls	NL	520	157	19	1	36	110	66	114	125	10	6	369	.302	.424	.550	.328	114		

If Edgar Martinez does retire, here's a new nominee for the most underrated player in the game. Gary Sheffield's career EqA of .316 is tenth among active players and 43rd all time. For any number of reasons, some his own making, he hasn't received proper credit. When the Dodgers win the NL West, he'll be the league MVP.

Joe Thurston — SS — Bats L — Age 21

YEAR	TEAM	LGE	AB	H	DB	TP	HR	BB	SO	R	RBI	SB	CS	OUT	BA	OBP	SLG	EQA	EQR	DEFENSE			
1999	Yakima	Nwn	277	63	8	2	0	15	38	24	20	8	7	221	.227	.286	.271	.184	16	67-SS	-1		
2000	San Bern	Cal	556	140	27	5	3	32	63	61	46	13	9	425	.252	.302	.335	.213	45	110-SS	1	28-2B	-4
2001	LosAngls	NL	328	84	13	2	1	21	47	35	28	10	7	251	.256	.301	.317	.215	27				

Joe Thurston got his break when 1999 #1 pick Jason Repko missed 2000 with an injury. Thurston is a very fast slap hitter, in the right organization for a shortstop of middling ability. Where the organization places Nunez and Thurston will be one of Dodgertown's better storylines this spring.

Devon White — CF — Bats B — Age 38

YEAR	TEAM	LGE	AB	H	DB	TP	HR	BB	SO	R	RBI	SB	CS	OUT	BA	OBP	SLG	EQA	EQR	DEFENSE	
1998	Arizona	NL	568	156	26	1	24	40	96	84	84	21	8	420	.275	.332	.451	.260	73	140-CF	6
1999	LosAngls	NL	479	129	21	2	14	33	83	58	65	15	5	355	.269	.330	.409	.250	56	122-CF	-5
2000	LosAngls	NL	160	43	4	1	4	7	28	25	12	3	6	123	.269	.303	.381	.219	14	35-CF	-2
2001	LosAngls	NL	269	63	8	0	9	22	50	31	30	9	4	210	.234	.292	.364	.229	26		

There was a case to be made, about a year or so ago, for Devon White as a useful fourth outfielder, especially on a team with Gary Sheffield. Now, he looks done; a torn rotator cuff wiped out the parts of the season in which he didn't suck. White was the gold standard for center-field defense between Dwayne Murphy and Andruw Jones.

PITCHERS (ERA: 4.50, H/9: 9.00, HR/9: 1.00, BB/9: 3.00, K/9: 6.00, KW: 1.00, PERA: 4.50)

Terry Adams — Throws R — Age 28

YEAR	TEAM	LGE	IP	H	ER	HR	BB	K	ERA	W	L	H/9	HR/9	BB/9	K/9	KW	PERA
1998	ChiCubs	NL	70.3	72	39	7	37	59	4.99	3	5	9.21	0.90	4.73	7.55	0.80	5.24
1999	ChiCubs	NL	63.7	58	30	8	23	48	4.24	3	4	8.20	1.13	3.25	6.79	1.04	4.28
2000	LosAngls	NL	81.7	78	40	6	34	47	4.41	4	5	8.60	0.66	3.75	5.18	0.69	4.23

Terry Adams is pretty much the ground-ball-inducing workhorse every team needs in the seventh and eighth innings. A 20-inning April preceded a rough patch, after which he was fine. He's never had consecutive good seasons, so tread carefully.

Kevin Brown — Throws R — Age 36

YEAR	TEAM	LGE	IP	H	ER	HR	BB	K	ERA	W	L	H/9	HR/9	BB/9	K/9	KW	PERA
1998	San Dieg	NL	244.3	222	79	9	48	209	2.91	18	9	8.18	0.33	1.77	7.70	2.18	2.92
1999	LosAngls	NL	242.0	203	97	20	52	186	3.61	15	12	7.55	0.74	1.93	6.92	1.79	3.02
2000	LosAngls	NL	220.3	178	76	21	41	180	3.10	15	9	7.27	0.86	1.67	7.35	2.20	2.89

National League

Kevin Brown is starting to move in the general direction of Hall of Fame consideration. Two years ago, *Baseball Prospectus 1999* touted the case of David Cone, who declined rapidly from that point and now needs a comeback just to get close. Brown is now the same age Cone was at that point; he has 170 wins and a career winning percentage of .599. He's pitching at a higher level now than had Cone was going into 1999. As a matter of fact, he was the second-best pitcher in the NL last season.

The bad news for Brown is that he doesn't have Cone's high points. No Cy Young Awards, just one 20-win season and just one world championship. His only black-ink markers are two ERA titles, a wins crown, and one time leading the league in innings pitched.

Greg Maddux, Roger Clemens, and Tom Glavine are the best starting pitchers of this era. It's not realistic to expect that they'll be the only Hall of Famers; some of Cone, Brown, Orel Hershiser, Mike Mussina, John Smoltz, and Jack Morris are going. Right now, Brown's resume looks like the second-best in that group, and he and Mussina are the only ones still at the top of their game.

Adrian Burnside — Throws L — Age 24

YEAR	TEAM	LGE	IP	H	ER	HR	BB	K	ERA	W	L	H/9	HR/9	BB/9	K/9	KW	PERA
1998	Yakima	Nwn	30.0	28	24	2	35	17	7.20	1	2	8.40	0.60	10.50	5.10	0.24	6.81
1998	San Bern	Cal	72.0	94	84	13	57	34	10.50	1	7	11.75	1.63	7.13	4.25	0.30	8.48
1999	San Bern	Cal	122.3	122	76	13	65	68	5.59	5	9	8.98	0.96	4.78	5.00	0.52	5.18
2000	SanAnton	Tex	84.0	74	51	12	65	50	5.46	3	6	7.93	1.29	6.96	5.36	0.38	5.82

While they lack great position-player prospects, the Dodgers are fairly deep in arms. Adrian Burnside was pitching reasonably well when he was shut down in July, suffering from elbow tendinitis. This effectively kept him from pitching for Australia in the Olympics, as well. If healthy, he should be up in September.

Robinson Checo — Throws R — Age 29

YEAR	TEAM	LGE	IP	H	ER	HR	BB	K	ERA	W	L	H/9	HR/9	BB/9	K/9	KW	PERA
1998	Pawtuckt	Int	50.0	49	33	11	26	31	5.94	2	4	8.82	1.98	4.68	5.58	0.60	6.13
1999	Albuquer	PCL	74.3	68	41	15	41	62	4.96	3	5	8.23	1.82	4.96	7.51	0.76	5.72
1999	LosAngls	NL	15.3	23	18	5	11	9	10.57	0	2	13.50	2.93	6.46	5.28	0.41	10.56
2000	Albuquer	PCL	82.3	78	37	13	32	57	4.04	4	5	8.53	1.42	3.50	6.23	0.89	4.88

The Dodgers did such a good job bringing in middle relief last off-season that they never had a chance to call up Robinson Checo, who had his best year since 1997. His reputation as a head case hurts, because there are a dozen guys just like him who don't come with that baggage. Paying Jose Mesa millions of dollars is stupid when there are pitchers like Checo available.

Allen Davis — Throws L — Age 25

YEAR	TEAM	LGE	IP	H	ER	HR	BB	K	ERA	W	L	H/9	HR/9	BB/9	K/9	KW	PERA
1998	Yakima	Nwn	15.3	10	4	0	4	7	2.35	1	1	5.87	0.00	2.35	4.11	0.88	1.81
1998	San Bern	Cal	28.7	32	16	4	9	17	5.02	1	2	10.05	1.26	2.83	5.34	0.94	5.36
1998	SanAnton	Tex	29.0	31	15	3	11	22	4.66	1	2	9.62	0.93	3.41	6.83	1.00	4.96
1999	SanAnton	Tex	119.3	138	100	24	59	54	7.54	3	10	10.41	1.81	4.45	4.07	0.46	6.80
2000	SanAnton	Tex	147.7	189	115	37	63	71	7.01	4	12	11.52	2.26	3.84	4.33	0.56	7.66

Allen Davis seems to have reached his level at Double-A San Antonio and has neither the stuff nor the performance record of a top prospect. The Expos took him in the Triple-A portion of the Rule 5 draft. It will be hard for Davis to make headway in an organization as loaded with pitching prospects as the Montreal.

Darren Dreifort — Throws R — Age 29

YEAR	TEAM	LGE	IP	H	ER	HR	BB	K	ERA	W	L	H/9	HR/9	BB/9	K/9	KW	PERA
1998	LosAngls	NL	171.3	169	88	14	55	137	4.62	8	11	8.88	0.74	2.89	7.20	1.25	4.11
1999	LosAngls	NL	172.7	172	103	21	67	118	5.37	7	12	8.97	1.09	3.49	6.15	0.88	4.79
2000	LosAngls	NL	186.0	173	103	31	76	136	4.98	8	13	8.37	1.50	3.68	6.58	0.89	4.94

One of the more inexplicable things in baseball is the idea that Darren Dreifort is a star. His won/loss record comes up as a negative, but there's much better evidence that he's overrated. He's never thrown 200 innings in a season. Despite a good fastball and a nasty slider, he's never put up good peripheral numbers. Or primary ones, for that matter. Five years and $55 million is a huge investment in a #3 starter, and the fact that there were worse contracts given out—Kevin Appier, anyone?—doesn't make this one any better.

Mike Fetters — Throws R — Age 36

YEAR	TEAM	LGE	IP	H	ER	HR	BB	K	ERA	W	L	H/9	HR/9	BB/9	K/9	KW	PERA
1998	Oakland	AL	46.7	45	23	3	18	31	4.44	2	3	8.68	0.58	3.47	5.98	0.86	4.07
1998	Anaheim	AL	11.3	13	7	2	3	8	5.56	0	1	10.32	1.59	2.38	6.35	1.33	5.64
1999	Baltimor	AL	31.0	33	19	4	18	21	5.52	1	2	9.58	1.16	5.23	6.10	0.58	5.92
2000	LosAngls	NL	48.3	35	18	7	22	33	3.35	3	2	6.52	1.30	4.10	6.14	0.75	3.84

Wow, he was injured for part of the year and fairly effective when healthy. That's never happened before. As he was in 2000, Mike Fetters will be the Dodger reliever who picks up saves when Jeff Shaw struggles. And Shaw will struggle.

Eric Gagne — Throws R — Age 25

YEAR	TEAM	LGE	IP	H	ER	HR	BB	K	ERA	W	L	H/9	HR/9	BB/9	K/9	KW	PERA
1998	Vero Bch	Fla	126.3	129	94	30	58	82	6.70	4	10	9.19	2.14	4.13	5.84	0.71	6.29
1999	SanAnton	Tex	151.0	132	80	31	81	115	4.77	7	10	7.87	1.85	4.83	6.85	0.71	5.49
1999	LosAngls	NL	29.0	18	8	3	13	25	2.48	2	1	5.59	0.93	4.03	7.76	0.96	2.95
2000	Albuquer	PCL	53.3	55	30	9	14	42	5.06	2	4	9.28	1.52	2.36	7.09	1.50	4.95
2000	LosAngls	NL	98.3	104	59	20	52	66	5.40	4	7	9.52	1.83	4.76	6.04	0.63	6.40

The Dodgers spent most of 2000 mishandling Eric Gagne, jerking him between L.A. and Albuquerque and never allowing him to get settled in a rotation. He didn't make it easier by throwing a ton of pitches on his way to averaging just over five innings per start. He'll go into camp in the same position as a year ago: battling Carlos Perez for the #5 starter's job.

Carlos Garcia — Throws R — Age 22

YEAR	TEAM	LGE	IP	H	ER	HR	BB	K	ERA	W	L	H/9	HR/9	BB/9	K/9	KW	PERA
2000	San Bern	Cal	171.0	155	58	11	52	57	3.05	12	7	8.16	0.58	2.74	3.00	0.55	3.50

It's hard to be down on the California League Pitcher of the Year, but Carlos Garcia's big season comes with a couple of caveats. One is his experience: he'd played two years with the Mexico City Reds, so the Cal League wasn't a big change for him. Another is his workload: he went at least six innings in 25 of his 27 starts and was second in innings pitched among all A-ball starters.

Matt Herges — Throws R — Age 31

YEAR	TEAM	LGE	IP	H	ER	HR	BB	K	ERA	W	L	H/9	HR/9	BB/9	K/9	KW	PERA
1998	Albuquer	PCL	85.0	109	60	9	38	48	6.35	3	6	11.54	0.95	4.02	5.08	0.63	6.38
1999	Albuquer	PCL	125.7	124	75	17	49	55	5.37	5	9	8.88	1.22	3.51	3.94	0.56	4.87
1999	LosAngls	NL	23.3	23	12	5	7	15	4.63	1	2	8.87	1.93	2.70	5.79	1.07	5.26
2000	LosAngls	NL	106.7	97	41	7	35	62	3.46	7	5	8.18	0.59	2.95	5.23	0.89	3.61

Gagne's inability to get past the fifth inning and Orel Hershiser's struggles left a lot of middle-inning work. Matt Herges stepped in and owned those innings, inducing ground ball after ground ball in getting games to Mike Fetters and Terry Adams. He should decline in 2001—this was his career year—while still being worth the roster spot. Another good reason to mock the Jose Mesa contract.

Orel Hershiser — Throws R — Age 42

YEAR	TEAM	LGE	IP	H	ER	HR	BB	K	ERA	W	L	H/9	HR/9	BB/9	K/9	KW	PERA
1998	San Fran	NL	192.3	194	106	25	80	102	4.96	8	13	9.08	1.17	3.74	4.77	0.64	5.03
1999	NY Mets	NL	173.3	166	85	14	67	75	4.41	9	10	8.62	0.73	3.48	3.89	0.56	4.19
2000	LosAngls	NL	24.3	41	34	5	12	11	12.58	0	3	15.16	1.85	4.44	4.07	0.46	9.67

Is Orel Hershiser a Hall of Famer? Tough call, but I think he eventually ends up in, thanks to a great public image and the memory of 1988. Whether he deserves it is another question; Greg Maddux and Roger Clemens are in, and among his contemporaries, Hershiser is behind at least Tom Glavine and David Cone, and may eventually end up behind John Smoltz. He doesn't have overly impressive black ink and just barely reached 200 wins. He's a perfect Veterans Committee pick, actually.

Mike Judd — Throws R — Age 26

YEAR	TEAM	LGE	IP	H	ER	HR	BB	K	ERA	W	L	H/9	HR/9	BB/9	K/9	KW	PERA
1998	Albuquer	PCL	91.7	92	55	16	42	53	5.40	4	6	9.03	1.57	4.12	5.20	0.63	5.59
1999	Albuquer	PCL	106.7	127	84	21	47	81	7.09	3	9	10.72	1.77	3.97	6.83	0.86	6.73
1999	LosAngls	NL	27.0	29	17	4	11	18	5.67	1	2	9.67	1.33	3.67	6.00	0.82	5.53
2000	Albuquer	PCL	136.0	144	79	14	60	62	5.23	6	9	9.53	0.93	3.97	4.10	0.52	5.13

The good news is that he bounced back from his horrific 1999 season. The bad news is that he's really not in the Dodgers' plans anymore. He'll be more successful with his next organization in 2002.

Onan Masaoka — Throws L — Age 23

YEAR	TEAM	LGE	IP	H	ER	HR	BB	K	ERA	W	L	H/9	HR/9	BB/9	K/9	KW	PERA
1998	SanAnton	Tex	100.3	111	90	18	76	62	8.07	2	9	9.96	1.61	6.82	5.56	0.41	7.29
1999	LosAngls	NL	64.7	54	32	8	42	51	4.45	3	4	7.52	1.11	5.85	7.10	0.61	4.91
2000	LosAngls	NL	26.3	23	12	2	13	23	4.10	1	2	7.86	0.68	4.44	7.86	0.88	4.11
2000	Albuquer	PCL	36.7	29	15	1	33	16	3.68	2	2	7.12	0.25	8.10	3.93	0.24	4.72

He's an effective pitcher whose struggles at the start of the season, paired with a Dodger roster crunch, doomed him to lots of time at Southwest Airlines gates. Onan Masaoka deserves better than a specialist role. How Jim Tracy, who watched Davey Johnson move away from LaRussian roles in 2000, uses him will be interesting to see.

Trever Miller — Throws L — Age 28

YEAR	TEAM	LGE	IP	H	ER	HR	BB	K	ERA	W	L	H/9	HR/9	BB/9	K/9	KW	PERA
1998	Houston	NL	51.0	55	20	4	19	24	3.53	3	3	9.71	0.71	3.35	4.24	0.63	4.76
1999	Houston	NL	48.7	56	27	6	25	31	4.99	2	3	10.36	1.11	4.62	5.73	0.62	6.09
2000	Philadel	NL	14.0	19	15	3	7	8	9.64	0	2	12.21	1.93	4.50	5.14	0.57	8.04
2000	Albuquer	PCL	55.7	57	28	6	20	26	4.53	3	3	9.22	0.97	3.23	4.20	0.65	4.71

The fact that Trever Miller isn't very good finally caught up to him after a couple of decent seasons in low-leverage relief. He's not good enough against left-handed hitters to be a specialist, so that leaves mop-up work... or attempts at starting. The Dodgers stuck Miller in the Albuquerque rotation after the Phillies released him, and he pitched well in nine starts. He's right about where Brian Bohanon was at 28.

Gregg Olson — Throws R — Age 34

YEAR	TEAM	LGE	IP	H	ER	HR	BB	K	ERA	W	L	H/9	HR/9	BB/9	K/9	KW	PERA
1998	Arizona	NL	66.0	55	24	4	22	45	3.27	4	3	7.50	0.55	3.00	6.14	1.02	3.22
1999	Arizona	NL	59.0	52	25	8	20	38	3.81	4	3	7.93	1.22	3.05	5.80	0.95	4.11
2000	LosAngls	NL	17.0	20	10	4	6	12	5.29	1	1	10.59	2.12	3.18	6.35	1.00	6.63

Gregg Olson had the world's worst strained right forearm in 2000, making the Dodgers' decision to give him a guaranteed two-year deal look a bit silly. They never missed him, thanks to Matt Herges and the return of Antonio Osuna. They won't notice when he misses half of 2001, either.

Antonio Osuna — Throws R — Age 28

YEAR	TEAM	LGE	IP	H	ER	HR	BB	K	ERA	W	L	H/9	HR/9	BB/9	K/9	KW	PERA
1998	LosAngls	NL	61.3	51	28	9	31	58	4.11	3	4	7.48	1.32	4.55	8.51	0.94	4.58
2000	LosAngls	NL	65.3	57	30	7	31	58	4.13	3	4	7.85	0.96	4.27	7.99	0.94	4.32

We've left 22 innings in 1999 out of his DT so you can see just how far back he came. Antonio Osuna is essentially the same pitcher he was before undergoing elbow ligament surgery in September 1999. He'll have better years than this, too, particularly if he gets more serious about conditioning. Masaoka and Osuna give the Dodgers two explode-on-the-league candidates.

Chan Ho Park — Throws R — Age 28

YEAR	TEAM	LGE	IP	H	ER	HR	BB	K	ERA	W	L	H/9	HR/9	BB/9	K/9	KW	PERA
1998	LosAngls	NL	209.3	196	105	19	94	155	4.51	10	13	8.43	0.82	4.04	6.66	0.82	4.40
1999	LosAngls	NL	188.3	204	119	33	89	146	5.69	7	14	9.75	1.58	4.25	6.98	0.82	6.07
2000	LosAngls	NL	219.0	173	90	21	108	180	3.70	13	11	7.11	0.86	4.44	7.40	0.83	3.85

Unlike Dreifort, Chan Ho Park has some years in his record that support his reputation. He's a better pitcher when he gets ahead with his fastball and sets up his excellent curveball, which helps him keep the ball in the park. His hit rates have been all over the place; see the Tom Glavine and Kevin Millwood comments for more on the significance of this.

Base stealers are just 39 for 84 against Park since 1996 (courtesy STATS, Inc.), despite his pitching to Todd Hundley and Mike Piazza He allowed just three stolen bases in 2000, which is Terry Mulholland territory.

Carlos Perez — Throws L — Age 30

YEAR	TEAM	LGE	IP	H	ER	HR	BB	K	ERA	W	L	H/9	HR/9	BB/9	K/9	KW	PERA
1998	Montreal	NL	156.0	168	75	12	30	67	4.33	8	9	9.69	0.69	1.73	3.87	1.12	4.06
1998	LosAngls	NL	73.3	66	32	11	29	37	3.93	4	4	8.10	1.35	3.56	4.54	0.64	4.57
1999	LosAngls	NL	86.7	111	74	24	35	34	7.68	2	8	11.53	2.49	3.63	3.53	0.49	7.84
1999	Albuquer	PCL	36.7	41	25	6	11	9	6.14	1	3	10.06	1.47	2.70	2.21	0.41	5.51
2000	LosAngls	NL	138.7	183	90	25	29	53	5.84	5	10	11.88	1.62	1.88	3.44	0.91	6.40

His interesting bloodlines and on-field antics aside, Carlos Perez is no different than any other pitcher of his ilk: if you don't strike people out, any success you have will be short-lived. Perez is Jeff Ballard with a better peak—that's all.

Luke Prokopec — Throws R — Age 23

YEAR	TEAM	LGE	IP	H	ER	HR	BB	K	ERA	W	L	H/9	HR/9	BB/9	K/9	KW	PERA
1998	San Bern	Cal	99.3	112	61	23	39	77	5.53	4	7	10.15	2.08	3.53	6.98	0.99	6.55
1998	SanAnton	Tex	23.7	16	7	2	16	17	2.66	2	1	6.08	0.76	6.08	6.46	0.53	3.83
1999	SanAnton	Tex	145.3	173	137	32	57	82	8.48	3	13	10.71	1.98	3.53	5.08	0.72	6.77
2000	SanAnton	Tex	119.3	120	48	15	26	77	3.62	7	6	9.05	1.13	1.96	5.81	1.48	4.24
2000	LosAngls	NL	20.3	18	9	2	8	10	3.98	1	1	7.97	0.89	3.54	4.43	0.63	4.01

The hard-throwing Aussie came back from a rough 1999 season to reach Dodger Stadium in 2000. He's a two-pitch pitcher right now but young enough to add the breaking ball he needs and have one heck of a career. At worst, he'll be a good setup man for a few years. Luke Prokopec is the kind of low-cost talent the Dodgers need in order to make up for the Perezes and Grudzielaneks.

Maximo Regalado — Throws R — Age 24

YEAR	TEAM	LGE	IP	H	ER	HR	BB	K	ERA	W	L	H/9	HR/9	BB/9	K/9	KW	PERA
1998	San Bern	Cal	43.0	46	35	8	28	22	7.33	1	4	9.63	1.67	5.86	4.60	0.39	6.75
1998	Vero Bch	Fla	14.0	18	18	5	15	8	11.57	0	2	11.57	3.21	9.64	5.14	0.27	11.07
1999	Vero Bch	Fla	79.7	115	82	32	59	34	9.26	1	8	12.99	3.62	6.67	3.84	0.29	11.15
2000	Vero Bch	Fla	28.0	18	5	0	10	24	1.61	3	0	5.79	0.00	3.21	7.71	1.20	2.02
2000	SanAnton	Tex	21.0	22	9	2	17	16	3.86	1	1	9.43	0.86	7.29	6.86	0.47	6.32

Converted to the bullpen, Maximo Regalado abused the Florida State League for four months. Give the Dodgers credit for identifying him as a two-pitch pitcher and putting him in a role in which he could succeed. Don't get too excited: the words "closer prospect" have all the value of the words "voter intent."

Al Reyes — Throws R — Age 30

YEAR	TEAM	LGE	IP	H	ER	HR	BB	K	ERA	W	L	H/9	HR/9	BB/9	K/9	KW	PERA
1998	Milwauke	NL	55.0	55	26	9	28	47	4.25	3	3	9.00	1.47	4.58	7.69	0.84	5.66
1999	Milwauke	NL	35.7	27	16	5	21	33	4.04	2	2	6.81	1.26	5.30	8.33	0.79	4.46
1999	Baltimor	AL	29.7	22	14	4	13	27	4.25	1	2	6.67	1.21	3.94	8.19	1.04	3.78
2000	Albuquer	PCL	36.7	33	20	6	20	26	4.91	2	2	8.10	1.47	4.91	6.38	0.65	5.24

His career ERA is 4.27, but he keeps getting caught in roster crunches. The Dodgers traded for Al Reyes solely because he had an option left and could be sent down to make room for Gregg Olson. Reyes is a sleeper closer candidate in the right situation.

Jeff Shaw — Throws R — Age 34

YEAR	TEAM	LGE	IP	H	ER	HR	BB	K	ERA	W	L	H/9	HR/9	BB/9	K/9	KW	PERA
1998	Cincnnti	NL	47.3	38	10	2	11	23	1.90	4	1	7.23	0.38	2.09	4.37	1.05	2.60
1998	LosAngls	NL	33.3	35	12	7	7	21	3.24	2	2	9.45	1.89	1.89	5.67	1.50	5.27
1999	LosAngls	NL	65.3	61	24	6	13	36	3.31	4	3	8.40	0.83	1.79	4.96	1.38	3.51
2000	LosAngls	NL	55.0	59	28	7	14	32	4.58	3	3	9.65	1.15	2.29	5.24	1.14	4.74

The decline continues, taking millions of dollars with it. Jeff Shaw's shoulder problems are just the tip of the iceberg. His creeping ineffectiveness is going to cost the Dodgers games if they insist on using him in high-leverage situations. His contract is costing them a lot, too.

Ismael Valdes — Throws R — Age 27

YEAR	TEAM	LGE	IP	H	ER	HR	BB	K	ERA	W	L	H/9	HR/9	BB/9	K/9	KW	PERA
1998	LosAngls	NL	165.0	167	85	20	64	99	4.64	8	10	9.11	1.09	3.49	5.40	0.77	4.86
1999	LosAngls	NL	195.3	205	96	34	51	120	4.42	10	12	9.45	1.57	2.35	5.53	1.18	5.09
2000	ChiCubs	NL	65.3	68	36	15	22	37	4.96	3	4	9.37	2.07	3.03	5.10	0.84	5.85
2000	LosAngls	NL	38.7	51	27	5	11	24	6.28	1	3	11.87	1.16	2.56	5.59	1.09	6.17

His location, velocity, mechanics, and confidence were shot by the time he came back to Los Angeles. Other than that, he looked pretty good. Ismael Valdes needs a good pitching coach and an iron-clad guarantee that he has a job. Even that might not be enough. He's that far gone.

Jeff Williams — Throws L — Age 29

YEAR	TEAM	LGE	IP	H	ER	HR	BB	K	ERA	W	L	H/9	HR/9	BB/9	K/9	KW	PERA
1998	SanAnton	Tex	38.0	42	23	6	17	21	5.45	1	3	9.95	1.42	4.03	4.97	0.62	5.90
1998	Albuquer	PCL	116.7	150	80	14	50	60	6.17	4	9	11.57	1.08	3.86	4.63	0.60	6.46
1999	Albuquer	PCL	121.0	138	69	14	49	54	5.13	5	8	10.26	1.04	3.64	4.02	0.55	5.55
1999	LosAngls	NL	17.0	12	10	2	8	6	5.29	1	1	6.35	1.06	4.24	3.18	0.38	3.58
2000	Albuquer	PCL	60.7	60	31	7	27	26	4.60	3	4	8.90	1.04	4.01	3.86	0.48	4.89

Jeff Williams has swing-man potential. He's someone who would be a useful pitcher on a heavily right-handed staff or on a team trying a different kind of pitcher usage scheme. I want to see if Jim Tracy creates a Terry Mulholland role for him.

Support-Neutral Statistics			LOS ANGELES DODGERS							Park Effect: -13.8%	
PITCHER	GS	IP	R	SNW	SNL	SNPCT	W	L	RA	APW	SNVA	SNWAR
Kevin Brown	33	230.0	76	17.3	7.1	.710	13	6	2.97	4.5	4.8	7.0
Darren Dreifort	32	192.7	105	11.3	11.7	.491	12	9	4.90	-0.3	-0.3	1.5
Eric Gagne	19	98.0	60	5.0	7.2	.408	4	6	5.51	-0.8	-1.0	-0.2
Matt Herges	4	23.0	15	0.8	1.8	.310	0	3	5.87	-0.3	-0.5	-0.3
Orel Hershiser	6	19.3	27	0.8	3.1	.210	1	4	12.57	-1.6	-1.1	-0.8
Mike Judd	1	4.0	7	0.0	0.8	.014	0	1	15.75	-0.5	-0.4	-0.4
Chan Ho Park	34	226.0	92	15.2	9.3	.621	18	10	3.66	2.7	2.7	4.8
Carlos Perez	22	118.7	90	5.6	9.8	.362	5	8	6.83	-2.6	-2.2	-1.0
Luke Prokopec	3	15.3	10	0.6	1.2	.350	1	1	5.87	-0.2	-0.2	-0.1
Ismael Valdes	8	39.0	29	1.9	3.4	.365	0	3	6.69	-0.8	-0.7	-0.3
TOTALS	162	966.0	511	58.5	55.3	.514	54	51	4.76	0.2	1.0	10.1

The great seasons by Kevin Brown and Chan Ho Park served to mask deeper problems with the Dodgers' rotation. Thanks to those two, the team's pitching stats looked respectable, but the Dodgers had the shallowest starting rotation in the majors in 2000.

If you rank 2000 starting rotations by just the performances of the best three starters on the staff (using Support-Neutral Wins Above Replacement), the Dodgers come out #2 in the majors, behind only the Braves. But if you rank rotations according to the performances by everyone other than the best three starters, the Dodgers were third-worst in the majors, ahead of only the Orioles and the Expos.

You could argue that this shallowness is good news, since the problem seems so reparable. If the Dodgers get the same aggregate performance from the trio of Brown, Park, and Darren Dreifort in 2001, and if they find league-average starters to plug into the other two slots, that alone would be enough to add about six wins above the Dodgers' 2000 total, according to SNVA.

Just in case they aren't able to find those average starters, Dodger fans should start working on a catchy chant along the lines of "Spahn and Sain and pray for rain." My suggestion: "Kevin and Chan Ho and the rest really blow."

For a quick explanation of SN stats, see page 7.

Reliever Evaluation Tools											
PITCHER	G	IP	R	ARA	APR	IRNR/G	EIRS/G	IRP	BRS	RRA	ARP
Terry Adams	66	84.3	42	4.87	3.1	0.39	0.12	1.4	4.3	5.30	-0.9
Jamie Arnold	2	6.7	3	4.40	0.6	1.00	0.48	-1.2	0.0	6.49	-1.0
Mike Fetters	51	50.0	18	3.52	9.3	0.25	0.08	3.4	0.3	3.03	12.1
Eric Gagne	1	3.3	2	5.87	-0.2	0.00	0.00	0.0	0.0	5.77	-0.2
Matt Herges	55	87.7	28	3.12	20.2	0.60	0.29	-1.9	0.7	3.40	17.5
Orel Hershiser	4	5.3	9	16.50	-6.7	0.50	0.09	0.4	-1.6	12.58	-4.4
Onan Masaoka	29	27.0	12	4.35	2.6	0.21	0.07	-0.5	0.3	4.72	1.4
Trever Miller	2	2.3	6	25.15	-5.2	0.00	0.00	0.0	0.7	26.28	-5.5
Alan Mills	18	25.7	12	4.57	1.8	0.22	0.11	-1.2	1.6	5.69	-1.4
Gregg Olson	13	17.7	11	6.09	-1.8	0.15	0.03	-1.8	0.3	7.33	-4.2
Antonio Osuna	46	67.3	30	4.36	6.3	0.28	0.10	0.2	1.6	4.45	5.6
Carlos Perez	8	25.3	5	1.93	9.2	1.00	0.37	-1.3	-0.7	2.35	8.0
Luke Prokopec	2	5.7	0	0.00	3.3	0.50	0.13	0.3	0.0	-0.34	3.5
Al Reyes	6	6.7	0	0.00	3.8	0.00	0.00	0.0	0.2	0.20	3.7
Jeff Shaw	60	57.3	29	4.95	1.6	0.15	0.03	2.3	-0.6	4.61	3.7
Ismael Valdes	1	1.0	0	0.00	0.6	0.00	0.00	0.0	0.0	0.00	0.6
Jeff Williams	7	5.7	11	18.98	-8.7	0.43	0.18	0.4	-1.2	17.64	-7.8
TOTALS	371	479.0	218	4.45	39.7	0.33	0.12			4.62	30.7

For a quick guide to RET, see page 10.

Milwaukee Brewers

As disastrous as 1999 was, at least the season ended on a hopeful note for the Brewers. The Dean Taylor regime began in September, and Davey Lopes was hired to manage soon thereafter. Their assignment was a tough one, with a limited budget and a farm system virtually devoid of talent. Taylor's hiring was lauded, as he seemed to possess actual credentials as opposed to convenient friendships. At the time, the consensus was that in light of the club's recent fortunes, any changes had to be for the better.

For the next ten months, things only got worse.

First, the new manager—whose only previous experience consisted of a couple of stints in the Arizona Fall League—announced that the club was going to run its way back into contention. Naturally, people wondered if Lopes had bothered to look at his roster before opening his mouth. At the time, Lopes might well have been the second-fastest man on the club; no Brewer besides Marquis Grissom had stolen more than seven bases in 1999. The statement also raised legitimate questions about whether the former stolen-base champion's entire understanding of offense was limited to aggressive baserunning. For many, the announcement blew a massive hole in Lopes's credibility before he'd even stepped onto the field.

Meanwhile, Taylor laid out his two main goals: to acquire a good defensive catcher and to remake the finesse-oriented pitching staff into a stable of hard throwers. Brewers fans, for their part, had gotten their fill of good-field, no-hit catchers while suffering through four years of Mike Matheny. As to the latter goal, it seemed a bit like planning to get rich by obtaining a lot of gold bricks. Nice plan, but where are they going to come from? There were no power arms in the upper levels of the farm system, and other clubs sure weren't giving them away.

Taylor wasted no time getting to work, overhauling the roster with a flurry of trades. Five deals scattered Mike Myers, Jeff Cirillo, Scott Karl, Fernando Vina, Cal Eldred, and Jose Valentin across the Central and Mountain time zones. The deals accomplished Taylor's goals: new Brewers Curtis Leskanic, Jimmy Haynes, Jamey Wright, Juan Acevedo, and John Snyder are "power arms" of varying quality, while catcher Henry Blanco brought with him from Colorado a strong arm and a good defensive reputation.

None of the deals, save the one that sent Cirillo to Colorado, seemed that bad for the Brewers. Taken as a whole, though, the team had swapped a starting infield and some spare parts for a collection of lottery tickets. Taylor had dealt Vina and Valentin—the Brewers starting double-play combination in April 1999—at their points of lowest trade value, and the return showed. If each of the deals was defensible on its face, the overall impact was strongly negative.

Things got worse. Taylor signed Jose Hernandez to a three-year, $11-million contract and named him Jeff Cirillo's successor at third base. This gave Hernandez a higher annual salary and a longer contract than the departed Cirillo and cost the dirt-farming Brewers their second-round pick in the upcoming draft. For a self-proclaimed cash-poor team, it meant one more mediocre player and $11 million less to spend on getting back into contention.

Taylor explained that Hernandez had been signed to lend right-handed power to a left-leaning lineup. Power? Hernandez, playing most of his career in Wrigley Field, had compiled a career slugging percentage 29 points below Cirillo's. His main asset was his ability to play several positions, including shortstop, something the Brewers apparently intended not to exploit.

Then, to rid themselves of a player who would become arbitration-eligible after the season, the Brewers dealt outfielder Alex Ochoa to the Reds for pinch-hitter Mark Sweeney. Ochoa would slug .586 for Cincinnati in a part-time role and cost about $2 million less than Hernandez, the ostensible "right-handed power."

With the roster overhaul complete, spring training began with the obligatory rash of injuries to the pitching staff. Jamey

Brewers Prospectus

2000 record: 73–89; Third place, NL Central
Pythagenport W/L: 73–89
Runs Scored: 740 (13th in NL)
Runs Allowed: 826 (10th in NL)
Team EqA: .246 (tied for 13th in NL)
2000 Batters' Age: 29.0 (7th youngest in NL)
2000 Pitchers' Age: 26.8 (tied for 3rd youngest in NL)
Ballpark: County Stadium; neutral park; Park Factor of .999; Moving to Miller Park for 2001 season.
2000: Dean Taylor kept busy without having much impact on the season.
2001: The offense is still a problem, but there are signs of life on the mound and in the system.

Wright was diagnosed with a partially torn labrum, although he was able to forgo surgery in favor of rehabilitation. Kyle Peterson, 1999's rookie hope, came down with a sore arm. Chad Fox, a revelation in '98 and a DL resident in '99, broke his elbow. John Snyder pulled a muscle in his side.

Things continued downhill after the bell rang. Hernandez was a Dale Sveum lowlight reel, making little contact at the plate or in the field. Kevin Barker, the rookie first baseman who had been rated the third-best prospect in the Brewers' system by *Baseball America*, struggled and was sent down after only 100 at-bats, never to be heard from again. Marquis Grissom, a marginal leadoff hitter at his best, was at his worst. Jaime Navarro, a throw-in in the Jose Valentin/Cal Eldred trade with the White Sox, allowed 31 runs in 18⅔ innings and was released. Geoff Jenkins broke a finger and missed three weeks. Steve Woodard, the most effective remaining starter from 1999, both pitched and acted like a man who knew that his days in Milwaukee were numbered.

In June, Mark Loretta got hurt. Jeff D'Amico, who'd pitched well after missing almost all of 1998 and 1999 with injuries, went back on the DL with shoulder tendinitis. Jimmy Haynes declined rapidly after a decent start and never recovered. Snyder soon followed. With no leadoff hitter, #2 hitter, or cleanup hitter, and with Jeromy Burnitz in a deep slump, the offense was impotent.

In July, Burnitz announced that he had cut off negotiations for a long-term contract. He was tired of playing for a loser, he said, and the lack of progress this season had convinced him to play out his contract in 2001. The club's top pick in the June draft, outfielder David Krynzel, suffered a season-ending injury in late July after playing only 34 games; Drew Olson's article in the *Milwaukee Journal-Sentinel* began, "It's official: David Krynzel is a Milwaukee Brewer."

D'Amico returned in July and went 5–0 to win the NL Pitcher of the Month award . . . but the team went 7–15 when he didn't start. The club hit bottom at the end of July, dropping eight of nine games to fall to 40–59, a stretch that culminated in a three-game sweep at the hands of the lowly Cubs.

Needless to say, what came five days later caught everyone by surprise. It someday may be regarded—if things work out—as a turning point in the franchise's history. The Brewers acquired Richie Sexson, plus pitchers Paul Rigdon and Kane Davis, and gave up no one who figured prominently in the club's future. The cost was closer and local favorite Bob Wickman, who had more than a year to go on his multi-million-dollar contract, Jason "Ball Three" Bere, and Woodard, the foundering finesse pitcher.

Taylor immediately declared Sexson a cornerstone of the club's rebuilding effort and announced his intent to sign the ex-Indian to a long-term deal. Meanwhile, Lopes returned the unnatural outfielder to his proper position, first base, and slotted him into the cleanup spot.

Some people remained understandably skeptical, seeing Sexson as a one-dimensional slugger, a right-handed-hitting first baseman whose only asset was power. Plenty of players with similarly narrow, albeit inferior, skills were freely available, they argued. Over the next two months, though, Sexson won over the skeptics, hitting .296/.398/.559 and playing impressive defense. Against all odds, the Brewers turned into a winning club, going 31–29 after the acquisition of Sexson.

The slugger got the lion's share of the credit, but the team's stunning turnaround truly was a group effort. D'Amico stayed strong through the end of the year and nearly captured the NL's ERA title. Curtis Leskanic stepped in as the new closer and allowed just six runs in the last two months. Ray King came out of nowhere to join Acevedo, Valerio de los Santos, and David Weathers in one of the league's best bullpens.

Suddenly, it was as if the entire organization was blessed. Their top prospect, right-hander Ben Sheets, threw a shutout in the gold-medal game in the Olympics, looking for all the world like he was ready to win in the majors. Burnitz was so impressed with the club's turnaround that he decided he might like to stay after all.

For now, the Brewers look good on paper. Ronnie Belliard is the only logical choice as the leadoff hitter, and Loretta will occupy his customary #2 spot. Jenkins, Sexson, and Burnitz form a potent and balanced middle of the order. The six through eight spots aren't especially strong, with Hernandez, Grissom, and Blanco, but with any luck the former two will rebound.

The pitching looks even better, with a rotation headed by D'Amico, Wright, and Ben Sheets. Rigdon and left-hander Horacio Estrada—who is out of options—are around to give Haynes and Snyder needed competition for the last two spots. The relievers remain in the roles they performed so well late last year. Leskanic is the closer, with Acevedo, de los Santos, and Weathers setting up. King is the situational left-hander.

Now, if the lineup and pitching staff still look this way in June, they might have something. But here's the rub: what will happen when the inevitable injuries hit? Remember, this is a club that would have trouble getting 120 games out of Cal Ripken. The history of the franchise has been one of constant injuries, from Rollie Fingers's arm injury that likely cost them the 1982 World Series and Pete Vuckovich's torn rotator cuff the next spring, to Paul Molitor spending half of his prime on the disabled list and Robin Yount's shoulder woes bringing a premature end to his days as a shortstop. Juan Nieves, Teddy Higuera, Cal Eldred, John Jaha, Jose Valentin, Fernando Vina . . . even Steve Sparks—a knuckleballer, for crying out loud—blew out his elbow.

The Brewers will go into 2001 with several potentially serious health concerns. The biggest one is the protruding disk in Belliard's lower back, a condition that rendered his bat useless over the second half of last season. When healthy, Belliard gets on base enough to be a decent leadoff man. If he's not able to play, Lopes will have few options in the leadoff spot and may be tempted to revert to Grissom. In other words, a potential fiasco awaits.

Henry Blanco's shoulder is also a concern. He missed most of September with a partially torn rotator cuff and narrowly avoided surgery. Though the club is optimistic, it's uncertain whether he'll be able to hold up in spring training. While the loss of Blanco probably wouldn't be as damaging as the club would like to believe, there's little additional catching talent on hand.

If health wasn't enough of a question mark, the Brewers signed Jeffrey Hammonds to a three-year deal in December. Hammonds is a talented outfielder who has never stayed healthy for a full season and is coming off a season of altitude-inflated statistics. He is going to be a disappointment to a team expecting a healthy, productive center fielder for its $7 million. And when he gets hurt, the Brewers are right back to Marquis Grissom.

It will be easier to cover injuries to the pitching staff. Even if Sheets begins the year in Triple-A, Rigdon, Snyder, and Estrada can contend for the final two spots in the rotation. In the event of a disaster, de los Santos or Acevedo could move into the rotation temporarily. A more serious problem could develop if Leskanic is unable to continue last season's success as the closer. Each of the other relievers will begin the season in a role he thrived in during 2000, so there won't be nearly as much in-season experimentation if everything goes according to plan.

There's good reason to look forward to a full year of Richie Sexson, but it won't necessarily mean a huge improvement at first base. Sexson should be able to match the power the Brewers got from the position in 2000 but probably won't approach the 97 walks Milwaukee's first basemen drew last year. The real improvement must come at third base and center field; in each case, the club is hopelessly tied to the current regular and can only hope for a rebound.

Should holes open up, the club almost certainly won't be in any position to fill them. There's very little useful talent in the upper levels of the farm system, particularly among position players. An injury to any key regular could be crippling.

Truth be told, the Brewers' best hope is that their pitching staff can hold up and perform the way it did last August and September. Specifically, they'll need D'Amico to pitch the way he did in 2000 and stay healthy all season. That's a lot to ask, considering that D'Amico hasn't been able to put in a full year since Little League. On the other hand, his workload last year wasn't necessarily damaging, as he worked efficiently and rarely ran up high pitch counts. After diligently rehabbing from two arm surgeries, his only injury was June's sore shoulder. He may have built himself back up to the point where he can reach 200 innings.

An equally important question is whether D'Amico really is this good or is simply a latter-day Don August. I'm willing to bet that D'Amico will prove to be no fluke. After all, he'd already shown signs he could pitch well in the big leagues, even before last year. Back in 1997, he put together a largely unnoticed string of impressive starts before he got hurt. From May 7 through July 18, he went 8-2 with a 3.84 ERA in 13 starts. In 84⅓ innings, a 21-year-old D'Amico allowed 78 hits, walked 21, and struck out 58.

To fulfill his promise, D'Amico will need to adjust properly to the Brewers' new home park, Miller Field. D'Amico is a fly-ball pitcher who's learned to pitch in forgiving County Stadium, so this could be a problem. The foul lines at Miller Park are going to be unusually deep, but the power alleys will be quite reachable, so longballs could be a concern. D'Amico probably has good enough command, however, to keep batters from hitting it to the wrong part of the park.

There are many legitimate reasons to be optimistic about this year's Brew Crew, apart from the obligatory hoopla surrounding the opening of the new park. And there also are plenty of good reasons to temper that enthusiasm. From this point, the next step is not to vault into contention; the next step is to weed out the non-bloomers, continue nurturing the youngsters, and keep moving forward. If that goes well, by next year at this time, we may legitimately ask whether the Brewers have a chance to shoot a hole in Bud Selig's theory that small-market teams are doomed to mediocrity.

HITTERS (BA: .270, OBP: .340, SLG: .440, EqA: .260)

Eliezer Alfonzo — C — Bats R — Age 22

YEAR	TEAM	LGE	AB	H	DB	TP	HR	BB	SO	R	RBI	SB	CS	OUT	BA	OBP	SLG	EQA	EQR	DEFENSE
1998	New Jrsy	NYP	177	39	4	0	2	4	52	12	14	0	0	138	.220	.241	.277	.155	7	22-C -7
1999	New Jrsy	NYP	180	47	10	1	2	1	42	10	18	1	2	135	.261	.271	.361	.202	12	23-C 0
2000	Peoria	Mid	178	47	9	0	5	2	39	21	15	1	0	131	.264	.283	.399	.223	15	40-C -3
2000	Beloit	Mid	224	53	5	0	5	3	64	17	20	1	1	172	.237	.251	.326	.182	12	35-C -10
2001	Milwauke	NL	318	84	9	0	9	9	87	27	38	2	1	235	.264	.284	.377	.219	26	

Eliezer Alfonzo was one of two borderline prospects acquired from St. Louis in the Fernando Vina deal. His pluses: he's young, he's a catcher, and he has a little power. The minuses: he has the speed and strike-zone judgment of Glenallen Hill after seven beers and apparently isn't much of a receiver. He caught only 78 games last year, making the rest of his appearances as a DH or pinch hitter.

Kevin Barker — 1B — Bats L — Age 25

YEAR	TEAM	LGE	AB	H	DB	TP	HR	BB	SO	R	RBI	SB	CS	OUT	BA	OBP	SLG	EQA	EQR	DEFENSE
1998	Louisvil	Int	463	115	21	3	19	26	96	49	77	1	3	351	.248	.292	.430	.234	47	105-1B 2
1999	Louisvil	Int	441	108	22	4	18	48	93	71	66	1	1	334	.245	.323	.435	.251	53	117-1B 8
1999	Milwauke	NL	117	32	2	0	3	8	18	12	21	1	0	85	.274	.320	.368	.233	11	30-1B 1
2000	Milwauke	NL	101	22	4	0	2	18	20	13	8	1	0	79	.218	.341	.317	.233	10	28-1B 0
2000	Indianap	Int	291	54	9	1	10	44	79	37	38	0	1	238	.186	.294	.326	.209	24	73-1B 2
2001	Milwauke	NL	414	97	18	1	16	53	101	53	59	1	1	318	.234	.321	.399	.244	47	

It's difficult to defend or even explain the Brewers' decision to demote Kevin Barker last May after just 100 at-bats. Before the season, he'd been ranked the third-best prospect in the Milwaukee system by *Baseball America*. Granted, that's not saying much, but he certainly was more important to the Brewers' future than Charlie Hayes or Tyler Houston, the two players who divvied up his playing time. With the acquisition of Richie Sexson, his future in the Milwaukee system is as bright as a telegraph operator's.

Jason Belcher — C — Bats L — Age 19

YEAR	TEAM	LGE	AB	H	DB	TP	HR	BB	SO	R	RBI	SB	CS	OUT	BA	OBP	SLG	EQA	EQR	DEFENSE
2000	Helena	Pio	161	39	12	1	2	10	29	16	18	1	1	123	.242	.288	.366	.215	13	23-C -6
2001	Milwauke	NL	88	22	4	0	2	6	46	9	10	0	0	66	.250	.298	.364	.222	8	

Jason Belcher was the Brewers' fifth-round pick last year and really cranked the ball in his pro debut in the Pioneer League. There are major questions about his defense, but the Brewers will find a place for his bat if he keeps hitting.

Ron Belliard — 2B — Bats R — Age 26

YEAR	TEAM	LGE	AB	H	DB	TP	HR	BB	SO	R	RBI	SB	CS	OUT	BA	OBP	SLG	EQA	EQR	DEFENSE
1998	Louisvil	Int	506	144	33	5	11	55	76	91	58	18	8	370	.285	.361	.435	.269	69	126-2B 0
1999	Louisvil	Int	108	24	2	0	1	11	13	10	6	8	3	87	.222	.298	.269	.202	8	26-2B -3
1999	Milwauke	NL	458	130	27	4	8	57	56	57	53	3	4	332	.284	.363	.413	.262	58	112-2B 4
2000	Milwauke	NL	575	148	28	8	8	72	79	78	50	6	5	432	.257	.343	.376	.244	64	149-2B 2
2001	Milwauke	NL	506	139	26	4	10	65	72	83	70	13	7	374	.275	.357	.401	.261	65	

Ronnie Belliard hasn't stolen bases the way he did in the minors, and he developed back problems late last year. That all just goes to show that it's hard to play major-league baseball—much less play second base and lead off—when you're fat. He's opted for rehab over surgery, which only makes it more crucial that he learn there's more at the gym than just vending machines. Belliard could go either way: he could do a half-assed rehab and have back problems for the rest of his career, or he could work hard, get into better shape, and become another Ray Durham.

Henry Blanco — C — Bats R — Age 29

YEAR	TEAM	LGE	AB	H	DB	TP	HR	BB	SO	R	RBI	SB	CS	OUT	BA	OBP	SLG	EQA	EQR	DEFENSE	
1998	Albuquer	PCL	132	28	5	0	4	18	27	13	17	1	0	104	.212	.307	.341	.221	12	31-C	2
1999	ColSprin	PCL	55	14	3	0	2	1	12	5	8	0	1	42	.255	.268	.418	.215	5	13-C	1
1999	Colorado	NL	258	52	11	2	5	29	36	26	22	1	1	207	.202	.285	.318	.201	19	83-C	7
2000	Milwauke	NL	286	66	18	0	8	32	56	27	29	0	3	223	.231	.308	.378	.226	27	81-C	13
2001	Milwauke	NL	219	49	7	0	6	27	42	23	25	0	1	171	.224	.309	.338	.220	19		

It took the Sal Bando regime four years to realize that the similarly skilled Mike Matheny simply wasn't worth it. Taylor's crew is completely enamored of Henry Blanco; how long do you think it will take them to learn? The answer, if the Brewers improve at all, could be "never," because Blanco's ability to shut down the running game will be cited as a major factor in the club's improvement. Just look at what happened to Matheny in St. Louis: during the playoffs, his teammates told anyone who would listen that Matheny was their MVP. Edgar Renteria, Darryl Kile, and Jim Edmonds must have brutal intangibles.

Kevin Brown — C — Bats R — Age 28

YEAR	TEAM	LGE	AB	H	DB	TP	HR	BB	SO	R	RBI	SB	CS	OUT	BA	OBP	SLG	EQA	EQR	DEFENSE	
1998	Toronto	AL	110	30	8	1	2	9	28	18	15	0	0	80	.273	.338	.418	.253	13	35-C	-1
1999	Syracuse	Int	294	67	15	1	10	15	80	30	38	0	1	228	.228	.269	.388	.212	24	80-C	-15
2000	Indianap	Int	83	19	1	0	2	4	26	4	6	0	0	64	.229	.271	.313	.189	5	21-C	1
2000	Syracuse	Int	178	51	12	1	5	5	50	21	22	0	0	127	.287	.306	.449	.247	19	47-C	1
2001	Milwauke	NL	239	63	10	0	8	16	72	26	34	0	0	176	.264	.310	.406	.239	25		

It looks like the Brewers intend to employ an offense/defense platoon behind the plate. Henry Blanco has the defensive half covered; apparently Kevin Brown will battle Raul Casanova for the hitter's job. Neither is all that impressive at the plate, mind you; the point is that they both can out-hit Blanco and thus could pinch-hit for him and remain in the game.

Jeromy Burnitz — RF — Bats L — Age 32

YEAR	TEAM	LGE	AB	H	DB	TP	HR	BB	SO	R	RBI	SB	CS	OUT	BA	OBP	SLG	EQA	EQR	DEFENSE	
1998	Milwauke	NL	617	161	23	1	40	67	148	93	124	6	4	460	.261	.337	.496	.271	88	153-RF	-2
1999	Milwauke	NL	468	122	31	2	31	83	117	82	93	5	3	349	.261	.389	.534	.301	87	122-RF	-3
2000	Milwauke	NL	568	129	28	2	29	89	113	86	90	5	4	443	.227	.344	.437	.261	77	149-RF	-1
2001	Milwauke	NL	500	123	24	1	29	87	115	86	94	6	2	379	.246	.358	.472	.278	77		

Jeromy Burnitz's right hand was broken by a Jose Rosado pitch on July 17, 1999. For a long time after that, he wasn't the same hitter. He had 26 homers in 343 at-bats at the time of the injury, then hit just seven more in 141 at-bats after returning a month later. He spent most of 2000 in a deep funk before getting hot over the final three weeks of the season. Hand injuries often linger, and we're betting that his late-season surge is a sign that he's finally over it. Hopefully the Brewers will sign him to an extension before the start of the season. Otherwise, trade rumors could be an ongoing distraction.

Raul Casanova — C — Bats B — Age 28

YEAR	TEAM	LGE	AB	H	DB	TP	HR	BB	SO	R	RBI	SB	CS	OUT	BA	OBP	SLG	EQA	EQR	DEFENSE	
1998	Toledo	Int	172	41	6	0	6	18	28	15	22	0	1	132	.238	.319	.378	.233	17	45-C	-1
1998	Detroit	AL	42	6	3	0	1	5	9	4	3	0	0	36	.143	.249	.286	.173	2	13-C	1
1999	Toledo	Int	161	32	5	0	6	4	29	17	20	0	0	129	.199	.222	.342	.173	8	29-C	-1
2000	Indianap	Int	74	19	1	0	4	5	11	8	9	0	1	56	.257	.310	.432	.240	8	18-C	-2
2000	Milwauke	NL	233	56	12	3	6	22	45	19	34	1	2	179	.240	.315	.395	.236	24	58-C	-4
2001	Milwauke	NL	245	58	11	1	8	24	47	27	32	0	1	188	.237	.305	.388	.232	24		

It gives little comfort to know that if and when Henry Blanco slumps his way back to the bench, his at-bats will go to Raul Casanova. What Casanova did last year is about all that can be expected from him. He hits a lot of ground balls and isn't a very good defensive catcher; he switch-hits, so he'll likely stick around.

Daryl Clark — 1B/3B — Bats L — Age 21

YEAR	TEAM	LGE	AB	H	DB	TP	HR	BB	SO	R	RBI	SB	CS	OUT	BA	OBP	SLG	EQA	EQR	DEFENSE			
2000	Ogden	Pio	216	49	7	1	8	40	62	26	28	1	2	169	.227	.349	.380	.249	26	34-3B	-10	20-1B	-4
2001	Milwauke	NL	114	27	3	0	5	26	47	19	19	0	1	88	.237	.379	.395	.268	16				

Daryl Clark is one of the better offensive prospects in the system, albeit one several years away. In the field, he's DH material. At the plate, he's a potential Burnitz, a left-handed hitter who hits for power and draws walks.

Pat Cline — C — Bats R — Age 26

YEAR	TEAM	LGE	AB	H	DB	TP	HR	BB	SO	R	RBI	SB	CS	OUT	BA	OBP	SLG	EQA	EQR	DEFENSE			
1998	Iowa	PCL	422	105	20	1	10	30	58	42	47	1	2	319	.249	.307	.372	.226	39	106-C	-21		
1999	Iowa	PCL	289	59	15	1	5	21	71	22	33	1	1	231	.204	.264	.315	.188	18	27-C	-10	16-RF	-3
2000	Dayton	Mid	116	25	3	0	4	16	21	10	10	0	0	91	.216	.317	.345	.226	11	21-C	-12		
2000	Huntsvil	Sou	53	8	4	0	0	4	12	2	4	0	0	45	.151	.224	.226	.124	1				
2000	Indianap	Int	37	8	1	0	1	2	5	3	5	0	0	29	.216	.256	.324	.186	2				
2001	Milwauke	NL	205	45	8	0	5	22	42	20	21	0	0	160	.220	.295	.332	.212	17				

Sign #37 that your farm system has serious problems: you start picking up failed Cubs' prospects. Pat Cline never progressed as a hitter and doesn't project as a major-league player, but you never know when injuries might simultaneously strike the top four receivers in the system.

Lou Collier — SS — Bats R — Age 27

YEAR	TEAM	LGE	AB	H	DB	TP	HR	BB	SO	R	RBI	SB	CS	OUT	BA	OBP	SLG	EQA	EQR	DEFENSE	
1998	Pittsbrg	NL	337	83	15	6	2	30	66	31	34	2	2	256	.246	.318	.344	.224	30	98-SS	-4
1999	Milwauke	NL	136	35	5	0	3	12	30	16	21	2	2	103	.257	.318	.360	.227	13	18-SS	-2
2000	Huntsvil	Sou	180	41	3	1	2	22	49	23	23	3	2	141	.228	.314	.289	.207	14	31-3B	-1
2000	Indianap	Int	57	13	3	1	0	9	10	6	9	1	1	46	.228	.341	.316	.226	6	10-CF	1
2000	Milwauke	NL	32	7	0	0	1	6	4	7	2	0	0	25	.219	.342	.313	.230	3		
2001	Milwauke	NL	239	56	9	1	4	31	55	30	25	3	1	184	.234	.322	.331	.227	23		

A knee injury cost Lou Collier most of 2000. The Brewers gave him some time in center field, trying to see if they could expand his versatility enough to make him worth keeping. He doesn't quite hit enough to make it solely as a backup infielder. If he reaches the 239 at-bats we've projected for him, it can only mean that the Brewers have had a dismal 2001.

Angel Echevarria — OF — Bats R — Age 30

YEAR	TEAM	LGE	AB	H	DB	TP	HR	BB	SO	R	RBI	SB	CS	OUT	BA	OBP	SLG	EQA	EQR	DEFENSE			
1998	ColSprin	PCL	292	76	17	1	9	11	49	35	39	0	1	217	.260	.291	.418	.231	28	41-1B	-4	26-RF	-2
1998	Colorado	NL	28	9	3	0	1	2	3	7	8	0	0	19	.321	.402	.536	.308	5				
1999	Colorado	NL	186	47	6	0	9	14	32	23	28	0	2	141	.253	.315	.430	.243	20	34-RF	-1		
2000	ColSprin	PCL	276	72	17	1	4	17	49	31	31	1	1	205	.261	.312	.373	.228	26	51-RF	-3	13-1B	-1
2000	Milwauke	NL	42	9	1	0	1	7	8	3	4	0	0	33	.214	.327	.310	.221	4				
2001	Milwauke	NL	243	62	9	0	7	19	46	26	31	0	0	181	.255	.309	.379	.232	23				

By relying so heavily on the bats of their corner outfielders, the Brewers make it difficult to get much out of players like Angel Echevarria, decent hitters who can play only the outfield corners. On the other hand, most fifth outfielders either bat left-handed or can play center field, with good reason.

Mark Ernster — SS — Bats R — Age 23

YEAR	TEAM	LGE	AB	H	DB	TP	HR	BB	SO	R	RBI	SB	CS	OUT	BA	OBP	SLG	EQA	EQR	DEFENSE	
2000	Mudville	Cal	209	46	7	1	3	6	42	23	17	1	1	164	.220	.247	.306	.173	10	59-SS	-13
2000	Huntsvil	Sou	214	48	6	0	5	27	48	23	23	5	3	169	.224	.313	.322	.218	19	47-SS	-6
2001	Milwauke	NL	199	47	4	0	6	18	51	21	22	3	1	153	.236	.300	.347	.220	17		

The club sent Mark Ernster to the Arizona Fall League, as if to prove they could fulfill their six-player allotment, dammit. With little power or speed, Ernster's absolute best-case scenario is to become a lower-class Mark Loretta.

Jose Fernandez — 3B — Bats R — Age 26

YEAR	TEAM	LGE	AB	H	DB	TP	HR	BB	SO	R	RBI	SB	CS	OUT	BA	OBP	SLG	EQA	EQR	DEFENSE	
1998	Harrisbg	Eas	372	93	17	1	14	27	74	45	45	9	4	283	.250	.311	.414	.242	41	83-3B	-5
1998	Ottawa	Int	60	15	3	1	0	4	14	7	3	2	1	46	.250	.297	.333	.212	5	10-3B	-4
1999	Ottawa	Int	464	113	26	2	11	23	135	58	53	9	5	356	.244	.285	.379	.219	40	109-3B	-6
1999	Montreal	NL	24	5	2	0	0	1	7	1	1	0	0	19	.208	.240	.292	.162	1		
2000	Indianap	Int	472	124	31	3	10	40	97	61	57	7	2	350	.263	.326	.405	.246	53	116-3B	5
2001	*Milwauke*	*NL*	*417*	*109*	*25*	*2*	*11*	*38*	*103*	*57*	*57*	*8*	*3*	*311*	*.261*	*.323*	*.410*	*.248*	*48*		

Last winter, the Brewers signed third baseman Jose *Hernandez* to an $11-million contract and signed third baseman Jose *Fernandez* as a minor-league free agent. The two had roughly equal 2000 seasons, and few would have noticed had the Talented Mr. Fernandez simply murdered and proceeded to impersonate his counterpart.

Chad Green — CF — Bats B — Age 26

YEAR	TEAM	LGE	AB	H	DB	TP	HR	BB	SO	R	RBI	SB	CS	OUT	BA	OBP	SLG	EQA	EQR	DEFENSE	
1998	Stockton	Cal	153	44	12	1	0	8	23	19	12	9	3	112	.288	.325	.379	.242	16	36-CF	0
1999	Huntsvil	Sou	427	91	19	2	7	32	119	40	33	13	7	343	.213	.270	.316	.195	29	104-CF	-2
2000	Huntsvil	Sou	327	71	19	1	3	19	93	35	23	9	4	260	.217	.261	.309	.187	20	83-CF	2
2000	Indianap	Int	124	24	6	2	3	8	37	15	9	4	2	102	.194	.247	.347	.194	8	34-CF	-1
2001	*SanDieg*	*NL*	*322*	*67*	*14*	*1*	*4*	*24*	*98*	*38*	*27*	*14*	*6*	*262*	*.208*	*.263*	*.295*	*.198*	*23*		

"Mr. Signability." Unwilling to shell out a hefty bonus in 1998, the club used its first-round pick on a third-round talent—Chad Green—and paid him second-round money. In trying to save some cash, they acquired a useless player and overpaid to boot. Granted, Green could have turned out to be a decent player and vindicated the club's thriftiness, but the whole thing smacked of a small-market team shooting itself in the foot to prove it can't keep up with the big guys. A major test of the Taylor regime over the next few years will be whether it takes the Chad Green approach with its first-round draft picks.

Marquis Grissom — CF — Bats R — Age 34

YEAR	TEAM	LGE	AB	H	DB	TP	HR	BB	SO	R	RBI	SB	CS	OUT	BA	OBP	SLG	EQA	EQR	DEFENSE	
1998	Milwauke	NL	547	148	24	1	12	23	73	58	60	12	8	407	.271	.302	.384	.227	50	137-CF	3
1999	Milwauke	NL	605	158	22	1	21	41	103	86	78	19	6	453	.261	.308	.405	.239	63	145-CF	-1
2000	Milwauke	NL	600	144	19	2	13	30	93	63	58	18	10	466	.240	.276	.343	.205	44	139-CF	1
2001	*Milwauke*	*NL*	*483*	*118*	*14*	*1*	*14*	*38*	*81*	*54*	*55*	*14*	*8*	*373*	*.244*	*.299*	*.364*	*.224*	*45*		

Kids, this is what toughness is all about. Marquis Grissom had leg problems all year, but did he ever complain? Did he ever take himself out of the lineup or ask for a day off? No! He went out there and played, consequences be damned. If he had only 27 percent to give on any particular day, then dammit, he gave all of that 27 percent. A team needs players like Grissom who aren't concerned about their own statistics and will suck it up and drag themselves out there no matter what. If he'd been a wuss and rested or rehabbed or something, it would have been a disaster—the Brewers probably would have had to play some zero who couldn't hit for power or get on base to save his life. Thank you, Marquis, for showing our children how to be a winner.

Creighton Gubanich — C — Bats R — Age 29

YEAR	TEAM	LGE	AB	H	DB	TP	HR	BB	SO	R	RBI	SB	CS	OUT	BA	OBP	SLG	EQA	EQR	DEFENSE	
1998	LasVegas	PCL	288	70	14	0	14	24	86	35	50	1	1	219	.243	.305	.438	.244	32	65-C	-9
1999	Pawtuckt	Int	92	23	1	0	4	4	24	9	7	0	0	69	.250	.281	.391	.220	8	22-C	0
1999	Boston	AL	47	13	3	1	1	2	12	4	11	0	0	34	.277	.330	.447	.257	6		
2000	Indianap	Int	383	94	20	0	14	26	106	38	55	0	1	290	.245	.296	.407	.231	37	75-C	0
2001	*Milwauke*	*NL*	*260*	*67*	*10*	*0*	*12*	*22*	*76*	*31*	*41*	*0*	*0*	*193*	*.258*	*.316*	*.435*	*.250*	*30*		

Creighton Gubanich has a little pop and would be a better backup than Raul Casanova or Kevin Brown, but the difference isn't enormous. Among Gubanich, Casanova, Brown, and Cline, it's hard to see how all of them will be able to get at-bats unless Cline gets pushed down to Double-A.

Cristian Guerrero   RF   Bats R   Age 20

YEAR	TEAM	LGE	AB	H	DB	TP	HR	BB	SO	R	RBI	SB	CS	OUT	BA	OBP	SLG	EQA	EQR	DEFENSE	
1999	Ogden	Pio	222	50	6	1	3	13	68	23	14	7	1	173	.225	.270	.302	.193	14	55-RF	-2
2000	Beloit	Mid	56	10	2	0	2	0	20	4	7	1	0	46	.179	.185	.321	.149	2	14-RF	-2
2000	Ogden	Pio	250	59	9	1	7	19	49	25	26	7	3	194	.236	.294	.364	.221	22	58-RF	1
2001	*Milwauke*	*NL*	*229*	*59*	*9*	*1*	*7*	*15*	*73*	*29*	*29*	*9*	*2*	*172*	*.258*	*.303*	*.397*	*.239*	*24*		

It's an interesting approach: if you can't identify good ballplayers, just wait for other teams to grab the good ones and then sign their siblings. Cristian Guerrero is Vladimir's cousin; he's bigger than Vlad—6′7″—and supposedly has tools comparable to Vlad's at age 19. Don't scarf up his baseball cards yet; plenty of toolsy guys never pan out, and the Brewers don't exactly have a reputation for getting the most out of their prospects. Guerrero must learn how not to be like his cousin and lay off pitches over his head or in the dirt.

Jose Hernandez   3B/SS   Bats R   Age 31

YEAR	TEAM	LGE	AB	H	DB	TP	HR	BB	SO	R	RBI	SB	CS	OUT	BA	OBP	SLG	EQA	EQR	DEFENSE			
1998	ChiCubs	NL	493	124	21	6	24	38	131	76	73	4	6	375	.252	.306	.465	.249	58	61-3B	2	39-SS	-2
1999	ChiCubs	NL	342	90	12	2	14	35	95	53	39	5	2	254	.263	.340	.433	.259	43	79-SS	8	13-CF	-3
1999	Atlanta	NL	167	42	7	0	4	10	42	21	18	3	1	126	.251	.294	.365	.220	14	40-SS	1		
2000	Milwauke	NL	449	107	20	1	11	35	117	48	55	2	7	349	.238	.301	.361	.217	38	91-3B	-2	33-SS	0
2001	*Milwauke*	*NL*	*441*	*111*	*17*	*1*	*16*	*42*	*124*	*54*	*62*	*4*	*3*	*333*	*.252*	*.317*	*.404*	*.242*	*48*				

The Brewers richly deserve every bit of abuse we've heaped on them for the Jose Hernandez signing, but in fairness, there were several factors that combined to make his season worse than it might have been. First, he's a pronounced hot-weather hitter, and Milwaukee had a very cool spring and a mild summer. Also, there was the late-season back injury that stopped his numbers in their tracks. That doesn't make his signing defensible, but it does raise the possibility that he'll rebound a bit, especially with the Brewers moving into (presumably heated) Miller Park.

Damon Hollins   OF   Bats R   Age 27

YEAR	TEAM	LGE	AB	H	DB	TP	HR	BB	SO	R	RBI	SB	CS	OUT	BA	OBP	SLG	EQA	EQR	DEFENSE	
1998	Richmond	Int	437	105	22	2	11	36	84	51	39	6	2	334	.240	.298	.375	.225	40	104-RF	0
1999	Indianap	Int	329	79	11	0	9	24	44	46	36	8	2	252	.240	.293	.356	.219	28	95-CF	7
2000	Indianap	Int	289	75	14	2	2	16	37	28	27	3	2	216	.260	.300	.343	.214	23	79-CF	7
2001	*Milwauke*	*NL*	*276*	*71*	*12*	*1*	*6*	*23*	*42*	*34*	*33*	*4*	*1*	*206*	*.257*	*.314*	*.373*	*.235*	*27*		

Jermaine Dye and Damon Hollins played side by side at Double-A Greenville in the Braves' system in 1995. Dye batted .285 with 15 homers and 71 RBI, and Hollins batted .247 with 18 homers and 77 RBI. *Baseball America* rated them the sixth- and seventh-best prospects in the Braves' system, respectively. The following year, Dye batted .281 for the Braves, and Hollins missed most of the season after dislocating a bone in his left wrist. Since then Hollins hasn't progressed an inch and is in danger of becoming a Triple-A lifer.

Tyler Houston   3B/C   Bats L   Age 30

YEAR	TEAM	LGE	AB	H	DB	TP	HR	BB	SO	R	RBI	SB	CS	OUT	BA	OBP	SLG	EQA	EQR	DEFENSE			
1998	ChiCubs	NL	257	66	7	1	9	12	50	27	32	2	2	193	.257	.290	.397	.224	23	55-C	-3		
1999	ChiCubs	NL	250	57	9	0	9	24	63	25	25	1	1	194	.228	.296	.372	.222	22	51-3B	-12	13-C	-2
1999	Clevelnd	AL	27	4	1	0	1	3	10	2	3	0	0	23	.148	.233	.296	.167	1				
2000	Milwauke	NL	286	70	12	0	18	13	67	28	40	2	1	217	.245	.278	.476	.242	31	29-1B	-1	21-3B	3
2001	*Milwauke*	*NL*	*252*	*60*	*7*	*0*	*13*	*18*	*64*	*25*	*37*	*1*	*1*	*193*	*.238*	*.289*	*.421*	*.234*	*26*				

There's always work for left-handed pitchers; a corollary is that there's always work for left-handed-hitting catchers who also can play third base. That's why it was so easy for Houston to parlay 142 decent rookie at-bats into three more years of service time. Perhaps he decided last year that he ought to put up another good month or two, just to make sure he'll qualify for a pension. Eighteen homers? He ought to be able to ride that one into his forties.

Buck Jacobsen — 1B — Bats R — Age 25

YEAR	TEAM	LGE	AB	H	DB	TP	HR	BB	SO	R	RBI	SB	CS	OUT	BA	OBP	SLG	EQA	EQR	DEFENSE			
1998	Beloit	Mid	519	123	16	1	21	61	143	70	68	2	1	397	.237	.322	.393	.240	56	129-RF	-3		
1999	Huntsvil	Sou	153	28	4	1	3	14	34	16	16	2	1	126	.183	.259	.281	.176	8	24-LF	-6	13-1B	-1
1999	Stockton	Cal	157	32	5	0	4	15	42	15	15	1	1	126	.204	.281	.312	.197	11	11-LF	-3		
2000	Huntsvil	Sou	281	67	10	0	14	39	73	36	38	2	1	215	.238	.336	.423	.255	35	75-1B	-9		
2001	Milwauke	NL	323	78	8	0	15	44	89	42	50	1	1	246	.241	.332	.406	.250	39				

This is for all the lonely power hitters, thinking that life has passed them by. Buck Jacobsen signed late and has been old for the leagues in which he's played. He reemerged as a viable power prospect last year before getting hurt. He's still too old to develop much further, and the demand for right-handed-hitting first basemen is limited, especially in Milwaukee.

Geoff Jenkins — LF — Bats L — Age 26

YEAR	TEAM	LGE	AB	H	DB	TP	HR	BB	SO	R	RBI	SB	CS	OUT	BA	OBP	SLG	EQA	EQR	DEFENSE	
1998	Louisvil	Int	214	63	7	3	6	10	39	31	42	1	1	152	.294	.337	.439	.257	25	49-LF	0
1998	Milwauke	NL	265	61	11	1	10	19	57	34	28	1	3	207	.230	.286	.392	.221	24	64-LF	0
1999	Milwauke	NL	448	136	41	3	20	29	82	67	75	4	1	313	.304	.355	.542	.290	71	118-LF	8
2000	Milwauke	NL	515	152	37	3	32	25	126	94	86	10	1	364	.295	.343	.565	.292	84	130-LF	4
2001	Milwauke	NL	463	139	34	2	28	35	109	81	98	10	1	325	.300	.349	.564	.297	78		

All signs are positive. Geoff Jenkins moved into the #3 spot last year and would have had better numbers if he hadn't broken his finger in May. He should improve his totals simply by staying healthy, and the new park could give him a boost, too. Jenkins has great power to all fields and should be able to take advantage of the short power alleys in Miller Park. He'll never walk, and he'll never fly, but he will hit.

Scott Kirby — RF — Bats R — Age 23

YEAR	TEAM	LGE	AB	H	DB	TP	HR	BB	SO	R	RBI	SB	CS	OUT	BA	OBP	SLG	EQA	EQR	DEFENSE			
1998	Beloit	Mid	371	69	15	1	7	34	117	40	31	2	2	304	.186	.260	.288	.177	20	50-3B	-2	20-2B	-3
1999	Beloit	Mid	252	60	8	0	12	32	64	35	28	1	1	193	.238	.327	.413	.248	29	67-3B	-2		
1999	Stockton	Cal	203	47	11	1	7	17	61	23	22	1	1	157	.232	.301	.399	.232	20	38-1B	-2	12-3B	-2
2000	Huntsvil	Sou	360	74	10	0	11	52	116	47	39	3	3	289	.206	.316	.325	.220	33	74-RF	-7	20-3B	-4
2001	Milwauke	NL	337	72	9	0	13	43	109	36	41	1	1	266	.214	.303	.356	.224	31				

After a fine 1999 season, Scott Kirby didn't handle the challenge of Double-A. Formerly a third baseman, he was moved to outfield in May. One good sign was that he drew 49 walks in his last 68 games after getting only 15 in his first 50.

David Krynzel — CF — Bats L — Age 19

YEAR	TEAM	LGE	AB	H	DB	TP	HR	BB	SO	R	RBI	SB	CS	OUT	BA	OBP	SLG	EQA	EQR	DEFENSE	
2000	Ogden	Pio	128	33	5	1	1	7	27	11	15	2	2	97	.258	.305	.336	.213	10	32-CF	-2
2001	Milwauke	NL	67	18	2	0	0	4	49	6	6	1	1	50	.269	.310	.299	.205	5		

The club's first pick in last year's draft, David Krynzel was named the top prospect in the Pioneer League by *Baseball America*. He's several years away but could become what Chad Green was supposed to be—a speedy center fielder who will hit well enough to bat leadoff.

Luis Lopez — SS/2B — Bats B — Age 30

YEAR	TEAM	LGE	AB	H	DB	TP	HR	BB	SO	R	RBI	SB	CS	OUT	BA	OBP	SLG	EQA	EQR	DEFENSE			
1998	NY Mets	NL	270	71	14	2	2	20	56	39	22	2	2	201	.263	.323	.352	.227	25	33-2B	-3	21-SS	-5
1999	NY Mets	NL	105	22	2	0	3	11	31	11	14	1	1	84	.210	.302	.314	.208	8	17-SS	-1		
2000	Milwauke	NL	203	53	9	0	7	6	33	22	26	1	2	152	.261	.297	.409	.230	19	36-SS	-4	14-2B	1
2001	Milwauke	NL	206	54	7	0	6	16	42	23	27	2	1	153	.262	.315	.383	.236	21				

For a few months last summer, he thought he was the other Luis Lopez and hit a bunch of home runs. Don't bet on a repeat. He could luck into some playing time if Belliard or Mark Loretta comes up lame.

Mickey Lopez — 2B — Bats B — Age 27

YEAR	TEAM	LGE	AB	H	DB	TP	HR	BB	SO	R	RBI	SB	CS	OUT	BA	OBP	SLG	EQA	EQR	DEFENSE			
1998	El Paso	Tex	451	98	21	3	1	31	69	54	41	6	5	358	.217	.269	.284	.179	24	113-2B	-6		
1999	Huntsvil	Sou	319	77	14	3	3	32	52	38	27	14	3	245	.241	.316	.332	.227	30	81-2B	-5		
1999	Louisvil	Int	180	49	14	1	4	31	25	33	23	7	5	136	.272	.383	.428	.274	27	47-2B	6		
2000	Huntsvil	Sou	221	59	16	3	3	21	36	31	19	7	4	166	.267	.331	.407	.247	25	50-2B	-1		
2000	Indianap	Int	211	49	10	1	2	31	28	31	18	9	5	167	.232	.339	.318	.230	21	41-2B	-6	12-SS	0
2001	*Milwauke*	*NL*	*415*	*101*	*25*	*2*	*6*	*54*	*67*	*65*	*44*	*18*	*8*	*322*	*.243*	*.330*	*.357*	*.240*	*45*				

Mickey Lopez probably could have an Adam Kennedy-type season if given the chance, but never would go much beyond that level. Like a box of old candles or a third flashlight, he's nice to have around in case of an emergency.

Mark Loretta — SS — Bats R — Age 29

YEAR	TEAM	LGE	AB	H	DB	TP	HR	BB	SO	R	RBI	SB	CS	OUT	BA	OBP	SLG	EQA	EQR	DEFENSE			
1998	Milwauke	NL	440	137	19	0	10	40	44	54	56	8	6	309	.311	.377	.423	.270	59	45-SS	5	41-1B	-2
1999	Milwauke	NL	589	166	35	4	5	44	56	89	62	3	1	424	.282	.342	.380	.245	63	70-SS	-5	56-1B	-2
2000	Milwauke	NL	354	97	19	1	7	32	36	46	37	0	3	260	.274	.336	.393	.243	38	81-SS	11		
2001	*Milwauke*	*NL*	*438*	*131*	*24*	*1*	*7*	*44*	*47*	*66*	*64*	*3*	*2*	*309*	*.299*	*.363*	*.406*	*.263*	*55*				

Mark Loretta is one of the best pure contact hitters in the majors, so it was shocking to see him occasionally break character and turn on inside pitches last year. Look for him to post career highs in doubles and/or home runs this season.

James Mouton — CF — Bats R — Age 32

YEAR	TEAM	LGE	AB	H	DB	TP	HR	BB	SO	R	RBI	SB	CS	OUT	BA	OBP	SLG	EQA	EQR	DEFENSE	
1998	LasVegas	PCL	187	52	12	2	2	13	33	25	20	9	1	136	.278	.327	.396	.250	21	40-LF	-4
1998	San Dieg	NL	64	13	2	1	0	7	10	8	7	4	3	54	.203	.282	.266	.184	4	16-OF	0
1999	Montreal	NL	123	32	5	1	2	16	29	17	12	5	2	93	.260	.354	.366	.251	15	26-LF	-3
2000	Milwauke	NL	160	36	7	1	2	27	40	26	16	12	4	128	.225	.346	.319	.240	18	40-OF	-1
2001	*Milwauke*	*NL*	*135*	*32*	*6*	*1*	*2*	*23*	*33*	*25*	*14*	*8*	*2*	*105*	*.237*	*.348*	*.341*	*.249*	*16*		

I used to hate James Mouton, who made it to the majors on the strength of his misinterpreted Pacific Coast League stats. Now that he's learned to draw a few walks, he's actually become somewhat underrated, thus leaving me conflicted. Regardless, he still can't hit right-handed pitchers, so he has limited value.

Lyle Mouton — OF — Bats R — Age 32

YEAR	TEAM	LGE	AB	H	DB	TP	HR	BB	SO	R	RBI	SB	CS	OUT	BA	OBP	SLG	EQA	EQR	DEFENSE	
1998	YKL	JpC	89	21	6	0	3	7	0	0	0	0	0	68	.236	.292	.404	.231	9		
1998	Rochestr	Int	137	37	7	1	5	10	33	18	23	1	1	101	.270	.326	.445	.254	16	27-RF	0
1999	Rochestr	Int	163	33	7	1	3	9	33	19	13	2	1	131	.202	.247	.313	.179	9	33-RF	-5
1999	Louisvil	Int	301	88	24	1	13	19	72	43	52	11	1	214	.292	.341	.508	.281	45	75-LF	9
2000	Indianap	Int	199	52	15	0	9	17	46	25	37	3	1	148	.261	.329	.472	.264	26	49-LF	-1
2000	Milwauke	NL	98	27	6	1	2	8	27	13	15	1	0	71	.276	.336	.418	.254	12	23-LF	0
2001	*Milwauke*	*NL*	*297*	*80*	*21*	*1*	*10*	*27*	*72*	*42*	*47*	*1*	*0*	*217*	*.269*	*.330*	*.448*	*.260*	*37*		

Lyle Mouton gets shockingly little respect for a guy who's produced in both the minors and majors. As Lopes emphasized the need for "accountability," Mouton got a mid-year demotion for not hitting left-handers well enough in the two dozen at-bats he was given. Atta boy, Davey. John Snyder has got to understand that unless he gets his butt in gear, one of these years he'll wake up and his job will be gone.

Santiago Perez — SS — Bats B — Age 25

YEAR	TEAM	LGE	AB	H	DB	TP	HR	BB	SO	R	RBI	SB	CS	OUT	BA	OBP	SLG	EQA	EQR	DEFENSE	
1998	El Paso	Tex	442	106	15	6	8	19	77	46	41	10	6	342	.240	.275	.355	.207	33	104-SS	-16
1998	Louisvil	Int	133	33	3	2	3	4	31	15	12	4	2	102	.248	.270	.368	.209	10	34-SS	-5
1999	Louisvil	Int	406	97	19	6	6	23	93	44	30	14	3	312	.239	.282	.360	.217	34	95-SS	-15
2000	Indianap	Int	412	105	24	5	5	36	100	62	29	21	6	314	.255	.316	.374	.237	43	100-SS	-14
2000	Milwauke	NL	52	9	1	0	0	8	8	7	2	4	0	43	.173	.293	.192	.187	3	14-SS	-2
2001	*San Dieg*	*NL*	*434*	*105*	*20*	*5*	*7*	*33*	*106*	*61*	*47*	*22*	*5*	*334*	*.242*	*.296*	*.359*	*.236*	*45*		

Santiago Perez is similar to ex-Brewer Jose Valentin, with many of the same weaknesses but without the strengths. At shortstop, he has good range but is error-prone and has gotten a "bad concentration" rap. He's a decent hitter from the left side but hopeless from the right. If Perez can learn to play a few more positions, he could be decent off the bench. The Padres traded a middle-relief prospect for him and are likely to give him their shortstop job.

Jeff Pickler   2B/3B   Bats L   Age 25

YEAR	TEAM	LGE	AB	H	DB	TP	HR	BB	SO	R	RBI	SB	CS	OUT	BA	OBP	SLG	EQA	EQR	DEFENSE	
1998	Ogden	Pio	270	67	7	0	4	19	30	24	24	6	4	207	.248	.299	.319	.207	20	64-2B	0
1999	Stockton	Cal	308	84	11	1	1	14	30	27	28	3	3	227	.273	.304	.325	.208	22	72-2B	-11
1999	Huntsvil	Sou	184	45	5	1	1	10	27	15	18	5	2	141	.245	.284	.299	.194	12	45-2B	0
2000	Huntsvil	Sou	263	69	7	0	1	22	30	27	22	7	6	200	.262	.321	.300	.210	20	66-2B	-4
2000	Indianap	Int	191	54	5	1	1	20	28	29	17	10	2	139	.283	.353	.335	.245	21	48-2B	-2
2001	Milwauke	NL	404	115	13	1	2	39	53	61	41	18	7	296	.285	.348	.337	.242	42		

Jeff Pickler is another potentially useful reserve infielder. He has little in common with Perez, though. Pickler is a Bill Mueller wannabe, a left-handed-hitting on-base guy with zero power. He can play second base and third base but not shortstop, but has a limited future.

Marcos Scutaro   2B   Bats R   Age 25

YEAR	TEAM	LGE	AB	H	DB	TP	HR	BB	SO	R	RBI	SB	CS	OUT	BA	OBP	SLG	EQA	EQR	DEFENSE			
1998	Akron	Eas	468	126	24	4	8	35	72	52	48	18	10	352	.269	.329	.389	.242	51	117-2B	0		
1998	Buffalo	Int	26	6	2	0	0	0	2	2	3	0	0	20	.231	.231	.308	.161	1				
1999	Buffalo	Int	465	117	23	1	6	50	69	61	41	14	5	353	.252	.330	.344	.233	46	118-2B	6		
2000	Buffalo	Int	431	110	16	4	5	51	55	58	47	6	5	326	.255	.344	.346	.237	45	109-2B	-2	17-SS	-5
2001	Milwauke	NL	377	98	17	2	7	46	55	57	46	11	4	284	.260	.340	.371	.247	43				

Marcos Scutaro was acquired from Cleveland in the Sexson deal for reasons that aren't readily apparent. It's not that he isn't a good player—he's a decent all-around second baseman and is young enough to get a little better. But he doesn't project as the type of player who has a reasonable chance of playing regularly for the Brewers in the future. Perhaps the club was just hedging its bets in case Belliard's back goes haywire again.

Richie Sexson   1B   Bats R   Age 26

YEAR	TEAM	LGE	AB	H	DB	TP	HR	BB	SO	R	RBI	SB	CS	OUT	BA	OBP	SLG	EQA	EQR	DEFENSE			
1998	Buffalo	Int	347	93	16	0	18	41	67	50	60	1	1	255	.268	.349	.470	.270	49	66-LF	2	17-1B	5
1998	Clevelnd	AL	173	54	13	1	12	6	37	28	35	1	1	120	.312	.345	.607	.299	29	39-1B	0		
1999	Clevelnd	AL	476	121	16	7	32	30	107	70	111	3	3	358	.254	.303	.519	.262	63	58-1B	6	39-LF	0
2000	Clevelnd	AL	321	82	15	1	16	21	87	42	41	1	0	239	.255	.309	.458	.252	38	47-LF	-3	25-1B	4
2000	Milwauke	NL	214	62	10	0	14	30	59	41	44	1	0	152	.290	.384	.533	.300	37	56-1B	9		
2001	Milwauke	NL	446	121	19	1	29	47	119	65	91	1	1	326	.271	.341	.513	.279	67				

One thing that projection doesn't take into account is that in coming from Cleveland, Richie Sexson has gone from a crowded lineup to a vacuum. He won't be batting seventh and battling Wil Cordero for playing time; he'll be batting cleanup and playing every day. Given that, he's likely to bat 600 times and approach 40 home runs and 120 RBI, even if he hits no better than he has in the past.

Mark Sweeney   PH   Bats L   Age 31

YEAR	TEAM	LGE	AB	H	DB	TP	HR	BB	SO	R	RBI	SB	CS	OUT	BA	OBP	SLG	EQA	EQR	DEFENSE			
1998	San Dieg	NL	196	48	9	3	2	26	35	18	15	1	2	150	.245	.336	.352	.234	20	24-RF	-2	16-1B	-3
1999	Indianap	Int	313	83	12	1	8	45	43	49	35	2	1	231	.265	.362	.387	.258	39	53-RF	-2	16-1B	-1
2000	Indianap	Int	55	23	5	0	2	8	9	10	11	0	0	32	.418	.492	.618	.366	13				
2000	Milwauke	NL	74	16	4	0	2	10	17	9	7	0	0	58	.216	.317	.351	.227	7				
2001	Milwauke	NL	177	50	9	1	5	27	33	31	29	1	0	127	.282	.377	.429	.278	26				

The Brewers got out from under Alex Ochoa's impending arbitration eligibility by dealing him for Sweeney. Then, at season's end, they cut Sweeney loose. Keeping Sweeney would have been kind of pointless anyway; you don't buy one of those fluffy covers for the toilet seat before you install the plumbing.

PITCHERS (ERA: 4.50, H/9: 9.00, HR/9: 1.00, BB/9: 3.00, K/9: 6.00, KW: 1.00, PERA: 4.50)

Juan Acevedo — Throws R Age 31

YEAR	TEAM	LGE	IP	H	ER	HR	BB	K	ERA	W	L	H/9	HR/9	BB/9	K/9	KW	PERA
1998	St Louis	NL	93.7	80	29	7	26	45	2.79	7	3	7.69	0.67	2.50	4.32	0.87	3.24
1999	St Louis	NL	100.0	109	64	16	40	44	5.76	4	7	9.81	1.44	3.60	3.96	0.55	5.69
2000	Milwauke	NL	80.3	74	34	10	25	42	3.81	5	4	8.29	1.12	2.80	4.71	0.84	4.13

Juan Acevedo pitched well in the second half last year, but can he continue? He had a history in St. Louis of failing to sustain his success in a given role from year to year. One thing he's got going for him now is that the Brewers seem pretty well convinced that he's cut out to be a setup man. The Cardinals, in contrast, seemed to redefine his role every time he had three poor outings in a row.

Mike Buddie — Throws R Age 30

YEAR	TEAM	LGE	IP	H	ER	HR	BB	K	ERA	W	L	H/9	HR/9	BB/9	K/9	KW	PERA
1998	Columbus	Int	40.3	35	16	1	15	20	3.57	2	2	7.81	0.22	3.35	4.46	0.67	3.22
1998	NY Yanks	AL	40.7	43	26	5	11	18	5.75	2	3	9.52	1.11	2.43	3.98	0.82	4.68
1999	Columbus	Int	74.7	78	29	2	23	46	3.50	5	3	9.40	0.24	2.77	5.54	1.00	3.86
2000	Columbus	Int	27.7	35	35	11	21	11	11.39	0	3	11.39	3.58	6.83	3.58	0.26	10.25
2000	Indianap	Int	54.3	40	22	5	31	28	3.64	3	3	6.63	0.83	5.13	4.64	0.45	3.83

Teams don't look for "good" long relievers. By definition, a long reliever's innings don't mean much to the team's performance, so they're used to get a wild kid some experience or get a struggling pitcher straightened out. If they simply went for the best available pitcher, Mike Buddie would have had a job long ago. He isn't quite good enough to be anything more than a middleman, so he gets stuck in Triple-A year after year.

Jeff D'Amico — Throws R Age 25

YEAR	TEAM	LGE	IP	H	ER	HR	BB	K	ERA	W	L	H/9	HR/9	BB/9	K/9	KW	PERA
1998	Huntsvil	Sou	57.0	79	62	19	33	29	9.79	1	5	12.47	3.00	5.21	4.58	0.44	9.59
2000	Indianap	Int	29.0	26	13	8	11	15	4.03	1	2	8.07	2.48	3.41	4.66	0.68	5.68
2000	Milwauke	NL	156.7	137	50	12	38	84	2.87	11	6	7.87	0.69	2.18	4.83	1.11	3.24

Brewers pitchers have a long history of major arm injuries, but none ever did what Jeff D'Amico has done: come all the way back and pitch even better than before. If you didn't see him last year, he really was as good as his numbers, living on the black and changing speeds like a veteran. He wasn't overworked, and there's little reason to expect another breakdown.

Kane Davis — Throws R Age 26

YEAR	TEAM	LGE	IP	H	ER	HR	BB	K	ERA	W	L	H/9	HR/9	BB/9	K/9	KW	PERA
1998	Carolina	Sou	69.7	100	86	19	37	24	11.11	1	7	12.92	2.45	4.78	3.10	0.32	9.08
1999	Altoona	Eas	87.3	94	57	9	49	31	5.87	3	7	9.69	0.93	5.05	3.19	0.32	5.68
1999	Nashvill	PCL	47.3	60	36	9	19	21	6.85	1	4	11.41	1.71	3.61	3.99	0.55	6.95
2000	Akron	Eas	18.3	18	10	4	6	8	4.91	1	1	8.84	1.96	2.95	3.93	0.67	5.43
2000	Buffalo	Int	28.0	29	17	3	13	13	5.46	1	2	9.32	0.96	4.18	4.18	0.50	5.12
2000	Clevelnd	AL	11.3	18	16	2	6	2	12.71	0	1	14.29	1.59	4.76	1.59	0.17	8.92
2000	Indianap	Int	19.0	19	9	3	7	9	4.26	1	1	9.00	1.42	3.32	4.26	0.64	5.07

Kane Davis can throw 90 mph, so of course the Brewers jumped at the opportunity to pick him up in the Sexson deal. Whether he can pitch in the majors remains an open question, but he'll be waiting in Triple-A if and when they want to find out.

Valerio de los Santos — Throws L Age 25

YEAR	TEAM	LGE	IP	H	ER	HR	BB	K	ERA	W	L	H/9	HR/9	BB/9	K/9	KW	PERA
1998	El Paso	Tex	64.3	78	31	2	24	41	4.34	3	4	10.91	0.28	3.36	5.74	0.85	5.01
1998	Milwauke	NL	20.7	11	7	4	2	15	3.05	1	1	4.79	1.74	0.87	6.53	3.75	2.17
2000	Milwauke	NL	72.0	71	39	13	27	58	4.88	3	5	8.88	1.63	3.38	7.25	1.07	5.24

More than any other major-league pitcher last year, Valerio de los Santos had his numbers ruined by a pair of lousy outings. He was bombed for nine hits—including five home runs—and eight runs in 3⅔ innings on April 9. On May 21, he was left in to absorb eight runs in two-thirds of an inning. Take away those two games and he had a 3.38 ERA in 69⅓ innings with 57 hits allowed, 28 walks, and 69 strikeouts. As a reverse-platooner with no breaking pitch, he's horribly miscast as a situational left-hander but has good potential as a setup man or even a starter. The back injury that cost him most of 1999 might have been the best thing that could have happened as far as his arm was concerned. Now he hasn't been overworked in five years. An excellent sleeper.

Horacio Estrada — Throws L — Age 25

YEAR	TEAM	LGE	IP	H	ER	HR	BB	K	ERA	W	L	H/9	HR/9	BB/9	K/9	KW	PERA
1998	El Paso	Tex	47.7	47	24	3	20	24	4.53	2	3	8.87	0.57	3.78	4.53	0.60	4.26
1998	Louisvil	Int	11.3	9	4	1	5	3	3.18	1	0	7.15	0.79	3.97	2.38	0.30	3.59
1999	Louisvil	Int	126.7	125	81	21	61	82	5.76	5	9	8.88	1.49	4.33	5.83	0.67	5.50
2000	Indianap	Int	150.3	146	66	18	45	77	3.95	9	8	8.74	1.08	2.69	4.61	0.86	4.30
2000	Milwauke	NL	24.3	29	15	4	16	11	5.55	1	2	10.73	1.48	5.92	4.07	0.34	7.23

The Brewers don't have a single left-hander in the rotation, and Horacio Estrada is out of options, so the math is fairly simple. He would have been called up sooner last year, but Indianapolis was in the playoffs.

Jose Garcia — Throws R — Age 23

YEAR	TEAM	LGE	IP	H	ER	HR	BB	K	ERA	W	L	H/9	HR/9	BB/9	K/9	KW	PERA
1998	Stockton	Cal	151.7	153	115	28	114	87	6.82	4	13	9.08	1.66	6.76	5.16	0.38	6.81
2000	Huntsvil	Sou	93.7	113	63	15	58	47	6.05	3	7	10.86	1.44	5.57	4.52	0.41	7.14

Jose Garcia missed all of 1999 with elbow surgery after throwing 155⅓ innings at age 19 and 169⅓ innings at age 20. His recovery last year was rocky at times, and he missed time early in the season and in July. Garcia pitched well at the end of the campaign, posting a 1.96 ERA in his last six starts. A curveballer, he's still building up his stamina and might need to break in as a reliever.

J.M. Gold — Throws R — Age 21

YEAR	TEAM	LGE	IP	H	ER	HR	BB	K	ERA	W	L	H/9	HR/9	BB/9	K/9	KW	PERA
1998	Ogden	Pio	17.0	20	11	2	7	7	5.82	1	1	10.59	1.06	3.71	3.71	0.50	5.74
1999	Beloit	Mid	100.7	129	102	33	61	49	9.12	2	9	11.53	2.95	5.45	4.38	0.40	9.08
2000	Beloit	Mid	30.7	30	17	2	18	17	4.99	1	2	8.80	0.59	5.28	4.99	0.47	4.89

What do you get when the Brewers spend a first-round draft pick on a high-school pitcher with a history of elbow problems? Right. J.M. Gold underwent Tommy John surgery last summer and will be out until at least mid-2001.

Jimmy Haynes — Throws R — Age 28

YEAR	TEAM	LGE	IP	H	ER	HR	BB	K	ERA	W	L	H/9	HR/9	BB/9	K/9	KW	PERA
1998	Oakland	AL	192.0	214	110	23	76	124	5.16	8	13	10.03	1.08	3.56	5.81	0.82	5.42
1999	Oakland	AL	141.7	148	96	18	65	88	6.10	5	11	9.40	1.14	4.13	5.59	0.68	5.35
2000	Milwauke	NL	195.0	218	115	19	82	73	5.31	8	14	10.06	0.88	3.78	3.37	0.45	5.32

A lot of people look at Jimmy Haynes and think that if they could just get their hands on him for a few weeks, they could straighten him out. Maybe that's the problem.

In his book *It's What You Learn after You Know It All That Counts,* Earl Weaver wrote about his experience as a minor-league manager with legendary wild man Steve Dalkowski. Poor Dalkowski was the ultimate guinea pig—everybody wanted to be the one to turn him around. People in the Orioles' system gave him all kinds of advice and kept trying to teach him a curveball. Weaver, on the other hand, observed that all the advice and instruction only served to confuse Dalkowski, who apparently was no mental giant. Weaver told him to forget everything and just throw his fastball and slider over the plate. These were instructions Dalkowski could understand. According to Weaver, in Dalkowski's final 57 innings that year he gave up one earned run, walked 11, and struck out 110.

(Jimmy Haynes *continued*)

Haynes is no Dalkowski by any stretch, but he's been similarly over-coached during his entire major-league career. They've fiddled with this, altered that, taken away this pitch, and taught him the other one. It's kind of crazy that we need to point this out, but it hasn't worked. Every team he's been on ultimately has thrown up its hands and shown him the door, and the Brewers soon could do the same if things keep going this way. What do they have to lose, at this point, by simply sending him out to the mound and letting him do what comes naturally?

Ray King — Throws L — Age 27

YEAR	TEAM	LGE	IP	H	ER	HR	BB	K	ERA	W	L	H/9	HR/9	BB/9	K/9	KW	PERA
1998	WestTenn	Sou	27.7	23	10	2	10	15	3.25	2	1	7.48	0.65	3.25	4.88	0.75	3.37
1998	Iowa	PCL	30.3	34	21	5	17	18	6.23	1	2	10.09	1.48	5.04	5.34	0.53	6.50
1999	Iowa	PCL	39.7	29	12	1	26	26	2.72	3	1	6.58	0.23	5.90	5.90	0.50	3.51
1999	ChiCubs	NL	10.7	11	7	2	8	4	5.91	0	1	9.28	1.69	6.75	3.38	0.25	6.96
2000	Indianap	Int	24.0	25	15	1	13	14	5.63	1	2	9.38	0.38	4.88	5.25	0.54	4.80
2000	Milwauke	NL	27.7	17	6	1	8	16	1.95	2	1	5.53	0.33	2.60	5.20	1.00	1.94

Here's a prediction: as soon as hitters start laying off his slider and sitting on his fastball, it will be all over for Ray King. In the meantime, it makes for a fun Strat card.

Jack Krawczyk — Throws R — Age 25

YEAR	TEAM	LGE	IP	H	ER	HR	BB	K	ERA	W	L	H/9	HR/9	BB/9	K/9	KW	PERA
1998	Beloit	Mid	36.0	42	33	8	14	21	8.25	1	3	10.50	2.00	3.50	5.25	0.75	6.67
1999	Stockton	Cal	70.3	89	60	17	25	37	7.68	2	6	11.39	2.18	3.20	4.73	0.74	7.24
2000	Mudville	Cal	78.7	66	17	6	12	38	1.94	7	2	7.55	0.69	1.37	4.35	1.58	2.78

There are plenty of reasons to downplay what Jack Krawczyk did last year. He was in A ball at age 24, he was repeating the league, etc. The facts are that he pitched very well and showed excellent control as a two-inning closer. If he can handle Double-A hitters half as well, the Brewers might have a decent middle reliever here.

Derek Lee — Throws L — Age 26

YEAR	TEAM	LGE	IP	H	ER	HR	BB	K	ERA	W	L	H/9	HR/9	BB/9	K/9	KW	PERA
1998	Stockton	Cal	121.7	141	93	23	65	68	6.88	4	10	10.43	1.70	4.81	5.03	0.52	6.84
1999	Huntsvil	Sou	128.7	143	82	27	59	45	5.74	5	9	10.00	1.89	4.13	3.15	0.38	6.50
2000	Huntsvil	Sou	119.0	126	61	13	49	47	4.61	6	7	9.53	0.98	3.71	3.55	0.48	5.09
2000	Indianap	Int	12.3	16	8	3	6	6	5.84	0	1	11.68	2.19	4.38	4.38	0.50	7.86

Derek Lee, a breaking-ball pitcher, got a little more play as a prospect than he deserved by putting together a flashy won-lost record as a 25-year-old Double-A repeater. His control improved over the course of the season; he walked just 24 batters in 93 1/3 innings over his last 15 starts.

Curtis Leskanic — Throws R — Age 33

YEAR	TEAM	LGE	IP	H	ER	HR	BB	K	ERA	W	L	H/9	HR/9	BB/9	K/9	KW	PERA
1998	Colorado	NL	75.7	73	30	6	29	45	3.57	4	4	8.68	0.71	3.45	5.35	0.78	4.21
1999	Colorado	NL	86.0	86	43	4	32	65	4.50	4	6	9.00	0.42	3.35	6.80	1.02	4.04
2000	Milwauke	NL	76.0	58	21	6	42	62	2.49	6	2	6.87	0.71	4.97	7.34	0.74	3.78

It went without saying that he was better than his Colorado ERAs showed, but did anyone really think Curtis Leskanic was this good? His road ERAs over the two previous years were 2.91 and 4.28, which gives no definitive answer. His walk rate remains high, but even so, he's pitched well enough to hold the closer job. Would you ever have guessed he's 33 years old? He doesn't look like it or pitch like it.

Allen Levrault — Throws R — Age 23

YEAR	TEAM	LGE	IP	H	ER	HR	BB	K	ERA	W	L	H/9	HR/9	BB/9	K/9	KW	PERA
1998	Stockton	Cal	88.3	82	47	19	34	45	4.79	4	6	8.35	1.94	3.46	4.58	0.66	5.31
1998	El Paso	Tex	60.3	73	47	8	17	30	7.01	2	5	10.89	1.19	2.54	4.48	0.88	5.63
1999	Huntsvil	Sou	92.3	80	53	17	35	52	5.17	4	6	7.80	1.66	3.41	5.07	0.74	4.65
1999	Louisvil	Int	33.0	47	34	9	15	24	9.27	1	3	12.82	2.45	4.09	6.55	0.80	8.73
2000	Indianap	Int	102.7	97	57	11	45	60	5.00	4	7	8.50	0.96	3.94	5.26	0.67	4.56
2000	Milwauke	NL	11.7	10	7	0	6	7	5.40	0	1	7.71	0.00	4.63	5.40	0.58	3.44

One of the best pitching prospects in the upper levels of the Brewers' farm system, Allen Levrault did his finest work after being sent back down in July following an uneventful June call-up. He had a 3.91 ERA in 11 starts with 50 strikeouts in 66⅔ innings. Between a broken nose in 1999 and the call-up last year, his workloads have been kept reasonable.

Jose Mieses — Throws R — Age 21

YEAR	TEAM	LGE	IP	H	ER	HR	BB	K	ERA	W	L	H/9	HR/9	BB/9	K/9	KW	PERA
1999	Helena	Pio	100.3	79	40	12	37	41	3.59	6	5	7.09	1.08	3.32	3.68	0.55	3.63
2000	Beloit	Mid	122.3	121	59	19	41	70	4.34	6	8	8.90	1.40	3.02	5.15	0.85	4.87
2000	Mudville	Cal	30.3	27	14	3	22	21	4.15	1	2	8.01	0.89	6.53	6.23	0.48	5.27

His stuff doesn't seem to impress people, but Jose Mieses doesn't do anything but win. A groundballer, he went 17-7 last year with an excellent strikeout-to-walk ratio. He's young and skinny, so we'll need to see how his arm holds up. Plus, he'll need to make the jump to Double-A, often a tough one for pitchers who rely more on savvy than stuff.

Nick Neugebauer — Throws R — Age 20

YEAR	TEAM	LGE	IP	H	ER	HR	BB	K	ERA	W	L	H/9	HR/9	BB/9	K/9	KW	PERA
1999	Beloit	Mid	71.3	60	53	8	91	66	6.69	2	6	7.57	1.01	11.48	8.33	0.36	7.19
2000	Mudville	Cal	66.3	48	53	3	105	63	7.19	2	5	6.51	0.41	14.25	8.55	0.30	7.06
2000	Huntsvil	Sou	45.7	39	35	4	50	34	6.90	1	4	7.69	0.79	9.85	6.70	0.34	6.33

Not quite Dalkowskiesque, Nick Neugebauer pitches with an upper-90s fastball and a compass. He faced 578 batters last year; more than half of them failed to put the ball in play (308; 134 walks and 174 strikeouts). An encouraging sign is that he had a 9.37 ERA over first seven starts but a 3.02 ERA over his next 21 while his walk rate went from 15.21 to 8.11. Opposing batters hit .179 and slugged .234 against him. His average start in 2000 went 4⅔ innings with three hits, five walks, and seven strikeouts. He pitched 128 innings and walked the leadoff man 34 times. Now it's a race to see if he can harness his stuff before he burns himself out.

Kyle Peterson — Throws R — Age 25

YEAR	TEAM	LGE	IP	H	ER	HR	BB	K	ERA	W	L	H/9	HR/9	BB/9	K/9	KW	PERA
1998	Stockton	Cal	88.0	102	64	10	42	55	6.55	3	7	10.43	1.02	4.30	5.63	0.65	5.90
1998	El Paso	Tex	41.3	39	22	2	16	22	4.79	2	3	8.49	0.44	3.48	4.79	0.69	3.84
1999	Louisvil	Int	104.3	88	49	13	39	69	4.23	6	6	7.59	1.12	3.36	5.95	0.88	3.95
1999	Milwauke	NL	74.7	82	42	3	21	29	5.06	3	5	9.88	0.36	2.53	3.50	0.69	4.16
2000	Beloit	Mid	12.7	14	8	5	5	8	5.68	0	1	9.95	3.55	3.55	5.68	0.80	7.99

Kyle Peterson, who pitched fairly well as a rookie in 1999, lost almost all of last season to a shoulder injury. The club blamed his poor mechanics, though it might be just as fair to finger his rather heavy workload in 1999. Admittedly, he does have one of the oddest deliveries around. He has a half-second pause in mid-delivery when he momentarily droops like a marionette with its strings cut but just as quickly snaps back to life. You have to wonder if the deception was one of the keys to his effectiveness. It will be a moot point unless he recovers.

Ryan Poe — Throws R — Age 23

YEAR	TEAM	LGE	IP	H	ER	HR	BB	K	ERA	W	L	H/9	HR/9	BB/9	K/9	KW	PERA
1998	Helena	Pio	37.7	52	31	8	17	21	7.41	1	3	12.42	1.91	4.06	5.02	0.62	7.90
1999	Beloit	Mid	87.7	104	61	19	18	57	6.26	3	7	10.68	1.95	1.85	5.85	1.58	6.02
2000	Mudville	Cal	73.7	66	32	15	26	51	3.91	4	4	8.06	1.83	3.18	6.23	0.98	4.91
2000	Huntsvil	Sou	19.3	19	10	2	10	12	4.66	1	1	8.84	0.93	4.66	5.59	0.60	5.00

Ryan Poe is a pure control pitcher, the type that could hit a wall at Double-A. He's one of the best of the type, though, with a career strikeout-to-walk ratio of 4.4 to 1 in 246⅓ innings.

Paul Rigdon — Throws R — Age 25

YEAR	TEAM	LGE	IP	H	ER	HR	BB	K	ERA	W	L	H/9	HR/9	BB/9	K/9	KW	PERA
1998	Kinston	Car	112.7	131	85	21	49	49	6.79	3	10	10.46	1.68	3.91	3.91	0.50	6.46
1999	Akron	Eas	46.3	20	6	3	11	15	1.17	5	0	3.88	0.58	2.14	2.91	0.68	1.32
1999	Buffalo	Int	98.7	108	57	13	28	44	5.20	4	7	9.85	1.19	2.55	4.01	0.79	5.01
2000	Buffalo	Int	67.3	70	27	5	18	31	3.61	4	3	9.36	0.67	2.41	4.14	0.86	4.12
2000	Clevelnd	AL	18.0	19	12	3	7	14	6.00	1	1	9.50	1.50	3.50	7.00	1.00	5.52
2000	Milwauke	NL	67.7	65	32	12	21	40	4.26	4	4	8.65	1.60	2.79	5.32	0.95	4.82

Acquired from Cleveland in the Sexson deal, Paul Rigdon looks like a smart pickup. He had Tommy John surgery in '97, returned in '98, and pitched fairly well in 1999 and 2000. The Brewers showed faith in him by immediately inserting him into the rotation. He rewarded their faith by pitching consistently in August and September.

Rafael Roque — Throws L — Age 29

YEAR	TEAM	LGE	IP	H	ER	HR	BB	K	ERA	W	L	H/9	HR/9	BB/9	K/9	KW	PERA
1998	El Paso	Tex	89.3	108	54	10	38	42	5.44	4	6	10.88	1.01	3.83	4.23	0.55	5.97
1998	Louisvil	Int	47.0	42	22	2	19	29	4.21	2	3	8.04	0.38	3.64	5.55	0.76	3.60
1998	Milwauke	NL	46.0	41	27	9	22	28	5.28	2	3	8.02	1.76	4.30	5.48	0.64	5.27
1999	Milwauke	NL	82.7	93	48	15	35	56	5.23	3	6	10.13	1.63	3.81	6.10	0.80	6.17
2000	Indianap	Int	123.0	130	76	24	67	79	5.56	5	9	9.51	1.76	4.90	5.78	0.59	6.40

Rafael Roque, the Brewers' 1999 Opening Day starter, apparently was a victim of the new regime's strong preference for power pitchers and spent almost all year in Triple-A. That's not to say he didn't necessarily belong there. He isn't all that tough on left-handed hitters, so even Ray King going down in flames may not help Roque resurface.

Bob Scanlan — Throws R — Age 34

YEAR	TEAM	LGE	IP	H	ER	HR	BB	K	ERA	W	L	H/9	HR/9	BB/9	K/9	KW	PERA
1998	New Orln	PCL	58.0	82	49	9	29	22	7.60	1	5	12.72	1.40	4.50	3.41	0.38	7.73
1998	Houston	NL	25.0	23	11	4	12	7	3.96	2	1	8.28	1.44	4.32	2.52	0.29	5.08
1999	New Orln	PCL	154.7	185	114	18	70	49	6.63	5	12	10.77	1.05	4.07	2.85	0.35	6.03
2000	Indianap	Int	56.3	41	17	5	19	16	2.72	4	2	6.55	0.80	3.04	2.56	0.42	2.97

The Brewers' 2000 media guide notes that Scanlan was named the fifth-best prospect in the Eastern League by *Baseball America*... in 1987. Other ex-prospects who pitched for the Brewers' Triple-A team in 2000 include Rod Bolton, Mike Busby, Joe Crawford, Tom Fordham, Tim Harikkala, Reggie Harris, Ricardo Jordan, and Eric Ludwick.

Ben Sheets — Throws R — Age 22

YEAR	TEAM	LGE	IP	H	ER	HR	BB	K	ERA	W	L	H/9	HR/9	BB/9	K/9	KW	PERA
1999	Stockton	Cal	25.7	23	13	2	17	15	4.56	1	2	8.06	0.70	5.96	5.26	0.44	4.91
2000	Huntsvil	Sou	65.7	59	22	8	27	36	3.02	4	3	8.09	1.10	3.70	4.93	0.67	4.35
2000	Indianap	Int	77.7	75	31	5	30	45	3.59	5	4	8.69	0.58	3.48	5.21	0.75	4.07

We heard he pitched pretty well in an international tournament last year. Ben Sheets doesn't get tons of strikeouts, but he throws hard, pitches inside, and gets a lot of weakly hit balls. A low strikeout rate is often a danger sign, but in Sheets's case, we're not worried at all. He has a good chance to be the NL Rookie of the Year.

John Snyder — Throws R — Age 26

YEAR	TEAM	LGE	IP	H	ER	HR	BB	K	ERA	W	L	H/9	HR/9	BB/9	K/9	KW	PERA
1998	Calgary	PCL	94.3	103	43	11	33	44	4.10	5	5	9.83	1.05	3.15	4.20	0.67	5.11
1998	ChiSox	AL	84.3	89	43	13	20	48	4.59	4	5	9.50	1.39	2.13	5.12	1.20	4.84
1999	ChiSox	AL	128.7	154	86	22	39	64	6.02	4	10	10.77	1.54	2.73	4.48	0.82	6.00
2000	Milwauke	NL	125.0	143	86	7	63	57	6.19	4	10	10.30	0.50	4.54	4.10	0.45	5.38

John Snyder knows he's right-handed, and that's about it. He doesn't know what his second-best pitch is. He doesn't know what his third-best pitch is. He doesn't know how to use them to set up hitters. He doesn't know if he should use them to try to get ground balls or to try to get hitters to go up the ladder. Every outing is continual trial and error, mostly the latter.

Everett Stull — Throws R — Age 29

YEAR	TEAM	LGE	IP	H	ER	HR	BB	K	ERA	W	L	H/9	HR/9	BB/9	K/9	KW	PERA
1998	Rochestr	Int	39.3	50	49	12	48	26	11.21	0	4	11.44	2.75	10.98	5.95	0.27	11.12
1999	Richmond	Int	131.3	124	77	19	74	86	5.28	5	10	8.50	1.30	5.07	5.89	0.58	5.38
2000	Indianap	Int	97.7	93	43	4	46	53	3.96	6	5	8.57	0.37	4.24	4.88	0.58	4.11
2000	Milwauke	NL	42.7	40	27	6	25	27	5.70	2	3	8.44	1.27	5.27	5.70	0.54	5.39

Everett Stull: the dark underside of the new regime's preoccupation with velocity. Well, that's not exactly fair; he did all right at Triple-A last year (for the first time in five tries) and survived in the bullpen for the Brewers in August and September. It's still fair to say that he never has shown acceptable command for more than a couple of months at a time.

Dave Weathers — Throws R — Age 31

YEAR	TEAM	LGE	IP	H	ER	HR	BB	K	ERA	W	L	H/9	HR/9	BB/9	K/9	KW	PERA
1998	Cincnnti	NL	60.3	84	45	3	24	41	6.71	2	5	12.53	0.45	3.58	6.12	0.85	6.24
1998	Milwauke	NL	45.7	43	22	3	13	35	4.34	2	3	8.47	0.59	2.56	6.90	1.35	3.61
1999	Milwauke	NL	90.7	98	45	13	32	62	4.47	4	6	9.73	1.29	3.18	6.15	0.97	5.31
2000	Milwauke	NL	74.3	71	26	6	26	42	3.15	5	3	8.60	0.73	3.15	5.09	0.81	4.05

You wouldn't know it just from perusing that stat line, but Dave Weathers took a big step forward last year. In the past, he's been limited to long relief by his need for a day off between appearances. Last year he moved into a middle relief/setup role and learned to deal with being used on consecutive days. He's much more valuable than he was a year ago but probably has gone as far as he can go.

Jamey Wright — Throws R — Age 26

YEAR	TEAM	LGE	IP	H	ER	HR	BB	K	ERA	W	L	H/9	HR/9	BB/9	K/9	KW	PERA
1998	Colorado	NL	205.0	223	113	15	68	70	4.96	9	14	9.79	0.66	2.99	3.07	0.51	4.60
1999	ColSprin	PCL	98.0	121	75	12	37	50	6.89	3	8	11.11	1.10	3.40	4.59	0.68	6.01
1999	Colorado	NL	95.7	105	40	6	36	41	3.76	6	5	9.88	0.56	3.39	3.86	0.57	4.72
2000	Milwauke	NL	161.0	152	73	11	72	80	4.08	9	9	8.50	0.61	4.02	4.47	0.56	4.22

Coors Field seemed to hurt Jamey Wright more than the average pitcher, which makes sense, since he relies almost entirely upon movement on his pitches. He was worked too hard for someone who was pitching with a partially torn labrum, so the Brewers will be lucky to get a full season out of him in 2001.

Support-Neutral Statistics						MILWAUKEE BREWERS					Park Effect: -7.7%	
PITCHER	GS	IP	R	SNW	SNL	SNPCT	W	L	RA	APW	SNVA	SNWAR
Jason Bere	20	115.0	66	6.8	6.9	.497	6	7	5.17	-0.3	-0.0	1.0
Jeff D'Amico	23	162.3	55	12.0	5.6	.682	12	7	3.05	3.3	3.1	4.5
Valerio de los Santos	2	8.7	9	0.5	0.9	.364	0	1	9.35	-0.4	-0.2	-0.1
Horacio Estrada	4	18.0	16	1.0	1.6	.385	2	0	8.00	-0.6	-0.3	-0.1
Jimmy Haynes	33	199.3	128	9.6	12.8	.430	12	13	5.78	-1.8	-1.5	0.1
Allen Levrault	1	6.0	4	0.2	0.5	.314	0	0	6.00	-0.1	-0.1	-0.1
Jaime Navarro	5	18.7	31	0.3	3.3	.077	0	5	14.95	-2.0	-1.5	-1.3
Paul Rigdon	12	69.7	37	3.6	4.1	.469	4	4	4.78	0.1	-0.2	0.3
John Snyder	23	127.0	95	6.3	9.9	.387	3	10	6.73	-2.4	-1.8	-0.6
Everett Stull	4	16.7	17	0.8	1.7	.305	1	3	9.18	-0.7	-0.4	-0.3
Steve Woodard	11	59.3	52	2.3	5.7	.284	1	6	7.89	-1.9	-1.7	-1.1
Jamey Wright	25	163.7	80	9.9	8.0	.554	7	9	4.40	0.9	0.9	2.3
TOTALS	163	964.3	590	53.3	61.1	.466	48	65	5.51	-5.8	-3.9	4.7

How good was Jeff D'Amico's 2000 season? Only three starters since 1979 have had as successful a season (measured by Support-Neutral Wins Above Replacement) in as few starts. All three of those seasons were during strike years: Randy Johnson and David Cone in 1994 and Nolan Ryan in 1981. D'Amico's performance is even more amazing given that he had just missed two years due to injury and had put together an undistinguished two-year career before that.

Trying to find comparable career patterns to D'Amico's, I looked for pitchers who were mediocre or worse (RA+ of less than 105) for two, three, or four years to start their careers and then had an outstanding season (RA+ greater than 140). I figured the resulting list would contain several superstars; unfortunately for D'Amico, I was wrong. The short list is heavy with one- and two-year wonders: Billy Hoeft, Steve McCatty, Jim Abbott, Kevin Millwood. Tom Glavine is the only unquestionably great pitcher on the list.

That doesn't mean that D'Amico can't go on to have a great career, of course. His ability to stay healthy will have a lot more to do with his future success than a short list of comparable pitchers. But the numbers show that seasons like D'Amico's 2000 turned out to be flukes more often than they turned out to be breakthrough years.

For a quick explanation of SN stats, see page 7.

Reliever Evaluation Tools											
PITCHER	G	IP	R	ARA	APR	IRNR/G	EIRS/G	IRP	BRS	RRA	ARP
Juan Acevedo	62	82.7	38	4.35	7.7	0.44	0.13	-0.7	1.7	4.74	4.2
Jim Bruske	15	16.7	15	8.52	-6.2	0.80	0.20	-3.1	0.9	10.64	-10.1
Mike Buddie	5	6.0	3	4.74	0.3	0.00	0.00	0.0	1.1	5.80	-0.4
Kane Davis	3	4.0	3	7.10	-0.8	0.00	0.00	0.0	2.0	12.01	-3.0
Valerio de los Santos	64	65.0	34	4.95	1.8	0.86	0.28	2.2	0.9	4.91	2.1
Horacio Estrada	3	6.3	2	2.99	1.6	0.00	0.00	0.0	1.5	5.26	-0.0
Ray King	36	28.7	7	2.31	9.2	0.58	0.17	2.3	-0.2	1.69	11.2
Curtis Leskanic	73	77.3	23	2.82	20.4	0.42	0.13	7.0	2.5	2.47	23.4
Allen Levrault	4	6.0	3	4.74	0.3	0.00	0.00	0.0	0.0	4.88	0.2
Horacio Ramirez	6	9.0	10	10.52	-5.3	0.00	0.00	0.0	-0.7	10.08	-4.9
Rafael Roque	4	5.3	6	10.66	-3.2	0.00	0.00	0.0	-0.4	10.72	-3.3
Bob Scanlan	2	1.7	6	34.10	-5.4	0.00	0.00	0.0	0.3	36.31	-5.8
Everett Stull	16	26.7	13	4.62	1.7	0.31	0.07	1.2	0.7	4.29	2.7
Dave Weathers	69	76.3	29	3.60	13.6	0.64	0.20	2.2	2.2	3.88	11.1
Bob Wickman	43	46.0	18	3.71	7.6	0.05	0.01	0.7	1.1	3.74	7.4
Matt Williams	11	9.0	7	7.37	-2.2	0.91	0.21	-4.0	1.1	12.68	-7.5
Steve Woodard	16	34.3	18	4.97	0.9	0.56	0.17	-3.6	1.4	6.23	-3.9
Jamey Wright	1	1.0	1	9.47	-0.5	0.00	0.00	0.0	0.0	9.75	-0.5
TOTALS	433	502.0	236	4.45	41.5	0.50	0.15			4.79	22.9

For a quick guide to RET, see page 10.

Montreal Expos

The dawning of the Age of Loria brought a lot of promise. It was hard not to get carried away as the Expos started doing very un-Expo-like things. They traded prospects for an established major leaguer for the first time in years. Before spring training opened, the Expos had signed four pitchers to multi-year deals: staff ace Dustin Hermanson, holdover relievers Steve Kline and Anthony Telford, and free-agent reliever Graeme Lloyd.

Enthusiasm reigned briefly. Ticket sales rose and artists' conceptions and plans for a new stadium closer to downtown Montreal were openly bandied about. The Expos picked up an option from the Canada Lands Corporation on the ideal site, and a potential name, Labatt Park, was kicked around. Things looked better than anyone could have anticipated a year before.

The honeymoon didn't last four months. Loria and his henchman/son-in-law David Samson seem to have acquired people skills by watching Dan Duquette's instructional video, *How to Alienate, Offend, and Annoy*. They fought a losing battle with Canadian television over broadcasting rights and fees, one in which each side accused the other of having unreasonable expectations. After the dust settled, local television had to stand by its boast that it would make more money broadcasting subtitled *Columbo* reruns than by carrying Expos games. Even more humiliating, Loria and Samson failed to secure a broadcast deal for the English radio broadcasts, having to settle for French. Between the television and radio snafus, the Expos suddenly started talking about how great webcasting is for lonely Expos fans in New Brunswick.

Optimism was dead by the end of May. The Loria/Samson duo went out of its way to antagonize local minority partners, culminating in a meeting at which they projected a cycle of salary inflation that would have the Expos spending more than $100 million annually in five years. Stephen Bronfman, Seagram's heir and son of the original Expos owner, responded by trying to organize the minority partners in an effort to buy out Loria. That effort was doomed because Loria wasn't about to sell. The minority partners responded punitively, refusing to lend Loria the money to cover expenses, a move that forced him to cough up $12 million out of his own pocket. Their bluff apparently called, the minority partners are now eagerly selling off their stakes to Loria.

Not satisfied with antagonizing the local media who might promote the team in Montreal and the business partners committed to keeping the team there, Loria and Samson were accused of trying to offend the closest thing to Expodom personified, manager Felipe Alou. By firing two of Alou's coaches shortly after the All-Star Break, they fueled speculation that they were trying to bully Alou into a resignation with a year left on his contract. General Manager Jim Beattie was supposed to be hanging on by a thread.

Loria and Samson declined to mention that they'd allowed their option on the potential downtown ballpark site to lapse in late August. Everything seemed set for Loria to finish buying the rest of the team and pull up stakes for 2001, but at the end of August, Loria made the surprising announcement that the team would be back in Montreal for another season.

It isn't hard to interpret Loria's moves in his first year as a devious attempt to make a case that baseball in Montreal can't work. From the start, Loria did things differently. He raised payroll through multi-year deals with players he inherited, signed one moderately expensive free agent, and traded for two veterans with seven-figure salaries. He didn't blow the bank on a big-ticket item. He did not spend so much that the threat of a postseason purge, à la the 1997 Marlins, materialized.

Loria played at being an owner, not in such a way that he'd field a significantly better team, but enough to mark out the difference between himself and Claude Brochu, who had made the Expos a dependent of the rest of MLB. Loria made it clear that he was your basic moderately ambitious baseball

Expos Prospectus

2000 record: 67–95; Fourth place, NL East
Pythagenport W/L: 65–97
Runs Scored: 738 (14th in NL)
Runs Allowed: 902 (14th in NL)
Team EqA: .254 (11th in NL)
2000 Batters' age: 26.1 (2nd youngest in NL)
2000 Pitchers' age: 26.0 (youngest in NL)
Ballpark: Olympic Stadium; slight pitchers' park; Park Factor of .976
2000: A new owner spent money aimlessly, but the homegrown talent was the best story.
2001: The core of a special baseball team is present. The Expos should jump to 80 or more wins this year.

owner intent on doing things commonly associated with making his team better. Attendance nearly doubled, but even offering the broadcast rights for free wasn't enough to get Expos games on local television.

Loria has essentially assembled a brief on why Montreal is a bad market: backbiting minority partners who conveniently make the local business community or a potential local ownership team look bad; a bad media market and the subsequently negligible advertising revenue streams; and attendance that might improve but cannot finance a major-league organization in the absence of other revenue streams. If the objective was to build consensus among major-league owners about the Expos leaving Montreal, it's a pretty good brief.

There's still the possibility that Loria is playing it straight, but that's irrelevant, no matter how much fun the Montreal media has had demonizing him as a Yank carpetbagger. Loria isn't the problem because any solution that involves keeping baseball in Montreal will depend on the commissioner's office and the other 29 owners creating a workable system for comprehensive revenue sharing.

For that reason, it would be premature to say baseball in Montreal is dead. It is on life support, and its survival depends entirely on the commissioner's office. Through the process of systematically rejecting or dismissing his local options, Loria has mapped out how baseball in Montreal could work, with or without him. The location for the new ballpark next to the Molson Center isn't about to disappear, even though Loria failed to renew his option on the property. The opportunity to assemble a local ownership group—with Stephen Bronfman at its center—and build a local stadium is there if the commissioner's office wishes it to be so.

There's precedent here. Bob Lurie originally bought the San Francisco Giants to save them from moving, and it was his subsequent attempt to move them that led to the intervention of baseball in assembling a local ownership group and sending Lurie packing. If baseball has to support a local effort to buy back the Expos, Loria could still make a great return on his initial investment.

Okay, so you can stop weeping over this tale of woe. What's going on with the organization? Did all of those moves make any difference on the field? In a word, no. Bringing in Graeme Lloyd and Hideki Irabu and Lee Stevens might have made sense to a team on the fringes of the playoff hunt and lacking internal options. As part of a quest for symbolic competitiveness, it did nothing to fuel the Expos' drive for mediocrity. Irabu was on the DL before the end of May, and Lloyd missed the entire season after the death of his wife. Stevens ended up missing September and was only so good as to make people forget Orlando Merced.

Losing both of their new "big-name" pitchers was just the beginning of the Expos' season-long pitching problems. When Ugueth Urbina suffered an injury after the first month, Alou hurt his rotation by bumping Dustin Hermanson back to the pen to close for almost a month. Carl Pavano and Tony Armas Jr. have both had cases of the fragiles which upset the timetable that should have made the Pedro Martinez trade look better.

Even so, the club managed to claw its way to 31–23 on June 5 and was still 42–42 at the All-Star break before the combination of journeyman pitching and a weak offense killed its season. Worst of all, the injuries to the pitching staff pushed the organization into making a bad deal to fill a temporary need. Flipping Rondell White for talent was the biggest opportunity Jim Beattie would have to add a good young shortstop or third baseman. Instead, the Expos got Scott Downs. At best, Downs might get to be the fifth starter in 2001, if the Expos trade someone or lose two starting pitchers.

That isn't Downs's fault. The Expos have a rotation that matches that of the Phillies in quantity of young talent. Getting full seasons out of Tony Armas Jr. and Carl Pavano and a good showing from Javier Vazquez would give the Expos a significant improvement in their starting pitching. Hermanson is already gone, and Hideki Irabu won't be around to see the Expos win 90 games, but the three young pitchers will.

The team should also see some offensive improvements this year. Brad Wilkerson will be up, giving the Expos an outstanding young four-man outfield in which Vladimir Guerrero is the old man at 25. Picking up Fernando Tatis on the cheap gives the Expos a third big bat to go with Guerrero and Jose Vidro. Michael Barrett will finally be catching regularly.

The lineup's problems are Orlando Cabrera and Lee Stevens. They're symptoms of the larger blind spot: the Expos don't understand how runs are produced. Any organization that places Brad Fullmer's limitations ahead of an appreciation of his strengths needs to be judged harshly. Alou, Beattie, and Loria all deserve blame, and Stevens will get to be the daily reminder of a squandered opportunity. Cabrera is about to enter his arbitration years, which is another way of saying that the Expos will have to choose between overpaying for Royce Clayton Lite or finding a better all-around player.

Expos player development has its strengths and weaknesses. Its biggest strength is Fred Ferreira, the team's VP/director of international operations. Ferreira makes his biggest impression through international free agents from the Dominican Republic and Venezuela, but his network has also given the Expos an advantage in scouting Puerto Rican talent, a major factor in making the team's draft record look adequate. The Expos have also made it a point to try things few other teams are exploring. They've built a relationship with the Dutch that has started to yield a couple of players in the lowest rungs of the minors; a third baseman named Vince Rooi is the best so far, but he's as raw as you'd expect. They've also started signing Japanese players, and while Japanese college player Yuji Nerei isn't a great hitting prospect, you have to start somewhere. Pitcher Eiji

Miyamoto showed something in his debut. The point is that the Expos are expending effort.

The weakness in player development has been in domestic scouting. A major problem has been the organization's general-manager shuffle. Jim Beattie may be entering his sixth year on the job, but the Expos had four general managers in the 1990s. Dave Dombrowski stepped down after 1991, followed by two-year stints from Dan Duquette and Kevin Malone before Beattie was given the job. The organization has lost more than just Dombrowski, the Duke, and the Sheriff. Frank Wren, Gary Hughes, Bill Geivett, Bill Stoneman, and Ed Creech are among the notables who have jumped ship. It isn't easy to maintain a consistent player-development program through that kind of turmoil, especially when it means your organization doesn't get to evaluate its mistakes but inherit them.

The Expos' young talent is outstanding. If they let Barrett settle in at catcher and don't get impatient with young players like Armas, Pavano, Wilkerson, Peter Bergeron, and Milton Bradley, they'll be able to field a great young team in 2002 and beyond. Where that team will play is something that Bud Selig, Jeff Loria, and the other 29 lords will have to decide.

HITTERS (BA: .270, OBP: .340, SLG: .440, EqA: .260)

Michael Barrett — C/3B — Bats R — Age 24

YEAR	TEAM	LGE	AB	H	DB	TP	HR	BB	SO	R	RBI	SB	CS	OUT	BA	OBP	SLG	EQA	EQR	DEFENSE			
1998	Harrisbg	Eas	454	122	26	1	14	19	44	61	65	4	3	335	.269	.300	.423	.237	46	77-C	-2	28-3B	2
1999	Montreal	NL	435	125	30	3	8	26	37	51	48	0	2	312	.287	.332	.425	.250	49	63-3B	-9	51-C	-6
2000	Ottawa	Int	120	38	5	0	2	11	10	18	16	1	0	82	.317	.381	.408	.272	16	24-3B	-1		
2000	Montreal	NL	274	59	15	1	1	19	33	27	21	0	1	216	.215	.268	.288	.178	15	47-3B	-10	25-C	-3
2001	Montreal	NL	440	125	26	2	8	36	48	58	62	1	1	316	.284	.338	.407	.255	52				

Michael Barrett's core skills are like those of a hockey goalie: he's all whip-snap reactions, bordering on downright twitchy. That kind of athleticism got him in trouble, because it was impressive enough to coax people into thinking he could play anywhere and everywhere when he's best left at catcher. He was shut down early with elbow problems that affected his throwing and batting. Barrett is a great bet to start meeting the expectations of a year ago, before the distractions about his position became a problem.

Peter Bergeron — OF — Bats L — Age 23

YEAR	TEAM	LGE	AB	H	DB	TP	HR	BB	SO	R	RBI	SB	CS	OUT	BA	OBP	SLG	EQA	EQR	DEFENSE	
1998	SanAnton	Tex	420	113	14	5	6	46	76	56	39	17	6	313	.269	.343	.369	.246	47	107-CF	5
1998	Harrisbg	Eas	136	29	6	4	0	13	27	17	8	4	2	109	.213	.282	.316	.201	10	31-CF	1
1999	Harrisbg	Eas	163	43	11	1	3	18	31	21	13	4	4	124	.264	.337	.399	.245	18	37-LF	0
1999	Ottawa	Int	193	53	12	2	2	19	40	28	15	9	6	146	.275	.342	.389	.246	22	38-LF	-1
2000	Montreal	NL	523	126	26	6	5	50	94	76	29	9	13	410	.241	.307	.342	.215	44	129-CF	3
2001	Montreal	NL	478	130	22	5	6	61	93	78	59	18	10	358	.272	.354	.377	.256	59		

Do guys with weak arms rack up lots of assists because people are running on them or because they can compensate for their shortcomings? Peter Bergeron's arm hasn't been the same since he hurt it a few years ago, but he racked up a major-league leading 15 assists as a center fielder, in part because of an instructional program instituted by coach Pete Mackanin. No good deed goes unpunished: Mackanin was fired after the season. While Milton Bradley is the better prospect, the Expos need Bergeron's on-base skills. He's far too young to be relegated to a fourth-outfielder role.

Geoff Blum — 3B — Bats B — Age 28

YEAR	TEAM	LGE	AB	H	DB	TP	HR	BB	SO	R	RBI	SB	CS	OUT	BA	OBP	SLG	EQA	EQR	DEFENSE			
1998	Harrisbg	Eas	140	34	9	2	4	13	26	18	14	1	1	107	.243	.319	.421	.245	16	14-3B	4	13-SS	0
1999	Ottawa	Int	269	63	13	1	7	29	40	34	28	4	1	207	.234	.312	.368	.231	26	54-SS	-7		
1999	Montreal	NL	134	32	7	1	8	15	24	20	17	1	0	102	.239	.315	.485	.262	18	32-SS	-6		
2000	Montreal	NL	346	96	21	2	10	21	56	38	42	1	4	254	.277	.324	.436	.248	39	48-3B	-2	29-SS	2
2001	Montreal	NL	315	83	19	1	11	33	56	44	49	1	1	233	.263	.333	.435	.260	40				

(Geoff Blum *continued*)

The Expos' acquisition of Fernando Tatis moves Geoff Blum back to the utility infielder role he fits so well. If Orlando Cabrera becomes too expensive, an offense/defense platoon of Blum and Tomas de la Rosa would be a cheap—and maybe even better—alternative.

Milton Bradley CF Bats B Age 23

YEAR	TEAM	LGE	AB	H	DB	TP	HR	BB	SO	R	RBI	SB	CS	OUT	BA	OBP	SLG	EQA	EQR	DEFENSE	
1998	CapeFear	SAL	285	68	16	2	4	17	60	35	32	5	4	221	.239	.286	.351	.210	22	49-CF	-4
1998	Jupiter	Fla	265	63	10	1	4	23	48	37	24	6	4	206	.238	.305	.328	.214	22	61-CF	4
1999	Harrisbg	Eas	347	94	18	3	9	23	64	46	36	7	6	259	.271	.319	.418	.243	38	73-CF	-5
2000	Ottawa	Int	344	92	17	1	5	37	58	50	24	7	10	262	.267	.340	.366	.236	35	87-CF	2
2000	Montreal	NL	156	35	8	1	2	11	30	19	15	2	1	122	.224	.279	.327	.201	11	38-CF	0
2001	Montreal	NL	395	110	20	2	9	43	76	60	55	10	8	293	.278	.349	.408	.259	50		

Like Albert Belle, Milton Bradley is intelligent and has a temper. That gets in print, he sees it and doesn't like it, so then he gets labeled as sulky. Alou had little patience for him initially, demoting him for not hustling when he was first called up. He has tremendous range and the arm for center field. With Wilkerson ready to slip into left field, Bradley will have to convince people that he's not the demon he's been portrayed as if he wants to beat out Bergeron.

Orlando Cabrera SS Bats R Age 27

YEAR	TEAM	LGE	AB	H	DB	TP	HR	BB	SO	R	RBI	SB	CS	OUT	BA	OBP	SLG	EQA	EQR	DEFENSE			
1998	Ottawa	Int	274	60	9	3	0	22	27	25	23	11	6	220	.219	.277	.274	.184	16	45-SS	-1	21-2B	0
1998	Montreal	NL	264	74	17	5	3	17	25	46	22	6	2	192	.280	.324	.417	.248	29	44-SS	-1	28-2B	-2
1999	Montreal	NL	384	96	22	5	8	13	36	46	37	1	2	290	.250	.280	.396	.219	33	102-SS	9		
2000	Montreal	NL	426	101	23	1	13	19	26	45	52	4	4	329	.237	.271	.387	.213	35	107-SS	11		
2001	Montreal	NL	401	100	22	3	11	30	32	48	51	8	5	306	.249	.302	.401	.237	42				

If Alex Gonzalez (the good one, from Toronto) is the great breakout tease, Orlando Cabrera is Alex Gonzalez Lite. For the second straight year, he got hurt just as he was getting hot at the plate. This time he dislocated his shoulder on July 15, which cost him a month. The Expos are dangling him in trade, which is a fine idea. He won't be as good as Alex Gonzalez, but he doesn't have a Sheehan-sized gorilla of great expectations on his shoulders.

Matt Cepicky OF Bats L Age 23

YEAR	TEAM	LGE	AB	H	DB	TP	HR	BB	SO	R	RBI	SB	CS	OUT	BA	OBP	SLG	EQA	EQR	DEFENSE	
1999	Vermont	NYP	328	79	9	2	9	13	52	34	34	3	4	253	.241	.271	.363	.204	24	51-LF	-3
2000	Jupiter	Fla	542	139	27	4	5	16	73	44	66	14	7	410	.256	.279	.349	.207	40	106-LF	-1
2001	Montreal	NL	326	90	15	1	5	14	57	37	37	7	3	239	.276	.306	.374	.232	31		

Matt Cepicky is a chunky ex-football player who gets high marks from scouts for his power potential after being a first-team All-American at Southwest Missouri State. After an inauspicious start, you could give him some benefit of the doubt. It was his first full season hitting with wood, and the Florida State League is a tough place to hit for power. Cepicky's lack of patience as a hitter is an enormous roadblock to success.

Tomas de la Rosa SS Bats R Age 23

YEAR	TEAM	LGE	AB	H	DB	TP	HR	BB	SO	R	RBI	SB	CS	OUT	BA	OBP	SLG	EQA	EQR	DEFENSE	
1998	Jupiter	Fla	396	89	16	1	3	27	69	39	34	11	4	311	.225	.280	.293	.193	25	116-SS	10
1999	Harrisbg	Eas	471	108	18	2	5	29	67	53	33	14	8	371	.229	.275	.308	.193	30	125-SS	3
2000	Ottawa	Int	343	69	9	1	1	25	45	24	33	7	2	276	.201	.259	.242	.161	14	95-SS	-9
2000	Montreal	NL	67	19	2	1	2	6	10	7	8	2	1	49	.284	.350	.433	.263	9	21-SS	-2
2001	Montreal	NL	411	100	15	1	4	38	63	52	35	18	6	317	.243	.307	.314	.220	36		

De la Rosa has good hands and range, a strong arm, anticipates the deuce, and comes across the bag well. The Expos realize he's got offensive limitations beyond struggling against breaking stuff, but Cabrera hasn't improved in his two years as a regular. The Expos wouldn't be killing themselves if they traded Cabrera for good stuff and just played de la Rosa until Albenis Machado or Brandon Phillips is ready.

Vladimir Guerrero — RF — Bats R — Age 25

YEAR	TEAM	LGE	AB	H	DB	TP	HR	BB	SO	R	RBI	SB	CS	OUT	BA	OBP	SLG	EQA	EQR	DEFENSE	
1998	Montreal	NL	631	201	35	6	39	40	89	108	106	10	9	439	.319	.365	.578	.299	107	146-RF	-5
1999	Montreal	NL	612	188	36	3	41	47	59	96	120	10	6	430	.307	.363	.577	.299	105	148-RF	-5
2000	Montreal	NL	576	193	27	10	42	49	69	95	113	8	10	393	.335	.394	.635	.320	114	138-RF	-3
2001	Montreal	NL	568	193	32	4	44	69	70	118	154	11	7	382	.340	.411	.643	.337	126		

I don't know where Wilton found the base runners to get Vladimir Guerrero 154 RBI, so let's take that as an expression of faith in the NL's best hitter for the next five years. I'm not sold on the jump in his walk rate: in 641 plate appearances last year he drew 35 walks by himself. The Expos have him signed for three more years. If they don't move, they'll lose him. Without him, they'll be a tougher sell in a new market and a worse sell in the old one.

Wilton Guerrero — Sibling — Bats R — Age 26

YEAR	TEAM	LGE	AB	H	DB	TP	HR	BB	SO	R	RBI	SB	CS	OUT	BA	OBP	SLG	EQA	EQR	DEFENSE			
1998	Albuquer	PCL	118	29	3	1	1	7	12	11	7	7	2	91	.246	.292	.314	.210	9	20-2B	-3		
1998	LosAngls	NL	183	54	5	3	0	4	31	23	8	5	2	131	.295	.314	.355	.225	16	26-2B	-3		
1998	Montreal	NL	224	63	11	6	2	10	28	30	20	3	0	161	.281	.312	.411	.242	23	52-2B	-7		
1999	Montreal	NL	316	90	15	6	2	10	36	39	28	5	5	231	.285	.311	.389	.230	29	40-2B	-14	14-LF	-3
2000	Montreal	NL	291	78	6	2	2	15	38	29	22	8	1	214	.268	.304	.323	.214	23	61-LF	-6		
2001	Cincnnti	NL	280	83	11	4	2	16	39	40	36	8	2	199	.296	.334	.386	.245	30				

In the pantheon of siblings who weren't as good as their brothers, Wilton Guerrero isn't quite up at the Joe Niekro end of the spectrum. Still, he belongs, because he also isn't all the way down at the other end of the scale with Stephen Larkin and Craig Griffey. He makes a fine pinch hitter; nobody should play him semi-regularly.

Scott Hodges — 3B — Bats L — Age 22

YEAR	TEAM	LGE	AB	H	DB	TP	HR	BB	SO	R	RBI	SB	CS	OUT	BA	OBP	SLG	EQA	EQR	DEFENSE	
1998	Vermont	NYP	269	63	10	1	3	6	63	24	24	3	1	207	.234	.252	.312	.179	14	37-3B	-3
1999	CapeFear	SAL	463	99	23	1	6	33	111	47	43	3	6	370	.214	.268	.307	.185	27	119-3B	1
2000	Jupiter	Fla	433	110	18	1	13	36	75	56	61	4	1	324	.254	.314	.390	.236	44	105-3B	5
2001	Montreal	NL	397	100	19	1	12	41	85	51	54	4	2	299	.252	.322	.395	.246	45		

Not every first-round pick out of high school has a Griffey-like waltz to the majors. Scott Hodges has come around slowly but steadily. His glove work has significantly improved, and he flashes a pretty good arm, but he's still playing third base a little flat-footed. He's got decent power potential, but strikes me as a guy who could benefit from some Charlie Lau/Walt Hriniak instruction on releasing his top hand. This is a big year for him: if he hits at Double-A, he could get a September cup of coffee and challenge for a big-league job in 2002. It's a safer bet that he won't be up to stay until the second half of 2002, especially now that Tatis is in the fold.

Terry Jones — CF — Bats R — Age 30

YEAR	TEAM	LGE	AB	H	DB	TP	HR	BB	SO	R	RBI	SB	CS	OUT	BA	OBP	SLG	EQA	EQR	DEFENSE	
1998	Ottawa	Int	280	62	4	3	0	24	50	26	18	20	5	223	.221	.283	.257	.192	18	78-CF	3
1998	Montreal	NL	214	47	8	2	1	21	43	31	15	15	4	171	.220	.289	.290	.205	16	59-CF	5
1999	Ottawa	Int	331	76	11	2	0	17	71	34	18	18	8	263	.230	.269	.275	.182	19	76-CF	-3
1999	Montreal	NL	63	16	1	1	0	3	13	4	3	1	2	49	.254	.288	.302	.187	4	17-CF	3
2000	Montreal	NL	170	43	7	2	0	7	30	29	12	7	2	129	.253	.282	.318	.203	12	42-LF	1
2001	Montreal	NL	239	53	7	2	0	19	50	27	13	15	5	191	.222	.279	.268	.195	16		

Terry Jones has no business being kept on a 40-man roster over the winter. What are the roster pressures in play here? To fill 25 spots, the team needs 11 pitchers, eight starting guys, a backup catcher, at least two backup infielders (probably Mike Mordecai and Andy Tracy), one non-Terry Jones outfielder, and supersub Geoff Blum. That's 24, and we haven't figured out what to do with Fenando Seguignol yet.

The depressing thing about the Expos isn't their revenue stream or whether they'll always be in Montreal. It's that Terry Jones has job security, which indicates that performance means nothing.

Albenis Machado   SS   Bats B   Age 22

YEAR	TEAM	LGE	AB	H	DB	TP	HR	BB	SO	R	RBI	SB	CS	OUT	BA	OBP	SLG	EQA	EQR	DEFENSE			
1998	Vermont	NYP	205	45	4	1	1	22	35	19	15	3	5	165	.220	.299	.263	.186	12	54-SS	0		
1999	CapeFear	SAL	462	91	14	3	1	77	81	62	25	7	11	382	.197	.315	.247	.193	31	104-SS	17		
2000	Jupiter	Fla	445	96	11	2	1	60	76	61	30	7	6	355	.216	.312	.256	.196	30	127-SS	-5		
2001	Montreal	NL	474	108	14	2	1	75	87	64	36	13	12	378	.228	.333	.272	.216	41				

Albenis Machado is the opposite of what the Expos seem to want in hitters: his one offensive skill is drawing walks. There have been shortstops who can make it with this one offensive skill: Jose Oquendo was the best, and while Eddie Joost and Steve Jeltz didn't excite people, they had good careers. Oquendo hit from an exaggerated crouch, while Machado takes a big open stance from the left side. A good year in Double-A could be enough to get him the job.

Henry Mateo   2B   Bats B   Age 24

YEAR	TEAM	LGE	AB	H	DB	TP	HR	BB	SO	R	RBI	SB	CS	OUT	BA	OBP	SLG	EQA	EQR	DEFENSE		
1998	CapeFear	SAL	424	96	15	3	3	29	117	48	29	8	7	335	.226	.286	.297	.193	28	104-2B	-11	
1999	Jupiter	Fla	454	101	24	4	4	33	129	49	43	14	8	361	.222	.282	.319	.201	33	100-2B	-23	
2000	Harrisbg	Eas	535	133	23	6	5	43	105	66	47	27	11	412	.249	.309	.342	.224	49	130-2B	-7	
2001	Montreal	NL	502	126	23	4	6	41	122	69	48	28	12	388	.251	.308	.349	.230	49			

Henry Mateo was named the fastest player in the Eastern League in *Baseball America*'s tools poll. Mateo is about as likely to move Jose Vidro as Scott Baio is, but a switch-hitting second baseman with alley power and speed ought to have value somewhere. Like Vidro, Mateo has a strong arm for second base, although he isn't a great glove at the position.

Josh McKinley   3B/2B   Bats B   Age 21

YEAR	TEAM	LGE	AB	H	DB	TP	HR	BB	SO	R	RBI	SB	CS	OUT	BA	OBP	SLG	EQA	EQR	DEFENSE				
1999	CapeFear	SAL	173	39	9	0	0	12	40	13	13	3	3	137	.225	.276	.277	.179	9	20-SS	-9			
1999	Vermont	NYP	292	61	11	1	3	22	55	34	22	3	2	233	.209	.265	.284	.178	16	44-SS	-10	16-2B	-3	
2000	CapeFear	SAL	495	108	28	2	4	38	107	48	47	15	8	395	.218	.276	.307	.195	33	94-3B	-17	18-2B	-9	
2001	Montreal	NL	499	121	29	1	4	43	114	64	43	21	8	386	.242	.303	.329	.221	45					

He's still so raw that he makes sushi look overdone, and he may not work out as an infielder. Still, he's making progress: unadjusted, you're talking about a 20-year-old who stole 46 bases, drew 54 walks, and hit 34 doubles in his first full year in a full-season league. Keep in mind it took Trot Nixon six years to make it, and he was considered a can't-miss high-school player. Josh McKinley has another year before he even needs to be added to the 40-man roster.

Mike Mordecai   IF   Bats R   Age 33

YEAR	TEAM	LGE	AB	H	DB	TP	HR	BB	SO	R	RBI	SB	CS	OUT	BA	OBP	SLG	EQA	EQR	DEFENSE				
1998	Montreal	NL	120	25	4	2	3	9	19	12	10	1	0	95	.208	.264	.350	.202	9	14-SS	0	10-2B	1	
1999	Montreal	NL	227	52	9	2	5	17	29	27	23	1	4	179	.229	.286	.352	.206	17	24-SS	4	22-3B	3	
2000	Montreal	NL	171	48	12	0	5	9	32	19	16	2	2	125	.281	.320	.439	.248	19	37-3B	-3			
2001	Montreal	NL	169	39	8	1	4	13	30	17	18	2	2	132	.231	.286	.361	.217	15					

Can you think of another utility infielder with this kind of job security? Going back to his Atlanta days, Mike Mordecai has been a utility infielder for seven years with no shot at ever becoming a regular. Even Alex Arias got a couple of months as a starter once. Is this what people are pining for when they say baseball was better before free agency? Mordecai gets job security, and the Expos get cost certainty. It's downright un-American, I tell you.

Talmadge Nunnari   1B/LF   Bats L   Age 26

YEAR	TEAM	LGE	AB	H	DB	TP	HR	BB	SO	R	RBI	SB	CS	OUT	BA	OBP	SLG	EQA	EQR	DEFENSE				
1998	CapeFear	SAL	298	72	8	0	3	30	46	35	37	1	2	228	.242	.312	.299	.206	22	72-1B	3			
1998	Jupiter	Fla	206	50	7	0	3	22	44	13	26	0	1	157	.243	.316	.320	.215	17	53-1B	5			
1999	Jupiter	Fla	265	76	11	1	4	19	43	28	31	4	0	189	.287	.338	.381	.246	28	43-1B	0			
1999	Harrisbg	Eas	241	64	12	1	4	29	50	33	20	3	1	178	.266	.346	.373	.247	27	38-1B	-2	20-LF	-1	
2000	Harrisbg	Eas	322	71	13	1	4	36	75	34	39	5	4	255	.220	.301	.304	.205	24	86-1B	3			
2000	Ottawa	Int	136	34	11	1	0	20	32	15	10	0	1	103	.250	.353	.346	.240	15	34-1B	-2			
2001	Montreal	NL	397	93	16	1	5	53	90	49	40	3	1	305	.234	.324	.317	.226	37					

One of the strangest things the Expos do is collect first basemen who don't have power. Beattie has traded for Jon Tucker and Ryan McGuire and has developed Talmadge Nunnari. While you might be able to understand the addiction to big pitchers because there have been successful big pitchers, collecting first baseman without power makes little sense. What possible payoff is there? Finding out which scouts can't identify power prospects?

Valentino Pascucci   OF   Bats R   Age 22

YEAR	TEAM	LGE	AB	H	DB	TP	HR	BB	SO	R	RBI	SB	CS	OUT	BA	OBP	SLG	EQA	EQR	DEFENSE	
1999	Vermont	NYP	272	72	13	1	6	37	49	39	32	5	1	201	.265	.364	.386	.260	35	65-RF	-3
2000	CapeFear	SAL	73	18	3	0	2	12	16	12	6	2	0	55	.247	.353	.370	.254	9	19-RF	0
2000	Jupiter	Fla	419	100	20	1	12	50	111	51	48	6	3	322	.239	.328	.377	.240	45	89-RF	-6
2001	Montreal	NL	289	79	11	0	10	43	90	48	46	5	1	211	.273	.367	.415	.273	41		

Look past the publicity over the Expos' pitching or the Peter Bergeron/Milton Bradley standoff and you'll discover the team has a pair of good hitting prospects for the outfield corners: Brad Wilkerson and Valentino Pascucci. As you might expect from the Expos, Pascucci is a more athletic version of Richie Sexson. Predominantly a pitcher at Oklahoma, he's got the arm for right field but doesn't move around well. Most importantly, he crushes the ball, and he'll take a walk.

Jarrod Patterson   3B   Bats L   Age 27

YEAR	TEAM	LGE	AB	H	DB	TP	HR	BB	SO	R	RBI	SB	CS	OUT	BA	OBP	SLG	EQA	EQR	DEFENSE			
1998	High Des	Cal	487	120	22	4	12	45	102	56	60	4	1	368	.246	.312	.382	.233	48	80-3B	-14	39-1B	0
1999	El Paso	Tex	244	67	17	1	5	36	51	40	30	1	1	178	.275	.369	.414	.266	33	58-3B	-5		
1999	Tucson	PCL	267	74	18	2	8	29	36	33	33	3	1	194	.277	.352	.449	.268	36	64-3B	-10		
2000	Nashvill	PCL	198	49	5	0	5	8	42	19	24	0	1	150	.247	.282	.348	.205	14	43-3B	1		
2000	Ottawa	Int	92	23	4	1	0	3	14	8	13	1	0	69	.250	.274	.315	.193	6	25-3B	-3		
2001	Detroit	AL	405	105	16	1	11	37	84	54	58	2	1	301	.259	.321	.385	.243	44				

Jarrod Patterson was a temporarily fashionable pick to surprise people in 2000, a case of overthinking. If the Pirates were unwilling to trust Aramis Ramirez, maybe a minor-league free agent like Patterson would slip in, right? Cam Bonifay was one step ahead and had the great Luis Sojo and Mike Benjamin already in place. Patterson could still be useful to a team with a right-handed-hitting regular at third base who needs a day or two off. The Tigers, with Dean Palmer, fit that.

Brandon Phillips   SS   Bats R   Age 20

YEAR	TEAM	LGE	AB	H	DB	TP	HR	BB	SO	R	RBI	SB	CS	OUT	BA	OBP	SLG	EQA	EQR	DEFENSE	
2000	CapeFear	SAL	495	104	12	5	10	26	104	53	53	8	4	395	.210	.255	.315	.185	29	121-SS	-8
2001	Montreal	NL	267	58	6	2	5	16	100	20	22	5	2	211	.217	.261	.311	.192	17		

The Expos like to talk about their depth at shortstop, but the guys who could turn out well are both in A ball: Albenis Machado and Brandon Phillips. A tools guy who generates power through great bat speed, Phillips spent most of the year hitting third in the lineup. That says a lot about the state of Expo prospectdom. Afield, he's got decent range, good hands, and a lot of work to do. Phillips gives me a Hubie Brooks vibe for reasons I don't understand. It must be the hitting third thing, because it isn't something I'd trust.

Josh Reding   SS   Bats R   Age 24

YEAR	TEAM	LGE	AB	H	DB	TP	HR	BB	SO	R	RBI	SB	CS	OUT	BA	OBP	SLG	EQA	EQR	DEFENSE	
1998	CapeFear	SAL	258	54	2	0	2	16	75	22	18	5	2	206	.209	.261	.240	.159	10	73-SS	5
1999	Jupiter	Fla	418	98	9	1	2	16	84	38	24	14	5	325	.234	.263	.275	.176	21	118-SS	1
2000	Harrisbg	Eas	464	95	12	3	2	44	119	45	39	14	4	373	.205	.282	.256	.184	27	127-SS	3
2001	Montreal	NL	370	81	8	1	1	36	96	38	22	16	4	293	.219	.288	.254	.193	24		

Anybody else remember Gary Green, Team USA's shortstop in the 1984 Olympics? Josh Reding is a similar player. He's a great shortstop, but he swings for the fences while generating little power. The only reason he's in the book is because the Expos might trade Cabrera. If they do, and if Reding has a good camp, he might sneak into the picture the way Geoff Blum did in 1999.

Wilken Ruan CF Bats R Age 21

YEAR	TEAM	LGE	AB	H	DB	TP	HR	BB	SO	R	RBI	SB	CS	OUT	BA	OBP	SLG	EQA	EQR	DEFENSE	
1999	CapeFear	SAL	403	84	15	2	1	13	84	30	38	11	8	327	.208	.238	.263	.153	15	110-CF	12
2000	CapeFear	SAL	581	143	23	6	1	16	80	60	37	23	7	445	.246	.270	.312	.195	37	131-CF	4
2001	Montreal	NL	431	104	18	3	1	20	72	45	30	22	7	334	.241	.275	.304	.201	30		

Wilken Ruan is a speed guy with some hope of panning out because he's a line-drive hitter, not a slapper. In the field, he has good range and a strong, accurate arm. Unfortunately, the Expos think he's a prototypical leadoff hitter when he's more like Brian Hunter. Sure, that doesn't sound like much, but it'll be enough to chase Terry Jones over the border someday.

Brian Schneider C Bats L Age 24

YEAR	TEAM	LGE	AB	H	DB	TP	HR	BB	SO	R	RBI	SB	CS	OUT	BA	OBP	SLG	EQA	EQR	DEFENSE	
1998	CapeFear	SAL	137	32	5	0	5	12	9	21	19	2	1	106	.234	.302	.380	.228	13	35-C	-1
1998	Jupiter	Fla	305	72	9	0	3	16	43	25	23	2	2	235	.236	.275	.295	.184	17	76-C	4
1999	Harrisbg	Eas	424	97	16	1	13	21	59	39	50	1	1	328	.229	.267	.363	.205	31	105-C	3
2000	Ottawa	Int	239	55	20	2	4	12	44	20	27	1	0	184	.230	.267	.381	.211	19	59-C	0
2000	Montreal	NL	116	27	6	0	0	6	22	6	11	0	1	90	.233	.270	.284	.174	6	32-C	-3
2001	Montreal	NL	368	89	19	1	10	25	63	37	44	1	1	280	.242	.290	.380	.226	34		

A decent backup catcher in the making, Brian Schneider compensates for his lack of arm strength behind the plate with quick footwork. It's a treat to watch; we're so used to rockets getting launched by the Ivan Rodriguezes and the Henry Blancos that we forget the difference that anticipation and quickness can make. Schneider's shot at backing up Barrett is endangered by the signing of Sandy Martinez. Laugh away, monkey boy, but this is serious as far as Schneider is concerned.

Fernando Seguignol 1B/LF Bats B Age 26

YEAR	TEAM	LGE	AB	H	DB	TP	HR	BB	SO	R	RBI	SB	CS	OUT	BA	OBP	SLG	EQA	EQR	DEFENSE			
1998	Harrisbg	Eas	284	70	10	0	18	21	79	41	50	3	1	215	.246	.307	.472	.254	35	53-1B	3	12-LF	-1
1998	Ottawa	Int	110	26	4	0	6	9	43	13	14	0	0	84	.236	.299	.436	.241	12	21-LF	-1		
1999	Ottawa	Int	312	78	14	2	18	32	95	42	55	2	6	240	.250	.335	.481	.262	42	48-1B	-6		
1999	Montreal	NL	106	27	5	0	6	3	31	13	10	0	0	79	.255	.318	.472	.258	13	21-1B	-2		
2000	Ottawa	Int	142	36	9	0	8	10	27	17	26	1	1	107	.254	.320	.486	.261	19	24-1B	0	12-RF	-3
2000	Montreal	NL	164	45	7	0	10	6	43	21	21	0	1	120	.274	.310	.500	.260	21	17-1B	-1	14-LF	-6
2001	Montreal	NL	359	94	15	0	22	31	103	47	66	2	2	267	.262	.321	.487	.267	49				

Fernando Seguignol has nothing left to prove in Ottawa, but he's far from a finished product. He's a guess hitter: he guesses he'll swing at everything and see what happens. Although Seguignol killed left-handed pitchers in his major-league trial, he has not been a platoon hitter in the minors, so it isn't an ideal platoon situation. Alou could be creative, maximizing the plate appearances of both Seguignol and Lee Stevens by rotating them as starters and aggressively double-switching them in a game-within-the-game of "hide the pitcher and the shortstop."

Terrmel Sledge OF Bats L Age 24

YEAR	TEAM	LGE	AB	H	DB	TP	HR	BB	SO	R	RBI	SB	CS	OUT	BA	OBP	SLG	EQA	EQR	DEFENSE	
1999	Everett	Nwn	230	55	5	2	3	14	39	23	17	3	3	178	.239	.292	.317	.202	16	57-RF	-6
2000	Lancastr	Cal	381	96	17	3	8	47	51	52	43	10	4	289	.252	.347	.375	.249	45	72-RF	0
2001	Montreal	NL	251	65	9	2	5	32	51	40	32	8	2	188	.259	.343	.371	.252	30		

The payoff for slipping Chris Widger into a "return to sender" envelope, Terrmel Sledge is a good hitter without platoon issues. He led the California League in OBP and batting average, winning both titles after his season ended a couple of weeks early with a sore shoulder. He'd already had surgery to fix a torn labrum, and there's concern he's torn it again. He's older than every Expos outfielder except Vlad and has only A-ball experience, so you can't really be optimistic about his chances.

National League

Lee Stevens — 1B — Bats L — Age 33

YEAR	TEAM	LGE	AB	H	DB	TP	HR	BB	SO	R	RBI	SB	CS	OUT	BA	OBP	SLG	EQA	EQR	DEFENSE	
1998	Texas	AL	341	90	15	4	21	30	83	52	57	0	2	253	.264	.323	.516	.269	47	27-1B	-1
1999	Texas	AL	510	142	28	1	25	47	120	72	76	2	3	371	.278	.339	.484	.269	69	120-1B	10
2000	Montreal	NL	453	119	26	2	21	41	98	58	70	0	0	334	.263	.326	.468	.261	58	118-1B	4
2001	Montreal	NL	418	112	19	1	22	52	101	62	78	0	1	307	.268	.349	.476	.276	62		

We once said that Brad Fullmer might turn into Lee Stevens. If, in doing so, we somehow created the karma that made the Expos go out and get the original, we apologize to Expos fans. What we failed to say is that the best years of Stevens's career were spent in Japan and Oklahoma City, similar to how Fullmer's prime was being spent in Felipe Alou's doghouse instead of in the big leagues. Fullmer got liberated, and the Expos got an adequate veteran on the downside of his career. To compound the error, Stevens was signed to a two-year contract extension.

Andy Tracy — 3B/1B — Bats L — Age 27

YEAR	TEAM	LGE	AB	H	DB	TP	HR	BB	SO	R	RBI	SB	CS	OUT	BA	OBP	SLG	EQA	EQR	DEFENSE			
1998	Jupiter	Fla	258	56	10	1	8	28	80	26	36	2	2	204	.217	.298	.357	.219	23	67-1B	3		
1998	Harrisbg	Eas	214	42	10	2	7	18	65	26	24	1	1	173	.196	.267	.360	.205	16	51-1B	-1		
1999	Harrisbg	Eas	500	111	20	1	24	49	154	69	83	3	1	390	.222	.296	.410	.234	51	108-3B	-7	16-1B	3
2000	Ottawa	Int	197	52	11	0	9	28	67	23	29	1	1	146	.264	.360	.457	.272	28	43-1B	-3	11-3B	1
2000	Montreal	NL	194	50	9	1	10	19	57	28	29	1	0	144	.258	.329	.469	.263	26	22-3B	-6	20-1B	1
2001	Montreal	NL	260	64	12	1	12	29	84	34	42	1	0	196	.246	.322	.438	.257	33				

Andy Tracy is a happy reminder that even in the Expos' system, a good minor-league hitter can create his own opportunity. He was the beneficiary of the organizational confusion over third base; if the Expos had made up their minds about Michael Barrett before the season, they might have brought in somebody else to play third. Now that the issue has been settled by Fernando Tatis, Tracy will battle Seguignol for a pinch-hitting role.

Jose Vidro — 2B — Bats B — Age 26

YEAR	TEAM	LGE	AB	H	DB	TP	HR	BB	SO	R	RBI	SB	CS	OUT	BA	OBP	SLG	EQA	EQR	DEFENSE			
1998	Ottawa	Int	236	62	13	1	2	18	25	30	27	3	1	175	.263	.323	.352	.230	22	30-2B	-1	23-3B	1
1998	Montreal	NL	208	47	13	0	0	26	31	25	18	2	2	163	.226	.323	.288	.211	17	44-2B	-2		
1999	Montreal	NL	496	146	43	2	12	23	48	65	55	0	3	353	.294	.331	.462	.258	60	107-2B	-4		
2000	Montreal	NL	611	198	45	2	24	40	65	95	91	4	4	417	.324	.367	.522	.289	94	148-2B	-4		
2001	Montreal	NL	527	166	37	2	20	45	59	87	102	4	2	363	.315	.369	.507	.292	84				

While the American League shortstops get the attention, the National League has a pretty sweet group of second basemen. Behind the famous old men (Jeff Kent and Craig Biggio), there's an outstanding trio in the prime of their careers in Edgardo Alfonzo, Luis Castillo, and Jose Vidro. Vidro has worked hard at improving his defense, making gains in his second full season at second base. I wouldn't move him. Like Kent, he plays acceptable defense and gives his team an opportunity to stock the lineup with another hitter at third base. Vidro struggled in September with a strained elbow that required surgery but is expected to be fine in spring training.

Brad Wilkerson — OF — Bats L — Age 24

YEAR	TEAM	LGE	AB	H	DB	TP	HR	BB	SO	R	RBI	SB	CS	OUT	BA	OBP	SLG	EQA	EQR	DEFENSE	
1999	Harrisbg	Eas	431	86	19	2	6	68	105	53	37	1	2	347	.200	.314	.295	.210	35	113-RF	-1
2000	Harrisbg	Eas	232	64	24	1	6	33	41	39	32	5	3	171	.276	.371	.466	.279	35	57-LF	0
2000	Ottawa	Int	215	48	9	1	10	38	62	34	28	3	3	170	.223	.346	.414	.255	28	62-LF	-1
2001	Montreal	NL	344	88	23	1	11	60	97	63	53	7	3	259	.256	.366	.424	.274	51		

Talk about nice problems to have: you've sent away Rondell White and you *still* have one good young outfielder too many? After plenty of people whined that Brad Wilkerson was too patient or too home-run-oriented, Wilkerson smacked nearly 70 extra-base hits between Harrisburg and Ottawa. Now nobody in the organization is worrying that 87 walks means something bad. The starting center fielder for Team USA in the Olympics, he's got an arm good enough for right field but will settle for a crack at left field in 2001. There's big-time power to come from his uppercut stroke. A bad shoulder may cost him April, but he'll be up before the end of the season.

PITCHERS (ERA: 4.50, H/9: 9.00, HR/9: 1.00, BB/9: 3.00, K/9: 6.00, KW: 1.00, PERA: 4.50)

Brandon Agamennone Throws R Age 25

YEAR	TEAM	LGE	IP	H	ER	HR	BB	K	ERA	W	L	H/9	HR/9	BB/9	K/9	KW	PERA
1998	Vermont	NYP	28.7	21	8	3	14	13	2.51	2	1	6.59	0.94	4.40	4.08	0.46	3.62
1998	CapeFear	SAL	32.3	26	20	4	8	13	5.57	1	3	7.24	1.11	2.23	3.62	0.81	3.33
1999	Jupiter	Fla	59.0	53	44	10	21	23	6.71	2	5	8.08	1.53	3.20	3.51	0.55	4.60
1999	Harrisbg	Eas	48.7	45	21	7	14	25	3.88	3	2	8.32	1.29	2.59	4.62	0.89	4.23
2000	Harrisbg	Eas	88.7	103	67	18	29	33	6.80	3	7	10.45	1.83	2.94	3.35	0.57	6.20

One of the ripple effects from the wave of injuries at the big-league level and at Ottawa was that Brandon Agamennone continued to be used in a swing role instead of out of the pen, which hurt his stats. He throws a big-bending "Krukow" curve with 12-to-6 action and a fastball that sometimes gets into the 90s. He may surface as a swing man in the majors if Carl Pavano or Tony Armas Jr. can't stay healthy.

Tony Armas Jr. Throws R Age 23

YEAR	TEAM	LGE	IP	H	ER	HR	BB	K	ERA	W	L	H/9	HR/9	BB/9	K/9	KW	PERA
1998	Jupiter	Fla	139.0	144	80	24	75	80	5.18	6	9	9.32	1.55	4.86	5.18	0.53	6.05
1999	Harrisbg	Eas	140.3	124	67	14	55	67	4.30	7	9	7.95	0.90	3.53	4.30	0.61	4.01
2000	Ottawa	Int	18.0	22	12	4	4	9	6.00	1	1	11.00	2.00	2.00	4.50	1.13	6.35
2000	Montreal	NL	92.3	72	44	9	42	49	4.29	5	5	7.02	0.88	4.09	4.78	0.58	3.68

Tony Armas Jr. has been handled pretty carefully, with the Expos monitoring even the number of types of pitches he's thrown. Nevertheless, nagging injuries keep interfering with his progress. He was bouncing back from a sprained elbow suffered over the winter when problems with shoulder tendinitis cropped up. Armas throws a sinker in the low 90s with a good change-up and slider; he tips his curve, so left-handed hitters sat on it. The assumption is that once he's physically mature, he can be turned loose and blossom into the star pitcher we keep expecting.

Matt Blank Throws L Age 25

YEAR	TEAM	LGE	IP	H	ER	HR	BB	K	ERA	W	L	H/9	HR/9	BB/9	K/9	KW	PERA
1998	CapeFear	SAL	123.7	124	51	12	33	52	3.71	8	6	9.02	0.87	2.40	3.78	0.79	4.14
1998	Jupiter	Fla	39.0	33	16	4	13	15	3.69	2	2	7.62	0.92	3.00	3.46	0.58	3.64
1999	Jupiter	Fla	81.0	68	38	13	26	37	4.22	4	5	7.56	1.44	2.89	4.11	0.71	4.07
1999	Harrisbg	Eas	79.0	94	46	20	27	26	5.24	3	6	10.71	2.28	3.08	2.96	0.48	6.90
2000	Montreal	NL	13.3	11	7	1	4	3	4.72	0	1	7.43	0.68	2.70	2.03	0.38	3.13

An organizational favorite because of his makeup, Matt Blank is your basic left-hander with four pitches he can throw for strikes, none of them fast. Called up to replace Graeme Lloyd in the bullpen at the start of the season, he was put on the DL in May with a strained forearm that turned out to be a hairline fracture. He should be 100% for 2001, but he's about eighth on the list of potential starters, and those strikeout rates do not bode well for his future.

Donnie Bridges Throws R Age 22

YEAR	TEAM	LGE	IP	H	ER	HR	BB	K	ERA	W	L	H/9	HR/9	BB/9	K/9	KW	PERA
1998	Vermont	NYP	62.3	68	41	5	47	19	5.92	2	5	9.82	0.72	6.79	2.74	0.20	6.25
1999	CapeFear	SAL	42.3	39	15	4	23	20	3.19	3	2	8.29	0.85	4.89	4.25	0.43	4.69
1999	Jupiter	Fla	91.0	112	58	12	46	38	5.74	3	7	11.08	1.19	4.55	3.76	0.41	6.57
2000	Jupiter	Fla	67.3	59	34	3	25	39	4.54	3	4	7.89	0.40	3.34	5.21	0.78	3.41
2000	Harrisbg	Eas	120.3	103	40	8	51	55	2.99	8	5	7.70	0.60	3.81	4.11	0.54	3.68

The Expos' best pitching prospect, Donnie Bridges is moving up quickly. Upon his promotion to Double-A, he tossed three shutouts in his first six starts. Bridges throws mid-90s heat and a sharp-breaking high-80s slider with good mechanics; his curve is developing. He telegraphs his change-up, but he's coachable, and pitching coach Brad Arnsberg knows the pitch. Bridges did some damage against left-handers as a hitter, so his manager at Harrisburg, Doug Sisson, wanted to DH him. That got Sisson fired.

National League

Scott Downs — Throws L — Age 25

YEAR	TEAM	LGE	IP	H	ER	HR	BB	K	ERA	W	L	H/9	HR/9	BB/9	K/9	KW	PERA
1998	Daytona	Fla	150.7	177	89	21	65	67	5.32	6	11	10.57	1.25	3.88	4.00	0.52	6.07
1999	Daytona	Fla	44.0	42	14	4	14	23	2.86	3	2	8.59	0.82	2.86	4.70	0.82	4.02
1999	WestTenn	Sou	74.0	60	15	3	31	62	1.82	7	1	7.30	0.36	3.77	7.54	1.00	3.23
2000	ChiCubs	NL	91.7	113	54	12	30	52	5.30	4	6	11.09	1.18	2.95	5.11	0.87	5.90

He's carved in the Greg Hibbard "battlin' lefty" mold, from his sweet curve to the sense of confidence he projects to the high-80s fastball with which he plays peek-a-boo. Scott Downs got into the spirit of things with the Expos pretty quickly, spraining his elbow in his debut. He's depending on injury or a trade to get him a shot at being the fifth starter. It's hard to get enthusiastic about left-handers without great stuff, but Downs has exceptional control, an improving strikeout rate, and a record of continuous improvement.

Scott Forster — Throws L — Age 29

YEAR	TEAM	LGE	IP	H	ER	HR	BB	K	ERA	W	L	H/9	HR/9	BB/9	K/9	KW	PERA
1998	Harrisbg	Eas	70.7	89	57	12	55	30	7.26	2	6	11.33	1.53	7.00	3.82	0.27	8.10
1999	Ottawa	Int	49.3	46	30	3	48	22	5.47	2	3	8.39	0.55	8.76	4.01	0.23	6.02
2000	Ottawa	Int	29.0	24	13	1	23	16	4.03	1	2	7.45	0.31	7.14	4.97	0.35	4.58
2000	Montreal	NL	31.7	28	29	5	21	19	8.24	1	3	7.96	1.42	5.97	5.40	0.45	5.59

An organizational soldier called up after Graeme Lloyd and his replacements all disappeared, Scott Forster was the sixth-round pick from Kevin Malone's first draft as GM in 1994. Javier Vazquez is the keeper from that draft. Geoff Blum and Mike Thurman, the next-best picks, and Hiram Bocachica might turn out all right. Malone's second draft produced Michael Barrett and Henry Mateo. And that's it. The Expos' player-development program has a great reputation, but that's a bad two-year run.

Josh Girdley — Throws L — Age 20

YEAR	TEAM	LGE	IP	H	ER	HR	BB	K	ERA	W	L	H/9	HR/9	BB/9	K/9	KW	PERA
2000	Vermont	NYP	70.3	70	49	15	33	33	6.27	2	6	8.96	1.92	4.22	4.22	0.50	5.95

He was the Expos' top pick in 1999. Unlike a lot of the "projectable" big pitchers with whom Beattie keeps rolling the dice, Josh Girdley already throws in the low 90s with a good curve and change-up. Because the Expos love to promote their pitching prospects during the season, Girdley will get pushed up if he has a good first half in the Sally League. He's still at least two years away from major-league radar screens, and anything could happen to him between now and then.

Bryan Hebson — Throws R — Age 25

YEAR	TEAM	LGE	IP	H	ER	HR	BB	K	ERA	W	L	H/9	HR/9	BB/9	K/9	KW	PERA
1998	CapeFear	SAL	64.0	74	55	17	40	26	7.73	1	6	10.41	2.39	5.63	3.66	0.32	7.88
1999	CapeFear	SAL	29.0	24	19	4	25	15	5.90	1	2	7.45	1.24	7.76	4.66	0.30	5.82
1999	Jupiter	Fla	93.3	88	45	13	36	44	4.34	5	5	8.49	1.25	3.47	4.24	0.61	4.67
2000	Harrisbg	Eas	156.7	180	124	41	74	54	7.12	4	13	10.34	2.36	4.25	3.10	0.36	7.25

Last year, we thought it would be interesting to compare how Donnie Bridges and Bryan Hebson did in 2000 at Harrisburg, because Hebson was a '97 first-rounder out of Auburn and Bridges was a '97 first-rounder out of high school. Hebson got his head handed to him. While high-school pitchers are invariably riskier development projects, mediocre college pitchers generally have little upside. Hebson wasn't added to the 40-man roster over the winter.

Dustin Hermanson — Throws R — Age 28

YEAR	TEAM	LGE	IP	H	ER	HR	BB	K	ERA	W	L	H/9	HR/9	BB/9	K/9	KW	PERA
1998	Montreal	NL	178.7	160	79	21	51	125	3.98	10	10	8.06	1.06	2.57	6.30	1.23	3.84
1999	Montreal	NL	209.7	214	101	19	58	122	4.34	11	12	9.19	0.82	2.49	5.24	1.05	4.20
2000	Montreal	NL	192.0	216	117	24	63	78	5.48	7	14	10.13	1.13	2.95	3.66	0.62	5.28

Be afraid. While the Expos want to brush aside his problems as a season-long bout of tendinitis, anybody whose strikeout rate drops by half in two years is someone to worry about. The one good thing that happened to Dustin Hermanson in 2000 was that he got some benefit from having Arnsberg join the staff, as he started perfecting a new change-up. His overall numbers were hurt by his brief fling as the team's closer after Ugueth Urbina went down: he surrendered ten runs in 10⅓ relief innings. He'll be the #4 starter for the Cardinals.

Hideki Irabu — Throws R — Age 32

YEAR	TEAM	LGE	IP	H	ER	HR	BB	K	ERA	W	L	H/9	HR/9	BB/9	K/9	KW	PERA
1998	NY Yanks	AL	169.3	139	71	25	67	116	3.77	10	9	7.39	1.33	3.56	6.17	0.87	4.13
1999	NY Yanks	AL	166.7	167	86	23	38	127	4.64	8	11	9.02	1.24	2.05	6.86	1.67	4.37
2000	Montreal	NL	53.0	74	42	8	12	35	7.13	1	5	12.57	1.36	2.04	5.94	1.46	6.58

No sooner was Hideki Irabu picked up than he needed surgery to remove bone spurs and bone chips in his elbow, which might explain the reputation the Yankees gave him for not being tough. Set aside "fat toad." It's insulting, but it's reportable. From what I understand, George Steinbrenner called him another word for kitty cat. In light of the injury, The Boss's remarks seem a bit unfair. Irabu is expected to be ready to pitch in camp.

Mike Johnson — Throws R — Age 25

YEAR	TEAM	LGE	IP	H	ER	HR	BB	K	ERA	W	L	H/9	HR/9	BB/9	K/9	KW	PERA
1998	Harrisbg	Eas	30.7	39	36	13	11	23	10.57	0	3	11.45	3.82	3.23	6.75	1.05	9.05
1998	Ottawa	Int	103.3	104	65	23	36	64	5.66	4	7	9.06	2.00	3.14	5.57	0.89	5.64
1999	Ottawa	Int	141.7	169	99	25	60	88	6.29	5	11	10.74	1.59	3.81	5.59	0.73	6.48
2000	Ottawa	Int	28.3	15	10	4	14	20	3.18	2	1	4.76	1.27	4.45	6.35	0.71	3.01
2000	Montreal	NL	99.0	104	67	17	44	58	6.09	3	8	9.45	1.55	4.00	5.27	0.66	5.76

The wave of injuries to the pitching staff gave three swing men the chance to pick up service time and pension money: Mike Johnson, Felipe Lira, and Julio Santana. That's a pretty good indicator of "replacement-level" talent. Santana throws hard, Johnson has a great curve, and Lira has the most experience. Everyone has to do something well to get this far. Johnson is proof that even if you can fool some of the people some of the time, other guys will sit on Uncle Charlie and go yard.

Steve Kline — Throws L — Age 28

YEAR	TEAM	LGE	IP	H	ER	HR	BB	K	ERA	W	L	H/9	HR/9	BB/9	K/9	KW	PERA
1998	Montreal	NL	69.0	62	25	4	37	62	3.26	5	3	8.09	0.52	4.83	8.09	0.84	4.21
1999	Montreal	NL	68.0	55	31	8	28	58	4.10	4	4	7.28	1.06	3.71	7.68	1.04	3.86
2000	Montreal	NL	79.7	85	34	7	23	53	3.84	5	4	9.60	0.79	2.60	5.99	1.15	4.46

Even having led the league in appearances in consecutive years, Steve Kline would have to top last year's 83 games by ten to break Mike Marshall's franchise record of 92 set in 1973. Did Marshall melt down? Not exactly; he appeared in 106 games in 1974, tossing more than 200 innings in relief, but did miss time in 1975 with a rib injury. I'm not going to advocate that anybody get used the same way, but I wouldn't worry about Kline's workload. He struggled against right-handed batters after we advocated he be used against them more often; sometimes you need to be careful what you wish for.

Felipe Lira — Throws R — Age 29

YEAR	TEAM	LGE	IP	H	ER	HR	BB	K	ERA	W	L	H/9	HR/9	BB/9	K/9	KW	PERA
1998	Tacoma	PCL	120.7	133	74	15	52	56	5.52	4	9	9.92	1.12	3.88	4.18	0.54	5.54
1998	Seattle	AL	15.7	21	9	5	4	15	5.17	1	1	12.06	2.87	2.30	8.62	1.88	8.02
1999	Toledo	Int	107.7	158	97	31	37	47	8.11	2	10	13.21	2.59	3.09	3.93	0.64	8.70
2000	Ottawa	Int	19.0	24	13	4	3	7	6.16	1	1	11.37	1.89	1.42	3.32	1.17	6.24
2000	Montreal	NL	99.0	123	65	10	30	42	5.91	3	8	11.18	0.91	2.73	3.82	0.70	5.58

He's several years removed from the day when he and Jose Lima were the closest things to pitching prospects in the Tigers' chain. Felipe Lira was a right-handed junk-baller then and still relies heavily on a cut fastball, slider, and change-up. He's still gifted with fine control but needs a pitch that will fool hitters or a striptease act to distract them. He didn't average even four innings in his seven starts.

Graeme Lloyd — Throws L — Age 34

YEAR	TEAM	LGE	IP	H	ER	HR	BB	K	ERA	W	L	H/9	HR/9	BB/9	K/9	KW	PERA
1997	NY Yanks	AL	48.0	51	22	6	17	24	4.13	2	3	9.56	1.13	3.19	4.50	0.71	5.03
1998	NY Yanks	AL	36.3	24	9	3	5	19	2.23	3	1	5.94	0.74	1.24	4.71	1.90	2.01
1999	Toronto	AL	71.0	63	30	9	18	45	3.80	4	4	7.99	1.14	2.28	5.70	1.25	3.77

Graeme Lloyd's wife died in the spring. Later, he had to have shoulder surgery, but he's supposed to be pitching in 2001. There's not much to say but that we wish him the best in getting his career back on track. I don't care who he's facing next, whether it's my favorite team or yours. I hope he wins.

Montreal Expos

Troy Mattes — Throws R — Age 25

YEAR	TEAM	LGE	IP	H	ER	HR	BB	K	ERA	W	L	H/9	HR/9	BB/9	K/9	KW	PERA
1998	Jupiter	Fla	67.7	71	38	9	25	24	5.05	3	5	9.44	1.20	3.33	3.19	0.48	5.10
1999	Jupiter	Fla	21.7	27	14	5	10	7	5.82	1	1	11.22	2.08	4.15	2.91	0.35	7.42
1999	Harrisbg	Eas	91.0	113	71	17	39	36	7.02	2	8	11.18	1.68	3.86	3.56	0.46	6.86
2000	Harrisbg	Eas	160.0	175	111	36	63	66	6.24	5	13	9.84	2.03	3.54	3.71	0.52	6.31

Frederick the Great's father collected tall guys, not to fill the roster of the royal basketball team, but to stock a regiment of impressive-looking bodyguards. If there's any evidence that Beattie was the King of Prussia in a previous life, it's his predilection for big guys: Troy Mattes stands 6'7". He's got a nifty slider, but he's another "project" of Beattie's who gives up home runs by the sackful. There isn't a whole lot separating Mattes from Bryan Hebson, except that Mattes keeps the ball on the ground a little more often. Neither are prospects at this point.

Trey Moore — Throws L — Age 28

YEAR	TEAM	LGE	IP	H	ER	HR	BB	K	ERA	W	L	H/9	HR/9	BB/9	K/9	KW	PERA
1998	Montreal	NL	58.7	75	35	5	15	28	5.37	2	5	11.51	0.77	2.30	4.30	0.93	5.44
2000	Ottawa	Int	55.0	56	39	5	19	31	6.38	2	4	9.16	0.82	3.11	5.07	0.82	4.47
2000	Montreal	NL	34.7	53	28	6	18	20	7.27	1	3	13.76	1.56	4.67	5.19	0.56	8.58

Trey Moore is almost all that's left in the organization from the Jeff Fassero deal. The Expos dumped Chris Widger for Termel Sledge and Sean Spencer, then put Spencer on waivers. A shoulder 'scope cost Moore all of 1999. Before that, he relied heavily on his slider to compensate for his lack of velocity. With the shoulder problem, he can't snap off his slider like he used to. While he's still on the 40-man roster, he has no great future. Now Braves property.

Guillermo Mota — Throws R — Age 27

YEAR	TEAM	LGE	IP	H	ER	HR	BB	K	ERA	W	L	H/9	HR/9	BB/9	K/9	KW	PERA
1998	Jupiter	Fla	38.0	17	6	0	9	14	1.42	4	0	4.03	0.00	2.13	3.32	0.78	1.03
1998	Harrisbg	Eas	15.7	11	2	0	2	11	1.15	2	0	6.32	0.00	1.15	6.32	2.75	1.60
1999	Montreal	NL	53.7	51	22	5	21	23	3.69	3	3	8.55	0.84	3.52	3.86	0.55	4.27
2000	Ottawa	Int	59.0	48	17	5	32	25	2.59	5	2	7.32	0.76	4.88	3.81	0.39	4.05
2000	Montreal	NL	29.0	26	20	3	10	20	6.21	1	2	8.07	0.93	3.10	6.21	1.00	3.91

Guillermo Mota's fastball gets rave reviews, but it lacks movement, and, as an ex-shortstop, he's still acquiring pitching instincts. Because of some past elbow problems he's had, I'd hold off trying to teach him a curve or slider. Maybe a change-up, maybe a forkball. Once he adds a second pitch and learns when and how to use it, he could be an effective setup man.

Carl Pavano — Throws R — Age 25

YEAR	TEAM	LGE	IP	H	ER	HR	BB	K	ERA	W	L	H/9	HR/9	BB/9	K/9	KW	PERA
1998	Montreal	NL	128.7	126	68	18	39	67	4.76	6	8	8.81	1.26	2.73	4.69	0.86	4.55
1999	Montreal	NL	101.0	111	61	8	29	59	5.44	4	7	9.89	0.71	2.58	5.26	1.02	4.54
2000	Montreal	NL	93.7	86	37	7	28	53	3.56	6	4	8.26	0.67	2.69	5.09	0.95	3.62

Expect to find Pavano's picture under the definition of "tendinitis." He's had it in both his shoulder and elbow, and it has kept him from a full season in each of the last three years. If he finally pitches a full season, he'll be one of the top 20 starters in the league—and very wealthy through arbitration or a multi-year deal. Elbow surgery will cost him April.

Jeremy Powell — Throws R — Age 25

YEAR	TEAM	LGE	IP	H	ER	HR	BB	K	ERA	W	L	H/9	HR/9	BB/9	K/9	KW	PERA
1998	Harrisbg	Eas	122.7	114	60	18	39	47	4.40	6	8	8.36	1.32	2.86	3.45	0.60	4.40
1998	Montreal	NL	24.0	26	24	5	10	11	9.00	0	3	9.75	1.88	3.75	4.13	0.55	6.18
1999	Ottawa	Int	87.3	82	34	5	35	53	3.50	6	4	8.45	0.52	3.61	5.46	0.76	3.93
1999	Montreal	NL	94.7	107	54	13	37	37	5.13	4	7	10.17	1.24	3.52	3.52	0.50	5.66
2000	Ottawa	Int	120.0	158	104	21	54	74	7.80	3	10	11.85	1.58	4.05	5.55	0.69	7.22
2000	Montreal	NL	25.3	34	26	6	8	16	9.24	0	3	12.08	2.13	2.84	5.68	1.00	7.48

Here's another one of Beattie's gentle giants. If you told the Expos they could pitch, the Expos would sign the Jolly Green Giant, Queen Latifah, and the Giant Chicken of Bristol. Jeremy Powell tries to live on a curve/forkball mix and occasionally tops 90 mph with his fastball. Things may be changing: Powell was dumped from the 40-man roster.

Julio Santana — Throws R — Age 27

YEAR	TEAM	LGE	IP	H	ER	HR	BB	K	ERA	W	L	H/9	HR/9	BB/9	K/9	KW	PERA
1998	TampaBay	AL	137.7	134	62	16	49	55	4.05	7	8	8.76	1.05	3.20	3.60	0.56	4.49
1999	TampaBay	AL	55.7	62	41	8	25	32	6.63	2	4	10.02	1.29	4.04	5.17	0.64	5.85
2000	Montreal	NL	65.0	68	42	10	28	48	5.82	2	5	9.42	1.38	3.88	6.65	0.86	5.52

A couple of years ago, converting position players to pitchers was the rage. While Felix Rodriguez has turned out okay, most proved no better than the original Clint Hartung. Julio Santana is one of the guys people were excited about, and there's still enough here for some prurient interest. He bounced to the Giants on waivers and then the Mets in the Rule 5 draft. He can be a useful swing man for long relief and spot starts against righty-heavy lineups.

James Serrano — Throws R — Age 25

YEAR	TEAM	LGE	IP	H	ER	HR	BB	K	ERA	W	L	H/9	HR/9	BB/9	K/9	KW	PERA
1998	CapeFear	SAL	21.0	23	14	4	21	13	6.00	1	1	9.86	1.71	9.00	5.57	0.31	8.21
1999	Jupiter	Fla	82.7	67	39	10	37	66	4.25	4	5	7.29	1.09	4.03	7.19	0.89	4.02
2000	Harrisbg	Eas	68.0	68	48	11	48	48	6.35	2	6	9.00	1.46	6.35	6.35	0.50	6.35

He's a 5'8" reliever who throws in the low 90s. That doesn't sound like much, but this is the Expos, where everyone is big and throws under 90 mph. Using James Serrano in relief of all of Beattie's big guys who he throws harder than might be interesting on paper, but Serrano wasn't unhittable in Double-A. He has a deceptive delivery, but control problems with his curve and change took a big chunk out of the momentum he had after 1999.

Scott Strickland — Throws R — Age 25

YEAR	TEAM	LGE	IP	H	ER	HR	BB	K	ERA	W	L	H/9	HR/9	BB/9	K/9	KW	PERA
1998	CapeFear	SAL	31.3	42	26	6	16	24	7.47	1	2	12.06	1.72	4.60	6.89	0.75	7.71
1998	Jupiter	Fla	63.0	65	35	11	26	29	5.00	3	4	9.29	1.57	3.71	4.14	0.56	5.57
1999	Jupiter	Fla	23.3	24	17	3	6	19	6.56	1	2	9.26	1.16	2.31	7.33	1.58	4.59
1999	Harrisbg	Eas	27.0	27	9	1	10	22	3.00	2	1	9.00	0.33	3.33	7.33	1.10	3.96
1999	Ottawa	Int	26.3	24	6	1	11	25	2.05	2	1	8.20	0.34	3.76	8.54	1.14	3.71
1999	Montreal	NL	17.7	15	9	3	9	19	4.58	1	1	7.64	1.53	4.58	9.68	1.06	4.89
2000	Montreal	NL	46.3	38	18	3	13	40	3.50	3	2	7.38	0.58	2.53	7.77	1.54	3.01

One of the season's weirdest footnotes was Scott Strickland's torn/not-torn labrum. He was put on the 60-day DL with what was supposed to be a season-ending injury that would require major surgery. Two months and a second opinion later, Strickland was pitching again, and it now appears he won't need surgery. The Expos don't have a track record like the Red Sox or Indians when it comes to screwing up medical evaluations, so maybe this is a one-time thing. Strickland dominates right-handed hitters with his fastball/slider combo, but until he starts fooling lefties, Alou will have to pick Strickland's spots carefully.

Anthony Telford — Throws R — Age 35

YEAR	TEAM	LGE	IP	H	ER	HR	BB	K	ERA	W	L	H/9	HR/9	BB/9	K/9	KW	PERA
1998	Montreal	NL	87.3	83	44	9	33	48	4.53	4	6	8.55	0.93	3.40	4.95	0.73	4.34
1999	Montreal	NL	93.7	107	48	3	32	58	4.61	4	6	10.28	0.29	3.07	5.57	0.91	4.53
2000	Montreal	NL	75.7	74	36	9	19	57	4.28	4	4	8.80	1.07	2.26	6.78	1.50	4.15

Anthony Telford is of the more unlikely beneficiaries of the five multi-year contracts handed out to pitchers just after Loria and Samson rode into town. He has been a junk-balling middle man for four years, and where else but Montreal would he be under contract for two more? Is there somebody who's going to stand up and say, "I'm in my thirties, and it's great to be an Expo"? He had his shoulder 'scoped at the end of September and is expected to be fine for 2001.

Mike Thurman — Throws R — Age 27

YEAR	TEAM	LGE	IP	H	ER	HR	BB	K	ERA	W	L	H/9	HR/9	BB/9	K/9	KW	PERA
1998	Ottawa	Int	100.3	105	51	15	48	54	4.57	5	6	9.42	1.35	4.31	4.84	0.56	5.65
1998	Montreal	NL	64.0	58	37	7	24	26	5.20	3	4	8.16	0.98	3.38	3.66	0.54	4.16
1999	Montreal	NL	142.0	133	77	16	44	71	4.88	6	10	8.43	1.01	2.79	4.50	0.81	4.10
2000	Montreal	NL	86.3	108	63	8	39	43	6.57	3	7	11.26	0.83	4.07	4.48	0.55	6.10

Mike Thurman is the most successful of the organization's big soft-tossing right-handers. Knee problems that started in 1998 are getting the better of him. Late in the season, he had no life on his stuff and was complaining of constant soreness. That couldn't have happened at a worse time for him or the Expos. He and Scott Downs are the sixth and seventh starters going into camp, and concerns about his knee will keep him from commanding any value in a trade.

T.J. Tucker — Throws R — Age 22

YEAR	TEAM	LGE	IP	H	ER	HR	BB	K	ERA	W	L	H/9	HR/9	BB/9	K/9	KW	PERA
1998	Vermont	NYP	30.3	25	9	0	19	15	2.67	2	1	7.42	0.00	5.64	4.45	0.39	3.68
1999	Jupiter	Fla	39.7	25	10	5	20	21	2.27	3	1	5.67	1.13	4.54	4.76	0.52	3.36
1999	Harrisbg	Eas	108.7	111	61	17	38	54	5.05	5	7	9.19	1.41	3.15	4.47	0.71	5.10
2000	Harrisbg	Eas	41.3	36	26	12	18	16	5.66	2	3	7.84	2.61	3.92	3.48	0.44	5.93

Since being a first-round pick in 1997, T.J. Tucker missed most of '97, '98, and 2000 with injuries. None have been major; this year it was a forearm strain that healed slowly. There have been constant complaints about Tucker's conditioning. When healthy, he throws in the low 90s with little or no movement; he's still perfecting a curve and change-up.

Ugueth Urbina — Throws R — Age 27

YEAR	TEAM	LGE	IP	H	ER	HR	BB	K	ERA	W	L	H/9	HR/9	BB/9	K/9	KW	PERA
1998	Montreal	NL	66.7	39	11	2	30	76	1.49	6	1	5.27	0.27	4.05	10.26	1.27	2.26
1999	Montreal	NL	73.7	60	34	6	30	84	4.15	4	4	7.33	0.73	3.67	10.26	1.40	3.54
2000	Montreal	NL	13.0	12	7	1	4	18	4.85	0	1	8.31	0.69	2.77	12.46	2.25	3.74

In April, Ugueth Urbina woke up with his elbow locked in position. He had to have surgery to have bone chips removed and a second surgery in July to remove another chip. He's supposed to be 100% in camp, but the Expos should take seriously any offers they get for him between now and the July deadline. Closers are the coin you use to fleece organizations inclined to give Jose Mesa a seven-figure contract, and saves are the baubles you shine in their eyes while lifting their wallets.

Javier Vazquez — Throws R — Age 25

YEAR	TEAM	LGE	IP	H	ER	HR	BB	K	ERA	W	L	H/9	HR/9	BB/9	K/9	KW	PERA
1998	Montreal	NL	165.3	192	119	32	61	113	6.48	5	13	10.45	1.74	3.32	6.15	0.93	6.27
1999	Ottawa	Int	40.7	45	23	7	15	34	5.09	2	3	9.96	1.55	3.32	7.52	1.13	5.76
1999	Montreal	NL	150.0	148	92	19	44	95	5.52	6	11	8.88	1.14	2.64	5.70	1.08	4.43
2000	Montreal	NL	211.0	241	99	22	51	163	4.22	11	12	10.28	0.94	2.18	6.95	1.60	4.85

The Expos deserve a lot of credit for taking a pitcher with only six games above A ball prior to 1998 and turning him into one of the best starters in the NL. Javier Vazquez has outstanding command of his fastball and uses his curve and change-up effectively. He ranked fifth in the NL in quality starts behind guys named Johnson, Maddux, Glavine, and Brown. Lousy run support translated into an MLB-high nine team losses when Vazquez posted quality starts. We should all expect good things from him, except there's concern that Felipe Alou worked him extremely hard down the stretch. Vazquez had topped 120 pitches only once going into September then averaged more than 120 in his six starts that month.

Justin Wayne — Throws R — Age 22

YEAR	TEAM	LGE	IP	H	ER	HR	BB	K	ERA	W	L	H/9	HR/9	BB/9	K/9	KW	PERA
2000	Jupiter	Fla	23.3	27	29	5	14	14	11.19	0	3	10.41	1.93	5.40	5.40	0.50	7.28

The Expos' top pick in 2000 after racking up a 30-4 record in three years at Stanford, Justin Wayne enjoys the reputation of a command pitcher. He's supposed to be able to throw four pitches for strikes with a balanced delivery, the best being a slider, and he doesn't throw especially hard. He's usually compared to Mike Mussina, which is a nice thing to say.

Support-Neutral Statistics — MONTREAL EXPOS — Park Effect: -0.2%

PITCHER	GS	IP	R	SNW	SNL	SNPCT	W	L	RA	APW	SNVA	SNWAR
Tony Armas Jr.	17	95.0	49	6.4	5.0	.559	7	9	4.64	0.5	0.7	1.5
Scott Downs	1	3.0	3	0.1	0.5	.163	0	0	9.00	-0.1	-0.2	-0.2
Dustin Hermanson	30	187.7	118	10.3	11.9	.464	10	14	5.66	-1.0	-0.7	0.9
Hideki Irabu	11	54.7	45	2.7	4.8	.358	2	5	7.41	-1.3	-1.0	-0.5
Mike Johnson	13	59.0	47	3.3	5.3	.383	4	6	7.17	-1.3	-1.0	-0.4
Felipe Lira	7	26.7	28	0.9	3.4	.206	0	6	9.45	-1.2	-1.2	-0.9
Trey Moore	8	35.3	31	1.1	4.1	.216	1	5	7.90	-1.0	-1.4	-1.1
Carl Pavano	15	97.0	40	6.4	3.9	.621	8	4	3.71	1.4	1.2	2.0
Jay Powell	4	17.0	20	0.6	2.1	.216	0	2	10.59	-1.0	-0.7	-0.6
Julio Santana	4	19.7	14	1.0	1.5	.387	0	2	6.41	-0.3	-0.3	-0.1
Mike Thurman	17	88.3	69	4.1	7.7	.346	4	8	7.03	-1.8	-1.7	-0.9
T.J. Tucker	2	7.0	9	0.1	1.1	.105	0	1	11.57	-0.5	-0.5	-0.4
Javier Vazquez	33	217.7	104	13.1	10.4	.557	11	9	4.30	1.9	1.2	3.1
TOTALS	162	908.0	577	50.0	61.8	.447	47	71	5.72	-5.6	-5.7	2.5

Despite a couple of encouraging performances by their young pitchers, the Expos had easily the worst starting staff in the majors, costing the team 5.7 wins compared to average pitching according to Support Neutral Value Added (SNVA). It may be a small consolation to Expos fans that the 2000 rotation wasn't as bad as other bottom-ranked rotations of the recent past. In fact, you could say that the Expos were the "best worst" rotation of the past 20 years. Their SNVA of –5.7 was better than any other starting staff that finished at the bottom of the major leagues since 1979, excluding the strike-shortened year of 1981. It's interesting that the rotation that the 2000 Expos surpassed in the "best worst" category came from just a year earlier—the 1999 Florida Marlins were last in the league with an SNVA of "only" –6.9.

Could it be that really putrid starting rotations—the kind that we've seen from the Marlins (1998), A's (1997), Tigers (1996), and Twins (1995) in recent years—is becoming a thing of the past? Probably not, but there are some signs throughout baseball of growing parity. A lot was made of the fact that 2000 was the first season in which no team finished above .600 and no team finished below .400. That same sort of narrowing gap seen between the top and bottom of the league was also evident among pitching rotations. The split between the best team SNVA (the Red Sox and Braves with 6.3) and the worst (the Expos with –5.7) was by far the smallest of the past 20 years.

For a quick explanation of SN stats, see page 7.

Reliever Evaluation Tools

PITCHER	G	IP	R	ARA	APR	IRNR/G	EIRS/G	IRP	BRS	RRA	ARP
Miguel Batista	4	8.3	14	15.33	-9.4	1.00	0.45	-2.2	0.2	17.93	-11.8
Matt Blank	13	14.0	8	5.21	-0.0	0.62	0.24	-1.3	-2.9	3.43	2.8
Scott Forster	42	32.0	31	8.84	-12.9	0.62	0.21	-3.9	-2.5	9.43	-15.0
Dustin Hermanson	8	10.3	10	8.83	-4.2	0.75	0.14	-1.2	-0.7	9.40	-4.8
Mike Johnson	28	42.3	26	5.60	-1.9	0.89	0.34	-0.9	-1.0	5.78	-2.8
Steve Kline	83	82.3	36	3.99	11.1	0.48	0.16	-5.7	3.9	5.04	1.4
Yovanny Lara	6	5.7	4	6.44	-0.8	1.17	0.57	-0.9	0.2	8.11	-1.8
Felipe Lira	46	75.0	43	5.23	-0.3	1.04	0.43	2.1	-0.9	4.73	3.9
David Moraga	3	1.7	7	38.32	-6.1	2.00	0.77	-3.6	-2.2	47.74	-7.9
Guillermo Mota	29	30.0	21	6.39	-4.0	0.59	0.22	0.4	-3.9	5.43	-0.8
Jim Poole	5	2.0	6	27.37	-4.9	0.40	0.15	-0.7	-0.9	30.43	-5.6
Jeremy Powell	7	9.0	7	7.10	-1.9	0.43	0.07	0.5	0.4	7.10	-1.9
Brad Rigby	6	5.3	5	8.55	-2.0	1.50	0.51	-3.2	0.1	14.57	-5.6
Julio Santana	32	47.0	31	6.02	-4.3	0.62	0.22	-0.3	-3.2	5.70	-2.7
Matt Skrmetta	6	5.3	10	17.11	-7.1	0.83	0.17	-0.4	-2.4	13.52	-4.9
Stan Spencer	8	6.7	4	5.47	-0.2	0.88	0.36	-2.5	0.4	9.54	-3.2
Scott Strickland	49	48.0	18	3.42	9.5	0.55	0.21	-0.5	-1.8	2.94	12.0
Anthony Telford	64	78.3	38	4.43	6.7	0.53	0.18	3.4	-3.3	3.59	14.0
Ugueth Urbina	13	13.3	6	4.11	1.6	0.54	0.17	0.3	1.1	4.86	0.5
TOTALS	452	516.7	325	5.74	-31.1	0.67	0.24			5.79	-34.1

For a quick guide to RET, see page 10.

New York Mets

If you're expecting to find an apology for our apathy towards the team that turned the World Series into a regional overcelebration and a television disaster, guess again.

Baseball Prospectus 2000 included a less-than-enthusiastic endorsement of the 2000 Mets. We expected the Mets to compete for a playoff slot in 2000 and maybe in 2001 as well. It was not a daring claim—Steve Phillips is playing for the short term. We generally don't give much benefit of the doubt to teams that take a short-term approach, and we're not shy about our preference for teams who know winning runs in cycles, teams who invest the time in trying to build organizations capable of sustained success. We like to see development at both the major- and minor-league levels and aggressive acquisition of pre-peak or at-peak talent whenever possible.

When the White Sox took a good look at the rosters of the Indians and other teams around the league in 1997, they saw that they'd be better off taking their future more seriously than their present. We were happy to give them credit for daring to do the right thing, investing their hope and faith—and that of their fans—in a long-term rebuilding project. It's a worthwhile goal, especially when you consider the sustained success of the Indians and Braves despite all the handicaps they were saddled with a dozen years ago.

Of course, Steve Phillips and Bobby Valentine could not afford to be exceedingly patient in 2000. Both were working on the last years of their contracts, and their core offensive players, Mike Piazza and Edgardo Alfonzo, are in their primes. If the Mets wanted to avoid the fate of the Ken Griffey/Alex Rodriguez Mariners, there is no time like the present.

After failing to make the playoffs in 1998, Phillips had done a great job of attacking the weaknesses of his team. He upgraded from Carlos Baerga to Robin Ventura at third base, brought in Roger Cedeno and Rickey Henderson to bolster the top of the order, and picked up Armando Benitez to balance a bullpen leaning to the left with John Franco and Dennis Cook.

After falling short in the NLCS in 1999, Phillips again had to assess his team. He'd built a great offense and a great bullpen, but the Mets lacked depth in the rotation. They had relied heavily on not merely old but ancient players like Henderson and Orel Hershiser. The team's broad offensive strength of 1999 had already taken a big hit with the departure of John Olerud; factor in the continued use of Rey Ordonez, and it looked like the Mets offense was going to decline significantly.

Rather than pack it in or bring back everyone to thank them for the memories (as the Cubs, Diamondbacks, and Yankees have done in recent years), Phillips again attacked his team's problems. To fix the starting pitching, he took a single-season roll of the dice on Mike Hampton. The '99 team had been weak against left-handed pitching, so in addition to getting Derek Bell in the Hampton deal, Phillips signed Todd Zeile to replace Olerud at first base. However, none of these moves seemed to add up to the stuff of Braves-killers. Despite these moves, the Mets still looked like a team that would end the year getting chewed up by the Braves.

But the Mets had a few happy accidents along the way, foremost among them the Rey Ordonez injury. Six months after Ordonez's limp bat had given Bobby Cox the rare thrill of exploiting a tactical advantage in a postseason series, the Mets entered the 2000 season with a weaker lineup. They could no longer afford to let Ordonez continue to cost them runs. He cooperated by breaking his left forearm in May and wiping out his season.

It was probably the most important piece of addition by subtraction enjoyed by any team in the 2000 season. Playing Ordonez would have cost the Mets several runs and a couple of games. That could have been the difference between the

---

Mets Prospectus

2000 record: 94–68; Second place, NL East; NL wild card; Lost to Yankees in World Series, 4–1

Pythagenport W/L: 88–74

Runs Scored: 807 (7th in NL)

Runs Allowed: 738 (3rd in NL)

Team EqA: .266 (tied for 4th in NL)

2000 Batters' Age: 30.3 (4th oldest in NL)

2000 Pitchers' Age: 30.6 (3rd oldest in NL)

Ballpark: Shea Stadium; moderate pitchers' park; Park Factor of .952

2000: They rode a good bullpen and a couple of great hitters all the way to October 25.

2001: Relying heavily on an ancient rotation, and certain to carry a couple of dead spots in the lineup. They'll be over .500, but not by much.

Reds trading away Denny Neagle at the All-Star break or—being closer to the Mets in the wild-card race—keeping Neagle and adding another starting pitcher.

While Ordonez's "breakthrough" 1999 had many people excited, he'd still barely cracked a 600 OPS and was one of the worst regulars in baseball. He opened the 2000 season worse than ever, hitting .188/.278/.226 at the time of his injury. Had he played the entire season, his bat would have cost the Mets between three and four games more than a replacement-level shortstop.

In his absence, the Mets patched together a Melvin Mora/Kurt Abbott solution, but both players were stretched in the more prominent role. At the trade deadline, the Mets picked up Mike Bordick from the Orioles. Bordick didn't hit as well as he did in the AL; nevertheless, his performance for the Mets was slightly above replacement level, and he provided better defense than did Mora and Abbott. It's fair to say, in light of his replacements, that Ordonez's injury was worth at least three wins to the team.

The Mets might want to consider life without Ordonez in 2001. Although Phillips failed to sign Alex Rodriguez, he made a couple of waiver-wire pickups in Desi Relaford and Jorge Velandia. Neither is a star in waiting, but both players could be as good or better than Ordonez, and both come considerably cheaper than St. Rey.

Ordonez's contract and injury status are barriers to a trade, but since there are a few teams, like the Mariners, in the market for shortstops, this could be a chance for the Mets to lighten their payroll and improve their everyday lineup. Sure, they'll have fewer SportsCenter highlights during the season, but they'll have a better chance of being showcased in October.

The absence of Rey Ordonez wasn't the only break the Mets caught in 2000. The Mets never did beat the Braves; it turned out they didn't have to. Instead, the Mets got to face a Cardinals team that couldn't hit left-handed pitching. Just like that, they were in the World Series.

Now that Steve Phillips has reached the Series and secured extensions for himself and Bobby Valentine, the time would seem to have come for him to focus a few years out, to begin planning the next good Mets team. He has chosen, instead, to try and squeeze another year or two out of the Alfonzo/Piazza/Al Leiter squad. Phillips re-signed Rick Reed and gave Kevin Appier and Steve Trachsel a combined $50 million to come pitch in Queens. The average age of the Mets' rotation after these moves is 72. The rest of the team isn't much younger; the only good Met under the age of 29 is Edgardo Alfonzo.

The team has a few pitching prospects on the lower levels and some upper-level hitters like Brian Cole and Alex Escobar who might give Jay Payton a run for the center-field job in 2002, but overall it's not a good system. Unlike the Braves, you can't look at the Mets' farm teams and find the players who will replace the guys currently making big money.

The problem is that the Mets are not going to get much better than they were in 1999 and 2000. If they insist on playing Ordonez and Timoniel Perez and Jay Payton, it will be nearly impossible for them to construct a lineup that can score 750 runs. If the declines of Todd Zeile and Robin Ventura continue, this could be the worst offense in the division.

While the Mets are getting older and more expensive, the rest of the teams in the division are either young and improving or better bets to sustain their levels. It's not hard to envision a scenario in which the Expos and Marlins chase the Mets into the bottom part of the NL East. The Expos and Marlins are good baseball teams with upside. If the Mets focus solely on 90 wins and the 2001 wild card, they're going to find themselves lapped by teams that are building to win 100 games and world championships—for a decade. In guys like Andruw Jones, Rafael Furcal, and Kevin Millwood even the Braves have more good young talent with upside than do the Mets.

Though we're coming down hard on a team playing for the short term, it's worth mentioning that we do admire the job Steve Phillips did for the Mets last year. He had a plan and executed it, which is far better than having no plan and just doing things willy-nilly, like Ed Wade and Cam Bonifay do. But short-term planning only works for a short time, and teams built this way eventually take hard falls. The Orioles of the mid-1990s are a great comp for the current Mets, from the aging roster to the spiraling payroll to the unproductive player-development program. If the Mets don't win in 2001—and they're at best the sixth- or seventh-best team in the league—the whole thing could come crashing down the way it did around Peter Angelos in 1998.

National League

HITTERS (BA: .270, OBP: .340, SLG: .440, EqA: .260)

Kurt Abbott — IF — Bats R — Age 32

YEAR	TEAM	LGE	AB	H	DB	TP	HR	BB	SO	R	RBI	SB	CS	OUT	BA	OBP	SLG	EQA	EQR	DEFENSE			
1998	Oakland	AL	123	34	8	1	2	10	30	18	9	2	1	90	.276	.335	.407	.249	14	25-SS	-7		
1998	Colorado	NL	70	16	4	0	3	2	18	8	13	0	0	54	.229	.259	.414	.217	6				
1999	Colorado	NL	280	67	14	2	7	12	65	35	34	2	2	215	.239	.271	.379	.210	22	52-2B	-5		
2000	NY Mets	NL	159	35	6	1	6	12	48	21	12	1	1	125	.220	.278	.384	.217	14	30-SS	-6	11-2B	-1
2001	Atlanta	NL	194	47	9	1	6	15	56	23	27	1	1	148	.242	.297	.392	.231	19				

He used to provide more power than the average shortstop. Now, Kurt Abbott is indistinguishable from a couple dozen other utility infielders. With Desi Relaford and Jorge Velandia in tow, the Mets released Abbott after the season, and he signed with the Braves. As Bobby Cox's bench players go, he's Rogers Hornsby.

Benny Agbayani — LF — Bats R — Age 29

YEAR	TEAM	LGE	AB	H	DB	TP	HR	BB	SO	R	RBI	SB	CS	OUT	BA	OBP	SLG	EQA	EQR	DEFENSE	
1998	Norfolk	Int	324	81	19	3	8	40	59	34	41	9	4	247	.250	.336	.401	.250	39	71-LF	-7
1999	Norfolk	Int	101	30	5	1	6	12	20	15	23	3	2	73	.297	.379	.545	.297	18	18-CF	-1
1999	NY Mets	NL	278	78	17	3	14	28	57	40	39	4	4	204	.281	.353	.514	.280	42	65-OF	-1
2000	NY Mets	NL	355	101	19	1	15	48	64	56	57	4	5	259	.285	.379	.470	.281	54	83-LF	-3
2001	NY Mets	NL	298	85	16	2	16	48	60	57	61	7	4	217	.285	.384	.513	.302	54		

If you were going to create a folk hero, you'd probably make him look less like a ballplayer than an average guy, have him hail from a faraway place, and let him do something memorable in a big situation. Benny Agbayani isn't a man; he's a fictional character, something Stephen King dreamed up one night on his way home from Fenway. Agbayani is also the Mets' starting left fielder for the foreseeable future and the team's third-best hitter.

Edgardo Alfonzo — 2B — Bats R — Age 27

YEAR	TEAM	LGE	AB	H	DB	TP	HR	BB	SO	R	RBI	SB	CS	OUT	BA	OBP	SLG	EQA	EQR	DEFENSE	
1998	NY Mets	NL	569	163	28	2	19	63	72	100	81	8	3	409	.286	.360	.443	.270	78	144-3B	-1
1999	NY Mets	NL	633	190	33	2	28	76	80	118	103	7	2	445	.300	.378	.491	.289	100	157-2B	-2
2000	NY Mets	NL	551	176	37	2	25	86	66	105	89	3	2	377	.319	.415	.530	.312	103	142-2B	-5
2001	NY Mets	NL	553	175	29	2	29	98	73	118	125	8	1	379	.316	.419	.533	.325	114		

Edgardo Alfonzo had the misfortune of exploding on the league in the same year that another second baseman on a successful team—the Giants' Jeff Kent—had an MVP season. Alfonzo is a phenomenal baseball player with few weaknesses. His peak is going to look a lot like those of Roberto Alomar and Ryne Sandberg, minus the speed but with better defense. The shame is that had Rey Ordonez never defected, Alfonzo might have stayed at shortstop and would now be mentioned in the same breath as the Trinity.

Chris Basak — SS — Bats R — Age 23

YEAR	TEAM	LGE	AB	H	DB	TP	HR	BB	SO	R	RBI	SB	CS	OUT	BA	OBP	SLG	EQA	EQR	DEFENSE	
2000	Pittsfld	NYP	260	74	14	2	1	16	40	28	12	10	6	192	.285	.329	.365	.235	26	57-SS	-3
2001	NY Mets	NL	147	43	6	1	0	13	39	25	14	10	4	108	.293	.350	.347	.251	17		

Chris Basak was a sixth-round pick from the University of Illinois. The Mets hope he will be their shortstop of the future, even though his fielding at the position isn't great. He's tall and has good speed, and scouts think he'll add some power. Basak did lead the team in doubles, and his home-run total of zero can be largely explained by his home park. Some perspective, though: Basak is just two years younger than Alex Rodriguez.

Derek Bell — RF — Bats R — Age 32

YEAR	TEAM	LGE	AB	H	DB	TP	HR	BB	SO	R	RBI	SB	CS	OUT	BA	OBP	SLG	EQA	EQR	DEFENSE	
1998	Houston	NL	643	205	39	2	25	49	118	116	111	12	3	441	.319	.370	.502	.289	99	141-RF	1
1999	Houston	NL	513	121	15	0	14	44	122	57	64	14	6	398	.236	.301	.347	.220	45	112-RF	-11
2000	NY Mets	NL	553	147	29	1	18	57	117	84	66	7	4	410	.266	.340	.420	.255	67	127-RF	-5
2001	Pittsbrg	NL	465	123	15	0	18	51	107	65	72	8	3	345	.265	.337	.413	.255	57		

(Derek Bell *continued*)

It's fair to say that Derek Bell belongs with Garret Anderson, Rey Ordonez, and Jaime Navarro on the list of people we've been pretty hard on over the years. Still, the Mets really could have used Bell—out with a sprained ankle—in the World Series, because Bobby Valentine didn't want to play Bubba Trammell, and Bell would have been a better option than the overmatched Timo Perez. Bell has been signed by the Pirates and will be their everyday right fielder. You go, Cam.

Mike Bordick   SS   Bats R   Age 35

YEAR	TEAM	LGE	AB	H	DB	TP	HR	BB	SO	R	RBI	SB	CS	OUT	BA	OBP	SLG	EQA	EQR	DEFENSE	
1998	Baltimor	AL	466	127	26	1	16	38	58	61	53	5	7	345	.273	.339	.436	.256	57	144-SS	4
1999	Baltimor	AL	630	181	36	7	11	48	93	92	76	13	4	453	.287	.342	.419	.257	76	156-SS	23
2000	Baltimor	AL	390	119	21	1	17	29	65	67	57	6	6	277	.305	.355	.495	.276	55	96-SS	-5
2000	NY Mets	NL	194	51	4	0	5	13	26	17	21	3	1	144	.263	.315	.361	.228	18	51-SS	-4
2001	Baltimor	AL	527	138	20	1	14	44	84	72	73	10	5	394	.262	.319	.383	.243	57		

Like Luis Gonzalez and Steve Finley, Mike Bordick's career path has been atypical, with a flat period during the usual peak years and a steady improvement in his thirties. It's probably time to redo the Bill James career-path study, published in the 1982 *Baseball Abstract*. There are 20 additional years of data and at least a mild perception that players may be peaking later or showing a slower decline in their thirties. We place a lot of importance on the idea of a career path centered on an age-27 peak; even a small shift in overall career-path patterns would have significant repercussions for player evaluation and expectation. Bordick returned to Baltimore for the 2001 season.

Brian Cole   OF   Bats B   Age 22

YEAR	TEAM	LGE	AB	H	DB	TP	HR	BB	SO	R	RBI	SB	CS	OUT	BA	OBP	SLG	EQA	EQR	DEFENSE	
1998	Kingsprt	App	227	51	10	3	3	2	27	18	19	4	4	180	.225	.231	.335	.175	11	48-CF	0
1999	Columbia	SAL	511	129	29	2	12	27	81	61	47	19	8	390	.252	.291	.387	.227	48	116-CF	4
2000	St Lucie	Fla	380	99	18	2	13	21	58	48	43	25	7	288	.261	.300	.421	.244	42	86-OF	-2
2000	Binghmtn	Eas	176	42	6	1	4	10	30	23	19	9	3	137	.239	.282	.352	.215	15	43-RF	-3
2001	NY Mets	NL	483	129	22	2	16	35	81	72	64	28	10	364	.267	.317	.420	.256	60		

Brian Cole is extremely fast, stealing 75 bases in 2000. He rarely walks, despite the team's effort to teach him the strike zone. While small (the Mets' claim that he is 5'9" is generous), he did rope 60 extra-base hits in each of the past two seasons, so there is evidence of power. Some in the organization like him better than Alex Escobar; they're too optimistic.

Alex Escobar   CF   Bats R   Age 22

YEAR	TEAM	LGE	AB	H	DB	TP	HR	BB	SO	R	RBI	SB	CS	OUT	BA	OBP	SLG	EQA	EQR	DEFENSE	
1998	Columbia	SAL	425	102	18	3	16	39	140	52	55	17	4	327	.240	.308	.409	.243	47	101-CF	-7
2000	Binghmtn	Eas	441	107	18	4	14	43	123	58	49	13	4	338	.243	.316	.397	.241	48	119-CF	0
2001	NY Mets	NL	294	73	11	2	9	32	91	44	38	13	2	223	.248	.322	.391	.253	36		

Alex Escobar is the crown jewel of the Mets' depleted farm system. After missing almost the entire 1999 season with a pair of injuries, Escobar played nearly every day in 2000 and didn't suffer any injuries until the second to last day of the playoffs. He was almost as good as advertised in Binghamton: he drew some walks, had good but not great power, and played a solid center field. The Mets were reportedly very pleased with his attitude and work ethic, despite rumors to the contrary. If he stays healthy, he'll be a star.

Matt Franco   PH   Bats L   Age 31

YEAR	TEAM	LGE	AB	H	DB	TP	HR	BB	SO	R	RBI	SB	CS	OUT	BA	OBP	SLG	EQA	EQR	DEFENSE			
1998	NY Mets	NL	165	46	9	2	1	22	24	22	13	0	1	120	.279	.367	.376	.254	20	10-LF	-2		
1999	NY Mets	NL	133	31	5	0	4	26	20	18	20	0	0	102	.233	.358	.361	.250	16				
2000	NY Mets	NL	136	33	4	0	2	19	21	9	14	0	0	103	.243	.335	.316	.226	12	12-1B	-2	11-3B	-3
2000	Norfolk	Int	52	8	2	0	0	2	11	3	1	0	0	44	.154	.185	.192	—	0				
2001	NY Mets	NL	143	34	2	0	3	24	24	18	17	0	0	109	.238	.347	.315	.240	15				

He's the Mets' answer to Dave Hansen, but when the team traded for Lenny Harris, Matt Franco found himself back in Triple-A. Pay no attention to the performance line; as we've said a thousand times, it's impossible to evaluate pinch hitters based on one season's numbers. Franco is a good early-inning pinch hitter who can spell a right-handed-hitting corner man twice a month.

Darryl Hamilton — CF — Bats L — Age 36

YEAR	TEAM	LGE	AB	H	DB	TP	HR	BB	SO	R	RBI	SB	CS	OUT	BA	OBP	SLG	EQA	EQR	DEFENSE	
1998	San Fran	NL	376	113	20	2	1	58	50	67	26	8	8	271	.301	.397	.372	.266	50	91-CF	-1
1998	Colorado	NL	189	56	8	1	4	22	19	27	21	3	1	134	.296	.372	.413	.269	25	45-CF	-1
1999	Colorado	NL	327	86	10	3	3	32	20	53	19	2	4	245	.263	.330	.339	.226	30	82-CF	2
1999	NY Mets	NL	169	56	7	1	5	17	17	18	20	1	3	116	.331	.396	.473	.286	25	45-CF	0
2000	NY Mets	NL	106	29	4	1	1	13	19	20	6	2	0	77	.274	.353	.358	.249	12	23-OF	-1
2001	*NY Mets*	*NL*	*278*	*72*	*9*	*2*	*4*	*39*	*34*	*39*	*34*	*3*	*3*	*209*	*.259*	*.350*	*.349*	*.248*	*32*		

A sprained left foot wiped out his first half and opened the door for Jay Payton to take his job. Darryl Hamilton doesn't have the arm for right field or the legs for center field, which means that even his good on-base skills might not be enough to warrant a roster spot.

Lenny Harris — PH — Bats L — Age 36

YEAR	TEAM	LGE	AB	H	DB	TP	HR	BB	SO	R	RBI	SB	CS	OUT	BA	OBP	SLG	EQA	EQR	DEFENSE	
1998	Cincnnti	NL	123	35	9	0	0	8	8	12	10	1	3	91	.285	.333	.358	.228	11	23-RF	-4
1998	NY Mets	NL	170	41	5	0	7	9	11	19	18	5	2	131	.241	.283	.394	.225	16	39-RF	3
1999	Colorado	NL	155	41	11	0	0	3	6	13	11	1	1	115	.265	.278	.335	.198	10	20-2B	-7
1999	Arizona	NL	29	11	0	0	1	0	1	2	6	1	0	18	.379	.379	.483	.292	4		
2000	Arizona	NL	86	16	2	1	1	2	5	9	13	4	0	70	.186	.205	.267	.147	3	17-3B	-2
2000	NY Mets	NL	140	42	6	3	3	15	16	21	12	7	1	99	.300	.368	.450	.280	21	16-3B	-5
2001	*NY Mets*	*NL*	*196*	*48*	*8*	*1*	*4*	*16*	*16*	*22*	*22*	*4*	*1*	*149*	*.245*	*.302*	*.357*	*.230*	*19*		

It took a few years, but we've caught on to the appeal of Lenny Harris. People think he's Tony Gwynn. He's a short, fat, left-handed hitter with no defensive value and all the power of a watch battery. In bad light, the only difference between them is the uniform.

Joe McEwing — UT — Bats R — Age 28

YEAR	TEAM	LGE	AB	H	DB	TP	HR	BB	SO	R	RBI	SB	CS	OUT	BA	OBP	SLG	EQA	EQR	DEFENSE			
1998	Arkansas	Tex	220	60	15	2	5	14	21	29	28	2	1	161	.273	.318	.427	.247	24	50-LF	9		
1998	Memphis	PCL	325	93	23	5	5	17	39	40	35	8	7	239	.286	.325	.434	.249	37	75-OF	4		
1999	St Louis	NL	515	138	27	4	9	34	82	62	41	5	4	381	.268	.320	.388	.237	52	84-2B	3	52-OF	0
2000	Norfolk	Int	172	39	9	1	4	13	37	23	14	5	2	135	.227	.281	.360	.214	14	16-CF	0	11-3B	1
2000	NY Mets	NL	155	35	14	1	2	3	27	20	19	3	1	121	.226	.245	.368	.198	11	20-LF	1		
2001	*NY Mets*	*NL*	*344*	*85*	*20*	*2*	*7*	*26*	*61*	*40*	*40*	*4*	*1*	*260*	*.247*	*.300*	*.378*	*.234*	*34*				

The plight of players without secondary skills is that they kill you when they hit for a low average. Joe McEwing is a useful bench player—kind of a Rex Hudler for the new millennium—but his aversion to walks and lack of power make him a lousy pinch hitter. Like Hudler, he'll bounce around for a while and have some pretty good years with the bat. Unlike Hudler, he's not clinically insane.

Rey Ordonez — SS — Bats R — Age 30

YEAR	TEAM	LGE	AB	H	DB	TP	HR	BB	SO	R	RBI	SB	CS	OUT	BA	OBP	SLG	EQA	EQR	DEFENSE	
1998	NY Mets	NL	512	132	22	2	1	22	56	50	43	3	6	386	.258	.290	.314	.196	33	145-SS	6
1999	NY Mets	NL	524	135	24	2	1	42	56	47	57	6	4	393	.258	.314	.317	.213	41	150-SS	8
2000	NY Mets	NL	135	26	6	0	0	15	15	10	9	0	0	109	.193	.273	.237	.164	6	40-SS	-3
2001	*NY Mets*	*NL*	*295*	*72*	*13*	*2*	*0*	*29*	*34*	*32*	*25*	*3*	*2*	*225*	*.244*	*.312*	*.302*	*.216*	*24*		

If you're looking for a positive, it's that Rey Ordonez's walk rate was continuing an upward trend when he got hurt. Regardless, he's an overpaid, overrated player who pushes a team away from, not towards, a championship. Trading him to the Mariners for an umbrella and a old Moose costume would help the Mets considerably.

Jay Payton — CF — Bats R — Age 28

YEAR	TEAM	LGE	AB	H	DB	TP	HR	BB	SO	R	RBI	SB	CS	OUT	BA	OBP	SLG	EQA	EQR	DEFENSE			
1998	Norfolk	Int	323	77	13	3	7	20	50	37	25	7	5	251	.238	.284	.362	.213	26	49-LF	-1	25-1B	-2
1998	NY Mets	NL	22	7	1	0	0	1	4	2	1	0	0	15	.318	.348	.364	.241	2				
1999	Norfolk	Int	142	47	11	1	6	9	13	20	25	1	1	96	.331	.374	.549	.298	23	33-LF	-2		
2000	NY Mets	NL	494	142	21	1	17	23	56	60	59	4	11	363	.287	.323	.437	.245	54	128-CF	1		
2001	NY Mets	NL	306	86	14	1	13	21	39	38	51	2	5	225	.281	.327	.461	.262	40				

It really all depends on what organization you call home. The Giants' Calvin Murray is a similar player to Jay Payton: both guys hit left-handers well and can play a good center field (although Payton can't throw). Because the Mets had no other options, Payton played every day and got some Rookie of the Year votes. Murray was Marvin Benard's Legs. Payton is stretched as a regular but would make a fantastic fourth outfielder.

Timoniel Perez — OF — Bats L — Age 24

YEAR	TEAM	LGE	AB	H	DB	TP	HR	BB	SO	R	RBI	SB	CS	OUT	BA	OBP	SLG	EQA	EQR	DEFENSE	
1998	HIR	JpC	234	65	6	1	5	17	0	0	0	4	0	169	.278	.327	.376	.242	24		
1999	HIR	JpW	165	48	9	3	1	26	1	15	19	4	0	117	.291	.420	.400	.292	27		
2000	St Lucie	Fla	31	8	2	0	1	2	1	2	5	1	2	25	.258	.314	.419	.229	3		
2000	Norfolk	Int	291	94	15	4	5	12	26	38	30	9	5	202	.323	.355	.454	.268	38	70-CF	8
2000	NY Mets	NL	50	14	4	1	1	2	5	11	3	1	1	37	.280	.319	.460	.252	6	13-OF	1
2001	NY Mets	NL	321	103	15	3	8	29	22	53	56	4	0	218	.321	.377	.461	.291	50		

If Timoniel Perez puts up a .291 EqA in 2001, Joe Sheehan will ride the 7 train wearing only a diaper and a "Timo Rocks" tattoo. Perez is another Met who would make a better bench player than regular, though he's not even as good as Melvin Mora for that role. He looks like a heck of a defensive outfielder; given the current makeup of the Mets' rotation, having him and Payton covering right-center might almost be worth the offensive sacrifice.

Mike Piazza — C — Bats R — Age 32

YEAR	TEAM	LGE	AB	H	DB	TP	HR	BB	SO	R	RBI	SB	CS	OUT	BA	OBP	SLG	EQA	EQR	DEFENSE	
1998	LosAngls	NL	152	44	6	0	9	11	25	21	30	0	0	108	.289	.337	.507	.274	21	37-C	-3
1998	NY Mets	NL	404	141	26	0	27	46	50	69	79	1	0	263	.349	.418	.614	.332	83	97-C	-5
1999	NY Mets	NL	538	160	22	0	40	44	66	97	116	1	2	380	.297	.352	.561	.291	87	131-C	-8
2000	NY Mets	NL	488	156	24	0	37	51	65	87	106	4	2	334	.320	.387	.596	.314	92	119-C	-9
2001	NY Mets	NL	489	146	21	0	33	60	68	82	111	1	1	344	.299	.375	.544	.306	89		

He becomes a Hall of Famer with his first at-bat in 2001. It's going to be very weird seeing "Florida Marlins" on his plaque; are there even any pictures of him in teal and black? Hell, Bill Daley spent more time in Florida than Mike Piazza did. Of course, Piazza won't need a recount. Forty games at first base every year wouldn't hurt.

Todd Pratt — C — Bats R — Age 34

YEAR	TEAM	LGE	AB	H	DB	TP	HR	BB	SO	R	RBI	SB	CS	OUT	BA	OBP	SLG	EQA	EQR	DEFENSE	
1998	Norfolk	Int	118	35	4	0	5	11	20	12	22	1	0	83	.297	.370	.458	.279	17	10-C	0
1998	NY Mets	NL	70	20	9	1	2	2	19	9	18	0	0	50	.286	.306	.529	.267	9	11-C	0
1999	NY Mets	NL	141	41	4	0	3	13	30	18	20	2	0	100	.291	.363	.383	.258	17	35-C	0
2000	NY Mets	NL	162	44	6	0	8	20	29	32	24	0	0	118	.272	.367	.457	.276	24	44-C	1
2001	NY Mets	NL	145	39	6	0	6	17	30	20	24	0	0	106	.269	.346	.434	.268	20		

Teams with a player this good as their backup catcher have an advantage over teams carrying Matt Walbeck and his ilk. Todd Pratt could have, maybe should have, had a ten-year career as a starter and been as good a player as Terry Steinbach or Don Slaught. He had the misfortune of coming up behind Darren Daulton and going into a slump at exactly the wrong time in 1994.

Marvin Seale — OF — Bats B — Age 22

YEAR	TEAM	LGE	AB	H	DB	TP	HR	BB	SO	R	RBI	SB	CS	OUT	BA	OBP	SLG	EQA	EQR	DEFENSE	
1999	Kingsprt	App	213	41	7	1	1	13	82	23	12	6	2	174	.192	.239	.249	.152	8	55-LF	-4
2000	Columbia	SAL	466	110	19	3	5	37	134	47	26	17	8	364	.236	.300	.322	.212	38	112-CF	-3
2000	St Lucie	Fla	17	4	0	0	1	2	7	4	1	0	0	13	.235	.316	.412	.242	2		
2001	NY Mets	NL	260	63	8	1	2	23	91	35	20	17	4	201	.242	.304	.304	.223	24		

National League

Marvin Seale was a fan favorite in Columbia, perhaps because he can hit a little, unlike most of his teammates. He doesn't possess much raw power but has a quick work ethic and good wrists, so he should add some. Seale has a strong enough glove to stay in center field for now; he won't have the bat to play a corner outfield spot. With the Mets' system as depleted as it is, Seale will get plenty of chances to become a prospect.

Tsuyoshi Shinjo — OF — Bats R — Age 29

YEAR	TEAM	LGE	AB	H	DB	TP	HR	BB	SO	R	RBI	SB	CS	OUT	BA	OBP	SLG	EQA	EQR	DEFENSE
2000	HAN	JpC	516	131	23	1	23	32	92	67	76	15	6	391	.254	.299	.436	.242	56	

The Mets signed Tsuyoshi Shinjo about two weeks after the Mariners reached an agreement with Ichiro Suzuki. Unlike Suzuki, Shinjo is a low-average slugger in the mold of Vinny Castilla. He is supposed to be a very good defensive outfielder, winning the Japanese version of the Gold Glove seven times.

Jorge Toca — 1B/LF — Bats R — Age 30

YEAR	TEAM	LGE	AB	H	DB	TP	HR	BB	SO	R	RBI	SB	CS	OUT	BA	OBP	SLG	EQA	EQR	DEFENSE			
1999	Binghmtn	Eas	280	66	10	1	12	21	49	40	41	2	2	216	.236	.295	.407	.231	28	49-LF	1	18-1B	0
1999	Norfolk	Int	174	49	10	1	3	3	25	19	20	0	2	127	.282	.296	.402	.225	15	43-1B	2		
2000	Norfolk	Int	453	108	20	2	9	11	81	47	55	6	6	351	.238	.261	.351	.196	30	77-1B	-8	18-LF	-6
2001	NY Mets	NL	284	69	11	1	7	14	60	25	31	0	0	215	.243	.279	.363	.217	24				
2001	NY Mets	NL	479	127	22	2	14	27	81	59	68	7	5	357	.265	.304	.407	.237	49				

The two Wilton projections reflect his two ages: he claims to be 26, not that it really matters. The second projection is for the 1975 birth date. After coming over as Hyped Cuban Signee #15, Jorge Toca hasn't hit enough to make us forget Orestes Destrade, much less to challenge Todd Zeile for a job in the big city.

Bubba Trammell — Batter's Box — Bats R — Age 29

YEAR	TEAM	LGE	AB	H	DB	TP	HR	BB	SO	R	RBI	SB	CS	OUT	BA	OBP	SLG	EQA	EQR	DEFENSE	
1998	Durham	Int	218	55	9	0	12	31	43	36	36	4	1	164	.252	.345	.459	.268	31	56-RF	-1
1998	TampaBay	AL	199	59	17	1	13	15	40	29	35	0	2	142	.296	.346	.588	.292	33	32-LF	-3
1999	TampaBay	AL	280	82	16	0	15	40	34	47	37	0	2	200	.293	.383	.511	.292	46	64-LF	6
1999	Durham	Int	186	44	7	0	6	11	38	19	24	0	0	142	.237	.279	.371	.213	15	41-LF	-2
2000	TampaBay	AL	187	52	11	2	7	19	27	18	31	3	0	135	.278	.351	.471	.275	27	39-LF	-2
2000	NY Mets	NL	57	13	3	0	3	7	18	9	12	1	0	44	.228	.313	.439	.251	7	13-RF	-1
2001	San Dieg	NL	308	80	18	1	13	42	59	46	49	4	1	229	.260	.349	.451	.279	47		

He gets less respect than Chris Kahrl at Pete Newell's Big Man Camp. Nevertheless, Bubba Trammell has hit well every time he's been given a regular job. He was traded to the Padres after the season, so they're well-situated for the mid-April injury to Tony Gwynn. Trammell is going to have a three- or four-year run of 900 OPSs once he finds a manager who will just play him.

Jorge Velandia — SS — Bats R — Age 26

YEAR	TEAM	LGE	AB	H	DB	TP	HR	BB	SO	R	RBI	SB	CS	OUT	BA	OBP	SLG	EQA	EQR	DEFENSE	
1998	Edmonton	PCL	482	120	25	1	5	30	51	50	44	6	4	366	.249	.298	.336	.212	38	125-SS	19
1999	Oakland	AL	48	9	1	0	0	2	12	4	2	2	0	39	.188	.234	.208	.136	1	17-2B	3
2000	Sacramen	PCL	302	75	14	1	8	26	53	44	44	3	2	229	.248	.316	.381	.233	30	81-SS	10
2000	Oakland	AL	24	3	1	0	0	0	5	1	2	0	0	21	.125	.161	.167	—	0		
2001	NY Mets	NL	255	57	7	0	7	24	45	25	26	3	1	199	.224	.290	.333	.217	22		

Take Rey Ordonez. Subtract the back story, the reputation, and some athleticism. Add more range, better hands, 15 doubles, and about $3 million in cash saved. Stir briskly in a wooden bowl, pour into a mold, and heat at 375 degrees for two hours. Congratulations, you've made a Jorge Velandia. He's a defensive replacement looking for an opportunity.

Robin Ventura — 3B — Bats L — Age 33

YEAR	TEAM	LGE	AB	H	DB	TP	HR	BB	SO	R	RBI	SB	CS	OUT	BA	OBP	SLG	EQA	EQR	DEFENSE	
1998	ChiSox	AL	590	161	31	4	23	78	99	87	92	1	1	430	.273	.359	.456	.272	83	153-3B	19
1999	NY Mets	NL	593	176	32	0	33	65	103	85	114	1	1	418	.297	.369	.518	.290	95	154-3B	18
2000	NY Mets	NL	475	110	21	1	24	68	85	59	80	3	5	370	.232	.330	.432	.252	59	120-3B	12
2001	NY Mets	NL	462	120	22	1	24	75	87	75	87	1	1	343	.260	.363	.468	.284	74		

(Robin Ventura *continued*)

Robin Ventura fought nagging injuries in 2000, so it's hard to say with certainty how much of last year's decline is permanent. Between injuries and off years, he's really been good at the plate only one season in the last four. That projection seems generous; his 1998 level is where the smart money is going.

Ty Wigginton   2B/3B   Bats R   Age 23

YEAR	TEAM	LGE	AB	H	DB	TP	HR	BB	SO	R	RBI	SB	CS	OUT	BA	OBP	SLG	EQA	EQR	DEFENSE	
1998	Pittsfld	NYP	279	59	12	2	6	10	77	26	19	4	1	221	.211	.240	.333	.183	16	49-2B -2	
1999	St Lucie	Fla	463	108	18	2	16	41	95	50	49	4	5	361	.233	.298	.384	.225	43	117-2B -10	
2000	Binghmtn	Eas	453	110	20	2	16	16	116	49	55	3	3	346	.243	.270	.402	.217	38	65-2B -11	45-3B -2
2001	*NY Mets*	*NL*	*392*	*97*	*14*	*1*	*15*	*30*	*102*	*42*	*54*	*3*	*2*	*297*	*.247*	*.301*	*.403*	*.240*	*42*		

Ty Wigginton looked like a decent prospect after his solid 1999, but his plate discipline dissolved when he reached Double-A in 2000. That, coupled with a late-season move to third base, probably kills any shot he had of a career as a starter because he doesn't hit enough to play third base every day. The Mets like his all-out style of playing, but if Double-A pitchers threw him for a loop, major-league pitchers will have him for an appetizer.

Todd Zeile   1B   Bats R   Age 35

YEAR	TEAM	LGE	AB	H	DB	TP	HR	BB	SO	R	RBI	SB	CS	OUT	BA	OBP	SLG	EQA	EQR	DEFENSE
1998	LosAngls	NL	161	42	6	1	8	9	22	24	29	1	1	120	.261	.304	.460	.248	18	36-3B -9
1998	Florida	NL	239	71	11	1	7	30	32	39	40	2	3	171	.297	.380	.439	.274	34	57-3B 4
1998	Texas	AL	178	46	15	1	6	28	29	26	27	1	0	132	.258	.362	.455	.274	26	50-3B -3
1999	Texas	AL	580	168	35	1	26	50	86	76	93	1	2	414	.290	.350	.488	.274	82	151-3B -6
2000	NY Mets	NL	551	147	36	3	21	66	80	65	75	3	4	408	.267	.347	.457	.266	74	142-1B 3
2001	*NY Mets*	*NL*	*511*	*134*	*27*	*1*	*21*	*67*	*79*	*76*	*85*	*2*	*2*	*379*	*.262*	*.348*	*.442*	*.271*	*72*	

Last year looks like a decent season, and for a third baseman—even one who fields like Todd Zeile—it would have been one. In 2000, though, offensive levels are such that a .266 EqA from your first baseman is a problem. It's not like Zeile saves a bunch of runs with his glove or the Mets get so much offense from other spots that they can carry him. Signing Zeile was a panic move in the wake of the loss of John Olerud; he's not pushing the Mets towards anything.

PITCHERS (ERA: 4.50, H/9: 9.00, HR/9: 1.00, BB/9: 3.00, K/9: 6.00, KW: 1.00, PERA: 4.50)

J.D. Arteaga   Throws L   Age 26

YEAR	TEAM	LGE	IP	H	ER	HR	BB	K	ERA	W	L	H/9	HR/9	BB/9	K/9	KW	PERA
1998	St Lucie	Fla	35.0	36	15	2	9	15	3.86	2	2	9.26	0.51	2.31	3.86	0.83	3.87
1998	Binghmtn	Eas	111.3	122	52	11	26	57	4.20	6	6	9.86	0.89	2.10	4.61	1.10	4.51
1999	Binghmtn	Eas	26.0	33	23	4	15	14	7.96	1	2	11.42	1.38	5.19	4.85	0.47	7.25
2000	Binghmtn	Eas	105.0	124	63	10	28	45	5.40	4	8	10.63	0.86	2.40	3.86	0.80	5.06

J.D. Arteaga returned from a lost season of shoulder injuries to do what he typically does: get guys out with his assortment of slop. Arteaga has a great change-up that isn't much different from his 81-mph fastball, so if he wasn't left-handed, he'd be a nonentity. His control probably isn't good enough to get him to the majors; that he's come even this far is an upset.

Armando Benitez   Throws R   Age 28

YEAR	TEAM	LGE	IP	H	ER	HR	BB	K	ERA	W	L	H/9	HR/9	BB/9	K/9	KW	PERA
1998	Baltimor	AL	67.3	46	26	9	34	80	3.48	4	3	6.15	1.20	4.54	10.69	1.18	3.68
1999	NY Mets	NL	76.0	43	17	4	35	108	2.01	6	2	5.09	0.47	4.14	12.79	1.54	2.36
2000	NY Mets	NL	74.0	41	24	10	33	88	2.92	5	3	4.99	1.22	4.01	10.70	1.33	2.90

Armando Benitez didn't get settled until after Memorial Day, carrying an ERA in the 4.00s and coughing up some ugly blown saves. Once in gear, he was the most unhittable pitcher in baseball—the skinny guy in Boston included—for three months. He's right behind Mariano Rivera and Trevor Hoffman as the third-best closer in baseball.

Eric Cammack — Throws R — Age 25

YEAR	TEAM	LGE	IP	H	ER	HR	BB	K	ERA	W	L	H/9	HR/9	BB/9	K/9	KW	PERA
1998	Columbia	SAL	28.0	21	21	4	17	22	6.75	1	2	6.75	1.29	5.46	7.07	0.65	4.47
1998	St Lucie	Fla	32.0	26	18	4	17	30	5.06	2	2	7.31	1.13	4.78	8.44	0.88	4.37
1999	Binghmtn	Eas	52.7	33	21	3	38	51	3.59	3	3	5.64	0.51	6.49	8.72	0.67	3.51
2000	Norfolk	Int	60.3	39	15	3	31	50	2.24	5	2	5.82	0.45	4.62	7.46	0.81	2.86
2000	NY Mets	NL	10.0	7	7	1	9	8	6.30	0	1	6.30	0.90	8.10	7.20	0.44	4.98

He's a strange case, a pitcher who has neither started a professional game nor been a full-time closer. Eric Cammack's minor-league performance has been astounding: he's a power ground-ball pitcher with great ratios and run prevention. With the Mets collecting middle relievers like Keith Law collects Pokèmon cards, it's hard to see where Cammack fits, but he's earned a chance at a job.

Dennis Cook — Throws L — Age 38

YEAR	TEAM	LGE	IP	H	ER	HR	BB	K	ERA	W	L	H/9	HR/9	BB/9	K/9	KW	PERA
1998	NY Mets	NL	64.7	61	23	6	26	64	3.20	4	3	8.49	0.84	3.62	8.91	1.23	4.29
1999	NY Mets	NL	61.0	50	27	11	23	57	3.98	4	3	7.38	1.62	3.39	8.41	1.24	4.36
2000	NY Mets	NL	57.3	62	34	8	27	44	5.34	2	4	9.73	1.26	4.24	6.91	0.81	5.71

Strange but true: last year marked the first time Dennis Cook had ever pitched for the same team in three consecutive seasons. He's miscast in the situational left-hander role, despite the fact that his innings per appearance have declined for five straight seasons. He drops down on occasion; the rest of the time he comes over the top and doesn't present the problems a Mike Myers does.

Mike Cox — Throws L — Age 23

YEAR	TEAM	LGE	IP	H	ER	HR	BB	K	ERA	W	L	H/9	HR/9	BB/9	K/9	KW	PERA
2000	Pittsfld	NYP	52.0	56	43	14	40	37	7.44	1	5	9.69	2.42	6.92	6.40	0.46	8.06

Mike Cox joined Pittsfield after the Mets selected him out of Pan American University in the 18th round of the 2000 draft. He didn't have much trouble adjusting to the pros. He can touch 90 mph but gets more hitters out with his breaking stuff and his off-speed pitch. Because of this, he often has to work deep into the count, which may hurt him at higher levels. He's a bit of a project, but the early signs are good.

John Franco — Throws L — Age 40

YEAR	TEAM	LGE	IP	H	ER	HR	BB	K	ERA	W	L	H/9	HR/9	BB/9	K/9	KW	PERA
1998	NY Mets	NL	62.0	65	29	5	28	48	4.21	3	4	9.44	0.73	4.06	6.97	0.86	4.92
1999	NY Mets	NL	39.7	39	13	1	16	35	2.95	3	1	8.85	0.23	3.63	7.94	1.09	3.87
2000	NY Mets	NL	54.0	46	23	6	22	47	3.83	3	3	7.67	1.00	3.67	7.83	1.07	4.00

His three-year deal, in addition to being kind of silly, should mean he'll retire as the career leader in appearances. He's about two seasons behind Jesse Orosco, who threw 2 1/3 innings in 2000 at the age of 91. John Franco will set up Armando Benitez until he slips a little more, then turn into... Orosco.

Dicky Gonzalez — Throws R — Age 22

YEAR	TEAM	LGE	IP	H	ER	HR	BB	K	ERA	W	L	H/9	HR/9	BB/9	K/9	KW	PERA
1998	Columbia	SAL	102.0	111	70	17	18	50	6.18	3	8	9.79	1.50	1.59	4.41	1.39	4.91
1998	St Lucie	Fla	42.0	49	29	15	16	13	6.21	1	4	10.50	3.21	3.43	2.79	0.41	7.91
1999	St Lucie	Fla	155.0	162	83	24	37	86	4.82	7	10	9.41	1.39	2.15	4.99	1.16	4.80
2000	Binghmtn	Eas	138.0	136	88	22	37	90	5.74	5	10	8.87	1.43	2.41	5.87	1.22	4.64

Dicky Gonzalez just keeps performing despite scouting reports that would appear to paint him as a minor-league lifer. He just touches 90 with his fastball, and his off-speed stuff isn't great, but his control is incredible. It allows him to work hitters inside and outside and rack up strikeouts. His 3.84 ERA in 2000 was his worst since 1997, though his indicators remained strong. He'll have to prove himself anew at every level.

Jeremy Griffiths — Throws R — Age 23

YEAR	TEAM	LGE	IP	H	ER	HR	BB	K	ERA	W	L	H/9	HR/9	BB/9	K/9	KW	PERA
1999	Kingsprt	App	69.0	72	49	14	46	29	6.39	2	6	9.39	1.83	6.00	3.78	0.32	6.85
2000	Columbia	SAL	113.3	137	116	30	51	64	9.21	2	11	10.88	2.38	4.05	5.08	0.63	7.51

Jeremy Griffiths is a big kid who hasn't quite yet figured out his physique. He has a hard fastball and a habit of throwing it to the next zip code: over the hitter's head, behind him, to the backstop, you name it. He's not Brad Pennington wild, so he can probably figure it out. The Mets might have something here if they teach Griffiths a more effective breaking pitch.

Mike Hampton — Throws L — Age 28

YEAR	TEAM	LGE	IP	H	ER	HR	BB	K	ERA	W	L	H/9	HR/9	BB/9	K/9	KW	PERA
1998	Houston	NL	202.0	220	92	20	77	111	4.10	11	11	9.80	0.89	3.43	4.95	0.72	5.04
1999	Houston	NL	231.3	198	80	12	87	149	3.11	16	10	7.70	0.47	3.38	5.80	0.86	3.39
2000	NY Mets	NL	210.7	189	84	10	85	126	3.59	13	10	8.07	0.43	3.63	5.38	0.74	3.65

There is no story in baseball this year more interesting than the Rockies' $180-million investment in their rotation. While Mike Hampton and Denny Neagle are on opposite ends of the ground-ball/fly-ball spectrum, they are both fastball/change-up pitchers, which is what the experiment is about.

Hampton's so-so peripherals are a concern; pitchers with his walk and strikeout data are poor bets to sustain success. Hampton has many of the characteristics of Tommy John pitchers—he gets a ton of ground balls, controls the running game, and doesn't give up home runs—which has allowed him to be successful while walking 80 men a year. The extra pitches he'll need to throw at altitude may be the proverbial back-breaking straw.

Bobby J. Jones — Throws R — Age 31

YEAR	TEAM	LGE	IP	H	ER	HR	BB	K	ERA	W	L	H/9	HR/9	BB/9	K/9	KW	PERA
1998	NY Mets	NL	185.3	186	96	26	50	93	4.66	9	12	9.03	1.26	2.43	4.52	0.93	4.56
1999	NY Mets	NL	57.3	65	35	3	10	26	5.49	2	4	10.20	0.47	1.57	4.08	1.30	4.09
2000	NY Mets	NL	149.3	164	85	24	42	71	5.12	6	11	9.88	1.45	2.53	4.28	0.85	5.30
2000	Norfolk	Int	22.0	31	16	7	4	13	6.55	1	1	12.68	2.86	1.64	5.32	1.63	8.03

Give Bobby Jones some credit: he took his June demotion very well for a seven-year veteran. After three starts at Norfolk, he returned and filled a big hole for the Mets at the back of their rotation, posting a 3.69 ERA in 19 starts. The Kevin Appier and Steve Trachsel signings leave him in limbo; he'll be a low-upside innings-muncher wherever he lands.

Bobby M. Jones — Throws L — Age 29

YEAR	TEAM	LGE	IP	H	ER	HR	BB	K	ERA	W	L	H/9	HR/9	BB/9	K/9	KW	PERA
1998	Colorado	NL	140.0	150	73	8	47	89	4.69	7	9	9.64	0.51	3.02	5.72	0.95	4.38
1999	Colorado	NL	116.0	125	66	14	51	62	5.12	5	8	9.70	1.09	3.96	4.81	0.61	5.40
2000	Norfolk	Int	124.3	122	73	17	61	71	5.28	5	9	8.83	1.23	4.42	5.14	0.58	5.22
2000	NY Mets	NL	21.0	18	11	2	12	17	4.71	1	1	7.71	0.86	5.14	7.29	0.71	4.45

The Mets' depth in the bullpen meant they had no real use for this Bobby Jones, who'd been acquired when the team dumped Masato Yoshii. Don't expect greatness, but keep in mind that he's at an age where left-handers of his ilk are prone to a Great Leap Forward. His performances have never really been bad, either. If given an opportunity, Jones could be a real surprise in the middle of a rotation.

Al Leiter — Throws L — Age 35

YEAR	TEAM	LGE	IP	H	ER	HR	BB	K	ERA	W	L	H/9	HR/9	BB/9	K/9	KW	PERA
1998	NY Mets	NL	184.0	149	56	9	68	141	2.74	14	6	7.29	0.44	3.33	6.90	1.04	3.13
1999	NY Mets	NL	206.7	202	101	19	80	136	4.40	10	13	8.80	0.83	3.48	5.92	0.85	4.40
2000	NY Mets	NL	201.0	174	82	19	65	166	3.67	12	10	7.79	0.85	2.91	7.43	1.28	3.62

The notion that a game should be a particular pitcher's "to win" should have died last October 26, but bad ideas are often resilient. Here's hoping Al Leiter's last ten pitches of 2000 don't overshadow the very good year he had. By some measures, it was the best season of his career. He's not a real strong bet to repeat at this level.

Pat Mahomes — Throws R — Age 30

YEAR	TEAM	LGE	IP	H	ER	HR	BB	K	ERA	W	L	H/9	HR/9	BB/9	K/9	KW	PERA
1999	Norfolk	Int	36.3	37	17	7	12	16	4.21	2	2	9.17	1.73	2.97	3.96	0.67	5.33
1999	NY Mets	NL	61.7	43	24	7	32	43	3.50	4	3	6.28	1.02	4.67	6.28	0.67	3.63
2000	NY Mets	NL	92.0	95	60	15	57	63	5.87	3	7	9.29	1.47	5.58	6.16	0.55	6.24

It was a rough season for Pat Mahomes, who rediscovered his love of watching baseballs travel a long, long way. Michael Wolverton's system pegs Mahomes as the third-worst reliever in baseball in 2000, a far cry from his career-saving 1999 performance. The Mets have a right-handed closer, two right-handed setup men, and a right-handed middle man ahead of Mahomes, so he'll need a lot of luck to even get a chance at returning to his 1999 level. Signed by Texas.

Jose Nunez — Throws L — Age 22

YEAR	TEAM	LGE	IP	H	ER	HR	BB	K	ERA	W	L	H/9	HR/9	BB/9	K/9	KW	PERA
1999	Kingsprt	App	64.7	78	41	14	19	24	5.71	2	5	10.86	1.95	2.64	3.34	0.63	6.44
2000	Columbia	SAL	85.3	93	51	14	29	53	5.38	3	6	9.81	1.48	3.06	5.59	0.91	5.50

Jose Nunez made a few spot starts for Capital City but spent most of the year in the bullpen, where he had more success. He doesn't have much pop to his fastball, so he succeeds by changing speeds and working both sides of the plate. The Dodgers took him in the Rule 5 draft; they have no established left-handed relievers, so he could stick. Tired of lukewarm reviews of pitching prospects? Flip ahead to the Cardinals' chapter.

Rick Reed — Throws R — Age 35

YEAR	TEAM	LGE	IP	H	ER	HR	BB	K	ERA	W	L	H/9	HR/9	BB/9	K/9	KW	PERA
1998	NY Mets	NL	201.0	204	89	34	28	124	3.99	11	11	9.13	1.52	1.25	5.55	2.21	4.41
1999	NY Mets	NL	144.3	156	73	23	41	87	4.55	7	9	9.73	1.43	2.56	5.42	1.06	5.21
2000	NY Mets	NL	176.7	185	86	27	29	101	4.38	9	11	9.42	1.38	1.48	5.15	1.74	4.52

Rick Reed has had one hellish career path, so it's hard to not feel good about him finally having a payday, but the three-year, $24 million contract he signed last November is a terrible risk for the Mets. Reed has suffered from nagging injuries the past couple of seasons, he works very close to the edge, and it's not like his performance since 1997 has been anything special.

Jerrod Riggan — Throws R — Age 27

YEAR	TEAM	LGE	IP	H	ER	HR	BB	K	ERA	W	L	H/9	HR/9	BB/9	K/9	KW	PERA
1998	Columbia	SAL	35.7	42	31	11	21	16	7.82	1	3	10.60	2.78	5.30	4.04	0.38	8.28
1999	St Lucie	Fla	65.0	72	44	10	33	35	6.09	2	5	9.97	1.38	4.57	4.85	0.53	6.13
2000	Binghmtn	Eas	60.0	47	11	3	20	46	1.65	6	1	7.05	0.45	3.00	6.90	1.15	2.89

Jerrod Riggan was a lousy starter in the Angels' organization when he asked for his release, got it, and signed with the Mets before the 1998 season. Converted to relief, he improved his performance dramatically, but nothing portended his 1.11 ERA in 2000 with no blown saves in 28 opportunities. Riggan can touch the low 90s with his fastball and has a decent slider; his split-fingered fastball is his out pitch. Despite the crowd in Queens, he should appear in the Mets' bullpen mix this summer.

Jason Roach — Throws R — Age 25

YEAR	TEAM	LGE	AB	H	DB	TP	HR	BB	SO	R	RBI	SB	CS	OUT	BA	OBP	SLG	EQA	EQR	DEFENSE		
1998	Columbia	SAL	380	84	18	1	12	21	127	38	45	1	0	296	.221	.267	.368	.208	29	32-3B -5	25-1B 0	
1999	St Lucie	Fla	413	80	13	0	13	22	141	38	46	3	0	333	.194	.242	.320	.180	23	86-3B 0	13-1B 0	

YEAR	TEAM	LGE	IP	H	ER	HR	BB	K	ERA	W	L	H/9	HR/9	BB/9	K/9	KW	PERA
2000	Pittsfld	NYP	24.0	19	12	0	10	11	4.50	1	2	7.13	0.00	3.75	4.13	0.55	2.80
2000	St Lucie	Fla	44.0	42	19	6	17	11	3.89	3	2	8.59	1.23	3.48	2.25	0.32	4.70

Jason Roach hit .215/.280/.377 as a third baseman for St. Lucie in 1999, at which point the Mets asked him if he wanted to try pitching. He jumped at the chance since he had pitched a bit for North Carolina-Wilmington. He now sports a 2.48 career ERA in 83⅓ innings thanks to a 91-mph fastball, a good change-up, and a feel for pitching. His strikeout rate dropped off when he moved back up to St. Lucie, so he still has some work to do.

Grant Roberts — Throws R — Age 23

YEAR	TEAM	LGE	IP	H	ER	HR	BB	K	ERA	W	L	H/9	HR/9	BB/9	K/9	KW	PERA
1998	St Lucie	Fla	64.3	78	49	21	45	41	6.85	2	5	10.91	2.94	6.30	5.74	0.46	9.05
1999	Binghmtn	Eas	123.7	134	83	12	48	59	6.04	4	10	9.75	0.87	3.49	4.29	0.61	5.01
1999	Norfolk	Int	27.0	32	15	1	11	22	5.00	1	2	10.67	0.33	3.67	7.33	1.00	5.10
2000	Norfolk	Int	150.0	150	66	7	62	88	3.96	9	8	9.00	0.42	3.72	5.28	0.71	4.20

With the Mets' signing of lots of pitchers born in the 1960s and their win-now focus, Grant Roberts is likely to get his first rotation job in another organization. He was the team's best pitching prospect about three years ago and is only now returning to his pre-surgery form. He'll help his new team starting in 2002.

Rich Rodriguez — Throws L — Age 38

YEAR	TEAM	LGE	IP	H	ER	HR	BB	K	ERA	W	L	H/9	HR/9	BB/9	K/9	KW	PERA
1998	San Fran	NL	62.7	67	29	8	19	36	4.16	3	4	9.62	1.15	2.73	5.17	0.95	4.92
1999	San Fran	NL	55.0	58	32	8	25	37	5.24	2	4	9.49	1.31	4.09	6.05	0.74	5.57
2000	NY Mets	NL	36.0	56	37	7	13	15	9.25	1	3	14.00	1.75	3.25	3.75	0.58	8.33
2000	Norfolk	Int	19.3	17	8	3	6	11	3.72	1	1	7.91	1.40	2.79	5.12	0.92	4.16

Rich Rodriguez was the second-worst reliever in baseball, just ahead of teammate Mahomes. The two ruined the performance statistics of what otherwise was actually a very good bullpen. Rodriguez is left-handed and only 38, so he's probably got 15 to 18 years left.

Glendon Rusch — Throws L — Age 26

YEAR	TEAM	LGE	IP	H	ER	HR	BB	K	ERA	W	L	H/9	HR/9	BB/9	K/9	KW	PERA
1998	KansasCy	AL	153.0	177	89	18	42	87	5.24	6	11	10.41	1.06	2.47	5.12	1.04	5.18
1999	Omaha	PCL	110.0	133	64	11	35	68	5.24	4	8	10.88	0.90	2.86	5.56	0.97	5.45
2000	NY Mets	NL	183.7	190	89	18	38	131	4.36	9	11	9.31	0.88	1.86	6.42	1.72	4.09

For the many people who think the only thing that matters in building a winner is money, recall that the Kansas City Royals gave Glendon Rusch to the Mets in exchange for something called Dan Murray. That's decision-making, not check-writing. Rusch could easily be the Mets' best pitcher in 2001. Something to watch: he pitched a hell of a lot better when he got an extra day's rest between starts.

Pat Strange — Throws — Age 20

YEAR	TEAM	LGE	IP	H	ER	HR	BB	K	ERA	W	L	H/9	HR/9	BB/9	K/9	KW	PERA
1999	Columbia	SAL	143.0	139	60	8	39	52	3.78	8	8	8.75	0.50	2.45	3.27	0.67	3.64
2000	St Lucie	Fla	80.0	80	59	10	39	45	6.64	2	7	9.00	1.13	4.39	5.06	0.58	5.19
2000	Binghmtn	Eas	52.7	60	29	3	31	23	4.96	2	4	10.25	0.51	5.30	3.93	0.37	5.69

Pat Strange has good stuff, but he's an injury waiting to happen. His delivery is about as violent as a Tarantino flick, and he has worse mechanics than a backwoods auto shop. He stayed healthy throughout 2000, but that's not likely to last unless he gets some quality instruction.

Tyler Walker — Throws R — Age 25

YEAR	TEAM	LGE	IP	H	ER	HR	BB	K	ERA	W	L	H/9	HR/9	BB/9	K/9	KW	PERA
1998	Columbia	SAL	104.0	126	75	18	51	50	6.49	3	9	10.90	1.56	4.41	4.33	0.49	6.79
1999	St Lucie	Fla	70.7	68	44	14	38	36	5.60	3	5	8.66	1.78	4.84	4.58	0.47	5.88
1999	Binghmtn	Eas	63.3	81	54	15	32	36	7.67	1	6	11.51	2.13	4.55	5.12	0.56	7.83
2000	Binghmtn	Eas	112.3	84	47	5	60	67	3.77	6	6	6.73	0.40	4.81	5.37	0.56	3.35
2000	Norfolk	Int	25.0	29	8	1	9	13	2.88	2	1	10.44	0.36	3.24	4.68	0.72	4.81

Tyler Walker recovered from a dismal 1999 in Double-A to post superb numbers in his second go-round, including an outstanding 82 hits allowed in 121 innings. He runs his fastball into the low 90s and has a terrific change-up. He had shoulder surgery after just two appearances in the Arizona Fall League; he's expected back for the start of the season.

National League

Turk Wendell — Throws R — Age 34

YEAR	TEAM	LGE	IP	H	ER	HR	BB	K	ERA	W	L	H/9	HR/9	BB/9	K/9	KW	PERA
1998	NY Mets	NL	73.0	61	26	5	31	47	3.21	5	3	7.52	0.62	3.82	5.79	0.76	3.60
1999	NY Mets	NL	83.0	78	30	9	32	65	3.25	5	4	8.46	0.98	3.47	7.05	1.02	4.35
2000	NY Mets	NL	80.0	59	34	9	35	61	3.83	5	4	6.64	1.01	3.94	6.86	0.87	3.53

He's been as consistent a middle reliever as you'll find in the age of specialization. Four of his last five seasons, including the three above, are pretty much indistinguishable from each other. He's back with the Mets for three years and a little over $9 million; if age catches up with him, the Mets have plenty of fallback positions.

Jae Weong Seo — Throws R — Age 24

YEAR	TEAM	LGE	IP	H	ER	HR	BB	K	ERA	W	L	H/9	HR/9	BB/9	K/9	KW	PERA
1998	St Lucie	Fla	33.7	33	22	4	13	23	5.88	1	3	8.82	1.07	3.48	6.15	0.88	4.60
1999	St Lucie	Fla	14.0	11	5	0	3	8	3.21	1	1	7.07	0.00	1.93	5.14	1.33	2.04

Jae Weong Seo is considered one of the Mets' top prospects despite making just 13 appearances in three seasons since coming to the States. He spent the entire 2000 season rehabbing from May 1999 Tommy John surgery. The Mets must have seen enough from him to think he's going to recover, because they added him to their 40-man roster in November. Before the surgery, he had electric stuff and good control. He's expected to start 2001 at Binghamton.

Rick White — Throws R — Age 32

YEAR	TEAM	LGE	IP	H	ER	HR	BB	K	ERA	W	L	H/9	HR/9	BB/9	K/9	KW	PERA
1998	Durham	Int	51.0	60	29	4	11	21	5.12	2	4	10.59	0.71	1.94	3.71	0.95	4.69
1998	TampaBay	AL	67.3	61	28	7	20	36	3.74	4	3	8.15	0.94	2.67	4.81	0.90	3.82
1999	TampaBay	AL	107.3	122	48	7	30	77	4.02	6	6	10.23	0.59	2.52	6.46	1.28	4.58
2000	TampaBay	AL	70.3	53	25	6	20	45	3.20	5	3	6.78	0.77	2.56	5.76	1.13	2.88
2000	NY Mets	NL	27.3	25	13	2	10	17	4.28	1	2	8.23	0.66	3.29	5.60	0.85	3.81

Rick White is a good example of the kind of capable pitcher who floats between Triple-A and the major leagues. The difference between him and people like Johnny Ruffin and Chad Bradford is that White got lucky. The difference between him and people like Ricky Bottalico and Jose Mesa is that White didn't rack up a bunch of saves five years ago. Labels should matter less than performance.

Support-Neutral Statistics — NEW YORK METS — Park Effect: -13.1%

PITCHER	GS	IP	R	SNW	SNL	SNPCT	W	L	RA	APW	SNVA	SNWAR
Mike Hampton	33	217.7	89	14.1	9.2	.606	15	10	3.68	2.6	2.3	4.2
Bobby J. Jones	27	154.7	90	8.9	9.7	.479	11	6	5.24	-0.7	-0.5	1.0
Bobby M. Jones	1	4.0	7	0.0	0.8	.048	0	1	15.75	-0.5	-0.4	-0.3
Al Leiter	31	208.0	84	13.5	8.8	.606	16	8	3.63	2.6	2.2	4.0
Pat Mahomes	5	27.0	19	1.3	2.1	.386	0	1	6.33	-0.4	-0.3	-0.1
Bill Pulsipher	2	6.7	9	0.1	1.3	.070	0	2	12.15	-0.5	-0.6	-0.5
Rick Reed	30	184.0	90	11.4	9.4	.548	11	5	4.40	0.8	0.9	2.5
Grant Roberts	1	1.3	7	0.0	0.9	.001	0	0	47.25	-0.6	-0.4	-0.4
Glendon Rusch	30	188.7	89	11.9	9.4	.558	10	11	4.25	1.1	1.1	2.8
Dennis Springer	2	11.3	11	0.2	1.3	.121	0	1	8.74	-0.5	-0.5	-0.5
TOTALS	162	1003.3	495	61.4	52.8	.538	63	45	4.44	3.9	3.8	12.9

Over the years, we at *Baseball Prospectus* have gotten some mileage out of the fact that left-handed pitchers always seem to have a job waiting for them in the majors simply by virtue of the "L" that appears on the back of their baseball cards. In some cases, it doesn't seem to matter whether they've actually demonstrated an ability to get major-league hitters out.

Most of those hangers-on are relievers, though; left-handed starters are another story entirely. In fact, left-handed starters as a group are far superior to their right-handed counterparts, and the gap is widening. Lefty starters have put up a better cumulative Support-Neutral Winning Percentage (SNPct) than righties every year since 1995. In 2000, lefty starters had a cumulative SNPct of .530, as compared to .496 for righties, the largest split in the 21 years for which we have data. This split suggests that in contrast to the above-mentioned stereotype for left-handed relievers, left-handed starters may be held to a higher standard than right-handers.

No one understands the value of left-handed starters better than the Mets. Last year, the Mets led the majors in production by left-handed starters (as measured by Support Neutral Wins Above Replacement), and they've been no lower than seventh in that category for the past four years.

For a quick explanation of SN stats, see page 7.

Reliever Evaluation Tools

PITCHER	G	IP	R	ARA	APR	IRNR/G	EIRS/G	IRP	BRS	RRA	ARP
Derek Bell	1	1.0	5	48.72	-4.8	0.00	0.00	0.0	0.0	54.43	-5.5
Armando Benitez	76	76.0	24	3.08	17.9	0.33	0.12	-3.0	0.8	3.61	13.4
Eric Cammack	8	10.0	7	6.82	-1.8	0.62	0.27	1.3	0.3	4.49	0.8
Dennis Cook	68	59.0	35	5.78	-3.8	0.72	0.23	3.0	1.6	5.79	-3.9
John Franco	62	55.7	24	4.20	6.2	0.37	0.09	0.4	-3.1	3.71	9.2
Bobby M. Jones	10	17.7	4	2.21	5.9	0.40	0.15	1.5	-0.4	1.26	7.7
Pat Mahomes	48	67.0	44	6.40	-9.0	0.73	0.27	-7.7	3.7	8.01	-21.0
Jim Mann	2	2.7	3	10.96	-1.7	0.00	0.00	0.0	0.0	11.89	-2.0
Jarrod Riggan	1	2.0	2	9.74	-1.0	0.00	0.00	0.0	0.0	10.36	-1.1
Grant Roberts	3	5.7	3	5.16	0.0	0.33	0.19	-0.5	0.0	5.93	-0.5
Rich Rodriguez	32	37.0	40	10.53	-21.9	0.56	0.18	0.3	0.1	10.69	-22.6
Glendon Rusch	1	2.0	2	9.74	-1.0	0.00	0.00	0.0	0.0	9.67	-1.0
Turk Wendell	77	82.7	36	4.24	8.8	0.52	0.17	5.8	-1.9	3.40	16.5
Rick White	22	28.3	14	4.81	1.2	0.68	0.28	1.4	2.1	5.14	0.2
TOTALS	411	446.7	243	5.30	-5.2	0.52	0.18			5.39	-9.7

For a quick guide to RET, see page 10.

Philadelphia Phillies

The revolutionaries have been left behind. Over the past few years, teams such as the Yankees, Astros, and A's have demonstrated the effectiveness of building an offense around high on-base-percentage hitters with strong but not overwhelming power. These teams are in many ways the legacy of the 1993 Phillies team that unexpectedly rode a bunch of walking fools to the World Series.

While other organizations learned from the success of that team, the Phillies have been stuck in a cycle of futility since then, suffering through seven straight losing seasons. The disastrous years were caused by a complete organizational meltdown in scouting, player development, and team management. In recent years, many of the flaws have been corrected, and the team now has an opportunity to make surprisingly rapid strides with some shrewd moves, but the actions of the Phillies' brass indicate that they are oblivious to their most significant flaw: the gaping on-base holes in their lineup.

One of the Phillies' most startling improvements is in the starting rotation. In the early 1990s, the Phillies were obsessed with large pitchers who could throw extremely hard. However, they lacked the coaching and training staff to properly develop those pitchers, so the result was guys like Jeff Juden who were ludicrously wild for a few months until they got hurt. Recently, however, the Phillies have quietly shuffled many of the incompetent pitching coaches out of the system and brought in some outstanding teachers to replace them, while at the same time changing the type of pitchers they're developing. These days, the Phillies are focused on pitchers who do not have overwhelming velocity but who throw a wide variety of pitches with different movements and speeds. Randy Wolf and Bruce Chen are already in the majors, while Evan Thomas and Nelson Figeroa spent last year at Triple-A and could do serviceable jobs in the majors this year.

The results so far have been positive. It's a well-guarded secret that last year's Phillies had a starting rotation that was well above average. They finished in the top quarter of the Support-Neutral Win/Loss standings and their starters put up quality starts in 51% of their games, well above the major-league average of 43%. Furthermore, the much–hyped and now departed trio of 1999 All-Stars (Andy Ashby, Paul Byrd, and Curt Schilling) actually brought the overall level of the staff down. The strength of the 2000 rotation emerged in younger pitchers such as Wolf, Chen, Robert Person, and Omar Daal. If they can stay healthy, they're all young enough to provide a solid rotation core for years to come.

Unfortunately, the Phils offered reason to be concerned about the health of their young pitchers. Randy Wolf was one of the best pitchers in the league in the first half of 2000, but he was also one of the most abused. Wolf had a number of high-pitch outings despite being just 23 years old. It's not surprising that he was less effective in the second half.

The wretched overuse of Wolf is not the only example of pitcher mismanagement. Terry Francona displayed a consistent lack of understanding of the finer points of handling a bullpen. Relievers frequently warmed up multiple times per game. Francona had a very slow hook, which meant that a reliever would spend 15-20 minutes more than necessary throwing in the bullpen while a tiring starter or ineffective reliever was left on the mound. Given this additional strain, it's hardly surprising that the bullpen wore down over the course of the season.

Francona is gone now, replaced by Larry Bowa, and there are enough other positive signs for the Phillies to be optimistic about their pitching. Daal and Chen came to the team in July, so there was much less time for them to be overworked by Francona. Person is the oldest of the lot, and while he was used fairly heavily, his workload was not excessive given his age and history. If a member of the current major-league rotation falters, there are pitchers at Triple-A like Evan Thomas waiting to step in.

Scranton/Wilkes-Barre pitching coach Gorm Heimueller has taken a very different approach from Francona's "work 'em until they drop" philosophy, instead championing an

Phillies Prospectus

2000 record: 65–97; Fifth place, NL East
Pythagenport W/L: 69–93
Runs Scored: 708 (16th in NL)
Runs Allowed: 830 (11th in NL)
Team EqA: .245 (16th in NL)
2000 Batters' Age: 28.4 (tied for 3rd youngest in NL)
2000 Pitchers' Age: 28.4 (tied for 7th oldest in NL)
Ballpark: Veterans Stadium; slight hitters' park; Park Factor of 1.028
2000: Spent the year putting together one hell of a rotation to go with three great hitters.
2001: Player acquisition is still unfocused and haphazard. The core talent is so good that it may not matter.

approach summarized by the adage "most of the time, a groundout on the third pitch is better than a strikeout on the sixth." As a result, the pitchers coming through Scranton/Wilkes-Barre have not been overworked and have shown good control of their pitches.

Even if there is no room right away in the major-league rotation for all the young pitchers, some may wind up taking Ramiro Mendoza-type roles in the bullpen. Though the bullpen was a disaster last year, it is much easier to construct a passable bullpen than it is to assemble a solid rotation. With some sensible off-season pickups (including a new pitching coach in Vern Ruhle) the Phils should have been able to piece together an average bullpen to go with the strong rotation.

But this winter, Ed Wade couldn't be bothered to "piece" together a bullpen, instead wasting a bunch of money on proven mediocrities Jose Mesa and Ricky Bottalico, as well as competent left-hander Rheal Cormier. Combined, these three pitchers will make about $7 million in 2001. Mesa and Bottalico are poster children for high-profile implosion, so it's hard to believe that Wade couldn't have found some better options internally or in the free-talent bins.

Still, the pitching staff is not a major problem for the Phillies. Their biggest problem is that their offense is wretched, and they are not taking the necessary steps to improve it. The experience of Omar Daal over the last six weeks of the season illustrates the Phillies' plight. In his last seven starts, Daal looked very much like the pitcher he was in 1998 and 1999, tossing a quality start in each of those games. Yet the Phillies won only the final one. In the middle of that stretch, Daal had to suffer through more than 20 straight innings with zero runs of support. It seems incredible that a team with hitters the quality of Bobby Abreu and Scott Rolen could finish last in the majors in runs scored, but the Phillies' 708 runs were 23 fewer than the next-worst team, the Florida Marlins.

The Phillies' problems are rather uncommon. It's far more usual to see a team with a lot of average players but a lack of top-tier players. In contrast, the Phillies have the core of a league-leading offense. Abreu and Rolen get on base and hit for power. They have consistently been among the best hitters at their positions. Over the past two years, Mike Lieberthal has joined them, and Pat Burrell is showing every sign of being the best hitter of the lot. The four of them are all still in their twenties, and three of the four (Lieberthal being the exception) should still have their best years ahead of them. This core needs only to be surrounded by players who will get on base so that there will be more runners on and fewer outs wasted. A judicious raiding of the contemporary Ken Phelps All-Stars could produce some truly remarkable results.

Instead, the Phillies seem to be focusing on assembling the Rey Ordonez All-Stars. Last year, while the top players on the team did their part, the rest of the lineup was a disaster.

In particular, the various combinations of Doug Glanville, Ron Gant, Mickey Morandini, and Marlon Anderson in the top two lineup spots produced outs at a rate that prohibited big innings. It's hardly a coincidence that the Phillies were last in the majors—by a substantial margin—in first-inning runs, scoring only 69, roughly 40 less than the major-league average.

If the new manager and coaching staff are any indication of where the team is headed, the Phillies' problems are not going to be solved in the near future. Manager Larry Bowa has succeeded in sounding remarkably like Francona by talking about how important it is to "play aggressively" and "do the little things right" and "respect the game." The Phillies seem to think that the reason this philosophy didn't work before was because Francona wasn't willing to chew out his players on a regular basis, unlike the fiery Bowa. The hand of senior advisor Dallas Green is clearly at work here, since he was a big advocate of the bluster approach in his days as a manager. A quick glance over Green's recent record hardly offers a ringing endorsement of this way of doing things, but the Phillies are still obsessed with the idea of Green as the only man to have managed the team to a World Series title. To them, he can do no wrong, so his stumping for Bowa was enough to put Larry in the manager's spot.

Beyond the hiring of Bowa, the Phillies are continuing to dig their own grave with the addition of Richie Hebner as the hitting coach. Hebner's record of developing hitters for the Pirates as hitting coach at Triple-A Nashville was abysmal, and his stated attitude towards hitting explains why. His idea of plate discipline is not striking out too much, even if it comes at the expense of walks.

Hebner's approach could do enormous damage if it takes hold with the established quality players. Scott Rolen's on-base percentage has dropped considerably over the past two years, but at the end of last season he said that he felt he had gotten too aggressive, was swinging at too many bad pitches, and was trying to correct the problem. It's exactly the sort of effort he should be making, even if it results in additional strikeouts, but that may lead him into conflict with Hebner.

In even more danger is Pat Burrell, who registered a very high strikeout rate in his rookie season but also a very good walk rate. If Burrell is pushed into being more "aggressive," he will wind up trading both strikeouts and walks for weak infield grounders. It's clearly not a good trade-off, but the Phillies' major-league staff shows no indication they understand.

Time is running out for the Phillies to win with this generation of players. Rolen and Lieberthal can be free agents after 2002 and Abreu the year after that. If the team continues to struggle, all will most likely bolt for greener pastures. The Phillies will improve over the next two years; they have far too much talent not to do so. However, if the organization doesn't wake up and fix its glaring problems, the team will make a serious playoff run only with a lot of luck.

The Phillies winning half their games in 2000 looks like a reasonable expectation, which would be appropriate for a team with half a clue.

HITTERS (BA: .270, OBP: .340, SLG: .440, EqA: .260)

Bobby Abreu — RF — Bats L — Age 27

YEAR	TEAM	LGE	AB	H	DB	TP	HR	BB	SO	R	RBI	SB	CS	OUT	BA	OBP	SLG	EQA	EQR	DEFENSE	
1998	Philadel	NL	505	154	28	5	18	82	125	68	72	17	10	361	.305	.402	.487	.296	86	145-RF	-1
1999	Philadel	NL	544	174	33	10	19	99	107	108	84	20	8	378	.320	.427	.522	.316	106	133-RF	-6
2000	Philadel	NL	576	174	41	8	23	89	109	95	71	25	8	410	.302	.396	.521	.304	104	151-RF	3
2001	Philadel	NL	518	175	38	7	24	97	109	142	118	31	9	352	.338	.442	.577	.334	114		

Bobby Abreu has been getting sniped at by some teammates for supposedly being a little too laid back and not working as hard as he could. Given that Abreu was far and away the most productive member of the Phillies' lineup last year, that criticism seems somewhat misplaced. He was our first choice for the cover this year, but circumstances intervened.

Marlon Anderson — 2B — Bats L — Age 27

YEAR	TEAM	LGE	AB	H	DB	TP	HR	BB	SO	R	RBI	SB	CS	OUT	BA	OBP	SLG	EQA	EQR	DEFENSE	
1998	Scran-WB	Int	575	161	31	10	13	19	76	86	70	14	8	422	.280	.309	.437	.245	63	132-2B	-11
1999	Philadel	NL	453	112	24	4	5	19	58	45	50	10	2	343	.247	.280	.351	.211	35	101-2B	3
2000	Scran-WB	Int	402	111	15	6	7	30	46	47	44	16	8	299	.276	.332	.396	.246	45	93-2B	-7
2000	Philadel	NL	163	37	7	1	1	9	21	9	14	2	2	128	.227	.267	.301	.182	9	40-2B	2
2001	Philadel	NL	516	143	24	7	9	40	68	77	66	21	7	380	.277	.329	.403	.248	58		

He was banished to Scranton at the start of last season, but the stated reasons were the wrong ones. Marlon Anderson's defense was blamed for his demotion, since he sometimes booted routine plays. However, the real problem was that he could not lay off pitches low and away, a weakness he has yet to address. Anderson is Pokey Reese without the speed and defense.

Alex Arias — IF — Bats R — Age 33

YEAR	TEAM	LGE	AB	H	DB	TP	HR	BB	SO	R	RBI	SB	CS	OUT	BA	OBP	SLG	EQA	EQR	DEFENSE	
1998	Philadel	NL	135	40	5	0	2	12	17	17	17	2	0	95	.296	.358	.378	.254	16	31-SS	-2
1999	Philadel	NL	347	101	19	1	4	31	29	40	44	1	2	248	.291	.356	.386	.252	39	82-SS	-3
2000	Philadel	NL	156	29	5	0	3	14	26	16	15	1	0	127	.186	.264	.276	.177	8	31-SS	1
2001	San Dieg	NL	178	43	3	0	4	20	24	21	22	1	0	135	.242	.318	.326	.232	17		

Mr. Arias, meet the cliff. The Phillies have gotten good mileage out of Alex Arias over the past few years by using him as a spot starter and pinch-hitter. Some players of his type see their skills decline sharply in their early thirties. Given how overmatched Arias was last year, it looks like this has happened to him. Kevin Towers to the rescue: Arias signed a two-year deal with the Padres.

Gary Bennett — C — Bats R — Age 29

YEAR	TEAM	LGE	AB	H	DB	TP	HR	BB	SO	R	RBI	SB	CS	OUT	BA	OBP	SLG	EQA	EQR	DEFENSE	
1998	Scran-WB	Int	284	66	12	0	9	19	42	28	33	0	0	218	.232	.284	.370	.215	23	64-C	2
1999	Philadel	NL	88	23	1	0	2	3	10	6	18	0	0	65	.261	.286	.341	.205	6	21-C	-2
2000	Scran-WB	Int	322	85	13	0	11	30	49	37	41	1	0	237	.264	.336	.407	.251	37	75-C	-5
2000	Philadel	NL	74	17	4	0	2	12	14	7	5	0	0	57	.230	.350	.365	.247	9	24-C	0
2001	Philadel	NL	299	80	10	0	14	34	49	40	52	0	0	219	.268	.342	.441	.261	38		

The Phillies wasted what will probably be the best year of Gary Bennett's career, sending him to Scranton solely because he had an option left. They'll use him as their backup catcher in 2001, but the results won't be as good as the numbers he put up in 2000.

Pat Burrell   1B/LF   Bats R   Age 24

YEAR	TEAM	LGE	AB	H	DB	TP	HR	BB	SO	R	RBI	SB	CS	OUT	BA	OBP	SLG	EQA	EQR	DEFENSE			
1998	Clearwtr	Fla	134	31	4	1	5	21	25	21	19	1	0	103	.231	.335	.388	.247	16	22-1B	0		
1999	Reading	Eas	421	114	22	3	20	60	108	63	61	1	2	309	.271	.362	.480	.278	63	80-1B	-6	25-LF	1
2000	Scran-WB	Int	146	39	11	1	4	28	37	27	21	1	1	108	.267	.385	.438	.279	22	29-LF	1		
2000	Philadel	NL	409	102	25	1	17	56	130	53	72	0	0	307	.249	.341	.440	.261	53	58-1B	-5	42-LF	-1
2001	Philadel	NL	436	127	25	2	24	75	130	86	96	2	1	310	.291	.395	.523	.302	77				

Pat Burrell didn't hit as well as was hoped in his rookie year, but he will get better. His knowledge of the strike zone is outstanding, and his ability to drive pitches to all parts of the field is amazing. Within three years he will be one of the best hitters in the game. Out in left field he looks horrible lumbering around but still tends to get the job done.

Rob Ducey   OF   Bats L   Age 36

YEAR	TEAM	LGE	AB	H	DB	TP	HR	BB	SO	R	RBI	SB	CS	OUT	BA	OBP	SLG	EQA	EQR	DEFENSE
1998	Seattle	AL	217	54	17	2	6	23	54	30	23	3	3	166	.249	.343	.429	.257	28	61-RF -2
1999	Philadel	NL	188	47	8	2	8	35	54	27	30	1	1	142	.250	.368	.441	.272	27	44-LF 0
2000	Philadel	NL	153	29	3	1	6	26	44	23	23	1	0	124	.190	.307	.340	.222	14	28-LF -6
2000	Toronto	AL	13	2	1	0	0	2	2	2	1	0	0	11	.154	.267	.231	.162	1	
2001	Philadel	NL	154	33	7	1	5	32	45	25	21	1	1	122	.214	.349	.370	.247	19	

Much was made of Rob Ducey essentially being traded for himself in late July and early August of last year, but no one seemed to be asking the crucial question: why on earth did the Phillies want him back? He has another year left on his contract and is at an age where you have to expect his 2000 performance to be the best you'll get.

Nate Espy   1B   Bats R   Age 23

YEAR	TEAM	LGE	AB	H	DB	TP	HR	BB	SO	R	RBI	SB	CS	OUT	BA	OBP	SLG	EQA	EQR	DEFENSE
1998	Martnsvl	App	232	57	10	0	7	32	65	26	27	0	1	176	.246	.341	.379	.245	26	56-1B -1
1999	Piedmont	SAL	309	64	13	1	8	36	59	27	27	1	1	246	.207	.291	.333	.209	25	70-1B 1
2000	Piedmont	SAL	476	114	21	1	15	74	112	63	56	2	0	362	.239	.344	.382	.249	56	128-1B 3
2001	Philadel	NL	360	96	12	0	14	60	87	58	61	1	0	264	.267	.371	.417	.269	49	

Nate Espy rebounded admirably from an injury-plagued 1999, showing excellent patience, power, and defense. He is also a perfect example of the Phillies leaving players at lower levels too long. At every level of the minors, their hitters are older than the league average. Perhaps they wanted to keep Espy out of the hands of the Clearwater coaching staff (who were all let go at the end of the year), but he is losing valuable development time.

Doug Glanville   CF   Bats R   Age 30

YEAR	TEAM	LGE	AB	H	DB	TP	HR	BB	SO	R	RBI	SB	CS	OUT	BA	OBP	SLG	EQA	EQR	DEFENSE
1998	Philadel	NL	685	191	27	7	9	40	83	107	49	21	6	500	.279	.324	.378	.239	70	153-CF 11
1999	Philadel	NL	627	198	37	5	11	40	77	93	67	26	2	431	.316	.362	.443	.276	86	148-CF 9
2000	Philadel	NL	640	171	27	6	7	21	71	82	48	27	8	477	.267	.292	.361	.221	55	149-CF 1
2001	Philadel	NL	573	170	24	5	7	40	70	91	71	28	6	409	.297	.343	.393	.253	66	

Doug Glanville is an analyst's nightmare because he has been spectacularly inconsistent over the past three years. In his good stretches, he has just enough plate discipline and power to complement a high batting average. In the bad stretches—your people call it "2000"—he's an incredibly feeble hacker. He could bounce back this year, but he's always going to be a crapshoot. If The Bad Mr. Glanville shows up, it's going to hurt the team considerably.

Brian R. Hunter   1B   Bats R   Age 33

YEAR	TEAM	LGE	AB	H	DB	TP	HR	BB	SO	R	RBI	SB	CS	OUT	BA	OBP	SLG	EQA	EQR	DEFENSE
1998	St Louis	NL	113	23	10	1	4	7	22	12	13	1	1	91	.204	.256	.416	.216	10	21-LF 0
1999	Atlanta	NL	182	44	12	1	6	28	38	27	28	0	1	139	.242	.355	.418	.260	24	51-1B 0
2000	Philadel	NL	139	29	3	0	7	17	37	12	21	0	1	111	.209	.295	.381	.223	13	22-1B 0
2001	Philadel	NL	137	30	6	0	6	20	34	17	20	0	0	107	.219	.318	.394	.239	15	

Picked up from the Braves in April, Brian Hunter promptly contracted the malaise that affected the entire Phillies bench. Either that or it was the realization that he'd have plenty of time to plan that Halloween party. Hunter would make an excellent platoon partner for Travis Lee.

Kevin Jordan — IF — Bats R — Age 31

YEAR	TEAM	LGE	AB	H	DB	TP	HR	BB	SO	R	RBI	SB	CS	OUT	BA	OBP	SLG	EQA	EQR	DEFENSE			
1998	Philadel	NL	252	70	8	0	4	8	28	23	28	0	0	182	.278	.305	.357	.220	21	20-1B	0	18-2B	-2
1999	Philadel	NL	347	96	15	3	4	20	32	34	47	0	0	251	.277	.327	.372	.235	34	46-3B	4	24-2B	3
2000	Philadel	NL	339	74	14	2	5	12	38	28	34	0	1	266	.218	.247	.316	.176	17	36-2B	1	34-3B	2
2001	Philadel	NL	278	68	10	1	4	18	32	24	27	0	0	210	.245	.291	.331	.205	20				

Kevin Jordan draws plaudits for his ability to foul off pitch after pitch, but he's missing the skill that would make that ability more useful: the judgment to lay off pitches not close to the strike zone. Many times last year he would bail out a wild pitcher by swinging at a first pitch up around his eyes, resulting in a pop-up. His inability to play shortstop makes him a marginal bench player.

Travis Lee — 1B — Bats L — Age 26

YEAR	TEAM	LGE	AB	H	DB	TP	HR	BB	SO	R	RBI	SB	CS	OUT	BA	OBP	SLG	EQA	EQR	DEFENSE			
1998	Arizona	NL	568	151	18	2	23	65	115	72	71	7	1	418	.266	.341	.426	.259	71	145-1B	4		
1999	Arizona	NL	376	87	15	2	9	52	47	53	47	13	3	292	.231	.325	.354	.236	40	101-1B	5		
2000	Arizona	NL	226	52	11	0	8	21	43	32	38	5	1	175	.230	.296	.385	.229	22	47-RF	4	15-1B	-2
2000	Philadel	NL	180	41	10	1	1	37	31	18	13	3	0	139	.228	.364	.311	.245	21	43-1B	4		
2001	Philadel	NL	369	93	16	1	11	53	67	57	52	7	1	277	.252	.346	.390	.253	44				

Travis Lee's offensive collapse is inexplicable. His strike-zone judgment remains impeccable, but his swing does not look smooth, and his power has completely vanished. The Phillies are hoping that lingering effects of his 1999 injuries are to blame and that Lee will have a Darin Erstad-like revival this year. It seems unlikely, but nothing about this situation is particularly normal.

Mike Lieberthal — C — Bats R — Age 29

YEAR	TEAM	LGE	AB	H	DB	TP	HR	BB	SO	R	RBI	SB	CS	OUT	BA	OBP	SLG	EQA	EQR	DEFENSE	
1998	Philadel	NL	316	81	14	3	9	16	41	40	45	2	1	236	.256	.306	.405	.236	32	83-C	1
1999	Philadel	NL	510	147	26	1	31	37	81	79	88	0	0	363	.288	.349	.525	.283	78	136-C	4
2000	Philadel	NL	390	104	23	0	16	34	50	51	67	2	0	286	.267	.334	.449	.260	49	102-C	5
2001	Philadel	NL	432	127	22	1	22	43	64	67	86	1	0	305	.294	.358	.502	.282	64		

In the first half of 2000, Mike Lieberthal proved that his 1999 production wasn't a fluke, but his second half raised serious questions about whether he can hold up for an entire season. He was plagued by bone spurs in his elbow and a sprained ankle that knocked down his final numbers considerably. Because he really doesn't hit right-handers that well, finding a quality left-handed-hitting backup should be a priority. Once Ed Wade finishes signing all the lousy relievers, of course.

Anderson Machado — SS — Bats B — Age 20

YEAR	TEAM	LGE	AB	H	DB	TP	HR	BB	SO	R	RBI	SB	CS	OUT	BA	OBP	SLG	EQA	EQR	DEFENSE
1999	Piedmont	SAL	62	12	4	1	0	5	21	5	5	1	0	50	.194	.259	.290	.181	3	17-SS -1
2000	Clearwtr	Fla	424	88	19	4	1	40	117	39	26	14	9	345	.208	.276	.278	.185	25	117-SS -10
2001	Philadel	NL	222	54	11	2	1	25	72	33	19	13	5	172	.243	.320	.324	.225	21	

He's the latest in a line of slick-fielding shortstops that the Phillies have been producing, but Anderson Machado's offense needs a lot of work. Given Jimmy Rollins's presence ahead of him, Machado may very well wind up as trade bait.

Rusty McNamara — UT — Bats R — Age 26

YEAR	TEAM	LGE	AB	H	DB	TP	HR	BB	SO	R	RBI	SB	CS	OUT	BA	OBP	SLG	EQA	EQR	DEFENSE			
1998	Clearwtr	Fla	526	127	23	1	8	16	50	55	67	5	3	402	.241	.274	.335	.199	35	117-3B	-21		
1999	Clearwtr	Fla	275	70	10	1	2	21	26	28	29	2	1	206	.255	.317	.320	.216	22	31-3B	-6	26-1B	-1
1999	Reading	Eas	179	38	6	1	4	11	24	20	15	0	2	143	.212	.266	.324	.188	11	28-3B	-7		
2000	Reading	Eas	470	114	19	3	11	30	47	59	53	2	2	358	.243	.302	.366	.222	42	46-3B	0	23-LF	-2
2001	Philadel	NL	500	123	22	1	10	41	54	54	55	4	2	379	.246	.303	.354	.219	43				

Rusty McNamara hasn't been left at one position long enough to really develop strong defensive skills, but his ability to play passably at a variety of positions makes him a potentially useful bench player for a few years. It's rough to be a utility man at 25, rougher still to be one for a Double-A team.

Tomas Perez — SS — Bats R — Age 27

YEAR	TEAM	LGE	AB	H	DB	TP	HR	BB	SO	R	RBI	SB	CS	OUT	BA	OBP	SLG	EQA	EQR	DEFENSE			
1998	Syracuse	Int	404	95	16	3	2	12	66	35	31	2	5	314	.235	.257	.304	.175	20	99-SS	36	17-2B	0
1999	Edmonton	PCL	291	65	13	1	3	15	42	24	30	1	1	227	.223	.265	.306	.183	16	70-SS	2	11-2B	2
2000	Scran-WB	Int	281	75	14	1	9	12	51	38	47	3	1	207	.267	.301	.420	.238	28	55-3B	0	14-SS	1
2000	Philadel	NL	141	31	6	1	1	9	28	16	12	1	1	111	.220	.267	.298	.182	8	41-SS	-5		
2001	Philadel	NL	392	98	20	1	9	26	73	42	45	4	2	296	.250	.297	.375	.222	34				

A hot first month masked the fact that Tomas Perez is still what he has always been: a sure-handed shortstop who can't hit enough to play at the major-league level. The Phillies recognize that Jimmy Rollins is the shortstop of the future, but they seem blind to the fact that they could easily find a better stopgap than Perez.

Tom Prince — C — Bats R — Age 36

YEAR	TEAM	LGE	AB	H	DB	TP	HR	BB	SO	R	RBI	SB	CS	OUT	BA	OBP	SLG	EQA	EQR	DEFENSE	
1998	LosAngls	NL	82	16	6	1	0	7	22	8	5	0	0	66	.195	.274	.293	.186	5	24-C	4
2000	Philadel	NL	123	28	6	0	3	11	29	13	16	1	0	95	.228	.300	.350	.219	11	35-C	0
2001	LosAngls	NL	93	18	1	0	3	12	23	9	11	0	0	75	.194	.286	.301	.205	7		

Like the rest of the Phillies' bench, Tom Prince put up awful numbers; unlike the rest of the bench, his performance is not a surprise. Francona's sense of loyalty led him to give Prince a large percentage of the starts once Lieberthal went down for the year, which contributed to the ugly results.

Nick Punto — SS — Bats B — Age 23

YEAR	TEAM	LGE	AB	H	DB	TP	HR	BB	SO	R	RBI	SB	CS	OUT	BA	OBP	SLG	EQA	EQR	DEFENSE	
1998	Batavia	NYP	291	62	9	2	1	29	51	33	14	7	4	233	.213	.285	.268	.186	17	69-SS	-8
1999	Clearwtr	Fla	406	98	16	3	1	50	61	46	33	7	3	311	.241	.327	.303	.219	35	105-SS	4
2000	Reading	Eas	465	105	14	2	5	53	77	58	37	19	7	367	.226	.307	.297	.210	37	118-SS	-9
2001	Philadel	NL	458	121	17	2	3	62	78	75	46	20	7	344	.264	.352	.330	.240	49		

Nick Punto didn't build on his offensive progress from last year, which somewhat diminishes his prospect status. With Jimmy Rollins ahead of him, the Phillies are considering moving Punto to second base next season, possibly as insurance in case Anderson doesn't work out.

Scott Rolen — 3B — Bats R — Age 26

YEAR	TEAM	LGE	AB	H	DB	TP	HR	BB	SO	R	RBI	SB	CS	OUT	BA	OBP	SLG	EQA	EQR	DEFENSE	
1998	Philadel	NL	610	173	43	4	32	90	132	121	108	13	7	444	.284	.385	.525	.297	107	157-3B	16
1999	Philadel	NL	421	109	24	1	25	60	108	68	70	9	2	314	.259	.355	.499	.282	66	112-3B	13
2000	Philadel	NL	484	139	32	5	24	43	93	82	80	7	1	346	.287	.351	.523	.285	75	125-3B	13
2001	Philadel	NL	448	133	32	2	24	63	101	91	95	10	2	317	.297	.384	.538	.301	79		

Scott Rolen's sore back continued to plague him last year. The hopeful party line is that the original injury in mid-1999 is one that often takes 18 months to fully heal, but there are worries that his pain will be chronic. The installation of the grass-like NeXturf is an attempt on the team's part to keep Rolen's back from getting worse, and they made sure Rolen tested it before agreeing to have the Vet playing surface redone. If he can come back at full strength, he's capable of an MVP season.

Jimmy Rollins — SS — Bats B — Age 22

YEAR	TEAM	LGE	AB	H	DB	TP	HR	BB	SO	R	RBI	SB	CS	OUT	BA	OBP	SLG	EQA	EQR	DEFENSE	
1998	Clearwtr	Fla	497	104	18	5	5	30	70	51	25	8	5	398	.209	.257	.296	.179	27	119-SS	-2
1999	Reading	Eas	536	126	19	6	8	35	49	61	42	11	7	417	.235	.283	.338	.206	40	132-SS	0
2000	Scran-WB	Int	476	122	27	8	11	40	57	58	59	16	6	360	.256	.316	.416	.245	54	129-SS	0
2000	Philadel	NL	53	17	0	1	0	1	7	5	5	3	0	36	.321	.333	.358	.245	5	12-SS	-2
2001	Philadel	NL	529	142	25	7	11	49	65	80	69	21	8	395	.268	.330	.405	.248	61		

Just like in 1999 at Double-A, Jimmy Rollins suffered through a hideous start both offensively and defensively while adjusting to the new level. Once he worked through it, he produced some outstanding results for the rest of the year. Rollins has good range in the field and more pop in his bat than you would expect from a 5'8" player. The Phillies will have to decide whether they want to risk exposing him to the Vet's boo-birds at the start of the season, but whenever he takes over, he'll fill a large hole in the lineup. He's a sleeper candidate for Rookie of the Year.

National League   193

Kevin Sefcik — UT — Bats R — Age 30

YEAR	TEAM	LGE	AB	H	DB	TP	HR	BB	SO	R	RBI	SB	CS	OUT	BA	OBP	SLG	EQA	EQR	DEFENSE	
1998	Philadel	NL	172	53	8	2	3	24	30	28	20	4	2	121	.308	.413	.430	.290	27	44-LF	1
1999	Philadel	NL	209	56	14	3	1	26	23	26	10	7	4	157	.268	.352	.378	.250	24	36-OF	-3
2000	Philadel	NL	154	36	5	2	0	10	18	14	9	4	2	120	.234	.288	.292	.195	10	35-OF	-1
2001	Philadel	NL	166	45	9	2	1	21	21	28	19	6	3	124	.271	.353	.367	.248	19		

Yet another Phillies' bench player who had a horrendous 2000 season. Given that Kevin Sefcik is 30 and arbitration-eligible, he may start bouncing between Triple-A and the majors for a few years. That's a shame, because he's a fun pest hitter who drove opposing pitchers nuts with his patience and his ability to slap the ball.

Reggie Taylor — CF — Bats L — Age 24

YEAR	TEAM	LGE	AB	H	DB	TP	HR	BB	SO	R	RBI	SB	CS	OUT	BA	OBP	SLG	EQA	EQR	DEFENSE	
1998	Reading	Eas	337	81	12	4	4	7	74	37	17	12	6	262	.240	.259	.335	.194	22	77-CF	-7
1999	Reading	Eas	526	122	16	6	12	9	83	54	46	18	12	416	.232	.247	.354	.193	34	122-CF	0
2000	Scran-WB	Int	425	108	9	6	14	16	90	51	37	16	9	326	.254	.284	.402	.226	39	98-CF	3
2001	Philadel	NL	424	109	12	5	12	20	90	52	50	24	10	325	.257	.291	.394	.229	41		

Reggie Taylor is an ugly legacy of the previous "development" process in the Phillies system. A number-one pick with the drool-worthy five tools, he hasn't gotten nearly enough coaching to turn those tools into skills. This year, the Scranton coaching staff tried to inject some sense of discipline into his approach at the plate; by the end of the year, it looked like it might be starting to take hold. If this had happened three years ago when he was in A ball, his future would be much brighter.

Chase Utley — 2B — Bats L — Age 22

YEAR	TEAM	LGE	AB	H	DB	TP	HR	BB	SO	R	RBI	SB	CS	OUT	BA	OBP	SLG	EQA	EQR	DEFENSE	
2000	Batavia	NYP	159	39	11	0	2	11	26	15	15	1	1	121	.245	.298	.352	.216	13	34-2B	2
2001	Philadel	NL	81	22	2	0	2	6	36	8	11	0	0	59	.272	.322	.370	.232	8		

The team's first-round draft pick in 2000, Chase Utley signed relatively quickly and put in a decent performance in short-season ball, leading his team on a late charge to the playoffs. There's some question about where he will play in the future, with speculation that he'll be moved to third base in case Scott Rolen leaves as a free agent after 2002. If that happens, or if Marlon Anderson continues to hit poorly, look for Utley move quickly up the ladder.

Eric Valent — OF — Bats L — Age 24

YEAR	TEAM	LGE	AB	H	DB	TP	HR	BB	SO	R	RBI	SB	CS	OUT	BA	OBP	SLG	EQA	EQR	DEFENSE	
1998	Piedmont	SAL	92	30	7	0	5	10	20	16	17	0	0	62	.326	.392	.565	.310	17	21-RF	-1
1998	Clearwtr	Fla	126	27	6	1	3	12	33	17	16	0	1	100	.214	.291	.349	.211	10	32-RF	1
1999	Clearwtr	Fla	524	122	22	4	16	42	127	65	71	2	1	403	.233	.293	.382	.223	48	127-RF	-3
2000	Reading	Eas	478	107	17	3	18	54	96	64	66	1	2	373	.224	.306	.385	.230	48	122-RF	2
2001	Philadel	NL	374	91	15	2	14	44	86	48	55	2	1	284	.243	.323	.406	.244	42		

Eric Valent put up a very strange platoon split last year, hitting left-handed pitchers far better than he did righties. This may be a result of stretches in which he tried to do too much against right-handers, attempting to pull everything. Against southpaws he was willing to be more patient and to use the whole field. If he learns to apply that selectiveness to all his at-bats, he'll move from an intriguing but raw prospect to a player with star potential.

PITCHERS (ERA: 4.50, H/9: 9.00, HR/9: 1.00, BB/9: 3.00, K/9: 6.00, KW: 1.00, PERA: 4.50)

Brad Baisley — Throws R — Age 21

YEAR	TEAM	LGE	IP	H	ER	HR	BB	K	ERA	W	L	H/9	HR/9	BB/9	K/9	KW	PERA
1998	Martnsvl	App	25.7	27	14	5	6	6	4.91	1	2	9.47	1.75	2.10	2.10	0.50	5.21
1999	Piedmont	SAL	133.7	116	65	10	75	51	4.38	7	8	7.81	0.67	5.05	3.43	0.34	4.30
2000	Clearwtr	Fla	81.0	98	57	19	39	35	6.33	3	6	10.89	2.11	4.33	3.89	0.45	7.34

The Phillies shut down Brad Baisley in the middle of the year, not because of a specific injury, but because they wanted to work on improving his overall strength and conditioning. While you have to question why they didn't work on those things in the off-season, their caution with a young pitcher is commendable.

Kent Bottenfield — Throws R — Age 32

YEAR	TEAM	LGE	IP	H	ER	HR	BB	K	ERA	W	L	H/9	HR/9	BB/9	K/9	KW	PERA
1998	St Louis	NL	128.3	125	70	13	52	80	4.91	6	8	8.77	0.91	3.65	5.61	0.77	4.54
1999	St Louis	NL	185.7	189	82	19	74	104	3.97	11	10	9.16	0.92	3.59	5.04	0.70	4.75
2000	Anaheim	AL	127.3	133	68	21	44	71	4.81	6	8	9.40	1.48	3.11	5.02	0.81	5.29
2000	Philadel	NL	43.0	40	21	4	17	26	4.40	2	3	8.37	0.84	3.56	5.44	0.76	4.19

This is exactly the sort of player a team like the Phillies does not need. He's a solid back-of-the-rotation pitcher, but a very expensive one. On a team with a limited budget and several cheaper options, there are far better ways to spend the money. After some initial talks, the Phillies wised up and let him walk. Signed by Houston to be a utility pitcher.

Jason Boyd — Throws R — Age 28

YEAR	TEAM	LGE	IP	H	ER	HR	BB	K	ERA	W	L	H/9	HR/9	BB/9	K/9	KW	PERA
1998	Tucson	PCL	20.7	26	22	5	15	8	9.58	0	2	11.32	2.18	6.53	3.48	0.27	8.59
1999	Tucson	PCL	72.0	70	39	6	29	38	4.88	3	5	8.75	0.75	3.63	4.75	0.66	4.33
2000	Clearwtr	Fla	10.3	11	4	0	5	6	3.48	1	0	9.58	0.00	4.35	5.23	0.60	4.33
2000	Scran-WB	Int	14.3	7	3	0	15	7	1.88	2	0	4.40	0.00	9.42	4.40	0.23	3.41
2000	Philadel	NL	34.0	39	26	2	19	27	6.88	1	3	10.32	0.53	5.03	7.15	0.71	5.62

After losing Jason Boyd in the 1997 expansion draft, the Phillies jumped at the chance to bring him back this year. They're now working on his control in a couple of different areas. They'd like him to be around the plate a little more. They'd also like him to calm his temper: he lost several weeks to a broken hand caused by slamming his glove on the bench.

Jeff Brantley — Throws R — Age 37

YEAR	TEAM	LGE	IP	H	ER	HR	BB	K	ERA	W	L	H/9	HR/9	BB/9	K/9	KW	PERA
1998	St Louis	NL	48.3	40	26	12	16	39	4.84	2	3	7.45	2.23	2.98	7.26	1.22	4.87
1999	Philadel	NL	8.7	5	6	0	7	9	6.23	0	1	5.19	0.00	7.27	9.35	0.64	3.11
2000	Philadel	NL	54.7	63	32	10	23	47	5.27	2	4	10.37	1.65	3.79	7.74	1.02	6.32

It looks like the end of the line may be near. Jeff Brantley slowly regained velocity over the course of the season, but he never regained the movement on his pitches and produced some truly ugly results. Signed by Texas.

Jason Brester — Throws L — Age 24

YEAR	TEAM	LGE	IP	H	ER	HR	BB	K	ERA	W	L	H/9	HR/9	BB/9	K/9	KW	PERA
1998	Shrevprt	Tex	105.3	113	63	17	51	52	5.38	4	8	9.66	1.45	4.36	4.44	0.51	5.93
1998	New Havn	Eas	21.0	22	9	2	8	9	3.86	1	1	9.43	0.86	3.43	3.86	0.56	4.79
1999	Carolina	Sou	55.7	71	48	12	27	28	7.76	1	5	11.48	1.94	4.37	4.53	0.52	7.53
1999	Reading	Eas	98.7	106	52	11	26	55	4.74	5	6	9.67	1.00	2.37	5.02	1.06	4.63
2000	Reading	Eas	107.0	105	69	12	97	47	5.80	4	8	8.83	1.01	8.16	3.95	0.24	6.54

His control disappeared last year, effectively burying any chance he had of making the majors and leading to some very bizarre outings. How many pitchers can claim to have won starts that included a 50-pitch inning?

Chris Brock — Throws R — Age 31

YEAR	TEAM	LGE	IP	H	ER	HR	BB	K	ERA	W	L	H/9	HR/9	BB/9	K/9	KW	PERA
1998	Fresno	PCL	108.7	108	49	13	36	72	4.06	6	6	8.94	1.08	2.98	5.96	1.00	4.54
1998	San Fran	NL	26.3	30	13	3	7	15	4.44	1	2	10.25	1.03	2.39	5.13	1.07	5.02
1999	San Fran	NL	103.3	120	67	19	36	64	5.84	4	7	10.45	1.65	3.14	5.57	0.89	6.12
2000	Philadel	NL	91.7	82	42	18	33	57	4.12	5	5	8.05	1.77	3.24	5.60	0.86	4.86

After a very shaky period as a starter, Chris Brock moved to the bullpen and became one of the Phillies' few effective relievers. He probably has a few years as a serviceable middle or short reliever, but the Phillies should not be afraid to cut him loose if he becomes ineffective or expensive.

Paul Byrd — Throws R — Age 30

YEAR	TEAM	LGE	IP	H	ER	HR	BB	K	ERA	W	L	H/9	HR/9	BB/9	K/9	KW	PERA
1998	Richmond	Int	96.3	91	47	11	37	57	4.39	5	6	8.50	1.03	3.46	5.33	0.77	4.42
1998	Philadel	NL	52.3	40	15	6	15	31	2.58	4	2	6.88	1.03	2.58	5.33	1.03	3.17
1999	Philadel	NL	194.3	194	105	30	57	89	4.86	9	13	8.98	1.39	2.64	4.12	0.78	4.76
2000	Philadel	NL	81.3	85	58	14	28	44	6.42	3	6	9.41	1.55	3.10	4.87	0.79	5.36
2000	Scran-WB	Int	24.3	20	7	3	7	7	2.59	2	1	7.40	1.11	2.59	2.59	0.50	3.58

His hunched-over, herky-jerky motion and some appearances out of the bullpen between starts finally caught up to Paul Byrd as his shoulder fell apart. The Phillies yanked him from the 40-man roster, which certainly indicates they don't expect him back. Look for him to resurface as a reliever.

Bruce Chen — Throws L — Age 24

YEAR	TEAM	LGE	IP	H	ER	HR	BB	K	ERA	W	L	H/9	HR/9	BB/9	K/9	KW	PERA
1998	Greenvil	Sou	131.7	113	61	16	42	105	4.17	7	8	7.72	1.09	2.87	7.18	1.25	3.80
1998	Richmond	Int	23.0	18	5	1	18	21	1.96	2	1	7.04	0.39	7.04	8.22	0.58	4.40
1998	Atlanta	NL	19.3	22	8	3	8	14	3.72	1	1	10.24	1.40	3.72	6.52	0.88	5.88
1999	Richmond	Int	74.7	74	36	10	25	66	4.34	4	4	8.92	1.21	3.01	7.96	1.32	4.69
1999	Atlanta	NL	49.7	37	30	11	23	38	5.44	2	4	6.70	1.99	4.17	6.89	0.83	4.68
2000	Atlanta	NL	38.7	34	14	4	16	27	3.26	2	2	7.91	0.93	3.72	6.28	0.84	4.09
2000	Philadel	NL	91.7	78	35	12	21	67	3.44	6	4	7.66	1.18	2.06	6.58	1.60	3.53

While a good development process is certainly key to building a franchise, highway robbery helps. Bruce Chen made the Phillies look good by being one of the best starters in the league over the last two months of the season. He was miraculously spared the worst of Francona's arm mangling. He's already very good, will get better, and should end talk of the Phillies needing an ace.

David Coggin — Throws R — Age 24

YEAR	TEAM	LGE	IP	H	ER	HR	BB	K	ERA	W	L	H/9	HR/9	BB/9	K/9	KW	PERA
1998	Reading	Eas	101.7	103	60	11	64	39	5.31	4	7	9.12	0.97	5.67	3.45	0.30	5.64
1999	Reading	Eas	39.3	55	39	11	20	13	8.92	1	3	12.58	2.52	4.58	2.97	0.32	8.89
2000	Clearwtr	Fla	30.7	25	12	2	16	14	3.52	2	1	7.34	0.59	4.70	4.11	0.44	3.80
2000	Reading	Eas	39.0	50	28	9	14	19	6.46	1	3	11.54	2.08	3.23	4.38	0.68	7.24
2000	Scran-WB	Int	43.0	34	28	3	33	21	5.86	2	3	7.12	0.63	6.91	4.40	0.32	4.60
2000	Philadel	NL	26.7	34	19	2	10	14	6.41	1	2	11.48	0.68	3.38	4.72	0.70	5.82

He's finally healthy; now he just needs the Phillies to leave him at one level so he can work on improving his pitches. David Coggin has a good range of pitches but needs to develop some consistency with his location. If they give him 28 starts at Triple-A, he should develop into a solid starter.

Joseph Cotton — Throws R — Age 26

YEAR	TEAM	LGE	IP	H	ER	HR	BB	K	ERA	W	L	H/9	HR/9	BB/9	K/9	KW	PERA
1998	Piedmont	SAL	66.3	87	78	31	23	34	10.58	1	6	11.80	4.21	3.12	4.61	0.74	9.59
1999	Clearwtr	Fla	62.0	45	26	11	20	23	3.77	4	3	6.53	1.60	2.90	3.34	0.57	3.65
2000	Clearwtr	Fla	14.7	17	9	2	3	7	5.52	1	1	10.43	1.23	1.84	4.30	1.17	5.15
2000	Reading	Eas	66.0	51	22	9	22	30	3.00	4	3	6.95	1.23	3.00	4.09	0.68	3.57

It's not that often that you see someone sneak this far up the ranks pitching almost exclusively in middle relief. Joseph Cotton always seems to be an afterthought in the organization, but if he keeps the base-runner count as far down as he has, he may force the team to consider him after all. That is, until the A's took him in the Triple-A portion of the Rule 5 draft first.

Omar Daal — Throws L — Age 29

YEAR	TEAM	LGE	IP	H	ER	HR	BB	K	ERA	W	L	H/9	HR/9	BB/9	K/9	KW	PERA
1998	Arizona	NL	156.0	143	58	12	45	107	3.35	10	7	8.25	0.69	2.60	6.17	1.19	3.60
1999	Arizona	NL	208.7	180	83	19	65	125	3.58	13	10	7.76	0.82	2.80	5.39	0.96	3.54
2000	Arizona	NL	94.0	121	78	15	34	37	7.47	2	8	11.59	1.44	3.26	3.54	0.54	6.59
2000	Philadel	NL	69.7	78	36	8	24	42	4.65	3	5	10.08	1.03	3.10	5.43	0.88	5.21

His luck got so absurdly bad last year that he probably would have interpreted a black cat running across the field as a good omen. His performance over the last six weeks of last year was similar to his 1998 and 1999 output, so he should bounce back with a strong season.

Brandon Duckworth — Throws R — Age 25

YEAR	TEAM	LGE	IP	H	ER	HR	BB	K	ERA	W	L	H/9	HR/9	BB/9	K/9	KW	PERA
1998	Piedmont	SAL	134.7	123	75	21	33	54	5.01	6	9	8.22	1.40	2.21	3.61	0.82	4.14
1998	Clearwtr	Fla	49.3	63	26	4	27	26	4.74	2	3	11.49	0.73	4.93	4.74	0.48	6.50
1999	Clearwtr	Fla	119.7	167	100	28	51	56	7.52	3	10	12.56	2.11	3.84	4.21	0.55	8.12
2000	Reading	Eas	150.0	160	95	31	60	107	5.70	6	11	9.60	1.86	3.60	6.42	0.89	6.02

Brandon Duckworth seemingly came out of nowhere to be the ace of Reading's staff, but having already thrown a lot of innings in winter ball, he wore down in August. If he manages to avoid getting hurt, he could wind up as a September call-up.

Nelson Figueroa — Throws R — Age 27

YEAR	TEAM	LGE	IP	H	ER	HR	BB	K	ERA	W	L	H/9	HR/9	BB/9	K/9	KW	PERA
1998	Binghmtn	Eas	113.0	140	88	27	49	65	7.01	3	10	11.15	2.15	3.90	5.18	0.66	7.37
1998	Tucson	PCL	39.3	43	21	9	16	20	4.81	2	2	9.84	2.06	3.66	4.58	0.63	6.36
1999	Tucson	PCL	121.7	120	57	17	44	67	4.22	7	7	8.88	1.26	3.25	4.96	0.76	4.80
2000	Tucson	PCL	107.0	96	38	10	27	53	3.20	7	5	8.07	0.84	2.27	4.46	0.98	3.53
2000	Arizona	NL	15.3	16	12	4	4	6	7.04	0	2	9.39	2.35	2.35	3.52	0.75	5.90
2000	Scran-WB	Int	46.3	52	35	13	12	25	6.80	1	4	10.10	2.53	2.33	4.86	1.04	6.51

One of the Phillies' baffle-them-with-location pitchers. Nelson Figueroa probably has the lowest velocity of the bunch, which makes him the most vulnerable to mistakes in location. He could very well turn into a one-year wonder somewhere along the way, but I doubt he'll be more than a fifth starter on a regular basis.

Wayne Gomes — Throws R — Age 28

YEAR	TEAM	LGE	IP	H	ER	HR	BB	K	ERA	W	L	H/9	HR/9	BB/9	K/9	KW	PERA
1998	Philadel	NL	89.7	93	48	9	32	70	4.82	4	6	9.33	0.90	3.21	7.03	1.09	4.69
1999	Philadel	NL	73.3	69	34	4	46	49	4.17	4	4	8.47	0.49	5.65	6.01	0.53	4.75
2000	Philadel	NL	72.3	70	37	5	28	41	4.60	3	5	8.71	0.62	3.48	5.10	0.73	4.15

Phillies fans have come to fear "The Look" when Wayne Gomes pitches. He will be sailing through an inning until he throws three consecutive pitches out of the strike zone or gives up a hit. Then he looks like a deer caught in the headlights. His control deteriorates rapidly, and the base-runners start piling up. He has the stuff to be an effective pitcher, but he may need a good sports psychologist to harness it.

Thomas Jacquez — Throws L — Age 25

YEAR	TEAM	LGE	IP	H	ER	HR	BB	K	ERA	W	L	H/9	HR/9	BB/9	K/9	KW	PERA
1998	Clearwtr	Fla	160.0	210	106	23	38	62	5.96	6	12	11.81	1.29	2.14	3.49	0.82	6.12
1999	Reading	Eas	114.3	149	91	28	33	42	7.16	3	10	11.73	2.20	2.60	3.31	0.64	7.22
2000	Reading	Eas	25.0	26	13	4	10	13	4.68	1	2	9.36	1.44	3.60	4.68	0.65	5.37
2000	Scran-WB	Int	51.7	51	15	4	21	25	2.61	4	2	8.88	0.70	3.66	4.35	0.60	4.38
2000	Philadel	NL	7.3	10	8	2	2	5	9.82	0	1	12.27	2.45	2.45	6.14	1.25	7.80

Thomas Jacquez found his niche once he was moved to the bullpen and put under the tutelage of Gorm Heimueller. His control improved considerably, despite the fact that he stopped using his change-up, which might be his best pitch. He should get a look in the major-league bullpen this year and could be useful if he keeps the improved control.

Jason Kershner — Throws L — Age 24

YEAR	TEAM	LGE	IP	H	ER	HR	BB	K	ERA	W	L	H/9	HR/9	BB/9	K/9	KW	PERA
1998	Clearwtr	Fla	88.0	107	62	15	29	38	6.34	3	7	10.94	1.53	2.97	3.89	0.66	6.19
1999	Reading	Eas	86.0	103	75	19	40	54	7.85	2	8	10.78	1.99	4.19	5.65	0.68	7.08
2000	Clearwtr	Fla	12.3	8	1	2	6	8	0.73	1	0	5.84	1.46	4.38	5.84	0.67	3.64
2000	Reading	Eas	110.0	129	59	26	27	51	4.83	5	7	10.55	2.13	2.21	4.17	0.94	6.28

Jason Kershner worked a lot more on mixing his pitches and improving his location, and it showed in the results. The fact that he disappears when he turns sideways makes you wonder if he'll hold up, and the drop in his velocity is a concern.

Brett Myers — Throws R — Age 20

YEAR	TEAM	LGE	IP	H	ER	HR	BB	K	ERA	W	L	H/9	HR/9	BB/9	K/9	KW	PERA
2000	Piedmont	SAL	159.0	167	91	17	89	66	5.15	7	11	9.45	0.96	5.04	3.74	0.37	5.57

The usual first-round-pick hype surrounds Brett Myers, which may prevent some people from taking an honest look at him. Don't be fooled by the blazing fastball; his control was awful, and if he doesn't improve, all the heat in the world won't help.

Doug Nickle — Throws R — Age 26

YEAR	TEAM	LGE	IP	H	ER	HR	BB	K	ERA	W	L	H/9	HR/9	BB/9	K/9	KW	PERA
1998	CedarRpd	Mid	63.0	68	34	5	26	28	4.86	3	4	9.71	0.71	3.71	4.00	0.54	4.93
1998	Lk Elsin	Cal	60.0	69	47	7	33	33	7.05	2	5	10.35	1.05	4.95	4.95	0.50	6.15
1999	Clearwtr	Fla	64.0	61	29	2	31	37	4.08	3	4	8.58	0.28	4.36	5.20	0.60	4.07
2000	Reading	Eas	71.0	57	31	8	26	34	3.93	4	4	7.23	1.01	3.30	4.31	0.65	3.62
2000	Philadel	NL	2.7	5	4	0	2	0	13.50	0	0	16.88	0.00	6.75	0.00	0.00	9.86

Doug Nickle puts a lot of effort into studying hitters and situations, and the work is starting to pay off. He could use at least a half-season at Triple-A, which should be just enough time for Jose Mesa and Ricky Bottalico to be booed out of the Eastern time zone.

Jimmy Osting — Throws L — Age 24

YEAR	TEAM	LGE	IP	H	ER	HR	BB	K	ERA	W	L	H/9	HR/9	BB/9	K/9	KW	PERA
1999	Macon	SAL	133.0	141	68	25	40	59	4.60	6	9	9.54	1.69	2.71	3.99	0.74	5.42
2000	Myrtle B	Car	21.3	25	8	0	7	8	3.38	1	1	10.55	0.00	2.95	3.38	0.57	4.39
2000	Greenvil	Sou	65.7	71	35	9	29	30	4.80	3	4	9.73	1.23	3.97	4.11	0.52	5.58
2000	Reading	Eas	53.3	51	17	2	28	20	2.87	4	2	8.61	0.34	4.73	3.38	0.36	4.29

More booty from the Andy Ashby heist, and yet another not-particularly-overpowering pitcher. If Jimmy Osting can get the walk rate down somewhat he'll be a much more viable prospect. Right now, he's buried under a pile of other arms. Not literally; that would be weird.

Vicente Padilla — Throws R — Age 23

YEAR	TEAM	LGE	IP	H	ER	HR	BB	K	ERA	W	L	H/9	HR/9	BB/9	K/9	KW	PERA
1999	High Des	Cal	48.3	50	26	4	17	30	4.84	2	3	9.31	0.74	3.17	5.59	0.88	4.49
1999	Tucson	PCL	91.0	96	40	6	24	39	3.96	5	5	9.49	0.59	2.37	3.86	0.81	4.11
2000	Tucson	PCL	17.7	22	8	2	7	16	4.08	1	1	11.21	1.02	3.57	8.15	1.14	6.05
2000	Arizona	NL	33.7	32	11	1	8	25	2.94	3	1	8.55	0.27	2.14	6.68	1.56	3.19
2000	Philadel	NL	30.0	39	21	3	14	17	6.30	1	2	11.70	0.90	4.20	5.10	0.61	6.47

Vicente Padilla appears intent on imitating the multi-armed Indian god Kali by throwing from several different angles. He would actually be better off if he focused on perfecting a couple of those angles; right now he's not consistent with any.

Robert Person — Throws R — Age 32

YEAR	TEAM	LGE	IP	H	ER	HR	BB	K	ERA	W	L	H/9	HR/9	BB/9	K/9	KW	PERA
1998	Syracuse	Int	55.3	40	20	11	29	37	3.25	4	2	6.51	1.79	4.72	6.02	0.64	4.59
1998	Toronto	AL	38.3	43	28	8	19	29	6.57	1	3	10.10	1.88	4.46	6.81	0.76	6.72
1999	Toronto	AL	11.3	9	10	1	12	11	7.94	0	1	7.15	0.79	9.53	8.74	0.46	5.86
1999	Philadel	NL	134.7	127	65	20	57	107	4.34	7	8	8.49	1.34	3.81	7.15	0.94	4.89
2000	Philadel	NL	170.3	144	66	11	76	136	3.49	11	8	7.61	0.58	4.02	7.19	0.89	3.69

His motto last year seemed to be "Why use three pitches to get an out when eight will do?" A frequent pattern found Person quickly getting two strikes on a batter then nibbling, running the count to full before finally retiring him. He needs Ruhle and Lieberthal leaning on him to just throw strikes.

Cliff Politte — Throws R — Age 27

YEAR	TEAM	LGE	IP	H	ER	HR	BB	K	ERA	W	L	H/9	HR/9	BB/9	K/9	KW	PERA
1998	Arkansas	Tex	62.0	57	29	9	19	37	4.21	3	4	8.27	1.31	2.76	5.37	0.97	4.29
1998	Memphis	PCL	48.0	68	47	12	27	28	8.81	1	4	12.75	2.25	5.06	5.25	0.52	8.91
1998	St Louis	NL	35.7	44	31	6	16	18	7.82	1	3	11.10	1.51	4.04	4.54	0.56	6.72
1999	Reading	Eas	100.0	117	54	18	36	56	4.86	4	7	10.53	1.62	3.24	5.04	0.78	6.16
2000	Scran-WB	Int	105.0	96	54	12	45	76	4.63	5	7	8.23	1.03	3.86	6.51	0.84	4.44
2000	Philadel	NL	58.0	54	22	7	22	42	3.41	3	3	8.38	1.09	3.41	6.52	0.95	4.42

Cliff Politte is now out of options, which is unfortunate since he just started adding a change-up to his mix of pitches, and he needs more time to polish it. He did well in eight major-league starts last year, but batters may begin to figure him out soon; without that extra pitch, he could be in trouble.

John Sneed — Throws R — Age 25

YEAR	TEAM	LGE	IP	H	ER	HR	BB	K	ERA	W	L	H/9	HR/9	BB/9	K/9	KW	PERA
1998	Hagerstn	SAL	144.3	139	78	16	75	96	4.86	6	10	8.67	1.00	4.68	5.99	0.64	5.00
1999	Dunedin	Fla	112.3	119	77	22	46	80	6.17	4	8	9.53	1.76	3.69	6.41	0.87	5.92
1999	Knoxvill	Sou	26.7	33	17	3	21	17	5.74	1	2	11.14	1.01	7.09	5.74	0.40	7.45
2000	Tennesse	Sou	110.3	132	96	15	58	55	7.83	2	10	10.77	1.22	4.73	4.49	0.47	6.49
2000	Reading	Eas	22.7	33	35	9	22	14	13.90	0	3	13.10	3.57	8.74	5.56	0.32	12.01

When the Phillies got John Sneed, they tried to tinker with his mechanics to reduce his wildness. The progress was sufficiently slow that they didn't want to keep him on the 40-man roster, but his fastball is strong enough that teams were lined up to grab him. He first was reclaimed by the Blue Jays; when they tried to slip him through waivers, the Twins grabbed him. Sleeper.

Amaury Telemaco — Throws R — Age 27

YEAR	TEAM	LGE	IP	H	ER	HR	BB	K	ERA	W	L	H/9	HR/9	BB/9	K/9	KW	PERA
1998	ChiCubs	NL	26.7	23	12	5	12	15	4.05	1	2	7.76	1.69	4.05	5.06	0.63	4.98
1998	Arizona	NL	116.0	121	59	13	29	49	4.58	6	7	9.39	1.01	2.25	3.80	0.84	4.42
1999	Tucson	PCL	17.0	20	11	1	7	11	5.82	1	1	10.59	0.53	3.71	5.82	0.79	5.29
1999	Philadel	NL	46.0	44	26	7	16	35	5.09	2	3	8.61	1.37	3.13	6.85	1.09	4.72
2000	Scran-WB	Int	114.3	116	71	22	46	63	5.59	4	9	9.13	1.73	3.62	4.96	0.68	5.61
2000	Philadel	NL	24.0	24	19	5	11	18	7.13	1	2	9.00	1.88	4.13	6.75	0.82	5.86

The team's attempt to improve his mechanics in spring training turned into a disaster, and Amaury Telemaco was sent to Triple-A where he eventually regained some control. Aside from demonstrating the relative abilities of the pitching coaches in question, Telemaco may have earned himself one more chance this year—but he's rapidly approaching his last.

Evan Thomas — Throws R — Age 27

YEAR	TEAM	LGE	IP	H	ER	HR	BB	K	ERA	W	L	H/9	HR/9	BB/9	K/9	KW	PERA
1998	Reading	Eas	146.7	182	74	17	49	75	4.54	7	9	11.17	1.04	3.01	4.60	0.77	5.83
1999	Reading	Eas	117.0	128	62	11	55	73	4.77	5	8	9.85	0.85	4.23	5.62	0.66	5.34
2000	Scran-WB	Int	159.3	164	81	24	55	90	4.58	8	10	9.26	1.36	3.11	5.08	0.82	5.08

Evan Thomas's strikeout rate dropped, but that was in large part due to an organizational attempt to reduce the number of pitches thrown by Scranton's staff. Thomas's walk rate dropped even more. He's an effective pitcher with several good pitches who gets overlooked because he's 5' 10" and doesn't throw 95 mph. Once he finally gets a chance in the majors, he'll be a solid starter.

Randy Wolf — Throws L — Age 24

YEAR	TEAM	LGE	IP	H	ER	HR	BB	K	ERA	W	L	H/9	HR/9	BB/9	K/9	KW	PERA
1998	Reading	Eas	23.0	18	6	1	4	20	2.35	2	1	7.04	0.39	1.57	7.83	2.50	2.36
1998	Scran-WB	Int	141.3	163	89	19	47	86	5.67	5	11	10.38	1.21	2.99	5.48	0.91	5.54
1999	Scran-WB	Int	73.3	72	36	9	29	53	4.42	4	4	8.84	1.10	3.56	6.50	0.91	4.74
1999	Philadel	NL	120.0	123	71	18	55	98	5.32	5	8	9.23	1.35	4.13	7.35	0.89	5.47
2000	Philadel	NL	201.7	204	96	21	66	133	4.28	10	12	9.10	0.94	2.95	5.94	1.01	4.47

Terry Francona's legacy may be the destruction of Randy Wolf's star potential. If he has survived the abuse, Wolf could be a fun pitcher to watch for years to come because he has four good pitches thrown at four different speeds. When he has the control to keep them near the plate, batters tend to look very silly. Unfortunately, Bowa will likely finish the job Francona started.

Support-Neutral Statistics				PHILADELPHIA PHILLIES							Park Effect: -0.1%	
PITCHER	GS	IP	R	SNW	SNL	SNPCT	W	L	RA	APW	SNVA	SNWAR
Andy Ashby	16	101.3	75	4.4	7.5	.373	4	7	6.66	-1.6	-1.5	-0.6
Kent Bottenfield	8	44.0	24	2.8	2.3	.547	1	2	4.91	0.1	0.2	0.6
Chris Brock	5	31.0	17	1.9	1.5	.549	0	3	4.94	0.1	0.2	0.4
Paul Byrd	15	80.7	61	4.1	6.6	.383	2	8	6.81	-1.4	-1.3	-0.5
Bruce Chen	15	94.3	39	6.7	3.7	.646	3	4	3.72	1.4	1.4	2.3
David Coggin	5	27.0	20	1.0	2.1	.312	2	0	6.67	-0.4	-0.6	-0.4
Omar Daal	12	71.0	40	3.9	3.9	.501	2	9	5.07	0.0	-0.1	0.6
Robert Person	28	173.3	73	11.7	7.5	.610	9	7	3.79	2.4	2.0	3.5
Cliff Politte	8	50.0	18	3.5	1.8	.666	4	3	3.24	1.0	0.9	1.3
Curt Schilling	16	112.7	49	7.4	4.9	.602	6	6	3.91	1.4	1.2	2.2
Amaury Telemaco	2	12.7	8	0.8	0.9	.480	0	2	5.68	-0.1	-0.0	0.1
Randy Wolf	32	206.3	107	12.7	10.2	.554	11	9	4.67	1.0	1.0	3.0
TOTALS	162	1004.3	531	61.0	52.9	.535	44	60	4.76	3.9	3.5	12.6

Among the many surprising things about the Phillies' great 2000 rotation, perhaps the most surprising is the sheer number of pitchers who put together good seasons. The Phillies weren't one of those teams who had a stable rotation all year; they used 12 different starters, eight of whom had Support-Neutral W/L records better than .500. The number of above-average starters is tied for fourth-most among all rotations since 1979. There were three teams that had nine above-average starters—the 1985 Red Sox, the 1993 Expos, and the 1987 Yankees.

I don't know that this says anything too profound; often all it means is that the team had to use several fill-in starters, and that a few of those had a handful of good starts. On the other hand, it certainly isn't a bad sign that two of the three teams just mentioned, the Red Sox and Expos, had terrific rotations the following year.

If we're going to conclude anything from across-the-board strong performances by a pitching staff, it might be just that the pitching coach had a good year. I'm not saying Galen Cisco is a genius or anything—he's typically presided over crummy staffs in the past—but just look at the cast of characters who suddenly became fine starters for the Phillies last year. If you can get Robert Person, Cliff Politte, and even Kent Bottenfield to put up good numbers, you must be doing something right.

For a quick explanation of SN stats, see page 7.

Reliever Evaluation Tools											
PITCHER	G	IP	R	ARA	APR	IRNR/G	EIRS/G	IRP	BRS	RRA	ARP
Scott Aldred	23	20.3	14	6.28	-2.4	0.48	0.16	-2.5	-1.8	6.62	-3.2
Jason Boyd	30	34.3	28	7.43	-8.5	0.23	0.11	0.3	-2.5	6.51	-5.0
Jeff Brantley	55	55.3	36	5.93	-4.5	0.15	0.03	0.6	5.0	6.66	-9.0
Chris Brock	58	62.3	31	4.53	4.6	0.45	0.10	2.2	0.3	4.59	4.2
Mark Brownson	2	5.0	4	7.29	-1.2	0.00	0.00	0.0	0.4	8.01	-1.6
Kirk Bullinger	3	3.3	2	5.47	-0.1	1.00	0.52	-0.4	0.0	6.60	-0.5
Paul Byrd	2	2.3	6	23.44	-4.7	0.00	0.00	0.0	0.0	22.90	-4.6
Rob Ducey	1	0.3	2	54.70	-1.8	0.00	0.00	0.0	0.0	55.71	-1.9
Wayne Gomes	64	73.3	39	4.85	2.8	0.59	0.19	-0.6	-1.7	4.93	2.1
Mark Holzemer	25	25.7	23	8.17	-8.5	0.56	0.21	-0.4	1.1	8.36	-9.0
Thomas Jacquez	9	7.3	9	11.19	-4.9	1.11	0.49	-0.8	-0.9	11.89	-5.5
Trever Miller	14	14.0	16	10.42	-8.1	0.36	0.14	-0.1	-0.9	9.78	-7.1
Doug Nickle	4	2.7	4	13.67	-2.5	0.00	0.00	0.0	-1.0	10.52	-1.6
Vicente Padilla	28	30.3	23	6.91	-5.8	0.68	0.24	0.9	-0.1	6.62	-4.8
Cliff Politte	4	9.0	6	6.08	-0.9	0.00	0.00	0.0	0.0	6.74	-1.5
Carlos Reyes	10	10.3	6	5.29	-0.1	0.60	0.12	-0.9	0.7	7.02	-2.1
Steve Schrenk	20	23.3	20	7.81	-6.8	0.15	0.03	-1.3	-1.6	7.65	-6.4
Amaury Telemaco	11	11.7	14	10.94	-7.4	0.36	0.07	-1.3	-1.0	11.18	-7.8
Ed Vosberg	31	24.0	11	4.18	2.7	0.55	0.19	0.7	0.4	4.02	3.1
Bryan Ward	20	19.3	5	2.36	6.1	0.35	0.16	-3.0	0.1	3.78	3.1
TOTALS	414	434.3	299	6.28	-52.1	0.43	0.14			6.42	-59.0

For a quick guide to RET, see page 10.

Pittsburgh Pirates

Imagine that one day you showed up for the same job you've had for years, only to find that the owner of your company has made a few changes. The brand-new Pentium III computer on your desk has been replaced by an XT, circa 1983. Your calculator is gone; in its stead you find a rickety abacus. Your phone is now one of those antique rotary models. Oh, and your secretary is gone.

A few months before all this, you had asked the owner for a little security—a contract extension, for example. He said no but wouldn't elaborate. When you asked permission to hunt for another job, he refused. Perhaps out of a misguided sense of loyalty, you decided to stick it out since there was just one more year in your employment agreement.

So you set about your job, knowing full well that the bell tolls for thee. You discover that most of the pens on your desk are out of ink. Your boss arranges for some extra help, but most of the employees sent in to work for you have been trained by barely-sentient trolls who toil in your company's remote offices. You realize that the phone isn't even plugged into the wall jack. Two months into the work year, IT comes along, steals your mouse and removes the "S" and "A" keys from your keyboard.

Welcome to Gene Lamont's final year as the Pirates' manager, although to be fair he had it even worse. Owner Kevin McClatchy belied his reputation as an enlightened owner when he refused to give Lamont a deserved extension and also refused to allow him to pursue managerial openings with other teams. Their meeting occurred in October 1999 and was widely reported, so Lamont had to live and work under a dark cloud four months before pitchers and catchers reported to spring training. And that only scratches the surface of the injustices done to Gene Lamont by the Pirates.

In the NFL, head coaches have realized that their job security depends more upon the competence of the men charged with assembling the rosters than upon their own abilities as football coaches. Bill Parcells, Mike Ditka, and Dan Reeves have made control over personnel decisions a prerequisite before taking head coaching positions.

In baseball, however, such a combination of responsibility and accountability in one position is rare. Whitey Herzog had it in St. Louis and produced three World Series appearances. Buck Showalter sort of had it in Arizona, but that turned into an abject lesson in the importance of getting pre-employment promises in writing. The list of managers who were fired for the sins of their bosses is long, and Gene Lamont can now be added to that list.

The fundamental problem with the Pirates the past few years is that their front office provided Lamont with very little talent. For starters, Lamont was asked to win with a roster full of mediocrities, some quite expensive, flanked by just two stars. Indeed, he was probably better off with the crowd of outcasts and discards he nearly rode to the division crown in 1997, the last gasp at glory this franchise has seen. That year, unbound by the piles of cash that have held the Orioles and Dodgers in check for the last five years, the Pirates meted out roles based on ability and performance, rather than on salary and reputation, and surprised nearly everyone by contending for the NL Central title into late September.

Then things got ugly. Owner Kevin McClatchy, no doubt thinking he was doing right by the team's growing fan base in western Pennsylvania, loosened the purse strings and allowed GM Cam Bonifay to triple the payroll. But a funny thing happens when you allow someone who has operated on a shoestring budget to spend more money. The incentive to maximize the production from every dollar spent diminishes. Suddenly, houses in Sewickley look inexpensive, and you stop complaining about the price gouging at Giant Eagle, and, before you know it, Pat Meares is on the payroll.

If Meares seems to come up a lot in this chapter, it's for a good reason. When Meares was a free agent after the 1998 season, Minnesota didn't even offer him arbitration—meaning any team could sign Meares without surrendering a draft pick or two as compensation. Meares received no multi-year offers and ultimately accepted a small one-year offer from

Pirates Prospectus

2000 record: 69–93; Fifth place, NL Central
Pythagenport W/L: 72–90
Runs Scored: 793 (9th in NL)
Runs Allowed: 888 (12th in NL)
Team EqA: .256 (tied for 9th in NL)
2000 Batters' Age: 28.4 (tied for 3rd youngest in NL)
2000 Pitchers' Age: 26.8 (tied for 3rd youngest in NL)
Ballpark: Three Rivers Stadium; neutral park; Park Factor of 1.002; Moving to PNC Park for 2001 season.
2000: The commitments to Kendall and Giles overshadowed a disappointing year on the field.
2001: There's a good baseball team hidden amongst the bad contracts. Let them play!

the Bucs. But about a month into the season, the Pirates inexplicably gave Meares a four-year, $16-million contract extension that would keep him with the club through 2002. At a time when neither Jason Kendall nor Brian Giles was signed for that long, it was incredibly irresponsible.

Yet the Pirates have repeatedly shown themselves to be sketchy at best when it comes to fiscal responsibility. Kevin Young is signed for two more years at big money. Wil Cordero got a three-year deal when no other team offered him anything more than a one-year contract; only the mercy of John Hart saved the Pirates from that albatross. Pete Schourek's two-year, $4 million deal turned into a one-year, $4-million deal when the Bucs cut him last spring (although it was the right move). Have we mentioned the Pat Meares fiasco?

While Gene Lamont was saddled with these expensive hitters of questionable value, he also had to cobble together a rotation around Kris Benson, the consensus preseason pick for breakthrough pitcher in the National League, and the tattered remains of 1997's what-could-have-been team. Jon Lieber, one of the three stars from the '97–'98 squads, was dipped in Belgian chocolate and handed to the Cubs as a goodwill gesture. The Cubs failed to reciprocate in handing the Pirates a stale outfielder named Brant Brown. Jason Schmidt had been overworked for years, though the blame for that might as easily be placed on Lamont. Francisco Cordova has always been fragile. Aside from Benson, the farm system hasn't produced any top pitching prospects in years, with both Jimmy Anderson and Bronson Arroyo struggling from the time they first reached Double-A.

Indeed, part of the reason the Bucs have dabbled in the treacherous waters of the free-agent market in the past few years is the fact that the Pirates' farm system has come up almost completely dry. Aside from Benson, the #1 overall draft pick in '96 and a multi-million-dollar signee, the Pirates haven't produced an everyday player or starting pitcher who might reasonably be called homegrown since Jason Kendall emerged in '96.

The problem with position players is particularly acute, as the Pirates de-emphasize patience at the plate throughout their system. For years, a massive obstacle has existed at Triple-A, where prospects with plate discipline would lose it entirely in their first season at the level. The list isn't pretty—Ron Wright, Freddy Garcia, Chad Hermansen, Tike Redman, Alex Hernandez, T.J. Staton—and the problem isn't new: we've been highlighting it here for years. In 2000, John Wehner led the Nashville Sounds, the Pirates' Triple-A club, with 56 walks. In '99, only one player drew more than 35 walks. Aramis Ramirez, whose high ceiling derives partly from his excellent strike-zone judgment, was told to cut down on his strikeouts and be more aggressive at the plate when he returned to Triple-A in 1999. (He still drew 79 walks to lead the team by a factor of more than two.) It's a good thing that the Pirates' minor-league coaches didn't get their hands on Brian Giles.

So Lamont was handed a roster with two bona fide hitters, one good starting pitcher, a few decent arms in the bullpen, little talent on the bench, and virtually no help on the farm. With this, he was expected to reach the playoffs. Even if the rotation had stayed intact, that was an impossible, illogical goal. With Schmidt and Cordova shelved and the likes of Dan Serafini, Bronson Arroyo, and Brian O'Connor pressed into service, 70 wins seemed a reach.

The right path for the Pirates is clear. An organization-wide instructional overhaul is necessary if this franchise ever wants to produce the hitters it needs to staff the big club inexpensively. Prospects should improve their walk rates as they mature while coaches who see their pupils' patience erode should be sacked. New managerial and coaching blood should be brought in, preferably from organizations with some record of success. The dead-weight contracts of Pat Meares and Kevin Young should be cleared or restructured if at all possible. The organization should start breaking in more young pitchers via the bullpen or swing-man roles while using minor-league veterans like Todd Ritchie to staff the rotation. The successful starters will make great trade bait, while the youngsters will get the valuable experience that eases the transition into the major leagues.

Unfortunately, early signs aren't positive. The Pirates interviewed nearly a dozen candidates for their managerial opening, from successful veterans (Buck Showalter) to deserving newcomers (Chris Chambliss). Instead of choosing from either category, they chose Lloyd McClendon, their hitting coach. Needless to say, McClendon is making all the right press-friendly noises about getting the team to play hard, but it's difficult to ignore his culpability in the Pirates' recent failures. In McClendon's tenure as hitting coach, only one rookie hitter has had even a moderately successful season, and Warren Morris had come from another organization.

Not content with misfiring on the managerial decision, the Pirates went shopping and signed Derek Bell and Terry Mulholland to free-agent contracts. Mulholland has some value as a swing man, particularly for a team developing younger pitchers, and he came cheap. But giving Derek Bell money to play for your baseball team is an idea cut from the same cloth as last winter's horrific Wil Cordero signing: paying a known mediocrity instead of your own younger players.

With the Bell signing, it's going to be nearly impossible for John Vander Wal and Chad Hermansen to get the playing time they deserve, and Bell won't do anything for the Pirates that Vander Wal and Hermansen couldn't. People clamoring for increased sharing of local revenue as a cure-all should examine the Pirates' last two off-seasons carefully and then try to explain how giving them additional millions would help the game of baseball.

The Pirates won't be contenders by the time their new ballpark opens. Instead of accepting that fact and making tough choices, they've taken the easy road and fired the manager. To make matters worse, they've replaced him with an internal candidate who presided over the stagnation of all of the team's top hitting prospects. It's a formula that works about as often as an early-model Yugo, and the results in Pittsburgh won't be any prettier.

HITTERS (BA: .270, OBP: .340, SLG: .440, EqA: .260)

Tony Alvarez — LF — Bats R — Age 22

YEAR	TEAM	LGE	AB	H	DB	TP	HR	BB	SO	R	RBI	SB	CS	OUT	BA	OBP	SLG	EQA	EQR	DEFENSE	
1999	Willmspt	NYP	202	50	11	0	5	14	38	23	29	10	4	156	.248	.316	.376	.236	21	33-3B	-11
2000	Hickory	SAL	451	104	17	2	12	27	99	45	52	16	11	358	.231	.283	.357	.212	37	101-LF	1
2001	Pittsbrg	NL	375	95	18	1	11	28	86	52	44	21	11	291	.253	.305	.395	.236	39		

Tony Alvarez took a smaller step forward than expected, losing some power and some patience with the jump to full-season ball. He gradually cooled off over the year, which dampened his numbers a bit, and he was moved to left field as questions about his abilities at second base continued to dog him, meaning he needs to kick up his offensive game even more. He has good tools and is young enough to improve.

Mike Benjamin — SS/2B — Bats R — Age 35

YEAR	TEAM	LGE	AB	H	DB	TP	HR	BB	SO	R	RBI	SB	CS	OUT	BA	OBP	SLG	EQA	EQR	DEFENSE			
1998	Boston	AL	348	97	15	0	7	14	65	45	40	3	0	251	.279	.317	.382	.235	34	76-2B	0	17-SS	5
1999	Pittsbrg	NL	370	90	27	6	1	15	85	40	34	8	1	281	.243	.276	.357	.211	29	86-SS	18	11-2B	0
2000	Pittsbrg	NL	235	62	18	2	2	8	42	26	18	4	4	177	.264	.296	.383	.222	21	24-3B	1	22-2B	3
2001	Pittsbrg	NL	288	70	16	1	4	17	61	29	28	4	1	219	.243	.285	.347	.212	23				

Mike Benjamin is another questionable acquisition. Guys like him can be had for the minimum salary as minor-league free agents, and there's not much Benjamin does that Abraham Nunez doesn't. But Benjamin holds that consecutive-hits record and has lots of major-league experience. Some GMs seem to value that stuff more than they value the money they could save by finding cheaper options.

Josh Bonifay — 2B — Bats R — Age 22

YEAR	TEAM	LGE	AB	H	DB	TP	HR	BB	SO	R	RBI	SB	CS	OUT	BA	OBP	SLG	EQA	EQR	DEFENSE	
1999	Willmspt	NYP	207	44	8	1	3	17	59	32	12	1	1	164	.213	.275	.304	.190	13	37-2B	-5
2000	Hickory	SAL	388	87	11	1	11	34	111	45	42	4	3	304	.224	.289	.343	.210	31	95-2B	-9
2001	Pittsbrg	NL	248	61	5	0	8	25	84	28	31	3	1	188	.246	.315	.363	.232	24		

Josh Bonifay originally seemed like a nepotista selection, but it turns out he has some good baseball skills. He was second on the Hickory squad in walks, one behind 25-year-old Jason Landreth. He gets decent marks for defense and has some pop in his bat, particularly to the opposite field. That said, he has chronic knee problems that will probably prevent him from making the majors. Hey, at least he outplayed Woody Woodward's kid.

Adrian Brown — CF — Bats B — Age 27

YEAR	TEAM	LGE	AB	H	DB	TP	HR	BB	SO	R	RBI	SB	CS	OUT	BA	OBP	SLG	EQA	EQR	DEFENSE	
1998	Nashvill	PCL	309	79	11	4	2	23	38	45	21	17	5	235	.256	.307	.337	.223	28	80-CF	7
1998	Pittsbrg	NL	153	43	5	1	0	9	17	21	6	4	0	110	.281	.321	.327	.225	13	37-CF	0
1999	Nashvill	PCL	55	15	1	1	0	10	8	7	3	4	1	41	.273	.385	.327	.261	7	15-LF	0
1999	Pittsbrg	NL	226	59	4	2	4	30	37	32	16	4	3	170	.261	.350	.350	.241	24	56-RF	-3
2000	Pittsbrg	NL	309	94	17	3	4	25	32	61	26	12	1	216	.304	.356	.417	.267	40	75-CF	-3
2001	Pittsbrg	NL	321	91	14	3	4	34	41	55	39	16	3	233	.283	.352	.383	.259	40		

If the Pirates have completely given up on Chad Hermansen, they could do worse than play this guy in center field. Adrian Brown isn't a star, but he draws a few walks, is a great base-stealer, and—here's the kicker—can actually field. That's a rarity in the 'burgh these days, so you can bet the Pirates' pitchers are secretly hoping he'll get the nod.

Emil Brown — OF — Bats R — Age 26

YEAR	TEAM	LGE	AB	H	DB	TP	HR	BB	SO	R	RBI	SB	CS	OUT	BA	OBP	SLG	EQA	EQR	DEFENSE
1998	Carolina	Sou	464	127	21	1	11	30	76	59	45	12	4	341	.274	.327	.394	.244	50	104-CF -7
1999	Nashvill	PCL	424	113	17	4	13	28	77	73	45	11	4	315	.267	.319	.417	.246	47	98-RF -9
2000	Nashvill	PCL	237	65	16	1	4	32	45	32	19	16	3	175	.274	.371	.401	.272	34	65-RF -1
2000	Pittsbrg	NL	120	26	4	0	3	9	32	12	15	3	1	95	.217	.286	.325	.206	9	29-OF 0
2001	Pittsbrg	NL	326	87	15	1	9	33	69	52	43	15	3	242	.267	.334	.402	.255	40	

On most teams, Emil Brown would have found a niche as a fourth outfielder and top pinch hitter. He has a good glove, a little pop, and draws plenty of walks. In his old organization, the A's, he'd have gold stars all over his file. In Pittsburgh, he got two weeks to show what he could do and was then benched. Anyone looking for a cheap center-field solution for the next two to three years should inquire with C. Bonifay, c/o Pittsburgh Pirates.

Jose Castillo — SS — Bats R — Age 20

YEAR	TEAM	LGE	AB	H	DB	TP	HR	BB	SO	R	RBI	SB	CS	OUT	BA	OBP	SLG	EQA	EQR	DEFENSE
2000	Hickory	SAL	535	128	23	4	12	20	114	67	47	5	6	413	.239	.272	.364	.206	40	121-SS -19
2001	Pittsbrg	NL	263	66	10	1	6	11	95	24	28	3	2	199	.251	.281	.365	.214	21	

The good: in his first year of full-season ball, Jose Castillo slugged .480 in the Sally League at age 19. He also has a great arm. The bad: he drew just 29 walks in more than 550 plate appearances, with 107 strikeouts. The ugly: he made 60 errors—yep, sixty—in all colors of the rainbow. The Bucs seem inclined to leave him at shortstop for now because he's young and raw, but there are too many holes in his game to get too excited this soon.

Humberto Cota — C — Bats R — Age 22

YEAR	TEAM	LGE	AB	H	DB	TP	HR	BB	SO	R	RBI	SB	CS	OUT	BA	OBP	SLG	EQA	EQR	DEFENSE
1998	Princetn	App	247	54	8	1	8	19	70	25	30	1	2	195	.219	.281	.356	.209	19	49-C -9
1999	Charl-SC	SAL	342	79	16	1	6	15	54	32	43	0	0	263	.231	.265	.336	.194	22	61-C -10
1999	Hickory	SAL	139	30	10	1	1	15	21	21	14	1	0	109	.216	.292	.324	.208	11	30-C 0
2000	Altoona	Eas	435	105	15	1	8	14	86	41	36	4	3	333	.241	.268	.336	.195	28	90-C -23
2001	Pittsbrg	NL	419	107	21	1	10	27	86	46	51	4	1	313	.255	.300	.382	.229	39	

The Pirates profess to be pleased with Humberto Cota's progress, even if it looks like regression to these eyes. Cota's walk rate and strikeout-to-walk ratios collapsed, and he hit for no power. He was young for Double-A, so we can cut him some slack, but the fundamental skills of offense aren't here. On defense, Cota has quickened his release to second base, in part to compensate for what isn't a great arm. The Bucs are spending a lot of time working with him; he seems to need it.

J.J. Davis — LF — Bats R — Age 22

YEAR	TEAM	LGE	AB	H	DB	TP	HR	BB	SO	R	RBI	SB	CS	OUT	BA	OBP	SLG	EQA	EQR	DEFENSE
1998	Erie	NYP	200	43	7	1	6	13	58	16	24	1	1	158	.215	.266	.350	.200	14	46-RF -4
1998	Augusta	SAL	107	20	2	0	4	2	25	8	9	0	1	88	.187	.202	.318	.148	4	21-RF -2
1999	Hickory	SAL	329	69	15	1	13	33	105	41	43	1	2	262	.210	.285	.380	.219	29	45-RF -8
2000	Lynchbrg	Car	498	105	22	1	17	36	178	60	59	4	2	395	.211	.267	.361	.206	38	119-RF -15
2001	Pittsbrg	NL	443	101	19	1	19	39	160	49	59	4	2	344	.228	.290	.404	.231	44	

J.J. Davis adjusted slowly to high-A ball, then hit 14 of his 20 homers in the second half and showed improved power to all fields. Scouts say he's susceptible to a good breaking ball low and away, and his strikeout-to-walk ratio of more than 3-to-1 reflects his still-embryonic command of the strike zone. Power like his doesn't grow on trees; if he can tighten his pitch selection, he'll become a top prospect.

Eddy Furniss — 1B — Bats L — Age 25

YEAR	TEAM	LGE	AB	H	DB	TP	HR	BB	SO	R	RBI	SB	CS	OUT	BA	OBP	SLG	EQA	EQR	DEFENSE
1998	Augusta	SAL	92	32	4	0	6	18	21	22	19	0	0	60	.348	.455	.587	.341	20	12-1B -1
1998	Lynchbrg	Car	113	20	3	0	3	14	39	6	10	0	0	93	.177	.271	.283	.183	7	28-1B -3
1999	Lynchbrg	Car	462	100	20	1	18	70	116	72	60	2	2	364	.216	.324	.381	.238	50	83-1B -3
2000	Altoona	Eas	361	76	10	1	10	53	91	40	41	2	2	287	.211	.314	.327	.219	32	76-1B -2
2001	Oakland	AL	358	82	12	1	13	60	97	54	53	1	1	277	.229	.340	.377	.252	44	

The clock is ticking. Eddy Furniss was a college draft pick in '98, but he hit a wall at Double-A and ended the season on the bench. Furniss had shown good power in the past, and while some of the drop is due to the tough pitchers' park at Altoona, he simply struggled with the better pitchers in the Eastern League. He's a mediocre defender at first base, so his bat will have to carry him; right now, it's not exactly load-bearing. Furniss was drafted by the A's in the Triple-A portion of the Rule 5 draft.

Brian Giles — RF/CF — Bats L — Age 30

YEAR	TEAM	LGE	AB	H	DB	TP	HR	BB	SO	R	RBI	SB	CS	OUT	BA	OBP	SLG	EQA	EQR	DEFENSE	
1998	Clevelnd	AL	348	95	15	0	18	72	67	55	66	8	5	258	.273	.401	.471	.293	60	86-LF	14
1999	Pittsbrg	NL	521	158	31	3	37	86	76	103	104	5	2	365	.303	.405	.587	.319	105	137-CF	-1
2000	Pittsbrg	NL	561	170	36	6	33	104	65	105	112	6	0	391	.303	.417	.565	.322	115	153-OF	1
2001	Pittsbrg	NL	529	163	30	2	35	110	74	121	133	6	2	368	.308	.427	.571	.328	114		

The antithesis of a modern Pirate hitter: patient, powerful, above average for his position, and an All-Star. The best hitter on the team, Brian Giles executed in every offensive category for the second year in a row, even improving his ability to get on base. He continued to play center field due to the Pirates' lack of faith in any of the Browns. With Derek Bell on board, Giles may stay in center field instead of moving to right field where he belongs. Giles will be a star for most of the '00s.

Kevin Haverbusch — "3B" — Bats R — Age 25

YEAR	TEAM	LGE	AB	H	DB	TP	HR	BB	SO	R	RBI	SB	CS	OUT	BA	OBP	SLG	EQA	EQR	DEFENSE			
1998	Lynchbrg	Car	185	51	9	1	6	7	34	20	29	2	1	135	.276	.313	.432	.246	20	32-SS	-6	12-3B	-1
1998	Carolina	Sou	166	51	5	0	3	6	21	20	20	1	1	116	.307	.339	.392	.245	17	40-3B	-8		
1999	Altoona	Eas	335	86	19	1	11	7	63	45	47	3	2	251	.257	.294	.418	.233	33	79-3B	-15		
2000	Altoona	Eas	143	35	3	1	4	7	17	18	16	1	1	109	.245	.285	.364	.213	11	30-3B	-12		
2001	Pittsbrg	NL	181	51	5	0	8	11	30	22	29	2	1	131	.282	.323	.442	.255	21				

It was a lost season in what is starting to look like a lost career. Kevin Haverbusch played just 43 games before he blew his shoulder out while throwing a helmet in disgust over his play. Haverbusch started out like a house afire in '98, but he hasn't hit well since. He has just 45 walks in more than 1,100 pro plate appearances. Footwork problems have made his throwing from third base positively Knoblauchian. Aramis Ramirez shouldn't be concerned.

Chad Hermansen — CF — Bats R — Age 23

YEAR	TEAM	LGE	AB	H	DB	TP	HR	BB	SO	R	RBI	SB	CS	OUT	BA	OBP	SLG	EQA	EQR	DEFENSE	
1998	Nashvill	PCL	457	104	21	3	22	41	150	62	59	15	3	356	.228	.295	.431	.242	51	102-LF	-6
1999	Nashvill	PCL	490	114	21	2	24	29	115	66	71	13	7	383	.233	.279	.431	.232	50	115-CF	1
1999	Pittsbrg	NL	60	14	0	0	2	6	18	5	3	2	2	48	.233	.313	.333	.217	5	14-OF	0
2000	Nashvill	PCL	295	62	10	1	9	18	91	36	30	10	3	236	.210	.271	.342	.206	23	74-OF	-2
2000	Pittsbrg	NL	109	21	3	1	2	4	35	11	8	0	0	88	.193	.221	.294	.152	4	23-CF	-3
2001	Pittsbrg	NL	462	113	18	3	22	38	143	61	69	15	5	354	.245	.302	.439	.248	54		

Last season was a complete disaster for Chad Hermansen, long considered the Pirates' top prospect by scouts. He came to the majors with no plate discipline and had trouble recognizing breaking balls. When he struggled early, the Pirates tinkered with his swing to get him to lift the ball more, throwing his mechanics off so badly that he couldn't hit at Nashville, either. He needs to learn to be selective in Triple-A before he'll have a shot at hitting in the majors.

Alex Hernandez — RF/1B — Bats L — Age 24

YEAR	TEAM	LGE	AB	H	DB	TP	HR	BB	SO	R	RBI	SB	CS	OUT	BA	OBP	SLG	EQA	EQR	DEFENSE			
1998	Carolina	Sou	454	103	18	4	7	23	86	45	34	6	2	353	.227	.264	.330	.194	29	106-CF	-4		
1999	Altoona	Eas	486	112	23	2	12	39	116	63	49	6	4	378	.230	.289	.360	.215	41	103-RF	-4		
2000	Altoona	Eas	202	59	11	1	4	9	45	23	26	1	1	144	.292	.322	.416	.244	21	39-CF	-3		
2000	Nashvill	PCL	275	68	15	1	7	7	61	23	29	4	2	209	.247	.268	.385	.213	22	43-1B	-3	23-RF	0
2000	Pittsbrg	NL	60	12	2	0	1	0	12	4	5	1	1	49	.200	.200	.283	.131	2	12-1B	-2		
2001	Pittsbrg	NL	431	110	23	2	10	27	102	47	53	4	1	322	.255	.299	.387	.230	41				

He regressed badly last year after slight progress in 1999. Alex Hernandez drew 11 walks in 285 Triple-A plate appearances, so while the Pirates have helped him make more contact via a "two-tap" open batting stance, it's still not enough. He is an excellent right fielder whom the Pirates have been toying with at first base, where his bat would have negative value. The scouts love him because he looks and swings like a real ballplayer, but someone has to teach him how to play the game.

J.R. House — C — Bats R — Age 21

YEAR	TEAM	LGE	AB	H	DB	TP	HR	BB	SO	R	RBI	SB	CS	OUT	BA	OBP	SLG	EQA	EQR	DEFENSE	
1999	Willmspt	NYP	102	24	4	0	1	6	22	9	9	0	0	78	.235	.278	.304	.189	6	14-C	0
2000	Hickory	SAL	430	115	16	1	16	32	97	55	57	0	1	316	.267	.322	.421	.246	47	77-C	-13
2001	Pittsbrg	NL	251	74	7	0	10	21	72	32	44	0	0	177	.295	.349	.442	.266	32		

J.R. House was perhaps the best player in the Sally League last year and a near-certain Triple Crown winner had he not missed a month with mononucleosis. House is a diligent worker who learned how to take pitches the other way this year, showing good power to the opposite field. He also improved his throwing from behind the plate, though some scouts wonder if he's big enough to stay there. His bat is sufficient to carry mediocre defense. House is the Pirates' best hitting prospect.

Adam Hyzdu — OF — Bats R — Age 29

YEAR	TEAM	LGE	AB	H	DB	TP	HR	BB	SO	R	RBI	SB	CS	OUT	BA	OBP	SLG	EQA	EQR	DEFENSE			
1998	Tucson	PCL	98	27	4	1	3	12	23	15	10	0	1	72	.276	.355	.429	.260	12	21-RF	-1		
1999	Altoona	Eas	352	89	18	1	16	27	70	45	51	4	2	265	.253	.309	.446	.248	41	55-LF	-3	18-1B	-2
1999	Nashvill	PCL	44	9	0	0	4	3	11	4	9	0	0	35	.205	.255	.477	.233	5	12-RF	1		
2000	Altoona	Eas	533	126	26	1	22	69	119	70	71	2	4	411	.236	.329	.413	.247	62	135-OF	-5		
2001	Pittsbrg	NL	490	124	20	1	26	63	117	70	87	1	1	367	.253	.338	.457	.265	66				

He's a minor-league lifer who finally got his first cup of coffee last season, three years after the Red Sox ignored him when he was hitting well in their system. Adam Hyzdu doesn't have much of a future in Pittsburgh, but he does have patience and power and can even play a little outfield. As long as there are guys like him kicking around, there's no reason for any team to pay more than the minimum for an average DH.

Jason Kendall — C — Bats R — Age 27

YEAR	TEAM	LGE	AB	H	DB	TP	HR	BB	SO	R	RBI	SB	CS	OUT	BA	OBP	SLG	EQA	EQR	DEFENSE	
1998	Pittsbrg	NL	542	174	35	3	13	49	48	95	74	24	5	373	.321	.406	.469	.299	91	144-C	-4
1999	Pittsbrg	NL	280	91	18	3	8	33	30	56	38	17	3	192	.325	.418	.496	.312	52	75-C	6
2000	Pittsbrg	NL	581	178	33	5	13	70	74	104	53	19	12	415	.306	.393	.448	.283	89	145-C	-1
2001	Pittsbrg	NL	522	178	32	5	15	68	66	121	98	29	9	353	.341	.417	.508	.313	96		

He's doomed to second-string All-Star status as long as Mike Piazza is behind the plate, but Jason Kendall has firmly landed himself on the list of the best players in baseball and is just entering his power peak. Signing him for $60 million over six years was an excellent decision. Considering where the market went after he signed, Kendall might be a bargain at $10 million per year.

Garrett Long — 1B — Bats R — Age 24

YEAR	TEAM	LGE	AB	H	DB	TP	HR	BB	SO	R	RBI	SB	CS	OUT	BA	OBP	SLG	EQA	EQR	DEFENSE			
1998	Lynchbrg	Car	323	76	20	1	6	40	85	37	33	3	1	248	.235	.322	.359	.233	32	61-1B	-5	12-LF	1
1998	Carolina	Sou	98	25	3	0	0	7	29	10	6	0	0	73	.255	.309	.286	.200	6	24-LF	-1		
1999	Altoona	Eas	366	80	10	3	14	48	105	49	43	3	3	289	.219	.316	.377	.233	38	46-LF	-1	45-1B	5
2000	Altoona	Eas	125	26	5	0	4	14	36	15	15	0	1	100	.208	.294	.344	.211	10	23-LF	0		
2001	Pittsbrg	NL	231	55	8	0	9	32	70	30	33	1	1	177	.238	.331	.390	.245	26				

Garrett Long hurt his back and neck while weight lifting one day near the end of March and wound up spending more than two months recuperating in extended spring training. He still wasn't 100% when he returned and had to repeat Double-A just to keep from falling further behind. Back problems and power hitters are about as good a combination as tomato sauce and chocolate ice cream. Long has to get healthy and have a hot start to get back into the Pirates' plans.

Rob Mackowiak — 2B/3B/OF — Bats L — Age 25

YEAR	TEAM	LGE	AB	H	DB	TP	HR	BB	SO	R	RBI	SB	CS	OUT	BA	OBP	SLG	EQA	EQR	DEFENSE			
1998	Augusta	SAL	73	15	2	0	1	10	20	11	6	2	1	59	.205	.306	.274	.201	5	16-RF	-1		
1998	Lynchbrg	Car	298	71	18	4	3	14	66	25	24	3	1	228	.238	.277	.356	.208	23	73-3B	-5		
1999	Lynchbrg	Car	267	69	6	2	6	11	59	38	22	4	2	200	.258	.296	.363	.219	22	58-2B	-2		
1999	Altoona	Eas	197	47	14	2	2	5	36	18	21	0	1	151	.239	.272	.360	.204	14	52-2B	-2		
2000	Altoona	Eas	532	139	29	2	11	14	106	64	66	10	3	396	.261	.287	.385	.223	46	69-2B	-6	33-RF	-4
2001	Pittsbrg	NL	453	123	24	2	11	23	99	57	58	11	2	332	.272	.307	.406	.241	47				

He's someone you want to root for. Rob Mackowiak was a 53rd-round pick in 1996 who plays hard, works his tail off, and can field three positions (four if the experiment with him behind the plate works). He even has a little pop in his bat, slugging .478 against right-handers. So what's the problem? Twenty-two walks last year, just eight off his career high, mean he's really no different than most of the Pirates' other bench options.

Pat Meares   SS   Bats R   Age 32

YEAR	TEAM	LGE	AB	H	DB	TP	HR	BB	SO	R	RBI	SB	CS	OUT	BA	OBP	SLG	EQA	EQR	DEFENSE	
1998	Minnesot	AL	540	141	26	3	10	23	77	56	69	6	4	403	.261	.298	.376	.223	47	149-SS	0
1999	Pittsbrg	NL	91	27	4	0	0	8	19	14	6	0	0	64	.297	.366	.341	.246	10	19-SS	0
2000	Pittsbrg	NL	466	111	22	2	12	29	85	52	44	1	0	355	.238	.293	.371	.220	40	119-SS	-2
2001	Pittsbrg	NL	379	91	16	1	9	29	71	39	42	3	1	289	.240	.294	.359	.220	33		

The Great Mistake. The biggest question of Cam Bonifay's tenure is why he signed Pat Meares, among the game's worst-hitting shortstops and a mediocre fielder, to a four-year deal when Meares hadn't received any multi-year offers as a free agent. One would hope that the acquisitions of Enrique Wilson and Jack Wilson will turn Meares into nothing more than an overpaid backup, starting in 2001.

Dan Meier   1B/LF   Bats L   Age 23

YEAR	TEAM	LGE	AB	H	DB	TP	HR	BB	SO	R	RBI	SB	CS	OUT	BA	OBP	SLG	EQA	EQR	DEFENSE	
1998	Sth Bend	Mid	59	10	3	0	0	8	21	6	4	0	0	49	.169	.269	.220	.156	2	16-1B	0
1999	High Des	Cal	412	82	15	2	15	48	143	52	50	0	0	330	.199	.289	.354	.215	35	93-1B	3
2000	Lynchbrg	Car	208	52	7	1	11	21	48	34	29	1	1	157	.250	.328	.452	.257	26	33-1B	-2
2000	El Paso	Tex	62	11	1	0	2	1	26	6	5	0	0	51	.177	.190	.290	.128	2	14-1B	1
2001	Pittsbrg	NL	351	81	13	1	15	41	114	42	50	0	0	270	.231	.311	.402	.240	38		

Cut loose by the Diamondbacks after he scuffled in a 62 at-bat trial at El Paso, Dan Meier was Lynchburg's best hitter in the second half of 2000. Meier isn't big, but he posted an OPS just under 1000 as a Hillcat, more than 200 points above that of J.J. Davis. Meier's problem is defense; he spent most of the year at first base before the Hillcats moved him to his college position of left field in August, where he was passable. Sleeper.

Warren Morris   2B   Bats L   Age 27

YEAR	TEAM	LGE	AB	H	DB	TP	HR	BB	SO	R	RBI	SB	CS	OUT	BA	OBP	SLG	EQA	EQR	DEFENSE	
1998	Carolina	Sou	151	40	4	2	4	15	37	18	19	2	1	112	.265	.334	.397	.247	17	38-2B	-5
1998	Tulsa	Tex	387	102	16	2	10	30	71	40	48	6	4	289	.264	.320	.393	.238	40	88-2B	-1
1999	Pittsbrg	NL	512	142	17	3	15	51	83	61	67	2	6	376	.277	.345	.410	.251	60	138-2B	-12
2000	Pittsbrg	NL	531	134	28	2	3	57	73	63	40	6	10	407	.252	.327	.330	.221	47	130-2B	-2
2001	Pittsbrg	NL	477	126	21	2	8	53	78	64	59	6	5	356	.264	.338	.367	.241	51		

"Sophomore slump" just doesn't describe it. Warren Morris maintained his ability to draw a walk; everything else from 1999 disappeared: his power, his average, and especially his skill at hitting left-handers (.336/.393/.464 in '99, .230/.309/.276 in 2000). He battled some nagging injuries but mostly seemed to be pressing at the plate. Morris has a good eye and a track record of hitting, so you can bet on a full recovery.

Abraham Nunez   SS   Bats B   Age 25

YEAR	TEAM	LGE	AB	H	DB	TP	HR	BB	SO	R	RBI	SB	CS	OUT	BA	OBP	SLG	EQA	EQR	DEFENSE			
1998	Nashvill	PCL	365	81	12	2	2	32	72	39	25	11	6	290	.222	.290	.282	.194	24	91-SS	-8		
1998	Pittsbrg	NL	53	11	2	0	1	11	13	6	2	4	2	44	.208	.344	.302	.233	6	20-SS	-3		
1999	Nashvill	PCL	57	15	0	0	0	4	8	9	2	1	0	42	.263	.311	.263	.197	4	15-SS	-2		
1999	Pittsbrg	NL	260	57	8	0	0	25	51	23	16	7	1	204	.219	.290	.250	.185	15	56-SS	-3	13-2B	1
2000	Nashvill	PCL	351	89	7	1	3	27	47	37	23	13	4	266	.254	.308	.305	.212	27	78-SS	0		
2000	Pittsbrg	NL	92	20	2	0	1	6	13	10	8	0	0	72	.217	.265	.272	.170	4	18-SS	-1		
2001	Pittsbrg	NL	339	83	6	0	3	36	56	43	28	14	2	258	.245	.317	.289	.217	28				

The Pirates appear to have lost interest in Abraham Nunez, one of just two prospects remaining in the system from the Orlando Merced trade with the Blue Jays in '96. Nunez is probably their best-fielding shortstop and has some ability with the bat, but he doesn't walk much and doesn't hit the ground balls the team wants to see. He belongs on someone's bench and is young enough that he might eventually start.

Keith Osik — C — Bats R — Age 32

YEAR	TEAM	LGE	AB	H	DB	TP	HR	BB	SO	R	RBI	SB	CS	OUT	BA	OBP	SLG	EQA	EQR	DEFENSE			
1998	Pittsbrg	NL	99	21	5	0	0	13	15	9	7	1	2	80	.212	.315	.263	.196	7	21-C	0		
1999	Pittsbrg	NL	168	31	4	1	2	9	28	12	13	0	0	137	.185	.230	.256	.141	5	42-C	1		
2000	Pittsbrg	NL	124	35	6	1	4	12	10	11	21	3	0	89	.282	.366	.444	.276	18	18-C	-1	10-3B	-3
2001	Pittsbrg	NL	135	30	5	1	3	15	17	16	14	3	0	105	.222	.300	.341	.222	12				

Keith Osik hit .186 and .214 in the years before last year's .293 performance, so unless you think he started using androstenedione, there's no explanation beyond random fluctuation. Anything more than a backup role is a stretch for Osik; with Kendall around, the Bucs won't ask any more of him than that.

Alex Ramirez — LF/RF — Bats R — Age 26

YEAR	TEAM	LGE	AB	H	DB	TP	HR	BB	SO	R	RBI	SB	CS	OUT	BA	OBP	SLG	EQA	EQR	DEFENSE	
1998	Buffalo	Int	521	144	19	6	28	9	100	80	84	4	3	380	.276	.294	.497	.254	61	109-RF	-5
1999	Buffalo	Int	305	85	17	1	10	12	52	40	39	3	4	224	.279	.312	.439	.244	33	65-RF	4
1999	Clevelnd	AL	96	29	6	1	3	2	24	11	17	1	1	68	.302	.322	.479	.260	12	16-RF	-4
2000	Clevelnd	AL	111	31	5	1	5	4	15	12	11	1	0	80	.279	.304	.477	.255	13	24-OF	-2
2000	Pittsbrg	NL	116	24	6	1	4	5	30	13	17	1	0	92	.207	.240	.379	.199	8	27-RF	-2

For most teams, Alex Ramirez would be a welcome pickup: a fourth outfielder with home-run power from the bench. For the Pirates, it's a chance to squander more at bats on a guy who never walks and who can't hit anything with a break, hook, bend, jump, or wiggle. Can I scare you? From 1997 to 1999, Alex Ramirez drew a mere 51 unintentional walks in 1,242 Triple-A at-bats. He could be a coach in this organization. Ramirez was sold to the Japanese Leagues for the 2001 season.

Aramis Ramirez — 3B — Bats R — Age 23

YEAR	TEAM	LGE	AB	H	DB	TP	HR	BB	SO	R	RBI	SB	CS	OUT	BA	OBP	SLG	EQA	EQR	DEFENSE	
1998	Nashvill	PCL	168	40	5	0	5	20	28	15	15	0	1	129	.238	.328	.357	.232	17	44-3B	-5
1998	Pittsbrg	NL	253	60	7	1	7	17	67	23	24	0	1	194	.237	.295	.356	.215	21	59-3B	-4
1999	Nashvill	PCL	454	127	24	1	16	60	54	69	55	3	2	329	.280	.371	.443	.274	65	120-3B	-17
1999	Pittsbrg	NL	56	10	1	1	0	6	8	2	6	0	0	46	.179	.258	.232	.152	2	16-3B	-4
2000	Nashvill	PCL	165	52	12	1	3	8	27	22	20	1	1	114	.315	.357	.455	.269	21	42-3B	-4
2000	Pittsbrg	NL	256	65	14	2	6	34	18	33	0	0	191	.254	.283	.395	.221	22	56-3B	-9	
2001	Pittsbrg	NL	436	128	21	2	18	39	69	65	79	3	1	309	.294	.352	.475	.275	61		

He got a second chance to claim the third-base job last April, but the Pirates persisted in their impatience and demoted him after a slow start. He got a third chance in August, began to hit, and separated his shoulder, effectively ending his season. Aramis Ramirez could certainly stand a little luck, because the Pirates are disinclined to use him, even though he has been their best third-base option since mid-'98. He's a future star if the Pirates just give him a chance.

Julian "Tike" Redman — OF — Bats L — Age 24

YEAR	TEAM	LGE	AB	H	DB	TP	HR	BB	SO	R	RBI	SB	CS	OUT	BA	OBP	SLG	EQA	EQR	DEFENSE	
1998	Lynchbrg	Car	535	121	23	6	6	27	75	54	37	15	7	421	.226	.264	.325	.194	35	125-CF	-6
1999	Altoona	Eas	543	132	20	9	2	37	55	66	48	14	9	420	.243	.293	.324	.207	41	133-CF	2
2000	Nashvill	PCL	506	119	24	8	3	22	75	48	39	15	12	399	.235	.270	.332	.196	34	119-CF	-6
2001	Pittsbrg	NL	489	125	23	7	6	36	72	64	52	20	10	374	.256	.307	.368	.229	47		

Tike Redman is everything this club values: he plays hard, has blazing speed, and is an excellent defensive outfielder. Unfortunately, what he has in tools he lacks in skills. He possesses minimal power and doesn't draw the walks that would still make him a valuable player. This isn't the organization where he'll learn that skill. He also hasn't leveraged his speed into good baserunning. Right now, Redman looks like he'll be an out machine if he gets any playing time in the majors.

John Vander Wal — LF — Bats L — Age 35

YEAR	TEAM	LGE	AB	H	DB	TP	HR	BB	SO	R	RBI	SB	CS	OUT	BA	OBP	SLG	EQA	EQR	DEFENSE			
1998	Colorado	NL	102	26	9	1	4	15	27	16	17	0	0	76	.255	.350	.480	.274	15	17-RF	-3		
1998	San Dieg	NL	26	7	3	0	0	6	5	3	1	0	0	19	.269	.406	.385	.279	4				
1999	San Dieg	NL	250	69	13	0	8	33	56	26	42	2	1	182	.276	.365	.424	.267	34	38-LF	1	19-1B	-1
2000	Pittsbrg	NL	386	112	23	0	24	65	86	69	87	10	2	276	.290	.395	.536	.307	72	70-RF	-4	27-1B	-5
2001	Pittsbrg	NL	293	82	14	0	15	57	70	59	59	4	1	212	.280	.397	.481	.298	51				

Pittsburgh Pirates

It was a great year... and totally out of sync with his career. John Vander Wal is 34 and nothing special in the field. He could easily have one or two more years like this, but with the glut of Quadruple-A outfielders the Pirates have hanging around PNC Park, they'd be better off turning Vander Wal into a prospect or two while the luster of his 973 OPS is still bright. They signed him to a two-year deal, of course. Trade bait now that Derek Bell has been signed.

Rico Washington — 3B/C — Bats L — Age 23

YEAR	TEAM	LGE	AB	H	DB	TP	HR	BB	SO	R	RBI	SB	CS	OUT	BA	OBP	SLG	EQA	EQR	DEFENSE			
1998	Erie	NYP	199	50	10	1	4	11	35	20	18	0	1	150	.251	.300	.372	.222	17	39-3B	4		
1998	Augusta	SAL	52	13	1	1	1	5	9	8	8	1	0	39	.250	.328	.365	.239	5				
1999	Hickory	SAL	300	82	8	1	9	36	48	49	34	2	1	219	.273	.358	.397	.258	37	54-C	-18		
1999	Lynchbrg	Car	211	50	4	0	6	22	46	24	23	2	1	162	.237	.315	.341	.223	19	31-3B	0	13-C	-3
2000	Altoona	Eas	515	120	21	4	8	42	80	63	47	2	5	400	.233	.295	.336	.208	40	73-3B	-4	61-2B	-12
2001	Pittsbrg	NL	463	121	16	2	11	45	82	56	60	3	2	344	.261	.327	.376	.239	48				

Rico Washington, like many Pirate prospects, disappointed in his first exposure to Double-A. His walk rate remained above par—he was the youngest Altoona player to draw at least 25 walks—while his power and average both dropped, although they improved as the season progressed. Part of the problem is his ever-changing position; he spent most of the year at third base, but he played some second base, and the Bucs worked with him at catcher in the Instructional League. Even though the Bucs released him, he's worth watching.

John Wehner — Who cares? — Bats R — Age 34

YEAR	TEAM	LGE	AB	H	DB	TP	HR	BB	SO	R	RBI	SB	CS	OUT	BA	OBP	SLG	EQA	EQR	DEFENSE			
1998	Charlott	Int	82	22	2	0	2	2	17	8	11	2	1	61	.268	.297	.366	.221	7	18-LF	-3		
1998	Florida	NL	89	21	3	0	0	7	11	11	5	1	0	68	.236	.292	.270	.188	5	14-OF	0		
1999	Nashvill	PCL	56	19	3	0	5	2	6	9	10	0	0	37	.339	.362	.661	.318	11	13-SS	-5		
1999	Pittsbrg	NL	65	12	2	0	1	6	11	6	4	1	0	53	.185	.254	.262	.167	3	12-LF	-1		
2000	Nashvill	PCL	429	92	13	0	13	41	72	40	45	8	3	340	.214	.287	.336	.210	34	92-2B	0	19-3B	-1
2000	Pittsbrg	NL	50	14	0	0	2	4	6	9	9	0	0	36	.280	.333	.400	.246	5	15-3B	-4		
2001	Pittsbrg	NL	280	61	7	0	10	33	48	30	33	4	1	220	.218	.300	.350	.223	26				

There has probably been a worse running gag on a Fox sitcom, but none comes to mind. The Pirates could have used John Wehner's 50 at-bats on any number of prospects and suspects this September. A career in coaching beckons him, and one would hope the Pirates nudge him towards it.

Paul Weichard — CF — Bats — Age 21

YEAR	TEAM	LGE	AB	H	DB	TP	HR	BB	SO	R	RBI	SB	CS	OUT	BA	OBP	SLG	EQA	EQR	DEFENSE	
1998	Lethbrid	Pio	187	39	7	1	0	21	53	17	14	6	2	150	.209	.288	.257	.187	11	53-CF	-1
1999	Hickory	SAL	324	65	6	2	4	21	97	31	29	9	4	263	.201	.249	.269	.166	15	88-CF	4
2000	Lynchbrg	Car	270	60	8	1	5	21	87	28	21	8	4	214	.222	.284	.315	.201	19	70-CF	-3
2001	Pittsbrg	NL	302	70	8	1	5	30	100	35	27	12	6	238	.232	.301	.315	.213	25		

Paul Weichard showed his first signs of improved plate discipline and power in 2000. His raw numbers, .251/.327/.365, are unimpressive, but he was just 20 years old in the high-A Carolina League and finished strong after a sub-.200 first half. He's built like a tank, so the Pirates expect him to add power to his excellent speed. He should also put up better numbers after off-season elbow surgery solves the nerve problem that troubled him all year.

Aron Weston — CF — Bats L — Age 20

YEAR	TEAM	LGE	AB	H	DB	TP	HR	BB	SO	R	RBI	SB	CS	OUT	BA	OBP	SLG	EQA	EQR	DEFENSE	
2000	Hickory	SAL	324	73	10	1	2	25	95	34	16	10	4	255	.225	.282	.281	.189	20	73-CF	-6
2001	Pittsbrg	NL	156	35	1	0	2	13	81	15	11	7	2	123	.224	.284	.269	.192	10		

Aron Weston is a huge kid who reminds scouts of Darryl Strawberry. Thus far, he has generated almost no power. He was only 19 and playing in a full-season league, so we'll cut him some slack. While we tend to advocate pushing players up through the system, Weston gives us pause. How does it affect the psyche of a lifelong star to hit .267, strike out in more than a quarter of his at-bats, and struggle in the field?

Craig Wilson — C/1B — Bats R — Age 24

YEAR	TEAM	LGE	AB	H	DB	TP	HR	BB	SO	R	RBI	SB	CS	OUT	BA	OBP	SLG	EQA	EQR	DEFENSE			
1998	Lynchbrg	Car	226	52	9	1	9	18	54	21	33	1	0	174	.230	.294	.398	.230	22	42-C	-5		
1998	Carolina	Sou	147	41	7	0	4	8	34	14	14	2	1	107	.279	.327	.408	.246	16	29-C	-6		
1999	Altoona	Eas	370	88	17	2	16	29	109	47	53	1	1	283	.238	.312	.424	.243	41	33-C	-11	13-1B	-3
2000	Nashvill	PCL	396	100	20	1	26	34	124	64	63	1	1	297	.253	.340	.505	.274	59	66-C	-6	28-1B	0
2001	Pittsbrg	NL	323	87	15	1	21	29	102	46	64	1	1	237	.269	.330	.517	.275	47				

We told you about him in *Baseball Prospectus 1999*, right after he had the same surgery that sidelined Todd Hundley for two years. Craig Wilson still needs to work on his footwork behind the plate, but pitchers like the game he calls, and he slugged .604 in Nashville with what passes for good strike-zone judgment in this organization. Given time, he could easily develop into enough of a defender to let his bat carry his glove. Note to major-league GMs: You passed over this guy in the 1999 Rule 5 draft.

Enrique Wilson — IF — Bats B — Age 25

YEAR	TEAM	LGE	AB	H	DB	TP	HR	BB	SO	R	RBI	SB	CS	OUT	BA	OBP	SLG	EQA	EQR	DEFENSE			
1998	Buffalo	Int	222	58	6	0	5	15	21	33	21	5	2	166	.261	.308	.356	.224	20	45-2B	0		
1998	Clevelnd	AL	90	29	4	0	3	3	7	12	12	1	4	65	.322	.350	.467	.257	11	17-2B	0		
1999	Clevelnd	AL	330	87	22	1	2	22	37	40	23	5	4	247	.264	.311	.355	.223	29	46-3B	1	23-SS	-3
2000	Clevelnd	AL	115	37	6	0	3	6	10	15	12	2	1	79	.322	.355	.452	.269	15				
2000	Pittsbrg	NL	123	32	5	1	3	9	12	10	14	0	1	92	.260	.311	.390	.231	12	14-3B	-3		
2001	Pittsbrg	NL	306	94	16	1	6	22	32	43	47	3	2	214	.307	.354	.425	.263	38				

Freedom? Maybe. The Pirates now have Enrique Wilson, Warren Morris, Aramis Ramirez, and Pat Meares spread among second base, shortstop, and third base. There's no guarantee they'll sit the right guy (Meares). Still, getting Wilson in the Cordero deal was a coup; he has a slick glove at shortstop, should hit .280-.290 with decent pop, and will cost the Pirates close to the minimum salary. He's a sleeper.

Jack Wilson — SS — Bats R — Age 23

YEAR	TEAM	LGE	AB	H	DB	TP	HR	BB	SO	R	RBI	SB	CS	OUT	BA	OBP	SLG	EQA	EQR	DEFENSE	
1998	JohnsnCy	App	234	59	11	1	2	9	35	22	14	6	3	178	.252	.284	.333	.205	17	57-SS	-10
1999	Peoria	Mid	251	68	17	2	2	8	25	30	18	4	2	185	.271	.296	.378	.223	22	63-SS	-9
1999	Potomac	Car	261	66	7	1	2	12	32	33	14	3	2	197	.253	.287	.310	.196	17	63-SS	-1
2000	Potomac	Car	48	10	1	1	1	4	10	6	4	1	1	40	.208	.269	.333	.194	3	13-SS	0
2000	Arkansas	Tex	344	85	16	5	5	24	62	49	24	1	1	260	.247	.302	.366	.222	30	88-SS	4
2000	Altoona	Eas	142	32	8	1	1	11	18	15	13	1	2	112	.225	.286	.317	.197	10	29-SS	1
2001	Pittsbrg	NL	416	113	20	2	5	31	67	51	48	6	2	305	.272	.322	.365	.235	41		

When Cam Bonifay was negotiating with the Cardinals in the Jason Christiansen trade, the Pirate coaches in Lynchburg campaigned for him to acquire Jack Wilson. He's a hard-working, scrappy type with a reputation as a slick glove man, and his bat looks like it will be at least adequate for a starting shortstop in the majors. He could stand to improve his plate discipline; aren't you sick of reading that in this chapter by now?

Kevin Young — 1B — Bats R — Age 32

YEAR	TEAM	LGE	AB	H	DB	TP	HR	BB	SO	R	RBI	SB	CS	OUT	BA	OBP	SLG	EQA	EQR	DEFENSE	
1998	Pittsbrg	NL	598	160	37	2	28	42	119	88	106	14	7	445	.268	.326	.477	.263	79	153-1B	-8
1999	Pittsbrg	NL	585	167	40	5	25	66	117	95	96	16	9	427	.285	.369	.499	.285	93	154-1B	-7
2000	Pittsbrg	NL	500	127	20	0	21	24	90	72	84	7	3	376	.254	.297	.420	.236	51	119-1B	-20
2001	Pittsbrg	NL	486	135	27	1	22	48	97	76	84	10	5	356	.278	.343	.473	.271	68		

Kevin Young was hurt all year, but since none of the injuries were to his eyes, it's hard to explain the immediate erosion of the just-as-suddenly-acquired plate discipline he demonstrated in '99. He'll bounce back some once he's healthy, but he's 32, expensive, and still ranks in the lower half of NL first basemen offensively. If the Pirates can find a taker, which isn't likely, they should trade Young posthaste.

National League

PITCHERS (ERA: 4.50, H/9: 9.00, HR/9: 1.00, BB/9: 3.00, K/9: 6.00, KW: 1.00, PERA: 4.50)

Paul Ah Yat — Throws L — Age 26

YEAR	TEAM	LGE	IP	H	ER	HR	BB	K	ERA	W	L	H/9	HR/9	BB/9	K/9	KW	PERA
1998	Lynchbrg	Car	91.7	102	55	19	18	37	5.40	4	6	10.01	1.87	1.77	3.63	1.03	5.50
1998	Carolina	Sou	78.7	85	48	16	20	37	5.49	3	6	9.72	1.83	2.29	4.23	0.93	5.50
1999	Altoona	Eas	86.7	90	52	11	36	53	5.40	4	6	9.35	1.14	3.74	5.50	0.74	5.16
1999	Nashvill	PCL	61.7	69	44	12	27	27	6.42	2	5	10.07	1.75	3.94	3.94	0.50	6.33
2000	Nashvill	PCL	103.3	106	61	21	40	41	5.31	4	7	9.23	1.83	3.48	3.57	0.51	5.72

Another year, another level, another low ERA. His ratios weren't great last year and he hits only 87 mph on the gun, but Paul Ah Yat is left-handed, keeps the ball down, and is extremely intelligent. Bad run support doomed him to a 3-8 record, which won't help him in the eyes of the Pirates. He'd need some adjustment time in the majors, then would eventually be an effective pitcher for a team willing to ignore the scouts and focus on the results.

Jimmy Anderson — Throws L — Age 25

YEAR	TEAM	LGE	IP	H	ER	HR	BB	K	ERA	W	L	H/9	HR/9	BB/9	K/9	KW	PERA
1998	Nashvill	PCL	118.3	130	82	10	77	44	6.24	4	9	9.89	0.76	5.86	3.35	0.29	5.95
1999	Nashvill	PCL	129.0	138	60	6	44	63	4.19	7	7	9.63	0.42	3.07	4.40	0.72	4.29
1999	Pittsbrg	NL	28.7	24	13	2	13	11	4.08	1	2	7.53	0.63	4.08	3.45	0.42	3.73
2000	Pittsbrg	NL	140.3	162	84	11	47	61	5.39	6	10	10.39	0.71	3.01	3.91	0.65	5.01

He continued to throw his sinker for strikes, retained his extreme ground-ball tendencies, improved after returning from a demotion (his ERAs were 5.89 before the break and 4.76 after), and was league-average on the whole. That's pretty good for a 24-year-old rookie with a spotty minor-league record. Jimmy Anderson is still too susceptible to the extra-base hit and needs to sharpen his control, but there's reason for cautious optimism here. For a player who looked like a lost cause two years ago, that's damn good, and the credit should go to pitching coach Pete Vukovich.

Bronson Arroyo — Throws R — Age 24

YEAR	TEAM	LGE	IP	H	ER	HR	BB	K	ERA	W	L	H/9	HR/9	BB/9	K/9	KW	PERA
1998	Carolina	Sou	120.0	158	95	28	48	58	7.13	3	10	11.85	2.10	3.60	4.35	0.60	7.60
1999	Altoona	Eas	141.0	167	83	25	64	63	5.30	6	10	10.66	1.60	4.09	4.02	0.49	6.55
2000	Nashvill	PCL	84.0	77	43	10	26	38	4.61	4	5	8.25	1.07	2.79	4.07	0.73	4.05
2000	Pittsbrg	NL	70.3	85	55	9	29	42	7.04	2	6	10.88	1.15	3.71	5.37	0.72	6.05

Bronson Arroyo is young, throws up to 91 mph, boasts four pitches he can throw for strikes, and sure looks like a ballplayer in that there uniform. So why doesn't he ever strike anyone out? For a guy the scouts took to like a Denny's customer to a $1.99 Hungry Klansman breakfast, Arroyo hasn't put up the numbers you'd expect. He needs to show he can fool Triple-A hitters before the Pirates rush him back to the majors.

Kris Benson — Throws R — Age 26

YEAR	TEAM	LGE	IP	H	ER	HR	BB	K	ERA	W	L	H/9	HR/9	BB/9	K/9	KW	PERA
1998	Nashvill	PCL	147.7	156	106	31	54	89	6.46	4	12	9.51	1.89	3.29	5.42	0.82	5.87
1999	Pittsbrg	NL	191.7	177	96	15	69	117	4.51	9	12	8.31	0.70	3.24	5.49	0.85	3.90
2000	Pittsbrg	NL	212.0	201	95	21	70	153	4.03	12	12	8.53	0.89	2.97	6.50	1.09	4.10

He took a 3.05 ERA and a 104-to-44 strikeout-to-walk ratio into the All-Star break, then slowly but consistently declined. The Pirates continued to work him hard as he struggled; fortunately, a fluke injury kept him out of several September starts, perhaps saving his arm for the time being. Kris Benson is a future Cy Young contender whom the Bucs should handle a lot more carefully.

Bobby Bradley — Throws R — Age 20

YEAR	TEAM	LGE	IP	H	ER	HR	BB	K	ERA	W	L	H/9	HR/9	BB/9	K/9	KW	PERA
2000	Hickory	SAL	74.0	74	45	7	27	56	5.47	3	5	9.00	0.85	3.28	6.81	1.04	4.47

Bobby Bradley has done nothing yet to shed the label of "Greg Maddux clone." He throws an incredible curveball, but the Pirates are trying to get him to rely more on his fierce 92–93 mph fastball. He works both sides of the plate, throws strikes,

(Bobby Bradley *continued*)

clearly knows what he's doing... so what's the catch? He missed eight weeks with a sore elbow that was never really diagnosed. There are rumors that he, like Kerry Wood, was overused in high school. Health is the only thing that could stop him from becoming a star.

Francisco Cordova — Throws R — Age 29

YEAR	TEAM	LGE	IP	H	ER	HR	BB	K	ERA	W	L	H/9	HR/9	BB/9	K/9	KW	PERA
1998	Pittsbrg	NL	211.0	198	88	22	62	128	3.75	12	11	8.45	0.94	2.64	5.46	1.03	3.97
1999	Pittsbrg	NL	156.3	158	76	15	49	82	4.38	8	9	9.10	0.86	2.82	4.72	0.84	4.34
2000	Pittsbrg	NL	92.7	103	58	11	31	55	5.63	3	7	10.00	1.07	3.01	5.34	0.89	5.16

Francisco Cordova suffered through another injury-plagued year, this one ending with August surgery to remove a bone spur from his right elbow. If that's all that's been bothering him, there's no reason he couldn't return to his '98 form. His career indicates that there's more damage to come. His sinker is the key: if Cordova can throw it hard and still get that drop at the end, he's a potential ace.

Wilson Guzman — Throws L — Age 23

YEAR	TEAM	LGE	IP	H	ER	HR	BB	K	ERA	W	L	H/9	HR/9	BB/9	K/9	KW	PERA
1998	Augusta	SAL	62.7	57	30	2	34	34	4.31	3	4	8.19	0.29	4.88	4.88	0.50	4.06
1999	Lynchbrg	Car	59.7	77	42	6	13	41	6.34	2	5	11.61	0.91	1.96	6.18	1.58	5.51
2000	Lynchbrg	Car	53.7	71	35	11	21	30	5.87	2	4	11.91	1.84	3.52	5.03	0.71	7.34
2000	Altoona	Eas	110.0	99	57	12	52	50	4.66	5	7	8.10	0.98	4.25	4.09	0.48	4.47

The Pirates' minor-league pitcher of the year, Wilson Guzman has moved up through the system slowly since he was signed as a non-drafted free agent out of the Dominican Republic in '97. He doesn't throw hard, so he doesn't get any press, but he has yet to post a full-season ERA above 3.50. His strikeout-to-walk ratio took a big tumble last year, so there's a 50% chance he'll get splattered in Nashville.

Clint Johnston — Throws L — Age 23

YEAR	TEAM	LGE	IP	H	ER	HR	BB	K	ERA	W	L	H/9	HR/9	BB/9	K/9	KW	PERA
1998	Augusta	SAL	50.7	46	29	9	45	32	5.15	2	4	8.17	1.60	7.99	5.68	0.36	6.71
1999	Hickory	SAL	80.7	100	84	24	66	44	9.37	1	8	11.16	2.68	7.36	4.91	0.33	9.35
2000	Lynchbrg	Car	34.0	49	31	6	17	12	8.21	1	3	12.97	1.59	4.50	3.18	0.35	8.11

This former #1 pick looks more and more like a bust. Arm problems limited Clint Johnston to 37 1/3 bad innings. He surrendered 28 runs (22 earned) and still hasn't found a delivery that works. His season ended in June after he had surgery to remove bone spurs in his elbow. We suggested last year that the Pirates return him to the outfield, where he starred at Vanderbilt, and it still seems like a good idea.

Rich Loiselle — Throws R — Age 29

YEAR	TEAM	LGE	IP	H	ER	HR	BB	K	ERA	W	L	H/9	HR/9	BB/9	K/9	KW	PERA
1998	Pittsbrg	NL	53.3	55	25	2	32	39	4.22	3	3	9.28	0.34	5.40	6.58	0.61	4.95
1999	Pittsbrg	NL	15.0	16	8	2	7	12	4.80	1	1	9.60	1.20	4.20	7.20	0.86	5.54
2000	Pittsbrg	NL	41.7	42	23	4	24	27	4.97	2	3	9.07	0.86	5.18	5.83	0.56	5.27

Rich Loiselle's season wasn't quite as awful as it looked—Lamont hung him out to dry in September, sending him to the mound for back-to-back 30-pitch outings, the second of which resulted in a six-run inning. True, it was his first year back after shoulder surgery, but Loiselle wasn't that good of a pitcher to begin with, possessing a straight fastball and middling control. Middle relief is his upside.

Jose Lopez — Throws R — Age 25

YEAR	TEAM	LGE	IP	H	ER	HR	BB	K	ERA	W	L	H/9	HR/9	BB/9	K/9	KW	PERA
1998	Hickory	SAL	40.0	48	33	18	22	15	7.43	1	3	10.80	4.05	4.95	3.38	0.34	9.62
1999	WnstnSlm	Car	24.7	36	22	2	16	5	8.03	1	2	13.14	0.73	5.84	1.82	0.16	7.80
2000	Hickory	SAL	66.7	58	39	8	50	30	5.27	3	4	7.83	1.08	6.75	4.05	0.30	5.44
2000	Lynchbrg	Car	33.3	32	20	5	24	18	5.40	1	3	8.64	1.35	6.48	4.86	0.38	6.12

National League

Here's a great story: Jose Lopez was 42-1 at a small high school in Corpus Christi, Texas, and wasn't drafted because of his (relatively) diminutive stature, despite a great curve and low-90s fastball. He started 2000 in Hickory's pen and was awful, then got pressed into service in the rotation and caught fire. In a six-start stretch, half in Hickory and half in Lynchburg, he gave up three runs in 48 innings. He wore down at season's end but has definitely emerged as a grade-C prospect.

Josias Manzanillo — Throws R — Age 33

YEAR	TEAM	LGE	IP	H	ER	HR	BB	K	ERA	W	L	H/9	HR/9	BB/9	K/9	KW	PERA
1998	Durham	Int	80.7	92	60	14	31	41	6.69	2	7	10.26	1.56	3.46	4.57	0.66	6.05
1998	Norfolk	Int	73.3	77	37	6	32	49	4.54	3	5	9.45	0.74	3.93	6.01	0.77	4.88
1999	NY Mets	NL	18.0	19	12	5	3	21	6.00	1	1	9.50	2.50	1.50	10.50	3.50	5.73
2000	Nashvll	PCL	21.7	19	10	1	7	16	4.15	1	1	7.89	0.42	2.91	6.65	1.14	3.27
2000	Pittsbrg	NL	57.3	49	20	5	26	32	3.14	4	2	7.69	0.78	4.08	5.02	0.62	3.96

Josias Manzanillo was arguably the Bucs' most effective reliever in 2000, logging a season not out of line with his best years with the Mets. He earned the minimum salary and didn't even require a 40-man roster spot until the Pirates called him up. Yet teams routinely hand out million-dollar contracts to middle relievers. Why?

Sam McConnell — Throws L — Age 25

YEAR	TEAM	LGE	IP	H	ER	HR	BB	K	ERA	W	L	H/9	HR/9	BB/9	K/9	KW	PERA
1998	Augusta	SAL	40.7	37	29	5	19	16	6.42	1	4	8.19	1.11	4.20	3.54	0.42	4.67
1998	Lynchbrg	Car	111.0	118	52	8	26	40	4.22	6	6	9.57	0.65	2.11	3.24	0.77	4.10
1999	Lynchbrg	Car	92.3	90	54	17	32	34	5.26	4	6	8.77	1.66	3.12	3.31	0.53	5.12
1999	Altoona	Eas	57.0	81	58	12	37	25	9.16	1	5	12.79	1.89	5.84	3.95	0.34	8.84
2000	Altoona	Eas	98.0	81	27	7	32	37	2.48	8	3	7.44	0.64	2.94	3.40	0.58	3.24
2000	Nashvll	PCL	46.3	55	37	11	17	16	7.19	1	4	10.68	2.14	3.30	3.11	0.47	6.83

Sam McConnell is a finesse left-hander who blew through Double-A as a repeater, then was pummeled by PCL hitters in his first exposure to Triple-A. Similar to Ah Yat in experience, McConnell doesn't have the assortment of breaking stuff or Ah Yat's control so his chances for success are slightly lower. A full year in Triple-A will tell the tale of whether he deserves a bullpen shot.

Brian O'Connor — Throws L — Age 24

YEAR	TEAM	LGE	IP	H	ER	HR	BB	K	ERA	W	L	H/9	HR/9	BB/9	K/9	KW	PERA
1998	Lynchbrg	Car	78.3	89	39	6	28	43	4.48	4	5	10.23	0.69	3.22	4.94	0.77	4.97
1998	Carolina	Sou	61.0	86	66	17	50	26	9.74	1	6	12.69	2.51	7.38	3.84	0.26	10.08
1999	Altoona	Eas	141.0	150	109	17	102	67	6.96	4	12	9.57	1.09	6.51	4.28	0.33	6.38
2000	Altoona	Eas	119.3	115	73	8	72	48	5.51	4	9	8.67	0.60	5.43	3.62	0.33	4.89
2000	Nashvll	PCL	25.0	28	22	3	14	14	7.92	1	2	10.08	1.08	5.04	5.04	0.50	6.03

Brian O'Connor has pitched in Double-A for parts of three seasons with an unsettling combined strikeout-to-walk ratio of 223-to-206 in nearly 350 innings. He's still around because he's young, left-handed, and has good movement on all four of his pitches, but at some point, you have to focus your resources on players who are making progress. That O'Connor got two call-ups last year and Paul Ah Yat got none is indicative of what's wrong with this organization.

Chris Peters — Throws L — Age 29

YEAR	TEAM	LGE	IP	H	ER	HR	BB	K	ERA	W	L	H/9	HR/9	BB/9	K/9	KW	PERA
1998	Pittsbrg	NL	142.0	138	61	13	49	84	3.87	8	8	8.75	0.82	3.11	5.32	0.86	4.21
1999	Nashvll	PCL	47.0	49	16	1	17	21	3.06	3	2	9.38	0.19	3.26	4.02	0.62	3.99
1999	Pittsbrg	NL	69.7	93	53	15	22	39	6.85	2	6	12.01	1.94	2.84	5.04	0.89	7.20
2000	Nashvll	PCL	49.7	67	38	9	29	22	6.89	2	4	12.14	1.63	5.26	3.99	0.38	7.96
2000	Pittsbrg	NL	27.7	22	8	2	11	13	2.60	2	1	7.16	0.65	3.58	4.23	0.59	3.34

You have to feel for the guy: After becoming the surprise star of the rotation in '98, Chris Peters hasn't been healthy since, with the latest ailment a bone spur in his left elbow that required arthroscopic surgery in September. At full strength, Peters has good control, a solid breaking pitch, and the ability to start or relieve as needed. He's a good #5-starter sleeper if healthy this spring.

Justin Reid — Throws R — Age 24

YEAR	TEAM	LGE	IP	H	ER	HR	BB	K	ERA	W	L	H/9	HR/9	BB/9	K/9	KW	PERA
1999	Willmspt	NYP	55.3	77	50	10	30	30	8.13	1	5	12.52	1.63	4.88	4.88	0.50	8.02
2000	Hickory	SAL	152.0	167	125	31	41	77	7.40	4	13	9.89	1.84	2.43	4.56	0.94	5.68

Justin Reid started the year in the bullpen, but when he joined the rotation right before Bradley went down, he became one of the team's saviors. He works quickly, keeps the ball down, and has excellent control of three pitches. He doesn't light up the gun, though, and he threw a ton of innings as a starter. A long shot, but the numbers are good so far.

Todd Ritchie — Throws R — Age 29

YEAR	TEAM	LGE	IP	H	ER	HR	BB	K	ERA	W	L	H/9	HR/9	BB/9	K/9	KW	PERA
1998	SaltLake	PCL	57.3	54	38	5	32	40	5.97	2	4	8.48	0.78	5.02	6.28	0.63	4.79
1998	Minnesot	AL	24.0	28	15	1	7	20	5.63	1	2	10.50	0.38	2.63	7.50	1.43	4.56
1999	Pittsbrg	NL	167.3	160	71	15	45	90	3.82	10	9	8.61	0.81	2.42	4.84	1.00	3.84
2000	Pittsbrg	NL	181.3	199	101	23	42	103	5.01	8	12	9.88	1.14	2.08	5.11	1.23	4.79

Regression to the mean has taken hold, especially of Todd Ritchie's ERA, since his last two seasons were similar in most respects. He was more hittable and homer-prone in 2000 and a lot less lucky. Most Pirate fans thought they had an ace here, but part of the reason he never broke through in Minnesota is that his fastball is as straight as Alex P. Keaton. What you saw in 2000 is what you get: a back-of-the-rotation innings eater.

Scott Sauerbeck — Throws L — Age 29

YEAR	TEAM	LGE	IP	H	ER	HR	BB	K	ERA	W	L	H/9	HR/9	BB/9	K/9	KW	PERA
1998	Norfolk	Int	152.0	172	83	10	71	81	4.91	7	10	10.18	0.59	4.20	4.80	0.57	5.27
1999	Pittsbrg	NL	66.3	52	17	5	31	46	2.31	5	2	7.06	0.68	4.21	6.24	0.74	3.56
2000	Pittsbrg	NL	75.0	78	34	4	50	69	4.08	4	4	9.36	0.48	6.00	8.28	0.69	5.41

As predicted, the second time around was worse. Scott Sauerbeck puts up good ERAs, largely because he inherits other people's messes and isn't charged with the runs he allows to score. His curve is his best pitch, but it's generally not in the strike zone, so hitters who lay off it tend to end up on first base. He should never be allowed to face a right-handed hitter, which limits his usefulness to LaRussian manipulations.

Jason Schmidt — Throws R — Age 28

YEAR	TEAM	LGE	IP	H	ER	HR	BB	K	ERA	W	L	H/9	HR/9	BB/9	K/9	KW	PERA
1998	Pittsbrg	NL	205.7	222	103	24	64	128	4.51	10	13	9.71	1.05	2.80	5.60	1.00	4.89
1999	Pittsbrg	NL	207.3	210	100	22	70	124	4.34	11	12	9.12	0.95	3.04	5.38	0.89	4.54
2000	Pittsbrg	NL	62.3	70	39	5	33	42	5.63	2	5	10.11	0.72	4.76	6.06	0.64	5.58

We told you last year he was a big breakdown risk, and break down he did, pitching poorly before he was sidelined by shoulder surgery. The Pirates piled a ton of innings on Jason Schmidt's arm and never saw the results they (or we) expected of someone with his talent. He's young, but his arm is in questionable shape, and he'll probably spend the first half of 2001 finding his mechanics again.

Dan Serafini — Throws L — Age 27

YEAR	TEAM	LGE	IP	H	ER	HR	BB	K	ERA	W	L	H/9	HR/9	BB/9	K/9	KW	PERA
1998	SaltLake	PCL	51.3	52	26	4	21	26	4.56	3	3	9.12	0.70	3.68	4.56	0.62	4.53
1998	Minnesot	AL	74.7	88	49	8	24	43	5.91	3	5	10.61	0.96	2.89	5.18	0.90	5.37
1999	ChiCubs	NL	61.3	81	45	8	26	14	6.60	2	5	11.89	1.17	3.82	2.05	0.27	6.73
2000	LasVegas	PCL	49.0	71	41	7	23	30	7.53	1	4	13.04	1.29	4.22	5.51	0.65	7.69
2000	Nashvill	PCL	43.7	37	18	6	20	15	3.71	3	2	7.63	1.24	4.12	3.09	0.38	4.40
2000	Pittsbrg	NL	60.7	67	31	8	21	27	4.60	3	4	9.94	1.19	3.12	4.01	0.64	5.29

Dan Serafini still hasn't developed into the pitcher some saw when he survived Salt Lake in 1997 and '98. Crafty left-handers often take years of incubation to develop. The Pirates certainly need arms in the bullpen to soak up innings, so it's worth working with Serafini to see if he can better harness his four-pitch arsenal, as long as they don't expect immediate results or put him in the rotation.

Jose Silva — Throws R — Age 27

YEAR	TEAM	LGE	IP	H	ER	HR	BB	K	ERA	W	L	H/9	HR/9	BB/9	K/9	KW	PERA
1998	Pittsbrg	NL	96.3	100	53	7	27	52	4.95	4	7	9.34	0.65	2.52	4.86	0.96	4.15
1999	Pittsbrg	NL	95.0	104	64	9	32	65	6.06	3	8	9.85	0.85	3.03	6.16	1.02	4.86
2000	Pittsbrg	NL	133.0	172	88	14	41	82	5.95	5	10	11.64	0.95	2.77	5.55	1.00	5.92

There's talent here, as evidenced by the eight-start, 3.55-ERA run he went on when he first entered the rotation in June, but the bottom keeps falling out. Jose Silva doesn't seem to have the endurance to throw 90 pitches every five days, much less 110 pitches, as he was asked to do in the last two of those eight starts. The closer role would be a waste of his skills, but Vuckovich has to find a usage pattern that maximizes Silva's abilities.

Matt Skrmetta — Throws R — Age 28

YEAR	TEAM	LGE	IP	H	ER	HR	BB	K	ERA	W	L	H/9	HR/9	BB/9	K/9	KW	PERA
1998	Mobile	Sou	71.0	72	42	16	33	45	5.32	3	5	9.13	2.03	4.18	5.70	0.68	6.15
1999	Mobile	Sou	33.3	44	33	5	28	26	8.91	1	3	11.88	1.35	7.56	7.02	0.46	8.44
1999	LasVegas	PCL	27.0	19	13	4	12	16	4.33	1	2	6.33	1.33	4.00	5.33	0.67	3.71
2000	Ottawa	Int	32.3	33	26	5	20	27	7.24	1	3	9.19	1.39	5.57	7.52	0.68	6.09

He's a spare right-hander who came over when the Pirates traded minor-league veteran third baseman Jarrod Patterson to the Expos last summer. Matt Skrmetta throws a fastball in the low to mid 90s and also boasts a hard slider but hasn't shown good control since he was in the Tigers' system in '96. He has an excellent splitter, too; the Padres discouraged him from using it, so he shows it only to left-handed batters. He needs a little more Triple-A time.

Brian Smith — Throws R — Age 28

YEAR	TEAM	LGE	IP	H	ER	HR	BB	K	ERA	W	L	H/9	HR/9	BB/9	K/9	KW	PERA
1998	Dunedin	Fla	10.0	8	4	0	4	5	3.60	1	0	7.20	0.00	3.60	4.50	0.63	2.83
1998	Knoxvill	Sou	66.7	72	40	10	24	29	5.40	2	5	9.72	1.35	3.24	3.92	0.60	5.39
1999	Knoxvill	Sou	32.7	42	27	6	7	15	7.44	1	3	11.57	1.65	1.93	4.13	1.07	6.27
1999	Syracuse	Int	43.7	45	23	8	24	31	4.74	2	3	9.27	1.65	4.95	6.39	0.65	6.14
2000	Altoona	Eas	25.0	14	7	0	10	13	2.52	2	1	5.04	0.00	3.60	4.68	0.65	1.80
2000	Pittsbrg	NL	4.3	6	5	1	2	3	10.38	0	0	12.46	2.08	4.15	6.23	0.75	8.38

Brian Smith is a Rule 5 draft pick who represents Cam Bonifay at his most clever. After selecting Smith in the draft, Bonifay non-tendered him and immediately signed him to a minor-league deal so the Pirates didn't have to keep him on the 25-man roster all year. Smith was excellent as Altoona's closer in 2000 despite off-season shoulder surgery. If the elbow soreness that shut him down in September isn't serious, he could probably be a league-average reliever for the Bucs in 2001.

Jeff Wallace — Throws L — Age 25

YEAR	TEAM	LGE	IP	H	ER	HR	BB	K	ERA	W	L	H/9	HR/9	BB/9	K/9	KW	PERA
1999	Nashvill	PCL	13.7	17	14	3	9	10	9.22	0	2	11.20	1.98	5.93	6.59	0.56	8.08
1999	Pittsbrg	NL	39.0	27	15	2	31	35	3.46	2	2	6.23	0.46	7.15	8.08	0.56	4.04
2000	Nashvill	PCL	13.0	11	1	1	6	8	0.69	1	0	7.62	0.69	4.15	5.54	0.67	3.82
2000	Pittsbrg	NL	35.7	42	29	4	28	22	7.32	1	3	10.60	1.01	7.07	5.55	0.39	7.15

Last year, Jeff Wallace was just 18 months removed from major arm surgery, so some control troubles would have been unsurprising. He has a good fastball but can't throw it or anything else for strikes. The Reds claimed Wallace off waivers in November, and he's expected to be in their bullpen. At 24, he has about two years before he turns into Keith Shepherd.

Marc Wilkins — Throws R — Age 30

YEAR	TEAM	LGE	IP	H	ER	HR	BB	K	ERA	W	L	H/9	HR/9	BB/9	K/9	KW	PERA
1998	Pittsbrg	NL	14.7	13	6	1	8	14	3.68	1	1	7.98	0.61	4.91	8.59	0.88	4.25
1999	Pittsbrg	NL	50.0	48	26	3	21	37	4.68	3	3	8.64	0.54	3.78	6.66	0.88	4.13
2000	Nashvill	PCL	35.0	33	26	6	27	22	6.69	1	3	8.49	1.54	6.94	5.66	0.41	6.39
2000	Pittsbrg	NL	59.3	53	31	4	35	31	4.70	3	4	8.04	0.61	5.31	4.70	0.44	4.47

He's a replaceable innings eater and more proof that no one should pay real money for tenth and 11th pitchers. Marc Wilkins hasn't pitched 60 major-league innings in a season since '97, and his control continues to worsen as the injuries take a cumulative toll. As long as he's willing to work for the minimum, though, he's worth having around.

Dave Williams — Throws L — Age 22

YEAR	TEAM	LGE	IP	H	ER	HR	BB	K	ERA	W	L	H/9	HR/9	BB/9	K/9	KW	PERA
1998	Erie	NYP	42.3	51	29	15	17	17	6.17	1	4	10.84	3.19	3.61	3.61	0.50	8.17
1999	Willmspt	NYP	41.3	37	23	5	14	21	5.01	2	3	8.06	1.09	3.05	4.57	0.75	4.06
1999	Hickory	SAL	53.7	46	31	10	15	21	5.20	2	4	7.71	1.68	2.52	3.52	0.70	4.27
2000	Hickory	SAL	151.7	167	98	33	49	91	5.82	5	12	9.91	1.96	2.91	5.40	0.93	6.01

Dave Williams obliterated the Sally League with an excellent slider, a plus splitter, and a good fastball. He ended the year as the youngest member of Lynchburg's pitching staff and the minor-league leader in strikeouts. Williams is left-handed and doesn't throw especially hard, so he'll have to prove himself again at every level; his coaches praised his poise and pitching knowledge, so he has a good chance.

Mike Williams — Throws R — Age 32

YEAR	TEAM	LGE	IP	H	ER	HR	BB	K	ERA	W	L	H/9	HR/9	BB/9	K/9	KW	PERA
1998	Nashvill	PCL	33.7	37	29	14	16	22	7.75	1	3	9.89	3.74	4.28	5.88	0.69	8.44
1998	Pittsbrg	NL	49.0	39	12	1	14	48	2.20	4	1	7.16	0.18	2.57	8.82	1.71	2.57
1999	Pittsbrg	NL	57.7	64	34	8	31	64	5.31	2	4	9.99	1.25	4.84	9.99	1.03	6.13
2000	Pittsbrg	NL	70.7	56	31	7	33	59	3.95	4	4	7.13	0.89	4.20	7.51	0.89	3.81

To his credit, Mike Williams pitched much better than the low save total indicates. Since he isn't likely to be part of the next good Pirate team, they need to trade him before the one-trick (slider) pony loses its charm, but that low save total may reduce his trade value. He was one of the Pirates' only effective relievers in 2000, and he'll remain the closer until he's dealt or completely implodes.

Support-Neutral Statistics — PITTSBURGH PIRATES — Park Effect: -3.6%

PITCHER	GS	IP	R	SNW	SNL	SNPCT	W	L	RA	APW	SNVA	SNWAR
Jimmy Anderson	26	141.0	92	8.1	10.0	.446	5	11	5.87	-1.2	-0.9	0.4
Bronson Arroyo	12	57.7	47	3.0	4.9	.380	2	4	7.34	-1.4	-0.9	-0.4
Kris Benson	32	217.7	104	14.1	10.3	.577	10	12	4.30	1.7	1.7	3.7
Francisco Cordova	17	93.0	60	5.3	6.4	.454	6	8	5.81	-0.7	-0.5	0.3
Brian O'Connor	1	2.0	6	0.0	0.9	.002	0	0	27.00	-0.5	-0.4	-0.4
Jose Parra	2	7.0	7	0.4	0.9	.289	0	1	9.00	-0.3	-0.3	-0.2
Todd Ritchie	31	187.0	111	10.1	11.2	.473	9	8	5.34	-0.6	-0.6	1.0
Jason Schmidt	11	63.3	43	2.9	4.2	.408	2	5	6.11	-0.7	-0.7	-0.1
Dan Serafini	11	62.3	35	3.4	4.0	.455	2	5	5.05	-0.0	-0.3	0.2
Jose Silva	19	96.3	76	5.9	7.9	.427	6	7	7.10	-2.1	-1.1	0.0
TOTALS	162	927.3	581	53.1	60.8	.466	42	61	5.64	-5.8	-3.9	4.7

Of the ten starters used by the Pirates in 2000, only one, Kris Benson, managed to put together a year that was above league average. On the face of it, that looks bad for the Pirates' future. When a team has only a single starter who shows much ability or promise in a year, you might expect a long rebuilding process before they can field enough quality starters to fill out a good rotation.

That isn't always the case. Since 1979, 33 teams met the "standard" of having only a single above-average starter in the rotation. Things generally got better the following year for those teams, a lot better in many cases. Of those 33 teams, 26 saw their starting-rotation performance improve the following year, and 11 of the rotations were actually above average. More impressive still is that several were among the top rotations in the league the following year, including the AL-best 1993 Chicago White Sox and the NL-best 1985 New York Mets.

I seriously doubt that the Pirates have pitchers in their system ready to duplicate the 1985 seasons of Dwight Gooden, Ron Darling, and Sid Fernandez, but history does indicate that the poor across-the-board performance of the 2000 Pirates doesn't necessarily doom them to years of mediocrity.

For a quick explanation of SN stats, see page 7.

Reliever Evaluation Tools

PITCHER	G	IP	R	ARA	APR	IRNR/G	EIRS/G	IRP	BRS	RRA	ARP
Jimmy Anderson	1	3.0	2	6.18	-0.3	0.00	0.00	0.0	0.0	6.01	-0.3
Bronson Arroyo	8	14.0	14	9.28	-6.3	0.88	0.22	1.8	1.1	8.69	-5.4
Jason Christiansen	44	38.0	22	5.37	-0.7	0.48	0.15	2.7	-2.2	4.19	4.3
Brad Clontz	5	7.0	4	5.30	-0.1	0.60	0.14	-0.3	0.9	6.71	-1.2
Francisco Cordova	1	2.0	3	13.91	-1.9	0.00	0.00	0.0	0.0	8.42	-0.7
Mike Garcia	13	11.3	15	12.28	-8.9	0.54	0.19	-0.7	-0.1	12.86	-9.6
Rich Loiselle	40	42.3	27	5.92	-3.4	0.55	0.19	-2.3	2.1	6.38	-5.5
Josias Manzanillo	43	58.7	23	3.64	10.2	0.77	0.27	1.6	-0.6	3.21	12.9
Brian O'Connor	5	10.3	5	4.49	0.8	0.80	0.42	0.9	0.6	4.34	1.0
Keith Osik	1	1.0	5	46.38	-4.6	0.00	0.00	0.0	0.0	46.68	-4.6
Jose Parra	4	4.7	2	3.98	0.6	0.50	0.17	-1.4	0.0	7.06	-1.0
Chris Peters	18	28.3	9	2.95	7.1	0.83	0.27	0.0	2.6	3.99	3.8
Scott Sauerbeck	75	75.7	36	4.41	6.6	0.65	0.23	-0.9	-0.7	4.41	6.6
Jose Silva	32	39.7	20	4.68	2.3	0.59	0.27	2.2	-0.1	4.26	4.1
Matt Skrmetta	8	9.3	12	11.93	-7.0	0.50	0.15	0.3	-0.8	10.54	-5.5
Brian Smith	3	4.3	5	10.70	-2.7	1.00	0.63	0.9	-0.5	7.12	-0.9
Steve Sparks	3	4.0	3	6.96	-0.8	1.67	0.57	-1.4	0.7	11.73	-2.9
Jeff Wallace	38	35.7	32	8.32	-12.4	0.61	0.20	-1.8	4.1	9.89	-18.6
Marc Wilkins	52	60.3	34	5.23	-0.2	0.65	0.21	0.0	-1.8	5.18	0.1
Mike Williams	72	72.0	34	4.38	6.5	0.21	0.06	-1.2	1.2	4.79	3.3
TOTALS	466	521.7	307	5.46	-15.2	0.57	0.20			5.55	-20.3

For a quick guide to RET, see page 10.

St. Louis Cardinals

In some ways, it's easy to admire the St. Louis Cardinals organization. They've done some really amazing things over the last few years, things that demonstrate an ability to make coherent long-term plans and execute them. In other ways, they can be an incredibly frustrating organization to watch. Grown men have been caught staring slack-jawed at the television as some inexplicable Cardinals news is announced on ESPN, usually involving a playing-time decision for another of Tony LaRussa's Anointed Ones. Fortunately, those same men, despondent over seeing Craig Paquette in the uniform of the team they love, can later spend hours oozing praise for the latest personnel move made by Walt Jocketty, the Cardinals' vice president and general manager.

The Cardinals have done one thing better than any other organization: market themselves within the industry. Using some creative landscaping and marketing savvy, they've managed to turn a cookie-cutter stadium along the lines of the atrocities in Pittsburgh and Cincinnati into a truly inviting ballpark. The dividends are clear: they can save money when they sign veteran players. Mark McGwire, Darryl Kile, and Jim Edmonds accepted long-term deals at less than market value in order to play in St. Louis. Edmonds would likely have demanded close to Shawn Green's $14 million per year if he'd tested the free-agent market; the Cardinals were instead able to sign him through 2006 at about $5 million less per year. Not only do they save money on the deal, but they're able to demonstrate to their considerable fan base that they're committed to winning, and that the fans should come out and see these familiar and productive faces on a regular basis.

But what about the other side of the coin? What aren't the Cardinals doing well? For starters, they're making some, well, intriguing decisions about on-field talent. We at *Baseball Prospectus* have had our problems with Tony LaRussa from time to time, and last year was no exception. We've been critical of his pitcher handling in the past, even before Alan Benes had his career derailed and Matt Morris went under the knife after blowing away the league in 1997 and 1998. In 2000, we were curious to see what LaRussa would do with one of the best pitching prospects ever, young Rick Ankiel.

Let's go back to the 2000 preseason. A few pundits and analysts cried Chicken Little, fearful that Ankiel's arm would be put into the LaRussa/Duncan meat grinder and go the way of Benes's and Morris's. Sensitive to this criticism and Ankiel's age, LaRussa assured the St. Louis fan base that he was acutely aware of the talent he had in Ankiel, and that he would be exceptionally careful with the fireballing prodigy, so that he didn't end up like Kerry Wood of the Cubs. LaRussa said that Ankiel wouldn't go more than "about 100" pitches in his starts and that he and pitching coach Dave Duncan would keep a careful eye on the health of Ankiel's arm.

So how did it shake down? In his first start on April 9, Ankiel pretty much made the Brewers look like a Little League team. (Okay, *more* like a Little League team.) He had a couple of games in which he was left in one batter too long, but that happens. Ankiel's start at home against San Diego on April 20 serves as a nice analog for his entire season. He was completely untouchable, giving up just two hits, but doled out seven walks and needed 112 pitches to get through five innings.

LaRussa let Ankiel toss more than 110 pitches four times in April and May, peaking with a May 25 game against Florida. Ankiel was excellent through six innings and was right at 100 pitches at the start of the seventh. It looked as if he would be yanked. It had been a good outing, one in which he hadn't walked a guy and showed stuff really comparable only to Randy Johnson. Guess again. Ankiel came back out for the seventh and struggled with his command. He gave up a couple of runs, ran his pitch count to 121, and was pulled, mercifully, before he could finish the inning.

The next day, ESPN.com ran a story about how Scott Boras (Ankiel's representative) was aggravated because Duncan and

Cardinals Prospectus

2000 record: 95–67; First place, NL Central; Lost to Mets in NLCS, 4-1

Pythagenport W/L: 92–70

Runs Acored: 887 (4th in NL)

Runs Allowed: 771 (7th in NL)

Team EqA: .270 (3rd in NL)

2000 Batters' Age: 29.8 (6th oldest in NL)

2000 Pitchers' Age: 29.0 (6th oldest in NL)

Ballpark: Busch Stadium; neutral park; Park Factor of 1.007

2000: Walt Jocketty's winter moves paid off handsomely, even with the first baseman missing half the season.

2001: They're the favorites in the Central this time, even without Fernando Tatis.

LaRussa had agreed to limit the pitcher's workload until he turned 22. The Scott Boras Corporation supposedly had contacted the Cardinals to gently remind them, and the next thing you know, Ligamentgate was on.

The Cardinal organization claimed to be primarily concerned with Ankiel's welfare and winning games. They knew what they were doing, they said. Basically, the message was, "Boras can get bent," to which Ankiel's reps responded with something to the effect of, "We don't want to interfere with the Cardinals' baseball operations, but this is pretty much a regime of war criminals we're dealing with; ask Benes or Morris."

Of course, Ankiel completely kicked tail for the balance of the year and was remarkably consistent, holding opponents to two runs or fewer in each of his starts after August 22. Everyone was happy, because he also didn't throw more than 112 pitches in any of those starts, leaving him rested and ready... for the postseason.

And what about that postseason? Ankiel had a difficult time, totally losing his control. He made two starts during which he set records for most wild pitches in an inning and in a game, and he dented the backstop more than once. The talk-show circuit had a field day, comparing him to Steve Blass, Mark Wohlers, and, in one particular lowlight, Helen Keller with an automatic weapon.

On October 16, with the final game of the NLCS pretty much decided, LaRussa and Duncan decided to put Ankiel on the mound in relief. The thinking was clear: let him mow down a couple of people so he doesn't spend the off-season thinking about losing his control and hearing passersby do bad Harry Doyle impersonations. It was a pretty reasonable plan, and if it had worked, the upside would have been huge. Unfortunately, it didn't. Ankiel unleashed a couple of pitches to the backstop and the Shea fans were less than supportive. Ankiel's final postseason line: seven runs in four innings, fueled primarily by 11 walks.

Ankiel appears to be one exceptional kid in a lot of ways, but his postseason was rough, and there are legitimate doubts about what's going to happen when he takes the mound this season. Is he a #1 starter, or is he Steve Blass? My money says #1 starter.

Why have we paid so much attention to one pitcher? After all, the Cardinals have a number of interesting things going on, from the signing of Jim Edmonds to the development of J.D. Drew, from a pretty good first baseman to Edgar Renteria, the NL's probable answer to the shortstop trinity. One reason we've focused on Ankiel is because he highlights the contrast between the Cardinals' uncommonly smart approach to player development and their less-than-stellar handling of those players once they reach the majors. They choose their prospects very carefully, pay them well, and try to minimize risk by focusing on guys who are really grade-A talent. It's a shame, then, that the other side of the house, major-league operations, abuses players and hinders their success once they actually arrive in the majors.

To some extent, this is endemic in the industry, because player development is necessarily focused on the long term, whereas Tony LaRussa is working towards winning the World Series this year. But the Cardinals have earned extra scrutiny on this front with their treatment of Morris, Benes, and Drew. Ankiel was actually handled fairly well on balance, but this is only his first year, and the real challenge may be making sure he's not overworked in 2002, when he'll have two years' experience and still be just 22.

Walt Jocketty is still doing an outstanding job of gathering and developing young talent. He made a pair of excellent deals that brought in Renteria and Fernando Tatis; the Cardinal organization also has a shiny new left-hander by the name of Bud Smith who has ripped up the minors. Smith is smallish but has posted ERAs and peripheral numbers that indicate a good chance of future success. The Cardinals could have a really tremendous rotation by mid-2002 if Ankiel comes back and can find the plate, if Matt Morris shows he's healthy, if Darryl Kile doesn't descend into reliving the Coors nightmare, and if Bud Smith pitches like he's capable. You'll forgive us for being a bit skeptical about the ability of LaRussa and Duncan to develop a young staff.

With a little bit better health, this is a team that could win a lot of games. The starting lineup should look something like this:

C	Mike Matheny
1B	Mark McGwire
2B	Fernando Vina
3B	Placido Polanco
SS	Edgar Renteria
LF	Ray Lankford
CF	Jim Edmonds
RF	J.D. Drew

That is absolutely a championship-quality offense. It was even better before Jocketty traded his All-Star-caliber third baseman, Tatis, for a #4 starter and a middle reliever. Still, combine the current lineup with a rotation that has a good chance to be the best in the division, and this is a club that can win upwards of 100 games. If LaRussa can avoid giving Craig Paquette 250 at-bats and resists the temptation to reactivate Scott Hemond, this team should coast to an NL Central win in 2001.

Unless the Cubs get their act together this century.

HITTERS (BA: .270, OBP: .340, SLG: .440, EqA: .260)

Stubby Clapp — 2B — Bats L — Age 28

YEAR	TEAM	LGE	AB	H	DB	TP	HR	BB	SO	R	RBI	SB	CS	OUT	BA	OBP	SLG	EQA	EQR	DEFENSE			
1998	Arkansas	Tex	517	113	23	5	7	61	116	74	36	8	5	409	.219	.307	.323	.215	44	129-2B	18		
1999	Memphis	PCL	391	86	20	1	10	43	95	54	45	5	5	310	.220	.300	.353	.218	35	56-2B	-4	30-LF	-1
2000	Memphis	PCL	507	118	23	5	1	60	95	66	38	6	3	392	.233	.318	.304	.214	42	127-2B	-9		
2001	*St Louis*	*NL*	*409*	*96*	*20*	*2*	*5*	*49*	*90*	*51*	*41*	*7*	*3*	*316*	*.235*	*.317*	*.330*	*.223*	*37*				

This is the second baseman whose power vanished in 2000, not the short-lived clown played by Lenny Bruce in the 1950s. Stubby Clapp can play and has the skill set of Frankie Menechino in Oakland; he can draw a walk, not kill you on defense, and hits the ball farther than you'd think. His poor showing in Memphis last year probably cost him a chance at a career as a utility guy.

Will Clark — 1B — Bats L — Age 37

YEAR	TEAM	LGE	AB	H	DB	TP	HR	BB	SO	R	RBI	SB	CS	OUT	BA	OBP	SLG	EQA	EQR	DEFENSE	
1998	Texas	AL	548	168	32	2	26	70	86	97	101	1	0	380	.307	.388	.515	.298	92	124-1B	-2
1999	Baltimor	AL	249	77	12	0	12	36	38	39	29	2	2	174	.309	.400	.502	.299	42	63-1B	4
2000	Baltimor	AL	254	79	13	1	10	44	41	47	27	4	2	177	.311	.421	.488	.306	46	70-1B	-1
2000	St Louis	NL	171	57	14	1	11	20	22	27	38	1	0	114	.333	.411	.620	.330	36	45-1B	1

I'll take "Rednecks Who Can Flat-Out Hit" for $200, Alex. Will Clark never got his ring, but he had a very good career and was a fun guy to root for and against. In his younger days, Clark was a hell of a defensive first baseman. He had the misfortune of peaking in a pitchers' park during a low-offense era. As such, Clark is one of a class of players who will be slighted in Hall of Fame voting. I'm not saying he should get in, but I am saying he'll be underappreciated; his numbers aren't as eye-popping as his performance actually was.

Eric Davis — RF — Bats R — Age 39

YEAR	TEAM	LGE	AB	H	DB	TP	HR	BB	SO	R	RBI	SB	CS	OUT	BA	OBP	SLG	EQA	EQR	DEFENSE	
1998	Baltimor	AL	453	155	25	1	32	43	96	83	92	6	6	303	.342	.405	.614	.323	90	68-RF	-5
1999	St Louis	NL	192	48	7	2	5	27	46	25	28	4	4	148	.250	.345	.385	.247	22	44-RF	0
2000	St Louis	NL	255	75	9	0	7	32	56	35	38	1	1	181	.294	.375	.412	.268	34	58-RF	-4
2001	*SanFran*	*NL*	*205*	*55*	*6*	*0*	*8*	*32*	*49*	*30*	*32*	*1*	*1*	*151*	*.268*	*.367*	*.415*	*.276*	*30*		

Who knows what his career numbers would look like if he could have stayed healthy? Eric Davis is still a graceful athlete who feasts on mistake pitches, but his various ailments keep him from helping a club beyond a couple hundred at-bats as a spot starter and platoon guy. He's still an exciting ballplayer to watch. Davis is likely to have his role reduced further in 2001.

J.D. Drew — RF/CF — Bats L — Age 25

YEAR	TEAM	LGE	AB	H	DB	TP	HR	BB	SO	R	RBI	SB	CS	OUT	BA	OBP	SLG	EQA	EQR	DEFENSE	
1998	SPL	Nth	112	31	6	1	5	14	0	0	0	3	1	82	.277	.357	.482	.281	17		
1998	Arkansas	Tex	67	18	1	0	4	10	17	12	7	1	1	50	.269	.369	.463	.275	10	18-CF	1
1998	Memphis	PCL	79	21	6	1	1	19	18	12	9	1	2	60	.266	.412	.405	.280	12	25-CF	1
1998	St Louis	NL	37	15	3	1	5	4	9	9	13	0	0	22	.405	.463	.946	.409	12		
1999	Memphis	PCL	86	22	5	1	1	7	19	8	11	4	1	65	.256	.322	.372	.240	9	21-CF	0
1999	St Louis	NL	370	88	15	5	13	44	73	67	36	15	3	285	.238	.328	.411	.253	46	96-CF	-1
2000	St Louis	NL	409	115	16	2	17	60	93	68	52	15	9	303	.281	.380	.455	.279	63	109-RF	-1
2001	*St Louis*	*NL*	*351*	*103*	*16*	*2*	*16*	*54*	*78*	*73*	*66*	*17*	*5*	*253*	*.293*	*.388*	*.487*	*.295*	*60*		

He'll completely obliterate that forecast if LaRussa lets him. J.D. Drew is probably eight years away from being old enough for Tony LaRussa to take him seriously, something TLR made more than clear during the 2000 season. The idea that Shawon Dunston or Craig Paquette ever played while Drew was still breathing boggles the mind. Drew can play any outfield spot well, which makes him a valuable guy to have when your other outfielders are notoriously injury-prone. He's still not the most loved guy in Philadelphia, but can you imagine a 3-4-5-6 featuring him, Pat Burrell, Bobby Abreu, and Scott Rolen?

National League

Shawon Dunston — UT — Bats R — Age 38

YEAR	TEAM	LGE	AB	H	DB	TP	HR	BB	SO	R	RBI	SB	CS	OUT	BA	OBP	SLG	EQA	EQR	DEFENSE	
1998	Clevelnd	AL	156	38	13	3	3	5	16	26	12	7	2	120	.244	.271	.423	.230	15	18-2B	0
1998	San Fran	NL	51	9	3	0	3	0	9	11	8	0	2	44	.176	.219	.412	.187	3		
1999	NY Mets	NL	93	31	6	1	0	0	15	11	15	3	1	63	.333	.347	.419	.258	11	21-CF	0
1999	St Louis	NL	150	45	4	2	5	1	22	22	23	5	3	108	.300	.318	.453	.252	17	17-OF	0
2000	St Louis	NL	218	54	11	2	11	3	44	27	39	3	1	165	.248	.266	.468	.236	22	39-LF	1
2001	San Fran	NL	187	44	7	1	5	5	35	18	22	4	2	145	.235	.255	.364	.211	15		

We receive a lot of deserved criticism at *Baseball Prospectus* for, well, basically for being jerks. We point out that guys just can't play ball when they are in fact among the best ballplayers on the planet. It's true—Dunston is among the best ballplayers on the planet. He shouldn't be blamed for not being optimal for the role he ends up playing. That blame belongs to a particular manager with a 1970s haircut and a reputation as a genius. Dunston isn't the worst problem on this team, but that doesn't mean he's good enough to play in the majors anymore. Players like this are the only things that stand between the Cardinals and the 2001 postseason. Dunston signed a free-agent contract with the Giants.

Jim Edmonds — CF — Bats L — Age 31

YEAR	TEAM	LGE	AB	H	DB	TP	HR	BB	SO	R	RBI	SB	CS	OUT	BA	OBP	SLG	EQA	EQR	DEFENSE	
1998	Anaheim	AL	597	187	35	2	29	56	102	116	92	6	5	415	.313	.373	.524	.292	96	153-CF	7
1999	Anaheim	AL	203	51	17	2	5	26	41	33	22	5	4	156	.251	.336	.429	.254	25	42-CF	6
2000	St Louis	NL	527	150	21	0	40	93	156	120	99	9	3	380	.285	.397	.552	.309	101	141-CF	3
2001	St Louis	NL	414	130	23	1	28	74	113	92	103	7	2	286	.314	.418	.577	.325	86		

Jim Edmonds signed a long-term deal through 2006 at well below market value because he likes St. Louis. He's a good, if over-rated, defensive center fielder and a vastly improved and terrifying hitter. The one problem with Edmonds is his fragility. He's missed fewer than 20 games just twice in his career, and he does have a tendency to run into rather inelastic and immobile objects. In the brief history of divisional play, has there ever been a division with stronger talent at one position?—Edmonds, Ken Griffey, Richard Hidalgo, Brian Giles, and soon Corey Patterson. (Apologies to you Marquis Grissom fans.)

Chris Haas — 3B/1B — Bats L — Age 24

YEAR	TEAM	LGE	AB	H	DB	TP	HR	BB	SO	R	RBI	SB	CS	OUT	BA	OBP	SLG	EQA	EQR	DEFENSE			
1998	Arkansas	Tex	446	100	19	2	14	55	142	53	56	1	1	347	.224	.316	.370	.232	45	102-3B	-4		
1999	Memphis	PCL	397	79	16	1	14	55	150	49	55	3	3	321	.199	.299	.350	.218	36	74-3B	5	28-1B	0
2000	Arkansas	Tex	293	67	11	0	13	28	88	38	40	0	0	226	.229	.301	.399	.232	29	61-3B	2	14-1B	-3
2000	Memphis	PCL	56	11	0	0	1	8	11	6	7	0	0	45	.196	.297	.250	.185	3				
2001	St Louis	NL	385	89	13	0	13	46	130	44	49	1	1	297	.231	.313	.366	.230	38				

He's a low-average, medium-power tweener. The trade of Fernando Tatis gives Chris Haas a semblance of a chance at a job because beating out Placido Polanco should be an easier task. Haas still faces an uphill battle.

Carlos Hernandez — C — Bats R — Age 34

YEAR	TEAM	LGE	AB	H	DB	TP	HR	BB	SO	R	RBI	SB	CS	OUT	BA	OBP	SLG	EQA	EQR	DEFENSE	
1998	San Dieg	NL	397	108	11	1	11	15	51	36	56	2	2	291	.272	.313	.388	.233	38	104-C	-3
2000	San Dieg	NL	194	50	9	0	3	13	24	16	26	1	3	147	.258	.313	.351	.219	17	50-C	-1
2000	St Louis	NL	51	14	3	0	1	4	8	6	9	1	0	37	.275	.338	.392	.250	6	14-C	-3
2001	St Louis	NL	163	42	3	0	5	14	33	17	21	1	1	122	.258	.316	.368	.231	16		

Another indistinguishable St. Louis catcher. Carlos Hernandez has some pop, is a solid catch-and-throw guy, and is pretty predictable, which fits Tony LaRussa's catcher preferences to a T. While he won't kill you as a backup, you're giving up ground if he's starting for you. A back injury may crimp his style at the start of the season.

Thomas Howard — PH/RF — Bats B — Age 36

YEAR	TEAM	LGE	AB	H	DB	TP	HR	BB	SO	R	RBI	SB	CS	OUT	BA	OBP	SLG	EQA	EQR	DEFENSE	
1998	LosAngls	NL	77	15	2	0	3	3	14	9	5	1	0	62	.195	.225	.338	.178	4	18-OF	1
1999	Memphis	PCL	117	33	8	1	1	10	22	17	14	1	1	85	.282	.342	.393	.247	13	28-CF	-2
1999	St Louis	NL	196	56	6	0	7	14	25	15	27	1	1	141	.286	.339	.423	.254	23	39-RF	-3
2000	St Louis	NL	134	28	3	1	6	5	32	12	26	1	0	106	.209	.242	.381	.200	10	20-RF	-6
2001	Pittsbrg	NL	171	39	5	0	4	14	35	18	20	1	1	133	.228	.286	.327	.205	13		

St. Louis Cardinals

(Thomas Howard *continued*)

Yes, there were times, even against right-handed pitchers, when Thomas Howard got to play while J.D. Drew sat on the bench. Howard is a defensive liability who can't run particularly well any more and can't outplay the average Triple-A outfielder. He's probably come to the end of a nice MLB career.

Ray Lankford — LF — Bats L — Age 34

YEAR	TEAM	LGE	AB	H	DB	TP	HR	BB	SO	R	RBI	SB	CS	OUT	BA	OBP	SLG	EQA	EQR	DEFENSE	
1998	St Louis	NL	542	157	29	1	34	84	141	95	105	25	5	390	.290	.388	.535	.305	100	137-CF	5
1999	St Louis	NL	423	125	29	1	15	43	104	72	58	11	4	302	.296	.364	.475	.280	62	103-LF	4
2000	St Louis	NL	394	96	15	3	24	63	139	68	59	4	6	304	.244	.353	.480	.272	58	97-LF	-6
2001	St Louis	NL	341	90	15	1	18	70	110	71	65	10	3	254	.264	.389	.472	.292	59		

Like a number of the other Cardinal outfielders, Ray Lankford is both tremendously productive and injury prone. Hamstring and knee problems slowed him in the field and at the plate, but he's likely to bounce back and should beat that projection handily. He's been the subject of intense trade talks and could well be dealt before spring training begins.

Lankford's brother was the victim of a homicide in July, and our condolences go out to him and his family. Ray Lankford has always been a paragon of what a ballplayer should be, on and off the field. We've said it before: the next time you hear someone whine about how players today are overpaid, inconsiderate, privileged jerks, remind them of Ray Lankford.

Tim Lemon — CF — Bats R — Age 20

YEAR	TEAM	LGE	AB	H	DB	TP	HR	BB	SO	R	RBI	SB	CS	OUT	BA	OBP	SLG	EQA	EQR	DEFENSE	
1998	JohnsnCy	App	190	35	6	1	2	8	59	13	13	3	1	156	.184	.217	.258	.137	5	45-CF	-6
1999	New Jrsy	NYP	249	46	6	1	4	15	66	17	23	4	7	210	.185	.238	.265	.149	9	66-CF	-4
2000	Peoria	Mid	475	100	21	3	9	7	116	47	40	11	6	381	.211	.226	.324	.172	23	115-CF	-6
2001	St Louis	NL	331	72	13	1	7	15	89	29	26	13	5	263	.218	.251	.326	.192	21		

He's a very raw physical talent with miles to go. Tim Lemon has all five tools, but so do a lot of guys. I'm not optimistic about his long-term future; occasionally, someone like this explodes into, well, Glenn Braggs.

Eli Marrero — C — Bats R — Age 27

YEAR	TEAM	LGE	AB	H	DB	TP	HR	BB	SO	R	RBI	SB	CS	OUT	BA	OBP	SLG	EQA	EQR	DEFENSE	
1998	Memphis	PCL	130	27	5	0	5	11	23	17	16	4	3	106	.208	.270	.362	.207	10	27-C	1
1998	St Louis	NL	257	63	17	1	5	27	39	29	21	6	2	196	.245	.317	.377	.236	26	70-C	3
1999	St Louis	NL	319	62	13	1	6	14	53	30	33	9	2	259	.194	.230	.298	.169	15	76-C	6
2000	St Louis	NL	103	23	2	1	5	7	15	20	16	5	0	80	.223	.289	.408	.239	11	27-C	4
2001	St Louis	NL	186	40	7	0	5	16	31	20	17	6	1	147	.215	.277	.333	.209	15		

Thyroid cancer cost him a year of development and catching has cost him some mobility and offense. Eli Marrero will be indistinguishable from the rest of the MLB catching corps for the remainder of his career. Until a torn ligament in his left thumb—the trailing thumb in his swing—fully heals, batting will be an adventure, and even after that there's no guarantee.

Mike Matheny — C — Bats R — Age 30

YEAR	TEAM	LGE	AB	H	DB	TP	HR	BB	SO	R	RBI	SB	CS	OUT	BA	OBP	SLG	EQA	EQR	DEFENSE	
1998	Milwauke	NL	323	78	9	0	8	10	59	25	28	1	0	245	.241	.278	.344	.204	23	87-C	-7
1999	Toronto	AL	163	36	3	0	4	10	34	15	17	0	0	127	.221	.270	.313	.189	10	53-C	1
2000	St Louis	NL	420	108	21	1	6	25	90	41	45	0	0	312	.257	.304	.355	.220	35	115-C	15
2001	St Louis	NL	259	66	7	0	7	17	58	25	31	0	0	193	.255	.301	.363	.222	22		

Thanks to other people's misfortune, Mike Matheny was finally given an opportunity to show what he was capable of doing. And that he did. He hit three times as many home runs as Rick Ankiel did in just seven times the at-bats. Matheny did have a strange year offensively, hitting .300 or better in three months and .217 or less in the other three. He's not someone who will help a club in anything more than a backup role.

Mark McGwire — 1B — Bats R — Age 37

YEAR	TEAM	LGE	AB	H	DB	TP	HR	BB	SO	R	RBI	SB	CS	OUT	BA	OBP	SLG	EQA	EQR	DEFENSE			
1998	St Louis	NL	522	154	24	0	69	160	145	133	143	1	0	368	.295	.465	.738	.370	154	150-1B	-7		
1999	St Louis	NL	522	140	22	1	60	123	133	112	131	0	0	382	.268	.410	.659	.333	123	142-1B	-7		
2000	St Louis	NL	236	69	9	0	29	71	73	56	65	1	0	167	.292	.466	.699	.364	67	66-1B	-3		
2001	St Louis	NL	330	90	14	0	37	110	97	90	106	0	0	240	.273	.455	.652	.352	88				

How eye-popping are those numbers? Mark McGwire's shortened season probably cost him his already slight chance at obliterating the career home-run record. It's well past time to start talking about Big Mac as the greatest first baseman ever, with all due respect to Lou Gehrig. The patellar tendinitis that knocked him out for so long can recur, but his surgery in October should mean there's no reason he can't play in 130 games this year and post his usual obscene numbers.

Craig Paquette — 3B/LF — Bats R — Age 32

YEAR	TEAM	LGE	AB	H	DB	TP	HR	BB	SO	R	RBI	SB	CS	OUT	BA	OBP	SLG	EQA	EQR	DEFENSE			
1998	Norfolk	Int	61	15	1	1	2	0	14	8	10	1	1	47	.246	.246	.393	.202	4				
1999	Norfolk	Int	281	66	16	2	10	6	50	29	37	2	0	215	.235	.256	.413	.217	23	35-3B	0	19-RF	1
1999	St Louis	NL	158	44	5	0	10	4	36	20	34	1	0	114	.278	.296	.500	.257	19	19-RF	-1		
2000	St Louis	NL	387	93	24	2	14	21	78	44	57	3	3	297	.240	.282	.421	.229	37	60-3B	-6	17-LF	-3
2001	St Louis	NL	372	90	21	1	14	20	79	39	49	3	1	283	.242	.281	.417	.229	36				

Craig Paquette is a more useful ballplayer than Dunston, primarily because he can still play the infield credibly. Paquette's plate discipline is non-existent, but that doesn't matter when you're a proven scrub who played under LaRussa in Oakland. Like Scott Hemond and Mike Gallego before him, Paquette has overcome the obstacle of having insufficient ability to perform.

Eduardo Perez — 1B/3B — Bats R — Age 31

YEAR	TEAM	LGE	AB	H	DB	TP	HR	BB	SO	R	RBI	SB	CS	OUT	BA	OBP	SLG	EQA	EQR	DEFENSE			
1998	Cincnnti	NL	174	42	4	0	4	20	42	20	30	0	1	133	.241	.326	.333	.224	16	38-1B	4		
1999	Memphis	PCL	411	105	18	0	13	34	96	46	56	5	5	311	.255	.318	.394	.237	42	80-1B	3	13-3B	1
1999	St Louis	NL	32	11	1	0	1	6	6	5	8	0	0	21	.344	.447	.469	.315	6				
2000	Memphis	PCL	278	66	8	2	13	31	53	39	43	6	2	214	.237	.315	.421	.246	32	34-1B	-1	20-3B	0
2000	St Louis	NL	91	26	4	0	3	4	18	9	9	1	0	65	.286	.334	.429	.256	11	19-1B	2		
2001	St Louis	NL	329	85	8	0	12	33	73	42	46	6	2	246	.258	.326	.392	.244	36				

He'a a similar but superior player to Paquette. Eduardo Perez can play either corner acceptably and provides some punch from the right side. Unlike Paquette or Dunston, he's still good enough that he can actually help a team win in the right situation. Is it time for me to let go of the whole "Paquette and Dunston got 600 at-bats" thing? Perhaps a nice 12-step program would help. Sold to the Japanese.

Placido Polanco — IF — Bats R — Age 25

YEAR	TEAM	LGE	AB	H	DB	TP	HR	BB	SO	R	RBI	SB	CS	OUT	BA	OBP	SLG	EQA	EQR	DEFENSE			
1998	Memphis	PCL	244	61	14	1	1	13	15	28	17	4	2	185	.250	.293	.328	.207	18	56-2B	2		
1998	St Louis	NL	115	30	3	2	1	5	8	10	11	2	0	85	.261	.297	.348	.218	9	23-SS	3	11-2B	-2
1999	Memphis	PCL	118	29	3	1	0	3	11	14	8	1	0	89	.246	.268	.288	.179	6	19-2B	5		
1999	St Louis	NL	221	60	9	3	1	12	23	23	18	1	3	164	.271	.309	.353	.217	18	47-2B	-1		
2000	St Louis	NL	325	100	10	3	5	11	24	46	36	3	4	229	.308	.332	.403	.243	33	37-2B	4	27-3B	2
2001	St Louis	NL	316	93	12	3	3	18	26	38	40	4	3	226	.294	.332	.380	.240	32				

He just had the season of his life; outside of that, he's still potentially useful. Placido Polanco can play any infield position pretty well, he's not slow, and he's young enough to actually hold onto some of that fluke batting average. In the proper role, this is a good guy to have on a club. As the everyday third baseman—his likely role in the absence of Fernando Tatis—he's lacking.

Albert Pujols — 3B — Bats R — Age 21

YEAR	TEAM	LGE	AB	H	DB	TP	HR	BB	SO	R	RBI	SB	CS	OUT	BA	OBP	SLG	EQA	EQR	DEFENSE	
2000	Peoria	Mid	407	108	22	4	13	24	41	46	56	1	2	301	.265	.310	.435	.244	44	104-3B	12
2000	Potomac	Car	83	20	5	1	2	4	8	8	8	0	1	64	.241	.276	.398	.215	7	20-3B	5
2001	St Louis	NL	281	85	18	2	10	18	43	40	51	0	0	196	.302	.344	.488	.274	39		

(Albert Pujols *continued*)

Albert Pujols is a very promising third-base prospect. It's probably early to call him grade-A, but he has one great year under his belt, a .324/.389/.585 performance at Peoria followed by a brief stint at Potomac in which he wasn't overmatched. He finished the season with three games in Memphis and will likely start the 2001 season at Double-A Arkansas. Pujols is not going to be a fast guy; he's already big at 205 pounds and has the frame of a power hitter. His defense is good enough that he can probably avoid the dreaded corner migration from third base to first base. This is someone to watch; he could be starting at a Cardinal corner sooner than anyone realizes.

Edgar Renteria — SS — Bats R — Age 25

YEAR	TEAM	LGE	AB	H	DB	TP	HR	BB	SO	R	RBI	SB	CS	OUT	BA	OBP	SLG	EQA	EQR	DEFENSE	
1998	Florida	NL	527	150	20	2	3	46	73	80	31	38	22	399	.285	.346	.347	.239	56	129-SS	-2
1999	St Louis	NL	587	158	34	2	11	45	77	84	59	28	7	436	.269	.323	.390	.245	65	147-SS	-12
2000	St Louis	NL	565	151	27	1	16	54	72	87	70	19	13	427	.267	.332	.404	.246	64	142-SS	-2
2001	St Louis	NL	533	155	25	1	13	57	73	101	71	39	13	390	.291	.359	.415	.268	73		

The next superstar. Edgar Renteria is ready to completely explode on the league, and he'll do so in a season in which the Cardinals are having enough success to draw national media attention. Three of us (Rany Jazayerli, a friend in a Scoresheet Baseball league, and I) each independently came up with the most fitting analog for Renteria: the Mets' Edgardo Alfonzo. Alfonzo started in the Mets' system at shortstop, so let's do a quick age comparison:

Edgardo Alfonzo	AVG/ OBP/ SLG	Edgar Renteria	AVG/ OBP /SLG
Age 22	.261/.304/.345	Age 22	.282/.347/.342
Age 23	.315/.391/.432	Age 23	.275/.334/.400
Age 24	.278/.355/.427	Age 24	.278/.346/.423

It's not perfect, but those Age 24 lines are nearly identical. If reports are correct that Renteria's age has been overstated by a year, he's even further ahead of the game. At age 25, Alfonzo busted out, posting a .304/.385/.502 year in a bad hitters' park. Renteria probably won't do that, but I expect him to smack 55 to 60 extra base hits, hit 25 home runs, and draw 75 walks a year starting in about 2003.

Fernando Tatis — 3B — Bats R — Age 26

YEAR	TEAM	LGE	AB	H	DB	TP	HR	BB	SO	R	RBI	SB	CS	OUT	BA	OBP	SLG	EQA	EQR	DEFENSE	
1998	Texas	AL	328	89	18	2	3	11	59	41	31	5	2	241	.271	.302	.366	.223	28	92-3B	5
1998	St Louis	NL	205	58	14	2	9	23	53	28	26	6	3	150	.283	.361	.502	.283	32	55-3B	-4
1999	St Louis	NL	538	154	29	2	32	74	121	97	97	16	8	392	.286	.388	.526	.299	96	144-3B	-1
2000	St Louis	NL	326	80	19	1	17	51	88	55	58	2	3	249	.245	.362	.466	.274	49	75-3B	-1
2001	Montreal	NL	425	115	23	1	19	58	112	70	69	12	5	314	.271	.358	.464	.279	65		

A very unfriendly torn groin put a real damper on Fernando Tatis's season. He's made tremendous strides offensively and, if healthy, will be one of the third-base stars of the '00s along with Troy Glaus, Eric Chavez, Adrian Beltre, and the like. He's a young veteran coming off an injury; look out. I think he'll step forward and completely obliterate that projection with the Expos. The Vladimir forecasting system shows him at .292/.390/.575.

Fernando Vina — 2B — Bats L — Age 32

YEAR	TEAM	LGE	AB	H	DB	TP	HR	BB	SO	R	RBI	SB	CS	OUT	BA	OBP	SLG	EQA	EQR	DEFENSE	
1998	Milwauke	NL	645	197	39	6	8	52	43	101	44	20	16	464	.305	.378	.422	.269	87	155-2B	24
1999	Milwauke	NL	155	41	3	0	2	11	6	15	16	4	2	116	.265	.329	.323	.224	14	37-2B	3
2000	St Louis	NL	489	143	23	5	4	29	34	75	29	9	8	354	.292	.361	.384	.253	57	118-2B	13
2001	St Louis	NL	420	122	21	2	5	35	30	59	53	10	9	307	.290	.345	.386	.247	46		

Fernando Vina is a very solid player. He plays defense pretty well, posts a reasonable average, and makes up for his impatience at the plate by sticking any convenient body part in front of breaking curves with amazing regularity. If he drew 20 more walks a year, he'd be a great leadoff man. Vina will probably show a bit more power than we're forecasting here. I wouldn't be surprised to see him hit 40 doubles, draw 40 walks, and get hit by 25 pitches. Thwap.

National League

Ernie Young — OF — Bats R — Age 31

YEAR	TEAM	LGE	AB	H	DB	TP	HR	BB	SO	R	RBI	SB	CS	OUT	BA	OBP	SLG	EQA	EQR	DEFENSE	
1998	Omaha	PCL	292	76	9	1	14	22	72	40	36	4	3	219	.260	.319	.442	.250	34	70-CF	5
1998	KansasCy	AL	53	10	3	0	1	2	8	3	3	2	1	44	.189	.231	.302	.170	3	16-RF	3
1999	Tucson	PCL	445	102	15	1	19	43	135	51	61	2	1	344	.229	.302	.396	.232	45	91-LF	-5
2000	Memphis	PCL	455	100	12	0	24	48	129	53	65	6	1	356	.220	.298	.404	.235	47	103-LF	-3
2001	*SanDieg*	*NL*	*366*	*81*	*8*	*0*	*17*	*38*	*113*	*42*	*52*	*4*	*1*	*286*	*.221*	*.295*	*.383*	*.237*	*39*		

Team USA hero, tweener, and someone who can help the right club. Ernie Young can pop the ball pretty well, play pretty good defense, and he busts his ass. He's a ballplayer, one of the easiest ones to root for in baseball. Young can probably have a pretty solid Lloyd McClendon-like career after his playing days are over. Signed by the Padres.

PITCHERS (ERA: 4.50, H/9: 9.00, HR/9: 1.00, BB/9: 3.00, K/9: 6.00, KW: 1.00, PERA: 4.50)

Rick Ankiel — Throws L — Age 21

YEAR	TEAM	LGE	IP	H	ER	HR	BB	K	ERA	W	L	H/9	HR/9	BB/9	K/9	KW	PERA
1998	Peoria	Mid	32.0	16	9	0	15	21	2.53	3	1	4.50	0.00	4.22	5.91	0.70	1.77
1998	Pr Willm	Car	110.0	110	74	17	51	93	6.05	4	8	9.00	1.39	4.17	7.61	0.91	5.41
1999	Arkansas	Tex	45.7	29	8	3	19	48	1.58	4	1	5.72	0.59	3.74	9.46	1.26	2.64
1999	Memphis	PCL	83.0	73	41	8	50	81	4.45	4	5	7.92	0.87	5.42	8.78	0.81	4.73
1999	St Louis	NL	32.0	26	12	2	12	33	3.38	2	2	7.31	0.56	3.38	9.28	1.38	3.27
2000	St Louis	NL	171.7	138	73	18	73	161	3.83	10	9	7.23	0.94	3.83	8.44	1.10	3.77

He's a tough SOB with a golden arm. Rick Ankiel demonstrates maturity well beyond his years both on and off the field. Few left-handed pitchers do a good job of working right-handed hitters inside with anything except "show me" fastballs. Ankiel, like Randy Johnson, has a nasty hard breaking ball that he uses down and in against righties with great effectiveness. Righties his .213 against him, lefties .253. There are a lot of young pitchers who are one walk per nine innings away from having a nice career. Ankiel is already a monster; he's one walk per nine innings away from turning into a left-handed Pedro Martinez.

There's a lot of speculation that his loss of command in the postseason is indicative of major troubles, à la Steve Blass or Mark Wohlers. We all hope not, but look at it this way. Let's say Ankiel has a complete psychological disaster and loses the strike zone for two years, then slowly makes his way back over the course of another year. Then he'd be Tim Hudson with better stuff. Personally, I don't think he'll miss a beat. There is no more fun pitcher to watch in baseball except possibly Martinez or Randy Johnson. Larry Walker is already figuring out ways to duck this guy.

Alan Benes — Throws R — Age 29

YEAR	TEAM	LGE	IP	H	ER	HR	BB	K	ERA	W	L	H/9	HR/9	BB/9	K/9	KW	PERA
1997	St Louis	NL	162.0	139	66	15	64	135	3.67	11	7	7.72	0.83	3.56	7.50	1.05	3.75
2000	Memphis	PCL	36.3	44	34	10	23	17	8.42	1	3	10.90	2.48	5.70	4.21	0.37	8.29
2000	St Louis	NL	45.0	52	30	6	19	22	6.00	2	3	10.40	1.20	3.80	4.40	0.58	5.87

He's still recovering from 1997. His strikeout rate hasn't rebounded, and he still looks tentative out there. Alan Benes will likely have a successful career, albeit out of the bullpen rather than in the rotation. He should be a setup guy in 2001 and has the potential to thrive in that role, like Jeff Nelson or Mike Jackson.

Andy Benes — Throws R — Age 33

YEAR	TEAM	LGE	IP	H	ER	HR	BB	K	ERA	W	L	H/9	HR/9	BB/9	K/9	KW	PERA
1998	Arizona	NL	222.0	215	108	25	66	133	4.38	11	14	8.72	1.01	2.68	5.39	1.01	4.22
1999	Arizona	NL	194.0	207	106	31	67	119	4.92	9	13	9.60	1.44	3.11	5.52	0.89	5.37
2000	St Louis	NL	162.3	169	86	26	55	114	4.77	7	11	9.37	1.44	3.05	6.32	1.04	5.21

Andy Benes is a plain old workhorse. He still has very good stuff but doesn't have that extra two mph he had when he was in his late twenties. Benes is remarkably durable and consistent and should rebound somewhat from a subpar 2000. He has gone 11 years without a major injury and has never really had a bad year in that span. With a little better luck, we could be talking about a Hall of Famer, but the run support wasn't there early in his career. He can still make it if he puts together three or four "next level" seasons. Don't rule it out.

Justin Brunette   Throws L   Age 25

YEAR	TEAM	LGE	IP	H	ER	HR	BB	K	ERA	W	L	H/9	HR/9	BB/9	K/9	KW	PERA
1999	Peoria	Mid	40.3	36	12	5	20	22	2.68	3	1	8.03	1.12	4.46	4.91	0.55	4.64
1999	Arkansas	Tex	16.7	22	15	5	8	14	8.10	0	2	11.88	2.70	4.32	7.56	0.88	8.51
2000	Memphis	PCL	32.0	40	26	5	15	19	7.31	1	3	11.25	1.41	4.22	5.34	0.63	6.76
2000	St Louis	NL	4.7	8	3	0	4	2	5.79	0	1	15.43	0.00	7.71	3.86	0.25	9.16

A rare bird. Justin Brunette is a reliever who came up pitching strictly as a setup guy in the minors. He has reasonable stuff but probably needs a year at Triple-A to pull together the physical development and pitching experience.

Jason Christiansen   Throws L   Age 31

YEAR	TEAM	LGE	IP	H	ER	HR	BB	K	ERA	W	L	H/9	HR/9	BB/9	K/9	KW	PERA
1998	Pittsbrg	NL	62.3	52	22	2	24	58	3.18	4	3	7.51	0.29	3.47	8.37	1.21	3.17
1999	Pittsbrg	NL	37.0	26	16	2	18	29	3.89	2	2	6.32	0.49	4.38	7.05	0.81	3.07
2000	Pittsbrg	NL	37.3	29	21	2	20	34	5.06	2	2	6.99	0.48	4.82	8.20	0.85	3.57
2000	St Louis	NL	9.7	13	7	1	2	10	6.52	0	1	12.10	0.93	1.86	9.31	2.50	5.84

Somewhere deep in slumber, Gene Lamont is mumbling something about getting Jason Christiansen up in the pen. He's a situational left-hander who lost a bit of stuff to injury in 2000 but should recover at some point this season. Christiansen is a smart pitcher who can relentlessly work that outside six inches of the strike zone. He's part of an alarming invasion of players named something like "Christenson." At least his first name's not Ryan.

Luther Hackman   Throws R   Age 26

YEAR	TEAM	LGE	IP	H	ER	HR	BB	K	ERA	W	L	H/9	HR/9	BB/9	K/9	KW	PERA
1998	New Havn	Eas	128.0	168	116	28	61	53	8.16	3	11	11.81	1.97	4.29	3.73	0.43	7.72
1999	Carolina	Sou	57.3	53	37	6	31	29	5.81	2	4	8.32	0.94	4.87	4.55	0.47	4.79
1999	ColSprin	PCL	97.7	98	43	6	43	58	3.96	6	5	9.03	0.55	3.96	5.34	0.67	4.43
1999	Colorado	NL	16.7	24	14	3	8	8	7.56	0	2	12.96	1.62	4.32	4.32	0.50	7.99
2000	Memphis	PCL	113.0	126	71	16	39	44	5.65	4	9	10.04	1.27	3.11	3.50	0.56	5.44

Luther Hackman made three disastrous starts for the Rockies before being rescued by the Cardinals. His future is pretty iffy; he'll have to step it up a notch to have a shot at a career. He doesn't throw hard enough to rely on his stuff, and big-league hitters eat guys like this. If he were left-handed, it would be a different story.

Pat Hentgen   Throws R   Age 32

YEAR	TEAM	LGE	IP	H	ER	HR	BB	K	ERA	W	L	H/9	HR/9	BB/9	K/9	KW	PERA
1998	Toronto	AL	175.3	193	94	24	59	87	4.83	8	11	9.91	1.23	3.03	4.47	0.74	5.30
1999	Toronto	AL	197.0	207	97	27	52	112	4.43	10	12	9.46	1.23	2.38	5.12	1.08	4.76
2000	St Louis	NL	190.0	195	96	21	72	98	4.55	9	12	9.24	0.99	3.41	4.64	0.68	4.81

He's another Cardinals' horse. Pat Hentgen's stuff has decayed badly due to very heavy workloads throughout his career, but he deserves a lot of credit. He continues to work inside despite the decline, and yes, he often pays for it. Still, Hentgen takes the ball every bloody time and gives his team a good chance to win games. He helps the bullpen get some rest and works hard to stay healthy. There's a lot of mileage on that arm; the chances of him surviving a long-term contract without a major physical breakdown are slim. The Orioles gave him a two-year deal.

Chad Hutchinson   Throws R   Age 24

YEAR	TEAM	LGE	IP	H	ER	HR	BB	K	ERA	W	L	H/9	HR/9	BB/9	K/9	KW	PERA
1998	New Jrsy	NYP	14.0	16	7	0	5	9	4.50	1	1	10.29	0.00	3.21	5.79	0.90	4.27
1998	Pr Willm	Car	24.7	24	20	8	15	16	7.30	1	2	8.76	2.92	5.47	5.84	0.53	7.40
1999	Arkansas	Tex	129.3	129	92	18	98	96	6.40	4	10	8.98	1.25	6.82	6.68	0.49	6.33
1999	Memphis	PCL	11.3	4	3	2	9	11	2.38	1	0	3.18	1.59	7.15	8.74	0.61	3.44
2000	Arkansas	Tex	44.7	41	24	2	29	33	4.84	2	3	8.26	0.40	5.84	6.65	0.57	4.63

Chad Hutchinson has a live arm despite being hampered in 2000 by elbow trouble. He throws hard and down, two good things. Hutchinson fought some nasty control problems early in the year but righted himself and pitched well in the Texas League. Most organizations would be willing to sacrifice livestock, children, and cliches to get this guy, Ankiel, and Bud

National League

Smith. He absolutely has #1-starter stuff and should be in St. Louis before the season's over, unless he spends too much time with Tyler Pope.

Mike James — Throws R — Age 33

YEAR	TEAM	LGE	IP	H	ER	HR	BB	K	ERA	W	L	H/9	HR/9	BB/9	K/9	KW	PERA
1998	Anaheim	AL	13.7	10	3	1	6	11	1.98	2	0	6.59	0.66	3.95	7.24	0.92	3.21
2000	St Louis	NL	50.0	39	19	6	19	34	3.42	3	3	7.02	1.08	3.42	6.12	0.89	3.61

Mike James is a reliable reliever with a penchant for shaving in the dark. He bounced back from two lost seasons to be the Cardinals' main right-handed setup guy and will have that same role in 2001.

Darryl Kile — Throws R — Age 32

YEAR	TEAM	LGE	IP	H	ER	HR	BB	K	ERA	W	L	H/9	HR/9	BB/9	K/9	KW	PERA
1998	Colorado	NL	228.3	247	114	18	68	128	4.49	11	14	9.74	0.71	2.68	5.05	0.94	4.49
1999	Colorado	NL	194.7	213	111	19	72	98	5.13	8	14	9.85	0.88	3.33	4.53	0.68	5.01
2000	St Louis	NL	225.0	208	100	29	47	160	4.00	13	12	8.32	1.16	1.88	6.40	1.70	3.82

Darryl Kile is a reliable front-of-the-order starting pitcher with a plus fastball and a delivery that makes it very difficult to identify his pitches. You think Kile was happy to get out of Coors Field? The damage that place does isn't just measured in the extra distance a ball flies. During his stint with the Rockies, Kile walked 205 hitters in two years. Last year? A career best, with 58 walks against 192 strikeouts in 232 1/3 innings. Timidity in a pitcher is a very bad thing.

Kile should continue to baffle hitters with his curveball for several years and will do so in St. Louis, having signed a three-year extension for $23 million, way less than he would have drawn as a free agent. Chalk up an even higher return on investment for management and its campaign to make St. Louis a great place for players to play. The rest of the league better hope some bigger markets don't figure out how to make themselves more attractive.

Matt Morris — Throws R — Age 26

YEAR	TEAM	LGE	IP	H	ER	HR	BB	K	ERA	W	L	H/9	HR/9	BB/9	K/9	KW	PERA
1998	St Louis	NL	108.7	98	36	8	38	64	2.98	8	4	8.12	0.66	3.15	5.30	0.84	3.71
2000	Memphis	PCL	14.0	19	14	3	7	5	9.00	0	2	12.21	1.93	4.50	3.21	0.36	8.07
2000	St Louis	NL	51.3	51	21	3	14	28	3.68	3	3	8.94	0.53	2.45	4.91	1.00	3.76

LaRussa has said that Matt Morris will either be in the rotation or fight for a spot in it in 2001; the trade for Dustin Hermanso decreases Morris's opportunity. Morris is a great pitcher, period. He knows how to pitch, throws hard, has good control, and can make great hitters look like bumbling rookies. If he's in the rotation, managed well, and can avoid being made into a closer, he can compete for the Cy Young Award as early as this year. People forget just how great this guy was before surgery, and by the end of this year, he should have a fully healed elbow. Hopefully, Duncan and LaRussa can avoid the temptation to use him like a damp rag.

Jesse Orosco — Throws L — Age 44

YEAR	TEAM	LGE	IP	H	ER	HR	BB	K	ERA	W	L	H/9	HR/9	BB/9	K/9	KW	PERA
1998	Baltimor	AL	55.7	44	19	6	25	46	3.07	4	2	7.11	0.97	4.04	7.44	0.92	3.82
1999	Baltimor	AL	32.0	27	18	4	16	33	5.06	2	2	7.59	1.13	4.50	9.28	1.03	4.41
2000	St Louis	NL	2.3	3	3	1	2	3	11.57	0	0	11.57	3.86	7.71	11.57	0.75	10.70

Elbow trouble knocked Orosco out for the season in early August, and the Cardinals declined to pick up his 2001 option. He is still left-handed and still breathing, so he could catch on with some team as a situational left-hander. More likely, this is the end of a Kent Tekulvesque run. I wonder how different his career would have been if the strike zone hadn't gotten squashed.

Josh Pearce — Throws R — Age 23

YEAR	TEAM	LGE	IP	H	ER	HR	BB	K	ERA	W	L	H/9	HR/9	BB/9	K/9	KW	PERA
1999	New Jrsy	NYP	68.0	90	67	22	26	35	8.87	1	7	11.91	2.91	3.44	4.63	0.67	8.41
2000	Potomac	Car	57.7	73	30	11	11	22	4.68	3	3	11.39	1.72	1.72	3.43	1.00	6.15
2000	Arkansas	Tex	90.7	115	75	21	37	39	7.44	2	8	11.42	2.08	3.67	3.87	0.53	7.35

He's a grade-C prospect with good control but Quadruple-A stuff. Josh Pearce will have to live on the edge to have a career; in this organization, he's not likely to get much of an opportunity to break through.

Scott Radinsky — Throws L — Age 33

YEAR	TEAM	LGE	IP	H	ER	HR	BB	K	ERA	W	L	H/9	HR/9	BB/9	K/9	KW	PERA
1998	LosAngls	NL	58.7	61	21	6	19	37	3.22	4	3	9.36	0.92	2.91	5.68	0.97	4.58
1999	St Louis	NL	27.3	26	15	2	15	14	4.94	1	2	8.56	0.66	4.94	4.61	0.47	4.69

His ulnar collateral ligament blew out, and he underwent Tommy John surgery in the middle of the year. Scott Radinsky probably won't be able to contribute until late in the 2001 season and would be wise to sit it out and heal fully. He should be able to bounce back pretty strong in 2002. Radinsky used to have tremendous stuff and has had some rough breaks in terms of health. Hopefully, this recovery will work out.

Britt Reames — Throws R — Age 27

YEAR	TEAM	LGE	IP	H	ER	HR	BB	K	ERA	W	L	H/9	HR/9	BB/9	K/9	KW	PERA
1999	Potomac	Car	33.0	34	24	4	26	10	6.55	1	3	9.27	1.09	7.09	2.73	0.19	6.47
2000	Arkansas	Tex	36.0	47	33	7	21	22	8.25	1	3	11.75	1.75	5.25	5.50	0.52	7.84
2000	Memphis	PCL	70.7	54	21	3	22	52	2.67	6	2	6.88	0.38	2.80	6.62	1.18	2.69
2000	St Louis	NL	40.0	30	15	3	19	26	3.38	2	2	6.75	0.68	4.28	5.85	0.68	3.44

Meet another of the Frank Jobe All-Stars. Britt Reames, like the overwhelming majority of pitchers in the Cardinals organization, has already had Tommy John surgery. He was pretty impressive in a late-season audition and, despite never impressing the scouts, has a chance at carving out a Pedro Astacio career. He doesn't throw hard, but he has a very slick curveball, and he's performed every time he's been given a shot. The Expos stole him; he should be in the back of their rotation, and pitching well, in 2001.

Jose Rodriguez — Throws L — Age 26

YEAR	TEAM	LGE	IP	H	ER	HR	BB	K	ERA	W	L	H/9	HR/9	BB/9	K/9	KW	PERA
1998	Peoria	Mid	35.0	46	36	3	26	14	9.26	1	3	11.83	0.77	6.69	3.60	0.27	7.44
1999	Peoria	Mid	14.3	15	9	2	11	7	5.65	1	1	9.42	1.26	6.91	4.40	0.32	6.67
1999	Arkansas	Tex	32.0	39	20	10	31	18	5.63	1	3	10.97	2.81	8.72	5.06	0.29	9.97
2000	Arkansas	Tex	10.3	7	3	0	5	5	2.61	1	0	6.10	0.00	4.35	4.35	0.50	2.60
2000	Memphis	PCL	44.3	46	22	6	21	25	4.47	2	3	9.34	1.22	4.26	5.08	0.60	5.45
2000	St Louis	NL	4.0	2	1	0	2	2	2.25	0	0	4.50	0.00	4.50	4.50	0.50	1.84

He's born and bred to be a situational lefty. With Orosco and Radinsky gone, Jose Rodriguez should have a pretty good shot to make the team. He might struggle even within a well-defined role but hasn't posted an ERA above 4.00 at any stop since Peoria in 1998.

Bud Smith — Throws L — Age 21

YEAR	TEAM	LGE	IP	H	ER	HR	BB	K	ERA	W	L	H/9	HR/9	BB/9	K/9	KW	PERA
1998	JohnsnCy	App	58.0	88	51	17	42	28	7.91	1	5	13.66	2.64	6.52	4.34	0.33	10.44
1999	Peoria	Mid	49.3	57	25	9	19	31	4.56	2	3	10.40	1.64	3.47	5.66	0.82	6.20
1999	Potomac	Car	96.0	94	50	4	35	49	4.69	5	6	8.81	0.38	3.28	4.59	0.70	3.87
2000	Arkansas	Tex	101.7	93	35	8	28	63	3.10	7	4	8.23	0.71	2.48	5.58	1.13	3.55
2000	Memphis	PCL	51.3	38	23	5	15	25	4.03	3	3	6.66	0.88	2.63	4.38	0.83	2.94

Bud Smith is an absolutely great pitching prospect, or at least as good as one can be when he's relatively small. Smith and Ryan Anderson are probably the best left-handed pitching prospects in baseball, and they're not really similar in how they get things done. Smith has nasty, but not overpowering, stuff, is difficult to read, and is already a master at completely messing up a hitter's timing. He'll probably start the year in Triple-A, He reminds me of Greg Maddux. Will he be that good? No, but he doesn't show any fear despite not having a tremendous fastball; sometimes, that's enough. I like him more than I should based on his numbers and velocity.

Gene Stechschulte — Throws R — Age 27

YEAR	TEAM	LGE	IP	H	ER	HR	BB	K	ERA	W	L	H/9	HR/9	BB/9	K/9	KW	PERA
1998	Peoria	Mid	59.0	61	32	3	30	31	4.88	3	4	9.31	0.46	4.58	4.73	0.52	4.76
1999	Arkansas	Tex	38.0	42	33	7	26	24	7.82	1	3	9.95	1.66	6.16	5.68	0.46	7.07
2000	Memphis	PCL	44.7	37	15	6	20	25	3.02	3	2	7.46	1.21	4.03	5.04	0.63	4.25
2000	St Louis	NL	25.3	23	19	5	14	10	6.75	1	2	8.17	1.78	4.97	3.55	0.36	5.65

Minor-league closers don't have a tremendous record of success in the majors. Gene Stechschulte has reasonable stuff, but he'll have to get an opportunity to make the club in spring training and totally blow away everyone in order to capitalize.

Garrett Stephenson — Throws R — Age 29

YEAR	TEAM	LGE	IP	H	ER	HR	BB	K	ERA	W	L	H/9	HR/9	BB/9	K/9	KW	PERA
1998	Scran-WB	Int	69.0	81	55	19	17	32	7.17	2	6	10.57	2.48	2.22	4.17	0.94	6.67
1998	Philadel	NL	22.3	30	23	3	17	14	9.27	0	2	12.09	1.21	6.85	5.64	0.41	8.10
1999	Memphis	PCL	24.0	20	9	3	8	12	3.38	2	1	7.50	1.13	3.00	4.50	0.75	3.72
1999	St Louis	NL	83.0	86	39	10	24	50	4.23	4	5	9.33	1.08	2.60	5.42	1.04	4.62
2000	St Louis	NL	194.7	200	94	27	51	102	4.35	10	12	9.25	1.25	2.36	4.72	1.00	4.64

Garrett Stephenson was a godsend, giving the Cardinals 200 above-average innings. His peripheral numbers don't jump out at you, but he could be a middle-of-the-rotation starter for a couple of years. He may have earned the coveted Tony LaRussa halo, which would prevent younger pitchers from having a chance to earn his job in a fair fight. The injury that knocked him out of the postseason doesn't appear to be serious, but the Hermanson trade may keep him out of the rotation.

Mike Timlin — Throws R — Age 35

YEAR	TEAM	LGE	IP	H	ER	HR	BB	K	ERA	W	L	H/9	HR/9	BB/9	K/9	KW	PERA
1998	Seattle	AL	77.3	72	22	4	14	55	2.56	6	3	8.38	0.47	1.63	6.40	1.96	3.09
1999	Baltimor	AL	62.0	48	26	8	19	48	3.77	4	3	6.97	1.16	2.76	6.97	1.26	3.42
2000	Baltimor	AL	34.7	34	18	5	12	25	4.67	2	2	8.83	1.30	3.12	6.49	1.04	4.73
2000	St Louis	NL	29.3	30	10	2	16	22	3.07	2	1	9.20	0.61	4.91	6.75	0.69	5.00

He's a solid reliever who was miscast in the role of closer. Mike Timlin has respectable stuff but suffers from a somewhat straight fastball and has been raked over the coals by fans who seem to think he always gives up the big hit at the wrong time. There's no reason he won't continue to be productive as a setup man. He's under contract for two more years. I'd make him a setup guy and leave him there.

Dave Veres — Throws R — Age 34

YEAR	TEAM	LGE	IP	H	ER	HR	BB	K	ERA	W	L	H/9	HR/9	BB/9	K/9	KW	PERA
1998	Colorado	NL	75.0	66	22	4	19	60	2.64	6	2	7.92	0.48	2.28	7.20	1.58	3.11
1999	Colorado	NL	78.0	84	35	8	25	60	4.04	4	5	9.69	0.92	2.88	6.92	1.20	4.78
2000	St Louis	NL	73.3	64	24	5	20	56	2.95	5	3	7.85	0.61	2.45	6.87	1.40	3.26

Dave Veres signed a big contract extension and will likely be the closer through 2002. He had some shoulder trouble in 2000, but it was nothing to worry about: he got hurt picking up his young son. I'd like to find some way to blame *that* on Dave Duncan. Veres has very good stuff, and he knows how to pitch. He'll be a solid closer for the foreseeable future.

Clint Weibl — Throws R — Age 26

YEAR	TEAM	LGE	IP	H	ER	HR	BB	K	ERA	W	L	H/9	HR/9	BB/9	K/9	KW	PERA
1998	Arkansas	Tex	129.3	156	92	32	61	55	6.40	4	10	10.86	2.23	4.24	3.83	0.45	7.41
1999	Arkansas	Tex	100.7	118	67	18	61	44	5.99	3	8	10.55	1.61	5.45	3.93	0.36	7.07
2000	Arkansas	Tex	51.0	61	48	18	22	29	8.47	1	5	10.76	3.18	3.88	5.12	0.66	8.20
2000	Memphis	PCL	112.7	96	50	16	40	62	3.99	7	6	7.67	1.28	3.20	4.95	0.77	4.09

Clint Weibl has dutifully moved through the organization and may have had a showing in 2000 that will lead him to a major-league career. He had 18 very good starts at Memphis, allowing only 98 hits in 120 innings with a very respectable 92-to-37 strikeout-to-walk ratio. He's not Bud Smith or Chad Hutchinson, but if this improvement is real, he'll likely get a start or two at some point in the next year or so.

Support-Neutral Statistics — ST. LOUIS CARDINALS — Park Effect: -3.6%

PITCHER	GS	IP	R	SNW	SNL	SNPCT	W	L	RA	APW	SNVA	SNWAR
Rick Ankiel	30	173.0	80	11.9	7.6	.610	11	7	4.16	1.6	2.0	3.6
Andy Benes	27	163.0	87	9.4	8.7	.519	12	8	4.80	0.4	0.1	1.7
Pat Hentgen	33	194.3	107	11.3	10.8	.510	15	12	4.96	0.2	0.0	1.9
Darryl Kile	34	232.3	109	14.9	10.7	.582	19	9	4.22	2.0	2.0	4.0
Britt Reames	7	38.7	17	2.5	1.6	.604	2	1	3.96	0.4	0.4	0.7
Garrett Stephenson	31	199.3	105	11.3	11.0	.508	16	9	4.74	0.6	0.2	1.8
TOTALS	162	1000.7	505	61.1	50.3	.548	75	46	4.54	5.3	4.6	13.8

Last year, we devoted this space to the success of veteran starters under the leadership of Tony LaRussa and Dave Duncan in St. Louis. In 2000, with the great Cardinal debut of Darryl Kile and the disastrous return to form by Darren Oliver upon leaving St. Louis, the tradition continued.

Through 2000, there are seven starters who had at least 20 Support-Neutral decisions under LaRussa and Duncan in St. Louis and who also had at least 20 career Support-Neutral decisions away from them. Five of those seven were dramatically better under LaRussa/Duncan. Andy Benes has a career .575 Support-Neutral Winning Percentage (SNPct) with them and .517 away from them. Kent Bottenfield's split is .505/.461. Darryl Kile's is .582/.494. Darren Oliver's is .543/.477. Todd Stottlemyre's is .514/.468 (the .514 includes a year with LaRussa/Duncan in Oakland). Pat Hentgen doesn't split in the same direction as the others; he was .510 in his first year with LaRussa/Duncan after going .552 away from them. On the other hand, last year was his best of the past three. The only unambiguous failure of a veteran pitcher under LaRussa/Duncan was Kent Mercker, who put up a terrible .429 SNPct in two years under them and has been a fine .517 away from them. Hey, nobody's perfect.

For a quick explanation of SN stats, see page 7.

Reliever Evaluation Tools

PITCHER	G	IP	R	ARA	APR	IRNR/G	EIRS/G	IRP	BRS	RRA	ARP
Rick Ankiel	1	2.0	0	0.00	1.2	0.00	0.00	0.0	0.0	0.00	1.2
Alan Benes	29	44.0	33	6.96	-8.6	0.38	0.14	1.3	0.2	6.40	-5.9
Andy Benes	3	3.0	8	24.73	-6.5	0.00	0.00	0.0	-0.9	21.57	-5.5
David Benham	1	2.0	0	0.00	1.2	0.00	0.00	0.0	0.0	0.00	1.2
Justin Brunette	4	4.7	3	5.96	-0.4	0.25	0.06	-0.5	1.1	9.16	-2.1
Jason Christiansen	21	10.0	7	6.49	-1.4	0.76	0.28	-0.8	1.1	8.23	-3.4
Luther Hackman	1	2.7	3	10.43	-1.6	0.00	0.00	0.0	0.4	11.48	-1.9
Darren Holmes	5	8.3	9	10.02	-4.5	1.00	0.36	-2.3	0.0	12.44	-6.7
Mike James	51	51.3	22	3.98	7.0	0.63	0.19	-0.7	-3.9	3.59	9.2
Mike Matthews	14	9.3	12	11.93	-7.0	0.93	0.36	-2.6	0.3	14.34	-9.5
Mike Mohler	22	19.0	20	9.76	-9.6	0.64	0.27	-2.5	-2.0	8.86	-7.7
Matt Morris	31	53.0	22	3.85	7.9	0.23	0.06	1.1	1.7	3.99	7.1
Jesse Orosco	6	2.3	3	11.93	-1.7	1.33	0.37	0.3	-0.9	7.13	-0.5
Scott Radinsky	1	0.0	0	NaN	0.0	2.00	1.10	0.0	0.3	Inf	-0.2
Britt Reames	1	2.0	0	0.00	1.2	0.00	0.00	0.0	0.0	0.00	1.2
Jose Rodriguez	6	4.0	2	4.64	0.2	0.50	0.26	0.5	0.0	3.41	0.8
Heathcliff Slocumb	43	49.7	32	5.98	-4.3	0.67	0.29	7.6	-2.1	4.16	5.7
Gene Stechschulte	20	25.7	22	7.95	-7.9	0.50	0.17	-1.7	0.0	8.75	-10.1
Garrett Stephenson	1	1.0	0	0.00	0.6	0.00	0.00	0.0	0.0	0.00	0.6
Mark Thompson	20	25.0	21	7.79	-7.2	0.50	0.15	-1.1	-1.4	7.40	-6.1
Mike Timlin	25	29.7	11	3.44	5.8	0.28	0.09	-3.0	1.7	4.95	0.8
Dave Veres	71	75.7	26	3.19	16.9	0.63	0.22	0.2	-0.0	3.34	15.6
David Wainhouse	9	8.7	10	10.70	-5.3	0.22	0.19	-0.2	-0.0	9.63	-4.3
TOTALS	386	433.0	266	5.70	-24.1	0.56	0.20			5.62	-20.5

For a quick guide to RET, see page 10.

San Diego Padres

A couple of very interesting things happened with the Padres organization in 2000. The first involved their new ballpark; the second involved a federal investigation of owner John Moores. Unfortunately for the team's faithful, neither had much to do with the on-field product, as the team limped to a last-place finish in the NL West.

As this is written, the Padres' new East Village ballpark figures prominently in the minds of San Diego voters. Hopefully, newly elected city officials, as well as the municipal governments of cities across the land considering new sports facilities, have been paying attention to the singular goings-on at the construction site, in the boardrooms, and in the courtrooms of San Diego.

On its surface, the ballpark deal seems simple enough. As stated by Proposition C and approved by the city council and Mayor Susan Golding in 1998, the San Diego Padres and the city government agreed to jointly construct a baseball-only stadium in a dilapidated warehouse district downtown. The Padres would contribute $115 million, and the city would kick in $300 million. Most of the public money was to be raised by a bond issue which would be repaid with increased hotel-tax revenues. Much of the tax revenue was expected to come from a brand-new bayfront hotel, to be built on a plot of land occupied by a vacant shipyard.

A key point of the agreement—one that will hopefully become standard in publicly-financed stadium agreements—was the Padres' commitment to fund hundreds of millions of dollars' worth of redevelopment to occur in the surrounding area as the stadium was being built. Instead of a stadium surrounded by dive bars and vacant lots with land barons trying to squeeze investors out of every last penny, the redevelopment of the area would be complete by the time the Padres were ready to move into the new park before the 2002 season.

Prop C was not without its detractors. Many, led by local legal gadfly Bruce Henderson, filed lawsuits once the terms of the agreement were made public. That was expected, and the city council had done its homework. All lawsuits were thrown out of court by August and none served to hold up construction at all.

Padres Prospectus

2000 record: 76–86; Fifth place, NL West
Pythagenport W/L: 75–87
Runs Scored: 752 (12th in NL)
Runs Allowed: 815 (9th in NL)
Team EqA: .257 (8th in NL)
2000 Batters' Age: 28.7 (5th youngest in NL)
2000 Pitchers' Age: 27.1 (5th youngest in NL)
Ballpark: Qualcomm Stadium; excellent pitchers' park; Park Factor of .918
2000: They're not even trying until they get their new park.
2001: They're not even trying until they get their new park.

Nevertheless, the Padres announced on October 2 that construction on the new ballpark was being suspended immediately. The problem was not strictly legal: rather, the ballpark project had run out of money, and the bond issue was being held up by a series of problems that made the future of the East Village ballpark very cloudy.

The environmental testing of the shipyard and the surrounding areas caused a snag. Toxin levels were found to be around three times higher than expected, making building on the land impossible without expensive cleanup operations. Cleanup still had not started as of December, and because tests show that extensive dredging of the bay is necessary, nobody is sure how long it will take. Though the city fathers make brave talk about finding alternative ways to fund the ballpark without the increased tourism (and the corresponding taxes) that the new hotel was to provide, the reality is that millions of dollars earmarked for the bond debt service have gone up in smoke. Making up the difference without raiding the city's general fund will be a feat in and of itself.

A considerably more important problem is the federal government's investigation into team owner John Moores and a rumored "pattern of gift-giving" that may or may not have compromised metropolitan officials, up to and including city council members. Not much is known about the extent of the investigation, but city council member Valerie Stallings has been questioned about the circumstances surrounding her holdings in Neon Systems, a company run by Moores. Stallings traded in Neon Systems stock in 1999 and profited from her involvement to the tune of about $14,000 before taxes.

If a $10,000 payout to a city council member is enough to swing his or her vote on a major issue, I'll take two, thanks. Chances are that rather than conspiring with Moores and the Padres, Stallings was simply naïve in managing her personal business. Unless the extent of the federal investigation becomes public, we may never know for sure.

What we do know is that the ballpark project, a given one year ago, is now on life support. With the uncertainty of the federal investigation and the problems with the bayfront hotel, the city cannot issue bonds to pay for its share of construction. The autumn breezes off the bay whistle through the silent construction site. If the federal investigation determines that the ballpark process was tainted, an entirely new council vote may be necessary to get it back on track.

Even that might not be as simple as it sounds. The two largest issues in the recently concluded local elections were the ballpark and the moronic deal the city signed with the San Diego Chargers to keep the team in town following the Super Bowl season of 1995. Not expecting that the Chargers would range from mediocre to terrible for the rest of the decade, the city had guaranteed a minimum number of tickets would be sold. Paying for thousands of unsold tickets to every Chargers home game is doing tremendous damage to the city's coffers, the public's perception of the Chargers, and the public's willingness to get into bed with major professional sports teams.

Proposition C passed comfortably in 1998, but there's no guarantee it would pass again in the current political climate. Negative press from the Chargers' attendance guarantee and the Padres' ballpark fiasco has already killed former Mayor Golding's aspirations for higher office. The next generation of civic leaders will think harder about footing any bills to keep the local franchises happy.

The Padres need to move because their current lease at Qualcomm Stadium is highly unfavorable. As part of the Chargers deal, the Padres agreed to give up half of their advertising revenue—as well as most of their ability to solicit advertisers at Qualcomm Stadium—to the Chargers. With the new ballpark on the way, this wasn't a big problem. Now it is, and the Chargers have shown no desire to renegotiate their deals with either the city or the Padres.

Supposedly, this revenue shortfall was the reason for the $10 million cash call the team made towards the end of the season. The move is no reason to panic. Three teams made similar moves last season, led by the Arizona Diamondbacks, a club that featured a king-sized payroll and mediocre attendance in 2000. It isn't a surprise—or a problem—that a team with the Snakes' players and salaries is having financial difficulty. It's a case of financial distress accompanying financial irresponsibility, and Jerry Colangelo has only himself to blame.

On the other side of the equation, we have the Montreal Expos. Though their payroll is not high, the Expos attendance woes and lack of reasonable TV and radio deals probably dooms them to bleed red ink. The off-season acquisitions of mediocre millionaires Graeme Lloyd, Hideki Irabu, and Lee Stevens certainly didn't help matters.

The Padres fall somewhere in between. They aren't hurting for attendance, in part because the team has been marketed deftly in the Moores era. The team has broken 2.4 million in attendance for three straight years, easily the best numbers in club history. Team payroll wasn't as high as that of the Diamondbacks, but it was still too high considering the team's performance; this year, it will be lower. Anyhow, a company taking out a loan isn't a notable or worrisome occurrence. Real corporations many times the size of baseball clubs have debits on their balance sheets at all times because they stand to make more money using the funds than they will lose when the loans are repaid.

With all the intrigue surrounding the business side of things, it is easy to forget that the Padres also played 162 baseball games last year. On the field, the team suffered through a season plagued with injuries. The team used an astounding 56 players in 2000, setting a new National League record and tying for most in major-league history with the 1915 Philadelphia Athletics. The disabled list was more loaded than Dean Martin; Padres players spent 1,408 games on the DL. Six position players bested 100 games played: of those, only Ryan Klesko and Phil Nevin were above average at their positions. Eleven different pitchers started games for San Diego; Matt Clement was the only one who managed to stay healthy and in the rotation all season. Padres head trainer Todd Hutcheson and his staff earned their pay and then some with this injury-plagued club.

The Padres' system isn't coughing up many position players. Sean Burroughs is the prize, one of the top five prospects in the game. 2000 second-round pick Xavier Nady actually made his major-league debut last September. An advanced hitting prospect, Nady is expected to contribute to the big-league team soon. The Padres did experience some unexpected success, both at the major- and minor-league levels, with pitcher development. While Clement struggled, rookie pitchers Adam Eaton and Brian Tollberg were called up as emergency plug-ins and were outstanding. The pitching staffs at Double-A Mobile, low-A Fort Wayne, and high-A Rancho Cucamonga were stacked. Young pitchers Gerik Baxter, Mike Bynum, Rickey Guttormson, Wascar Serrano, in-season steal Dennis Tankersley, and organizational Pitchers of the Year Brian Lawrence and Jacob Peavy all had solid seasons.

There's no question several of these pitchers will have major-league futures. What ballpark they'll call home is another matter. In one of the more amusing exchanges of the year, Mayor Golding noted after the work stoppage at the ballpark site that perhaps a "time out" was in order while the city explored legal and financial issues. Alan Petrasek, project executive, curtly noted that construction jobs don't have "time outs."

All projects of this magnitude are subject to the laws of inertia, and lost construction time has already made a 2002 debut of the new ballpark impossible. Hopefully, the city of San Diego will be able to work out the details of its agreement with the Padres and get the new ballpark back on track. If they fail, John Moores and company may be forced to do something they really want to avoid: finance and build a new park all by themselves.

National League

HITTERS (BA: .270, OBP: .340, SLG: .440, EqA: .260)

Gabe Alvarez 3B Bats R Age 27

YEAR	TEAM	LGE	AB	H	DB	TP	HR	BB	SO	R	RBI	SB	CS	OUT	BA	OBP	SLG	EQA	EQR	DEFENSE			
1998	Toledo	Int	251	63	13	1	16	24	59	31	46	2	1	189	.251	.318	.502	.265	34	64-3B	3		
1998	Detroit	AL	199	47	7	0	7	17	58	16	31	1	3	155	.236	.302	.377	.223	18	55-3B	-12		
1999	Toledo	Int	412	106	17	0	18	47	79	57	53	1	2	308	.257	.340	.430	.256	51	84-3B	-12	18-RF	1
2000	Toledo	Int	246	47	11	1	7	39	56	33	29	0	1	200	.191	.304	.329	.215	21	31-1B	-2	10-3B	-6
2000	LasVegas	PCL	139	34	6	0	7	26	46	23	18	1	0	105	.245	.374	.439	.277	21	31-1B	-2		
2001	Cincnnti	NL	383	94	16	0	19	60	98	58	65	1	1	290	.245	.348	.436	.262	51				

He plays defense like Godzilla—the guy-in-a-rubber-suit model, not the CGI one. Gabe Alvarez was a shortstop in college but has gotten much slower and more hesitant as he's aged. He hit well at Las Vegas after coming over from the Tigers in July. Outrighted; there are worse players on benches across the land. A Rule 5 pick by the Reds, who really will give him a shot.

Bret Boone 2B Bats R Age 32

YEAR	TEAM	LGE	AB	H	DB	TP	HR	BB	SO	R	RBI	SB	CS	OUT	BA	OBP	SLG	EQA	EQR	DEFENSE	
1998	Cincnnti	NL	588	154	32	1	26	46	97	76	94	6	4	438	.262	.319	.452	.253	71	154-2B	10
1999	Atlanta	NL	612	152	32	1	21	39	106	96	60	10	8	468	.248	.299	.407	.232	61	147-2B	-2
2000	San Dieg	NL	471	121	19	2	19	43	91	60	73	7	4	354	.257	.325	.427	.250	55	123-2B	-7
2001	Seattle	AL	457	110	19	1	17	42	88	59	66	5	2	349	.241	.305	.398	.244	51		

The Original Warning-Track Commando: accept no imitations. Bret Boone can be a useful player; he's got a little pop for a middle infielder, and he's solid defensively. Because of his counting stats, though, he's consistently regarded as more valuable than he actually is. The Mariners have signed him for 2001; Safeco could make him look terrible.

Sean Burroughs 3B Bats R Age 20

YEAR	TEAM	LGE	AB	H	DB	TP	HR	BB	SO	R	RBI	SB	CS	OUT	BA	OBP	SLG	EQA	EQR	DEFENSE	
1999	Ft Wayne	Mid	433	120	21	1	4	50	64	42	51	6	7	320	.277	.361	.358	.246	48	115-3B	-6
2000	Mobile	Sou	409	106	25	3	2	44	47	41	35	3	4	307	.259	.333	.350	.232	40	106-3B	-4
2001	San Dieg	NL	317	91	17	1	3	45	56	53	41	4	4	230	.287	.376	.375	.270	43		

Sean Burroughs had an off year compared to 1999.Nevertheless, considering he was the youngest player in all of Double-A, he certainly wasn't overmatched, and he brought home the gold to boot. The Padres currently have a logjam at third base; Burroughs will be moving Nady and Nevin to other positions—or other cities—sooner rather than later.

Mike Darr LF/RF Bats L Age 25

YEAR	TEAM	LGE	AB	H	DB	TP	HR	BB	SO	R	RBI	SB	CS	OUT	BA	OBP	SLG	EQA	EQR	DEFENSE	
1998	Mobile	Sou	524	139	32	2	5	39	84	72	63	14	5	390	.265	.320	.363	.233	51	129-RF	-4
1999	LasVegas	PCL	375	92	16	0	10	41	100	41	47	7	2	285	.245	.324	.368	.237	39	88-RF	1
2000	LasVegas	PCL	358	104	19	3	7	33	56	58	46	8	4	258	.291	.353	.419	.260	45	89-CF	0
2000	San Dieg	NL	209	57	15	4	1	20	42	21	30	8	1	153	.273	.336	.397	.253	25	54-RF	5
2001	San Dieg	NL	482	131	26	3	9	49	101	75	61	16	3	354	.272	.339	.394	.263	63		

With Al Martin and his wives leaving town, Mike Darr should have left field all to himself in 2001. He wasn't devastating at Las Vegas, and he's not going to do much for the Padres offensively without a serious development spike. He goes through spurts in which he tries to pull everything and becomes markedly less productive. In his favor, Darr has youth, the right price, and a good glove.

Ben Davis C Bats B Age 24

YEAR	TEAM	LGE	AB	H	DB	TP	HR	BB	SO	R	RBI	SB	CS	OUT	BA	OBP	SLG	EQA	EQR	DEFENSE	
1998	Mobile	Sou	435	107	23	1	11	24	64	47	52	2	1	329	.246	.291	.379	.222	38	115-C	10
1999	LasVegas	PCL	196	50	13	1	5	20	40	20	31	3	1	147	.255	.328	.408	.248	23	57-C	-3
1999	San Dieg	NL	270	67	15	1	5	21	66	29	29	2	1	204	.248	.302	.367	.223	24	69-C	-1
2000	LasVegas	PCL	219	48	10	1	6	30	44	28	29	3	1	172	.219	.315	.356	.229	22	59-C	-5
2000	San Dieg	NL	132	30	4	0	4	12	33	12	15	1	1	103	.227	.292	.348	.212	11	34-C	-1
2001	San Dieg	NL	364	89	18	1	10	41	83	47	47	4	1	276	.245	.321	.382	.249	43		

(Ben Davis *continued*)

Ben Davis is headed for a career with two or three solidly above-average years, and that's certainly something. However, he's still got enough of that shiny top-prospect sheen that he might bring more than he's worth in trade, which is something the Padres should be and have been exploring. Davis has the inside track to start for the Padres in 2001.

Kory DeHaan   OF   Bats L   Age 24

YEAR	TEAM	LGE	AB	H	DB	TP	HR	BB	SO	R	RBI	SB	CS	OUT	BA	OBP	SLG	EQA	EQR	DEFENSE	
1998	Augusta	SAL	493	123	32	5	5	50	120	55	51	11	6	376	.249	.324	.365	.234	50	121-CF	-4
1999	Lynchbrg	Car	302	81	15	3	6	25	65	37	30	13	6	226	.268	.328	.397	.246	34	75-CF	-4
1999	Altoona	Eas	193	47	13	1	2	7	48	20	19	7	3	149	.244	.274	.352	.208	15	44-OF	-2
2000	San Dieg	NL	105	22	5	0	3	3	37	19	14	4	2	85	.210	.231	.343	.184	6	24-RF	1
2001	San Dieg	NL	282	70	15	2	5	25	79	37	31	10	5	217	.248	.309	.369	.240	31		

The Padres managed to keep Rule 5 pick Kory DeHaan on the roster all season, retaining his rights. What remains to be seen is if his development suffers from a year of playing sporadically. He got some playing time in the AFL. As a fleet left-handed hitter who can handle center field, he'll have plenty of chances to play.

Kevin Eberwein   1B/3B   Bats R   Age 24

YEAR	TEAM	LGE	AB	H	DB	TP	HR	BB	SO	R	RBI	SB	CS	OUT	BA	OBP	SLG	EQA	EQR	DEFENSE	
1998	Clinton	Mid	254	62	15	1	8	18	71	30	26	1	1	193	.244	.301	.406	.233	25	51-3B	0
1999	R Cucmng	Cal	416	87	23	2	12	28	144	45	43	3	2	331	.209	.268	.361	.206	32	91-3B	0
2000	Mobile	Sou	386	92	14	0	16	33	80	51	58	1	1	295	.238	.300	.399	.231	38	91-1B	-3
2001	San Dieg	NL	364	84	15	1	14	34	103	39	48	1	1	281	.231	.296	.393	.239	39		

For several years, Kevin Eberwein has been the only real power prospect in the system, Pete Tucci decidedly notwithstanding. Eberwein led Mobile in home runs in 2000 while moving to first base. He is obviously not destined for stardom, but he could stick around the majors for a year or two; his ability to handle third base helps.

Vince Faison   CF   Bats L   Age 20

YEAR	TEAM	LGE	AB	H	DB	TP	HR	BB	SO	R	RBI	SB	CS	OUT	BA	OBP	SLG	EQA	EQR	DEFENSE	
2000	Ft Wayne	Mid	468	96	16	1	11	13	176	48	30	9	3	375	.205	.230	.314	.172	23	114-CF	-10
2001	San Dieg	NL	251	54	5	0	6	10	115	18	19	8	2	199	.215	.245	.307	.191	16		

Although Vince Faison and the Padres had "an understanding" that he wouldn't pursue football, the organization's 1999 top pick is now reported to be doing his best to attend the University of Georgia and chase success on the gridiron. Faison isn't exactly polished, and splitting his attention in this fashion is unlikely to be good for his career.

Chris Gomez   SS   Bats R   Age 30

YEAR	TEAM	LGE	AB	H	DB	TP	HR	BB	SO	R	RBI	SB	CS	OUT	BA	OBP	SLG	EQA	EQR	DEFENSE	
1998	San Dieg	NL	460	128	33	3	5	49	81	59	41	1	3	335	.278	.354	.396	.253	54	136-SS	2
1999	San Dieg	NL	237	61	8	1	1	24	46	20	15	1	2	178	.257	.328	.312	.218	20	68-SS	1
2000	San Dieg	NL	55	13	0	0	0	6	5	4	3	0	0	42	.236	.311	.236	.185	3	13-SS	-1
2001	San Dieg	NL	116	30	3	0	2	15	23	14	14	0	1	87	.259	.344	.336	.243	13		

The Padres payroll stood at $51.3 million to start the 2000 season, only $2.7 million less than the Giants. The teams finished 21 games apart, so obviously performance isn't solely a function of payroll. Rather, the Giants got production from the guys with multi-million dollar contracts while the Padres got Chris Gomez, Carlos Hernandez, and a few games of Tony Gwynn. To be fair, Gomez was injured and didn't play much, but he'll have a tough time living up to the big contract he signed in the afterglow of 1998.

Wiki Gonzalez   C   Bats R   Age 27

YEAR	TEAM	LGE	AB	H	DB	TP	HR	BB	SO	R	RBI	SB	CS	OUT	BA	OBP	SLG	EQA	EQR	DEFENSE	
1998	R Cucmng	Cal	294	68	14	1	8	18	57	35	39	0	0	226	.231	.278	.367	.212	23	43-C	3
1999	Mobile	Sou	227	61	11	1	7	19	31	27	32	0	0	166	.269	.336	.419	.252	27	51-C	5
2000	San Dieg	NL	289	69	15	1	5	26	29	25	30	1	2	222	.239	.307	.349	.219	25	76-C	1
2001	San Dieg	NL	295	79	15	1	9	27	37	37	44	0	1	217	.268	.329	.417	.259	37		

National League

It was a disappointing season at the plate for Wiki Gonzalez, but he's almost certainly better than he played in 2000. At worst, he's a defensively excellent second catcher, and, entering his prime, he could be more than that. The fans still love him, and it's always nice to have a guy on the roster who doesn't leave until the last autograph is signed.

Tony Gwynn — RF — Bats L — Age 41

YEAR	TEAM	LGE	AB	H	DB	TP	HR	BB	SO	R	RBI	SB	CS	OUT	BA	OBP	SLG	EQA	EQR	DEFENSE			
1998	San Dieg	NL	472	155	28	0	20	34	17	68	73	3	1	318	.328	.375	.515	.292	73	89-RF	-8		
1999	San Dieg	NL	416	141	18	0	13	24	13	57	62	6	2	277	.339	.378	.476	.285	60	81-RF	-6		
2000	San Dieg	NL	129	42	9	0	2	7	4	16	17	0	1	88	.326	.364	.442	.267	16	20-RF	-3		
2001	San Dieg	NL	209	56	5	0	6	19	7	24	28	1	1	154	.268	.329	.378	.249	24				

If you include the $2 million buyout, the Padres paid Tony Gwynn $8.3 million for 127 at-bats in 2000. His health is a more serious issue than ever, so the team was pleased when he accepted an incentive-based contract for 2001. Although his age and conditioning are really hurting his effectiveness, somehow Gwynn donning another team's colors just didn't seem right.

Damian Jackson — 2B/SS — Bats R — Age 27

YEAR	TEAM	LGE	AB	H	DB	TP	HR	BB	SO	R	RBI	SB	CS	OUT	BA	OBP	SLG	EQA	EQR	DEFENSE			
1998	Indianap	Int	521	125	35	7	5	49	124	84	41	14	7	403	.240	.314	.363	.230	51	127-SS	-9		
1999	San Dieg	NL	393	90	21	2	9	48	99	53	38	27	9	312	.229	.317	.361	.237	43	92-SS	-10	16-2B	1
2000	San Dieg	NL	478	124	30	5	6	55	101	67	36	26	6	360	.259	.339	.381	.251	57	83-SS	3	33-2B	3
2001	San Dieg	NL	452	109	27	4	8	59	109	78	49	29	8	351	.241	.329	.372	.256	58				

A below-average arm victimizes Damian Jackson at shortstop; he has to hurry everything, and that trashes his technique and leads to errors in bunches. After failing another audition at shortstop in 2000, it appears Jackson will have a new lease on life with the Padres as the starting second baseman in 2001. His defense at second base looked at least adequate, and his relatively small contract is just what the Padres want in the infield in 2001.

Ben Johnson — OF — Bats R — Age 20

YEAR	TEAM	LGE	AB	H	DB	TP	HR	BB	SO	R	RBI	SB	CS	OUT	BA	OBP	SLG	EQA	EQR	DEFENSE	
1999	JohnsnCy	App	201	44	4	0	6	16	62	17	25	3	2	159	.219	.282	.328	.202	15	49-RF	1
2000	Peoria	Mid	345	73	13	1	11	36	86	41	33	7	4	275	.212	.290	.351	.215	30	86-RF	-5
2000	Ft Wayne	Mid	112	21	4	1	3	4	28	9	10	0	1	92	.188	.225	.321	.165	5	29-RF	2
2001	San Dieg	NL	294	63	10	1	10	29	100	31	33	5	2	233	.214	.285	.357	.226	28		

The Padres made the mistake of re-signing Carlos Hernandez for three years and $6 million but salvaged the deal when they turned him into Ben Johnson at the deadline. Johnson has an interesting skill set. He runs well, has reasonable plate discipline already and can pop the ball out of the park. He needs to refine his defense a bit, but he does have some upside. If he can boost his batting average a little, he has more than a bit of Rob Deer potential. Rob Deer's bat with a good glove in center field will be worth a few million bucks.

Ryan Klesko — 1B — Bats L — Age 30

YEAR	TEAM	LGE	AB	H	DB	TP	HR	BB	SO	R	RBI	SB	CS	OUT	BA	OBP	SLG	EQA	EQR	DEFENSE			
1998	Atlanta	NL	434	119	25	1	20	54	62	70	71	5	3	318	.274	.358	.475	.276	63	94-LF	-3		
1999	Atlanta	NL	406	118	27	2	20	47	65	53	74	4	2	290	.291	.367	.515	.288	65	60-1B	-7	37-LF	-2
2000	San Dieg	NL	503	143	32	2	26	84	76	86	89	22	7	367	.284	.388	.511	.298	89	123-1B	-1		
2001	San Dieg	NL	449	125	24	1	25	87	73	97	89	17	4	328	.278	.396	.503	.313	90				

Easily having the best year of his career, Ryan Klesko hit .316/.405/.625 before the All-Star break. He blamed injuries for his less-than-stellar second half, but overall he still turned in his best campaign since 1995. He posted career highs in playing time and performance against left-handed pitching. Klesko looked much more comfortable at first base than he did in the outfield and will be playing there full-time in 2001.

Greg LaRocca — IF — Bats R — Age 28

YEAR	TEAM	LGE	AB	H	DB	TP	HR	BB	SO	R	RBI	SB	CS	OUT	BA	OBP	SLG	EQA	EQR	DEFENSE			
1998	LasVegas	PCL	298	79	19	3	6	15	47	42	29	5	3	222	.265	.317	.409	.241	32	19-2B	-6	18-SS	-3
2000	LasVegas	PCL	475	113	33	4	6	39	67	62	53	7	3	365	.238	.307	.362	.226	44	103-3B	-6	20-2B	-3
2001	San Dieg	NL	332	77	20	2	7	28	52	39	36	7	2	257	.232	.292	.367	.232	33				

(Greg LaRocca *continued*)

He has less chance at a career than Kato Kaelin, really, but it was nice to see organizational soldier Greg LaRocca get a cup of coffee last year. He's re-signed for 2001. Where he's going to play is an open question; he's most comfortable at third base, but the Padres have three better options there, so he'll probably move around a lot.

John Mabry — UT — Bats L — Age 30

YEAR	TEAM	LGE	AB	H	DB	TP	HR	BB	SO	R	RBI	SB	CS	OUT	BA	OBP	SLG	EQA	EQR	DEFENSE			
1998	St Louis	NL	381	96	15	0	12	29	71	42	48	0	2	287	.252	.306	.386	.229	36	51-LF	0	27-3B	-7
1999	Seattle	AL	261	65	12	0	10	18	55	33	32	2	1	197	.249	.297	.410	.233	26	35-RF	4	24-3B	-8
2000	Seattle	AL	103	26	3	0	2	9	28	17	7	0	1	78	.252	.325	.340	.223	9	11-3B	-1	10-RF	0
2000	San Dieg	NL	125	29	6	0	8	3	36	17	25	0	0	96	.232	.250	.472	.229	12	25-RF	-1		
2001	StLouis	NL	237	57	8	0	9	21	62	27	35	0	1	181	.241	.302	.388	.229	23				

Acquired in the Al Martin trade, John Mabry slugged .549 in August. For fans of a team not paying attention, such a hot streak can be really worrisome: you know Mabry's bat sucks, and I know Mabry's bat sucks, but did anyone tell the front office? Fortunately, Mabry returned to earth over the rest of the season, making the question moot, and is now a free agent.

Dave Magadan — 3B/1B — Bats L — Age 38

YEAR	TEAM	LGE	AB	H	DB	TP	HR	BB	SO	R	RBI	SB	CS	OUT	BA	OBP	SLG	EQA	EQR	DEFENSE			
1998	Oakland	AL	109	36	6	0	2	13	11	12	14	0	1	74	.330	.402	.440	.284	16	24-3B	1		
1999	San Dieg	NL	252	70	12	1	2	41	34	20	29	1	3	185	.278	.379	.357	.255	30	36-3B	1	24-1B	-1
2000	San Dieg	NL	135	37	5	0	3	30	22	13	22	0	0	98	.274	.406	.378	.277	20	18-3B	-1		
2001	San Dieg	NL	143	36	5	0	2	30	22	23	18	0	1	108	.252	.382	.329	.262	19				

A team's bench is traditionally defined by what the players can do defensively, but should it be? Dave Magadan is very tough on right-handed hitters and can do a lot for a team with his bat, and it's silly that his services aren't more in demand. There are a million guys out there who can field, but guys who work the count and get on base at a 40% clip are rare indeed.

Xavier Nady — 3B — Bats R — Age 22

Xavier Nady became the 14th amateur in history to sign a major-league contract when he finally inked a deal with the Padres in September. He was arguably the top collegiate hitter in the country, outslugging Mark McGwire's conference record at Cal. Nady also sports a good batting eye. He will likely move to first base, assuming he can't handle a corner outfield spot.

Phil Nevin — 3B — Bats R — Age 30

YEAR	TEAM	LGE	AB	H	DB	TP	HR	BB	SO	R	RBI	SB	CS	OUT	BA	OBP	SLG	EQA	EQR	DEFENSE			
1998	Anaheim	AL	237	56	7	1	9	16	60	28	27	0	0	181	.236	.297	.388	.227	22	63-C	-6		
1999	San Dieg	NL	388	105	24	0	25	46	77	52	82	1	0	283	.271	.349	.526	.284	61	58-3B	9	24-C	-1
2000	San Dieg	NL	548	168	30	1	32	51	113	85	104	2	0	380	.307	.369	.540	.296	90	136-3B	-14		
2001	San Dieg	NL	460	131	17	0	28	55	103	71	94	1	0	329	.285	.361	.504	.296	78				

Phil Nevin was the second-best third baseman in the league last season, behind only Chipper Jones, and it wasn't a fluke. He's become an outstanding solution to the hole at third base, and, unlike Klesko, his contract is very advantageous to the team. Even though the Brewers trade flopped, there's no guarantee he'll start 2001 with the Padres.

Kevin Nicholson — SS — Bats B — Age 25

YEAR	TEAM	LGE	AB	H	DB	TP	HR	BB	SO	R	RBI	SB	CS	OUT	BA	OBP	SLG	EQA	EQR	DEFENSE
1998	Mobile	Sou	494	98	25	2	4	28	121	49	40	5	3	399	.198	.244	.281	.165	22	130-SS -14
1999	Mobile	Sou	493	122	29	2	10	31	98	62	59	8	3	374	.247	.296	.375	.224	44	123-SS 0
2000	LasVegas	PCL	322	77	19	2	5	26	63	35	32	2	3	248	.239	.300	.357	.218	27	84-SS -13
2000	San Dieg	NL	99	23	6	1	1	2	29	7	8	1	0	76	.232	.254	.343	.193	6	22-SS 6
2001	San Dieg	NL	392	91	21	2	7	29	91	41	39	5	2	303	.232	.285	.349	.222	35	

Kevin Nicholson got his first big-league action because of injuries, not because of anything he did. He could use some more time in Triple-A but on a straight effectiveness basis deserves a shot at the shortstop job for the Padres in 2001. Again, that's more an indictment of the team's fun bunch of middle infielders than anything else.

National League

Eric Owens — OF — Bats R — Age 30

YEAR	TEAM	LGE	AB	H	DB	TP	HR	BB	SO	R	RBI	SB	CS	OUT	BA	OBP	SLG	EQA	EQR	DEFENSE			
1998	Louisvil	Int	253	72	10	2	4	26	31	35	31	11	4	185	.285	.351	.387	.254	30	34-RF	1	25-3B	-1
1999	San Dieg	NL	446	121	23	3	9	32	47	52	59	26	7	332	.271	.324	.397	.248	51	95-OF	1		
2000	San Dieg	NL	593	175	21	6	6	37	59	85	49	27	15	433	.295	.340	.381	.244	64	144-OF	5		
2001	San Dieg	NL	503	139	19	3	7	39	56	72	56	26	11	375	.276	.328	.368	.250	58				

He had the season of his life in 2000 and was rewarded with a two-year, $3.5 million contract extension, which begs the question: what does Eric Owens want from his career? His success last year arguably hurts his chance at being a component of a really good team. The problem: Owens does a lot of good things for a team in a reserve role but even in his best year was plainly overmatched as a starting outfielder. Any well-run organization will avoid making a utility man a multi-millionaire, and the teams that actually think Owens can be a starter are, well, the Orioles and the Brewers.

Jeremy Owens — CF — Bats R — Age 24

YEAR	TEAM	LGE	AB	H	DB	TP	HR	BB	SO	R	RBI	SB	CS	OUT	BA	OBP	SLG	EQA	EQR	DEFENSE	
1998	IdahoFls	Pio	283	59	10	2	5	17	96	27	26	10	4	228	.208	.261	.311	.190	18	63-CF	-1
1999	Ft Wayne	Mid	522	122	22	7	7	41	167	66	44	25	8	408	.234	.295	.343	.219	46	128-CF	0
2000	R Cucmng	Cal	579	127	23	5	14	37	190	61	42	17	5	457	.219	.269	.349	.207	44	138-CF	17
2001	San Dieg	NL	488	105	20	3	8	40	172	53	40	22	8	390	.215	.275	.318	.213	41		

Co-Minor League Player of the Year for the Padres in 2000, Jeremy Owens is an A-ball outfielder with speed and defense to burn, but he might have the worst strike-zone judgment in the system. He has enough pop that he'd make a useful fifth outfielder right now; defensive replacements who can occasionally poke one over the wall are nice to have.

Desi Relaford — SS — Bats B — Age 27

YEAR	TEAM	LGE	AB	H	DB	TP	HR	BB	SO	R	RBI	SB	CS	OUT	BA	OBP	SLG	EQA	EQR	DEFENSE	
1998	Philadel	NL	499	124	23	3	6	31	81	46	41	8	5	380	.248	.296	.343	.213	40	136-SS	-12
1999	Philadel	NL	212	50	10	2	1	16	32	29	24	3	3	165	.236	.307	.316	.210	17	63-SS	2
2000	Philadel	NL	254	54	11	3	3	43	42	27	28	5	0	200	.213	.344	.315	.236	27	78-SS	-11
2000	San Dieg	NL	160	34	3	0	2	24	24	26	16	8	0	126	.213	.325	.269	.220	14	42-SS	1
2001	NY Mets	NL	319	72	12	2	5	42	55	47	34	10	2	249	.226	.316	.323	.231	32		

Desi Relaford suddenly learned how to take a walk. He also forgot how to field his position in a frustrating season that saw him waived by two teams in three months. Relaford established a career high with 75 walks, but 31 errors was a pretty good indication of his defensive play. He was claimed by the Mets; if they're executing Plan B of Operation Alex Rodriguez, expect fans to be mildly disappointed.

Ruben Rivera — CF — Bats R — Age 27

YEAR	TEAM	LGE	AB	H	DB	TP	HR	BB	SO	R	RBI	SB	CS	OUT	BA	OBP	SLG	EQA	EQR	DEFENSE	
1998	LasVegas	PCL	104	14	1	0	3	9	41	7	9	3	0	90	.135	.204	.231	.126	3	27-CF	0
1998	San Dieg	NL	176	39	6	2	7	27	49	33	31	5	1	138	.222	.331	.398	.250	22	50-RF	2
1999	San Dieg	NL	417	83	15	1	24	49	135	63	47	14	7	341	.199	.291	.412	.233	45	123-CF	4
2000	San Dieg	NL	430	93	19	6	17	38	128	61	56	7	4	341	.216	.293	.407	.232	44	121-CF	4
2001	San Dieg	NL	398	79	16	2	14	43	131	45	42	13	4	323	.198	.277	.354	.224	38		

Few other teams would have blown 1,000 major-league at-bats on a player of this apparent skill level. Ruben Rivera has the best situation he could hope for in San Diego. The last thing management wants to do is dump him and watch him hit 40 bombs somewhere else, and there isn't a good candidate on the roster to take over center field, so it'll probably be more of the same next year.

John Roskos — OF/1B — Bats R — Age 26

YEAR	TEAM	LGE	AB	H	DB	TP	HR	BB	SO	R	RBI	SB	CS	OUT	BA	OBP	SLG	EQA	EQR	DEFENSE			
1998	Charlott	Int	413	103	18	1	8	33	83	45	49	0	2	312	.249	.308	.356	.221	36	70-1B	-6		
1999	Calgary	PCL	489	127	23	0	19	42	108	59	63	1	1	363	.260	.321	.423	.247	55	65-LF	-7	26-1B	-1
2000	LasVegas	PCL	370	99	17	0	15	41	68	55	53	1	3	274	.268	.343	.435	.258	46	46-LF	-7	26-1B	-4
2001	San Dieg	NL	426	106	16	0	16	54	94	55	63	1	1	321	.249	.333	.399	.258	54				

(John Roskos *continued*)

It looked like it'd be a good year for John Roskos. He was the team's best hitter in Cactus League action, and, over the season's first week, the Padres lost more outfielders than they did games. Roskos managed to go only 1-for-27 before being sent out again. He knows a team with a weak outfield when he sees it and has re-signed with the Padres for 2001.

Troy Schader — 3B — Bats R — Age 24

YEAR	TEAM	LGE	AB	H	DB	TP	HR	BB	SO	R	RBI	SB	CS	OUT	BA	OBP	SLG	EQA	EQR	DEFENSE			
1999	IdahoFls	Pio	265	63	10	3	10	20	87	30	32	0	1	203	.238	.295	.411	.231	26	28-3B	-6	19-SS	-1
2000	Ft Wayne	Mid	288	73	17	1	10	18	79	37	36	2	1	216	.253	.304	.424	.240	30	73-3B	0		
2001	San Dieg	NL	204	52	9	1	8	16	75	24	30	1	0	152	.255	.309	.426	.255	25				

Despite logging only 279 at-bats before an injury knocked him out for the year, Troy Schader led Fort Wayne in homers and was second in doubles. He's handled the pitching everywhere he's played; given his age, it'd be a good gamble to goose his career by having him skip high-A ball entirely.

Ed Sprague — 3B/1B — Bats R — Age 33

YEAR	TEAM	LGE	AB	H	DB	TP	HR	BB	SO	R	RBI	SB	CS	OUT	BA	OBP	SLG	EQA	EQR	DEFENSE	
1998	Toronto	AL	381	93	15	0	20	24	65	50	52	0	2	290	.244	.306	.441	.244	42	105-3B	-4
1999	Pittsbrg	NL	491	126	25	2	21	43	88	67	74	2	5	370	.257	.337	.444	.257	62	132-3B	-22
2000	San Dieg	NL	160	43	9	0	11	10	37	18	27	0	0	117	.269	.322	.531	.274	23	22-1B	-6
2000	Boston	AL	110	24	3	0	2	11	16	10	8	0	0	86	.218	.289	.300	.196	7	26-3B	1
2001	San Dieg	NL	331	77	12	1	13	30	65	34	44	0	1	255	.233	.296	.393	.238	35		

Not every free-agent signing is a terrible move, even if the signing involves a terrible player. Witness Ed Sprague: San Diego management turned a few hot weeks of Sprague into Dennis Tankersley, Cesar Saba, and a nifty screw-you move in which the Pads picked up Sprague again after the Red Sox waived him.

Joe Vitiello — 1B — Bats R — Age 31

YEAR	TEAM	LGE	AB	H	DB	TP	HR	BB	SO	R	RBI	SB	CS	OUT	BA	OBP	SLG	EQA	EQR	DEFENSE	
1998	Omaha	PCL	372	85	15	1	12	30	72	31	48	0	0	287	.228	.292	.371	.220	33	83-1B	-1
1999	Omaha	PCL	439	109	18	1	18	51	88	47	63	2	3	333	.248	.330	.417	.249	51	39-1B	-2
2000	LasVegas	PCL	267	73	15	0	9	19	65	28	30	1	0	194	.273	.325	.431	.251	31	62-1B	0
2000	San Dieg	NL	53	14	3	0	2	9	8	7	8	0	0	39	.264	.371	.434	.273	8	10-1B	-3
2001	San Dieg	NL	321	78	12	0	11	32	73	36	43	0	0	243	.243	.312	.383	.243	36		

His legs are in worse shape than a *Survivor* contestant's, but Joe Vitiello battled back to hit well at Las Vegas and with the Padres last season. He's lost much of his prodigious power, yet still flashes a dangerous bat. Defensively, he's near valueless; his on-base skills should give him a chance at a pinch-hitting spot with the Padres in 2001.

PITCHERS (ERA: 4.50, H/9: 9.00, HR/9: 1.00, BB/9: 3.00, K/9: 6.00, KW: 1.00, PERA: 4.50)

Carlos Almanzar — Throws R — Age 27

YEAR	TEAM	LGE	IP	H	ER	HR	BB	K	ERA	W	L	H/9	HR/9	BB/9	K/9	KWH	PERA
1998	Syracuse	Int	48.0	45	23	8	13	38	4.31	2	3	8.44	1.50	2.44	7.13	1.46	4.48
1998	Toronto	AL	28.3	32	16	3	7	19	5.08	1	2	10.16	0.95	2.22	6.04	1.36	4.85
1999	LasVegas	PCL	21.3	31	25	12	9	11	10.55	0	2	13.08	5.06	3.80	4.64	0.61	11.54
1999	San Diego	NL	36.0	46	30	6	13	25	7.50	1	3	11.50	1.50	3.25	6.25	0.96	6.57
2000	San Diego	NL	67.0	72	36	13	22	47	4.84	3	4	9.67	1.75	2.96	6.31	1.07	5.67

The Mad Bomber. Carlos Almanzar went through a tragic streak near the start of the season in which every appearance culminated in a three-run jack. The runners were always someone else's responsibility; Almanzar was terrible at keeping inherited runners from scoring, and his season was significantly worse than the numbers above indicate. Bruce Bochy never lost faith, and Almanzar ended the season strong, but I'm not looking for much this year.

National League

Gerik Baxter — Throws R — Age 21

YEAR	TEAM	LGE	IP	H	ER	HR	BB	K	ERA	W	L	H/9	HR/9	BB/9	K/9	KWH	PERA
1999	IdahoFls	Pio	21.0	23	19	7	22	14	8.14	0	2	9.86	3.00	9.43	6.00	0.32	9.78
2000	Ft Wayne	Mid	90.7	91	62	13	51	55	6.15	3	7	9.03	1.29	5.06	5.46	0.54	5.70

Prior to taking a baseball to the head, Gerik Baxter was having a good season at Fort Wayne. The Padres' top pitching draft pick in 1999, Baxter needs to work on his control but benefits from a full toolbox: a nasty slider, good fastball, and serviceable change-up.

Brian Boehringer — Throws R — Age 31

YEAR	TEAM	LGE	IP	H	ER	HR	BB	K	ERA	W	L	H/9	HR/9	BB/9	K/9	KWH	PERA
1998	San Dieg	NL	72.3	75	41	12	44	54	5.10	3	5	9.33	1.49	5.47	6.72	0.61	6.25
1999	San Dieg	NL	90.7	93	38	11	32	54	3.77	5	5	9.23	1.09	3.18	5.36	0.84	4.81
2000	San Dieg	NL	15.0	17	14	4	9	7	8.40	0	2	10.20	2.40	5.40	4.20	0.39	7.61

Brian Boehringer never got out of the gate in 2000. He began the year in the rotation, which he left after three marginal starts. He then managed 2⅓ relief innings in May before he was gone for the season, a victim of his cranky shoulder. Boehringer might make a nice pickup for the Yankees this year; if he's healthy, he's got another season like 1999 in him.

Mike Bynum — Throws L — Age 23

YEAR	TEAM	LGE	IP	H	ER	HR	BB	K	ERA	W	L	H/9	HR/9	BB/9	K/9	KWH	PERA
1999	R Cucmng	Cal	36.0	35	18	2	9	24	4.50	2	2	8.75	0.50	2.25	6.00	1.33	3.55
2000	R Cucmng	Cal	116.0	105	61	9	55	67	4.73	5	8	8.15	0.70	4.27	5.20	0.61	4.20
2000	Mobile	Sou	31.0	33	15	4	17	16	4.35	1	2	9.58	1.16	4.94	4.65	0.47	5.82

He cruised through the season as Rancho Cucamonga's ace, making the California League All-Star team and striking out more than a batter per inning. Mike Bynum is a power left-hander with a high-draft-pick pedigree and a live fastball. He should make Triple-A Portland this year.

Buddy Carlyle — Throws R — Age 23

YEAR	TEAM	LGE	IP	H	ER	HR	BB	K	ERA	W	L	H/9	HR/9	BB/9	K/9	KWH	PERA
1998	Mobile	Sou	173.3	173	78	21	45	62	4.05	9	10	8.98	1.09	2.34	3.22	0.69	4.31
1999	LasVegas	PCL	154.3	168	91	25	42	94	5.31	6	11	9.80	1.46	2.45	5.48	1.12	5.22
1999	San Dieg	NL	36.3	35	28	8	15	24	6.94	1	3	8.67	1.98	3.72	5.94	0.80	5.63
2000	LasVegas	PCL	145.3	159	89	28	41	92	5.51	6	10	9.85	1.73	2.54	5.70	1.12	5.59
2000	San Dieg	NL	3.0	6	7	0	3	2	21.00	0	0	18.00	0.00	9.00	6.00	0.33	11.43

Buddy Carlyle was sent to the Hanshin Tigers in what qualifies as a very strange move. It isn't that the Padres are hurting for pitching, but Carlyle pitched well for a 22-year-old in Las Vegas last season: by comparison, Junior Herndon was quite a bit worse with the Stars, and Mike Bynum experienced success in high-A ball at the same age. The upside? Maybe Towers and company took PlayStation 2 consoles in lieu of cash, which would make holiday shopping a snap.

Matt Clement — Throws R — Age 26

YEAR	TEAM	LGE	IP	H	ER	HR	BB	K	ERA	W	L	H/9	HR/9	BB/9	K/9	KWH	PERA
1998	LasVegas	PCL	164.3	150	90	12	85	111	4.93	7	11	8.22	0.66	4.66	6.08	0.65	4.36
1999	San Dieg	NL	174.7	184	104	19	78	114	5.36	7	12	9.48	0.98	4.02	5.87	0.73	5.19
2000	San Dieg	NL	198.3	192	129	23	111	141	5.85	7	15	8.71	1.04	5.04	6.40	0.64	5.22

Matt Clement won the Triple Crown of wildness, setting club records in walks, wild pitches, and hit batsmen during the regular season before taking over as Rick Ankiel's personal pitching coach for the playoffs. He struggled with his control after starting the season hot, leading the team to explore trading him. That would have been a huge mistake; there was little chance of getting appropriate value, and the Padres have to let Clement-type talents take their time. He still brings the fastball with overwhelming movement.

Will Cunnane — Throws R — Age 27

YEAR	TEAM	LGE	IP	H	ER	HR	BB	K	ERA	W	L	H/9	HR/9	BB/9	K/9	KWH	PERA
1998	LasVegas	PCL	34.7	42	24	1	19	20	6.23	1	3	10.90	0.26	4.93	5.19	0.53	5.62
1999	LasVegas	PCL	34.0	32	6	1	17	34	1.59	3	1	8.47	0.26	4.50	9.00	1.00	4.04
1999	San Dieg	NL	29.7	33	19	9	11	18	5.76	1	2	10.01	2.73	3.34	5.46	0.82	7.06
2000	LasVegas	PCL	92.7	94	45	8	26	66	4.37	5	5	9.13	0.78	2.53	6.41	1.27	4.15
2000	San Dieg	NL	37.0	35	21	2	19	28	5.11	2	2	8.51	0.49	4.62	6.81	0.74	4.36

He had another chance to stick with the Padres last year and didn't quite get it done. Although he finished the season strong, with a 3.60 ERA in September, Will Cunnane's fastball is probably too straight to ever make him a top-shelf reliever. Still, he's not a head case, and with his willingness to go after hitters, he won't walk in the tying run. Traded to the Brewers.

Tom Davey — Throws R — Age 27

YEAR	TEAM	LGE	IP	H	ER	HR	BB	K	ERA	W	L	H/9	HR/9	BB/9	K/9	KWH	PERA
1998	Knoxvill	Sou	72.7	72	35	3	49	46	4.33	4	4	8.92	0.37	6.07	5.70	0.47	5.05
1999	Syracuse	Int	32.0	28	14	1	19	14	3.94	2	2	7.88	0.28	5.34	3.94	0.37	4.04
1999	Toronto	AL	44.0	38	24	4	21	40	4.91	2	3	7.77	0.82	4.30	8.18	0.95	4.13
1999	Seattle	AL	21.0	22	13	1	11	16	5.57	1	1	9.43	0.43	4.71	6.86	0.73	4.88
2000	Tacoma	PCL	87.3	101	65	16	42	52	6.70	3	7	10.41	1.65	4.33	5.36	0.62	6.57
2000	LasVegas	PCL	15.0	26	13	1	7	11	7.80	0	2	15.60	0.60	4.20	6.60	0.79	8.43
2000	San Dieg	NL	12.0	11	1	0	2	5	0.75	1	0	8.25	0.00	1.50	3.75	1.25	2.55

A very solid audition by the big right-hander has the Padres hoping for good things in 2001. The problem? The audition lasted only 12 innings, and Tom Davey was up to his usual tricks with Tacoma and Las Vegas, walking hitters in bunches. The smart money is on someone else.

Adam Eaton — Throws R — Age 23

YEAR	TEAM	LGE	IP	H	ER	HR	BB	K	ERA	W	L	H/9	HR/9	BB/9	K/9	KWH	PERA
1998	Clearwtr	Fla	123.0	148	71	17	55	52	5.20	5	9	10.83	1.24	4.02	3.80	0.47	6.26
1999	Clearwtr	Fla	64.7	78	39	4	28	30	5.43	2	5	10.86	0.56	3.90	4.18	0.54	5.50
1999	Reading	Eas	71.7	63	35	12	28	42	4.40	4	4	7.91	1.51	3.52	5.27	0.75	4.61
2000	Mobile	Sou	52.0	52	26	6	19	35	4.50	3	3	9.00	1.04	3.29	6.06	0.92	4.66
2000	San Dieg	NL	130.0	130	62	15	54	75	4.29	7	7	9.00	1.04	3.74	5.19	0.69	4.84

Another desperation call-up, Adam Eaton logged 12 quality starts in 22 outings for the Padres. Even better, he averaged fewer than 100 pitches a game despite the horror show that was the Padres' bullpen. Many young starters' careers have been placed at risk by managers who succumb to the temptation to overwork them like Al Gore rides his legal team, so kudos to Bruce Bochy and Dave Smith for a job well done.

Rickey Guttormson — Throws R — Age 24

YEAR	TEAM	LGE	IP	H	ER	HR	BB	K	ERA	W	L	H/9	HR/9	BB/9	K/9	KWH	PERA
1998	Clinton	Mid	144.3	164	82	23	51	72	5.11	6	10	10.23	1.43	3.18	4.49	0.71	5.75
1999	R Cucmng	Cal	163.0	161	93	28	42	66	5.13	7	11	8.89	1.55	2.32	3.64	0.79	4.73
2000	Mobile	Sou	73.3	92	56	18	39	21	6.87	2	6	11.29	2.21	4.79	2.58	0.27	7.88

Rickey Guttormson moved on to Mobile without missing a beat. At some point, the lack of a strikeout pitch is going to become a serious problem. You can count on one hand the guys in the majors who have success with only great control; even Greg Maddux brings the heat and strikes people out. For every Bob Tewksbury, there are a hundred Mike Birkbecks and Jeff Ballards.

Junior Herndon — Throws R — Age 22

YEAR	TEAM	LGE	IP	H	ER	HR	BB	K	ERA	W	L	H/9	HR/9	BB/9	K/9	KWH	PERA
1998	Clinton	Mid	122.3	120	63	8	42	51	4.63	6	8	8.83	0.59	3.09	3.75	0.61	4.02
1998	R Cucmng	Cal	36.0	39	23	10	15	15	5.75	1	3	9.75	2.50	3.75	3.75	0.50	6.82
1999	Mobile	Sou	151.3	172	110	38	56	55	6.54	5	12	10.23	2.26	3.33	3.27	0.49	6.70
2000	LasVegas	PCL	131.0	140	79	14	60	55	5.43	5	10	9.62	0.96	4.12	3.78	0.46	5.28

He struggled a little bit with his control at Las Vegas and generally didn't find the PCL to his liking. Junior Herndon is very young to be in Triple-A and needs to be concerned about all the recent draft picks who are sitting hitters down at the lower levels of the chain. He will probably spend the whole season at Portland.

Sterling Hitchcock — Throws L — Age 30

YEAR	TEAM	LGE	IP	H	ER	HR	BB	K	ERA	W	L	H/9	HR/9	BB/9	K/9	KWH	PERA
1998	San Dieg	NL	166.7	170	92	34	47	128	4.97	7	12	9.18	1.84	2.54	6.91	1.36	5.31
1999	San Dieg	NL	198.0	198	100	31	68	163	4.55	10	12	9.00	1.41	3.09	7.41	1.20	4.97
2000	San Dieg	NL	63.3	69	39	13	23	51	5.54	2	5	9.81	1.85	3.27	7.25	1.11	6.00

With the trade of Andy Ashby, the Padres were counting on Sterling Hitchcock to lead the staff in 2000, but even before going down with an elbow sprain in May, Hitchcock was very uneven. He was probably even more marketable than Ashby last off-season when the trade rumors swirled, but it's tough to blame the Padres for wanting to hold onto their most established remaining starter. He may be pitching by midseason. Maybe.

Trevor Hoffman — Throws R — Age 33

YEAR	TEAM	LGE	IP	H	ER	HR	BB	K	ERA	W	L	H/9	HR/9	BB/9	K/9	KWH	PERA
1998	San Dieg	NL	69.3	42	13	2	20	70	1.69	7	1	5.45	0.26	2.60	9.09	1.75	1.87
1999	San Dieg	NL	64.3	47	23	5	13	61	3.22	4	3	6.58	0.70	1.82	8.53	2.35	2.45
2000	San Dieg	NL	69.0	61	30	7	10	71	3.91	4	4	7.96	0.91	1.30	9.26	3.55	3.16

It was an off year by Trevor Hoffman's extremely high standards, one which had a few numbskulls calling for his head. He had an uncharacteristic seven blown saves but none after August 26. Were the Padres contenders, Hoffman would be a clutch performer; since they sucked, nobody noticed. Ahh, the vagaries of the fireman's job.

Brian Lawrence — Throws R — Age 25

YEAR	TEAM	LGE	IP	H	ER	HR	BB	K	ERA	W	L	H/9	HR/9	BB/9	K/9	KWH	PERA
1998	Clinton	Mid	72.7	75	49	13	17	39	6.07	2	6	9.29	1.61	2.11	4.83	1.15	4.96
1999	R Cucmng	Cal	165.0	173	74	12	37	83	4.04	9	9	9.44	0.65	2.02	4.53	1.12	3.99
2000	Mobile	Sou	114.7	109	54	12	32	66	4.24	6	7	8.56	0.94	2.51	5.18	1.03	3.98
2000	LasVegas	PCL	44.7	47	13	7	7	33	2.62	3	2	9.47	1.41	1.41	6.65	2.36	4.57

Brian Lawrence was the best pitcher in Mobile last season, following a good campaign with the Quakes in 1998. Lawrence shared the Padres' Minor League Pitcher of the Year Award and could get a shot at a starting spot with the Padres in 2001. He's another in the procession of Padres pitching prospects who struck out a batter per inning in 2000.

Carlton Loewer — Throws R — Age 27

YEAR	TEAM	LGE	IP	H	ER	HR	BB	K	ERA	W	L	H/9	HR/9	BB/9	K/9	KWH	PERA
1998	Scran-WB	Int	89.3	86	34	6	22	49	3.43	6	4	8.66	0.60	2.22	4.94	1.11	3.59
1998	Philadel	NL	118.0	147	82	18	35	47	6.25	4	9	11.21	1.37	2.67	3.58	0.67	6.06
1999	Philadel	NL	87.3	94	48	8	21	40	4.95	4	6	9.69	0.82	2.16	4.12	0.95	4.37

Carlton Loewer fell out of a tree while hunting not long after being acquired, and Kevin Towers' anticipated rotation hit dirt at the same time. Loewer, who the Padres were counting on to replace Andy Ashby, never did make it to the team. The Padres will be counting on him again in 2001; if he pitches the way he did in his last year as a Phillie, the Ashby trade looks like even more of a steal.

Rodrigo Lopez — Throws R — Age 25

YEAR	TEAM	LGE	IP	H	ER	HR	BB	K	ERA	W	L	H/9	HR/9	BB/9	K/9	KWH	PERA
1999	Mobile	Sou	157.7	187	100	22	64	85	5.71	6	12	10.67	1.26	3.65	4.85	0.66	6.03
2000	LasVegas	PCL	105.3	118	62	10	43	71	5.30	4	8	10.08	0.85	3.67	6.07	0.83	5.26
2000	San Dieg	NL	24.0	39	23	5	12	14	8.63	1	2	14.63	1.88	4.50	5.25	0.58	9.39

Rodrigo Lopez took a couple of turns through the revolving door before getting booted, and he wasn't really successful. Then again, we're talking about three games, including one in which he pitched well and another in which a bunch of guys hit seeing-eye grounders and soft drives that fell in front of charging outfielders. Having to evaluate pitchers on the fly is a tough job.

Dave Maurer — Throws L — Age 26

YEAR	TEAM	LGE	IP	H	ER	HR	BB	K	ERA	W	L	H/9	HR/9	BB/9	K/9	KWH	PERA
1998	R Cucmng	Cal	75.0	57	32	2	59	45	3.84	4	4	6.84	0.24	7.08	5.40	0.38	4.13
1999	Mobile	Sou	65.7	61	38	12	30	35	5.21	3	4	8.36	1.64	4.11	4.80	0.58	5.25
2000	Mobile	Sou	24.0	18	14	4	4	15	5.25	1	2	6.75	1.50	1.50	5.63	1.88	3.14
2000	LasVegas	PCL	42.0	46	19	6	15	30	4.07	2	3	9.86	1.29	3.21	6.43	1.00	5.38
2000	San Dieg	NL	14.0	15	8	2	4	11	5.14	1	1	9.64	1.29	2.57	7.07	1.38	4.96

The crafty left-hander with a heavy fastball did a good job for the Padres and Stars last year. Dave Maurer's strikeout rates climbed in 2000; it's just bad luck on his part that the left-hander the Padres have lusted after for years turned out to be Kevin Walker.

Jason Middlebrook — Throws R — Age 26

YEAR	TEAM	LGE	IP	H	ER	HR	BB	K	ERA	W	L	H/9	HR/9	BB/9	K/9	KWH	PERA
1998	R Cucmng	Cal	136.7	163	116	23	80	64	7.64	3	12	10.73	1.51	5.27	4.21	0.40	7.01
1999	Mobile	Sou	58.3	78	68	15	35	22	10.49	1	5	12.03	2.31	5.40	3.39	0.31	8.69
2000	Mobile	Sou	105.7	143	122	32	62	41	10.39	2	10	12.18	2.73	5.28	3.49	0.33	9.15

Jason Middlebrook's control never came around, and he struggled at Double-A Mobile. He was slated to play in the Arizona Fall League, but the Padres attempted to slip him through waivers at the last second, and he was claimed by the Mets. It was a very good move by Steve Phillips; the talent is still there, and it isn't like Middlebrook will be counted on or paid much in 2001.

Steve Montgomery — Throws R — Age 30

YEAR	TEAM	LGE	IP	H	ER	HR	BB	K	ERA	W	L	H/9	HR/9	BB/9	K/9	KWH	PERA
1998	Rochestr	Int	82.0	80	58	18	25	45	6.37	3	6	8.78	1.98	2.74	4.94	0.90	5.29
1999	Philadel	NL	63.3	52	22	9	25	46	3.13	4	3	7.39	1.28	3.55	6.54	0.92	4.07
2000	San Dieg	NL	5.3	6	6	3	3	2	10.13	0	1	10.13	5.06	5.06	3.38	0.33	10.13

The Padres were counting on him heavily last year—probably too heavily, considering he's had one good season in the last three—but a bum shoulder kept him from contributing at all. Only in the unpredictable domain of relief pitching can a guy have one good season and change from a nobody to a respected setup man.

Randy Myers — Throws L — Age 38

YEAR	TEAM	LGE	IP	H	ER	HR	BB	K	ERA	W	L	H/9	HR/9	BB/9	K/9	KWH	PERA
1998	Toronto	AL	41.7	41	18	3	16	29	3.89	3	2	8.86	0.65	3.46	6.26	0.91	4.22
1998	San Dieg	NL	13.7	15	10	2	7	7	6.59	1	1	9.88	1.32	4.61	4.61	0.50	6.09

Randy Myers's contract is finally up, so if he can pitch in 2001, it will be for much less money. Beware the trial ballooning, spin doctoring, and unadulterated propaganda that surround players with big contracts and big injuries: the rumors going around in spring training that Myers was throwing off a mound and was a week from rejoining the team were as laughable then as they are now.

Rodney Myers — Throws R — Age 32

YEAR	TEAM	LGE	IP	H	ER	HR	BB	K	ERA	W	L	H/9	HR/9	BB/9	K/9	KWH	PERA
1998	Iowa	PCL	93.7	82	54	13	53	55	5.19	4	6	7.88	1.25	5.09	5.28	0.52	4.98
1999	Iowa	PCL	29.0	27	19	4	13	15	5.90	1	2	8.38	1.24	4.03	4.66	0.58	4.81
1999	ChiCubs	NL	62.3	68	31	9	21	35	4.48	3	4	9.82	1.30	3.03	5.05	0.83	5.33
2000	San Dieg	NL	2.0	2	1	0	0	3	4.50	0	0	9.00	0.00	0.00	13.50	-1.00	2.50

Does anyone have a better case for hating Cinergy Field's artificial turf than Rod Myers? He's a mediocre pitcher who needs all the breaks he can get, and what better break for a guy looking to build up some pension time than the mangled Padres pitching staff of 2000? If Myers could have pulled off a career season, he would have become a commodity. Unfortunately, the turf had other ideas; a torn patellar tendon ended his season—and his best chance at a career—before it started.

National League

Jacob Peavy — Throws R — Age 20

YEAR	TEAM	LGE	IP	H	ER	HR	BB	K	ERA	W	L	H/9	HR/9	BB/9	K/9	KWH	PERA
1999	IdahoFls	Pio	10.3	5	0	0	1	6	0.00	1	0	4.35	0.00	0.87	5.23	3.00	0.82
2000	Ft Wayne	Mid	119.7	124	84	15	61	87	6.32	4	9	9.33	1.13	4.59	6.54	0.71	5.49

He was one of the youngest and best starters in the Midwest League, leading the Wizards with 13 wins and placing eighth in the league with a 2.90 ERA. With a strikeout fastball and deceptive delivery, Jacob Peavy was the #7 prospect in the league according to *Baseball America*. He's certainly one of the biggest steals in the 1999 draft at this point.

Wascar Serrano — Throws R — Age 23

YEAR	TEAM	LGE	IP	H	ER	HR	BB	K	ERA	W	L	H/9	HR/9	BB/9	K/9	KWH	PERA
1998	Clinton	Mid	142.7	156	86	15	67	73	5.43	6	10	9.84	0.95	4.23	4.61	0.54	5.45
1999	R Cucmng	Cal	122.7	111	67	18	49	70	4.92	6	8	8.14	1.32	3.60	5.14	0.71	4.57
1999	Mobile	Sou	39.3	48	30	8	18	18	6.86	1	3	10.98	1.83	4.12	4.12	0.50	7.01
2000	Mobile	Sou	101.0	105	59	21	45	67	5.26	4	7	9.36	1.87	4.01	5.97	0.74	6.04
2000	LasVegas	PCL	13.0	25	23	6	9	14	15.92	0	1	17.31	4.15	6.23	9.69	0.78	14.15

Futures Game alum Wascar Serrano had a solid season with Double-A Mobile, tying for the team lead in wins and putting up a 2.80 ERA, good for eighth in the league. He's got a live fastball with great movement, so the PCL will be a good test for him next year. He'll be a full-time starter at Portland.

Heathcliff Slocumb — Throws R — Age 35

YEAR	TEAM	LGE	IP	H	ER	HR	BB	K	ERA	W	L	H/9	HR/9	BB/9	K/9	KWH	PERA
1998	Seattle	AL	67.3	68	36	5	38	47	4.81	3	4	9.09	0.67	5.08	6.28	0.62	5.07
1999	St Louis	NL	52.3	48	15	3	25	40	2.58	4	2	8.25	0.52	4.30	6.88	0.80	4.10
2000	St Louis	NL	48.7	48	28	8	19	28	5.18	2	3	8.88	1.48	3.51	5.18	0.74	5.13
2000	San Dieg	NL	18.3	19	12	1	12	10	5.89	1	1	9.33	0.49	5.89	4.91	0.42	5.38

He was a closer the last time I looked. Heathcliff Slocumb managed to get a multi-year contract out of the Cards following his good work there last year and was acquired by the Padres in the Carlos Hernandez deal. He's lost a lot of velocity and isn't any better than a back-of-the-bullpen pitcher at this point. Outrighted, so he could be anywhere when you read this.

Stan Spencer — Throws R — Age 31

YEAR	TEAM	LGE	IP	H	ER	HR	BB	K	ERA	W	L	H/9	HR/9	BB/9	K/9	KWH	PERA
1998	LasVegas	PCL	129.3	118	70	19	45	87	4.87	6	8	8.21	1.32	3.13	6.05	0.97	4.43
1999	LasVegas	PCL	52.0	65	33	6	16	31	5.71	2	4	11.25	1.04	2.77	5.37	0.97	5.76
1999	San Dieg	NL	37.0	55	45	12	10	30	10.95	0	4	13.38	2.92	2.43	7.30	1.50	8.90
2000	LasVegas	PCL	34.7	29	9	2	7	27	2.34	3	1	7.53	0.52	1.82	7.01	1.93	2.77
2000	San Dieg	NL	47.7	43	22	7	17	33	4.15	2	3	8.12	1.32	3.21	6.23	0.97	4.40

Stan Spencer has made it through one season in the past five without an injury; in 2000, he hit the 60-day DL with a strained elbow just when the Padres needed him most. Spencer has had stretches of effectiveness when healthy; he's just too fragile to count on. He could put up another season like 1998, which would certainly be useful.

Dennis Tankersley — Throws R — Age 22

YEAR	TEAM	LGE	IP	H	ER	HR	BB	K	ERA	W	L	H/9	HR/9	BB/9	K/9	KWH	PERA
2000	Augusta	SAL	66.7	77	54	11	43	35	7.29	2	5	10.40	1.49	5.81	4.73	0.41	6.99
2000	Ft Wayne	Mid	58.7	60	41	13	29	46	6.29	2	5	9.20	1.99	4.45	7.06	0.79	6.30

Stolen from the Red Sox for four really bad weeks of Ed Sprague, Dennis Tankersley owned the Midwest League following his acquisition. Along with Peavy and Baxter, he struck out more than a batter per inning and will be moving on to Lake Elsinore next season. Given the fame and fortune of "the Eck," "the Tank" is basically his preordained nickname.

Brian Tollberg — Throws R — Age 28

YEAR	TEAM	LGE	IP	H	ER	HR	BB	K	ERA	W	L	H/9	HR/9	BB/9	K/9	KWH	PERA
1998	Mobile	Sou	37.7	34	14	5	4	26	3.35	2	2	8.12	1.19	0.96	6.21	3.25	3.37
1998	LasVegas	PCL	104.3	135	86	24	29	70	7.42	3	9	11.65	2.07	2.50	6.04	1.21	6.99
1999	LasVegas	PCL	28.7	32	16	3	7	15	5.02	1	2	10.05	0.94	2.20	4.71	1.07	4.78
2000	LasVegas	PCL	72.7	69	27	6	11	40	3.34	5	3	8.55	0.74	1.36	4.95	1.82	3.34
2000	San Dieg	NL	113.3	122	57	14	31	63	4.53	6	7	9.69	1.11	2.46	5.00	1.02	4.80

He became the first Frontier League vet to see major-league action when the Padres called him up on June 19. By June 26, Brian Tollberg had his first Player of the Week award. Despite missing most of 1999 to an elbow sprain, Tollberg has had success in the minors, thanks largely to his good-to-excellent control. He'll have a full-time job in San Diego next season, and he hasn't let long odds beat him yet.

Kevin Walker — Throws L — Age 24

YEAR	TEAM	LGE	IP	H	ER	HR	BB	K	ERA	W	L	H/9	HR/9	BB/9	K/9	KWH	PERA
1998	R Cucmng	Cal	112.0	123	72	21	57	49	5.79	4	8	9.88	1.69	4.58	3.94	0.43	6.42
1999	R Cucmng	Cal	36.0	34	21	4	22	18	5.25	1	3	8.50	1.00	5.50	4.50	0.41	5.22
2000	San Dieg	NL	64.3	49	34	5	34	47	4.76	3	4	6.85	0.70	4.76	6.58	0.69	3.69

Desperation Double-A call-ups at the beginning of the season generally exhibit less stick than Ozzie Guillen on Valium, but Kevin Walker improbably spent the rest of the season as the left-handed reliever Bruce Bochy had been seeking for years.

Donne Wall — Throws R — Age 33

YEAR	TEAM	LGE	IP	H	ER	HR	BB	K	ERA	W	L	H/9	HR/9	BB/9	K/9	KWH	PERA
1998	San Dieg	NL	66.7	50	19	7	31	46	2.57	5	2	6.75	0.95	4.19	6.21	0.74	3.24
1999	San Dieg	NL	67.3	57	29	12	21	45	3.88	4	3	7.62	1.60	2.81	6.01	1.07	3.79
2000	San Dieg	NL	51.3	35	17	4	19	24	2.98	4	2	6.14	0.70	3.33	4.21	0.63	2.47

He had a very good season last year. Donne Wall is the comparatively rare reliever who emerged from obscurity to pitch well and continued on that path without regression. He improved on his performance by keeping the ball in the park. Traded to the Mets, he's behind Armando Benitez and Turk Wendell in the pecking order, so his innings in 2001 will be low-leverage.

Woody Williams — Throws R — Age 34

YEAR	TEAM	LGE	IP	H	ER	HR	BB	K	ERA	W	L	H/9	HR/9	BB/9	K/9	KWH	PERA
1998	San Dieg	NL	66.7	50	21	7	31	46	2.84	5	2	6.75	0.95	4.19	6.21	0.74	3.65
1999	San Dieg	NL	67.3	57	32	12	21	45	4.28	3	4	7.62	1.60	2.81	6.01	1.07	4.26
2000	San Dieg	NL	51.3	35	19	4	19	24	3.33	4	2	6.14	0.70	3.33	4.21	0.63	2.78

The Davy Crockett of pitchers: Woody Williams returned from an aneurysm to pitch as well as he ever has, with an ERA of 3.30 after the break. The difference? His fastball had more movement, and his willingness to work inside kept opposing hitters from getting good swings. He probably killed a bear when he was only three years old, too.

Jay Witasick — Throws R — Age 28

YEAR	TEAM	LGE	IP	H	ER	HR	BB	K	ERA	W	L	H/9	HR/9	BB/9	K/9	KWH	PERA
1998	Edmonton	PCL	139.3	126	82	22	54	99	5.30	5	10	8.14	1.42	3.49	6.39	0.92	4.64
1999	KansasCy	AL	159.7	178	89	18	64	97	5.02	7	11	10.03	1.01	3.61	5.47	0.76	5.38
2000	KansasCy	AL	90.0	101	52	11	29	64	5.20	4	6	10.10	1.10	2.90	6.40	1.10	5.22
2000	San Dieg	NL	58.7	68	41	9	31	45	6.29	2	5	10.43	1.38	4.76	6.90	0.73	6.46

Jay Witasick was stolen from the Royals for Brian "Pitching Machine" Meadows at the trade deadline. No, it isn't like Witasick is any great shakes, but at least he's got a live arm, whereas Meadows will always be Meadows. Witasick gets tattooed when he leaves the ball up; he gave up lots of bombs last year, which was no surprise.

Support-Neutral Statistics — SAN DIEGO PADRES — Park Effect: -17.3%

PITCHER	GS	IP	R	SNW	SNL	SNPCT	W	L	RA	APW	SNVA	SNWAR
Brian Boehringer	3	13.3	14	0.8	1.3	.363	0	3	9.45	-0.7	-0.3	-0.1
Matt Clement	34	205.0	131	10.5	13.7	.432	13	17	5.75	-2.4	-1.6	0.2
Will Cunnane	3	13.3	14	0.6	1.5	.292	0	1	9.45	-0.7	-0.5	-0.3
Adam Eaton	22	135.0	63	8.6	6.6	.566	7	4	4.20	0.7	1.0	2.1
Sterling Hitchcock	11	65.7	38	3.3	4.1	.447	1	6	5.21	-0.4	-0.5	0.2
Rodrigo Lopez	6	24.7	24	1.1	2.9	.277	0	3	8.76	-1.1	-0.8	-0.6
Brian Meadows	22	124.7	80	5.4	10.2	.349	7	8	5.78	-1.5	-2.2	-1.2
Stan Spencer	8	49.7	22	2.6	2.7	.491	2	2	3.99	0.4	-0.0	0.4
Brian Tollberg	19	118.0	58	7.4	5.8	.560	4	5	4.42	0.3	0.7	1.8
Woody Williams	23	168.0	74	9.8	8.0	.552	10	8	3.96	1.3	0.8	2.3
Jay Witasick	11	60.7	42	2.7	5.1	.347	3	2	6.23	-1.0	-1.2	-0.6
TOTALS	162	978.0	560	52.8	61.8	.461	47	59	5.15	-4.9	-4.5	4.1

Bill James's "Devil's Theory of Park Effects" (detailed in the 1986 *Baseball Abstract*) is that "teams tend to develop those characteristics which are least favored by the park in which they play." Applied to pitching, the theory suggests that a team that plays in a strong pitchers' park won't recognize when they have a problem with pitching because the park will make a crummy pitching staff appear average, or an average one appear great. As a result, James wrote, "Teams which play in great pitchers' parks tend to develop mediocre pitching staffs." James used a number of examples to support the theory, and the crummy recent Padre rotations—who have pitched in arguably the most pitcher-friendly park of the 20th century—can be added to those supporting examples.

However, if James's theory held true in general, you'd expect to see a high percentage of pitching staffs that pitched in extreme pitchers' parks have below-average park-adjusted numbers, and you'd expect to see the converse for hitters' parks. That isn't the case. Of the 53 20th-century teams with a *Total Baseball* Pitchers' Park Factor (PPF) of 92 or lower, only 22 (or 42%) had a below-average pitching staff, measured by Adjusted Pitching Wins (APW). Of the 67 20th-century teams with a PPF of 109 or higher, only 29 (or 43%) had an above-average pitching staff. Using different thresholds for the pitchers' or hitters' parks gives slightly different results but always right around a 50-50 split between above-average staffs and below-average ones. Overall, no statistical correlation exists between teams' park factors and their APWs.

The bottom line: there's no reason to assume that San Diego's lousy pitching is due to management being fooled by the pitcher-friendly park.

For a quick explanation of SN stats, see page 7.

Reliever Evaluation Tools

PITCHER	G	IP	R	ARA	APR	IRNR/G	EIRS/G	IRP	BRS	RRA	ARP
Carlos Almanzar	62	69.7	35	5.01	1.5	0.71	0.26	-6.4	3.1	6.38	-9.2
Brian Boehringer	4	2.3	1	4.27	0.2	0.00	0.00	0.0	0.4	6.05	-0.2
Buddy Carlyle	4	3.0	7	23.25	-6.0	0.00	0.00	0.0	-1.3	8.89	-1.2
Will Cunnane	24	25.0	7	2.79	6.7	0.62	0.24	-1.2	-3.7	2.18	8.4
Tom Davey	11	12.7	1	0.79	6.2	0.18	0.03	-0.8	1.2	2.21	4.2
Todd Erdos	22	29.7	24	8.06	-9.4	0.50	0.19	-0.5	-0.2	8.54	-11.0
Domingo Guzman	1	1.0	1	9.97	-0.5	0.00	0.00	0.0	-0.6	3.64	0.2
Trevor Hoffman	70	72.3	29	4.00	9.7	0.29	0.09	1.7	0.6	3.93	10.2
Brandon Kolb	11	14.0	8	5.69	-0.8	1.09	0.41	1.9	1.6	5.56	-0.6
Dave Maurer	14	14.7	8	5.44	-0.4	0.36	0.12	0.7	-2.2	3.06	3.5
Steve Montgomery	7	5.7	6	10.55	-3.4	0.43	0.11	0.6	-0.0	10.18	-3.1
Rodney Myers	3	2.0	1	4.98	0.0	0.00	0.00	0.0	0.4	6.06	-0.2
Vincente Palacios	7	10.7	10	9.34	-4.9	0.71	0.40	-1.1	-1.4	8.88	-4.4
Carlos Reyes	12	18.0	12	6.64	-2.9	0.75	0.29	-2.0	-1.7	6.81	-3.2
Dan Serafini	2	2.0	3	14.95	-2.2	0.00	0.00	0.0	1.1	20.12	-3.3
Wascar Serrano	1	1.0	3	29.90	-2.7	0.00	0.00	0.0	0.0	31.09	-2.9
Heathcliff Slocumb	22	19.0	11	5.77	-1.2	0.64	0.21	-4.5	2.6	9.07	-8.2
Kevin Walker	69	65.3	35	5.34	-1.0	0.65	0.17	-2.4	-3.8	5.11	0.7
Donne Wall	45	55.0	20	3.62	9.6	0.58	0.18	2.3	-1.5	2.96	13.7
Matt Whisenant	26	22.3	13	5.80	-1.5	0.69	0.24	-1.0	1.7	6.80	-4.0
Matt Whiteside	26	36.0	20	5.54	-1.4	0.73	0.26	0.9	0.1	5.33	-0.5
TOTALS	443	481.3	255	5.28	-4.4	0.56	0.19			5.41	-11.2

For a quick guide to RET, see page 10.

San Francisco Giants

A banner reading "No More Candlestick" hung between two very proud fifth-graders the day Pacific Bell Park opened. For fans who had spent 40 years freezing their collective buttocks off at a crappy football stadium, this was the best free-agent acquisition they could imagine. For $319,000,000 in private money, Giants fans had not simply a state-of-the-art ballpark, but a real baseball cathedral. Never mind that there were enough ads in the place to make Andy Warhol break into spontaneous giggling; Pac Bell Park was everything it was supposed to be—great sight lines, warmer than Candlestick, walking distance from downtown, beautiful grass, interesting architecture that works with the surroundings, and a really cool cove in which to hit home runs.

There were naysayers, of course. Parking was going to be sparse, and public and private officials clamored for fans to take BART and Muni, which were running extra trains, buses, and shuttles to games. Tickets were expensive. Disabled access was dependent on the goodwill of beer-swilling baseball fans. Scalpers charged a fortune for tickets, and all sorts of human ugliness was displayed outside the park, where a small section of wall is cut away to allow a view of the game through a chain-link fence. I actually observed one guy physically move a ten-year-old kid out of the way so he could watch the game. Why, if that guy weren't a *Baseball Prospectus* investor, I would have turned him over to San Francisco's finest.

So yes, Pac Bell Park rocks. It is, as advertised, a great place to watch a game.

But what about the product on the field? If you had seen only the home opener, you would have been convinced that Tommy Lasorda had cut a deal with the devil. The hated Dodgers came to town and ruined the most anticipated Giants game in San Francisco history, beating the Giants behind three home runs by Kevin F-ing Elster. The Giants had a terrible stretch of luck in their first week at Pac Bell, bad enough that local news radio started wisecracking about tearing down the park and returning to Candlestick. Every time the opposing team hit a slicing line drive, it would just nick the chalk for an extra-base hit. Completely washed-up pitchers would get calls on pitches just outside Tom Glavine's Personal Strike Zone™. Anything that could go wrong for the Giants in those first six games did.

Then they finally broke the park in, started to hit a little, and didn't quit for five months. The Giants became a devastating offensive machine on the shoulders of Jeff Kent, Barry Bonds, and Ellis Burks. The team turned Pac Bell Park into its own little sandbox, where they routinely drubbed the opposition into compete and utter submission. The Giants went 55–26 at home, a record that would have been unimaginable in mid-April. The perfect ballpark is now officially broken in, and the headlines are earned by the players on the field. Which is as it should be.

Those of us on the *Baseball Prospectus* staff have taken some criticism over the years. One complaint that has stuck—largely because there's a grain of truth to it—is that we can be pretty hard on players and even occasionally go over the line and get personally negative. I would argue that we've come across that way because we haven't adequately explained all our comments over the years.

There really is no such thing as a bad baseball player in the majors. So how come we make negative comments from time to time? The answer is simple, and it doesn't lie with the player—it lies with management.

Let's take the example of Brian Hunter, journeyman outfielder. In *Baseball Prosepctus 2000,* we wrote: "Although I don't know if a two-by-four would help as a tool of instruction, Hunter would undoubtedly be tastier on the grill than in the lineup." Now, we're not advocating battery or cannibalism here. What can Hunter do well? He can play defense and pinch-run. In the right organization, he may be of use as a fifth or sixth outfielder, or as a designated runner in September, once rosters expand to 40 guys. Our criticism is not of Hunter per se, but of a management team that has put

> **Giants Prospectus**
>
> **2000 record:** 97–65; First place, NL West; Lost to Mets in Division Series, 3-1
> **Pythagenport W/L:** 98–64
> **Runs Scored:** 925 (3rd in NL)
> **Runs Allowed:** 747 (4th in NL)
> **Team EqA:** .286 (1st in NL)
> **2000 Batters' Age:** 30.2 (5th oldest in NL)
> **2000 Pitchers' Age:** 28.2 (8th youngest in NL)
> **Ballpark:** Pac Bell Park; excellent pitchers' park; Park Factor of .925
> **2000:** The best offense in baseball and a fantastic managing job garnered them a divisional title.
> **2001:** They have a chance in weak division, although it's hard to see how they can do much better than they did last year.

him in a role beyond his capabilities. Having him start for your club is sheer lunacy, based on what wins games and what Hunter can realistically be expected to do.

How is this relevant to the San Francisco Giants?

The Giants didn't have a single Brian Hunter last year. Dusty Baker crafted a tremendous season using the talent available to him, particularly in managing the offense. Baker put his players in situations suited to their skill sets. He didn't ask them to do more than they were capable of doing, and he took advantage of the things they could do well. He found ways to get the platoon advantage while strategically resting his players. He found youngsters to team with veterans to minimize injuries and keep the bench fresh. He had a deep, diverse set of skills at his disposal, and he used them exceptionally well.

Need a defensive replacement who can pinch-run and hit left-handers? Poof! There's Calvin Murray. Need to rest J.T. Snow because he's played a ton of innings and a nasty left-handed starter is scheduled? No problem. Run Ramon Martinez out there, put him at second base, and move Jeff Kent to first base. Effectively utilizing players isn't rocket science, but it does require consistency and trust from your players. Baker did it all year long.

Nowhere was it more obvious than with Ellis Burks in right field. Burks has tremendous talent and has been a good player throughout his career, but he's fragile. Back injuries and balky knees have kept him out of the lineup for at least 20 games a year for most of his career. When he has been healthy enough to play, he's often been so dinged up that his performance has suffered.

In the past, clubs tried to run Burks out there every day, often in center field, where his knees took a beating. Dusty Baker didn't make that mistake. What can Burks do? Hit, catch the ball, and run quickly, but only a limited amount each day. What can't he do? Cover a lot of ground, play several games in a row, or play well when dinged up. So how did Dusty deal with this? He and the team medical staff worked up a plan for Burks's playing time, sitting him when it made the most sense—against tough right-handers, when a game was out of hand, or when Burks had played three or four straight days. Instead of 135 to 145 pretty good games, Baker got 122 great ones from Burks. This usage pattern also gave Armando Rios some much deserved playing time. Burks stayed hot all year, and the Giants buried the NL West by mid-September.

It wasn't just Burks; most of the Giants were used exceptionally well. The team didn't have a true center fielder, so Marvin Benard covered what ground he could, held his own with the bat, and got occasional help from Calvin Murray. Ramon Martinez was a great utility infielder, providing defense and a lot of power from that spot. Russ Davis's severe limitations were dodged while his strengths were utilized.

Davis hit .311/.355/.544 against southpaws, but his fielding percentage wasn't far from his OPS, and his range factor at third base looked like Pedro Martinez's ERA against Ray Charles. Baker maximized Davis's opportunities to face left-handers and minimized his time in the field.

Few Giants fans would argue that Baker was anything less than brilliant with the hitters in 2000, yet many weren't thrilled with the idea of Baker being Manager of the Year. Why not?

Because Dusty Baker works his starting pitchers damn hard. Livan Hernandez threw 240 innings after being injured and ineffective following overuse in Florida. Shawn Estes was allowed to finish meaningless blowouts while throwing 127 pitches. Dusty Baker's pitchers tied for the NL lead in 120-pitch starts with 25; only Terry Francona was as dedicated to testing the limits of rotator cuffs. If Hernandez had a tracking stock for his future success, Giants fans would be shorting it.

The GM duties in San Francisco are performed by the quote machine that is Brian Sabean. Just three years after he delighted baseball fans with "I am not an idiot" (a phrase that adorns several hundred T-shirts in the Bay Area), Sabean followed that up this year with the always-to-be-remembered "Don't talk to me about on-base percentage. That sabermetric stuff gives me a headache."

It would be easy to take a few cheap shots here, but it wouldn't be fair. Sure, the Giants' farm system is a shining example of Sabean's bumper-sticker philosophy, but let's give credit where credit is due. Sabean may not approach player evaluation in the same fashion we do, but he put together an offense and bench that really did the job. He signed a pair of National League MVPs to unbelievably cheap contracts. He refused to give a 36-year-old Ellis Burks a three-year deal. He robbed the Phillies of Bobby Estalella in exchange for Chris Brock. Sabean has been a pretty good general manager, and you know he cringes every time he sees Keith Foulke pitch.

These days, he has his work cut out for him. The Giants are both good and young. But the good players aren't young, and the young players aren't good. Jeff Kent is 33. Barry Bonds is 36. There are some young veterans who can be very good players provided they're in the right roles—specifically Estalella, Rios, and Martinez—and players like Rich Aurilia are right in their prime.

The farm system, though, is in real trouble. The organization is very high on young pitchers Kurt Ainsworth and Ryan Vogelsong, but neither looks like a legitimate front-line starter. Jerome Williams is probably the pitching prospect with the highest upside, and he's down in A ball still developing. The offensive side of the ledger looks like something from MicroStrategy's accounting firm—a complete disaster. The organization and fans are high on guys like Pedro Feliz and Tony Torcato, a pair of third-base prospects with live bats, but they're not players who would draw attention in another organization. Up and down the minors, the Giants' prospects have miserable plate discipline. It's better to have one or two drop-dead nasty prospects than a bunch of guys who might be contributors in the majors if they're lucky. The Giants have neither. Their farm system is dilapidated and will require not only a major infusion of talent, but a complete overhaul of the way it works.

The Giants are in an easy division, but they're in trouble. Their window is closing, and there's competition all around them. Their stadium debt is reminiscent of the sword of Damocles; if things go wrong three or four years down the road, it could be difficult to dig out. The key for the Giants is to make sure they keep winning. Given the age of the talent base and the state of the farm system, they need to start thinking about 2002 and beyond.

HITTERS (BA: .270, OBP: .340, SLG: .440, EqA: .260)

Rich Aurilia — SS — Bats R — Age 29

YEAR	TEAM	LGE	AB	H	DB	TP	HR	BB	SO	R	RBI	SB	CS	OUT	BA	OBP	SLG	EQA	EQR	DEFENSE	
1998	San Fran	NL	420	115	27	2	10	30	58	57	50	3	3	308	.274	.325	.419	.247	46	100-SS	8
1999	San Fran	NL	564	158	21	1	23	35	67	67	77	1	3	409	.280	.328	.443	.253	66	145-SS	2
2000	San Fran	NL	517	142	25	2	20	47	84	67	77	1	2	377	.275	.335	.447	.258	64	136-SS	8
2001	San Fran	NL	473	129	20	1	17	47	74	62	75	1	1	345	.273	.338	.427	.266	63		

This is a shortstop who pushes a club towards a championship. Rich Aurilia's defense doesn't spin my wheels, despite the numbers above, but he's not a complete disaster out there, and he can hit. I expect him to be an above-average hitter this year. He'll take the field every day, play good enough defense to help the club, and play hard. The Giants have signed him to a three-year extension.

Marvin Benard — CF — Bats L — Age 30

YEAR	TEAM	LGE	AB	H	DB	TP	HR	BB	SO	R	RBI	SB	CS	OUT	BA	OBP	SLG	EQA	EQR	DEFENSE	
1998	San Fran	NL	293	96	19	1	4	33	37	42	37	11	4	201	.328	.399	.440	.287	44	63-RF	-7
1999	San Fran	NL	568	163	35	5	16	47	92	94	61	20	13	418	.287	.348	.451	.264	75	138-CF	-3
2000	San Fran	NL	569	151	30	5	12	55	91	100	54	20	7	425	.265	.336	.399	.250	67	141-CF	-1
2001	San Fran	NL	521	145	29	4	13	57	88	84	75	17	8	384	.278	.349	.424	.271	73		

Marvin Benard is a scrappy little ballplayer who works hard to cover the mammoth center field in Pac Bell Park. He's a mistake hitter, smacking hard line drives that occasionally attain enough loft to get over the fence. Benard is also a very solid and smart base runner and a fan favorite. He's a very easy player to like; a center fielder who can be a league-average hitter while playing acceptable defense is a good thing to have.

Barry Bonds — LF — Bats L — Age 36

YEAR	TEAM	LGE	AB	H	DB	TP	HR	BB	SO	R	RBI	SB	CS	OUT	BA	OBP	SLG	EQA	EQR	DEFENSE	
1998	San Fran	NL	568	171	44	6	39	129	86	123	122	26	12	409	.301	.437	.606	.334	132	155-LF	4
1999	San Fran	NL	359	93	21	2	33	68	59	88	78	12	2	268	.259	.381	.604	.314	74	92-LF	-1
2000	San Fran	NL	489	150	28	4	48	110	72	126	101	10	3	342	.307	.436	.675	.348	122	125-LF	3
2001	San Fran	NL	416	116	21	1	36	109	68	104	108	12	3	303	.279	.429	.594	.342	104		

He has now passed Rickey Henderson as the second-best left fielder of all time and will probably pass Ted Williams either this year or next. I have never seen a player have such a bipolar relationship with a team or a city. Everything that goes wrong with the Giants eventually gets blamed on Barry Bonds, and he's absolutely savaged on talk radio throughout the Bay Area.

My guess is that after he's been retired for ten years, he'll be adequately respected. As it is today, people focus on the fact that he has a really cool recliner in the clubhouse instead of the fact that he's the greatest ballplayer of his generation by a wide margin. He's still an outstanding defender in left field, a great base runner, and has the most powerful left-handed swing in baseball. There is no better ballplayer not named Alex Rodriguez.

Ellis Burks — RF — Bats R — Age 36

YEAR	TEAM	LGE	AB	H	DB	TP	HR	BB	SO	R	RBI	SB	CS	OUT	BA	OBP	SLG	EQA	EQR	DEFENSE	
1998	Colorado	NL	350	87	17	4	15	37	75	48	46	2	6	269	.249	.324	.449	.250	42	90-CF	-4
1998	San Fran	NL	150	46	5	1	6	19	29	23	23	8	1	105	.307	.395	.473	.297	25	39-CF	1
1999	San Fran	NL	394	110	16	0	31	64	81	70	90	5	5	289	.279	.388	.556	.303	73	93-RF	2
2000	San Fran	NL	400	138	21	4	24	50	46	73	92	5	1	263	.345	.419	.598	.329	82	92-RF	2
2001	Clevelnd	AL	381	110	15	1	21	59	61	68	75	5	2	273	.289	.384	.499	.292	63		

Ellis Burks is a fine ballplayer when healthy, and Dusty Baker and his staff have been masterful at managing him. They rationed his playing time very carefully, making sure to keep the knee swelling and back pain to a minimum instead of running him out there every day and getting reduced production for 150 games. Burks still brings a solid bat to the ballpark and can help a team with realistic expectations. Of course, realistic expectations don't usually accompany a three-year, $20-million contract, which is what the Cleveland Indians gave him.

Giuseppe Chiaramonte — C — Bats R — Age 25

YEAR	TEAM	LGE	AB	H	DB	TP	HR	BB	SO	R	RBI	SB	CS	OUT	BA	OBP	SLG	EQA	EQR	DEFENSE
1998	San Jose	Cal	511	118	22	1	18	33	142	63	61	2	1	394	.231	.281	.384	.218	44	105-C -11
1999	Shrevprt	Tex	404	87	16	1	14	31	95	42	54	2	1	318	.215	.278	.364	.212	33	86-C -21
2000	Fresno	PCL	438	96	24	4	18	35	83	52	55	1	1	343	.219	.280	.416	.227	42	109-C -20
2001	San Fran	NL	403	89	19	1	16	37	93	42	51	1	1	315	.221	.286	.392	.234	42	

He's kind of Mickey Tettleton Really Lite. Guiseppe Chiaramonte is going to have some value, but it's a question of where. His defensive reputation isn't great, but he can hit the ball hard on a pretty consistent basis, his strikeout rate has dropped significantly, and he's at least able to play catcher. He will start the season at Triple-A and isn't going to displace Bobby Estalella during this reality. If his defense and offense both improve 5%, he'll have a major-league career.

Julio Cordido — 3B — Bats R — Age 20

YEAR	TEAM	LGE	AB	H	DB	TP	HR	BB	SO	R	RBI	SB	CS	OUT	BA	OBP	SLG	EQA	EQR	DEFENSE
1999	Salem OR	Nwn	243	52	7	1	1	16	49	21	17	3	2	193	.214	.267	.263	.170	11	67-3B -1
2000	Bakrsfld	Cal	465	100	16	1	8	26	103	49	43	4	4	369	.215	.262	.305	.182	26	128-3B 16
2001	San Fran	NL	277	64	4	0	5	20	69	22	24	3	2	215	.231	.283	.300	.202	20	

He's an athletic third baseman who played reasonably well in the California League at age 19. Julio Cordido will have an opportunity to show what he can do in Double-A but is clearly behind Tony Torcato in the organization at the moment.

Felipe Crespo — UT — Bats B — Age 28

YEAR	TEAM	LGE	AB	H	DB	TP	HR	BB	SO	R	RBI	SB	CS	OUT	BA	OBP	SLG	EQA	EQR	DEFENSE	
1998	Toronto	AL	130	35	9	1	1	14	24	11	15	3	3	98	.269	.349	.377	.245	15	24-RF 2	
1999	Fresno	PCL	377	99	18	3	16	62	72	67	55	11	5	283	.263	.373	.454	.278	58	65-1B 4	22-OF -2
2000	San Fran	NL	133	39	6	1	4	8	22	17	28	3	2	96	.293	.349	.444	.263	17	15-LF -3	
2001	San Fran	NL	175	47	8	1	6	24	34	29	27	5	2	130	.269	.357	.429	.276	26		

A great tool for a manager to have, Felipe Crespo can play pretty much anywhere without embarrassing himself except shortstop and catcher, and he's turned into a pretty reasonable pinch hitter. The proper marriage of a utility player and a manager makes both of them look good, and that was certainly the case last year for Crespo and Baker.

Russ Davis — 3B — Bats R — Age 31

YEAR	TEAM	LGE	AB	H	DB	TP	HR	BB	SO	R	RBI	SB	CS	OUT	BA	OBP	SLG	EQA	EQR	DEFENSE
1998	Seattle	AL	502	135	27	1	23	33	119	70	84	3	3	370	.269	.318	.464	.255	61	130-3B -7
1999	Seattle	AL	431	108	17	1	22	28	101	54	57	3	3	326	.251	.303	.448	.245	48	112-3B -2
2000	San Fran	NL	183	49	5	0	9	6	27	27	23	0	3	137	.268	.297	.443	.236	19	26-3B -4
2001	San Fran	NL	267	68	8	0	13	23	58	31	42	2	2	201	.255	.314	.431	.255	33	

This is not a good third baseman. Cue Tony Iommi: I...am...Ironglove! Russ Davis is a low-OBP pseudo-slugger who simply can't play defense. In other words, he's a good complement to Bill Mueller, which won't do the Cubs any good. Davis has some value as a tweener and right-handed bat off the bench, but beyond that role—say, starting for the Giants in 2001—he doesn't help a club.

Bobby Estalella — C — Bats R — Age 26

YEAR	TEAM	LGE	AB	H	DB	TP	HR	BB	SO	R	RBI	SB	CS	OUT	BA	OBP	SLG	EQA	EQR	DEFENSE	
1998	Scran-WB	Int	245	62	12	0	14	56	49	42	39	0	0	183	.253	.395	.473	.292	42	67-C	-1
1998	Philadel	NL	166	32	6	1	8	13	46	17	20	0	0	134	.193	.255	.386	.208	13	45-C	-6
1999	Scran-WB	Int	390	83	21	2	12	45	99	48	50	3	1	308	.213	.300	.369	.225	37	100-C	5
2000	San Fran	NL	304	72	22	3	14	53	86	45	51	3	0	232	.237	.353	.467	.274	46	95-C	-1
2001	San Fran	NL	344	81	19	1	18	56	97	53	60	1	0	263	.235	.343	.453	.276	52		

It's the Gabe Kapler of the catching profession! Bobby Estalella is a fine ballplayer who is only going to get better. Defensively, he's perfectly acceptable if not a virtuoso, and he can definitely smack the crap out of the ball. He's shown a bunch of skills in the majors and minors, and I see no reason to think that he can't start consolidating a few of those skills in single seasons for a few years. He will be at least a reasonable MVP candidate at some point during the next five years.

Pedro Feliz — 3B — Bats R — Age 24

YEAR	TEAM	LGE	AB	H	DB	TP	HR	BB	SO	R	RBI	SB	CS	OUT	BA	OBP	SLG	EQA	EQR	DEFENSE	
1998	Shrevprt	Tex	362	84	17	1	9	4	68	29	36	0	1	279	.232	.243	.359	.189	22	92-3B	0
1999	Shrevprt	Tex	492	111	22	3	10	13	98	41	58	2	1	382	.226	.248	.343	.189	30	126-3B	7
2000	Fresno	PCL	494	126	23	1	26	20	96	62	74	1	1	369	.255	.286	.464	.242	53	121-3B	2
2001	San Fran	NL	440	106	17	1	19	23	92	42	59	1	1	335	.241	.279	.414	.235	45		

A borderline prospect at third base, Pedro Feliz is a true low-OBP slugger. I was doing a local radio show on which talk turned to the Giants' farm system. We were discussing the lack of position players when a number of people called in and read me the riot act for not being high on Feliz. The reason I'm not is simple: he's a shaky defensive third baseman who has drawn a grand total of 105 unintentional walks in seven minor-league seasons. You want to be a good player in the majors? Get on base. You want to get on base while drawing less than a walk a week? Hit .350. Feliz won't.

Mike Glendenning — OF/1B — Bats R — Age 24

YEAR	TEAM	LGE	AB	H	DB	TP	HR	BB	SO	R	RBI	SB	CS	OUT	BA	OBP	SLG	EQA	EQR	DEFENSE			
1998	San Jose	Cal	181	39	5	0	8	17	68	19	23	0	1	143	.215	.283	.376	.216	15	47-LF	-1		
1998	Shrevprt	Tex	256	53	11	1	5	27	63	21	24	0	0	203	.207	.289	.316	.203	19	62-LF	-5		
1999	San Jose	Cal	373	74	15	1	16	51	116	46	50	3	2	301	.198	.303	.373	.228	37	55-LF	1		
1999	Shrevprt	Tex	107	24	4	0	4	9	33	11	14	1	1	84	.224	.288	.374	.218	9	25-LF	0		
2000	Shrevprt	Tex	294	66	9	0	13	25	92	38	39	1	1	229	.224	.292	.388	.224	27	26-LF	-7	19-1B	-2
2000	Fresno	PCL	139	24	6	0	5	9	42	13	14	0	1	116	.173	.227	.324	.169	7	34-LF	0		
2001	San Fran	NL	451	96	14	0	18	51	149	46	55	1	1	356	.213	.293	.364	.229	45				

He's trying to build a career as a right-handed Mark Sweeney. Mike Glendenning has some offensive skills, but he doesn't hit for average and can't play defense at a tough position. He had a rough go in Fresno last year, where he'll be again unless rescued by another organization. He's still young enough to have a big-league career; it just may not happen for a while.

Joe Jester — 2B — Bats R — Age 22

YEAR	TEAM	LGE	AB	H	DB	TP	HR	BB	SO	R	RBI	SB	CS	OUT	BA	OBP	SLG	EQA	EQR	DEFENSE			
1999	Salem OR	Nwn	263	58	10	1	5	31	64	35	21	4	3	208	.221	.309	.323	.215	22	44-SS	-3	24-2B	3
2000	San Jose	Cal	439	99	11	2	4	46	78	62	32	7	3	343	.226	.311	.308	.213	36	105-2B	-2		
2001	San Fran	NL	282	65	7	1	5	36	65	34	28	5	2	219	.230	.318	.316	.229	27				

This is an underrated prospect. Joe Jester is still learning to play second base, but he's shown some pretty decent athleticism and is quickly picking up the footwork and positioning. He's got a pretty quick bat and a good eye, is a smart base runner, has a little pop, and can run well. He'll likely see time at both Double-A and Triple-A this year but could surprise and move up rapidly. He probably deserves a few extra points for having a really cool baseball name.

Jeff Kent — 2B — Bats R — Age 33

YEAR	TEAM	LGE	AB	H	DB	TP	HR	BB	SO	R	RBI	SB	CS	OUT	BA	OBP	SLG	EQA	EQR	DEFENSE	
1998	San Fran	NL	536	161	35	3	33	47	103	98	129	9	4	379	.300	.366	.562	.298	92	134-2B	-5
1999	San Fran	NL	516	148	38	2	23	54	106	83	95	10	6	374	.287	.360	.502	.282	79	127-2B	-6
2000	San Fran	NL	597	198	42	6	32	82	100	111	118	11	9	408	.332	.419	.583	.322	120	141-2B	5
2001	San Fran	NL	516	150	33	2	26	66	100	91	102	8	6	372	.291	.371	.514	.299	91		

National League

Jeff Kent is a great ballplayer with no weaknesses to speak of in his game. He used to have subpar plate discipline, but that fault appears to have been addressed. Kent hits for average and power, plays defense, stays healthy, and gives the media what they want. He pushes a club towards a championship and is a deserving MVP.

Terrell Lowery — OF — Bats R — Age 30

YEAR	TEAM	LGE	AB	H	DB	TP	HR	BB	SO	R	RBI	SB	CS	OUT	BA	OBP	SLG	EQA	EQR	DEFENSE	
1998	Iowa	PCL	245	61	11	1	8	21	65	30	35	3	1	185	.249	.311	.400	.238	26	62-CF	6
1999	Durham	Int	275	76	15	3	10	33	66	49	38	6	4	203	.276	.355	.462	.270	39	64-CF	-6
1999	TampaBay	AL	184	48	16	1	2	17	48	24	16	0	2	138	.261	.326	.391	.238	19	44-CF	1
2000	Fresno	PCL	301	51	7	1	11	26	97	33	30	3	1	251	.169	.240	.309	.177	16	75-LF	-5
2000	San Fran	NL	35	16	1	0	2	6	7	12	6	1	0	19	.457	.546	.657	.404	10		
2001	San Fran	NL	336	77	13	1	11	39	103	41	42	5	1	260	.229	.309	.372	.241	37		

If you saw him play only during 2000 in San Francisco, you'd swear he was the illegitimate child of Stan Musial, Kirby Puckett, and Joe DiMaggio. I know it was only about 10 games worth of plate appearances, but every time I looked up, this guy was hitting scalding line drives with an absolutely beautiful swing. Terrell Lowery can definitely help a club as an extra outfielder/pinch hitter.

Ramon Martinez — IF — Bats R — Age 28

YEAR	TEAM	LGE	AB	H	DB	TP	HR	BB	SO	R	RBI	SB	CS	OUT	BA	OBP	SLG	EQA	EQR	DEFENSE			
1998	Fresno	PCL	358	95	16	1	11	31	41	45	45	0	2	265	.265	.326	.408	.243	39	95-2B	2		
1999	Fresno	PCL	111	30	5	1	1	8	17	9	12	1	0	81	.270	.319	.360	.230	10	22-SS	-1		
1999	San Fran	NL	146	38	4	0	6	12	16	21	19	1	2	110	.260	.316	.411	.239	15	23-2B	3		
2000	San Fran	NL	192	59	12	2	6	12	21	29	24	3	2	135	.307	.351	.484	.274	26	26-SS	2	18-2B	-2
2001	San Fran	NL	203	57	9	1	7	19	25	27	33	1	1	147	.281	.342	.438	.270	28				

Ballplayer. Ramon Martinez swings hard and can play any infield position well enough to be a defensive replacement. On another team, I'd be clamoring for him to at least receive a shot at the starting shortstop or second-base jobs; here, he's stuck behind two great players. Martinez can fill in for either without the club losing much, which is saying a lot.

Juan Melo — SS/2B — Bats B — Age 24

YEAR	TEAM	LGE	AB	H	DB	TP	HR	BB	SO	R	RBI	SB	CS	OUT	BA	OBP	SLG	EQA	EQR	DEFENSE			
1998	LasVegas	PCL	460	109	18	1	5	19	90	47	37	7	6	357	.237	.271	.313	.189	28	123-SS	-13		
1999	LasVegas	PCL	167	31	2	1	2	5	33	14	11	1	1	137	.186	.215	.246	.122	4	43-SS	-10		
1999	Syracuse	Int	141	30	9	1	2	7	31	16	10	5	3	114	.213	.254	.333	.191	9	38-SS	1		
2000	Fresno	PCL	410	102	20	4	9	25	91	42	35	8	8	316	.249	.295	.383	.222	37	70-SS	-15	46-2B	0
2001	San Fran	NL	355	84	15	2	7	24	83	38	35	10	4	275	.237	.285	.349	.223	32				

He's unburdened by excessive plate discipline. Juan Melo has some serious pop and can play second base without hurting a team but hasn't developed the skills to play shortstop and probably never will. His swing has holes in it the size of grapefruits; that's not likely to change unless he switches organizations or batting coaches or something.

Doug Mirabelli — C — Bats R — Age 30

YEAR	TEAM	LGE	AB	H	DB	TP	HR	BB	SO	R	RBI	SB	CS	OUT	BA	OBP	SLG	EQA	EQR	DEFENSE			
1998	Fresno	PCL	264	55	9	1	9	42	57	32	36	1	0	209	.208	.321	.352	.231	27	83-C	4		
1998	San Fran	NL	17	4	2	0	1	2	6	2	4	0	0	13	.235	.316	.529	.270	2				
1999	Fresno	PCL	314	75	15	1	9	37	58	42	33	5	1	240	.239	.320	.379	.238	33	61-C	-2	17-1B	2
1999	San Fran	NL	88	22	4	0	2	8	24	10	11	0	0	66	.250	.319	.364	.230	8	23-C	3		
2000	San Fran	NL	234	55	11	2	6	32	53	23	28	1	0	179	.235	.331	.376	.241	26	65-C	-1		
2001	San Fran	NL	225	46	7	1	6	34	53	26	24	1	0	179	.204	.309	.324	.228	22				

Doug Mirabelli can hit better than he showed in 2000. He's about two seasons away from being a certified backup catcher, a role for which he's well suited.

San Francisco Giants

Bill Mueller — 3B — Bats B — Age 30

YEAR	TEAM	LGE	AB	H	DB	TP	HR	BB	SO	R	RBI	SB	CS	OUT	BA	OBP	SLG	EQA	EQR	DEFENSE	
1998	San Fran	NL	546	165	18	0	13	78	78	96	63	3	3	384	.302	.390	.407	.274	75	133-3B	-1
1999	San Fran	NL	418	121	15	0	5	59	49	58	36	3	2	299	.289	.381	.361	.259	51	109-3B	-1
2000	San Fran	NL	569	156	29	4	10	44	58	96	54	4	2	415	.274	.332	.392	.244	61	136-3B	-1
2001	ChiCubs	NL	449	126	19	1	8	56	54	67	63	3	1	324	.281	.360	.381	.257	54		

It was off season for Bill Mueller, as he slipped everywhere except in power. He's a reasonable defensive third baseman and was very much a fan favorite in San Francisco. Mueller couldn't hit from the right side particularly well in 2000, but he should rebound with the Cubs this year; that improvement will be exaggerated by the change in ballpark.

Calvin Murray — CF — Bats R — Age 29

YEAR	TEAM	LGE	AB	H	DB	TP	HR	BB	SO	R	RBI	SB	CS	OUT	BA	OBP	SLG	EQA	EQR	DEFENSE	
1998	Shrevprt	Tex	340	80	16	3	4	41	54	38	24	15	8	268	.235	.323	.335	.227	33	88-CF	-1
1998	Fresno	PCL	90	18	3	1	2	9	18	12	4	2	1	73	.200	.273	.322	.198	6	17-LF	-2
1999	Fresno	PCL	534	142	24	4	15	38	90	82	49	25	10	402	.266	.317	.410	.245	60	129-CF	-1
1999	San Fran	NL	19	5	2	0	0	2	4	1	3	1	0	14	.263	.333	.368	.249	2		
2000	San Fran	NL	197	48	13	1	2	26	31	34	22	8	3	152	.244	.340	.350	.241	22	56-CF	0
2001	San Fran	NL	277	67	10	2	7	32	49	41	32	15	6	216	.242	.320	.368	.247	33		

Calvin Murray was a defensive replacement for much of the season and provided a right-handed bat off the bench. He can help a team in that role but will have to fight for a job every spring for the foreseeable future. He tailed off badly at the plate during the second half and looked a little lost. Murray is capable of doing more than he showed at the plate in 2000. If forced into a larger role, he might surprise some people.

Lance Niekro — 3B — Bats R — Age 22

YEAR	TEAM	LGE	AB	H	DB	TP	HR	BB	SO	R	RBI	SB	CS	OUT	BA	OBP	SLG	EQA	EQR	DEFENSE	
2000	Salem OR	Nwn	199	57	10	2	4	4	26	19	27	1	0	142	.286	.306	.417	.239	20	29-3B	-1
2001	San Fran	NL	103	32	4	1	2	3	50	11	16	0	0	71	.311	.330	.427	.261	12		

He was old for the league, yes, but he still hit .362. Lance Niekro didn't really show much other than the ability to hit for average with moderate power. That isn't bad for your first stint in the pros. He will move up at least to the California League this season; if he can retain his consistency at the plate, there will be opportunities for him in this organization. If he were in a system that knew how to teach plate discipline, he might be scary.

Armando Rios — RF — Bats L — Age 29

YEAR	TEAM	LGE	AB	H	DB	TP	HR	BB	SO	R	RBI	SB	CS	OUT	BA	OBP	SLG	EQA	EQR	DEFENSE	
1998	Fresno	PCL	439	110	15	1	19	44	74	61	74	11	4	333	.251	.321	.419	.248	51	102-LF	-3
1999	Fresno	PCL	107	24	1	0	3	9	22	17	15	2	1	84	.224	.300	.318	.210	8	18-OF	-2
1999	San Fran	NL	152	49	6	0	8	21	33	30	28	5	4	107	.322	.408	.520	.302	27	38-RF	3
2000	San Fran	NL	237	64	15	5	10	27	40	38	49	3	2	175	.270	.345	.502	.276	35	58-RF	2
2001	San Fran	NL	259	70	11	1	12	35	51	42	45	5	2	191	.270	.357	.459	.283	41		

Yes, Armando Rios is available for base-running clinics. One of our staff wrote a piece for www.baseballprospectus.com suggesting that Rios's base-running blunder against the Mets was actually not horrible and may even have been a defensible risk. Rubbish. Rios brain-locked, the play was unbelievably stupid, and he knows it. Major-league shortstops—American Legion shortstops—don't botch that play.

That said, Rios was a big part of why the Giants even reached the playoffs, and he earned the right to make a mistake. In his role as Ellis Burks's legs, he played good defense and hit for a reasonable average and power, particularly when pitchers fell behind. Throwing a 3-1 pitch to Rios was a very dangerous endeavor: he slugged 1.038 when ahead in the count. Yikes.

Rios underwent extensive elbow surgery in October and is in a race against time to heal up. Players don't get many chances to win an everyday job, and Rios doesn't want to miss his opportunity. The recovery time from his surgery would normally take him through March.

National League

Scott Servais — C — Bats R — Age 34

YEAR	TEAM	LGE	AB	H	DB	TP	HR	BB	SO	R	RBI	SB	CS	OUT	BA	OBP	SLG	EQA	EQR	DEFENSE	
1998	ChiCubs	NL	328	73	14	1	8	25	48	36	37	1	0	255	.223	.287	.345	.210	26	89-C	-2
1999	San Fran	NL	200	54	8	0	6	11	29	21	21	0	0	146	.270	.317	.400	.239	20	53-C	-4
2000	ColSprin	PCL	64	15	1	1	2	2	9	5	8	0	1	50	.234	.265	.375	.202	5	12-C	0
2000	Colorado	NL	100	19	1	0	2	5	15	5	12	0	1	82	.190	.235	.260	.142	3	31-C	-1
2000	San Fran	NL	8	2	0	0	0	2	1	1	0	0	0	6	.250	.400	.250	.244	1		
2001	San Fran	NL	181	39	4	0	5	14	28	14	17	0	0	142	.215	.272	.320	.204	13		

Scrub, but with the gleam that comes from being a "proven major leaguer." Scott Servais is as good as some backup catchers, better than a few others, and worse than most. For some reason, he strikes me as the sort who'll get 75 to 100 at-bats for the Detroit Tigers. I would apologize to the Tigers, but they haven't earned it.

J.T. Snow — 1B — Bats L — Age 33

YEAR	TEAM	LGE	AB	H	DB	TP	HR	BB	SO	R	RBI	SB	CS	OUT	BA	OBP	SLG	EQA	EQR	DEFENSE	
1998	San Fran	NL	443	113	27	1	17	57	79	68	82	1	2	332	.255	.340	.436	.258	56	117-1B	6
1999	San Fran	NL	576	156	25	2	24	78	114	92	93	0	3	423	.271	.363	.446	.270	80	152-1B	11
2000	San Fran	NL	545	157	33	2	19	58	121	81	94	1	3	391	.288	.367	.461	.275	77	143-1B	-1
2001	San Fran	NL	520	134	28	1	20	72	105	76	84	0	2	388	.258	.348	.431	.271	74		

He is probably no longer on the Benitez family's Christmas card list. J.T. Snow is a replacement-level first baseman with a reliable glove and a little pop. He will probably hit 17 to 23 home runs as long as he has a job, and if he can hit .280 with 75 walks, he *will* have a job. Defensively, Snow is very well regarded and with good reason. Overall, he's not horrible, but first basemen have gotten so good offensively that even a .275 EqA isn't enough to push a club towards a championship; it's only enough to keep a team from losing significant ground. The Giants can carry him because of Aurilia, Bonds, Kent, and Estalella, but imagine the offense with a true bomber at first base like Jason Giambi, Carlos Delgado, or Frank Thomas. Brrr.

Tony Torcato — 3B — Bats R — Age 21

YEAR	TEAM	LGE	AB	H	DB	TP	HR	BB	SO	R	RBI	SB	CS	OUT	BA	OBP	SLG	EQA	EQR	DEFENSE	
1998	Salem OR	Nwn	220	51	12	1	2	6	43	19	26	1	1	170	.232	.256	.323	.184	12	49-3B	-2
1999	Bakrsfld	Cal	417	99	9	0	6	18	70	33	41	1	0	318	.237	.271	.302	.186	24	79-3B	-10
2000	San Jose	Cal	494	134	28	1	6	22	64	52	59	6	2	362	.271	.306	.368	.226	44	104-3B	-16
2001	San Fran	NL	408	109	12	1	8	23	64	41	48	3	1	300	.267	.306	.360	.233	39		

Tony Torcato is a good athlete who performed fairly well as a 20-year-old in the California League, hitting a promising 37 doubles. There's an overriding problem here, though, and I don't mean just with Torcato, but rather throughout the Giant organization: these guys have no plate discipline! Torcato's defense is pretty suspect, so if he makes the majors to stay, it's likely to be as a first baseman. If he wants to be a major-league first baseman, though, he's going to have to learn to control the strike zone, and that's not an adequate priority in this organization. I wonder what Torcato would look like at this point if drafted by, say, the Athletics.

PITCHERS (ERA: 4.50, H/9: 9.00, HR/9: 1.00, BB/9: 3.00, K/9: 6.00, KW: 1.00, PERA: 4.50)

Kurt Ainsworth — Throws R — Age 22

YEAR	TEAM	LGE	IP	H	ER	HR	BB	K	ERA	W	L	H/9	HR/9	BB/9	K/9	KW	PERA
1999	Salem OR	Nwn	41.3	38	21	2	20	32	4.57	2	3	8.27	0.44	4.35	6.97	0.80	4.07
2000	Shrevprt	Tex	146.3	139	78	20	68	81	4.80	7	9	8.55	1.23	4.18	4.98	0.60	4.97

He's probably the Giants' best prospect. Kurt Ainsworth has plus stuff, his control is coming along, and he's well regarded in terms of his ability to pitch out of trouble. He is likely to start the season at Fresno but could be in San Francisco late in the year. His peripheral numbers are good but not great. Many Giants fans think he's a prospect à la Rick Ankiel or Ryan Anderson. He's not, and he's not close.

Luke Anderson — Throws R — Age 23

YEAR	TEAM	LGE	IP	H	ER	HR	BB	K	ERA	W	L	H/9	HR/9	BB/9	K/9	KW	PERA
2000	Salem OR	Nwn	27.0	27	9	3	11	24	3.00	2	1	9.00	1.00	3.67	8.00	1.09	4.76

Yes, he's old for the league. Yes, he's a closer in low-A ball. Yes, those facts make future success somewhat unlikely. But take a look at the actual performance here. Luke Anderson was completely dominant, allowing 19 hits and ten walks in 31 innings while striking out 55 guys. That's 16 guys per nine innings. Let's see what happens when he moves up a level or two. It makes sense to pay attention to usage patterns to forecast future performance, but it also makes sense to see if this guy is different.

Ryan Cox — Throws R — Age 24

YEAR	TEAM	LGE	IP	H	ER	HR	BB	K	ERA	W	L	H/9	HR/9	BB/9	K/9	KW	PERA
1999	Salem OR	Nwn	33.0	36	11	2	11	10	3.00	3	1	9.82	0.55	3.00	2.73	0.45	4.50
1999	Bakrsfld	Cal	31.0	46	25	11	3	16	7.26	1	2	13.35	3.19	0.87	4.65	2.67	8.47
2000	San Jose	Cal	97.0	125	84	30	33	27	7.79	2	9	11.60	2.78	3.06	2.51	0.41	7.95
2000	Shrevprt	Tex	31.3	52	39	9	6	15	11.20	0	3	14.94	2.59	1.72	4.31	1.25	9.18

Already polished, Ryan Cox is dominating young hitters with great command and passable stuff. Still, there's nothing in his performance record to suggest that he's got a good chance at a career in the majors as a starter. He's likely to end up as a Quadruple-A pitcher barring the development of a new pitch or the marked improvement of his current arsenal.

Robbie Crabtree — Throws R — Age 28

YEAR	TEAM	LGE	IP	H	ER	HR	BB	K	ERA	W	L	H/9	HR/9	BB/9	K/9	KW	PERA
1998	San Jose	Cal	49.3	44	9	3	11	31	1.64	4	1	8.03	0.55	2.01	5.66	1.41	3.12
1998	Shrevprt	Tex	49.0	32	16	7	21	33	2.94	3	2	5.88	1.29	3.86	6.06	0.79	3.37
1999	Shrevprt	Tex	58.0	51	26	4	24	38	4.03	3	3	7.91	0.62	3.72	5.90	0.79	3.79
1999	Fresno	PCL	32.7	36	23	2	11	25	6.34	1	3	9.92	0.55	3.03	6.89	1.14	4.59
2000	Fresno	PCL	121.7	122	64	9	31	78	4.73	6	8	9.02	0.67	2.29	5.77	1.26	3.88

He'a solid reliever who could probably help the Giants out of the pen this year. Robbie Crabtree has great but inconsistent stuff with breaking pitches that absolutely punish right-handed batters. He reminds me a little bit of Jeff Nelson, and his 2000 performance bears out the comparison: left-handed batters hit over .300 against him while he held righties to a .238 average. Crabtree will receive a careful look during spring training, in part because what he lacks in experience he makes up for in affordability.

Miguel del Toro — Throws R — Age 29

YEAR	TEAM	LGE	IP	H	ER	HR	BB	K	ERA	W	L	H/9	HR/9	BB/9	K/9	KW	PERA
1999	Fresno	PCL	67.3	73	42	12	32	45	5.61	2	5	9.76	1.60	4.28	6.01	0.70	6.12
1999	San Fran	NL	23.0	24	11	5	10	17	4.30	1	2	9.39	1.96	3.91	6.65	0.85	6.17
2000	Fresno	PCL	106.7	115	82	20	41	66	6.92	3	9	9.70	1.69	3.46	5.57	0.80	5.83
2000	San Fran	NL	16.7	17	10	3	5	13	5.40	1	1	9.18	1.62	2.70	7.02	1.30	5.14

An extremely skinny right-hander with a funky delivery, Miguel Del Toro came up and made a start to cover for the Giants' tired pitching staff, despite posting a rather terrifying 6.01 ERA in Triple-A. (Hey, it's the Pacific Coast League.) Del Toro pitched creditably and will receive an extended look in spring training. He's a long shot to have a major-league career.

National League

Alan Embree — Throws L — Age 31

YEAR	TEAM	LGE	IP	H	ER	HR	BB	K	ERA	W	L	H/9	HR/9	BB/9	K/9	KW	PERA
1998	Atlanta	NL	18.0	23	14	2	9	15	7.00	0	2	11.50	1.00	4.50	7.50	0.83	6.59
1998	Arizona	NL	33.7	32	18	5	12	20	4.81	2	2	8.55	1.34	3.21	5.35	0.83	4.70
1999	San Fran	NL	56.7	41	21	6	23	45	3.34	4	2	6.51	0.95	3.65	7.15	0.98	3.31
2000	San Fran	NL	58.0	61	33	4	22	41	5.12	2	4	9.47	0.62	3.41	6.36	0.93	4.55

Alan Embree has been a consistent reliever but didn't pitch particularly well last year, at least in the early and late parts of the season. He occasionally serves up a complete freaking meatball. Embree's velocity is solid and he should be healthy, so he'll be on the mound for 60-70 games, face a bunch of left-handed hitters, and enjoy the vast expanse of Pac Bell's outfield. He had minor arthroscopic surgery in late November but should be 100% by spring training.

Shawn Estes — Throws L — Age 28

YEAR	TEAM	LGE	IP	H	ER	HR	BB	K	ERA	W	L	H/9	HR/9	BB/9	K/9	KW	PERA
1998	San Fran	NL	142.7	148	91	16	75	110	5.74	5	11	9.34	1.01	4.73	6.94	0.73	5.41
1999	San Fran	NL	197.3	203	117	22	99	134	5.34	8	14	9.26	1.00	4.52	6.11	0.68	5.29
2000	San Fran	NL	184.3	189	94	11	95	113	4.59	9	11	9.23	0.54	4.64	5.52	0.59	4.82

Shawn Estes and Dusty Baker seem to have come to an agreement: Baker doesn't completely shred his arm, and Estes responds by throwing 190-200 consistent, dependable innings. Estes has very good stuff that induces a whole bunch of ground balls to Jeff Kent. If his strikeout rate was about 10% higher, he'd be a tremendous breakout candidate, particularly in that home park. Estes has had a history of twinges in his elbow and shoulder that forced him to miss a start here and there. I sometimes wonder if some guys save their careers that way, while "tough guys" end up on Dr. James Andrews's Christmas card list.

Aaron Fultz — Throws L — Age 27

YEAR	TEAM	LGE	IP	H	ER	HR	BB	K	ERA	W	L	H/9	HR/9	BB/9	K/9	KW	PERA
1998	Shrevprt	Tex	56.7	57	48	7	37	37	7.62	1	5	9.05	1.11	5.88	5.88	0.50	5.85
1998	Fresno	PCL	15.3	20	9	2	2	9	5.28	1	1	11.74	1.17	1.17	5.28	2.25	5.47
1999	Fresno	PCL	128.7	140	91	35	56	95	6.37	4	10	9.79	2.45	3.92	6.65	0.85	6.88
2000	San Fran	NL	66.7	66	38	8	25	51	5.13	3	4	8.91	1.08	3.38	6.89	1.02	4.68

Aaron Fultz rocks. He's a left-hander with decent stuff who gets a lot of ground balls and occasionally leaves an 87-mph pitch in the middle of the plate at approximately mid-thigh. The result is extremely entertaining baseball. You may get to watch the defense make a graceful play, see Fultz strike out someone by getting them off balance, or gaze in awe as Brian Giles hits a pitch at 185 mph into dead center field.

Mark Gardner — Throws R — Age 39

YEAR	TEAM	LGE	IP	H	ER	HR	BB	K	ERA	W	L	H/9	HR/9	BB/9	K/9	KW	PERA
1998	San Fran	NL	201.3	199	109	32	61	123	4.87	9	13	8.90	1.43	2.73	5.50	1.01	4.78
1999	San Fran	NL	134.0	137	100	28	50	72	6.72	4	11	9.20	1.88	3.36	4.84	0.72	5.70
2000	San Fran	NL	143.0	149	70	17	37	77	4.41	7	9	9.38	1.07	2.33	4.85	1.04	4.51

What an incredibly tough old bastard. Mark Gardner is a true pitcher. It's amazing to see the looks of stunned disbelief on the faces of people like Gary Sheffield when they watch a 3–2 pitch go right over the heart of the plate at 82 mph. Gardner's stuff is all but gone, but he keeps the ball down, seems to completely own about half the hitters who come to the plate, and changes speeds and location enough to prevent even the best hitters from just waiting on his "fastball." Back with the Giants in 2001, he's not likely to repeat his 2000 performance.

Doug Henry — Throws R — Age 37

YEAR	TEAM	LGE	IP	H	ER	HR	BB	K	ERA	W	L	H/9	HR/9	BB/9	K/9	KW	PERA
1998	Houston	NL	67.7	55	26	10	33	48	3.46	5	3	7.32	1.33	4.39	6.38	0.73	4.44
1999	Houston	NL	39.7	44	23	8	21	30	5.22	1	3	9.98	1.82	4.76	6.81	0.71	6.67
2000	Houston	NL	52.7	38	21	8	21	38	3.59	3	3	6.49	1.37	3.59	6.49	0.90	3.68
2000	San Fran	NL	24.7	18	10	2	19	13	3.65	2	1	6.57	0.73	6.93	4.74	0.34	4.45

(Doug Henry *continued*)

There are probably only about four places Doug Henry should consider playing now: Montreal, Oakland, Los Angeles, and San Francisco. He's a fly-ball pitcher who has lost that critical 2 mph off his fastball. Henry wisely got tentative in 2000, keeping the ball out of the middle of the plate, and the results weren't encouraging. Henry walked 49 men in 78 innings and was one of the luckiest pitchers on the planet late in the season, when he walked 21 and struck out 16 in 25 innings and, despite himself, posted an ERA of about two and a half. He's on the edge, and the Royals may be in for a nasty surprise.

Livan Hernandez — Throws R — Age 26

YEAR	TEAM	LGE	IP	H	ER	HR	BB	K	ERA	W	L	H/9	HR/9	BB/9	K/9	KW	PERA
1998	Florida	NL	223.3	260	137	42	99	132	5.52	9	16	10.48	1.69	3.99	5.32	0.67	6.52
1999	Florida	NL	132.0	154	74	17	48	82	5.05	6	9	10.50	1.16	3.27	5.59	0.85	5.66
1999	San Fran	NL	61.3	63	30	6	18	39	4.40	3	4	9.24	0.88	2.64	5.72	1.08	4.35
2000	San Fran	NL	230.7	245	111	23	65	137	4.33	12	14	9.56	0.90	2.54	5.35	1.05	4.53

Agradezca Al Dios! He escapado los embragues del él que destroza cartílago! Libertad Dulce! Por dos años, me he estado recuperando del daño hecho por Jim Leyland. Finalmente, santuario, donde mi encargado se ocupará de los mejores intereses de mí y del club no haciendo que eche 240 turnos! Agradezca a Jesús dulce que los tiempos oscuros están en un extremo!

Some pitchers should make sure they write their contracts carefully, perhaps giving some money back to their clubs if they pitch 180 innings three years down the road. Beware of implosion.

Ryan Jensen — Throws R — Age 25

YEAR	TEAM	LGE	IP	H	ER	HR	BB	K	ERA	W	L	H/9	HR/9	BB/9	K/9	KW	PERA
1998	Bakrsfld	Cal	153.7	169	109	29	73	83	6.38	5	12	9.90	1.70	4.28	4.86	0.57	6.29
1999	Fresno	PCL	150.0	151	91	17	69	102	5.46	6	11	9.06	1.02	4.14	6.12	0.74	5.03
2000	Fresno	PCL	131.0	160	98	20	59	81	6.73	4	11	10.99	1.37	4.05	5.56	0.69	6.51

He's a not-so-young pitcher who is still struggling to find his command. Ryan Jensen has pretty reasonable stuff and might have a shot at a major-league career, provided he can learn to throw his entire repertoire for strikes. If the Giants get hit by an injury or two in the rotation, Jensen could get a brief audition. Being a short right-hander, he'd be wise to take advantage of the opportunity by not allowing a run. Or a hit. And maybe curing a major disease.

John Johnstone — Throws R — Age 32

YEAR	TEAM	LGE	IP	H	ER	HR	BB	K	ERA	W	L	H/9	HR/9	BB/9	K/9	KW	PERA
1998	San Fran	NL	83.7	72	34	11	36	70	3.66	5	4	7.75	1.18	3.87	7.53	0.97	4.31
1999	San Fran	NL	63.0	47	24	8	18	47	3.43	4	3	6.71	1.14	2.57	6.71	1.31	3.20
2000	San Fran	NL	48.0	62	34	11	11	31	6.38	1	4	11.63	2.06	2.06	5.81	1.41	6.77

John Johnstone's nightmare season has finally ended. Nothing went right for the guy in 2000: his velocity was down, he was leaving the ball up, and whenever he missed with a pitch, it was clobbered like an Al Gore spin doctor. Johnstone's bulging disc gave him trouble all year, and it showed. If he's healthy in 2001, he'll rebound significantly.

Joe Nathan — Throws R — Age 26

YEAR	TEAM	LGE	IP	H	ER	HR	BB	K	ERA	W	L	H/9	HR/9	BB/9	K/9	KW	PERA
1998	San Jose	Cal	106.3	113	81	33	65	57	6.86	3	9	9.56	2.79	5.50	4.82	0.44	7.77
1999	Fresno	PCL	70.7	66	45	12	38	54	5.73	3	5	8.41	1.53	4.84	6.88	0.71	5.47
1999	San Fran	NL	87.0	81	43	18	40	45	4.45	4	6	8.38	1.86	4.14	4.66	0.56	5.50
2000	San Fran	NL	90.3	87	60	12	56	51	5.98	3	7	8.67	1.20	5.58	5.08	0.46	5.57

The Giants' designated bubble guy. Every club has at least one player like this, the Terry Felton/Doug Johns/Jody Treadwell type who's brought in for an audition in spring training and occasionally pops up when there's an injury. Occasionally, such players will stretch their auditions long enough to qualify for nice pensions, but with Joe Nathan's shoulder twinges, Dusty Baker probably isn't the right guy with whom to be working. Nathan will be in the mix for a bottom-of-the-rotation/swing-man spot.

National League

Robb Nen — Throws R — Age 31

YEAR	TEAM	LGE	IP	H	ER	HR	BB	K	ERA	W	L	H/9	HR/9	BB/9	K/9	KW	PERA
1998	San Fran	NL	84.3	60	22	4	24	89	2.35	7	2	6.40	0.43	2.56	9.50	1.85	2.41
1999	San Fran	NL	70.0	77	35	8	24	65	4.50	4	4	9.90	1.03	3.09	8.36	1.35	5.09
2000	San Fran	NL	63.3	38	16	4	17	76	2.27	5	2	5.40	0.57	2.42	10.80	2.24	2.01

He bounced back nicely from a subpar 1999. Robb Nen was lights out all year with surprisingly little fanfare. Nobody hit him, nobody walked off him, and Baker used him judiciously. Nen gave up a total of three earned runs in the second half of the season and had a strikeout-to-walk ratio of 50 to 4 at home. There's no closer in baseball I'd rather have going into 2001, including Mariano Rivera.

Russ Ortiz — Throws R — Age 27

YEAR	TEAM	LGE	IP	H	ER	HR	BB	K	ERA	W	L	H/9	HR/9	BB/9	K/9	KW	PERA
1998	Fresno	PCL	48.0	35	10	3	23	40	1.88	4	1	6.56	0.56	4.31	7.50	0.87	3.23
1998	San Fran	NL	84.3	89	52	12	43	61	5.55	3	6	9.50	1.28	4.59	6.51	0.71	5.74
1999	San Fran	NL	201.7	185	106	25	110	138	4.73	9	13	8.26	1.12	4.91	6.16	0.63	4.98
2000	San Fran	NL	189.3	190	115	29	99	139	5.47	7	14	9.03	1.38	4.71	6.61	0.70	5.62

Russ Ortiz was pitching like Don Knotts on a Ritalin binge for the first half of the season. The only thing rising faster than the line drives he was giving up was his ERA. During May and June, he threw perhaps ten pitches that didn't come back faster than they went in, and most of those ten were return throws from Estalella after walks.

In the second half, Ortiz found his release point and threw pretty well, posting a 3.22 ERA after the All-Star break. Ortiz has worked a fair number of innings but was very strong in the second half and showed no signs of fatigue down the stretch. He could be a very capable #2 starter for a few years.

Todd Ozias — Throws R — Age 24

YEAR	TEAM	LGE	IP	H	ER	HR	BB	K	ERA	W	L	H/9	HR/9	BB/9	K/9	KW	PERA
1998	Salem OR	Nwn	41.7	45	34	13	13	26	7.34	1	4	9.72	2.81	2.81	5.62	1.00	6.77
1999	Bakrsfld	Cal	51.3	51	27	11	29	35	4.73	2	4	8.94	1.93	5.08	6.14	0.60	6.33
2000	San Jose	Cal	46.3	55	39	10	20	30	7.58	1	4	10.68	1.94	3.88	5.83	0.75	6.86

He has a good pitcher's build, solid stuff, and great numbers thus far. Todd Ozias has struck out more than a batter per inning at each stop, all in relief. He's likely to start the season in Double-A but could get a September call-up and is on track to have a career as a setup guy in the bigs. Minor-league closers, as a group, don't have great track records; Ozias nevertheless bears watching.

Mike Riley — Throws L — Age 26

YEAR	TEAM	LGE	IP	H	ER	HR	BB	K	ERA	W	L	H/9	HR/9	BB/9	K/9	KW	PERA
1998	Bakrsfld	Cal	116.7	130	85	18	73	53	6.56	4	9	10.03	1.39	5.63	4.09	0.36	6.61
1999	Shrevprt	Tex	100.0	81	45	11	68	63	4.05	5	6	7.29	0.99	6.12	5.67	0.46	4.77
2000	Fresno	PCL	121.7	138	91	25	53	77	6.73	4	10	10.21	1.85	3.92	5.70	0.73	6.49

His strong 1999 earned him a promotion to Fresno, where experienced hitters and a lively offensive environment beat him senseless. Mike Riley has basically one year to pitch well and avoid the flypaper of Quadruple-A pitcherdom. It's a long shot.

Felix Rodriguez — Throws R — Age 28

YEAR	TEAM	LGE	IP	H	ER	HR	BB	K	ERA	W	L	H/9	HR/9	BB/9	K/9	KW	PERA
1998	Arizona	NL	42.7	44	30	5	26	29	6.33	1	4	9.28	1.05	5.48	6.12	0.56	5.77
1999	San Fran	NL	64.3	65	31	6	26	46	4.34	3	4	9.09	0.84	3.64	6.44	0.88	4.66
2000	San Fran	NL	79.0	66	29	5	37	79	3.30	5	4	7.52	0.57	4.22	9.00	1.07	3.71

He pitched well out of the pen. Felix Rodriguez reminds me a great deal of LaTroy Hawkins of Minnesota. They have similar deliveries with those long forearms that just whip the ball. Rodriguez throws hard and works high in the strike zone, and he's added about an inch of movement to his fastball. He had a breakthrough season in 2000 and is a good bet to have continued success. He did appear in 76 games but looked strong all year and was still throwing peas in late September. He will be the primary setup guy for Robb Nen in 2001.

Kirk Rueter — Throws L — Age 30

YEAR	TEAM	LGE	IP	H	ER	HR	BB	K	ERA	W	L	H/9	HR/9	BB/9	K/9	KW	PERA
1998	San Fran	NL	178.3	187	102	30	54	83	5.15	8	12	9.44	1.51	2.73	4.19	0.77	5.19
1999	San Fran	NL	178.0	208	112	29	48	79	5.66	7	13	10.52	1.47	2.43	3.99	0.82	5.65
2000	San Fran	NL	176.7	195	88	24	55	59	4.48	9	11	9.93	1.22	2.80	3.01	0.54	5.20

Tom Glavine Lite. Kirk Rueter has no velocity and doesn't strike anybody out; he just nibbles hitters to death. Rueter can throw on the outer three to six inches of the strike zone all day long and seldom gives in and throws a batting-practice fastball on a hitters' count. He's not a good bet for long-term success, but he knows how to pitch, fields his position well, can take the mound every fifth day, and is capable of throwing 180 generic innings. Damn few teams don't need a guy like that. In Pac Bell Park, his numbers will look pretty darn reasonable.

Ryan Vogelsong — Throws R — Age 23

YEAR	TEAM	LGE	IP	H	ER	HR	BB	K	ERA	W	L	H/9	HR/9	BB/9	K/9	KW	PERA
1998	Salem OR	Nwn	51.3	44	22	11	18	34	3.86	3	3	7.71	1.93	3.16	5.96	0.94	4.80
1998	San Jose	Cal	16.7	27	24	7	5	13	12.96	0	2	14.58	3.78	2.70	7.02	1.30	10.63
1999	San Jose	Cal	63.7	40	34	6	32	46	4.81	3	4	5.65	0.85	4.52	6.50	0.72	3.09
1999	Shrevprt	Tex	25.7	41	30	12	18	15	10.52	0	3	14.38	4.21	6.31	5.26	0.42	12.47
2000	Shrevprt	Tex	143.3	156	97	26	75	91	6.09	5	11	9.80	1.63	4.71	5.71	0.61	6.35

Ryan Vogelsong's numbers and stuff are both promising, but if you watch him pitch, it's hard to imagine him having a really bright future. He puts forth a hell of an effort with a jerky, awkward motion. Sure, there are successful pitchers who can get away with that, but the stresses this guy is putting on his body are astonishing. I hope he doesn't get hurt before he learns to pull it all together. He has the stuff to be a front-of-the-rotation starter, but that's not enough. He needs a year in Triple-A, perhaps two, with a great pitching coach.

Jerome Williams — Throws R — Age 19

YEAR	TEAM	LGE	IP	H	ER	HR	BB	K	ERA	W	L	H/9	HR/9	BB/9	K/9	KW	PERA
1999	Salem OR	Nwn	35.0	29	13	2	12	17	3.34	2	2	7.46	0.51	3.09	4.37	0.71	3.20
2000	San Jose	Cal	115.3	94	64	14	52	62	4.99	5	8	7.34	1.09	4.06	4.84	0.60	4.06

Jerome Williams pitched exceptionally well in the California League, posting a 2.54 ERA and striking out about eight guys per nine innings. For an 18-year-old, that's pretty impressive. Even more impressive is allowing only six home runs in more than 120 innings. Unlike Vogelson, Williams has sound mechanics and an easy motion from which he throws four solid pitches, including a plus fastball. The Giants are aware of what a potential gem they have in Williams and will take their time with him. He'll likely spend the entire year in Double-A; he could well be the best pitcher in the Texas League. I prefer Williams to Ainsworth; if he can avoid the dreaded injury nexus, I think he'll have a major-league career.

Support-Neutral Statistics — SAN FRANCISCO GIANTS — Park Effect: -16.8%

PITCHER	GS	IP	R	SNW	SNL	SNPCT	W	L	RA	APW	SNVA	SNWAR
Shawn Estes	30	190.3	99	11.8	9.7	.548	15	6	4.68	0.1	0.9	2.6
Mark Gardner	20	126.3	54	8.4	6.2	.575	10	5	3.85	1.2	1.0	2.2
Livan Hernandez	33	240.0	114	14.4	11.4	.558	17	11	4.28	1.1	1.3	3.4
Joe Nathan	15	81.0	55	4.8	5.3	.476	5	2	6.11	-1.2	-0.3	0.5
Russ Ortiz	32	189.7	116	10.2	12.8	.444	13	12	5.50	-1.6	-1.3	0.4
Kirk Rueter	31	181.7	92	10.2	10.6	.492	10	9	4.56	0.3	-0.2	1.4
Miguel del Toro	1	5.0	4	0.1	0.5	.161	1	0	7.20	-0.1	-0.2	-0.2
TOTALS	162	1014.0	534	59.9	56.5	.515	71	45	4.74	-0.4	1.2	10.4

While teams all over the major leagues have starting rotations that closely resemble casting calls or hospital wards, Dusty Baker's group was once again a model of stability. Only a mid-season injury to Joe Nathan and a makeup doubleheader start by Miguel del Toro kept Baker from using just five starters all year. That wasn't a one-year fluke; it's Baker's standard operating procedure. Over the past five years, the Giants are second only to the Braves in rotation stability, averaging just 8.4 starters per season. Over the past three years, the Giants had the majors' most stable rotation (tied with the Braves), averaging just 6.7 different starters per year.

There are two reasons for this stability. The first is that Baker exercises great patience with his starters, sticking with them even when they hit extended rough patches. Baker's patience with Russ Ortiz during his struggles in the first half of 2000 reminded me of Larry Dierker and his patience with a struggling and unproven Mike Hampton during his disastrous first half in 1997. The second reason for this stability is that Baker manages to keep his starters healthy. I don't know if he has a magic formula or if he just lives a charmed life, but Baker's recent record with starting-pitcher health has got to be the envy of every other manager in the league.

For a quick explanation of SN stats, see page 7.

Reliever Evaluation Tools

PITCHER	G	IP	R	ARA	APR	IRNR/G	EIRS/G	IRP	BRS	RRA	ARP
Alan Embree	63	60.0	34	5.63	-2.9	0.63	0.22	-2.3	1.0	5.67	-3.1
Aaron Fultz	58	69.3	38	5.45	-1.9	0.72	0.31	-1.8	-3.3	4.71	3.8
Mark Gardner	10	22.7	18	7.89	-6.8	0.70	0.33	-1.1	-0.3	6.86	-4.2
Doug Henry	27	25.3	10	3.92	3.6	0.63	0.17	-0.0	-0.8	4.02	3.3
John Johnstone	47	50.0	35	6.96	-9.8	0.57	0.20	-1.3	1.9	7.23	-11.3
Scott Linebrink	3	2.3	3	12.78	-2.0	1.00	0.61	-1.3	1.4	22.71	-4.5
Joe Nathan	5	12.3	8	6.45	-1.7	0.40	0.16	1.0	0.4	6.12	-1.3
Robb Nen	68	66.0	15	2.26	21.5	0.26	0.10	1.6	0.4	2.20	22.0
Russ Ortiz	1	6.0	1	1.66	2.4	0.00	0.00	0.0	0.0	1.81	2.3
Felix Rodriguez	76	81.7	29	3.53	15.1	0.66	0.21	-5.2	-0.7	4.05	10.4
Kirk Rueter	1	2.3	0	0.00	1.3	1.00	0.23	0.2	0.0	-0.56	1.5
Miguel del Toro	8	12.3	6	4.84	0.5	0.25	0.09	0.7	0.0	4.63	0.8
Ryan Vogelsong	4	6.0	0	0.00	3.5	0.00	0.00	0.0	0.0	0.00	3.5
Ben Weber	9	8.0	13	16.15	-9.7	0.89	0.20	0.8	-3.9	11.85	-5.9
Chad Zerbe	4	6.0	3	4.97	0.2	0.00	0.00	0.0	0.0	5.35	-0.1
TOTALS	384	430.3	213	4.92	13.3	0.57	0.20			4.84	17.1

For a quick guide to RET, see page 10.

Anaheim Angels

The Angels are going to hell, not for disobedience but rather apathy. They're doomed for not caring about their farm system, for their inability to build a team around the talent at hand, and possibly as retribution for Disney's atrocities against cinema. As their aging core of not-that-good players declines, this franchise will turn into the Los Angeles Clippers, a .300 team unable to rebuild, hoping vainly for a rescue or redemption that won't come.

The Angels' farm system had the worst winning percentage of any organization (.426) while fielding old teams on nearly every level. They lost five minor-league affiliates, some of them quite eager to ditch the parent club. Even in an offseason that featured a lot of musical chairs, the Angels' losses are cause for concern, as one of the things new GM Bill Stoneman was going to bring to the club was a focus on player development and a quality farm system. It would seem that he has supplied neither in his first year.

Looking at the organization's pitcher performance records is like reading itineraries for trips bought on Priceline.com: Anaheim, by way of Erie and Edmonton; Erie, by way of Butte and Cedar Rapids. About 30 of 80 pitchers in the Angels' organization spent significant time at more than one level last year. That's ridiculous, a giant flashing neon sign that blinks "clue" and then "less." It makes me feel bad for John Lackey, a talented young pitcher who was excited when he signed, said all the right things about how happy he was to join the organization, and now has to be hoping he'll be tossed into the next ill-advised Ron Gant trade rather than spend another season at three levels.

The Angels advance their hitters much more slowly; that's because they're all stiffs. Some can steal bases, but none can hit. Only 25 position players in the organization drew 40 or more walks, while there were 11 guys stealing 25 or more bases. Guess which group is touted as prospects. The Angels aren't drafting Vladimir Guerrero-type bad-ball contact hitters, either; they are, as an organization, devoid of hitting talent.

> **Angels Prospectus**
>
> **2000 record:** 82–80; Third place, AL West
> **Pythagenport W/L:** 81–81
> **Runs Scored:** 864 (7th in AL)
> **Runs Allowed:** 869 (9th in AL)
> **Team EqA:** .268 (5th in AL)
> **2000 Batters' Age:** 27.6 (tied for 5th youngest in AL)
> **2000 Pitchers' Age:** 28.5 (5th youngest in AL)
> **Ballpark:** Edison International Field; neutral park; Park Factor of .997
> **2000:** A good offense and some pitching surprises kept the Halos above .500.
> **2001:** They did almost nothing over the winter; that won't get it done in the AL West.

Table 1 breaks down the Angels' minor-leaguers by their performance at the level at which they spent the most time in 2000.

Two hitters in the entire organization hit for an EqA of .250 or better. One was minor-league veteran Steve Decker, who posted a .257 at Triple-A Edmonton. The other was Shawn Wooten, who hit .257 at Edmonton (following 191 at-bats at Double-A Erie in which he hit .218). A sustained .260 or higher EqA in the minors indicates a possible legitimate prospect. The Angels have no such players.

The Angels aren't deep in pitching, either. Just nine Angels' farmhands threw 50 or more innings with an adjusted ERA of 5.00 or better. Two, Seth Etherton and Brett Hinchliffe, are no longer with the Angels. Two others, Gilbert Landestoy and David Wolensky, were making their professional debuts. In the entire system, then, there are no hitting prospects and only two pitching prospects—Scott Shields and Francisco Rodriguez—who can be taken seriously. Two prospects.

The Angels' draft last year was pitching-heavy, and they were aggressive in getting their picks signed: nine of their top ten and 17 of their top 20. That's good, because their minor-league teams are old and bad. To get any semblance of depth in the system, the Angels need to draft well, and they will also need to make good minor-league free-agent signings, pick role players off of waivers, and work the Rule 5 draft for more Derrick Turnbow-style prospects. Pumping money into international scouting and development instead of Mo Vaughn's bar tabs would help, too, but you know how Vaughn gets when he's cut off.

What this organization really seems to need is direction. Not that the Angels have to copy the A's—though they should—but if they want to develop players, they need to figure out how they're going to do it. They don't know where they want their players to be, for how long, or what they're supposed to

Table 1: Performance Level (EqA) of Angels' Minor League Players for Most of 2000

Performance Level	No. of Players
EqA of .000–.150:	14
EqA of .150–.174:	26
EqA of .175–.199:	30
EqA of .200–.249:	33
EqA of .250 or above:	2

learn. As a result, players are slow to develop if they develop at all.

The Angels are going to spend the next decade as the stepchild of the AL West, a division with a potential rising dynasty in the A's, a newly cash-rich Mariner franchise, and a Rangers team built around the best player in the game. Certainly, this team, the Troy Glaus/Darin Erstad version, is better than the Jim Edmonds/Chuck Finley/Gary DiSarcina Angels. They've finally had a season with a team OBP above .350 (.352) and have a set of young hitters on the rise. Still, they're not as smart or as good as the A's are (much less as good as the A's are going to get), while the Mariners have money, guile, and are willing to cheat.

There are two ways the Angels can go: one is to play the part of the media-owned, mismanaged franchise and to bumble to a late-1960s Yankee-style collapse. The Angels can play .500 ball for a couple years, hoping their hitters all get hot at the same time their young pitchers put together a great year while Seattle, Oakland, and all of the AL wild-card contenders have bad years. This is what a lot of clubs do, in a low-profile, talk-about-competing way, and it's exactly the course the Angels will take. Their other choice is to act now and try and win it all before Glaus and Co. hit their free-agent years, at which point this franchise will self-destruct regardless of what happens in the meantime unless its farm system gets real good, real quickly.

Now is the time for bold moves, including a complete revamping of the offense. Tim Salmon's trade value is as high as it's going to get, so he should be the consolation prize for the loser of the Manny Ramirez sweepstakes. Garret Anderson hit a lot of home runs in 2000 and is strangely well-regarded; he could net a couple of useful pieces and a fruit basket. If the Yankees really are fixated on Mo Vaughn, the Angels need to trade him for either D'Angelo Jimenez or Nick Johnson, dumping salary and improving at the same time. They'll be blasted in the press, but it's that kind of crazy, risk-taking move that will give this franchise its best chance of winning division titles.

The risks are huge, but if a team has only three years, do you wager it all and—if you're wrong—go to seed a year or two early, or do you sit around and twiddle your thumbs?

Disney didn't make a risky movie about the atrocities of European colonialism; they made *Pocahontas*, with talking animals and cheery songs. They're going to sit tight.

What's more, the Angels are unable to make the small moves. Picking up high-salaried Ron Gant last year made no sense, especially for a team having just solved the too-many-outfielders problem. They seem to get outsmarted on the transaction front like few teams this side of the Royals, picking up a David Eckstein only to lose a Mike Colangelo. Their free-agent signing record has been abysmal of late. They couldn't see that Gary DiSarcina would break down again and were also unable to pick up anyone who could hit to replace him, leading to an ugly bottom-of-the-order scarcely better than the one they had in 1999.

In a world where both Larry Bowa and Bob Boone can get major-league managing jobs, it's important to remember that last year the Angels hired a good manager in Mike Scioscia. Scioscia was responsible for much of what the Angels did well last year. He's not a Phil Garner-style glad-handing press-indulgent manager, but he does give simple, honest answers to questions, even when they go against conventional wisdom.

After one game, he was asked why he didn't have Garret Anderson sacrifice in a particular situation; Scioscia responded that it never occurred to him. His team stole bases, but he wasn't stuck on it; they managed a decent success rate with the bulk of the stealing done by Darin Erstad and Adam Kennedy (28 and 22). Just five players even attempted five steals. He's not a great manager, however—he batted Anderson fifth for almost the entire season, leaving Troy Glaus to hit with the bases empty far too often.

Sixteen pitchers made starts for the Angels last season, the most of any major-league team. Tim Belcher was injured and mostly bad when sort of healthy. Kent Bottenfield was bad but managed to pitch three times as many innings as Belcher. The Angels' best starter turned out to be Jarrod Washburn, who spent some quality time on the DL as well. Even in the chaos of the collapse, the nucleus of a good, young staff emerged. Ramon Ortiz, Jarrod Washburn, Matt Wise, and Scott Schoeneweis are already in the majors. Once Edmonton pitching coach Greg Minton turns Scot Shields into an effective pitcher—and it's only a matter of time—they'll have to find a place for him. Five of these guys will comprise a killer rotation that costs less than they paid Belcher last year to read magazines in waiting rooms.

Nevertheless, Designated Team Leader Mo Vaughn has made noises that this is a team that needs to acquire some quality veteran pitching to contend. Such remarks not only prove that he's not a very adept team leader, but also that he absolutely failed to learn any lessons from the Belcher and Ken Hill meltdowns. It's going to take some guts to tell Vaughn that he's being a moron, but that's exactly what the team must do. The Angels may not have old pitching, but

American League

they have good pitching that will get better. Sticking to the development of that pitching is going to be at times rocky but the most rewarding path.

Having a strong relief corps will help that commitment. Scioscia inherited a deep and effective bullpen and managed it well, paying little attention to traditional roles while running many of his relievers out for more than one inning. Only two Angel relievers had more appearances than innings pitched. Scioscia didn't get particularly hung up on platoon splits or hot hands. As a result, the bullpen was third-best in the major leagues and did a lot to contain the damage done by the starting rotation, which was third-worst in the majors. Of the relievers who threw more than 20 innings, just two allowed more than one Adjusted Run Prevented. (See the chart at the back of this chapter for the data.) Only lefty specialist Mike Holtz was particularly misused, as he continued to be helpless against right-handed hitters but was forced to see them all too often. Bullpens are one of the areas a manager's influence is felt strongly. Scioscia should be praised for his excellent work in keeping the bullpen productive despite a rotation that left games early and with runners on.

In the same vein, he kept Erstad in one position, returned Orlando Palmeiro to the fourth-outfielder role he fits best, and generally managed roles calmly and intelligently. Scioscia handled crises and breakdowns evenly, without panicking and slagging his players in the press as Mt. Piniella is fond of doing. All told, he kept his team above .500 in what could have been a total collapse under a different manager.

The Angels now have a chance to be a factor in 2001 and for a couple years after that. Whether Scioscia will be able to mount a serious challenge lies in the hands of the front office, which will hem and haw and wait until the opportunity has passed.

HITTERS (BA: .270, OBP: .340, SLG: .440, EqA: .260)

Alfredo Amezaga   2B/SS   Bats R   Age 23

YEAR	TEAM	LGE	AB	H	DB	TP	HR	BB	SO	R	RBI	SB	CS	OUT	BA	OBP	SLG	EQA	EQR	DEFENSE			
1999	Butte	Pio	33	7	1	0	0	3	6	5	3	2	1	27	.212	.285	.242	.182	2				
1999	Boise	Nwn	203	50	5	3	1	13	32	27	17	4	1	154	.246	.298	.315	.208	15	39-2B	-3	10-SS	-1
2000	Lk Elsin	Cal	429	102	12	3	3	41	73	50	30	23	9	336	.238	.307	.301	.212	35	90-2B	-4	14-SS	3
2001	Anaheim	AL	234	57	6	2	1	21	48	31	18	12	4	181	.244	.306	.299	.214	19				

In his first full season of pro ball, Alfredo Amezaga didn't hit for average, take walks, or show power. He can steal bases but was old for the California League and struggled. The Angels still have Amezaga at shortstop in the hopes he can fill their yawning void at the position in 2003. He's a better bet to get hung up at Double-A and never be seen again.

Garret Anderson   CF   Bats L   Age 29

YEAR	TEAM	LGE	AB	H	DB	TP	HR	BB	SO	R	RBI	SB	CS	OUT	BA	OBP	SLG	EQA	EQR	DEFENSE	
1998	Anaheim	AL	621	187	41	7	17	28	71	63	79	7	3	437	.301	.332	.472	.264	78	134-RF	15
1999	Anaheim	AL	616	189	35	2	22	28	74	86	77	3	4	431	.307	.337	.477	.266	78	153-CF	13
2000	Anaheim	AL	645	186	38	3	37	16	79	88	112	7	7	466	.288	.306	.529	.265	84	140-CF	2
2001	Anaheim	AL	618	181	35	2	30	31	81	90	116	8	4	441	.293	.327	.502	.273	86		

The home runs were the only thing to go up; his already-low OBP fell and even his batting average dropped. Because of this, his nominal career year really wasn't much better than his typical one. Garret Anderson will be able to hit like this for as long as he gets regular playing time. Look for about the same performance every year until, as with *Full House*, someone mercifully pulls the plug while no one is watching.

Larry Barnes   1B   Bats L   Age 26

YEAR	TEAM	LGE	AB	H	DB	TP	HR	BB	SO	R	RBI	SB	CS	OUT	BA	OBP	SLG	EQA	EQR	DEFENSE	
1998	Lk Elsin	Cal	187	40	7	1	6	15	50	23	24	1	0	147	.214	.274	.358	.209	15	46-1B	-3
1998	Midland	Tex	241	52	12	2	4	21	60	20	23	2	1	190	.216	.280	.332	.203	18	56-1B	2
1999	Erie	Eas	498	117	21	5	14	33	107	53	69	6	2	383	.235	.286	.382	.221	44	114-1B	12
2000	Edmonton	PCL	394	87	19	7	6	37	83	43	39	2	4	311	.221	.288	.350	.210	31	93-1B	-1
2001	Anaheim	AL	370	78	15	3	6	33	88	35	32	3	3	295	.211	.275	.316	.197	26		

(Larry Barnes *continued*)

He's not a prospect. Larry Barnes doesn't hit anywhere near as well as a first baseman must, and there's little evidence that he can. He was sent to the Arizona Fall League for no reason and didn't make himself a prospect there. The lack of depth in this organization buys him time.

Justin Baughman   SS   Bats R   Age 26

YEAR	TEAM	LGE	AB	H	DB	TP	HR	BB	SO	R	RBI	SB	CS	OUT	BA	OBP	SLG	EQA	EQR	DEFENSE			
1998	Vancouvr	PCL	223	62	9	3	0	10	28	28	13	19	6	167	.278	.317	.345	.232	22	46-2B	10		
1998	Anaheim	AL	196	52	10	1	1	5	32	23	20	8	4	148	.265	.287	.342	.209	15	55-2B	-3		
2000	Erie	Eas	126	30	2	1	1	5	23	10	5	6	1	97	.238	.270	.294	.192	8	18-2B	-2	13-SS	0
2000	Edmonton	PCL	301	64	7	1	1	23	42	32	28	17	4	241	.213	.280	.252	.186	18	74-SS	-4		
2001	*Anaheim*	*AL*	*268*	*63*	*9*	*2*	*1*	*18*	*56*	*27*	*20*	*7*	*2*	*207*	*.235*	*.283*	*.295*	*.197*	*18*				

Justin Baughman is an outstanding base stealer with blazing speed and good instincts. He reads opposing starters as easily as he does the *USA Today* children's edition. He just needs to learn to get on base any way he can—including taking ball four—to become the leadoff hitter the Angels need. It's not the kind of learning that takes place in this organization.

Mike Colangelo   OF   Bats R   Age 24

YEAR	TEAM	LGE	AB	H	DB	TP	HR	BB	SO	R	RBI	SB	CS	OUT	BA	OBP	SLG	EQA	EQR	DEFENSE	
1998	CedarRpd	Mid	86	20	5	0	3	8	17	9	5	2	1	67	.233	.305	.395	.234	9	13-LF	-2
1998	Lk Elsin	Cal	146	43	8	1	4	9	25	23	14	1	3	106	.295	.350	.445	.259	18	35-CF	3
1999	Erie	Eas	109	30	7	2	1	10	23	17	9	1	1	81	.275	.348	.404	.252	13	24-RF	-4
1999	Edmonton	PCL	102	31	5	1	0	11	17	10	7	1	1	72	.304	.379	.373	.259	12	20-LF	-1
2001	*SanDieg*	*NL*	*89*	*27*	*5*	*1*	*2*	*9*	*18*	*13*	*14*	*1*	*1*	*63*	*.303*	*.367*	*.449*	*.283*	*13*		

Once considered a future star, Mike Colangelo has missed the last season and a half to thumb and shoulder injuries. The Angels took him off the DL in October and lost him on waivers to the Padres two days later. Like the Angels, the Padres could use a real leadoff hitter, so there's opportunity if there's health.

Steve Decker   C/3B   Bats R   Age 35

YEAR	TEAM	LGE	AB	H	DB	TP	HR	BB	SO	R	RBI	SB	CS	OUT	BA	OBP	SLG	EQA	EQR	DEFENSE			
1998	Nashvill	PCL	62	8	2	0	2	4	15	4	4	0	0	54	.129	.182	.258	.106	1	18-C	0		
1998	Norfolk	Int	356	93	12	0	10	41	52	43	46	0	1	264	.261	.342	.379	.245	39	66-1B	1	20-C	-3
1999	Edmonton	PCL	223	49	13	1	9	34	40	34	31	0	0	174	.220	.328	.408	.248	27	32-3B	-1	14-1B	1
1999	Anaheim	AL	62	15	6	0	0	13	8	5	5	0	0	47	.242	.381	.339	.256	8	13-C	-1		
2000	Edmonton	PCL	161	38	7	1	5	30	24	20	22	0	0	123	.236	.361	.385	.257	21	15-C	-2		
2000	Sacramen	PCL	244	56	5	0	4	25	44	16	32	1	1	189	.230	.301	.299	.202	17	33-1B	0	11-C	-2

Steve Decker had the best on-base percentage of any Angels minor leaguer who got significant playing time above rookie ball, and he had some power to boot. He finished the season with the Sacramento RiverCats, the A's Triple-A affiliate. Decker, as he's been for years, would be a great addition to a team needing a right-handed-hitting backup at a few positions—the 2000 Mariners, for instance. It's now irrelevant, as Decker retired in the off season.

Gary DiSarcina   SS   Bats R   Age 33

YEAR	TEAM	LGE	AB	H	DB	TP	HR	BB	SO	R	RBI	SB	CS	OUT	BA	OBP	SLG	EQA	EQR	DEFENSE	
1998	Anaheim	AL	550	162	41	3	3	20	45	73	55	9	6	394	.295	.328	.396	.242	57	157-SS	3
1999	Anaheim	AL	271	63	8	1	1	12	29	31	28	2	2	210	.232	.270	.280	.175	14	81-SS	4
2000	Anaheim	AL	38	15	2	0	1	0	3	6	10	0	1	24	.395	.411	.526	.300	6	12-SS	2
2001	*Anaheim*	*AL*	*298*	*81*	*14*	*1*	*3*	*19*	*32*	*34*	*34*	*3*	*3*	*220*	*.272*	*.315*	*.356*	*.227*	*27*		

A bum shoulder limited him to 12 games, after which Gary DiSarcina finally had surgery and spent the rest of the season on the DL. If he's healthy, he'll be a replacement-level player. If he's injured, the Angels will be playing Benji Gil. Pick your poison.

American League

David Eckstein — 2B — Bats R — Age 26

YEAR	TEAM	LGE	AB	H	DB	TP	HR	BB	SO	R	RBI	SB	CS	OUT	BA	OBP	SLG	EQA	EQR	DEFENSE			
1998	Sarasota	Fla	511	126	26	2	2	65	58	64	40	16	8	393	.247	.346	.317	.233	52	110-2B	3	13-SS	5
1999	Trenton	Eas	495	131	20	3	4	67	52	80	39	15	7	371	.265	.368	.341	.250	58	126-2B	2		
2000	Pawtuckt	Int	427	98	9	0	4	50	47	66	29	8	6	335	.230	.332	.279	.214	35	112-2B	6		
2000	Edmonton	PCL	51	14	4	0	3	7	1	12	6	3	2	39	.275	.399	.529	.300	10	13-2B	-3		
2001	Anaheim	AL	439	104	17	1	6	58	49	63	43	15	9	344	.237	.326	.321	.227	42				

Claimed on waivers from Boston in August, David Eckstein is an average defensive second baseman with good plate discipline and no power. Unless Adam Kennedy breaks something, Eckstein will be labeled a career minor leaguer. Eckstein/Kennedy would be a good gestalt second baseman.

Darin Erstad — LF — Bats L — Age 27

YEAR	TEAM	LGE	AB	H	DB	TP	HR	BB	SO	R	RBI	SB	CS	OUT	BA	OBP	SLG	EQA	EQR	DEFENSE			
1998	Anaheim	AL	536	162	39	3	21	42	69	84	82	16	5	379	.302	.359	.504	.284	82	64-LF	-2	58-1B	0
1999	Anaheim	AL	582	149	23	5	13	42	92	81	50	12	7	440	.256	.307	.380	.229	55	71-1B	7	69-LF	18
2000	Anaheim	AL	668	239	37	6	26	55	75	116	94	30	9	438	.358	.407	.548	.315	122	136-LF	16		
2001	Anaheim	AL	529	164	28	3	16	45	72	96	91	17	5	370	.310	.364	.465	.282	78				

Darin Erstad had a great season, finally managing to hit for power while controlling the strike zone. Keeping him in the outfield helped; anyone would get tired of being moved between left field and first base, year after year, while trying to shake off a nagging hamstring injury. I think the projection is low.

Ron Gant — LF — Bats R — Age 36

YEAR	TEAM	LGE	AB	H	DB	TP	HR	BB	SO	R	RBI	SB	CS	OUT	BA	OBP	SLG	EQA	EQR	DEFENSE	
1998	St Louis	NL	388	93	16	1	27	50	86	62	67	8	0	295	.240	.329	.495	.272	57	87-LF	-3
1999	Philadel	NL	516	129	28	4	16	77	106	100	70	10	3	390	.250	.348	.413	.259	67	126-LF	7
2000	Philadel	NL	344	84	15	1	19	31	68	50	34	4	4	264	.244	.308	.459	.249	41	83-LF	-1
2000	Anaheim	AL	81	19	2	1	6	19	16	14	15	1	2	64	.235	.380	.506	.286	14	20-LF	0
2001	Colorado	NL	389	111	20	2	20	63	83	75	79	6	2	280	.285	.385	.501	.268	52		

After years of carrying four starting outfielders, the Angels traded Jim Edmonds for Adam Kennedy, solving two problems. Later in the season, insecure, adrift, and not sure if they were contending or rebuilding, they made a trade for an old excess outfielder. Maybe Disney's *The Legend of Stoneman*, in the summer of 2002, will clear this up for us. Ron Gant signed with the Rockies, where he'll put up good raw numbers that amount to a .250 EqA.

Benji Gil — SS — Bats R — Age 28

YEAR	TEAM	LGE	AB	H	DB	TP	HR	BB	SO	R	RBI	SB	CS	OUT	BA	OBP	SLG	EQA	EQR	DEFENSE	
1998	Calgary	PCL	453	95	19	3	11	33	89	60	51	7	3	361	.210	.267	.338	.200	32	112-SS	-21
1999	Calgary	PCL	401	90	19	1	12	21	100	51	44	11	4	315	.224	.271	.367	.212	32	98-SS	-11
2000	Anaheim	AL	300	73	14	1	6	26	54	26	22	10	7	234	.243	.315	.357	.226	28	81-SS	-2
2001	Anaheim	AL	315	71	13	1	7	27	71	36	31	9	4	248	.225	.287	.340	.214	26		

"Woof woof!" "What's that, boy? Trouble up the middle?" It's sad that Benji Gil has to endure this kind of cheap humor, but did you know his real name is Romar? Beats Benji in my book. Anyway, this is what happens when you break the glass and deploy the emergency middle infielder for the whole season.

Troy Glaus — 3B — Bats R — Age 24

YEAR	TEAM	LGE	AB	H	DB	TP	HR	BB	SO	R	RBI	SB	CS	OUT	BA	OBP	SLG	EQA	EQR	DEFENSE	
1998	Midland	Tex	185	43	8	1	11	29	45	32	29	2	1	143	.232	.340	.465	.266	26	48-3B	-1
1998	Vancouvr	PCL	221	62	10	0	14	17	54	26	34	2	2	161	.281	.337	.516	.275	32	57-3B	3
1998	Anaheim	AL	165	38	6	0	2	14	45	19	24	1	0	127	.230	.291	.303	.199	11	45-3B	2
1999	Anaheim	AL	548	134	24	0	32	65	130	83	78	5	1	415	.245	.330	.464	.263	73	150-3B	8
2000	Anaheim	AL	555	158	32	1	49	105	148	113	96	14	13	410	.285	.400	.611	.316	115	151-3B	3
2001	Anaheim	AL	550	151	25	1	38	81	152	102	124	5	3	402	.275	.368	.531	.296	96		

(Troy Glaus *continued*)

Troy Glaus will soon be one of the best hitters in the AL as long as he continues to ignore the advice of hitting coach Mickey Hatcher. Hatcher told anyone who would listen that Glaus needed to become more "aggressive" at the plate, like success story Garret Anderson. Glaus took 112 walks and hit 47 home runs last season. Hatcher took 134 walks and hit 38 home runs... in his 11-year career.

Elpidio Guzman   CF   Bats L   Age 22

YEAR	TEAM	LGE	AB	H	DB	TP	HR	BB	SO	R	RBI	SB	CS	OUT	BA	OBP	SLG	EQA	EQR	DEFENSE
1998	Butte	Pio	287	65	11	2	5	8	52	28	28	12	5	227	.226	.249	.331	.190	18	69-CF -4
1999	CedarRpd	Mid	529	120	22	7	4	24	92	45	32	20	9	418	.227	.262	.318	.192	34	127-CF -11
2000	Lk Elsin	Cal	541	129	17	9	9	37	120	59	49	17	6	418	.238	.289	.353	.216	46	133-CF -1
2001	Anaheim	AL	489	122	19	6	7	37	108	63	52	17	7	374	.249	.302	.356	.226	46	

Elpidio Guzman is a fast and graceful player, but though he is improving, he's still not a serious prospect. He's a great base runner who hit almost as many triples as doubles. As long as he keeps working on his strike-zone judgment and power, he'll make strides in this thin organization.

Nathan Haynes   CF   Bats L   Age 21

YEAR	TEAM	LGE	AB	H	DB	TP	HR	BB	SO	R	RBI	SB	CS	OUT	BA	OBP	SLG	EQA	EQR	DEFENSE
1998	Modesto	Cal	514	114	14	3	1	38	142	59	30	19	10	409	.222	.278	.267	.183	29	112-CF -13
1999	Lk Elsin	Cal	109	28	5	2	1	8	20	11	9	4	2	83	.257	.310	.367	.229	10	26-CF -1
1999	Visalia	Cal	144	35	5	0	1	11	28	17	9	5	4	113	.243	.303	.299	.202	10	34-CF -1
2000	Erie	Eas	458	102	15	2	5	24	116	41	32	21	12	368	.223	.269	.297	.188	28	112-CF -10
2001	Anaheim	AL	408	96	15	2	4	29	109	47	33	18	7	319	.235	.286	.311	.207	31	

The Angels' hopes that Haynes would be their center fielder and leadoff hitter in 2001 were tempered as the young outfielder took a step back last year. In his first full season after groin surgery, he reverted to hitting at his unimpressive 1998 level.

Bret Hemphill   C   Bats B   Age 29

YEAR	TEAM	LGE	AB	H	DB	TP	HR	BB	SO	R	RBI	SB	CS	OUT	BA	OBP	SLG	EQA	EQR	DEFENSE
1998	Vancouvr	PCL	156	36	10	1	3	10	33	13	9	0	1	121	.231	.277	.365	.208	12	36-C -5
1999	Edmonton	PCL	241	60	13	1	4	24	59	21	21	1	0	181	.249	.324	.361	.233	24	52-C -1
2000	Edmonton	PCL	146	33	6	1	4	15	31	15	14	0	0	113	.226	.298	.363	.221	13	35-C -5
2000	Erie	Eas	209	41	6	2	3	15	48	24	17	0	1	169	.196	.252	.287	.169	10	52-C -6
2001	Anaheim	AL	286	62	10	1	5	30	71	28	27	0	0	224	.217	.291	.311	.205	21	

Bret Hemphill didn't get a whole lot of respect from the Angels before his 1998 shoulder injury. Since then, he's been passed by Ben Molina and Shawn Wooten in the organization. He'd make a decent backup catcher but needs to get lucky to have a shot at a career.

Gary Johnson   LF   Bats L   Age 25

YEAR	TEAM	LGE	AB	H	DB	TP	HR	BB	SO	R	RBI	SB	CS	OUT	BA	OBP	SLG	EQA	EQR	DEFENSE
1999	Boise	Nwn	262	62	12	1	1	20	49	33	27	2	1	201	.237	.293	.302	.198	18	66-RF -5
2000	Lk Elsin	Cal	270	71	13	1	9	26	63	35	37	4	2	201	.263	.332	.419	.251	32	66-LF -6
2000	Erie	Eas	260	60	8	2	8	26	70	33	39	2	2	202	.231	.305	.369	.225	24	60-LF -9
2001	Anaheim	AL	334	85	16	1	9	37	94	47	46	3	2	251	.254	.329	.389	.246	38	

Gary Johnson preyed on high-A pitching, but those kids were five to seven years his junior. Promoted to Double-A, he slipped noticeably. He needs to prove he can hit against his age group before he'll be taken seriously outside of the Angels organization.

American League

Adam Kennedy — 2B — Bats L — Age 25

YEAR	TEAM	LGE	AB	H	DB	TP	HR	BB	SO	R	RBI	SB	CS	OUT	BA	OBP	SLG	EQA	EQR	DEFENSE			
1998	Pr Willm	Car	71	17	5	0	0	4	12	7	6	2	1	55	.239	.280	.310	.196	5	15-2B	-2		
1998	Arkansas	Tex	203	48	10	1	4	5	23	25	17	3	1	156	.236	.259	.355	.199	14	49-SS	-4		
1998	Memphis	PCL	302	81	18	5	3	9	41	28	32	11	3	224	.268	.291	.391	.228	28	59-SS	1	14-2B	-1
1999	Memphis	PCL	361	102	19	3	7	24	35	52	47	13	4	263	.283	.332	.410	.251	42	50-2B	-8	19-SS	-2
1999	St Louis	NL	103	26	10	1	1	1	8	12	15	0	1	78	.252	.273	.398	.214	8	27-2B	-5		
2000	Anaheim	AL	596	160	31	11	10	21	66	78	69	23	9	445	.268	.297	.408	.235	59	146-2B	4		
2001	Anaheim	AL	549	148	30	7	9	28	65	76	67	19	6	407	.270	.305	.399	.240	57				

For all the hoopla surrounding his performance, this wasn't a good season for Adam Kennedy. While he hit a lot of doubles, he didn't hit home runs, and he took a walk about once every five games. He isn't going to learn plate discipline unless he starts taking instruction from Troy Glaus instead of his "hitting" coach. Kennedy is young and should improve, hitting for a higher average and a little more power.

Keith Luuloa — IF — Bats R — Age 26

YEAR	TEAM	LGE	AB	H	DB	TP	HR	BB	SO	R	RBI	SB	CS	OUT	BA	OBP	SLG	EQA	EQR	DEFENSE			
1998	Midland	Tex	468	120	32	4	11	55	60	56	63	3	3	351	.256	.340	.412	.252	56	58-2B	-7	30-3B	5
1999	Edmonton	PCL	389	93	16	1	3	36	51	40	34	5	5	301	.239	.309	.308	.208	30	61-2B	0	37-3B	0
2000	Edmonton	PCL	268	56	16	1	6	23	31	30	32	1	2	214	.209	.275	.343	.202	20	27-3B	5	27-SS	1
2001	SanDieg	NL	319	74	13	1	7	34	42	39	38	3	1	246	.232	.306	.345	.231	32				

He never did hit in Triple-A but ended up with the Angels as a utility man. Keith Luuloa can play well at any infield position, so he'll stick around for a while. He was traded to the Cubs in August and signed with the Padres in December.

Ben Molina — C — Bats R — Age 26

YEAR	TEAM	LGE	AB	H	DB	TP	HR	BB	SO	R	RBI	SB	CS	OUT	BA	OBP	SLG	EQA	EQR	DEFENSE	
1998	Midland	Tex	149	41	4	0	6	10	8	18	24	0	0	108	.275	.328	.423	.250	17	33-C	-4
1998	Vancouvr	PCL	184	50	7	1	1	4	14	11	19	1	1	135	.272	.287	.337	.203	13	44-C	-3
1999	Edmonton	PCL	236	57	10	0	6	12	16	21	31	1	1	180	.242	.290	.360	.214	19	53-C	5
1999	Anaheim	AL	101	26	3	0	2	5	5	8	10	0	1	76	.257	.304	.347	.214	8	30-C	1
2000	Anaheim	AL	471	134	19	2	15	18	30	57	68	1	0	337	.285	.319	.429	.248	51	125-C	6
2001	Anaheim	AL	403	108	16	1	13	23	28	46	58	1	0	295	.268	.308	.409	.241	42		

While Ben Molina's translated statistics don't look good, consider that he was about average for his position offensively, played good defense, and is still improving. A left-handed-hitting backup would help, as Molina hit for much less power against righties. The Angels have invited Jorge Fabregas to spring training, hardly a solution.

Scott Morgan — LF — Bats R — Age 27

YEAR	TEAM	LGE	AB	H	DB	TP	HR	BB	SO	R	RBI	SB	CS	OUT	BA	OBP	SLG	EQA	EQR	DEFENSE	
1998	Akron	Eas	464	114	26	3	17	42	130	74	65	2	3	353	.246	.315	.425	.244	52	103-RF	-1
1999	Akron	Eas	349	81	18	1	18	26	106	52	47	3	1	269	.232	.287	.444	.239	38	80-LF	2
1999	Buffalo	Int	172	40	7	0	7	14	38	26	25	1	2	134	.233	.299	.395	.228	17	41-LF	3
2000	Buffalo	Int	34	11	3	0	0	5	7	4	3	1	0	23	.324	.422	.412	.295	5		
2000	Edmonton	PCL	318	68	19	1	7	23	78	39	39	5	2	252	.214	.271	.346	.204	24	82-LF	1
2001	Anaheim	AL	382	89	20	1	13	37	108	47	50	3	2	295	.233	.301	.393	.234	39		

Scott Morgan is a tall guy who has hit for some power in the past. A waiver pickup from the Indians, Morgan got through his second stint in Triple-A without much improvement. They say three times is a charm. It won't be. Designated for assignment by the Angels.

Orlando Palmeiro   LF   Bats L   Age 32

YEAR	TEAM	LGE	AB	H	DB	TP	HR	BB	SO	R	RBI	SB	CS	OUT	BA	OBP	SLG	EQA	EQR	DEFENSE	
1998	Vancouvr	PCL	142	37	9	2	1	12	11	16	22	2	1	106	.261	.318	.373	.233	14	34-CF	1
1998	Anaheim	AL	164	53	8	2	0	20	10	28	20	4	4	115	.323	.397	.396	.270	22	43-LF	1
1999	Anaheim	AL	314	88	12	1	1	36	27	44	22	5	5	231	.280	.364	.334	.242	33	73-LF	2
2000	Anaheim	AL	240	73	15	3	1	35	18	35	24	4	1	168	.304	.397	.404	.279	34	55-LF	0
2001	Anaheim	AL	228	63	10	1	1	34	20	39	27	4	3	168	.276	.370	.342	.252	27		

Ahhh, sweet lacquered bench. Returned to his fourth-outfielder role, Orlando Palmeiro's hitting returned to its 1998 level, and he continued to play average defense. He'll be a good role player for years to come.

Tim Salmon   RF   Bats R   Age 32

YEAR	TEAM	LGE	AB	H	DB	TP	HR	BB	SO	R	RBI	SB	CS	OUT	BA	OBP	SLG	EQA	EQR	DEFENSE	
1998	Anaheim	AL	461	143	25	1	29	89	89	86	89	0	1	319	.310	.425	.557	.322	94	19-RF	1
1999	Anaheim	AL	349	94	22	2	18	60	75	58	66	4	1	256	.269	.377	.499	.290	58	84-RF	6
2000	Anaheim	AL	560	165	34	2	35	97	127	103	92	0	2	397	.295	.404	.550	.311	107	119-RF	0
2001	Anaheim	AL	466	126	23	1	27	90	110	94	101	1	1	341	.270	.388	.498	.299	83		

Tim Salmon poured it on after the All-Star break, hitting .320/.415/.591 to wind up the second most valuable right fielder in the AL; no one noticed. He's healthy, so he's back to his 1998 level of performance, which is a great asset to the Angels' offense. His trade value will never be higher.

Scott Spiezio   UT   Bats B   Age 28

YEAR	TEAM	LGE	AB	H	DB	TP	HR	BB	SO	R	RBI	SB	CS	OUT	BA	OBP	SLG	EQA	EQR	DEFENSE			
1998	Oakland	AL	406	109	20	1	10	43	50	56	51	1	3	300	.268	.341	.397	.247	46	111-2B	0		
1999	Vancouvr	PCL	105	35	7	1	4	12	16	21	20	0	0	70	.333	.408	.533	.311	19	24-2B	1		
1999	Oakland	AL	246	61	18	0	11	27	33	30	34	0	0	185	.248	.327	.455	.258	31	34-2B	7	23-3B	-2
2000	Anaheim	AL	295	72	12	2	17	37	51	45	46	1	2	225	.244	.334	.471	.263	40	19-1B	-5	11-3B	-1
2001	Anaheim	AL	326	87	18	1	16	49	54	58	63	1	1	240	.267	.363	.475	.282	51				

He started just 26 games last year, most of them at first base, where his offensive numbers look terrible. Scott Spiezio also took turns starting at third base and in left field and subbed at second base and in right field. The Angels regard him as a sort of super-sub; we can thank Mike Scioscia that he didn't decide to play Spiezio at every position in one game.

Kevin Stocker   SS   Bats B   Age 31

YEAR	TEAM	LGE	AB	H	DB	TP	HR	BB	SO	R	RBI	SB	CS	OUT	BA	OBP	SLG	EQA	EQR	DEFENSE	
1998	TampaBay	AL	336	73	10	3	7	26	71	37	25	4	3	266	.217	.288	.327	.205	25	103-SS	14
1999	TampaBay	AL	252	76	11	2	1	21	37	37	26	8	7	183	.302	.364	.373	.250	29	76-SS	-9
2000	TampaBay	AL	112	29	7	1	2	18	25	19	7	1	2	85	.259	.371	.393	.259	15	32-SS	-3
2000	Anaheim	AL	228	45	14	3	0	29	49	20	15	0	3	186	.197	.294	.285	.192	15	62-SS	7
2001	Anaheim	AL	307	71	14	2	3	39	66	39	30	4	5	241	.231	.318	.319	.219	27		

One team's release is another team's starting shortstop. Hits lefties not quite as badly as he hits righties. That the Angels were excited to pick up Stocker off the transaction wire speaks volumes about the problem-solving ability of the organization.

E.J. t'Hoen   SS/3B   Bats R   Age 25

YEAR	TEAM	LGE	AB	H	DB	TP	HR	BB	SO	R	RBI	SB	CS	OUT	BA	OBP	SLG	EQA	EQR	DEFENSE			
1998	CedarRpd	Mid	453	87	12	1	15	35	138	42	40	4	2	368	.192	.255	.322	.188	28	125-SS	-19		
1999	Erie	Eas	188	36	8	1	2	9	55	14	17	3	1	153	.191	.235	.277	.159	8	15-3B	-2	15-SS	-4
2000	Erie	Eas	200	38	6	0	6	18	60	18	20	4	1	163	.190	.263	.310	.191	13				
2000	Edmonton	PCL	120	23	4	0	3	5	37	10	8	1	1	98	.192	.228	.300	.161	5	15-3B	2	14-SS	0
2001	Anaheim	AL	164	31	4	0	4	12	53	11	11	2	1	134	.189	.244	.287	.171	8				

To answer your question, he's from the Netherlands. E.J. t'Hoen showed promise back in 1998. Since then, he's split time between Double- and Triple-A and been successful at neither level. In most organizations, he never would have escaped A ball.

Mo Vaughn — 1B — Bats L — Age 33

YEAR	TEAM	LGE	AB	H	DB	TP	HR	BB	SO	R	RBI	SB	CS	OUT	BA	OBP	SLG	EQA	EQR	DEFENSE	
1998	Boston	AL	605	207	30	2	42	59	128	108	113	0	0	398	.342	.407	.607	.325	120	131-1B	12
1999	Anaheim	AL	520	148	18	0	35	49	116	62	105	0	0	372	.285	.357	.521	.286	81	67-1B	-3
2000	Anaheim	AL	609	168	25	0	39	72	165	89	113	2	0	441	.276	.366	.509	.287	98	143-1B	-18
2001	Anaheim	AL	536	151	20	0	34	69	145	90	117	0	0	385	.282	.364	.509	.291	88		

He's entering the third year of his six-year, $80-million contract, good money for a "268-pound," below-average first baseman who won't reach a .300 EqA again. Mo Vaughn's walks came back and his strikeouts kept increasing. The decline will continue; if his health goes, it will accelerate rapidly. He's already grumbling about how he wants to be traded back to the East Coast, where all his favorite strip clubs and lenient jurors are. The Angels can't replace him, so he won't be leaving. Worse yet, that projection is bunk now that we know he's going to miss at least the first three months with a ruptured tendon in his left arm.

Matt Walbeck — C — Bats B — Age 31

YEAR	TEAM	LGE	AB	H	DB	TP	HR	BB	SO	R	RBI	SB	CS	OUT	BA	OBP	SLG	EQA	EQR	DEFENSE	
1998	Anaheim	AL	337	89	14	2	7	30	61	42	46	1	1	249	.264	.328	.380	.238	34	102-C	-2
1999	Anaheim	AL	287	70	9	1	3	23	42	25	21	2	3	220	.244	.306	.314	.207	21	75-C	0
2000	Anaheim	AL	146	30	5	0	6	5	20	16	11	0	1	117	.205	.237	.363	.188	9	36-C	2
2001	Cincnnti	NL	206	49	6	0	5	18	33	23	26	1	1	158	.238	.299	.340	.213	17		

As Ben Molina's backup, he's been good at making Molina look impressive. Matt Walbeck won't be back in Anaheim, as the Angels have filled the backup-catcher-with-no-power-and-lousy-OBP slot by bringing in Jorge Fabregas. Walbeck, like most lifeless bodies, will resurface somewhere. Signed by Cincinnati, where he might back up.

Shawn Wooten — C — Bats R — Age 28

YEAR	TEAM	LGE	AB	H	DB	TP	HR	BB	SO	R	RBI	SB	CS	OUT	BA	OBP	SLG	EQA	EQR	DEFENSE	
1998	Lk Elsin	Cal	400	94	14	0	13	25	88	38	49	0	1	307	.235	.283	.368	.213	32	77-1B	4
1999	Erie	Eas	518	120	16	1	13	33	116	49	59	1	1	399	.232	.284	.342	.207	39	123-3B	7
2000	Erie	Eas	191	44	9	1	6	12	35	22	22	2	1	148	.230	.280	.382	.218	16	38-C	0
2000	Edmonton	PCL	246	71	16	2	7	12	41	30	27	0	0	175	.289	.327	.455	.257	29	47-C	-1
2001	Anaheim	AL	391	93	17	1	10	28	82	40	45	0	0	298	.238	.289	.363	.219	33		

Shawn Wooten is listed at 5'10", 205 pounds, and he looks like a big man behind the plate, more Damian Miller than Dan Wilson. He served time in the Tigers' system and the independent leagues before working all the way up through the Anaheim system for a cup of joe this year. He'd be well served by learning to hit left-handed to complement Molina. Heck, that might not be enough of a challenge for a guy who went from Moose Jaw to The Show.

PITCHERS (ERA: 4.50, H/9: 9.00, HR/9: 1.00, BB/9: 3.00, K/9: 6.00, KW: 1.00, PERA: 4.50)

Tim Belcher — Strains R — Age 39

YEAR	TEAM	LGE	IP	H	ER	HR	BB	K	ERA	W	L	H/9	HR/9	BB/9	K/9	KW	PERA
1998	KansasCy	AL	230.3	228	107	31	61	120	4.18	12	14	8.91	1.21	2.38	4.69	0.98	4.42
1999	Anaheim	AL	131.3	154	87	22	37	50	5.96	5	10	10.55	1.51	2.54	3.43	0.68	5.77
2000	Anaheim	AL	40.7	42	26	7	17	21	5.75	2	3	9.30	1.55	3.76	4.65	0.62	5.56

Tim Belcher made $4.6 million from the comfort of his home, spending most of the season on the 60-day DL repeatedly with elbow problems, for which he underwent surgery in July. The Angels wisely swallowed a $1-million pill in buying out the remaining year on his contract rather than paying him $5.1 million for an encore presentation.

Brian Cooper — Throws R — Age 26

YEAR	TEAM	LGE	IP	H	ER	HR	BB	K	ERA	W	L	H/9	HR/9	BB/9	K/9	KW	PERA
1998	Midland	Tex	153.7	210	134	41	61	91	7.85	4	13	12.30	2.40	3.57	5.33	0.75	8.17
1999	Erie	Eas	146.3	153	72	23	30	84	4.43	7	9	9.41	1.41	1.85	5.17	1.40	4.70
1999	Edmonton	PCL	29.3	29	18	1	10	21	5.52	1	2	8.90	0.31	3.07	6.44	1.05	3.74
1999	Anaheim	AL	27.7	22	12	2	14	14	3.90	2	1	7.16	0.65	4.55	4.55	0.50	3.72
2000	Edmonton	PCL	58.3	83	49	15	18	25	7.56	1	5	12.81	2.31	2.78	3.86	0.69	8.05
2000	Anaheim	AL	86.7	97	55	15	28	34	5.71	3	7	10.07	1.56	2.91	3.53	0.61	5.70

Batters scorched Brian Cooper from both sides of the plate, even in his Triple-A starts. The Angels should hand him the fifth starter job and let him sink or swim. Having him pitch at three levels for a third consecutive year is not going to do him any good, and if he can work out his inconsistency, he'll help this team.

Seth Etherton — Throws R — Age 24

YEAR	TEAM	LGE	IP	H	ER	HR	BB	K	ERA	W	L	H/9	HR/9	BB/9	K/9	KW	PERA
1998	Midland	Tex	46.0	55	34	10	12	23	6.65	1	4	10.76	1.96	2.35	4.50	0.96	6.27
1999	Erie	Eas	157.3	157	78	18	41	97	4.46	8	9	8.98	1.03	2.35	5.55	1.18	4.25
1999	Edmonton	PCL	20.3	24	12	7	6	13	5.31	1	1	10.62	3.10	2.66	5.75	1.08	7.53
2000	Edmonton	PCL	56.0	58	29	7	18	36	4.66	3	3	9.32	1.13	2.89	5.79	1.00	4.79
2000	Anaheim	AL	60.0	62	31	13	17	31	4.65	3	4	9.30	1.95	2.55	4.65	0.91	5.49

Tendinitis in his throwing shoulder put Seth Etherton on the DL in early August, and he never came back. The Reds would be well-advised to keep Etherton on a tight leash to prevent the problem from recurring. Taken care of, he'll be a solid pitcher and should come around this year. He's the high-upside candidate at the back of Cincinnati's rotation, fighting Elmer Dessens and Osvaldo Fernandez, among others.

Mike Fyhrie — Throws R — Age 31

YEAR	TEAM	LGE	IP	H	ER	HR	BB	K	ERA	W	L	H/9	HR/9	BB/9	K/9	KW	PERA
1998	Norfolk	Int	94.7	111	86	15	47	41	8.18	2	9	10.55	1.43	4.47	3.90	0.44	6.48
1999	Edmonton	PCL	107.3	87	49	9	44	71	4.11	6	6	7.30	0.75	3.69	5.95	0.81	3.56
1999	Anaheim	AL	51.3	56	27	7	17	25	4.73	2	4	9.82	1.23	2.98	4.38	0.74	5.21
2000	Edmonton	PCL	14.7	6	4	1	12	6	2.45	1	1	3.68	0.61	7.36	3.68	0.25	2.91
2000	Anaheim	AL	52.3	50	12	3	12	41	2.06	5	1	8.60	0.52	2.06	7.05	1.71	3.43

Mike Fyhrie's strikeout rate spiked, which helped him turn in a great season of relief in which he threw almost two innings an outing. There's talk that he may become a traditional setup man in 2001, but he's more valuable in his present role.

Shigetoshi Hasegawa — Throws R — Age 32

YEAR	TEAM	LGE	IP	H	ER	HR	BB	K	ERA	W	L	H/9	HR/9	BB/9	K/9	KW	PERA
1998	Anaheim	AL	95.3	80	32	12	27	67	3.02	7	4	7.55	1.13	2.55	6.33	1.24	3.62
1999	Anaheim	AL	76.7	74	38	12	27	42	4.46	4	5	8.69	1.41	3.17	4.93	0.78	4.82
2000	Anaheim	AL	95.0	93	36	9	30	56	3.41	6	5	8.81	0.85	2.84	5.31	0.93	4.17

A shade more than half of his appearances lasted longer than one inning. That suits Shigetoshi Hasegawa, who has done his best work in long relief. His only bad season came when the Angels tried to make him an eighth-inning setup man. As evidence that sample sizes are important, Hasegawa had a great year pitching at home, contravening three years of being significantly better away from Edison Field.

Anaheim Angels

American League

Mike Holtz — Throws L — Age 28

YEAR	TEAM	LGE	IP	H	ER	HR	BB	K	ERA	W	L	H/9	HR/9	BB/9	K/9	KW	PERA
1998	Anaheim	AL	30.0	37	16	1	13	27	4.80	1	2	11.10	0.30	3.90	8.10	1.04	5.40
1999	Edmonton	PCL	25.3	21	8	4	12	25	2.84	2	1	7.46	1.42	4.26	8.88	1.04	4.55
1999	Anaheim	AL	22.7	25	18	3	12	16	7.15	1	2	9.93	1.19	4.76	6.35	0.67	6.02
2000	Anaheim	AL	41.0	35	22	3	14	38	4.83	2	3	7.68	0.66	3.07	8.34	1.36	3.45

Mike Holtz should be a great left-handed specialist. Because he gets hung out to dry against right-handed hitters too often, his overall numbers look pretty bad. It's a shame, because used as an anti-lefty device, he's devastating.

John Lackey — Throws R — Age 22

YEAR	TEAM	LGE	IP	H	ER	HR	BB	K	ERA	W	L	H/9	HR/9	BB/9	K/9	KW	PERA
1999	Boise	Nwn	75.0	83	63	14	55	39	7.56	2	6	9.96	1.68	6.60	4.68	0.35	7.27
2000	CedarRpd	Mid	28.0	21	8	2	6	11	2.57	2	1	6.75	0.64	1.93	3.54	0.92	2.54
2000	Lk Elsin	Cal	91.7	98	69	21	46	40	6.77	3	7	9.62	2.06	4.52	3.93	0.43	6.62
2000	Erie	Eas	53.7	59	25	9	9	28	4.19	3	3	9.89	1.51	1.51	4.70	1.56	4.94

He led the Angels' organization in innings pitched (188) and faced 782 batters. Other than giving up too many hits, John Lackey posted decent ratios pitching at three levels. His workload is the only concern; if healthy, he's right behind Matt Wise and Scot Shields in this system.

Gilbert Landestoy — Throws R — Age 24

YEAR	TEAM	LGE	IP	H	ER	HR	BB	K	ERA	W	L	H/9	HR/9	BB/9	K/9	KW	PERA
2000	Boise	Nwn	58.3	50	32	3	25	22	4.94	2	4	7.71	0.46	3.86	3.39	0.44	3.57

Gilbert Landestoy is a 37th-round draft pick who put up an impressive line in his first season, which makes him a prospect in an organization this shallow. You'll note he's old for his level. He throws a high-80s fastball, a change-up, a slurve from a three-quarters delivery, and a sidearm slider. The Angels had a terrible rotation at Boise but used Landestoy as a setup man.

Al Levine — Throws R — Age 33

YEAR	TEAM	LGE	IP	H	ER	HR	BB	K	ERA	W	L	H/9	HR/9	BB/9	K/9	KW	PERA
1998	Oklahoma	PCL	50.0	48	35	9	19	19	6.30	2	4	8.64	1.62	3.42	3.42	0.50	5.11
1998	Texas	AL	57.0	62	25	5	13	18	3.95	3	3	9.79	0.79	2.05	2.84	0.69	4.34
1999	Anaheim	AL	83.3	70	33	11	23	35	3.56	5	4	7.56	1.19	2.48	3.78	0.76	3.66
2000	Anaheim	AL	95.0	91	36	8	39	40	3.41	6	5	8.62	0.76	3.69	3.79	0.51	4.32

In another overlooked middle-relief performance, Al Levine stranded inherited runners all season long and was quietly the best reliever in one of baseball's best bullpens. He will lead the revolt if the front office signs another Belcher/Hill type, thus further increasing his workload.

Matt Lubozynski — Throws L — Age 24

YEAR	TEAM	LGE	IP	H	ER	HR	BB	K	ERA	W	L	H/9	HR/9	BB/9	K/9	KW	PERA
1998	Boise	Nwn	26.3	18	6	2	8	11	2.05	2	1	6.15	0.68	2.73	3.76	0.69	2.59
1998	CedarRpd	Mid	17.7	24	21	15	6	6	10.70	0	2	12.23	7.64	3.06	3.06	0.50	13.51
1999	Lk Elsin	Cal	36.7	31	11	2	21	10	2.70	3	1	7.61	0.49	5.15	2.45	0.24	4.07
2000	Erie	Eas	77.7	90	52	14	27	42	6.03	3	6	10.43	1.62	3.13	4.87	0.78	6.06

While allowing a lot of hits, Matt Lubozynski cut down his walks and struck out more batters. He has spent time on two levels every year but 2000, when he was converted from relieving to starting. This is nearly as good as it gets for Angels prospects.

Mark Lukasiewicz — Throws L — Age 28

YEAR	TEAM	LGE	IP	H	ER	HR	BB	K	ERA	W	L	H/9	HR/9	BB/9	K/9	KW	PERA
1998	Syracuse	Int	44.7	38	19	9	24	20	3.83	3	2	7.66	1.81	4.84	4.03	0.42	5.32
1999	Syracuse	Int	92.7	107	59	22	41	52	5.73	3	7	10.39	2.14	3.98	5.05	0.63	6.94
2000	Syracuse	Int	38.7	37	20	9	25	37	4.66	2	2	8.61	2.09	5.82	8.61	0.74	6.61

Plucked from the Blue Jays, Mark Lukasiewicz has been throwing middle relief in the minors for years without sustained success. His strikeout numbers have always been good, reflecting his good stuff, but he has also walked a lot of hitters, belying his poor control. He's a decent gamble in case the team gets tired of Holtz.

Kent Mercker — Throws L — Age 33

YEAR	TEAM	LGE	IP	H	ER	HR	BB	K	ERA	W	L	H/9	HR/9	BB/9	K/9	KW	PERA
1998	St Louis	NL	155.3	189	93	11	48	58	5.39	6	11	10.95	0.64	2.78	3.36	0.60	5.17
1999	St Louis	NL	101.7	119	66	15	42	54	5.84	4	7	10.53	1.33	3.72	4.78	0.64	6.04
1999	Boston	AL	25.3	22	11	1	10	16	3.91	2	1	7.82	0.36	3.55	5.68	0.80	3.40
2000	Anaheim	AL	48.7	53	29	10	23	29	5.36	2	3	9.80	1.85	4.25	5.36	0.63	6.39

Kent Mercker turned down a $1.75-million option with the Red Sox for the lure of free-agent riches then ended up taking a minor-league deal with the Angels. He didn't like working from the bullpen, suffered a cerebral hemorrhage, and strained his rotator cuff in September, so by Labor Day that $1.75 million must have looked pretty good. Mercker hasn't been effective since 1997, and there's no sign he'll be able to turn it around.

Elvin Nina — Throws R — Age 25

YEAR	TEAM	LGE	IP	H	ER	HR	BB	K	ERA	W	L	H/9	HR/9	BB/9	K/9	KW	PERA
1998	Visalia	Cal	119.3	138	87	18	73	66	6.56	4	9	10.41	1.36	5.51	4.98	0.45	6.74
1999	Modesto	Cal	67.0	57	35	4	51	37	4.70	3	4	7.66	0.54	6.85	4.97	0.36	4.82
1999	Midland	Tex	28.3	34	21	1	19	11	6.67	1	2	10.80	0.32	6.04	3.49	0.29	6.07
1999	Erie	Eas	22.7	20	13	3	15	12	5.16	1	2	7.94	1.19	5.96	4.76	0.40	5.28
2000	Erie	Eas	53.7	50	33	5	26	18	5.53	2	4	8.39	0.84	4.36	3.02	0.35	4.54

Lucky as much as he was effective in Erie, Elvin Nina allowed two base runners an inning in three games at Edmonton but escaped with a 2.89 ERA and prospect status. He's pretty far back in line among Angels' pitchers, though the team may want to see him succeed as justification for the Randy Velarde/Omar Olivares dump that brought him here.

Ramon Ortiz — Throws R — Age 25

YEAR	TEAM	LGE	IP	H	ER	HR	BB	K	ERA	W	L	H/9	HR/9	BB/9	K/9	KW	PERA
1998	Midland	Tex	44.3	51	31	11	16	35	6.29	1	4	10.35	2.23	3.25	7.11	1.09	6.70
1999	Erie	Eas	95.0	91	42	16	39	53	3.98	6	5	8.62	1.52	3.69	5.02	0.68	5.10
1999	Edmonton	PCL	50.7	45	26	7	19	43	4.62	3	3	7.99	1.24	3.38	7.64	1.13	4.30
1999	Anaheim	AL	48.3	47	30	6	20	42	5.59	2	3	8.75	1.12	3.72	7.82	1.05	4.77
2000	Anaheim	AL	111.0	89	57	15	44	70	4.62	5	7	7.22	1.22	3.57	5.68	0.80	3.93
2000	Edmonton	PCL	85.0	72	48	8	36	54	5.08	3	6	7.62	0.85	3.81	5.72	0.75	3.89

Ramon Ortiz throws 95-mph heat, a deadly slider, and a good change-up. After his July recall, he was a completely different pitcher, throwing more first-pitch strikes and relying less on his fastball. Ortiz could break out this year, but a great 2002 season is certain.

Troy Percival — Throws R — Age 31

YEAR	TEAM	LGE	IP	H	ER	HR	BB	K	ERA	W	L	H/9	HR/9	BB/9	K/9	KW	PERA
1998	Anaheim	AL	66.0	44	27	4	31	80	3.68	4	3	6.00	0.55	4.23	10.91	1.29	2.89
1999	Anaheim	AL	56.3	35	19	7	17	55	3.04	4	2	5.59	1.12	2.72	8.79	1.62	2.63
2000	Anaheim	AL	50.3	40	23	6	24	47	4.11	3	3	7.15	1.07	4.29	8.40	0.98	4.04

Troy Percival came back from minor shoulder surgery to repair tears in his rotator cuff, labrum, and supraspinatus. He looked good before losing time and effectiveness to elbow inflammation and a persistent neck problem. If he can get healthy, we'll see a return to his glory days, but the injury bug seems to have acquired a particular taste for Percival.

Mark Petkovsek — Throws R — Age 35

YEAR	TEAM	LGE	IP	H	ER	HR	BB	K	ERA	W	L	H/9	HR/9	BB/9	K/9	KW	PERA
1998	St Louis	NL	101.7	125	60	9	33	45	5.31	4	7	11.07	0.80	2.92	3.98	0.68	5.47
1999	Anaheim	AL	81.3	78	32	5	17	41	3.54	5	4	8.63	0.55	1.88	4.54	1.21	3.40
2000	Anaheim	AL	79.7	79	33	7	18	30	3.73	5	4	8.92	0.79	2.03	3.39	0.83	3.85

He doesn't have much of a fastball, but it does move well, and his change-up is sweet. Mark Petkovsek is a good multi-purpose bullpen arm, another unrecognized player who makes his team better without appearing to do so. Signed by the Rangers, where the unsettled bullpen situation makes him a sleeper candidate for some saves.

Lou Pote — Throws R — Age 29

YEAR	TEAM	LGE	IP	H	ER	HR	BB	K	ERA	W	L	H/9	HR/9	BB/9	K/9	KW	PERA
1998	Midland	Tex	145.7	187	109	23	60	70	6.73	4	12	11.55	1.42	3.71	4.32	0.58	6.75
1999	Edmonton	PCL	143.3	160	77	21	45	74	4.83	7	9	10.05	1.32	2.83	4.65	0.82	5.39
1999	Anaheim	AL	29.0	22	8	1	10	19	2.48	2	1	6.83	0.31	3.10	5.90	0.95	2.74
2000	Edmonton	PCL	29.0	26	13	2	14	19	4.03	1	2	8.07	0.62	4.34	5.90	0.68	4.09
2000	Anaheim	AL	50.0	48	19	3	13	42	3.42	3	3	8.64	0.54	2.34	7.56	1.62	3.56

Another nice season by Lou Pote, building on a promising 1999. Pote spent eight years in the minors before his debut. Next time you hear someone lament the weakness of modern bullpens, remember that there are dozens of pitchers like Pote (and Ben Weber, below) waiting patiently.

Francisco Rodriguez — Throws R — Age 19

YEAR	TEAM	LGE	IP	H	ER	HR	BB	K	ERA	W	L	H/9	HR/9	BB/9	K/9	KW	PERA
1999	Butte	Pio	48.3	36	22	2	23	33	4.10	2	3	6.70	0.37	4.28	6.14	0.72	3.12
2000	Lk Elsin	Cal	58.3	47	35	5	35	42	5.40	2	4	7.25	0.77	5.40	6.48	0.60	4.22

Francisco Rodriguez had his second straight good season while advancing a level, though he put enough runners on to raise eyebrows. He throws a fastball reported to have hit 97 mph—more consistently around the mid 90s—and a sharp breaking slider, along with a decent curve and change-up. He's another one of these guys who is listed as six feet tall because there's prejudice against small right-handed pitchers. That's not at all important: Rodriguez can pitch.

Scott Schoeneweis — Throws L — Age 27

YEAR	TEAM	LGE	IP	H	ER	HR	BB	K	ERA	W	L	H/9	HR/9	BB/9	K/9	KW	PERA
1998	Vancouvr	PCL	167.3	179	115	28	72	90	6.19	6	13	9.63	1.51	3.87	4.84	0.63	5.76
1999	Edmonton	PCL	34.3	54	33	7	13	18	8.65	1	3	14.16	1.83	3.41	4.72	0.69	8.61
1999	Anaheim	AL	39.0	44	23	3	11	21	5.31	1	3	10.15	0.69	2.54	4.85	0.95	4.68
2000	Anaheim	AL	168.7	169	94	18	53	75	5.02	7	12	9.02	0.96	2.83	4.00	0.71	4.40

He made more starts than any other Angel as the veteran free agents fell apart. Scott Schoeneweis had a 3.15 ERA in April and never had a month below 5.40 afterwards. Schoeneweis would pitch very well for the first couple of innings (up to about 40 pitches), then get hit much harder as the game went on. He would be a great long-relief candidate if the Angels didn't have so many better options.

Scot Shields — Throws R — Age 25

YEAR	TEAM	LGE	IP	H	ER	HR	BB	K	ERA	W	L	H/9	HR/9	BB/9	K/9	KW	PERA
1998	CedarRpd	Mid	65.7	70	46	12	36	40	6.30	2	5	9.59	1.64	4.93	5.48	0.56	6.34
1999	Lk Elsin	Cal	99.3	88	39	2	50	57	3.53	6	5	7.97	0.18	4.53	5.16	0.57	3.71
1999	Erie	Eas	69.3	62	31	13	26	50	4.02	4	4	8.05	1.69	3.38	6.49	0.96	4.83
2000	Edmonton	PCL	156.0	154	111	19	79	111	6.40	5	12	8.88	1.10	4.56	6.40	0.70	5.18

Inconsistent and unpredictable, Scot Shields will follow a shelling with a three-hit shutout. He will throw a single pitch until an authority figure snaps him to. His palm ball, like Britney Spears, can be transfixing. And sometimes, like Spears, it asks to be hit just one more time. If he gets his head together with a little better control, he'll be outstanding.

Derrick Turnbow — Throws R — Age 23

YEAR	TEAM	LGE	IP	H	ER	HR	BB	K	ERA	W	L	H/9	HR/9	BB/9	K/9	KW	PERA
1998	Martnsvl	App	62.0	68	59	18	38	19	8.56	1	6	9.87	2.61	5.52	2.76	0.25	7.77
1999	Piedmont	SAL	144.3	139	87	20	72	69	5.42	6	10	8.67	1.25	4.49	4.30	0.48	5.18
2000	Anaheim	AL	39.0	34	17	6	29	24	3.92	2	2	7.85	1.38	6.69	5.54	0.41	5.77

A Rule 5 draftee from the Phillies, Derrick Turnbow had pitched only one inning above high-A ball before 2000. Instead of letting Turnbow ride the pine all year or cursing him with a variety of Rule 5-related maladies such as Chris Kahrl Narcoleptic Dementia Disorder, the Angels let him pitch. He gave up a hit and a walk about every inning, mixed in with some promising moments. He'll return to the minors, most likely Double-A, and resume his career as a starter.

Jarrod Washburn Throws L Age 26

YEAR	TEAM	LGE	IP	H	ER	HR	BB	K	ERA	W	L	H/9	HR/9	BB/9	K/9	KW	PERA
1998	Vancouvr	PCL	85.3	85	49	11	52	46	5.17	3	6	8.96	1.16	5.48	4.85	0.44	5.69
1998	Anaheim	AL	72.7	65	35	10	23	44	4.33	4	4	8.05	1.24	2.85	5.45	0.96	4.13
1999	Edmonton	PCL	56.0	47	30	6	18	36	4.82	2	4	7.55	0.96	2.89	5.79	1.00	3.58
1999	Anaheim	AL	61.0	57	31	5	21	37	4.57	3	4	8.41	0.74	3.10	5.46	0.88	3.93
2000	Edmonton	PCL	29.3	33	12	2	13	13	3.68	2	1	10.13	0.61	3.99	3.99	0.50	5.16
2000	Anaheim	AL	83.3	59	30	13	29	47	3.24	5	4	6.37	1.40	3.13	5.08	0.81	3.46

Jarrod Washburn got his crack at the starting rotation and managed to spend significant time on the DL fighting problems with biceps, a rib-cage muscle, and a nasty stress fracture in his shoulder blade. Washburn was effective when healthy. He needs a rotation spot and excessive mothering by the team doctor.

Ben Weber Throws R Age 31

YEAR	TEAM	LGE	IP	H	ER	HR	BB	K	ERA	W	L	H/9	HR/9	BB/9	K/9	KW	PERA
1999	Fresno	PCL	82.0	73	34	7	31	42	3.73	5	4	8.01	0.77	3.40	4.61	0.68	3.87
2000	Fresno	PCL	74.3	70	30	8	20	45	3.63	4	4	8.48	0.97	2.42	5.45	1.13	3.94
2000	San Fran	NL	8.0	16	13	0	4	5	14.63	0	1	18.00	0.00	4.50	5.63	0.63	9.56
2000	Anaheim	AL	14.0	12	8	1	2	8	5.14	1	1	7.71	0.64	1.29	5.14	2.00	2.82

After wandering through the minor leagues and international ball for a decade and change, Ben Weber got a chance and acquitted himself well while in Anaheim. He will hang around, contributing as a one-plus inning reliever. Trust us: modeling isn't the guy's second career option.

Matt Wise Throws R Age 25

YEAR	TEAM	LGE	IP	H	ER	HR	BB	K	ERA	W	L	H/9	HR/9	BB/9	K/9	KW	PERA
1998	Midland	Tex	160.7	188	105	26	46	87	5.88	6	12	10.53	1.46	2.58	4.87	0.95	5.72
1999	Erie	Eas	92.0	103	52	13	24	44	5.09	4	6	10.08	1.27	2.35	4.30	0.92	5.16
2000	Edmonton	PCL	119.0	115	50	12	25	58	3.78	7	6	8.70	0.91	1.89	4.39	1.16	3.78
2000	Anaheim	AL	37.0	37	19	6	10	19	4.62	2	2	9.00	1.46	2.43	4.62	0.95	4.75

During one Triple-A start last season, Matt Wise struggled in the first inning, then figured out the strike zone's liberal size and set down 18 of the next 21 batters. He didn't walk any of them, got ahead of all but two, and went to three-ball counts just twice. Wise displayed amazing control with three pitches: a basic fastball, a great breaking ball, and a criminally deceptive change-up. He nailed the front corners of the plate with the breaking stuff and came right down the middle with the change to get batters swinging. He was able to adapt and make adjustments pitch-to-pitch and batter-to-batter.

Wise was shut down with elbow problems, which bodes ill, because he missed about half the 1999 season after straining his right elbow.

American League

Support-Neutral Statistics — ANAHEIM ANGELS — Park Effect: +3.8%

PITCHER	GS	IP	R	SNW	SNL	SNPCT	W	L	RA	APW	SNVA	SNWAR
Tim Belcher	9	40.7	31	2.6	3.6	.414	4	5	6.86	-0.6	-0.5	-0.1
Kent Bottenfield	21	127.7	82	6.1	8.2	.424	7	8	5.78	-0.5	-0.9	-0.0
Brian Cooper	15	87.0	66	4.2	6.8	.382	4	8	6.83	-1.3	-1.2	-0.5
Jason Dickson	6	28.0	20	1.9	2.3	.459	2	2	6.43	-0.3	-0.1	0.1
Seth Etherton	11	60.3	38	3.4	3.6	.488	5	1	5.67	-0.2	-0.1	0.4
Ken Hill	16	78.7	59	3.7	6.4	.368	5	7	6.75	-1.1	-1.2	-0.6
Scott Karl	4	16.3	17	0.6	2.0	.233	0	2	9.37	-0.7	-0.6	-0.5
Al Levine	5	18.3	13	1.2	1.5	.437	0	0	6.38	-0.2	-0.2	0.0
Kent Mercker	7	26.7	18	1.5	2.1	.420	1	2	6.08	-0.2	-0.3	-0.0
Ramon Ortiz	18	111.3	69	6.7	6.4	.512	8	6	5.58	-0.2	0.2	1.1
Mark Petkovsek	1	4.3	2	0.3	0.1	.730	0	0	4.15	0.1	0.1	0.1
Lou Pote	1	4.3	1	0.5	0.1	.866	0	0	2.08	0.1	0.2	0.2
Scott Schoeneweis	27	170.0	112	8.9	11.2	.443	7	9	5.93	-1.0	-1.2	0.4
Derrick Turnbow	1	3.7	0	0.5	0.0	.928	0	0	0.00	0.2	0.2	0.3
Jarrod Washburn	14	84.3	38	6.2	3.6	.632	7	2	4.06	1.1	1.2	2.0
Matt Wise	6	34.3	23	2.0	2.3	.463	3	3	6.03	-0.2	-0.2	0.2
TOTALS	162	896.0	589	50.2	60.2	.455	53	55	5.92	-5.0	-4.6	3.3

The Angels' rotation was not exactly a model of stability in 2000. By trying 16 different starters last year, Anaheim used the most since the Pirates' 18 starters in 1996. We might look at a rotation in disarray and see the instability as a sign of more bad things to come. That's not necessarily the case.

The Indians used 18 different starters in their terrible rotation of 1993; a year later, they began a run of fine starting pitching that has continued to the present. The Royals used 16 different starters in 1992; within a year they were consistently fielding rotations that were among the best in the game. In fact, if you take the 16 teams since 1992 that used 14 or more different starters and look at what they did the following seasons, you get some pretty surprising results. The unstable rotations, on average, improved by an impressive 5.7 wins the following years, going from an average SNVA of –4.3 during their unstable years to an average SNVA of 1.4 the following years. Needless to say, the Angels will be quite happy if that trend continues in 2001.

For a quick explanation of SN stats, see page 7.

Reliever Evaluation Tools

PITCHER	G	IP	R	ARA	APR	IRNR/G	EIRS/G	IRP	BRS	RRA	ARP
Juan Alvarez	11	6.0	9	13.07	-5.3	0.91	0.29	-1.1	0.9	16.90	-7.8
Mike Fyhrie	32	52.7	14	2.32	16.9	0.91	0.32	-0.1	1.5	2.81	14.0
Shigetoshi Hasegawa	66	95.7	43	3.92	13.6	0.55	0.21	-1.9	2.9	4.51	7.3
Brett Hinchliffe	2	1.7	1	5.23	-0.0	0.00	0.00	0.0	-0.6	1.57	0.7
Mike Holtz	61	41.0	26	5.53	-1.5	0.97	0.32	4.6	-5.8	3.30	8.6
Scott Karl	2	5.3	4	6.54	-0.8	1.00	0.21	0.4	0.0	5.60	-0.2
Al Levine	46	77.0	31	3.51	14.4	0.67	0.22	4.1	0.2	3.16	17.4
Kent Mercker	14	21.7	17	6.84	-4.0	0.64	0.17	-1.1	-1.2	6.73	-3.7
Troy Percival	54	50.0	27	4.71	2.7	0.06	0.03	-0.6	2.1	5.29	-0.5
Mark Petkovsek	63	76.7	37	4.21	8.4	0.68	0.25	0.9	1.2	4.48	6.1
Lou Pote	31	46.0	22	4.17	5.3	0.74	0.29	-1.0	-0.2	4.37	4.2
Derrick Turnbow	23	34.3	21	5.33	-0.5	0.70	0.28	1.0	2.0	5.78	-2.2
Bryan Ward	7	8.0	6	6.54	-1.2	0.14	0.03	0.2	0.4	6.56	-1.2
Eric Weaver	17	18.3	16	7.61	-4.9	0.47	0.15	-1.7	-1.2	8.05	-5.8
Ben Weber	10	14.7	6	3.57	2.7	1.20	0.44	1.8	1.2	3.33	3.0
Matt Wise	2	3.0	0	0.00	1.7	0.00	0.00	0.0	0.0	0.00	1.7
TOTALS	441	552.0	280	4.42	47.6	0.64	0.23			4.52	41.6

For a quick guide to RET, see page 10.

Baltimore Orioles

Finally, several years too late and with great reluctance, the Orioles faced up to the need to rebuild the team. They started the 2000 season still relying on the same cast of players who had carried them to the AL East title in 1997. Even in 1997 they were an old team, the perfect example of one that needed to win now, and until fan interference by Jeffrey Maier cost them ALCS Game 2, they were on their way to the World Series. Roberto Alomar and Jeffrey Hammonds were the only regulars on that team under 30; the only players under 25 to appear in even a half-dozen games were Armando Benitez, Mike Johnson, and David Dellucci.

None of those players remain in the organization. Dellucci was left unprotected in the expansion draft and taken by the Diamondbacks. Alomar departed as a free agent. Hammonds and Mike Johnson were traded for Willie Greene and Everett Stull, respectively, neither of whom is still with the Orioles. Only Benitez, by being traded for Charles Johnson, contributed in any way, shape, or form to the 2000 Orioles.

In 1998, motivated perhaps by a plea from Cal Ripken, the Orioles tried to keep going with the same old team. The only position-player changes in 1998 were replacing Hammonds with Eric Davis in the outfield and Geronimo Berroa with Harold Baines at DH, thereby adding 15 years of age to the club. The more important change was replacing Davey Johnson with Ray Miller as manager, the result of a power struggle in the front office. Johnson lost, as did the Miller-led Orioles.

After the '98 season, the Orioles had no choice but to make some changes. Alomar, Davis, and Rafael Palmeiro were allowed to leave as free agents, while Chris Hoiles's bad back forced him into retirement. Although the Orioles had very little talent in their system, what little they had was at the positions vacated by Palmeiro and Alomar: first baseman Calvin Pickering and second baseman Jerry Hairston, both coming off good years at Double-A Bowie. Another club might have given one or both a chance, but the Birds instead decided to sign free agents Will Clark and Delino DeShields. Then, because it looked like the Yankees might get him, they signed Albert Belle to play right field, even though what they really needed was a center fielder so that Brady Anderson could move to a corner spot. Miller ran Benitez out of town (at least netting the team a new catcher), forcing the Orioles to pick up Mike Timlin to fill the now-vacant closer role. Taken together, the moves did almost nothing to offset the team's main problem: age.

The age problem carried right into year 2000. The Orioles started the season with the same team that had led them to fourth place in 1999, with the exception of an all-new but unimproved bullpen. The main problems with a team being this old are threefold.

First, old teams can't field. While older players tend to not make many errors (and the especially lenient official scoring at Camden Yards saves them from more), their range is diminished. Where this absolutely killed the Orioles was in the outfield, with their inability to hold runners to singles.

One indicator of this problem is the ratio between doubles/triples and hits. While the Orioles ratio of .217 looks no different from the league average of .216, the problem is disguised by their home park; last year, there were 46% more doubles and triples in Oriole road games than in Oriole home games. In road games only, the Orioles had by far the worst ratio in the league. As you can see in Table 1, the difference between them and next-to-last was larger than the spread between next-to-last and fourth.

Second, old teams are completely unable to manufacture runs and have no choice but to wait on home runs. We tend to downplay little-ball skills, and in strategic terms, it is a reasonable prejudice. However, the 2000 Orioles demonstrated just how boring, lifeless, and joyless a pure station-to-station approach can be. A team that hits only homers is

Orioles Prospectus

2000 record: 74–88; Fourth place, AL East
Pythagenport W/L: 70–92
Runs Scored: 794 (11th in AL)
Runs Allowed: 913 (12th in AL)
Team EqA: .258 (9th in AL)
2000 Batters' Age: 32.2 (oldest in AL)
2000 Pitchers' Age: 28.7 (tied for 7th oldest in AL)
Ballpark: Oriole Park at Camden Yards; moderate pitchers' park; Park Factor of .969
2000: The aging team continued to falter and was broken up at the trade deadline.
2001: The youth movement lasted less than four months. More money, more old players, more 75-win seasons.

Table 1: Comparison of Doubles/Triples-to-Hits Ratio in the American League

Team	DB+TP	Per H
Baltimore	203	.250
Seattle	172	.231
New York	164	.228
Tampa Bay	171	.227
Texas	188	.225
Boston	134	.223
Toronto	168	.221
Minnesota	166	.217
Kansas City	157	.216
Detroit	166	.216
Oakland	170	.213
Anaheim	147	.200
Chicago	149	.198
Cleveland	144	.197

not going to be very good, unless it hits a huge number of them.

You can estimate how many runs a team gets from home runs by using the following formula:

Runs on homers = HR * (1+OBP+OBP2+OBP3)

I should clarify that this isn't ordinary OBP, but a special left-on-base OBP: home runs and caught stealing are subtracted, yielding the formula

(H−HR+BB+HBP−CS)/(AB+BB+HBP−HR)

Call runs on homers ROH. A team's non-homer run efficiency would then be something like

(R−ROH)/(H+BB+HBP−ROH).

Under current conditions, this is normally around .290 or .300. For the Birds, it's been more like .280, as Table 2 shows. "Norm" is the team's run efficiency divided by the league's, and "Rank" is the normalized rank among all major-league teams (28 in 1997, otherwise 30). The 2000 Orioles just weren't able to piece together an offense, though, as you can see, there was some improvement after the deals at the trade deadline.

Third, old players are expensive. The way the major leagues are structured, young players are underpaid for their production while older players are overpaid. In order to get a reasonable return on investment, you have to offset the large salaries of older players with the very cheap production you get from rookies and other homegrown players.

At the moment, the salary structure of baseball makes itself conducive to a fairly simple analysis. We frequently use a statistic called "Runs Above Replacement" for evaluating

Table 2: Orioles' Non-Homer Run Efficiency, 1997–2000

Year	NHRE	Norm	Rank
1997	.282	.975	20
1998	.271	.914	29
1999	.282	.954	25
April–July 2000	.282	.940	25
August–Sept. 2000	.293	.977	19

players. It is a combination of their offensive and defensive ratings, weighted by position. By this yardstick, an average player is worth about 40 RAR for a full season. The best player in a given year is usually around 110, a little less than three times more than the average player; the worst players that manage to play for most of the year tend to score around 10–15, or about 30% of average.

The average salary in 2000 was just under $2 million. The minimum salary was $200,000, about a tenth the league average, while the maximum salary was around $16 million, or eight times the average. This means we have a structure in which the ratio of the salary to an average player is roughly the square of the ratio of the RAR to average, as Table 3 shows.

Table 3

Salary	RAR Value
$200K	13
$2000K	40
$16000K	113

Obviously, this is a very simplistic model. It is not meant to be a detailed system for setting actual salaries, but a quick approach to estimating value. For better or worse, players have generally been able to set their salaries based on their best season, not their average one. (For what it's worth, the method projects Alex Rodriguez to be worth $21 million per season, based on his 2000 performance).

Table 4 shows how the 2000 Opening Day Orioles stack up, using their best 1997-99 season to set their salaries.

You can apply this tool to the projected season rosters listed in the *Baseball Weekly* preview issue last spring, changing it only when BW clearly missed on who would be the primary player at the position. By this mark, the Orioles' –9 million score was the worst in the AL, though they were beaten out by the Dodgers, Cubs, and Rockies for overall honors. The best team was the A's, at +19,795; the Cardinals, Mariners, Royals, and White Sox completed the top five.

Table 4

Player	Best RAR	Value (000s)	2000 Salary (000s)	Value-Salary (000s)
Mike Bordick	71	6301	3083	3218
Albert Belle	108	14580	13000	1580
B.J. Surhoff	67	5611	4333	1278
Harold Baines	38	1805	2000	-195
Brady Anderson	72	6480	7200	-720
Jeff Conine	28	980	2500	-1520
Charles Johnson	43	2311	4600	-2289
Will Clark	51	3251	6000	-2749
Delino DeShields	33	1361	4333	-2972
Cal Ripken	36	1620	6300	-4680
Total				-9049

The real blowout for the Orioles is Cal Ripken. Of course, there's a pretty fair argument that he's worth far more to the team right now as an icon than as a player, so his salary isn't so far out of line. Mike Bordick was the only serious bargain, and a lucky one at that, as his performance prior to 1998 justified a mere $1.5 million salary.

Every player in Table 4 had a best season that was well removed from his three-year average. Not only were the Orioles overpaying for each player's best season, they were generally getting a performance far below that peak. Brady Anderson, for instance, had seasons of 38 and 39 RAR to go with his 72; B.J. Surhoff had a 47 and a 37; Albert Belle had an 81 and a 39; Will Clark had a 28. That's what comes of acquiring old players: it's buying into a declining market.

Compare the Orioles to the Yankees. Sure, the Bronx Bombers are overpaying for Paul O'Neill and Tino Martinez and even Bernie Williams. But Jorge Posada and Derek Jeter are both bargains, and the Yankees started the year with a very cheap DH (Jim Leyritz was signed for only $1 million) and left fielder (Ricky Ledee at $240,000). They didn't get much production from those spots, but didn't overpay for what they got.

At the end of July, with the Orioles below .500 and well out of contention, they finally committed to a player purge. Will Clark, Mike Bordick, Mike Timlin, B.J. Surhoff, Charles Johnson, and Harold Baines made their ways into the playoffs by leaving town. The Orioles weren't able to get much in return: all of the departing players were old, several would be free agents at the end of the season, and none of the ones who weren't had a good (from a buyer's perspective) contract for the future. The Orioles came out of the purge with a serviceable catcher, a decent utility player, one solid but injury-prone pitching prospect, and a pile of hope-they-turn-outs; they then spent the last two months of the season using a collection of not-readies from their minor-league system.

In some ways, it was a more interesting team after the breakup. They could score runs the old-fashioned way, for instance, even if they didn't do so very often. Their run scoring was down 10% compared to the first half, and to do even that well they needed two routs in the closing days of the season. They started stealing bases much more often and wound up leading the American League in that department. The defense was much improved; Orioles' pitchers gave up a run and a hit less per game in August and September than before.

It isn't really worth analyzing the post-breakup team in detail, however, because it is so unlikely that anything like it will be allowed into Camden Yards again. The Orioles were unable to sign any premier free agents over the winter, and they lost their own Mike Mussina. Rather than see if the minor successes of late 2000 could be replicated in 2001, the Birds went back to their old playbook, signing mid-market, aging, past-peak free agents David Segui, Mike Bordick, and Pat Hentgen for a combined $15 million per year.

Peter Angelos, the Orioles' owner, made his substantial fortune as a labor attorney, most notably as the lead attorney in a class-action suit brought by shipyard employees and others regarding asbestos exposure. Whether consciously or not, he appears to bring several philosophies from the labor field into his role as owner.

First, he is willing to pay his employees handsomely. The Orioles have been one of the highest-salaried teams in baseball year-in and year-out since Angelos bought the team. Labor lesson: good management doesn't try to shortchange employees' compensation. Second, he seems to regard the fans who come to Camden Yards as if they were employees at the Oriole factory, not customers. Labor lesson: good management doesn't close down a plant. Both are pretty good lessons from a fan's point of view, but sometimes factories, like ballclubs, need to be re-tooled.

Angelos's third carryover from labor is more problematic. He apparently believes that something like a union salary scale, driven by seniority but without much range, is an appropriate model for the baseball industry. His willingness to carry a large payroll for the team does not translate into a willingness to pay top dollar for premium talent. Instead, the Orioles have repeatedly paid premium prices for veterans who have "paid their dues" in the majors like Clark, DeShields, and Anderson. In only one instance—Albert Belle—did Angelos pay the going rate for a legitimate star, and it now looks like Belle's hip is going to turn that into a very bad deal.

American League

That philosophy is behind Angelos's off-season statement, regarding Mussina, that the team can't "place such a large percentage of our resources in one player." The statement also removed the Orioles from competition for Alex Rodriguez or Manny Ramirez. Angelos, having been recently burned, is in no mood to accept any risk.

But you have to take risks; otherwise you become the Minnesota Twins. The trick is in telling the difference between a good risk and a bad risk. Players with no histories of injury, players signed to good-value contracts, players under 30 who have had a good year or two (even if last year was bad) on cheap contracts—those are reasonable risks. Bad risks are players with lengthy DL rap sheets, players over 30 showing signs of slippage, players coming off years like they've never had before and may never have again, and players who receive over-sized contracts in the hope that they'll play up to them.

There's no reason to believe the Orioles know the difference between good and bad risks, and therefore no reason to believe they will be competitive in the near future.

HITTERS (BA: .270, OBP: .340, SLG: .440, EqA: .260)

Brady Anderson — OF — Bats L — Age 37

YEAR	TEAM	LGE	AB	H	DB	TP	HR	BB	SO	R	RBI	SB	CS	OUT	BA	OBP	SLG	EQA	EQR	DEFENSE	
1998	Baltimor	AL	480	120	27	3	21	74	69	86	53	18	6	366	.250	.366	.450	.276	73	122-CF	-6
1999	Baltimor	AL	560	163	29	4	26	91	96	106	80	34	7	404	.291	.409	.496	.307	106	136-CF	0
2000	Baltimor	AL	503	132	19	0	22	86	94	85	49	17	11	382	.262	.379	.431	.274	75	122-CF	-3
2001	Baltimor	AL	458	109	15	1	19	88	87	85	71	12	3	352	.238	.361	.400	.270	67		

After the salary purge, Brady Anderson was moved out of center field in favor of Luis Matos and Eugene Kingsale. It should be a permanent move; while he still has enough range to play a corner outfield spot, he's lost too much speed to cut off balls in the gap from center field. He might make it through one more year at the top of the order, but it's hard to believe he can continue much longer in such a high-profile role.

Albert Belle — RF/DH — Bats R — Age 34

YEAR	TEAM	LGE	AB	H	DB	TP	HR	BB	SO	R	RBI	SB	CS	OUT	BA	OBP	SLG	EQA	EQR	DEFENSE	
1998	ChiSox	AL	608	207	42	2	55	80	75	116	155	5	4	405	.340	.418	.688	.343	140	151-LF	4
1999	Baltimor	AL	606	186	31	1	41	95	75	106	117	16	3	423	.307	.406	.564	.317	120	135-RF	0
2000	Baltimor	AL	557	160	33	1	26	46	62	69	101	0	6	403	.287	.346	.490	.271	77	101-RF	-6
2001	Baltimor	AL	473	133	23	1	28	69	60	86	102	3	3	343	.281	.373	.512	.297	82		

Albert Belle began to complain of hip problems last spring and was eventually forced out of the lineup for six weeks. Neither he nor the Orioles seem willing to talk about it, but it appears to be a condition similar to the one that ended Bo Jackson's football career. Last year, it was clearly sapping Belle's power and his ability to run. If it is in fact a degenerative condition, then it's not likely to get any better. At the least, it would keep him from playing the field; at worst, it could cost him his career and his chance at the Hall of Fame.

There's the secondary issue of his contract and the insurance that covers it if he is unable to play at all. Given a choice, the Orioles might encourage him to sit out rather than play crippled.

Larry Bigbie — OF — Bats L — Age 23

YEAR	TEAM	LGE	AB	H	DB	TP	HR	BB	SO	R	RBI	SB	CS	OUT	BA	OBP	SLG	EQA	EQR	DEFENSE	
1999	Delmarva	SAL	174	39	8	2	1	22	44	14	19	1	0	135	.224	.311	.310	.213	14	32-LF	0
2000	Frederck	Car	207	53	4	0	3	17	35	25	22	3	2	156	.256	.313	.319	.213	16	53-RF	-1
2000	Bowie	Eas	114	26	5	0	0	8	30	9	4	2	0	88	.228	.279	.272	.184	6	30-LF	0
2001	Baltimor	AL	208	50	2	0	3	24	56	23	20	2	1	159	.240	.319	.293	.217	17		

Larry Bigbie, along with Keith Reed, Brian Roberts, Rich Stahl, and Mike Paradis, was among the Orioles' seven first-round draft picks in 1999. So far, he's a wasted pick: lousy batting average, strikes out too much, very little power, no speed. Worst of all, he showed absolutely no improvement from 1999 and was badly overmatched when he was rushed up to Double-A Bowie.

Carlos Casimiro IF Bats R Age 24

YEAR	TEAM	LGE	AB	H	DB	TP	HR	BB	SO	R	RBI	SB	CS	OUT	BA	OBP	SLG	EQA	EQR	DEFENSE			
1998	Frederck	Car	486	102	19	5	13	22	100	37	48	4	3	387	.210	.245	.350	.190	30	110-2B	-6	14-3B	3
1999	Bowie	Eas	533	108	17	1	15	26	106	61	51	4	6	431	.203	.242	.323	.177	29	133-2B	-12		
2000	Bowie	Eas	293	68	9	1	6	17	71	36	25	1	2	227	.232	.276	.331	.197	20	84-3B	-8		
2000	Rochestr	Int	82	18	2	0	4	3	17	8	9	0	0	64	.220	.247	.390	.204	6	11-2B	0	10-3B	-1
2001	Baltimor	AL	376	82	13	1	10	24	89	31	37	1	1	295	.218	.265	.338	.202	27				

Another hitter who's making no progress at all. The only reason Carlos Casimiro played for the Orioles last year is that he was a warm, available body at nearby Bowie on July 31 when the Birds traded away a half-dozen players and needed to field a team. Casimiro has fair power for a middle infielder, but his isolated power numbers are trending downwards, and his strike-zone judgment indicators are flat.

Howie Clark UT Bats L Age 27

YEAR	TEAM	LGE	AB	H	DB	TP	HR	BB	SO	R	RBI	SB	CS	OUT	BA	OBP	SLG	EQA	EQR	DEFENSE			
1998	Bowie	Eas	279	68	9	0	8	22	44	30	36	1	1	212	.244	.304	.362	.222	25	44-LF	-3		
1998	Rochestr	Int	96	21	4	1	2	7	11	12	6	1	1	76	.219	.272	.344	.201	7				
1999	Bowie	Eas	127	32	2	0	2	7	13	12	9	1	0	95	.252	.300	.315	.207	9				
1999	Rochestr	Int	280	74	16	3	5	28	24	27	22	1	1	207	.264	.333	.396	.245	31	61-RF	0		
2000	Bowie	Eas	53	14	4	0	1	2	7	8	6	0	0	39	.264	.298	.396	.228	5				
2000	Rochestr	Int	192	51	4	0	4	21	15	21	19	2	1	142	.266	.340	.349	.237	19	23-2B	-4	13-RF	-1
2001	Baltimor	AL	268	68	8	1	5	25	29	30	32	1	1	201	.254	.317	.347	.230	26				

Howie Clark is an organization man who, after five years in Bowie, should consider finding a nice girl, buying a house, and settling down. He can play any position, a "gamer" in every sense of the word who just doesn't offer much offense. Clark might have caught on as a utility man; now he's a six-year free agent who's probably run out of time.

Ivanon Coffie 3B/SS Bats L Age 24

YEAR	TEAM	LGE	AB	H	DB	TP	HR	BB	SO	R	RBI	SB	CS	OUT	BA	OBP	SLG	EQA	EQR	DEFENSE			
1998	Frederck	Car	488	108	13	1	14	39	111	50	60	7	5	385	.221	.281	.338	.205	37	52-3B	-14	50-SS	-5
1999	Frederck	Car	283	68	14	2	9	19	64	26	38	3	2	217	.240	.293	.399	.228	27	51-3B	-2	12-SS	-6
1999	Bowie	Eas	199	36	7	2	3	14	48	18	19	1	1	164	.181	.237	.281	.160	8	49-3B	-1		
2000	Bowie	Eas	346	81	16	2	8	27	57	40	33	1	2	267	.234	.294	.361	.217	29	73-SS	-9		
2000	Rochestr	Int	79	18	1	1	0	1	22	4	9	0	0	61	.228	.245	.266	.151	3				
2000	Baltimor	AL	60	14	4	1	0	4	10	6	6	1	0	46	.233	.293	.333	.212	5	12-3B	2		
2001	Baltimor	AL	471	106	18	2	10	39	105	46	48	3	2	367	.225	.284	.335	.212	38				

Like several other Oriole farmhands, Ivanon Coffie was rushed up from Bowie to fill in when both Ryan Minor and Cal Ripken were injured. He lasted about a month before heading down to Rochester, then came back up when rosters expanded. He's shown some power at lower levels but doesn't make contact often enough.

Jeff Conine 3B/1B/OF Bats R Age 35

YEAR	TEAM	LGE	AB	H	DB	TP	HR	BB	SO	R	RBI	SB	CS	OUT	BA	OBP	SLG	EQA	EQR	DEFENSE			
1998	KansasCy	AL	307	79	19	0	11	26	61	30	44	3	0	228	.257	.319	.427	.249	35	62-LF	3	11-1B	-1
1999	Baltimor	AL	443	133	28	1	15	26	36	53	75	0	3	313	.300	.343	.470	.265	57	91-1B	-2		
2000	Baltimor	AL	408	119	20	2	14	31	48	51	45	4	4	293	.292	.345	.453	.263	52	38-3B	2	37-1B	1
2001	Baltimor	AL	381	102	14	0	14	31	48	48	58	1	2	281	.268	.323	.415	.251	44				

Jeff Conine's role expanded last season when he was forced to be a third baseman, with Cal Ripken hurt and the parade of minor leaguers not cutting it. His performance against right-handers fell off considerably, from a steady EqA of .260ish to .235, but he made up for it by pounding left-handers for a .320 EqA. He doesn't have a recent history of large platoon splits, though if you go back to the early 1990s, you'll see he crushed lefties.

American League

Delino DeShields — LF/2B — Bats L — Age 32

YEAR	TEAM	LGE	AB	H	DB	TP	HR	BB	SO	R	RBI	SB	CS	OUT	BA	OBP	SLG	EQA	EQR	DEFENSE			
1998	St Louis	NL	427	122	22	7	8	54	57	75	44	24	10	315	.286	.366	.426	.270	59	102-2B	-6		
1999	Baltimor	AL	329	88	13	2	6	34	47	45	33	10	8	249	.267	.338	.374	.240	35	85-2B	-9		
2000	Baltimor	AL	558	169	42	5	11	62	75	82	83	40	12	401	.303	.374	.455	.282	85	90-2B	-7	39-LF	-2
2001	*Baltimor*	*AL*	*461*	*122*	*25*	*4*	*7*	*60*	*69*	*82*	*57*	*20*	*10*	*349*	*.265*	*.349*	*.382*	*.258*	*59*				

You know how you get "tied" to a certain player for a year? How one player always seems to play well when you're at the ballpark? Delino DeShields was that player for me last year. He did return to being the good DeShields last year, in keeping with a schizophrenic stretch of seasons in which he has bounced from the .230s to the .280s. His fielding is totally shot, so he's probably through with second base. He didn't look good in the outfield, either, but then again, he'd never played there before.

Brook Fordyce — C — Bats R — Age 31

YEAR	TEAM	LGE	AB	H	DB	TP	HR	BB	SO	R	RBI	SB	CS	OUT	BA	OBP	SLG	EQA	EQR	DEFENSE
1998	Cincnnti	NL	147	37	6	0	4	11	26	8	14	0	1	111	.252	.304	.374	.223	13	41-C 0
1999	ChiSox	AL	331	100	24	1	10	18	44	35	48	2	0	231	.302	.343	.471	.269	44	92-C -2
2000	Charlott	Int	67	14	2	0	2	6	15	7	10	0	1	54	.209	.274	.328	.193	4	12-C -3
2000	ChiSox	AL	124	34	7	1	5	5	21	17	20	0	0	90	.274	.313	.468	.255	15	37-C 3
2000	Baltimor	AL	176	58	10	0	10	9	25	22	27	0	0	118	.330	.369	.557	.299	29	48-C -7
2001	*Baltimor*	*AL*	*302*	*81*	*12*	*0*	*11*	*21*	*51*	*36*	*46*	*0*	*0*	*221*	*.268*	*.316*	*.417*	*.250*	*34*	

Let's see: the Orioles had Charles Johnson, who would be a free agent after the 2000 season and was, the Orioles felt, unsignable. So they traded him for Brook Fordyce, who doesn't hit or field as well as Johnson and is older. Then they rewarded a half-season of great hitting with a three-year deal. By 2004, Fordyce will probably be hitting like Dan Wilson.

Karim Garcia — OF — Bats L — Age 25

YEAR	TEAM	LGE	AB	H	DB	TP	HR	BB	SO	R	RBI	SB	CS	OUT	BA	OBP	SLG	EQA	EQR	DEFENSE
1998	Arizona	NL	335	75	9	7	10	17	73	40	43	5	4	264	.224	.261	.382	.208	26	83-RF 3
1998	Tucson	PCL	104	27	3	1	7	13	24	15	18	4	1	78	.260	.342	.510	.280	16	27-RF 1
1999	Detroit	AL	287	69	10	3	14	17	61	37	30	2	4	222	.240	.283	.443	.232	29	66-RF 3
2000	Toledo	Int	156	43	5	1	13	8	33	26	31	1	1	114	.276	.321	.571	.281	24	39-CF -2
2000	Rochestr	Int	274	71	12	1	12	28	73	33	46	2	2	205	.259	.331	.442	.255	34	62-RF -3
2001	*Clevelnd*	*AL*	*339*	*86*	*10*	*2*	*19*	*33*	*85*	*47*	*62*	*2*	*1*	*254*	*.254*	*.320*	*.463*	*.256*	*42*	

The would-be prospect continues to fail completely in every major-league opportunity. The Orioles picked him up from the Tigers for "future considerations"; when they called him up in September, they had the cheap thrill of waiting out a suspension he'd earned as a Tiger in April. Karim Garcia is a free agent. Wherever he ends up, he'll be merely a Triple-A insurance policy against injury to a real outfielder.

Jerry Hairston — 2B — Bats R — Age 25

YEAR	TEAM	LGE	AB	H	DB	TP	HR	BB	SO	R	RBI	SB	CS	OUT	BA	OBP	SLG	EQA	EQR	DEFENSE			
1998	Frederck	Car	302	73	19	2	4	23	33	44	26	5	3	232	.242	.308	.358	.224	28	65-SS	10	14-2B	1
1998	Bowie	Eas	224	62	10	2	4	15	26	33	29	3	2	164	.277	.331	.393	.243	24	54-2B	0		
1999	Rochestr	Int	413	109	20	4	6	23	50	51	39	12	7	311	.264	.324	.375	.236	42	88-2B	-4	17-SS	-2
1999	Baltimor	AL	175	48	14	1	4	9	22	25	17	8	4	131	.274	.320	.434	.250	20	50-2B	6		
2000	Rochestr	Int	204	55	11	1	4	25	33	37	18	4	3	152	.270	.360	.392	.256	25	52-2B	1		
2000	Baltimor	AL	179	47	5	0	5	19	20	26	18	8	6	138	.263	.353	.374	.248	21	49-2B	9		
2001	*Baltimor*	*AL*	*487*	*129*	*24*	*2*	*9*	*44*	*68*	*67*	*61*	*9*	*5*	*363*	*.265*	*.326*	*.378*	*.244*	*53*				

He's the closest thing to a phenom the Orioles have. For two years in a row, injuries have kept him from challenging for the starting second-base job in spring training. In 2001, the job is his. Jerry Hairston Jr. is a solid contact hitter who showed much-improved patience last year. If he keeps it up, he'll become a legitimate leadoff option and a more valuable player.

Eugene Kingsale   CF   Bats B   Age 24

YEAR	TEAM	LGE	AB	H	DB	TP	HR	BB	SO	R	RBI	SB	CS	OUT	BA	OBP	SLG	EQA	EQR	DEFENSE			
1998	Bowie	Eas	435	103	10	4	1	36	81	54	29	16	8	340	.237	.307	.285	.204	32	111-CF	5		
1998	Rochestr	Int	55	12	0	1	0	3	8	2	2	2	2	45	.218	.268	.255	.165	3	16-CF	2		
1999	Bowie	Eas	273	57	12	3	2	24	48	34	18	7	5	221	.209	.274	.297	.189	17	67-CF	2		
1999	Rochestr	Int	191	53	3	0	3	10	23	24	17	7	7	145	.277	.321	.340	.219	16	47-CF	0		
1999	Baltimor	AL	85	21	3	0	0	4	12	9	7	1	3	67	.247	.295	.282	.183	5	20-CF	0		
2000	Baltimor	AL	88	21	3	1	0	1	13	13	9	1	2	69	.239	.247	.295	.162	4	24-CF	-1		
2001	*Baltimor*	*AL*	*253*	*64*	*6*	*1*	*2*	*17*	*44*	*23*	*24*	*1*	*1*	*190*	*.253*	*.300*	*.308*	*.208*	*19*				

Like some strange sort of lycanthrope, Eugene Kingsale is looking more and more like Curtis Goodwin. The slender Aruban has a history of being brittle; he missed most of 1996 and 1997 with injuries, and a torn leg muscle sidelined him through July last year. He's an asset in center field but overmatched at the plate.

Mike Kinkade   3B   Bats R   Age 28

YEAR	TEAM	LGE	AB	H	DB	TP	HR	BB	SO	R	RBI	SB	CS	OUT	BA	OBP	SLG	EQA	EQR	DEFENSE			
1998	Louisvil	Int	290	79	20	4	6	29	52	46	37	6	1	212	.272	.348	.431	.264	38	53-3B	-3	16-1B	0
1998	Norfolk	Int	125	33	4	0	1	1	24	10	16	4	1	93	.264	.291	.320	.206	9	28-3B	0		
1999	Norfolk	Int	311	85	18	1	5	15	32	41	37	4	1	227	.273	.314	.386	.235	30	33-3B	0	13-C	-1
1999	NY Mets	NL	46	9	1	1	2	3	8	3	5	1	0	37	.196	.273	.391	.223	4				
2000	Binghmtn	Eas	316	87	17	1	7	24	45	43	42	9	4	233	.275	.336	.402	.249	36	64-C	0	13-3B	-2
2000	Rochestr	Int	56	18	3	0	1	9	12	8	8	0	1	39	.321	.422	.429	.288	9				
2001	*Baltimor*	*AL*	*306*	*76*	*18*	*1*	*6*	*27*	*50*	*38*	*37*	*1*	*0*	*230*	*.248*	*.309*	*.373*	*.235*	*31*				

Mike Kinkade is a fair hitter, just not nearly as good as his lifetime .335 batting average in the minors suggests. He's always been old for his league (like last year; 27-year-olds shouldn't be playing in Double-A, even if they're winning batting titles), and his secondary skills are below average. His defensive reputation is hideous, but the numbers, surprisingly, don't look bad at all. He was in Double-A trying to relearn catching, a position he played in college, and threw out a respectable 43% of runners.

Jose Leon   3B   Bats R   Age 24

YEAR	TEAM	LGE	AB	H	DB	TP	HR	BB	SO	R	RBI	SB	CS	OUT	BA	OBP	SLG	EQA	EQR	DEFENSE			
1998	Pr Willm	Car	454	112	23	2	16	44	140	63	56	2	1	343	.247	.319	.412	.244	50	114-3B	3		
1999	Arkansas	Tex	337	69	11	0	14	18	124	28	40	2	2	270	.205	.253	.362	.198	24	67-3B	-2		
2000	Arkansas	Tex	297	69	12	2	11	9	69	31	29	1	1	229	.232	.262	.397	.212	24	46-3B	-4	18-1B	-4
2000	Bowie	Eas	69	16	1	0	1	2	14	5	5	3	1	54	.232	.265	.290	.185	4	16-3B	1		
2001	*Baltimor*	*AL*	*329*	*74*	*13*	*1*	*10*	*22*	*99*	*32*	*36*	*2*	*1*	*256*	*.225*	*.274*	*.362*	*.215*	*27*				

The Orioles went to market with Will Clark, and this is all they could get? It's a shame they didn't have a clause stipulating they would get more if Clark played well for his new team. Jose Leon has had exactly one year in his career, 1998, in which he played like a legitimate prospect; not coincidentally, it is the only year his strikeout-to-walk ratio was under 6 to 1. Basically, he's Ryan Minor without the memories of a neat basketball career.

Mark Lewis   UT   Bats R   Age 31

YEAR	TEAM	LGE	AB	H	DB	TP	HR	BB	SO	R	RBI	SB	CS	OUT	BA	OBP	SLG	EQA	EQR	DEFENSE			
1998	Philadel	NL	524	132	20	2	10	46	104	54	54	3	3	395	.252	.316	.355	.226	48	139-2B	-2		
1999	Cincnnti	NL	173	43	11	0	7	5	23	17	27	0	0	130	.249	.270	.434	.227	16	34-3B	-2		
2000	Baltimor	AL	163	45	12	0	4	10	28	18	22	8	3	121	.276	.322	.423	.250	19	17-2B	1	17-3B	-1
2001	*Baltimor*	*AL*	*191*	*45*	*6*	*0*	*6*	*16*	*36*	*21*	*23*	*3*	*1*	*147*	*.236*	*.295*	*.361*	*.226*	*18*				

Mark Lewis is a generic utility infielder. The Reds let him go after a slow start, and the Orioles claimed him on waivers. Was he better than Jesse Garcia, who started the year as their utility man? Yes. Did it matter?

American League

Fernando Lunar — C — Bats R — Age 24

YEAR	TEAM	LGE	AB	H	DB	TP	HR	BB	SO	R	RBI	SB	CS	OUT	BA	OBP	SLG	EQA	EQR	DEFENSE	
1998	DanvillC	Car	288	62	4	0	4	6	53	17	26	0	0	226	.215	.246	.271	.157	11	80-C	6
1999	Greenvil	Sou	342	70	14	1	2	5	68	27	27	0	0	272	.205	.231	.269	.147	11	86-C	0
2000	Greenvil	Sou	104	19	4	0	0	5	16	6	4	0	0	85	.183	.220	.221	.109	2	30-C	8
2000	Atlanta	NL	55	11	1	0	0	2	14	5	5	0	2	46	.200	.262	.218	.132	1	18-C	-1
2000	Bowie	Eas	81	21	5	1	0	4	9	9	6	0	0	60	.259	.308	.346	.219	7	21-C	3
2001	*Baltimor*	*AL*	*265*	*53*	*5*	*0*	*3*	*13*	*52*	*12*	*13*	*0*	*0*	*212*	*.200*	*.237*	*.253*	*.149*	*9*		

Behind the plate, he's Ivan Rodriguez; 54% of would-be base stealers in 2000 didn't make it. At the plate, he's Ivan the Terrible. His .152 EqA over the last three seasons undercuts even the great Bill Bergen's career .158 EqA.

Luis Matos — CF — Bats R — Age 22

YEAR	TEAM	LGE	AB	H	DB	TP	HR	BB	SO	R	RBI	SB	CS	OUT	BA	OBP	SLG	EQA	EQR	DEFENSE	
1998	Delmarva	SAL	512	116	20	4	5	27	95	46	43	15	7	403	.227	.270	.311	.193	33	131-CF	-2
1999	Frederck	Car	279	71	10	1	6	12	36	27	30	12	4	212	.254	.288	.362	.219	24	63-CF	1
1999	Bowie	Eas	286	62	11	1	7	9	41	32	29	7	3	227	.217	.242	.336	.186	17	66-CF	0
2000	Rochestr	Int	35	6	1	0	0	3	8	2	1	1	0	29	.171	.252	.200	.144	1		
2000	Bowie	Eas	183	43	7	3	2	13	25	19	25	8	5	145	.235	.296	.339	.214	15	48-CF	-1
2000	Baltimor	AL	182	42	6	3	1	10	27	20	16	14	5	145	.231	.282	.313	.207	14	57-CF	7
2001	*Baltimor*	*AL*	*493*	*117*	*18*	*4*	*8*	*30*	*81*	*53*	*47*	*15*	*7*	*383*	*.237*	*.281*	*.339*	*.213*	*40*		

He's been rushed. Following a reasonably strong half-season at Frederick two years ago, Luis Matos struggled after a promotion to Bowie. Nevertheless, the front office decided to move him up again, to Rochester, to start the 2000 season. He struggled there. They sent him back to Bowie, and he struggled there. When he righted himself for a month, boom, up to Baltimore and more struggling. He did look fabulous in center field, and while he doesn't walk much, he doesn't strike out much either. That's a combination that, historically, bodes better-than-average progress. Regardless, Matos should spend some more time in Triple-A.

Darnell McDonald — RF — Bats R — Age 22

YEAR	TEAM	LGE	AB	H	DB	TP	HR	BB	SO	R	RBI	SB	CS	OUT	BA	OBP	SLG	EQA	EQR	DEFENSE	
1998	Delmarva	SAL	535	120	21	3	4	24	123	57	32	13	6	421	.224	.261	.297	.182	30	108-LF	-7
1999	Frederck	Car	522	122	21	3	5	43	95	60	55	11	5	405	.234	.295	.314	.206	39	108-RF	-8
2000	Bowie	Eas	463	104	11	3	6	21	94	48	35	7	3	362	.225	.262	.300	.182	26	104-RF	-9
2001	*Baltimor*	*AL*	*485*	*114*	*15*	*2*	*6*	*36*	*107*	*49*	*43*	*10*	*4*	*375*	*.235*	*.288*	*.311*	*.207*	*37*		

His sheer athleticism is the only reason Darnell McDonald is still listed as a prospect. He went backwards in nearly every way possible last year: batting average down, strikeouts up, walks down, power down, defense worse. The sand is almost out of the hourglass.

Ryan Minor — 3B — Bats R — Age 27

YEAR	TEAM	LGE	AB	H	DB	TP	HR	BB	SO	R	RBI	SB	CS	OUT	BA	OBP	SLG	EQA	EQR	DEFENSE			
1998	Bowie	Eas	527	117	18	2	13	24	159	60	56	1	2	412	.222	.267	.338	.196	35	124-3B	-1		
1999	Rochestr	Int	385	91	17	1	18	29	118	45	53	2	1	295	.236	.296	.426	.237	40	75-3B	-1	14-1B	2
1999	Baltimor	AL	124	25	4	0	4	7	39	12	10	1	0	99	.202	.244	.331	.185	7	39-3B	1		
2000	Rochestr	Int	245	65	8	1	11	26	61	28	38	1	3	183	.265	.345	.441	.259	31	61-3B	-8		
2000	Baltimor	AL	85	11	2	0	0	2	18	4	3	0	0	74	.129	.160	.153	—	-2	22-3B	-2		
2001	*Montreal*	*NL*	*394*	*89*	*13*	*1*	*15*	*33*	*118*	*43*	*54*	*1*	*0*	*305*	*.226*	*.286*	*.378*	*.224*	*36*				

Even the Oriole front office has quit believing the hype over Ryan Minor, as they chose to play Ivanon Coffie and Carlos Casimiro over Minor at midseason. He did turn in a pretty nice year at Rochester, though, so maybe he'll brighten enough to produce a useful season or two. Traded to the Expos, he's now trapped behind Fernando Tatis.

Melvin Mora   SS/OF   Bats R   Age 29

YEAR	TEAM	LGE	AB	H	DB	TP	HR	BB	SO	R	RBI	SB	CS	OUT	BA	OBP	SLG	EQA	EQR	DEFENSE			
1998	St Lucie	Fla	55	12	0	0	0	4	11	4	6	0	0	43	.218	.271	.218	.149	2				
1999	Norfolk	Int	304	78	13	1	6	32	56	40	26	11	6	232	.257	.337	.365	.241	33	48-SS	-9	27-CF	-1
1999	NY Mets	NL	31	5	0	0	0	4	7	6	1	2	1	27	.161	.277	.161	.152	1				
2000	NY Mets	NL	218	57	12	2	6	15	45	33	29	6	3	164	.261	.314	.417	.243	24	37-SS	-3	16-CF	-3
2000	Norfolk	Int	28	8	2	0	0	5	3	5	5	1	0	20	.286	.394	.357	.272	4				
2000	Baltimor	AL	198	58	9	3	2	15	29	24	16	5	9	149	.293	.355	.399	.246	22	52-SS	0		
2001	Baltimor	AL	366	89	16	2	5	38	71	47	38	7	4	281	.243	.314	.339	.228	35				

Melvin Mora had the unenviable task of replacing the idolized Rey Ordonez in the Met lineup. Even though there was little difference in their fielding statistics (Mora made six fewer plays in the same number of games as St. Rey) and even though Mora outhit Ordonez by a wide margin (.243-.164 in EqA), he was run out of town. He's a useful player; the signing of Mike Bordick means he'll return to the outfield or a super-sub role in 2001.

Willie Morales   C   Bats R   Age 28

YEAR	TEAM	LGE	AB	H	DB	TP	HR	BB	SO	R	RBI	SB	CS	OUT	BA	OBP	SLG	EQA	EQR	DEFENSE	
1998	Edmonton	PCL	241	43	8	0	5	14	46	20	25	0	1	199	.178	.225	.274	.147	8	54-C	-3
1999	Midland	Tex	339	74	13	0	11	16	63	28	45	1	0	265	.218	.261	.354	.200	24	68-C	-2
2000	Rochestr	Int	251	58	10	1	5	8	63	18	19	0	2	195	.231	.255	.339	.187	15	65-C	-10
2001	Baltimor	AL	269	58	6	0	7	14	65	18	23	0	1	212	.216	.254	.316	.186	16		

Willie Morales got to start the season in Baltimore when Greg Myers went on the DL with a hamstring injury. Given the light April schedule and the durability of Charles Johnson, he rarely got to play. Morales has a solid defensive reputation that is not supported by the numbers and has no ability to hit at all, so the only way he'll get back to Baltimore is to take the Tonya Harding route.

Greg Myers   C   Bats L   Age 35

YEAR	TEAM	LGE	AB	H	DB	TP	HR	BB	SO	R	RBI	SB	CS	OUT	BA	OBP	SLG	EQA	EQR	DEFENSE	
1998	San Dieg	NL	175	45	9	0	5	16	34	20	21	0	1	131	.257	.319	.394	.237	18	40-C	0
1999	San Dieg	NL	130	38	2	0	4	11	13	9	15	0	0	92	.292	.348	.400	.253	15	30-C	-2
1999	Atlanta	NL	72	16	1	0	2	12	15	9	8	0	0	56	.222	.333	.319	.227	7	22-C	3
2000	Baltimor	AL	125	29	3	0	4	7	26	8	12	0	0	96	.232	.273	.352	.204	9	27-C	-1
2001	Baltimor	AL	127	27	2	0	4	15	25	12	14	0	0	100	.213	.296	.323	.214	11		

Greg Myers is strictly a platoon player; over the last five years, he's had just 102 at-bats against left-handers, a mere eight last season. The .204 EqA was a career low; because the Orioles signed him to a two-year contract, he'll be back in 2001.

Ntema Ndungidi   LF   Bats L   Age 22

YEAR	TEAM	LGE	AB	H	DB	TP	HR	BB	SO	R	RBI	SB	CS	OUT	BA	OBP	SLG	EQA	EQR	DEFENSE	
1998	Bluefld	App	211	43	8	2	3	21	61	13	17	1	2	170	.204	.277	.303	.190	13	42-LF	-6
1999	Delmarva	SAL	231	41	9	1	0	37	57	23	20	7	1	191	.177	.295	.225	.185	14	47-LF	-2
1999	Frederck	Car	200	45	9	2	0	30	44	32	13	2	1	156	.225	.331	.290	.218	17	54-LF	-3
2000	Frederck	Car	328	79	12	2	9	44	86	40	44	6	3	252	.241	.333	.372	.241	36	82-LF	-8
2000	Bowie	Eas	139	29	3	0	3	20	36	13	11	1	1	111	.209	.316	.295	.210	11	36-LF	-3
2001	Baltimor	AL	444	101	18	2	6	66	123	63	45	7	3	346	.227	.327	.318	.231	44		

He's called "Papy" because North Americans can't pronounce his name, and he comes to us via Montreal after being born in the Congo. Ntema Ndungidi's experience with baseball is limited, making him even more of a project player than most high-school athletes. Given that, it's surprising how well he handles the strike zone. He's a fabulous athlete, the kind who gets scouts squirming in their seats, and has been making steady progress as a baseball player. In his case, it's probably all right to be a little more optimistic than the basic stats suggest.

But Ndungidi's prospect status took a hit in November when he displayed some bizarre behavior near the end of his Arizona Fall League stay, reportedly talking to his locker and attempting to practice in his street clothes. He followed it up by being arrested for marijuana possession. The impact of these incidents, as well as the extent of any help he's receiving, is unknown as we go to press.

American League

Richard Paz — 2B/3B — Bats R — Age 23

YEAR	TEAM	LGE	AB	H	DB	TP	HR	BB	SO	R	RBI	SB	CS	OUT	BA	OBP	SLG	EQA	EQR	DEFENSE			
1998	Delmarva	SAL	342	84	9	3	3	55	44	35	38	7	3	261	.246	.357	.316	.239	36	88-3B	1		
1998	Frederck	Car	149	32	4	0	4	17	22	25	7	3	1	118	.215	.304	.322	.215	13	25-3B	-2		
1999	Frederck	Car	172	37	8	0	0	36	28	19	14	6	3	138	.215	.354	.262	.225	17	47-3B	1		
1999	Bowie	Eas	279	70	9	1	2	39	37	30	16	5	2	211	.251	.350	.312	.233	28	66-3B	-3		
2000	Frederck	Car	284	71	6	0	5	54	49	40	36	6	4	217	.250	.373	.324	.247	33	70-2B	-1		
2000	Bowie	Eas	140	34	7	2	1	22	30	14	13	2	1	107	.243	.350	.343	.242	15	17-2B	1	10-3B	0
2001	Baltimor	AL	403	100	14	1	4	67	72	65	43	7	5	308	.248	.355	.318	.243	45				

Richard Paz is easily overlooked. That's not a short joke, though he is 5'8". As you'd expect for a small player, he won't hit for power. What he will do is play reasonable defense, steal a couple of bases, and walk, walk, walk. He's drawn 373 of them in the last five seasons, increasing his rate as he's moved up the ladder. Surprisingly, this type of hitter has progressed about as well as the DTs indicate. You'd think such hitters would be overmatched as they advance, but that rarely happens.

Calvin Pickering — 1B — Bats L — Age 24

YEAR	TEAM	LGE	AB	H	DB	TP	HR	BB	SO	R	RBI	SB	CS	OUT	BA	OBP	SLG	EQA	EQR	DEFENSE	
1998	Bowie	Eas	502	132	23	1	23	77	121	75	86	2	3	373	.263	.369	.450	.274	73	117-1B	0
1998	Baltimor	AL	21	5	1	0	2	3	4	4	3	1	0	16	.238	.333	.571	.293	4		
1999	Rochestr	Int	374	96	14	0	14	50	98	52	50	1	2	280	.257	.357	.406	.258	48	94-1B	-4
1999	Baltimor	AL	40	5	1	0	1	11	15	4	5	0	0	35	.125	.314	.225	.195	3		
2000	Rochestr	Int	201	42	8	0	6	31	73	18	27	1	2	161	.209	.317	.338	.222	19	56-1B	-3
2001	Baltimor	AL	273	68	8	0	13	45	88	44	47	1	1	206	.249	.355	.421	.269	39		

Another disastrous year for the big Virgin Islander. Calvin Pickering struggled through the cold spring—as he always does—then didn't break out when the weather warmed up. His season came to an early end thanks to a torn quadriceps muscle; his persistent weight problem is a likely culprit. His only value right now is for salvage.

Tim Raines Jr. — CF — Bats B — Age 21

YEAR	TEAM	LGE	AB	H	DB	TP	HR	BB	SO	R	RBI	SB	CS	OUT	BA	OBP	SLG	EQA	EQR	DEFENSE	
1999	Delmarva	SAL	437	92	24	4	1	53	137	52	36	18	8	353	.211	.298	.291	.204	33	115-CF	-4
2000	Frederck	Car	475	107	20	2	2	48	110	59	31	33	12	380	.225	.305	.288	.211	39	124-CF	-3
2001	Baltimor	AL	364	83	16	2	1	48	103	59	26	24	7	288	.228	.318	.291	.225	35		

Like his father, Tim Raines Jr. relies on speed, swiping 81 bases at Frederick. The biggest drawback in his game is the strikeout rate; it shouldn't be this high given his complete lack of power. A lot of the strikeouts come from trying to bat left-handed, so he may need to go back to his natural right side full-time. He did improve his strikeout rate last year, though, and would appear to be on a major-league track. Unlike young Bonds or Griffey, he has little chance of surpassing his father. Here are his dad's lines for the same ages as Junior in 1999 and 2000:

YEAR	TEAM	LGE	AB	H	DB	TP	HR	BB	SO	R	RBI	SB	CS	OUT	BA	OBP	SLG	EQA	EQR
1979	Memphis	Sou	561	143	26	6	5	62	67	75	39	30	10	426	.258	.332	.353	.239	59
1980	Denver	AA	418	126	22	6	6	44	N/A	N/A	N/A	41	12	303	.301	.368	.426	.278	62

Keith Reed — RF — Bats R — Age 22

YEAR	TEAM	LGE	AB	H	DB	TP	HR	BB	SO	R	RBI	SB	CS	OUT	BA	OBP	SLG	EQA	EQR	DEFENSE	
1999	Delmarva	SAL	247	54	11	2	3	17	56	28	18	1	1	194	.219	.273	.316	.192	16	52-RF	-4
2000	Delmarva	SAL	277	66	9	1	9	17	60	29	41	7	2	213	.238	.287	.375	.222	25	65-RF	-1
2000	Frederck	Car	250	54	7	1	7	14	60	26	24	4	1	197	.216	.263	.336	.197	17	60-RF	-6
2001	Baltimor	AL	296	68	11	1	8	19	75	29	32	4	2	230	.230	.276	.355	.214	24		

Another 1999 draftee, Keith Reed was celebrated for his improvement in 2000, but it looks hollow. His best performance, last year at Delmarva, projects to only a .255 or so EqA at his peak. That's not major-league caliber for a corner outfielder. His strike-zone judgment is unacceptable and actually got worse in 2000. As with virtually every other player in the Oriole system, if he develops normally from here, he won't have a career.

Chris Richard   1B   Bats L   Age 27

YEAR	TEAM	LGE	AB	H	DB	TP	HR	BB	SO	R	RBI	SB	CS	OUT	BA	OBP	SLG	EQA	EQR	DEFENSE			
1998	Arkansas	Tex	89	15	7	0	1	7	11	6	11	0	0	74	.169	.234	.281	.158	4	22-1B	-4		
1999	Arkansas	Tex	444	105	19	2	18	30	86	53	60	3	3	342	.236	.292	.410	.230	43	117-1B	-5		
2000	Memphis	PCL	375	91	14	1	13	38	73	48	56	6	2	286	.243	.317	.389	.238	40	82-RF	3	11-1B	1
2000	Baltimor	AL	199	56	13	2	14	12	35	37	35	7	6	149	.281	.335	.578	.284	32	51-1B	-7		
2001	Baltimor	AL	478	117	23	1	21	48	97	63	75	1	1	362	.245	.314	.429	.252	58				

Picked up from St. Louis for Mike Timlin, Chris Richard hit much better than expected during his stay in Baltimore. Maybe the performance revealed his real ability; more likely it was an effect of pitchers testing an unknown with fastballs and getting burned. That theory is supported by the fact that he hit much better with the bases empty (.295 EqA) than with men on (.268), when pitchers were presumably more careful. The best strategy for the Birds would be to run out a Richard/Conine platoon. The David Segui acquisition and Albert Belle's probable need to DH may lock Richard out of a job.

Cal Ripken   3B   Bats R   Age 40

YEAR	TEAM	LGE	AB	H	DB	TP	HR	BB	SO	R	RBI	SB	CS	OUT	BA	OBP	SLG	EQA	EQR	DEFENSE	
1998	Baltimore	AL	602	170	24	1	17	50	61	67	63	0	2	434	.282	.341	.410	.251	69	156-3B	-3
1999	Baltimore	AL	331	116	22	0	21	10	28	50	57	0	1	216	.350	.374	.607	.311	58	72-3B	-5
2000	Baltimore	AL	309	81	13	0	17	19	34	42	56	0	0	228	.262	.311	.469	.255	37	73-3B	7
2001	Baltimor	AL	279	71	8	0	12	22	30	32	42	0	0	208	.254	.309	.412	.245	31		

He got his 3000th hit in 2000 while continuing to battle injuries: the back still aches, some bone chips the surgeon missed got inflamed and, at one point, he had to be carried off the field. As in 1999, though, he played quite well once he rested and recovered, posting a translated .320/.378/.493 with a .289 EqA. His career may be winding down, but it is pretty clear that Cal Ripken is going to hang in there until someone forces him out.

Brian Roberts   SS   Bats B   Age 23

YEAR	TEAM	LGE	AB	H	DB	TP	HR	BB	SO	R	RBI	SB	CS	OUT	BA	OBP	SLG	EQA	EQR	DEFENSE	
1999	Delmarva	SAL	175	37	9	1	0	20	44	14	17	6	3	141	.211	.294	.274	.195	12	46-SS	5
2000	Frederck	Car	170	42	6	2	0	20	25	20	12	5	5	133	.247	.328	.306	.216	14	42-SS	-7
2001	Baltimor	AL	135	32	5	1	0	19	42	20	11	5	3	106	.237	.331	.289	.224	13		

Brian Roberts missed most of 2000 after having surgery to remove bone chips in his elbow, then he had to drop out of the Arizona Fall League because the elbow was bothering him again. He was drafted and signed out of college in 1999, so there's not a lot of professional performance to evaluate. What performance there is suggests he can eventually be an average major-league shortstop. Even if his bat doesn't develop, his glove willl likely be good enough for him to make the majors as a backup. Ed Rogers should give him a challenge, if he needs the motivation.

Ed Rogers   SS   Bats R   Age 19

YEAR	TEAM	LGE	AB	H	DB	TP	HR	BB	SO	R	RBI	SB	CS	OUT	BA	OBP	SLG	EQA	EQR	DEFENSE	
2000	Delmarva	SAL	339	80	12	3	4	15	67	31	30	10	4	263	.236	.268	.324	.196	22	80-SS	-13
2000	Bowie	Eas	49	12	2	0	1	2	16	3	6	1	1	38	.245	.275	.347	.201	3	12-SS	-3
2001	Baltimor	AL	216	53	5	1	3	9	80	22	18	8	3	166	.245	.276	.319	.205	16		

A scout's dream, Ed Rogers is held up as one of those blessed five-tool prospects. That's premature; he doesn't hit for power, at least not yet. Like many tools prospects, he has real problems with the strike zone, with far too few walks and too many strikeouts. There also appear to be holes in his defense. He's a good prospect, especially if the age is true, but we should wait a little while before the coronation.

Jayson Werth   C   Bats R   Age 22

YEAR	TEAM	LGE	AB	H	DB	TP	HR	BB	SO	R	RBI	SB	CS	OUT	BA	OBP	SLG	EQA	EQR	DEFENSE	
1998	Delmarva	SAL	420	92	15	2	6	36	97	47	37	7	3	331	.219	.293	.307	.203	31	107-C	-2
1999	Frederck	Car	244	63	7	0	3	27	38	29	22	7	2	183	.258	.336	.324	.231	23	61-C	-7
1999	Bowie	Eas	123	30	3	1	1	13	27	13	9	3	1	94	.244	.322	.309	.219	11	29-C	-2
2000	Frederck	Car	86	21	2	0	2	7	16	12	15	2	1	66	.244	.301	.337	.215	7	16-C	-2
2000	Bowie	Eas	284	58	13	1	5	42	54	37	21	5	2	228	.204	.312	.310	.215	25	76-C	-12
2001	Toronto	AL	400	101	14	1	8	49	82	63	51	10	4	303	.252	.334	.352	.238	42		

American League

On one hand, Jayson Werth had a disappointing season. He started at Bowie and was demoted to Frederick, and his EqA declined. On the other hand, his isolated power was up a little, his walks continued to increase, and there was no increase in his strikeout rate. That performance indicates that the foundation of his hitting skills is solid, giving him a better than average chance of rebounding in 2001. His throwing arm isn't good, which is why his catcher rating is so low; a move to the outfield might free up his hitting development. Werth was traded to the Blue Jays in November for a middle-relief prospect, a fairly inexplicable move.

PITCHERS (ERA: 4.50, H/9: 9.00, HR/9: 1.00, BB/9: 3.00, K/9: 6.00, KW: 1.00, PERA: 4.50)

Lesli Brea — Throws R — Age 22? 26?

YEAR	TEAM	LGE	IP	H	ER	HR	BB	K	ERA	W	L	H/9	HR/9	BB/9	K/9	KW	PERA
1998	Wisconsn	Mid	51.0	53	34	3	51	43	6.00	2	4	9.35	0.53	9.00	7.59	0.42	6.70
1999	St Lucie	Fla	106.3	98	83	9	90	76	7.03	3	9	8.29	0.76	7.62	6.43	0.42	5.74
2000	Binghmtn	Eas	85.0	90	63	17	67	52	6.67	2	7	9.53	1.80	7.09	5.51	0.39	7.36
2000	Bowie	Eas	11.7	12	7	2	11	2	5.40	0	1	9.26	1.54	8.49	1.54	0.09	7.63
2000	Rochestr	Int	18.0	26	18	4	8	10	9.00	0	2	13.00	2.00	4.00	5.00	0.63	8.25
2000	Baltimor	AL	9.3	12	10	1	8	5	9.64	0	1	11.57	0.96	7.71	4.82	0.31	8.01

Whose age is it, anyway? A supposed 22-year-old picked up in the Mike Bordick deal, Lesli Brea told Baltimore newsmen that he was 26; the next day he said it was a joke—he was really 22. Uh-huh. The scary part is that Oriole GM Syd Thrift said it didn't matter how old Brea was. Thrift may have been blowing smoke to cover the situation, but there's plenty of evidence to suggest that he really believes it.

Scott Erickson — Throws R — Age 33

YEAR	TEAM	LGE	IP	H	ER	HR	BB	K	ERA	W	L	H/9	HR/9	BB/9	K/9	KW	PERA
1998	Baltimor	AL	246.3	265	113	22	61	172	4.13	13	14	9.68	0.80	2.23	6.28	1.41	4.38
1999	Baltimor	AL	227.0	226	109	24	81	101	4.32	12	13	8.96	0.95	3.21	4.00	0.62	4.51
2000	Baltimor	AL	92.7	118	69	12	39	39	6.70	3	7	11.46	1.17	3.79	3.79	0.50	6.45

In 1999, Scott Erickson turned in a wretched half-season and a good half-season; last year, the whole season was just bad. In the spring, he had bone chips removed from his elbow. He came back to pitch two months later and was horrible, giving up more runs than innings pitched in seven of 16 starts. Anything in the strike zone was drilled. Finally, in July, he came down with a torn ulnar collateral ligament in his elbow. He had Tommy John surgery and should miss the entire 2001 season.

Juan Figueroa — Throws R — Age 22

YEAR	TEAM	LGE	IP	H	ER	HR	BB	K	ERA	W	L	H/9	HR/9	BB/9	K/9	KW	PERA
1998	Bristol	App	69.7	102	82	31	29	44	10.59	1	7	13.18	4.00	3.75	5.68	0.76	10.45
1999	Burlingt	Mid	106.0	110	62	15	47	74	5.26	4	8	9.34	1.27	3.99	6.28	0.79	5.40
1999	WnstnSlm	Car	52.3	68	49	4	21	26	8.43	1	5	11.69	0.69	3.61	4.47	0.62	6.01
2000	WnstnSlm	Car	47.0	65	38	6	9	35	7.28	1	4	12.45	1.15	1.72	6.70	1.94	6.17
2000	Birmnghm	Sou	50.3	60	31	8	26	25	5.54	2	4	10.73	1.43	4.65	4.47	0.48	6.64
2000	Bowie	Eas	36.0	47	26	5	23	27	6.50	1	3	11.75	1.25	5.75	6.75	0.59	7.51

He has a good arm but was hardly a top White Sox prospect before being traded for Charles Johnson. In the Oriole system, he's near the top of the list. His strikeout rate seems to drop every time he moves up a level, but so far he has recovered shortly thereafter, which is an OK sign. Still, a pitcher with his gopher-ball tendencies is going to have real trouble in Camden Yards.

Buddy Groom — Throws L — Age 35

YEAR	TEAM	LGE	IP	H	ER	HR	BB	K	ERA	W	L	H/9	HR/9	BB/9	K/9	KW	PERA
1998	Oakland	AL	56.3	58	27	4	17	33	4.31	3	3	9.27	0.64	2.72	5.27	0.97	4.17
1999	Oakland	AL	45.3	45	26	1	15	30	5.16	2	3	8.93	0.20	2.98	5.96	1.00	3.65
2000	Baltimor	AL	58.7	58	31	4	17	42	4.76	3	4	8.90	0.61	2.61	6.44	1.24	3.88

Baltimore Orioles

(Buddy Groom *continued*)

For relief pitchers, it's easy to build up a large margin between an actual ERA and what the stats say it "should have" been, something Buddy Groom has now done two years in a row. Groom's ERA doesn't reflect how well he's pitched. He is best suited to being a one-batter specialist. His platoon splits have gotten steadily worse, and he did extremely well last year when he had to face only one batter (1-for-15).

Juan Guzman — Throws R — Age 23

YEAR	TEAM	LGE	IP	H	ER	HR	BB	K	ERA	W	L	H/9	HR/9	BB/9	K/9	KW	PERA
1998	Bluefld	App	23.3	23	13	2	9	11	5.01	1	2	8.87	0.77	3.47	4.24	0.61	4.39
1999	Delmarva	SAL	109.7	135	67	21	61	62	5.50	4	8	11.08	1.72	5.01	5.09	0.51	7.32
2000	Frederck	Car	16.3	12	4	0	5	10	2.20	2	0	6.61	0.00	2.76	5.51	1.00	2.25
2000	Bowie	Eas	91.3	110	60	9	50	37	5.91	3	7	10.84	0.89	4.93	3.65	0.37	6.27

Three impressive games at Frederick got the converted catcher a fast promotion to Bowie, and he was doing pretty well there before coming down with an elbow injury. Juan Guzman wasn't nearly the same pitcher when he returned:

Bowie, before injury:			54.7	63	29	5	22	24	4.77	3	3	10.37	0.82	3.62	3.95	0.55	5.40
Bowie, after injury:			36.7	48	32	4	28	13	7.85	1	3	11.78	0.98	6.87	3.19	0.23	7.73

His strikeout rate was disappointing even before the injury. Nevertheless, he has a good shot at pitching for the Orioles this September if his elbow heals.

Jason Johnson — Throws R — Age 27

YEAR	TEAM	LGE	IP	H	ER	HR	BB	K	ERA	W	L	H/9	HR/9	BB/9	K/9	KW	PERA
1998	TampaBay	AL	59.3	69	33	8	23	33	5.01	3	4	10.47	1.21	3.49	5.01	0.72	5.79
1999	Rochestr	Int	41.0	36	21	7	29	32	4.61	2	3	7.90	1.54	6.37	7.02	0.55	5.81
1999	Baltimor	AL	114.3	112	64	14	45	68	5.04	5	8	8.82	1.10	3.54	5.35	0.76	4.73
2000	Rochestr	Int	51.0	33	14	3	23	40	2.47	4	2	5.82	0.53	4.06	7.06	0.87	2.72
2000	Baltimor	AL	107.7	111	81	19	49	75	6.77	3	9	9.28	1.59	4.10	6.27	0.77	5.73

The good luck finally deserted Jason Johnson. Statistically, his performance wasn't much different from his 1998 and 1999 seasons, except that the timing changed. The ratio of his EqA with men on base to his EqA with the bases empty was a very good .983 coming into the 2000 season. The ratio jumped to a horrific 1.240 last year. Unless the experience broke his confidence completely, he'll return to his normal self: a pitcher who is 0.50-1.00 runs per game worse than average.

Ryan Kohlmeier — Throws R — Age 24

YEAR	TEAM	LGE	IP	H	ER	HR	BB	K	ERA	W	L	H/9	HR/9	BB/9	K/9	KW	PERA
1998	Bowie	Eas	44.7	58	50	20	18	34	10.07	1	4	11.69	4.03	3.63	6.85	0.94	9.54
1999	Bowie	Eas	57.0	51	32	15	31	49	5.05	2	4	8.05	2.37	4.89	7.74	0.79	6.19
2000	Rochestr	Int	44.0	34	16	5	16	38	3.27	3	2	6.95	1.02	3.27	7.77	1.19	3.47
2000	Baltimor	AL	26.3	28	8	1	12	16	2.73	2	1	9.57	0.34	4.10	5.47	0.67	4.59

Like most minor-league closers, Ryan Kohlmeier didn't look like an especially good prospect. But last year, he took some advice from fellow Red Wing Mike Grace on how to grip his slider, and he suddenly had a great complement to his fastball. (Note to front office: If Grace does this once every couple of years, you should let him pitch in Rochester for as long as he wants.) Kohlmeier took over the closing role in Baltimore following Mike Timlin's departure and saved 13 games in a row before finally blowing one. They weren't easy saves, though; "Full Pack" Kohlemeier did a high-wire act, repeatedly putting tying and winning runs on base but always—well, $^{13}/_{14}$ths of the time—getting the last out just in time.

Chuck McElroy — Throws L — Age 33

YEAR	TEAM	LGE	IP	H	ER	HR	BB	K	ERA	W	L	H/9	HR/9	BB/9	K/9	KW	PERA
1998	Colorado	NL	67.0	67	20	2	17	50	2.69	5	2	9.00	0.27	2.28	6.72	1.47	3.48
1999	Colorado	NL	42.0	46	21	5	19	31	4.50	2	3	9.86	1.07	4.07	6.64	0.82	5.52
1999	NY Mets	NL	13.0	11	4	0	7	6	2.77	1	0	7.62	0.00	4.85	4.15	0.43	3.45
2000	Baltimor	AL	63.0	56	31	5	28	48	4.43	3	4	8.00	0.71	4.00	6.86	0.86	4.03

A good relief pitcher for 12 years and 603 games, Chuck McElroy was given a desperation start by the Orioles last September and pitched so well that he was given another. He pitched so well again (six hits, three walks, and one run in 11 innings over the two starts) that he may enter spring training as a possible rotation member.

American League

Jose Mercedes — Throws R — Age 30

YEAR	TEAM	LGE	IP	H	ER	HR	BB	K	ERA	W	L	H/9	HR/9	BB/9	K/9	KW	PERA
1998	Milwauke	NL	30.7	40	24	5	8	9	7.04	1	2	11.74	1.47	2.35	2.64	0.56	6.34
1999	LasVegas	PCL	84.7	101	53	15	22	36	5.63	3	6	10.74	1.59	2.34	3.83	0.82	5.88
1999	Calgary	PCL	25.3	27	11	2	3	8	3.91	2	1	9.59	0.71	1.07	2.84	1.33	3.78
1999	Norfolk	Int	30.3	34	14	2	11	13	4.15	1	2	10.09	0.59	3.26	3.86	0.59	4.78
2000	Baltimor	AL	144.0	139	61	13	52	67	3.81	8	8	8.69	0.81	3.25	4.19	0.64	4.22

Jose Mercedes was signed by the Orioles because a scout liked the way he pitched in winter ball in the Dominican Republic. That scout looked good while Mercedes was flying through spring training, then looked bad for the next two months. Mercedes was beaten up in four starts and three relief appearances to the tune of 41 hits and 21 runs in 26 innings. He began pitching well in relief in June, got back into the rotation in July, and sailed through the rest of the season, running up a gaudy 11–3 record in the second half. The O's are counting on him to do it again next year, but they need to remember a name from their own history: Jeff Ballard.

Alan Mills — Throws R — Age 34

YEAR	TEAM	LGE	IP	H	ER	HR	BB	K	ERA	W	L	H/9	HR/9	BB/9	K/9	KW	PERA
1998	Baltimor	AL	75.7	52	29	8	44	53	3.45	5	3	6.19	0.95	5.23	6.30	0.60	3.74
1999	LosAngls	NL	70.0	68	31	10	38	41	3.99	4	4	8.74	1.29	4.89	5.27	0.54	5.43
2000	LosAngls	NL	25.0	30	11	3	14	15	3.96	2	1	10.80	1.08	5.04	5.40	0.54	6.48
2000	Baltimor	AL	24.0	24	14	5	15	17	5.25	1	2	9.00	1.88	5.63	6.38	0.57	6.51

The PERA column is the one to look at; Alan Mills has been falling backwards like a champion platform diver on a reverse-two-and-a-half tuck. He finally gave up at the end of August and had his shoulder operated on to clean up bone chips and repair a partial rotator-cuff tear. Since he's signed for next year and supposed to be doing well in rehab, he'll be back.

Mike Mussina — Throws R — Age 32

YEAR	TEAM	LGE	IP	H	ER	HR	BB	K	ERA	W	L	H/9	HR/9	BB/9	K/9	KW	PERA
1998	Baltimor	AL	201.0	177	77	21	36	162	3.45	13	9	7.93	0.94	1.61	7.25	2.25	3.29
1999	Baltimor	AL	200.0	192	77	14	43	164	3.46	13	9	8.64	0.63	1.94	7.38	1.91	3.50
2000	Baltimor	AL	234.0	218	92	25	37	201	3.54	15	11	8.38	0.96	1.42	7.73	2.72	3.48

In a fair world, Mike Mussina might have been runner-up to Pedro Martinez for the Cy Young Award. He was third in the league in ERA, second in OBP allowed, eighth in slugging average allowed, and second in Support-Neutral Winning Percentage. Unfortunately, instead of Tim Hudson's 7.34 runs per game of support, he had a league-worst 3.71 runs per game, .30 less than the next worst. Even with that kind of support, you'd have expected a 12–14 record instead of his 11–15. With Hudson's support, he'd have been 20–6. He didn't have it, he didn't win, and the Orioles let one of the best pitchers they've ever had walk away.

Mark Nussbeck — Throws R — Age 27

YEAR	TEAM	LGE	IP	H	ER	HR	BB	K	ERA	W	L	H/9	HR/9	BB/9	K/9	KW	PERA
1998	Pr Willm	Car	74.3	85	66	24	24	29	7.99	2	6	10.29	2.91	2.91	3.51	0.60	7.23
1998	Arkansas	Tex	38.7	43	35	11	22	13	8.15	1	3	10.01	2.56	5.12	3.03	0.30	7.63
1999	Memphis	PCL	95.7	137	102	29	44	52	9.60	2	9	12.89	2.73	4.14	4.89	0.59	9.09
2000	Memphis	PCL	117.7	121	72	16	48	51	5.51	4	9	9.25	1.22	3.67	3.90	0.53	5.17
2000	Rochestr	Int	17.3	21	9	3	4	9	4.67	1	1	10.90	1.56	2.08	4.67	1.13	5.78

It's pretty amazing that Mark Nussbeck stayed in the minor leagues through last season; most pitchers who are his age and who pitch like he has for the past two years start learning to install satellite dishes. He spent the 1999 off-season in the instructional league learning a new change-up and re-learning his curveball. For 11 games he was unhittable, turning in a performance that translates to:

2000	Memphis	PCL	71.0	54	27	6	30	34	3.42	5	3	6.85	0.76	3.80	4.31	0.57	3.38

After that, the scouting reports caught up, his arm went dead, or Mr. Applegate gave him his soul back, because it was the same old Nussbeck until he was shut down with tendinitis.

Mike Paradis — Throws R — Age 23

YEAR	TEAM	LGE	IP	H	ER	HR	BB	K	ERA	W	L	H/9	HR/9	BB/9	K/9	KW	PERA
2000	Delmarva	SAL	85.3	97	67	14	67	37	7.07	2	7	10.23	1.48	7.07	3.90	0.28	7.41
2000	Frederck	Car	41.7	54	24	2	28	17	5.18	2	3	11.66	0.43	6.05	3.67	0.30	6.74

Mike Paradis has been something of a disappointment so far. The 1999 first-rounder was supposed to be pretty well polished coming out of college, but the pros haven't treated him kindly. His coaches are still trying to get his mechanics straight, which might explain his strikeout-to-walk ratios.

John Parrish — Throws L — Age 23

YEAR	TEAM	LGE	IP	H	ER	HR	BB	K	ERA	W	L	H/9	HR/9	BB/9	K/9	KW	PERA
1998	Frederck	Car	73.7	82	50	10	35	42	6.11	2	6	10.02	1.22	4.28	5.13	0.60	5.87
1999	Frederck	Car	32.7	39	23	8	13	23	6.34	1	3	10.74	2.20	3.58	6.34	0.88	7.01
1999	Bowie	Eas	51.3	49	30	6	45	27	5.26	2	4	8.59	1.05	7.89	4.73	0.30	6.32
2000	Bowie	Eas	15.0	12	3	0	8	10	1.80	2	0	7.20	0.00	4.80	6.00	0.63	3.25
2000	Rochestr	Int	97.7	86	61	14	57	67	5.62	4	7	7.92	1.29	5.25	6.17	0.59	5.11
2000	Baltimor	AL	37.0	38	27	5	28	27	6.57	1	3	9.24	1.22	6.81	6.57	0.48	6.43

He was promoted rapidly, but aside from the three dominant starts at Bowie, nothing screamed "get him to Baltimore." John Parrish became an Oriole because when the team needed an arm, every other pitcher in the system was hurt. After a highly successful debut against the Yankees, his problems—particularly control—came to the fore. He needs more experience in Triple-A.

Sidney Ponson — Throws R — Age 24

YEAR	TEAM	LGE	IP	H	ER	HR	BB	K	ERA	W	L	H/9	HR/9	BB/9	K/9	KW	PERA
1998	Baltimor	AL	132.3	146	73	18	37	79	4.96	6	9	9.93	1.22	2.52	5.37	1.07	5.08
1999	Baltimor	AL	207.0	210	102	31	66	107	4.43	10	13	9.13	1.35	2.87	4.65	0.81	4.89
2000	Baltimor	AL	219.7	207	108	27	67	145	4.42	11	13	8.48	1.11	2.75	5.94	1.08	4.20

A solid, if unspectacular, year. Sidney Ponson's primary contribution to the Orioles is his ability to chew up innings. He's a tough pitcher to describe, because almost everything about his stat line is so... average. He has neither a platoon split (.249 EqA vs LHB, .251 RHB) nor a windup/stretch split (.250 EQA with bases empty, .248 with men on). The only reason there's much of a home/road split (.260/.240) is that he allowed 21 of his 30 homers in Camden Yards. There's still some worry about his pitch counts.

Pat Rapp — Throws R — Age 33

YEAR	TEAM	LGE	IP	H	ER	HR	BB	K	ERA	W	L	H/9	HR/9	BB/9	K/9	KW	PERA
1998	KansasCy	AL	187.7	196	100	20	89	122	4.80	9	12	9.40	0.96	4.27	5.85	0.69	5.22
1999	Boston	AL	145.7	137	66	11	54	86	4.08	8	8	8.46	0.68	3.34	5.31	0.80	4.00
2000	Baltimor	AL	173.3	189	108	16	67	101	5.61	6	13	9.81	0.83	3.48	5.24	0.75	5.00

You didn't really think he'd pitch again like he did in Boston, did you? Pat Rapp was one of the very few players the Orioles had signed for only one year. He is now an Angel. Another 1999 is outside his range. Really, the Angels shouldn't even be wasting time on him, given their pitching depth.

Matt Riley — Throws L — Age 21

YEAR	TEAM	LGE	IP	H	ER	HR	BB	K	ERA	W	L	H/9	HR/9	BB/9	K/9	KW	PERA
1998	Delmarva	SAL	71.7	52	30	2	60	64	3.77	4	4	6.53	0.25	7.53	8.04	0.53	4.15
1999	Frederck	Car	46.3	41	30	10	16	31	5.83	2	3	7.96	1.94	3.11	6.02	0.97	4.94
1999	Bowie	Eas	116.0	120	65	20	44	83	5.04	5	8	9.31	1.55	3.41	6.44	0.94	5.44
1999	Baltimor	AL	11.3	16	8	4	11	6	6.35	0	1	12.71	3.18	8.74	4.76	0.27	11.37
2000	Bowie	Eas	67.7	78	67	16	53	43	8.91	1	7	10.37	2.13	7.05	5.72	0.41	8.19

How many things can a prospect do wrong before you can call him released? Matt Riley's cocky antics reached a new level last year, culminating with his being suspended from the team in spring training following a bar altercation with police. Note to Matt: the better you pitch, the more you can get away with, and vice versa. He was smacked in spring training, rocked in Rochester, and finally bowed out in Bowie with a blown elbow, all of which may or may not have anything to do with his pitching while hurt in September 1999. He'll miss the entire 2001 season with Tommy John surgery. After that, who knows?

Luis Rivera — Throws R — Age 23

YEAR	TEAM	LGE	IP	H	ER	HR	BB	K	ERA	W	L	H/9	HR/9	BB/9	K/9	KW	PERA
1998	Macon	SAL	82.0	88	71	15	52	55	7.79	2	7	9.66	1.65	5.71	6.04	0.53	6.70
1999	Myrtle B	Car	59.3	52	38	8	29	43	5.76	2	5	7.89	1.21	4.40	6.52	0.74	4.65
2000	Richmond	Int	21.3	28	19	3	17	9	8.02	0	2	11.81	1.27	7.17	3.80	0.26	8.14

The Orioles got Luis Rivera from Atlanta for B.J. Surhoff. It's hard to figure out Rivera because he's been so seldom seen: back problems in 1998, blister problems in 1999, and, most worrisome, shoulder tendinitis for most of 2000. He looked very good in Atlanta in April. While he's been a starter throughout his career, it's possible that a move to the bullpen would be easier on him.

B.J. Ryan — Throws L — Age 25

YEAR	TEAM	LGE	IP	H	ER	HR	BB	K	ERA	W	L	H/9	HR/9	BB/9	K/9	KW	PERA
1998	Billings	Pio	15.7	16	4	0	6	12	2.30	2	0	9.19	0.00	3.45	6.89	1.00	3.80
1998	Chattang	Sou	15.3	14	4	0	6	13	2.35	1	1	8.22	0.00	3.52	7.63	1.08	3.31
1999	Chattang	Sou	39.0	34	14	1	18	28	3.23	2	2	7.85	0.23	4.15	6.46	0.78	3.54
1999	Rochestr	Int	13.7	9	5	2	4	15	3.29	1	1	5.93	1.32	2.63	9.88	1.88	3.01
1999	Baltimor	AL	18.0	10	7	1	10	26	3.50	1	1	5.00	0.50	5.00	13.00	1.30	2.64
2000	Rochestr	Int	23.0	24	16	6	9	21	6.26	1	2	9.39	2.35	3.52	8.22	1.17	6.35
2000	Baltimor	AL	43.0	34	24	6	25	39	5.02	2	3	7.12	1.26	5.23	8.16	0.78	4.57

B.J. Ryan, a tall sidearmer, shot through the minors at a miraculous pace for a 17th-round draft pick but finally hit a wall in May. He started out strong in Baltimore's bullpen, giving up just one run in his first 11 appearances. In his next nine, he allowed two or more runs seven times, lowlighted by a game against the Red Sox in which he walked all four batters he faced on 17 pitches. After two months of continuing struggle in Rochester, he endured a few more poundings before straightening out and looking great for the final six weeks. It was probably just growing pains; he'll be fine.

Jay Spurgeon — Throws R — Age 24

YEAR	TEAM	LGE	IP	H	ER	HR	BB	K	ERA	W	L	H/9	HR/9	BB/9	K/9	KW	PERA
1998	Delmarva	SAL	122.7	113	61	17	66	48	4.48	6	8	8.29	1.25	4.84	3.52	0.36	5.11
1999	Frederck	Car	133.3	180	115	30	61	45	7.76	3	12	12.15	2.03	4.12	3.04	0.37	7.91
2000	Frederck	Car	80.7	87	74	20	38	45	8.26	2	7	9.71	2.23	4.24	5.02	0.59	6.74
2000	Bowie	Eas	36.3	33	12	5	8	17	2.97	3	1	8.17	1.24	1.98	4.21	1.06	3.87
2000	Rochestr	Int	12.7	5	1	1	9	8	0.71	1	0	3.55	0.71	6.39	5.68	0.44	2.55
2000	Baltimor	AL	24.0	24	13	4	12	11	4.88	1	2	9.00	1.50	4.50	4.13	0.46	5.63

Jay Spurgeon jumped all the way from the Carolina League to the majors in 2000, though at first glance it's hard to understand how he got out of Frederick. The first glance is deceptive; he had back-to-back May starts in which he was hammered for eight runs apiece and was promoted to Bowie after allowing just six hits in his last three games and 20 innings in the Carolina League. He posted very impressive records (8–2 at Frederick, 3–0 Bowie, 2–0 Rochester, 1–1 Baltimore), succeeding with only an average fastball but a sharp-breaking slider. All of his numbers indicate that he's a fairly extreme fly-ball pitcher, which is going to be dangerous in Camden Yards.

Rich Stahl — Throws L — Age 20

YEAR	TEAM	LGE	IP	H	ER	HR	BB	K	ERA	W	L	H/9	HR/9	BB/9	K/9	KW	PERA
2000	Delmarva	SAL	79.0	97	54	8	68	39	6.15	3	6	11.05	0.91	7.75	4.44	0.29	7.58

A 1999 first-rounder, Rich Stahl is very tall and thin, with the best arm in the Oriole farm system. His fastball reaches the upper 90s, and his curve is knee-buckling. As far as knowing how to pitch—well, he's a year out of high school. He has two problems to overcome: lousy mechanics that ruin his control and an achy lower back (possibly the result of problem #1). His translated stat line looked a lot better before his back started acting up:

	IP	H	ER	HR	BB	K	ERA	W	L	H/9	HR/9	BB/9	K/9	KW	PERA
First 14 starts:	60.0	61	33	3	53	32	4.95	3	4	9.15	0.45	7.95	4.80	0.30	6.04
Last six starts:	19.0	35	21	5	15	8	9.95	0	2	16.58	2.37	7.11	3.79	0.27	12.09

Even so, the strikeout and walk numbers are disturbing.

John Stephens — Throws R — Age 21

YEAR	TEAM	LGE	IP	H	ER	HR	BB	K	ERA	W	L	H/9	HR/9	BB/9	K/9	KW	PERA
1998	Delmarva	SAL	30.3	28	16	6	18	19	4.75	1	2	8.31	1.78	5.34	5.64	0.53	5.87
1999	Delmarva	SAL	151.7	170	106	21	50	101	6.29	5	12	10.09	1.25	2.97	5.99	1.01	5.38
2000	Frederck	Car	108.0	128	54	11	25	65	4.50	5	7	10.67	0.92	2.08	5.42	1.30	5.02

The young Australian has made a remarkable recovery from a serious neck injury in 1998 to become one of the brighter stars in the Oriole constellation. (Admittedly, that constellation won't be confused with Orion anytime soon. Can you say "Coma Berenices"? Gooood.) John Stephens's fastball, which topped out at 82 mph or so when he first returned from the injury, continues to improve. In the meantime, he's relied on a Gregg Olson–like curve and outstanding control.

Josh Towers — Throws R — Age 24

YEAR	TEAM	LGE	IP	H	ER	HR	BB	K	ERA	W	L	H/9	HR/9	BB/9	K/9	KW	PERA
1998	Frederck	Car	132.0	147	75	22	12	63	5.11	6	9	10.02	1.50	0.82	4.30	2.63	4.73
1998	Bowie	Eas	17.0	19	9	2	4	4	4.76	1	1	10.06	1.06	2.12	2.12	0.50	4.81
1999	Bowie	Eas	175.7	206	99	39	27	67	5.07	8	12	10.55	2.00	1.38	3.43	1.24	5.81
2000	Rochestr	Int	139.7	156	70	23	22	78	4.51	7	9	10.05	1.48	1.42	5.03	1.77	4.99

"Hi. I'm B.B. King, and I'm here to talk about a terrible tragedy that could be could be occurring right in your community: Pitchers Without Fastballs. In the past, these poor souls have been destined to fail. You could find them fooling some hitters in A ball, but the real men at the higher levels terrorized them, and then where would did they end up? On our streets—destitute, homeless, hungry.

"You can help pitchers like Josh overcome their handicaps by making a generous donation to the Tewksbury Vocational Institute, where they can learn how to spot their pitches, keep hitters off-stride, and be proud, productive members of their communities. After all, a change-up is a terrible thing to waste."

Mike Trombley — Throws R — Age 34

YEAR	TEAM	LGE	IP	H	ER	HR	BB	K	ERA	W	L	H/9	HR/9	BB/9	K/9	KW	PERA
1998	Minnesot	AL	96.0	84	34	13	34	82	3.19	7	4	7.88	1.22	3.19	7.69	1.21	4.15
1999	Minnesot	AL	87.3	86	35	12	22	78	3.61	6	4	8.86	1.24	2.27	8.04	1.77	4.38
2000	Baltimor	AL	72.0	63	29	13	31	69	3.63	4	4	7.88	1.63	3.88	8.63	1.11	4.86

The Orioles thought Mike Trombley would be a good backup closer, in case Timlin's 1999 problems continued into 2000. They did, but Trombley didn't help, going 4-for-11 in save opportunities. In all but one of his blown saves, the culprit was a home run. If Kohlmeier struggles in 2001—hardly out of the question—Trombley would be the next in line for the closer role once again, so you fantasy players might want to consider him in the later rounds.

Support-Neutral Statistics — BALTIMORE ORIOLES — Park Effect: -3.2%

PITCHER	GS	IP	R	SNW	SNL	SNPCT	W	L	RA	APW	SNVA	SNWAR
Lesli Brea	1	3.3	6	0.0	0.7	.038	0	1	16.20	-0.4	-0.3	-0.3
Scott Erickson	16	92.7	81	3.5	8.4	.295	5	8	7.87	-2.6	-2.5	-1.6
Jason Johnson	13	75.0	65	3.2	6.2	.339	0	8	7.80	-2.0	-1.5	-0.8
Calvin Maduro	2	9.0	10	0.2	1.1	.184	0	0	10.00	-0.4	-0.4	-0.3
Chuck McElroy	2	11.0	1	1.1	0.1	.945	2	0	0.82	0.5	0.5	0.6
Jose Mercedes	20	121.3	59	8.1	6.0	.576	13	5	4.38	1.0	1.0	2.1
Mike Mussina	34	237.7	105	16.3	9.4	.634	11	15	3.98	3.0	3.3	5.4
John Parrish	8	36.3	32	1.5	4.0	.268	2	4	7.93	-1.0	-1.2	-0.9
Sidney Ponson	32	222.0	125	12.8	11.5	.528	9	13	5.07	0.3	0.6	2.5
Pat Rapp	30	172.0	123	8.2	12.4	.398	9	12	6.44	-2.2	-2.1	-0.6
Jay Spurgeon	4	19.0	15	0.9	1.7	.329	1	1	7.11	-0.4	-0.4	-0.2
TOTALS	162	999.3	622	55.9	61.5	.476	52	67	5.60	-4.3	-3.1	6.0

Everyone knows Mike Mussina is great, but I'm not sure everyone appreciates just how great. Mussina's career park-adjusted runs allowed average (RA+) is 138, meaning he's been 38% better at preventing runs than an average pitcher over his career. That's the 15th best RA+ since 1900 among pitchers with at least 1,000 innings pitched.

Nearly all of the pitchers ahead of him on that list are either Hall-of-Famers (Walter Johnson, Lefty Grove, Mordecai Brown, Sandy Koufax, Ed Walsh, Pete Alexander, Cy Young, and Christy Mathewson) or likely future Hall-of-Famers (Pedro Martinez, Greg Maddux, Roger Clemens, and Randy Johnson). The two exceptions are Smokey Joe Wood and Harry Brecheen, each of whom edged Mussina with a career RA+ of 139 and each of whom pitched too few innings to merit much consideration for the Hall. Wood's career was essentially over before he turned 30, while Brecheen's didn't get started until he was almost 30.

Granted, ranking an active player in an all-time list based on a rate stat is potentially deceptive, because the active player hasn't yet gone through the decline phase of his career. If you rank pitchers based on RA+ through the year they turned 32, Mussina falls a few spots to number 20 and has a few more non-HOFers ahead of him (Tiny Bonham, Ron Guidry, Babe Adams, and Tex Hughson). Still, there are many more HOFers than non-HOFers surrounding Mussina on the list, and there are many more reasons to be optimistic about Mussina than there would have been about, say, Tiny Bonham or Tex Hughson at age 32.

For a quick explanation of SN stats, see page 7.

Reliever Evaluation Tools

PITCHER	G	IP	R	ARA	APR	IRNR/G	EIRS/G	IRP	BRS	RRA	ARP
Lesli Brea	5	5.7	5	7.96	-1.7	0.60	0.17	-2.2	0.0	11.95	-4.3
Buddy Groom	70	59.3	37	5.63	-2.8	0.84	0.27	5.5	0.3	4.96	1.6
Darren Holmes	8	8.7	13	13.54	-8.0	0.25	0.09	-1.3	0.5	15.43	-9.8
Jason Johnson	12	32.7	30	8.29	-11.2	0.92	0.34	-1.0	-1.7	8.06	-10.4
Ryan Kohlmeier	25	26.3	9	3.08	6.2	0.08	0.04	-1.0	0.9	3.56	4.8
Calvin Maduro	13	14.3	15	9.45	-6.8	0.92	0.22	0.8	0.4	9.29	-6.5
Chuck McElroy	41	52.3	35	6.04	-4.9	0.71	0.28	-1.2	0.2	6.26	-6.2
Jose Mercedes	16	24.3	12	4.45	2.0	0.69	0.31	-1.3	1.0	5.50	-0.8
Alan Mills	23	23.7	17	6.48	-3.4	0.61	0.17	1.8	0.2	5.86	-1.7
Gabe Molina	9	13.0	14	9.72	-6.5	0.11	0.06	-0.5	0.0	10.49	-7.6
Pat Rapp	1	2.0	2	9.03	-0.9	0.00	0.00	0.0	0.0	9.01	-0.8
Al Reyes	13	13.0	10	6.94	-2.5	1.15	0.63	0.0	-2.4	5.33	-0.2
Luis Rivera	1	0.7	0	0.00	0.4	0.00	0.00	0.0	0.4	3.93	0.1
B.J. Ryan	42	42.7	29	6.13	-4.4	0.88	0.27	-4.9	-1.8	7.14	-9.2
Jay Spurgeon	3	5.0	1	1.81	1.9	0.67	0.35	1.1	0.0	-0.04	2.9
Mike Timlin	37	35.0	22	5.67	-1.9	0.30	0.10	-1.4	2.1	6.74	-6.0
Mike Trombley	74	71.0	34	4.32	6.9	0.61	0.22	1.1	1.7	4.53	5.3
Tim Worrell	5	7.3	6	7.38	-1.8	0.20	0.05	0.2	2.1	9.63	-3.6
TOTALS	398	437.0	291	6.01	-39.5	0.64	0.23			6.28	-52.6

For a quick guide to RET, see page 10.

Boston Red Sox

The Red Sox went into 2000 as playoff contenders and, arguably, favorites for a world championship (or so said *Sports Illustrated*). They boasted the best pitcher in baseball, one of the game's best-hitting shortstops, a great new center fielder, an on-base machine in the leadoff spot, a rising talent at catcher, the AL's best pitching coach, a pretty good manager, and a productive farm system. As long as the team could fill in its blanks well enough to reach the playoffs, Pedro Martinez made a victory in any series, even against the hated Yankees, possible. Yet the further into the season the Sox went, the more the team began to show its holes and fall out of any sort of playoff contention.

Indeed, many in Red Sox Nation traced the end of the team's season to the offense's dismal performance in a critical four-game set against the Yankees in September, with the first three games coming in Fenway. While the Sox's season was in jeopardy for months before that—credit Jimy Williams, Joe Kerrigan, and Pedro Martinez for keeping the Sox in contention as long as they did—nearly everything wrong with the Red Sox came to light in that three-game stretch. Facing the Yankees, a team with a similarly bloated payroll, the Sox began an amateur-hour performance that would spotlight just how thoroughly they had squandered the opportunity that Pedro Martinez had given them with his historic season.

"Yankees Suck" signs and T-shirts were out in full force as Roger Clemens came to town to start the first game for the Bombers, but he was surprisingly unfazed, tossing the first eight innings of a shutout. The Yanks beat Pedro Martinez the next day, holding the Sox to just one run until Boston scored two meaningless tallies in the ninth, then won 6-2 in the Fenway finale behind Randy Keisler's first major-league start. Four runs in three days had left the Sox nine games behind the Yankees in the loss column and in fourth place in the wild-card scrum. Their season was in tatters.

The offense was the primary cause of the Red Sox's woes in 2000. Despite the team spending nearly all of its season's-end $70-million payroll on hitters, exactly two Red Sox hitters produced above-average seasons for their positions: Nomar Garciaparra and Carl Everett, and even Everett was a nonentity after the All-Star break.

In the series with the Yanks, the holes were gaping. The team's starting third baseman was fan favorite Lou Merloni, who had been released by a Japanese team a month earlier for his poor hitting. At second base was water bug Donnie Sadler, a player with no discernible talents on offense. The left fielder was Troy O'Leary, a waiver-wire snag from 1996 who should have disappeared the moment he was eligible for arbitration. The first baseman was Jose Offerman, playing the one position on his résumé where his hitting talents—which were AWOL in 2000 anyway—are subpar. And the designated hitter, in the final insult, was newly acquired Dante Bichette, complete with a contract that pays him more than $6 million this season, even though he does nothing better than in-house options like Morgan Burkhart and Israel Alcantara. Sitting on the bench were expensive mediocrities Rico Brogna, Bernard Gilkey, and Mike Lansing.

Third base, in fact, was a black hole for the Sox the entire season. Regular third baseman John Valentin, who is no longer much with the stick even when he's healthy, hurt his knee, missed a month, then blew out the knee entirely, ending his season after 35 at-bats. Wilton Veras was called up but couldn't hit or field and was demoted when GM Dan Duquette gave up two prospects for the best third baseman he could get—Ed Sprague. That's the same Ed Sprague who had gotten only a minor-league offer from the Padres in the spring. Sprague didn't hit, and his fielding was as dismal as ever. Sean Berry came, played one game at third base, went 0-for-4, and was waived.

So down the stretch in a pennant race, Boston's third-base situation consisted of Lou Merloni and Manny Alexander, two utility infielders who came into 2000 with a combined 13 home runs in 1,226 major-league at-bats. With all the free talent available in the high minors and on major-league benches—Dave Hansen and Scott McClain come to

Red Sox Prospectus

2000 record: 85–77; Second place, AL East
Pythagenport W/L: 86–76
Runs Scored: 792 (12th in AL)
Runs Allowed: 745 (1st in AL)
Team EqA: .249 (12th in AL)
2000 Batters' Age: 29.3 (7th oldest in AL)
2000 Pitchers' Age: 30.1 (2nd oldest in AL)
Ballpark: Fenway Park; slight hitters' park; Park Factor of 1.021
2000: One legendary pitcher, one superstar shortstop, 23 other guys fall just short.
2001: Signing of Manny Ramirez, addition of pitching depth may put them over the top.

mind—there is simply no excuse for the Red Sox playing a cast of out machines at an important offensive position.

Despite a reputation for turning out top-notch talent, the Boston farm system has shown itself wildly unable to produce position players. Nomar Garciaparra is the last productive hitter to come out of the system, though most analysts believe Trot Nixon will eventually develop into a quality right fielder. Top hitting prospects repeatedly hit walls in the Boston farm system, from Dernell Stenson to Steve Lomasney to Michael Coleman to Astro farmhand Adam Everett. The team rushes to promote players who can't hit, like Veras, while waiving players who can hit but don't excite the scouts, like David Eckstein (now with Anaheim). Plate discipline is supposedly used as a criterion for advancement, but it isn't taught in the system and isn't applied consistently in evaluation.

Compounding the problem of the anemic offense was Jimy Williams's eccentric managing style, which was significantly more effective when he didn't have so many expensive toys with which to play. Brian Daubach inexplicably spent most of the Yankee series on the bench, and Morgan Burkhart had only one at-bat. Trot Nixon sat out two games against left-handers—one of whom was Keisler, who isn't exactly Randy Johnson—in favor of Darren Lewis. Instead of using all the tools at his disposal, Williams shuffled expensive cards in and out of the deck, running the Sox out of at least one game and playing them out of another.

In fact, Williams's refusal to use all of the arrows in his quiver was an issue throughout the season. When Duquette recalled Israel Alcantara in late June, Alcantara made two errors in his sixth game and put up one of the least impressive displays on both sides of the ball in recent memory. Williams then refused to play him again. This sparked a battle of wills in which Duquette refused to option Alcantara. The dual obstinacy led to a 14-day span during which the Sox played with a de facto 24-man roster and a 22-day span when Alcantara played just once.

Even the vaunted Red Sox pitching staff, which posted strong numbers all season, showed its weaknesses in the fateful Yankee series. Beyond the World's Greatest Pitcher, Boston had only one starter, Rolando Arrojo, capable of even the occasional six-inning start—and they didn't get him until the last week of July. Red Sox starting pitchers recorded the fewest outings of six or more innings (77) of any staff in the majors in the last three seasons, despite Pedro pitching six-plus innings in 27 of his 29 starts. Even when the starter wasn't blown out by the third inning, the bullpen still entered the picture by the sixth, placing undue strain on the team's generally strong relief corps.

After the first few months of overuse, that bullpen began to disintegrate. Rich Garces came up lame in late August, as did Hipolito Pichardo. Aside from the steady Derek Lowe, Jimy Williams had no one in the pen whom he could rely upon to relieve a starter who'd left in the fourth inning to catch the early-bird special at Brigham's. When you're counting on Rod Beck to fill a key bullpen role, it's time to worry.

It's almost as if Pedro Martinez's greatness lulled the Red Sox into a false sense of security this year. Given a near-automatic win every fifth day, they could build a team good enough to win just half of the remaining games and make the playoffs. But Martinez received no run support and suffered another minor injury at midseason, so the Sox didn't fare as well as they should have in the games he started while generally failing to stop the opposing team from scoring when he wasn't on the mound. No one can be sure how long Pedro will remain at this phenomenal level, but if the Sox don't turn the ship around soon, they'll be wasting the best years of an all-time great.

All of the Sox's problems in 2000 were foreseeable, and most of them were preventable. Dan Duquette has long been an advocate of using his Triple-A affiliate as a taxi squad where he can stash borderline talents, both hitting (Alcantara, Burkhart, Curtis Pride) and pitching (Pichardo, Julio Santana, Mel Rojas) for use on the big club during the season. But such a strategy works only if the manager is on board with it, and if the GM doesn't get an endorphin rush from putting the team name in the daily transactions column. With Williams unwilling to use the cheap talent Duquette was always able to provide, the Sox were boxed into a corner where they had to acquire short-term fixes with dire long-term costs.

Behind these questionable moves lay a possible ulterior motive: the quest for a new, partially subsidized stadium. Given the team's undeserved reputation as being unwilling to spend money to acquire talent, it seems plausible that John Harrington (managing partner of the Yawkey Trust, which owned 53% of the team and is selling its stake as of this writing) ordered Duquette to make some moves that involved taking on salary to demonstrate to the fans and the politicians of Boston that the team was serious. Of course, if the politicians are savvy, they'll question why taxpayer money should go to pay the salary of a hack like Dante Bichette, but that's another story.

The Red Sox ended the 2000 season with $79 million already committed to 15 players for 2001—more than any other team in baseball—not counting arbitration raises for Jason Varitek and Trot Nixon. Even with all that money misallocated, though, the Sox were one of four lucky winners in the Superstar Lottery, signing Manny Ramirez to an eight-year, $160 million contract. Ramirez addresses the Sox biggest need, another hitter to go with Garciaparra and Everett. The move also energized the team's fan base.

Most importantly, signing Ramirez closed the already small gap between the Sox and the Yankees. The Boston Red Sox are still a flawed team, but one good enough to win the division this year.

HITTERS (BA: .270, OBP: .340, SLG: .440, EqA: .260)

Israel Alcantara — RF — Bats R — Age 28

YEAR	TEAM	LGE	AB	H	DB	TP	HR	BB	SO	R	RBI	SB	CS	OUT	BA	OBP	SLG	EQA	EQR	DEFENSE	
1998	St Pete	Fla	144	37	4	0	6	15	35	14	16	0	0	107	.257	.332	.410	.249	16	25-3B	-3
1998	Reading	Eas	203	50	9	1	10	12	40	26	30	0	1	154	.246	.293	.448	.240	22	15-1B	-2
1999	Trenton	Eas	297	71	16	1	13	18	89	34	39	2	1	227	.239	.287	.431	.235	30	50-LF	3
1999	Pawtuckt	Int	81	19	2	0	7	7	30	10	17	0	0	62	.235	.312	.519	.267	11	12-LF	0
2000	Pawtuckt	Int	300	80	11	1	22	19	92	47	56	1	1	221	.267	.317	.530	.271	42	46-RF	-3
2000	Boston	AL	45	13	2	0	4	2	6	9	7	0	0	32	.289	.319	.600	.288	7		
2001	Boston	AL	336	84	13	0	19	27	103	42	58	1	1	253	.250	.306	.458	.250	40		

Israel Alcantara will forever be remembered for one game in Chicago on July 1 when he committed two errors, loafed on a ball that permitted the opposing catcher to score from first base, and failed to run out a grounder. Alcantara has some value: he has great power against left-handers and a pretty good arm. He might not be expensive enough to make this team, though.

Manny Alexander — 3B — Bats R — Age 30

YEAR	TEAM	LGE	AB	H	DB	TP	HR	BB	SO	R	RBI	SB	CS	OUT	BA	OBP	SLG	EQA	EQR	DEFENSE			
1998	ChiCubs	NL	266	61	8	1	6	17	62	35	25	4	1	206	.229	.278	.335	.204	19	30-SS	-4	21-2B	-2
1999	ChiCubs	NL	177	47	10	2	0	8	36	16	14	3	0	130	.266	.297	.345	.216	14	18-SS	1	12-3B	-4
2000	Boston	AL	193	41	4	3	4	11	37	28	18	2	0	152	.212	.255	.326	.189	12	44-3B	-2	11-SS	1
2001	Boston	AL	187	43	6	1	3	11	41	17	16	3	0	144	.230	.273	.321	.198	13				

Ah, what might have been. Had Manny Alexander not loaned his car to the Red Sox's bat boy, had the bat boy not been driving with a suspended license, had the cops not found Alexander's steroids in the glove compartment, then His Mannyness might have been the next Brady Anderson, popping 55 home runs in 2001. Alexander will likely face criminal charges and be suspended for a few games this season, after which he'll put up his typical season of no walks, no power, and lots of boneheaded baserunning.

Dante Bichette — DH — Bats R — Age 37

YEAR	TEAM	LGE	AB	H	DB	TP	HR	BB	SO	R	RBI	SB	CS	OUT	BA	OBP	SLG	EQA	EQR	DEFENSE	
1998	Colorado	NL	648	191	38	2	21	26	71	87	106	12	4	461	.295	.323	.457	.257	77	144-LF	5
1999	Colorado	NL	577	150	30	1	29	45	79	87	106	4	5	432	.260	.316	.466	.254	70	132-LF	-4
2000	Cincnnti	NL	462	132	25	2	15	34	65	62	70	4	2	332	.286	.339	.446	.261	58	108-RF	-1
2000	Boston	AL	113	33	4	0	7	7	20	12	13	0	0	80	.292	.333	.513	.274	16		
2001	Boston	AL	478	124	19	1	18	37	72	60	71	4	2	356	.259	.313	.416	.243	52		

After coming over from Cincinnati, Dante Bichette won a few fans in Boston with some timely home runs and an adequate performance, but the fact is that he was more overpriced than anything in Copley Square Mall. Bichette cost the Sox two top pitching prospects—former #2 pick Chris Reitsma and former #1 pick John Curtice—and Bichette's contract calls for him to receive $6.5 million in 2001. When you consider that the Sox already had Alcantara, Morgan Burkhart, Curtis Pride, and Brian Daubach—all of whom could hit as well as Bichette and also play the field—the Bichette acquisition was simply bizarre. It's quite likely the acquisition was ordered by owner John Harrington, who wanted to earn support for a new stadium by demonstrating a commitment to winning.

Tony Blanco — 3B — Bats R — Age 19

YEAR	TEAM	LGE	AB	H	DB	TP	HR	BB	SO	R	RBI	SB	CS	OUT	BA	OBP	SLG	EQA	EQR	DEFENSE
2000	Lowell	NYP	29	5	2	0	0	1	13	1	1	0	0	24	.172	.211	.241	.116	1	

A native of the Dominican Republic, Tony Blanco hit .384/.442/.668 with 13 home runs in 190 at-bats as an 18-year-old in the rookie-level Gulf Coast League, making the circuit's All-Star team. He's still a raw toolsy player but boasts an excellent arm at the hot corner. The mere mention of his name gets scouts all aflutter. Like teammate Rick Asadoorian, he's a prospect for the distant future.

American League

Rico Brogna   1B   Bats L   Age 31

YEAR	TEAM	LGE	AB	H	DB	TP	HR	BB	SO	R	RBI	SB	CS	OUT	BA	OBP	SLG	EQA	EQR	DEFENSE	
1998	Philadel	NL	571	150	35	3	21	47	117	78	103	6	7	428	.263	.319	.445	.250	67	144-1B	15
1999	Philadel	NL	620	166	27	4	23	45	125	85	93	6	4	458	.268	.319	.435	.249	71	153-1B	11
2000	Philadel	NL	130	32	10	0	2	5	26	11	13	1	0	98	.246	.283	.369	.216	11	31-1B	0
2000	Boston	AL	56	11	1	0	2	2	12	7	9	0	0	45	.196	.224	.321	.167	3	18-1B	-1
2001	*Atlanta*	*NL*	*333*	*86*	*16*	*1*	*11*	*29*	*72*	*43*	*49*	*3*	*2*	*249*	*.258*	*.318*	*.411*	*.247*	*38*		

Rico Brogna's tenure with the Sox is more notable for front-office shenanigans than on-field performance. Dan Duquette wisely held firm when the Phillies, clearly desperate to move Brogna, tried to pry away an actual prospect from Boston; the Phils eventually waived Brogna, and Boston got him for nothing. But then the Sox refused to play Brogna, allegedly fearing he'd reach incentive clauses in his contract. So, one wonders, why did they acquire him in the first place?

Morgan Burkhart   LF/1B   Bats B   Age 29

YEAR	TEAM	LGE	AB	H	DB	TP	HR	BB	SO	R	RBI	SB	CS	OUT	BA	OBP	SLG	EQA	EQR	DEFENSE			
1999	Sarasota	Fla	248	65	9	0	14	25	41	34	38	2	1	184	.262	.336	.468	.265	33	56-1B	-3		
1999	Trenton	Eas	245	49	11	1	8	21	49	30	29	1	0	196	.200	.278	.351	.209	20	24-1B	-1		
2000	Pawtuckt	Int	360	78	12	1	17	54	100	47	57	0	0	282	.217	.333	.397	.248	43	60-1B	2	14-LF	-2
2000	Boston	AL	72	21	2	0	4	16	23	15	16	0	0	51	.292	.446	.486	.318	15				
2001	*Boston*	*AL*	*298*	*71*	*9*	*0*	*17*	*48*	*94*	*47*	*54*	*0*	*0*	*227*	*.238*	*.344*	*.440*	*.264*	*41*				

The original draft of our Boston chapter didn't include a comment for Morgan Burkhart, but we told Jimy Williams to go back and write one anyway. What Williams has against Burkhart is beyond us: the Red Sox had a screaming need for an outfielder with sock and patience, and Burkhart showed both in Pawtucket and in Boston last year. There's no reason for the Sox to spend money on a first baseman or left fielder with Burkhart around.

Jim Chamblee   2B   Bats R   Age 26

YEAR	TEAM	LGE	AB	H	DB	TP	HR	BB	SO	R	RBI	SB	CS	OUT	BA	OBP	SLG	EQA	EQR	DEFENSE			
1998	Trenton	Eas	500	109	29	2	13	48	147	58	52	5	3	394	.218	.300	.362	.222	46	129-2B	-5		
1999	Pawtuckt	Int	463	113	18	2	19	34	125	67	67	3	2	352	.244	.309	.415	.240	49	99-2B	-7	21-3B	-7
2000	Pawtuckt	Int	411	98	21	3	15	41	134	62	47	6	2	315	.238	.316	.414	.244	46	107-RF	0		
2001	*Boston*	*AL*	*408*	*96*	*19*	*1*	*14*	*40*	*134*	*52*	*54*	*6*	*2*	*314*	*.235*	*.304*	*.390*	*.233*	*41*				

Here's an illustration of the axiom that says a player who has a great season repeating a low-A league usually isn't a prospect. Jim Chamblee looked good as the second baseman for Michigan in 1997, but he was already 22 at the time and playing in his second year in the Midwest League. Now he's in left field, where his bat is below average, and he's trying to scratch out a spot as a Jeff Frye-type utility man. The trade of Donnie Sadler helps him, especially if Chris Stynes has to play third base every day.

Michael Coleman   CF   Bats R   Age 25

YEAR	TEAM	LGE	AB	H	DB	TP	HR	BB	SO	R	RBI	SB	CS	OUT	BA	OBP	SLG	EQA	EQR	DEFENSE	
1998	Pawtuckt	Int	340	78	9	0	12	21	91	38	30	7	6	268	.229	.286	.362	.213	28	79-CF	-1
1999	Pawtuckt	Int	467	112	24	1	24	40	127	74	56	9	5	360	.240	.303	.450	.246	54	108-CF	4
2000	Pawtuckt	Int	66	16	4	1	5	2	24	9	12	2	0	50	.242	.265	.561	.263	9	14-CF	-4
2001	*Cincnnti*	*NL*	*305*	*81*	*16*	*1*	*17*	*26*	*91*	*47*	*52*	*12*	*5*	*229*	*.266*	*.323*	*.492*	*.266*	*42*		

Michael Coleman returned to Triple-A for a third year, which made him about as happy as Judge Maria Lopez in a room full of talk-radio hosts. He started the season with still more power but fewer walks, probably in an attempt to impress the Sox into recalling him. Unfortunately, Coleman fractured and dislocated his left wrist in June, ending his season. He's been traded to the Reds, who have a decent center fielder and a lot of outfield prospects reaching the upper levels.

Midre Cummings — PH/OF   Bats L   Age 29

YEAR	TEAM	LGE	AB	H	DB	TP	HR	BB	SO	R	RBI	SB	CS	OUT	BA	OBP	SLG	EQA	EQR	DEFENSE			
1998	Boston	AL	119	34	6	0	6	17	17	19	15	2	3	88	.286	.383	.487	.284	19	12-RF	-4		
1999	New Brit	Eas	95	28	3	0	2	12	16	19	11	1	1	68	.295	.380	.389	.264	12	24-CF	0		
1999	SaltLake	PCL	253	63	14	2	8	18	44	34	43	3	2	192	.249	.304	.415	.237	26	56-LF	-8		
2000	Minnesot	AL	179	49	6	0	5	9	23	25	21	0	0	130	.274	.320	.391	.237	18	33-RF	-4		
2001	Arizona	NL	223	60	5	0	7	21	35	28	33	1	0	163	.269	.332	.386	.245	24				

Did the Red Sox not have enough spare outfielders by the end of August? Midre Cummings is a useful pinch hitter for a team that doesn't have a bench laden with Morgan Burkhart, Trot Nixon, and a cast of spare outfielders to make Tony LaRussa jealous. Here, he was just superfluous.

Brian Daubach — 1B   Bats L   Age 29

YEAR	TEAM	LGE	AB	H	DB	TP	HR	BB	SO	R	RBI	SB	CS	OUT	BA	OBP	SLG	EQA	EQR	DEFENSE			
1998	Charlott	Int	493	130	36	2	25	63	116	78	89	5	2	365	.264	.360	.497	.282	77	86-RF	-9	24-1B	1
1999	Boston	AL	378	112	32	3	22	32	84	59	70	0	1	267	.296	.355	.571	.295	63	53-1B	-1		
2000	Boston	AL	492	123	29	2	22	38	118	52	72	1	1	370	.250	.312	.451	.250	58	77-1B	0		
2001	Boston	AL	443	117	27	1	23	47	113	69	83	1	1	327	.264	.335	.485	.270	62				

He dropped off enough from his excellent rookie season that Jimy Williams started using him less down the stretch, which didn't do anything to shake Brian Daubach's post-April slump. Daubach's shoulder injury in the Tampa Bay mêlée in late August didn't help, as he barely hit at all during September. He's better than he showed in 2000 but not as good as he was the year before. That gives him one more season of usefulness before he hits arbitration.

Juan Diaz — 1B   Bats R   Age 25

YEAR	TEAM	LGE	AB	H	DB	TP	HR	BB	SO	R	RBI	SB	CS	OUT	BA	OBP	SLG	EQA	EQR	DEFENSE	
1998	Vero Bch	Fla	250	58	7	1	12	15	59	23	33	0	1	193	.232	.281	.412	.225	23	54-1B	-3
1998	SanAnton	Tex	189	44	10	0	9	11	50	19	21	0	0	145	.233	.279	.429	.230	18	41-1B	-11
1999	SanAnton	Tex	257	67	15	1	7	20	83	33	39	0	0	190	.261	.319	.409	.242	27	60-1B	-4
2000	Sarasota	Fla	52	12	2	0	3	2	17	5	8	0	0	40	.231	.266	.442	.228	5	14-1B	0
2000	Trenton	Eas	200	54	10	1	12	6	62	27	36	0	0	146	.270	.291	.510	.256	24	35-1B	-4
2000	Pawtuckt	Int	43	11	1	0	5	5	9	9	12	1	0	32	.256	.333	.628	.301	8	10-1B	0
2001	Boston	AL	289	77	13	1	17	19	91	39	54	1	0	212	.266	.312	.495	.263	38		

Juan Diaz bludgeoned the ball like it was George Steinbrenner's head until yet another horrific Red Sox injury (a broken and dislocated right ankle) ended his season. Before then, he had hit 28 home runs in 290 at-bats at three levels. His plate discipline isn't great; however, it is good enough to make him a cheap fill-in at first base and DH for the Sox, unless they'd rather call Ed Sprague again.

Carl Everett — CF   Bats B   Age 30

YEAR	TEAM	LGE	AB	H	DB	TP	HR	BB	SO	R	RBI	SB	CS	OUT	BA	OBP	SLG	EQA	EQR	DEFENSE	
1998	Houston	NL	476	141	33	4	16	43	96	74	76	13	12	347	.296	.358	.483	.273	68	123-CF	11
1999	Houston	NL	467	148	32	3	24	44	89	81	100	21	6	326	.317	.388	.552	.307	85	121-CF	-1
2000	Boston	AL	490	147	31	3	35	46	103	77	101	11	5	348	.300	.370	.590	.305	89	121-CF	-2
2001	Boston	AL	482	142	31	2	25	56	106	95	99	15	6	346	.295	.368	.523	.293	80		

Carl Everett was incredible before the All-Star break, merely good after it. His infamous tirade against umpire Ron Kulpa (and subsequent, less-known explosion against *Boston Globe* writer Dan Shaughnessy) took him out of the lineup for ten critical games in August. So, despite what looks like a stellar Boston debut, two questions remain: was his second-half dive a harbinger of the future, and can he control himself enough to stay in the game?

Nomar Garciaparra — SS   Bats R   Age 27

YEAR	TEAM	LGE	AB	H	DB	TP	HR	BB	SO	R	RBI	SB	CS	OUT	BA	OBP	SLG	EQA	EQR	DEFENSE	
1998	Boston	AL	601	196	36	8	37	31	55	111	120	10	5	410	.326	.366	.597	.306	106	143-SS	-11
1999	Boston	AL	525	189	41	4	28	45	36	99	99	13	3	339	.360	.418	.613	.332	108	133-SS	0
2000	Boston	AL	519	194	48	3	22	54	46	98	90	5	2	327	.374	.435	.605	.337	108	133-SS	-7
2001	Boston	AL	569	201	37	2	30	59	51	126	141	12	2	370	.353	.414	.583	.328	114		

American League

Nomar Garciaparra is perhaps the best bad-ball hitter in the AL, particularly on anything up around the letters that he can just yank into left field. He might post a small power spike in the next year or two, but he seems fully developed at the plate. The best thing that could happen to him and to the Sox would be a move to third base, as folks are finally realizing that the ability to make the play deep in the hole (Garciaparra's forte) is not as important as turning the double play or making the routine throw to first, two tasks that have proven more difficult for him.

Bernard Gilkey   RF   Bats R Age 34

YEAR	TEAM	LGE	AB	H	DB	TP	HR	BB	SO	R	RBI	SB	CS	OUT	BA	OBP	SLG	EQA	EQR	DEFENSE	
1998	NY Mets	NL	269	64	12	0	6	31	62	35	31	5	1	206	.238	.325	.349	.233	27	67-LF	5
1998	Arizona	NL	102	25	0	0	1	11	13	8	5	4	2	79	.245	.324	.275	.210	8	25-LF	1
1999	Arizona	NL	204	58	13	1	8	26	40	26	36	1	2	148	.284	.370	.475	.279	30	47-RF	-3
2000	Arizona	NL	74	8	2	0	2	6	15	6	6	0	0	66	.108	.175	.216	.053	0	16-RF	-1
2000	Boston	AL	90	21	4	1	1	9	11	10	8	0	0	69	.233	.324	.333	.225	8	20-RF	-1
2001	StLouis	NL	200	44	5	0	6	26	39	26	25	3	1	157	.220	.310	.335	.222	18		

Another of the team's more questionable acquisitions, in the way that getting gonorrhea on a trip to Haiti would be a questionable acquisition. Bernard Gilkey went 3-for-4 with a home run in his first game for the Sox, then hit .218 without homering the rest of the way. Oh, and Jimy Williams barely used him. How many old, immobile, out-making outfielders does one team need?

Julio Guerrero   RF   Bats R Age 20

YEAR	TEAM	LGE	AB	H	DB	TP	HR	BB	SO	R	RBI	SB	CS	OUT	BA	OBP	SLG	EQA	EQR	DEFENSE	
2000	Lowell	NYP	151	34	4	1	0	7	29	13	10	6	2	119	.225	.261	.265	.173	7	39-RF	-1
2001	Boston	AL	83	18	2	0	0	4	59	7	3	4	1	66	.217	.253	.241	.161	3		

Vladimir's little brother may have started to turn the corner in 2000 as he stopped trying to pull everything and started to use the whole field, but he still looks more like Wilton than Vlad, with few walks and no power. Julio Guerrero has a good arm, and he has settled in right field for now, which probably fits his profile better and will reduce the wear and tear he faced at shortstop.

Scott Hatteberg   C   Bats L Age 31

YEAR	TEAM	LGE	AB	H	DB	TP	HR	BB	SO	R	RBI	SB	CS	OUT	BA	OBP	SLG	EQA	EQR	DEFENSE	
1998	Boston	AL	357	100	20	1	14	42	52	46	43	0	0	257	.280	.363	.459	.275	51	100-C	0
1999	Boston	AL	81	23	2	0	2	17	13	11	12	0	0	58	.284	.414	.383	.281	12	19-C	-3
2000	Boston	AL	232	62	12	0	9	36	36	20	35	0	1	171	.267	.366	.435	.269	32	43-C	-11
2001	Boston	AL	203	53	7	0	8	31	34	33	34	0	0	150	.261	.359	.414	.264	27		

He could start for at least half the teams in baseball. Scott Hatteberg brings plenty to the table offensively—he bats left-handed, draws walks, and has some pop—and is a solid defensive catcher. He's also about to get expensive, as is Varitek, so the Sox would be wise to trade the older player to a team in desperate need of a receiver, like the Brewers or Padres.

Mike Lansing   2B   Bats R Age 33

YEAR	TEAM	LGE	AB	H	DB	TP	HR	BB	SO	R	RBI	SB	CS	OUT	BA	OBP	SLG	EQA	EQR	DEFENSE	
1998	Colorado	NL	574	141	30	2	12	37	82	66	57	9	3	436	.246	.297	.368	.222	51	145-2B	-2
1999	Colorado	NL	141	39	6	0	4	5	21	20	13	1	0	102	.277	.306	.404	.236	14	35-2B	2
2000	Colorado	NL	358	80	13	4	9	25	46	51	37	6	2	280	.223	.274	.358	.209	28	86-2B	-19
2000	Boston	AL	139	27	5	0	0	5	24	10	13	0	0	112	.194	.222	.230	.115	3	35-2B	1
2001	Boston	AL	339	74	11	1	7	25	52	30	30	4	1	266	.218	.272	.319	.196	23		

True, Mike Lansing's $6.5-million salary next year represents part of the price for Arrojo since the Rockies wouldn't trade the pitcher without Lansing. But he also takes up a spot on the bench that would be better used on a player who can hit or field, and the Sox are unlikely to swallow Lansing's salary and cut him outright this winter. If Boston could simply learn the principle of sunk costs, they'd be a lot better off when it comes to eliminating stiffs like Lansing.

Darren Lewis — OF — Bats R — Age 33

YEAR	TEAM	LGE	AB	H	DB	TP	HR	BB	SO	R	RBI	SB	CS	OUT	BA	OBP	SLG	EQA	EQR	DEFENSE	
1998	Boston	AL	582	159	24	3	9	69	84	92	62	24	11	434	.273	.357	.371	.252	69	152-CF	9
1999	Boston	AL	467	113	14	6	2	41	47	60	38	15	10	364	.242	.309	.310	.211	37	130-CF	3
2000	Boston	AL	268	64	6	0	4	19	31	41	17	11	6	210	.239	.297	.306	.205	20	68-OF	1
2001	*Boston*	*AL*	*314*	*75*	*9*	*1*	*3*	*34*	*39*	*39*	*28*	*10*	*6*	*245*	*.239*	*.313*	*.303*	*.212*	*25*		

Darren Lewis is Trot Nixon's platoon-mate, for no reason apparent to any member of the Boston media, to anyone in Red Sox Nation, to this writer, or to Butch from the Cape. Darren Lewis has no offensive talents, and his defensive abilities were overrated before age chipped away at them. The Red Sox need to toss all these outfielders in a bag, take them to a Star Market, put them into the Spare Outfielder Drop, and take the tax write-off.

Steve Lomasney — C — Bats R — Age 23

YEAR	TEAM	LGE	AB	H	DB	TP	HR	BB	SO	R	RBI	SB	CS	OUT	BA	OBP	SLG	EQA	EQR	DEFENSE	
1998	Sarasota	Fla	449	90	15	1	16	44	163	52	43	5	2	361	.200	.285	.345	.211	37	79-C	-5
1999	Sarasota	Fla	192	43	7	0	6	19	66	24	19	2	1	150	.224	.306	.354	.223	18	41-C	0
1999	Trenton	Eas	156	33	5	0	9	24	46	18	23	3	3	126	.212	.336	.417	.251	20	46-C	-5
2000	Trenton	Eas	237	52	12	1	7	18	88	24	21	2	4	189	.219	.294	.367	.217	21	60-C	-10
2001	*Boston*	*AL*	*290*	*65*	*11*	*0*	*11*	*33*	*111*	*34*	*38*	*2*	*2*	*227*	*.224*	*.303*	*.376*	*.228*	*28*		

Steve Lomasney had a year to forget in 2000. He hit under .200 for the first two months of the year, fractured a toe in late May, and missed nearly a month in late summer due to a strained hamstring. In the time he did play after June 1, he started to hit again and finished up the year .245/.343/.425. The Sox have said publicly that they're pleased with his progress; Jason Varitek doesn't have to worry just yet.

Lou Merloni — 3B — Bats R — Age 30

YEAR	TEAM	LGE	AB	H	DB	TP	HR	BB	SO	R	RBI	SB	CS	OUT	BA	OBP	SLG	EQA	EQR	DEFENSE			
1998	Pawtuckt	Int	87	27	3	1	5	13	14	13	15	1	1	61	.310	.432	.540	.319	18	11-SS	-2		
1998	Boston	AL	96	28	3	0	2	6	18	10	16	1	0	68	.292	.345	.385	.250	11	25-2B	-1		
1999	Pawtuckt	Int	229	53	12	1	4	23	41	34	25	1	1	177	.231	.318	.345	.225	21	27-SS	-4	26-3B	3
1999	Boston	AL	125	32	4	0	2	7	15	17	13	0	0	93	.256	.305	.336	.214	10	19-SS	-1		
2000	Yokohama	JpC	95	20	3	0	1	7	15	10	4	0	0	75	.211	.272	.274	.175	5				
2000	Boston	AL	127	41	11	2	0	2	20	9	17	1	0	86	.323	.339	.441	.260	15	34-3B	-2		
2001	*Boston*	*AL*	*208*	*59*	*12*	*1*	*4*	*17*	*34*	*30*	*30*	*1*	*1*	*150*	*.284*	*.338*	*.409*	*.251*	*24*				

He's a fan favorite—The Governor—and a moderately useful 25th man if he doesn't cost you anything and if you don't have a better internal option. Unfortunately, the Red Sox came up empty in three-month search for a third baseman, and as a hitter, Lou Merloni was way over his head starting at the hot corner. He's not a lock to make the team in 2000, but he'll happily go to Pawtucket and wait.

Trot Nixon — RF — Bats L — Age 27

YEAR	TEAM	LGE	AB	H	DB	TP	HR	BB	SO	R	RBI	SB	CS	OUT	BA	OBP	SLG	EQA	EQR	DEFENSE	
1998	Pawtuckt	Int	509	139	24	3	18	61	80	78	58	15	9	379	.273	.355	.438	.265	69	115-RF	-7
1999	Boston	AL	377	103	20	5	16	49	68	65	50	3	1	275	.273	.361	.480	.279	56	103-RF	-8
2000	Boston	AL	421	116	28	8	12	58	77	63	56	8	1	306	.276	.366	.466	.280	63	105-RF	0
2001	*Boston*	*AL*	*361*	*98*	*20*	*4*	*12*	*52*	*69*	*69*	*61*	*9*	*2*	*265*	*.271*	*.363*	*.449*	*.276*	*53*		

Trot Nixon was again unable to play a full season, courtesy of a hamstring pull that kept him out for a month and occasional aches and pains. More aggravating to Sox fans was Jimy Williams's insistence on sitting Nixon against left-handers in favor of nonentity Darren Lewis. Nixon didn't even play against the Mark Mulders and Randy Keislers, so it's not as if he was getting to practice against weak left-handers so he could build up his skills. In the case for firing Jimy Williams, this is Exhibit A.

American League

Troy O'Leary — LF — Bats L — Age 31

YEAR	TEAM	LGE	AB	H	DB	TP	HR	BB	SO	R	RBI	SB	CS	OUT	BA	OBP	SLG	EQA	EQR	DEFENSE	
1998	Boston	AL	608	167	34	8	25	35	96	96	82	2	2	443	.275	.319	.480	.260	76	154-LF	3
1999	Boston	AL	591	167	35	4	29	50	83	81	99	1	2	426	.283	.342	.503	.275	84	153-LF	4
2000	Boston	AL	509	133	28	4	14	38	69	64	66	0	2	378	.261	.315	.415	.241	54	129-LF	1
2001	*Boston*	*AL*	*468*	*127*	*28*	*2*	*16*	*40*	*71*	*66*	*76*	*0*	*1*	*342*	*.271*	*.329*	*.442*	*.256*	*57*		

He was hurt, he went through a difficult divorce, he had a rough childhood—who cares? All the excuses in the world can't hide the fact that Troy O'Leary is barely above a replacement-level ballplayer. He doesn't walk, he has moderate power, and he's not a good fielder in the easiest spot in the outfield. The Red Sox should have discarded him when he became expensive but instead signed him to one of those albatross contracts that are fast becoming a Duquette trademark.

Jose Offerman — Um... — Bats B — Age 32

YEAR	TEAM	LGE	AB	H	DB	TP	HR	BB	SO	R	RBI	SB	CS	OUT	BA	OBP	SLG	EQA	EQR	DEFENSE			
1998	KansasCy	AL	602	192	27	13	8	88	86	98	64	37	11	421	.319	.410	.447	.296	100	150-2B	-3		
1999	Boston	AL	578	170	37	11	8	90	72	102	65	17	12	420	.294	.391	.438	.280	87	126-2B	-13		
2000	Boston	AL	446	113	14	3	9	64	64	68	38	0	9	342	.253	.348	.359	.237	47	75-2B	-8	31-1B	1
2001	*Boston*	*AL*	*484*	*132*	*23*	*6*	*7*	*77*	*72*	*89*	*68*	*11*	*10*	*362*	*.273*	*.373*	*.388*	*.261*	*63*				

Jose Offerman suffered through a lost season in which he didn't hit or draw walks while playing through a groin injury and a deep knee bruise that bothered him for the last four months of the season. Offerman wound up at first base for much of the time he was on the field; he was by far the AL's least productive player at the position. He's not this bad of a hitter and could easily return to his 1999 form. Unless Williams accepts Offerman's glove at second base, though, Offerman is another failed investment.

Curtis Pride — OF — Bats L — Age 32

YEAR	TEAM	LGE	AB	H	DB	TP	HR	BB	SO	R	RBI	SB	CS	OUT	BA	OBP	SLG	EQA	EQR	DEFENSE	
1998	Richmond	Int	79	16	3	1	1	12	18	8	4	4	0	63	.203	.308	.304	.221	7	14-RF	0
1998	Atlanta	NL	108	27	7	1	3	9	27	20	9	4	0	81	.250	.324	.417	.254	13	22-RF	0
2000	Albuquer	PCL	131	30	5	1	4	14	41	19	10	4	3	104	.229	.303	.374	.226	13	33-CF	-4
2000	Pawtuckt	Int	157	40	6	1	7	30	35	33	23	8	1	118	.255	.377	.439	.283	25	43-CF	-4
2001	*Montreal*	*NL*	*177*	*41*	*6*	*1*	*5*	*30*	*71*	*27*	*24*	*1*	*0*	*136*	*.232*	*.343*	*.362*	*.249*	*21*		

He hit .303/.450/.573 in limited time at Pawtucket, almost completely against right-handers. His defensive skills aren't outstanding, allegedly because of his hearing impairment, but O'Leary is no better and doesn't have the medical excuse. Curtis Pride should have gotten a better shot at playing time with Boston, but until teams overcome their bias against Pride's deafness, he's stuck in Triple-A.

Donnie Sadler — 2B/SS — Bats R — Age 26

YEAR	TEAM	LGE	AB	H	DB	TP	HR	BB	SO	R	RBI	SB	CS	OUT	BA	OBP	SLG	EQA	EQR	DEFENSE			
1998	Pawtuckt	Int	132	27	3	1	2	22	23	20	9	7	1	106	.205	.318	.288	.220	12	32-2B	0		
1998	Boston	AL	124	29	5	4	3	5	25	21	15	3	0	95	.234	.279	.411	.230	12	38-2B	-3		
1999	Pawtuckt	Int	171	44	10	3	1	13	36	18	13	3	2	129	.257	.318	.368	.231	16	36-SS	-3		
1999	Boston	AL	106	30	5	1	0	4	18	17	5	2	1	77	.283	.309	.349	.220	9				
2000	Pawtuckt	Int	317	61	6	4	5	38	62	40	21	7	1	257	.192	.285	.284	.196	22	49-CF	0	34-SS	3
2000	Boston	AL	99	22	2	0	2	4	16	13	10	3	1	78	.222	.260	.303	.185	6	13-SS	3		
2001	*Cincnnti*	*NL*	*367*	*83*	*11*	*4*	*6*	*42*	*75*	*51*	*41*	*9*	*2*	*286*	*.226*	*.306*	*.327*	*.218*	*32*				

Donnie Sadler is 25 years old and still hasn't learned to hit. He doesn't hit left-handers, he doesn't hit right-handers, he swings for the fences but has no power, he never walks, and he can be a real dimwit on the bases. The Sox supposedly wanted him to hit the ball on the ground more, which at best would turn him into Vince Coleman Lite. He's been traded to the Reds and will fight for Chris Stynes's old job this spring.

Freddy Sanchez   SS   Bats R   Age 23

YEAR	TEAM	LGE	AB	H	DB	TP	HR	BB	SO	R	RBI	SB	CS	OUT	BA	OBP	SLG	EQA	EQR	DEFENSE	
2000	Lowell	NYP	136	33	10	1	1	5	18	17	9	0	2	105	.243	.276	.353	.200	9	32-SS	1
2000	Augusta	SAL	113	29	6	0	0	7	20	12	11	1	0	84	.257	.302	.310	.206	8	30-SS	0
2001	Boston	AL	134	34	8	0	0	6	45	11	11	0	1	101	.254	.286	.313	.194	8		

He's a raw shortstop prospect who rates very highly with the Sox front office. An 11th-round pick in 2000 out of Oklahoma City University (where he hit .434 in his last year), Freddy Sanchez gets very high marks for his range and his throwing arm. He isn't projected to hit for much power, so he needs to sharpen his plate discipline if he wants to become more than a defensive replacement.

Angel Santos   2B   Bats B   Age 21

YEAR	TEAM	LGE	AB	H	DB	TP	HR	BB	SO	R	RBI	SB	CS	OUT	BA	OBP	SLG	EQA	EQR	DEFENSE			
1999	Augusta	SAL	488	110	22	1	11	46	93	58	40	9	5	383	.225	.295	.342	.214	41	45-SS	-1	41-2B	-2
2000	Trenton	Eas	281	65	15	1	3	24	65	25	25	10	5	221	.231	.294	.324	.210	22	79-2B	0		
2001	Boston	AL	280	69	13	1	5	31	71	41	31	8	3	214	.246	.322	.354	.233	28				

A .258/.335/.367 season by a Double-A second baseman wouldn't usually get a guy into this book. Angel Santos makes it because of one fact: He was 20 years old in 2000, one of the youngest regulars in the Eastern League. He jumped from the Sally League and still managed to show some patience at the plate. Santos really should start 2001 at Double-A, but the fact that he survived the leap in 2000 marks him as a sleeper.

Dernell Stenson   1B   Bats L   Age 23

YEAR	TEAM	LGE	AB	H	DB	TP	HR	BB	SO	R	RBI	SB	CS	OUT	BA	OBP	SLG	EQA	EQR	DEFENSE			
1998	Trenton	Eas	519	118	16	1	19	67	138	74	57	3	2	403	.227	.327	.372	.237	55	124-LF	0		
1999	Pawtuckt	Int	440	107	25	1	14	44	118	51	63	1	1	334	.243	.318	.400	.240	47	110-1B	-18		
2000	Pawtuckt	Int	383	94	11	0	20	37	103	52	59	0	0	289	.245	.317	.431	.248	44	65-1B	-3	21-LF	-1
2001	Boston	AL	419	106	15	0	21	49	121	58	73	0	0	313	.253	.331	.439	.257	53				

The bad news: Dernell Stenson scuffled at the plate all year, partly due to a pulled hamstring and a strained rib cage that never really healed. The good news: his fielding improved dramatically in his second season at first base. Stenson is not a good bet for immediate success, but anyone who can hit Triple-A pitching at age 21 like he did in 1999 is a real prospect. Brian Daubach should polish his resumé.

John Valentin   3B   Bats R   Age 34

YEAR	TEAM	LGE	AB	H	DB	TP	HR	BB	SO	R	RBI	SB	CS	OUT	BA	OBP	SLG	EQA	EQR	DEFENSE	
1998	Boston	AL	585	146	35	2	27	76	73	113	74	3	5	444	.250	.344	.455	.264	79	150-3B	17
1999	Boston	AL	447	114	26	1	13	36	62	56	68	0	1	334	.255	.316	.405	.239	47	109-3B	9
2000	Boston	AL	35	9	1	0	2	1	5	5	3	0	1	27	.257	.278	.457	.228	3		
2001	Boston	AL	193	46	8	0	8	23	28	26	31	0	1	148	.238	.319	.404	.242	21		

John Valentin's season ended after just 35 at-bats when he ruptured a knee tendon while fielding a ground ball, sending the Sox into a third-base tailspin from which they never recovered. Valentin's future is murky. He's 33, brittle, hasn't hit well since 1997, and will earn $5 million this year. It'll be tough for the Sox to peddle him, but if they can give even half his contract away, it will help.

Jason Varitek   C   Bats B   Age 29

YEAR	TEAM	LGE	AB	H	DB	TP	HR	BB	SO	R	RBI	SB	CS	OUT	BA	OBP	SLG	EQA	EQR	DEFENSE	
1998	Boston	AL	220	56	9	0	9	17	40	31	34	2	2	166	.255	.313	.418	.241	24	56-C	-5
1999	Boston	AL	479	130	37	2	21	42	77	68	73	1	2	351	.271	.332	.489	.267	65	133-C	-12
2000	Boston	AL	444	110	29	1	11	54	77	52	62	1	1	335	.248	.337	.392	.247	51	119-C	-9
2001	Boston	AL	425	113	26	1	17	54	76	70	74	1	1	313	.266	.349	.452	.268	58		

Although Jason Varitek's season appears to be a disappointment, rumors abound that he was playing with a sore right hand and wrist that affected his swing and robbed him of most of his power. If he is healed by April, he's in line for a breakthrough year at the plate and a big raise after the season.

American League

Wilton Veras — 3B — Bats R — Age 23

YEAR	TEAM	LGE	AB	H	DB	TP	HR	BB	SO	R	RBI	SB	CS	OUT	BA	OBP	SLG	EQA	EQR	DEFENSE	
1998	Trenton	Eas	473	122	22	3	13	10	67	58	54	3	2	353	.258	.279	.400	.221	41	124-3B	0
1999	Trenton	Eas	479	121	20	1	9	13	58	53	59	3	3	361	.253	.276	.355	.205	34	115-3B	13
1999	Boston	AL	117	34	5	1	2	4	13	13	12	0	2	85	.291	.324	.402	.236	11	30-3B	1
2000	Pawtuckt	Int	219	46	4	0	4	9	19	16	24	0	1	174	.210	.246	.283	.162	9	56-3B	7
2000	Boston	AL	163	39	8	1	0	6	18	20	13	0	0	124	.239	.275	.301	.186	9	47-3B	-2
2001	*Boston*	*AL*	*436*	*114*	*17*	*1*	*10*	*19*	*53*	*43*	*52*	*1*	*1*	*323*	*.261*	*.292*	*.374*	*.220*	*37*		

When John Valentin went down with his knee injury, Wilton Veras supporters were thrilled to see him get the job—until they discovered that Emperor Veras has no clothes. His slashing stroke can't compensate for his swinging at anything in the Kenmore Square area and the fact that he seems to wear a ceramic glove. He was banished to Pawtucket and didn't return in September. Veras is only 23, so someone will take a chance on him. He's a project at best.

PITCHERS (ERA: 4.50, H/9: 9.00, HR/9: 1.00, BB/9: 3.00, K/9: 6.00, KW: 1.00, PERA: 4.50)

Rolando Arrojo — Throws R — Age 32

YEAR	TEAM	LGE	IP	H	ER	HR	BB	K	ERA	W	L	H/9	HR/9	BB/9	K/9	KW	PERA
1998	TampaBay	AL	198.3	182	73	18	55	141	3.31	13	9	8.26	0.82	2.50	6.40	1.28	3.69
1999	TampaBay	AL	140.7	151	71	19	48	102	4.54	7	9	9.66	1.22	3.07	6.53	1.06	5.16
2000	Colorado	NL	102.3	116	58	7	29	67	5.10	4	7	10.20	0.62	2.55	5.89	1.16	4.62
2000	Boston	AL	70.7	62	34	8	17	42	4.33	4	4	7.90	1.02	2.17	5.35	1.24	3.57

The one Red Sox trade that really worked out last year brought the team its first decent non-Pedro Martinez starter in Arrojo, who posted five quality starts (plus two good not-quite-six-inning outings) in his two months with Boston. Arrojo's age and the soundness of his arm are in question, but if he can last the 2001 season, as seems likely, he and Martinez will be a potent one-two punch.

Brad Baker — Throws R — Age 20

YEAR	TEAM	LGE	IP	H	ER	HR	BB	K	ERA	W	L	H/9	HR/9	BB/9	K/9	KW	PERA
2000	Augusta	SAL	124.0	126	67	8	74	60	4.86	6	8	9.15	0.58	5.37	4.35	0.41	5.11

Brad Baker, a supplemental pick from 1999, is off to a great start as a professional. He posted a 3.07 ERA with 126 strikeouts and 55 walks in 138 innings in his first full pro season. Baker features a 95-mph fastball and a nearly major-league curve that has scouts salivating like Chris Kahrl at a surplus pork rinds auction. Baker also gets points for his intelligence and poise. If he stays healthy, he's a star in the making.

Rod Beck — Throws R — Age 32

YEAR	TEAM	LGE	IP	H	ER	HR	BB	K	ERA	W	L	H/9	HR/9	BB/9	K/9	KW	PERA
1998	ChiCubs	NL	77.0	85	33	11	18	66	3.86	5	4	9.94	1.29	2.10	7.71	1.83	4.98
1999	ChiCubs	NL	29.3	38	22	4	11	11	6.75	1	2	11.66	1.23	3.38	3.38	0.50	6.44
2000	Boston	AL	40.3	32	13	2	9	34	2.90	3	1	7.14	0.45	2.01	7.59	1.89	2.60

Shooting blanks, I'd say. Rod Beck's fastball has lost enough speed to make it look as big as a softball to opposing hitters. While Beck did pitch reasonably well around his DL time, it's extremely unlikely to happen again.

Hector Carrasco — Throws R — Age 31

YEAR	TEAM	LGE	IP	H	ER	HR	BB	K	ERA	W	L	H/9	HR/9	BB/9	K/9	KW	PERA
1998	Minnesot	AL	61.7	71	26	3	25	43	3.79	4	3	10.36	0.44	3.65	6.28	0.86	4.98
1999	Minnesot	AL	48.7	45	24	2	14	33	4.44	2	3	8.32	0.37	2.59	6.10	1.18	3.34
2000	Minnesot	AL	72.3	70	31	4	25	54	3.86	4	4	8.71	0.50	3.11	6.72	1.08	3.87

Hector Carrasco was just a live arm for a tired pen in September, with a low cost (Boston obtained him in exchange for Lew Ford, a speedy 24-year-old outfielder who hadn't gotten past the Sally League yet). If the Sox continue to employ the retread-rotation strategy for slots three through five, Carrasco should come in handy in preventing more bullpen burnout in the summer of 2001.

Jin Ho Cho — Throws R — Age 25

YEAR	TEAM	LGE	IP	H	ER	HR	BB	K	ERA	W	L	H/9	HR/9	BB/9	K/9	KW	PERA
1998	Sarasota	Fla	30.0	33	15	2	6	17	4.50	1	2	9.90	0.60	1.80	5.10	1.42	4.11
1998	Trenton	Eas	68.3	60	25	6	22	37	3.29	5	3	7.90	0.79	2.90	4.87	0.84	3.62
1999	Pawtuckt	Int	105.0	96	44	13	28	59	3.77	6	6	8.23	1.11	2.40	5.06	1.05	3.94
1999	Boston	AL	38.7	41	22	6	6	15	5.12	2	2	9.54	1.40	1.40	3.49	1.25	4.57
2000	Trenton	Eas	54.0	78	55	16	10	19	9.17	1	5	13.00	2.67	1.67	3.17	0.95	8.08
2000	Pawtuckt	Int	67.7	75	38	11	13	28	5.05	3	5	9.98	1.46	1.73	3.72	1.08	5.03

Jin Ho Cho was the first in the current wave of Boston's Asian pitching prospects to reach the majors. Since then, he has been consistently inconsistent. After back trouble sidelined him early in 2000, Cho returned and had his worst season yet. His control remains strong, and he still has the good fastball, but his command is lousy, and he is acquiring a reputation as a head case. The arm is there, but he needs help.

Rheal Cormier — Throws L — Age 34

YEAR	TEAM	LGE	IP	H	ER	HR	BB	K	ERA	W	L	H/9	HR/9	BB/9	K/9	KW	PERA
1999	Boston	AL	62.3	56	28	3	14	37	4.04	3	4	8.09	0.43	2.02	5.34	1.32	3.05
2000	Boston	AL	67.7	68	34	6	13	41	4.52	4	4	9.04	0.80	1.73	5.45	1.58	3.81

Rheal Cormier was moderately less effective in 2000 than in 1999, as Williams relied on him for more long stints (including six of 30 or more pitches). Before his comeback, Cormier had missed two years due to injuries. Given the workload his fragile arm has carried, further decline should be expected. He's covered if that happens: the Phillies gave him a three-year deal.

Paxton Crawford — Throws R — Age 23

YEAR	TEAM	LGE	IP	H	ER	HR	BB	K	ERA	W	L	H/9	HR/9	BB/9	K/9	KW	PERA
1998	Trenton	Eas	99.7	104	62	13	44	50	5.60	4	7	9.39	1.17	3.97	4.52	0.57	5.31
1999	Trenton	Eas	151.3	151	92	19	64	70	5.47	6	11	8.98	1.13	3.81	4.16	0.55	4.96
2000	Trenton	Eas	48.7	52	24	6	7	35	4.44	2	3	9.62	1.11	1.29	6.47	2.50	4.27
2000	Pawtuckt	Int	58.0	47	33	7	21	36	5.12	2	4	7.29	1.09	3.26	5.59	0.86	3.71
2000	Boston	AL	28.7	24	14	1	10	16	4.40	1	2	7.53	0.31	3.14	5.02	0.80	3.08

After starting his third year in Trenton, Paxton Crawford finally broke through to Triple-A and had a strong summer at Pawtucket, including a seven-inning no-hitter in July. Crawford's fastball is only adequate, but on nights when he's hitting spots with it as well as his slider and change-up, he's solid. Expectations that Crawford can be a rotation savior are as overblown for 2001 as they were in 2000.

Rich Croushore — Throws R — Age 30

YEAR	TEAM	LGE	IP	H	ER	HR	BB	K	ERA	W	L	H/9	HR/9	BB/9	K/9	KW	PERA
1998	Memphis	PCL	26.3	22	20	4	10	26	6.84	1	2	7.52	1.37	3.42	8.89	1.30	4.14
1998	St Louis	NL	52.0	44	31	6	26	38	5.37	2	4	7.62	1.04	4.50	6.58	0.73	4.34
1999	St Louis	NL	70.3	68	39	8	36	74	4.99	3	5	8.70	1.02	4.61	9.47	1.03	5.00
2000	ColSprin	PCL	35.7	39	28	4	30	20	7.07	1	3	9.84	1.01	7.57	5.05	0.33	6.91
2000	Pawtuckt	Int	19.7	17	9	1	11	16	4.12	1	1	7.78	0.46	5.03	7.32	0.73	4.11

American League

An unusual throw-in in the trade that brought Arrojo and Lansing to Boston, Rich Croushore is a screwballer capable of some league-average innings if he's healthy. It's unclear why the Rockies, a team that needs a pretty full bullpen at all times, would give away someone like that, though the fact that Dan O'Dowd's former employer (the Indians) was in a heated battle with Boston at the time of the deal might have had something to do with it.

Jeff Fassero — Throws L — Age 38

YEAR	TEAM	LGE	IP	H	ER	HR	BB	K	ERA	W	L	H/9	HR/9	BB/9	K/9	KW	PERA
1998	Seattle	AL	220.3	208	102	30	57	163	4.17	12	12	8.50	1.23	2.33	6.66	1.43	4.17
1999	Seattle	AL	140.0	175	105	29	59	96	6.75	4	12	11.25	1.86	3.79	6.17	0.81	7.07
2000	Boston	AL	130.0	142	61	13	39	92	4.22	7	7	9.83	0.90	2.70	6.37	1.18	4.76

It was a better season than 1999, which is about the best you can say of Fassero's performance. Aside from a five-start stretch in May, he was a pretty lousy pitcher last year. His pitches don't have the drop they had in his halcyon days with Montreal, and he pitched seven innings only once all year. Lousy-and-durable has its place. Lousy-and-fragile should spell retirement. Or "Cub."

Bryce Florie — Throws R — Age 31

YEAR	TEAM	LGE	IP	H	ER	HR	BB	K	ERA	W	L	H/9	HR/9	BB/9	K/9	KW	PERA
1998	Detroit	AL	131.3	132	69	14	50	90	4.73	6	9	9.05	0.96	3.43	6.17	0.90	4.66
1999	Detroit	AL	51.3	57	27	5	16	38	4.73	2	4	9.99	0.88	2.81	6.66	1.19	4.89
1999	Boston	AL	30.0	31	17	2	12	24	5.10	1	2	9.30	0.60	3.60	7.20	1.00	4.50
2000	Boston	AL	49.3	53	25	4	15	32	4.56	2	3	9.67	0.73	2.74	5.84	1.07	4.52

Bryce Florie's hard-luck season turned gruesome on September 8 when a Ryan Thompson line drive hit him in the face, breaking three bones in his eye socket and damaging his retina. Thankfully, his eyeball wasn't crushed and his retina wasn't detached. His playing career is probably over, though that is a secondary concern at this point. We're just hoping he makes a recovery that enables him to live a normal life.

Casey Fossum — Throws L — Age 23

YEAR	TEAM	LGE	IP	H	ER	HR	BB	K	ERA	W	L	H/9	HR/9	BB/9	K/9	KW	PERA
1999	Lowell	NYP	12.7	8	4	3	7	7	2.84	1	0	5.68	2.13	4.97	4.97	0.50	4.63
2000	Sarasota	Fla	136.7	154	87	17	44	82	5.73	5	10	10.14	1.12	2.90	5.40	0.93	5.26

One of four Red Sox farmhands to throw no-hitters in 2000—along with Tomokazu Ohka (perfect game), Paxton Crawford, and Eric Glaser—Casey Fossum made the jump from the New York-Penn League to the Florida State League without missing a beat. The supplemental-round pick (for losing Greg Swindell—ha!) doesn't throw hard but has a plus curve and excellent control. He could be in the Fenway rotation by 2003.

Jerome Gamble — Throws R — Age 21

YEAR	TEAM	LGE	IP	H	ER	HR	BB	K	ERA	W	L	H/9	HR/9	BB/9	K/9	KW	PERA
1999	Lowell	NYP	22.7	22	11	3	12	17	4.37	1	2	8.74	1.19	4.76	6.75	0.71	5.30
2000	Augusta	SAL	71.0	69	29	3	43	34	3.68	4	4	8.75	0.38	5.45	4.31	0.40	4.70

Jerome Gamble is a tall right-hander once described by a Boston scout as "better than sex," which raises all sorts of questions better left for another time. The team's second-round pick in '99, Gamble has three plus pitches, including a nasty curve, and good control. He was limited by injuries to 15 starts after beginning the year in extended spring training, so the Sox need to handle him carefully. His upside is high.

Rich Garces — Throws R — Age 30

YEAR	TEAM	LGE	IP	H	ER	HR	BB	K	ERA	W	L	H/9	HR/9	BB/9	K/9	KW	PERA
1998	Boston	AL	45.7	34	16	5	23	31	3.15	3	2	6.70	0.99	4.53	6.11	0.67	3.80
1999	Pawtuckt	Int	26.0	24	12	6	10	16	4.15	1	2	8.31	2.08	3.46	5.54	0.80	5.40
1999	Boston	AL	40.0	24	8	1	14	31	1.80	3	1	5.40	0.22	3.15	6.97	1.11	1.99
2000	Boston	AL	74.0	59	23	6	18	66	2.80	5	3	7.18	0.73	2.19	8.03	1.83	2.91

El Guapo rode his fastball and pinpoint control to another stellar season before overwork caught up to him in late August, prompting Jimy Williams to shut him down as a precautionary measure. Assuming the injury isn't major, he should remain one of the AL's top setup men and is a viable closer for the Sox if Lowe has to return to the rotation.

Eric Glaser — Throws R — Age 23

YEAR	TEAM	LGE	IP	H	ER	HR	BB	K	ERA	W	L	H/9	HR/9	BB/9	K/9	KW	PERA
1999	Lowell	NYP	69.0	76	57	19	34	37	7.43	2	6	9.91	2.48	4.43	4.83	0.54	7.20
2000	Augusta	SAL	107.0	123	94	39	47	55	7.91	2	10	10.35	3.28	3.95	4.63	0.59	8.09

Eric Glaser came to the Sox as a compensation pick they received for losing Roger Clemens to the Blue Jays after the 1996 season; so far the returns are good. Glaser is a big right-hander (6'6", 239 pounds) who turned down a scholarship from Michigan State to sign with Boston. He threw a no-hitter against Hagerstown in late August and should see time in Sarasota in 2001.

Tom Gordon — Throws R — Age 33

YEAR	TEAM	LGE	IP	H	ER	HR	BB	K	ERA	W	L	H/9	HR/9	BB/9	K/9	KW	PERA
1997	Boston	AL	180.3	147	66	8	63	146	3.29	12	8	7.34	0.40	3.14	7.29	1.16	2.71
1998	Boston	AL	77.7	52	19	2	21	72	2.20	7	2	6.03	0.23	2.43	8.34	1.71	1.82
1999	Boston	AL	18.0	16	8	2	9	23	4.00	1	1	8.00	1.00	4.50	11.50	1.28	3.98

His recovery from Tommy John surgery continues to go slowly, and his 2001 season remains in doubt at this point. That didn't keep about a half-dozen teams from bidding on Tom Gordon, who signed a two-year deal with the Cubs. Even if Gordon pitches this year, an immediate return to form is unlikely: think Kerry Wood.

Andy Hazlett — Throws L — Age 25

YEAR	TEAM	LGE	IP	H	ER	HR	BB	K	ERA	W	L	H/9	HR/9	BB/9	K/9	KW	PERA
1998	Sarasota	Fla	151.0	153	78	8	31	77	4.65	7	10	9.12	0.48	1.85	4.59	1.24	3.58
1999	Trenton	Eas	151.7	159	100	24	45	76	5.93	5	12	9.44	1.42	2.67	4.51	0.84	5.07
2000	Trenton	Eas	83.7	92	59	18	28	51	6.35	3	6	9.90	1.94	3.01	5.49	0.91	6.03

Andy Hazlett is a soft-tossing left-hander who moved to the bullpen last year when he repeated Double-A. He pitched well, raising his strikeout rate a bit before being pounded in three Triple-A appearances. He's tough on left-handed hitters, holding them to .228/.273/.386.

Sun Woo Kim — Throws R — Age 23

YEAR	TEAM	LGE	IP	H	ER	HR	BB	K	ERA	W	L	H/9	HR/9	BB/9	K/9	KW	PERA
1998	Sarasota	Fla	140.3	166	109	34	48	78	6.99	4	12	10.65	2.18	3.08	5.00	0.81	6.75
1999	Trenton	Eas	137.7	165	101	25	47	82	6.60	4	11	10.79	1.63	3.07	5.36	0.87	6.25
2000	Pawtuckt	Int	128.0	168	101	21	41	89	7.10	3	11	11.81	1.48	2.88	6.26	1.09	6.62

Sun Woo Kim looked like he might step right into the rotation after an impressive spring performance with the big club and a 5-0 start at Pawtucket, but a midseason slump and fisticuffs with then-teammate Tomo Ohka derailed that train. Still, he has a live arm, good movement on his pitches, and two important fans in Jimy Williams and Joe Kerrigan. A year in the Boston bullpen would do wonders for his development, as he has struggled after each promotion.

Mauricio Lara — Throws L — Age 22

YEAR	TEAM	LGE	IP	H	ER	HR	BB	K	ERA	W	L	H/9	HR/9	BB/9	K/9	KW	PERA
2000	Lowell	NYP	77.3	76	26	4	26	39	3.03	6	3	8.84	0.47	3.03	4.54	0.75	3.87
2000	Augusta	SAL	28.0	28	16	5	18	16	5.14	1	2	9.00	1.61	5.79	5.14	0.44	6.31

Mauricio Lara came out of Mexico and exploded on the New York-Penn League last year, finishing fourth in ERA and strikeouts. Lara throws hard, but instead of overpowering hitters, he gets them out by changing speeds and using his off-speed stuff effectively. He's a long way from Fenway, so check back next year.

Bryan Leach — Throws R — Age 23

YEAR	TEAM	LGE	IP	H	ER	HR	BB	K	ERA	W	L	H/9	HR/9	BB/9	K/9	KW	PERA
1999	Lowell	NYP	39.3	48	35	11	24	23	8.01	1	3	10.98	2.52	5.49	5.26	0.48	8.33
2000	Augusta	SAL	63.7	54	40	11	28	40	5.65	2	5	7.63	1.55	3.96	5.65	0.71	4.68

He's a 14th-round pick from 1999 who went to the bullpen full-time this year and took to it like Joan Kennedy to a gin and tonic, earning 40 saves and allowing just 65 base runners in 72⅓ innings while striking out 87 hitters. He finished second in the minors in the Rolaids Relief Man standings behind San Diego's J.J. Trujillo. Minor-league closers aren't usually prospects; Leach has an outside shot.

American League

Sang-Hoon Lee Throws L Age 30

YEAR	TEAM	LGE	IP	H	ER	HR	BB	K	ERA	W	L	H/9	HR/9	BB/9	K/9	KW	PERA
2000	Pawtuckt	Int	66.3	53	27	7	25	52	3.66	4	3	7.19	0.95	3.39	7.06	1.04	3.57
2000	Boston	AL	11.7	10	3	2	4	6	2.31	1	0	7.71	1.54	3.09	4.63	0.75	4.36

He has a remarkably smooth and fluid motion compared to most of the Asian pitchers who have made the trek across the Pacific. After early expectations of his immediate move into the Boston bullpen faded, Sang-Hoon Lee adjusted to life in the States and posted a solid year in Triple-A. He boasts excellent control, though his fastball still doesn't have the life that some claimed it did before he arrived. He should spend 2001 as the #2 left-hander in the pen.

Derek Lowe Throws R Age 28

YEAR	TEAM	LGE	IP	H	ER	HR	BB	K	ERA	W	L	H/9	HR/9	BB/9	K/9	KW	PERA
1998	Boston	AL	121.0	118	56	4	35	71	4.17	6	7	8.78	0.30	2.60	5.28	1.01	3.52
1999	Boston	AL	107.0	78	30	6	20	76	2.52	9	3	6.56	0.50	1.68	6.39	1.90	2.26
2000	Boston	AL	90.3	83	23	5	17	75	2.29	8	2	8.27	0.50	1.69	7.47	2.21	3.09

The second-best pitcher on the Boston staff had another excellent year in the bullpen, but could he have done more? From April through August, the Sox had a bullpen overflowing with good arms and a rotation from the Island of Misfit Toys. Derek Lowe, a former starter, never got the call to join the rotation. If he ever gets the chance, he'll be their best mortal starter. Danger sign: Lowe has pitched more than 90 relief innings in three straight years, and he went on the annual exhibition tour of Japan that some blamed for Billy Wagner's injury.

Pedro Martinez Throws R Age 29

YEAR	TEAM	LGE	IP	H	ER	HR	BB	K	ERA	W	L	H/9	HR/9	BB/9	K/9	KW	PERA
1998	Boston	AL	230.0	177	71	22	56	232	2.78	18	8	6.93	0.86	2.19	9.08	2.07	2.91
1999	Boston	AL	210.7	151	49	7	29	298	2.09	18	5	6.45	0.30	1.24	12.73	5.14	1.91
2000	Boston	AL	213.3	119	37	14	25	271	1.56	21	3	5.02	0.59	1.05	11.43	5.42	1.47

The best pitcher in the world. Pedro Martinez has been the American League's most valuable player the last two years, no matter what some moron writer from New York tells you. When Martinez is on—approximately every fifth day—he spots all three of his pitches for strikes with so much movement on them that he's nearly impossible to hit. In his 18 wins, he pitched 216 innings and gave up just 13 earned runs; he had eight quality starts in which he was tagged with a loss or no decision. If the Sox could just reach the playoffs, Martinez could pitch them into the second round and probably the World Series given just a modicum of support and one more solid starting pitcher. This team can't even provide that, which is just criminal.

Ramon Martinez Throws R Age 33

YEAR	TEAM	LGE	IP	H	ER	HR	BB	K	ERA	W	L	H/9	HR/9	BB/9	K/9	KW	PERA
1998	LosAngls	NL	96.3	76	44	9	40	74	4.11	5	6	7.10	0.84	3.74	6.91	0.93	3.56
1999	Boston	AL	20.3	13	7	2	6	14	3.10	1	1	5.75	0.89	2.66	6.20	1.17	2.49
2000	Boston	AL	128.7	134	78	13	52	85	5.46	5	9	9.37	0.91	3.64	5.95	0.82	4.90

The projections for Ramon Martinez that ran so high in spring training were dashed with his first start: four outs, seven earned runs. Boston's easiest decision this off-season was declining his $8 million option. He went more than six innings in only four of his 27 starts and his control—never great—was generally horrible. Part of his problem comes from the natural process of recovery from major shoulder surgery, but part comes from the fact that this is Ramon Martinez, not Pedro. Expectations should be set accordingly. He's back in Los Angeles this spring.

Tomokazu Ohka Throws R Age 25

YEAR	TEAM	LGE	IP	H	ER	HR	BB	K	ERA	W	L	H/9	HR/9	BB/9	K/9	KW	PERA
1999	Trenton	Eas	65.7	66	34	15	28	33	4.66	3	4	9.05	2.06	3.84	4.52	0.59	5.99
1999	Pawtuckt	Int	65.3	59	17	5	11	46	2.34	5	2	8.13	0.69	1.52	6.34	2.09	3.14
2000	Pawtuckt	Int	123.0	110	57	19	23	58	4.17	7	7	8.05	1.39	1.68	4.24	1.26	3.82
2000	Boston	AL	68.7	64	21	6	20	38	2.75	5	3	8.39	0.79	2.62	4.98	0.95	3.76

Tomokazu Ohka was the team's only reliable starter beyond Pedro Martinez and Rolando Arrojo, which isn't saying much. Ohka improved his command in his second time around with Boston, allowing him to use his outstanding curve more effectively. Some scouts say he is nothing more than a fifth starter, but his minor-league track record is strong enough that he should easily become a #3 starter in the next two seasons.

Jesus Pena — Throws L — Age 26

YEAR	TEAM	LGE	IP	H	ER	HR	BB	K	ERA	W	L	H/9	HR/9	BB/9	K/9	KW	PERA
1998	WnstnSlm	Car	27.7	23	17	4	16	18	5.53	1	2	7.48	1.30	5.20	5.86	0.56	4.83
1998	Birmnghm	Sou	21.3	22	15	5	10	18	6.33	1	1	9.28	2.11	4.22	7.59	0.90	6.32
1999	Birmnghm	Sou	41.7	33	16	4	21	29	3.46	3	2	7.13	0.86	4.54	6.26	0.69	3.90
1999	ChiSox	AL	21.0	21	13	3	18	19	5.57	1	1	9.00	1.29	7.71	8.14	0.53	6.77
2000	Birmnghm	Sou	18.7	23	14	4	7	14	6.75	1	1	11.09	1.93	3.38	6.75	1.00	6.89
2000	Charlott	Int	16.3	10	6	1	10	13	3.31	1	1	5.51	0.55	5.51	7.16	0.65	3.10
2000	ChiSox	AL	23.7	23	14	5	12	18	5.32	1	2	8.75	1.90	4.56	6.85	0.75	5.91

He's a hard thrower with shaky control who continues to make appearances in the majors to do one thing: swat down left-handed hitters like the insects they are. Because right-handed hitters have touched Jesus Pena for an OPS around 950 in his brief major-league tenure, there is no extended role in his immediate future. If you see him facing a lot of rightis in 2001, you know the Red Sox are in dire straits.

Juan Pena — Throws R — Age 24

YEAR	TEAM	LGE	IP	H	ER	HR	BB	K	ERA	W	L	H/9	HR/9	BB/9	K/9	KW	PERA
1997	Sarasota	Fla	83.0	75	51	17	28	52	5.53	3	6	8.13	1.84	3.04	5.64	0.93	4.36
1997	Trenton	Eas	89.7	100	57	18	33	50	5.72	3	7	10.04	1.81	3.31	5.02	0.76	5.42
1998	Pawtuckt	Int	133.3	141	66	18	48	106	4.46	7	8	9.52	1.22	3.24	7.16	1.10	4.56
1999	Pawtuckt	Int	45.7	45	25	8	12	45	4.93	2	3	8.87	1.58	2.36	8.87	1.88	4.23
1999	Boston	AL	12.7	9	1	1	2	14	0.71	1	0	6.39	0.71	1.42	9.95	3.50	2.00

From *Baseball Prospectus 1997*: "... [Juan Pena] averaged 7⅓ innings a start this year [1996], a frightening number for a 19-year-old. He'll probably get hurt in the next 16 months." Apparently, someone in the Boston front office read that, because when Pena went down this spring with a torn ligament in his elbow after years of smaller injuries, the Red Sox claimed it was because he had been hit in the arm with a soft line drive. The explanation was about as believable as Al Gore's iced-tea defense. Pena was overworked for years and broke down, and the Red Sox are 100% culpable.

Hipolito Pichardo — Throws R — Age 31

YEAR	TEAM	LGE	IP	H	ER	HR	BB	K	ERA	W	L	H/9	HR/9	BB/9	K/9	KW	PERA
1998	KansasCy	AL	110.7	117	62	9	36	51	5.04	5	7	9.52	0.73	2.93	4.15	0.71	4.49
2000	Boston	AL	64.3	59	25	1	20	35	3.50	4	3	8.25	0.14	2.80	4.90	0.88	3.17

Hipolito Pichardo was a year removed from Tommy John surgery, so expectations weren't high. Nevertheless, his fastball reached 94 mph with better movement than he had before the operation, and he was arguably one of the top 20 relievers in baseball in 2000. A sore forearm took his slider away in September, but he's expected to be 100% for 2001. Like Garces, Pichardo is part of a good case for returning Lowe to the rotation.

Bret Saberhagen — Throws R — Age 37

YEAR	TEAM	LGE	IP	H	ER	HR	BB	K	ERA	W	L	H/9	HR/9	BB/9	K/9	KW	PERA
1998	Boston	AL	171.0	167	69	18	24	92	3.63	10	9	8.79	0.95	1.26	4.84	1.92	3.63
1999	Boston	AL	116.3	111	37	9	9	77	2.86	9	4	8.59	0.70	0.70	5.96	4.28	3.07
2000	Pawtuckt	Int	12.0	14	9	3	4	6	6.75	0	1	10.50	2.25	3.00	4.50	0.75	6.65

The Sox counted on a Bret Saberhagen return in the second half of 2000 and never prepared for the likelihood that he wouldn't pitch at all. Saberhagen says he'll try again in 2001, but one would hope that the Sox aren't going to sit around holding their collective breath again.

Pete Schourek — Throws L — Age 32

YEAR	TEAM	LGE	IP	H	ER	HR	BB	K	ERA	W	L	H/9	HR/9	BB/9	K/9	KW	PERA
1998	Boston	AL	43.3	42	18	6	12	33	3.74	3	2	8.72	1.25	2.49	6.85	1.38	4.39
1998	Houston	NL	76.3	80	43	11	34	48	5.07	3	5	9.43	1.30	4.01	5.66	0.71	5.48
1999	Pittsbrg	NL	110.7	124	68	18	40	79	5.53	4	8	10.08	1.46	3.25	6.42	0.99	5.74
2000	Boston	AL	106.7	106	55	14	29	60	4.64	5	7	8.94	1.18	2.45	5.06	1.03	4.42

American League

You have to give Pete Schourek credit: he knew the Red Sox needed him, so despite tears in his shoulder and elbow that will require surgery, he came back in September and gave the team a good start when they were desperate for one. At this point, the arm is shot, the curve doesn't break like it did in '95, and the Sox have some alternatives. He needs to hang 'em up.

Seung Song — Throws R — Age 21

YEAR	TEAM	LGE	IP	H	ER	HR	BB	K	ERA	W	L	H/9	HR/9	BB/9	K/9	KW	PERA
2000	Lowell	NYP	65.0	72	33	4	25	44	4.57	3	4	9.97	0.55	3.46	6.09	0.88	4.78

Seung Song is already drawing comparisons to fellow Sox farmhand Sun-Woo Kim. Song has a compact delivery, an overpowering fastball, a plus curve, and he throws strikes. At 21, he has a ways to go, but the Sox haven't been afraid to push their Korean and Japanese prospects up the chain once they get their feet wet in the American pros.

Rob Stanifer — Throws R — Age 29

YEAR	TEAM	LGE	IP	H	ER	HR	BB	K	ERA	W	L	H/9	HR/9	BB/9	K/9	KW	PERA
1998	Charlott	Int	38.0	38	19	1	12	20	4.50	2	2	9.00	0.24	2.84	4.74	0.83	3.67
1998	Florida	NL	46.0	52	33	6	21	24	6.46	1	4	10.17	1.17	4.11	4.70	0.57	5.84
1999	Pawtuckt	Int	37.3	33	21	6	15	20	5.06	2	2	7.96	1.45	3.62	4.82	0.67	4.58
2000	Pawtuckt	Int	48.7	41	15	8	21	30	2.77	3	2	7.58	1.48	3.88	5.55	0.71	4.53
2000	Boston	AL	13.0	20	15	2	3	3	10.38	0	1	13.85	1.38	2.08	2.08	0.50	7.37

He's a sinker/slider/change-up artist who is adequate against right-handed hitters but throws batting practice to lefties. He's certainly not a bad guy to have at the back of the pen, but he could use some adjustment time in the majors to hone his control. Boston isn't the place for that.

Tim Wakefield — Throws R — Age 34

YEAR	TEAM	LGE	IP	H	ER	HR	BB	K	ERA	W	L	H/9	HR/9	BB/9	K/9	KW	PERA
1998	Boston	AL	212.7	196	104	25	66	135	4.40	11	13	8.29	1.06	2.79	5.71	1.02	4.06
1999	Boston	AL	140.0	136	77	15	57	99	4.95	6	10	8.74	0.96	3.66	6.36	0.87	4.58
2000	Boston	AL	159.3	156	86	25	50	97	4.86	7	11	8.81	1.41	2.82	5.48	0.97	4.75

He started just 17 games but ranked third on the team with nine stints of at least six innings. Nevertheless, the Sox sent him to the bullpen at every opportunity, and the inconsistent usage wore on him. Given regular work and the occasional Phil Niekro pep talk, Wakefield can be a league-average starter at worst and a good team's #4 starter with a little luck. Despite all the fighting in 2000, he re-signed with the Sox for 2001.

Tim Young — Throws L — Age 27

YEAR	TEAM	LGE	IP	H	ER	HR	BB	K	ERA	W	L	H/9	HR/9	BB/9	K/9	KW	PERA
1998	Harrisbg	Eas	32.3	33	25	5	11	29	6.96	1	3	9.19	1.39	3.06	8.07	1.32	5.06
1998	Ottawa	Int	25.3	27	15	1	12	24	5.33	1	2	9.59	0.36	4.26	8.53	1.00	4.71
1999	Trenton	Eas	40.7	40	33	2	31	30	7.30	1	4	8.85	0.44	6.86	6.64	0.48	5.42
2000	Pawtuckt	Int	38.7	37	16	7	13	31	3.72	2	2	8.61	1.63	3.03	7.22	1.19	4.98

Tim Young is a reliever with superb control who is effective against both left-handed and right-handed batters. The Sox grabbed him from the Expos when he blew out his elbow, held him through his rehab year in 1999, and now have a third good left-hander for their pen in 2001. That sure beats giving up Mike Judd to get Billy Brewer.

Support-Neutral Statistics — BOSTON RED SOX — Park Effect: +10.8%

PITCHER	GS	IP	R	SNW	SNL	SNPCT	W	L	RA	APW	SNVA	SNWAR
Rolando Arrojo	13	71.3	41	4.5	4.1	.526	5	2	5.17	0.3	0.2	0.9
Hector Carrasco	1	2.0	0	0.3	0.0	1.000	0	0	0.00	0.1	0.1	0.2
Paxton Crawford	4	23.0	11	1.8	0.8	.681	2	1	4.30	0.3	0.4	0.7
Jeff Fassero	23	113.7	65	6.9	7.0	.500	8	7	5.15	0.5	0.1	1.0
Pedro Martinez	29	217.0	44	19.9	3.1	.867	18	6	1.82	8.1	8.1	10.2
Ramon Martinez	27	127.7	94	6.9	10.1	.408	10	8	6.63	-1.4	-1.4	-0.3
Tomokazu Ohka	12	68.0	25	5.0	2.4	.680	3	6	3.31	1.5	1.3	1.9
Steve Ontiveros	1	1.0	6	0.0	0.8	.006	0	1	54.00	-0.5	-0.4	-0.3
Hipolito Pichardo	1	4.0	4	0.1	0.4	.236	0	1	9.00	-0.1	-0.2	-0.1
Brian Rose	12	49.7	37	3.0	4.6	.397	3	5	6.70	-0.6	-0.8	-0.2
Pete Schourek	21	107.3	67	6.7	6.3	.514	3	10	5.62	-0.1	0.3	1.2
Tim Wakefield	17	97.7	73	4.5	7.1	.392	4	6	6.73	-1.1	-1.2	-0.4
John Wasdin	1	4.0	5	0.1	0.6	.133	0	1	11.25	-0.2	-0.2	-0.2
TOTALS	162	886.3	472	60.0	47.1	.560	56	54	4.79	6.7	6.3	14.5

The Red Sox starters were the beneficiaries of some of the best bullpen support in the majors last year. When Boston starters were taken out of the game with runners on base, their relievers generally did a good job of stranding those runners. Boston starters left 119 runners on base for their relievers during 2000. Given where those runners were and how many outs there were at the time the starters left, you would expect an average of 51.2 of them to score. Only 43 of them did score, so the bullpen saved the starters 8.2 runs. Jeff Fassero, Tomokazu Ohka, Brian Rose, Ramon Martinez, and Rolando Arrojo each had two or more runs saved by the bullpen, with all but Martinez finishing among the majors' top 15 in bullpen support. (The bulk of Arrojo's bullpen support and some of Rose's came while they were pitching for the Rockies.) Pete Schourek was the only Boston starter who received poor bullpen support.

Fassero is by far the major league's leading recipient of bullpen help over the five years I've been tracking the numbers. Since 1996, Expos, Mariners, Rangers, and Red Sox relievers have saved Fassero around 16 runs in his starts, lowering his RA during that time by about .15.

For a quick explanation of SN stats, see page 7.

Reliever Evaluation Tools

PITCHER	G	IP	R	ARA	APR	IRNR/G	EIRS/G	IRP	BRS	RRA	ARP
Rod Beck	34	40.7	15	3.11	9.4	0.38	0.15	-0.8	0.1	3.32	8.5
Hector Carrasco	7	4.7	8	14.44	-4.8	0.29	0.10	-1.2	-0.5	16.00	-5.6
Rheal Cormier	64	68.3	40	4.93	2.0	0.45	0.17	-0.5	-3.3	4.53	5.1
Paxton Crawford	3	6.0	4	5.61	-0.3	0.33	0.28	-0.2	0.0	6.37	-0.8
Rich Croushore	5	4.7	3	5.41	-0.1	1.00	0.38	1.8	0.4	3.51	0.9
Jeff Fassero	15	16.3	7	3.61	2.9	0.47	0.16	-0.6	0.2	4.30	1.6
Bryce Florie	29	49.3	30	5.12	0.4	0.66	0.31	2.5	0.6	4.96	1.3
Rich Garces	64	74.7	28	3.16	16.9	0.67	0.26	1.6	-2.5	2.78	20.1
Sang-Hoon Lee	9	11.7	4	2.89	3.0	0.67	0.18	1.5	1.1	2.67	3.3
Derek Lowe	74	91.3	27	2.49	27.5	0.22	0.08	-1.1	0.9	2.71	25.2
Tomokazu Ohka	1	1.3	0	0.00	0.8	2.00	0.41	-0.5	0.0	4.13	0.2
Steve Ontiveros	2	4.3	0	0.00	2.5	0.50	0.12	-0.7	0.0	1.57	1.7
Jesus Pena	2	3.0	1	2.81	0.8	0.00	0.00	0.0	0.0	2.96	0.7
Hipolito Pichardo	37	61.0	25	3.45	11.8	0.84	0.38	4.0	0.3	3.02	14.8
Brian Rose	3	3.3	0	0.00	1.9	0.33	0.05	0.1	0.0	-0.21	2.0
Dan Smith	2	3.3	3	7.58	-0.9	1.50	0.35	0.7	0.0	7.96	-1.0
Rob Stanifer	8	13.0	19	12.31	-10.3	0.12	0.06	0.4	-0.3	11.47	-9.1
Tim Wakefield	34	61.7	34	4.64	3.8	0.62	0.23	1.6	0.6	4.48	4.9
John Wasdin	24	40.7	20	4.14	4.8	0.83	0.36	-5.2	0.2	5.63	-1.9
Tim Young	8	7.0	5	6.02	-0.6	0.38	0.09	-1.5	-0.6	7.04	-1.4
TOTALS	425	566.3	273	4.06	71.6	0.53	0.21			4.08	70.4

For a quick guide to RET, see page 10.

Chicago White Sox

Sometimes waiting can make even the most patient of us cranky. Last year, we allowed for the possibility that the Sox could win the AL Central were the Indians to "collapse under the weight of too many ill-advised long-term contracts... but better things await the Sox in 2001 and 2002 if they're prepared to enter the coming winter as major players in the free-agent market." We also pointed out how much sense it would make to have Alex Rodriguez playing on Chicago's South Side.

The Tribe did collapse in a wave of big contracts, panicky trades, and febrile mood swings that look to get only worse in the years to come. The Sox did win the division. However, Alex Rodriguez is now a Texas Ranger and the Sox weren't major players in the free-agent market. Despite that, things still look good for the Sox in 2001 and 2002, at least up to a point.

The major reason the Sox elected to not enter the A-Rod bidding was the big year they got from Jose Valentin. Valentin was stolen from the Brewers pretty easily; after all, the Brew Crew just had to make space for Jose Hernandez. While nobody could have anticipated Valentin having a season this good, it wasn't too dissimilar from his breakout year in 1996. The Sox have since managed to sign Valentin relatively cheaply. A-Rod is the player to have, but when the difference between the best shortstop in baseball and the (arguably) fifth-best shortstop is nearly $20 million per year, it's clear that the Sox shopped pretty wisely. The decision reflected a lack of ambition, but you can understand the logic.

The future is rosy because the White Sox won the AL Central with a young team. On the strength of some of the best pitching talent in the minors today, they won *Baseball America*'s Organization of the Year Award. Half of the lineup and the core of the pitching staff are built around players who have broken into the majors since 1998. The oldest key players are Valentin (30) and Frank Thomas (33).

Clearly, this would appear to be a team poised on the edge of bigger and better things, though the White Sox aren't getting much attention going into this season because there's no "story" here. It seems to be the White Sox's lot in life to play second banana in almost any discussion. In Chicago, they're less snuggly than the Cubbies. In the AL Central, the Indians make headlines as they thrash around angrily trying to cheat Father Time. The Athletics dominate conversations about teams with great futures.

The lack of attention is unfair, because the Sox are a good example of how a team can profit from a long-term plan even before that plan has been fully executed. First, a team has to believe it can build a worthwhile multi-year program and reasonably project its collection of young talent coming together. The Sox were able to do so with core players like Frank Thomas, Ray Durham, and Magglio Ordonez. A team also must be flexible enough to fill the gaps with trades along the way and as opportunities present themselves. When the chance to get an outstanding young power hitter like Paul Konerko or an underappreciated shortstop like Jose Valentin arose, Ron Schueler seized the moment. A multi-year program usually means punting a couple of years so that the team can evaluate its players and start identifying what it'll need to shop for in order to complete the roster.

The White Sox's basic problem was one of perception. The year in which they initially reaped the benefit of the rebuilding effort that began in 1997 happened to coincide with the year that the rebuilt Athletics spent all summer in the headlines and a tight playoff race. The Sox were hurt by the speed with which they ascended into the winner's circle; they produced more disbelief than acceptance. The White Sox had a ten-game lead on the Tribe by July 1, and starting with Bobby Higginson's laughable comment that the Sox would fold and finish behind the always-dangerous Tigers, the focus shifted too quickly from how the Sox got to first place to how they might screw up.

As it turned out, the White Sox didn't screw up so much as they were screwed over by rotten luck. Going into the postseason, they were badly hampered by injuries to their pitching staff, none of which could have been anticipated or

White Sox Prospectus

2000 record: 95–67; First place, AL Central; Lost to Mariners in Division Series, 3–0
Pythagenport W/L: 94–68
Runs Scored: 978 (1st in AL)
Runs Allowed: 839 (7th in AL)
Team EqA: .269 (4th in AL)
2000 Batters' Age: 27.6 (tied for 4th youngest in AL)
2000 Pitchers' Age: 26.4 (3rd youngest in AL)
Ballpark: Comiskey Park; slight hitters' park; Park Factor of 1.012
2000: The surprise team of the year, at least until the Division Series.
2001: They hurt themselves in the off-season; they might still be the favorites. Might.

prevented. James Baldwin simply broke down as the season progressed. Cal Eldred's bad elbow got worse, which is news only on those slow days when the national telecasts have to close with shots of puppies or babies or panda bears. Mike Sirotka hyperextended his elbow in his last start of the season. Bill Simas and Jim Parque also got hurt down the stretch. By the time October 1 rolled around, there were doubts about all of the Sox starters.

Normally, a rash of pitcher injuries is reason to start wondering about a team's manager and the workloads and stress he places upon his pitchers. However, accusations of pitcher abuse don't stand up in the case of Jerry Manuel. By any of the measures we have, Manuel is one of the managers least likely to overwork his starters. While he did allow left-handed reliever Kelly Wunsch appear in a league-leading 83 games, the Sox have had deep and effective pens during Manuel's three seasons as manager. Where more famous managers have struggled to break in young pitchers, Manuel and pitching coach Nardi Contreras have done an exceptional job.

So Baldwin and Parque and Sirotka pitched hurt in the playoffs, and while that was a handicap, it was the Sox offense that wilted and helped crank out a sweep for the Mariners. After the Sox led the league in runs scored and finished fourth in Equivalent Average, more was expected, but they aren't the first strong offensive team to wilt in the postseason. While there were the usual attempts to label Frank Thomas a "choker," Magglio Ordonez, Paul Konerko, and Carlos Lee were all pretty invisible. It was three games, for Pete's sake. Anything can happen in three games, and as Wunsch or Keith Foulke or Josh Paul can attest, it usually does.

The quick playoff exit has created some anxiety in the organization, heightened by Ron Schueler's decision to resign shortly after the Division Series. While it has been apparent for a couple of years that Kenny Williams was being groomed for the GM role, the Sox's choice of Williams cost them their well-regarded assistant GM, Dan Evans. Schueler made a tough decision in stepping back out of the limelight. It was Schueler who made the hard call to finally break with the team of the early '90s and start over, and it is Schueler who deserves a large part of the credit for turning the organization around quickly enough to be in a position to take the division in 2000. Williams comes into the job realizing that the next five years will be judged a failure if the Sox don't win a World Series.

To make that happen, there are five issues the organization must address. The first issue is tactical: the Sox need to give more thought to their roster composition. Other than a one-week stretch in August after they'd acquired Charles Johnson and Harold Baines, the Sox carried 12 pitchers all season. It was a decision that hurt them in the playoffs, because it made Greg Norton ineligible for the postseason roster, which left them with only a badly injured Herb Perry to man third base.

Twelve pitchers is one too many under any circumstance, but even moreso when you have playoff roster considerations to worry about. Even with a situational reliever or two who may not see more than two or three batters per night, you should be able to cover the back half of games with six relievers. In the critical month of August, the Sox cycled Aaron Myette, Rocky Biddle, Ken Hill, Matt Ginter, and Kevin Beirne through the fifth rotation slot and the seventh spot in the pen. None of them got enough time to prove anything one way or another. This might be a team with too many options spending time reviewing all of them instead of making a choice.

On the last day of August, the Sox did make room for an extra position player: third catcher Josh Paul. This was about as smart as giving a postseason roster spot to a season-ticket holder.

The second issue that the Sox must address also involves the roster: deciding how to handle the first base/designated hitter situation. Acquiring Harold Baines might have been a nice nostalgic gesture, but he had no business playing in front of Paul Konerko. Never mind Baines's iconic value to management as a tie to 1983; it was a roster spot blown on a backup DH. Baines might be back with the Sox in 2001, but he'll have a reduced role. That should end talk of trading Konerko and should leave Frank Thomas where he belongs, at DH. First base is only going to get more crowded when Joe Crede comes up to play third base, because then the Sox will have to do something with Perry. There's really only one wrong answer here, which is to give up on Konerko.

The third issue the Sox have to consider is the reconfiguration of Comiskey this year. They're expanding seating in the bleachers and down the lines by moving the bullpens onto the field in the corners, parallel to and behind the outfield walls. It's a good business decision, in that more people are likely to pay to sit in the bleachers than in the upper deck. But the moves cut down on foul territory and will bring the fences in 17 feet down the left-field line and 12 feet down the right-field line, with some minor adjustments to the power alleys. For a dead pull hitter like Paul Konerko, that could be sweet news. For all of the ChiSox pitchers, it's a really bad break. There isn't a lot the team can do about the reconfiguration in terms of who's on the roster and who isn't, but the ballpark's new dimensions have to be taken into consideration in terms of how the Sox evaluate their players.

The fourth and fifth issues the Sox have to address are attendance and public relations. Jerry Manuel and Jim Parque complained about home attendance during a season in which the Sox were winning. I can only imagine the front office cringed, because attendance increased by 45.5% last season, which is phenomenal. The picture looks extremely

American League

rosy when you consider that attendance spikes for contenders are usually year-after phenomena. The Sox stand a really good chance of drawing 2.5 million people in 2001, but they need to encourage their players and staff to stop firing on the fans.

What the White Sox can look forward to is not worrying about being second-best any more. The example they offer to other baseball franchises is one that will command wider currency within the industry for the very reasons that it attracts less attention than Billy Beane's Athletics.

The Athletics are an analyst's dream team because they have put into practice the ideas about player value, evaluation, and development that serious seamheads espouse. That's to their credit, we love them for it, but it's still a controversial approach which isn't especially well-understood within the game.

The White Sox have been similar to the A's in the breadth of their drive to acquire talent. Both teams have relied primarily on the same three player-acquisition streams: overseas scouting, the draft, and trades. However, unlike the Athletics, the White Sox's approach doesn't bring with it theoretical baggage that can frighten or confuse the pat assumptions of your average journalist. What the Sox have done instead is tilt so heavily towards developing pitchers that they'll easily satisfy the "pitching is 90% of the game" believers.

The organization's pitcher development is fronted by the draft class of 1999, featuring six top picks who all throw hard. That's just the highlight of the best pitching system in baseball. Even with the number of blowouts and disappointments that come with developing pitching, the Sox look like they'll have a good supply in the years to come. The organization's position players are a little more dicey. There's one ready prospect in Joe Crede and a big maybe in top 2000 pick Joe Borchard; overall, the Sox are extremely weak.

With the pitching they have on hand and more coming up, the Sox should be able to continue to improve their staff, even if the reconfigured park hides the extent of the progress. Manuel and Contreras seem like the ideal manager/pitching coach team to handle the young staff. Their weakness is the offense; you can expect some of the hitters to slip, and the Sox have lost Charles Johnson and will continue to rely on Chris Singleton. They could lose a good 75 runs from last season's total. They should win the division, but it will be much closer this time around. The Tigers look like they're finally going to field a real team, and the Indians will continue to be a factor until they burn out entirely. With the new schedule weighted towards divisional games, it will be a tight race, one in which the Sox have the power to help themselves.

HITTERS (BA: .270, OBP: .340, SLG: .440, EqA: .260)

Jeff Abbott — OF — Bats R — Age 28

YEAR	TEAM	LGE	AB	H	DB	TP	HR	BB	SO	R	RBI	SB	CS	OUT	BA	OBP	SLG	EQA	EQR	DEFENSE	
1998	ChiSox	AL	244	70	13	1	13	9	25	33	41	2	3	177	.287	.312	.508	.262	31	58-OF	-5
1999	ChiSox	AL	57	9	1	0	2	4	11	5	6	1	1	49	.158	.213	.281	.146	2	12-LF	-1
1999	Charlott	Int	273	74	17	1	7	11	27	31	27	1	2	201	.271	.299	.418	.234	26	63-CF	-3
2000	ChiSox	AL	213	58	16	1	3	19	35	30	27	2	1	156	.272	.338	.399	.249	24	51-OF	-6
2001	Florida	NL	207	53	11	1	5	16	31	25	28	1	1	155	.256	.309	.391	.240	22		

While Jeff Abbott did not hit for the kind of power that was expected of him, Sox fans will remember his game-winning pinch-hit home run in the bottom of the ninth on May 13 as one of the most important moments of the season. In team lore, it's almost up there with Jerry Dybzinski's great month in 1983. Abbott is now Marlins' property after being traded for Julio Ramirez. He could get playing time in left field after Cliff Floyd's next injury.

Harold Baines — DH — Bats L — Age 42

YEAR	TEAM	LGE	AB	H	DB	TP	HR	BB	SO	R	RBI	SB	CS	OUT	BA	OBP	SLG	EQA	EQR	DEFENSE
1998	Baltimor	AL	294	92	12	0	12	31	36	41	60	0	0	202	.313	.380	.476	.286	44	
1999	Baltimor	AL	343	113	17	1	25	40	35	57	79	1	2	232	.329	.399	.603	.319	67	
1999	Clevelnd	AL	84	23	2	0	1	10	9	5	15	0	0	61	.274	.351	.333	.237	8	
2000	Baltimor	AL	221	61	6	0	11	26	36	23	29	0	0	160	.276	.352	.452	.268	30	
2000	ChiSox	AL	61	13	3	0	2	6	10	3	10	0	0	48	.213	.284	.361	.213	5	
2001	ChiSox	AL	272	68	7	0	11	37	40	38	43	0	0	204	.250	.340	.397	.252	32	

(Harold Baines *continued*)

Harold Baines is 145 hits from 3,000 and 16 home runs from 400. Those targets are essential to his shot at the Hall of Fame, and it will take him at least two years to reach them. Acquiring Baines was a fine gesture by the Sox toward one of the franchise's greatest players, but perhaps the move was partially motivated by the hope that Baines will think of himself as a White Sock when he retires. After spending most of his career in a White Sox uniform, Carlton Fisk ignored his fans in Chicago at his Hall of Fame induction. Never mind that Fisk owed the White Sox for letting him set the games-caught record years after he could no longer catch. Baines is in camp with the Sox as an NRI.

Joe Borchard — OF — Bats B — Age 22

YEAR	TEAM	LGE	AB	H	DB	TP	HR	BB	SO	R	RBI	SB	CS	OUT	BA	OBP	SLG	EQA	EQR	DEFENSE	
2000	WnstnSlm	Car	53	13	0	0	2	5	9	5	5	0	0	40	.245	.321	.358	.230	5	13-RF	0
2000	Birmnghm	Sou	23	5	0	1	0	2	8	3	3	0	0	18	.217	.280	.304	.192	1		

It took $5.3 million over the next two-and-a-half years to keep Joe Borchard away from football at Stanford. He's credited with a strong arm and the athleticism to play center field and has been compared to Larry Walker and Dale Murphy. In 1990, just a year after he was drafted, Frank Thomas was called up as soon as he had a hundred games at Double-A under his belt. Borchard may be on a similarly accelerated schedule because of the team's current options in center field.

Mike Caruso — SS — Bats L — Age 24

YEAR	TEAM	LGE	AB	H	DB	TP	HR	BB	SO	R	RBI	SB	CS	OUT	BA	OBP	SLG	EQA	EQR	DEFENSE			
1998	ChiSox	AL	523	166	17	6	6	13	34	81	55	19	6	363	.317	.342	.407	.254	59	130-SS	-16		
1999	ChiSox	AL	528	133	12	4	2	15	33	57	33	11	14	409	.252	.276	.301	.184	30	127-SS	-10		
2000	Charlott	Int	309	70	11	4	0	17	24	33	22	3	5	244	.227	.272	.288	.179	16	66-SS	0	19-2B	-2
2001	ChiSox	AL	382	104	10	3	2	17	28	40	37	9	7	285	.272	.303	.330	.212	29				

After a rough season, he was finally put out of his misery in August, going down with a bulging disk in his back. The Sox have taken Mike Caruso off of the 40-man roster, and even with the current shortage of shortstops, he was not claimed. More than any other A-ball-to-majors player, Caruso was the talented athlete who failed to make adjustments. The lack of upper-level experience killed him, and he hasn't been coachable.

McKay Christensen — CF — Bats L — Age 25

YEAR	TEAM	LGE	AB	H	DB	TP	HR	BB	SO	R	RBI	SB	CS	OUT	BA	OBP	SLG	EQA	EQR	DEFENSE	
1998	WnstnSlm	Car	375	90	15	4	3	43	55	53	25	8	4	289	.240	.327	.325	.226	35	95-CF	-1
1999	Birmnghm	Sou	297	76	7	5	2	22	49	39	21	9	3	224	.256	.317	.333	.224	27	74-CF	3
1999	ChiSox	AL	53	12	2	0	1	3	6	10	6	2	1	42	.226	.268	.321	.195	4	17-CF	-1
2000	Charlott	Int	337	81	11	1	6	25	53	40	25	19	5	261	.240	.294	.332	.217	29	83-CF	-7
2001	ChiSox	AL	323	80	10	2	6	34	56	47	35	14	4	247	.248	.319	.347	.233	32		

McKay Christensen is labeled a prospect because the team's starting center fielder is Chris Singleton. The White Sox have been extremely patient with Christensen, and it hasn't worked. He swings from his heels without hitting for power. The Sox want him to be a leadoff type, but he doesn't get on base well enough. He might make it as a pinch runner and defensive replacement.

Joe Crede — 3B — Bats R — Age 23

YEAR	TEAM	LGE	AB	H	DB	TP	HR	BB	SO	R	RBI	SB	CS	OUT	BA	OBP	SLG	EQA	EQR	DEFENSE	
1998	WnstnSlm	Car	507	130	24	2	15	43	100	73	65	4	3	380	.256	.322	.400	.241	54	124-3B	10
1999	Birmnghm	Sou	294	66	12	1	3	15	50	31	32	1	3	231	.224	.264	.303	.179	16	71-3B	-5
2000	Birmnghm	Sou	554	152	21	0	21	40	115	74	80	2	2	404	.274	.332	.426	.252	64	135-3B	-9
2001	ChiSox	AL	498	136	17	0	20	44	108	66	82	2	2	364	.273	.332	.428	.255	60		

Playing without pain for the first time since 1998, Joe Crede won his second league MVP award in three years. He's being compared to Scott Rolen, and while Crede will be good, the comparison is an overstatement. Crede gets credit for his defensive tools if not for consistent glove work. He hits with power to all fields and is starting to learn which pitches he can jerk down the line—a useful skill in the newly reconfigured Comiskey. He's a good candidate for Rookie of the Year, especially if the Sox move Paul Konerko to create playing time for him.

American League

Jason Dellaero — SS — Bats R — Age 24

YEAR	TEAM	LGE	AB	H	DB	TP	HR	BB	SO	R	RBI	SB	CS	OUT	BA	OBP	SLG	EQA	EQR	DEFENSE	
1998	WnstnSlm	Car	434	84	18	2	9	21	150	38	41	5	2	352	.194	.235	.306	.171	21	117-SS	-29
1999	WnstnSlm	Car	188	38	8	0	3	12	61	16	16	4	2	152	.202	.256	.293	.178	10	54-SS	-4
1999	Birmnghm	Sou	274	65	9	2	8	8	81	30	32	3	4	213	.237	.263	.372	.203	20	78-SS	-6
2000	Birmnghm	Sou	448	87	16	1	8	12	147	35	41	5	3	364	.194	.220	.288	.152	16	118-SS	0
2001	ChiSox	AL	498	110	19	2	11	27	163	52	56	5	2	390	.221	.261	.333	.195	33		

Jason Dellaero's primary accomplishment was providing Mike Caruso with job security before the Jose Valentin trade. As a hitter, Dellaero is completely hopeless against anything that wiggles, and he's gulled by any change of speeds. He can pick it at shortstop and throws in the 90s, which has led to speculation that he might start pitching.

Ray Durham — 2B — Bats B — Age 29

YEAR	TEAM	LGE	AB	H	DB	TP	HR	BB	SO	R	RBI	SB	CS	OUT	BA	OBP	SLG	EQA	EQR	DEFENSE	
1998	ChiSox	AL	635	187	34	8	22	72	94	126	68	30	8	456	.294	.371	.477	.285	99	154-2B	7
1999	ChiSox	AL	607	181	30	7	14	67	96	104	57	32	11	437	.298	.371	.440	.276	87	148-2B	0
2000	ChiSox	AL	608	170	32	9	18	67	96	114	70	26	15	453	.280	.358	.451	.269	85	145-2B	0
2001	ChiSox	AL	588	167	28	7	17	69	99	107	95	20	10	431	.284	.359	.442	.271	83		

Excelling in obscurity, Ray Durham logged another season as the second-best second baseman in the league. He doesn't have the greatest range, but he's outstanding on the deuce and at running down pop-ups and flares. As a hitter, he pastes outside pitches into the opposite-field corner from both sides of the plate. Durham hasn't really lost a step on the bases; the decline in his basestealing is due more to Jose Valentin not being the ideal #2 hitter when it comes to protecting the plate. The logical answer would be to have Durham steal less and score more.

Tony Graffanino — IF — Bats R — Age 29

YEAR	TEAM	LGE	AB	H	DB	TP	HR	BB	SO	R	RBI	SB	CS	OUT	BA	OBP	SLG	EQA	EQR	DEFENSE				
1998	Atlanta	NL	292	63	13	1	6	23	64	33	23	1	4	233	.216	.277	.329	.196	20	78-2B	-2			
1999	Durham	Int	344	91	20	5	6	28	48	48	42	9	6	259	.265	.324	.404	.243	38	84-2B	-1			
1999	TampaBay	AL	129	41	9	4	2	8	20	19	18	3	2	90	.318	.362	.496	.280	19	17-2B	4	16-SS	-2
2000	ChiSox	AL	146	39	5	1	2	20	23	23	15	7	5	112	.267	.359	.356	.246	17	16-SS	4	15-2B	2
2001	ChiSox	AL	287	72	12	2	6	33	51	39	37	3	2	217	.251	.328	.369	.238	30				

Tony Graffanino is your basic hard-nosed utility man, one of the best because he's almost good enough to play regularly. He hits better than the Husons or Alexanders, and as Robbie Alomar will attest, he has a nice take-out slide. Graffy proved he could play shortstop well enough to hold the utility role, which was important because he was asked to spot Valentin against tough left-handers.

Tim Hummel — SS/3B — Bats R — Age 22

YEAR	TEAM	LGE	AB	H	DB	TP	HR	BB	SO	R	RBI	SB	CS	OUT	BA	OBP	SLG	EQA	EQR	DEFENSE	
2000	Burlingt	Mid	148	39	6	1	1	14	22	15	15	3	2	111	.264	.329	.338	.227	14	33-SS	-1
2000	WnstnSlm	Car	101	28	4	0	1	9	12	11	7	0	1	74	.277	.342	.347	.232	10	25-3B	-3
2001	ChiSox	AL	129	35	0	0	2	13	41	15	15	1	1	95	.271	.338	.318	.227	12		

A second-round pick in the 2000 draft, Old Dominion star Tim Hummel was considered by *Baseball America* to be one of the best pure hitters coming out of college. He's a big guy who will probably move to third base, but the Sox are willing play him at shortstop until he proves he can't handle it. Hummel is already one of the better players in a weak field of hitting prospects, but he's more than a year away from entering the major-league picture.

Jeff Inglin — OF — Bats R — Age 25

YEAR	TEAM	LGE	AB	H	DB	TP	HR	BB	SO	R	RBI	SB	CS	OUT	BA	OBP	SLG	EQA	EQR	DEFENSE	
1998	Birmnghm	Sou	502	107	18	3	19	53	107	56	69	2	1	396	.213	.292	.375	.222	46	113-LF	-2
1999	Birmnghm	Sou	439	111	21	3	11	42	66	46	46	10	2	330	.253	.323	.390	.242	48	94-LF	-2
2000	Birmnghm	Sou	255	66	12	2	4	25	46	37	33	2	1	190	.259	.330	.369	.237	26	15-LF	0
2000	Charlott	Int	145	39	6	1	4	10	18	16	25	2	0	106	.269	.323	.407	.246	16	36-LF	0
2001	ChiSox	AL	421	104	22	2	10	43	76	56	54	4	1	318	.247	.317	.380	.237	44		

(Jeff Inglin *continued*)

You know your career has stalled when you win the MVP award in the Southern League's All-Star Game in consecutive years. Jeff Inglin is handicapped by an arm that's really suitable only for left field, which hurts his shot at a fourth-outfielder job. In an organization overloaded with right-handed-hitting outfielders, Inglin's future lies someplace else.

Charles Johnson   C   Bats R   Age 29

YEAR	TEAM	LGE	AB	H	DB	TP	HR	BB	SO	R	RBI	SB	CS	OUT	BA	OBP	SLG	EQA	EQR	DEFENSE	
1998	Florida	NL	115	26	3	0	8	16	28	13	24	0	1	90	.226	.321	.461	.254	15	30-C	0
1998	LosAngls	NL	352	80	11	0	14	28	93	33	37	0	1	273	.227	.286	.378	.218	30	97-C	6
1999	Baltimor	AL	425	110	17	1	18	51	97	57	54	0	0	315	.259	.343	.431	.259	54	125-C	6
2000	Baltimor	AL	285	86	14	0	23	28	63	51	54	2	0	199	.302	.364	.593	.305	51	78-C	0
2000	ChiSox	AL	133	44	8	0	10	18	34	23	34	0	0	89	.331	.415	.617	.329	28	36-C	2
2001	Florida	NL	455	127	19	0	26	57	116	65	84	1	0	328	.279	.359	.492	.288	73		

What gets said about catchers and what they do for a team's pitching is always good for a chuckle. Charles Johnson's reputation as a handler of pitchers is like a dot-com stock, bouncing from good to bad to all points in between. He was no more or less effective at stopping the running game than Brook Fordyce or Mark Johnson. His primary asset isn't his glove, it's his bat, and he finally had the kind of season that has been expected of him. Johnson signed a five-year deal with the Marlins for just $35 million.

Mark Johnson   C   Bats L   Age 25

YEAR	TEAM	LGE	AB	H	DB	TP	HR	BB	SO	R	RBI	SB	CS	OUT	BA	OBP	SLG	EQA	EQR	DEFENSE	
1998	Birmnghm	Sou	389	92	13	2	7	77	77	50	41	0	0	297	.237	.368	.334	.249	46	99-C	-18
1999	ChiSox	AL	205	47	9	0	5	34	53	26	16	3	1	159	.229	.344	.346	.241	23	67-C	0
2000	ChiSox	AL	212	48	9	0	4	24	36	27	23	3	2	166	.226	.308	.325	.215	18	69-C	5
2001	ChiSox	AL	234	53	8	1	6	36	50	32	29	2	1	182	.226	.330	.346	.235	24		

Mark Johnson is out of favor. He's considered too passive a hitter, but drawing walks is his primary offensive skill. Unlike Josh Paul, he's never been one of Kenny Williams's guys, even though he is an outstanding catcher and plate blocker. If the Sox weren't so stubborn about Paul, Johnson would give them 60 walks and a dozen home runs in the ninth slot as a semi-regular. Now, he'll wait for the inevitable Sandy Alomar injury.

Paul Konerko   1B   Bats R   Age 25

YEAR	TEAM	LGE	AB	H	DB	TP	HR	BB	SO	R	RBI	SB	CS	OUT	BA	OBP	SLG	EQA	EQR	DEFENSE	
1998	LosAngls	NL	146	33	2	0	4	10	28	15	16	0	1	114	.226	.284	.322	.198	10	20-1B	2
1998	Cincnnti	NL	74	17	3	0	3	5	9	7	13	0	0	57	.230	.287	.392	.223	7		
1998	Indianap	Int	150	44	5	0	7	16	18	21	32	1	0	106	.293	.367	.467	.279	22	32-3B	-2
1999	ChiSox	AL	509	152	31	4	25	40	62	70	78	1	0	357	.299	.352	.523	.284	77	88-1B	6
2000	ChiSox	AL	519	155	27	1	23	41	66	80	93	1	0	364	.299	.362	.487	.281	76	120-1B	-3
2001	ChiSox	AL	519	164	25	1	29	52	72	92	119	1	0	355	.316	.378	.536	.301	89		

You've read this before in this space, but it goes double now that the Sox are moving the fences in: if the Sox hold on to Paul Konerko, he's going to outhit that projection. He'll unleash a projectile shower that'll give the left-field grandstand at Comiskey some hokey name like Konerko's Korner. He's entering a great four-year run, so if the Sox deal him now, when his value is relatively low, they'll be making a big mistake. Considering they benched Konerko for Baines last year, it wouldn't be a total surprise.

Carlos Lee   LF   Bats R   Age 25

YEAR	TEAM	LGE	AB	H	DB	TP	HR	BB	SO	R	RBI	SB	CS	OUT	BA	OBP	SLG	EQA	EQR	DEFENSE	
1998	Birmnghm	Sou	551	143	24	1	17	20	58	55	74	6	3	411	.260	.287	.399	.225	49	124-3B	-16
1999	Charlott	Int	92	28	4	0	3	6	14	12	15	1	1	65	.304	.352	.446	.264	12	12-3B	-1
1999	ChiSox	AL	490	145	32	2	17	9	66	65	81	4	2	347	.296	.313	.473	.256	58	95-LF	-2
2000	ChiSox	AL	567	171	27	2	25	31	86	102	87	14	5	401	.302	.341	.489	.273	78	138-LF	4
2001	ChiSox	AL	531	161	23	1	28	31	81	84	105	12	3	373	.303	.342	.508	.281	78		

Like Konerko, Carlos Lee is a power hitter coming into his own, but while Konerko isn't appreciated, Lee is given the benefit of the doubt about his defense and on-base skills. While he has improved in the field, Lee managed just 37 unintentional

American League

walks, matching his career high in Birmingham in 1998. A lot of rookies shed a bit of patience in their first year and regain it once they're established. While Lee superficially seems to have made progress, he won't really be valuable until he improves beyond a level that he's already achieved.

Jeff Liefer — 1B — Bats L — Age 26

YEAR	TEAM	LGE	AB	H	DB	TP	HR	BB	SO	R	RBI	SB	CS	OUT	BA	OBP	SLG	EQA	EQR	DEFENSE			
1998	Birmnghm	Sou	475	118	26	3	16	39	133	61	60	1	1	358	.248	.313	.417	.242	52	91-1B	-4		
1999	ChiSox	AL	113	28	8	1	0	7	25	8	14	2	0	85	.248	.292	.336	.212	9	13-LF	0	11-1B	3
1999	Charlott	Int	168	49	11	1	7	17	26	27	25	1	1	120	.292	.359	.494	.280	25	23-1B	4	15-LF	-2
2000	Charlott	Int	445	111	21	1	26	43	111	62	71	1	2	336	.249	.318	.476	.258	57	61-1B	4	16-LF	-1
2001	ChiSox	AL	380	96	21	1	17	37	100	53	63	2	1	285	.253	.319	.447	.255	47				

Jeff Liefer's future isn't in his hands. If the White Sox trade Konerko, Liefer has a shot at sharing playing time with Frank Thomas at DH and getting some spot duty at first base and left field. Because the Sox lineup is so heavily right-handed, Liefer might be a useful bench player. Still, his usefulness doesn't make a Konerko trade a good idea. In Liefer's favor, he isn't a platoon hitter.

Terrell Merriman — CF — Bats L — Age 23

YEAR	TEAM	LGE	AB	H	DB	TP	HR	BB	SO	R	RBI	SB	CS	OUT	BA	OBP	SLG	EQA	EQR	DEFENSE	
1998	Bristol	App	130	24	5	0	1	10	39	12	9	3	1	107	.185	.243	.246	.153	5	35-CF	-1
1999	Burlingt	Mid	386	90	12	4	11	47	92	46	51	10	3	299	.233	.318	.370	.235	40	97-CF	-18
2000	WnstnSlm	Car	458	90	16	5	11	71	113	47	49	11	4	372	.197	.309	.325	.220	42	131-CF	-3
2001	ChiSox	AL	341	74	12	2	8	50	91	49	37	10	3	270	.217	.317	.334	.228	34		

Hitting .232 in the Carolina League is a pretty good way to avoid getting talked up as a prospect. Nevertheless, Terrell Merriman is a nifty bundle of the skills you measure using Bill James's old Secondary Average: 94 walks, 43 extra-base hits, and 28 stolen bases add up to a .435 SA. He's improved significantly on defense. In a weak field, Merriman could be the organization's best outfield prospect behind Borchard.

Greg Norton — 3B/1B — Bats B — Age 28

YEAR	TEAM	LGE	AB	H	DB	TP	HR	BB	SO	R	RBI	SB	CS	OUT	BA	OBP	SLG	EQA	EQR	DEFENSE			
1998	ChiSox	AL	299	73	18	2	10	26	69	39	37	2	3	229	.244	.308	.418	.239	32	64-1B	6	11-3B	-4
1999	ChiSox	AL	432	111	21	0	18	65	85	60	49	4	4	325	.257	.356	.431	.264	58	110-3B	0		
2000	ChiSox	AL	199	49	6	1	6	24	43	24	26	1	0	150	.246	.333	.377	.242	22	36-3B	-6	11-1B	0
2000	Charlott	Int	98	23	3	0	4	19	25	15	13	1	0	75	.235	.367	.388	.263	13	24-3B	3		
2001	Colorado	NL	320	96	12	0	17	52	72	60	67	3	1	225	.300	.398	.497	.272	43				

Demonized for his defense at third base, Greg Norton is still a useful utility infielder. The Sox blew their opportunity to have him around to back up Herb Perry in the 2000 postseason. Signed by the Rockies, where he'll be used as a pinch-hitter and bench player.

Magglio Ordonez — RF — Bats R — Age 27

YEAR	TEAM	LGE	AB	H	DB	TP	HR	BB	SO	R	RBI	SB	CS	OUT	BA	OBP	SLG	EQA	EQR	DEFENSE	
1998	ChiSox	AL	535	156	24	2	16	27	47	71	66	7	6	385	.292	.335	.434	.254	63	140-RF	2
1999	ChiSox	AL	620	188	35	3	31	41	58	97	112	12	6	438	.303	.347	.519	.281	92	146-RF	0
2000	ChiSox	AL	581	184	33	2	33	53	58	97	118	19	5	402	.317	.376	.551	.302	101	140-RF	-6
2001	ChiSox	AL	574	179	30	2	31	50	60	105	123	14	5	400	.312	.367	.533	.296	96		

One of the things about being a prodigious GIDP guy is that it takes two to tango. Just as Ben Grieve would have had a hard time hitting into 32 double plays if he was an Expo, Magglio Ordonez couldn't have finished second with 28 if it wasn't for the Big Hurt lumbering down to second base in front of him.

Consider the fate of an outfielder who came up at age 24 in 1998. Ordonez is arbitration-eligible for the first time this winter. His agent might have to fight and yell for three consecutive years. Ordonez will be a free agent after 2003, when he's 30, at which time the best years of his career will be behind him. Normally, the Sox would be deciding whether or not to offer him a four-year contract, but this is the last year of the old CBA, and who knows if four-year free agency is coming.

Josh Paul — C — Bats R — Age 26

YEAR	TEAM	LGE	AB	H	DB	TP	HR	BB	SO	R	RBI	SB	CS	OUT	BA	OBP	SLG	EQA	EQR	DEFENSE	
1998	WnstnSlm	Car	454	101	14	4	10	31	93	51	50	8	4	357	.222	.276	.337	.203	33	106-C	-2
1999	Birmnghm	Sou	323	77	16	2	3	19	74	36	31	3	3	249	.238	.287	.328	.202	23	81-C	-1
2000	Charlott	Int	168	37	4	0	4	10	39	23	16	4	2	133	.220	.270	.315	.193	11	47-C	-1
2000	ChiSox	AL	71	20	4	2	1	4	15	15	8	1	0	51	.282	.329	.437	.256	8	21-C	2
2001	*ChiSox*	*AL*	*226*	*53*	*7*	*1*	*4*	*16*	*54*	*21*	*22*	*3*	*2*	*175*	*.235*	*.285*	*.327*	*.204*	*17*		

Organizational favorites get perks, and Josh Paul got his. He was placed on the postseason roster after a 71-at-bat season, and not even a baserunning mistake in his pinch-running appearance was enough to hurt his popularity. Paul has trouble staying healthy for consecutive weeks, and while playing through injuries sometimes weakens a player's projection, don't bet on Paul being one of those guys. He'll get every opportunity to make the big leagues and play.

Herb Perry — 3B/1B — Bats R — Age 31

YEAR	TEAM	LGE	AB	H	DB	TP	HR	BB	SO	R	RBI	SB	CS	OUT	BA	OBP	SLG	EQA	EQR	DEFENSE	
1999	Durham	Int	102	27	4	0	4	4	22	15	14	0	0	75	.265	.301	.422	.237	10		
1999	TampaBay	AL	208	54	11	1	6	14	38	28	31	0	0	154	.260	.333	.409	.249	24	41-3B	0
2000	ChiSox	AL	380	118	27	1	13	17	62	65	58	4	1	263	.311	.355	.489	.279	54	99-3B	4
2001	*ChiSox*	*AL*	*318*	*88*	*12*	*0*	*11*	*19*	*60*	*39*	*48*	*1*	*0*	*230*	*.277*	*.318*	*.418*	*.247*	*35*		

Herb Perry was a waiver-wire steal, but the bad wheels that got him waived in the first place came back to haunt the Sox in August after they'd demoted Greg Norton. Perry's inability to run hurt the team in the playoffs. As a third baseman, he starts double plays and moves to his left well, which is considerably more than anyone with five knee operations is expected to do. If Konerko gets moved and Crede comes up, Perry could split a lot of time at first base with Liefer.

Jackie Rexrode — 2B — Bats L — Age 22

YEAR	TEAM	LGE	AB	H	DB	TP	HR	BB	SO	R	RBI	SB	CS	OUT	BA	OBP	SLG	EQA	EQR	DEFENSE			
1998	Sth Bend	Mid	186	45	7	1	0	34	33	21	7	8	2	143	.242	.361	.290	.238	20	49-2B	-10		
1998	High Des	Cal	207	53	4	2	1	33	43	31	15	8	1	155	.256	.358	.309	.242	22	42-2B	-7	11-3B	-2
1999	Birmnghm	Sou	217	52	6	4	0	20	32	25	20	7	2	167	.240	.304	.304	.210	17	61-2B	0		
1999	El Paso	Tex	142	34	7	1	1	22	17	21	7	3	1	109	.239	.341	.324	.234	14	34-2B	-9		
2000	Birmnghm	Sou	356	93	7	2	1	53	40	51	14	10	6	269	.261	.359	.301	.234	35	88-2B	-6		
2001	*ChiSox*	*AL*	*387*	*105*	*13*	*2*	*1*	*55*	*54*	*65*	*41*	*11*	*4*	*286*	*.271*	*.362*	*.323*	*.245*	*42*				

If anyone is going to give the Sox incentive to finally follow through on their threats to move Ray Durham to center, it should be an on-base machine like Jackie Rexrode. Though he isn't a great second baseman, he hangs tough on the double play. He's ready to be the Wally Backman half of a platoon, perhaps with Graffanino playing Tim Teufel. He wasn't added to the 40-man roster, so he might be helping somebody else score runs by the time you read this.

Liu Rodriguez — IF — Bats B — Age 24

YEAR	TEAM	LGE	AB	H	DB	TP	HR	BB	SO	R	RBI	SB	CS	OUT	BA	OBP	SLG	EQA	EQR	DEFENSE			
1998	WnstnSlm	Car	432	102	22	2	2	37	41	50	34	6	4	334	.236	.303	.310	.207	33	91-2B	1	10-SS	-1
1999	Birmnghm	Sou	247	64	9	1	2	15	37	33	28	3	2	185	.259	.306	.328	.212	19	35-2B	-6	20-SS	2
1999	ChiSox	AL	92	22	2	2	1	12	10	8	11	0	0	70	.239	.344	.337	.236	9	13-2B	1	11-SS	-2
2000	Charlott	Int	396	96	18	2	3	45	40	38	37	2	5	305	.242	.328	.321	.220	35	75-2B	0	45-SS	-5
2001	*ChiSox*	*AL*	*390*	*98*	*17*	*1*	*3*	*44*	*46*	*49*	*40*	*4*	*5*	*297*	*.251*	*.327*	*.323*	*.223*	*35*				

Liu Rodriguez is seriously old school—dead-ball-era old school—in that his offensive weapons are getting on base and bunting. He'd make a good utility man for several teams, though the Sox correctly identified Graffanino as a better all-around player. Rodriguez is a minor-league free agent, so he should be able to pick up and go to a team that could use him.

Aaron Rowand — RF — Bats R — Age 23

YEAR	TEAM	LGE	AB	H	DB	TP	HR	BB	SO	R	RBI	SB	CS	OUT	BA	OBP	SLG	EQA	EQR	DEFENSE	
1998	Hickory	SAL	221	58	11	2	3	15	37	28	21	2	1	164	.262	.318	.371	.232	21	46-RF	1
1999	WnstnSlm	Car	519	122	27	2	18	21	97	70	60	6	5	402	.235	.274	.399	.219	45	98-RF	-3
2000	Birmnghm	Sou	548	132	22	4	18	26	121	68	83	11	4	420	.241	.284	.394	.225	50	138-RF	7
2001	*ChiSox*	*AL*	*473*	*123*	*23*	*2*	*17*	*31*	*107*	*62*	*69*	*9*	*3*	*353*	*.260*	*.306*	*.425*	*.244*	*52*		

American League

This draft pick isn't turning out as hoped. Scouts emphasize Aaron Rowand's tremendous bat speed and great arm, but a corner outfielder with this much trouble getting on base has no future in the majors as a regular. He struggled around the Mendoza line with no home runs against left-handed pitchers, so a platoon role isn't an option. In a couple of years, he could be ready to be a fourth outfielder on a team with a good everyday center fielder.

Brian Simmons   CF   Bats B   Age 27

YEAR	TEAM	LGE	AB	H	DB	TP	HR	BB	SO	R	RBI	SB	CS	OUT	BA	OBP	SLG	EQA	EQR	DEFENSE	
1997	Birmnghm	Sou	550	120	24	7	11	65	134	76	49	9	7	437	.218	.302	.347	.219	49		
1998	Calgary	PCL	348	83	17	3	9	33	81	53	36	7	4	269	.239	.306	.382	.230	34	85-CF	0
1999	Charlott	Int	283	67	7	0	9	30	60	40	34	5	2	218	.237	.318	.357	.230	28	73-CF	-3
1999	ChiSox	AL	126	29	4	3	4	8	27	14	16	4	0	97	.230	.276	.405	.229	12	32-LF	1
2001	Toronto	AL	141	35	4	1	5	16	32	21	21	3	1	107	.248	.325	.397	.246	16		

While there might be a number of guys you'd nominate for luckiest player in baseball, Brian Simmons is almost certainly the unluckiest. He'd won the center-field job in 1999, only to get hurt just before the start of the season. Last year he was a lock to win the fourth-outfielder job before he blew out his knee in camp. Traded to the Blue Jays in the Wells–Sirotka deal, where he'll get a slot as the fourth outfielder—if he can avoid another bad break.

Chris Singleton   CF   Bats L   Age 28

YEAR	TEAM	LGE	AB	H	DB	TP	HR	BB	SO	R	RBI	SB	CS	OUT	BA	OBP	SLG	EQA	EQR	DEFENSE	
1998	Columbus	Int	414	98	18	7	5	19	77	47	38	5	2	318	.237	.275	.350	.206	31	115-CF	-2
1999	ChiSox	AL	494	150	30	6	18	17	41	70	69	19	5	349	.304	.328	.498	.271	67	127-CF	15
2000	ChiSox	AL	508	129	23	5	11	29	77	79	58	23	8	387	.254	.296	.384	.229	49	145-CF	9
2001	ChiSox	AL	446	114	21	5	11	28	65	60	56	15	5	337	.256	.300	.399	.236	46		

One way of looking at players and lineups is by asking, "If Fred Mertz were the worst hitter in your lineup, would that be good or bad?" With Chris Singleton, the answer is unclear. Neither corner outfielder covers a lot of ground, so the Sox need a good defensive center fielder and Singleton is their best glove. His hitting and fielding suffered when he played through a dislocated finger in May, so I agree with Wilton that he'll bounce back, probably even more than this projection indicates.

Frank Thomas   1B   Bats R   Age 33

YEAR	TEAM	LGE	AB	H	DB	TP	HR	BB	SO	R	RBI	SB	CS	OUT	BA	OBP	SLG	EQA	EQR	DEFENSE	
1998	ChiSox	AL	584	161	34	2	32	110	83	112	111	6	0	423	.276	.395	.505	.300	105	13-1B	-1
1999	ChiSox	AL	480	148	26	0	19	82	60	71	76	3	3	335	.308	.417	.481	.303	84	48-1B	-6
2000	ChiSox	AL	571	189	34	0	46	104	86	107	135	1	4	386	.331	.438	.632	.340	130	30-1B	-1
2001	ChiSox	AL	558	163	25	0	34	111	86	121	131	2	2	397	.292	.410	.520	.311	107		

He had to have endured one of the worst years imaginable in 1999: Frank Thomas got divorced, his agent died on Payne Stewart's plane, both of his business ventures flopped, and his dad went on dialysis while struggling with heart failure.

    Thomas paid Walt Hriniak out of his own pocket to help him get his groove back, and it seems to have worked, though he started tinkering with an open stance that eventually reduced his swing to all arms and left him looking weak in the playoffs. As far as stars bringing in their own coaches, I'm surprised we don't see more of it. Not every coach has the flexibility to address each player's strengths and weaknesses, and not every player can learn from every coach. Teams are investing a lot of money in star players, and there are some pretty bad coaches in the game. We'll be seeing more of this practice in the future, not less.

Jose Valentin   SS   Bats B   Age 31

YEAR	TEAM	LGE	AB	H	DB	TP	HR	BB	SO	R	RBI	SB	CS	OUT	BA	OBP	SLG	EQA	EQR	DEFENSE	
1998	Milwauke	NL	434	97	20	0	18	61	98	66	50	9	7	344	.224	.320	.394	.239	48	121-SS	-8
1999	Milwauke	NL	257	57	8	4	10	44	49	42	35	2	2	202	.222	.340	.401	.250	32	77-SS	-12
2000	ChiSox	AL	563	154	36	6	26	52	97	103	87	20	2	411	.274	.339	.497	.278	83	139-SS	0
2001	ChiSox	AL	444	111	25	2	17	60	87	78	69	13	3	336	.250	.339	.430	.263	60		

Freed from the miseries of Milwaukee and the thumb injury he played through in 1999, Jose Valentin busted out even better than we expected, flashing all of his strengths and weaknesses to their fullest. He has power and patience and a complete inability to hit left-handers. He's aggressive on the bases and in the field, and Ray Durham credited him with being the best

(Jose Valentin *continued*)

feeder on the deuce with whom he'd ever played. Chew on that, Ozzeroo fans. Valentin is a booter, though, so he's mistaken for a bad defensive player. The Sox appeciate him for his strengths, giving him a three-year contract, but he'll play some third base and outfield now that they've got Royce Clayton.

Mario Valenzuela — OF — Bats R — Age 24

YEAR	TEAM	LGE	AB	H	DB	TP	HR	BB	SO	R	RBI	SB	CS	OUT	BA	OBP	SLG	EQA	EQR	DEFENSE	
1998	Bristol	App	232	54	10	0	5	13	58	23	23	1	2	180	.233	.277	.341	.201	16	59-RF	1
1999	Burlingt	Mid	476	119	23	3	7	26	84	57	43	5	3	360	.250	.293	.355	.215	39	112-LF	-3
2000	WnstnSlm	Car	538	120	21	1	17	41	114	68	61	5	2	420	.223	.279	.361	.212	43	138-RF	-5
2001	*ChiSox*	*AL*	*478*	*114*	*19*	*1*	*15*	*40*	*106*	*53*	*60*	*3*	*2*	*366*	*.238*	*.297*	*.377*	*.226*	*44*		

A strong-armed Mexican outfielder with a bit of power, Mario Valenzuela has been compared to Magglio Ordonez because Ordonez also made slow progress through the system. Valenzuela's progress has been slower. By 24, Ordonez had played full seasons at both Double-A and Triple-A, and had gotten his first taste of the majors. Valenzuela will turn 24 in March, before he plays his first game at Double-A. He's older than Aaron Rowand.

Craig Wilson — IF — Bats R — Age 30

YEAR	TEAM	LGE	AB	H	DB	TP	HR	BB	SO	R	RBI	SB	CS	OUT	BA	OBP	SLG	EQA	EQR	DEFENSE			
1998	Calgary	PCL	422	103	15	1	9	28	43	48	47	3	1	320	.244	.294	.348	.214	34	48-2B	-7	26-SS	3
1999	ChiSox	AL	251	61	8	1	4	21	20	27	25	1	1	191	.243	.301	.331	.211	20	54-3B	8	16-SS	-2
2000	ChiSox	AL	73	19	4	0	0	4	10	12	4	1	0	54	.260	.308	.315	.212	6				
2000	Charlott	Int	228	68	12	1	2	24	29	33	25	0	1	161	.298	.372	.386	.259	28	27-3B	1	25-SS	-1
2001	*KansasCy*	*AL*	*276*	*76*	*7*	*0*	*7*	*28*	*33*	*38*	*42*	*1*	*1*	*201*	*.275*	*.342*	*.377*	*.243*	*29*				

Not every White Sox player had a Cinderella story to tell in 2000. Craig Wilson hurt his back in June, lost his job to Graffanino, and was cut after the season. He pastes lefty junk, which would have made him a good platoon mate for Valentin or Norton. He's been signed by the Royals, with whom he'll be a fine utility infielder.

PITCHERS (ERA: 4.50, H/9: 9.00, HR/9: 1.00, BB/9: 3.00, K/9: 6.00, KW: 1.00, PERA: 4.50)

James Baldwin — Throws R — Age 29

YEAR	TEAM	LGE	IP	H	ER	HR	BB	K	ERA	W	L	H/9	HR/9	BB/9	K/9	KW	PERA
1998	ChiSox	AL	156.3	164	90	16	52	100	5.18	6	11	9.44	0.92	2.99	5.76	0.96	4.67
1999	ChiSox	AL	198.0	203	100	28	65	117	4.55	10	12	9.23	1.27	2.95	5.32	0.90	4.91
2000	ChiSox	AL	177.0	170	79	28	46	111	4.02	10	10	8.64	1.42	2.34	5.64	1.21	4.47

James Baldwin finally had a good first half, but despite Manuel's careful use, his arm wore down faster than his manager's patience for the first time. The initial sign of trouble was a drop in velocity in June, followed by early-inning problems in July. By September, he needed a month off and a cortisone shot. After giving the Sox a gutty Division Series start, he had offseason surgery to remove a bone chip in his elbow. J.B. is one year away from free agency and has been the epitome of unpredictability. A good year will make him a very wealthy guy, probably in a different city.

Lorenzo Barcelo — Throws R — Age 23

YEAR	TEAM	LGE	IP	H	ER	HR	BB	K	ERA	W	L	H/9	HR/9	BB/9	K/9	KW	PERA
1999	Birmnghm	Sou	18.7	13	8	0	7	9	3.86	1	1	6.27	0.00	3.38	4.34	0.64	2.27
2000	Charlott	Int	94.7	111	52	21	15	48	4.94	4	7	10.55	2.00	1.43	4.56	1.60	5.81
2000	ChiSox	AL	38.3	31	14	4	7	25	3.29	2	2	7.28	0.94	1.64	5.87	1.79	2.96

The original prize of the 1997 trade with the Giants, Lorenzo Barcelo had to first endure a pair of elbow surgeries, including the Tommy John procedure that cost him 1998 and most of 1999. He now has less velocity—down around 94 mph after he used to flirt with 100—but his fastball tails nicely, and he's not wild. His slider and change-up are for show. The Sox seem content to leave him in the bullpen; he's the leading candidate to replace Keith Foulke as the closer someday.

Kevin Beirne — Throws R — Age 27

YEAR	TEAM	LGE	IP	H	ER	HR	BB	K	ERA	W	L	H/9	HR/9	BB/9	K/9	KW	PERA
1998	Birmnghm	Sou	153.7	148	93	23	94	91	5.45	6	11	8.67	1.35	5.51	5.33	0.48	5.71
1999	Charlott	Int	108.7	127	68	14	35	43	5.63	4	8	10.52	1.16	2.90	3.56	0.61	5.53
2000	Charlott	Int	31.7	39	13	3	7	20	3.69	2	2	11.08	0.85	1.99	5.68	1.43	5.18
2000	ChiSox	AL	49.7	46	33	7	16	39	5.98	2	4	8.34	1.27	2.90	7.07	1.22	4.35

Kevin Beirne was called up in early May to replace Kip Wells and spent the year as the team's 12th pitcher. He has low-90s heat and a big overhand curve. Although his improved control ought to bring him a little more attention, Beirne is one of the guys likely to get pushed aside by the coming wave of young pitchers. He's got a good chance of going Todd Ritchie on us if he gets a chance to start. Traded to Toronto as a throw-in on the Sirotka–Wells trade.

Rocky Biddle — Throws R — Age 25

YEAR	TEAM	LGE	IP	H	ER	HR	BB	K	ERA	W	L	H/9	HR/9	BB/9	K/9	KW	PERA
1998	WnstnSlm	Car	72.7	95	67	14	58	36	8.30	2	6	11.77	1.73	7.18	4.46	0.31	8.66
2000	Birmnghm	Sou	130.7	149	86	22	64	65	5.92	5	10	10.26	1.52	4.41	4.48	0.51	6.37
2000	ChiSox	AL	22.7	28	20	4	6	7	7.94	1	2	11.12	1.59	2.38	2.78	0.58	6.10

The Sox had six first-round picks in 1997. Rocky Biddle, a pitcher at Long Beach State, was the last of them. Last season was Biddle's first after the Tommy John surgery that cost him 1999. He took his rehab seriously and came back throwing in the low 90s with a plus curve. He had a 27⅔ scoreless-innings streak for the Barons before getting promoted. He's behind Jon Garland and Kip Wells and about to be passed up by Jon Rauch. A good year in Charlotte will do wonders for his future.

Chad Bradford — Throws R — Age 26

YEAR	TEAM	LGE	IP	H	ER	HR	BB	K	ERA	W	L	H/9	HR/9	BB/9	K/9	KW	PERA
1998	Calgary	PCL	49.3	46	11	3	11	19	2.01	4	1	8.39	0.55	2.01	3.47	0.86	3.34
1998	ChiSox	AL	29.3	25	15	1	6	10	4.60	1	2	7.67	0.31	1.84	3.07	0.83	2.65
1999	Charlott	Int	71.3	61	18	2	14	40	2.27	6	2	7.70	0.25	1.77	5.05	1.43	2.62
2000	Charlott	Int	50.7	38	18	2	12	30	3.20	4	2	6.75	0.36	2.13	5.33	1.25	2.37
2000	ChiSox	AL	13.0	12	5	1	1	8	3.46	1	0	8.31	0.69	0.69	5.54	4.00	2.88

It's clear that the Sox have too much pitching talent because they discarded Chad Bradford to the A's. Among the BP staff, there's an argument over whether Bradford is the next Dan Quisenberry or just the next Jeff Tam. The big submariner didn't give up a home run to a right-handed batter last year, kept his ground-ball/fly-ball ratio around 4 to 1, and was voted the guy International League hitters least wanted to face. He's going to be a great setup man.

Mark Buehrle — Throws L — Age 22

YEAR	TEAM	LGE	IP	H	ER	HR	BB	K	ERA	W	L	H/9	HR/9	BB/9	K/9	KW	PERA
1999	Burlingt	Mid	92.0	109	55	15	17	48	5.38	4	6	10.66	1.47	1.66	4.70	1.41	5.42
2000	Birmnghm	Sou	108.3	101	49	16	19	41	4.07	6	6	8.39	1.33	1.58	3.41	1.08	3.91
2000	ChiSox	AL	51.0	51	23	4	15	35	4.06	3	3	9.00	0.71	2.65	6.18	1.17	4.05

Mark Buehrle isn't really a 38th-rounder, just an old-fashioned draft-and-follow. He throws four pitches for strikes and owns a pickoff move that would make Terry Mulholland blush. Buehrle was named the best pitcher in the Southern League. He'll fight Kip Wells and Jon Garland for the fifth spot in the rotation and looks like the best choice. If he isn't there, look for Manuel to again use him effectively as a long reliever, as opposed to bumping him into situational relief.

Carlos Chantres — Throws R — Age 25

YEAR	TEAM	LGE	IP	H	ER	HR	BB	K	ERA	W	L	H/9	HR/9	BB/9	K/9	KW	PERA
1998	WnstnSlm	Car	76.7	79	61	19	53	43	7.16	2	7	9.27	2.23	6.22	5.05	0.41	7.30
1998	Birmnghm	Sou	49.3	59	37	9	42	31	6.75	1	4	10.76	1.64	7.66	5.66	0.37	8.15
1999	Birmnghm	Sou	129.7	124	77	22	69	65	5.34	5	9	8.61	1.53	4.79	4.51	0.47	5.56
2000	Charlott	Int	136.3	132	57	13	50	64	3.76	8	7	8.71	0.86	3.30	4.22	0.64	4.30

Carlos Chantres was one of the winter's best minor-league free agents. He's been in the top ten in ERA in his leagues each of the last two years, and his sinker/slider combo keeps improving with experience. He signed with the Brewers after being heavily courted by the A's. I don't know what he or his agent was thinking, but with a choice between having a shot to be the fifth starter for a division winner or for the Brewers, I know which team I'd pick.

Cal Eldred — Throws R — Age 33

YEAR	TEAM	LGE	IP	H	ER	HR	BB	K	ERA	W	L	H/9	HR/9	BB/9	K/9	KW	PERA
1998	Milwauke	NL	128.3	152	79	14	55	70	5.54	5	9	10.66	0.98	3.86	4.91	0.64	5.82
1999	Milwauke	NL	80.7	97	67	17	38	50	7.48	2	7	10.82	1.90	4.24	5.58	0.66	7.03
2000	ChiSox	AL	112.3	97	51	10	46	93	4.09	6	6	7.77	0.80	3.69	7.45	1.01	3.87

For the first time in eons, Cal Eldred almost had consistent command of his curve and fastball. Then he strained his troublesome elbow in July. After two months of hoping it would get better, he had a screw surgically implanted to stabilize a stress fracture. This being his first good year since before we knew who Monica Lewinsky was, he tried to pitch though the injury. Eldred has had stress fractures before, but his elbow problems will never let him pitch a full season, let alone pitch consistently. He's the guy who didn't bounce back from Tommy John surgery; while he made an impressive effort last year, you can't count on him. The Sox have re-signed him to a one-year contract.

Scott Eyre — Throws L — Age 29

YEAR	TEAM	LGE	IP	H	ER	HR	BB	K	ERA	W	L	H/9	HR/9	BB/9	K/9	KW	PERA
1998	ChiSox	AL	106.0	107	69	22	56	68	5.86	4	8	9.08	1.87	4.75	5.77	0.61	6.20
1999	Charlott	Int	65.3	74	31	3	22	43	4.27	3	4	10.19	0.41	3.03	5.92	0.98	4.60
1999	ChiSox	AL	25.3	35	18	5	12	16	6.39	1	2	12.43	1.78	4.26	5.68	0.67	7.85
2000	ChiSox	AL	19.3	27	12	2	9	15	5.59	1	1	12.57	0.93	4.19	6.98	0.83	6.98
2000	Charlott	Int	45.3	33	18	1	20	33	3.57	3	2	6.55	0.20	3.97	6.55	0.82	2.77

Scott Eyre was traded to the Blue Jays in November to give the Sox some roster space. What the Blue Jays plan to do with him is a mystery. He's their fourth left-handed reliever behind Pedro Borbon, Dan Plesac, and Lance Painter. All three of those guys are situational types, while Eyre throws hard and could be handy in long relief. He's looking at another fun summer mailing postcards from some very familiar cities around the International League.

Josh Fogg — Throws R — Age 24

YEAR	TEAM	LGE	IP	H	ER	HR	BB	K	ERA	W	L	H/9	HR/9	BB/9	K/9	KW	PERA
1998	Hickory	SAL	37.3	37	21	8	17	14	5.06	2	2	8.92	1.93	4.10	3.38	0.41	5.89
1999	WnstnSlm	Car	95.0	100	51	6	37	56	4.83	4	7	9.47	0.57	3.51	5.31	0.76	4.55
1999	Birmnghm	Sou	51.0	67	43	13	20	25	7.59	1	5	11.82	2.29	3.53	4.41	0.63	7.77
2000	Birmnghm	Sou	176.3	196	81	15	50	79	4.13	10	10	10.00	0.77	2.55	4.03	0.79	4.66

Although he was a closer in college, Josh Fogg is not a power pitcher. He gets into the low 90s once in a while but relies heavily on a quality slider and change-up. Fogg is more the typical college pitcher, using a good sense of how to set people up instead of dominating with pure stuff. In some organizations, he'd get talked up; with the Sox, he's just another guy.

Keith Foulke — Throws R — Age 28

YEAR	TEAM	LGE	IP	H	ER	HR	BB	K	ERA	W	L	H/9	HR/9	BB/9	K/9	KW	PERA
1998	ChiSox	AL	63.7	48	27	8	17	53	3.82	4	3	6.79	1.13	2.40	7.49	1.56	3.15
1999	ChiSox	AL	103.3	67	24	9	17	117	2.09	9	2	5.84	0.78	1.48	10.19	3.44	2.07
2000	ChiSox	AL	87.0	61	25	7	17	87	2.59	7	3	6.31	0.72	1.76	9.00	2.56	2.34

Well, that tears it. Now that Keith Foulke has a 30-save season to his credit, he's probably damned and doomed to spend the rest of his career closing instead of pitching 200 good innings. We know that guys need lighter workloads early in their professional careers, and we have a pretty good sense that pitchers who make it into their late twenties uninjured last longer. We also know closers have an almost negligible impact on their team's success as compared to starting pitchers. When are we going to see somebody follow the opposite-Eck career path, starting off as a quality reliever, then moving on to become a top quality starter? When asked, Foulke says he'd love to go back to starting.

Jon Garland — Throws R — Age 21

YEAR	TEAM	LGE	IP	H	ER	HR	BB	K	ERA	W	L	H/9	HR/9	BB/9	K/9	KW	PERA
1998	Rockford	Mid	95.7	129	86	28	56	36	8.09	2	9	12.14	2.63	5.27	3.39	0.32	9.01
1998	Hickory	SAL	24.3	35	21	4	17	9	7.77	1	2	12.95	1.48	6.29	3.33	0.26	8.71
1999	WnstnSlm	Car	110.0	112	63	13	42	44	5.15	5	7	9.16	1.06	3.44	3.60	0.52	4.84
1999	Birmnghm	Sou	36.0	39	26	7	20	17	6.50	1	3	9.75	1.75	5.00	4.25	0.43	6.56
2000	Charlott	Int	99.7	95	26	3	29	48	2.35	8	3	8.58	0.27	2.62	4.33	0.83	3.39
2000	ChiSox	AL	70.3	77	46	8	31	40	5.89	3	5	9.85	1.02	3.97	5.12	0.65	5.44

Jon Garland throws a heavy, low-90s sinker that draws comparisons to Kevin Brown's, and despite his youth, he knows how to set up his great change-up. His slider and curve are developing and look like they'll be good pitches. While his translations aren't special, keep in mind that he's usually been one of the youngest players in his league and has gotten promoted at the first sign of success. There isn't a whole lot for him to learn at Triple-A, so the Sox need to figure out what to do with him next. He has options, so he probably won't be in the majors to stay until Eldred's elbow goes on hiatus again.

Matt Ginter — Throws R — Age 23

YEAR	TEAM	LGE	IP	H	ER	HR	BB	K	ERA	W	L	H/9	HR/9	BB/9	K/9	KW	PERA
1999	Burlingt	Mid	37.3	39	22	6	20	15	5.30	1	3	9.40	1.45	4.82	3.62	0.38	5.98
2000	Birmnghm	Sou	165.0	158	84	12	66	75	4.58	8	10	8.62	0.65	3.60	4.09	0.57	4.17

After pitching for Mississippi State, Matt Ginter was part of the first-round bounty of '99. The Sox saw that he needed a minor mechanical adjustment to improve his stuff. He now throws in the mid 90s with a slider in the high 80s, but he has yet to master a decent change-up. If he doesn't pick one up, he may get moved to closer.

Matt Guerrier — Throws R — Age 22

YEAR	TEAM	LGE	IP	H	ER	HR	BB	K	ERA	W	L	H/9	HR/9	BB/9	K/9	KW	PERA
1999	Bristol	App	23.0	21	12	2	18	14	4.70	1	2	8.22	0.78	7.04	5.48	0.39	5.53
2000	WnstnSlm	Car	31.7	28	17	2	13	19	4.83	2	2	7.96	0.57	3.69	5.40	0.73	3.75
2000	Birmnghm	Sou	21.0	18	11	2	13	11	4.71	1	1	7.71	0.86	5.57	4.71	0.42	4.62

The White Sox's 1999 draft is already famed for the number of young power pitchers who are making quick progress. Matt Guerrier is one of the closest things to a sleeper from that draft. Picked in the tenth-round out of Kent, he throws a sharp slider and gets over 90 mph with his fastball. He's a year away from having to be added to the 40-man roster. Generally speaking, closer designates aren't prospects, but Guerrier is moving up relatively quickly.

Bobby Howry — Throws R — Age 27

YEAR	TEAM	LGE	IP	H	ER	HR	BB	K	ERA	W	L	H/9	HR/9	BB/9	K/9	KW	PERA
1998	Calgary	PCL	30.3	23	11	2	10	15	3.26	2	1	6.82	0.59	2.97	4.45	0.75	2.90
1998	ChiSox	AL	53.0	35	17	6	16	47	2.89	4	2	5.94	1.02	2.72	7.98	1.47	2.73
1999	ChiSox	AL	68.0	55	29	7	30	76	3.84	4	4	7.28	0.93	3.97	10.06	1.27	3.82
2000	ChiSox	AL	70.3	50	21	5	23	57	2.69	6	2	6.40	0.64	2.94	7.29	1.24	2.71

The save rule sucks because it changes people's perceptions of talent. If you don't believe that, consider Bobby Howry's predicament. He didn't do anything wrong but is now a flamethrowing ex-closer going into his arbitration years. If you take a look at Michael Wolverton's relief tools, you'll notice that Howry was one of the ten best relievers in the league. Howry had his shoulder 'scoped this winter; the Sox believe it won't be a problem in 2001.

Sean Lowe — Throws R — Age 30

YEAR	TEAM	LGE	IP	H	ER	HR	BB	K	ERA	W	L	H/9	HR/9	BB/9	K/9	KW	PERA
1998	Memphis	PCL	142.7	140	62	22	71	73	3.91	8	8	8.83	1.39	4.48	4.61	0.51	5.42
1999	ChiSox	AL	95.0	84	33	8	37	59	3.13	7	4	7.96	0.76	3.51	5.59	0.80	3.86
2000	ChiSox	AL	71.3	73	39	8	30	51	4.92	3	5	9.21	1.01	3.79	6.43	0.85	4.96

Sean Lowe had one of those tough years after his breakthrough in 1999: he played through a fractured cheek suffered in April, then finally went on the DL at the end of July with an inflamed shoulder. He was asked to come back and start and didn't embarrass himself despite problems with left-handed hitters and the absence of a good second pitch to go with his sinking fastball. He'll be back as the long man and should have a better year.

Gary Majewski — Throws R — Age 21

YEAR	TEAM	LGE	IP	H	ER	HR	BB	K	ERA	W	L	H/9	HR/9	BB/9	K/9	KW	PERA
1999	Bristol	App	69.3	72	40	9	47	35	5.19	3	5	9.35	1.17	6.10	4.54	0.37	6.17
2000	Burlingt	Mid	122.3	96	70	17	72	73	5.15	5	9	7.06	1.25	5.30	5.37	0.51	4.57
2000	WnstnSlm	Car	34.3	32	22	2	19	13	5.77	1	3	8.39	0.52	4.98	3.41	0.34	4.48

A Texas right-hander drafted in 1998? The White Sox drafted pitchers in years other than 1999? Sheesh. Gary Majewski throws hard and throws wild, making him more frightening than a Beatles reunion. He beaned 20 guys, including eight in his six starts in the Carolina League, and yet he tossed just four wild pitches all season. He allowed only nine home runs and a .195 batting average, so it's not like he had reasons to retaliate.

Aaron Myette Throws R Age 23

YEAR	TEAM	LGE	IP	H	ER	HR	BB	K	ERA	W	L	H/9	HR/9	BB/9	K/9	KW	PERA
1998	Hickory	SAL	92.7	88	51	8	40	48	4.95	4	6	8.55	0.78	3.88	4.66	0.60	4.37
1998	WnstnSlm	Car	39.3	37	21	8	18	28	4.81	2	2	8.47	1.83	4.12	6.41	0.78	5.52
1999	Birmnghm	Sou	150.7	144	95	32	85	85	5.67	6	11	8.60	1.91	5.08	5.08	0.50	6.09
1999	ChiSox	AL	16.0	16	9	2	11	10	5.06	1	1	9.00	1.13	6.19	5.63	0.45	5.93
2000	Charlott	Int	107.0	102	57	19	51	65	4.79	5	7	8.58	1.60	4.29	5.47	0.64	5.41

Aaron Myette lost time to injury, but it wasn't the elbow that bugged him in 1998: he broke his hand punching a dugout wall after a bad outing in spring training. That cost him his chance to win a spot on the roster. He can change speeds and locate his sinking fastball well, getting it anywhere from the high 80s to the mid 90s, and he has a nice curve and slider. Myette could use a year in the bullpen working on pitch selection and a change-up; the Rangers, who acquired him for Royce Clayton, may need him in the rotation.

Jim Parque Throws L Age 26

YEAR	TEAM	LGE	IP	H	ER	HR	BB	K	ERA	W	L	H/9	HR/9	BB/9	K/9	KW	PERA
1998	Calgary	PCL	46.3	45	23	7	24	21	4.47	2	3	8.74	1.36	4.66	4.08	0.44	5.40
1998	ChiSox	AL	111.7	126	64	13	43	71	5.16	5	7	10.16	1.05	3.47	5.72	0.83	5.43
1999	ChiSox	AL	173.3	195	94	19	63	106	4.88	8	11	10.13	0.99	3.27	5.50	0.84	5.26
2000	ChiSox	AL	186.0	192	87	17	55	106	4.21	10	11	9.29	0.82	2.66	5.13	0.96	4.34

Is Jim Parque lucky? The Sox were 51–14 when they got quality starts, including a combined 20–0 for Baldwin and Eldred and 15–5 for Mike Sirotka. When Parque tossed a quality start, they went 9-6. But he got the best run support on the team, which helped the Sox win a MLB-leading 13 games in which they did not get quality starts from Parque. One bout of control problems in August and it seemed like everyone was ready to toss him into Lake Michigan. He's cocky and outspoken, which is kind of fun coming from a finesse left-hander. He's good and getting better.

Rob Purvis Throws R Age 23

YEAR	TEAM	LGE	IP	H	ER	HR	BB	K	ERA	W	L	H/9	HR/9	BB/9	K/9	KW	PERA
1999	Burlingt	Mid	10.3	10	5	2	4	4	4.35	0	1	8.71	1.74	3.48	3.48	0.50	5.21
2000	WnstnSlm	Car	153.7	141	90	13	97	59	5.27	6	11	8.26	0.76	5.68	3.46	0.30	4.92

In another organization, Rob Purvis would be getting all sorts of publicity as a college first rounder, but with the Sox, he's just another one of the talented class of '99. He throws in the low 90s with good breaking stuff. Control is sort of a problem; he tossed 22 wild pitches to go with that poor KW. We don't usually cover a lot of A-ball pitchers, but it's remarkable to see this many young pitchers translate well so early in their careers.

Jon Rauch Throws R Age 22

YEAR	TEAM	LGE	IP	H	ER	HR	BB	K	ERA	W	L	H/9	HR/9	BB/9	K/9	KW	PERA
1999	Bristol	App	52.0	69	49	9	20	26	8.48	1	5	11.94	1.56	3.46	4.50	0.65	7.01
2000	WnstnSlm	Car	99.0	116	67	21	36	66	6.09	3	8	10.55	1.91	3.27	6.00	0.92	6.49
2000	Birmnghm	Sou	50.7	42	28	8	18	38	4.97	2	4	7.46	1.42	3.20	6.75	1.06	4.13

Baseball America's Player of the Year, he'll be the tallest major-leaguer once he's promoted. Jon Rauch dropped in the draft after scouts wondered about all the fuss over a guy who seemed weak all the time and didn't throw very hard. Viral meningitis isn't fun. After Rauch recovered, the Sox had a steal on their hands. He'll get attention because of his size and demeanor and is going to dominate with outstanding control of a great slider and an overhand curve that comes at you like a dive-bomber. It doesn't hurt that he throws in the mid 90s. The ace of Team USA in the Olympics, Rauch is a pretty good bet to be up before the end of the year.

Mark Roberts Throws R Age 25

YEAR	TEAM	LGE	IP	H	ER	HR	BB	K	ERA	W	L	H/9	HR/9	BB/9	K/9	KW	PERA
1998	WnstnSlm	Car	147.0	175	112	29	65	71	6.86	4	12	10.71	1.78	3.98	4.35	0.55	6.74
1999	Birmnghm	Sou	114.7	109	77	19	46	52	6.04	4	9	8.56	1.49	3.61	4.08	0.57	5.01
2000	Birmnghm	Sou	54.0	69	35	9	20	26	5.83	2	4	11.50	1.50	3.33	4.33	0.65	6.64
2000	Charlott	Int	61.3	57	16	8	19	28	2.35	5	2	8.36	1.17	2.79	4.11	0.74	4.24

American League

A fourth-round pick in 1996, Mark Roberts has the misfortune of being just ahead of the wave of '99 picks moving up through the organization and just behind the guys acquired from the Giants in '97. Shifting into a swing role, he's picked up some velocity and movement on his fastball, but he doesn't throw hard; he does have a good slider. After struggling in the Arizona Fall League, he was traded to the Marlins.

Brian Schmack — Throws R — Age 27

YEAR	TEAM	LGE	IP	H	ER	HR	BB	K	ERA	W	L	H/9	HR/9	BB/9	K/9	KW	PERA
1998	WnstnSlm	Car	54.0	51	31	6	24	24	5.17	2	4	8.50	1.00	4.00	4.00	0.50	4.61
1999	Birmnghm	Sou	58.0	61	37	6	22	32	5.74	2	4	9.47	0.93	3.41	4.97	0.73	4.88
2000	Charlott	Int	85.7	83	34	12	28	60	3.57	6	4	8.72	1.26	2.94	6.30	1.07	4.58

Brian Schmack signed as an undrafted free agent out of Northern Illinois University in 1996 and hasn't had a bad season yet. Sure, he's been pitching in relief in the minors, and he's been older than the competition at most levels, but he's got good control and keeps the ball low or in the infield. He's not a prospect.

Bill Simas — Throws R — Age 29

YEAR	TEAM	LGE	IP	H	ER	HR	BB	K	ERA	W	L	H/9	HR/9	BB/9	K/9	KW	PERA
1998	ChiSox	AL	69.0	51	26	11	19	52	3.39	5	3	6.65	1.43	2.48	6.78	1.37	3.40
1999	ChiSox	AL	71.3	68	31	5	26	39	3.91	4	4	8.58	0.63	3.28	4.92	0.75	4.00
2000	ChiSox	AL	67.3	64	22	7	17	47	2.94	5	2	8.55	0.94	2.27	6.28	1.38	3.89

Bill Simas picked up some of the velocity that went missing the year before and enjoyed a much better season. He'll have to hold the memories dear, because he won't be on a mound again until 2002: elbow surgery will wipe out his 2001 season. The Sox, who are hip-deep in relievers, won't miss him much.

Mike Sirotka — Throws L — Age 30

YEAR	TEAM	LGE	IP	H	ER	HR	BB	K	ERA	W	L	H/9	HR/9	BB/9	K/9	KW	PERA
1998	ChiSox	AL	207.3	236	121	27	41	118	5.25	8	15	10.24	1.17	1.78	5.12	1.44	4.91
1999	ChiSox	AL	206.3	217	92	20	46	119	4.01	11	12	9.47	0.87	2.01	5.19	1.29	4.23
2000	ChiSox	AL	195.7	187	84	19	54	122	3.86	11	11	8.60	0.87	2.48	5.61	1.13	3.93

In the American League, three guys tossed 20 or more quality starts (six innings, three runs): Pedro Martinez, Mike Mussina, and Mike Sirotka. He doesn't pitch for the Yankees or breathe fire out of his nostrils or whatever, so when people talk about staff aces, his name never comes up. Of all the bad breaks the Sox suffered in September, Sirotka's hyperextended elbow in his last start of the regular season was probably the worst. Traded to Toronto, just before questions about his shoulder were made public.

Ken Vining — Throws L — Age 26

YEAR	TEAM	LGE	IP	H	ER	HR	BB	K	ERA	W	L	H/9	HR/9	BB/9	K/9	KW	PERA
1998	Birmnghm	Sou	162.7	183	104	14	93	83	5.75	6	12	10.13	0.77	5.15	4.59	0.45	5.81
1999	Birmnghm	Sou	10.7	19	17	2	11	5	14.34	0	1	16.03	1.69	9.28	4.22	0.23	11.98
2000	Birmnghm	Sou	41.3	39	35	4	22	22	7.62	1	4	8.49	0.87	4.79	4.79	0.50	4.80

One of the less famous players in the '97 trade with the Giants, Ken Vining has been coming back slowly from elbow surgery, finally pitching his way onto the 40-man roster. He's got a great curve and good velocity and had a fine AFL last fall. If Buehrle is in the rotation instead of the pen, Vining might get a shot as the second left-hander behind Wunsch.

Kip Wells — Throws R — Age 24

YEAR	TEAM	LGE	IP	H	ER	HR	BB	K	ERA	W	L	H/9	HR/9	BB/9	K/9	KW	PERA
1999	WnstnSlm	Car	78.0	85	47	8	38	49	5.42	3	6	9.81	0.92	4.38	5.65	0.64	5.47
1999	Birmnghm	Sou	65.0	49	28	8	34	28	3.88	4	3	6.78	1.11	4.71	3.88	0.41	4.02
1999	ChiSox	AL	35.3	31	15	2	12	28	3.82	2	2	7.90	0.51	3.06	7.13	1.17	3.41
2000	ChiSox	AL	100.0	118	63	12	45	68	5.67	4	7	10.62	1.08	4.05	6.12	0.76	5.98
2000	Charlott	Int	59.7	66	38	11	25	29	5.73	2	5	9.96	1.66	3.77	4.37	0.58	6.10

Kip Wells was supposed to contend for the Rookie of the Year Award last year. He was demoted after three bad months, struggled in Charlotte before having a good August, and then was recalled down the stretch while injuries were wiping out the

(Kip Wells *continued*)

staff. He hides his pitches well with a deceptive delivery, tossing a nasty curve—sometimes even for strikes. He also had some arm problems late in 2000, and after logging 191 ⅔ innings as a 22-year-old in his first pro season, there's reason for concern. He must be taking fielding tips from Matt Young, because he has seven errors and eight assists in his brief major-league career.

Brian West — Throws R — Age 20

YEAR	TEAM	LGE	IP	H	ER	HR	BB	K	ERA	W	L	H/9	HR/9	BB/9	K/9	KW	PERA
1999	Bristol	App	15.7	28	30	9	18	7	17.23	0	2	16.09	5.17	10.34	4.02	0.19	16.20
2000	Burlingt	Mid	137.7	146	80	6	78	48	5.23	6	9	9.54	0.39	5.10	3.14	0.31	5.05

He was all set to go to Texas A&M and become a defensive lineman when the Sox picked him in the first round in 1999. Brian West throws in the mid 90s with a good curve, but not a lot of control.

What's going to happen when somebody rushes the mound on him? Maybe something to make people forget that great Dave Stewart/Pat Corrales stomping in 1986, or the time Dave Collins got tackled from behind by Lance Parrish as he was trying to rush Jack Morris in 1985. Not that I want to suggest those incidents were funny. That would be wrong. But as long as the rules don't provide a potent deterrent against charging the mound, maybe some basic intimidation will do the trick.

Danny Wright — Throws R — Age 23

YEAR	TEAM	LGE	IP	H	ER	HR	BB	K	ERA	W	L	H/9	HR/9	BB/9	K/9	KW	PERA
1999	Bristol	App	16.3	15	9	2	11	7	4.96	1	1	8.27	1.10	6.06	3.86	0.32	5.43
2000	WnstnSlm	Car	122.0	138	70	9	56	55	5.16	5	9	10.18	0.66	4.13	4.06	0.49	5.32
2000	Birmnghm	Sou	39.0	31	21	6	26	19	4.85	2	2	7.15	1.38	6.00	4.38	0.37	5.06

Unlike most of the organization's hard-throwing right-handers, Danny Wright's main breaking pitch is a good curve instead of a slider; like almost all of them, he throws in the mid 90s. While he was supposed to be very rough coming out of the University of Arkansas, he's now credited with having good mechanics.

Kelly Wunsch — Throws L — Age 28

YEAR	TEAM	LGE	IP	H	ER	HR	BB	K	ERA	W	L	H/9	HR/9	BB/9	K/9	KW	PERA
1998	El Paso	Tex	96.3	121	77	13	34	42	7.19	3	8	11.30	1.21	3.18	3.92	0.62	6.16
1998	Louisvil	Int	49.0	52	24	7	15	24	4.41	2	3	9.55	1.29	2.76	4.41	0.80	5.03
1999	Huntsvil	Sou	46.7	39	14	2	27	20	2.70	3	2	7.52	0.39	5.21	3.86	0.37	3.92
1999	Louisvil	Int	40.0	49	21	4	14	14	4.72	2	2	11.03	0.90	3.15	3.15	0.50	5.65
2000	ChiSox	AL	61.0	47	18	3	23	49	2.66	5	2	6.93	0.44	3.39	7.23	1.07	2.98

Kelly Wunsch is a guy we've been pulling for over the years, because if Mike Myers could make good money as a sidearming situational left-hander who couldn't dent bread, then Kelly Wunsch deserved a shot. Jerry Manuel made up for all those years without a lefty reliever, using Wunsch a league-leading 83 times. If you're a Sox fan, what's nice about the pickup of guys like Wunsch or Singleton is that it demonstrates that the Sox are doing a good job scouting other team's systems to find hidden value. You'd be surprised how few teams invest the time.

Support-Neutral Statistics — CHICAGO WHITE SOX — Park Effect: +5.7%

PITCHER	GS	IP	R	SNW	SNL	SNPCT	W	L	RA	APW	SNVA	SNWAR
James Baldwin	28	174.0	95	11.5	9.2	.555	14	6	4.91	0.9	1.1	2.7
Lorenzo Barcelo	1	4.0	5	0.1	0.5	.173	0	0	11.25	-0.2	-0.2	-0.1
Kevin Beirne	1	5.0	3	0.2	0.3	.423	0	1	5.40	0.0	-0.0	-0.0
Rocky Biddle	4	22.7	25	0.5	2.6	.158	1	2	9.93	-1.0	-1.0	-0.8
Mark Buehrle	3	15.7	10	0.9	1.0	.483	1	0	5.74	-0.1	-0.0	0.1
Cal Eldred	20	112.0	61	7.3	6.1	.546	10	2	4.90	0.6	0.5	1.6
Scott Eyre	1	3.7	2	0.1	0.3	.348	0	0	4.91	0.0	-0.0	-0.0
Jon Garland	13	65.7	55	3.0	5.5	.354	4	8	7.54	-1.4	-1.3	-0.6
Ken Hill	1	2.3	6	0.0	0.7	.016	0	1	23.14	-0.4	-0.3	-0.3
Sean Lowe	5	24.3	11	2.0	1.2	.638	1	0	4.07	0.3	0.4	0.7
Jim Parque	32	185.0	105	10.9	9.6	.533	13	6	5.11	0.6	0.6	2.2
Mike Sirotka	32	197.0	101	13.6	9.1	.597	15	10	4.61	1.6	2.1	3.9
Tanyon Sturtze	1	5.0	3	0.3	0.2	.560	0	1	5.40	0.0	-0.0	0.1
Kip Wells	20	98.7	76	4.6	8.0	.363	6	9	6.93	-1.5	-1.5	-0.8
TOTALS	162	915.0	558	55.1	54.3	.504	65	46	5.49	-0.6	0.4	8.6

The White Sox had the second worst rotation among postseason qualifiers. The only playoff team with a worse rotation was the team that swept them, the Mariners, but starting pitching nevertheless played a big role in the White Sox's turnaround between 1999 and 2000. Entering 2000, Chicago was coming off three consecutive years of horrible starting pitching, with Support-Neutral Value Added totals of –6.1, -9.4, and –5.2 wins, respectively. The performance by the 2000 starting rotation may have been nothing to celebrate, but with an SNVA of 0.4, it was still a huge improvement over the previous three years.

So what has happened to past teams with track records comparable to the White Sox, those with an established pattern of awful rotations that suddenly become average or better? There have been 16 teams in the past 20 years that have had two consecutive seasons of crummy starting pitching (-3 SNVA or worse in years one and two) followed by a season of above-average starting pitching (0 SNVA or better in year three). The fourth-year performances of those teams provides the White Sox with mixed news. On the one hand, the rotations did regress a fair amount, dropping an average of two wins from their year-three levels. On the other hand, the rotations were above average (0.7 average SNVA) despite the decline and came nowhere near the abysmal level of years one and two. That doesn't mean that Chicago will follow the same script in 2001, of course, but Sox fans can take comfort in the somewhat encouraging history.

For a quick explanation of SN stats, see page 7.

Reliever Evaluation Tools

PITCHER	G	IP	R	ARA	APR	IRNR/G	EIRS/G	IRP	BRS	RRA	ARP
James Baldwin	1	4.0	1	2.16	1.4	0.00	0.00	0.0	0.0	2.13	1.4
Lorenzo Barcelo	21	35.0	12	2.96	8.7	0.86	0.34	1.2	0.3	2.81	9.3
Kevin Beirne	28	44.7	38	7.34	-10.6	0.75	0.30	-2.5	-4.2	7.00	-9.0
Chad Bradford	12	13.7	4	2.53	4.1	0.58	0.17	1.9	0.1	1.53	5.6
Mark Buehrle	25	35.7	17	4.11	4.3	0.92	0.48	-0.1	1.8	4.51	2.7
Scott Eyre	12	15.3	13	7.32	-3.6	0.50	0.19	-2.6	1.2	9.68	-7.6
Keith Foulke	72	88.0	31	3.04	21.1	0.32	0.09	2.9	0.0	2.81	23.3
Jon Garland	2	4.0	0	0.00	2.3	0.00	0.00	0.0	0.0	0.00	2.3
Matt Ginter	7	9.3	14	12.95	-8.0	0.29	0.06	-1.5	0.0	14.17	-9.3
Ken Hill	1	0.7	2	25.89	-1.5	2.00	0.60	-0.5	-1.3	21.67	-1.2
Bobby Howry	65	71.0	26	3.16	16.1	0.58	0.24	0.7	-1.4	2.97	17.5
Sean Lowe	45	46.3	36	6.71	-7.8	0.96	0.34	0.7	0.4	6.74	-7.9
Aaron Myette	2	2.7	0	0.00	1.5	0.00	0.00	0.0	0.3	0.76	1.3
Jim Parque	1	2.0	0	0.00	1.2	0.00	0.00	0.0	0.0	0.00	1.2
Juan Pena	20	23.3	18	6.66	-3.8	0.80	0.37	-0.7	0.6	7.22	-5.2
Bill Simas	60	67.7	27	3.44	13.2	0.72	0.27	-0.8	4.2	4.26	7.1
Tanyon Sturtze	9	10.7	20	16.18	-13.0	0.33	0.14	-0.7	-0.1	17.10	-14.1
Kelly Wunsch	83	61.3	22	3.10	14.3	0.84	0.30	3.7	6.2	3.58	11.1
TOTALS	466	535.3	281	4.53	39.7	0.68	0.26			4.72	28.3

For a quick guide to RET, see page 10.

Cleveland Indians

Some organizations cannot understand the possibility of failure. Some things are just too big to be allowed to fail, no matter how glaring the mistake or how fundamental the problem. Whether it's Bill Clinton's foreign policy or the Spice Girls or Long-Term Capital Management or *Saturday Night Live* or New Coke, so much time, money, blood, silicone and corn syrup gets shed that the very notion of a setback is unacceptable.

Let's use *Saturday Night Live* as the example here, because it's the least depressing. Maybe this is difficult to accept, but there was a time when SNL was very funny, with an entire cast of people who could make you laugh. Yes, even Garrett Morris. But what started off as a funny show featuring funny people on a program crafted to make you laugh eventually turned into a brand name and a corporate farm for studiously unfunny people doing tediously dull sketches stretched to maximum length to fill 90 minutes so that they could avoid having to write more tediously dull sketches.

With so much invested in SNL, accepting that something might be wrong is impossible. So instead of changing anything or attempting to go back to what made the show successful in the first place, more money gets committed to mediocrity, and we wind up with *Superstar* or *It's Pat* or *A Night at the Roxbury* to convince advertisers and corporate parents that SNL still has star power. Somewhere, there's a warehouse with a million copies of *Stuart Saves His Family*, waiting to disgorge its horrors on unsuspecting future generations. The entire concept of SNL is now a triumph of form over content, because at the end of the day nobody in the boardroom can stand up and say, "Hey, this isn't any good." There's too much at stake to accept that a terrible mistake is being made.

John Hart and the Cleveland Indians are in the same boat, but no amount of advertising, lying, or mass dumping of videos or CDs or bad cola can hide the Indians' failure. The Tribe has committed so much to their scripted storyline of success and to maintaining their self-image as a team about to win the World Series that their failure to actually win it needs to be acknowledged as a triumph of reality over spin-doctoring.

Having lost the World Series in 1997, the ALCS in 1998, and the ALDS in 1999, the Indians punished manager Mike Hargrove where previously Hart had held only pitching coaches and scouting directors accountable. The firing was long overdue—Hart had inherited Hargrove as an interim manager from his predecessor, Hank Peters. Keeping Hargrove over the years had only given Grover time to dig in like a blood tick, cultivating relationships with the media and putting Hart in the uncomfortable position taking a PR hit whenever he finally got out the axe. Hargrove's performance in the 1995 World Series should have been enough to get him canned, but firing the first Indians manager since Al Lopez to reach the World Series would have been even more unpopular than the subsequent decision to dump Carlos Baerga before it was too late in 1996.

By scapegoating the Human Rain Delay, the Tribe did not repudiate whatever master plan John Hart had convinced himself he'd followed since 1995. Hiring Charlie Manuel was merely the crowning of Hart's hand-picked manager from within the organization.

However, there were nagging problems that needed to be addressed if the myth of invincibility was going to be maintained. Hart had already hurt the organization in the past with his trades for pitching (John Smiley, Dave Burba, Ricardo Rincon), and he still needed to shore up his staff. He bought Chuck Finley after failing to trade for him five months earlier, when it might have made a difference to the 1999 team. Hart also blew a big chunk of change on Cuban mystery Danys Baez. After molesting Jaret Wright right out of the 1999 season, Hart was hoping one starter was all the Indians would need, but now with Finley and Baez they had two, just in case. The Indians also blew some petty cash on Scott Kamieniecki and Bobby Witt, just to make sure everyone noticed that this pitching stuff was being taken very seriously.

Indians Prospectus

2000 record: 90–72; Second place, AL Central
Pythagenport W/L: 93–69
Runs Scored: 950 (2nd in AL)
Runs Allowed: 816 (5th in AL)
Team EqA: .271 (3rd in AL)
2000 Batters' Age: 30.2 (tied for 4th oldest in AL)
2000 Pitchers' Age: 30.0 (3rd oldest in AL)
Ballpark: Jacobs Field; moderate hitters' park; Park Factor of 1.046
2000: The resurgence ends with a whimper and a ton of transactions.
2001: Could squeeze out one more division title before becoming the Orioles.

The Tribe's overconfidence is probably best reflected in their decision to ignore the void in center field. During the winter, the Indians believed that Kenny Lofton would not be fully healed from his shoulder surgery in spring training and unavailable for the first couple of months of the 2000 season. Rather than find a possible replacement, Hart made the token gesture of signing a washed-up Lance Johnson. If Lofton couldn't play, what did it matter? The Tribe had won the division by 22 games in 1999. Why worry about the front half of the season when the Indians had a standing invitation to the playoffs thanks to the perennially weak AL Central?

The plan began to go awry early on when the White Sox made it clear that they weren't going to just mail in another second-place finish. The previous margin for error was gone, and the Tribe could no longer count on winning the division just by finishing above .500. Second, the Indians had to handle a raft of pitching injuries that they really should have anticipated. Bartolo Colon hit the DL early after showing up in camp ridiculously out of shape. Then on May 18, Injury Day, Hart had to place Charles Nagy, Jaret Wright, and Ricky Rincon on the DL. This was not a turning point so much as a reminder that the Indians hadn't been paying attention. Nagy may have had a workhorse reputation coming into the season, but he'd neglected to mention that his arm had been hurting for a year. There were clues, like the drop in his velocity and his over-reliance on his forkball in 1999. Still, as much as the Indians deserve to be blamed for not noticing the problem, Nagy needs to be held responsible for blithely assuming there was nothing at stake beyond his consecutive-starts streak. Wright's breakdown was easy to anticipate, considering how badly he'd been handled in 1999.

Such losses aren't the end of the world. Colon was back in short order, while Wright and Nagy were only the team's fourth and fifth starters. As long as the team had invested in a good sixth starter, they'd be fine. But Hart hadn't done that. He'd brought in Bobby Witt, who was finished, and Scott Kamieniecki, who couldn't start, and Baez, who wasn't ready for Double-A. Dipping into the minors yielded one good start by Paul Rigdon, which encouraged Hart to go to the well again, bringing up Jim Brower and Tim Drew. Brower is your basic journeyman, while Drew had less than six weeks of experience above A ball. After Drew got shelled and demoted, the Indians began a three-month cycle of considering all of their options while sticking with none. The Indians looked at Scott Sanders, Andrew Lorraine, Tyler Green, and Brian Williams. When Rick Behenna refused to pick up the phone, they had to reach for the lowest of the low and trot out Jaime Navarro. When a team goes through that kind of "talent," it reflects an organizational problem bigger than just an injury or two.

The real problem was that this team couldn't survive Manny Ramirez's hamstring injury. Losing pitchers merely highlighted the organization's failure to actually shore up its pitching. Losing Ramirez brought attention to the team's lack of offensive depth and its overreliance on a core group of aging hitters. After scoring a thousand runs in 1999, the Indians should have anticipated a decline, even with Kenny Lofton surprising everyone and playing on Opening Day. As we pointed out last year, the chance of Lofton, Roberto Alomar, and Omar Vizquel putting together the seasons they'd enjoyed in 1999 was historically remote. All three players declined. Add their struggles to those of the pitching staff, cap it off with the loss of Ramirez for six weeks, and you've got trouble too big for the Tribe to handle.

The Indians were a game and a half behind the White Sox when Ramirez hit the DL on June 2. Three weeks later, they were 8½ games out of first place. Hart started flailing. First, he began rousting the team's conditioning and medical programs, which only showed that he was freaking out and had time on his hands. Then he discarded David Justice for asking out of one game too many. Then "unnamed sources" started whining that Ramirez was dogging it for actually taking six weeks to recover, which was how long the Tribe's own physicians had said it would take his hamstring to heal. When Ramirez finally did return (on schedule), assistant Mark Shapiro couldn't resist firing on him once more: "We felt he needed more time... I think his agent may have told him it's time to get back." Well, either Ramirez was dogging it or he was ready to play after six weeks or he was still hurt—the Indians were ready to have it every way as long as it made Ramirez look bad.

Caught between failure and trying to live the life of a contender, Hart decided to make a desperate push for the wild card. He traded Richie Sexson to the Brewers and Enrique Wilson to the Pirates. "You can stockpile all your prospects and look good in *Baseball America*," he sniffled, "or you can continue to run up banners at Jacobs Field. Part of what you do as a championship organization is play for championships." Soon enough, Hart wouldn't have prospects, banners, championships, the wild card, or even a first-round playoff defeat to brag about, but he would have some swell journeymen like David Segui, Jason Bere, Wil Cordero, and Bob Wickman. The Tribe finished with a flurry, going 46–30 down the stretch, but ran out of season faster than they could make up for having squandered its first four months.

So now the Indians are left playing a guessing game: what killed them in 2000? Was it the game they lost while starting Mark Whiten in center field? Was it the game in which Jason Bere blew a seven-run lead? Was it the three doubleheaders played in a six-day stretch in September? It's a fool's errand, because every team, manager, and general manager makes mistakes during the course of six months and 162 games. You may as well ask why Mays made the catch in '54. The Indians lost because they failed to anticipate a more competitive division and failed to do enough to improve themselves over the winter. John Hart had operated on the assumption that his team was a perennial winner, and he didn't bother to insure against the injuries that every team endures.

Suddenly, the good times are over, and no amount of bluster or arrogance is going to bring them back. There's no safety net here, no federal insurance program. Manny Ramirez is gone, the team is old and getting worse, and the farm system is so empty that Shapiro has to rely on bold statements like "We use minor-league stats as little as possible." Sure, the damned things give you nothing but bad news, so who needs them?

Tribe fans can only hope that this team, like the 1972 Tigers, has one last gasp left. The AL Central will be a fistfight, one the White Sox seem determined to enter with new disadvantages like Royce Clayton and Sandy Alomar. When Hart and Richard Jacobs started saving this franchise a decade ago, they never anticipated they'd be relying on the mistakes of others to keep from falling too far behind.

Hart is now facing the same situation Ron Schueler confronted in 1996. He's three years removed from his team's high-water mark and fighting against younger, better competition. Schueler had the support of his owner when he decided to rebuild. Hart has less with which to rebuild, a worse scouting and player-development infrastructure, and an owner in Larry Dolan who bought the entire mess believing he'd acquired a team too big to founder.

While the Indians should be able to win more than 80 games and stay close on the strength of a good rotation, one bad streak could be enough to destabilize the entire organization in a flurry of firings and trades. In baseball, no organization is too big to fail.

HITTERS (BA: .270, OBP: .340, SLG: .440, EqA: .260)

Roberto Alomar   2B   Bats B   Age 33

YEAR	TEAM	LGE	AB	H	DB	TP	HR	BB	SO	R	RBI	SB	CS	OUT	BA	OBP	SLG	EQA	EQR	DEFENSE	
1998	Baltimor	AL	589	175	31	2	17	58	62	88	58	16	5	419	.297	.362	.443	.272	81	144-2B	-3
1999	Clevelnd	AL	553	179	39	3	25	93	87	131	114	34	6	380	.324	.426	.541	.324	114	148-2B	3
2000	Clevelnd	AL	600	184	35	2	20	56	75	105	82	42	5	421	.307	.372	.472	.289	95	148-2B	-7
2001	Clevelnd	AL	511	150	27	1	19	68	72	106	90	22	4	365	.294	.377	.462	.284	79		

You're probably wailing about those Prospectus Fielding Runs. Sure, he's good. Everyone in the majors is good. But how do you *know* he's good? Because Harold Reynolds told you so? If *SportsCenter* had been around in the 1920s, we would have been watching the plays Rogers Hornsby made every night and not seeing the many he didn't. Television is no substitute for performance analysis using scouting and data, especially not two-second snippets selected to reinforce the popular opinion that the best all-around player at a position is the best at everything. Take Roberto Alomar for what he is: an outstanding player with some strengths and some weaknesses.

Sandy Alomar Jr.   C   Bats R   Age 35

YEAR	TEAM	LGE	AB	H	DB	TP	HR	BB	SO	R	RBI	SB	CS	OUT	BA	OBP	SLG	EQA	EQR	DEFENSE	
1998	Clevelnd	AL	408	97	26	2	7	17	40	46	44	0	2	314	.238	.273	.363	.205	30	109-C	0
1999	Clevelnd	AL	136	42	10	0	7	3	21	18	24	0	1	95	.309	.324	.537	.273	19	35-C	-6
2000	Clevelnd	AL	353	101	17	2	7	11	37	41	39	2	2	254	.286	.315	.405	.238	35	88-C	-7
2001	ChiSox	AL	268	70	14	1	7	15	31	32	39	0	1	199	.261	.300	.399	.232	26		

America loves Kennedys and Bushes beyond all common sense. Ozzie Guillen was rarely judged on his abilities but accepted because he happened to be named Ozzie. Maybe we're just too lazy to evaluate people for what they do, and not for what somebody with the same name did. Sandy Alomar has been an All-Star five times and is the recipient of awards and acclaim, but what you've really got is Rick Cerone under an assumed name. He's hit 20 home runs once. He might be a nice guy, but his knees are shot. Replacing him in Cleveland was overdue. The Sox signing him was a bonus for the Tribe.

Russ Branyan   Slugger   Bats L   Age 25

YEAR	TEAM	LGE	AB	H	DB	TP	HR	BB	SO	R	RBI	SB	CS	OUT	BA	OBP	SLG	EQA	EQR	DEFENSE			
1998	Akron	Eas	168	42	8	2	12	27	59	28	34	1	1	127	.250	.354	.536	.286	28	38-3B	-1		
1999	Buffalo	Int	399	77	9	1	25	43	186	42	53	5	2	324	.193	.276	.409	.226	39	99-3B	0		
2000	Buffalo	Int	232	53	8	1	18	23	97	40	49	1	1	180	.228	.302	.504	.259	31	35-3B	-2	19-LF	0
2000	Clevelnd	AL	191	45	6	2	16	20	69	30	35	0	0	146	.236	.321	.539	.275	29	32-LF	-2		
2001	Clevelnd	AL	332	76	11	1	24	40	148	48	63	3	1	257	.229	.312	.485	.258	44				

American League

Russ Branyan gets compared to Dave Kingman for his strikeouts, and like Kong he also has the gift for making himself unloved. Upon his last promotion from Buffalo, a local reporter wrote about how great the move was for the Bisons. Branyan fought with Kenny Lofton in July and has irritated all of his minor-league managers. With Manny Ramirez gone and the Tribe employing a bunch of expensive outfield temps, Branyan will DH if he isn't added to the list of traded prospects.

Jolbert Cabrera   UT   Bats R   Age 28

YEAR	TEAM	LGE	AB	H	DB	TP	HR	BB	SO	R	RBI	SB	CS	OUT	BA	OBP	SLG	EQA	EQR	DEFENSE			
1998	Buffalo	Int	497	143	18	1	9	55	70	76	38	14	10	364	.288	.370	.382	.258	61	121-SS	-2		
1999	Buffalo	Int	280	67	12	3	0	20	44	34	22	13	3	216	.239	.293	.304	.207	21	38-CF	3	20-SS	-2
2000	Buffalo	Int	74	22	5	1	2	4	9	14	8	1	1	53	.297	.340	.473	.265	10	12-CF	0		
2000	Clevelnd	AL	174	43	3	1	2	6	14	25	14	6	5	136	.247	.280	.310	.193	11	37-OF	4		
2001	Clevelnd	AL	291	75	10	1	5	24	39	39	31	12	6	222	.258	.314	.351	.225	27				

The Indians attack their roster with Homer Simpson's problem-solving skills. Jolbert Cabrera isn't really a fourth outfielder, but after Jacob Cruz went down, that's what the Indians needed. Forget reading the instructions; the Indians pull out the hammer and make things work. The Indians almost never bench their infield regulars in-game, so having a utility infielder who can play the outfield is fine as long as he doesn't have to play when Lofton takes a day off.

Wil Cordero   OF   Bats R   Age 29

YEAR	TEAM	LGE	AB	H	DB	TP	HR	BB	SO	R	RBI	SB	CS	OUT	BA	OBP	SLG	EQA	EQR	DEFENSE	
1998	ChiSox	AL	341	94	16	2	15	21	59	60	50	2	1	248	.276	.323	.466	.259	42	72-1B	14
1999	Clevelnd	AL	192	58	12	0	9	13	34	33	31	2	0	134	.302	.363	.505	.286	29	29-LF	-2
2000	Pittsbrg	NL	350	96	23	3	15	20	54	44	47	1	2	256	.274	.320	.486	.261	44	73-LF	-7
2000	Clevelnd	AL	147	38	12	2	0	5	16	17	16	0	0	109	.259	.297	.367	.220	12	38-LF	3
2001	Clevelnd	AL	375	105	23	1	13	29	61	54	62	1	1	271	.280	.332	.451	.257	45		

Wil Cordero resembles a useful ballplayer in the same way that Spam is sort of a meat. Not the good spam, but that Spam Lite stuff for the diet-conscious Spam lover on the go. "Look honey, it fits in pita bread, and it tastes like the real thing!" Cordero is signed through 2002, which is reason enough for the Indians to vote for a very long lockout.

Chris Coste   C/1B/3B   Bats R   Age 28

YEAR	TEAM	LGE	AB	H	DB	TP	HR	BB	SO	R	RBI	SB	CS	OUT	BA	OBP	SLG	EQA	EQR	DEFENSE	
2000	Akron	Eas	241	65	17	2	1	10	38	24	21	1	1	177	.270	.305	.369	.223	21	20-1B	0
2000	Buffalo	Int	96	26	2	0	3	2	13	13	6	0	1	71	.271	.291	.385	.218	8	20-C	1
2001	Clevelnd	AL	155	40	6	1	2	6	42	13	16	0	1	116	.258	.286	.348	.204	11		

Chris Coste led the organization's full-season players in batting average. He's a Northern League All-Star catcher from the 1998 Fargo-Moorhead team that upset the big-market St. Paul Saints, sending Bill "the Boss" Murray-brenner weeping into his foie gras and Dom Perignon. Okay, maybe his cheese fries. The other stars from that team? Darryl Motley of the '85 Royals, Ozzie Canseco, Jeff Bittiger, and the great Northern League slugger, Forry Wells.

Jacob Cruz   OF   Bats L   Age 28

YEAR	TEAM	LGE	AB	H	DB	TP	HR	BB	SO	R	RBI	SB	CS	OUT	BA	OBP	SLG	EQA	EQR	DEFENSE	
1998	Fresno	PCL	338	86	14	2	13	37	56	45	45	8	4	255	.254	.337	.423	.255	42	81-RF	-4
1998	Buffalo	Int	169	50	7	1	11	10	26	27	29	1	2	121	.296	.338	.544	.280	25	38-OF	-3
1999	Buffalo	Int	203	50	8	1	5	16	40	23	23	2	1	154	.246	.308	.369	.227	19	40-LF	-3
1999	Clevelnd	AL	87	28	6	1	3	4	12	14	16	0	2	61	.322	.358	.517	.277	12	21-CF	1
2000	Clevelnd	AL	29	7	4	0	0	4	4	3	5	1	0	22	.241	.354	.379	.258	4		
2001	Clevelnd	AL	234	67	17	2	9	26	37	40	42	1	1	168	.286	.358	.491	.278	34		

After blowing out his knee in May, Jacob Cruz is rehabbing over the winter in the hope he'll be ready by spring. This is the second straight season he's lost to injury, so it's hard to know what to expect. With Cordero, Ellis Burks and Juan Gonzalez all batting right-handed and having limitations, Cruz could get the chance to be as valuable as that projection suggests.

Einar Diaz   C   Bats R   Age 28

YEAR	TEAM	LGE	AB	H	DB	TP	HR	BB	SO	R	RBI	SB	CS	OUT	BA	OBP	SLG	EQA	EQR	DEFENSE	
1998	Buffalo	Int	416	120	18	2	7	14	33	54	53	2	2	298	.288	.319	.392	.236	40	112-C	1
1999	Clevelnd	AL	389	110	21	1	3	20	37	41	30	10	4	283	.283	.325	.365	.234	38	110-C	2
2000	Clevelnd	AL	248	67	13	2	4	8	26	27	23	4	2	183	.270	.315	.387	.235	24	74-C	3
2001	Clevelnd	AL	326	91	14	1	6	18	34	41	41	5	2	237	.279	.317	.383	.233	31		

Einar Diaz is a hustling catch-and-throw guy who doesn't get the bat knocked out of his hands. He's a good choice for baseball's best backup catcher. Eddie Taubensee's defensive limitations should get Diaz the right amount of playing time. However, the Indians are talking about making Taubensee the backup and playing Diaz regularly, something their offense can no longer afford.

Mike Edwards   3B   Bats R   Age 24

YEAR	TEAM	LGE	AB	H	DB	TP	HR	BB	SO	R	RBI	SB	CS	OUT	BA	OBP	SLG	EQA	EQR	DEFENSE	
1998	Columbus	SAL	506	116	27	2	5	47	100	54	53	5	3	393	.229	.297	.320	.207	38	113-3B	-11
1999	Kinston	Car	478	116	21	2	13	70	120	59	64	3	2	364	.243	.345	.377	.247	55	122-3B	-15
2000	Akron	Eas	490	126	19	1	10	52	93	57	48	4	2	366	.257	.332	.361	.236	50	131-3B	-9
2001	Clevelnd	AL	512	135	26	1	12	61	114	77	72	5	2	379	.264	.342	.389	.247	58		

Mike Edwards is the organization's best—arguably its only—hitting prospect. He made the jump to Double-A and survived while showing improved fielding skills. Edwards has always had the arm for third base but needs to improve his footwork. He posted an enormous backwards platoon split last year, hitting .320 with all of his power against right handers and .236 with no power against lefties. Good coaching will fix that. Keep in mind that Travis Fryman is under contract through 2002 with an option for 2003.

Travis Fryman   3B   Bats R   Age 32

YEAR	TEAM	LGE	AB	H	DB	TP	HR	BB	SO	R	RBI	SB	CS	OUT	BA	OBP	SLG	EQA	EQR	DEFENSE	
1998	Clevelnd	AL	554	160	31	2	30	43	111	74	94	8	7	401	.289	.343	.514	.276	81	144-3B	-2
1999	Clevelnd	AL	320	82	16	2	10	22	52	43	45	2	1	239	.256	.306	.412	.238	33	81-3B	2
2000	Clevelnd	AL	563	179	38	4	22	65	101	87	98	1	1	385	.318	.390	.517	.299	94	152-3B	4
2001	Clevelnd	AL	474	137	25	1	19	51	93	77	88	2	2	339	.289	.358	.466	.272	66		

Travis Fryman is a good defensive third baseman now, but it didn't happen overnight, and it wasn't automatic. He was a solid shortstop, but Sparky Anderson's early attempts to move him to third base didn't take. Fryman had bad footwork, didn't anticipate the double play well, and was terrible at guarding the line. He could have settled for being Dean Palmer, but he worked and got better, all at the major-league level. Getting Fryman for Matt Williams was a great move at the time, and it looks even better now.

Nate Grindell   3B   Bats R   Age 24

YEAR	TEAM	LGE	AB	H	DB	TP	HR	BB	SO	R	RBI	SB	CS	OUT	BA	OBP	SLG	EQA	EQR	DEFENSE	
1998	Watertwn	NYP	85	18	4	0	1	11	10	9	9	0	1	68	.212	.302	.294	.199	6	21-RF	0
1999	MahngVal	NYP	276	69	14	1	4	16	42	30	32	2	2	209	.250	.295	.351	.214	22	66-3B	-6
2000	Columbus	SAL	510	115	23	2	13	38	79	55	64	6	1	396	.225	.284	.355	.213	42	113-3B	-17
2001	Clevelnd	AL	394	98	18	1	9	33	65	46	48	2	1	297	.249	.307	.368	.224	35		

He's like the original monster of the fjords—you'll spend more time talking about him than seeing him. Nate Grindell was the Sally League's All-Star third baseman, and he led the Indians' minor leaguers in RBI. But he was old for the league, and he scuffled through a 39-error season. He'll have a hard time passing Edwards or staying ahead of 2000 draft pick Corey Smith.

Jon Hamilton   OF   Bats L   Age 23

YEAR	TEAM	LGE	AB	H	DB	TP	HR	BB	SO	R	RBI	SB	CS	OUT	BA	OBP	SLG	EQA	EQR	DEFENSE	
1998	Columbus	SAL	500	102	17	6	10	57	137	57	46	7	4	402	.204	.290	.322	.207	39	124-CF	-2
1999	Kinston	Car	490	118	23	3	11	43	117	58	48	4	2	374	.241	.303	.367	.224	45	121-CF	-3
2000	Akron	Eas	502	112	22	2	7	47	126	46	44	7	4	394	.223	.292	.317	.204	37	129-LF	-5
2001	Clevelnd	AL	480	116	21	2	10	51	130	61	56	6	3	367	.242	.315	.356	.226	44		

American League

The Tribe tried a cadre concept, promoting Edwards, Jon Hamilton, Scott Pratt, and Zach Sorensen to Akron as a group. It didn't work. Hamilton is young enough to rebound from a bad first year in Double-A, but hitting .236 and slugging .346 off of right-handed pitching is a good way to kill one's future as a corner outfielder.

Eric Johnson — OF — Bats R — Age 23

YEAR	TEAM	LGE	AB	H	DB	TP	HR	BB	SO	R	RBI	SB	CS	OUT	BA	OBP	SLG	EQA	EQR	DEFENSE	
1999	BlngtnNC	App	152	29	7	0	2	15	32	13	13	4	1	124	.191	.273	.276	.186	9	39-RF	6
1999	MahngVal	NYP	111	25	4	0	1	12	18	14	8	4	1	87	.225	.305	.288	.208	9	25-CF	-2
2000	Columbus	SAL	269	66	8	1	3	26	52	36	30	13	4	207	.245	.319	.316	.223	24	64-RF	11
2000	Kinston	Car	221	45	5	1	2	19	49	18	18	6	3	179	.204	.274	.262	.178	12	53-CF	6
2001	*Clevelnd*	*AL*	*297*	*71*	*8*	*1*	*3*	*33*	*70*	*42*	*25*	*15*	*4*	*230*	*.239*	*.315*	*.303*	*.217*	*25*		

Eric Johnson is a tools guy who was an all-conference defensive back at Western Carolina. He's been batting second and working on bunting, activities that usually scream out "non-prospect," but Johnson drew 64 walks and stole 56 bases (at an 82% success rate) in his first full season. He has a great arm, and he can fly in center field. He's a different type of player than Brian Jordan but could develop better than expected, like Jordan.

Kenny Lofton — CF — Bats L — Age 34

YEAR	TEAM	LGE	AB	H	DB	TP	HR	BB	SO	R	RBI	SB	CS	OUT	BA	OBP	SLG	EQA	EQR	DEFENSE	
1998	Clevelnd	AL	596	171	32	6	13	86	71	98	63	45	9	434	.287	.378	.426	.281	91	147-CF	0
1999	Clevelnd	AL	458	138	28	6	7	74	76	104	37	23	6	326	.301	.404	.434	.291	74	116-CF	0
2000	Clevelnd	AL	534	146	21	5	15	72	66	100	67	31	8	396	.273	.364	.416	.270	75	135-CF	5
2001	*Clevelnd*	*AL*	*490*	*130*	*24*	*4*	*9*	*76*	*70*	*96*	*65*	*22*	*8*	*368*	*.265*	*.364*	*.386*	*.259*	*63*		

Shoulder surgery was supposed to keep him from playing in the first half, but Kenny Lofton came back in time for Opening Day and put together a good year. In the first half, he hit for more power; in the second, he started going with the pitch and hitting to the opposite field. His BA and OBP went up while his walk rate remained consistent. If he sticks to getting on base, he'll justify the Tribe's decision to pick up his 2001 option.

Jeff Manto — 1B/3B — Bats R — Age 36

YEAR	TEAM	LGE	AB	H	DB	TP	HR	BB	SO	R	RBI	SB	CS	OUT	BA	OBP	SLG	EQA	EQR	DEFENSE			
1998	Buffalo	Int	213	54	7	0	16	46	51	34	44	2	1	160	.254	.388	.512	.296	38	34-1B	-2	10-3B	-1
1999	Buffalo	Int	207	51	8	0	15	53	50	34	29	2	1	157	.246	.405	.502	.302	39	51-1B	-5		
2000	Buffalo	Int	331	61	12	1	10	40	108	33	37	0	0	270	.184	.272	.317	.195	23	13-3B	0		

This is last time Jeff Manto will appear in the book, which is a sad landmark. I still remember his great '88 season at Midland. He's been on some of the most interesting teams of the last ten years, always for cups of coffee: the '93 Phillies, '97 Indians, and '99 Yankees. He's played in more than 1,300 minor-league games. He's played in Japan. He was good enough to have had more of a big-league career, and he ought to get a pension out of the game. Manto has retired and taken a coaching job in the Phillies' organziation.

John McDonald — SS — Bats R — Age 26

YEAR	TEAM	LGE	AB	H	DB	TP	HR	BB	SO	R	RBI	SB	CS	OUT	BA	OBP	SLG	EQA	EQR	DEFENSE	
1998	Akron	Eas	521	113	16	1	2	32	62	57	38	10	4	412	.217	.267	.263	.173	26	132-SS	14
1999	Akron	Eas	228	59	5	0	2	13	28	23	21	4	2	171	.259	.302	.307	.205	16	55-SS	1
1999	Buffalo	Int	237	69	8	2	0	7	23	24	21	4	2	170	.291	.316	.342	.221	19	58-SS	2
2000	Buffalo	Int	288	73	16	1	1	17	30	33	31	3	2	217	.253	.297	.326	.207	21	67-SS	-1
2001	*Clevelnd*	*AL*	*330*	*84*	*13*	*1*	*1*	*24*	*40*	*35*	*29*	*3*	*1*	*247*	*.255*	*.305*	*.309*	*.205*	*24*		

John McDonald is a great defensive player and slap hitter. The Indians could use him as a defensive replacement at second base and shortstop, but doing so would mean acknowledging that there are better defensive players than Roberto Alomar and Omar Vizquel. His real position is boogeyman in the nightmares of the Kansas sabermetric mafia, who are appropriately frightened that the Royals might covet the second coming of Rey Sanchez.

Billy Munoz   1B   Bats L   Age 26

YEAR	TEAM	LGE	AB	H	DB	TP	HR	BB	SO	R	RBI	SB	CS	OUT	BA	OBP	SLG	EQA	EQR	DEFENSE	
1998	Columbus	SAL	428	89	17	1	8	49	110	43	39	1	1	340	.208	.290	.308	.201	31	105-1B	6
1999	Kinston	Car	391	86	16	1	8	34	114	36	41	1	1	306	.220	.283	.327	.202	28	99-1B	-4
2000	Kinston	Car	219	55	7	1	8	14	50	21	26	0	0	164	.251	.300	.402	.232	21	47-1B	-1
2000	Akron	Eas	285	65	12	1	11	21	75	31	33	1	0	220	.228	.286	.393	.224	26	71-1B	-1
2001	Clevelnd	AL	435	98	14	1	13	44	122	46	51	1	0	337	.225	.296	.352	.215	36		

Billy Munoz tied for the organizational lead in home runs and won the organization's Player of the Year Award. As gestures go, it's great that the organization gave the award to a lifer instead of a prospect. Munoz is a month older than Alex Rodriguez and hasn't worked his way past Double-A yet. He's a minor-league slugger with a good defensive reputation.

Danny Peoples   1B   Bats R   Age 26

YEAR	TEAM	LGE	AB	H	DB	TP	HR	BB	SO	R	RBI	SB	CS	OUT	BA	OBP	SLG	EQA	EQR	DEFENSE	
1998	Akron	Eas	226	55	12	0	7	22	62	24	26	1	1	172	.243	.312	.389	.234	23	42-LF	-2
1999	Akron	Eas	502	110	18	2	16	38	153	59	58	1	1	393	.219	.277	.359	.209	39	88-1B	3
2000	Buffalo	Int	426	102	15	1	19	53	127	60	62	1	3	327	.239	.328	.413	.247	49	112-1B	-6
2001	Clevelnd	AL	350	81	14	1	13	41	113	44	49	1	1	270	.231	.312	.389	.233	35		

He was the organization's first-round pick in 1996 out of the University of Texas. From the 1990s crop of Indians of the future—from Tim Costo to David Miller to Scott Morgan to Brian Giles to Herb Perry to Sean Casey—Danny Peoples is what's left. He didn't have a great year, but he hurt left-handers, and he can move around first base or left field about as well as Richie Sexson did. The Indians could do worse than go with a Branyan/Peoples platoon at DH.

Scott Pratt   2B   Bats L   Age 24

YEAR	TEAM	LGE	AB	H	DB	TP	HR	BB	SO	R	RBI	SB	CS	OUT	BA	OBP	SLG	EQA	EQR	DEFENSE	
1998	Watertwn	NYP	184	49	9	1	2	24	28	23	9	5	4	139	.266	.358	.359	.246	21	33-2B	-1
1999	Kinston	Car	506	112	25	3	8	56	98	61	42	20	7	401	.221	.303	.330	.219	45	127-2B	-31
2000	Akron	Eas	506	109	17	3	7	29	106	53	41	13	8	405	.215	.259	.302	.182	29	123-2B	-16
2001	Clevelnd	AL	424	103	17	2	7	41	93	61	42	21	7	328	.243	.310	.342	.224	39		

Like fellow 1998 pick Zach Sorensen, Scott Pratt came out of a top college program (Auburn) and has been pushed up at a steady level-per-season pace. His background didn't prepare him for the toughest jump in baseball, from A-ball to Double-A. He didn't hit left-handers at all, his patience evaporated, and he continued to show poor range and bad hands. While he recovered some with a nice Arizona Fall League performance, he's as likely to replace Roberto Alomar as Duane Kuiper is.

Manny Ramirez   RF   Bats R   Age 29

YEAR	TEAM	LGE	AB	H	DB	TP	HR	BB	SO	R	RBI	SB	CS	OUT	BA	OBP	SLG	EQA	EQR	DEFENSE	
1998	Clevelnd	AL	567	169	31	2	48	75	108	108	143	4	3	401	.298	.385	.614	.316	112	139-RF	-2
1999	Clevelnd	AL	512	171	34	3	44	90	119	126	155	2	4	345	.334	.444	.670	.349	124	132-RF	-2
2000	Clevelnd	AL	427	148	31	2	38	79	107	85	112	1	1	280	.347	.452	.696	.359	108	80-RF	-9
2001	Boston	AL	473	165	30	1	43	93	114	98	121	1	1	309	.349	.456	.689	.363	123		

Manny Ramirez became the Indians' slugging version of what Lenny Dykstra was to the Phillies in the early '90s: without him, they're a pretty crummy team. Now that he's in Boston, do you want to bet he'll have a bigger impact on the 2001 playoff picture than Alex Rodriguez? He may not fix the Red Sox's problems against left-handed pitching by himself; even with one of the best lefty-killers around, the Tribe finished last season with an even worse record than did the Sox against southpaws. Replacing 120 games of Manny Ramirez with 120 games of Ellis Burks will cost the Indians a good 40 runs.

Alex Requena   CF   Bats B   Age 20

YEAR	TEAM	LGE	AB	H	DB	TP	HR	BB	SO	R	RBI	SB	CS	OUT	BA	OBP	SLG	EQA	EQR	DEFENSE	
1999	MahngVal	NYP	225	48	8	1	0	26	68	24	14	13	6	183	.213	.301	.258	.197	16	56-CF	-3
2000	Columbus	SAL	495	109	5	4	1	46	146	50	18	29	12	398	.220	.290	.253	.189	31	118-CF	-4
2001	Clevelnd	AL	341	81	5	2	0	36	125	48	21	25	8	268	.238	.310	.264	.205	25		

Alex Requena is one of the products of the Indians' Venezuelan program. He was voted the fastest player in the Sally League in *Baseball America*'s tools poll after stealing 87 bases and hitting into only one double play. For a speedster, he made a valiant attempt at being a Three True Outcomes (homeruns, walks, and strikeouts) guy by not putting the ball into play 37.5% of the time. His patience may not be that impressive because he has an extremely hard time getting the ball out of the infield. Once he starts facing pitchers with some command, he'll struggle if he doesn't improve.

Dave Roberts — OF — Bats L — Age 29

YEAR	TEAM	LGE	AB	H	DB	TP	HR	BB	SO	R	RBI	SB	CS	OUT	BA	OBP	SLG	EQA	EQR	DEFENSE	
1998	Jacksnvl	Sou	281	71	12	2	3	34	68	43	25	9	5	215	.253	.337	.342	.234	29	49-LF	1
1998	Akron	Eas	231	64	9	3	4	25	33	32	22	14	4	171	.277	.349	.394	.258	29	56-CF	-1
1999	Buffalo	Int	353	84	12	7	1	33	54	47	30	25	3	272	.238	.306	.320	.225	33	87-CF	6
1999	Clevelnd	AL	142	34	1	0	3	8	15	25	12	11	3	111	.239	.280	.310	.206	11	35-CF	2
2000	Buffalo	Int	468	118	14	2	10	45	76	71	43	24	9	358	.252	.320	.355	.233	47	118-CF	0
2001	Clevelnd	AL	466	118	12	3	8	51	81	71	51	22	6	354	.253	.327	.343	.233	46		

He was supposed to be the guy who would play center field while Lofton missed the first couple of months, but it was clear the Indians didn't have a lot of faith in him when they hauled Lance Johnson into camp. After losing Jacob Cruz to injury, they still didn't call up Dave Roberts. Maybe Buffalo's entire marketing campaign was built around Dave Roberts batting leadoff.

Osmany Santana — OF — Bats L — Age 24

YEAR	TEAM	LGE	AB	H	DB	TP	HR	BB	SO	R	RBI	SB	CS	OUT	BA	OBP	SLG	EQA	EQR	DEFENSE	
1998	Watertwn	NYP	81	18	3	1	2	8	9	11	8	1	1	64	.222	.292	.358	.215	7	19-CF	3
1999	Columbus	SAL	135	35	4	0	0	7	22	14	12	5	3	103	.259	.298	.289	.197	9	35-CF	1
1999	Kinston	Car	148	33	6	0	3	5	27	12	16	3	0	115	.223	.251	.324	.188	9	38-CF	1
2000	Kinston	Car	195	55	11	1	0	10	28	20	11	5	2	142	.282	.317	.349	.226	17	35-CF	-2
2000	Akron	Eas	192	49	2	0	2	8	25	12	19	8	1	144	.255	.287	.297	.201	13	43-CF	-1
2001	Clevelnd	AL	273	74	9	1	3	17	42	37	28	11	2	201	.271	.314	.344	.226	24		

One of the organization's Cubans, Osmany Santana lost time in 1998 with rotator cuff and knee injuries. Nevertheless, he's retained his mobility, so much so that the Tribe considers him the best defensive outfielder in the system. He isn't really a prospect, just a potential fourth outfielder if Jacob Cruz breaks down and they don't bring in anyone else.

David Segui — 1B — Bats B — Age 34

YEAR	TEAM	LGE	AB	H	DB	TP	HR	BB	SO	R	RBI	SB	CS	OUT	BA	OBP	SLG	EQA	EQR	DEFENSE	
1998	Seattle	AL	522	164	32	1	22	48	71	81	85	3	1	359	.314	.372	.506	.289	81	119-1B	29
1999	Seattle	AL	343	102	21	3	10	29	39	42	38	1	2	243	.297	.354	.464	.270	46	78-1B	10
1999	Toronto	AL	94	30	3	0	6	7	15	14	13	0	0	64	.319	.366	.543	.295	15		
2000	Texas	AL	344	114	25	1	12	29	46	48	53	0	1	231	.331	.383	.515	.295	54	38-1B	0
2000	Clevelnd	AL	219	72	10	0	9	16	30	38	43	0	0	147	.329	.377	.498	.289	33	34-1B	5
2001	Baltimor	AL	465	143	23	1	18	45	65	70	83	1	1	323	.308	.369	.477	.288	72		

Remember Bill James's comments about the great young first basemen coming up in the mid-'80s, the new Willie McCoveys? David Segui reflects a different age: he's wrestling with Mark Grace to be remembered as the new Vic Power. The Orioles have given him a four-year, $28-million contract to spearhead their youth movement. He is just 34.

Bill Selby — UT — Bats L — Age 31

YEAR	TEAM	LGE	AB	H	DB	TP	HR	BB	SO	R	RBI	SB	CS	OUT	BA	OBP	SLG	EQA	EQR	DEFENSE			
1998	Akron	Eas	77	24	4	1	2	1	12	11	7	0	0	53	.312	.326	.468	.260	9	13-RF	0		
1998	Buffalo	Int	338	75	15	1	11	28	53	36	41	2	0	263	.222	.281	.370	.216	28	26-3B	3	13-LF	-1
1999	Buffalo	Int	450	112	25	3	14	43	67	55	60	2	2	340	.249	.316	.411	.242	49	24-3B	0	14-RF	-1
2000	Buffalo	Int	389	93	16	4	16	37	68	55	65	1	1	297	.239	.309	.424	.242	43	49-3B	1	27-LF	-2
2000	Clevelnd	AL	46	11	1	0	0	0	8	6	4	0	0	35	.239	.256	.261	.155	2				
2001	Cincnnti	NL	382	95	19	2	12	41	68	51	57	1	1	288	.249	.322	.403	.242	41				

If you need a Jeff Manto fix in the future, we direct you to Bill Selby. He's played only 845 minor-league games, so he'll need at least five years to catch up to Manto. Like Manto, Selby spent time in Japan, which is usually Bobby Valentine's cue to sign you. He slugged .560 against right-handed pitching in Buffalo. Remember, Keith Lockhart didn't make it until he was past 30. Selby can play second base as well as third base and the outfield, so he'd be a good last man on the bench.

Zach Sorensen   SS   Bats B   Age 24

YEAR	TEAM	LGE	AB	H	DB	TP	HR	BB	SO	R	RBI	SB	CS	OUT	BA	OBP	SLG	EQA	EQR	DEFENSE	
1998	Watertwn	NYP	210	49	7	3	4	25	37	24	17	5	2	163	.233	.315	.352	.228	20	52-SS	-1
1999	Kinston	Car	525	113	15	4	7	44	130	60	47	10	7	419	.215	.277	.299	.191	33	127-SS	1
2000	Akron	Eas	388	90	14	2	6	32	67	48	30	9	4	302	.232	.292	.325	.208	30	96-SS	2
2000	Buffalo	Int	38	9	1	1	0	3	9	5	2	1	0	29	.237	.293	.316	.209	3	12-SS	3
2001	*Clevelnd*	*AL*	*432*	*105*	*13*	*3*	*7*	*47*	*95*	*59*	*45*	*15*	*6*	*333*	*.243*	*.317*	*.336*	*.224*	*39*		

After being picked in the second round of the 1998 draft, Zach Sorensen was expected to move up quickly. Instead, he's another one of the Kinston cadre of '99 who tried to jump across to Double-A and ended up like so much organizational roadkill. On the plus side, he cut down on his strikeouts, still played good defense, and scraped himself off the pavement to have a good AFL season. Vizquel is signed through 2002, and Sorensen has always-injured organizational favorite Maicer Izturis behind him, so he needs a good year as a hitter to make progress.

Jim Thome   1B   Bats L   Age 30

YEAR	TEAM	LGE	AB	H	DB	TP	HR	BB	SO	R	RBI	SB	CS	OUT	BA	OBP	SLG	EQA	EQR	DEFENSE	
1998	Clevelnd	AL	437	131	32	2	32	87	126	90	84	1	0	306	.300	.420	.602	.329	95	117-1B	-2
1999	Clevelnd	AL	485	135	28	2	33	121	156	98	102	0	0	350	.278	.426	.548	.321	102	107-1B	7
2000	Clevelnd	AL	545	145	26	1	38	111	156	98	98	1	0	400	.266	.394	.527	.303	101	104-1B	4
2001	*Clevelnd*	*AL*	*512*	*136*	*26*	*1*	*33*	*115*	*162*	*113*	*119*	*1*	*0*	*376*	*.266*	*.400*	*.514*	*.302*	*95*		

It's hard to believe that four years ago he was part of a lineup in which he was just one of the guys. Now he's the last guy. But wait, we forget that Cleveland is one of the "big market" teams that are supposed to be the only ones who can afford to re-sign their own free agents. So Albert Belle and Manny Ramirez never left, right? With Ramirez gone, I wouldn't be surprised if opposing teams quit juggling their rotations and simply let their right-handers start against the Indians, which might allow Jim Thome to set the franchise record for home runs in style.

Omar Vizquel   SS   Bats B   Age 34

YEAR	TEAM	LGE	AB	H	DB	TP	HR	BB	SO	R	RBI	SB	CS	OUT	BA	OBP	SLG	EQA	EQR	DEFENSE	
1998	Clevelnd	AL	573	168	32	6	2	61	57	83	49	30	11	416	.293	.365	.380	.259	71	150-SS	11
1999	Clevelnd	AL	566	189	36	4	5	59	46	106	62	39	9	386	.334	.398	.438	.290	87	141-SS	-7
2000	Clevelnd	AL	603	170	26	3	7	79	66	94	60	23	11	444	.282	.370	.370	.257	74	151-SS	-4
2001	*Clevelnd*	*AL*	*491*	*134*	*23*	*2*	*4*	*72*	*53*	*92*	*56*	*20*	*9*	*366*	*.273*	*.366*	*.352*	*.251*	*58*		

If you play with the Player Cards at www.baseballprospectus.com, you can come up with a pretty interesting comparison between Ozzie Smith and Omar Vizquel. Both started off terrible hitters, with Smith being slightly better. Both players had the finest years of their careers at 32, Smith posting a .291 EqA, Vizquel logging the 1999 season you see above. Smith had a better year at 33 (.278 EqA) than Vizquel did last year, but Leetle-O is not too far behind. If he can come close to matching Smith's longevity, he'll be a worthy Hall of Famer, even with those other shortstops in the AL today.

    Entertaining typo of the year from the Indians' postseason media guide: Vizquel "is the first AL SS to win 76 straight Gold Gloves since the award's inception in 1957."

Mark Whiten   Hit 4 HRs in a Game Once   Bats B   Age 34

YEAR	TEAM	LGE	AB	H	DB	TP	HR	BB	SO	R	RBI	SB	CS	OUT	BA	OBP	SLG	EQA	EQR	DEFENSE	
1998	Clevelnd	AL	225	65	10	0	8	28	53	31	30	2	1	161	.289	.374	.440	.275	32	53-LF	5
1999	Buffalo	Int	176	42	6	0	5	17	41	24	14	2	1	135	.239	.306	.358	.223	16	35-RF	2
2000	Buffalo	Int	358	86	20	1	8	25	81	47	31	3	2	274	.240	.290	.369	.218	30	76-RF	-8
2001	*Clevelnd*	*AL*	*247*	*57*	*8*	*0*	*6*	*26*	*61*	*27*	*27*	*1*	*1*	*191*	*.231*	*.304*	*.336*	*.213*	*20*		

Whoops, what's he doing here? Must be Homer Simpson with that hammer again. You...will...be...a...center fielder. THWACK! D'oh! In the countdown of single games that made the difference between the Indians going to the playoffs and going fishing, Mark Whiten's game-losing start in center on May 3 deserves footnote status.

American League

PITCHERS (ERA: 4.50, H/9: 9.00, HR/9: 1.00, BB/9: 3.00, K/9: 6.00, KW: 1.00, PERA: 4.50)

Mike Bacsik — Throws L — Age 23

YEAR	TEAM	LGE	IP	H	ER	HR	BB	K	ERA	W	L	H/9	HR/9	BB/9	K/9	KW	PERA
1998	Kinston	Car	146.0	160	94	38	50	66	5.79	5	11	9.86	2.34	3.08	4.07	0.66	6.45
1999	Akron	Eas	138.0	166	96	36	49	53	6.26	4	11	10.83	2.35	3.20	3.46	0.54	7.08
2000	Kinston	Car	59.3	77	45	10	9	29	6.83	2	5	11.68	1.52	1.37	4.40	1.61	5.95
2000	Akron	Eas	67.0	60	24	5	16	29	3.22	4	3	8.06	0.67	2.15	3.90	0.91	3.30
2000	Buffalo	Int	27.0	31	22	9	7	7	7.33	1	2	10.33	3.00	2.33	2.33	0.50	7.13

Mike Bacsik is a left-handed control artist with your standard fastball/curve/change-up assortment. He bounced back to A ball to recover from a miserable '99, then moved up on merit almost as much as he was sucked upwards by the vortex of arm death that beset the organization. The higher he went, the more often hitters hammered his mistakes, so he shouldn't be ready for this year's rotation shuffle.

Danny Baez — Throws R — Age 23

YEAR	TEAM	LGE	IP	H	ER	HR	BB	K	ERA	W	L	H/9	HR/9	BB/9	K/9	KW	PERA
2000	Kinston	Car	43.7	53	44	12	24	29	9.07	1	4	10.92	2.47	4.95	5.98	0.60	8.03
2000	Akron	Eas	96.0	99	52	11	35	50	4.88	4	7	9.28	1.03	3.28	4.69	0.71	4.83

America's Cuba policy leaves much to be desired. While we do business with every other Communist regime on the planet, we punish Cuba for showing us up 40 years ago. A side effect is that one of Castro country's top commodities, pitchers, can sign in this country on the basis of a false birth date, a fast gun-reading, and the right agent. Danys Baez was supposed to be 19. He's probably 25. He was supposed to throw 97 mph, but he's usually around 93 and doesn't have a reliable second pitch. The Indians signed him to a four-year, $14.5 million major-league contract. One year down, and he didn't exactly dominate in the Eastern League. If you want to do something about this, move to North Carolina and vote Jesse Helms out of existence. We have to start somewhere. Baez may get pressed into the fifth rotation spot; don't expect greatness.

Jason Bere — Throws R — Age 30

YEAR	TEAM	LGE	IP	H	ER	HR	BB	K	ERA	W	L	H/9	HR/9	BB/9	K/9	KW	PERA
1998	ChiSox	AL	83.3	93	63	13	50	49	6.80	2	7	10.04	1.40	5.40	5.29	0.49	6.55
1998	Cincnnti	NL	42.0	38	19	3	18	25	4.07	2	3	8.14	0.64	3.86	5.36	0.69	3.99
1999	Cincnnti	NL	43.7	55	32	5	32	24	6.60	1	4	11.34	1.03	6.60	4.95	0.38	7.41
1999	Milwauke	NL	22.7	22	14	3	8	16	5.56	1	2	8.74	1.19	3.18	6.35	1.00	4.59
2000	Milwauke	NL	113.0	113	60	17	52	82	4.78	5	8	9.00	1.35	4.14	6.53	0.79	5.35
2000	Clevelnd	AL	55.0	61	35	5	20	42	5.73	2	4	9.98	0.82	3.27	6.87	1.05	5.02

With the Tribe, Jason Bere had only one quality start against teams with an above-.500 record. The team that signs him needs to take off the beer goggles, but it's already the morning after, Bere is awake, and it's too late for Cubs GM Andy MacPhail to chew off his own arm. Now MacPhail needs to find a way to make Bere leave without having to give him his phone number. A jacktastic fly-ball pitcher going to Wrigley? Better get those DJ Stewie Scott "Boo-yahs!" pre-recorded, because he's going to wear himself out calling Cubs' highlights.

Jamie Brewington — Throws R — Age 29

YEAR	TEAM	LGE	IP	H	ER	HR	BB	K	ERA	W	L	H/9	HR/9	BB/9	K/9	KW	PERA
1999	Kinston	Car	70.7	82	61	15	49	38	7.77	2	6	10.44	1.91	6.24	4.84	0.39	7.66
2000	Buffalo	Int	22.0	20	10	4	13	18	4.09	1	1	8.18	1.64	5.32	7.36	0.69	5.67
2000	Clevelnd	AL	45.7	52	23	2	14	33	4.53	2	3	10.25	0.39	2.76	6.50	1.18	4.49

A minor-league journeyman, Jamie Brewington blew his chance of sticking around by going on a golf outing in the Texas heat before a game on the last day of August. When he was called to the mound, he coughed up five runs. Manuel found out about the trip to the links, and Brewington pitched just three more times before being dumped. He throws hard and did well against right-handers in the mop-up role, but neither skill is that rare.

Jim Brower — Throws R — Age 28

YEAR	TEAM	LGE	IP	H	ER	HR	BB	K	ERA	W	L	H/9	HR/9	BB/9	K/9	KW	PERA
1998	Akron	Eas	143.7	140	69	15	46	50	4.32	7	9	8.77	0.94	2.88	3.13	0.54	4.26
1999	Buffalo	Int	150.0	158	105	29	64	52	6.30	5	12	9.48	1.74	3.84	3.12	0.41	5.92
1999	Clevelnd	AL	25.7	25	10	6	8	17	3.51	2	1	8.77	2.10	2.81	5.96	1.06	5.47
2000	Buffalo	Int	95.0	97	45	10	26	48	4.26	5	6	9.19	0.95	2.46	4.55	0.92	4.33
2000	Clevelnd	AL	62.7	74	36	8	23	31	5.17	3	4	10.63	1.15	3.30	4.45	0.67	5.74

Jim Brower has a nice slider and a bunch of stuff that isn't a nice slider. Pressed into the rotation when Charles Nagy and Jaret Wright broke down on Injury Day, he was an adequate replacement through June (4.89 ERA) before collapsing in July (13.09 ERA). He won't kill you as your mop-up man and emergency starter. Brower has been traded to the Reds with Rob Pugmire for Eddie Taubensee. Hart 1, Bowden 0.

Jamie Brown — Throws R — Age 24

YEAR	TEAM	LGE	IP	H	ER	HR	BB	K	ERA	W	L	H/9	HR/9	BB/9	K/9	KW	PERA
1998	Kinston	Car	153.7	172	122	27	60	76	7.15	4	13	10.07	1.58	3.51	4.45	0.63	5.97
1999	Akron	Eas	128.7	140	79	16	41	62	5.53	5	9	9.79	1.12	2.87	4.34	0.76	5.04
2000	Akron	Eas	89.0	99	62	22	29	36	6.27	3	7	10.01	2.22	2.93	3.64	0.62	6.38

This organizational favorite was asked to repeat Double-A, got hurt in the early going, and failed to build on his 1999 season. Jamie Brown gets good marks for smarts, mechanics, an adequate fastball, a nasty change-up, and even a working curve. He did improve the sinking action on his fastball, but it was a bad year to spend repeating a level when everyone producing carbon dioxide got a trip to Cleveland.

Dave Burba — Throws R — Age 34

YEAR	TEAM	LGE	IP	H	ER	HR	BB	K	ERA	W	L	H/9	HR/9	BB/9	K/9	KW	PERA
1998	Clevelnd	AL	200.7	195	85	25	58	122	3.81	12	10	8.75	1.12	2.60	5.47	1.05	4.32
1999	Clevelnd	AL	219.3	196	93	24	75	166	3.82	13	11	8.04	0.98	3.08	6.81	1.11	3.96
2000	Clevelnd	AL	193.0	187	81	14	69	172	3.78	11	10	8.72	0.65	3.22	8.02	1.25	4.07

Dave Burba is probably baseball's best #3 starter, including either Andy Pettite or Orlando Hernandez. The forkball gets a bad rap because of people like Kelly Downs, but it's the pitch that sets up Burba's four-pitch assortment: two-seam and four-seam heat, the splitter, and a great change-up. Considering what the pitch did for Burba and Dave Stewart and Mike Scott, I'd think you'd see more of it. Burba should be able to handle this workload through the two years left on his contract.

Bartolo Colon — Throws R — Age 26

YEAR	TEAM	LGE	IP	H	ER	HR	BB	K	ERA	W	L	H/9	HR/9	BB/9	K/9	KW	PERA
1998	Clevelnd	AL	201.3	192	79	13	66	146	3.53	12	10	8.58	0.58	2.95	6.53	1.11	3.81
1999	Clevelnd	AL	203.3	172	80	19	59	153	3.54	13	10	7.61	0.84	2.61	6.77	1.30	3.40
2000	Clevelnd	AL	190.0	154	69	16	74	202	3.27	13	8	7.29	0.76	3.51	9.57	1.36	3.49

Bartolo Colon can be a menace to himself, but he's worth the trouble. He came into camp looking like he'd spent his winter out-eating Rich Garces then had to log three weeks on the DL getting into playing shape. He spent the last months of the season fighting with Jerry Manuel and Dick Pole about his endurance after pulling himself out of three starts. When you consider he had four five-inning, one-run starts, you can understand the frustration. If he shows up in camp in shape, he'll be the second-best pitcher in the league behind Pedro Martinez.

Zach Day — Throws R — Age 23

YEAR	TEAM	LGE	IP	H	ER	HR	BB	K	ERA	W	L	H/9	HR/9	BB/9	K/9	KW	PERA
1998	Greensbr	SAL	33.0	36	24	2	8	17	6.55	1	3	9.82	0.55	2.18	4.64	1.06	4.15
1998	Tampa	Fla	94.0	136	89	10	40	41	8.52	2	8	13.02	0.96	3.83	3.93	0.51	7.18
2000	Greensbr	SAL	74.7	83	44	16	41	47	5.30	3	5	10.00	1.93	4.94	5.67	0.57	6.88
2000	Tampa	Fla	30.7	35	29	5	19	21	8.51	1	2	10.27	1.47	5.58	6.16	0.55	6.82
2000	Akron	Eas	43.0	38	21	2	23	28	4.40	2	3	7.95	0.42	4.81	5.86	0.61	4.04

Zach Day missed most of 1998 following surgery to repair his rotator cuff and spent 1999 putting himself back together. He earns high good marks for knowing what he's doing on the mound, because he gets by with only a good sinker and a change-up, mixing in breaking stuff for show. He keeps the ball on the ground and doesn't get hit hard. Jake Westbrook's talent makes him better-known, but Day looks like the best prospect from the David Justice deal.

Sean DePaula — Throws R — Age 27

YEAR	TEAM	LGE	IP	H	ER	HR	BB	K	ERA	W	L	H/9	HR/9	BB/9	K/9	KW	PERA
1998	Kinston	Car	42.7	54	29	3	28	27	6.12	1	4	11.39	0.63	5.91	5.70	0.48	6.74
1998	Akron	Eas	15.3	16	12	0	18	10	7.04	0	2	9.39	0.00	10.57	5.87	0.28	6.85
1999	Kinston	Car	43.3	48	34	15	22	35	7.06	1	4	9.97	3.12	4.57	7.27	0.80	7.94
1999	Akron	Eas	25.0	22	15	3	20	18	5.40	1	2	7.92	1.08	7.20	6.48	0.45	5.70
1999	Clevelnd	AL	11.7	8	5	0	2	17	3.86	1	0	6.17	0.00	1.54	13.11	4.25	1.68
2000	Clevelnd	AL	17.3	19	9	2	11	15	4.67	1	1	9.87	1.04	5.71	7.79	0.68	6.20

The hero of the 1999 playoffs, Sean DePaula is rehabbing this winter after missing most of 2000 with elbow tendinitis. He's expected to be 100% by camp. If DePaula is ready to go, they Indians will have six good right-handed relievers, counting Steve Karsay, so DePaula's spring will have a major impact on the gamble of making Karsay a starter.

Tim Drew — Throws R — Age 22

YEAR	TEAM	LGE	IP	H	ER	HR	BB	K	ERA	W	L	H/9	HR/9	BB/9	K/9	KW	PERA
1998	Columbus	SAL	65.0	70	50	9	33	30	6.92	2	5	9.69	1.25	4.57	4.15	0.45	5.84
1998	Kinston	Car	79.3	109	74	20	42	35	8.39	2	7	12.37	2.27	4.76	3.97	0.42	8.57
1999	Kinston	Car	153.7	162	99	26	70	66	5.80	5	12	9.49	1.52	4.10	3.87	0.47	5.80
2000	Akron	Eas	49.0	39	18	2	16	14	3.31	3	2	7.16	0.37	2.94	2.57	0.44	2.86
2000	Buffalo	Int	90.3	118	70	15	31	41	6.97	2	8	11.76	1.49	3.09	4.08	0.66	6.69
2000	Clevelnd	AL	9.3	16	10	1	6	5	9.64	0	1	15.43	0.96	5.79	4.82	0.42	9.37

The Tribe loves Tim Drew because he's picking up velocity as he fills out. Add that to a good slider and change-up, and you see reasons to get excited. He throws from about any arm angle, which is fun when you're talking about some geezer like Luis Tiant, but strange when you're talking about a young prospect. The decision to call him up was indefensible and cost the Tribe a spot on the 40-man roster a half-season early.

Chuck Finley — Throws L — Age 38

YEAR	TEAM	LGE	IP	H	ER	HR	BB	K	ERA	W	L	H/9	HR/9	BB/9	K/9	KW	PERA
1998	Anaheim	AL	221.0	199	85	17	93	196	3.46	14	11	8.10	0.69	3.79	7.98	1.05	3.99
1999	Anaheim	AL	212.3	185	99	19	75	190	4.20	11	13	7.84	0.81	3.18	8.05	1.27	3.71
2000	Clevelnd	AL	219.0	197	87	17	76	180	3.58	13	11	8.10	0.70	3.12	7.40	1.18	3.72

Chuck Finley had a better year than John Hart should have expected. Nevertheless, Hart is disappointed. Like Barry Bonds, Finley won't get credit for his clutch performance down the stretch; he made six quality starts in seven tries in September, including two on three days' rest.

Chris Haney — Throws L — Age 32

YEAR	TEAM	LGE	IP	H	ER	HR	BB	K	ERA	W	L	H/9	HR/9	BB/9	K/9	KW	PERA
1998	KansasCy	AL	96.3	115	66	15	30	47	6.17	3	8	10.74	1.40	2.80	4.39	0.78	5.86
1999	Buffalo	Int	55.0	48	26	5	24	25	4.25	3	3	7.85	0.82	3.93	4.09	0.52	4.02
1999	Clevelnd	AL	40.0	40	18	2	13	21	4.05	2	2	9.00	0.45	2.93	4.72	0.81	3.92
2000	Buffalo	Int	86.3	87	30	11	18	50	3.13	6	4	9.07	1.15	1.88	5.21	1.39	4.22

Chris Haney staged a great comeback, coming off the surgeon's table, to log a fine half-season after having a nerve in his elbow relocated in April. His struggles in '97 and '98 resulted from non-arm injuries. He's always known how to dish slop, so he's a better bet to be a useful fourth or fifth starter than Steve Avery is. Invited to camp with the Rangers, where he could finally sneak back into the big leagues.

Steve Karsay — Throws R — Age 29

YEAR	TEAM	LGE	IP	H	ER	HR	BB	K	ERA	W	L	H/9	HR/9	BB/9	K/9	KW	PERA
1998	Buffalo	Int	74.7	87	41	7	16	43	4.94	3	5	10.49	0.84	1.93	5.18	1.34	4.76
1998	Clevelnd	AL	24.0	29	15	3	5	12	5.63	1	2	10.88	1.13	1.88	4.50	1.20	5.30
1999	Clevelnd	AL	78.0	66	24	5	23	65	2.77	6	3	7.62	0.58	2.65	7.50	1.41	3.16
2000	Clevelnd	AL	76.3	73	28	4	19	63	3.30	5	3	8.61	0.47	2.24	7.43	1.66	3.44

His overall save numbers don't look good (20 saves, nine blown), but he was 19-for-24 in save opportunities before the Bob Wickman trade, logging four blown saves in middle relief after the deal. Steve Karsay's real problem was an overreliance on his fastball, on which right-handed hitters sat. He's cranky about not closing, so the Tribe is considering moving him into the rotation. That means the experience of 1999 (Karsay starts, Karsay gets hurt) taught them nothing. Maybe we all have habits we can't break, but this is one of those hand-in-the-blender-is-bad lessons that you expect memory or Darwinian selection to have sorted out by now.

Andrew Lorraine — Throws L — Age 28

YEAR	TEAM	LGE	IP	H	ER	HR	BB	K	ERA	W	L	H/9	HR/9	BB/9	K/9	KW	PERA
1998	Tacoma	PCL	74.0	89	49	15	44	45	5.96	2	6	10.82	1.82	5.35	5.47	0.51	7.41
1999	Iowa	PCL	135.0	139	70	21	41	61	4.67	6	9	9.27	1.40	2.73	4.07	0.74	4.98
1999	ChiCubs	NL	60.3	68	38	8	18	34	5.67	2	5	10.14	1.19	2.69	5.07	0.94	5.26
2000	ChiCubs	NL	31.3	35	22	4	15	21	6.32	1	2	10.05	1.15	4.31	6.03	0.70	5.81
2000	Buffalo	Int	85.0	95	40	11	26	36	4.24	4	5	10.06	1.16	2.75	3.81	0.69	5.20

Andrew Lorraine continued his nomadic existence in 2000, getting dumped by the Cubs after opening the season in their rotation, then moving on to a competitive team—the Bisons. Anybody with a shutout in the last two seasons is going to get as many chances as Pauly Shore, but Haney is the better choice as a sixth starter.

Tom Martin — Throws L — Age 31

YEAR	TEAM	LGE	IP	H	ER	HR	BB	K	ERA	W	L	H/9	HR/9	BB/9	K/9	KW	PERA
1998	Buffalo	Int	33.7	46	27	5	14	24	7.22	1	3	12.30	1.34	3.74	6.42	0.86	7.10
1998	Clevelnd	AL	15.0	27	18	3	10	8	10.80	0	2	16.20	1.80	6.00	4.80	0.40	10.81
2000	Clevelnd	AL	33.3	30	13	2	11	20	3.51	2	2	8.10	0.54	2.97	5.40	0.91	3.52

Situational left-handers are like beers: too many of them are bad for you, but you can't have just one. Last year was the closest Tom Martin has come since 1997 to having a full season in the majors, but he still missed almost two months with shoulder tendinitis. He's your basic second lefty. Traded to the Mets.

Willie Martinez — Throws R — Age 23

YEAR	TEAM	LGE	IP	H	ER	HR	BB	K	ERA	W	L	H/9	HR/9	BB/9	K/9	KW	PERA
1998	Akron	Eas	143.0	169	104	23	48	71	6.55	4	12	10.64	1.45	3.02	4.47	0.74	5.94
1999	Akron	Eas	136.7	164	93	30	47	58	6.12	4	11	10.80	1.98	3.10	3.82	0.62	6.63
1999	Buffalo	Int	21.3	26	15	3	7	9	6.33	1	1	10.97	1.27	2.95	3.80	0.64	5.89
2000	Buffalo	Int	127.7	131	77	21	67	73	5.43	5	9	9.23	1.48	4.72	5.15	0.54	5.86

Though he has stayed relatively healthy for the last two seasons, Willie Martinez has failed to make much progress. Despite plenty of time in Akron and Buffalo, he still lives and dies with an adequate fastball, and his breaking stuff remains rudimentary. He's been claimed on waivers by the Twins, with whom he'll get a shot at a bullpen job.

Charles Nagy — Throws R — Age 34

YEAR	TEAM	LGE	IP	H	ER	HR	BB	K	ERA	W	L	H/9	HR/9	BB/9	K/9	KW	PERA
1998	Clevelnd	AL	207.3	231	118	29	55	111	5.12	9	14	10.03	1.26	2.39	4.82	1.01	5.12
1999	Clevelnd	AL	200.3	219	101	21	46	120	4.54	10	12	9.84	0.94	2.07	5.39	1.30	4.55
2000	Clevelnd	AL	57.7	65	42	11	16	39	6.55	2	4	10.14	1.72	2.50	6.09	1.22	5.74

Jason Bere's blowing a seven-run lead makes for an easy target, but it was Charles Nagy's insistence on pitching in September that cost the Indians three games they couldn't afford to lose. He'd spent most of the season trying to rush back from May elbow surgery that had come after he hid a sore arm for almost a year. He ought to be suspended for this kind of selfishness, but the Indians are too busy firing on their better players to single out real problems. Nagy's ability to contribute is up in the air, but he'll be pitching before Jaret Wright will.

American League

Chris Nichting — Throws R — Age 35

YEAR	TEAM	LGE	IP	H	ER	HR	BB	K	ERA	W	L	H/9	HR/9	BB/9	K/9	KW	PERA
1998	Buffalo	Int	90.3	105	60	12	39	66	5.98	3	7	10.46	1.20	3.89	6.58	0.85	5.94
1999	Columbus	Int	120.0	134	83	26	49	75	6.22	4	9	10.05	1.95	3.68	5.63	0.77	6.40
2000	Buffalo	Int	61.7	66	35	8	17	43	5.11	3	4	9.63	1.17	2.48	6.28	1.26	4.83
2000	Clevelnd	AL	9.0	12	6	0	4	7	6.00	0	1	12.00	0.00	4.00	7.00	0.88	5.57

Who else would be the idol of the Knights Who Say Nichting? Chris logged a win or save in 19 straight games at Buffalo. A Northwestern grad drafted by the Dodgers in 1987, Nichting lost two years to a torn rotator cuff back in the bad old Dan Opperman/Kiki Diaz days when every Dodgers draft pick was blowing out his arm within weeks of joining the organization. He has no real future outside of coaching.

Roy Padilla — Throws L — Age 25

YEAR	TEAM	LGE	IP	H	ER	HR	BB	K	ERA	W	L	H/9	HR/9	BB/9	K/9	KW	PERA
1999	Columbus	SAL	53.0	55	33	6	37	24	5.60	2	4	9.34	1.02	6.28	4.08	0.32	6.08
1999	Kinston	Car	11.3	10	9	2	13	3	7.15	0	1	7.94	1.59	10.32	2.38	0.12	7.66
2000	Kinston	Car	20.0	15	27	0	27	15	12.15	0	2	6.75	0.00	12.15	6.75	0.28	5.85
2000	Akron	Eas	21.0	19	17	0	29	11	7.29	0	2	8.14	0.00	12.43	4.71	0.19	6.83

Roy Padilla is a big Panamanian who throws in the high 90s. He's been added to the 40-man roster after an AFL stint in which he put 30 men on base in 18 innings, but not without frightening all of them. He's a prime example of the Indians taking pride in farm players who have physical talent but dubious performance records. He'll have a hard time becoming the new John Rocker; Rocker was better than this in the minors.

Steve Reed — Throws R — Age 35

YEAR	TEAM	LGE	IP	H	ER	HR	BB	K	ERA	W	L	H/9	HR/9	BB/9	K/9	KW	PERA
1998	San Fran	NL	52.0	30	10	4	18	41	1.73	5	1	5.19	0.69	3.12	7.10	1.14	2.25
1998	Clevelnd	AL	25.3	24	16	3	7	21	5.68	1	2	8.53	1.07	2.49	7.46	1.50	4.08
1999	Clevelnd	AL	61.3	64	28	8	16	42	4.11	3	4	9.39	1.17	2.35	6.16	1.31	4.66
2000	Clevelnd	AL	56.0	54	24	5	16	37	3.86	3	3	8.68	0.80	2.57	5.95	1.16	3.95

A good sinker/slider guy with a handy change-up, Steve Reed had an absolutely awful first half (6.04 ERA) but was part of the team-wide rally down the stretch. The slow start kind of left the Tribe wondering how to use him, so Reed spent most of the year pitching in lost causes. He's a likely target for a spring trade if everyone else is healthy.

Ricardo Rincon — Throws L — Age 31

YEAR	TEAM	LGE	IP	H	ER	HR	BB	K	ERA	W	L	H/9	HR/9	BB/9	K/9	KW	PERA
1998	Pittsbrg	NL	62.3	50	31	6	26	52	4.48	3	4	7.22	0.87	3.75	7.51	1.00	3.65
1999	Clevelnd	AL	44.7	38	18	5	19	29	3.63	3	2	7.66	1.01	3.83	5.84	0.76	4.06
2000	Clevelnd	AL	20.3	16	6	1	10	19	2.66	1	1	7.08	0.44	4.43	8.41	0.95	3.43

While Brian Giles kept going on to bigger and better things, Ricardo Rincon went into the elbow surgery bin on Injury Day, coming back to pitch in the last six weeks of the season. It hurts that the Indians will never use him in anything more than a super-situational role. Whereas most left-handed setup men still see right-handed hitters about half the time, Rincon faced twice as many left-handers as right-handers, being used only in situations where Manuel was almost absolutely certain that he'd face a left-handed batter. When a manager is too aware of platoon issues, he ends up needing 12 pitchers, which makes it hard to give relievers good workloads and costs you a position player. A bad trade gets turned into a tactical handicap.

David Riske — Throws R — Age 24

YEAR	TEAM	LGE	IP	H	ER	HR	BB	K	ERA	W	L	H/9	HR/9	BB/9	K/9	KW	PERA
1998	Kinston	Car	47.3	55	23	9	21	35	4.37	2	3	10.46	1.71	3.99	6.65	0.83	6.55
1999	Akron	Eas	22.0	6	7	1	14	21	2.86	1	1	2.45	0.41	5.73	8.59	0.75	1.66
1999	Buffalo	Int	26.0	14	3	1	7	16	1.04	3	0	4.85	0.35	2.42	5.54	1.14	1.62
1999	Clevelnd	AL	14.3	19	14	2	5	15	8.79	0	2	11.93	1.26	3.14	9.42	1.50	6.63

(David Riske *continued*)

David Riske missed 2000 with what was initially termed a back injury but turned out to be a shoulder injury. The Indians are loaded with relievers who have had good stretches. J.D. Brammer has a great curve and no control. Padilla has great heat and no control. DePaula has the best stuff but got hurt. Riske had the best control before he got hurt. All of them will probably show up in Cleveland at some point in 2001.

C.C. Sabathia — Throws L — Age 20

YEAR	TEAM	LGE	IP	H	ER	HR	BB	K	ERA	W	L	H/9	HR/9	BB/9	K/9	KW	PERA
1999	MahngVal	NYP	17.3	10	6	0	16	12	3.12	1	1	5.19	0.00	8.31	6.23	0.38	3.48
1999	Columbus	SAL	15.0	9	3	2	6	9	1.80	2	0	5.40	1.20	3.60	5.40	0.75	2.88
1999	Kinston	Car	28.3	32	28	7	22	15	8.89	1	2	10.16	2.22	6.99	4.76	0.34	8.10
2000	Kinston	Car	49.7	56	33	9	28	37	5.98	2	4	10.15	1.63	5.07	6.70	0.66	6.72
2000	Akron	Eas	83.3	79	49	11	52	59	5.29	3	6	8.53	1.19	5.62	6.37	0.57	5.51

C.C. Sabathia is the best prospect in the organization. There aren't a whole lot of left-handers who flirt with 100 mph on any gun and fewer still who add a nice curve and change-up. What elbow troubles he had were addressed quickly. The Indians yanked him off of Team USA once it became clear Tommy Lasorda had lied about how he planned on using Sabathia. Considering his youth and the fact that he will be the first Indians' top draft pick since Jaret Wright to turn into something, you can understand their caution. Calling him up before the end of the year cost the Tribe a roster spot, but he may not need more than a half-season at Buffalo.

Paul Shuey — Throws R — Age 30

YEAR	TEAM	LGE	IP	H	ER	HR	BB	K	ERA	W	L	H/9	HR/9	BB/9	K/9	KW	PERA
1998	Clevelnd	AL	50.7	42	16	5	21	54	2.84	4	2	7.46	0.89	3.73	9.59	1.29	3.80
1999	Clevelnd	AL	82.0	65	31	6	31	98	3.40	5	4	7.13	0.66	3.40	10.76	1.58	3.27
2000	Clevelnd	AL	64.0	48	20	3	23	66	2.81	5	2	6.75	0.42	3.23	9.28	1.43	2.81

Paul Shuey still has the big "can't close" monkey riding on his back. Treat that criticism with derision, because he throws in the mid 90s with a good curve and forkball. Shuey missed a month with yet another injury, notching his eighth stint on the DL. If the Indians make the mistake of getting frustrated with him, he'll make some other team very happy.

Justin Speier — Throws R — Age 27

YEAR	TEAM	LGE	IP	H	ER	HR	BB	K	ERA	W	L	H/9	HR/9	BB/9	K/9	KW	PERA
1998	Iowa	PCL	48.3	52	35	13	21	33	6.52	1	4	9.68	2.42	3.91	6.14	0.79	6.80
1998	Florida	NL	18.3	25	19	8	11	12	9.33	0	2	12.27	3.93	5.40	5.89	0.55	10.50
1999	Richmond	Int	39.7	50	27	4	22	26	6.13	1	3	11.34	0.91	4.99	5.90	0.59	6.60
1999	Atlanta	NL	28.0	27	17	8	11	19	5.46	1	2	8.68	2.57	3.54	6.11	0.86	6.20
2000	Clevelnd	AL	68.3	53	22	7	21	66	2.90	5	3	6.98	0.92	2.77	8.69	1.57	3.19

A 55th-round draft choice and the son of former Giants and Expos infielder Chris Speier, Justin Speier finally got an extended opportunity to prove he belongs in the majors and ran with it. He throws hard and can handle a middle-relief role. Don't raise your expectations any higher than that. He's allowed an eye-popping 24 home runs in 117⅔ major league innings. Until he comes up with some change of pace, he won't have hitters guessing on timing, only location.

Jason Stanford — Throws L — Age 24

YEAR	TEAM	LGE	IP	H	ER	HR	BB	K	ERA	W	L	H/9	HR/9	BB/9	K/9	KW	PERA
2000	Columbus	SAL	72.0	85	37	7	26	32	4.63	3	5	10.63	0.88	3.25	4.00	0.62	5.42
2000	Kinston	Car	63.7	70	25	5	21	29	3.53	4	3	9.90	0.71	2.97	4.10	0.69	4.69

A nifty pickup as an undrafted free agent from UNC-Charlotte, Jason Stanford went a combined 12–7 with a 2.62 ERA in his debut season. That was enough to win the organization's Pitcher of the Year Award.

American League

Jake Westbrook — Throws R — Age 23

YEAR	TEAM	LGE	IP	H	ER	HR	BB	K	ERA	W	L	H/9	HR/9	BB/9	K/9	KW	PERA
1998	Jupiter	Fla	157.3	163	80	24	76	46	4.58	7	10	9.32	1.37	4.35	2.63	0.30	5.64
1999	Harrisbg	Eas	164.3	176	90	19	63	57	4.93	7	11	9.64	1.04	3.45	3.12	0.45	5.11
2000	Columbus	Int	85.0	91	52	4	37	47	5.51	3	6	9.64	0.42	3.92	4.98	0.64	4.64

When you see him, Jake Westbrook's talent jumps out at you. He has a fastball with a natural boring, sinking action and a good slider. He needs to pick up a solid change-up. The Expos wanted him to add a splitter, but with Westbrook going through his third organization in less than a year, it's impossible to know if he's going to master it any time soon. A broken rib kept him from pitching for Buffalo. He has an outside chance at the fifth slot in the rotation depending on how quickly the Karsay experiment breaks down.

Bob Wickman — Throws R — Age 32

YEAR	TEAM	LGE	IP	H	ER	HR	BB	K	ERA	W	L	H/9	HR/9	BB/9	K/9	KW	PERA
1998	Milwauke	NL	79.3	78	37	5	35	58	4.20	4	5	8.85	0.57	3.97	6.58	0.83	4.36
1999	Milwauke	NL	72.7	73	29	6	32	50	3.59	4	4	9.04	0.74	3.96	6.19	0.78	4.66
2000	Milwauke	NL	44.7	37	17	1	16	37	3.43	3	2	7.46	0.20	3.22	7.46	1.16	2.96
2000	Clevelnd	AL	26.3	26	12	1	9	10	4.10	1	2	8.89	0.34	3.08	3.42	0.56	3.80

Shortly after he joined the Indians, Bob Wickman was described as being built like a middle linebacker, which I guess makes Marlon Brando a nose tackle. Bob Wickman is many things: a proud Cheesehead, someone who can advise people that while it worked for him, losing a fingertip doesn't give everyone a good sinker. But a middle linebacker? His greatest value isn't the quality of his pitching, it's the needed sense of security he brings to the Indians.

Steve Woodard — Throws R — Age 26

YEAR	TEAM	LGE	IP	H	ER	HR	BB	K	ERA	W	L	H/9	HR/9	BB/9	K/9	KW	PERA
1998	Milwauke	NL	158.3	166	82	19	30	110	4.66	8	10	9.44	1.08	1.71	6.25	1.83	4.31
1999	Milwauke	NL	179.3	207	93	21	30	100	4.67	8	12	10.39	1.05	1.51	5.02	1.67	4.76
2000	Milwauke	NL	91.7	120	64	14	27	54	6.28	3	7	11.78	1.37	2.65	5.30	1.00	6.40
2000	Clevelnd	AL	53.3	51	27	8	8	33	4.56	3	3	8.61	1.35	1.35	5.57	2.06	3.94

Getting Steve Woodard was the saving grace of the Brewers' trade. New managers have a way of coming to snap judgments, and Davey Lopes's was that Woodard is useless. Given the lousy alternatives the Brewers had, let's just call that decision premature. Woodard has outstanding command and fools people with a great change-up and good breaking stuff. He owns the only Indians' win against Pedro Martinez in ten games. He may be a six-inning guy, but he'll give the Tribe 30 starts and a league-average ERA. They need that a lot more than they need to haul Doc Gooden back.

Jaret Wright — Throws R — Age 25

YEAR	TEAM	LGE	IP	H	ER	HR	BB	K	ERA	W	L	H/9	HR/9	BB/9	K/9	KW	PERA
1998	Clevelnd	AL	191.0	194	94	19	73	129	4.43	9	12	9.14	0.90	3.44	6.08	0.88	4.66
1999	Clevelnd	AL	134.3	135	81	14	60	87	5.43	5	10	9.04	0.94	4.02	5.83	0.73	4.88
2000	Clevelnd	AL	52.0	41	22	5	21	34	3.81	3	3	7.10	0.87	3.63	5.88	0.81	3.54

The hope was that if you put Jaret Wright together with Dick Pole, it would undo the years of damage and misinformation that come from having suffered an odd collection of pitching coaches. Unfortunately, a legacy of the Hargrove Era came home when Wright broke down. The Tribe is claiming that he'll be throwing in December and might miss only April. Don't believe them: the Tribe blows sunshine about injuries. When Wright was first hurt, Hart said he'd be fine. Hart said the same thing in 1999 when Wright was rushed back and repeatedly reinjured. Wright's career and future are in trouble. He's not so good that he can afford to lose his fastball to surgery, and that's a risk with shoulder injuries.

Support-Neutral Statistics				CLEVELAND INDIANS						Park Effect: +7.1%		
PITCHER	GS	IP	R	SNW	SNL	SNPCT	W	L	RA	APW	SNVA	SNWAR
Jason Bere	11	54.3	41	3.0	4.5	.401	6	3	6.79	-0.7	-0.7	-0.2
Jim Brower	11	51.0	37	3.2	4.1	.436	2	3	6.53	-0.6	-0.3	0.1
Dave Burba	32	191.3	99	12.4	9.2	.575	16	6	4.66	1.5	1.7	3.2
Bartolo Colon	30	188.0	86	13.3	7.5	.640	15	8	4.12	2.5	2.7	4.5
Kane Davis	2	7.0	13	0.0	1.5	.026	0	2	16.71	-0.8	-0.7	-0.6
Tim Drew	3	9.0	12	0.4	1.4	.223	1	0	12.00	-0.6	-0.5	-0.4
Chuck Finley	34	218.0	108	14.2	9.3	.605	16	11	4.46	2.2	2.4	4.2
Charles Nagy	11	57.0	53	2.3	5.3	.306	2	7	8.37	-1.7	-1.4	-0.9
Jaime Navarro	2	8.0	9	0.2	1.2	.132	0	1	10.13	-0.4	-0.5	-0.4
Paul Rigdon	4	16.7	15	0.9	2.0	.320	1	1	8.10	-0.4	-0.5	-0.3
Bobby Witt	2	5.7	9	0.1	1.2	.086	0	1	14.29	-0.5	-0.5	-0.4
Steve Woodard	11	52.0	34	3.4	3.9	.470	3	3	5.88	-0.2	-0.2	0.3
Jaret Wright	9	51.7	27	3.9	2.7	.593	3	4	4.70	0.4	0.5	1.1
TOTALS	162	909.7	543	57.5	53.6	.517	65	50	5.37	0.8	2.1	10.3

There's plenty of discussion these days about which current pitchers will go into the Hall of Fame. Roger Clemens and Greg Maddux are no-brainers, but after them, there's room for debate. Plenty of names are bandied about, among them Randy Johnson, Tom Glavine, Kevin Brown, David Cone, John Smoltz, Orel Hershiser, and Dwight Gooden. That's not counting younger guys like Pedro Martinez and Mike Mussina who are, to say the least, off to good starts.

One name you never hear mentioned is Chuck Finley. After posting the fourth-best season of his career in 2000, Finley now has a career Support-Neutral record of 175–132. Among the names mentioned above, Finley's record is as good or better than those of Hershiser (185–150), Smoltz (154–110), and Gooden (168–135). Finley also looks pretty good compared to Cone (174–119) when you take into account that the former is still going strong while the latter may be finished. Finally, while Finley has to be considered a level below Johnson (170–101), Glavine (190–134), and Brown (172–114), he is closer than you might expect.

I'm not saying I would vote for Chuck Finley if his career ended today (I wouldn't), and I'm certainly not saying that the BBWAA might vote him in (they won't). I am saying that if Cone and Hershiser are going to be part of the discussion, then Finley deserves to be mentioned as well, and that we should watch the rest of Finley's career carefully to see just how strong a case he makes for himself.

For a quick explanation of SN stats, see page 7.

Reliever Evaluation Tools											
PITCHER	G	IP	R	ARA	APR	IRNR/G	EIRS/G	IRP	BRS	RRA	ARP
Jamie Brewington	26	45.3	28	5.30	-0.5	1.15	0.46	1.1	1.6	5.40	-1.0
Jim Brower	6	11.0	8	6.23	-1.3	0.83	0.43	0.4	1.2	7.19	-2.4
Cameron Cairncross	15	9.3	4	3.67	1.6	1.47	0.52	0.1	-0.7	3.27	2.0
Kane Davis	3	4.0	8	17.15	-5.3	0.00	0.00	0.0	-2.3	10.76	-2.5
Sean DePaula	13	16.7	11	5.66	-0.9	0.85	0.41	-1.0	2.1	7.26	-3.8
Scott Kamieniecki	26	33.3	22	5.66	-1.7	0.38	0.12	2.0	3.6	6.12	-3.4
Steve Karsay	72	76.7	33	3.69	12.8	0.46	0.15	-4.1	1.2	4.33	7.4
Andrew Lorraine	10	9.3	4	3.67	1.6	0.70	0.24	-0.5	-0.0	4.33	0.9
Tom Martin	31	33.3	16	4.12	4.0	0.77	0.28	3.7	0.2	3.24	7.2
Jaime Navarro	5	6.7	4	5.14	0.0	1.20	0.77	0.8	0.0	4.08	0.8
Chris Nichting	7	9.0	7	6.67	-1.5	0.57	0.27	-0.1	1.5	8.48	-3.3
Steve Reed	57	56.0	30	4.59	3.8	0.63	0.22	4.9	-2.9	3.57	10.1
Ricardo Rincon	35	20.0	7	3.00	4.9	0.71	0.19	3.5	2.2	2.37	6.3
Paul Shuey	57	63.7	25	3.37	12.9	0.70	0.26	-1.0	-1.7	3.51	11.9
Justin Speier	47	68.3	27	3.39	13.7	0.81	0.24	-1.1	4.8	4.31	6.7
Mark Watson	6	6.3	7	9.48	-3.0	0.67	0.12	-1.3	-0.4	11.18	-4.2
Bob Wickman	26	26.7	12	3.86	4.0	0.31	0.10	-0.3	2.3	4.77	1.3
Brian Williams	7	18.0	9	4.29	1.8	1.71	0.76	1.3	-0.3	3.51	3.4
Bobby Witt	5	9.7	4	3.55	1.8	0.60	0.21	1.1	0.7	3.61	1.7
TOTALS	462	532.7	273	4.39	47.5	0.69	0.25			4.58	36.6

For a quick guide to RET, see page 10.

Detroit Tigers

Great expectations often produce great disappointments, regardless of whether the expectations were justified. In the case of the 2000 Detroit Tigers, they were not. Coming off a 69–92 season that left them three-and-a-half games above the basement floor in 1999, the team made but two noteworthy changes prior to last season: hiring deposed Brewers' manager Phil Garner and acquiring enigmatic slugger Juan Gonzalez.

These two moves were more than enough to fire up the Detroit scribes, who are accustomed to following a squad as riveting as the local Kiwanis Club Kapers. Garner stirred the pot some more in spring training when he proclaimed—prophetically, as it turned out—that the Indians were ripe for a fall. Gonzalez pranced around the fields of Lakeland like a newborn colt, telling anybody within earshot how happy he was. Camp was humming with talk of the new ballpark. Team owner Mike Ilitch got so caught up in the moment that he extended General Manager Randy Smith's contract through 2003, even though the team hadn't had a winning season on his four-year watch. It was only March, but the Tigers were ready to print playoff tickets.

Then came April. The Tigers' impatient offense completely collapsed, averaging a run-and-a-half less than the next-worst team in the league. Players spent their idle time bad-mouthing the vast dimensions of Comerica Park. At the end of the month, Detroit was 6–17, ten games behind the division-leading White Sox. Though the Tigers recovered somewhat in late August and put on a brave face about winning the wild card, their season was effectively over by May Day.

The team's 79–83 final record was merely confirmation that the latest ill-conceived plot of Illitch and Smith had failed. Motown's version of *Pinky and the Brain* are constantly dreaming up ideas to assume control of the baseball world, but, like the two laboratory mice run amok, their plans always fail. However, unlike previous schemes, which were short on both planning and execution, this one was hatched years ago and looked promising on paper. It went something like this: 1) Have the city build a new ballpark; 2) Hire a feisty, proven manager; 3) Acquire a superstar hitter to improve the offense and draw fans; 4) Use the new stadium and increased revenues to sign big-name free agents; and 5) Hang championship banners from the rafters.

The plan seemed straightforward enough. Similar plans had even been used successfully by other thriving franchises. Unfortunately, it fell apart due to some miscalculations by the Tigers' brass. Examining each of the plan's five points reveals some of the flaws that doomed it to failure.

Tigers Prospectus

2000 record: 79–83; Third place, AL Central
Pythagenport W/L: 81–81
Runs Scored: 823 (10th in AL)
Runs Allowed: 827 (6th in AL)
Team EqA: .259 (8th in AL)
2000 Batters' Age: 28.7 (7th youngest in AL)
2000 Pitchers' Age: 28.9 (6th oldest in AL)
Ballpark: Comerica Park; slight pitchers' park; Park Factor of .973
2000: Lousy start masked their best season in years.
2001: They had the best winter of any AL Central team, and are a viable 87-win threat.

1. Have the City Build a New Ballpark

Getting a new ballpark in Detroit was not a monumental task for the Tigers, notwithstanding delays that caused Comerica Park to open two years later than the team had hoped. Detroit has economic woes the equal of any city in the country, but these woes have never prevented Motown from supporting its sports teams. Intentional neglect of venerable Tiger Stadium only helped fuel the fire for a new ballpark. Mayor Dennis Archer saw new stadiums and casinos as the mechanism to spur redevelopment of the blighted downtown, so he donated the land. As with virtually every new stadium deal, it was a good one for the team owner. Though Ilitch is scheduled to kick in nearly $200 million in private money, lucrative parking rights granted by the city will cover most of the bill.

Naturally, a new stadium is supposed to provide both the facility and revenue stream that will attract and retain premium players. While Comerica Park is a pleasant ballpark, the team didn't draw as well as expected. The Tigers' disappointing performance and the typically miserable springtime weather around the Great Lakes conspired to keep crowds small. Though turnout improved over the summer, overall attendance ranked tenth among the 13 baseball stadiums that have opened since 1989.

No discussion of Comerica Park is complete without a mention of its dimensions, which are the largest of any field not a mile high. Smith felt that constructing a unique park would give the Tigers a marked home-field advantage. However, the prevailing wisdom is that Comerica's proportions best suit a team that is fast, good defensively, has strong pitching, and gets on base, none of which describes the 2000 Tigers. There is plenty of speed and defense in the organization's farm system, but the Tigers have a distinct shortage of the two most important components—starting pitching and players who get on base.

2. Hire a Feisty, Proven Manager

This was another easy part of the master plan. Since the corpse of Leo Durocher was not scheduled for exhumation anytime soon, Smith went with his backup choice and hired Garner, who was fleeing the purge being carried out in Milwaukee by Czar Bud's daughter. It was a smart public-relations move. Baseball writers adore Garner because he treats them like old pals, and he talks tough, which makes for good copy.

Garner is proven, too. He has proven that he doesn't win very often. Garner managed only one above-.500 team in eight seasons in Milwaukee. While his backers are quick to point out that he never had the players, any manager who is with one club for such a long time has input into personnel decisions; in eight years, Garner should have *gotten* the players. He showed his inability to evaluate talent last year, regularly playing Luis Polonia, Gregg Jefferies, and Shane Halter, then hauling in the ghost of Hal Morris to man first base when better options were but a phone call away in Toledo.

Garner's managerial skill isn't going to make much difference in the win/loss column. It was silly for baseball writers to tout him as a key component in helping the Tigers win the extra 20 games they needed to be in the playoff chase.

3. Acquire a Superstar Hitter to Improve the Offense and Draw Fans

Smith's heart was in the right place when he acquired Juan Gonzalez from the Rangers, even if his head wasn't. The Tigers had been limping along for years without a superstar in the lineup or on the horizon. While it's debatable whether Gonzalez merits the label of "superstar," he is an extremely good hitter. To obtain his services, however, the team overpaid and assumed the huge risk of trying to sign him to a new contract before he became a free agent after the season.

The plan to sign Gonzalez was simple: accommodate him in every way and then overwhelm him with an outlandish sum of money. The Tigers executed it to perfection. Gonzalez reported to camp on time, with Ilitch personally greeting him. He was allowed to get ready at his own pace, wasn't asked to make any long bus trips, and enjoyed one of his best springs ever. Gonzalez himself said he couldn't remember being happier or more relaxed. Smith pounced in mid-March, proffering the alleged eight-year, $140-million package. Gonzalez said he wanted to see how he liked the team and the city of Detroit before signing.

One peek at Comerica Park probably answered all of Gonzalez's questions. After all, this is a man who can't get past the fact that The Ballpark in Arlington may have cost him home runs, a man who once spent the better part of a game taunting the press box after an official scorer's ruling cost him two RBI.

It was all downhill from Opening Day. One nagging injury followed another, causing Gonzalez's performance to suffer. If fans were at the park specifically to see Gonzalez, it was to boo him mercilessly. Nothing in any of Gonzalez's subsequent words or actions indicated that he had any intention of re-signing with the Tigers. The deal had proven to be a high-stakes gamble that didn't pay.

4. Use the New Stadium and Increased Revenues to Sign Big-Name Free Agents

This is probably the biggest miscalculation made by Ilitch and Smith. Including the new stadiums in Milwaukee and Pittsburgh, 15 ballparks have opened since 1989, seven since the groundbreaking for Comerica Park in the fall of 1997. In the early days of Camden Yards and Jacobs Field, modern facilities could help a team lure players; however, that's no longer the case since half the teams in the majors boast similar facilities. These days, the top free agents are generally after two things: an armored truck full of large-denomination bills and a winning ballclub. The Tigers have the cash if they want to spend it, but they haven't set foot in the upper division since 1993.

Furthermore, no winning team is built by signing free agents. The best organizations rely on player development and use the free-agent system judiciously to fill in a missing piece here and there. The cost of building through free agency is prohibitive, and the amount of talent on the market too limited. For example, before last season, the free-agent class of 2000 was anticipated to be the best ever. But, as always, many of the big names signed long-term contracts with their teams. This reduced the number of top-tier players to a handful and drove up their prices. While there is a lower strata of free agents who can help a team, none of those players are worth more than a game or two in the standings, and all cost more than they can be expected to return.

American League

Talent mined through scouting and player development is still the foundation of every good team. Smith has received a lot of praise for overhauling and improving the Tigers' prospect base since he arrived after the 1995 season. Ilitch's previous GM, Joe Klein, ran the system into the ground; there's no doubt it was the worst in the game at the time he was fired. Though things have improved under Smith, the Tigers' farm system remains in the bottom quartile of baseball.

Some of Smith's worst decisions have occurred in his highest-leverage situations. The Tigers had a top-three selection in both the 1997 and 1999 drafts. They picked Matt Anderson in 1997 despite the terrible track record of college closers, and in 1999, they chose catcher Eric Munson and then immediately slashed his value by moving him to first base.

The Tigers don't have anybody in their system who could be labeled a sure-fire star. Most other organizations have, at minimum, many promising prospects in the low minors, some of whom wilt when they reach Double-A. The Tigers' pipeline is dry even at those levels, save a few decent arms.

5. Hang Championship Banners from the Rafters

Oh, well. It seems obvious that five years of Randy Smith at the controls have produced a lot of motion, but no real progress. A rational owner would see the situation for what it is, fire off a pink slip, and bring in the wrecking ball. Instead, Mike Ilitch has decided to partner with his sidekick for three more years. They haven't revealed their latest plot, but everybody knows their goal: taking over the world.

HITTERS (BA: .270, OBP: .340, SLG: .440, EqA: .260)

Brad Ausmus — C — Bats R — Age 32

YEAR	TEAM	LGE	AB	H	DB	TP	HR	BB	SO	R	RBI	SB	CS	OUT	BA	OBP	SLG	EQA	EQR	DEFENSE	
1998	Houston	NL	420	117	9	4	7	52	56	65	47	10	3	306	.279	.362	.369	.254	50	118-C	4
1999	Detroit	AL	454	125	26	6	9	46	65	59	51	11	9	338	.275	.358	.419	.260	58	121-C	5
2000	Detroit	AL	520	142	23	3	8	63	72	72	49	12	6	384	.273	.358	.375	.253	62	142-C	13
2001	Houston	NL	442	126	24	3	6	58	65	78	60	13	8	324	.285	.368	.394	.255	53		

Brad Ausmus has never been on the disabled list in 13 professional seasons and started a career-high 140 games in 2000. Combining his durability with good defense, good baserunning, and an adequate bat yields a solid total package. Ausmus is at the age and position where his offense could nose-dive, but I expect more of a slow burn that dovetails neatly with the emergence of the organizational catching prospects. He's been traded to the Astros, making Jeff Bagwell happy.

Rich Becker — OF — Bats L — Age 29

YEAR	TEAM	LGE	AB	H	DB	TP	HR	BB	SO	R	RBI	SB	CS	OUT	BA	OBP	SLG	EQA	EQR	DEFENSE	
1998	NY Mets	NL	102	20	5	2	3	21	39	16	10	3	1	83	.196	.333	.373	.245	12	29-OF	2
1998	Baltimor	AL	113	25	2	0	3	22	30	23	11	2	0	88	.221	.357	.319	.243	13	27-RF	1
1999	Milwauke	NL	139	34	4	2	5	31	36	14	15	4	0	105	.245	.382	.410	.278	21	33-OF	-2
1999	Oakland	AL	124	33	1	0	2	24	39	20	10	3	2	93	.266	.392	.323	.256	15	33-CF	-1
2000	Detroit	AL	236	59	8	0	9	53	64	46	34	1	2	179	.250	.388	.398	.271	34	60-RF	-6
2001	Detroit	AL	238	56	8	1	8	51	74	46	35	4	1	183	.235	.370	.378	.269	34		

Rich Becker signed with the Tigers in mid-May after being released by the A's because he couldn't cut the mustard defensively and made it plain that he wasn't happy. He's a very handy fourth outfielder who will always be underrated because so much of his value lies in the stealth weapon, bases on balls. Becker was a free agent as of mid-January.

Javier Cardona — C — Bats R — Age 25

YEAR	TEAM	LGE	AB	H	DB	TP	HR	BB	SO	R	RBI	SB	CS	OUT	BA	OBP	SLG	EQA	EQR	DEFENSE	
1998	Jacksnvl	Sou	163	46	11	1	3	8	31	22	27	0	0	117	.282	.318	.417	.244	17	34-C	-1
1998	Toledo	Int	163	31	2	0	5	6	32	11	15	0	0	132	.190	.222	.294	.154	6	42-C	-1
1999	Jacksnvl	Sou	422	110	20	0	20	32	74	62	65	2	1	313	.261	.320	.450	.253	51	88-C	-8
2000	Toledo	Int	219	56	7	0	10	12	34	25	36	0	1	164	.256	.299	.425	.236	22	50-C	-4
2000	Detroit	AL	40	7	1	0	1	0	8	1	2	0	0	33	.175	.196	.275	.123	1	11-C	-1
2001	Detroit	AL	301	75	10	0	13	21	57	33	44	0	0	226	.249	.298	.412	.240	32		

(Javier Cardona *continued*)

Robert Fick's separated shoulder hurt in more ways than one; it forced the Tigers to recall Javier Cardona even though he likely would see very limited playing time. He sat on the bench, and his hitting suffered as a result. The acquisition of Mitch Meluskey should squeeze Cardona out of the organization. Randy Smith probably had planned to trade him over the winter, but with 40 at-bats suggesting he can't hit big-league pitching, his market value dropped. He could be a steal for a team looking for a decent part-time catcher.

Tony Clark   1B   Bats B   Age 29

YEAR	TEAM	LGE	AB	H	DB	TP	HR	BB	SO	R	RBI	SB	CS	OUT	BA	OBP	SLG	EQA	EQR	DEFENSE	
1998	Detroit	AL	600	178	29	0	39	62	114	85	105	2	3	425	.297	.365	.540	.292	98	140-1B	-1
1999	Detroit	AL	531	150	25	0	33	58	121	71	96	2	1	382	.282	.359	.516	.285	83	129-1B	7
2000	Detroit	AL	207	58	13	0	14	22	46	31	36	0	0	149	.280	.349	.546	.288	33	53-1B	5
2001	Detroit	AL	366	101	13	0	25	46	84	60	80	0	1	266	.276	.357	.516	.291	61		

In Motown-speak, Tony Clark cut an EP last year. The abbreviated release used the same formula as his recent LPs; it started out slowly and heated up in the middle tracks before settling into an acceptable but uninspiring groove. A bulging disc in his back ended last year's session and gives rise to doubts about whether he'll be able to survive the 2001 summer tour. The Tigers are banking that Eric Munson will be ready to replace Clark in the limelight when Clark's contract ends this year.

Deivi Cruz   SS   Bats R   Age 25

YEAR	TEAM	LGE	AB	H	DB	TP	HR	BB	SO	R	RBI	SB	CS	OUT	BA	OBP	SLG	EQA	EQR	DEFENSE	
1998	Detroit	AL	453	120	22	3	6	12	49	53	45	2	4	337	.265	.288	.366	.213	35	130-SS	17
1999	Detroit	AL	516	147	25	0	17	7	52	61	58	1	4	373	.285	.299	.432	.237	51	147-SS	16
2000	Detroit	AL	583	181	46	5	11	6	39	66	80	1	5	407	.310	.322	.463	.254	66	150-SS	8
2001	Detroit	AL	486	143	28	1	14	13	44	57	75	1	3	346	.294	.313	.442	.252	55		

Deivi Cruz has developed into a far better offensive player than we thought possible—he actually helps the team. Cruz's unwillingness to take pitches is legendary. No one in history had ever played more than 135 games in four straight seasons and drawn fewer than 68 walks (Hal Lanier, from 1965 to 1968), but Cruz demolished that record, managing only 52 free passes in his four-year career. The local media has it bass-ackwards, exalting his batting exploits while criticizing his play at shortstop. Cruz is now an average hitter, and while his range has diminished since he bulked up, he remains a brilliant fielder. It's hard to imagine him improving on last year's numbers, but we've been wrong about him before.

Damion Easley   2B   Bats R   Age 31

YEAR	TEAM	LGE	AB	H	DB	TP	HR	BB	SO	R	RBI	SB	CS	OUT	BA	OBP	SLG	EQA	EQR	DEFENSE			
1998	Detroit	AL	592	164	36	2	30	38	100	84	101	12	5	433	.277	.336	.497	.272	83	131-2B	24	19-SS	-7
1999	Detroit	AL	545	146	27	1	22	46	113	80	63	10	3	402	.268	.343	.442	.263	72	140-2B	11	11-SS	-3
2000	Detroit	AL	462	122	27	2	15	50	72	74	56	14	5	345	.264	.350	.429	.264	62	120-2B	9		
2001	Detroit	AL	464	118	21	1	18	50	87	68	71	8	3	349	.254	.327	.420	.257	58				

Damion Easley was the beneficiary of a Randy Smith public-relations maneuver in 1999 when his contract was extended through 2004 as Smith demonstrated how the new ballpark would allow the team to attract and retain quality players. While Easley is a nice supporting player, he's not the kind of guy to which a team should shackle itself for six years. Easley will probably fulfill his obligation, but he'll be a drag on the Tigers by the time the deal is done. Jermaine Clark, acquired in the Rule 5 draft, could free the team to trade Easley.

Juan Encarnacion   CF   Bats R   Age 25

YEAR	TEAM	LGE	AB	H	DB	TP	HR	BB	SO	R	RBI	SB	CS	OUT	BA	OBP	SLG	EQA	EQR	DEFENSE	
1998	Toledo	Int	357	95	16	2	7	22	84	44	35	14	3	265	.266	.322	.381	.241	38	80-RF	-1
1998	Detroit	AL	163	54	9	3	8	7	28	30	21	6	4	113	.331	.362	.571	.296	27	31-OF	-1
1999	Detroit	AL	508	130	29	6	20	9	103	59	71	30	12	390	.256	.280	.455	.241	56	117-LF	6
2000	Detroit	AL	546	161	26	6	15	23	82	74	70	17	5	390	.295	.332	.447	.260	67	138-CF	0
2001	Detroit	AL	455	129	21	3	15	24	86	68	68	17	5	331	.284	.319	.442	.261	57		

One of the team's chief concerns entering the 2000 season was how Juan Encarnacion would handle the transition from left field to center field. The move went off without a hitch. A greater concern should have been his woeful lack of plate discipline.

American League

Encarnacion made strides in that department, too, doubling his walk rate to a still-ridiculous once-every-20-plate appearances and cutting his strikeouts by not chasing bad pitches. He isn't going to emerge as the dominant force that the Tigers hoped for and so desperately need. If they lower their sights a little, they should have a pretty good center fielder for the next five years.

Robert Fick — C/1B — Bats L — Age 27

YEAR	TEAM	LGE	AB	H	DB	TP	HR	BB	SO	R	RBI	SB	CS	OUT	BA	OBP	SLG	EQA	EQR	DEFENSE
1998	Jacksnvl	Sou	516	134	34	3	13	45	91	69	73	4	2	384	.260	.324	.413	.246	58	79-C -17
1999	Toledo	Int	48	13	0	2	1	7	5	9	6	1	0	35	.271	.372	.417	.273	7	
1999	Detroit	AL	41	9	1	0	3	6	5	6	10	1	0	32	.220	.319	.463	.261	6	
2000	Toledo	Int	69	10	5	0	1	5	14	5	7	1	0	59	.145	.219	.261	.146	2	
2000	Detroit	AL	162	42	8	2	3	20	36	18	21	2	1	121	.259	.344	.389	.250	19	25-1B -1
2001	Detroit	AL	234	56	14	2	5	26	49	32	29	2	1	179	.239	.315	.380	.240	25	

For the second consecutive season, Robert Fick missed significant time with a shoulder injury. Fick is an effective left-handed hitter with extra-base wallop and a good eye, but his talents are wasted if he is used strictly as a backup catcher. If Garner has the stones to risk being caught short-handed at catcher and gives Fick an additional 200 at-bats at first base and designated hitter, I think he would be pleasantly surprised. Finding a taker for Tony Clark would help.

Alejandro Freire — 1B/OF — Bats R — Age 26

YEAR	TEAM	LGE	AB	H	DB	TP	HR	BB	SO	R	RBI	SB	CS	OUT	BA	OBP	SLG	EQA	EQR	DEFENSE
1998	Jacksnvl	Sou	496	119	16	0	15	16	88	57	57	2	1	378	.240	.279	.363	.211	39	121-1B 9
1999	Jacksnvl	Sou	245	61	12	0	8	15	48	33	30	1	0	184	.249	.301	.396	.232	24	31-1B 0
2000	Jacksnvl	Sou	491	116	10	0	20	50	121	60	59	1	2	377	.236	.317	.379	.233	50	58-1B -2
2001	Detroit	AL	369	88	7	0	13	37	90	40	48	1	1	282	.238	.308	.363	.231	36	

Alejandro Freire displayed newfound knowledge of the strike zone and led the Southern League in home runs. Then again, it was his third year at Jacksonville, and he's 26 years old. Like almost all of the top power sources in the upper levels of the Tigers' organization, Freire is too old and too limited afield to be taken seriously as a prospect.

Richard Gomez — OF — Bats R — Age 23

YEAR	TEAM	LGE	AB	H	DB	TP	HR	BB	SO	R	RBI	SB	CS	OUT	BA	OBP	SLG	EQA	EQR	DEFENSE
1999	W Michgn	Mid	489	122	22	6	7	35	133	53	54	26	6	373	.249	.306	.362	.231	48	109-LF -8
2000	Lakeland	Fla	461	106	16	5	8	37	116	51	41	21	5	360	.230	.293	.338	.218	40	117-LF -9
2001	Detroit	AL	361	88	14	4	4	32	105	52	34	19	4	277	.244	.305	.338	.231	35	

The lower reaches of the Tigers' farm system are infested with pesky, fleet outfielders, not unlike the swarm of flying ants that descended on Comerica Park last August. Richard Gomez is the best of the lot other than Andres Torres. Not only does he have speed that makes the Tigers foam at the mouth, but he also has a fair mix of on-base skills and power. Even with his tools, Gomez is not good defensively, which will hurt him in his efforts to be a fourth outfielder, because his bat alone isn't strong enough to cover his glove.

Juan Gonzalez — RF — Bats R — Age 31

YEAR	TEAM	LGE	AB	H	DB	TP	HR	BB	SO	R	RBI	SB	CS	OUT	BA	OBP	SLG	EQA	EQR	DEFENSE
1998	Texas	AL	600	191	44	2	48	45	112	110	153	2	1	410	.318	.371	.638	.316	116	105-RF -8
1999	Texas	AL	553	179	32	1	40	45	96	108	120	3	3	377	.324	.378	.602	.311	102	119-RF -11
2000	Detroit	AL	460	137	31	2	23	26	77	68	65	1	2	325	.298	.338	.524	.278	66	59-RF -4
2001	Clevelnd	AL	483	151	29	1	32	45	87	79	105	1	2	334	.313	.371	.576	.302	84	

Juan Gonzalez let his feelings be known about the oversized dimensions of Comerica Park, but the difference between his home and road OPSs, 95 points, isn't out of line with normal fluctuation or even his 1999 campaign with Texas. His frustration had more to do with a succession of injuries that caused him to have his worst year since 1994. A trade that looked bad when it was announced could go down as one of the worst ever. Gonzalez is a dangerous hitter, but the oft-reported eight-year, $140 million deal that Randy Smith dangled was preposterous. If those reports are accurate, last season probably cost Gonzalez $40 million. The Tigers are off the hook, as Gonzalez signed with the Indians, where he'll DH.

Shane Halter — UT — Bats R — Age 31

YEAR	TEAM	LGE	AB	H	DB	TP	HR	BB	SO	R	RBI	SB	CS	OUT	BA	OBP	SLG	EQA	EQR	DEFENSE			
1998	Omaha	PCL	95	24	2	1	1	5	16	10	9	3	1	72	.253	.290	.326	.208	7	15-SS	-2		
1998	KansasCy	AL	203	45	10	0	3	12	34	16	13	1	5	163	.222	.268	.315	.183	12	47-SS	6		
1999	Norfolk	Int	476	109	18	2	4	45	96	56	25	11	12	379	.229	.296	.300	.198	33	66-SS	-8	28-CF	-4
2000	Detroit	AL	238	64	13	2	3	11	45	25	26	5	2	176	.269	.304	.378	.228	22	35-3B	0	18-1B	2
2001	Detroit	AL	327	78	12	1	4	28	69	36	30	7	6	255	.239	.299	.318	.212	26				

When local newspapers issue their obligatory team report cards after the season, why are the Shane Halters of the world invariably awarded a "B?" Does that imply that if Tom Veryzer were pried from his Barcalounger, he would be an above-average player? It's hard to accept that the Tigers are close to contending when they willingly grant Halter 250 plate appearances.

Bobby Higginson — LF — Bats L — Age 30

YEAR	TEAM	LGE	AB	H	DB	TP	HR	BB	SO	R	RBI	SB	CS	OUT	BA	OBP	SLG	EQA	EQR	DEFENSE	
1998	Detroit	AL	610	177	35	4	28	62	90	94	86	2	3	436	.290	.361	.498	.281	91	140-RF	8
1999	Detroit	AL	373	89	13	0	14	60	60	49	45	4	6	290	.239	.347	.386	.248	44	81-RF	-2
2000	Detroit	AL	593	183	43	4	32	67	90	101	99	16	4	413	.309	.381	.556	.305	106	145-LF	10
2001	Detroit	AL	533	154	34	2	26	75	88	104	109	8	3	382	.289	.377	.507	.299	93		

The Motor City's favorite Bengal halted a three-year slide into mediocrity, re-establishing himself as one of the top outfielders in the American League. Hitting coach Bill Madlock says that everything clicked offensively when Higginson moved off the plate, which freed up his swing. I hope it's that simple, because when he's right, Higginson is a dynamite player with both the bat and the glove, and he is a vital part of any success the Tigers will have.

Omar Infante — SS — Bats R — Age 19

YEAR	TEAM	LGE	AB	H	DB	TP	HR	BB	SO	R	RBI	SB	CS	OUT	BA	OBP	SLG	EQA	EQR	DEFENSE	
2000	W Michgn	Mid	50	12	0	0	0	3	8	5	5	0	0	38	.240	.295	.240	.174	2	12-SS	1
2000	Lakeland	Fla	261	62	5	0	3	14	33	25	19	5	3	202	.238	.278	.291	.186	15	76-SS	1
2001	Detroit	AL	163	40	2	0	1	8	39	12	12	2	1	124	.245	.281	.276	.186	9		

Omar Infante is the youngest player in the history of the Arizona Fall League and the brother of former Tigers' pitching prospect Asdrubal Infante, who was murdered in Venezuela over the 1999 off-season. Infante is advanced defensively but needs to add upper-body strength so that he can start driving the ball. He jumped three levels last year, and while he didn't embarrass himself at Lakeland, neither his performance nor the middle-infield situation in Detroit justifies rushing him.

Brandon Inge — C — Bats B — Age 24

YEAR	TEAM	LGE	AB	H	DB	TP	HR	BB	SO	R	RBI	SB	CS	OUT	BA	OBP	SLG	EQA	EQR	DEFENSE	
1998	Jamestwn	NYP	195	37	5	0	7	12	57	15	19	3	4	162	.190	.246	.323	.180	11	34-C	-3
1999	W Michgn	Mid	361	77	19	1	7	25	95	37	32	6	2	286	.213	.267	.330	.197	25	94-C	3
2000	Jacksnvl	Sou	307	74	19	1	6	18	76	34	46	5	2	235	.241	.283	.368	.216	25	67-C	2
2000	Toledo	Int	192	41	7	2	5	12	53	21	17	1	1	152	.214	.263	.349	.198	13	49-C	4
2001	Detroit	AL	370	84	19	1	9	26	106	38	39	4	2	288	.227	.278	.357	.215	31		

The Golden Boy. Moved from shortstop to catcher immediately after being snared in the second round of the 1998 draft, Brandon Inge has developed rapidly and was named the top defensive backstop in the Southern League. He skyrocketed up the prospect chart after leading the now-defunct California Fall League in OPS in 1999, though his offensive skills trail his defense. Ironically, the player he most closely resembles, projection-wise, is the guy the Tigers just dealt, Brad Ausmus.

Gregg Jefferies — HB — Bats B — Age 33

YEAR	TEAM	LGE	AB	H	DB	TP	HR	BB	SO	R	RBI	SB	CS	OUT	BA	OBP	SLG	EQA	EQR	DEFENSE			
1998	Philadel	NL	488	143	20	3	9	28	25	66	48	10	3	348	.293	.333	.402	.248	53	100-LF	-1		
1999	Detroit	AL	205	41	6	0	7	11	10	21	18	3	4	168	.200	.253	.332	.186	13				
2000	Detroit	AL	141	39	6	0	3	15	9	17	14	0	2	104	.277	.346	.383	.243	15	18-1B	2	12-2B	-1

"Home Builder." Gregg Jefferies was on pace for more than 450 plate appearances when he mercifully tore his hamstring in late May. Before going on the disabled list, he was regularly batting in the top third of the order and had started more than a dozen games at second base, flashing range that had fans misty for Big Daddy Fielder. The decision to start Jefferies is the kind of stunt that helps explain why Garner hasn't managed a winner in eight years. Jefferies, just 33 years old, has retired.

American League

Neil Jenkins — 3B/OF — Bats R — Age 20

YEAR	TEAM	LGE	AB	H	DB	TP	HR	BB	SO	R	RBI	SB	CS	OUT	BA	OBP	SLG	EQA	EQR	DEFENSE
2000	W Michgn	Mid	427	96	14	2	12	23	167	46	49	0	0	331	.225	.265	.351	.200	30	99-3B -17
2001	Detroit	AL	204	44	3	0	6	11	94	14	18	0	0	160	.216	.256	.319	.189	12	

Neil Jenkins's diabetes scared teams and caused him to fall to the third round of the 1999 draft. He and Nate Cornejo are exactly the type of low-risk, high-upside picks the Tigers need in order to stock their barren farm system. Jenkins is the organization's one legitimate slugger below Double-A, but he has some mighty big holes in his swing. As if fixing his swing wasn't enough of a project, he'll also be learning how to play the outfield this year after committing 46 errors at third base last season.

Rodney Lindsey — CF — Bats R — Age 25

YEAR	TEAM	LGE	AB	H	DB	TP	HR	BB	SO	R	RBI	SB	CS	OUT	BA	OBP	SLG	EQA	EQR	DEFENSE
1998	Clinton	Mid	159	37	3	2	4	12	58	18	13	13	3	125	.233	.292	.352	.226	15	39-CF -3
1998	W Michgn	Mid	165	39	7	2	3	16	45	23	13	8	4	130	.236	.322	.358	.233	17	44-CF -1
1999	Lakeland	Fla	485	111	20	4	6	17	149	51	37	25	10	384	.229	.267	.324	.199	34	117-CF -1
2000	Jacksnvl	Sou	406	91	9	3	1	26	106	43	19	23	8	323	.224	.279	.268	.189	25	114-CF 3
2001	Detroit	AL	472	103	15	4	4	31	145	49	32	27	11	380	.218	.266	.292	.195	32	

Phil Garner cut his teeth in the big leagues with the Swingin' A's of the early 1970s, where one of his teammates was the legendary Herb Washington. When the rosters expanded last September, Garner fondly recalled those early days and decided that he needed a designated runner, too. Rodney Lindsey is in the first stage of Eugene Kingsale's career.

Wendell Magee — OF — Bats R — Age 28

YEAR	TEAM	LGE	AB	H	DB	TP	HR	BB	SO	R	RBI	SB	CS	OUT	BA	OBP	SLG	EQA	EQR	DEFENSE
1998	Scran-WB	Int	509	134	26	5	20	36	101	72	58	4	5	380	.263	.315	.452	.250	59	124-CF -2
1998	Philadel	NL	76	22	6	1	1	7	10	9	11	0	0	54	.289	.349	.434	.262	10	18-LF -1
1999	Scran-WB	Int	568	143	26	2	16	43	126	75	61	6	6	431	.252	.306	.389	.230	55	128-CF 1
2000	Detroit	AL	186	52	3	2	8	8	26	30	31	1	0	134	.280	.309	.446	.248	21	40-RF 1
2001	Detroit	AL	316	82	15	1	10	25	65	40	45	2	2	236	.259	.314	.408	.245	35	

Wendell Magee was acquired in March as an insurance policy in case Juan Encarnacion flopped in center field. He can handle all three outfield spots and offers a little bit of everything offensively but not enough of anything to deserve a starting job. Not to damn Magee with faint praise, but he's a significant upgrade over Kimera Bartee on the Tiger bench.

Billy McMillon — OF/DH — Bats L — Age 29

YEAR	TEAM	LGE	AB	H	DB	TP	HR	BB	SO	R	RBI	SB	CS	OUT	BA	OBP	SLG	EQA	EQR	DEFENSE
1998	Scran-WB	Int	269	62	14	1	10	27	60	34	30	3	2	209	.230	.306	.401	.235	28	67-LF 3
1999	Scran-WB	Int	467	122	31	3	11	51	83	74	62	7	2	347	.261	.339	.411	.254	56	119-LF -4
2000	Toledo	Int	385	110	21	1	10	56	73	48	38	2	1	276	.286	.378	.423	.273	54	100-LF 0
2000	Detroit	AL	122	38	7	1	4	18	17	19	23	1	0	84	.311	.404	.484	.300	21	14-RF -1
2001	Detroit	AL	426	110	22	1	10	64	84	69	61	3	1	317	.258	.355	.385	.261	55	

A minor-league free agent after the 1999 season, Billy McMillon weighed the offers, swallowed his pride, and packed his bags for Toledo. The Tigers recalled him when they'd had their fill of Luis Polonia's hack-happy ways. McMillon opened some eyes with his ability to get on base and hit the ball hard, the same skills that he had always shown while toiling needlessly in Triple-A for four-and-a-half years. Garner spent a fair amount of time last year yammering to reporters about the importance of on-base percentage. If he wasn't just blowing smoke, he'll find a way to get McMillon 400 at-bats this season.

Eric Munson — 1B — Bats L — Age 23

YEAR	TEAM	LGE	AB	H	DB	TP	HR	BB	SO	R	RBI	SB	CS	OUT	BA	OBP	SLG	EQA	EQR	DEFENSE
1999	W Michgn	Mid	259	58	10	1	10	25	51	29	28	1	1	202	.224	.303	.386	.230	26	32-1B 0
2000	Jacksnvl	Sou	378	88	19	3	13	28	100	45	57	2	1	291	.233	.302	.402	.234	38	74-1B -2
2001	Detroit	AL	254	61	12	1	10	27	74	33	38	1	0	193	.240	.313	.413	.249	30	

This isn't what Randy Smith envisioned when he took Eric Munson with the third pick of the 1999 draft. Though the ex-Trojan has buffed up his body, his numbers still sag like an auto worker's midsection. Unless Munson has a breakout season, Smith may have to find a makeshift solution at first base in 2002, since he had planned on Munson being ready to inherit Tony

(Eric Munson *continued*)

Clark's job. In my opinion, the organization was too hasty in stripping Munson of the tools of ignorance; catcher is the only position he can handle at which he projects to be much of an asset offensively.

Dean Palmer 3B Bats R Age 32

YEAR	TEAM	LGE	AB	H	DB	TP	HR	BB	SO	R	RBI	SB	CS	OUT	BA	OBP	SLG	EQA	EQR	DEFENSE	
1998	KansasCy	AL	569	160	26	2	36	47	119	85	117	7	2	411	.281	.342	.524	.281	86	117-3B -17	
1999	Detroit	AL	556	147	24	2	39	51	139	89	96	3	3	412	.264	.336	.525	.277	83	141-3B -3	
2000	Detroit	AL	522	137	21	2	31	60	133	71	99	4	2	387	.262	.343	.489	.273	75	107-3B -11	14-1B -3
2001	Detroit	AL	510	130	20	1	28	65	137	78	94	3	2	382	.255	.339	.463	.272	73		

The Tigers should borrow from Al Davis and emblazon the words "Commitment to Mediocrity" under their logo. Nothing better symbolizes that commitment than the five-year contract Randy Smith bestowed upon Dean Palmer. Sure, he's a decent power hitter, but when you count the dozen runs a year he costs the team with his ham-handed glove work, he's barely average at the hot corner. With no third-base prospects in the minors and another three years left on Palmer's hefty contract, the mediocrity will continue.

Mike Rivera C Bats R Age 24

YEAR	TEAM	LGE	AB	H	DB	TP	HR	BB	SO	R	RBI	SB	CS	OUT	BA	OBP	SLG	EQA	EQR	DEFENSE
2000	Lakeland	Fla	244	58	12	2	9	12	51	22	36	1	0	186	.238	.275	.414	.225	22	56-C 0
2000	Jacksnvl	Sou	153	30	8	1	2	4	31	10	8	0	0	123	.196	.217	.301	.152	6	31-C -6
2001	Detroit	AL	207	45	9	1	6	7	71	15	20	0	0	162	.217	.243	.357	.196	14	

It's a credit to roving catching instructor Glenn Ezell that the Tigers have a bushel of fair catching prospects while hopefuls at other positions die on the vine. This abundance may help rationalize—but certainly doesn't validate—moving Munson to first base. Mike Rivera's bat is his ticket to The Show, so his initial dislike of Double-A pitching isn't encouraging. He needs to learn to be more selective at the plate, a course of study that hasn't been a prerequisite to playing in Comerica Park.

Pedro Santana 2B Bats R Age 24

YEAR	TEAM	LGE	AB	H	DB	TP	HR	BB	SO	R	RBI	SB	CS	OUT	BA	OBP	SLG	EQA	EQR	DEFENSE
1998	W Michgn	Mid	449	107	21	4	4	19	100	50	35	24	5	347	.238	.276	.330	.208	34	110-2B -6
1999	Jacksnvl	Sou	515	127	29	4	4	22	104	64	37	17	6	394	.247	.280	.342	.208	39	118-2B 0
2000	Jacksnvl	Sou	462	121	18	3	6	26	86	49	46	20	5	346	.262	.303	.353	.225	42	109-2B -13
2001	Detroit	AL	423	107	21	3	5	26	90	58	41	23	6	322	.253	.296	.352	.229	40	

Pedro Santana is a burner who, by all accounts, can pick it at second base. However, he showed no appreciable progress with the bat in his second season at Jacksonville. It would be easy to label Santana a future utility man, even though he probably won't fill that role with the Tigers. After all, they already have Speedy Utility Man 1.0 in Jose Macias. Santana could be 2.0, but even though he's faster, he offers less power and flexibility. Why bother with the upgrade?

Ramon Santiago SS Bats B Age 19

YEAR	TEAM	LGE	AB	H	DB	TP	HR	BB	SO	R	RBI	SB	CS	OUT	BA	OBP	SLG	EQA	EQR	DEFENSE
1999	Oneonta	NYP	51	14	0	1	1	1	13	5	5	2	0	37	.275	.294	.373	.228	5	11-SS 1
2000	W Michgn	Mid	393	99	13	1	1	21	66	47	34	16	7	301	.252	.299	.298	.204	28	74-SS 7
2001	Detroit	AL	236	64	6	1	1	16	60	32	21	13	4	176	.271	.317	.318	.228	22	

Warning: Ramon Santiago flashes more leather than the drag queens at the Male Box. Not that there's anything wrong with that. It's just that fielding wizardry can become an organizational fetish to the point that teams excuse a player's shortcomings. Santiago's biggest offensive asset right now is his age, though he does seem to understand that his job is to get on base. If he does so with any regularity, he can become a very special player.

Rob Sasser 3B/1B Bats R Age 26

YEAR	TEAM	LGE	AB	H	DB	TP	HR	BB	SO	R	RBI	SB	CS	OUT	BA	OBP	SLG	EQA	EQR	DEFENSE	
1998	Tulsa	Tex	417	95	18	1	6	45	108	39	43	9	6	328	.228	.306	.319	.212	34	110-3B -7	
1999	Jacksnvl	Sou	430	102	26	2	5	40	110	44	44	4	3	331	.237	.305	.342	.217	36	109-3B 8	
2000	Toledo	Int	491	121	22	0	23	43	110	67	53	5	4	374	.246	.309	.432	.244	55	108-3B -8	16-1B 2
2001	Detroit	AL	467	112	17	1	16	50	120	59	63	3	2	357	.240	.313	.383	.240	50		

American League

Last summer, when Tigers' first basemen were dropping like dot-com stocks and Palmer's shoulder ached so much that he couldn't even throw the ball, why wasn't Rob Sasser promoted? The power that had been missing from his arsenal bloomed in spades at Toledo, and he's always been able to draw a walk. Yes, his defense is inconsistent, but even if it were Carney Lansford bad, it wouldn't warrant giving those at-bats to Halter or Macias.

Andres Torres — CF — Bats B — Age 23

YEAR	TEAM	LGE	AB	H	DB	TP	HR	BB	SO	R	RBI	SB	CS	OUT	BA	OBP	SLG	EQA	EQR	DEFENSE	
1998	Jamestwn	NYP	198	40	2	4	1	17	54	18	15	5	1	159	.202	.267	.268	.178	11	46-CF	-4
1999	W Michgn	Mid	425	86	16	3	2	65	127	46	25	15	9	348	.202	.315	.268	.205	33	112-CF	-2
2000	Lakeland	Fla	406	100	10	7	3	47	93	52	24	28	9	315	.246	.328	.328	.233	41	104-CF	9
2000	Jacksnvl	Sou	56	11	0	0	0	3	15	3	1	1	0	45	.196	.237	.196	.117	1	14-CF	0
2001	Detroit	AL	400	89	7	5	2	58	111	58	31	19	7	318	.222	.321	.280	.220	36		

Ninety-two bases on balls at West Michigan in 1999 indicated that Andres Torres could mature into a respectable hitter. A year later, it happened. Torres added 62 points to his batting average while maintaining his plate discipline in the Florida State League, a tough loop for hitters. The Tigers see him as their leadoff man of the future, a great defensive center fielder who can fly. I'll hold off on handing him the keys to Comerica Park until he conquers Double-A. Torres is going to have to post an OBP close to .400 to pull his weight in the majors, because his slap-and-dash style doesn't generate any power.

Chris Wakeland — OF — Bats L — Age 27

YEAR	TEAM	LGE	AB	H	DB	TP	HR	BB	SO	R	RBI	SB	CS	OUT	BA	OBP	SLG	EQA	EQR	DEFENSE	
1998	Lakeland	Fla	491	114	19	3	12	48	129	54	56	6	6	383	.232	.304	.356	.221	44	119-LF	-3
1999	Jacksnvl	Sou	215	54	12	2	8	25	59	29	22	3	3	164	.251	.335	.437	.255	27	54-LF	-4
2000	Toledo	Int	497	121	20	1	23	49	158	55	60	3	4	380	.243	.315	.427	.244	56	122-RF	-13
2001	Detroit	AL	374	91	17	1	15	39	121	50	55	4	3	286	.243	.315	.414	.248	44		

Chris Wakeland has bruised the ball everywhere he's been since being picked in the 15th round of the 1996 draft. He wasn't even rewarded with an autumn cup of coffee in Detroit after a rock-solid season in the International League. Though he and Sasser aren't blue-chip prospects, the club's apathy towards them stems from a mistaken belief that speed and defense are more valuable in the new ballpark than scoring runs. The Tigers' prediction that Comerica Park would be a haven for pitchers is self-fulfilling.

PITCHERS (ERA: 4.50, H/9: 9.00, HR/9: 1.00, BB/9: 3.00, K/9: 6.00, KW: 1.00, PERA: 4.50)

Matt Anderson — Throws R — Age 24

YEAR	TEAM	LGE	IP	H	ER	HR	BB	K	ERA	W	L	H/9	HR/9	BB/9	K/9	KW	PERA
1998	Lakeland	Fla	24.0	19	4	0	9	20	1.50	3	0	7.13	0.00	3.38	7.50	1.11	2.66
1998	Detroit	AL	44.0	37	14	3	26	41	2.86	3	2	7.57	0.61	5.32	8.39	0.79	4.23
1999	Detroit	AL	39.0	31	21	6	28	31	4.85	2	2	7.15	1.38	6.46	7.15	0.55	5.26
1999	Toledo	Int	36.0	33	28	10	31	26	7.00	1	3	8.25	2.50	7.75	6.50	0.42	7.64
2000	Detroit	AL	74.3	58	37	7	36	68	4.48	4	4	7.02	0.85	4.36	8.23	0.94	3.76

Labeled the team's closer of the future when he was drafted, Matt Anderson is the Tigers' mop-up man of the present. He was so inconsistent last season that Garner went weeks without using him when the team had a lead. Anderson has eased off on his fastball to improve his control but still has no reliable second pitch. You can't give up on an arm like his, but the Tigers' questionable decision to use the first overall pick in the June 1997 draft on a closer looks even worse now.

Adam Bernero — Throws R — Age 24

YEAR	TEAM	LGE	IP	H	ER	HR	BB	K	ERA	W	L	H/9	HR/9	BB/9	K/9	KW	PERA
1999	W Michgn	Mid	86.3	83	54	20	29	41	5.63	3	7	8.65	2.08	3.02	4.27	0.71	5.46
2000	Jacksnvl	Sou	55.0	59	36	12	26	27	5.89	2	4	9.65	1.96	4.25	4.42	0.52	6.41
2000	Toledo	Int	44.7	34	17	6	10	28	3.43	3	2	6.85	1.21	2.01	5.64	1.40	3.12
2000	Detroit	AL	34.0	31	16	3	11	19	4.24	2	2	8.21	0.79	2.91	5.03	0.86	3.84

(Adam Bernero *continued*)

His rise to the majors was the most improbable of any player's in the game last season. Adam Bernero was signed as an undrafted free agent out of a Division II school, yet Barry Zito was the only hurler from the 1999 draft class to reach the majors faster. Bernero throws four pitches for strikes, his high-80s fastball being the weakest in his repertoire. The Tigers are going to give him an opportunity to crack the rotation in spring training, but given their desire to contend, he'll probably begin the season in long relief or at Toledo.

Willie Blair Throws R Age 35

YEAR	TEAM	LGE	IP	H	ER	HR	BB	K	ERA	W	L	H/9	HR/9	BB/9	K/9	KW	PERA
1998	Arizona	NL	141.0	158	87	27	45	58	5.55	5	11	10.09	1.72	2.87	3.70	0.64	5.85
1998	NY Mets	NL	27.0	23	11	5	9	17	3.67	2	1	7.67	1.67	3.00	5.67	0.94	4.39
1999	Detroit	AL	133.7	155	88	23	35	78	5.93	5	10	10.44	1.55	2.36	5.25	1.11	5.67
2000	Detroit	AL	154.0	169	77	18	28	71	4.50	8	9	9.88	1.05	1.64	4.15	1.27	4.50

Willie Blair lives the axiom that it's better to be lucky than good. Last year was just the third time in 11 major-league seasons that he managed anything resembling league-average innings, but just like the last time, 1997, it happened to be his walk year. The Tigers were interested in bringing him back but declined to offer arbitration. He's a free agent.

David Borkowski Throws R Age 24

YEAR	TEAM	LGE	IP	H	ER	HR	BB	K	ERA	W	L	H/9	HR/9	BB/9	K/9	KW	PERA
1998	Jacksnvl	Sou	167.3	203	108	41	53	62	5.81	6	13	10.92	2.21	2.85	3.33	0.58	6.85
1999	Toledo	Int	120.0	116	59	18	43	69	4.43	6	7	8.70	1.35	3.23	5.18	0.80	4.79
1999	Detroit	AL	77.0	80	48	8	31	48	5.61	3	6	9.35	0.94	3.62	5.61	0.77	4.89
2000	Toledo	Int	44.0	44	30	11	14	22	6.14	1	4	9.00	2.25	2.86	4.50	0.79	5.76

David Borkowski's year was marred by a series of injuries, the most serious being bone chips in his elbow that led to surgery. It probably wasn't a quirk of fate that the injuries followed a 1999 season in which he threw more than 200 innings as a 22-year-old. When healthy, he's basically a one-trick pony, employing a sinking fastball up to 75% of the time. Though the Tigers project him as a starter, Borkowski is better suited to relief right now, where his limited repertoire isn't as likely to catch up to him.

Doug Brocail Throws R Age 34

YEAR	TEAM	LGE	IP	H	ER	HR	BB	K	ERA	W	L	H/9	HR/9	BB/9	K/9	KW	PERA
1998	Detroit	AL	61.3	44	20	2	15	51	2.93	5	2	6.46	0.29	2.20	7.48	1.70	2.21
1999	Detroit	AL	81.0	56	20	6	20	74	2.22	7	2	6.22	0.67	2.22	8.22	1.85	2.41
2000	Detroit	AL	50.3	53	21	4	11	39	3.75	3	3	9.48	0.72	1.97	6.97	1.77	4.07

Doug Brocail hurt his arm in May when he altered his mechanics so that he could pitch with a sore knee. Despite intense pain, he posted above-average numbers until the Tigers shut him down in September to have his elbow cleaned. He's expected to be back at 100% by spring training, ready to résumé his role as one of the top setup men in the game, this time for the Astros.

Calvin Chipperfield Throws R Age 23

YEAR	TEAM	LGE	IP	H	ER	HR	BB	K	ERA	W	L	H/9	HR/9	BB/9	K/9	KW	PERA
1999	Oneonta	NYP	70.0	63	48	14	43	37	6.17	2	6	8.10	1.80	5.53	4.76	0.43	5.85
2000	W Michgn	Mid	123.7	118	81	35	82	78	5.89	4	10	8.59	2.55	5.97	5.68	0.48	7.13

The native Australian led the Midwest League in ERA as the nominal ace of a very good West Michigan staff. Calvin Chipperfield doesn't have overpowering stuff, instead keeping batters off balance by effectively locating his fastball, curve, and change-up at any point in the count. While Chipperfield was old for the league, and while his lack of a big heater may cause him to struggle at the upper levels, any pitcher who can post the ratios that he posted last year bears watching.

Nate Cornejo Throws R Age 21

YEAR	TEAM	LGE	IP	H	ER	HR	BB	K	ERA	W	L	H/9	HR/9	BB/9	K/9	KW	PERA
1999	W Michgn	Mid	162.3	167	89	10	82	66	4.93	7	11	9.26	0.55	4.55	3.66	0.40	4.82
2000	Lakeland	Fla	70.0	69	45	11	36	35	5.79	3	5	8.87	1.41	4.63	4.50	0.49	5.52
2000	Jacksnvl	Sou	83.7	94	62	12	46	36	6.67	2	7	10.11	1.29	4.95	3.87	0.39	6.26

American League   355

Randy Smith's small gamble in the 1998 draft is paying off handsomely. Nate Cornejo's knees, the poor condition of which made him available with the 34th pick, have held up. His workload—more than 340 innings the last two seasons—leaves one to wonder if his arm will. His best pitch is a heavy, low-90s, sinking, two-seam fastball that is as tough to launch as a Delta III rocket. Cornejo's timetable has been accelerated; if he makes small gains with his off-speed pitches, he could be auditioning at Comerica Park in September.

Nelson Cruz — Throws R — Age 28

YEAR	TEAM	LGE	IP	H	ER	HR	BB	K	ERA	W	L	H/9	HR/9	BB/9	K/9	KW	PERA
1998	Calgary	PCL	121.7	150	80	19	41	65	5.92	4	10	11.10	1.41	3.03	4.81	0.79	6.18
1999	Toledo	Int	59.0	46	21	6	23	28	3.20	4	3	7.02	0.92	3.51	4.27	0.61	3.51
1999	Detroit	AL	66.3	68	36	9	18	44	4.88	3	4	9.23	1.22	2.44	5.97	1.22	4.63
2000	Toledo	Int	48.7	55	43	12	18	28	7.95	1	4	10.17	2.22	3.33	5.18	0.78	6.62
2000	Detroit	AL	40.7	36	13	4	11	33	2.88	3	2	7.97	0.89	2.43	7.30	1.50	3.59

Nelson Cruz doesn't have the stamina to work deep into the game as a starter, nor does he have the dominant out pitch that clubs want in a closer. He does, however, throw five adequate pitches for strikes, and he thrived in the bullpen after being recalled from Toledo. He's not as good as last year's line, but if he keeps the ball down, he should be swell in long and middle relief for the Astros, who added him in the Meluskey trade.

Shane Heams — Throws R — Age 25

YEAR	TEAM	LGE	IP	H	ER	HR	BB	K	ERA	W	L	H/9	HR/9	BB/9	K/9	KW	PERA
1998	Jamestwn	NYP	41.7	51	35	3	21	32	7.56	1	4	11.02	0.65	4.54	6.91	0.76	5.96
1999	W Michgn	Mid	60.3	47	37	3	52	50	5.52	2	5	7.01	0.45	7.76	7.46	0.48	4.72
2000	Jacksnvl	Sou	49.0	42	26	8	39	37	4.78	2	3	7.71	1.47	7.16	6.80	0.47	5.96

Due to his age, Shane Heams was advanced two levels to Jacksonville, where he continued to blow batters away. The Mariners drafted him as an outfielder, but unlike most converted position players, Heams boasts more than just a good fastball. In addition to mid-90s gas, he has a devastating slider and a change-up for show. His biggest challenge is throwing strikes consistently. It would be good to see Heams work long stretches of about 50 pitches every third or fourth game so that he gets the reps needed to iron out his control problems.

Erik Hiljus — Throws R — Age 30

YEAR	TEAM	LGE	IP	H	ER	HR	BB	K	ERA	W	L	H/9	HR/9	BB/9	K/9	KW	PERA
1998	Jacksnvl	Sou	59.3	57	44	13	38	49	6.67	2	5	8.65	1.97	5.76	7.43	0.64	6.48
1999	Toledo	Int	55.3	51	35	6	17	49	5.69	2	4	8.30	0.98	2.77	7.97	1.44	3.96
2000	Toledo	Int	66.3	69	37	4	21	58	5.02	3	4	9.36	0.54	2.85	7.87	1.38	4.17

This is what can happen when a struggling, hard-throwing starter is moved to the bullpen. Free to go right after hitters, Erik Hiljus halved his walk rate and boosted his strikeouts after the Tigers switched him to relief. His next daunting obstacle will be overcoming the stigma of ten years of carrying his own bags and getting a real opportunity in The Show. It probably won't happen in Detroit, but I think he can help a team.

Todd Jones — Throws R — Age 33

YEAR	TEAM	LGE	IP	H	ER	HR	BB	K	ERA	W	L	H/9	HR/9	BB/9	K/9	KW	PERA
1998	Detroit	AL	62.7	55	33	6	30	53	4.74	3	4	7.90	0.86	4.31	7.61	0.88	4.23
1999	Detroit	AL	66.7	61	26	6	28	61	3.51	4	3	8.24	0.81	3.78	8.24	1.09	4.20
2000	Detroit	AL	63.7	63	24	5	20	64	3.39	4	3	8.91	0.71	2.83	9.05	1.60	4.06

His saves were up by a dozen from 1999, due more to opportunity than performance. Despite a lot of blather by the local press about his vastly improved slider and brand-spanking-new change-up, Todd Jones wasn't appreciably better than he'd been in previous seasons. It will be interesting to see if the Tigers recognize that when they extend his contract. Ilitch isn't exactly penurious and may offer Trevor Hoffman/Mariano Rivera money. While Jones is a pretty good pitcher, he's nowhere near that level.

Kris Keller — Throws R — Age 23

YEAR	TEAM	LGE	IP	H	ER	HR	BB	K	ERA	W	L	H/9	HR/9	BB/9	K/9	KW	PERA
1998	Jamestwn	NYP	28.7	34	17	8	20	18	5.34	1	2	10.67	2.51	6.28	5.65	0.45	8.43
1999	W Michgn	Mid	68.3	70	40	15	44	46	5.27	3	5	9.22	1.98	5.80	6.06	0.52	6.81
2000	Jacksnvl	Sou	62.0	61	28	2	47	36	4.06	3	4	8.85	0.29	6.82	5.23	0.38	5.24

Prior to Heams's August promotion to Toledo, he and Kris Keller had been joined at the hip since 1998. They're very similar pitchers. Keller throws a little harder, possessing the best fastball in the system except for Matt Anderson's. After previously splitting the closer's role, Keller had it all to himself at Jacksonville, perhaps because he's better at keeping the ball down: he didn't allow a home run in 68 innings. Like Heams, Keller has to better harness his stuff before he'll be ready to help the Tigers.

Shane Loux — Throws R — Age 21

YEAR	TEAM	LGE	IP	H	ER	HR	BB	K	ERA	W	L	H/9	HR/9	BB/9	K/9	KW	PERA
1998	W Michgn	Mid	140.3	189	122	38	69	45	7.82	3	13	12.12	2.44	4.43	2.89	0.33	8.45
1999	W Michgn	Mid	42.7	59	50	12	20	23	10.55	1	4	12.45	2.53	4.22	4.85	0.57	8.69
1999	Lakeland	Fla	82.7	91	55	16	56	31	5.99	3	6	9.91	1.74	6.10	3.38	0.28	7.11
2000	Jacksnvl	Sou	143.3	161	100	23	59	78	6.28	5	11	10.11	1.44	3.70	4.90	0.66	5.91

After two years of teasing scouts with his potential, Shane Loux emerged as a force last season. For the Tigers' second-round pick in 1997, it's never been a question of having the pitches or the command, but of getting rattled when things don't break his way. He matured after being pushed aggressively to Jacksonville and is now considered the top starting-pitcher prospect in the system. Loux would benefit from a full year at Toledo, but continued success could find him in the Motor City.

Tommy Marx — Throws L — Age 21

YEAR	TEAM	LGE	IP	H	ER	HR	BB	K	ERA	W	L	H/9	HR/9	BB/9	K/9	KW	PERA
1999	Oneonta	NYP	19.3	22	19	5	17	9	8.84	0	2	10.24	2.33	7.91	4.19	0.26	8.69
2000	W Michgn	Mid	86.7	83	51	17	62	44	5.30	4	6	8.62	1.77	6.44	4.57	0.35	6.50

He and Fernando Rodney supplied the juice in the West Michigan rotation. Tommy Marx is another of the host of Tiger farmhands who can run it up to the plate in a hurry without any confidence that it's going to arrive at the desired destination. In Marx's case, it may just take a few years to get the far-flung parts of his gangly body working in concert. Given the rampant wildness among hard throwers in the organization, the Tigers may need to examine their coaching methods.

Matt Miller — Throws L — Age 26

YEAR	TEAM	LGE	IP	H	ER	HR	BB	K	ERA	W	L	H/9	HR/9	BB/9	K/9	KW	PERA
1998	W Michgn	Mid	85.3	63	25	3	37	48	2.64	6	3	6.64	0.32	3.90	5.06	0.65	2.90
1998	Jacksnvl	Sou	57.3	70	51	10	50	31	8.01	1	5	10.99	1.57	7.85	4.87	0.31	8.27
1999	Lakeland	Fla	95.7	111	77	21	61	43	7.24	3	8	10.44	1.98	5.74	4.05	0.35	7.52
1999	Jacksnvl	Sou	37.7	42	25	5	14	15	5.97	-1	3	10.04	1.19	3.35	3.58	0.54	5.44
2000	Jacksnvl	Sou	109.0	137	68	21	38	54	5.61	4	8	11.31	1.73	3.14	4.46	0.71	6.70

The former Texas A&M Aggie is fully recovered from the Tommy John surgery that kept him on the sidelines for the 1997 season. Featuring a 90-mph fastball with good sink, a nice curve, and a change-up to keep batters honest, Matt Miller could be a passable fifth starter. However, because he's already 26 years old and the Tigers are short on lefty-getters, I think he'll ultimately drop anchor in the bullpen.

Dave Mlicki — Throws R — Age 33

YEAR	TEAM	LGE	IP	H	ER	HR	BB	K	ERA	W	L	H/9	HR/9	BB/9	K/9	KW	PERA
1998	NY Mets	NL	54.3	66	38	9	24	32	6.29	2	4	10.93	1.49	3.98	5.30	0.67	6.56
1998	LosAngls	NL	117.7	117	68	18	37	63	5.20	5	8	8.95	1.38	2.83	4.82	0.85	4.80
1999	Detroit	AL	190.3	193	90	19	55	113	4.26	10	11	9.13	0.90	2.60	5.34	1.03	4.30
2000	Detroit	AL	118.3	132	68	15	36	54	5.17	5	8	10.04	1.14	2.74	4.11	0.75	5.16

The three-year, $15.5 million contract given to Dave Mlicki after the 1999 season was part of the club's ongoing corporate initiative to embrace mediocrity. Mlicki has long had a reputation of having good stuff, but his strikeout rate has decreased in each of the last five seasons to the point where he's not fooling anybody except the Tigers.

American League

Brian Moehler — Throws R — Age 29

YEAR	TEAM	LGE	IP	H	ER	HR	BB	K	ERA	W	L	H/9	HR/9	BB/9	K/9	KW	PERA
1998	Detroit	AL	216.3	203	88	26	47	114	3.66	13	11	8.45	1.08	1.96	4.74	1.21	3.84
1999	Detroit	AL	194.3	211	98	18	46	101	4.54	10	12	9.77	0.83	2.13	4.68	1.10	4.42
2000	Detroit	AL	175.7	204	86	18	32	98	4.41	9	11	10.45	0.92	1.64	5.02	1.53	4.71

Some players can't make the adjustment when their bread-and-butter move is taken away. Ross Barnes was never the same hitter after the fair-foul rule was revoked. Although his dream of being a spokesperson for Western Garnet was dashed, Brian Moehler appears to have survived having the scuff ball removed from his arsenal. He compensated for being more hittable last season by lowering his walk rate into the Maddux Zone. Moehler walks a thin line but should be an acceptable back-of-the-rotation guy for a few more years.

C.J. Nitkowski — Throws L — Age 28

YEAR	TEAM	LGE	IP	H	ER	HR	BB	K	ERA	W	L	H/9	HR/9	BB/9	K/9	KW	PERA
1998	Houston	NL	56.7	48	27	4	22	36	4.29	3	3	7.62	0.64	3.49	5.72	0.82	3.55
1999	Detroit	AL	81.7	59	36	9	35	63	3.97	5	4	6.50	0.99	3.86	6.94	0.90	3.42
2000	Detroit	AL	109.3	116	68	11	40	77	5.60	4	8	9.55	0.91	3.29	6.34	0.96	4.85

Seven promising starts at the tail end of 1999 put C.J. Nitkowski on many roto sleeper lists heading into last season. Not even the broad expanse of Comerica Park could save him when he left pitches up and over the plate. Nitkowski has a career ERA of 3.79 as a reliever versus 6.84 as a starter, mainly because he doesn't need his fickle change-up in relief. He'll work out of the bullpen as long as he wears Tiger stripes. As the only portsider on the staff, he has job security matched only by William Rehnquist and his eight cronies.

Hideo Nomo — Throws R — Age 32

YEAR	TEAM	LGE	IP	H	ER	HR	BB	K	ERA	W	L	H/9	HR/9	BB/9	K/9	KW	PERA
1998	LosAngls	NL	64.3	58	42	9	37	59	5.88	2	5	8.11	1.26	5.18	8.25	0.80	5.16
1998	NY Mets	NL	85.3	74	51	12	53	76	5.38	3	6	7.80	1.27	5.59	8.02	0.72	5.14
1999	Milwauke	NL	172.3	168	89	25	65	136	4.65	8	11	8.77	1.31	3.39	7.10	1.05	4.85
2000	Detroit	AL	189.7	179	88	27	72	173	4.18	10	11	8.49	1.28	3.42	8.21	1.20	4.67

Hideo Nomo tailed Phil Garner's Mayflower van out of Suds City all the way to Detroit. The combination of decreased movement and command has reduced "The Tornado" to more of a Midwest dust devil, though he was still the team's second-best starter. He can help the Red Sox, his new team, as an innings-munching fourth starter, and he's relatively low-priced.

Danny Patterson — Throws R — Age 30

YEAR	TEAM	LGE	IP	H	ER	HR	BB	K	ERA	W	L	H/9	HR/9	BB/9	K/9	KW	PERA
1998	Texas	AL	60.0	59	25	9	15	31	3.75	4	3	8.85	1.35	2.25	4.65	1.03	4.47
1999	Texas	AL	60.3	71	32	4	14	41	4.77	3	4	10.59	0.60	2.09	6.12	1.46	4.63
2000	Detroit	AL	56.0	63	23	4	11	28	3.70	3	3	10.13	0.64	1.77	4.50	1.27	4.27

Danny Patterson was the equivalent of Styrofoam peanuts when he arrived in the package from Texas that contained Juan Gonzalez. To everyone's surprise, he ended up being Detroit's most effective reliever. Patterson thinks he has some of the best stuff in the league, but he actually has evolved into an extreme finesse pitcher, something that can't be considered a positive sign.

Adam Pettyjohn — Throws L — Age 24

YEAR	TEAM	LGE	IP	H	ER	HR	BB	K	ERA	W	L	H/9	HR/9	BB/9	K/9	KW	PERA
1998	W Michgn	Mid	44.7	54	23	9	12	33	4.63	2	3	10.88	1.81	2.42	6.65	1.38	6.24
1999	Lakeland	Fla	55.7	62	37	4	13	30	5.98	2	4	10.02	0.65	2.10	4.85	1.15	4.36
1999	Jacksnvl	Sou	118.3	134	84	21	38	58	6.39	4	9	10.19	1.60	2.89	4.41	0.76	5.79
2000	Jacksnvl	Sou	45.7	48	28	8	13	26	5.52	2	3	9.46	1.58	2.56	5.12	1.00	5.22
2000	Toledo	Int	37.0	44	35	6	22	18	8.51	1	3	10.70	1.46	5.35	4.38	0.41	6.97

Marx has a higher ceiling, but Adam Pettyjohn has mastered the Double-A test track and has better control. Nevertheless, he had difficulty hitting his spots in his brief stint with the Mud Hens, which caused problems since his fastball tops out in the high 80s. The Tigers are eager to add a southpaw to their rotation, so a decent showing at Toledo should put him on I-75 north to Detroit sometime after the All-Star game. Once there, nobody will mistake him for Rick Ankiel.

Victor Santos — Throws R — Age 24

YEAR	TEAM	LGE	IP	H	ER	HR	BB	K	ERA	W	L	H/9	HR/9	BB/9	K/9	KW	PERA
1998	Lakeland	Fla	92.7	90	45	16	28	43	4.37	5	5	8.74	1.55	2.72	4.18	0.77	4.81
1998	Jacksnvl	Sou	34.7	40	20	3	15	24	5.19	1	3	10.38	0.78	3.89	6.23	0.80	5.45
1999	Jacksnvl	Sou	160.7	154	101	25	63	92	5.66	6	12	8.63	1.40	3.53	5.15	0.73	4.93

Undrafted out of high school because of a bum ankle, Victor Santos produced a string of good performances at each rung of the ladder that landed him a spot on the Tigers' 40-man roster following the 1999 season. Last year, after not missing a start in five years, he blew out his elbow and underwent Tommy John surgery. While his 90-mph fastball should eventually return, his best chance to have a significant career is gone.

Steve Sparks — Throws R — Age 35

YEAR	TEAM	LGE	IP	H	ER	HR	BB	K	ERA	W	L	H/9	HR/9	BB/9	K/9	KW	PERA
1998	Anaheim	AL	127.0	122	57	12	49	83	4.04	7	7	8.65	0.85	3.47	5.88	0.85	4.33
1999	Anaheim	AL	147.7	154	84	17	65	70	5.12	6	10	9.39	1.04	3.96	4.27	0.54	5.17
2000	Toledo	Int	84.7	84	57	11	43	31	6.06	3	6	8.93	1.17	4.57	3.30	0.36	5.28
2000	Detroit	AL	102.3	99	47	6	24	51	4.13	5	6	8.71	0.53	2.11	4.49	1.06	3.51

For a guy with just five years in the big leagues, it seems that Steve Sparks has made more comebacks than Sugar Ray Leonard. He says that the latest revival is due to him changing speeds on his floater, an adjustment he made on a recommendation from the Grand Sheik of the Knuckleballers Lodge, Phil Niekro. Sparks is first in line to inherit Hideo Nomo's spot in the rotation. Consult your Ouija board for insight as to what happens next.

Andy Van Hekken — Throws L — Age 21

YEAR	TEAM	LGE	IP	H	ER	HR	BB	K	ERA	W	L	H/9	HR/9	BB/9	K/9	KW	PERA
1999	Oneonta	NYP	44.7	49	23	8	21	22	4.63	2	3	9.87	1.61	4.23	4.43	0.52	6.17
2000	W Michgn	Mid	145.0	144	54	9	45	67	3.35	9	7	8.94	0.56	2.79	4.16	0.74	3.92

The Tigers could have gotten nothing for Brian L. Hunter and come out ahead; instead, Woody Woodward gave them a quality left-hander. Andy Van Hekken throws a live heater that kisses 90 mph, but the thing that makes his fastball special is his uncanny ability to locate it. He sets it up nicely with his off-speed pitches while occasionally abandoning them if they're not clicking early in the game. It may seem ludicrous for us to try and project a hurler from low-A ball since so much can happen in the next few years, but it beats rehashing the career of Mike Oquist.

Jeff Weaver — Throws R — Age 24

YEAR	TEAM	LGE	IP	H	ER	HR	BB	K	ERA	W	L	H/9	HR/9	BB/9	K/9	KW	PERA
1999	Detroit	AL	162.7	162	86	22	44	109	4.76	7	11	8.96	1.22	2.43	6.03	1.24	4.47
2000	Detroit	AL	197.0	189	88	23	42	130	4.02	11	11	8.63	1.05	1.92	5.94	1.55	3.90

The most exciting player on the Tigers (and not just because he led the league in hit batsmen), Jeff Weaver has absolutely electric stuff. Pitchers are constantly tinkering with things, but Weaver is in the early stages of his career, when such adjustments can pay off handsomely. Weaver's biggest physical change was the addition of a cut fastball that resulted in a 137-point drop in the OPS left-handed hitters posted against him. Maybe even more important was his increased maturity on the mound. Pay no attention to the 11–15 record; according to Michael Wolverton's Support-Neutral work, Weaver was the sixth-unluckiest pitcher in the majors last year.

American League

Support-Neutral Statistics — DETROIT TIGERS — Park Effect: -3.8%

PITCHER	GS	IP	R	SNW	SNL	SNPCT	W	L	RA	APW	SNVA	SNWAR
Adam Bernero	4	21.7	12	1.1	1.3	.457	0	1	4.98	0.0	-0.1	0.1
Willie Blair	17	100.3	61	4.7	6.3	.427	8	3	5.47	-0.3	-0.8	0.0
David Borkowski	1	1.7	8	0.0	0.8	.005	0	1	43.20	-0.7	-0.4	-0.3
Mark Johnson	3	10.3	15	0.3	1.6	.156	0	1	13.06	-0.8	-0.6	-0.5
Dave Mlicki	21	114.3	79	6.8	8.2	.453	6	11	6.22	-1.2	-0.7	0.4
Brian Moehler	29	178.0	99	10.3	9.5	.521	12	9	5.01	0.3	0.4	1.9
C.J. Nitkowski	11	53.0	53	1.8	5.5	.250	2	7	9.00	-2.1	-1.8	-1.3
Hideo Nomo	31	189.0	102	11.7	10.0	.538	8	12	4.86	0.6	0.7	2.5
Steve W. Sparks	15	97.3	53	5.7	5.2	.520	7	5	4.90	0.3	0.3	1.0
Jeff Weaver	30	199.0	98	12.7	9.6	.568	11	15	4.43	1.5	1.5	3.2
TOTALS	162	964.7	580	55.0	58.1	.487	54	65	5.41	-2.5	-1.5	7.0

For a lot of clubs, a rotation performance like the Tigers' in 2000 would be considered a disappointing year. For the Tigers, it was their second-best rotation since the Reagan administration. Since 1989, Detroit has featured by far the worst starting pitching in the majors, costing the team about 68 wins compared to average pitching, according to Support-Neutral Value Added (SNVA). That's 26 wins worse than the next-worst team over that span, Minnesota. In fact, Detroit's recent run of pitching ineptitude is one of historic proportions. In the postwar era, only the Padres' 1969–78 pitching staffs put together a worse decade than the Tigers of 1989–98, measured by Adjusted Pitching Wins.

So after two straight years of improvement, are the Tigers finally building a decent rotation? Anything is possible, but keep in mind that they fooled us once before with a fine 1997, only to sink back toward the basement the next season.

For a quick explanation of SN stats, see page 7.

Reliever Evaluation Tools

PITCHER	G	IP	R	ARA	APR	IRNR/G	EIRS/G	IRP	BRS	RRA	ARP
Matt Anderson	69	74.3	44	5.36	-1.3	0.68	0.24	-1.3	-2.0	5.48	-2.3
Adam Bernero	8	12.7	6	4.29	1.3	0.38	0.13	1.0	-1.9	2.33	4.0
Willie Blair	30	56.3	28	4.50	4.4	0.97	0.45	-0.5	-4.3	3.95	7.8
David Borkowski	1	3.7	5	12.35	-2.9	2.00	1.21	1.1	0.4	9.20	-1.6
Doug Brocail	49	50.7	25	4.47	4.1	0.43	0.15	1.6	1.1	4.48	4.0
Nelson Cruz	27	41.0	14	3.09	9.6	1.00	0.30	-5.9	0.5	4.66	2.4
Shane Halter	1	0.0	0	NaN	0.0	0.00	0.00	0.0	0.4	Inf	-0.4
Erik Hiljus	3	3.7	3	7.41	-0.9	0.33	0.07	-0.8	0.3	10.04	-2.0
Mark Johnson	6	13.7	8	5.30	-0.2	0.83	0.30	-1.2	-0.9	5.63	-0.7
Todd Jones	67	64.0	28	3.96	8.8	0.42	0.14	2.3	1.2	3.83	9.7
Masao Kida	2	2.7	3	10.19	-1.5	2.50	0.62	1.2	0.6	7.23	-0.6
Allan McDill	13	10.0	9	8.15	-3.3	0.69	0.26	-1.2	0.3	9.72	-5.0
Dave Mlicki	3	5.0	0	0.00	2.9	0.00	0.00	0.0	0.0	0.00	2.9
C.J. Nitkowski	56	56.7	26	4.15	6.6	1.20	0.47	-1.4	1.7	4.82	2.4
Hideo Nomo	1	1.0	0	0.00	0.6	0.00	0.00	0.0	0.0	0.00	0.6
Danny Patterson	58	56.7	26	4.15	6.6	0.76	0.28	1.6	-4.3	3.38	11.5
Jim Poole	18	8.7	8	8.36	-3.0	1.28	0.59	-4.0	0.5	12.89	-7.4
Sean Runyan	3	3.0	2	6.04	-0.3	1.33	0.62	-0.5	-0.5	6.16	-0.3
Steve W. Sparks	5	6.7	2	2.72	1.8	0.20	0.06	0.3	0.0	2.51	2.0
Kevin Tolar	5	3.0	1	3.02	0.7	1.00	0.41	-0.5	-0.2	3.34	0.6
Brandon Villafuerte	3	4.3	5	10.45	-2.5	0.33	0.14	-0.6	0.0	12.24	-3.4
Jeff Weaver	1	1.0	4	36.22	-3.4	0.00	0.00	0.0	0.0	39.00	-3.8
TOTALS	429	478.7	247	4.67	27.9	0.75	0.28			4.81	20.4

For a quick guide to RET, see page 10.

Kansas City Royals

No matter what you hear, no team in baseball is so "small market" that it can't create a window of opportunity for itself. Not every team can be like the Yankees, who have paid to have their window enlarged and bolted open, but no team is so poor that it can't wiggle its way into contention with some innovation, some creativity, and some risk.

The Royals have been building toward a contending season, in fits and starts, for five years now. And while their fans, players, and front-office personnel are optimistic about a better and brighter future, we at BP are here to douse them with the ice water of reason. The Royals' window of opportunity is already closing fast.

Johnny Damon is no longer a Royal. Mike Sweeney and Jermaine Dye are due for free agency at the end of 2002. The Royals' dreams of wild-card contention are inextricably linked to these three players. The loss of Damon hurts, but does not cripple, the team; if Sweeney and Dye were to follow, though, the entire rebuilding process would begin again.

It's easy to argue that the Royals brought this crunch time upon themselves. You don't need to be a genius to realize that the Royals could have locked up all three players a year ago after their breakout seasons and spent the next few years surrounding their stars with a supporting cast worthy of a postseason berth. A year ago, however, the Royals were still looking for an owner, and their desire to reduce operating costs (such as future contract commitments) to make the team more attractive to buyers, even at the expense of future profits, is a standard business practice. Herk Robinson was still GM, and for Robinson to be bold and forward-thinking would have been out of character.

The Royals now have an owner. They have a new GM with new ideas for the future. What they don't have is time. We cannot drill this point home with too much force: in the new order of baseball, time is the most valuable commodity a small-market team has—namely, the six years prior to free agency in which a team can avoid paying its players market value. Once upon a time, when the disparity in payrolls was not nearly so great, low-spending teams could compete with their high-spending competitors simply by passing on overpriced veterans (i.e., not spending $5 million a year on Marquis Grissom). Those days are over. Today, when the Yankees spend nearly four times as much money on player salaries as the Royals, it's not enough for small-market teams to avoid overpaying for talent. They must learn the art of underpaying for talent, and the best way to do this is to make good use of a player before he gains full leverage.

A team that understands the value of service time can manipulate it advantageously. By waiting until May to bring up its latest phenom instead of putting him in the lineup on Opening Day, a team can delay the onset of free agency by a full year. An organization that believes in the players it develops can buy out a player's first year or two of free agency, at a salary well below market value, by offering him a long-term contract early in his career. This is how the Indians, for example, got away with paying Manny Ramirez $4 million last year. The epitome of small-market finance, the Oakland Athletics, have locked up virtually their entire core of talent to long-term deals. Ben Grieve, Eric Chavez, Tim Hudson, and Miguel Tejada are all signed for years at a fraction of their market values.

Thanks to their youth movement, the Royals have been able to pay their core players much less than they're worth. This is about to change. As a player with five years of service time, Damon can compare himself to free agents in an arbitration case, essentially guaranteeing himself a one-year contract at market value. That was a motivation behind the Royals' dealing him to the A's. Sweeney and Dye will reach the same point next year. By not offering long-term deals when they had the leverage, the Royals deprived themselves of additional bargain years from their maturing stars. The problem now is that the Royals can't pay Damon, Sweeney,

> **Royals Prospectus**
>
> **2000 record:** 77–85; Fourth place, AL Central
> **Pythagenport W/L:** 76–86
> **Runs Scored:** 879 (5th in AL)
> **Runs Allowed:** 930 (13th in AL)
> **Team EqA:** .253 (11th in AL)
> **2000 Batters' Age:** 27.5 (3rd youngest in AL)
> **2000 Pitchers' Age:** 25.5 (youngest in AL)
> **Ballpark:** Kauffman Stadium; moderate hitters' park; Park Factor of 1.042
> **2000:** They scored some runs, developed some pitchers and settled on an owner.
> **2001:** With a soft division and a decent talent core, 2001 might be their best chance. Really.

and Dye what they're worth and still afford to fill the holes on their roster.

To beat this predicament, the Royals will have to work fast. They still have Sweeney and Dye under obligation though 2002, possibly longer if they belatedly ink both players to long-term deals. Together, they form an effective, albeit expensive, core around which to build. Around them, the Royals have a new generation of players, the Mark Quinns and Carlos Beltrans and a pitching staff of Blake Steins and Dan Reicherts, none of whom are eligible for arbitration. By 2003, however, all will be well into their arbitration years, and unless David Glass can tolerate a payroll north of $60 million, the dismantling of the team will have already begun.

That gives the Royals just two years to ripen their talent into a championship ballclub. And since the 2002 season has had the Sword of Damocles hanging over it since the last Bargaining Agreement was signed, the Royals' best shot at winning may be now. That isn't to say that the Royals won't be competitive in 2002 or 2003, or that they won't be able to sign the stars that develop from their new class of youngsters. But if the Royals understand the importance of using long-term deals to keep their homegrown talent under contract an extra couple of years, they sure have a funny way of showing it.

Take a player like Beltran, the 1999 Rookie of the Year. Beltran has a chance to be a superstar and make an absurd amount of money in this game, a point no doubt reinforced by his agent, Scott Boras, on a regular basis. For Beltran to accept a long-term deal that may cap his earning potential for years, he will expect security in return—not just the financial security of a guaranteed contract, but also the security of playing for an organization that he trusts, one that he feels is looking out for his best interests. When the Royals suspended Beltran last summer and created a national story over a matter so trivial as where he should rehabilitate his gimpy knee, they sent him a message. The Royals thought their message read "no player is more important than the team," but Beltran interpreted the message as "you are not important to us." Any player would feel insecure under such circumstances.

The incident with Beltran is hardly an isolated one; the Royals have an unparalleled history of going out of their way to remind their best players who is in control. In just the past year, they have suspended Beltran, sent Mark Quinn to the minors for a month to punish a perceived lack of effort, suspended top prospect Dee Brown for a few days for failing to run out a ground ball, suspended Brown's teammate, Kit Pellow, for unspecified reasons, and traded both Jeremy Giambi and Sal Fasano to the Athletics for beans because neither player was willing to kiss up to Tony Muser. Even Mike Sweeney, who has become the most popular Royal since George Brett, was treated callously early in his career.

The Royals now claim they knew all along that Sweeney had superstar potential, which is a remarkable piece of revisionist history: they had no idea, and any team in baseball could have acquired him for a song just two years ago.

Which brings us back to the Royals' predicament. If they aren't willing to invest in their players, financially and emotionally, on a long-term basis, then they might as well go all out to win this year, because they may not have a better chance before they have to rebuild.

It is a daunting task, but not an impossible one. All the talk about having to replace Damon obscures the fact that the Royals' offense is already playoff-caliber. They ranked fifth in the AL with 879 runs last year, their highest ranking since 1982. The loss of Damon will hurt less if Carlos Beltran recovers from a disastrous sophomore season. Whatever drop-off there is should be countered by the maturation of Quinn, a rebound by a hopefully healthy Carlos Febles, and the improvement of a bench that can't possibly be worse than it was last season.

If the Royals fail to contend this year, it will have nothing to do with the offense and everything to do with a pitching staff that has finished last and next-to-last in runs allowed the last two seasons. Some pitching staffs are bad because they have a two or three effective pitchers weighed down by a truly awful back end, something you might see on an over-the-hill team going nowhere (think Mike Mussina and the Orioles). That's a relatively easy problem to fix, as pitchers who can give you average innings to support your strong top end are available.

The Royals' staffs the past two seasons have instead featured a bland sameness throughout, which is what you would expect from a rebuilding team conducting open try-outs for fuzzy-cheeked hurlers in the hopes that the youngsters might one day become effective pitchers. The Royals' pitching woes cannot, therefore, be fixed by simply jettisoning their worst pitchers and signing a free agent or two.

Part of the problem is, it's not entirely clear who the Royals' worst starter is. Every member of the final rotation finished with a Support-Neutral Value Added between zero and one win. The Red Sox were the only other team in the league to have five average-or-better starters make ten starts each. What the Royals have in depth, though, they lack in quality. Their best starter in 2000, Mac Suzuki, had no prior history of success and faces an uncertain future after minor shoulder surgery in the off-season. Their ace, Jose Rosado, missed almost the entire season with rotator-cuff problems; their interim ace, Jeff Suppan, needed a shutout in his final start to bring his ERA under 5.00.

Still, the Royals have reason to hope for dramatic improvement, because they had the youngest pitching staff in baseball last year. Their staff could vault into the top half of the league if they get breakout seasons from one or two pitchers, or if they experience even a modest across-the-board improvement.

Because of the need for across-the-board improvement, the single most important person to a Royals' pitching revival isn't Dan Reichert or Jeff Suppan or whatever free-agent closer the Royals scrounge up. It's pitching coach Brent Strom.

Since taking over the job a year ago, Strom has received a lot of credit for his communication skills, which, combined with unorthodox teaching methods and his willingness to scour the Internet looking for an edge for his pitchers, has given Strom more influence in the success or failure of his pitchers than most pitching coaches wield. In particular, Strom's "fastball-first" philosophy—which stresses learning to use the fastball the majority of the time, no matter what a pitcher's particular strength is—has caught him a lot of flak despite the Royals having one of the softest-tossing staffs in baseball (they have ranked 30th and 28th in strikeouts the last two seasons). The staff did not take to his teachings at all during the first half of 2000, with a major-league-worst 5.87 ERA at the All-Star break. But the team's ERA dropped 83 points in the second half of the season, compared to an AL average drop of just 16 points, and the organization continues to believe in Strom.

The Royals are, for the most part, ignoring their lack of #1 and #2 starters and instead focusing their attention on the bullpen, which was the worst in history in 1999 and still awfully bad last year. Superficially, it seems a reasonable focus. The problem is that relievers, even good relievers, are so unpredictable from year to year that acquiring one based on past performance is almost certain to be a losing proposition. Only five relievers have made even 40 appearances with ERAs under 3.50 in each of the last three years: Danny Graves, Trevor Hoffman, Mariano Rivera, John Rocker, and Donne Wall. The Royals signed Ricky Bottalico last year on the basis of his previous good performances, and he rewarded them with a 4.83 ERA. Roberto Hernandez, acquired for Johnny Damon, isn't likely to push the Royals over .500, much less into contention.

Another reason the Royals should be careful when spending finite resources on bullpen help is that the bullpen is the one part of a roster where players with little major-league experience routinely perform as well as their veteran counterparts. Furthermore, the Royals' prime organizational strength currently lies in their quantity of live arms. Kris Wilson and Scott Mullen both pitched well for the Royals late in the season, and they represent only the Royals' second-tier prospects. Shawn Sonnier is one of the best closers in the minor leagues, Robbie Morrison and Junior Guerrero could both be assets in middle relief, and in Chris George, the Royals have one of the best starting-pitcher prospects in the minors, someone who could be eased into the majors with a year of long-relief work. The Royals already have the talent on hand to turn a liability into a strength.

The Future is Now. Play the Kids. If ever those contradictory statements held true for one team, it is these Kansas City Royals.

HITTERS (BA: .270, OBP: .340, SLG: .440, EqA: .260)

Carlos Beltran — CF — Bats B — Age 24

YEAR	TEAM	LGE	AB	H	DB	TP	HR	BB	SO	R	RBI	SB	CS	OUT	BA	OBP	SLG	EQA	EQR	DEFENSE	
1998	Wilmngtn	Car	201	48	8	0	5	20	40	25	26	5	3	156	.239	.311	.353	.225	19	50-CF	3
1998	Wichita	Tex	179	50	11	1	9	17	33	33	28	3	1	130	.279	.344	.503	.277	26	42-CF	-4
1998	KansasCy	AL	58	16	6	3	0	3	11	12	7	2	0	42	.276	.322	.483	.268	8	14-CF	2
1999	KansasCy	AL	656	190	27	6	23	40	112	106	102	25	8	474	.290	.334	.454	.263	84	150-CF	4
2000	KansasCy	AL	369	91	14	4	7	30	63	46	41	14	0	278	.247	.303	.363	.231	36	88-CF	1
2001	KansasCy	AL	482	135	22	4	15	41	91	77	76	13	2	349	.280	.337	.436	.260	60		

This is not what anyone had in mind for Carlos Beltran's second season. The silver lining of trading Johnny Damon is that it may show Beltran that he has the organization's support as the team's center fielder. His problems last year stemmed almost entirely from a lack of confidence, and if the Royals can't restore his confidence and develop him into the five-tool star everyone thought he would be, they don't deserve to make the playoffs anyway.

Dee Brown — LF — Bats L — Age 23

YEAR	TEAM	LGE	AB	H	DB	TP	HR	BB	SO	R	RBI	SB	CS	OUT	BA	OBP	SLG	EQA	EQR	DEFENSE	
1998	Wilmngtn	Car	461	106	24	1	9	43	117	51	48	11	5	360	.230	.301	.345	.219	40	96-LF	-15
1999	Wilmngtn	Car	232	59	8	1	10	33	58	34	32	8	4	177	.254	.352	.427	.263	31	55-LF	0
1999	Wichita	Tex	234	65	12	1	8	27	44	41	37	5	4	173	.278	.357	.440	.265	31	61-LF	-2
2000	Omaha	PCL	478	116	21	4	19	26	114	57	53	12	2	364	.243	.285	.423	.235	49	108-LF	-8
2001	KansasCy	AL	490	130	24	2	19	52	125	77	80	8	2	362	.265	.336	.439	.259	62		

American League

Despite Dee Brown's outstanding 1999 performance at two levels, the Royals correctly told anyone who would listen that Brown was still far from being a polished hitter and needed another full year in the minor leagues. Brown has a history of struggling for about two months after each promotion, but it took him all season to adjust to Triple-A journeymen who consistently throw off-speed pitches for strikes. He's one of those guys for whom the ball simply sounds different coming off his bat, and he's publicly admitted his need to lay off pitches outside the strike zone. He may have a bit too much confidence, though, and he was suspended for a few days for not running out a ground ball. He's got a world of talent, but more and more observers think he isn't fully committed to becoming a great player. This is the year he must prove them wrong.

Joe Caruso — UT — Bats R — Age 26

YEAR	TEAM	LGE	AB	H	DB	TP	HR	BB	SO	R	RBI	SB	CS	OUT	BA	OBP	SLG	EQA	EQR	DEFENSE			
1998	Lansing	Mid	427	93	18	3	8	43	65	49	42	8	4	338	.218	.299	.330	.213	35	63-3B	-3	43-2B	2
1999	Wilmngtn	Car	372	79	13	3	5	23	72	48	29	2	2	295	.212	.266	.304	.184	22	63-2B	-6	33-RF	0
2000	Wichita	Tex	396	97	17	1	9	20	50	45	43	4	2	301	.245	.296	.361	.219	34	63-LF	-2	19-3B	-2
2001	KansasCy	AL	360	84	15	1	6	29	58	37	35	4	2	278	.233	.290	.331	.206	27				

An organizational soldier, Joe Caruso took advantage of the favorable hitting conditions at Wichita to have a semi-productive season. His ability to play every non-battery position is something he needs to keep at the top of his résumé if he has any hope of becoming the next Bill Pecota.

Mike Curry — CF — Bats L — Age 24

YEAR	TEAM	LGE	AB	H	DB	TP	HR	BB	SO	R	RBI	SB	CS	OUT	BA	OBP	SLG	EQA	EQR	DEFENSE	
1998	Spokane	Nwn	232	47	5	1	1	30	47	27	16	10	4	189	.203	.297	.246	.191	15	66-CF	1
1999	Charl-WV	SAL	333	84	11	2	0	36	61	40	19	21	7	256	.252	.332	.297	.226	31	85-CF	2
1999	Wilmngtn	Car	209	45	5	1	1	25	40	22	13	11	5	169	.215	.301	.263	.198	15	47-CF	-4
2000	Wichita	Tex	462	109	15	4	3	68	104	68	36	25	9	362	.236	.337	.305	.230	46	120-CF	-3
2001	KansasCy	AL	490	122	18	3	1	63	111	79	41	25	9	377	.249	.335	.304	.226	46		

Mike Curry rarely gets a mention on the list of prospects who fit the classic Brett Butler mold of left-handed-hitting center fielders and leadoff hitters. Over the last two seasons, he has averaged 69 stolen bases and 88 walks, and he posted a .413 OBP in Double-A last year. He's not particularly young, and his four homers last season were a career high, but I expect he will have a long career as a fourth outfielder at the very least. If the Royals find themselves in contention in 2001, they will likely cash in Curry at the trading deadline for whatever holes they need to fill.

Johnny Damon — CF/LF — Bats L — Age 27

YEAR	TEAM	LGE	AB	H	DB	TP	HR	BB	SO	R	RBI	SB	CS	OUT	BA	OBP	SLG	EQA	EQR	DEFENSE	
1998	KansasCy	AL	638	178	28	10	20	57	75	102	65	21	11	471	.279	.342	.448	.262	83	158-CF	0
1999	KansasCy	AL	574	175	37	9	15	61	46	95	73	33	6	405	.305	.374	.479	.289	91	133-LF	9
2000	KansasCy	AL	644	208	40	10	16	57	55	128	81	48	10	446	.323	.379	.491	.294	105	133-CF	8
2001	Oakland	AL	600	187	32	10	17	66	56	116	95	32	8	421	.312	.380	.483	.299	103		

Johnny Damon had exactly the season the Royals thought he would, though they can be forgiven for thinking he would have it in 1996 and not in 2000, a year away from free agency. The end of his career in Kansas City means that the Damon/Sweeney combination will be split apart before it can be seen as one of the most productive duos in recent history. Despite having a complete non-entity batting between them, Damon set a team record for runs while Sweeney did the same for RBI. On 58 different occasions, Sweeney drove in Damon to score a run. Our play-by-play records go back to 1979, and in that span, no player has driven in a teammate as many times in one season:

Year	Team	Set the Table	Cleared the Table	Times
2000	KC	Johnny Damon	Mike Sweeney	58
1985	NYY	Rickey Henderson	Don Mattingly	56
1983	MON	Tim Raines	Andre Dawson	55
1996	MIN	Chuck Knoblauch	Paul Molitor	55
1992	CLE	Kenny Lofton	Carlos Baerga	47

Wilson Delgado   SS/2B   Bats B   Age 25

YEAR	TEAM	LGE	AB	H	DB	TP	HR	BB	SO	R	RBI	SB	CS	OUT	BA	OBP	SLG	EQA	EQR	DEFENSE	
1998	Fresno	PCL	506	120	19	1	9	42	91	67	48	6	3	389	.237	.298	.332	.212	40	126-SS	-4
1999	Fresno	PCL	209	53	7	2	1	14	34	21	25	3	1	157	.254	.300	.321	.209	16	56-SS	-7
1999	San Fran	NL	72	18	3	1	0	4	8	7	3	1	0	54	.250	.298	.319	.209	5	13-SS	-1
2000	KansasCy	AL	82	22	0	0	0	5	15	12	6	1	1	61	.268	.310	.268	.192	5	17-2B	7
2001	KansasCy	AL	201	52	3	0	3	16	37	21	21	3	1	150	.259	.313	.318	.214	16		

Wilson Delgado was a shrewd pickup by Allard Baird, who took advantage of the Yankees' overbooked 40-man roster to grab him for journeyman Nick Ortiz (who re-signed with the Royals after the season). Delgado switch-hits and will take a walk, which makes him a nice backup for Rey Sanchez, who does neither. He's also young enough that the Royals can hope he'll fill the gap once Sanchez leaves.

Joe Dillon   3B   Bats R   Age 25

YEAR	TEAM	LGE	AB	H	DB	TP	HR	BB	SO	R	RBI	SB	CS	OUT	BA	OBP	SLG	EQA	EQR	DEFENSE			
1998	Lansing	Mid	274	57	11	1	11	26	61	25	28	3	1	218	.208	.277	.376	.216	24	45-1B	5	13-3B	1
1999	Wilmngtn	Car	521	121	23	1	14	41	128	58	68	4	3	403	.232	.293	.361	.217	44	111-3B	3	12-1B	0
2000	Wichita	Tex	219	55	10	1	7	27	41	24	27	0	0	164	.251	.344	.402	.253	26	50-3B	3		
2000	Omaha	PCL	149	37	10	1	1	13	27	15	8	1	0	112	.248	.315	.349	.225	14	35-3B	3		
2001	KansasCy	AL	344	83	16	1	9	33	78	41	43	2	1	262	.241	.308	.372	.227	32				

Another organization man, Joe Dillon developed into a genuine prospect in 2000. He has no single outstanding skill, but he plays excellent defense, will hit for a good average, take some walks, and hit for gap power. In other words, he's indistinguishable from the guy ahead of him on the depth chart, Joe Randa. Dillon has minimal star potential but has value to the Royals because they have no other options should Randa get injured. He struggled mightily in the Arizona Fall League.

Todd Dunwoody   OF   Bats L (as in "Lousy")   Age 26

YEAR	TEAM	LGE	AB	H	DB	TP	HR	BB	SO	R	RBI	SB	CS	OUT	BA	OBP	SLG	EQA	EQR	DEFENSE	
1998	Charlott	Int	101	26	4	2	5	10	28	15	17	2	1	76	.257	.342	.485	.271	15	28-CF	5
1998	Florida	NL	440	114	27	7	6	20	106	56	29	5	1	327	.259	.297	.393	.229	41	102-CF	10
1999	Florida	NL	188	42	6	3	2	9	39	19	19	2	4	150	.223	.263	.319	.183	11	44-CF	-2
1999	Calgary	PCL	240	53	13	5	6	7	54	25	25	5	5	192	.221	.247	.392	.203	18	64-CF	4
2000	KansasCy	AL	178	37	7	0	2	5	38	11	23	3	0	141	.208	.234	.281	.160	7	37-OF	-3
2001	ChiCubs	NL	276	62	12	2	6	17	68	31	31	6	3	217	.225	.270	.348	.206	21		

If the Royals want to take the next step in the rebuilding process, they have to stop using their major-league roster as an extension of their minor-league operations. That means no longer giving Todd Dunwoody 178 at-bats to prove that he has no business being in the major leagues. Tim Allen fumbles with his tools less than Dunwoody, whose .238 OBP was the lowest by a Royals outfielder (minimum: 150 at-bats) in team history.

Jermaine Dye   RF   Bats R   Age 27

YEAR	TEAM	LGE	AB	H	DB	TP	HR	BB	SO	R	RBI	SB	CS	OUT	BA	OBP	SLG	EQA	EQR	DEFENSE	
1998	Omaha	PCL	155	39	4	0	9	16	29	22	25	5	0	116	.252	.324	.452	.262	20	35-RF	4
1998	KansasCy	AL	213	50	5	0	6	11	41	24	23	2	2	165	.235	.275	.343	.201	15	59-RF	8
1999	KansasCy	AL	600	175	42	8	28	52	108	92	112	2	3	428	.292	.349	.528	.283	91	153-RF	10
2000	KansasCy	AL	590	188	36	2	34	62	90	100	109	0	1	403	.319	.386	.559	.306	104	135-RF	-8
2001	KansasCy	AL	583	175	37	2	28	69	102	108	124	3	1	409	.300	.374	.515	.292	94		

By hitting just one home run after September 1, Jermaine Dye ensured that Steve Balboni's team-record 36 homers would stand for another year as an embarrassment to the organization. That was about the only fault one can find with his season. The only person to make a more startling transformation from wild youth to distinguished veteran is George W. Bush. Six Royals qualified for the batting title; Dye was the only one who didn't rank in the bottom quartile of the AL in pitches seen per plate appearance. Damon and Mike Sweeney get more press, but Dye is the best overall player on the team.

American League

Mark Ellis — SS/2B — Bats R — Age 24

YEAR	TEAM	LGE	AB	H	DB	TP	HR	BB	SO	R	RBI	SB	CS	OUT	BA	OBP	SLG	EQA	EQR	DEFENSE	
1999	Spokane	Nwn	280	67	7	0	5	29	45	35	26	7	3	216	.239	.313	.318	.217	24	71-SS	5
2000	Wilmngtn	Car	507	133	22	2	6	57	75	64	49	10	4	378	.262	.341	.349	.238	52	127-SS	1
2001	Oakland	AL	365	95	11	1	6	44	68	57	45	10	3	273	.260	.340	.345	.245	41		

Mark Ellis was drafted as a college senior in 1999, which left many observers skeptical that he could translate his impressive pro debut into production at higher rungs on the ladder. He won converts after skipping a level and posting a .404 OBP at Wilmington. The Royals remain unsure that he can play shortstop in the majors, so they moved him to second base during a late-season call-up to Double-A, even though some observers likened his sturdy defensive work to that of Mike Bordick. Mark Loretta is a better comparison. Ellis could be an asset at either middle-infield position. A throw-in to Oakland in the Damon trade.

Jorge Fabregas — C — Bats L — Age 31

YEAR	TEAM	LGE	AB	H	DB	TP	HR	BB	SO	R	RBI	SB	CS	OUT	BA	OBP	SLG	EQA	EQR	DEFENSE
1998	Arizona	NL	152	31	1	0	2	13	24	8	16	0	0	121	.204	.271	.250	.167	7	40-C 7
1999	Florida	NL	225	47	10	2	3	23	25	20	20	0	0	178	.209	.288	.311	.200	16	69-C 7
2000	Omaha	PCL	129	28	3	1	1	8	10	6	14	1	1	102	.217	.263	.279	.172	6	22-C -2
2000	KansasCy	AL	141	40	4	0	3	6	10	12	16	1	0	101	.284	.313	.376	.231	13	38-C 2
2001	Anaheim	AL	208	47	5	1	3	18	20	22	23	0	0	161	.226	.288	.303	.199	14	

He's a left-handed-hitting catcher who has thrown out 41% of attempted base stealers over the last two seasons. But his 693 OPS in 2000 was a career high, and there's no evidence to suggest that his modest success was anything more than a sample-size fluke. That should matter little to Fabregas, as catchers have been known to prolong their careers for years on the basis of a single good performance. Remember Rick Cerone? Fabregas is like the ball on a roulette table; you don't know where he's going to end up, you just know he'll drop in somewhere. On this spin, he landed back in Anaheim, where he'll back up Ben Molina.

Carlos Febles — 2B — Bats R — Age 25

YEAR	TEAM	LGE	AB	H	DB	TP	HR	BB	SO	R	RBI	SB	CS	OUT	BA	OBP	SLG	EQA	EQR	DEFENSE
1998	Wichita	Tex	428	110	22	4	10	60	77	69	34	24	9	327	.257	.357	.397	.261	57	112-2B -16
1999	KansasCy	AL	448	114	23	9	10	43	83	67	50	18	4	338	.254	.331	.413	.254	55	122-2B 6
2000	KansasCy	AL	335	84	12	1	2	32	44	56	26	18	7	258	.251	.335	.310	.228	32	92-2B -4
2001	KansasCy	AL	437	115	18	4	9	48	77	74	55	21	7	329	.263	.336	.384	.247	50	

He doesn't turn 25 until May, but he looks less like a phenom and more like a Comeback Player of the Year candidate every day. Repetitive shoulder injuries have robbed him of his power—he had a lower slugging average than Rey Sanchez—and his defense slipped from excellent to merely adequate. Febles has All-Star ability at second base, but if you look at the top-echelon second baseman like Roberto Alomar and Edgardo Alfonzo, you'll notice that they have a knack for avoiding injury while playing one of the game's most dangerous positions. Febles, for whatever reason, lacks that ability. Unless he develops it quickly, it's going to render his talent useless.

Alexis Gomez — CF — Bats L — Age 20

YEAR	TEAM	LGE	AB	H	DB	TP	HR	BB	SO	R	RBI	SB	CS	OUT	BA	OBP	SLG	EQA	EQR	DEFENSE
2000	Wilmngtn	Car	476	112	13	3	1	32	126	51	27	9	6	370	.235	.285	.282	.187	28	119-CF -6
2001	KansasCy	AL	244	57	4	1	0	17	86	19	15	4	3	190	.234	.284	.258	.174	12	

A raw, wiry 19-year-old, Alexis Gomez was one of the youngest regulars in the Carolina League last year. He's not even in the top five on the organizational center-field depth chart, so he makes for an interesting high-risk/high-reward opportunity for any GM looking to cash in on some excess pitching.

Pat Hallmark — OF/1B — Bats R — Age 27

YEAR	TEAM	LGE	AB	H	DB	TP	HR	BB	SO	R	RBI	SB	CS	OUT	BA	OBP	SLG	EQA	EQR	DEFENSE	
1998	Wilmngtn	Car	381	89	15	1	4	36	74	44	28	13	8	300	.234	.304	.310	.209	30	27-C -3	16-CF -4
1999	Wichita	Tex	241	55	7	1	3	15	71	23	16	6	3	190	.228	.282	.303	.195	16	50-OF -9	
2000	Wichita	Tex	474	119	18	2	6	32	84	48	49	17	7	362	.251	.313	.335	.222	42	89-LF -3	
2001	KansasCy	AL	392	92	13	1	4	35	85	46	32	16	7	307	.235	.297	.304	.205	29		

(Pat Hallmark *continued*)

An unfortunate victim of Prospect's Disease, it took Pat Hallmark five years to develop his bat enough to make it as a backup catcher—the same five years it took for him to lose the ability to play the position. He can still catch in a pinch, and that might be his only route to the majors. His skill set as an outfielder became obsolete about the time Whitey Herzog retired.

Ken Harvey   1B   Bats R   Age 23

YEAR	TEAM	LGE	AB	H	DB	TP	HR	BB	SO	R	RBI	SB	CS	OUT	BA	OBP	SLG	EQA	EQR	DEFENSE	
1999	Spokane	Nwn	199	57	8	0	6	13	33	26	22	2	1	143	.286	.339	.417	.253	23	34-1B	-1
2000	Wilmngtn	Car	169	48	6	0	4	10	30	16	19	0	1	122	.284	.336	.391	.243	18	18-1B	-1
2001	KansasCy	AL	148	46	6	0	5	10	34	21	27	0	0	102	.311	.354	.453	.268	19		

Last off-season, the Royals foolishly failed to seek medical treatment for Ken Harvey's nagging toe injury. It ended Ken Harvey's 2000 campaign after just 46 games and cost him power while he played. He's not going to be Frank Thomas, but he's quite capable of graduating from Double-A in four months, much as Thomas did in his rookie season. If he gets healthy and stays healthy—and there's no reason he can't—Harvey is the best hitting prospect in the minors who no one knows.

Dave McCarty   1B   Bats R   Age 31

YEAR	TEAM	LGE	AB	H	DB	TP	HR	BB	SO	R	RBI	SB	CS	OUT	BA	OBP	SLG	EQA	EQR	DEFENSE			
1998	Tacoma	PCL	401	105	23	2	7	45	91	54	37	6	4	300	.262	.342	.382	.246	45	62-OF	3	37-1B	0
1999	Toledo	Int	470	107	19	2	21	54	118	63	53	4	4	367	.228	.311	.411	.239	51	104-1B	16	16-OF	0
2000	KansasCy	AL	267	74	13	2	12	19	62	32	49	0	0	193	.277	.325	.476	.262	34	54-1B	7		
2001	KansasCy	AL	330	85	13	1	13	38	85	47	53	2	2	247	.258	.334	.421	.251	39				

For much of the season, Dave McCarty was essentially the only decent hitter the Royals had on their bench. Since McCarty's sole reason for existence was to fill the Tony Muser Memorial Roster Spot, you can only wonder how bad the Royals' bench would have been had McCarty not begun to hit in the major leagues for the first time. His offense was exactly what his minor-league track record indicated he was capable of . . . nine years ago. He has value as long as he's used solely against left-handers, whom he hit as if he were Vladimir Guerrero. Against right-handers, he hit like Orlando Cabrera.

Luis Ordaz   SS/2B   Bats R   Age 25

YEAR	TEAM	LGE	AB	H	DB	TP	HR	BB	SO	R	RBI	SB	CS	OUT	BA	OBP	SLG	EQA	EQR	DEFENSE			
1998	Memphis	PCL	213	55	7	1	5	12	20	23	27	2	2	160	.258	.300	.371	.221	18	58-SS	-5		
1998	St Louis	NL	155	33	6	0	0	11	17	10	8	2	0	122	.213	.265	.252	.167	7	44-SS	4		
1999	Memphis	PCL	358	89	20	3	1	19	39	24	36	2	3	272	.249	.292	.330	.204	26	100-SS	0		
2000	KansasCy	AL	104	23	2	0	0	3	9	16	10	4	2	83	.221	.250	.240	.153	4	17-SS	-7	12-2B	-1
2001	KansasCy	AL	172	42	7	1	1	11	19	18	14	3	2	132	.244	.290	.314	.199	12				

Picked up on waivers from the Diamondbacks on April 5, Luis Ordaz played like Rey Sanchez's younger brother, with steady defense that hardly made up for a .221 average with two extra-base hits and five walks. He's a terrible fit for this ball club because he contributes nothing that Sanchez doesn't. His presence on the roster this season would be a sign that the Royals still aren't playing to win.

Hector Ortiz   C   Bats R   Age 31

YEAR	TEAM	LGE	AB	H	DB	TP	HR	BB	SO	R	RBI	SB	CS	OUT	BA	OBP	SLG	EQA	EQR	DEFENSE			
1998	Omaha	PCL	189	38	6	0	0	7	28	14	10	0	0	151	.201	.232	.233	.126	4	52-C	-10		
1999	SanAnton	Tex	123	26	4	0	0	7	20	9	11	0	0	97	.211	.254	.244	.150	4	33-C	0		
1999	Albuquer	PCL	159	38	3	0	5	5	28	14	14	1	2	123	.239	.265	.352	.197	11	28-C	-3	12-1B	-1
2000	Omaha	PCL	225	60	6	0	5	15	20	21	17	2	2	167	.267	.314	.360	.225	20	48-C	-3		
2000	KansasCy	AL	86	33	6	0	0	7	7	14	5	0	0	53	.384	.436	.453	.306	14	23-C	0		
2001	KansasCy	AL	287	72	6	0	4	22	36	28	28	1	1	216	.251	.304	.314	.205	21				

Prior to 2000, Hector Ortiz's career average in 12 minor-league seasons was .233. Then he hit .322 at Omaha and .386 in 88 at-bats with the Royals. It could be a manifestation of Jazayerli's Rule: given enough opportunities, eventually a backup catcher will have a good season purely by chance. But there are other markers: after hitting just three home runs in his first 11 pro seasons, he's hit 12 in his last two. He's not a .386 hitter, but I think he could be a .286 hitter with enough doubles and defense to make for a worthwhile package.

Kit Pellow — 1B — Bats R — Age 27

YEAR	TEAM	LGE	AB	H	DB	TP	HR	BB	SO	R	RBI	SB	CS	OUT	BA	OBP	SLG	EQA	EQR	DEFENSE	
1998	Wichita	Tex	371	81	18	0	19	18	121	46	46	2	2	292	.218	.261	.420	.220	33	83-3B	-9
1999	Omaha	PCL	466	114	22	2	26	16	113	65	71	4	3	355	.245	.287	.468	.244	52	123-3B	-8
2000	Omaha	PCL	421	93	13	2	17	28	93	46	54	4	3	331	.221	.288	.382	.221	38	114-1B	2
2001	*KansasCy*	*AL*	*431*	*100*	*17*	*1*	*21*	*29*	*113*	*49*	*61*	*5*	*2*	*333*	*.232*	*.280*	*.422*	*.229*	*42*		

Kit Pellow moved from third base to first base for the 2000 season, officially killing his prospect status. Previously famous only for his Phil Hiatt impersonation, Pellow made news for a different reason last year, getting suspended for the final month of the season after an alleged run-in with his manager. The incident occurred just days after Pellow was quoted in *Sports Illustrated* as saying that he had witnessed former teammates using steroids. Regardless of the real reason for Pellow's suspension, if the Royals continue to use 1960s tactics to discipline ballplayers in the 2000s, they're going to get burnt.

Paul Phillips — C — Bats R — Age 24

YEAR	TEAM	LGE	AB	H	DB	TP	HR	BB	SO	R	RBI	SB	CS	OUT	BA	OBP	SLG	EQA	EQR	DEFENSE	
1998	Spokane	Nwn	234	57	8	1	3	9	22	31	15	4	1	178	.244	.277	.325	.199	16	47-C	-1
1999	Wichita	Tex	391	89	17	1	2	19	41	44	41	4	4	306	.228	.266	.292	.178	20	93-C	0
2000	Wichita	Tex	289	70	10	3	3	13	23	37	21	2	2	221	.242	.276	.329	.197	19	69-C	2
2001	*KansasCy*	*AL*	*289*	*73*	*10*	*2*	*3*	*15*	*28*	*27*	*28*	*2*	*2*	*218*	*.253*	*.289*	*.332*	*.203*	*20*		

Just two years after converting from the outfield, Paul Phillips has become an asset behind the plate defensively. He repeated Double-A last year, but his small-but-significant gains shouldn't be discounted because he had previously skipped a level of A ball. He's the closest thing the Royals have to a catching prospect, and while he played okay in the AFL, his outlook is more second-string than first. His upside might be Brian Harper with a better arm.

Scott Pose — OF — Bats L — Age 34

YEAR	TEAM	LGE	AB	H	DB	TP	HR	BB	SO	R	RBI	SB	CS	OUT	BA	OBP	SLG	EQA	EQR	DEFENSE	
1998	Columbus	Int	490	124	20	7	2	38	77	56	36	25	10	375	.253	.312	.335	.224	44	98-LF	-4
1999	KansasCy	AL	135	38	3	0	0	19	20	25	11	6	2	99	.281	.370	.304	.243	14	20-LF	-3
2000	KansasCy	AL	48	9	0	0	0	5	12	5	1	0	1	40	.188	.264	.188	.124	1		

Like Ordaz, Scott Pose spent all but three days on the Royals' active roster and played even less than the backup infielder: just 47 games and 48 at-bats. He's a favorite of Muser because he does his job (or more accurately, doesn't) without complaint, and who can blame him? He was 32 years old and had spent just a few months in the majors when Muser made him a fifth outfielder, earning him two years of major-league salary. You can't waste a bench spot on a player who plays in less than one-third of your games; the Royals need to clear out guys like Ordaz and Pose and quit playing with a 23-man roster.

Mark Quinn — LF — Bats R — Age 27

YEAR	TEAM	LGE	AB	H	DB	TP	HR	BB	SO	R	RBI	SB	CS	OUT	BA	OBP	SLG	EQA	EQR	DEFENSE	
1998	Wichita	Tex	366	99	20	3	10	30	61	54	53	2	1	268	.270	.335	.423	.254	43	81-RF	-3
1999	Omaha	PCL	416	126	15	0	20	22	67	49	62	5	6	296	.303	.348	.483	.270	56	97-RF	5
1999	KansasCy	AL	59	19	4	1	6	4	10	11	17	1	0	40	.322	.374	.729	.336	13	13-LF	0
2000	KansasCy	AL	494	144	30	2	21	29	83	71	73	5	2	352	.291	.335	.488	.269	66	81-LF	1
2000	Omaha	PCL	59	19	1	0	3	0	8	5	10	0	1	41	.322	.322	.492	.258	7	11-RF	1
2001	*KansasCy*	*AL*	*507*	*151*	*26*	*1*	*23*	*35*	*89*	*76*	*97*	*3*	*2*	*358*	*.298*	*.343*	*.489*	*.272*	*69*		

In case you hadn't heard, Mark Quinn is, uh, confident in himself. He also has ridiculously good hand-eye coordination, which is what it takes to hit .290 while corkscrewing yourself into the ground on every swing. The Royals' Rookie of the Year disappointments have fans a little skittish about the future of any Royals rookie. Whether you call it arrogance or self-assuredness, confidence is a necessary ingredient in the success of virtually any star player and is why I think that Quinn, despite his age, has better days ahead of him.

Joe Randa   3B   Bats R   Age 31

YEAR	TEAM	LGE	AB	H	DB	TP	HR	BB	SO	R	RBI	SB	CS	OUT	BA	OBP	SLG	EQA	EQR	DEFENSE			
1998	Detroit	AL	459	119	21	2	10	40	62	56	50	6	6	346	.259	.327	.379	.237	47	106-3B	7	13-2B	1
1999	KansasCy	AL	620	194	35	7	17	44	73	88	79	5	4	430	.313	.361	.474	.276	86	153-3B	2		
2000	KansasCy	AL	605	183	28	4	15	29	60	82	98	6	3	425	.302	.341	.436	.259	72	155-3B	6		
2001	KansasCy	AL	503	146	25	2	12	40	59	73	77	5	3	360	.290	.343	.419	.254	59				

Batting fifth or sixth all season, Joe Randa had plenty of RBI opportunities; the last player to drive in more runs with fewer extra-base hits was Lee May in 1976. Randa lost about 15 walks and 10 doubles from his 1999 season, which is the difference between a very good year and a year that, at age 31, hints at the decline to come. At his salary, he's still an asset.

Jeff Reboulet   IF   Bats R   Age 37

YEAR	TEAM	LGE	AB	H	DB	TP	HR	BB	SO	R	RBI	SB	CS	OUT	BA	OBP	SLG	EQA	EQR	DEFENSE			
1998	Baltimor	AL	126	33	3	0	2	19	30	20	9	0	1	94	.262	.367	.333	.244	14	17-SS	3	14-2B	2
1999	Baltimor	AL	154	27	4	0	0	31	26	24	4	1	0	127	.175	.320	.201	.188	10	29-3B	1	24-2B	6
2000	KansasCy	AL	180	43	7	0	0	21	29	27	13	3	1	138	.239	.318	.278	.207	13	41-2B	5		
2001	KansasCy	AL	142	31	4	0	0	25	26	19	10	2	1	112	.218	.335	.246	.206	11				

Jeff Reboulet didn't slug .188 again, and he drove in more runners (14) than he had the last two years combined (12). But he hasn't had a triple or home run since 1998, he slugged just .186 after the All-Star break, he no longer has the range for shortstop or the arm for third base, and he turns 37 in April. All of this is just a polite way of saying that after fashioning a far greater career for himself than most thought possible, it might be time for Reboulet to retire and start working on his second career: he's widely considered future manager material.

Rey Sanchez   SS   Bats R   Age 33

YEAR	TEAM	LGE	AB	H	DB	TP	HR	BB	SO	R	RBI	SB	CS	OUT	BA	OBP	SLG	EQA	EQR	DEFENSE			
1998	San Fran	NL	321	94	15	2	2	15	44	46	30	0	0	227	.293	.332	.371	.237	31	61-SS	2	21-2B	5
1999	KansasCy	AL	475	140	18	6	2	17	44	62	53	10	5	340	.295	.324	.371	.234	45	131-SS	24		
2000	KansasCy	AL	505	137	17	2	1	22	50	63	35	7	3	371	.271	.307	.319	.210	38	133-SS	25		
2001	KansasCy	AL	408	110	16	2	1	24	45	45	39	5	2	300	.270	.310	.326	.213	31				

He's everything that the other Rey—the one whose greatest contribution to the Mets was missing most of 2000—is supposed to be. Sanchez has outstanding range, positions himself well, made just four errors all year, and spearheaded a middle infield that ranked first in the majors by converting 64% of its double-play opportunities. Despite that, it's still difficult to argue that he's an asset, because his .210 EqA was the second-lowest in baseball (minimum: 400 plate appearances). Batting Sanchez second between two players who would go on to set team records for runs scored and RBI may be the silliest thing Tony Muser has ever done.

Mike Sweeney   1B   Bats R   Age 27

YEAR	TEAM	LGE	AB	H	DB	TP	HR	BB	SO	R	RBI	SB	CS	OUT	BA	OBP	SLG	EQA	EQR	DEFENSE	
1998	KansasCy	AL	281	74	13	0	10	23	34	32	35	2	3	210	.263	.323	.416	.244	31	83-C	-2
1999	KansasCy	AL	567	182	42	2	23	48	44	97	97	6	1	386	.321	.383	.524	.299	94	69-1B	-10
2000	KansasCy	AL	606	201	23	0	31	63	61	98	135	8	3	408	.332	.408	.523	.309	108	110-1B	5
2001	KansasCy	AL	547	179	24	0	31	62	56	107	129	7	2	370	.327	.396	.541	.307	97		

Fans outside of Kansas City are only beginning to get a glimpse of Mike Sweeney's character, which may be more remarkable than his talent. The man is unfailingly polite to his manager, reporters, fans, and the guy who cleans out the urinals in the clubhouse. It is simply impossible to find anyone who has a bad thing to say about him. Of course, Paul Molitor was a pillar of Christian values right up to the moment he admitted he was a cocaine addict. Nevertheless, if Mike Sweeney is ever caught with a prostitute, or smoking crack, or smoking crack with a prostitute, I may swear off the game permanently. Sweeney can play a little baseball, too. He hits the ball harder than any Royal since George Brett and is a better bet than Dye to smack 40 home runs this year.

American League

Gregg Zaun — C — Bats B — Age 30

YEAR	TEAM	LGE	AB	H	DB	TP	HR	BB	SO	R	RBI	SB	CS	OUT	BA	OBP	SLG	EQA	EQR	DEFENSE
1998	Florida	NL	303	60	12	2	6	34	49	20	31	5	2	245	.198	.281	.310	.199	22	84-C -1
1999	Texas	AL	92	23	1	1	1	9	6	11	11	1	0	69	.250	.317	.315	.217	8	26-C 2
2000	KansasCy	AL	230	62	7	0	8	40	31	33	31	7	4	172	.270	.385	.404	.272	33	65-C -6
2001	KansasCy	AL	196	47	6	0	5	30	27	29	24	4	3	152	.240	.341	.347	.236	20	

It was a good year for the Practically Perfect Backup Catcher. Gregg Zaun was actually the closest thing to a first-stringer on the Royals, and you would think a .390 OBP would garner him more consideration as a possible starter for 2001. Instead, the Royals are looking to trade for Ben Davis or some other defensive whiz who's a non-factor at the plate. Zaun threw out just 19% of base stealers, though in his defense he missed six weeks early in the season with a torn elbow ligament. A team as right-handed as the Royals are can't afford to throw away a switch-hitter who can give them 300 quality at-bats while playing a key defensive position.

PITCHERS (ERA: 4.50, H/9: 9.00, HR/9: 1.00, BB/9: 3.00, K/9: 6.00, KW: 1.00, PERA: 4.50)

Jeff Austin — Throws R — Age 24

YEAR	TEAM	LGE	IP	H	ER	HR	BB	K	ERA	W	L	H/9	HR/9	BB/9	K/9	KW	PERA
1999	Wilmngtn	Car	100.3	118	71	23	47	50	6.37	3	8	10.58	2.06	4.22	4.49	0.53	7.07
1999	Wichita	Tex	32.7	37	17	1	12	13	4.68	2	2	10.19	0.28	3.31	3.58	0.54	4.54
2000	Wichita	Tex	40.3	33	17	4	4	19	3.79	2	2	7.36	0.89	0.89	4.24	2.38	2.70
2000	Omaha	PCL	121.0	140	81	21	35	41	6.02	4	9	10.41	1.56	2.60	3.05	0.59	5.76

Two years after the Royals gave him the biggest signing bonus in team history, Jeff Austin is a greater enigma than ever. He was supposed to have the stuff of a #3 starter but the mind of an ace; his pitches are slightly better than advertised, but a guy with a feel for pitching should know how to punch out more than 57 Triple-A batters in 127 innings. You wouldn't expect a #1 pick two years out of college to be sent to the instructional league, but Austin is clearly missing something. The Royals were hoping that Brent Strom could help him find it.

Ryan Baerlocher — Throws R — Age 23

YEAR	TEAM	LGE	IP	H	ER	HR	BB	K	ERA	W	L	H/9	HR/9	BB/9	K/9	KW	PERA
1999	Spokane	Nwn	69.0	80	47	14	36	34	6.13	2	6	10.43	1.83	4.70	4.43	0.47	6.92
2000	Charl-WV	SAL	100.7	102	66	16	45	64	5.90	3	8	9.12	1.43	4.02	5.72	0.71	5.46
2000	Wilmngtn	Car	45.7	40	28	8	21	28	5.52	2	3	7.88	1.58	4.14	5.52	0.67	4.92

Ryan Baerlocher was a sixth-round pick in 1999. All he did in his first full professional season was record the second-most strikeouts (193) in the minor leagues. He's still in the low minors, but keep in mind that unlike hitters, pitchers frequently make the jump from A ball to the major leagues in less than a year. Realistically, Baerlocher is unlikely to make any sort of contribution to the Royals in 2001, but he remains one of the best sleeper pitching prospects in baseball.

Ricky Bottalico — Throws R — Age 31

YEAR	TEAM	LGE	IP	H	ER	HR	BB	K	ERA	W	L	H/9	HR/9	BB/9	K/9	KW	PERA
1998	Philadel	NL	42.0	53	30	7	23	22	6.43	1	4	11.36	1.50	4.93	4.71	0.48	7.26
1999	St Louis	NL	72.3	81	41	7	41	55	5.10	3	5	10.08	0.87	5.10	6.84	0.67	5.87
2000	KansasCy	AL	73.3	60	31	9	31	53	3.80	4	4	7.36	1.10	3.80	6.50	0.85	3.98

A lot was made of the fact that Ricky Bottalico's ERA was below 2.00 in outings of two innings or more, a statistic that ignores a huge selection bias: Bottalico would stay in the game to pitch a second inning only if he had thrown well in the first. He terrified Royals fans all season with his taterrific tendencies (surrendering five homers to first batters faced), but his RRE value—one of Michael Wolverton's metrics—was the highest on the team. While it wouldn't have been a terrible decision to bring him back, the Royals will be better served by taking a chance with their youngsters. Bottalico signed with the Phillies and could close for them once Jose Mesa fails.

Kiko Calero — Throws R — Age 27

YEAR	TEAM	LGE	IP	H	ER	HR	BB	K	ERA	W	L	H/9	HR/9	BB/9	K/9	KW	PERA
1998	Wilmngtn	Car	80.7	80	54	18	79	41	6.02	3	6	8.93	2.01	8.81	4.57	0.26	7.93
1999	Wichita	Tex	119.0	140	75	22	69	53	5.67	4	9	10.59	1.66	5.22	4.01	0.38	7.06
2000	Wichita	Tex	141.0	144	87	25	72	73	5.55	5	11	9.19	1.60	4.60	4.66	0.51	5.90

Kiko Calero has pitched for the Wranglers for four straight seasons; Joe Sheehan likes to make fun of minor leaguers who have been consigned to spend years in places like Little Rock, Arkansas, or Midland, Texas, but I grew up in Wichita, so there will be no jokes here. Calero had always shown flashes of major-league stuff in the past; his breakthrough in 2000 came because he found a way to eliminate the 30% of starts in which he got ripped apart like a Firestone tire. He saved his best start, a one-hit shutout, for the Texas League playoffs. Even at his age, I think he'll sip some coffee before all is said and done.

Jared Camp — Throws R — Age 26

YEAR	TEAM	LGE	IP	H	ER	HR	BB	K	ERA	W	L	H/9	HR/9	BB/9	K/9	KW	PERA
1998	Akron	Eas	79.3	82	42	12	35	25	4.76	4	5	9.30	1.36	3.97	2.84	0.36	5.47
1999	Kinston	Car	48.7	53	20	5	21	27	3.70	3	2	9.80	0.92	3.88	4.99	0.64	5.26
2000	Akron	Eas	15.0	31	29	12	8	8	17.40	0	2	18.60	7.20	4.80	4.80	0.50	17.48
2000	Omaha	PCL	11.7	19	26	6	14	9	20.06	0	1	14.66	4.63	10.80	6.94	0.32	14.91

The prize of last season's Rule 5 draft after being clocked at 98 mph in the AFL in 1999, Jared Camp wasn't able to stick with the Marlins and ended up pitching in the Indians' and Rangers' systems before he was claimed by Kansas City. To their credit, the Royals gave him more than six weeks to work out his control problems and sent him back to the AFL for a brief, successful stint. He's a gamble, but one worth taking: you won't find many 26-year-old prospects with an upside this high.

Jeff D'Amico — Throws R — Age 26

YEAR	TEAM	LGE	IP	H	ER	HR	BB	K	ERA	W	L	H/9	HR/9	BB/9	K/9	KW	PERA
1999	Midland	Tex	42.7	52	32	5	18	23	6.75	1	4	10.97	1.05	3.80	4.85	0.64	6.06
2000	Omaha	PCL	85.0	87	45	23	28	44	4.76	4	5	9.21	2.44	2.96	4.66	0.79	6.12
2000	KansasCy	AL	14.3	18	12	2	11	9	7.53	0	2	11.30	1.26	6.91	5.65	0.41	7.70

On the continuum between "thrower" and "pitcher," this Jeff D'Amico (not to be confused with the Brewers' hurler) is a lot closer to the former. He's finally figured out that the batter doesn't have to swing if the pitch isn't a strike, but the lessons on changing speeds and keeping the ball down still haven't taken. If he can learn either lesson, he may yet have a future as a reliever, though it might require several years and several organizations for him to reach that point.

Chad Durbin — Throws R — Age 23

YEAR	TEAM	LGE	IP	H	ER	HR	BB	K	ERA	W	L	H/9	HR/9	BB/9	K/9	KW	PERA
1998	Wilmngtn	Car	128.7	138	81	22	81	84	5.67	5	9	9.65	1.54	5.67	5.88	0.52	6.57
1999	Wichita	Tex	147.0	153	97	28	54	78	5.94	5	11	9.37	1.71	3.31	4.78	0.72	5.60
2000	KansasCy	AL	73.3	84	57	11	32	35	7.00	2	6	10.31	1.35	3.93	4.30	0.55	6.01
2000	Omaha	PCL	69.0	72	38	13	22	39	4.96	3	5	9.39	1.70	2.87	5.09	0.89	5.41

His four-pitch repertoire and preternatural poise notwithstanding, Chad Durbin became yet another data point for the argument that rookie pitchers—all of them—belong in long relief. Durbin became more and more tentative with each start, allowing two base runners an inning after giving up just one hit in his first outing. He caught his breath at Omaha—remember, he made the rotation straight out of Double-A—so his future is still bright.

Chris Fussell — Throws R — Age 25

YEAR	TEAM	LGE	IP	H	ER	HR	BB	K	ERA	W	L	H/9	HR/9	BB/9	K/9	KW	PERA
1998	Bowie	Eas	84.3	91	67	20	58	51	7.15	2	7	9.71	2.13	6.19	5.44	0.44	7.44
1998	Rochestr	Int	55.7	49	31	5	27	37	5.01	2	4	7.92	0.81	4.37	5.98	0.69	4.21
1999	Omaha	PCL	77.3	63	35	12	28	54	4.07	4	5	7.33	1.40	3.26	6.28	0.96	4.04
1999	KansasCy	AL	57.0	68	43	7	28	35	6.79	2	4	10.74	1.11	4.42	5.53	0.63	6.24
2000	KansasCy	AL	71.3	70	40	14	33	44	5.05	3	5	8.83	1.77	4.16	5.55	0.67	5.69

Here's another example of a pitcher with major-league stuff who hurt his arm before he learned how to use it. Chris Fussell has frustrated the Royals since he was acquired for Jeff Conine. He can be dominant for stretches of an inning or two but has yet to find anything resembling consistency. He tweaked his arm midseason and missed two months; when he was recalled in September, Muser went out of his way to avoid using him. His future in this organization is probably over.

Chris George — Throws L — Age 21

YEAR	TEAM	LGE	IP	H	ER	HR	BB	K	ERA	W	L	H/9	HR/9	BB/9	K/9	KW	PERA
1999	Wilmngtn	Car	131.3	151	80	18	62	75	5.48	5	10	10.35	1.23	4.25	5.14	0.60	6.05
2000	Wichita	Tex	92.0	90	41	7	51	50	4.01	5	5	8.80	0.68	4.99	4.89	0.49	4.88
2000	Omaha	PCL	42.3	46	31	11	20	20	6.59	1	4	9.78	2.34	4.25	4.25	0.50	6.91

Chris George is a rare phenomenon. Despite his superficially unimpressive performance record, analysts and scouts are almost universally in agreement that he is one awesome prospect. After wowing everyone in 1999 with his understanding of how to pitch, he showed up last year with a couple mph added to his fastball. Despite episodic battles with control—like an adolescent struggling with his coordination after a growth spurt—he ascended to the top of the class among left-handed pitching prospects. His supporting role on the U.S. Olympic team has the Royals thinking that he is almost ready to be unleashed on major-league hitters. If the Royals do their best impression of the 1991 Braves in the next year or two, here's their Steve Avery.

Jimmy Gobble — Throws L — Age 19

YEAR	TEAM	LGE	IP	H	ER	HR	BB	K	ERA	W	L	H/9	HR/9	BB/9	K/9	KW	PERA
2000	Charl-WV	SAL	131.3	153	99	26	45	54	6.78	4	11	10.48	1.78	3.08	3.70	0.60	6.25

Like George, Jimmy Gobble is a left-handed pitcher drafted out of high school in the first supplemental round. His performance in his first full season, while not as impressive as George's, was still plenty good. He was dominant in the second half (8–3, 2.61 ERA, 71 to 15 strikeout-to-walk ratio after June 19). He throws a little harder and with better control than George did a year ago, but he lacks George's knack for changing speeds and moving the ball around. He's only two years away, so prepare now for more lame turkey jokes than you ever thought possible.

Junior Guerrero — Throws R — Age 21

YEAR	TEAM	LGE	IP	H	ER	HR	BB	K	ERA	W	L	H/9	HR/9	BB/9	K/9	KW	PERA
1999	Charl-WV	SAL	91.7	97	52	13	62	52	5.11	4	6	9.52	1.28	6.09	5.11	0.42	6.37
1999	Wilmngtn	Car	46.0	35	15	5	31	36	2.93	3	2	6.85	0.98	6.07	7.04	0.58	4.49
2000	Wichita	Tex	122.7	152	99	36	68	49	7.26	3	11	11.15	2.64	4.99	3.60	0.36	8.33

We labeled him the best pitching prospect in the system a year ago, which in hindsight was pretty damn foolish. Julio Guerrero is essentially a one-pitch pitcher, never mind that said pitch is a fastball with plus-plus velocity and movement. He pitched well after going to the bullpen in August, a move reminiscent of ex-phenom Orber Moreno, who went from failed starter to Jeff Montgomery's heir apparent in a year before missing the last two seasons following Tommy John surgery. As a reliever, Guerrero could arrive sometime this year and has the ability to make an immediate impact.

Andy Larkin — Throws R — Age 27

YEAR	TEAM	LGE	IP	H	ER	HR	BB	K	ERA	W	L	H/9	HR/9	BB/9	K/9	KW	PERA
1998	Charlott	Int	52.0	54	37	8	29	29	6.40	2	4	9.35	1.38	5.02	5.02	0.50	5.96
1998	Florida	NL	71.7	98	86	13	52	35	10.80	1	7	12.31	1.63	6.53	4.40	0.34	8.58
2000	Louisvil	Int	39.0	31	15	5	17	28	3.46	2	2	7.15	1.15	3.92	6.46	0.82	3.95
2000	KansasCy	AL	19.7	27	16	4	8	16	7.32	0	2	12.36	1.83	3.66	7.32	1.00	7.59

The former Marlin prospect was claimed on waivers from the Reds in July. Despite an ERA approaching 9.00, he survived the season in Kansas City. For those of us who still cringe at the memory of the Tim Pugh Transaction War fought between the Reds and Royals in 1998, that's just as well. Larkin has little or no future. Signed by the Rockies, so he's now closer to "no" than "little."

Brett Laxton — Throws R — Age 27

YEAR	TEAM	LGE	IP	H	ER	HR	BB	K	ERA	W	L	H/9	HR/9	BB/9	K/9	KW	PERA
1998	Huntsvil	Sou	121.7	105	64	7	82	49	4.73	6	8	7.77	0.52	6.07	3.62	0.30	4.53
1998	Edmonton	PCL	44.0	41	34	7	25	14	6.95	1	4	8.39	1.43	5.11	2.86	0.28	5.46
1999	Vancouvr	PCL	150.7	144	71	12	63	70	4.24	8	9	8.60	0.72	3.76	4.18	0.56	4.28
2000	Omaha	PCL	102.3	111	69	6	67	59	6.07	3	8	9.76	0.53	5.89	5.19	0.44	5.65

(Brett Laxton *continued*)

Tony Muser's greatest weakness as a manager is his unwillingness to accept that some players have value despite, not because of, their work ethic. As disappointing as Giambi's season was, the Royals' atrocious bench missed him desperately, while Laxton was little more than the Golden Spikes' #3 starter for most of the season. Laxton's freakish ability to keep the ball down—he allowed just four home runs in 2000—is the one thing on his résumé that portends success.

Mike MacDougal — Throws R — Age 24

YEAR	TEAM	LGE	IP	H	ER	HR	BB	K	ERA	W	L	H/9	HR/9	BB/9	K/9	KW	PERA
1999	Spokane	Nwn	42.3	47	30	6	20	28	6.38	1	4	9.99	1.28	4.25	5.95	0.70	5.91
2000	Wilmngtn	Car	128.0	121	103	13	97	64	7.24	3	11	8.51	0.91	6.82	4.50	0.33	5.71

Here's a great example of how success in the minor leagues is gauged differently than in the majors. Mike MacDougal's performance in 2000 left something to be desired, but the Royals don't mind. His slider was the class of the 1999 draft, but the Royals insisted he work on developing his other pitches, and he finished the season with people raving about the late, heavy sink on his new-and-improved fastball. The movement on his pitches can sometimes be a problem (he led the organization with 22 wild pitches), but the Royals are ecstatic about his progress, as he was promoted to Double-A late in the season and finished by pitching well in the Texas League playoffs.

Brian Meadows — Throws R — Age 25

YEAR	TEAM	LGE	IP	H	ER	HR	BB	K	ERA	W	L	H/9	HR/9	BB/9	K/9	KW	PERA
1998	Florida	NL	166.3	212	104	22	44	71	5.63	6	12	11.47	1.19	2.38	3.84	0.81	5.90
1999	Florida	NL	172.3	202	109	31	49	61	5.69	6	13	10.55	1.62	2.56	3.19	0.62	5.89
2000	San Dieg	NL	120.0	144	77	25	45	44	5.78	4	9	10.80	1.88	3.38	3.30	0.49	6.65
2000	KansasCy	AL	70.7	76	32	6	11	25	4.08	4	4	9.68	0.76	1.40	3.18	1.14	4.00

The challenge trade of Jay Witasick for Brian Meadows was a peculiar one, with the Royals essentially swapping a high-risk, high-upside pitcher for a guy who peaked in his rookie season. For now, the Royals can claim they made a good deal, as Meadows cut his walks in half after the trade and kept his ERA under 5.00. If Meadows keeps giving up fewer than two walks per nine innings, he'll continue to have value as a fifth starter/long reliever, but the Padres may end up thanking the Royals this year for doing the dirty work of developing Jay Witasick into an effective pitcher.

Robbie Morrison — Throws R — Age 24

YEAR	TEAM	LGE	IP	H	ER	HR	BB	K	ERA	W	L	H/9	HR/9	BB/9	K/9	KW	PERA
1998	Spokane	Nwn	22.7	18	11	5	20	17	4.37	1	2	7.15	1.99	7.94	6.75	0.43	6.47
1999	Wilmngtn	Car	39.3	35	19	5	16	24	4.35	2	2	8.01	1.14	3.66	5.49	0.75	4.35
1999	Wichita	Tex	21.0	26	8	1	8	13	3.43	1	1	11.14	0.43	3.43	5.57	0.81	5.36
2000	Wichita	Tex	57.3	58	33	9	29	30	5.18	2	4	9.10	1.41	4.55	4.71	0.52	5.64

Robbie Morrison has been the supposed closer-in-waiting ever since he was drafted in the second round in 1998, the highest draft pick the Royals had ever used on a reliever. He stumbled a little bit in Double-A last year; his strikeouts were down, a bigger concern than the hits and walks he gave up. He's been passed by Shawn Sonnier on the reliever depth chart, but he's still a very good prospect. The Royals have a number of cheap, effective alternatives to spending millions on free agents to help their bullpen.

Scott Mullen — Throws L — Age 26

YEAR	TEAM	LGE	IP	H	ER	HR	BB	K	ERA	W	L	H/9	HR/9	BB/9	K/9	KW	PERA
1998	Wilmngtn	Car	75.7	69	38	10	37	27	4.52	4	4	8.21	1.19	4.40	3.21	0.36	4.81
1998	Wichita	Tex	65.7	63	35	9	29	27	4.80	3	4	8.63	1.23	3.97	3.70	0.47	4.94
1999	Wichita	Tex	46.0	44	28	3	21	18	5.48	2	3	8.61	0.59	4.11	3.52	0.43	4.27
1999	Omaha	PCL	114.3	139	86	26	56	58	6.77	3	10	10.94	2.05	4.41	4.57	0.52	7.34
2000	Wichita	Tex	67.7	65	30	8	28	34	3.99	4	4	8.65	1.06	3.72	4.52	0.61	4.64

After falling so far off the prospect map that he was removed from the 40-man roster last winter, Scott Mullen converted to relief as a last resort. When a starter moves into the bullpen and thrives, it's supposed to be because he can use just one or two pitches, or because he has the mentality of an everyday player, or because he can't focus for more than an inning at a time. None of those things apply to Mullen, but the conversion worked anyway, as he finished the year the top left-hander in the Royals' bullpen. He's everything Tim Byrdak was supposed to be: a lefty specialist with a three-quarters delivery that neutralizes left-handed hitters and enough stuff to keep right-handed hitters in check.

Dan Murray — Throws R — Age 27

YEAR	TEAM	LGE	IP	H	ER	HR	BB	K	ERA	W	L	H/9	HR/9	BB/9	K/9	KW	PERA
1998	Binghmtn	Eas	151.3	159	77	19	60	89	4.58	7	10	9.46	1.13	3.57	5.29	0.74	5.14
1999	Norfolk	Int	136.7	145	92	26	73	65	6.06	5	10	9.55	1.71	4.81	4.28	0.45	6.33
2000	Omaha	PCL	131.0	145	108	31	65	69	7.42	3	12	9.96	2.13	4.47	4.74	0.53	6.87
2000	KansasCy	AL	19.7	18	7	5	8	15	3.20	1	1	8.24	2.29	3.66	6.86	0.94	5.70

The "bounty" from the trades of Jeremy Giambi and Glendon Rusch was on display in Omaha all year, boldly proclaiming that the Royals' era of being ripped off in trades hardly ended with Ed Hearn and Felix Jose. Unlike Laxton, Dan Murray can't even keep the ball down (he gave up six homers in six innings during a June call-up). The Royals recalled him in September with the excuse that his fastball had gained velocity with improved mechanics. While he did pitch better, you can't help but think that Rusch's breakout season with the Mets embarrassed the Royals enough to pull Murray out of the minor leagues.

Dan Reichert — Throws R — Age 24

YEAR	TEAM	LGE	IP	H	ER	HR	BB	K	ERA	W	L	H/9	HR/9	BB/9	K/9	KW	PERA
1998	Lansing	Mid	32.3	27	20	2	23	18	5.57	1	3	7.52	0.56	6.40	5.01	0.39	4.57
1998	Wichita	Tex	34.0	50	39	9	31	16	10.32	1	3	13.24	2.38	8.21	4.24	0.26	10.64
1999	Omaha	PCL	106.3	89	51	9	52	84	4.32	6	6	7.53	0.76	4.40	7.11	0.81	3.98
1999	KansasCy	AL	37.7	46	33	2	25	19	7.88	1	3	10.99	0.48	5.97	4.54	0.38	6.38
2000	KansasCy	AL	154.7	147	74	11	69	90	4.31	8	9	8.55	0.64	4.02	5.24	0.65	4.28

The Royals began the season with two highly-touted rookies on their pitching staff. Chad Durbin got shelled in two different stints in the rotation. Dan Reichert, who was awful during a rotation trial in 1999, started in the bullpen and pitched so well that he was promoted to the rotation in June. This is not a coincidence, friends. Reichert has the most electrifying and exasperating stuff on the team, best exhibited when he walked nine Yankees in one start without allowing a run. If Jose Rosado is healthy, the Royals may benefit by once again using Reichert as a middle-relief weapon. Reichert had the highest ground-ball/fly-ball ratio of any pitcher in baseball (minimum: 150 innings) and has the highest upside of any pitcher in the organization.

Jose Rosado — Throws L — Age 26

YEAR	TEAM	LGE	IP	H	ER	HR	BB	K	ERA	W	L	H/9	HR/9	BB/9	K/9	KW	PERA
1998	KansasCy	AL	172.3	168	90	21	47	125	4.70	8	11	8.77	1.10	2.45	6.53	1.33	4.24
1999	KansasCy	AL	206.3	182	84	19	55	134	3.66	13	10	7.94	0.83	2.40	5.84	1.22	3.49
2000	KansasCy	AL	27.7	27	15	3	7	14	4.88	1	2	8.78	0.98	2.28	4.55	1.00	4.09

In an era when even small-market teams have payrolls higher than $25 million a year, how much money should a team invest in protecting its assets from injury? Jose Rosado made $3 million last season. Would you spend $1,500 to insure a $3-million asset? That's how much an MRI exam costs. Rosado complained of a tired arm in late April, but the Royals shook it off as a normal reaction to losing part of spring training to a hamstring problem. Rosado took the mound for his next start, willed his way to a win, and his arm came up dead. *Then* the Royals got the MRI. Rosado rested for two months, eventually had surgery, and everyone is holding their breath to see whether he'll be back at full strength this season. In any other business, a management team that showed such careless disregard for one of its prime assets would be sacked at the first opportunity. In baseball, they get promoted.

Brian Sanches — Throws R — Age 22

YEAR	TEAM	LGE	IP	H	ER	HR	BB	K	ERA	W	L	H/9	HR/9	BB/9	K/9	KW	PERA
1999	Spokane	Nwn	31.0	36	23	4	14	26	6.68	1	2	10.45	1.16	4.06	7.55	0.93	5.98
2000	Wilmngtn	Car	142.0	140	100	22	82	65	6.34	5	11	8.87	1.39	5.20	4.12	0.40	5.76

Like MacDougal, Brian Sanches was a high draft pick in 1999. The two were teammates at Wilmington last year. Sanches is the more polished pitcher and did perform better than MacDougal, tossing a no-hitter early in the season. His upside isn't as high as MacDougal's; how Double-A hitters respond to his thus-far dominant curveball should tell us just how high it is.

Jose Santiago — Throws R — Age 26

YEAR	TEAM	LGE	IP	H	ER	HR	BB	K	ERA	W	L	H/9	HR/9	BB/9	K/9	KW	PERA
1998	Wichita	Tex	68.0	74	36	12	30	20	4.76	3	5	9.79	1.59	3.97	2.65	0.33	5.99
1999	KansasCy	AL	46.7	42	18	5	11	14	3.47	3	2	8.10	0.96	2.12	2.70	0.64	3.61
2000	KansasCy	AL	68.7	65	27	5	20	42	3.54	4	4	8.52	0.66	2.62	5.50	1.05	3.73

This is where relievers come from. Jose Santiago, a 70th-round draft pick in 1994, was thoroughly mediocre throughout his minor-league career and has now posted two solid seasons as the Royals' setup man. His bread and butter is a fastball with average velocity but a nice sink. He was briefly demoted to Omaha when he lost faith in the pitch and started going to his slider instead. Getting performances like this from non-arbitration-eligible players is what lower-revenue teams need to stay in the hunt.

Shawn Sonnier — Throws R — Age 24

YEAR	TEAM	LGE	IP	H	ER	HR	BB	K	ERA	W	L	H/9	HR/9	BB/9	K/9	KW	PERA
1999	Wilmngtn	Car	53.7	51	25	2	23	38	4.19	3	3	8.55	0.34	3.86	6.37	0.83	3.91
2000	Wichita	Tex	59.0	47	29	9	26	55	4.42	3	4	7.17	1.37	3.97	8.39	1.06	4.21

From modest beginnings as a non-drafted free agent, Shawn Sonnier has risen to become the rarest of breeds, a minor-league closer who is also a real prospect. He saved 21 games for the Wranglers last year with more than twice as many strikeouts (90) as hits allowed (41). A strikeout-to-hit ratio of greater than 2 to 1 is a prerequisite for a closer prospect; Armando Benitez was regularly above 3 to 1. Sonnier was outstanding in the AFL; if the Royals drop him into their bullpen this April, he's got a chance to be their Jeff Zimmerman.

Paul Spoljaric — Throws L — Age 30

YEAR	TEAM	LGE	IP	H	ER	HR	BB	K	ERA	W	L	H/9	HR/9	BB/9	K/9	KW	PERA
1998	Seattle	AL	83.0	81	60	13	48	82	6.51	2	7	8.78	1.41	5.20	8.89	0.85	5.72
1999	Toronto	AL	62.3	59	35	7	26	60	5.05	3	4	8.52	1.01	3.75	8.66	1.15	4.56
2000	Omaha	PCL	47.7	45	20	7	21	38	3.78	3	2	8.50	1.32	3.97	7.17	0.90	4.96

The Royals were so desperate for pitching from the left side that they had Ralph Nader outfitted for a uniform; their total of 54 innings by left-handed pitchers was the fewest by an AL team since 1947. This makes their snub of Spoljaric all the more puzzling. He got a call-up in mid-May that lasted less than two innings before he was sent down, and Muser angrily snapped that he was brought up only because it was mandated in his contract. Meanwhile, Tim Byrdak got multiple chances to prove that he isn't a major-league pitcher. Spoljaric signed with the Devil Rays and will one day be an integral part of a deep, effective bullpen.

Blake Stein — Throws R — Age 27

YEAR	TEAM	LGE	IP	H	ER	HR	BB	K	ERA	W	L	H/9	HR/9	BB/9	K/9	KW	PERA
1998	Oakland	AL	116.0	110	81	20	61	82	6.28	4	9	8.53	1.55	4.73	6.36	0.67	5.51
1999	Vancouvr	PCL	100.3	91	66	14	55	70	5.92	3	8	8.16	1.26	4.93	6.28	0.64	5.07
1999	KansasCy	AL	70.7	55	27	8	32	41	3.44	5	3	7.00	1.02	4.08	5.22	0.64	3.82
2000	KansasCy	AL	108.7	91	45	15	43	75	3.73	6	6	7.54	1.24	3.56	6.21	0.87	4.13

Blake Stein is practically all that the Royals got for Kevin Appier, yet he alone may justify the trade. The line drive that broke his arm in spring training and cost him half a season may be a blessing in the long term, as he was worked pretty hard after he returned. Stein has that rare rising fastball that hitters will chase, only occasionally dumping it into the bleachers. He is a big guy and, at 28, the old man in the rotation, so the Royals would do well to ride him for 35 starts and 240 innings this year.

Jeff Suppan — Throws R — Age 26

YEAR	TEAM	LGE	IP	H	ER	HR	BB	K	ERA	W	L	H/9	HR/9	BB/9	K/9	KW	PERA
1998	Arizona	NL	63.7	79	53	12	19	32	7.49	2	5	11.17	1.70	2.69	4.52	0.84	6.40
1998	Tucson	PCL	64.7	71	27	4	17	43	3.76	4	3	9.88	0.56	2.37	5.98	1.26	4.30
1999	KansasCy	AL	206.3	203	92	22	48	98	4.01	11	12	8.85	0.96	2.09	4.27	1.02	4.00
2000	KansasCy	AL	217.0	220	97	28	63	122	4.02	12	12	9.12	1.16	2.61	5.06	0.97	4.58

Jeff Suppan highlights the pros and cons of Brent Strom's approach. Forced to use his curveball and fosh change-up as secondary pitches, he struggled most of the season. In September, his fastball started breaking 90 mph regularly for the first time in his career, and he went 8–3 with a 3.99 ERA after the All-Star break. Suppan's performance this year is probably the best litmus test for whether Strom's ideas are inspired or just insane.

Mac Suzuki — Throws R — Age 26

YEAR	TEAM	LGE	IP	H	ER	HR	BB	K	ERA	W	L	H/9	HR/9	BB/9	K/9	KW	PERA
1998	Tacoma	PCL	122.3	126	78	26	80	81	5.74	5	9	9.27	1.91	5.89	5.96	0.51	6.82
1998	Seattle	AL	26.3	32	21	3	13	18	7.18	1	2	10.94	1.03	4.44	6.15	0.69	6.29
1999	KansasCy	AL	68.0	71	37	7	23	34	4.90	3	5	9.40	0.93	3.04	4.50	0.74	4.67
1999	Seattle	AL	42.7	45	40	6	27	31	8.44	1	4	9.49	1.27	5.70	6.54	0.57	6.19
2000	KansasCy	AL	190.0	181	80	20	71	129	3.79	11	10	8.57	0.95	3.36	6.11	0.91	4.34

The case for Brent Strom rides primarily on Mac Suzuki, who hadn't posted a successful season since he pitched for San Bernardino in 1993, then emerged as the Royals' quasi-ace last year. It's not coincidental that Suzuki's fastball was the best on the staff, but there was more than that to his success: Strom had Suzuki slow down his delivery in spring training; while base runners took advantage (27 of 28 on steal attempts), the consistency in his delivery made his splitter that much more believable. Suzuki had his rotator cuff cleaned up after the season. He's probably not going to get better than he was in 2000 unless he develops a real off-speed pitch.

Corey Thurman — Throws R — Age 22

YEAR	TEAM	LGE	IP	H	ER	HR	BB	K	ERA	W	L	H/9	HR/9	BB/9	K/9	KW	PERA
1998	Spokane	Nwn	56.7	71	35	7	35	25	5.56	2	4	11.28	1.11	5.56	3.97	0.36	7.02
1998	Lansing	Mid	55.7	53	42	13	34	31	6.79	2	4	8.57	2.10	5.50	5.01	0.46	6.43
1999	Wilmngtn	Car	134.7	169	109	25	75	69	7.28	3	12	11.29	1.67	5.01	4.61	0.46	7.40
2000	Wilmngtn	Car	104.3	103	43	15	54	51	3.71	6	6	8.88	1.29	4.66	4.40	0.47	5.42
2000	Wichita	Tex	46.3	49	40	14	24	29	7.77	1	4	9.52	2.72	4.66	5.63	0.60	7.32

How do you know that an organization has pitching depth? When a guy like Corey Thurman, who went 10–5 with a 2.26 ERA for Wilmington, hardly gets mentioned, you have pitching depth. Despite being in his fifth professional season, Thurman is actually younger than both MacDougal and Sanches. He attributed his breakout season to improved focus on the mound, which sounds a lot better than, "Well, I was only 20 last year, and I'm still developing physically." The Royals need to see another year in the minor leagues to know whether his future is as a starter or as a reliever.

Kris Wilson — Throws R — Age 24

YEAR	TEAM	LGE	IP	H	ER	HR	BB	K	ERA	W	L	H/9	HR/9	BB/9	K/9	KW	PERA
1998	Lansing	Mid	109.3	121	55	15	17	38	4.53	5	7	9.96	1.23	1.40	3.13	1.12	4.65
1999	Wilmngtn	Car	43.7	28	10	2	13	23	2.06	4	1	5.77	0.41	2.68	4.74	0.88	2.14
1999	Wichita	Tex	70.3	88	52	15	15	29	6.65	2	6	11.26	1.92	1.92	3.71	0.97	6.35
2000	Wichita	Tex	96.0	98	57	17	21	42	5.34	4	7	9.19	1.59	1.97	3.94	1.00	4.81
2000	KansasCy	AL	34.0	35	13	2	8	16	3.44	2	2	9.26	0.53	2.12	4.24	1.00	3.81

The gutsiest decision Allard Baird made after taking over as GM was to promote Kris Wilson, who was starting in Double-A, directly to the Royals' bullpen. Wilson has never overpowered hitters but does a good job of moving his fastball around and throwing strikes with it. In the long term, Wilson still projects as a starter; for this season, the Royals hope he can give them something they haven't had since Rusty Meacham in 1992: 100 innings of high-leverage relief, delivered two innings at a time.

Support-Neutral Statistics — KANSAS CITY ROYALS — Park Effect: +6.1%

PITCHER	GS	IP	R	SNW	SNL	SNPCT	W	L	RA	APW	SNVA	SNWAR
Miguel Batista	9	48.0	39	1.7	4.2	.288	1	6	7.31	-0.9	-1.2	-0.8
Jeff M. D'Amico	1	2.0	8	0.0	0.8	.003	0	1	36.00	-0.6	-0.4	-0.4
Chad Durbin	16	72.3	71	3.2	7.7	.293	2	5	8.83	-2.5	-2.1	-1.4
Chris Fussell	9	44.3	33	2.6	3.2	.450	4	1	6.70	-0.6	-0.3	0.1
Brett Laxton	1	3.3	6	0.0	0.7	.024	0	1	16.20	-0.4	-0.3	-0.3
Brian Meadows	10	65.0	38	3.8	3.4	.528	5	2	5.26	0.1	0.2	0.7
Dan Reichert	18	108.7	66	6.6	6.1	.520	5	6	5.47	-0.0	0.2	1.2
Jose Rosado	5	27.7	18	1.5	1.7	.469	2	2	5.86	-0.1	-0.1	0.1
Blake Stein	17	107.7	57	6.6	5.8	.533	8	5	4.76	0.7	0.5	1.3
Jeff Suppan	33	212.7	115	12.9	11.1	.537	10	9	4.87	1.2	0.9	2.7
Mac Suzuki	29	177.7	98	10.6	9.1	.538	8	10	4.96	0.8	0.9	2.2
Jay Witasick	14	74.3	56	3.3	6.1	.355	3	7	6.78	-1.0	-1.3	-0.7
TOTALS	162	943.7	605	52.9	60.0	.469	48	55	5.77	-3.3	-3.2	4.9

It may be hard to remember this now, but the Royals have an outstanding long-term track record with starting rotations. In the years for which I have the Support-Neutral data (every year since 1979 except 1991), Kansas City starters have the fifth-best cumulative Support-Neutral Value Added (SNVA) total. Royal rotations were worth 30.4 wins above average during those years according to SNVA, ranking them behind only Atlanta (55.5), Boston (49.3), Los Angeles (39.1), and Toronto (38.0).

Unfortunately for the Royals, their tradition of strong rotations seems to have died—or at least gone on hiatus—for the past three seasons. In fact, if you exclude the past three years from the above analysis and rank starting rotations based only on the period 1979-1997 (again excluding 1991), the Royals were the second-best rotation during that time, behind only the Expos(!).

Are the Royal rotations going to return to their former greatness anytime soon? It's hard to say. Jeff Suppan, Dan Reichert, Blake Stein, and Mac Suzuki make for a promising young core, but one of them will have to emerge as the next Bret Saberhagen or Kevin Appier in order for Royals fans to get the kind of rotation they've grown accustomed to over the past two decades.

For a quick explanation of SN stats, see page 7.

Reliever Evaluation Tools

PITCHER	G	IP	R	ARA	APR	IRNR/G	EIRS/G	IRP	BRS	RRA	ARP
Miguel Batista	5	9.0	15	14.36	-9.2	0.40	0.23	1.1	0.0	13.09	-7.9
Doug Bochtler	6	8.3	6	6.20	-0.9	0.50	0.27	-1.3	1.4	9.34	-3.8
Ricky Bottalico	62	72.7	40	4.74	3.7	0.35	0.12	3.5	-0.1	4.52	5.4
Tim Byrdak	12	6.3	8	10.88	-4.0	1.33	0.65	-1.6	0.4	14.03	-6.2
Jeff M. D'Amico	6	11.7	6	4.43	1.0	0.33	0.07	0.4	0.7	4.58	0.8
Chris Fussell	11	25.7	19	6.38	-3.4	1.00	0.30	0.3	0.6	6.37	-3.4
Andy Larkin	18	19.3	20	8.91	-8.0	0.83	0.32	-0.2	1.5	9.82	-9.9
Brett Laxton	5	13.3	9	5.82	-0.9	0.60	0.24	1.1	-1.4	4.04	1.7
Brian Meadows	1	6.7	1	1.29	2.9	2.00	1.06	0.1	0.0	1.28	2.9
Scott Mullen	11	10.3	5	4.17	1.2	0.82	0.26	0.9	0.2	3.70	1.7
Dan Murray	10	19.3	10	4.46	1.6	0.60	0.20	0.9	2.1	4.88	0.7
Jason Rakers	11	21.7	22	8.75	-8.6	0.91	0.36	0.8	-1.2	8.16	-7.1
Dan Reichert	26	44.7	26	5.02	0.9	0.42	0.22	0.7	-0.3	4.78	2.0
Brad Rigby	4	8.3	16	16.54	-10.5	1.00	0.32	0.2	0.2	17.92	-11.8
Jose Santiago	45	69.0	33	4.12	8.2	0.73	0.32	-6.7	4.0	5.57	-2.9
Paul Spoljaric	13	9.7	7	6.24	-1.1	1.31	0.56	4.7	0.8	2.87	2.5
Jerry Spradlin	50	75.0	49	5.63	-3.6	0.56	0.25	5.1	-0.9	4.99	1.7
Jeff Suppan	2	4.3	6	11.93	-3.2	0.00	0.00	0.0	0.0	11.14	-2.9
Mac Suzuki	3	11.0	2	1.57	4.4	1.67	0.97	-2.0	0.7	3.72	1.8
Kris Wilson	20	34.3	16	4.02	4.5	0.80	0.33	0.7	-1.3	3.79	5.4
Jay Witasick	8	15.0	9	5.17	0.0	0.75	0.28	-0.7	0.4	5.96	-1.3
TOTALS	329	495.7	325	5.65	-24.9	0.67	0.28			5.75	-30.5

For a quick guide to RET, see page 10.

Minnesota Twins

Even in our sixth year, we at *Baseball Prospectus* have some blind spots. We haven't had much respect for the Mets and what they've tried to accomplish over the years. We keep railing about wasted opportunities in Toronto. And then there are the Twins. Probably more than anybody, even the Twins themselves, we like to give them credit for what they achieve, especially in player development. One year, we got silly enough to say they had a shot at the postseason. Keep that bias in mind, because we're going to review again why the Twins—as a baseball team, as an organization, and as a business—deserve more credit than they get. We apologize in advance if you end up sharing the delusion.

What is the one complaint we hear, year after year, from analysts and commentators who fail to make allowances for current offensive levels? The absence of pitching. We hear that pitching is 90% of the game, or 115%, or that it's more important than you think or more than we know or more than anyone could believe. Over and over we're told that good teams need starting pitching, and good starting pitching equals winning. If there's any truth to this, then the Twins have already assembled the most basic component of a good team—the front half of a strong rotation. With Brad Radke and Eric Milton, they arguably have the best front half in the league.

Look around at the rest of the American League. Few teams can make a similar claim. Yes, the Yankees' tandem of Mike Mussina and Roger Clemens is the strongest on paper—as long as neither of them get a case of the olds. The Red Sox might have a claim, too, because anything that starts with Pedro Martinez looks good, but their claim depends on Frank Castillo not turning back into a pumpkin. The Athletics have a good case, because like the Twins they have a pair of young starters in Tim Hudson and Barry Zito. Their argument relies heavily on Barry Zito being as good over a full season as he was in his two months as a rookie.

Move into the AL Central and the pickings get really slim. The White Sox? The Tigers? Each has one good major-league starter. The Royals and the White Sox have young guys with promise; lots of organizations do. They're also crossing their fingers while trotting out Brian Meadows and Cal Eldred. The Indians probably have the best front duo in the division, but they're relying on the improvement of Bartolo Colon's eating habits and Chuck Finley's ability to stay effective beyond age 37. If you include third starters and compare teams in order of Support-Neutral Value Added, the Twins look good with a front three of Radke, Milton, and Mark Redman. On the basis of 2000 performance, they're behind only the Yankees' front three of Mussina, Clemens, and Orlando Hernandez, the Indians' trio of Colon, Finley, and Dave Burba, and Boston's Martinez, Castillo, and Tomo Ohka (though it should be noted that Pedro Martinez and two non-Sean Bergmans wind up ahead of almost everybody, courtesy of Maximum Pedrocity).

> **Twins Prospectus**
>
> **2000 record:** 69–93; Fifth place, AL Central
> **Pythagenport W/L:** 68–94
> **Runs Scored:** 748 (13th in AL)
> **Runs Allowed:** 880 (10th in AL)
> **Team EqA:** .241 (13th in AL)
> **2000 Batters' Age:** 26.4 (youngest in AL)
> **2000 Pitchers' Age:** 26.1 (2nd youngest in AL)
> **Ballpark:** Metrodome; good hitters' park; Park Factor of 1.053
> **2000:** Tying revenue-sharing money to payroll keeps Carl Pohlad's wallet closed.
> **2001:** There's a good rotation here and some young hitters on the way. Hope and faith, in other words.

So the AL Central has weak pitching. The Tigers and Royals are getting better. The White Sox haven't done anything to build on last season's division winner. The Tribe is getting older when it isn't busy getting worse with each big contract and short-sighted trade. Everyone in the division is moving towards .500, and you've got a new unbalanced schedule that will increase the number of games played against divisional opponents. The Twins managed to play right around .500 against divisional opponents in 2000 (24–26), and now they'll get to play 76 games against that group in 2001.

The Twins have done the hard part. They've developed a pair of top starters and assembled a group of supporting pitchers who will keep them in games more often than not. There's a chance that pitchers like Matt Kinney and Adam Johnson could give the Twins the best top-to-bottom rotation in the league, though it's no sure thing.

In addition to having a pretty good rotation, Tom Kelly has always done a solid job of cobbling together functional bullpens from spare parts like Carl Willis, Terry Leach, and Bob Wells, or resurrections like Juan Berenguer and Greg Swindell, or converted starters like Rick Aguilera, Mark

Guthrie, and Eddie Guardado. It isn't hard to envision this pitching staff finishing in the middle of the league or higher.

Of course, as Michael Wolverton points out at the end of the chapter, none of this will matter unless the Twins quit hurting themselves with the bottom of their rotation. But what if that bad habit is coming to an end? Kinney, Joe Mays, and J.C. Romero aren't your basic Bergmans, after all. When you consider the solid work of Mays, the talent of Kinney and Romero, and the fact that Tom Kelly has always done a good job of not overworking his pitchers, it isn't hard to envision some improvement.

The Twins' real problem is that they're a pitching staff in search of an offense. What Terry Ryan should be doing is assembling an offense that can score 850 runs. If he did that, the Twins would contend in the AL Central right now. Sound ludicrous? One of the great things about baseball research today is that while pitching is a relative mystery, we really do understand how offense works. It's not just the BP staff or people who read books like this. Several major-league teams grasp the basic operating principle of offense: OBP is life.

The Twins have the beginnings of an effective OBP offense. David Ortiz, Matt Lawton, and Corey Koskie aren't stars, but they're good on-base guys in their primes. The team has made a commitment to develop current OBP sinkhole Cristian Guzman, and in 2000, Guzman gave everyone reason to believe he can improve. The Twins have plenty of options at catcher involving players with different potential offensive capabilities, whether it's Matt LeCroy's right-handed power or A.J. Pierzynski's line-drive bat or Danny Ardoin's patience and limited sock. Even if LeCroy, the best long-term prospect of the group, isn't ready on Opening Day, the Twins will have a decent hitter catching and manning the bottom of the order as long as they avoid giving playing time to Chad Moeller.

Where the Twins cost themselves offense is at first base, second base, and whatever spots in the outfield Matt Lawton isn't playing. The Twins don't have the money for premium free-agent hitting talent at high-profile offensive positions like left field or first base, but that isn't a handicap in itself. Matt Stairs wasn't initially expensive when the A's took a look at him. The Twins can't afford to play Ron Coomer or Doug Mientkiewicz every day or to discard somebody like Mario Valdez. Bobby Kielty has good on-base skills, so if they can't buy power, the Twins can try improving their team OBP with someone like him. Torii Hunter and Jacque Jones need not be discarded; they can be used to advantage. Both can play center field. Hunter has more long-term upside while Jones has enough power to bat behind the on-base guys. Using both players along with Kielty—and not somebody like Chad Allen—would help produce some runs.

Platooning is one of the more basic ways the Twins can help themselves offensively. It's true that running platoons chews up roster space, which can limit a manager's ability to carry spare parts. A lineup takes nine men, and a roster needs a backup catcher, infielder, and outfielder. There are two, maybe three spots that a manager can use at his discretion; if he's running two platoons, he has none. But the Twins don't have this problem, thanks to Denny Hocking, one of the best utility men in the game. Count him as an infielder or an outfielder—either way the Twins have the roster space to platoon at two positions. The Twins can't afford to stock first base and left field with Jones and Koskie. They can be good offensive contributors in center field and at third base, respectively, but as a left fielder and first baseman, they become part of the problem.

Upgrading at second base is a different proposition, especially in light of the Twins' decision to cut loose Todd Walker. There was friction between Walker and Kelly, and generally speaking, it's easier to replace a manager than a talented player, but this was a situation where it wasn't very hard to accept the organization's loss of faith in Walker. Platoon second basemen with defensive limitations aren't that difficult to scare up. Having traded Walker, the Twins could have nabbed somebody like Jackie Rexrode in the Rule 5 draft. They did not, but as long as they commit the playing time to a long-term investment in Luis Rivas, they'll be helping themselves.

Admittedly, we're painting an optimistic picture, and the Twins chances in 2001 are slight. Teams built on good rotations and lousy offenses can usually count on having crummy records. Take the 1984 Pirates. They led the National League in ERA. They had four starters with ERAs better than the league average (Rick Rhoden, John Candelaria, John Tudor, and Larry McWilliams). They had a good bullpen. But they were tenth in a 12-team league in scoring and finished last in the NL East. Are the Twins doomed even if the bottom of the rotation improves to the point that the staff ranks in the upper half of the league in runs allowed? Let's not forget the 1985 Royals, who finished second in the AL in ERA and next-to-last in runs scored. They won the World Series by using everything and everyone they had as well as they could.

From a business standpoint, the Twins must quit buying into the current popular misunderstanding of the game's economic conditions. The mountain of economic misinformation and the race to grant victimhood to poorer franchises will reach epic proportions as we gear up for the next labor spat. Tune in for the Sally Struthers infomercial on the plight of billionaires used by their employees.

As attendance figures from the late 1980s and early 1990s show, fans support winning in any market, especially in Minnesota. More fans equals better television contracts. The Twins are strictly dependent on their local revenues and revenue-sharing cash only to the extent that billionaire Carl

American League

Pohlad is still trying to avoid spending his own money by finding someone else to pick up the tab. If Pohlad really wanted a new stadium that would allow the Twins to escape their real financial handicap—a miserable lease with the Metrodome—he should have invested in the franchise and generated a cycle of winning that would have cranked out popular support for everything, up to and including a new stadium. Given the examples set by Cleveland, Houston, and Seattle, he'd more than recoup his money.

Now, even that opportunity might be lost. We are confronted with the possibility that the Twins will have to move not because of the Twin Cities' viability as a big-league market, but because Pohlad took too long to build support for a new stadium. The Twins may be kicked out of the Metrodome as part of a plan to convert it to a football-only facility by 2004. If the plan becomes reality, the Twins will have nowhere to play in the Twin Cities after 2003.

The scenario creates a few possibilities. The Twins could scramble to another market, such as the North Carolina Triad area or Washington, D.C. though chances are they'd be racing the Expos, because there aren't many markets with viable stadiums. It's also possible that the football-only Metrodome proposal could generate just the kind of crisis needed to mobilize governmental support for a new stadium. Between the labor war on the horizon and Pohlad's notorious inability to drum up allies, however, the chances of a "neighborhood" park going up in the parking lot next to the Target Center in three years seems slight.

Finally, there are the proposals to fold a pair of franchises. The Twins keep getting mentioned as a likely candidate, but the problem is not the market so much as the ownership and its relationship to the market. If the Twins folded, it seems more likely that a franchise owned by somebody not named Carl Pohlad would move to Minneapolis from a less-viable market (Tampa Bay?) and would probably have an easier time drumming up local support because of the absence of a shared history.

However, the Twins are showing signs of progress, from the money committed in four-year contracts to Brad Radke and Cristian Guzman to the signing bonuses given to top picks B.J. Garbe and Adam Johnson. The ludicrous claims that the Twins threatened the game's integrity by punting a replacement-level talent like Pat Meares have been laid to rest. The Twins need to stop putting themselves down. Talking about how uncompetitive you are, how hopeless your season is, how your stadium sucks, and how everything won't get better until somebody else helps you is a great way to make people stay away from your ballpark. This team has several young stars and is a lot closer to being competitive than the Orioles or Devil Rays or Diamondbacks. Nobody can do a better sales job for the Twins than the Twins. Nobody is going to help the Twins more than the Twins. Snap to it, gents.

HITTERS (BA: .270, OBP: .340, SLG: .440, EqA: .260)

Chad Allen OF Bats R Age 26

YEAR	TEAM	LGE	AB	H	DB	TP	HR	BB	SO	R	RBI	SB	CS	OUT	BA	OBP	SLG	EQA	EQR	DEFENSE	
1998	New Brit	Eas	515	122	26	5	7	38	80	57	68	12	6	399	.237	.294	.348	.216	43	114-LF	-4
1999	Minnesot	AL	476	130	22	3	10	33	81	66	43	13	7	353	.273	.323	.395	.241	50	122-LF	6
2000	SaltLake	PCL	380	99	16	3	7	22	74	51	47	6	1	282	.261	.302	.374	.227	35	81-LF	-4
2000	Minnesot	AL	49	14	3	0	0	3	13	2	6	0	2	37	.286	.340	.347	.221	4	12-RF	1
2001	Minnesot	AL	432	113	18	2	9	40	86	60	54	9	3	322	.262	.324	.375	.236	43		

Fast and accident-prone, Chad Allen isn't our idea of a good corner outfielder. If he's the kind of player held back by Tom Kelly, then the world needs to cut the practitioners of tough love some slack. No amount of warm fuzzies or self-esteem-boosting is going to get him to hit for power. Allen was left off of the 40-man roster over the winter.

Danny Ardoin C Bats R Age 26

YEAR	TEAM	LGE	AB	H	DB	TP	HR	BB	SO	R	RBI	SB	CS	OUT	BA	OBP	SLG	EQA	EQR	DEFENSE			
1998	Huntsvil	Sou	367	77	12	0	13	43	93	47	43	4	2	292	.210	.300	.349	.220	33	80-C	-3		
1999	Vancouvr	PCL	338	77	11	1	7	43	75	43	37	2	2	263	.228	.326	.328	.225	31	74-C	5		
2000	Sacramen	PCL	234	58	12	1	5	27	74	32	26	4	0	176	.248	.340	.372	.247	27	41-C	-2	11-1B	0
2000	Minnesot	AL	32	4	1	0	1	7	9	4	5	0	0	28	.125	.282	.250	.183	2	12-C	1		
2001	Minnesot	AL	266	61	9	0	8	35	80	33	33	1	1	206	.229	.319	.353	.226	25				

One of the fun things about the Twins' catching situation (where fun = unpredictable) is that Kelly can do anything that strikes his fancy. He could build a lefty/righty platoon, a job-sharing arrangement, or an offense/defense platoon with almost any of the catchers on hand. As long as Matt LeCroy doesn't rot on the bench, the only outright wrong answer is playing Chad Moeller regularly. Ardoin is a nimble and strong-armed catcher with the trademark Athletics patience and a little power. He can be a good backup catcher if Kelly wants him to be.

John Barnes — OF — Bats R — Age 25

YEAR	TEAM	LGE	AB	H	DB	TP	HR	BB	SO	R	RBI	SB	CS	OUT	BA	OBP	SLG	EQA	EQR	DEFENSE	
1998	Trenton	Eas	387	93	12	0	12	31	48	44	29	2	5	299	.240	.300	.364	.219	33	80-RF	-7
1998	New Brit	Eas	73	17	4	1	0	7	9	8	7	1	1	57	.233	.306	.315	.209	6	17-RF	3
1999	New Brit	Eas	461	109	16	1	11	35	42	50	46	5	1	353	.236	.294	.347	.215	38	122-OF	-2
2000	SaltLake	PCL	426	126	28	3	10	43	49	76	59	4	4	304	.296	.367	.446	.271	58	111-CF	-2
2000	Minnesot	AL	36	12	4	0	0	2	5	5	2	0	1	25	.333	.400	.444	.277	5	11-RF	2
2001	Minnesot	AL	450	128	22	1	10	41	53	65	67	3	2	324	.284	.344	.404	.250	51		

John Barnes was a throw-in on the Swindell trade that netted Matt Kinney and has turned into someone who will make it. He'll play center field when asked, and he's got a decent arm. Everyone loves his work ethic, and with Kelly, playing the game a certain way means everything. Barnes is only slightly better than Allen in terms of results, but it's enough of a difference to make him the Twins' fourth outfielder.

Casey Blake — 3B — Bats R — Age 27

YEAR	TEAM	LGE	AB	H	DB	TP	HR	BB	SO	R	RBI	SB	CS	OUT	BA	OBP	SLG	EQA	EQR	DEFENSE	
1998	Dunedin	Fla	338	90	20	1	8	21	94	41	41	3	3	251	.266	.318	.402	.239	35	86-3B	3
1998	Knoxvill	Sou	168	48	10	2	5	13	27	25	23	4	0	120	.286	.342	.458	.269	22	44-3B	-4
1999	Syracuse	Int	387	84	14	1	17	51	81	54	56	6	4	307	.217	.316	.390	.237	42	109-3B	0
2000	Syracuse	Int	106	21	3	1	2	7	24	8	6	0	2	87	.198	.263	.302	.177	6	29-3B	-2
2000	SaltLake	PCL	286	72	18	1	8	29	62	41	34	4	1	215	.252	.330	.406	.248	33	64-3B	-9
2001	Minnesot	AL	430	105	21	1	13	46	102	56	59	1	0	325	.244	.317	.388	.235	43		

Not a lot of guys like Casey Blake make the book, but we're in Ron Coomer territory here, and natural laws of selection don't always apply. Blake has helped himself by playing a little bit of shortstop and first base. The Twins already have a good set of utility men, and getting a platoon mate for Koskie isn't that high a priority or even necessary. Blake will need a break to have as much of a career as Archi Cianfrocco or Craig Paquette.

Rob Bowen — C — Bats B — Age 20

YEAR	TEAM	LGE	AB	H	DB	TP	HR	BB	SO	R	RBI	SB	CS	OUT	BA	OBP	SLG	EQA	EQR	DEFENSE	
2000	Elizbthn	App	76	16	1	0	3	6	21	11	12	0	0	60	.211	.268	.342	.199	5	19-C	1

Rob Bowen was the team's second-round pick in the 1999 draft out of an Indiana high school. Wait two years before you start wondering how he's doing. If Matt LeCroy doesn't work out, Bowen might be the Opening Day catcher by 2004. He's already advanced for his age as a hitter and catcher. He's also the main reason why Justin Morneau will probably be moved to first base.

Brian Buchanan — OF — Bats R — Age 27

YEAR	TEAM	LGE	AB	H	DB	TP	HR	BB	SO	R	RBI	SB	CS	OUT	BA	OBP	SLG	EQA	EQR	DEFENSE	
1998	SaltLake	PCL	491	116	24	2	12	29	89	55	60	9	2	377	.236	.287	.367	.219	42	122-RF	-3
1999	SaltLake	PCL	381	94	18	1	7	22	82	48	43	7	1	289	.247	.298	.354	.220	33	88-RF	0
2000	SaltLake	PCL	356	86	14	1	18	30	79	56	66	3	1	271	.242	.304	.438	.245	40	74-RF	-5
2000	Minnesot	AL	81	19	2	0	1	7	20	9	7	0	0	64	.235	.304	.296	.194	5	17-RF	-1
2001	Minnesot	AL	365	87	13	1	13	30	85	43	47	6	2	280	.238	.296	.386	.226	34		

Brian Buchanan is turning out to be the extra guy in the Chuck Knoblauch trade, but as part of the four-for-one deal, he got his obligatory cup of coffee last year. As much as you sympathize with him for coming back from an injury similar to Jason Kendall's, he's never hit .300 in his three years at Salt Lake. Some coaches could unretire and hit .300 at Salt Lake.

Jay Canizaro — 2B — Bats R — Age 27

YEAR	TEAM	LGE	AB	H	DB	TP	HR	BB	SO	R	RBI	SB	CS	OUT	BA	OBP	SLG	EQA	EQR	DEFENSE	
1998	Shrevprt	Tex	286	54	5	0	9	40	52	34	22	3	1	233	.189	.293	.301	.203	22	75-2B	3
1998	Fresno	PCL	106	21	4	1	5	14	23	17	11	0	1	86	.198	.295	.396	.227	11	21-2B	1
1999	Fresno	PCL	358	84	15	1	19	40	76	56	55	11	4	278	.235	.315	.441	.252	44	97-2B	-10
2000	SaltLake	PCL	98	28	7	1	4	12	18	14	20	2	1	71	.286	.368	.500	.285	15	21-2B	2
2000	Minnesot	AL	342	91	20	1	7	20	52	40	37	4	2	253	.266	.309	.392	.233	33	78-2B	-8
2001	Minnesot	AL	400	104	20	1	13	44	76	60	60	6	2	298	.260	.333	.412	.249	46		

American League

The good thing about entering the replacement-level second-baseman market is that your options are as plentiful and as interchangeable as a casting call for *Baywatch*. You don't want to get stuck with a high-maintenance type like Pamela Anderson or Todd Walker. They get too big for their thongs, wanting everything their way. When you're the Twins, you're better off with people who are just happy to be there. That's Jay Canizaro. Once Luis Rivas wins the job, Canizaro won't stick around for long. Minor-league-veteran second basemen don't often make it in a utility role.

Ron Coomer 1B/3B Bats R Age 34

YEAR	TEAM	LGE	AB	H	DB	TP	HR	BB	SO	R	RBI	SB	CS	OUT	BA	OBP	SLG	EQA	EQR	DEFENSE			
1998	Minnesot	AL	526	146	18	1	17	17	64	54	71	2	2	382	.278	.300	.413	.234	50	73-3B	3	42-1B	7
1999	Minnesot	AL	463	121	23	1	17	26	63	51	62	2	1	343	.261	.302	.425	.239	48	60-1B	5	49-3B	5
2000	Minnesot	AL	538	143	26	1	17	30	46	60	76	2	0	395	.266	.310	.413	.240	55	121-1B	6		
2001	ChiCubs	NL	489	130	14	0	19	32	55	55	76	1	0	359	.266	.311	.411	.242	52				

Is there anyone who loves being a Twin as much as Ron Coomer? He makes no bones about his wanting to stay. He had surgery on his foot last year and was playing four days later. He should never get 500 at-bats again, especially not hitting cleanup. As a pinch hitter, defensive replacement, and spot starter at either corner, he'll be helpful, and the Twins will be better. He's signed a one-year deal with the Cubs.

Mike Cuddyer 3B Bats R Age 22

YEAR	TEAM	LGE	AB	H	DB	TP	HR	BB	SO	R	RBI	SB	CS	OUT	BA	OBP	SLG	EQA	EQR	DEFENSE	
1998	Ft Wayne	Mid	514	119	28	4	10	44	115	60	57	6	3	398	.232	.298	.360	.220	45	122-SS	-23
1999	Ft Myers	Fla	480	118	19	2	13	57	105	63	58	6	2	364	.246	.332	.375	.241	52	125-3B	-14
2000	New Brit	Eas	500	118	27	5	6	41	100	59	48	3	2	384	.236	.303	.346	.218	43	137-3B	-20
2001	Minnesot	AL	503	135	27	3	13	49	113	74	74	5	1	369	.268	.333	.412	.249	57		

Michael Cuddyer had a slow start in his introduction to Double-A, but he regrouped. If anything, Cuddyer's problem seems to be that his hands are too quick, both at the plate and in the field. He's still learning how to pull the ball and hits too many grounders. Defensively, he has good skills (strong arm, great range) and a funny ability to avoid converting them into outs. Cuddyer is a year away from being ready for the full-time job at third base.

Lew Ford CF Bats R Age 24

YEAR	TEAM	LGE	AB	H	DB	TP	HR	BB	SO	R	RBI	SB	CS	OUT	BA	OBP	SLG	EQA	EQR	DEFENSE	
1999	Lowell	NYP	256	58	11	2	6	13	37	32	23	5	1	199	.227	.269	.355	.207	19	55-CF	3
2000	Augusta	SAL	531	136	29	7	7	37	89	80	51	18	3	398	.256	.311	.377	.235	53	124-CF	14
2001	Minnesot	AL	346	94	18	2	6	28	73	53	47	8	1	253	.272	.326	.387	.241	36		

Lew Ford was swiped from the Red Sox for loaning the Duke a couple weeks of with Hector Carrasco. He had a good first full season, hitting over .300 with power and some patience while swiping 52 bases, but he was old for the Sally League. The Twins expect to push him to Double-A in 2001, which will give them a good read on whether or not he'll need to be added to the 40-man roster after the season.

B.J. Garbe CF Bats R Age 20

YEAR	TEAM	LGE	AB	H	DB	TP	HR	BB	SO	R	RBI	SB	CS	OUT	BA	OBP	SLG	EQA	EQR	DEFENSE	
1999	Elizbthn	App	173	40	2	0	3	11	37	18	19	1	0	133	.231	.278	.295	.188	10	37-CF	-9
2000	Quad Cit	Mid	495	106	10	2	5	42	101	48	41	6	4	393	.214	.282	.273	.184	28	131-CF	-18
2001	Minnesot	AL	290	69	5	1	3	28	70	29	26	3	1	222	.238	.305	.293	.201	20		

B.J. Garbe started slowly and struggled with back problems in his full-season debut. Like a lot of the Twins' talent, he was one of the youngest players in his league. Garbe is reputed to have great range in center field and a better arm, but there are whispers he'll need to move to right field.

It's hard to look at the performances of the Twins' minor-league hitters and not start thinking there's something wrong with their hitting instruction. Garbe needs to learn how to drive the ball, but this hasn't been an organization that teaches hitters how to work their way into cripple counts and then kill pitches.

Cristian Guzman   SS   Bats B   Age 23

YEAR	TEAM	LGE	AB	H	DB	TP	HR	BB	SO	R	RBI	SB	CS	OUT	BA	OBP	SLG	EQA	EQR	DEFENSE	
1998	New Brit	Eas	572	146	24	4	1	13	113	56	34	14	9	435	.255	.273	.316	.192	35	138-SS	0
1999	Minnesot	AL	418	94	13	3	1	18	82	44	25	8	7	331	.225	.261	.278	.171	20	123-SS	-4
2000	Minnesot	AL	626	152	23	20	8	38	92	83	49	29	11	485	.243	.288	.382	.225	59	148-SS	-8
2001	Minnesot	AL	538	139	20	9	4	36	96	71	54	22	9	408	.258	.305	.351	.221	47		

A September slump hurt his overall numbers, but up to then, his OBP topped .300, and he was slugging better than .400. That's lousy for somebody batting first or second all year, but impressive for a 22-year-old shortstop. He still doesn't have a sense of what to do in the field when the ball isn't hit at him. That may not sound like much of a problem until you consider the cutoff plays and throws that a shortstop has to back up. Nevertheless, Kelly seems to love him for his work ethic and willingness to learn. If he improves only defensively, he'll be Neifi Perez; if his offensive progress continues, he'll be as valuable as Greg Gagne was.

Denny Hocking   UT   Bats B   Age 31

YEAR	TEAM	LGE	AB	H	DB	TP	HR	BB	SO	R	RBI	SB	CS	OUT	BA	OBP	SLG	EQA	EQR	DEFENSE			
1998	Minnesot	AL	197	40	6	1	3	16	39	32	14	2	1	158	.203	.263	.289	.179	11	20-2B	-3	16-LF	4
1999	Minnesot	AL	383	101	19	2	7	18	49	45	38	10	7	289	.264	.301	.379	.225	35	37-SS	-4	34-2B	-2
2000	Minnesot	AL	366	107	24	4	4	43	70	48	43	7	6	265	.292	.367	.413	.263	47	34-OF	-1	32-2B	-4
2001	Minnesot	AL	318	86	16	2	4	35	59	49	39	7	5	237	.270	.343	.371	.241	34				

Although Denny Hocking isn't going to be a star, he can be a roster management MVP. He started games at all seven non-catcher positions, something that gives a manager tremendous flexibility when it comes to designing his roster. It usually means a lot of innings for Hocking while the team struggles offensively. His playing time will decline as a symptom of a better lineup, but he's the kind of spare part Kelly uses effectively.

Torii Hunter   CF   Bats R   Age 25

YEAR	TEAM	LGE	AB	H	DB	TP	HR	BB	SO	R	RBI	SB	CS	OUT	BA	OBP	SLG	EQA	EQR	DEFENSE	
1998	New Brit	Eas	312	78	19	2	5	14	65	34	26	7	6	239	.250	.288	.372	.217	26	79-CF	0
1998	SaltLake	PCL	89	25	2	0	4	1	13	11	15	2	2	65	.281	.294	.438	.237	9	23-CF	0
1999	Minnesot	AL	381	97	17	2	9	22	66	49	33	9	6	290	.255	.304	.381	.228	36	105-CF	11
2000	Minnesot	AL	333	92	13	7	5	14	62	41	40	4	3	244	.276	.310	.402	.235	33	96-CF	9
2000	SaltLake	PCL	202	63	13	1	13	7	29	41	41	7	2	141	.312	.342	.579	.294	33	48-CF	-1
2001	Minnesot	AL	453	126	22	3	16	27	85	64	71	9	4	331	.278	.319	.446	.250	52		

Torii Hunter spent two months in Salt Lake as a midseason reminder that more is expected of him than a homerless .207/.243/.300 start. Kelly could go either way with him. On one hand, Hunter irritates Kelly with his need for instruction. On the other hand, he's a serious fly-catcher with a great arm. Because of his glove, he'll have value no matter how the Twins sort out their power shortage. This year will determine whether Hunter will end up like Ryan Thompson or Rondell White. If he gets a full year and hits anything like this projection, choose the White path.

Marcus Jensen   C   Bats B   Age 28

YEAR	TEAM	LGE	AB	H	DB	TP	HR	BB	SO	R	RBI	SB	CS	OUT	BA	OBP	SLG	EQA	EQR	DEFENSE	
1998	Louisvil	Int	231	47	8	0	9	27	63	24	27	0	2	186	.203	.289	.355	.212	19	65-C	-2
1999	Memphis	PCL	235	58	13	3	6	24	59	28	32	0	0	177	.247	.323	.404	.244	26	56-C	-2
2000	Minnesot	AL	137	28	7	1	3	22	33	15	13	0	1	110	.204	.314	.336	.220	13	40-C	1
2000	SaltLake	PCL	54	12	2	0	1	8	11	7	8	0	1	43	.222	.337	.315	.222	5	11-C	0
2001	LosAngls	NL	167	36	6	1	5	25	45	22	22	0	1	132	.216	.318	.353	.235	18		

Marcus Jensen was the catcher for Team USA in the 1999 Pan Am Games and the 2000 Sydney Olympics. Now that those games are out of the way, he can get back to the business of being a solid backup catcher for some team. The Twins had their worst CERA with him behind the plate, but that's what happens when you're the one catching the Bergmans and Lincolns in the first half.

Jacque Jones — OF — Bats L — Age 26

YEAR	TEAM	LGE	AB	H	DB	TP	HR	BB	SO	R	RBI	SB	CS	OUT	BA	OBP	SLG	EQA	EQR	DEFENSE	
1998	New Brit	Eas	526	138	33	2	16	27	137	63	67	11	7	395	.262	.302	.424	.238	55	127-RF	8
1999	SaltLake	PCL	193	48	11	1	3	7	35	24	19	6	1	146	.249	.275	.363	.214	15	52-CF	6
1999	Minnesot	AL	319	91	25	2	9	14	57	52	41	3	4	232	.285	.322	.461	.254	38	86-CF	7
2000	Minnesot	AL	518	146	25	5	19	19	101	61	70	7	6	377	.282	.307	.459	.249	58	137-LF	7
2001	Minnesot	AL	415	115	25	2	14	21	89	59	63	11	4	304	.277	.312	.448	.249	47		

Jacque Jones is stuck in that range where he can be appreciated for what he does or drive you ape with what he doesn't do. He can play center field, so if he's there, he's valuable. He can't hit left-handers, but as a platoon player, he can still be valuable. As a regular in left field, he's as useful as a pet pig. Sure, he's grateful, but you ought to be doing better things with him.

Bobby Kielty — OF — Bats B — Age 24

YEAR	TEAM	LGE	AB	H	DB	TP	HR	BB	SO	R	RBI	SB	CS	OUT	BA	OBP	SLG	EQA	EQR	DEFENSE	
1999	Quad Cit	Mid	251	59	9	0	9	29	61	33	27	5	2	194	.235	.318	.378	.236	26	56-CF	3
2000	New Brit	Eas	466	106	25	2	12	78	118	64	50	3	2	363	.227	.342	.367	.243	53	121-CF	-13
2000	SaltLake	PCL	33	7	3	0	0	5	10	6	1	0	0	26	.212	.316	.303	.213	3		
2001	Minnesot	AL	304	75	14	0	10	50	86	50	46	2	1	230	.247	.353	.391	.253	37		

Bobby Kielty struggled with allergy and contact-lens problems in 1999, after which he had LASIK surgery, skipped a level, and handled Double-A just fine. He's a true switch-hitter, batting well from both sides of the plate. In center field, he gets good jumps and seems to cover the alleys well, but range is an issue. He has a Dave Henderson problem, too: his throws to the plate tail up the third-base line. With Hunter and Jones able to play center field, Kielty will move to a corner when he's called up this year. There's a lot to like here, and while he may not solve the team's power problems, he will give them another useful bat.

Corey Koskie — 3B — Bats L — Age 28

YEAR	TEAM	LGE	AB	H	DB	TP	HR	BB	SO	R	RBI	SB	CS	OUT	BA	OBP	SLG	EQA	EQR	DEFENSE			
1998	SaltLake	PCL	495	125	24	3	19	41	103	66	75	10	5	375	.253	.316	.428	.247	57	128-3B	-12		
1999	Minnesot	AL	337	104	14	0	13	36	66	39	56	4	4	237	.309	.383	.466	.282	50	68-3B	7	13-RF	-1
2000	Minnesot	AL	464	137	30	4	9	71	95	73	59	5	5	332	.295	.393	.435	.281	69	135-3B	0		
2001	Minnesot	AL	403	116	20	2	11	54	88	71	68	4	3	290	.288	.372	.429	.269	54				

It's the Twins' version of Mark Grace: put him at the top of the order and they could score some runs. Corey Koskie doesn't have tremendous range, and he'll never make people forget Scott Brosius coming in on bunts, but he can handle third base and does a good job starting the double play. Talk about moving him to first base is premature.

Matt Lawton — OF — Bats L — Age 29

YEAR	TEAM	LGE	AB	H	DB	TP	HR	BB	SO	R	RBI	SB	CS	OUT	BA	OBP	SLG	EQA	EQR	DEFENSE	
1998	Minnesot	AL	552	154	35	6	22	85	57	89	75	13	7	405	.279	.388	.484	.290	92	151-RF	13
1999	Minnesot	AL	401	103	12	0	9	53	38	54	52	25	4	302	.257	.351	.354	.252	48	84-RF	6
2000	Minnesot	AL	549	164	41	3	13	83	57	78	80	24	8	393	.299	.398	.455	.291	90	134-RF	-9
2001	Minnesot	AL	524	153	33	2	14	80	57	116	85	23	7	378	.292	.386	.443	.282	80		

Matt Lawton laid to rest any concerns about long-term problems from his shattered eyesocket and earned his first All-Star appearance in 2000. Anywhere else in baseball, he would be a top-of-the-order star, but with the Twins, he's a #3 hitter. Off-season discussions about trading him for power will work for the Twins only if they get a slugger at the start of his career. Any Twins' offensive boost will come by making Ron Coomer a memory, not by trading Lawton.

Matt LeCroy — C — Bats R — Age 25

YEAR	TEAM	LGE	AB	H	DB	TP	HR	BB	SO	R	RBI	SB	CS	OUT	BA	OBP	SLG	EQA	EQR	DEFENSE	
1998	Ft Wayne	Mid	234	54	11	1	7	25	48	25	28	0	0	180	.231	.315	.376	.233	24	48-C	-4
1998	Ft Myers	Fla	203	50	7	0	9	16	40	24	34	1	0	153	.246	.308	.414	.240	22	44-C	-6
1999	Ft Myers	Fla	341	79	14	1	15	31	59	41	47	0	0	262	.232	.298	.411	.234	35	62-C	-9
1999	SaltLake	PCL	116	29	3	1	7	4	21	17	21	0	1	88	.250	.279	.474	.239	12	16-C	-2
2000	Minnesot	AL	166	28	7	0	6	15	35	16	16	0	0	138	.169	.246	.319	.182	10	47-C	-1
2000	New Brit	Eas	200	48	8	1	8	22	38	25	28	0	0	152	.240	.326	.410	.246	23	42-C	-6
2000	SaltLake	PCL	63	16	3	0	4	3	11	11	10	0	0	47	.254	.288	.492	.250	7		
2001	Minnesot	AL	392	90	16	1	17	45	82	49	58	0	0	302	.230	.309	.406	.236	41		

Matt LeCroy had a great exhibition season, so even though he had just 32 games of experience above A ball, keeping him to start the season looked like a worthwhile risk. In retrospect, it seems clear he could have used a half-season in the minors. Give LeCroy credit for sorting out the office politics quickly enough: he refused to complain about his demotion and went so far as to blame himself for the pitching staff's problems. While ideally you want him to win the job and give the Twins the right-handed power they need, the Twins should let him play every day at the level for which he's ready and move the other catchers around accordingly. If they don't push, he'll be more than just the next Tim Laudner.

Jason Maxwell — IF — Bats R — Age 29

YEAR	TEAM	LGE	AB	H	DB	TP	HR	BB	SO	R	RBI	SB	CS	OUT	BA	OBP	SLG	EQA	EQR	DEFENSE			
1998	Iowa	PCL	481	123	33	2	11	42	94	66	45	5	1	359	.256	.322	.401	.243	52	101-2B	-14	18-SS	-8
1999	Toledo	Int	423	88	14	1	12	41	91	47	47	4	2	337	.208	.280	.331	.204	32	62-SS	1	35-2B	0
2000	Minnesot	AL	110	26	3	0	2	8	29	13	11	2	1	85	.236	.294	.318	.206	8	19-2B	2	10-3B	1
2001	Minnesot	AL	242	55	6	0	7	25	58	26	27	2	1	188	.227	.300	.339	.212	20				

Jason Maxwell's role was to platoon with and play defensive replacement for Todd Walker. Once Walker was demoted, both of Maxwell's possible jobs were gone. He was released this winter and re-signed as a minor-league free agent. With Hocking around, there are better ways to use the last roster spot than on a backup utility infielder.

Doug Mientkiewicz — 1B — Bats L — Age 27

YEAR	TEAM	LGE	AB	H	DB	TP	HR	BB	SO	R	RBI	SB	CS	OUT	BA	OBP	SLG	EQA	EQR	DEFENSE			
1998	New Brit	Eas	519	139	27	0	15	75	61	75	70	6	3	383	.268	.365	.407	.263	68	130-1B	2		
1999	Minnesot	AL	324	74	21	3	2	40	46	33	30	1	1	251	.228	.320	.330	.222	29	97-1B	7		
2000	SaltLake	PCL	472	126	25	2	12	44	71	67	63	5	3	349	.267	.332	.405	.247	53	81-1B	8	36-3B	-1
2001	Minnesot	AL	441	116	23	1	9	54	66	67	60	4	2	327	.263	.343	.381	.245	49				

Of the four angry Buzz, Doug Mientkiewicz was the most muted about Kelly. Probably not coincidentally, he is the only one likely to stick with the organization. The Twins took the Olympics seriously, so Minky was the first baseman for Team USA. As good as Mientkiewicz is defensively, he still isn't somebody to whom I'd hand a job. He's older than Mario Valdez, who should have gotten this opportunity. Stil, Mientkiewicz will get first crack at the first-base job. That's improvement through toe-wiggling, not taking a step forward.

Chad Moeller — C — Bats R — Age 26

YEAR	TEAM	LGE	AB	H	DB	TP	HR	BB	SO	R	RBI	SB	CS	OUT	BA	OBP	SLG	EQA	EQR	DEFENSE	
1998	Ft Myers	Fla	258	68	16	1	5	23	42	28	27	1	1	191	.264	.328	.391	.241	27	57-C	-15
1998	New Brit	Eas	192	42	5	0	6	18	42	17	20	1	1	151	.219	.293	.339	.210	15	54-C	-5
1999	New Brit	Eas	254	57	11	2	3	14	47	24	19	0	0	197	.224	.274	.319	.194	16	75-C	-11
2000	SaltLake	PCL	164	40	9	1	4	5	46	22	14	0	1	125	.244	.266	.384	.208	12	40-C	-8
2000	Minnesot	AL	127	26	3	1	1	8	30	12	8	1	0	101	.205	.252	.268	.164	5	39-C	0
2001	Minnesot	AL	291	70	13	1	6	21	72	30	32	1	1	222	.241	.292	.354	.211	23		

Chad Moeller did what he had to do by impressing Tom Kelly quickly. Kelly said he liked the way Moeller called a game, though his Catcher ERA wasn't any better than the other catchers'. You can tell Moeller knows how slender his opportunity is, because after tearing up his knee in August, he rushed back rather than get lost in the shuffle behind Matt LeCroy and A.J. Pierzynski. Moeller's future depends on things going badly for everybody else while he keeps up the apple-on-teacher's-desk routine.

American League

David Ortiz — DH — Bats L — Age 25

YEAR	TEAM	LGE	AB	H	DB	TP	HR	BB	SO	R	RBI	SB	CS	OUT	BA	OBP	SLG	EQA	EQR	DEFENSE	
1998	Minnesot	AL	276	77	13	0	12	38	64	46	47	1	0	199	.279	.375	.457	.280	41	58-1B	5
1999	SaltLake	PCL	463	118	24	2	21	64	102	60	75	1	1	346	.255	.348	.451	.266	63	99-1B	-7
2000	Minnesot	AL	408	113	33	1	11	52	74	55	59	1	0	295	.277	.359	.444	.269	56	25-1B	1
2001	*Minnesot*	*AL*	*413*	*116*	*26*	*1*	*18*	*65*	*90*	*80*	*82*	*1*	*0*	*297*	*.281*	*.379*	*.479*	*.285*	*64*		

After being demoted in 1999 because of questions about his attitude, David Ortiz made a point of not getting cranky about sitting during the first half. That made a good impression, but he still has a long way to go as far as conditioning and preparation. If you start reading stories about him coming into camp in great shape, that projection is low. If he doesn't, he'll have a hard time matching it. Kelly is never going to play him regularly at first base, so he has to hit to stick.

A.J. Pierzynski — C — Bats L — Age 24

YEAR	TEAM	LGE	AB	H	DB	TP	HR	BB	SO	R	RBI	SB	CS	OUT	BA	OBP	SLG	EQA	EQR	DEFENSE	
1998	New Brit	Eas	214	57	5	0	4	7	26	25	15	0	1	158	.266	.294	.346	.209	16	54-C	0
1998	SaltLake	PCL	205	45	8	1	5	7	24	23	22	2	1	161	.220	.245	.341	.187	12	53-C	-2
1999	SaltLake	PCL	223	49	4	0	2	13	28	22	20	0	0	174	.220	.263	.265	.165	10	58-C	-7
2000	New Brit	Eas	230	62	13	1	4	4	24	29	27	0	0	168	.270	.297	.387	.225	20	46-C	-6
2000	SaltLake	PCL	151	43	10	1	3	2	22	16	18	1	1	109	.285	.297	.424	.235	15	38-C	-2
2000	Minnesot	AL	87	26	5	1	2	4	13	11	10	1	0	61	.299	.344	.448	.265	11	24-C	1
2001	*Minnesot*	*AL*	*345*	*99*	*18*	*1*	*8*	*13*	*47*	*40*	*49*	*0*	*0*	*246*	*.287*	*.313*	*.414*	*.238*	*34*		

A.J. Pierzynski has the Greg Myers skill set: he's a left-handed-hitting line-drive machine with a strong arm. He'd make a nice caddy for LeCroy if LeCroy wins the job and a nice platoon mate for Ardoin if LeCroy doesn't. If the Twins keep Moeller, Pierzyski could get 400 plate appearances. The Twins are divided into a group of left-handed hitters who get on base, left-handed hitters who hit for good averages, and Ron Coomer. Pierzynski just adds another body to group two.

Mike Restovich — OF — Bats R — Age 22

YEAR	TEAM	LGE	AB	H	DB	TP	HR	BB	SO	R	RBI	SB	CS	OUT	BA	OBP	SLG	EQA	EQR	DEFENSE	
1998	Elizbthn	App	248	60	11	0	7	33	69	35	32	1	1	189	.242	.340	.371	.243	27	57-RF	-4
1998	Ft Wayne	Mid	46	16	4	1	0	3	13	7	4	0	0	30	.348	.388	.478	.289	7		
1999	Quad Cit	Mid	502	124	22	3	13	50	109	61	66	3	4	382	.247	.323	.380	.236	52	122-RF	-10
2000	Ft Myers	Fla	489	111	23	5	8	45	114	55	48	8	4	382	.227	.295	.344	.215	41	127-RF	-10
2001	*Minnesot*	*AL*	*400*	*105*	*20*	*2*	*11*	*43*	*100*	*59*	*58*	*4*	*2*	*297*	*.262*	*.334*	*.405*	*.247*	*45*		

Mike Restovich is a large human being who showed up in camp out of shape and became another slow starter among the team's prospects. He's got a little bit of the Andy Allanson problem: how does anyone 6′5″ not throw hard or hit tons of home runs? In his defense, he's very young, and the Florida State League is no place to try to make a living hitting for power. He may repeat the FSL, but a good start will get him to Double-A quickly.

Luis Rivas — 2B/SS — Bats R — Age 21

YEAR	TEAM	LGE	AB	H	DB	TP	HR	BB	SO	R	RBI	SB	CS	OUT	BA	OBP	SLG	EQA	EQR	DEFENSE	
1998	Ft Myers	Fla	464	115	20	3	3	9	85	40	38	13	5	354	.248	.265	.323	.193	29	124-SS	-20
1999	New Brit	Eas	535	123	29	4	6	28	97	61	39	15	8	420	.230	.270	.333	.199	37	119-SS	-17
2000	New Brit	Eas	334	75	21	4	3	28	44	45	31	6	3	262	.225	.289	.338	.210	27	73-2B	-5
2000	SaltLake	PCL	153	40	11	1	2	9	21	23	17	4	2	115	.261	.309	.386	.232	15	32-2B	0
2000	Minnesot	AL	57	17	4	1	0	2	4	8	5	2	0	40	.298	.322	.404	.248	6	14-2B	-2
2001	*Minnesot*	*AL*	*497*	*132*	*27*	*3*	*7*	*35*	*81*	*64*	*59*	*9*	*4*	*369*	*.266*	*.314*	*.374*	*.229*	*46*		

The Twins love Luis Rivas's reactions on the deuce now that they've moved him to second base. If Guzman makes progress, Twins pitchers might have a middle-infield combination they can brag about. Rivas has a quick bat and a tendency to try to pull everything, but he managed 51 walks and 55 extra-base hits as a 20-year-old playing at three high levels. If he wins the second-base job, he'll outhit that projection. Think Carlos Baerga with a glove, hopefully without Baerga's taste for living large.

Mike Ryan — OF/2B — Bats L — Age 23

YEAR	TEAM	LGE	AB	H	DB	TP	HR	BB	SO	R	RBI	SB	CS	OUT	BA	OBP	SLG	EQA	EQR	DEFENSE			
1998	Ft Wayne	Mid	425	110	19	3	8	31	99	52	50	2	1	316	.259	.311	.374	.229	40	104-3B	-13		
1999	Ft Myers	Fla	518	120	22	3	7	48	69	67	52	1	2	400	.232	.300	.326	.209	40	123-2B	-20		
2000	New Brit	Eas	487	120	21	5	10	25	85	53	53	2	2	369	.246	.285	.372	.215	40	102-LF	-3	16-2B	-6
2001	Minnesot	AL	469	120	19	2	12	36	86	55	61	2	1	350	.256	.309	.382	.228	44				

Mike Ryan is one of the new brand of tweeners: guys who can't field well enough to stick in the infield but who do enough as hitters to make their organizations move them to the outfield, where they have no chance of competing with the real prospects. Ryan had a big platoon split in Double-A, which could be enough to get him a career as a utility man in the Andy Fox mold. Most of these guys wind up like David Newhan or Chad Meyers.

Ruben Salazar — 2B — Bats R — Age 23

YEAR	TEAM	LGE	AB	H	DB	TP	HR	BB	SO	R	RBI	SB	CS	OUT	BA	OBP	SLG	EQA	EQR	DEFENSE			
1999	Elizbthn	App	264	72	13	1	7	28	47	33	31	3	2	194	.273	.346	.409	.254	32	27-2B	-2	16-3B	-1
2000	Ft Myers	Fla	508	134	13	0	11	26	92	62	48	1	2	376	.264	.301	.354	.217	41	100-2B	-9		
2001	Minnesot	AL	322	93	6	0	10	22	76	38	50	1	1	230	.289	.334	.401	.244	34				

Ruben Salazar is one of the organization's Venezuelans. He first drew attention by hitting .401 in the Appalachian League in 1999. The Twins promoted him aggressively, and after hitting .311 in the Florida State League, he's a certified hackmaster. His quick hands are his lone asset; Salazar has no range at second base, so third base may be his eventual position. He's a year older than Cuddyer, but he could have a career if he hits above .300 in Double-A.

Eric Sandberg — 1B — Bats L — Age 21

YEAR	TEAM	LGE	AB	H	DB	TP	HR	BB	SO	R	RBI	SB	CS	OUT	BA	OBP	SLG	EQA	EQR	DEFENSE	
1999	Elizbthn	App	261	57	9	1	8	27	56	33	30	1	1	205	.218	.293	.352	.215	22	64-1B	-2
2000	Quad Cit	Mid	448	97	7	0	13	68	79	57	43	0	0	351	.217	.325	.319	.223		41127-1B	5
2001	Minnesot	AL	286	68	6	0	9	46	70	40	39	0	0	218	.238	.343	.353	.238	30		

Another growing boy from the Pacific Northwest, Eric Sandberg is the brother of the D-Rays' Jared and Ryno's other nephew. He did things we like in his first full season. He drew 95 walks, and his 15 home runs were more than twice as many as anybody else on the team. With Justin Morneau coming up behind him, he needs to improve in the Florida State League this year, which won't be easy.

Todd Sears — 1B — Bats L — Age 25

YEAR	TEAM	LGE	AB	H	DB	TP	HR	BB	SO	R	RBI	SB	CS	OUT	BA	OBP	SLG	EQA	EQR	DEFENSE			
1998	Ashevlle	SAL	466	102	20	1	7	52	94	47	52	3	2	366	.219	.301	.311	.207	36	97-3B	-17		
1999	Salem VA	Car	397	93	13	0	12	42	102	43	43	5	1	305	.234	.311	.358	.227	38	47-1B	-2	29-3B	-16
2000	Carolina	Sou	314	78	11	0	11	56	81	43	56	6	2	238	.248	.364	.389	.261	41	80-1B	-12		
2000	New Brit	Eas	143	38	5	1	3	13	44	12	12	1	0	105	.266	.329	.378	.240	15	34-1B	-3		
2001	Minnesot	AL	453	111	14	0	16	62	125	63	66	1	0	342	.245	.336	.382	.242	49				

Need more power? Don't go to Sears. As athletic as he might be for a big man, Todd Sears's career as a third baseman is over. At first base, his defense gets good marks from scouts. He played at the University of Nebraska, so he'll have to cope with Tom Kelly's apparent bias against college players. Sears can only hope the bias doesn't apply to the school that has "N" on its helmets for knowledge. He has a shot at being the next Mientkiewicz.

Javier Valentin — C — Bats B — Age 25

YEAR	TEAM	LGE	AB	H	DB	TP	HR	BB	SO	R	RBI	SB	CS	OUT	BA	OBP	SLG	EQA	EQR	DEFENSE	
1998	Minnesot	AL	161	32	7	1	3	11	27	11	17	0	0	129	.199	.250	.311	.178	9	47-C	-5
1999	Minnesot	AL	216	53	13	1	5	20	36	21	26	0	0	163	.245	.312	.384	.233	21	65-C	5
2000	SaltLake	PCL	135	40	12	1	5	7	28	18	23	1	0	95	.296	.334	.511	.275	19	24-C	1
2001	Minnesot	AL	159	43	12	1	6	12	32	23	27	0	0	116	.270	.322	.472	.258	20		

American League

After Javier Valentin spent two years caddying for Terry Steinbach, it was a bit of a surprise that he was not the Opening Day catcher in 2000. He managed to offend Tom Kelly in spring training by assuming that the job was his and lost his spot on the big-league team for not hustling. It wasn't particularly fair, but summary judgments rarely are. Valentin injured his knee at Salt Lake so badly that he couldn't catch, then was removed from the 40-man roster this winter. Once he recovers, his shot at a career with the Twins depends on whether he can outlast Kelly.

PITCHERS (ERA: 4.50, H/9: 9.00, HR/9: 1.00, BB/9: 3.00, K/9: 6.00, KW: 1.00, PERA: 4.50)

Grant Balfour — Throws R — Age 23

YEAR	TEAM	LGE	IP	H	ER	HR	BB	K	ERA	W	L	H/9	HR/9	BB/9	K/9	KW	PERA
1998	Elizbthn	App	68.7	76	51	18	39	32	6.68	2	6	9.96	2.36	5.11	4.19	0.41	7.39
1999	Quad Cit	Mid	83.0	74	55	16	43	50	5.96	3	6	8.02	1.73	4.66	5.42	0.58	5.40
2000	Ft Myers	Fla	78.3	100	66	21	44	52	7.58	2	7	11.49	2.41	5.06	5.97	0.59	8.32

Grant Balfour is one of the Australians the Twins have picked up through the efforts of scout Howard Norsetter. After struggling as a starter, he's been moved to the pen. He relies on a sinker he can get into the low 90s, plus a developing slider and change-up. He's probably in the best shape of any player in the organization. Despite his struggles in the Florida State League, the Twins are high on him.

Jack Cressend — Throws R — Age 26

YEAR	TEAM	LGE	IP	H	ER	HR	BB	K	ERA	W	L	H/9	HR/9	BB/9	K/9	KW	PERA
1998	Trenton	Eas	137.0	170	101	21	64	77	6.64	4	11	11.17	1.38	4.20	5.06	0.60	6.68
1999	New Brit	Eas	132.7	156	95	17	59	73	6.44	4	11	10.58	1.15	4.00	4.95	0.62	6.02
2000	SaltLake	PCL	83.0	85	37	3	37	59	4.01	4	5	9.22	0.33	4.01	6.40	0.80	4.34
2000	Minnesot	AL	13.7	19	8	1	5	6	5.27	1	1	12.51	0.66	3.29	3.95	0.60	6.38

Nabbed on a waiver claim from the Red Sox at the start of 1999, Jack Cressend isn't a guy who impresses speed guns. What he does is command four pitches, getting a lot of ground balls and being hard to drive. He's in the mix for one of the last two spots in the bullpen. His value as a long reliever will largely depend upon on how quickly Rivas and Guzman gel.

Peter Fisher — Throws — Age 23

YEAR	TEAM	LGE	IP	H	ER	HR	BB	K	ERA	W	L	H/9	HR/9	BB/9	K/9	KW	PERA
1998	Elizbthn	App	60.0	89	57	23	13	24	8.55	1	6	13.35	3.45	1.95	3.60	0.92	9.24
1999	Ft Myers	Fla	134.3	169	86	24	49	55	5.76	5	10	11.32	1.61	3.28	3.68	0.56	6.62
2000	Ft Myers	Fla	77.3	84	53	24	48	38	6.17	3	6	9.78	2.79	5.59	4.42	0.40	7.94
2000	New Brit	Eas	57.3	86	56	8	16	23	8.79	1	5	13.50	1.26	2.51	3.61	0.72	7.22

A 1998 fourth-round pick from Alabama, Peter Fisher gets good marks for his command of a decent sinker and slider. Both the organization and opposing hitters like him. The problem is politely described as "too much command," but you need some ricochet sound effects to really understand. With Fisher, Stanford left-hander Brent Hoard, Auburn ace Brent Schoening, and Ryan Mills, the Twins have a lot of college stars who aren't turning out well.

Chris Garza — Throws L — Age 25

YEAR	TEAM	LGE	IP	H	ER	HR	BB	K	ERA	W	L	H/9	HR/9	BB/9	K/9	KW	PERA
1998	Ft Myers	Fla	73.7	70	38	7	60	36	4.64	3	5	8.55	0.86	7.33	4.40	0.30	5.86
1999	Ft Myers	Fla	36.0	35	19	3	25	17	4.75	2	2	8.75	0.75	6.25	4.25	0.34	5.44
1999	New Brit	Eas	27.3	17	16	2	21	25	5.27	1	2	5.60	0.66	6.91	8.23	0.60	3.79
2000	New Brit	Eas	39.3	36	26	2	31	31	5.95	1	3	8.24	0.46	7.09	7.09	0.50	5.16
2000	SaltLake	PCL	20.3	27	17	1	12	13	7.52	0	2	11.95	0.44	5.31	5.75	0.54	6.63

The Twins already have a good pair of left-handed relievers in Eddie Guardado and Travis Miller, plus they have to sort out what to do with J.C. Romero and Johan Santana. They have another good southpaw reliever on tap in Chris Garza. He owns left-handers with his breaking stuff, but he becomes a factor only if the Twins deal Guardado, or if the Opening Day roster makeup leaves Miller in a numbers crunch.

Eddie Guardado — Throws L — Age 30

YEAR	TEAM	LGE	IP	H	ER	HR	BB	K	ERA	W	L	H/9	HR/9	BB/9	K/9	KW	PERA
1998	Minnesot	AL	65.3	62	29	8	23	49	3.99	4	3	8.54	1.10	3.17	6.75	1.07	4.42
1999	Minnesot	AL	48.3	35	20	5	19	48	3.72	3	2	6.52	0.93	3.54	8.94	1.26	3.26
2000	Minnesot	AL	62.0	50	20	10	19	50	2.90	5	2	7.26	1.45	2.76	7.26	1.32	3.86

Eddie Guardado had the kind of season you get only by pitching for Tom Kelly. He pitched in long relief, situational relief, and closed some games. He came in with men on, he came in with the bases clear. He came in when the Twins were down or the score was tied, but rarely did he come in when the Twins had a lead. Of course, this is the Twins, so how often could that happen, anyway? Continue to expect the unexpected.

LaTroy Hawkins — Throws R — Age 28

YEAR	TEAM	LGE	IP	H	ER	HR	BB	K	ERA	W	L	H/9	HR/9	BB/9	K/9	KW	PERA
1998	Minnesot	AL	188.0	210	106	22	50	97	5.07	8	13	10.05	1.05	2.39	4.64	0.97	4.93
1999	Minnesot	AL	174.7	219	112	22	46	98	5.77	6	13	11.28	1.13	2.37	5.05	1.07	5.73
2000	Minnesot	AL	87.3	79	28	5	24	56	2.89	7	3	8.14	0.52	2.47	5.77	1.17	3.33

Sometimes the worst of intentions reward you in the strangest of ways. The Twins finally quit on LaTroy Hawkins as a starter after he was awful in spring training, keeping him on the roster just to avoid another Todd Ritchie-type embarrassment. So what happened? Hawkins did a good job with inherited runners, converting all 14 of his save opportunities. Now what? It's always cheaper to create your own closer, and somebody with a closer rep is incredibly valuable in trade. Keeping Hawkins in the role will make him a commodity, and even if the Twins don't deal him, his past miseries could make him easy to sign to a multi-year contract so that the team can avoid spending top dollar on a reliever for several years to come.

Adam Johnson — Throws R — Age 21

YEAR	TEAM	LGE	IP	H	ER	HR	BB	K	ERA	W	L	H/9	HR/9	BB/9	K/9	KW	PERA
2000	Ft Myers	Fla	62.7	51	29	5	25	54	4.16	3	4	7.32	0.72	3.59	7.76	1.08	3.50

Adam Johnson was given a $2.5-million bonus after being the second pick overall in the 2000 draft, but he was considered a signability pick. He quickly made the point moot by blowing through the Florida State League, flashing a mid-90s fastball and a good, hard slider. Some want to make him a closer, which would be a waste, but starting or relieving, he'll be in the majors by the end of the season. Johnson is considered cocky and starred at Cal State Fullerton. College players with attitudes seem to be the guys Kelly cuts down a peg.

Matt Kinney — Throws R — Age 24

YEAR	TEAM	LGE	IP	H	ER	HR	BB	K	ERA	W	L	H/9	HR/9	BB/9	K/9	KW	PERA
1998	Ft Myers	Fla	33.7	32	23	2	23	23	6.15	1	3	8.55	0.53	6.15	6.15	0.50	5.05
1998	Sarasota	Fla	111.0	106	76	9	90	56	6.16	4	8	8.59	0.73	7.30	4.54	0.31	5.75
1999	New Brit	Eas	55.7	71	63	13	39	32	10.19	1	5	11.48	2.10	6.31	5.17	0.41	8.51
2000	New Brit	Eas	78.7	80	41	14	40	59	4.69	4	5	9.15	1.60	4.58	6.75	0.74	5.88
2000	SaltLake	PCL	53.3	42	24	5	23	43	4.05	3	3	7.09	0.84	3.88	7.26	0.93	3.62
2000	Minnesot	AL	42.7	38	20	5	19	23	4.22	2	3	8.02	1.05	4.01	4.85	0.61	4.39

Matt Kinney started flashing mid-90s velocity in the Arizona Fall League last year, then showed improved command of his slider and change-up during the 2000 season. He's gone from being just another pitcher to being a pretty good rookie for 2001. Kinney had some bone chips removed from his elbow in 1998, but it didn't set him back. His smooth delivery means that the elbow isn't expected to be a chronic problem. While he may technically be fighting for the fifth starter's job, he'll have more job security in the rotation than Joe Mays. Decent run support could put him in the running for Rookie of the Year.

Mike Lincoln — Throws R — Age 26

YEAR	TEAM	LGE	IP	H	ER	HR	BB	K	ERA	W	L	H/9	HR/9	BB/9	K/9	KW	PERA
1998	New Brit	Eas	160.7	179	93	22	41	64	5.21	7	11	10.03	1.23	2.30	3.59	0.78	5.06
1999	SaltLake	PCL	57.7	75	46	12	21	26	7.18	1	5	11.71	1.87	3.28	4.06	0.62	7.15
1999	Minnesot	AL	76.0	94	48	8	20	26	5.68	3	5	11.13	0.95	2.37	3.08	0.65	5.45
2000	SaltLake	PCL	71.3	66	30	4	15	25	3.79	4	4	8.33	0.50	1.89	3.15	0.83	3.19
2000	Minnesot	AL	21.7	33	20	8	10	14	8.31	0	2	13.71	3.32	4.15	5.82	0.70	10.24

American League

Mike Lincoln might be finished after reinjuring his elbow, which required another surgery. The Twins tell their pitchers to yelp at the first sign of trouble and almost never lose pitchers to major injuries. Lincoln neglected to tell management he was hurt, and looks it like he ruined what shot he had at a career. Released in January.

Kyle Lohse — Throws R — Age 22

YEAR	TEAM	LGE	IP	H	ER	HR	BB	K	ERA	W	L	H/9	HR/9	BB/9	K/9	KW	PERA
1998	Rockford	Mid	156.3	162	89	20	56	62	5.12	6	11	9.33	1.15	3.22	3.57	0.55	4.95
1999	Daytona	Fla	48.7	49	25	8	19	25	4.62	2	3	9.06	1.48	3.51	4.62	0.66	5.26
1999	Ft Myers	Fla	37.3	50	39	12	12	20	9.40	1	3	12.05	2.89	2.89	4.82	0.83	8.26
1999	New Brit	Eas	65.0	87	55	14	25	26	7.62	2	5	12.05	1.94	3.46	3.60	0.52	7.48
2000	New Brit	Eas	153.0	203	149	43	61	81	8.76	3	14	11.94	2.53	3.59	4.76	0.66	8.09

You can lead a horse to water, push his muzzle into the bucket, and threaten to turn him into glue and dog food, but if he doesn't want to learn, he won't. Kyle Lohse can get into the low 90s, has a good slider, and can use his change-up effectively. Unfortunately, he's a pump-and-puke pitcher, using himself up by the fourth inning, after which he gets lit. Despite his youth, he has considerable pro experience and should know better by now. He seems more likely to succeed as a reliever.

Joe Mays — Throws R — Age 25

YEAR	TEAM	LGE	IP	H	ER	HR	BB	K	ERA	W	L	H/9	HR/9	BB/9	K/9	KW	PERA
1998	Ft Myers	Fla	86.7	104	56	16	30	48	5.82	3	7	10.80	1.66	3.12	4.98	0.80	6.31
1998	New Brit	Eas	53.3	63	46	7	24	27	7.76	1	5	10.63	1.18	4.05	4.56	0.56	6.09
1999	Minnesot	AL	170.7	166	76	19	52	110	4.01	9	10	8.75	1.00	2.74	5.80	1.06	4.26
2000	Minnesot	AL	161.3	179	85	15	50	97	4.74	7	11	9.99	0.84	2.79	5.41	0.97	4.83

Joe Mays may end up being a great test case for what the new unbalanced schedule could mean for individuals; he owns the White Sox to the point that they call him "Cy." Mays picked up a change-up from Brad Radke and started using it in the second half, but he didn't have much opportunity to show it off after Tom Kelly gave up on him, sending him to the pen and then to Salt Lake. Left alone, he'll be a good fifth starter, but how many fifth starters have job security?

Travis Miller — Throws L — Age 28

YEAR	TEAM	LGE	IP	H	ER	HR	BB	K	ERA	W	L	H/9	HR/9	BB/9	K/9	KW	PERA
1998	SaltLake	PCL	54.7	59	34	3	33	42	5.60	2	4	9.71	0.49	5.43	6.91	0.64	5.41
1998	Minnesot	AL	23.0	24	10	1	9	21	3.91	2	1	9.39	0.39	3.52	8.22	1.17	4.29
1999	Minnesot	AL	49.3	51	15	2	12	38	2.74	3	2	9.30	0.36	2.19	6.93	1.58	3.69
2000	Minnesot	AL	67.7	78	29	3	24	59	3.86	4	4	10.37	0.40	3.19	7.85	1.23	4.75

Sliderboy is getting a wee bit predictable, as right-handed hitters teed off on him, and he allowed far too many inherited runners to score for a situational left-hander. A change of leagues would probably do him some good. As long as he doesn't have to pitch too often and put his arm at risk, he can keep doing this for another ten years.

Ryan Mills — Throws L — Age 23

YEAR	TEAM	LGE	IP	H	ER	HR	BB	K	ERA	W	L	H/9	HR/9	BB/9	K/9	KW	PERA
1999	Ft Myers	Fla	83.7	114	122	15	113	42	13.12	1	8	12.26	1.61	12.16	4.52	0.19	10.88
2000	Quad Cit	Mid	107.0	109	68	13	76	57	5.72	4	8	9.17	1.09	6.39	4.79	0.38	6.10
2000	New Brit	Eas	28.7	47	55	11	38	14	17.27	0	3	14.76	3.45	11.93	4.40	0.18	14.18

When I was younger, I designed a game. It was a fun game, but designed so that you couldn't win. It was entertaining enough that people tried and failed and kept wondering about how much fun it would be if they won.

Ryan Mills is a similar puzzle. The organization is ecstatic over his work at Quad City, but after starring in college, Mills should own the Midwest League. The latest spin is that he struggled with his mechanics and focused too hard on his release point in 1999, and that these problems were a thing of the past in 2000. Once he got to Double-A, they were a thing of the present again. He was smacked around in the AFL. Anybody who throws 95 mph is tantalizing, but after a certain point, you start thinking there's nothing to be won.

Eric Milton — Throws L — Age 25

YEAR	TEAM	LGE	IP	H	ER	HR	BB	K	ERA	W	L	H/9	HR/9	BB/9	K/9	KW	PERA
1998	Minnesot	AL	171.0	181	94	20	57	99	4.95	8	11	9.53	1.05	3.00	5.21	0.87	4.86
1999	Minnesot	AL	204.7	175	90	22	48	155	3.96	12	11	7.70	0.97	2.11	6.82	1.61	3.38
2000	Minnesot	AL	198.7	186	97	26	33	153	4.39	10	12	8.43	1.18	1.49	6.93	2.32	3.74

He's in a hitters' park, can count on crummy run support, and there are worries about his shoulder and elbow, but any team would love to have Eric Milton. He's become an effective four-pitch left-hander, with everything working off of a fastball that has great movement. He'll have starts in which teams are lucky to get good wood on anything. It would have been nice if the Twins had shut him down for September after he experienced some bursitis in his knee. He's about to be recognized as one of the best starters in the league.

Danny Mota — Throws R — Age 25

YEAR	TEAM	LGE	IP	H	ER	HR	BB	K	ERA	W	L	H/9	HR/9	BB/9	K/9	KW	PERA
1998	Ft Wayne	Mid	28.3	28	21	5	10	19	6.67	1	2	8.89	1.59	3.18	6.04	0.95	5.10
1998	Ft Myers	Fla	42.3	46	27	7	29	28	5.74	2	3	9.78	1.49	6.17	5.95	0.48	6.78
1999	Ft Myers	Fla	17.0	19	5	0	7	12	2.65	1	1	10.06	0.00	3.71	6.35	0.86	4.34
2000	Ft Myers	Fla	42.0	40	29	3	33	27	6.21	1	4	8.57	0.64	7.07	5.79	0.41	5.56
2000	New Brit	Eas	25.7	22	19	2	10	24	6.66	1	2	7.71	0.70	3.51	8.42	1.20	3.68

The Knoblauch trade has given the Twins their #2 starter and a starting shortstop. Danny Mota is the player who will determine whether Terry Ryan got two starters and two throw-ins, or three major-leaguers. Mota throws 94 mph with a plus slider, but his elbow makes it hard to count on him. He has a chance to make the big-league bullpen this year. Behind Hawkins, he has the highest upside of any right-hander in the pen.

Brad Radke — Throws R — Age 28

YEAR	TEAM	LGE	IP	H	ER	HR	BB	K	ERA	W	L	H/9	HR/9	BB/9	K/9	KW	PERA
1998	Minnesot	AL	210.0	220	93	19	35	135	3.99	12	11	9.43	0.81	1.50	5.79	1.93	3.95
1999	Minnesot	AL	215.3	218	80	22	34	115	3.34	14	10	9.11	0.92	1.42	4.81	1.69	3.84
2000	Minnesot	AL	225.0	238	96	20	38	135	3.84	13	12	9.52	0.80	1.52	5.40	1.78	3.99

The minor resurgence in Brad Radke's strikeout rate makes the decision to give him a four-year contract a little less worrisome. Hittable aces are a tricky proposition, but outside of Pedro Martinez and Mike Mussina, there probably isn't a more reliable starter in the AL. Some people think Radke has had a couple of bad years, but he's been working with spotty infield defense and miserable run support in a high-offense era. In addition to his 16 quality starts, he had eight others in which he pitched six or more innings and gave up four runs. He didn't win any of them. By comparison, Kevin Appier got three wins in similar starts, as did Tim Hudson. Milton is poised to become the staff ace, but that's not a reason to be disappointed in Radke.

Mark Redman — Throws L — Age 27

YEAR	TEAM	LGE	IP	H	ER	HR	BB	K	ERA	W	L	H/9	HR/9	BB/9	K/9	KW	PERA
1998	New Brit	Eas	42.7	43	15	5	21	29	3.16	3	2	9.07	1.05	4.43	6.12	0.69	5.20
1998	SaltLake	PCL	95.3	105	70	13	41	59	6.61	3	8	9.91	1.23	3.87	5.57	0.72	5.63
1999	SaltLake	PCL	128.0	132	83	12	54	72	5.84	4	10	9.28	0.84	3.80	5.06	0.67	4.84
2000	Minnesot	AL	151.0	154	65	16	34	112	3.87	9	8	9.18	0.95	2.03	6.68	1.65	4.16

Making the roster as a mop-up man was Mark Redman's most important victory, because a month into the season, he got an opportunity to start and ran with it. While he isn't a hard thrower, he flirts with the 90s and works the inside corner, which is more than adequate for a left-hander with a nice curve. He's at the right age to be coming into his own and cranked out 14 quality starts in 24 tries. On a good team, he'd be a fourth starter; on the Twins, he's a solid third.

Juan Rincon — Throws R — Age 22

YEAR	TEAM	LGE	IP	H	ER	HR	BB	K	ERA	W	L	H/9	HR/9	BB/9	K/9	KW	PERA
1998	Ft Wayne	Mid	85.0	88	66	16	69	38	6.99	2	7	9.32	1.69	7.31	4.02	0.28	7.21
1999	Quad Cit	Mid	150.0	151	78	18	77	81	4.68	7	10	9.06	1.08	4.62	4.86	0.53	5.29
2000	Ft Myers	Fla	69.7	68	32	8	29	32	4.13	4	4	8.78	1.03	3.75	4.13	0.55	4.72
2000	New Brit	Eas	81.7	99	65	17	43	51	7.16	2	7	10.91	1.87	4.74	5.62	0.59	7.26

Another Twins' pitcher under six feet tall who can throw hard, Juan Rincon pumps gas into the mid 90s and has a good slider. He's butting heads with the organization because he has ideas of his own about how to throw a change-up, and they haven't worked. He also had the misfortune of getting called up in time to participate in New Britain's godawful season, and he pitched a lot of innings in winter ball. He's very young and already at risk.

Saul Rivera — Throws R — Age 23

YEAR	TEAM	LGE	IP	H	ER	HR	BB	K	ERA	W	L	H/9	HR/9	BB/9	K/9	KW	PERA
1998	Elizbthn	App	29.3	28	21	10	27	28	6.44	1	2	8.59	3.07	8.28	8.59	0.52	8.62
1999	Quad Cit	Mid	63.0	49	16	2	42	54	2.29	5	2	7.00	0.29	6.00	7.71	0.64	3.85
2000	Ft Myers	Fla	33.3	36	21	3	25	26	5.67	1	3	9.72	0.81	6.75	7.02	0.52	6.28
2000	New Brit	Eas	33.7	30	20	2	24	30	5.35	1	3	8.02	0.53	6.42	8.02	0.63	4.80

The Twins take the time to look at talent that other organizations might simply ignore. Saul Rivera is a Puerto Rican drafted out of the University of Mobile. He's short (5'11") for someone who throws over 90 mph with a good slider. A creative organization can scare up relievers from all sorts of places. Rivera had no trouble with Double-A, and a good camp will help get him into the majors sometime this summer. The Twins have another good young Puerto Rican reliever with college experience in Juan Padilla, who is also short and effective.

J.C. Romero — Throws L — Age 25

YEAR	TEAM	LGE	IP	H	ER	HR	BB	K	ERA	W	L	H/9	HR/9	BB/9	K/9	KW	PERA
1998	New Brit	Eas	71.0	50	35	5	50	48	4.44	4	4	6.34	0.63	6.34	6.08	0.48	3.95
1999	New Brit	Eas	48.0	54	31	10	38	33	5.81	2	3	10.13	1.88	7.13	6.19	0.43	7.81
1999	SaltLake	PCL	19.0	17	10	1	14	14	4.74	1	1	8.05	0.47	6.63	6.63	0.50	4.90
2000	SaltLake	PCL	63.0	56	35	6	23	27	5.00	3	4	8.00	0.86	3.29	3.86	0.59	3.90
2000	Minnesot	AL	58.7	67	41	6	22	48	6.29	2	5	10.28	0.92	3.38	7.36	1.09	5.31

J.C. Romero started the season on the DL with a strained shoulder but came back flashing his same nice assortment: low-90s heat, a slurve, a cutter, and a change-up. He may get pushed into situational relief because left-handed hitters struggle to do anything against him. While Romero will compete with Kinney for the last rotation slot, he'd be better off in the pen, getting spot starts against teams like the A's.

Jason Ryan — Throws R — Age 25

YEAR	TEAM	LGE	IP	H	ER	HR	BB	K	ERA	W	L	H/9	HR/9	BB/9	K/9	KW	PERA
1998	WestTenn	Sou	138.3	175	107	33	55	77	6.96	4	11	11.39	2.15	3.58	5.01	0.70	7.36
1999	WestTenn	Sou	41.7	31	14	2	16	33	3.02	3	2	6.70	0.43	3.46	7.13	1.03	2.87
1999	New Brit	Eas	46.0	50	36	10	27	26	7.04	1	4	9.78	1.96	5.28	5.09	0.48	6.92
1999	SaltLake	PCL	52.7	52	31	7	23	23	5.30	2	4	8.89	1.20	3.93	3.93	0.50	5.02
1999	Minnesot	AL	40.7	42	18	7	13	14	3.98	3	2	9.30	1.55	2.88	3.10	0.54	5.21
2000	SaltLake	PCL	93.0	89	46	16	28	47	4.45	4	6	8.61	1.55	2.71	4.55	0.84	4.73
2000	Minnesot	AL	26.3	34	19	6	7	18	6.49	1	2	11.62	2.05	2.39	6.15	1.29	6.89

The improved control Jason Ryan has shown for the past year-and-a-half seems to be the product of finally getting fitted for glasses. He can throw four pitches for strikes, but he doesn't have a lot of velocity. Signed by the Pirates, he's in the mix for one of the last spots in the bullpen; if others flop in camp or during the season, he might start a few games. If there's a staff-filler career track, he's on it. Then again, that's the job that gave Redman his big opportunity.

Johan Santana — Throws L — Age 22

YEAR	TEAM	LGE	IP	H	ER	HR	BB	K	ERA	W	L	H/9	HR/9	BB/9	K/9	KW	PERA
1998	Auburn	NYP	77.3	94	74	23	26	39	8.61	2	7	10.94	2.68	3.03	4.54	0.75	7.43
1999	Michigan	Mid	147.7	170	110	28	61	80	6.70	4	12	10.36	1.71	3.72	4.88	0.66	6.34
2000	Minnesot	AL	87.7	96	51	8	40	61	5.24	4	6	9.86	0.82	4.11	6.26	0.76	5.27

One of the Twins' best moves of the year was the decision to retain Johan Santana as a Rule 5 pick instead of keeping Bobby Ayala on the roster. In developing talent, there is no substitute for playing time, and Kelly made a great decision in letting Santana pitch instead of leaving him to rot in the bullpen like the Angels did with Derrick Turnbow. Santana has a good fastball, curve, and change-up. He'll probably spend 2001 in the rotation at either New Britain or Edmonton, but he could win a bullpen job or even the fifth starter's job in camp.

Brent Schoening   Throws R   Age 23

YEAR	TEAM	LGE	IP	H	ER	HR	BB	K	ERA	W	L	H/9	HR/9	BB/9	K/9	KW	PERA
1999	Quad Cit	Mid	10.0	8	4	2	6	6	3.60	1	0	7.20	1.80	5.40	5.40	0.50	5.33
2000	Ft Myers	Fla	63.0	63	35	8	35	33	5.00	3	4	9.00	1.14	5.00	4.71	0.47	5.49

A fifth-round pick in the 1999 draft, Brent Schoening had a better junior year at Auburn in 1999 than Chris Bootcheck did in 2000, going 13–1 with a 3.32 ERA while allowing less than a hit per inning and striking out 151 batters in 138 innings. Elbow troubles have hampered his pro career, but he hasn't needed surgery, and he pitched well in the second half of 2000. Schoening can get into the low 90s, has good breaking stuff, and knows how to use it. He's not a prospect so much as evidence that the Twins spend a lot of time picking pitchers from top college programs and not just affordable guys or Third World kids.

Brent Stentz   Throws R   Age 25

YEAR	TEAM	LGE	IP	H	ER	HR	BB	K	ERA	W	L	H/9	HR/9	BB/9	K/9	KW	PERA
1998	New Brit	Eas	53.7	46	16	5	32	39	2.68	4	2	7.71	0.84	5.37	6.54	0.61	4.53
1999	SaltLake	PCL	25.3	40	30	6	20	16	10.66	0	3	14.21	2.13	7.11	5.68	0.40	10.45
1999	New Brit	Eas	28.3	27	19	5	13	27	6.04	1	2	8.58	1.59	4.13	8.58	1.04	5.35
2000	New Brit	Eas	23.0	34	17	4	6	16	6.65	1	2	13.30	1.57	2.35	6.26	1.33	7.39
2000	SaltLake	PCL	44.7	31	13	6	12	33	2.62	3	2	6.25	1.21	2.42	6.65	1.38	2.96

Brent Stentz is a big guy who throws in the low 90s and supplements the heat with a decent slider. He depends on a herky-herky motion to keep hitters from picking up the ball. Minor-league closers are bad risks. Stentz could turn into a useful middle reliever, but in this organization, he may just be the ghost of Gus Gandarillases yet to come.

Brad Thomas   Throws L   Age 23

YEAR	TEAM	LGE	IP	H	ER	HR	BB	K	ERA	W	L	H/9	HR/9	BB/9	K/9	KW	PERA
1998	Ft Wayne	Mid	137.7	154	87	24	57	64	5.69	5	10	10.07	1.57	3.73	4.18	0.56	6.03
1999	Ft Myers	Fla	139.3	182	117	27	59	65	7.56	3	12	11.76	1.74	3.81	4.20	0.55	7.25
2000	Ft Myers	Fla	59.0	65	42	8	21	33	6.41	2	5	9.92	1.22	3.20	5.03	0.79	5.36
2000	New Brit	Eas	70.0	80	51	6	51	43	6.56	2	6	10.29	0.77	6.56	5.53	0.42	6.50

An Aussie and an Olympian (for them, not us), Brad Thomas has been clocked as high as 95 mph but is more consistently in the low 90s. In addition to the heat, he has a good change-up and a working curve. He needs to set up his pitches more effectively if he wants to continue to start, but his future looks good. How did the Twins get him? The Dodgers had him signed in 1997, but a visa screw-up made him a free agent. The Twins knew who he was and grabbed him.

Bob Wells   Throws R   Age 34

YEAR	TEAM	LGE	IP	H	ER	HR	BB	K	ERA	W	L	H/9	HR/9	BB/9	K/9	KW	PERA
1998	Seattle	AL	50.7	50	33	11	14	27	5.86	2	4	8.88	1.95	2.49	4.80	0.96	5.23
1999	Minnesot	AL	86.0	73	34	6	22	42	3.56	6	4	7.64	0.63	2.30	4.40	0.95	3.11
2000	Minnesot	AL	85.3	73	30	10	11	72	3.16	6	3	7.70	1.05	1.16	7.59	3.27	3.10

Last year, we wondered if Boomer had a specific skill as far as pitching with men on base. This year, despite his 11 blown saves, he once again stranded more than two-thirds of the runners he inherited. He came into 24 games with two or three men on base and didn't allow a man to score in 13 of them. Compare that to Hawkins, who saw eight of those situations and didn't allow anyone to score in seven of them, and to Eddie Guardado, who inherited multiple runners 14 times and sent the opposition away disappointed nine times. Is Bob Wells good at this "ice water in his veins" thing or not? Whatever the case, he's getting more opportunities. That isn't meant as a putdown of Wells: he and the Twins have been good for each other.

Support-Neutral Statistics — MINNESOTA TWINS — Park Effect: +13.2%

PITCHER	GS	IP	R	SNW	SNL	SNPCT	W	L	RA	APW	SNVA	SNWAR
Sean Bergman	14	67.3	72	2.4	7.3	.249	4	5	9.62	-2.7	-2.2	-1.7
Matt Kinney	8	42.3	26	2.7	2.4	.523	2	2	5.53	0.0	0.0	0.5
Mike Lincoln	4	13.7	22	0.1	2.7	.045	0	3	14.49	-1.2	-1.2	-1.1
Joe Mays	28	155.7	102	9.2	9.9	.484	7	15	5.90	-0.4	-0.3	1.1
Eric Milton	33	200.0	123	12.9	10.9	.541	13	10	5.54	0.2	0.9	2.7
Brad Radke	34	226.7	119	14.7	10.1	.593	12	16	4.73	2.0	2.1	4.1
Mark Redman	24	136.0	73	9.5	7.0	.576	11	9	4.83	1.1	1.2	2.5
J.C. Romero	11	53.7	46	2.7	4.8	.362	2	7	7.71	-1.1	-1.0	-0.5
Jason Ryan	1	3.0	5	0.0	0.6	.072	0	1	15.00	-0.3	-0.3	-0.2
Johan Santana	5	22.0	24	1.1	2.1	.334	0	3	9.82	-0.9	-0.5	-0.3
TOTALS	162	920.3	612	55.3	57.7	.489	51	71	5.98	-3.3	-1.2	7.3

The Twins had quite a few bright spots in 2000: a fine season by Brad Radke, the second good year in a row by Eric Milton, and a debut season by Mark Redman that should have gotten him more votes for Rookie of the Year than it did. But the Twins rotation as a whole was pulled down by a couple of awful performances. Sean Bergman was the third-worst starter in the league by Support Neutral Wins Above Replacement, and Mike Lincoln was 13th-worst.

We might expect that a team's having near-league-worst performances in the rotation would point to improvement for the rotation next year, on the theory that the offenders will be gone the following season. (See the Marlins Support-Neutral comment for some empirical support for this theory.) I wonder if the Twins aren't the exception to that rule, though. The thing with the Twins is that they manage to have near-league-worst performances in their rotation almost every year. Of the worst 30 seasons since 1994 by Support-Neutral Wins Above Replacement, five are by Twins. Of the worst 100 seasons, 13 are by Twins. It makes you wonder who the Twins will find next year to follow in the proud tradition of Jim Deshaies, Pat Mahomes, Scott Aldred, LaTroy Hawkins, Dan Perkins, and Sean Bergman. Chances are good that Tom Kelly will unearth someone who can't get anyone out, then leave him in the rotation for about ten starts too many, hoping he'll remedy his problems. In the Giants' SN comment, we point out how patience is a virtue for managers like Dusty Baker and Larry Dierker. With Tom Kelly it might be a vice—he seems to show patience with guys who just never get any better.

For a quick explanation of SN stats, see page 7.

Reliever Evaluation Tools

PITCHER	G	IP	R	ARA	APR	IRNR/G	EIRS/G	IRP	BRS	RRA	ARP
Sean Bergman	1	0.7	4	49.94	-3.3	0.00	0.00	0.0	0.2	49.67	-3.3
Hector Carrasco	61	72.0	38	4.39	6.4	0.80	0.30	-4.3	2.0	5.36	-1.3
Jack Cressend	11	13.7	8	4.87	0.5	0.91	0.47	-0.9	-0.0	5.61	-0.6
Eddie Guardado	70	61.7	27	3.64	10.6	0.70	0.28	1.1	1.9	3.83	9.4
LaTroy Hawkins	66	87.7	34	3.23	19.2	0.50	0.16	3.8	5.1	3.39	17.6
Mike Lincoln	4	7.0	3	3.57	1.3	0.00	0.00	0.0	0.0	3.43	1.4
Joe Mays	3	4.7	3	5.35	-0.1	0.33	0.16	0.4	0.0	4.43	0.4
Travis Miller	67	67.0	35	4.35	6.3	0.70	0.27	-3.5	2.5	5.14	0.4
Danny Mota	4	5.3	5	7.80	-1.5	2.00	1.12	-1.1	0.4	10.21	-3.0
Mark Redman	8	15.3	8	4.34	1.5	1.00	0.45	-1.2	-0.6	4.70	0.8
J.C. Romero	1	4.0	5	10.40	-2.3	1.00	0.48	-0.5	-1.2	8.15	-1.3
Jason Ryan	15	23.0	19	6.88	-4.3	0.47	0.17	-3.2	-0.5	7.88	-6.8
Johan Santana	25	64.0	40	5.20	-0.0	0.08	0.02	0.4	-0.1	5.42	-1.6
Bob Wells	76	86.3	39	3.76	13.8	0.92	0.38	8.5	1.2	3.17	19.4
TOTALS	412	512.3	268	4.35	48.0	0.69	0.28			4.64	31.5

For a quick guide to RET, see page 10.

New York Yankees

Regardless of where the 1996-2000 Yankees rank among the great teams in baseball lore, what's clear is that they are one of the greatest *postseason* teams in history. They've run a gauntlet over the past five seasons that is unsurpassed in baseball and may be unmatched in all of professional sports.

Since 1996, the Yankees have played 13 postseason series, winning 12. They have been forced to a deciding game just twice, in the 1997 Division Series against the Indians (the Yankees' only series loss) and in the 2000 Division Series against the Athletics. So not only have they won four championships, they've been seriously challenged only twice, and never after the Division Series. Table 1 breaks down the Yankees' record from 1996 through 2000 by playoff level.

Against the very best competition, the Yankees have played just shy of .750 postseason ball in a five-season span. That's phenomenal. The only teams that can approach that kind of performance are the Chicago Bulls of the 1990s (who look even more impressive if you count just the Michael Jordan years) and the Montreal Canadiens of the mid-1970s. Before that, of course, the playoff systems in all sports were considerably smaller, making comparisons less valid.

In *Baseball Prospectus,* we often suggest that luck is a significant factor in the postseason, and that the result of a short series doesn't really tell you much about the relative quality of the teams. So why is the Yankees team essay opening with a paean to their play in October? After all, they weren't even one of the four best teams in their league last season, and, thanks to that short-series factor, didn't even have to play the best team in the AL, the White Sox, to get to the World Series.

Pitcher won/lost records provide the best comparison for postseason won/loss records. Over the course of a season, the support a pitcher gets from his team's offense and bullpen can yield for him a won/lost record that does not accurately reflect the quality of his pitching. This is the reason we prefer to use ERA or, better still, Support-Neutral measures, to evaluate a pitcher's performance. Over the course of many years, however, run and bullpen support should even out, and we find it acceptable to look at wins and losses in evaluating careers. Even in career evaluations though, the won/loss record is not a perfect tool—pitchers who were saddled with lousy teams, like Walter Johnson and Phil Niekro, can lose in the comparison—but career won/lost record is nevertheless an infinitely better tool than seasonal won/lost record. Time evens out the breaks.

Similarly, in any given season, a team can win the World Series without being the best performer over the long haul. Baseball doesn't give out rings for regular-season records, but rather for winning three best-ofs in four weeks, so there can be a difference between being the best team in a season and being its champion. Some people don't like that fact—maybe even some people reading this book—but the distinction is a legitimate one. Short series are unpredictable because broken bats and bad bounces don't necessarily even out over the course of a week. Additionally, baseball's postseason teams tend to be of sufficiently similar quality that true differences between them can't be determined in seven or fewer games.

But over a span of years, it's not likely that one team would be consistently luckier in the postseason than others. The same breaks that even out over years and cause pitcher won/lost records to become a better measure of performance should also even out to cause postseason play to be a legitimate measure of team quality. That the Yankees have gone 46–16 in the postseason over five years is a valid indicator of their greatness in October.

In many years, the Braves have had teams as good as or better than the Yankees, yet they have just one world championship. The Indians appeared in five straight postseasons from 1995 to 1999 without ever winning a title. What has made the Yankees so good in the playoffs? Three reasons:

Yankees Prospectus

2000 record: 87–74; First place, AL East; Beat Mets in World Series, 4-1

Pythagenport W/L: 86–75

Runs Scored: 871 (6th in AL)

Runs Allowed: 814 (4th in AL)

Team EqA: .267 (6th in AL)

2000 Batters' Age: 31.2 (3rd oldest in AL)

2000 Pitchers' Age: 31.6 (oldest in AL)

Ballpark: Yankee Stadium; moderate pitchers' park; Park Factor of .952

2000: Good in-season maneuvering got them to October; pitching got them through it.

2001: They didn't get any younger in the offseason, falling behind the Red Sox.

Table 1: Yankees' Postseason Record 1996–2000

Division Series:	14–6
League Championship Series:	16–7
World Series:	16–3
Overall:	46–16

1. Frontline pitching. The Yankees have had good-to-great starting pitching and excellent bullpens for the entirety of their run. The postseason is a test of frontline talent, and the Yankees' frontline pitching—the six or seven hurlers who pitch 95% of their October innings—has been exceptional. You can count on two hands the number of bad starts they've gotten during their run—even fewer appendages needed if you exclude Kenny Rogers—and their bullpen, built around Mariano Rivera, has earned its mythic status.

2. OBP. The Yankees' offense during this run has been built largely around high-OBP hitters who draw a fair amount of walks. Facing the top halves of playoff-caliber pitching staffs, the ability to get on base becomes a bigger factor. The Yankees' plate discipline (not uniform, but collectively above average) has had two impacts: more base runners and more work for the opposition frontline pitching.

   The importance of OBP cannot be understated, particularly when you consider its effect on opposing staffs. The Yankees almost never go deeper than seven pitchers in the postseason. Meanwhile, their opponents have often been forced to use the eighth through 11th men. Each season, you can point to games the Yankees won because they were facing the bottom of a pitching staff. Steve Avery in Game Four of the 1996 World Series and Mark Langston in Game One of the 1998 World Series stand out as examples.

3. Luck. Even over five seasons, luck plays a factor, and the Yankees have had more than their share. From David Weathers and Jim Leyritz in 1996 to Jose Vizcaino in 2000, the Yankees have squeezed a century's worth of unlikely heroes into one five-year run. (Of course, Orioles fans will also mention Jeffrey Maier, and Mets fans will invoke Timo Perez and Todd Zeile.)

   The Yankees have also had the luxury of facing the Padres in the 1998 World Series and the Mets in 2000, instead of superior NL teams that could have presented tougher matchups. Last year, not only did they miss the White Sox, but they played the Division Series against an A's team that was off its rotation. All of these factors helped make it possible for them to go 46–16.

What's next for the dynasty? The Yankees return pretty much the same team in 2001 that partied into the New York night last October 25. Mike Mussina has been added to bolster a rotation that suffered through David Cone's collapse in 2000. D'Angelo Jimenez will replace Jose Vizcaino as the sixth infielder and may begin to push Scott Brosius for playing time at third base. There will be some new faces in the bullpen, with Jeff Nelson having returned to the Mariners.

After the Mussina signing, the consensus—bucked by the notable exception of Bob Klapisch at ESPN.com—was that the Yankees were clear favorites for a fourpeat. This prediction, of course, ignores the fact that the aging 87–74 team of 2000 is a year older without any real prospects for improvement in the starting lineup. A typical Mussina season will be worth anywhere from four to six wins above what Cone provided, but that might be enough only to cancel out the declines the team is likely to see at all four corner positions—where production is already inadequate—as well as at catcher and center field, where great players are likely to decline from excellent seasons. Jorge Posada is a longtime BP favorite, but you won't find anyone on our staff who thinks he can run a 944 OPS again.

Part of the groupthink among prognosticators stems from the Yankees' free-spending ways. A lot has been made of their ability to support a payroll much higher than that of the competition. In fact, the Yankees' high payroll and high success is primarily what drives the arguments that baseball is somehow in trouble. For teams other than the Yankees, the payroll/performance relationship is a dubious one. Most arguments for revenue sharing, at their core, look like "get the Yankees" schemes.

That said, the Yankees are clearly operating in a different economic environment. Their massive local-television contract, as well as the high demand for Yankee tickets in a large and affluent market, affords them a revenue stream unmatched in the sport. The Yankees do not have to worry much about the cost of in-season acquisitions, even if they must commit millions of dollars in future salaries. The David Justice deal, and, to a lesser extent, the Glenallen Hill pickup, are examples of this. No doubt, the Yankees' revenue stream does give them an advantage. It's not an insurmountable one—the Yankees had the fifth-best record in the AL last season—but it does mean they play by different rules.

The problem is that you can't implement a solution to that affects only one team. The Yankees are an outlier in all categories: market, revenue, success, payroll. Solutions that might force them to change their behavior would almost certainly invoke The Law of Unintended Consequences on many other teams.

The Collective Bargaining Agreement reached in 1996 implemented a revenue-sharing system that tied disbursements to payroll. The plan was intended to help low-payroll teams compete. The effect was to incentivize not spending money. To the justified howls of George Steinbrenner, the Expos and Twins pared their payrolls to the bone and pocketed the revenue-sharing money as profit.

In retrospect, tying eligibility for revenue sharing to expenditures was the flaw in the plan. It severed the relationship between success and marginal revenue that had existed for some time: to make more money, win more. Now, a team could make more money by not trying win than by trying and having only moderate success.

In tying revenue sharing to payroll, MLB used a flawed approach. The relationships among market, payroll, success, revenue, and—the forgotten factor—capitalization are much more complex than your average team owner or local sportscaster wants you to believe. Salaries don't drive ticket prices, demand does. Nevertheless, the lie about greedy players taking money out of Joe Sixpack's pocket gets told every single day in some sports section somewhere.

MLB also wants you to believe that teams in large markets have the highest payrolls and win all the time. That isn't true. There are large-market teams with low payrolls. There are small-market teams that win. There are small-market teams that have large revenue streams. Teams in a variety of markets are owned by corporations or high-net-worth individuals. Some of them invest in their teams (Tom Hicks, Rangers), and some of them don't (Carl Pohlad, Twins).

MLB is desperate to win its shady PR battle because any careful examination of the issues will lead to all kinds of unpleasant conclusions. Already, we've seen owners sign off on a plan—one transferring revenue based on expenditures—with significant negative consequences. A switch to a more logical system that transfers revenue based on revenue would lead to absurdities like well run small-market teams giving money to poorly run large-market teams.

Transferring revenue based on actual revenue generated would also force owners to open their books. They don't want to do that, because every time an economist has looked at their books, the owners have gotten their heads handed to them. The baseball industry is not losing money; some teams are, if not as many as The Lords would have you believe. All teams can compete if they so desire, and more teams are competitive today than have been for most of baseball's history. Competitive balance is historically high, not low.

That the Yankees have had a lot of success while plowing their revenues back into their team is not a reason to damn the system; it's a reason to celebrate it.

HITTERS (BA: .270, OBP: .340, SLG: .440, EqA: .260)

Erick Almonte — SS — Bats R — Age 23

YEAR	TEAM	LGE	AB	H	DB	TP	HR	BB	SO	R	RBI	SB	CS	OUT	BA	OBP	SLG	EQA	EQR	DEFENSE
1998	Greensbr	SAL	457	89	8	0	6	20	127	41	27	2	1	369	.195	.231	.252	.140	14	119-SS -38
1999	Tampa	Fla	232	51	6	1	5	14	57	28	19	1	1	182	.220	.267	.319	.190	14	61-SS -1
2000	Norwich	Eas	461	112	14	2	14	25	139	45	60	7	2	351	.243	.284	.373	.218	39	125-SS -18
2001	NY Yanks	AL	356	82	10	1	10	25	111	34	39	4	1	275	.230	.281	.348	.214	29	

Erick Almonte shot up the prospect lists with a big season in the Arizona Fall League. Don't be fooled: he's not even the best shortstop prospect with lousy plate discipline in this organization. With Derek Jeter, D'Angelo Jimenez, and Alfonso Soriano ahead of him, look for Almonte to be part of a deal to acquire a hitter. He's not a top prospect.

Clay Bellinger — UT — Bats B — Age 32

YEAR	TEAM	LGE	AB	H	DB	TP	HR	BB	SO	R	RBI	SB	CS	OUT	BA	OBP	SLG	EQA	EQR	DEFENSE			
1998	Columbus	Int	399	80	18	2	6	25	84	28	31	3	2	321	.201	.254	.301	.178	21	30-1B	-5	24-SS	-1
1999	Columbus	Int	142	30	9	1	1	9	34	15	11	4	0	112	.211	.265	.310	.194	9	21-3B	0		
1999	NY Yanks	AL	45	9	2	0	1	1	9	9	2	1	0	36	.200	.217	.311	.165	2	11-3B	1		
2000	NY Yanks	AL	184	39	9	2	6	15	44	32	20	5	0	145	.212	.290	.380	.228	18	23-CF	0	12-3B	1
2001	NY Yanks	AL	219	45	8	1	5	18	54	22	19	5	0	174	.205	.266	.320	.202	16				

Clay Bellinger made at least five appearances at seven different positions in 2000. He's a good spare part who, by learning how to play the outfield, has earned himself two World Series rings and a lot of money. He'll stay in this role for at least a couple more years.

American League

Scott Brosius — 3B — Bats R — Age 34

YEAR	TEAM	LGE	AB	H	DB	TP	HR	BB	SO	R	RBI	SB	CS	OUT	BA	OBP	SLG	EQA	EQR	DEFENSE	
1998	NY Yanks	AL	531	166	26	0	24	51	86	87	103	9	8	372	.313	.383	.497	.289	84	150-3B	17
1999	NY Yanks	AL	473	121	25	1	19	35	67	64	71	9	3	355	.256	.314	.433	.248	55	130-3B	14
2000	NY Yanks	AL	469	110	17	0	18	40	66	55	63	0	3	362	.235	.298	.386	.225	43	126-3B	16
2001	NY Yanks	AL	453	110	14	0	17	40	71	52	61	4	3	346	.243	.304	.386	.235	47		

Even with the dramatic decline from his 1998 peak, Scott Brosius does things that would make him an asset in a reduced role. He plays good defense at third base and hits for some power against left-handers. It's up to the Yankees to find someone to take 250 of Brosius's at-bats; D'Angelo Jimenez would be a great choice.

Jose Canseco — DH — Bats R — Age 36

YEAR	TEAM	LGE	AB	H	DB	TP	HR	BB	SO	R	RBI	SB	CS	OUT	BA	OBP	SLG	EQA	EQR	DEFENSE	
1998	Toronto	AL	582	139	23	0	49	64	142	96	106	23	15	458	.239	.320	.531	.270	87	68-LF	-9
1999	TampaBay	AL	426	120	18	1	35	54	123	73	91	3	0	306	.282	.371	.575	.304	78		
2000	TampaBay	AL	215	55	10	0	11	38	59	29	29	2	0	160	.256	.378	.456	.282	34		
2000	NY Yanks	AL	110	27	4	0	6	22	34	16	18	0	0	83	.245	.371	.445	.276	17		
2001	Anaheim	AL	314	72	10	0	20	54	92	50	57	3	1	243	.229	.342	.452	.269	46		

Jose Canseco should never play the field again, which puts him about where Harold Baines was a decade ago. Like Baines, Canseco is a good enough hitter that he can help a team win a championship. Canseco has played more than 131 games just twice since his MVP season of 1988 and still has managed 446 home runs. Had he been blessed with a stronger back, he would be approaching 600 bombs and immortality. Here's hoping people don't forget just how great a player he was with the A's.

Glenallen Hill — DH — Bats R — Age 36

YEAR	TEAM	LGE	AB	H	DB	TP	HR	BB	SO	R	RBI	SB	CS	OUT	BA	OBP	SLG	EQA	EQR	DEFENSE	
1998	Seattle	AL	259	78	18	2	14	13	40	38	34	1	1	182	.301	.341	.548	.285	39	60-LF	-6
1998	ChiCubs	NL	133	46	5	0	8	13	32	26	22	0	0	87	.346	.404	.564	.315	24	29-LF	2
1999	ChiCubs	NL	253	73	8	1	19	19	58	40	50	4	1	181	.289	.338	.553	.286	40	48-LF	-9
2000	ChiCubs	NL	169	43	5	1	10	8	40	22	26	0	1	127	.254	.288	.473	.244	19	25-LF	-2
2000	NY Yanks	AL	131	45	6	0	16	8	30	22	28	0	0	86	.344	.386	.756	.345	30	10-LF	-1
2001	NY Yanks	AL	265	72	10	1	17	23	64	38	54	1	1	194	.272	.330	.509	.278	39		

Clay Davenport's Prospectus Fielding Runs just don't do justice to the way Glenallen Hill plays left field. He misjudges most balls, so his first step is tentative. When he finally sticks his glove up, it's with all the confidence of the class nerd asking the cute girl in the second row for a date. The only thing that makes him a better choice out there than Canseco is that Hill can play defense without ending up on the DL. Hill has a limited role—lefty-mashing—and does it as well as anyone in the game.

Derek Jeter — SS — Bats R — Age 27

YEAR	TEAM	LGE	AB	H	DB	TP	HR	BB	SO	R	RBI	SB	CS	OUT	BA	OBP	SLG	EQA	EQR	DEFENSE	
1998	NY Yanks	AL	627	213	24	9	21	56	106	129	86	26	6	420	.340	.398	.507	.303	106	148-SS	-3
1999	NY Yanks	AL	622	223	37	9	26	85	106	132	100	18	8	407	.359	.444	.572	.333	131	156-SS	-12
2000	NY Yanks	AL	588	204	31	4	16	61	90	116	70	24	5	389	.347	.419	.495	.310	104	146-SS	-22
2001	NY Yanks	AL	611	206	31	6	19	74	106	134	121	22	7	412	.337	.409	.501	.312	112		

Yes, his defense really is that bad. No, it doesn't mean he should be moved. His offense is still more than enough to make him a championship-caliber player, and none of the Yankees' shortstop prospects are superior fielders. Derek Jeter still has a power spike coming; like Barry Larkin, his plate discipline and power will keep improving into his thirties.

D'Angelo Jimenez — IF — Bats B — Age 23

YEAR	TEAM	LGE	AB	H	DB	TP	HR	BB	SO	R	RBI	SB	CS	OUT	BA	OBP	SLG	EQA	EQR	DEFENSE	
1998	Norwich	Eas	156	36	6	1	2	20	27	18	17	3	3	123	.231	.323	.321	.220	14	40-SS	-1
1998	Columbus	Int	346	80	16	3	7	37	66	46	42	3	4	270	.231	.307	.355	.221	31	87-SS	-4
1999	Columbus	Int	524	151	27	5	11	48	74	75	67	16	10	383	.288	.349	.422	.258	65	116-SS	-5
1999	NY Yanks	AL	20	8	3	0	0	3	4	3	4	0	0	12	.400	.478	.550	.346	4		
2000	Tampa	Fla	43	8	1	0	1	6	8	6	2	0	0	35	.186	.286	.279	.190	3		
2000	Columbus	Int	74	17	2	1	1	5	12	9	5	1	0	57	.230	.286	.324	.205	5	13-2B	-7
2001	NY Yanks	AL	276	74	12	2	5	33	48	42	37	5	4	206	.268	.346	.380	.253	33		

(D'Angelo Jimenez *continued*)

D'Angelo Jimenez is a finalist in the "Best Season After an Off-Season Broken Neck" balloting. Forget the value of the performance and just tip your cap to him for playing so soon after suffering the injury in a January car accident. Healthy again, he's one of the better prospects in baseball. Jimenez will be with the Yankees this year; whether he plays second base or third base is yet to be determined.

Brian Johnson   C   Bats R   Age 33

YEAR	TEAM	LGE	AB	H	DB	TP	HR	BB	SO	R	RBI	SB	CS	OUT	BA	OBP	SLG	EQA	EQR	DEFENSE	
1998	San Fran	NL	313	76	8	1	14	27	63	36	35	0	2	239	.243	.312	.409	.238	33	88-C	1
1999	Cincnnti	NL	117	26	6	0	5	8	29	11	17	0	0	91	.222	.272	.402	.219	10	30-C	0
2000	KansasCy	AL	125	26	3	0	5	2	26	8	18	0	0	99	.208	.220	.352	.176	6	36-C	-3
2000	Memphis	PCL	48	10	3	0	2	3	11	4	5	0	0	38	.208	.274	.396	.219	4	12-C	-2
2000	Columbus	Int	69	13	3	0	1	6	10	10	5	0	0	56	.188	.253	.275	.167	3	18-C	-7
2001	LosAngls	NL	210	43	7	0	7	14	46	19	24	0	0	167	.205	.254	.338	.199	15		

You know your career is in trouble when you get released in favor of Jorge Fabregas. Brian Johnson didn't hit (.176 EqA) or throw (13% of base-stealers gunned) while in Kansas City. He's pretty bad defensively but still has pop against left-handers. He'll be in the majors in 2001.

Nick Johnson   1B   Bats L   Age 22

YEAR	TEAM	LGE	AB	H	DB	TP	HR	BB	SO	R	RBI	SB	CS	OUT	BA	OBP	SLG	EQA	EQR	DEFENSE	
1997	Greensbr	SAL	457	102	15	1	12	58	107	55	53	5	2	357	.223	.324	.339	.228	45		
1998	Tampa	Fla	312	78	10	1	12	52	86	50	38	0	2	236	.250	.376	.404	.266	43	89-1B	-1
1999	Norwich	Eas	434	125	26	3	11	98	93	89	65	4	3	312	.288	.441	.438	.306	81	127-1B	0
2001	NY Yanks	AL	391	122	20	2	16	72	90	74	73	3	3	272	.312	.419	.496	.313	75		

Nick Johnson, our #1 prospect a year ago, missed the entire 2000 season with an undiagnosed injury to his left hand. He's working out over the winter and is expected to be ready for spring training. If he's healthy, he goes right back near the top of all prospect lists. There's a lot of reason to worry, though: hand injuries can eliminate a hitter's power, and Johnson wasn't a pillar of health even before this.

David Justice   LF/DH   Bats L   Age 35

YEAR	TEAM	LGE	AB	H	DB	TP	HR	BB	SO	R	RBI	SB	CS	OUT	BA	OBP	SLG	EQA	EQR	DEFENSE	
1998	Clevelnd	AL	537	152	35	2	24	75	87	94	88	7	3	388	.283	.371	.490	.285	84	20-LF	-1
1999	Clevelnd	AL	422	121	16	0	22	89	82	72	84	1	3	304	.287	.413	.481	.300	75	91-LF	-2
2000	Clevelnd	AL	245	64	13	1	21	35	45	43	54	1	1	182	.261	.354	.580	.295	43	45-OF	-3
2000	NY Yanks	AL	273	86	16	0	21	35	38	42	58	1	0	187	.315	.395	.604	.319	54	62-LF	-1
2001	NY Yanks	AL	449	121	18	0	26	79	82	85	93	2	1	329	.269	.379	.483	.294	77		

The trade of the year was the one that brought David Justice to the Yankees for Ricky Ledee and pitching prospects. Justice gave the Yankees the fourth good hitter they desperately needed, and in the current market, his $6.5-million salary is peanuts. He's an affordable bat through 2002.

Roberto Kelly   OF   Bats R   Age 36

YEAR	TEAM	LGE	AB	H	DB	TP	HR	BB	SO	R	RBI	SB	CS	OUT	BA	OBP	SLG	EQA	EQR	DEFENSE	
1998	Texas	AL	255	82	6	3	17	7	41	48	45	0	2	175	.322	.346	.569	.290	39	61-OF	3
1999	Texas	AL	286	85	18	1	8	18	52	39	35	5	1	202	.297	.348	.451	.268	37	71-OF	-1
2000	NY Yanks	AL	25	3	1	0	1	1	5	4	1	0	0	22	.120	.186	.280	.127	1		
2001	Colorado	NL	121	38	5	0	6	9	23	20	24	2	0	83	.314	.362	.504	.261	14		

Roberto Kelly wasn't a bad choice as a fourth outfielder considering the Yankees had two left-handed hitters on the corners to start the season. A sprain of his ulnar collateral ligament ended his year in April and started a parade of lousy outfielders. Lance Johnson, Felix Jose, and Ryan Thompson were among the players who wore pinstripes in 2000.

American League

Chuck Knoblauch — 2B — Bats R — Age 32

YEAR	TEAM	LGE	AB	H	DB	TP	HR	BB	SO	R	RBI	SB	CS	OUT	BA	OBP	SLG	EQA	EQR	DEFENSE	
1998	NY Yanks	AL	604	168	25	4	19	75	62	117	65	26	11	447	.278	.373	.427	.273	87	149-2B	8
1999	NY Yanks	AL	600	181	38	4	19	78	52	118	67	26	9	428	.302	.398	.473	.295	101	149-2B	-16
2000	NY Yanks	AL	398	114	24	2	5	41	41	73	25	16	8	292	.286	.365	.394	.260	50	78-2B	-14
2001	NY Yanks	AL	492	134	24	2	12	66	52	90	69	19	9	367	.272	.358	.402	.266	67		

The pivotal decision for the Yankees heading into 2001 is whether they continue to keep Chuck Knoblauch at second base or put Jimenez there while making Knoblauch the DH. Neither option is particularly vibrant: Knoblauch won't hit enough to be a good DH, but playing him at second base sets up a potential circus. Anywhere he plays, he's going to be overpriced. It's a shame his career has gone this way, because Knoblauch was a superior second baseman from 1992–96.

Donny Leon — 3B — Bats B — Age 25

YEAR	TEAM	LGE	AB	H	DB	TP	HR	BB	SO	R	RBI	SB	CS	OUT	BA	OBP	SLG	EQA	EQR	DEFENSE	
1998	Tampa	Fla	387	94	18	1	8	16	72	42	42	0	0	293	.243	.280	.357	.208	29	99-3B	-21
1999	Norwich	Eas	463	122	26	1	17	22	107	56	76	0	0	341	.263	.299	.434	.240	48	109-3B	-20
2000	Columbus	Int	206	48	7	1	8	16	51	26	22	2	2	160	.233	.293	.393	.226	19	58-3B	2
2000	Tampa	Fla	80	15	2	0	2	5	27	4	12	0	0	65	.188	.240	.287	.163	3		
2001	NY Yanks	AL	284	70	12	0	10	22	75	32	39	1	0	214	.246	.301	.394	.237	29		

Donny Leon should not be on the list of possible platoon partners for Brosius. He just doesn't put enough runs on the board, and there are still questions about his defensive ability. His prospect status is mostly a function of the organization's lack of quality position players.

Tino Martinez — 1B — Bats L — Age 33

YEAR	TEAM	LGE	AB	H	DB	TP	HR	BB	SO	R	RBI	SB	CS	OUT	BA	OBP	SLG	EQA	EQR	DEFENSE	
1998	NY Yanks	AL	532	156	29	1	32	60	74	95	127	2	1	377	.293	.371	.532	.294	88	142-1B	5
1999	NY Yanks	AL	588	161	27	2	30	63	78	95	104	3	4	431	.274	.347	.480	.271	82	151-1B	17
2000	NY Yanks	AL	568	151	37	4	17	45	67	67	88	4	1	418	.266	.329	.435	.254	68	144-1B	1
2001	NY Yanks	AL	469	122	25	1	18	47	64	66	75	1	1	348	.260	.328	.433	.259	59		

Even when he was poking 44 home runs in 1997, we were never that high on Tino Martinez, mostly because he didn't walk enough. That said, this is a very steep decline. It's hard to lose 20 points of EqA a year and keep your job. Martinez is being brought back for 2001, primarily because Nick Johnson missed all of last season; he could be jobless by July.

Paul O'Neill — RF — Bats L — Age 38

YEAR	TEAM	LGE	AB	H	DB	TP	HR	BB	SO	R	RBI	SB	CS	OUT	BA	OBP	SLG	EQA	EQR	DEFENSE	
1998	NY Yanks	AL	603	199	37	2	28	56	92	97	120	13	1	405	.330	.389	.537	.306	105	148-RF	-2
1999	NY Yanks	AL	595	174	40	4	20	61	81	69	107	10	9	430	.292	.360	.474	.274	85	142-RF	-4
2000	NY Yanks	AL	564	163	19	0	21	44	82	75	98	15	11	412	.289	.340	.434	.256	69	124-RF	2
2001	NY Yanks	AL	510	138	22	1	18	52	80	76	80	7	4	376	.271	.338	.424	.261	65		

Like Martinez, Paul O'Neill is declining rapidly, the difference being that O'Neill is five years older. He, too, has been brought back for 2001. O'Neill was expected to move to left field this year, but because the Yankees never acquired a right fielder, he will stay in right field. He's no longer an asset on defense. A lineup with Brosius, Martinez, and O'Neill is going to struggle to be league-average.

David Parrish — C — Bats R — Age 22

YEAR	TEAM	LGE	AB	H	DB	TP	HR	BB	SO	R	RBI	SB	CS	OUT	BA	OBP	SLG	EQA	EQR	DEFENSE	
2000	StatenIs	NYP	227	46	11	1	4	15	60	21	20	0	0	181	.203	.257	.313	.183	13	51-C	-2
2001	NY Yanks	AL	110	21	1	0	3	9	47	7	8	0	0	89	.191	.252	.282	.174	6		

The Yankees' #1 pick in the 2000 draft is the son of former Tiger, Phillie, and Angel catcher Lance Parrish. Like his father, David Parrish has a great defensive reputation. He lacks his dad's power, though, and as a college draftee (Michigan), he needs to develop quickly to maintain his prospect status. Parrish is the best of a number of good-field, no-hit catchers in the Yankees' system.

Wily Mo Pena — CF — Bats R — Age 19

YEAR	TEAM	LGE	AB	H	DB	TP	HR	BB	SO	R	RBI	SB	CS	OUT	BA	OBP	SLG	EQA	EQR	DEFENSE	
2000	Greensbr	SAL	254	47	5	1	8	13	97	32	21	2	3	210	.185	.231	.307	.165	12	57-CF	-4
2000	StatenIs	NYP	73	18	2	1	0	1	26	5	6	1	0	55	.247	.272	.301	.188	4	20-CF	0
2001	NY Yanks	AL	146	27	2	1	3	6	74	6	7	1	1	120	.185	.217	.274	.146	5		

It was a brutal year for the Dominican signee. Wily Mo Pena was completely overmatched in the South Atlantic League and had to be sent back to low-A ball in July. His physical tools get scouts excited, and it was a lot to ask an 18-year-old to start in a middle-A league, so there's no reason to panic, even if he does swing at everything.

Luis Polonia — LF — Bats L — Age 36

YEAR	TEAM	LGE	AB	H	DB	TP	HR	BB	SO	R	RBI	SB	CS	OUT	BA	OBP	SLG	EQA	EQR	DEFENSE	
1998	MCT	Mex	345	97	13	6	8	29	0	0	0	23	8	255	.281	.337	.423	.261	44		
1999	Toledo	Int	160	43	5	1	2	7	30	14	16	8	2	119	.269	.299	.350	.223	14	34-LF	0
1999	Detroit	AL	330	106	22	8	10	13	29	44	30	15	9	233	.321	.350	.527	.282	49	38-LF	-1
2000	Detroit	AL	266	74	11	5	6	19	23	36	24	8	6	198	.278	.329	.425	.249	31	23-RF	-2
2000	NY Yanks	AL	77	22	2	0	2	6	6	10	5	4	2	57	.286	.337	.390	.247	9	16-LF	-2
2001	NY Yanks	AL	337	86	12	3	6	28	32	44	38	12	8	259	.255	.312	.362	.232	34		

It's strange, when you look at the players who actually did get traded at midseason, that the Tigers couldn't get anything for Luis Polonia. He's certainly not a stathead favorite, but he's a good pinch hitter who can drive the ball once in a while, pinch-run, and play left field better than Glenallen Hill. Hell, Ed Sprague netted two good prospects.

Jorge Posada — C — Bats B — Age 29

YEAR	TEAM	LGE	AB	H	DB	TP	HR	BB	SO	R	RBI	SB	CS	OUT	BA	OBP	SLG	EQA	EQR	DEFENSE	
1998	NY Yanks	AL	358	100	19	0	20	47	82	58	65	0	1	259	.279	.363	.500	.283	55	92-C	6
1999	NY Yanks	AL	378	96	19	2	13	50	83	50	56	1	0	282	.254	.345	.418	.258	48	102-C	-7
2000	NY Yanks	AL	499	147	30	1	31	101	138	89	84	2	2	354	.295	.421	.545	.317	100	135-C	2
2001	NY Yanks	AL	388	106	20	1	22	76	108	80	84	1	1	283	.273	.392	.500	.303	72		

That'll do. Jorge Posada was the best catcher in the AL last year. Even with Ivan Rodriguez healthy, Posada shouldn't slip further than second, maybe third if Mitch Meluskey plays a lot. Posada tired a bit in September and is not a big guy, so playing him in 151 games again would be a mistake. Then again, with Joe Oliver as the backup, maybe Posada should go for 162.

Juan Rivera — RF — Bats — Age 22

YEAR	TEAM	LGE	AB	H	DB	TP	HR	BB	SO	R	RBI	SB	CS	OUT	BA	OBP	SLG	EQA	EQR	DEFENSE	
1998	Oneonta	NYP	18	4	1	0	0	1	4	1	1	0	0	14	.222	.263	.278	.171	1		
1999	Tampa	Fla	429	96	14	1	12	19	77	38	56	2	2	335	.224	.260	.345	.195	28	91-RF	-2
2000	Norwich	Eas	63	13	3	0	2	5	16	7	10	0	0	50	.206	.265	.349	.200	4	13-RF	-1
2000	Tampa	Fla	416	98	16	1	12	23	64	46	50	5	4	322	.236	.281	.365	.212	33	115-RF	-5
2001	NY Yanks	AL	368	92	14	1	13	27	69	43	51	3	1	277	.250	.301	.399	.239	38		

Lost in the rhetoric about the advantage big-revenue teams enjoy in signing foreign free agents is the fact that most of these guys don't succeed. People like us may get all excited about Glenn Williams or Jackson Melian or Wily Mo Pena, but the bottom line is lots of money is thrown at players about whom very little is known. Juan Rivera got his head handed to him at Double-A, then didn't impress in a repeat run through the Florida State League.

Scott Seabol — 3B — Bats R — Age 26

YEAR	TEAM	LGE	AB	H	DB	TP	HR	BB	SO	R	RBI	SB	CS	OUT	BA	OBP	SLG	EQA	EQR	DEFENSE			
1998	Greensbr	SAL	213	50	7	0	5	9	42	17	22	1	1	164	.235	.271	.338	.197	14	17-LF	0		
1999	Greensbr	SAL	558	138	40	3	9	33	99	61	58	2	2	422	.247	.294	.378	.222	49	133-3B	1		
2000	Norwich	Eas	500	124	30	1	16	30	123	61	55	1	2	378	.248	.294	.408	.230	48	77-3B	-8	13-LF	-3
2001	NY Yanks	AL	428	102	24	1	13	31	102	47	54	1	1	327	.238	.290	.390	.230	41				

Scott Seabol is a late-blooming doubles factory; he's produced 100 in the past two seasons. Normally, a Double-A player this old wouldn't get noticed, but Seabol made the jump from A ball without a hitch. The Yankees added him to the 40-man roster over the winter. If something were to happen to Brosius, Seabol would be a better choice than Leon to pick up the playing time.

American League

Luis Sojo — IF — Bats R — Age 35

YEAR	TEAM	LGE	AB	H	DB	TP	HR	BB	SO	R	RBI	SB	CS	OUT	BA	OBP	SLG	EQA	EQR	DEFENSE			
1998	NY Yanks	AL	147	35	4	1	0	4	13	17	14	1	0	112	.238	.258	.279	.168	7	17-SS	-1	13-1B	0
1999	NY Yanks	AL	127	33	4	0	3	3	15	20	17	1	0	94	.260	.277	.362	.210	9	17-3B	0	14-2B	1
2000	Pittsbrg	NL	177	49	7	0	6	9	15	13	19	1	0	128	.277	.315	.418	.244	19	43-3B	-3		
2000	NY Yanks	AL	125	37	8	1	2	4	5	19	16	1	0	88	.296	.318	.424	.246	13	19-2B	2		
2001	*NY Yanks*	*AL*	*195*	*48*	*5*	*0*	*4*	*11*	*16*	*18*	*20*	*1*	*0*	*147*	*.246*	*.286*	*.333*	*.211*	*15*				

Why the Pirates signed him is a bit of a mystery, but no matter. Luis Sojo found his way back to the Yankees in time to be the regular at second base in the postseason. He's overrated thanks to good hands and good batting averages; the Yankees really need to give his roster spot to Jimenez. He's very popular, both in the clubhouse and in the city, and is back for 2001.

Alfonso Soriano — IF — Bats R — Age 23

YEAR	TEAM	LGE	AB	H	DB	TP	HR	BB	SO	R	RBI	SB	CS	OUT	BA	OBP	SLG	EQA	EQR	DEFENSE			
1999	Norwich	Eas	366	95	18	2	11	22	71	42	50	11	8	279	.260	.306	.410	.235	38	87-SS	-2		
1999	Columbus	Int	82	14	3	1	2	4	18	7	9	1	1	69	.171	.209	.305	.153	3	11-SS	0		
2000	Columbus	Int	461	123	28	4	11	18	88	78	56	10	5	343	.267	.298	.416	.235	46	64-SS	-20	40-2B	-5
2000	NY Yanks	AL	50	9	3	0	2	1	14	5	3	2	0	41	.180	.196	.360	.180	3				
2001	*NY Yanks*	*AL*	*361*	*94*	*20*	*2*	*11*	*17*	*81*	*44*	*49*	*6*	*2*	*269*	*.260*	*.294*	*.418*	*.241*	*38*				

Alfonso Soriano has excellent power for a middle infielder and good physical skills. The erosion in his walk rate and strikeout-to-walk ratio is a concern, but there are some extenuating circumstances. Soriano has been jerked around by the Yankees, splitting time between shortstop and second base at Columbus, then moving to the majors for two weeks and doing on-the-job training at third base. It's not surprising that his offense regressed under those conditions.

Among Soriano, Jimenez, Sojo, and the three starters in New York, the Yankees have to sort out who is going to play where at what level and commit. Having Soriano and/or Jimenez split time at multiple positions and levels is going to hurt both of them in the long run. Soriano has the biggest gap between actual and perceived value, so trading him to help clear up the logjam is the best option.

Shane Spencer — LF — Bats R — Age 29

YEAR	TEAM	LGE	AB	H	DB	TP	HR	BB	SO	R	RBI	SB	CS	OUT	BA	OBP	SLG	EQA	EQR	DEFENSE			
1998	Columbus	Int	342	96	21	1	14	32	60	53	51	1	2	248	.281	.346	.471	.268	46	65-RF	-4	12-1B	0
1998	NY Yanks	AL	67	26	4	0	11	5	11	18	27	0	1	42	.388	.431	.940	.388	20	14-RF	0		
1999	NY Yanks	AL	205	49	7	0	9	16	46	25	20	0	4	160	.239	.300	.405	.227	20	55-LF	2		
1999	Columbus	Int	50	15	0	0	2	7	8	13	8	0	0	35	.300	.386	.420	.276	7	12-LF	0		
2000	NY Yanks	AL	247	71	10	3	10	16	41	32	39	1	2	178	.287	.336	.474	.264	32	40-LF	0		
2001	*NY Yanks*	*AL*	*248*	*67*	*12*	*1*	*11*	*21*	*48*	*34*	*43*	*0*	*2*	*183*	*.270*	*.327*	*.460*	*.263*	*32*				

Shane Spencer got the regular playing time he'd long wanted and proved that he's not cut out for a starting job. He was providing inadequate offense before blowing out a knee in June. With Glenallen Hill—a better version of Spencer—on board, it's hard to see Spencer contributing very much to the 2001 Yankees.

Chris Turner — C — Bats R — Age 32

YEAR	TEAM	LGE	AB	H	DB	TP	HR	BB	SO	R	RBI	SB	CS	OUT	BA	OBP	SLG	EQA	EQR	DEFENSE			
1998	Omaha	PCL	195	47	8	1	1	29	38	22	11	4	2	150	.241	.345	.308	.230	19	52-C	-9		
1999	Buffalo	Int	233	54	5	0	7	26	48	27	24	1	1	180	.232	.311	.343	.221	21	52-C	0	13-1B	0
2000	Columbus	Int	44	11	0	0	2	2	12	4	3	0	0	33	.250	.283	.386	.219	4				
2000	NY Yanks	AL	89	21	1	0	2	9	19	8	7	0	1	69	.236	.313	.315	.210	7	25-C	-2		
2001	*Philadel*	*NL*	*135*	*31*	*2*	*0*	*4*	*15*	*32*	*16*	*17*	*1*	*1*	*105*	*.230*	*.307*	*.333*	*.215*	*11*				

Cipher. Chris Turner is a catch-and-throw guy whose value was in not being Joe Girardi. There's a reason Posada caught the third-most innings of anyone in baseball. "Name the bench players on the 2000 Yankees" is going to be a great trivia question someday. Hell, it may already be.

Jose Vizcaino — IF — Bats B — Age 33

YEAR	TEAM	LGE	AB	H	DB	TP	HR	BB	SO	R	RBI	SB	CS	OUT	BA	OBP	SLG	EQA	EQR	DEFENSE			
1998	LosAngls	NL	242	67	7	0	4	16	33	32	31	7	3	178	.277	.324	.355	.231	23	60-SS	1		
1999	LosAngls	NL	269	69	3	0	3	17	22	26	30	2	1	201	.257	.303	.301	.202	19	39-SS	0	21-2B	1
2000	LosAngls	NL	94	20	2	1	0	9	14	9	4	1	0	74	.213	.287	.255	.182	5	13-SS	2		
2000	NY Yanks	AL	174	48	7	2	0	10	26	22	10	5	8	134	.276	.315	.339	.211	14	43-2B	3		
2001	*Houston*	*NL*	*193*	*47*	*6*	*1*	*1*	*17*	*27*	*25*	*19*	*4*	*3*	*149*	*.244*	*.305*	*.301*	*.199*	*13*				

While he didn't play as well as Sojo did in 2000, Jose Vizcaino is actually a better bench player. He runs better, has a bit more plate discipline, and is a good fielder at three positions. Being a switch-hitter is a nice bonus. He'll help the Astros, who signed him to a small one-year contract.

Bernie Williams — CF — Bats B — Age 32

YEAR	TEAM	LGE	AB	H	DB	TP	HR	BB	SO	R	RBI	SB	CS	OUT	BA	OBP	SLG	EQA	EQR	DEFENSE	
1998	NY Yanks	AL	500	175	30	5	29	73	72	103	99	12	8	333	.350	.434	.604	.333	106	123-CF	3
1999	NY Yanks	AL	586	204	29	6	26	95	86	114	111	8	10	392	.348	.440	.551	.324	117	155-CF	4
2000	NY Yanks	AL	533	167	36	6	32	64	77	105	117	14	6	372	.313	.392	.583	.313	102	134-CF	0
2001	*NY Yanks*	*AL*	*495*	*151*	*28*	*3*	*25*	*82*	*77*	*108*	*109*	*9*	*5*	*349*	*.305*	*.404*	*.525*	*.313*	*96*		

You wouldn't think it possible that the All-Star center fielder for a team in New York that wins four World Series in five years could be underrated. Williams has been the best center fielder in baseball over the past four years and may be the best at the moment, depending on how much credit you give Andruw Jones for his defense. Despite all of that, Williams has received very little attention in the MVP voting, and most people still think Ken Griffey is a better player.

Tom Wilson — C — Bats — Age 30

YEAR	TEAM	LGE	AB	H	DB	TP	HR	BB	SO	R	RBI	SB	CS	OUT	BA	OBP	SLG	EQA	EQR	DEFENSE			
1998	Tucson	PCL	365	90	13	2	8	31	84	42	38	2	1	276	.247	.313	.359	.226	34	83-C	-18	10-1B	-2
1999	Orlando	Sou	106	24	1	0	5	12	39	8	15	0	0	82	.226	.315	.377	.233	11	18-C	-4		
1999	Durham	Int	217	49	12	0	11	39	63	29	29	0	1	169	.226	.344	.433	.259	29	57-C	-1		
2000	Columbus	Int	337	78	14	0	15	58	128	50	52	1	1	260	.231	.348	.407	.256	43	76-C	-12		
2001	*Oakland*	*AL*	*208*	*46*	*6*	*0*	*16*	*40*	*97*	*33*	*41*	*0*	*0*	*162*	*.221*	*.347*	*.481*	*.280*	*34*				

He's overqualified for a major-league job, even if you dock him for his defensive problems. As a backup who can pinch-hit or even DH a few times a week, Wilson would be a tremendous player for $200,000. He's 30 and has migrated to the A's: if it's gonna happen, now is the time.

American League

PITCHERS (ERA: 4.50, H/9: 9.00, HR/9: 1.00, BB/9: 3.00, K/9: 6.00, KW: 1.00, PERA: 4.50)

Ricardo Aramboles — Throws R — Age 19

YEAR	TEAM	LGE	IP	H	ER	HR	BB	K	ERA	W	L	H/9	HR/9	BB/9	K/9	KW	PERA
1999	Greensbr	SAL	31.3	26	11	2	17	16	3.16	2	1	7.47	0.57	4.88	4.60	0.47	3.96
2000	Greensbr	SAL	121.7	166	111	31	61	71	8.21	3	11	12.28	2.29	4.51	5.25	0.58	8.43

One of the "Oops, did I say I was *16*?" free agents, Ricardo Aramboles cashed in for $1.5 million, then had elbow surgery that kept him out for most of 1999. He started slowly before closing strong at Greensboro, a sign that his performance is improving as his health does. He's still a bit off radar and is here only as part of our platform to push for a worldwide draft.

Ryan Bradley — Throws R — Age 25

YEAR	TEAM	LGE	IP	H	ER	HR	BB	K	ERA	W	L	H/9	HR/9	BB/9	K/9	KW	PERA
1998	Tampa	Fla	85.7	65	42	11	39	64	4.41	5	5	6.83	1.16	4.10	6.72	0.82	3.85
1998	Norwich	Eas	23.0	9	6	2	9	15	2.35	2	1	3.52	0.78	3.52	5.87	0.83	1.71
1998	NY Yanks	AL	12.7	12	9	2	8	12	6.39	0	1	8.53	1.42	5.68	8.53	0.75	5.84
1998	Columbus	Int	15.3	15	12	4	12	9	7.04	0	2	8.80	2.35	7.04	5.28	0.38	7.47
1999	Columbus	Int	138.7	159	108	31	71	86	7.01	4	11	10.32	2.01	4.61	5.58	0.61	7.01
2000	Columbus	Int	68.7	82	55	14	52	40	7.21	2	6	10.75	1.83	6.82	5.24	0.38	8.00

When the Yankees called up Ryan Bradley in August 1998, he had a 2.03 ERA as a professional. Since then, his ERA is 5.74. Correlation doesn't imply causation, but he has been a complete disaster for a little more than two years. His 2000 season was his first as a full-time reliever. Bradley's stuff still receives raves, so when the switch gets flipped, he'll be very good.

Randy Choate — Throws L — Age 25

YEAR	TEAM	LGE	IP	H	ER	HR	BB	K	ERA	W	L	H/9	HR/9	BB/9	K/9	KW	PERA
1998	Greensbr	SAL	36.3	45	21	2	10	15	5.20	1	3	11.15	0.50	2.48	3.72	0.75	5.02
1998	Tampa	Fla	64.0	83	66	13	28	31	9.28	1	6	11.67	1.83	3.94	4.36	0.55	7.32
1999	Tampa	Fla	43.3	55	35	10	32	35	7.27	1	4	11.42	2.08	6.65	7.27	0.55	8.55
2000	Columbus	Int	33.3	34	9	3	14	28	2.43	3	1	9.18	0.81	3.78	7.56	1.00	4.71
2000	NY Yanks	AL	17.0	13	9	3	7	12	4.76	1	1	6.88	1.59	3.71	6.35	0.86	4.22

Randy Choate is a lefty specialist who looks the part, coming from the side with average stuff. He did his job in September with the Yankees, so he should be back as the second left-hander in the pen this year. Choate isn't $3 million worse than Rheal Cormier or Graeme Lloyd.

Roger Clemens — Throws R — Age 38

YEAR	TEAM	LGE	IP	H	ER	HR	BB	K	ERA	W	L	H/9	HR/9	BB/9	K/9	KW	PERA
1998	Toronto	AL	231.0	162	70	10	75	251	2.73	18	8	6.31	0.39	2.92	9.78	1.67	2.46
1999	NY Yanks	AL	186.3	174	89	18	74	155	4.30	10	11	8.40	0.87	3.57	7.49	1.05	4.25
2000	NY Yanks	AL	203.0	172	83	23	68	180	3.68	12	11	7.63	1.02	3.01	7.98	1.32	3.74

Roger Clemens possesses as healthy an arm as there is in baseball, a neat trick for a 38-year-old. Clemens has had problems with his right groin, however, and because he gets so much of his power from his legs, the injury has shown up in his performance. In 2000, his ERA was 4.76 prior to a June DL trip for the groin and 3.58 after. If the high strike really is back, Clemens is a threat to have a big season.

David Cone — Throws R — Age 38

YEAR	TEAM	LGE	IP	H	ER	HR	BB	K	ERA	W	L	H/9	HR/9	BB/9	K/9	KW	PERA
1998	NY Yanks	AL	203.3	175	81	19	52	193	3.59	13	10	7.75	0.84	2.30	8.54	1.86	3.36
1999	NY Yanks	AL	191.3	154	73	19	74	168	3.43	12	9	7.24	0.89	3.48	7.90	1.14	3.58
2000	NY Yanks	AL	155.7	180	107	22	66	115	6.19	5	12	10.41	1.27	3.82	6.65	0.87	5.96

At this writing, all we know is that David Cone won't be a Yankee. He's likely to sign for a low base salary and lots of incentives wherever he lands. He's a good risk: while the degradation of his strikeout and walk rates continued, the real problem was the .306 average he surrendered. That figure will come down closer to his career rate (in the .240s) in 2001. He still has a year or two left, maybe more, as an average pitcher. Speculation that Cone could become a reliever is misguided; his problem isn't in-game stamina but rebounding after an appearance. Signed by Boston, where he's supposed to start.

Randy Flores — Throws L — Age 25

YEAR	TEAM	LGE	IP	H	ER	HR	BB	K	ERA	W	L	H/9	HR/9	BB/9	K/9	KW	PERA
1998	Tampa	Fla	21.3	27	26	4	21	9	10.97	0	2	11.39	1.69	8.86	3.80	0.21	9.11
1998	Greensbr	SAL	118.0	126	60	13	46	63	4.58	6	7	9.61	0.99	3.51	4.81	0.68	5.07
1999	Norwich	Eas	23.0	32	23	2	12	12	9.00	0	3	12.52	0.78	4.70	4.70	0.50	7.03
1999	Tampa	Fla	123.0	117	65	10	51	55	4.76	6	8	8.56	0.73	3.73	4.02	0.54	4.26
2000	Norwich	Eas	129.0	138	75	16	70	58	5.23	5	9	9.63	1.12	4.88	4.05	0.41	5.77
2000	Columbus	Int	22.3	41	21	4	7	12	8.46	0	2	16.52	1.61	2.82	4.84	0.86	9.48

Randy Flores is a small left-hander out of USC who, in 2000, managed for the first time in a few years to avoid getting demoted. The Yankees helped by not pushing him up to Columbus after he finally mastered the Florida State League in 1999. There will be more adjustments, but Flores will eventually have some good years in the majors.

Dwight Gooden — Throws R — Age 36

YEAR	TEAM	LGE	IP	H	ER	HR	BB	K	ERA	W	L	H/9	HR/9	BB/9	K/9	KW	PERA
1998	Clevelnd	AL	132.0	126	51	11	43	77	3.48	9	6	8.59	0.75	2.93	5.25	0.90	3.98
1999	Clevelnd	AL	116.0	119	74	14	52	84	5.74	4	9	9.23	1.09	4.03	6.52	0.81	5.15
2000	TampaBay	AL	37.3	43	25	11	15	22	6.03	1	3	10.37	2.65	3.62	5.30	0.73	7.30
2000	NY Yanks	AL	63.3	61	24	7	17	30	3.41	4	3	8.67	0.99	2.42	4.26	0.88	4.07

He's nothing more than an 11th pitcher now, someone who can handle mop-up relief and start the second game of a doubleheader. The Yankees have invited him to spring training to compete for that job. As bad as he's been since 1994 or so, Dwight Gooden has 194 wins and a career ERA of 3.51. Nevertheless, he'll need a serious comeback for a shot at the Hall of Fame.

Alex Graman — Throws L — Age 23

YEAR	TEAM	LGE	IP	H	ER	HR	BB	K	ERA	W	L	H/9	HR/9	BB/9	K/9	KW	PERA
1999	Statenls	NYP	73.7	83	39	15	19	38	4.76	3	5	10.14	1.83	2.32	4.64	1.00	5.77
2000	Tampa	Fla	129.0	122	79	15	73	64	5.51	5	9	8.51	1.05	5.09	4.47	0.44	5.12

Alex Graman is a college left-hander (Indiana State) with a great pitchers' build and three solid pitches, including a splitter. He's the best pitching prospect in the Yankees' system, which means he has a good chance to be in someone else's rotation in 2003.

Jason Grimsley — Throws R — Age 33

YEAR	TEAM	LGE	IP	H	ER	HR	BB	K	ERA	W	L	H/9	HR/9	BB/9	K/9	KW	PERA
1998	Buffalo	Int	82.3	76	45	13	61	46	4.92	4	5	8.31	1.42	6.67	5.03	0.38	6.06
1999	NY Yanks	AL	74.0	62	34	6	33	47	4.14	4	4	7.54	0.73	4.01	5.72	0.71	3.79
2000	NY Yanks	AL	95.3	93	50	9	34	51	4.72	5	6	8.78	0.85	3.21	4.81	0.75	4.30

Very heavy use in the season's first two months ruined Jason Grimsley, who after May had an ERA of 6.68 and walked more men then he struck out. He missed the postseason with elbow pain and will be injured and/or ineffective in 2001. The Yankees have released him, and he'll be in the Royals' camp.

Adrian Hernandez — Throws R — Age 25

YEAR	TEAM	LGE	IP	H	ER	HR	BB	K	ERA	W	L	H/9	HR/9	BB/9	K/9	KW	PERA
2000	Norwich	Eas	33.0	36	20	2	20	29	5.45	1	3	9.82	0.55	5.45	7.91	0.73	5.54
2000	Columbus	Int	29.0	24	18	2	18	22	5.59	1	2	7.45	0.62	5.59	6.83	0.61	4.25

He might be 21. He might be 25. For all we know, he might be Elian Gonzalez. Adrian Hernandez is another data point in the case for a worldwide draft. He signed a four-year, $4-million contract with the Yankees before shooting through their system last year. He is expected to compete for their fifth-starter job. He's not ready yet, but he could be by the beginning of 2002.

While Hernandez shares a last name and a nationality with El Duque and emulates his pitching style, the two are not related.

Orlando Hernandez — Throws R — Age 35

YEAR	TEAM	LGE	IP	H	ER	HR	BB	K	ERA	W	L	H/9	HR/9	BB/9	K/9	KW	PERA
1998	Columbus	Int	39.7	44	22	2	17	40	4.99	2	2	9.98	0.45	3.86	9.08	1.18	4.87
1998	NY Yanks	AL	138.0	107	48	10	46	121	3.13	9	6	6.98	0.65	3.00	7.89	1.32	3.05
1999	NY Yanks	AL	211.0	175	94	21	72	149	4.01	11	12	7.46	0.90	3.07	6.36	1.03	3.55
2000	NY Yanks	AL	192.7	171	89	30	41	135	4.16	10	11	7.99	1.40	1.92	6.31	1.65	3.89

El Duque arrested his decline by tightening his control and posting the best walk rate and strikeout-to-walk ratios of his career. He gave up some extra power in the process (34 home runs, 74 extra-base hits), and the overall effect was basically neutral. Since we have no real idea of how much his arm has endured, it's hard to say what he might do in 2001 and beyond.

Randy Keisler — Throws L — Age 25

YEAR	TEAM	LGE	IP	H	ER	HR	BB	K	ERA	W	L	H/9	HR/9	BB/9	K/9	KW	PERA
1999	Greensbr	SAL	19.0	17	12	2	15	18	5.68	1	1	8.05	0.95	7.11	8.53	0.60	5.62
1999	Tampa	Fla	80.7	66	52	5	54	43	5.80	3	6	7.36	0.56	6.02	4.80	0.40	4.32
1999	Norwich	Eas	40.3	45	26	3	19	20	5.80	1	3	10.04	0.67	4.24	4.46	0.53	5.30
2000	Norwich	Eas	66.0	66	37	8	41	42	5.05	3	4	9.00	1.09	5.59	5.73	0.51	5.68
2000	Columbus	Int	107.0	103	46	11	42	64	3.87	6	6	8.66	0.93	3.53	5.38	0.76	4.44
2000	NY Yanks	AL	11.0	15	13	1	7	6	10.64	0	1	12.27	0.82	5.73	4.91	0.43	7.45

He's rising faster than Jeff Bower's temperature upon hearing the words "Christina Aguilera." After jumping four levels in two seasons, Randy Keisler debuted in the major leagues by beating the Red Sox in Fenway Park to essentially end their 2000 season. His best pitch is a curveball, but he also has a change-up and throws his fastball in the low 90s. Keisler vs. Adrian Hernandez for the Yankees' fifth-starter slot will be a great battle this spring.

Brandon Knight — Throws R — Age 25

YEAR	TEAM	LGE	IP	H	ER	HR	BB	K	ERA	W	L	H/9	HR/9	BB/9	K/9	KW	PERA
1998	Tulsa	Tex	80.3	94	60	16	42	57	6.72	2	7	10.53	1.79	4.71	6.39	0.68	6.96
1998	Oklahoma	PCL	62.0	95	74	19	31	36	10.74	1	6	13.79	2.76	4.50	5.23	0.58	9.82
1999	Oklahoma	PCL	155.7	159	92	26	51	66	5.32	6	11	9.19	1.50	2.95	3.82	0.65	5.13
2000	Columbus	Int	174.0	172	115	27	61	103	5.95	6	13	8.90	1.40	3.16	5.33	0.84	4.92

Brandon Knight led all Triple-A pitchers in innings last year. That calls to mind *Bull Durham* and the mixed emotions with which Crash Davis approached the minor-league home-run record. Sure, it's your name on top of a list, but what it really means is you spent a lot of years never reaching your real goal. The Yankees didn't want him in New York. He needs another expansion, but settled for the next-best thing, getting picked by the Twins in the Rule 5 draft.

Sam Marsonek — Throws R — Age 22

YEAR	TEAM	LGE	IP	H	ER	HR	BB	K	ERA	W	L	H/9	HR/9	BB/9	K/9	KW	PERA
1999	Charlott	Fla	83.0	111	81	18	34	37	8.78	2	7	12.04	1.95	3.69	4.01	0.54	7.58
2000	Greensbr	SAL	102.0	116	79	20	66	37	6.97	3	8	10.24	1.76	5.82	3.26	0.28	7.19

Along with Knight, Sam Marsonek came to the Yankees from the Rangers as the solution to their Chad problem. Neither pitcher is a prospect; both are listed here just to show how little the Yankees got for someone who had hit a World Series game-winning home run just three months prior. Maybe Royce Clayton had a point.

Ramiro Mendoza — Throws R — Age 29

YEAR	TEAM	LGE	IP	H	ER	HR	BB	K	ERA	W	L	H/9	HR/9	BB/9	K/9	KW	PERA
1998	NY Yanks	AL	126.7	121	44	8	26	52	3.13	9	5	8.60	0.57	1.85	3.69	1.00	3.39
1999	NY Yanks	AL	121.3	130	60	12	22	76	4.45	6	7	9.64	0.89	1.63	5.64	1.73	4.19
2000	NY Yanks	AL	64.7	61	28	8	16	29	3.90	4	3	8.49	1.11	2.23	4.04	0.91	4.01

What started out as shoulder tendinitis was later diagnosed as a torn labrum, repaired by arthroscopic surgery in September. With the way the Yankees' pitching staff is structured, Ramiro Mendoza, if healthy, will probably split setup duties with Mike Stanton. Mendoza is more valuable to the team in the sixth and seventh innings, but there are no other setup-man candidates in camp.

Denny Neagle — Throws L Age 32

YEAR	TEAM	LGE	IP	H	ER	HR	BB	K	ERA	W	L	H/9	HR/9	BB/9	K/9	KW	PERA
1998	Atlanta	NL	200.7	192	91	26	55	134	4.08	11	11	8.61	1.17	2.47	6.01	1.22	4.23
1999	Cincnnti	NL	108.7	90	47	20	32	64	3.89	6	6	7.45	1.66	2.65	5.30	1.00	4.13
2000	Cincnnti	NL	115.0	108	43	13	40	73	3.37	8	5	8.45	1.02	3.13	5.71	0.91	4.25
2000	NY Yanks	AL	90.3	91	52	14	25	55	5.18	4	6	9.07	1.39	2.49	5.48	1.10	4.74

The idea that a change-up/location pitcher has the best chance of success at altitude is supported in research by Craig Wright. The Rockies' signing of Mike Hampton, albeit for a lot of years and a lot of money, is a move that makes some sense. In addition to having the repertoire for Coors, Hampton is an extreme ground-ball pitcher. Plus, he's in his prime.

Denny Neagle, on the other hand, is all the way at the other end of the scale. He's an extreme fly-ball pitcher, someone who already has a problem with the long ball. The fly balls on which Neagle relies will travel 9% further when he pitches at home. His prime was spent with the Braves and ended in 1998. Give credit to Dan O'Dowd for taking the gamble, then go shopping for Kevlar.

Jeff Nelson — Throws R Age 34

YEAR	TEAM	LGE	IP	H	ER	HR	BB	K	ERA	W	L	H/9	HR/9	BB/9	K/9	KW	PERA
1998	NY Yanks	AL	40.0	42	16	1	19	32	3.60	2	2	9.45	0.22	4.28	7.20	0.84	4.49
1999	NY Yanks	AL	30.3	26	12	2	18	33	3.56	2	1	7.71	0.59	5.34	9.79	0.92	4.27
2000	NY Yanks	AL	69.7	42	20	2	36	68	2.58	6	2	5.43	0.26	4.65	8.78	0.94	2.51

Healthy for the first time in three years, Jeff Nelson was one of the best relievers in the AL. His frisbee slider just embarrasses right-handed hitters and may have more movement than any non-knuckleball pitch in baseball. He signed a three-year deal with the Mariners; his role will be the same, and his unadjusted numbers could look even better thanks to Safeco.

Todd Noel — Throws R Age 22

YEAR	TEAM	LGE	IP	H	ER	HR	BB	K	ERA	W	L	H/9	HR/9	BB/9	K/9	KW	PERA
1998	KaneCnty	Mid	34.3	43	24	2	21	13	6.29	1	3	11.27	0.52	5.50	3.41	0.31	6.35
1998	Rockford	Mid	82.0	81	46	3	46	36	5.05	3	6	8.89	0.33	5.05	3.95	0.39	4.57
1999	Tampa	Fla	86.0	99	60	7	41	48	6.28	3	7	10.36	0.73	4.29	5.02	0.59	5.55

Todd Noel missed almost the entire season with a variety of minor injuries (biceps, groin, shoulder). As odd as it sounds, having a ten-inning season could be a good thing for Noel. Pitchers are at risk of overwork in their early 20s because their arms are not fully developed; taking a year off lessens the chance of a major elbow or shoulder problem. Look for Noel to re-emerge in 2001.

Christian Parker — Throws R Age 25

YEAR	TEAM	LGE	IP	H	ER	HR	BB	K	ERA	W	L	H/9	HR/9	BB/9	K/9	KW	PERA
1998	Harrisbg	Eas	118.7	121	71	13	50	44	5.38	5	8	9.18	0.99	3.79	3.34	0.44	4.92
1999	Ottawa	Int	10.3	9	8	0	7	4	6.97	0	1	7.84	0.00	6.10	3.48	0.29	4.06
1999	Harrisbg	Eas	82.3	86	42	15	38	28	4.59	4	5	9.40	1.64	4.15	3.06	0.37	5.89
2000	Norwich	Eas	188.7	195	96	16	70	89	4.58	9	12	9.30	0.76	3.34	4.25	0.64	4.56

The third player acquired in the Hideki Irabu trade, Christian Parker had the best year of anyone involved. Parker bumped his fastball into the low 90s, which helped him post his best strikeout rate since 1996. Even with that improvement, the Yankees left him in Norwich all season. Danger: he averaged nearly 7⅓ innings per start.

Andy Pettitte — Throws L Age 29

YEAR	TEAM	LGE	IP	H	ER	HR	BB	K	ERA	W	L	H/9	HR/9	BB/9	K/9	KW	PERA
1998	NY Yanks	AL	212.3	211	98	19	76	135	4.15	12	12	8.94	0.81	3.22	5.72	0.89	4.35
1999	NY Yanks	AL	190.0	201	92	18	74	115	4.36	10	11	9.52	0.85	3.51	5.45	0.78	4.86
2000	NY Yanks	AL	202.7	203	96	15	65	119	4.26	11	12	9.01	0.67	2.89	5.28	0.92	4.12

Is Andy Pettitte consistent or inconsistent? His actual won/loss records the past three years are 16–11, 14–11, and 19–9, which would lead you to believe he's inconsistent. A peek at his translated ratios tells you he is actually one of the most consistent pitchers in baseball. But his Support-Neutral Wins Above Replacement totals from 1998–2000 are 2.4, 1.6 and 3.0. What's a stathead to do?

American League

Any single fact has the potential to be misleading. It's important, in evaluating performances, to look at as much good information as you can find, as well as to understand what different metrics do and don't do. Insisting that Player A is better than Player B based solely on EqA is just as wrong as taking the same closed-minded approach with a lesser metric like RBI. It's no different than people within the game ignoring plate discipline while worshiping "tools."

Judging whether Andy Pettitte is consistent or inconsistent based on DT-ERA would give you a completely different result than making a decision based on SNWAR. So the best move is to consider all the information. Andy Pettitte is a consistently above-average pitcher who can be a top starter in his best years.

Mariano Rivera — Throws R — Age 31

YEAR	TEAM	LGE	IP	H	ER	HR	BB	K	ERA	W	L	H/9	HR/9	BB/9	K/9	KW	PERA
1998	NY Yanks	AL	59.3	45	12	3	15	33	1.82	6	1	6.83	0.46	2.28	5.01	1.10	2.54
1999	NY Yanks	AL	67.0	40	13	2	15	49	1.75	6	1	5.37	0.27	2.01	6.58	1.63	1.67
2000	NY Yanks	AL	74.3	54	22	3	20	55	2.66	6	2	6.54	0.36	2.42	6.66	1.38	2.38

The words "Mariano Rivera" and "Hall of Fame" have been mentioned together a few times this winter, which is patently absurd. Not because Rivera's performance to date hasn't been worthy, but because he still has to play four more seasons just to reach eligibility. The career paths of many top closers have included a high, relatively brief peak not unlike Rivera's last five seasons. He has benefited from the constant postseason exposure, but even with points for his October success, he needs at least one or two more seasons of quality work just to get his raw numbers into the gray area for Hall of Fame consideration, and then he needs to spend some years adding to those numbers while avoiding the kind of decline many top-tier closers have experienced.

At this point, Mariano Rivera doesn't look so much different than Gregg Olson after 1993 or John Wetteland after 1998, and no one is offering those names up for immortality. Anyway, you'd first want to compare Rivera and Trevor Hoffman to see if Rivera is even the best closer in today's game. Rivera is a great pitcher who has played on great teams, but talking about Cooperstown is wildly optimistic.

Mike Stanton — Throws L — Age 34

YEAR	TEAM	LGE	IP	H	ER	HR	BB	K	ERA	W	L	H/9	HR/9	BB/9	K/9	KW	PERA
1998	NY Yanks	AL	77.3	67	46	12	23	64	5.35	3	6	7.80	1.40	2.68	7.45	1.39	4.09
1999	NY Yanks	AL	61.7	66	26	4	15	56	3.79	4	3	9.63	0.58	2.19	8.17	1.87	4.10
2000	NY Yanks	AL	67.7	64	28	4	19	72	3.72	4	4	8.51	0.53	2.53	9.58	1.89	3.56

The emergence of Randy Choate and the loss of Jeff Nelson could be boons to Mike Stanton. He's better suited to pitching complete innings or even two innings at a time, and he isn't so devastating to left-handed hitters that he should be used just to get them out. Expanding Stanton's role to that of a setup man will allow him to have his best season since his big 1997.

Jay Tessmer — Throws R — Age 29

YEAR	TEAM	LGE	IP	H	ER	HR	BB	K	ERA	W	L	H/9	HR/9	BB/9	K/9	KW	PERA
1998	Norwich	Eas	45.0	53	10	2	16	31	2.00	4	1	10.60	0.40	3.20	6.20	0.97	4.88
1998	Columbus	Int	17.3	8	2	1	1	10	1.04	2	0	4.15	0.52	0.52	5.19	5.00	0.97
1999	Columbus	Int	53.7	51	23	5	13	28	3.86	3	3	8.55	0.84	2.18	4.70	1.08	3.76
2000	Columbus	Int	62.3	71	38	7	20	28	5.49	2	5	10.25	1.01	2.89	4.04	0.70	5.19
2000	NY Yanks	AL	6.7	8	5	3	1	5	6.75	0	1	10.80	4.05	1.35	6.75	2.50	8.12

After six professional seasons, Jay Tessmer has 166 saves in the minor leagues and a whopping 22 major-league innings pitched. He's a sidearming ground-baller who could help a number of teams in the fifth and sixth innings. The Yankees skipped over him to call up Craig Dingman last year, so he needs a new organization right about now. Tessmer was traded to the Rockies in January.

Support-Neutral Statistics — NEW YORK YANKEES — Park Effect: -2.7%

PITCHER	GS	IP	R	SNW	SNL	SNPCT	W	L	RA	APW	SNVA	SNWAR
Roger Clemens	32	204.3	96	13.7	9.4	.592	13	8	4.23	2.0	2.0	3.8
David Cone	29	153.7	120	7.9	11.8	.401	4	14	7.03	-2.9	-2.0	-0.5
Ben Ford	2	8.3	9	0.4	1.1	.264	0	1	9.72	-0.4	-0.4	-0.2
Dwight Gooden	5	26.3	11	1.9	1.3	.594	3	1	3.76	0.4	0.3	0.5
Jason Grimsley	4	17.3	10	1.0	1.3	.434	1	0	5.19	0.0	-0.1	0.0
Orlando Hernandez	29	195.7	104	12.7	9.7	.566	12	13	4.78	0.8	1.3	3.2
Randy Keisler	1	5.0	1	0.5	0.0	.927	1	0	1.80	0.2	0.2	0.3
Ramiro Mendoza	9	53.3	25	3.8	2.5	.599	5	3	4.22	0.5	0.6	1.1
Denny Neagle	15	90.7	59	5.3	6.1	.463	7	7	5.86	-0.6	-0.3	0.4
Andy Pettitte	32	204.7	111	13.2	10.8	.551	19	9	4.88	0.7	1.2	3.0
Jake Westbrook	2	4.3	10	0.0	1.3	.035	0	2	20.77	-0.7	-0.6	-0.5
Ed Yarnall	1	1.0	5	0.0	0.6	.015	0	0	45.00	-0.4	-0.3	-0.3
TOTALS	161	964.7	561	60.3	55.9	.519	65	58	5.23	-0.4	1.9	10.9

Last year was not a good one for David Cone. Still, it wasn't as bad a season as a superficial glance at his numbers would suggest. Bad luck conspired to damage Cone's standard pitching line in a couple of different ways.

First, Cone had terrible support from the Yankee bullpen. He left 17 runners on base for his relievers during the year. Given the position of the runners and the number of outs, about 6.5 of those 17 would be expected to score with average relief. Cone's relievers allowed 13 to score, costing Cone an extra 6.5 runs. That's the third-worst bullpen support of any starter since I began tracking the numbers five years ago. If Cone had gotten average bullpen support, his RA as a starter would have been 6.65 instead of the 7.03 he actually recorded. Second, Cone was victimized by the Yankee offense, which didn't score for him even on those occasions when he did pitch well. As a result, his W/L record of 4–14 was much worse than his Support-Neutral record of around 8–12.

I'm not arguing that Cone is poised for a big comeback. A 6.65 RA and an 8–12 Support-Neutral record are still bad, any way you slice it. So are the reports of poor velocity that haunted him throughout 2000. But in evaluating Cone's comeback chances and his career, it's good to know that the 2000 season wasn't quite the disaster that the media and the traditional pitching stats make it out to be.

For a quick explanation of SN stats, see page 7.

Reliever Evaluation Tools

PITCHER	G	IP	R	ARA	APR	IRNR/G	EIRS/G	IRP	BRS	RRA	ARP
Randy Choate	22	17.0	10	5.30	-0.2	0.77	0.22	-1.2	-0.3	5.81	-1.2
David Cone	1	1.3	4	27.02	-3.2	0.00	0.00	0.0	0.7	32.05	-4.0
Craig Dingman	10	11.0	8	6.55	-1.7	1.30	0.54	-0.5	-0.4	6.81	-2.0
Darrell Einertson	11	12.7	9	6.40	-1.7	1.00	0.44	0.8	-0.2	5.83	-0.9
Todd Erdos	14	25.0	14	5.04	0.4	1.00	0.44	0.9	2.2	5.59	-1.1
Ben Ford	2	2.7	2	6.75	-0.5	2.00	1.16	-0.7	0.0	9.50	-1.3
Dwight Gooden	13	38.0	17	4.03	4.9	0.62	0.16	-1.9	-0.2	4.49	3.0
Jason Grimsley	59	79.0	48	5.47	-2.4	0.80	0.26	-4.0	-2.0	5.88	-6.0
Randy Keisler	3	5.7	13	20.66	-9.7	0.33	0.21	0.6	-1.5	17.75	-7.9
Ted Lilly	7	8.0	6	6.75	-1.4	0.71	0.18	-1.8	-0.0	8.72	-3.1
Ramiro Mendoza	5	12.3	7	5.11	0.1	0.80	0.40	0.1	0.1	4.77	0.6
Denny Neagle	1	0.7	2	27.02	-1.6	0.00	0.00	0.0	0.4	31.81	-2.0
Jeff Nelson	73	69.7	24	3.10	16.2	0.64	0.24	0.5	-0.4	3.07	16.4
Mariano Rivera	66	75.7	26	3.09	17.7	0.36	0.12	-1.9	0.9	3.53	14.0
Mike Stanton	69	68.0	32	4.24	7.2	0.59	0.19	2.8	-0.9	3.79	10.7
Jay Tessmer	7	6.7	6	8.11	-2.2	0.71	0.29	-0.9	0.0	9.76	-3.4
Allen Watson	17	22.0	25	10.23	-12.3	0.41	0.11	-3.1	1.6	12.44	-17.7
Jake Westbrook	1	2.3	0	0.00	1.3	3.00	0.69	0.7	0.0	-2.45	2.0
Ed Yarnall	1	2.0	0	0.00	1.2	0.00	0.00	0.0	0.0	0.00	1.2
TOTALS	382	459.7	253	4.96	12.3	0.66	0.23			5.25	-2.6

For a quick guide to RET, see page 10.

Oakland Athletics

The Athletics made the playoffs. After one round, the Athletics exited the playoffs. They didn't leave graciously, saying they were just happy to get there. Rather, Billy Beane ended the A's season with a declaration of war on the status quo by stating that the 2000 A's were the worst team he expects to field over the next five years.

The Athletics have demonstrated that the name of the game is quality talent evaluation, not money. Through player development and through the major leagues' best effort at scouting and collecting "free" talent—the players you can get on waivers, through the Rule 5 draft, as minor-league free agents, or through trades—the A's built a division champion. By identifying the skills that matter (for hitters, getting on base; for pitchers, getting people out), the Athletics enjoy the advantage of shopping in a different market than the annual winter spending frenzy. While other teams spend top dollar on "valuable" free-agent assets like Jose Mesa or Marquis Grissom, the Athletics limit themselves to digging up Jeff Tam or Olmedo Saenz or two dozen teenagers in the Dominican Republic. If you accept that the result of any short series borders on random, then the facade of Yankee invincibility rests entirely on a first-inning fly ball that an injured A's player, fighting the sun's glare during a game whose time was determined by network scheduling priorities, could not catch. Such is the slender margin on which the already tottering paradigm of "large-market" dominance rests.

However, if you're a bottom-line guy, a single division title is just that, and you might argue that even a blind dog finds a bone once in awhile. No sooner had Eric Chavez popped up the last pitch of the season to Tino Martinez than people started wailing that the A's are doomed because they're a "small-market" club. The tired refrain is that the A's won't be able to afford to keep their own talent and therefore won't be able to compete. Over the winter, the A's lost Kevin Appier, Randy Velarde, and Matt Stairs, and critics were quickly regurgitating the conventional wisdom that teams that don't spend more than successful franchises like the Orioles and Dodgers are doomed to failure. Of course, the wailing came after the A's had already locked up Ben Grieve, Miguel Tejada, Tim Hudson, and Eric Chavez with four-year contracts. Perhaps the team's unwillingness to pay Kevin Appier $10 million per year can be mistaken for an inability to afford him, but the reality is that Beane has the core of a good young team signed to multi-year deals.

Big money is just that—big. As the overblown anguish over Alex Rodriguez's contract showed, big money focuses people's attention, but mostly it just draws attention away from more important factors involved in the operation of a successful ballclub. As long as teams such as the Pirates and Phillies are accumulating bad talent at top dollar, smarter ball clubs can purchase useful talent at the price they want to pay. When the Athletics trade away Matt Stairs at the point that he becomes arbitration-eligible, financial considerations clearly play a part in the decision, but the A's made the move with the knowledge that the next Matt Stairs can be nabbed for almost nothing. The A's have a better player than Stairs in Mario Valdez. Valdez cost the A's just one player, Danny Ardoin, who might turn into a good backup catcher if the Twins want him to do so. If you're the A's, that's a trade worth making every time.

Another example of the Athletics' shrewd use of talent evaluation was their decision to bring in reliever Jeff Tam as a non-roster invitee. Tam has some obvious weaknesses: he struggles with left-handed hitters, and he'll never match anyone's idealized image of the big flame-throwing reliever. But he has outstanding command of his fastball, keeps the ball in the infield, and is death on right-handed hitters. If pitching is supposed to be so rare that people are throwing money at Darren Holmes and Ricky Bottalico, why not dump your preconceptions and get a guy with some basic skills? Why venture out into the free-agent market when one of the season's best relievers is available for the minimum salary?

Athletics Prospectus

2000 record: 91–70; First place, AL West; Lost to Yankees in Division Series, 3-2

Pythagenport W/L: 93–68

Runs Scored: 947 (3rd in AL)

Runs Allowed: 813 (3rd in AL)

Team EqA: .272 (2nd in AL)

2000 Batters' Age: 27.2 (2nd youngest in AL)

2000 Pitchers' Age: 29.3 (4th oldest in AL)

Ballpark: Network Associates Coliseum; moderate pitchers' park; Park Factor of .968

2000: Proved 1999 wasn't a fluke by adding a great closing kick.

2001: They cleared some dead weight, freed up money and opened up playing time for studs. The favorite by three lengths.

The Athletics' recognition that they don't have to pay "market" prices is not a permanent advantage. Other teams have figured out that arbitration with supporting players is something to be avoided and that it's smart to ink young stars to multi-year deals that sidestep the arbitration process. Some teams even recognize the three-year bargains you can get from players like Stairs or Olmedo Saenz or Gil Heredia. However, Oakland has a greater strength than manipulating the balance between a team's cost and talent. Oakland has theory.

Offensive theory is pretty straightforward, because it goes back to the origins of the game itself. Sabermetricians and analysts didn't invent the idea that getting on base is the game's most important offensive skill. Bill James drew attention to managers like Earl Weaver and Whitey Herzog, who favored on-base skills first and foremost; they viewed power or defense as secondary characteristics whose value was determined by individual tastes or ballparks. Beyond Weaver or Herzog, you can just as easily invoke Dick Williams or Joe McCarthy or Casey Stengel or Al Lopez.

What works on offense is timeless: get on base, score runs. It's a strategy of attrition: Work the opposing starting pitcher, wearing him down with high-pitch at-bats, and you'll either face a tiring starter in a key situation or you'll get to pick from the guys at the bottom of the staff. Beane and the A's think of winning games, series, and seasons in exactly these terms. While they deserve credit for a sound approach, it's not as if they've discovered a great secret. Getting on base is simply how you score runs, whether you're going to bat against Joe McGinnity or Roger Clemens. Period.

Pitching theory, though, has changed over the years. In today's game, effective management of a pitching staff requires a keen awareness of the uneasy balance between what you need at the moment and how to best protect a pitcher's future. Athletics' pitching coach Rick Peterson and the A's player-development staff demonstrate this awareness. They monitor everything: pitch counts, warm-up pitches, bullpen sessions, and side work. Despite the pressure of a pennant race, the A's avoided the temptation to overwork Tim Hudson and Barry Zito in 2000. Managing the staff will be trickier in 2001. This year's rotation won't be able to count on 200 league-average innings from Kevin Appier. Barry Zito will likely struggle to pitch as well over an entire season as he did down the stretch, Gil Heredia's problems with opponents who are familiar with him may get worse, and Mark Mulder might not improve. The fifth starter's slot could be a season-long problem.

Perhaps in anticipation of a rougher ride for their starters, the Athletics have assembled one of the best bullpens in the league. Jim Mecir, Jeff Tam, and Chad Bradford will never be household names, but each of them has specific skills that add up to a great bullpen. Mecir has been one of the most effective setup men in baseball for three years, while Tam and now Bradford are examples of the Athletics making use of unheralded minor-league relievers who keep the ball in the infield. Art Howe will have a fine crew with which to mix and match, stretching games backwards from closer Jason Isringhausen into the sixth inning and lowering the pressure on the rotation.

The A's are more shaky when it comes to defensive theory. Within the organziation, there exists debate. Should the team punt defense altogether and simply go for as many runs as possible? Should they make Ben Grieve go away because of his obvious limitations as an outfielder? There are no easy answers here, and it's an issue because weak defense cost the A's the third game in the Division Series.

The A's are very close to striking the right balance, so digging up glove men for second base or center field or catcher shouldn't be part of the plan. Acquiring Johnny Damon for Ben Grieve is the kind of move that upgrades the defense while not saddling the lineup with an offensive zero. They do need to see defensive improvements from young players like Eric Chavez, Miguel Tejada, Jose Ortiz, and Terrence Long.

Quibbling about defense aside, the A's are poised for bigger and better things. Chavez and Tejada give them great pre-peak hitting talent. Zito and Hudson give them the best pair of young starters in the American League, and you already know about the reinforced bullpen.

The A's have an effective player-development team. They've successfully implemented an organizational approach to hitter and pitcher development. They teach plate discipline. They do a good job scouting college talent. Lots of organizations have similar strengths. What differentiates the A's from the rest of baseball? First, they do a better job of scouting other teams' minor-league talent, allowing them to find valuable minor-league veterans from years gone by (like Geronimo Berroa) or ones with future value (like Chad Bradford or Tom Wilson). The A's second strength is more basic: from the management team all the way down to the coaching staffs in the rookie leagues, these guys are on the same page. The Athletics don't have organizational meetings because they don't need glorified winter golf outings to sort out a confusion of philosophies and approaches among their staff. Planning is a hell of a lot simpler when there's a shared vision of how to teach, use, and evaluate players.

We have the seen the future, and it starts now. In 20 years, high-school pitchers will be using Rick Peterson's latest instructional DVD. Competitive balance in the game will be tight, thanks to the influence of a generation of GMs like Billy Beane, Paul DePodesta, Dan O'Dowd, Brian Cashman, and Dave Dombrowski. We'll see some really hard-fought pennant races, brilliant rebuilding programs, and everything in between. And most of all, it will be fun.

American League

HITTERS (BA: .270, OBP: .340, SLG: .440, EqA: .260)

Mark Bellhorn — UT — Bats B — Age 26

YEAR	TEAM	LGE	AB	H	DB	TP	HR	BB	SO	R	RBI	SB	CS	OUT	BA	OBP	SLG	EQA	EQR	DEFENSE			
1998	Edmonton	PCL	308	65	16	3	7	52	89	43	32	4	1	244	.211	.332	.351	.237	33	44-3B	-3	32-2B	7
1999	Midland	Tex	57	13	1	0	2	8	14	8	6	0	0	44	.228	.323	.351	.230	6	15-2B	-2		
2000	Sacramen	PCL	438	103	14	7	20	76	124	83	54	12	4	339	.235	.353	.436	.267	62	90-3B	-4	10-2B	1
2001	Oakland	AL	266	58	10	2	9	45	82	42	36	5	1	209	.218	.331	.372	.250	32				

After losing most of '98 and '99 to injury, Mark Bellhorn had dropped off of our radar. Shame on us, because he's still a player with patience, power, and a lot of middle-infield experience. He was a shortstop at Auburn, and he's played a lot of short and second base in his pro career. He was going to play some outfield over the winter, but an emergency appendectomy ended the experiment. He has a shot at the second-base job, but if he loses to Jose Ortiz, he could still help the team as a utility man, starting at four or five positions several times a week.

Angel Berroa — SS — Bats R — Age 21

YEAR	TEAM	LGE	AB	H	DB	TP	HR	BB	SO	R	RBI	SB	CS	OUT	BA	OBP	SLG	EQA	EQR	DEFENSE
2000	Visalia	Cal	432	101	21	3	8	14	73	42	41	3	3	334	.234	.266	.352	.200	30	120-SS -26
2001	KansasCy	AL	297	77	18	1	7	13	75	35	42	1	1	221	.259	.290	.397	.224	26	

Oh, good, another power-hitting Dominican shortstop, just what this organization didn't need, except for trades. The A's aren't overly tools-oriented, but Angel Berroa is a very rough player who has power, speed, and a strong arm. While he's been extremely error-prone (54 boots in 2000), the A's love his work ethic and expect improvement. He hasn't really learned how to pull the ball yet, which is reason to believe he'll add power as he matures. He's the key player to the Damon trade.

Eric Byrnes — OF — Bats R — Age 25

YEAR	TEAM	LGE	AB	H	DB	TP	HR	BB	SO	R	RBI	SB	CS	OUT	BA	OBP	SLG	EQA	EQR	DEFENSE	
1998	So Oregn	Nwn	168	40	5	1	5	9	18	20	17	2	1	129	.238	.280	.369	.214	14	39-LF	-1
1998	Visalia	Cal	108	36	6	1	3	13	15	16	14	5	1	73	.333	.408	.491	.305	19	29-LF	3
1999	Modesto	Cal	362	94	15	1	5	40	38	50	42	11	4	272	.260	.340	.348	.239	38	89-LF	-5
1999	Midland	Tex	164	33	7	0	2	12	35	17	18	3	2	133	.201	.264	.280	.177	9	35-LF	-4
2000	Midland	Tex	257	59	19	1	3	30	41	32	23	10	5	203	.230	.311	.346	.225	24	66-RF	-3
2000	Sacramen	PCL	242	71	15	1	8	24	31	41	36	8	4	175	.293	.361	.463	.274	34	50-LF	0
2001	Oakland	AL	473	121	23	1	10	45	72	63	59	6	2	354	.256	.320	.372	.241	51		

Eric Byrnes is your basic hustle player. After smacking 48 doubles in 2000, he showed improved power during his Arizona Fall League stint. Add that to 74 walks and you start thinking that our projection for him may be a bit conservative. He has a good arm and runs well, but he's still picking up the finer points of outfield defense. Byrnes is a good fourth outfielder in the making who keeps improving.

Eric Chavez — 3B — Bats L — Age 23

YEAR	TEAM	LGE	AB	H	DB	TP	HR	BB	SO	R	RBI	SB	CS	OUT	BA	OBP	SLG	EQA	EQR	DEFENSE	
1998	Huntsvil	Sou	334	90	17	1	16	27	65	44	55	6	2	246	.269	.325	.470	.262	43	71-3B	-4
1998	Edmonton	PCL	191	53	11	0	9	9	32	29	30	2	2	140	.277	.312	.476	.255	23	44-3B	-8
1999	Oakland	AL	355	90	21	2	14	42	51	46	49	1	1	266	.254	.332	.442	.257	44	95-3B	-5
2000	Oakland	AL	499	143	22	4	28	56	86	87	84	2	2	358	.287	.360	.515	.285	78	134-3B	-5
2001	Oakland	AL	485	145	26	2	25	56	88	86	103	1	1	341	.299	.372	.515	.298	83		

Eric Chavez is catching some flak for opening his mouth before the last game against the Yankees, but if Terrence Long makes that catch in the first inning, Chavez has a shot at being baseball's Charles Barkley. Why shouldn't he feel confident? If you're Eric Chavez, life is sweet. He still isn't hitting left-handers, but losing Olmedo Saenz and John Jaha gave the A's a chance to see if Chavez can be an everyday player. It's worth trying when you consider how much progress Jason Giambi has made. Chavez still plays third base a little too upright and flat-footed, but he's got the arm for the position. He has things to work on, but so what? This guy rocks.

Ryan Christenson — CF — Bats R — Age 27

YEAR	TEAM	LGE	AB	H	DB	TP	HR	BB	SO	R	RBI	SB	CS	OUT	BA	OBP	SLG	EQA	EQR	DEFENSE	
1998	Oakland	AL	370	98	22	2	6	35	94	57	41	4	5	278	.265	.330	.384	.238	38	107-CF	4
1999	Oakland	AL	267	57	13	1	4	36	53	40	23	6	5	215	.213	.309	.315	.212	22	85-CF	-1
1999	Vancouvr	PCL	128	39	5	1	1	19	20	23	13	5	2	90	.305	.395	.383	.274	18	33-CF	1
2000	Oakland	AL	128	32	3	2	4	18	30	30	17	1	2	98	.250	.347	.398	.250	15	40-LF	1
2001	Oakland	AL	224	52	8	1	4	29	53	30	24	5	3	175	.232	.320	.330	.230	22		

Ryan Christenson isn't exactly a cautionary tale for guys like Byrnes or Mike Lockwood or Rusty Keith, but he's close. He broke out in 1997 with a 105-walk, 59 extra-base-hit season as a 23-year-old, shooting through three levels of the farm system. He hasn't made much progress since, but he also hasn't played every day since 1998. He can play a mean center field, so somebody is going to shake loose some roster space for him.

Mario Encarnacion — RF — Bats R — Age 23

YEAR	TEAM	LGE	AB	H	DB	TP	HR	BB	SO	R	RBI	SB	CS	OUT	BA	OBP	SLG	EQA	EQR	DEFENSE	
1998	Huntsvil	Sou	360	82	12	1	11	41	131	49	41	6	4	282	.228	.311	.358	.226	34	89-CF	-7
1999	Midland	Tex	350	85	15	2	12	35	93	48	46	5	4	269	.243	.313	.400	.237	37	71-CF	-12
1999	Vancouvr	PCL	145	32	3	0	3	5	43	15	14	4	3	116	.221	.253	.303	.178	8	37-RF	4
2000	Sacramen	PCL	301	72	12	2	11	28	97	38	46	9	5	234	.239	.309	.402	.237	32	74-RF	4
2001	Oakland	AL	326	77	12	1	11	36	110	44	42	7	3	252	.236	.312	.380	.240	36		

It would be easy to be disappointed with his struggles, but he was 22 in Triple-A, and a sprained wrist didn't help matters. Mario Encarnacion is an interesting project in that he's a tools player in an organization that stresses core offensive skills. Long learning curves aren't debilitating when your pro career starts at 16. Encarnacion may not blossom into a superstar, but if he begins to shine, it will be easier to let Damon go.

Sal Fasano — C — Bats R — Age 29

YEAR	TEAM	LGE	AB	H	DB	TP	HR	BB	SO	R	RBI	SB	CS	OUT	BA	OBP	SLG	EQA	EQR	DEFENSE	
1998	KansasCy	AL	215	50	9	0	9	10	50	21	31	1	0	165	.233	.311	.400	.238	23	65-C	6
1999	Omaha	PCL	277	61	9	0	14	33	70	42	32	2	1	217	.220	.339	.404	.252	35	81-C	-7
1999	KansasCy	AL	59	14	1	0	5	7	15	10	15	0	1	46	.237	.376	.508	.285	10	23-C	0
2000	Oakland	AL	126	28	4	0	8	13	43	20	19	0	0	98	.222	.310	.444	.248	15	38-C	0
2001	Oakland	AL	208	44	4	0	12	24	64	23	31	0	0	164	.212	.293	.404	.237	22		

Acquired for nothing from a Royals team that could have used him to platoon with Gregg Zaun, Sal Fasano spent most of the year as Kevin Appier's personal catcher. He has a good defensive reputation, but his primary asset behind the plate is a strong arm. He's on the Mark Parent career track, where he'll do a team some good if they want a backup catcher who can pop a home run.

Esteban German — 2B — Bats R — Age 22

YEAR	TEAM	LGE	AB	H	DB	TP	HR	BB	SO	R	RBI	SB	CS	OUT	BA	OBP	SLG	EQA	EQR	DEFENSE	
1999	Modesto	Cal	501	121	15	6	3	72	133	65	33	15	7	387	.242	.340	.313	.230	49	110-2B	-27
2000	Midland	Tex	76	14	0	0	1	13	22	8	5	2	2	64	.184	.312	.224	.187	5	18-2B	-3
2000	Visalia	Cal	435	101	14	6	2	39	89	45	24	25	5	339	.232	.299	.306	.214	36	106-2B	-19
2001	Oakland	AL	339	80	9	3	2	48	89	53	29	15	4	263	.236	.331	.298	.231	34		

Esteban German had an outstanding 1999, drawing 102 walks and stealing 40 bases, so the A's pushed him to Midland. He struggled and kept struggling when he went back to the California League. Defensively, he's error-prone and a little gun-shy about covering the bag, but the A's have no intention of moving him to the outfield. That's appropriate, considering the numerous second base-to-outfield failures littering other organizations. Most do not turn out as well as Eric Owens or Andy Fox; even those players are stretched as regulars anywhere but second base.

American League

Jason Giambi — 1B — Bats L — Age 30

YEAR	TEAM	LGE	AB	H	DB	TP	HR	BB	SO	R	RBI	SB	CS	OUT	BA	OBP	SLG	EQA	EQR	DEFENSE	
1998	Oakland	AL	561	172	21	0	32	81	91	95	114	2	2	391	.307	.398	.515	.302	98	135-1B	2
1999	Oakland	AL	569	184	31	1	36	99	96	112	121	1	1	386	.323	.429	.571	.327	118	126-1B	4
2000	Oakland	AL	502	172	25	1	46	130	87	104	133	2	0	330	.343	.485	.671	.371	138	123-1B	-5
2001	Oakland	AL	528	163	20	0	38	117	97	124	141	1	1	366	.309	.434	.563	.336	119		

Jason Giambi has become the A's riff on Tony Gwynn: he's a diligent student of hitting, working, studying, and recording what pitchers try to do to him. One of the payoffs has been his dramatic improvement against left-handed pitching, but I guess an MVP award isn't such a bad payoff either. Whether the A's should sign him long-term is an emotional decision for everybody involved. The organization has a lot of confidence in its ability to identify, develop, and acquire hitting talent, so if push comes to shove, few teams are as well qualified to move on, public image be damned. Do the A's want to risk alienating fans? Does Giambi want to be just another clueless rich guy, like Mo Vaughn? It will take compromise to kill the big-market/small-market paradigm.

Jeremy Giambi — OF — Bats L — Age 26

YEAR	TEAM	LGE	AB	H	DB	TP	HR	BB	SO	R	RBI	SB	CS	OUT	BA	OBP	SLG	EQA	EQR	DEFENSE			
1998	Omaha	PCL	319	99	18	1	14	46	63	50	47	5	3	223	.310	.403	.505	.301	56	60-LF	-4		
1999	KansasCy	AL	284	81	13	1	3	37	61	32	32	0	0	203	.285	.373	.370	.258	34	24-1B	-3		
1999	Omaha	PCL	124	36	5	1	8	26	29	23	19	1	1	89	.290	.416	.540	.313	24	20-LF	2	14-1B	1
2000	Oakland	AL	259	68	9	2	11	29	56	41	49	0	0	191	.263	.344	.440	.262	33	44-RF	-6		
2001	Oakland	AL	293	83	14	1	10	43	68	52	52	2	1	211	.283	.375	.440	.283	45				

Jeremy Giambi continues to be a tantalizing mystery. Even with our corrections for league difficulty levels, he has still hit significantly below what you'd expect based on his minor-league performance. It would be interesting to see what would happen if he finally got 400 to 500 plate appearances, but he may get only 300. His near-term future depends heavily on John Jaha's health; his long-term future depends on how soon Encarnacion is ready.

Ben Grieve — LF — Bats L — Age 25

YEAR	TEAM	LGE	AB	H	DB	TP	HR	BB	SO	R	RBI	SB	CS	OUT	BA	OBP	SLG	EQA	EQR	DEFENSE	
1998	Oakland	AL	582	174	38	2	21	84	110	96	91	2	2	410	.299	.395	.479	.293	95	123-RF	-3
1999	Oakland	AL	484	132	17	0	31	58	98	79	86	4	0	352	.273	.359	.500	.283	75	112-LF	5
2000	Oakland	AL	591	170	34	2	30	66	118	89	102	3	0	421	.288	.362	.504	.285	91	129-LF	-4
2001	TampaBay	AL	575	178	30	1	35	79	120	100	121	3	0	397	.310	.393	.548	.310	106		

The A's willingness to trade Ben Grieve from two of his weaknessess you don't see here. First is his defense. When a ball is hit to Ben Grieve in left field, the home crowd shows all the nervous silence of a golf gallery, complete with relieved clapping if the ball is actually caught. Second, his grounding into 32 double plays doesn't fly in an organization built on getting on base and stretching innings. There's some speculation that Grieve's hitting won't get any better, but I know I felt that way about Carlos Delgado after 1998. Grieve frustrates you with at-bats in which he commits himself too soon, producing weak tappers to second base. He can correct that impatience, but whether he can improve defensively is an open question. Given the D-Rays' notorious affection for athletes, Grieve may find himself at DH quite a bit.

Jason Hart — 1B — Bats R — Age 23

YEAR	TEAM	LGE	AB	H	DB	TP	HR	BB	SO	R	RBI	SB	CS	OUT	BA	OBP	SLG	EQA	EQR	DEFENSE	
1998	So Oregn	Nwn	298	60	11	0	13	20	76	35	38	0	0	238	.201	.255	.369	.202	22	66-1B	2
1999	Modesto	Cal	545	130	30	1	14	37	109	63	77	1	2	417	.239	.289	.374	.218	46	127-1B	1
2000	Midland	Tex	539	140	29	2	21	45	118	68	78	2	0	399	.260	.321	.438	.251	63	126-1B	-5
2001	Oakland	AL	481	117	22	1	19	42	115	58	70	1	0	364	.243	.304	.412	.244	53		

Jason Hart gets a lot of prospect billing because he's a big slugger in an organization known for bigness and sluggerness—and also because he's won three RBI titles in three pro seasons. Compare Hart's 2000 with Adam Piatt's 1999 at Midland. He still gets himself out too often and doesn't always kill pitches on which he commits. Since he shortened his swing and stopped striding into the pitch, he's done a better job identifying pitches. Hart tied with Hee Seop Choi for the AFL home-run title. He needs to improve, but he's young and plays for an organization that can help him do it.

Ramon Hernandez — C — Bats R — Age 25

YEAR	TEAM	LGE	AB	H	DB	TP	HR	BB	SO	R	RBI	SB	CS	OUT	BA	OBP	SLG	EQA	EQR	DEFENSE			
1998	Huntsvil	Sou	480	120	16	1	12	36	65	59	68	2	3	363	.250	.319	.363	.229	45	50-C	-5	21-1B	-4
1999	Vancouvr	PCL	291	69	9	3	10	19	36	31	43	1	1	223	.237	.295	.392	.227	27	44-C	1	11-3B	-4
1999	Oakland	AL	135	39	4	0	4	17	10	12	21	1	0	96	.289	.372	.407	.268	18	40-C	-3		
2000	Oakland	AL	419	104	16	0	16	33	58	50	61	1	0	315	.248	.314	.401	.239	44	122-C	-2		
2001	Oakland	AL	437	113	15	1	16	38	62	54	65	1	1	325	.259	.318	.407	.248	50				

The organization's Venezuelan scouting effort doesn't get as much attention as its commitment to the Dominican Republic, but this year it cranked out the team's starting catcher. Spending most of the season in the ninth slot, Hernandez had a solid campaign, consistent with his career and age. Don't be surprised if he outhits that projection. His defense is rough, but so was Terry Steinbach's in his early years.

A.J. Hinch — C — Bats R — Age 27

YEAR	TEAM	LGE	AB	H	DB	TP	HR	BB	SO	R	RBI	SB	CS	OUT	BA	OBP	SLG	EQA	EQR	DEFENSE	
1998	Oakland	AL	337	81	7	0	11	29	79	35	36	3	0	256	.240	.307	.359	.226	31	103-C	2
1999	Oakland	AL	205	45	3	1	8	9	37	26	24	6	2	162	.220	.258	.361	.204	15	60-C	-4
1999	Vancouvr	PCL	60	20	1	0	2	3	12	7	6	1	1	41	.333	.372	.450	.272	8	12-C	0
2000	Sacramen	PCL	417	98	18	1	5	34	70	50	35	3	3	322	.235	.300	.319	.207	32	86-C	-4
2001	KansasCy	AL	345	85	8	0	10	31	66	44	47	4	2	262	.246	.309	.357	.223	31		

Sometimes, a guy gets demoted and he regroups. More often, he goes down and tries to belt his way back. A.J. Hinch has degenerated into a hacker, and only organizations like the Pirates or Twins will be impressed. The name may have value in trade this spring after somebody loses a starting catcher, but the A's brought in Tom Wilson as a minor-league free agent and have Cody McKay ready for the bright lights of Sacramento. Hinch has played his way to Kansas City, where the competition isn't nearly as rough.

Josh Hochgesang — 3B — Bats R — Age 24

YEAR	TEAM	LGE	AB	H	DB	TP	HR	BB	SO	R	RBI	SB	CS	OUT	BA	OBP	SLG	EQA	EQR	DEFENSE	
1999	So Oregn	Nwn	73	10	2	0	1	9	26	7	6	0	0	63	.137	.245	.205	.135	2		
2000	Visalia	Cal	454	92	18	1	15	61	140	51	51	6	4	366	.203	.302	.346	.219	41	113-3B	-6
2001	Oakland	AL	248	49	8	0	8	40	95	30	28	2	1	200	.198	.309	.327	.224	24		

Josh Hochgesang is a big third baseman selected in the seventh round of the '99 draft. Generally speaking, it's hard to take a guy seriously if he hits like Rob Deer in the minors, and with Chavez ahead of him Hochgesang doesn't really have an ideal future. He'll have to work his way to Midland and beyond quickly if he's going to make it at all. He's improved defensively, no longer playing third base by standing erect and waving at balls as they whistle past him.

Daylan Holt — OF — Bats R — Age 22

YEAR	TEAM	LGE	AB	H	DB	TP	HR	BB	SO	R	RBI	SB	CS	OUT	BA	OBP	SLG	EQA	EQR	DEFENSE	
2000	Vancouvr	Nwn	123	30	4	0	2	6	27	13	13	0	0	93	.244	.284	.325	.200	8	27-RF	-3
2001	Oakland	AL	65	15	2	0	1	4	34	5	6	0	0	50	.231	.275	.308	.196	4		

A third-round pick in the 2000 draft, Daylan Holt led the country wth 34 home runs while playing for Texas A&M in 1999 but slumped in his junior season before entering the draft. There's some feeling that he struggled on a bad team (A&M fell from 52–18 to 23–35) and was pressing to fulfill expectations. He has the arm for right field and is already considered one of the potential steals of the draft.

John Jaha — DH/DL — Bats R — Age 35

YEAR	TEAM	LGE	AB	H	DB	TP	HR	BB	SO	R	RBI	SB	CS	OUT	BA	OBP	SLG	EQA	EQR	DEFENSE	
1998	Milwauke	NL	220	46	5	1	8	47	62	30	39	1	3	177	.209	.362	.350	.247	27	51-1B	-6
1999	Oakland	AL	453	129	21	0	37	96	117	91	109	2	0	324	.285	.418	.576	.323	96		
2000	Oakland	AL	96	17	2	0	1	32	35	14	5	1	0	79	.177	.397	.229	.245	12		
2001	Oakland	AL	205	43	5	0	12	53	64	39	37	1	0	162	.210	.372	.410	.277	33		

Basically unable to swing the bat last year, John Jaha became a hulking latter-day Eddie Gaedel. Rumors of Hoss's death are as exaggerated as they are expected. He's back from shoulder surgery and rehabbing, and he'll be in camp. If he can swing the bat in October, he can be Oakland's variation on Yankees' postseason ringer Darryl Strawberry.

American League

Rusty Keith — OF — Bats R — Age 23

YEAR	TEAM	LGE	AB	H	DB	TP	HR	BB	SO	R	RBI	SB	CS	OUT	BA	OBP	SLG	EQA	EQR	DEFENSE	
1999	Visalia	Cal	446	107	20	1	7	57	61	56	38	4	3	342	.240	.330	.336	.229	43	106-CF	-1
2000	Midland	Tex	61	11	0	0	1	7	12	6	4	0	0	50	.180	.271	.230	.161	3	13-LF	-1
2000	Modesto	Cal	394	99	14	1	6	56	75	56	39	3	1	296	.251	.347	.338	.238	41	78-LF	-7
2001	Oakland	AL	313	79	7	0	6	46	66	43	39	1	1	235	.252	.348	.332	.243	34		

As they did with Esteban German, the A's challenged Rusty Keith with a Double-A assignment to open the year, and he worked his way back down to the California League. His core skill is getting on base, and he's young enough to still pick up the power he needs in order to be a prospect. If he doesn't, he'll end up like Justin Bowles, with his own table in every diner within 30 miles of a Texas League ballpark.

Mike Lockwood — OF — Bats L — Age 24

YEAR	TEAM	LGE	AB	H	DB	TP	HR	BB	SO	R	RBI	SB	CS	OUT	BA	OBP	SLG	EQA	EQR	DEFENSE	
1999	So Oregn	Nwn	251	66	12	3	4	22	55	26	26	2	2	187	.263	.329	.382	.239	26	64-RF	0
2000	Modesto	Cal	162	39	6	0	5	33	26	26	22	3	1	124	.241	.376	.370	.262	22	43-LF	-3
2000	Midland	Tex	233	59	11	1	3	13	35	32	21	0	0	174	.253	.302	.348	.217	19	55-LF	-2
2000	Sacramen	PCL	126	29	1	0	1	14	14	11	10	0	1	98	.230	.311	.262	.192	8	29-LF	0
2001	Oakland	AL	311	79	11	1	6	32	70	38	38	1	1	233	.254	.324	.354	.236	31		

A 23rd rounder drafted in 1999 out of Ohio State, Mike Lockwood is a tweener. It doesn't look like he can play center field regularly, and he hasn't shown the power for a corner. However, he works hard in the cages and on his fielding, he doesn't need a lot of coaching on fundamentals, and he drew 77 unintentional walks. Should he start showing more power, he could be like Billy McMillon and shine if ever given a chance.

Terrence Long — CF — Bats L — Age 25

YEAR	TEAM	LGE	AB	H	DB	TP	HR	BB	SO	R	RBI	SB	CS	OUT	BA	OBP	SLG	EQA	EQR	DEFENSE	
1998	Binghmtn	Eas	459	113	18	6	12	47	107	52	43	12	7	353	.246	.318	.390	.238	49	119-RF	-5
1999	Norfolk	Int	302	87	17	4	5	18	41	32	36	9	5	220	.288	.330	.421	.250	34	75-RF	7
1999	Vancouvr	PCL	154	35	3	2	2	8	28	12	18	5	4	123	.227	.268	.312	.189	9	38-CF	0
2000	Sacramen	PCL	59	20	2	0	3	3	4	8	11	0	2	41	.339	.371	.525	.280	9	13-CF	-3
2000	Oakland	AL	583	173	35	4	19	36	70	102	78	5	0	410	.297	.339	.468	.267	76	137-CF	-9
2001	Oakland	AL	526	149	29	3	15	45	78	79	83	5	2	379	.283	.340	.435	.266	69		

He led off because that's what he was asked to do, but it clearly isn't his ideal role. Terrence Long spent a large chunk of the season playing hurt with a variety of injuries and lingering leg problems, but nobody called him tough or scrappy. He really couldn't run with a wrenched knee by the time the playoffs rolled around, but just as Jose Canseco was put on the spot in the 1990 World Series, Long was in the lineup in 2000. The difference between now and then is that Long's manager didn't try to scapegoat him. The key decision was to play him at all, and hopefully the A's learned a lesson. He'll do the team a little more good if he drops lower in the lineup, but he'll do them a lot more good if he improves in the outfield. He will if his wheels are sound.

Ryan Ludwick — CF — Bats R — Age 22

YEAR	TEAM	LGE	AB	H	DB	TP	HR	BB	SO	R	RBI	SB	CS	OUT	BA	OBP	SLG	EQA	EQR	DEFENSE	
1999	Modesto	Cal	170	37	10	1	3	13	47	19	22	1	0	133	.218	.279	.341	.206	13	39-CF	-1
2000	Modesto	Cal	500	108	19	1	21	43	133	58	63	3	2	394	.216	.284	.384	.220	45	118-CF	8
2001	Oakland	AL	282	61	8	0	13	26	85	29	37	1	1	222	.216	.282	.383	.225	27		

The A's love his work ethic, which will be important for his development because he's short a tool or two. Ryan Ludwick lacks great wheels, but he gets excellent jumps and he's a very instinctive center fielder. He has tremendous bat speed but is nowhere close to being as patient as the A's want him to be. He struggled early in 2000 and in the AFL, but he also spent most of the year fighting a pulled muscle or two. Don't be surprised if he adjusts slowly to Double-A, and don't forget about him.

Cody McKay   C   Bats L   Age 27

YEAR	TEAM	LGE	AB	H	DB	TP	HR	BB	SO	R	RBI	SB	CS	OUT	BA	OBP	SLG	EQA	EQR	DEFENSE			
1998	Modesto	Cal	406	94	15	1	5	28	65	42	40	1	2	314	.232	.297	.310	.202	29	93-C	0	12-3B	-4
1998	Edmonton	PCL	57	11	3	0	0	6	5	5	4	1	0	46	.193	.291	.246	.186	3				
1999	Midland	Tex	330	75	13	1	4	27	46	41	29	1	1	256	.227	.295	.309	.202	24	54-C	-6	22-3B	-1
2000	Midland	Tex	423	100	22	1	3	44	61	46	54	1	2	325	.236	.316	.314	.214	35	84-C	-16		
2000	Sacramen	PCL	58	12	2	0	1	4	15	6	5	0	0	46	.207	.266	.293	.181	3				
2001	Oakland	AL	372	79	13	1	4	38	62	34	29	1	1	294	.212	.285	.285	.195	25				

Cody McKay is making a case for himself as a Jamie Quirk kind of guy. He's a line-drive hitter without any platoon problems, and he can catch or man either infield corner. It could be enough to get him onto the roster as a third catcher. He got his AFL assignment only after Miguel Olivo hurt himself, so his presence in the AFL is not a signal that the A's will set aside a roster spot for him.

Frank Menechino   2B   Bats R   Age 30

YEAR	TEAM	LGE	AB	H	DB	TP	HR	BB	SO	R	RBI	SB	CS	OUT	BA	OBP	SLG	EQA	EQR	DEFENSE			
1998	Edmonton	PCL	377	84	9	4	7	55	78	52	28	6	6	299	.223	.331	.324	.226	36	68-2B	-5		
1999	Vancouvr	PCL	504	129	24	7	9	57	101	75	62	3	3	378	.256	.338	.385	.245	56	52-3B	3	39-SS	7
2000	Sacramen	PCL	38	10	2	0	1	4	4	6	2	1	0	28	.263	.333	.395	.250	4				
2000	Oakland	AL	144	37	10	1	6	19	41	30	25	1	5	112	.257	.348	.465	.259	19	37-2B	4		
2001	Oakland	AL	248	59	11	2	5	34	59	34	31	2	3	192	.238	.330	.359	.240	27				

Frankie Menechino is the default option at second base if Bellhorn or Jose Ortiz has a bad camp, and he's not a bad fallback. He has some power and patience and a better glove than he gets credit for. On an organizational level, having him around is like having a good sixth starter or a spare tire. You'd rather not use him, but if you have to, it isn't the end of the world. He's a throwback player in that looking at him, you'd swear he stepped right out of a team picture from the thirties.

Miguel Olivo   C   Bats R   Age 22

YEAR	TEAM	LGE	AB	H	DB	TP	HR	BB	SO	R	RBI	SB	CS	OUT	BA	OBP	SLG	EQA	EQR	DEFENSE	
1999	Modesto	Cal	241	58	10	3	6	13	62	30	25	2	2	185	.241	.282	.382	.217	20	63-C	-6
2000	Modesto	Cal	228	54	11	2	4	8	55	28	23	2	1	175	.237	.266	.355	.202	16	50-C	-2
2000	Midland	Tex	59	12	1	0	1	3	16	6	7	0	0	47	.203	.242	.271	.155	2	13-C	-4
2001	ChiSox	AL	182	46	7	1	3	10	59	20	23	1	1	137	.253	.292	.352	.214	14		

Miguel Olivo might be the best-throwing catcher in the minors, and he's a good receiver and plate-blocker as well. He's also a very impatient hitter, and there are some concerns about his attitude. For the second straight year, he lost time to injury, this time a broken hamate bone. He's been traded to the White Sox for Chad Bradford; while he may need another year in A ball, he's Chicago's best catching prospect.

Jose Ortiz   2B   Bats R   Age 24

YEAR	TEAM	LGE	AB	H	DB	TP	HR	BB	SO	R	RBI	SB	CS	OUT	BA	OBP	SLG	EQA	EQR	DEFENSE			
1998	Huntsvil	Sou	356	84	19	1	5	31	67	48	39	11	5	277	.236	.303	.337	.218	31	55-2B	-2	34-SS	-11
1999	Vancouvr	PCL	377	97	24	2	7	24	48	52	36	9	3	283	.257	.312	.387	.236	38	95-SS	-5		
2000	Sacramen	PCL	513	159	30	3	19	35	65	81	80	13	6	360	.310	.357	.491	.279	74	75-2B	-3	48-SS	-9
2001	Oakland	AL	429	118	22	2	12	36	63	66	62	11	3	314	.275	.331	.420	.260	54				

The MVP of the Pacific Coast League, Jose Ortiz is the odds-on favorite to win the second-base job. He has a strong arm for a second baseman, and it's thought that he'll improve there now that he's playing the position full-time. He's being compared to Tony Batista, but he's more of a spark plug like Menechino or Miguel Tejada. Offensively, he won't be the answer to the team's leadoff-hitter question. Normally, I'd tout him for a Rookie of the Year Award, but Ichiro Suzuki should have that locked up. Let's put it this way: Ortiz will still be playing ten years from now.

American League

Adam Piatt — 3B/OF/1B Bats R Age 25

YEAR	TEAM	LGE	AB	H	DB	TP	HR	BB	SO	R	RBI	SB	CS	OUT	BA	OBP	SLG	EQA	EQR	DEFENSE			
1998	Modesto	Cal	510	118	26	2	15	58	101	61	71	9	3	395	.231	.310	.378	.233	52	118-3B	-27		
1999	Midland	Tex	472	126	28	2	26	70	109	86	85	3	2	348	.267	.367	.500	.285	75	111-3B	-14	10-SS	1
2000	Sacramen	PCL	254	64	8	0	8	19	58	28	33	2	1	191	.252	.311	.378	.231	24	21-3B	-2	19-RF	-1
2000	Oakland	AL	156	48	6	5	5	21	40	23	22	0	1	109	.308	.393	.506	.296	26	22-RF	-3		
2001	Oakland	AL	445	114	22	2	18	61	110	73	74	5	2	333	.256	.346	.436	.269	63				

Adam Piatt didn't stick until his third call-up, but he gave the A's some needed punch against left-handers. Keep in mind that full-season notation can mask breakthroughs. Piatt started hitting for big power in the second half of 1998, which is reason to believe he'll outhit our projection if he gets regular playing time. He's going to eventually be a good or at least adequate outfielder, because he isn't tentative or afraid to run the ball down.

Olmedo Saenz — 3B/1B Bats R Age 30

YEAR	TEAM	LGE	AB	H	DB	TP	HR	BB	SO	R	RBI	SB	CS	OUT	BA	OBP	SLG	EQA	EQR	DEFENSE			
1998	Calgary	PCL	455	113	16	0	20	35	51	60	68	2	2	344	.248	.320	.415	.245	51	113-3B	-4		
1999	Oakland	AL	254	72	14	0	13	20	43	40	41	1	1	183	.283	.366	.492	.283	39	44-3B	-1	16-1B	3
2000	Oakland	AL	213	69	10	2	10	22	36	38	32	1	0	144	.324	.405	.531	.309	38	16-3B	-2	14-1B	-1
2001	Oakland	AL	268	75	9	0	13	29	45	40	50	1	0	193	.280	.350	.459	.277	39				

No sophomore slump here, even with him missing August and having to play on one leg during the second half. Olmedo Saenz is the corner-infield variation on a Geronimo Berroa theme. He'll be a handy extra bat as long as he can play third base once in a while, or up to the point that arbitration-inspired salary inflation makes him an Oriole.

Oscar Salazar — UT Bats R Age 23

YEAR	TEAM	LGE	AB	H	DB	TP	HR	BB	SO	R	RBI	SB	CS	OUT	BA	OBP	SLG	EQA	EQR	DEFENSE			
1998	So Oregn	Nwn	101	23	4	0	3	10	25	10	15	1	1	79	.228	.297	.356	.217	9				
1999	Modesto	Cal	520	122	23	8	13	24	110	64	64	6	3	401	.235	.269	.385	.213	42	29-2B	-2	28-3B	-9
2000	Midland	Tex	422	103	18	1	10	25	75	50	39	2	2	321	.244	.288	.363	.214	34	93-SS	-17		
2001	Oakland	AL	452	112	20	2	12	30	94	50	56	4	2	342	.248	.295	.381	.230	43				

Another Venezuelan, Oscar Salazar is compared to Mike Bordick. He's being used as a utility infielder so far, but he might end up as a full-time shortstop. Hey, it worked for Melvin Mora despite his limited range. Salazar made the right impression on the organization by working hard and becoming a lot less careless at the plate and in the field this year, but he isn't patient, and he struggled against left-handed pitchers. He'll needs to continue to improve across the board, but guys who can play six or seven positions have a way of getting opportunities.

Matt Stairs — OF/1B Bats L Age 33

YEAR	TEAM	LGE	AB	H	DB	TP	HR	BB	SO	R	RBI	SB	CS	OUT	BA	OBP	SLG	EQA	EQR	DEFENSE	
1998	Oakland	AL	523	160	29	1	30	58	83	90	109	7	3	366	.306	.381	.537	.299	90	12-LF	1
1999	Oakland	AL	528	139	27	3	39	84	113	93	99	2	7	396	.263	.366	.547	.291	90	127-RF	-6
2000	Oakland	AL	474	111	21	0	24	73	111	71	80	5	2	365	.234	.338	.430	.258	61	96-RF	-7
2001	ChiCubs	NL	459	116	19	0	29	82	107	74	86	4	2	345	.253	.366	.484	.284	74		

After coming into camp in shape in 1999, Matt Stairs spent the next off-season following the Rod Beck conditioning program. It made him a hero to the Superfans on Sheffield and Addison, not to mention a few BP writers, but it hurt his play in 2000. Traded to the Cubs for a waiver claim on Eric Ireland, he'll play first base as long as Sammy Sosa is in the fold. Stairs will huff and puff and hustle wherever he plays, but like John Kruk, he's a good bet to fade quickly.

Mike Stanley — 1B Bats R Age 38

YEAR	TEAM	LGE	AB	H	DB	TP	HR	BB	SO	R	RBI	SB	CS	OUT	BA	OBP	SLG	EQA	EQR	DEFENSE	
1998	Toronto	AL	340	84	11	0	24	55	77	50	47	2	1	257	.247	.359	.491	.280	53	21-1B	0
1998	Boston	AL	155	45	8	0	9	26	38	25	33	1	0	110	.290	.398	.516	.303	28	13-1B	-1
1999	Boston	AL	422	120	18	0	21	65	86	57	70	0	0	302	.284	.392	.476	.291	69	97-1B	6
2000	Boston	AL	183	40	3	0	11	28	40	21	27	0	0	143	.219	.322	.415	.247	22	33-1B	2
2000	Oakland	AL	96	26	5	0	5	13	19	10	18	0	0	70	.271	.364	.479	.279	14	16-1B	-1
2001	Oakland	AL	328	77	10	0	16	61	76	53	56	0	0	251	.235	.355	.412	.268	47		

Oakland Athletics

(Mike Stanley *continued*)

It's been an epic career for Mike Stanley, but all good things must come to an end. When Stanley first came up, he barely survived Geno Petralli's nefarious campaign of mafioso extortion and violence that ran off or rubbed out Don Slaught, Darrell Porter, Orlando Mercado, Jim Sundberg, Chad Kreuter, and John Russell. Anybody who tried to move in on Petralli's piece of the action ended up sleeping with the shin guards. Geno got sloppy and lost out to some new kid named Ivan from Latin America just after he started trying to convert himself over to legitimate business. Sheesh, ain't that the American dream? Ease up and get whacked. Adios, Mickey.

Miguel Tejada — SS — Bats R — Age 25

YEAR	TEAM	LGE	AB	H	DB	TP	HR	BB	SO	R	RBI	SB	CS	OUT	BA	OBP	SLG	EQA	EQR	DEFENSE	
1998	Oakland	AL	365	88	18	1	13	27	77	54	46	4	6	283	.241	.305	.403	.232	37	104-SS	0
1999	Oakland	AL	591	152	34	4	22	52	86	91	82	7	7	446	.257	.327	.440	.252	71	157-SS	4
2000	Oakland	AL	605	171	28	1	33	59	93	102	113	7	0	434	.283	.350	.496	.279	89	157-SS	-4
2001	*Oakland*	*AL*	*599*	*168*	*29*	*2*	*29*	*65*	*102*	*97*	*114*	*6*	*3*	*434*	*.280*	*.351*	*.481*	*.282*	*91*		

He's clearly the fourth-best shortstop in the league, but it's a strange group of guys to rank. Alex Rodriguez belongs on his own plane as far and away the best of the bunch, offensively and defensively. He's also the youngest. Miguel Tejada is actually older than Rodriguez by a couple of months. Among the non-A-Rods, Tejada is the slugger and the best defender. He's also coming off of a huge second half, improving from .250/.314/.443 to .305/.389/.524. At his age, that's growth, which should end up putting him at the head of the group behind Rodriguez.

Mario Valdez — 1B — Bats L — Age 26

YEAR	TEAM	LGE	AB	H	DB	TP	HR	BB	SO	R	RBI	SB	CS	OUT	BA	OBP	SLG	EQA	EQR	DEFENSE			
1998	Calgary	PCL	437	119	18	0	16	48	101	62	59	1	1	319	.272	.354	.423	.262	56	107-1B	4		
1999	Charlott	Int	400	94	14	1	20	62	90	61	56	1	0	306	.235	.350	.425	.262	54	81-1B	5	17-LF	-1
2000	SaltLake	PCL	306	91	16	1	13	44	47	54	57	1	1	216	.297	.389	.484	.291	49	38-1B	2		
2000	Sacramen	PCL	61	13	1	0	2	7	13	8	9	0	0	48	.213	.309	.328	.217	5	14-1B	0		
2001	*Oakland*	*AL*	*414*	*110*	*12*	*0*	*20*	*65*	*87*	*68*	*77*	*1*	*0*	*304*	*.266*	*.365*	*.440*	*.279*	*63*				

Mario Valdez was named the PCL's top hitting prospect in *Baseball America*'s tools poll. Valdez has 430 games of experience at Triple-A, which isn't his fault. His situation isn't quite as bad as Steve Balboni winning minor-league player of the month awards in different decades, but it is unfortunate. Valdez should have been up to stay by now. A broken hamate bone suffered just after his August call-up blew his shot at postseason glory, but he'll be playing some outfield over the winter to help his chances of making the team in the spring.

Randy Velarde — 2B — Bats R — Age 38

YEAR	TEAM	LGE	AB	H	DB	TP	HR	BB	SO	R	RBI	SB	CS	OUT	BA	OBP	SLG	EQA	EQR	DEFENSE	
1998	Anaheim	AL	187	50	14	1	4	34	37	29	25	6	2	139	.267	.383	.417	.276	28	48-2B	-1
1999	Anaheim	AL	372	115	13	4	10	40	51	55	46	12	4	261	.309	.381	.446	.281	55	95-2B	10
1999	Oakland	AL	253	85	12	3	7	25	38	47	27	10	4	172	.336	.399	.490	.298	42	59-2B	0
2000	Oakland	AL	483	138	17	0	15	49	87	79	41	10	4	349	.286	.355	.414	.261	61	117-2B	10
2001	*Texas*	*AL*	*361*	*96*	*12*	*1*	*8*	*49*	*64*	*60*	*51*	*7*	*4*	*269*	*.266*	*.354*	*.371*	*.246*	*41*		

Some are calling the decision to trade Randy Velarde to the Rangers a salary dump, but it made room on the roster and in the lineup for more talent. Velarde is starting to make a habit of leaving too soon: he parted with the Yankees after '95, just before the good times started to roll and just after a disappointing first-round playoff exit.

American League

PITCHERS (ERA: 4.50, H/9: 9.00, HR/9: 1.00, BB/9: 3.00, K/9: 6.00, KW: 1.00, PERA: 4.50)

Kevin Appier — Throws R — Age 33

YEAR	TEAM	LGE	IP	H	ER	HR	BB	K	ERA	W	L	H/9	HR/9	BB/9	K/9	KW	PERA
1998	Omaha	PCL	30.3	39	25	8	13	14	7.42	1	2	11.57	2.37	3.86	4.15	0.54	7.83
1998	KansasCy	AL	15.0	20	12	3	4	8	7.20	0	2	12.00	1.80	2.40	4.80	1.00	6.92
1999	KansasCy	AL	139.3	141	66	14	39	74	4.26	7	8	9.11	0.90	2.52	4.78	0.95	4.26
1999	Oakland	AL	68.3	72	44	8	27	50	5.80	3	5	9.48	1.05	3.56	6.59	0.93	5.07
2000	Oakland	AL	194.3	187	93	20	83	123	4.31	10	12	8.66	0.93	3.84	5.70	0.74	4.57

As good as it is to see Kevin Appier get a major payday after years of giving himself up for the greater glory of the hopeless Herk Robinson Royals, his contract with the Mets is a pretty heavy burden for them to carry. Even with the National League being a slightly more pitcher-friendly environment and Shea Stadium being a nice pitchers' park, he's coming off a couple of seasons of allowing 300 base runners. That's a lot of pitches for a guy with a delivery that's always going to make people think he's an injury risk.

Todd Belitz — Throws L — Age 25

YEAR	TEAM	LGE	IP	H	ER	HR	BB	K	ERA	W	L	H/9	HR/9	BB/9	K/9	KW	PERA
1998	Charl-SC	SAL	115.7	105	59	17	66	56	4.59	6	7	8.17	1.32	5.14	4.36	0.42	5.24
1998	St Pete	Fla	40.7	41	37	7	18	23	8.19	1	4	9.07	1.55	3.98	5.09	0.64	5.55
1999	Orlando	Sou	148.0	173	134	37	71	73	8.15	3	13	10.52	2.25	4.32	4.44	0.51	7.27
2000	Durham	Int	44.3	33	24	1	28	34	4.87	2	3	6.70	0.20	5.68	6.90	0.61	3.47
2000	Sacramen	PCL	11.7	12	7	3	5	7	5.40	0	1	9.26	2.31	3.86	5.40	0.70	6.43

The A's were initially expecting Todd Belitz to take the second left-hander role in the big-league pen, but he scuffled after coming over from the Devil Rays then got lit up in the AFL. He relies heavily on a slider, and he doesn't throw particularly hard. He's here because he's left-handed and because there isn't anything more to say about guys like Tim Kubinski.

Scott Chiasson — Throws R — Age 23

YEAR	TEAM	LGE	IP	H	ER	HR	BB	K	ERA	W	L	H/9	HR/9	BB/9	K/9	KW	PERA
1999	So Oregn	Nwn	65.0	78	50	11	42	26	6.92	2	5	10.80	1.52	5.82	3.60	0.31	7.28
2000	Visalia	Cal	141.0	160	85	36	61	78	5.43	6	10	10.21	2.30	3.89	4.98	0.64	6.96

Scott Chiasson has a decent fastball and a good curve, but he hasn't been consistent with his command. He pitched at East Connecticut State University before being drafted by the Royals in '98. He was traded to the A's for Jay Witasick. The A's had to decide whether he'd be on the 40-man roster, because roster-management rules say college players have to go on or get exposed after three pro years, whether they went to Stanford or East Connecticut State. The Cubs snagged him in the Rule 5 draft. It will be a bit of a surprise if they keep him without faking an injury to him.

Chad Harville — Throws R — Age 24

YEAR	TEAM	LGE	IP	H	ER	HR	BB	K	ERA	W	L	H/9	HR/9	BB/9	K/9	KW	PERA
1998	Visalia	Cal	64.0	60	27	2	36	40	3.80	4	3	8.44	0.28	5.06	5.63	0.56	4.27
1999	Midland	Tex	20.7	15	7	1	9	22	3.05	1	1	6.53	0.44	3.92	9.58	1.22	2.94
1999	Vancouvr	PCL	23.7	24	6	1	13	24	2.28	2	1	9.13	0.38	4.94	9.13	0.92	4.69
1999	Oakland	AL	14.3	17	10	2	8	14	6.28	1	1	10.67	1.26	5.02	8.79	0.88	6.54
2000	Sacramen	PCL	60.0	54	39	11	36	56	5.85	2	5	8.10	1.65	5.40	8.40	0.78	5.64

Chad Harville is a mighty mite who can blast gas in the high 90s, but the A's want him to get a little less exciting by throwing a two-seamer with some sink on it. He also has a high-80s slider that he can get to move like two different pitches. What Harville really needs is consistency, especially in his delivery, and to do a better job of putting batters away quickly. Calling him up to sit in the bullpen without pitching for two weeks has to be one of the Athletics' strangest decisions of the year, especially when you consider the amount of time wasted on Scott Service.

Gil Heredia — Throws R — Age 35

YEAR	TEAM	LGE	IP	H	ER	HR	BB	K	ERA	W	L	H/9	HR/9	BB/9	K/9	KW	PERA
1998	Edmonton	PCL	138.0	145	67	15	20	64	4.37	7	8	9.46	0.98	1.30	4.17	1.60	4.05
1998	Oakland	AL	41.3	40	13	4	3	25	2.83	3	2	8.71	0.87	0.65	5.44	4.17	3.29
1999	Oakland	AL	196.3	209	103	19	28	111	4.72	9	13	9.58	0.87	1.28	5.09	1.98	4.00
2000	Oakland	AL	195.7	197	91	21	54	96	4.19	11	11	9.06	0.97	2.48	4.42	0.89	4.29

Gil Heredia is a junk-baller whose act is wearing thin. The drop in his strikeout rate and the jump in his walk rate are ominous. Each of the four times he made consecutive starts against the same opponent in 2000, he got hammered in the latter outing. In first games, he allowed 3.7 runs per nine innings; in second games, 11.3. He made four starts against the Twins and went from two quality starts to two starts in which he couldn't get through the fifth inning. When he beat the Yankees in Game One of the AL Division Series and then had to start Game Five, the writing was on the wall. The new unbalanced schedule creates lots of situations in which starters will see the same opponents in consecutive starts. Heredia is a magician with only so many tricks, so the A's should worry.

Tim Hudson — Throws R — Age 25

YEAR	TEAM	LGE	IP	H	ER	HR	BB	K	ERA	W	L	H/9	HR/9	BB/9	K/9	KW	PERA
1998	Modesto	Cal	34.0	22	15	2	22	24	3.97	2	2	5.82	0.53	5.82	6.35	0.55	3.38
1998	Huntsvil	Sou	127.0	137	89	21	68	67	6.31	4	10	9.71	1.49	4.82	4.75	0.49	6.19
1999	Vancouvr	PCL	45.7	37	18	3	25	42	3.55	3	2	7.29	0.59	4.93	8.28	0.84	3.88
1999	Oakland	AL	135.3	114	49	7	50	126	3.26	9	6	7.58	0.47	3.33	8.38	1.26	3.30
2000	Oakland	AL	200.0	158	86	21	67	161	3.87	11	11	7.11	0.94	3.02	7.24	1.20	3.39

Tim Hudson changes speeds aggressively and well, his sinker moves, and his forkball drops on batters like an anvil on Wile E. Coyote. The key is that his release point is almost identical for every pitch, making it incredibly difficult for hitters to figure out what's coming. Here's a benefit of a potent offense: the A's went 17–0 when Hudson gave them six or more innings and allowed three runs or fewer. Hudson isn't the best prospect among good young pitchers, but he may have the best future, considering the care with which he's been managed and the support he'll get from the offense.

Jason Isringhausen — Throws R — Age 28

YEAR	TEAM	LGE	IP	H	ER	HR	BB	K	ERA	W	L	H/9	HR/9	BB/9	K/9	KW	PERA
1999	Norfolk	Int	48.0	34	20	5	21	35	3.75	3	2	6.38	0.94	3.94	6.56	0.83	3.35
1999	NY Mets	NL	38.3	42	28	7	19	26	6.57	1	3	9.86	1.64	4.46	6.10	0.68	6.30
1999	Oakland	AL	25.0	20	5	2	10	19	1.80	2	1	7.20	0.72	3.60	6.84	0.95	3.46
2000	Oakland	AL	68.7	63	29	5	26	54	3.80	4	4	8.26	0.66	3.41	7.08	1.04	3.89

So far, Jason Isringhausen has been an adequate closer who has moments of maximum fright-inducement. When he's on, his curve can be nasty, and he almost never shows up without high-90s heat. The question is whether he'll ever become less frightening and more consistent. The answer should be yes. If John Wetteland can triumph over wildness and Tommy Lasorda, Izzy ought to be able to put Dallas Green in his rear-view mirror.

Doug Jones — Throws R — Ageless

YEAR	TEAM	LGE	IP	H	ER	HR	BB	K	ERA	W	L	H/9	HR/9	BB/9	K/9	KW	PERA
1998	Milwauke	NL	51.7	64	32	15	10	35	5.57	2	4	11.15	2.61	1.74	6.10	1.75	6.97
1998	Clevelnd	AL	30.7	32	11	2	5	26	3.23	2	1	9.39	0.59	1.47	7.63	2.60	3.69
1999	Oakland	AL	102.0	98	38	9	20	60	3.35	6	5	8.65	0.79	1.76	5.29	1.50	3.60
2000	Oakland	AL	72.3	79	29	5	15	51	3.61	4	4	9.83	0.62	1.87	6.35	1.70	4.12

He retired, but even though space is at a premium, let's tip our caps to Yosemite Sam. His rookie season was 1987, a tough year for pitchers. He was about to turn 30, his out pitch was his change-up and he was toiling for the ill-fated *Sports Illustrated*-cover Indians. Phil Niekro was on that team, as was Steve Carlton. A handful of other survivors from that team are still playing: Jay Bell, Greg Swindell, and I'm willing to bet Scott Bailes is pitching somewhere on this planet.

American League

Marcus Jones — Throws R — Age 26

YEAR	TEAM	LGE	IP	H	ER	HR	BB	K	ERA	W	L	H/9	HR/9	BB/9	K/9	KW	PERA
1998	Visalia	Cal	121.3	154	86	17	56	54	6.38	4	9	11.42	1.26	4.15	4.01	0.48	6.69
1999	Modesto	Cal	28.0	33	27	10	18	17	8.68	1	2	10.61	3.21	5.79	5.46	0.47	8.97
1999	Visalia	Cal	83.7	101	63	14	41	39	6.78	2	7	10.86	1.51	4.41	4.20	0.48	6.72
2000	Midland	Tex	21.7	23	8	1	1	7	3.32	1	1	9.55	0.42	0.42	2.91	3.50	3.21
2000	Sacramento	PCL	95.7	100	56	10	40	34	5.27	4	7	9.41	0.94	3.76	3.20	0.43	4.99

The life of an organizational soldier has its ups and downs. Marcus Jones is big and doesn't throw especially hard, relying more on breaking stuff, but he finds ways to avoid being buried. Promoted to Midland to fill in, he managed to stick around, then repeated the routine with Sacramento. Jones even lucked into a major-league debut/random act of cruelty by getting to make a spot start in Coors Field. He's not a prospect but a survivor.

Justin Lehr — Throws R — Age 23

YEAR	TEAM	LGE	IP	H	ER	HR	BB	K	ERA	W	L	H/9	HR/9	BB/9	K/9	KW	PERA
1999	So Oregn	Nwn	40.3	61	34	6	18	20	7.59	1	3	13.61	1.34	4.02	4.46	0.56	8.00
2000	Modesto	Cal	162.3	164	79	21	49	72	4.38	8	10	9.09	1.16	2.72	3.99	0.73	4.62

Justin Lehr has relatively little pitching experience. He was a catcher at UC Santa Barbara before transferring to USC as a junior. As a senior, he was the #2 starter behind some guy named Zito before getting picked in the same draft by the same organization as his college teammate. Unlike most position-player conversions, he isn't somebody who throws hard, but a control pitcher who can throw a sinker, slider, and change-up for strikes. He's working on a forkball.

Mike Magnante — Throws L — Age 36

YEAR	TEAM	LGE	IP	H	ER	HR	BB	K	ERA	W	L	H/9	HR/9	BB/9	K/9	KW	PERA
1998	Houston	NL	49.7	54	27	2	25	32	4.89	2	4	9.79	0.36	4.53	5.80	0.64	4.93
1999	Anaheim	AL	68.7	64	26	2	23	42	3.41	5	3	8.39	0.26	3.01	5.50	0.91	3.44
2000	Oakland	AL	39.7	46	19	3	16	16	4.31	2	2	10.44	0.68	3.63	3.63	0.50	5.29

Signing Mike Magnante was a bad move. If there's something the union and the owners ought to be able to agree on, it's that the free-agent compensation system is wacky. Any scheme that makes a replacement-level talent like Magnante worth a first-round draft pick is a joke, but more importantly, it can hurt a player's value while sticking his original club with the potential hassle of an arbitration case. He's under contract and left-handed, so he'll be around.

Tim Manwiller — Throws R — Age 26

YEAR	TEAM	LGE	IP	H	ER	HR	BB	K	ERA	W	L	H/9	HR/9	BB/9	K/9	KW	PERA
1998	Modesto	Cal	144.0	150	80	18	59	62	5.00	6	10	9.38	1.13	3.69	3.88	0.53	5.14
1999	Midland	Tex	80.0	91	43	8	27	34	4.84	4	5	10.24	0.90	3.04	3.83	0.63	5.13
1999	Vancouvr	PCL	51.3	67	44	13	17	20	7.71	1	5	11.75	2.28	2.98	3.51	0.59	7.47
2000	Midland	Tex	106.0	122	73	24	38	45	6.20	4	8	10.36	2.04	3.23	3.82	0.59	6.49
2000	Sacramen	PCL	24.3	34	26	9	13	15	9.62	0	3	12.58	3.33	4.81	5.55	0.58	9.82

Remember that old Bob Feller footage in which Rapid Robert fires a fastball through a paper target just ahead of a speeding motorcycle? Tim Manwiller would have to square off against a bicycle and tissue paper, and I wouldn't bet against the bicycle. He has nothing, but he hides the ball well with his lead arm, shows an adequate slider and change-up, and knows what he's doing. He doesn't have much of a future, but neither did Doug Jones until he was 30.

T.J. Mathews — Throws R — Age 31

YEAR	TEAM	LGE	IP	H	ER	HR	BB	K	ERA	W	L	H/9	HR/9	BB/9	K/9	KW	PERA
1998	Oakland	AL	71.3	66	38	5	25	49	4.79	3	5	8.33	0.63	3.15	6.18	0.98	3.79
1999	Oakland	AL	58.0	43	24	8	16	40	3.72	3	3	6.67	1.24	2.48	6.21	1.25	3.23
2000	Oakland	AL	59.7	68	35	9	20	40	5.28	3	4	10.26	1.36	3.02	6.03	1.00	5.63

T.J. Mathews allowed runs in more than half of his 50 appearances, so his missing three weeks in August with elbow tendinitis wasn't exactly a setback for the team. How he managed to strand more than 70% of inherited base runners while getting lit up like this is beyond me. Mathews is the remaining prize from the Mark McGwire trade, but the A's will get a couple of draft picks from the Mets for Kevin Appier, who was acquired with a package built around Blake Stein. Mathews is under contract for 2001 and will be fighting left-handed people for the last spot in the pen.

Jim Mecir — Throws R — Age 31

YEAR	TEAM	LGE	IP	H	ER	HR	BB	K	ERA	W	L	H/9	HR/9	BB/9	K/9	KW	PERA
1998	TampaBay	AL	82.7	64	26	5	28	71	2.83	6	3	6.97	0.54	3.05	7.73	1.27	2.96
1999	TampaBay	AL	20.3	15	7	1	11	14	3.10	1	1	6.64	0.44	4.87	6.20	0.64	3.35
2000	TampaBay	AL	49.3	33	14	2	17	32	2.55	4	1	6.02	0.36	3.10	5.84	0.94	2.37
2000	Oakland	AL	35.0	33	12	2	11	35	3.09	3	1	8.49	0.51	2.83	9.00	1.59	3.63

Jim Mecir was one of the major plums swapped at the trade deadline, along with fellow D-Rays middle man Rick White. They were both among the most effective relievers in baseball at the time they were dealt. Why Billy Beane had to give up Jesus Colome while the Mets only had to cough up Jason friggin' Tyner should strike A's fans as random injustice. Mecir relies heavily on a screwball and also has good heat. If Izzy struggles, Mecir is the guy most likely to close.

Justin Miller — Throws R — Age 23

YEAR	TEAM	LGE	IP	H	ER	HR	BB	K	ERA	W	L	H/9	HR/9	BB/9	K/9	KW	PERA
1998	Ashevlle	SAL	151.0	180	95	23	48	66	5.66	6	11	10.73	1.37	2.86	3.93	0.69	5.85
1999	Salem VA	Car	33.7	38	23	6	12	18	6.15	1	3	10.16	1.60	3.21	4.81	0.75	5.90
2000	Midland	Tex	82.0	75	52	11	39	51	5.71	3	6	8.23	1.21	4.28	5.60	0.65	4.79
2000	Sacramen	PCL	52.0	40	18	4	13	25	3.12	4	2	6.92	0.69	2.25	4.33	0.96	2.79

Justin Miller was the payoff for trading Jimmy Haynes. Since he had missed most of 1999 with an impinged nerve in his elbow, there were some concerns about whether the A's were getting anything. Miller throws a hard sinker, splitter, and slider, and he's working on a change-up. He topped off his year with a pretty good AFL campaign. He isn't just the dark horse but the pitch-black horse for the last spot in the rotation. If they don't trade for anybody and either Olivares or Heredia breaks down, a good camp and fast start will bring Miller to Oakland.

Mark Mulder — Throws L — Age 23

YEAR	TEAM	LGE	IP	H	ER	HR	BB	K	ERA	W	L	H/9	HR/9	BB/9	K/9	KW	PERA
1999	Vancouvr	PCL	122.3	139	69	18	37	55	5.08	5	9	10.23	1.32	2.72	4.05	0.74	5.45
2000	Oakland	AL	153.3	177	91	19	56	84	5.34	6	11	10.39	1.12	3.29	4.93	0.75	5.56

Mark Mulder is finally throwing in the low 90s after complaining about having a dead arm in 1999. He's still learning the finer points of a change-up, and his curve needs work. Mulder gave the A's quality starts in 13 of 27 attempts (using three runs instead of three earned runs as the definition)—13 of 23 if you could somehow make his starts against the Yankees and Rangers disappear (he allowed 32 runs in 16⅓ innings in those four starts). A herniated disk in September kept him off of the playoff roster, but he's expected to be fine in camp.

Omar Olivares — Throws R — Age 33

YEAR	TEAM	LGE	IP	H	ER	HR	BB	K	ERA	W	L	H/9	HR/9	BB/9	K/9	KW	PERA
1998	Anaheim	AL	180.7	177	80	17	77	104	3.99	10	10	8.82	0.85	3.84	5.18	0.68	4.57
1999	Anaheim	AL	129.0	125	52	9	39	47	3.63	8	6	8.72	0.63	2.72	3.28	0.60	3.85
1999	Oakland	AL	74.0	76	37	7	26	34	4.50	4	4	9.24	0.85	3.16	4.14	0.65	4.56
2000	Oakland	AL	108.0	125	74	9	49	54	6.17	4	8	10.42	0.75	4.08	4.50	0.55	5.52

"Folks, we close tonight's awards banquet with the Golden Fleece Award, given to the player who exemplified addition by subtraction. Going onto the DL in June for two months with a strained shoulder was probably the best thing this pitcher could have done for the A's, because it created an opportunity to call up Barry Zito. Let's give Omar Olivares a big round of applause." Under contract for another year, Olivares will have to fight to win the fifth spot in the rotation. If he loses, he'll be dealt to an appropriately desperate team or cut.

Juan Pena — Throws L — Age 22

YEAR	TEAM	LGE	IP	H	ER	HR	BB	K	ERA	W	L	H/9	HR/9	BB/9	K/9	KW	PERA
1998	So Oregn	Nwn	43.7	46	21	4	11	19	4.33	2	3	9.48	0.82	2.27	3.92	0.86	4.28
1998	Modesto	Cal	31.3	49	24	4	8	17	6.89	1	2	14.07	1.15	2.30	4.88	1.06	7.36
1999	Visalia	Cal	124.3	158	103	18	68	58	7.46	3	11	11.44	1.30	4.92	4.20	0.43	7.04
2000	Modesto	Cal	142.0	142	95	14	77	95	6.02	5	11	9.00	0.89	4.88	6.02	0.62	5.16

American League

Juan Pena is another product of the organization's Dominican program. He's adding velocity as he fills out, and his breaking stuff is just starting to develop. He tied for the Cal League strikeout title. He'll move up more slowly than Ramos or the college pitchers, but he has the most upside among the organization's A-ball starters.

Ariel Prieto — Throws R — Age 34

YEAR	TEAM	LGE	IP	H	ER	HR	BB	K	ERA	W	L	H/9	HR/9	BB/9	K/9	KW	PERA
1998	Edmonton	PCL	49.7	45	20	4	13	32	3.62	3	3	8.15	0.72	2.36	5.80	1.23	3.47
2000	Sacramen	PCL	106.3	105	53	13	34	53	4.49	5	7	8.89	1.10	2.88	4.49	0.78	4.48
2000	Oakland	AL	31.7	39	19	3	11	18	5.40	1	3	11.08	0.85	3.13	5.12	0.82	5.65

Ariel Prieto had a pretty good season bouncing back from Tommy John surgery and moving back and forth as the team's sixth starter. Prieto is technically a candidate for the fifth spot in the rotation. They say he's 31, and they said he was throwing 94 in winter ball. If they said a Cuban had a cure for cancer and a fastball, he'd probably get a big-league contract first and the Nobel Prize second. Waived during the winter.

Mario Ramos — Throws L — Age 23

YEAR	TEAM	LGE	IP	H	ER	HR	BB	K	ERA	W	L	H/9	HR/9	BB/9	K/9	KW	PERA
2000	Modesto	Cal	141.0	134	68	13	53	70	4.34	7	9	8.55	0.83	3.38	4.47	0.66	4.22
2000	Midland	Tex	25.7	24	7	1	6	12	2.45	2	1	8.42	0.35	2.10	4.21	1.00	3.20

The A's love Mario Ramos, a small left-hander from Rice whom they picked in the sixth-round of the '99 draft. He throws in the high 80s with a good change-up, and his breaking stuff is still developing. He gets very high marks for his approach to bullpen sessions and sidework, his intelligence, his command, and his pitching know-how. Nothing is out of the question. He could move up quickly, possibly even into the big-league bullpen sometime this year.

Jon Ratliff — Throws R — Age 29

YEAR	TEAM	LGE	IP	H	ER	HR	BB	K	ERA	W	L	H/9	HR/9	BB/9	K/9	KW	PERA
1998	Richmond	Int	142.7	168	97	22	67	97	6.12	5	11	10.60	1.39	4.23	6.12	0.72	6.37
1999	Richmond	Int	149.3	152	90	27	45	88	5.42	6	11	9.16	1.63	2.71	5.30	0.98	5.14
2000	Sacramen	PCL	100.3	99	52	17	34	49	4.66	5	6	8.88	1.52	3.05	4.40	0.72	5.00

Jon Ratliff, the man drafted with the infamous "Greg Maddux pick" the Cubs received as compensation when Larry Himes blew it, finally pitched his first major-league inning. Ratliff has a nice slider and spots a slow fastball and change-up well. He's organization insurance, sort of like Larry Luebbers, and he's been re-signed. He's definitely a long shot for the fifth spot behind Olivares and Prieto.

Scott Service — Throws R — Age 34

YEAR	TEAM	LGE	IP	H	ER	HR	BB	K	ERA	W	L	H/9	HR/9	BB/9	K/9	KW	PERA
1998	KansasCy	AL	82.0	67	31	6	28	88	3.40	5	4	7.35	0.66	3.07	9.66	1.57	3.27
1999	KansasCy	AL	76.3	82	42	10	32	65	4.95	3	5	9.67	1.18	3.77	7.66	1.02	5.41
2000	Sacramen	PCL	39.0	27	8	1	12	34	1.85	3	1	6.23	0.23	2.77	7.85	1.42	2.23
2000	Oakland	AL	37.0	42	27	4	16	34	6.57	1	3	10.22	0.97	3.89	8.27	1.06	5.58

Scott Service's slider has officially wandered off, so he spent the summer trying to perfect a change-up to freeze left-handers. We basically try to include in the book every person who played a decent amount of time in the majors, but Service is one of those guys who we should think about ignoring. After his last two seasons, he'll either be an Oriole or pitching in the Atlantic League in 2001.

Bert Snow — Throws R — Age 24

YEAR	TEAM	LGE	IP	H	ER	HR	BB	K	ERA	W	L	H/9	HR/9	BB/9	K/9	KW	PERA
1998	So Oregn	Nwn	42.7	51	36	4	20	18	7.59	1	4	10.76	0.84	4.22	3.80	0.45	5.88
1999	Visalia	Cal	58.7	59	52	7	46	47	7.98	1	6	9.05	1.07	7.06	7.21	0.51	6.29
1999	Midland	Tex	19.3	16	5	4	9	20	2.33	1	1	7.45	1.86	4.19	9.31	1.11	4.95
2000	Midland	Tex	62.7	65	39	8	35	59	5.60	2	5	9.34	1.15	5.03	8.47	0.84	5.69

Bert Snow was a tenth-rounder in the 1998 draft from a lousy Vanderbilt team. He has a low-90s fastball, a dynamite slider that left-handed hitters can barely touch, and he's been tinkering with a splitter. The A's rely pretty heavily on scout John Poloni's SEC recommendations. Snow should eventually be a good big-league reliever once he tackles the same problems with inconsistent command and mechanics that have dimmed Harville's star in the organization.

Keith Surkont   Throws R   Age 24

YEAR	TEAM	LGE	IP	H	ER	HR	BB	K	ERA	W	L	H/9	HR/9	BB/9	K/9	KW	PERA
1999	So Oregn	Nwn	70.7	80	43	10	39	19	5.48	3	5	10.19	1.27	4.97	2.42	0.24	6.32
2000	Visalia	Cal	114.3	109	71	14	60	61	5.59	4	9	8.58	1.10	4.72	4.80	0.51	5.06

A fourth-round pick out of Williams College in 1999, Keith Surkont won the Cal League ERA title, but more than a third of his runs allowed were unearned. He has a reputation for being a guy who doesn't rattle. Surkont is in that area between soft-tosser and flame-thrower, but his core skill is command of heat in the low 90s, along with a good slurve and change-up. The A's have a lot of command guys, so remember that more of them will turn out like Tim Manwiller than like Tim Hudson.

Jeff Tam   Throws R   Age 30

YEAR	TEAM	LGE	IP	H	ER	HR	BB	K	ERA	W	L	H/9	HR/9	BB/9	K/9	KW	PERA
1998	Norfolk	Int	60.3	42	15	4	6	37	2.24	5	2	6.27	0.60	0.90	5.52	3.08	1.94
1999	Norfolk	Int	19.3	22	6	1	3	7	2.79	1	1	10.24	0.47	1.40	3.26	1.17	3.97
1999	NY Mets	NL	10.7	6	4	3	3	7	3.38	1	0	5.06	2.53	2.53	5.91	1.17	3.63
1999	Buffalo	Int	24.3	22	9	2	9	9	3.33	2	1	8.14	0.74	3.33	3.33	0.50	3.87
2000	Oakland	AL	84.0	79	26	3	19	44	2.79	6	3	8.46	0.32	2.04	4.71	1.16	3.16

Jeff Tam was more valuable than Kazuhiro Sasaki, which makes for a pretty good case for Rookie of the Year. And he should have been a rookie in 2000, considering that he'd pitched all of 25 games and 26 innings. The BBWAA and the Elias Sports Bureau do some pretty wacky things with rookie eligibility. When it suits them, they make exceptions to the rules: Larry Walker was granted rookie status so that he could win the Rookie of the Year Award in 1990, even though he had more than a year's worth of service thanks to time spent on the DL. Lance Berkman's rookie status was taken from him last year on a technicality.

    Before 2000, Tam had 31 days of active big-league service on the 25-man roster. That's less than the 45 stipulated in the eligibility "rule." As was the case with Walker, most of Tam's major-league "career" had been spent on the DL, on rehab assignment, or on the roster after September 1, all of which by rule or by precedent aren't supposed to count. The punchline is that Elias and the writers are making it up as they go along.

Eric Thompson   Throws R   Age 23

YEAR	TEAM	LGE	IP	H	ER	HR	BB	K	ERA	W	L	H/9	HR/9	BB/9	K/9	KW	PERA
1998	So Oregn	Nwn	52.3	65	40	15	27	26	6.88	2	4	11.18	2.58	4.64	4.47	0.48	8.14
1999	Visalia	Cal	119.7	143	91	16	63	59	6.84	3	10	10.75	1.20	4.74	4.44	0.47	6.47
2000	Visalia	Cal	50.7	54	41	11	19	32	7.28	1	5	9.59	1.95	3.38	5.68	0.84	6.00
2000	Midland	Tex	96.3	103	50	7	22	49	4.67	5	6	9.62	0.65	2.06	4.58	1.11	4.11

Like Lockwood, Eric Thompson is an Ohio State product. He has a good arm, developing breaking stuff, and a great change-up. The absence of an eye-popping fastball kept him from drawing enough attention to get snagged in the Rule 5 draft this winter, but guys who post ERAs under 4.00 with 4-to-1 strikeout-to-walk ratios at Midland bear watching.

Luis Vizcaino   Throws R   Age 24

YEAR	TEAM	LGE	IP	H	ER	HR	BB	K	ERA	W	L	H/9	HR/9	BB/9	K/9	KW	PERA
1998	Modesto	Cal	93.3	76	49	11	51	56	4.72	4	6	7.33	1.06	4.92	5.40	0.55	4.37
1998	Huntsvil	Sou	36.0	45	31	13	21	17	7.75	1	3	11.25	3.25	5.25	4.25	0.40	9.15
1999	Midland	Tex	98.7	119	75	22	50	56	6.84	3	8	10.85	2.01	4.56	5.11	0.56	7.30
1999	Vancouvr	PCL	12.3	11	4	0	7	5	2.92	1	0	8.03	0.00	5.11	3.65	0.36	3.76
2000	Oakland	AL	19.3	23	15	2	9	17	6.98	0	2	10.71	0.93	4.19	7.91	0.94	5.88
2000	Sacramen	PCL	46.0	46	26	5	21	30	5.09	2	3	9.00	0.98	4.11	5.87	0.71	4.93

Luis Vizcaino hasn't mastered any of the various changes of pace to his mid-90s heat that he's experimented with in the last couple of years. His slider impresses people but gets seen about as often as a Brigitte Nielsen feature film. His attempt to learn a change-up has been almost as successful as a Brigitte Nielsen feature film. *Red Sonja,* anyone?

Denny Wagner Throws R Age 24

YEAR	TEAM	LGE	IP	H	ER	HR	BB	K	ERA	W	L	H/9	HR/9	BB/9	K/9	KW	PERA
1999	Modesto	Cal	106.3	112	60	13	49	52	5.08	5	7	9.48	1.10	4.15	4.40	0.53	5.36
1999	Midland	Tex	26.7	26	20	1	15	8	6.75	1	2	8.78	0.34	5.06	2.70	0.27	4.56
2000	Midland	Tex	171.3	199	102	18	62	66	5.36	7	12	10.45	0.95	3.26	3.47	0.53	5.41

The organization really hoped Denny Wagner would take a step forward, but it looks like he'll be moving to the bullpen. His failure to develop consistency through repetition—basically the failure to learn—was a problem. You can have some sympathy for him when you consider it's hard to learn in a ballpark where innings explode like artillery salvos. There are some signs of hope. He managed a ground-ball/fly-ball ratio of almost 3-to-1, and he still has good movement on his fastball.

Barry Zito Throws L Age 23

YEAR	TEAM	LGE	IP	H	ER	HR	BB	K	ERA	W	L	H/9	HR/9	BB/9	K/9	KW	PERA
1999	Visalia	Cal	36.7	25	18	5	25	34	4.42	2	2	6.14	1.23	6.14	8.35	0.68	4.37
1999	Midland	Tex	20.7	23	16	1	11	19	6.97	0	2	10.02	0.44	4.79	8.27	0.86	5.23
2000	Sacramen	PCL	96.7	84	43	5	46	66	4.00	5	6	7.82	0.47	4.28	6.14	0.72	3.80
2000	Oakland	AL	91.7	60	25	5	37	74	2.45	7	3	5.89	0.49	3.63	7.27	1.00	2.59

Barry Zito doesn't have great velocity, but he's smart, even-keeled, and he's got an incredible overhand curve. He also wasn't exactly your typical rookie in that he'd already received some coaching from A's pitching coach Rick Peterson (as a consultant) before he was even drafted. Watching him carve up the Yankees in Game Four of the ALDS was probably the highlight of the A's season. He may have a rough patch in the first half of 2001, but he's in the right organization to break through it.

Support-Neutral Statistics — OAKLAND ATHLETICS — Park Effect: -2.5%

PITCHER	GS	IP	R	SNW	SNL	SNPCT	W	L	RA	APW	SNVA	SNWAR
Kevin Appier	31	195.3	109	11.3	10.8	.510	15	11	5.02	0.4	0.2	1.9
Gil Heredia	32	198.7	106	11.9	10.9	.522	15	11	4.80	0.8	0.5	2.2
Tim Hudson	32	202.3	100	13.8	10.2	.575	20	6	4.45	1.6	1.8	3.6
Marcus Jones	1	2.3	4	0.1	0.5	.103	0	0	15.43	-0.2	-0.2	-0.2
Ron Mahay	2	7.3	11	0.1	1.3	.062	0	1	13.50	-0.6	-0.6	-0.5
Mark Mulder	27	154.0	106	8.6	10.1	.460	9	10	6.19	-1.6	-0.8	0.7
Omar Olivares	16	90.0	69	3.6	7.2	.333	4	8	6.90	-1.6	-1.8	-1.0
Ariel Prieto	6	28.7	20	1.6	2.0	.441	1	2	6.28	-0.3	-0.3	0.1
Barry Zito	14	92.7	30	6.7	2.9	.693	7	4	2.91	2.2	1.8	2.6
TOTALS	161	971.3	555	57.5	55.9	.507	71	53	5.14	0.6	0.7	9.3

With outstanding performances by Tim Hudson and Barry Zito and a passable one by Mark Mulder, the Athletics' 2000 rotation featured one of the best collections of young starters in recent years. Last year's A's got the fourth best Support-Neutral Wins Above Replacement out of starters younger than 25 since 1992. They finished behind the 1993 and 1994 Chicago White Sox (Alex Fernandez, Wilson Alvarez, and Jason Bere) and the 1992 Baltimore Orioles (Mike Mussina, Ben McDonald, and Arthur Rhodes). They finished just ahead of the 1992 Royals (Kevin Appier and Hipolito Pichardo) and the 1998 Indians (Bartolo Colon and Jaret Wright).

It should come as no surprise that the long-term record of these young rotations is generally good. The Orioles had a very successful run of starting rotations after 1992, with Mussina and McDonald playing large roles. The Royals, led by Appier, had a rotation that was second only to the Braves from 1993 to 1996. The Indians have had above-average rotations since 1998, with Colon playing a key role. Only the White Sox failed to maintain a thriving pitching staff after their youngsters emerged, though Fernandez and Alvarez continued to pitch well. Good, young starting pitching is just one of many reasons that the future looks rosy for the A's.

For a quick explanation of SN stats, see page 7.

Reliever Evaluation Tools

PITCHER	G	IP	R	ARA	APR	IRNR/G	EIRS/G	IRP	BRS	RRA	ARP
Todd Belitz	5	3.3	2	5.40	-0.1	0.40	0.07	-1.7	0.7	12.09	-2.6
Jason Isringhausen	66	69.0	34	4.43	5.9	0.24	0.09	-0.3	0.0	4.26	7.2
Doug Johns	1	0.3	0	0.00	0.2	0.00	0.00	0.0	0.0	1.67	0.1
Doug Jones	53	73.0	34	4.19	8.2	0.89	0.36	-0.1	2.8	4.51	5.5
Mike Magnante	55	39.7	22	4.99	0.9	0.87	0.33	2.7	4.3	4.92	1.2
Ron Mahay	3	8.7	7	7.26	-2.0	1.00	0.42	0.2	-1.2	5.38	-0.2
T.J. Mathews	50	59.7	40	6.03	-5.5	0.70	0.27	3.1	2.9	5.60	-2.7
Jim Mecir	25	35.3	14	3.56	6.4	1.00	0.43	1.8	1.2	3.68	5.9
Frank Menechino	1	1.0	4	35.98	-3.4	2.00	2.33	0.2	0.0	20.40	-1.7
Omar Olivares	5	18.0	17	8.49	-6.6	0.80	0.29	1.5	-0.6	7.30	-4.2
Ariel Prieto	2	3.0	1	3.00	0.7	0.00	0.00	0.0	0.0	3.56	0.5
Jon Ratliff	1	1.0	0	0.00	0.6	0.00	0.00	0.0	0.0	0.00	0.6
Rich Sauveur	10	10.3	5	4.35	1.0	1.60	0.71	-0.5	1.1	6.10	-1.0
Scott Service	20	36.7	31	7.60	-9.8	0.90	0.37	1.2	-2.0	6.85	-6.7
Jeff Tam	72	85.7	30	3.15	19.5	0.86	0.31	5.2	0.3	2.79	22.9
Luis Vizcaino	12	19.3	17	7.91	-5.8	0.83	0.31	-1.9	-0.8	8.30	-6.7
TOTALS	381	464.0	258	5.00	10.1	0.76	0.30			4.84	18.2

For a quick guide to RET, see page 10.

Seattle Mariners

The axiom "the only constant is change" is especially appropriate for the workings of a major-league baseball team. Every club is constantly making changes to improve some aspect of its performance, whether it's the bean counters' bottom line or the team's on-field success, present or future. With personnel changes on the field and in the front office and philosophical changes at the managerial and organizational levels, the Seattle Mariners have undergone as many alterations as any team in the game since the conclusion of the 1999 season.

First, the Mariners hired Pat Gillick for the GM job in October 1999. Previous GM Woody Woodward was notorious for his lack of long-term vision and his tendency to make reactive moves. Most of his big trades were consummated during the season, frequently just before the trading deadline when the team was most vulnerable. While Gillick doesn't always get the best of a deal, he doesn't paint himself into corners. He prefers to identify the team's shortcomings and address them during the off-season, when there is more time and less urgency.

Maybe it was coincidence or maybe it was confidence in their new GM, but Mariners' ownership loosened the purse strings after Woodward's departure. Gillick was able to sign six free agents, filling vacancies in the bullpen (Kazuhiro Sasaki and Arthur Rhodes), rotation (Aaron Sele), and at first base (John Olerud) while adding outfield depth (Stan Javier and Mark McLemore). The signings meant the Mariners didn't have a pick until the fourth round of the June draft, but they mitigated the damage by selecting and reaching an agreement with first-round talent Sam Hays and later signing South Korean prodigy Shin-Soo Choo.

While the six new free agents represented a nearly 25% roster turnover from the previous season's 79–83 team, undoubtedly the biggest change was the absence of #24 in center field. Ken Griffey Jr. had been the brightest star in the Northwest since his arrival in 1989. However, as an impending free agent and a player with ten-and-five rights, he had privilege of dictating where he wanted to play the rest of his career. Despite his thorny negotiating position, Gillick was able to obtain decent value from the Reds for Griffey. Mike Cameron and Brett Tomko played significant roles on last year's playoff team, while 19-year-old minor leaguer Antonio Perez looks like he could develop into an All-Star shortstop.

Overall, the off-season acquisitions fit nicely with the existing team. The new players not only filled positions that needed shoring up, but, just as importantly, only Cameron and Tomko were under 30 years of age. In most organizations, being on the wrong side of 30 wouldn't be considered a positive, but the only thing that aggravates manager Lou Piniella more than inexperience is Major League Baseball's ban on smoking in the dugout.

Piniella's intolerance for youngsters has been the target of a fair amount of criticism within these pages over the years. For the most part, he has avoided doling out playing time to young position players; however, the attrition rate among pitchers has forced Piniella to use the Mariners' young arms rather than leaving them in the bullpen or in the minors. The results have been disastrous. When he wasn't destroying the confidence of his young pitchers, he was risking their futures by having them throw too many pitches on the occasions when they did pitch well. Prior to last year, Ken Cloude was the only pitcher the Mariners had developed who had managed to total 300 innings with the team since Piniella became manager in 1993.

In 2000, Freddy Garcia and John Halama tripled the membership in that group. It wasn't merely happenstance. Last year saw a fundamental change in the way Piniella operates. He recognized that handling pitchers is his Achilles' heel, and hedelegated much of the responsibility to his new pitching coach, Bryan Price.

Price was the ideal man for the job. He is comfortable working with youngsters, having spent ten years coaching at nearly every level in the Mariners' farm system before becoming the team's minor-league pitching coordinator in

---

Mariners Prospectus

2000 record: 91–71; Second place, AL West; AL wild card; Lost to Yankees in ALCS, 4-2

Pythagenport W/L: 93–69

Runs Scored: 907 (4th in AL)

Runs Allowed: 780 (2nd in AL)

Team EqA: .274 (1st in AL)

2000 Batters' Age: 31.4 (2nd oldest in AL)

2000 Pitchers' Age: 29.0 (5th oldest in AL)

Ballpark: Safeco Field; excellent pitchers' park; Park Factor of .922

2000: Capped the A-Rod era with a trip to the LCS.

2001: Some young pitching, but far too many lineup holes to catch the A's.

1998. His career was cut short due to shoulder problems that stemmed from carrying too heavy a workload at a young age. He is familiar with Craig Wright's revolutionary study on pitcher usage and injury in *The Diamond Appraised* and is a firm believer in using pitch counts to monitor and regulate a pitcher's workload. Of course, in years past, Price's expertise wouldn't have amounted to a hill of beans, as Piniella would have simply ignored virtually everything Price said. That's not the case anymore.

"For me, it's a great working environment," Price said in a *Baseball Prospectus* interview last July. "With the history of what has happened in the past here, or at least what has been chronicled, that wasn't always the case. I can only speak for myself, but the working relationship [with Piniella] has been fantastic."

The results were fantastic, too. The Mariners' team ERA, which ranked second-worst in the league in 1999 at 5.25, dropped to 4.49, second-best in the junior circuit. Some of that drop was attributable to the team's first full season in pitcher-friendly Safeco Field, but such improvement can't be credited to park effect alone. Only once in 2000 did a Mariners' starter throw more than 120 pitches in a game. Garcia alone topped that mark nine times in 1999. No other team in baseball came close to showing as much restraint, the Expos posting the next-lowest figure with five. In fact, PAP data shows that the Mariners went from annually being one of the most-abused rotations to having the lowest starter workload of any team in the major leagues last season.

The Mariners can expect even bigger payoffs in the near future. The team already has strict workload limits in place in the minor leagues (no pitcher is to begin an inning if he has thrown more than 90 pitches). Prospects Ryan Anderson and Joel Pineiro will likely join Garcia and Gil Meche as part of the under-25 crowd in Seattle at some juncture this season. Twelve months ago, those pitchers would have needed a cadre of psychologists and surgeons, but the Safeco Field mound is a much safer place than it used to be. Piniella's willingness to adapt was and will continue to be a critical factor in the success of the pitching staff.

The other major change in organizational philosophy came at the plate. Seattle had finished in the top three in home runs in the American League every year from 1994 through 1999. Last year, prompted by Griffey's exodus and a more spacious ballpark, the Mariners restructured their attack around on-base percentage. Imports Olerud, Cameron, McLemore, and Rickey Henderson all possess a keen eye at the plate, and Alex Rodriguez saw the light, dramatically boosting his walk total. The Mariners finished the season with five batters (Olerud, Rodriguez, McLemore, Cameron, and Edgar Martinez) in the top 25 in the league in bases on balls. They also became just the tenth team since 1950 to increase their walk rate by more than one a game over the previous season. It isn't as if they were a bunch of free swingers previously: of the ten teams, the Mariners are the only one to have drawn more than 600 walks in the first of the two seasons.

The net result was that Seattle's offense ranked fourth in the league in runs scored, despite the team playing half its games in the toughest hitters' ballpark in the circuit. Though the club finished 12th in batting average and seventh in home runs, its .274 Equivalent Average led the league.

While there will be more changes this year, the team's commitment to Lou Piniella through the 2003 season rules out the possibility of rebuilding what has become a very old ball club. He never would have returned as manager without assurances that the Mariners are planning to field a competitive team. Piniella has never been part of a rebuilding effort, and his personality would be as ill-suited to the task as Jim Leyland's was after the Marlins gutted their 1997 World Series winner.

Instead, Gillick will embark on a large-scale retooling mission. The Mariners have decided that they are now a "large market" team, so instead of shedding payroll to guarantee profitability, they will take the higher-risk/higher-reward route of spending money to make money. It's a good thing they've chosen that course, because if they plan on being competitive, up to six of the lineup slots from the team that faced the New York Yankees in the ALCS should be occupied by different faces this season. Ichiro Suzuki has been signed out of the Japanese Leagues to man one of the outfield corners, and Gillick is in hot pursuit of another corner outfielder and a power-hitting third baseman.

Of course, the biggest change from last season will be at shortstop. Alex Rodriguez has taken his All-World skills to Texas, becoming the richest baseball player in history. He joins Griffey and Randy Johnson as the third surefire Hall-of-Famer to leave the Emerald City in 30 months.

To their credit, the Mariners did everything possible to re-sign Rodriguez. They assembled a team that played deep into October and let it be known that Rodriguez was its undisputed leader. They honored his desire to stay in Seattle for the 2000 campaign without engaging in trade talks or contract negotiations, and they encouraged the press to show restraint in their questioning him about his leaving.

When the season ended, they signed Piniella to a new three-year deal and exercised the no-brainer club option on Martinez, a player whom Rodriguez greatly admires and respects. Before other clubs got deep into negotiations with Rodriguez's agent, Scott Boras, the Mariners proactively signed Suzuki to demonstrate their commitment to winning. They expressed a willingness to bring in the fences in Safeco's power alleys. And, of course, they said that their dollar offer would be in the same neighborhood as any other team's. Unfortunately, all those things didn't entice him to stay.

American League

Obviously, it isn't going to be easy to replace Rodriguez. Gillick's natural tendency is to check the list of available free agents, but he might as well keep his wallet in his pocket. A more workable solution would be to shift Carlos Guillen back to shortstop, the position he played while in the Astros' organization, and pick up a utility infielder on the cheap.

Last year, the Oakland Athletics took the final step in their ascent to the divisional throne. It appears that they will rule the AL West for a few years. The only way the Mariners can begin to keep pace is to continue to make changes, both in personnel and operating philosophy. They are charting a far better course than they did under the previous regime, but without Rodriguez in the fold, a September dogfight for the wild-card berth is about the best they can hope for.

HITTERS (BA: .270, OBP: .340, SLG: .440, EqA: .260)

David Bell   3B/2B   Bats R   Age 28

YEAR	TEAM	LGE	AB	H	DB	TP	HR	BB	SO	R	RBI	SB	CS	OUT	BA	OBP	SLG	EQA	EQR	DEFENSE			
1998	Clevelnd	AL	339	90	20	2	11	21	48	38	41	0	3	252	.265	.312	.434	.243	37	96-2B	5		
1998	Seattle	AL	80	27	8	0	0	5	7	11	8	0	0	53	.338	.376	.438	.275	10	14-2B	2		
1999	Seattle	AL	594	162	32	2	22	52	82	90	76	6	4	436	.273	.333	.444	.257	73	149-2B	-8		
2000	Seattle	AL	455	118	25	2	12	37	60	56	47	2	4	341	.259	.324	.402	.241	49	78-3B	2	39-2B	-2
2001	Seattle	AL	375	94	20	1	10	36	56	49	50	2	1	282	.251	.316	.389	.246	42				

The Mariners opted to suffer with David Bell's lack of production at the hot corner rather than import an unknown quantity. Now that Alex Rodriguez is gone, the team is going to have to compensate by getting more offense at other lineup spots; Bell simply can't shoulder his share of the load. Though limited by an inability to play shortstop, he isn't the worst guy to have on the bench. If Bell gets another 500 at-bats, Pat Gillick didn't do his job over the winter.

Willie Bloomquist   2B   Bats R   Age 23

YEAR	TEAM	LGE	AB	H	DB	TP	HR	BB	SO	R	RBI	SB	CS	OUT	BA	OBP	SLG	EQA	EQR	DEFENSE			
1999	Everett	Nwn	177	39	8	2	1	12	28	18	15	5	2	140	.220	.271	.305	.192	11	34-2B	-6		
2000	Lancastr	Cal	251	70	17	2	1	23	28	36	28	6	4	185	.279	.339	.375	.242	27	49-2B	-2	11-SS	-1
2000	Tacoma	PCL	192	42	4	1	1	4	29	14	20	3	0	150	.219	.235	.266	.151	7	50-2B	0		
2001	Seattle	AL	251	61	11	2	1	21	44	30	22	6	2	192	.243	.301	.315	.219	22				

Willie Bloomquist is a local kid who became the apple of Piniella's eye in spring training with his work ethic and feisty play. He does all the little things that coaches love but that don't have much bearing on the outcome of a game. Bloomquist is being fast-tracked, and it's possible that he could emerge with the keystone job this April, even though he's not ready to contribute offensively and may never be.

Jay Buhner   RF   Bats R   Age 36

YEAR	TEAM	LGE	AB	H	DB	TP	HR	BB	SO	R	RBI	SB	CS	OUT	BA	OBP	SLG	EQA	EQR	DEFENSE	
1998	Seattle	AL	244	61	8	1	16	37	63	34	46	0	0	183	.250	.351	.488	.276	37	65-RF	-4
1999	Seattle	AL	263	60	9	0	15	67	91	36	37	0	0	203	.228	.393	.433	.284	43	67-RF	-4
2000	Seattle	AL	363	96	17	0	29	56	89	49	82	0	2	269	.264	.369	.551	.295	64	85-RF	-4
2001	Seattle	AL	294	63	9	0	16	64	87	50	50	0	0	231	.214	.355	.408	.271	44		

He was back with a bang following bone-spur removal in both his shoulder and ankle, the latest in a long list of off-season surgeries. Lou Piniella was steadfast about resting him, and Jay Buhner responded with his best season since 1997. He's still a presence in the middle of the lineup. The game of baseball will be a little less rich when Bone finally hangs up his spikes.

Mike Cameron   CF   Bats R   Age 28

YEAR	TEAM	LGE	AB	H	DB	TP	HR	BB	SO	R	RBI	SB	CS	OUT	BA	OBP	SLG	EQA	EQR	DEFENSE	
1998	ChiSox	AL	396	87	16	5	9	36	90	52	44	22	10	319	.220	.294	.354	.221	36	116-CF	6
1999	Cincnnti	NL	542	133	32	8	20	71	137	84	59	28	11	420	.245	.339	.445	.263	75	146-CF	1
2000	Seattle	AL	542	151	28	4	21	73	121	96	77	26	8	399	.279	.374	.461	.282	84	148-CF	4
2001	Seattle	AL	485	113	23	5	16	70	123	86	64	25	10	382	.233	.330	.400	.259	65		

(Mike Cameron *continued*)

When Ken Griffey jilted the citizens of Seattle, their reaction could have run the gamut from a desire for revenge to a strong urge to make it with someone else. Mike Cameron's bubbly personality and better-than-Griffey play in center field made it easy for Mariners' fans to put away their guns and choose the latter. With the release of Rickey Henderson, the Mariners are searching for a leadoff hitter and could do much worse than Cameron. Using him, however, would require them to realize that a strikeout is basically the same as any other kind of out. That translation is way low: Wilton doesn't factor in Cameron's eager tutelage at the feet of Edgar Martinez.

Ryan Christianson — C — Bats R — Age 20

YEAR	TEAM	LGE	AB	H	DB	TP	HR	BB	SO	R	RBI	SB	CS	OUT	BA	OBP	SLG	EQA	EQR	DEFENSE	
1999	Everett	Nwn	106	22	3	0	5	8	35	10	9	1	0	84	.208	.270	.377	.214	9	11-C	-4
2000	Wisconsn	Mid	433	94	11	0	12	32	108	47	44	0	3	342	.217	.274	.326	.194	29	94-C	-4
2001	Seattle	AL	262	59	6	0	9	24	74	25	31	0	1	204	.225	.290	.351	.221	23		

Last year didn't shed much light on whether Ryan Christianson can buck the trend of high-school catchers who are drafted high and then fail. His performance was disappointing compared to 1999 but doesn't look so bad in isolation. He's never going to hit for average, but if he can belt home runs and maintain his walk rate, he'll help a team offensively. Given the Mariners' morass behind the plate, Christianson can't reach The Show fast enough, but mid-2003 is an optimistic ETA.

Jermaine Clark — 2B — Bats L — Age 24

YEAR	TEAM	LGE	AB	H	DB	TP	HR	BB	SO	R	RBI	SB	CS	OUT	BA	OBP	SLG	EQA	EQR	DEFENSE	
1998	Wisconsn	Mid	462	121	20	7	6	42	69	54	39	14	7	348	.262	.325	.374	.237	48	111-2B	-16
1999	Lancastr	Cal	491	116	21	3	4	38	83	65	36	12	6	381	.236	.292	.316	.205	36	117-2B	6
2000	New Havn	Eas	461	120	23	6	2	68	75	60	35	21	6	347	.260	.365	.349	.254	56	127-2B	-2
2001	Detroit	AL	431	113	20	3	4	59	74	77	49	16	6	324	.262	.351	.350	.252	51		

Jermaine Clark is the Ralph Nader of Seattle second basemen—he may well be the best choice, but nobody pays him much attention. In fact, just like the major political parties, the Mariners set up roadblocks to his candidacy. They said he wasn't good defensively. Clark took extra infield practice and has become solid with the glove. They said he wouldn't play hurt. He led New Haven in games played. They said he wasn't a gamer. He was named MVP of the Eastern League playoffs. They promoted Bloomquist ahead of him and now say he doesn't hit for enough power to be an everyday player. I expect that he'll bulk up and hit at least ten home runs this year. Sometimes organizations are willing to go the extra mile to screw a player out of a career. Hopefully the Tigers, who selected Clark in the Rule 5 draft, will treat him better.

Carlos Guillen — IF — Bats B — Age 25

YEAR	TEAM	LGE	AB	H	DB	TP	HR	BB	SO	R	RBI	SB	CS	OUT	BA	OBP	SLG	EQA	EQR	DEFENSE			
1998	New Orln	PCL	374	98	15	3	10	25	60	54	41	2	3	279	.262	.314	.398	.235	38	97-SS	-8		
1998	Tacoma	PCL	92	19	0	1	1	8	17	7	3	1	1	74	.207	.270	.261	.170	4	23-2B	0		
2000	Tacoma	PCL	87	23	2	1	2	10	17	15	9	3	1	65	.264	.345	.379	.250	10	13-3B	-1		
2000	Seattle	AL	288	77	15	2	8	25	48	44	42	1	4	215	.267	.330	.417	.246	32	68-3B	-8	17-SS	-2
2001	Seattle	AL	255	65	11	1	6	27	48	33	34	1	1	191	.255	.326	.376	.247	29				

Carlos Guillen primarily played third base last season because he can't stay out of harm's way. Often, a run of injuries isn't due to frailty, but just bad luck. Tony Fernandez was nicknamed "Glass" in the minor leagues but became one of the most durable middle infielders in the game. Closer to home, Jay Buhner repeatedly lost battles with inanimate objects during his first three seasons, then averaged 150 games the next three. Since Guillen can be an effective everyday player on either side of second base, he should be given every opportunity to break his body another time or two before being consigned to a utility role.

Rickey Henderson — LF — Bats R — Age 42

YEAR	TEAM	LGE	AB	H	DB	TP	HR	BB	SO	R	RBI	SB	CS	OUT	BA	OBP	SLG	EQA	EQR	DEFENSE	
1998	Oakland	AL	541	134	16	0	16	118	102	98	58	56	12	419	.248	.387	.366	.275	83	130-LF	15
1999	NY Mets	NL	441	135	20	1	14	75	77	81	40	29	13	319	.306	.409	.451	.293	74	97-LF	-4
2000	NY Mets	NL	97	21	0	0	0	24	19	16	3	5	2	78	.216	.381	.216	.231	10	22-LF	-3
2000	Seattle	AL	323	80	14	2	4	60	50	58	29	34	11	253	.248	.369	.341	.258	43	83-LF	1
2001	Seattle	AL	410	85	11	1	7	83	76	71	36	22	12	337	.207	.341	.290	.236	46		

American League

Having been released by the Mariners, Major League Baseball's version of the *Antique Road Show* could be stopping in a town near you. Rickey Henderson has his sights set on breaking the career records for walks and runs scored as well as reaching 3,000 hits. Any team that signs him and plays him regularly probably has an anemic offense, so the impending 2002 work stoppage casts a long shadow over Henderson's chances of scoring the 69 runs needed to overtake the Georgia Peach.

Raul Ibanez — OF/1B — Bats L — Age 29

YEAR	TEAM	LGE	AB	H	DB	TP	HR	BB	SO	R	RBI	SB	CS	OUT	BA	OBP	SLG	EQA	EQR	DEFENSE			
1998	Tacoma	PCL	192	38	6	1	5	19	48	20	20	1	1	155	.198	.270	.318	.193	13	42-LF	0		
1998	Seattle	AL	98	26	8	1	2	5	20	13	12	0	0	72	.265	.301	.429	.239	10	10-1B	0		
1999	Seattle	AL	208	55	5	0	10	15	29	22	27	5	1	154	.264	.314	.433	.249	24	38-RF	0	16-1B	0
2000	Seattle	AL	140	33	6	0	3	13	23	20	15	2	0	107	.236	.305	.343	.221	12	36-RF	2		
2001	KansasCy	AL	166	41	4	0	6	16	29	23	24	2	0	125	.247	.313	.380	.234	16				

Cattle mutilation. Crop circles. Spontaneous human combustion. Watching golf on television. Add Piniella's fascination with Ibanez to the list of unexplained mysteries. He's now eligible for arbitration and out of options. Hopefully you caught this phenomenon on film before it disappears forever.

Stan Javier — OF — Bats B — Age 37

YEAR	TEAM	LGE	AB	H	DB	TP	HR	BB	SO	R	RBI	SB	CS	OUT	BA	OBP	SLG	EQA	EQR	DEFENSE	
1998	San Fran	NL	427	127	13	5	5	63	59	65	51	20	5	305	.297	.389	.386	.273	60	106-RF	-3
1999	San Fran	NL	336	93	15	1	3	25	52	46	29	10	6	249	.277	.329	.354	.232	32	76-LF	-1
1999	Houston	NL	64	21	4	1	0	8	8	11	4	2	1	44	.328	.403	.422	.283	9	16-OF	0
2000	Seattle	AL	342	99	17	5	6	38	58	59	40	4	4	247	.289	.361	.421	.262	44	72-OF	-3
2001	Seattle	AL	319	78	11	3	3	40	56	43	33	5	4	245	.245	.329	.326	.234	32		

Stan Javier was a 22-year-old rookie with the Athletics when I had season tickets for the Green and Gold in 1986. Fifteen years later, he looks virtually the same. I sure don't. Despite reaching the majors at a young age, Javier has always been cast as a fourth outfielder; he's been a regular just four seasons in his long career. That's a fairly unique résumé. However, two of the skills that have served him well, speed and outfield defense, are disappearing. He'll be a real liability if he approaches the nearly 400 plate appearances he had last year.

Craig Kuzmic — UT — Bats B — Age 24

YEAR	TEAM	LGE	AB	H	DB	TP	HR	BB	SO	R	RBI	SB	CS	OUT	BA	OBP	SLG	EQA	EQR	DEFENSE			
1998	Everett	Nwn	187	39	10	1	5	21	62	21	24	1	1	149	.209	.296	.353	.217	16	25-3B	-3	14-LF	1
1999	Lancastr	Cal	108	18	3	0	3	14	45	12	9	1	0	90	.167	.265	.278	.181	6	13-C	-2		
1999	Wisconsn	Mid	332	65	10	1	8	43	92	33	37	3	2	269	.196	.290	.304	.201	24	42-3B	2	20-LF	-2
2000	Lancastr	Cal	520	120	20	4	14	44	129	70	61	1	3	403	.231	.297	.365	.219	45	78-1B	-2	25-2B	2
2001	Seattle	AL	424	91	16	1	10	46	125	43	44	1	1	334	.215	.291	.328	.216	36				

Yes, he invented the Veg-o-Matic and the Rhinestone and Stud Setter, but marketing legend Ron Popeil himself couldn't have devised a more useful baseball player than Craig Kuzmic. Kuzmic can legitimately handle every position on the field except shortstop and center field, he switch-hits, has good plate discipline, and can hit the ball out of the yard. He's still at least a year away, but Piniella has to be licking his chops at the prospect of further cultivating his dubious reputation as a master of in-game maneuvering.

Tom Lampkin — C — Bats L — Age 37

YEAR	TEAM	LGE	AB	H	DB	TP	HR	BB	SO	R	RBI	SB	CS	OUT	BA	OBP	SLG	EQA	EQR	DEFENSE	
1998	St Louis	NL	219	51	11	1	7	23	30	26	29	3	2	170	.233	.324	.388	.240	24	55-C	-2
1999	Seattle	AL	205	60	10	2	10	11	29	28	33	1	3	148	.293	.342	.507	.272	29	49-C	5
2000	Seattle	AL	103	27	5	1	8	8	15	15	23	0	0	76	.262	.334	.563	.285	17	24-C	0
2001	Seattle	AL	143	32	8	1	6	14	23	18	20	1	1	112	.224	.293	.420	.243	16		

Tom Lampkin injured his elbow last spring and played in severe pain for a few months. It didn't hurt him to swing a bat, but his usually accurate throwing was very erratic. He had Tommy John surgery in late June and optimistically proclaims that he'll be fit when pitchers and catchers report in February. It's just as likely that his career is over, which would be a shame, because after years of being an automatic out, he had become a bona fide threat at the plate.

Justin Leone — 3B/SS — Bats R — Age 24

YEAR	TEAM	LGE	AB	H	DB	TP	HR	BB	SO	R	RBI	SB	CS	OUT	BA	OBP	SLG	EQA	EQR	DEFENSE			
1999	Everett	Nwn	205	40	9	1	4	19	55	19	19	2	1	166	.195	.266	.307	.188	13	37-3B	1	15-SS	-4
2000	Wisconsn	Mid	393	88	23	1	14	56	118	56	42	4	1	306	.224	.328	.394	.245	46	69-3B	-5	17-SS	-2
2001	Seattle	AL	230	49	8	0	9	32	77	29	30	2	1	182	.213	.309	.365	.238	25				

Keep Justin Leone's name filed away in the back of your mind. Seattle's 13th-round pick in 1999 was a part-time player with the Timber Rattlers the first six weeks of the campaign when suddenly everything came together. He ended up finishing in the top ten in the Midwest League in both OBP and slugging average, though to be fair, he was older than most of the competition. A converted shortstop, Leone is solid in the field. Most of his errors came on throws, something the coaching staff feels is correctable.

Robert Machado — C — Bats R — Age 28

YEAR	TEAM	LGE	AB	H	DB	TP	HR	BB	SO	R	RBI	SB	CS	OUT	BA	OBP	SLG	EQA	EQR	DEFENSE	
1998	Calgary	PCL	235	53	11	0	4	16	33	23	21	1	1	183	.226	.280	.323	.198	16	61-C	6
1998	ChiSox	AL	111	24	4	0	4	7	20	14	16	0	0	87	.216	.263	.360	.202	8	33-C	0
1999	Charlott	Int	54	10	1	0	2	3	13	3	6	0	0	44	.185	.247	.315	.179	3	16-C	2
1999	Ottawa	Int	74	16	4	0	0	0	13	5	2	0	1	59	.216	.231	.270	.139	2	20-C	-1
2000	Tacoma	PCL	330	85	12	0	8	20	46	31	43	1	3	248	.258	.304	.367	.221	28	71-C	6
2001	Seattle	AL	270	63	7	0	8	19	46	24	30	0	1	208	.233	.284	.348	.216	23		

Robert Machado has been one of the best catch-and-throw guys in the minors for years. Though his front hip still tends to fly out, his hitting has improved enough that he could help a number of teams as a backup receiver. His biggest problem is that he feels he should be starting every day and lets it be known. Repeatedly. Why did you think a catcher with Machado's defensive skills is with his fourth organization in three years, while Josh Paul is hailed as a wunderkind?

Al Martin — OF — Bats L — Age 33

YEAR	TEAM	LGE	AB	H	DB	TP	HR	BB	SO	R	RBI	SB	CS	OUT	BA	OBP	SLG	EQA	EQR	DEFENSE	
1998	Pittsbrg	NL	444	106	14	2	13	31	85	58	47	19	3	341	.239	.295	.367	.227	42	101-LF	2
1999	Pittsbrg	NL	542	146	36	7	23	42	112	91	58	15	3	399	.269	.323	.489	.267	74	120-LF	-12
2000	San Dieg	NL	352	108	14	5	11	23	51	60	26	5	8	252	.307	.352	.469	.266	46	74-LF	-4
2000	Seattle	AL	135	33	3	4	4	6	28	19	9	4	1	103	.244	.287	.415	.233	14	33-LF	1
2001	Seattle	AL	453	111	18	4	14	39	89	57	60	7	5	347	.245	.305	.395	.242	50		

The Mariners made a travesty of their "Refuse to Abuse" campaign when they acquired Al Martin at the trading deadline. At the time of the deal, he was accused of hitting his backup wife, a charge to which he pled guilty last November. Martin not only arrived in Seattle with an arrest warrant but also a contract which will pay him $5 million in 2001. Because of that, he'll probably return to Safeco Field this season, giving me more opportunities to practice my heckling.

Edgar Martinez — DH — Bats R — Age 38

YEAR	TEAM	LGE	AB	H	DB	TP	HR	BB	SO	R	RBI	SB	CS	OUT	BA	OBP	SLG	EQA	EQR	DEFENSE
1998	Seattle	AL	555	185	38	2	34	105	86	88	105	1	1	371	.333	.442	.593	.337	122	
1999	Seattle	AL	495	169	29	1	27	92	90	83	84	7	2	328	.341	.450	.568	.336	107	
2000	Seattle	AL	553	187	26	0	41	90	87	98	144	3	0	366	.338	.435	.608	.338	121	
2001	Seattle	AL	489	137	21	0	26	96	87	99	103	2	1	353	.280	.398	.483	.307	92	

Talk about consistency—look at those EqAs! Edgar Martinez is constantly tinkering with his swing and evolving as a hitter, as evidenced by the fact that his ratio of doubles to home runs has reversed over the past five years. It's astonishing how someone who has been a truly great batsman for more than a decade can suddenly find the intangibles the media believes are required to be an "RBI man." Martinez will likely retire after this season, though he would still be a productive hitter when he is 40.

Mark McLemore — 2B/LF — Bats B — Age 36

YEAR	TEAM	LGE	AB	H	DB	TP	HR	BB	SO	R	RBI	SB	CS	OUT	BA	OBP	SLG	EQA	EQR	DEFENSE			
1998	Texas	AL	456	113	13	1	6	88	57	77	52	10	4	347	.248	.372	.320	.248	53	120-2B	2		
1999	Texas	AL	557	150	20	7	6	77	72	99	42	15	8	415	.269	.358	.363	.249	64	134-2B	6		
2000	Seattle	AL	480	122	25	1	3	76	71	71	45	32	17	374	.254	.357	.329	.243	54	123-2B	0	12-LF	0
2001	Seattle	AL	430	96	16	2	3	69	65	62	37	13	12	346	.223	.331	.291	.225	42				

In addition to walks, a major benefit of plate discipline is that it increases the likelihood that a batter will get a pitch he can handle and hit the ball hard. Mark McLemore's hitting has sunk to the point where that benefit is virtually non-existent. The base on balls is his only offensive skill. His club option automatically vested at 475 plate appearances, so he'll be back to provide everybody's favorite intangible, veteran leadership, but little else.

Mike Neill — OF/DH — Bats L — Age 31

YEAR	TEAM	LGE	AB	H	DB	TP	HR	BB	SO	R	RBI	SB	CS	OUT	BA	OBP	SLG	EQA	EQR	DEFENSE	
1998	Edmonton	PCL	369	88	15	2	6	50	97	51	32	4	3	284	.238	.331	.339	.230	36	89-OF	-6
1999	Vancouvr	PCL	368	91	18	2	6	44	101	44	43	6	3	280	.247	.330	.356	.235	37	74-OF	-4
2000	Tacoma	PCL	401	102	25	2	8	56	116	49	44	5	3	302	.254	.352	.387	.252	48	76-LF	-1
2001	Boston	AL	312	76	16	1	6	48	93	53	40	5	1	237	.244	.344	.359	.246	35		

He was only 30 miles to the south, but the Mariners turned over every stone from here to Hoboken looking for a left-handed bat for the stretch drive. They settled for Al Martin and sent Mike Neill to Sydney, even though he is Martin's equal in every legal way. Combine this latest oversight with the scouts' dislike for Neill's body and doubles power, and it becomes readily apparent that it's time for him to find a new line of work.

John Olerud — 1B — Bats L — Age 32

YEAR	TEAM	LGE	AB	H	DB	TP	HR	BB	SO	R	RBI	SB	CS	OUT	BA	OBP	SLG	EQA	EQR	DEFENSE	
1998	NY Mets	NL	574	204	37	4	24	95	68	96	95	2	2	372	.355	.450	.559	.334	120	151-1B	11
1999	NY Mets	NL	585	171	29	0	22	116	62	103	93	2	0	414	.292	.418	.455	.300	102	154-1B	14
2000	Seattle	AL	563	167	33	0	20	96	87	81	106	0	2	398	.297	.403	.462	.292	92	152-1B	17
2001	Seattle	AL	549	152	23	0	22	107	81	106	103	1	1	398	.277	.395	.439	.295	94		

John Olerud was the biggest name among the six free agents Gillick signed for the 2000 season, inking a three-year deal for the bargain price of $20 million. He wasn't much above average offensively at his position, but the Gold Glove was legitimate. His 133 assists were 42 more than the next best AL first baseman, and nobody is better at turning the 3–6–3 double play. For some reason, I think Olerud has another .325 EqA performance lurking somewhere beneath that placid exterior.

Joe Oliver — C — Bats R — Age 35

YEAR	TEAM	LGE	AB	H	DB	TP	HR	BB	SO	R	RBI	SB	CS	OUT	BA	OBP	SLG	EQA	EQR	DEFENSE	
1998	Detroit	AL	155	36	6	0	5	6	29	8	23	0	1	120	.232	.261	.368	.201	11	42-C	2
1998	Seattle	AL	85	20	3	0	2	10	13	12	10	1	0	65	.235	.316	.341	.226	8	24-C	-1
1999	Durham	Int	217	56	12	1	5	4	54	20	31	1	0	161	.258	.276	.392	.218	18	55-C	-8
1999	Pittsbrg	NL	135	27	5	0	2	8	31	9	13	2	0	108	.200	.245	.281	.168	6	39-C	-2
2000	Tacoma	PCL	62	12	2	0	0	3	13	2	7	0	0	50	.194	.239	.226	.129	1	16-C	-2
2000	Seattle	AL	200	55	12	1	11	12	35	32	35	2	1	146	.275	.316	.510	.266	27	55-C	-1
2001	NY Yanks	AL	263	58	8	0	9	19	56	28	34	1	0	205	.221	.273	.354	.212	21		

Lou Piniella's relationship with Joe Oliver dates back to the days when Lou didn't need a full-length mirror to see his shoes. The bug-eyed backstop was signed as a minor-league free agent before the season, purely as an insurance policy. The move paid off in spades when Lampkin went down, and Oliver had a career year at age 34. The Yankees signed Oliver to back up Jorge Posada.

Antonio Perez — SS/2B — Bats R — Age 19

YEAR	TEAM	LGE	AB	H	DB	TP	HR	BB	SO	R	RBI	SB	CS	OUT	BA	OBP	SLG	EQA	EQR	DEFENSE			
1999	Rockford	Mid	390	90	17	1	5	27	87	42	26	13	11	311	.231	.291	.318	.203	29	53-SS	-10	53-2B	-11
2000	Lancastr	Cal	396	85	23	3	12	36	103	53	37	8	6	317	.215	.287	.379	.220	36	92-SS	-2		
2001	Seattle	AL	300	73	15	1	8	26	87	39	36	8	5	232	.243	.304	.380	.238	32				

Gillick pulled a Houdini in lifting Antonio Perez from under Jim Bowden's nose while being bent over a barrel in the Griffey negotiations. Perez was voted the top prospect in the California League last year, leading the circuit with a .527 slugging average after missing 30 games with a broken hand. Perez has more tools than the *New Yankee Workshop*, and he supplements them with good patience at the plate. There are questions about his age, but even if it is off by a couple of years, the Mariners will need to clear a space in the middle infield in 2003.

Bo Robinson — 3B — Bats R — Age 25

YEAR	TEAM	LGE	AB	H	DB	TP	HR	BB	SO	R	RBI	SB	CS	OUT	BA	OBP	SLG	EQA	EQR	DEFENSE			
1998	Everett	Nwn	205	43	9	1	3	13	39	21	16	0	0	162	.210	.260	.307	.182	11	33-3B	-6	13-1B	-2
1999	Wisconsn	Mid	510	129	30	2	10	76	82	68	64	2	1	382	.253	.352	.378	.251	60	83-3B	-6	17-1B	2
2000	Lancastr	Cal	512	123	16	0	9	38	74	61	60	1	2	391	.240	.296	.324	.206	38	130-3B	-6		
2001	Seattle	AL	443	103	11	0	10	45	74	45	48	1	1	341	.233	.303	.325	.221	39				

Bo Robinson was last year what Justin Leone is this year: a 24-year-old third baseman fresh off an unexpectedly productive campaign in low-A ball. He was unable to build on it with Lancaster; his park-inflated performance didn't come close to matching his raw numbers with Wisconsin. It seems that before too long, not only will Bo know baseball, he'll know the blue-plate special at every greasy spoon in Tacoma, City of Destiny.

Alex Rodriguez — SS — Bats R — Age 25

YEAR	TEAM	LGE	AB	H	DB	TP	HR	BB	SO	R	RBI	SB	CS	OUT	BA	OBP	SLG	EQA	EQR	DEFENSE	
1998	Seattle	AL	685	218	34	5	45	44	108	121	124	38	12	479	.318	.367	.580	.304	122	157-SS	0
1999	Seattle	AL	499	144	22	0	44	51	99	107	107	20	7	362	.289	.360	.597	.303	92	127-SS	6
2000	Seattle	AL	551	183	34	2	44	94	110	134	131	17	5	373	.332	.436	.641	.343	129	146-SS	15
2001	Texas	AL	586	211	36	2	53	90	117	132	143	32	9	384	.360	.445	.700	.357	146		

Alex Rodriguez added the only weapon missing from his arsenal last year by doubling his career walk rate. He is the first player in the 25-year history of free agency to be established as one of the game's top few players and still have his peak seasons ahead of him at the time he entered the market. The move to The Ballpark in Arlington is going to bump Rodriguez's raw stats enough that he may finally get the MVP awards he's been denied so far.

Anthony Sanders — OF — Bats R — Age 27

YEAR	TEAM	LGE	AB	H	DB	TP	HR	BB	SO	R	RBI	SB	CS	OUT	BA	OBP	SLG	EQA	EQR	DEFENSE	
1998	Syracuse	Int	210	38	9	1	4	16	64	20	17	3	1	173	.181	.246	.290	.173	11	60-CF	7
1999	Syracuse	Int	495	108	19	4	14	36	110	55	45	11	7	395	.218	.274	.358	.208	39	117-CF	6
2000	Tacoma	PCL	428	115	16	2	16	23	114	55	59	6	5	318	.269	.313	.428	.243	46	95-RF	-5
2001	Seattle	AL	399	92	14	1	11	29	111	42	43	7	4	311	.231	.283	.353	.220	35		

Of the quartet of players that the organization sent to mine Olympic gold, Anthony Sanders is the only one with a fair chance of breaking camp on the major-league roster. He runs well, totes a solid glove out to any of the outfield positions, and has pretty good life in his bat. On the other hand, he tends to be streaky, a trait that won't serve him well playing twice a week.

Juan Silvestre — LF/RF — Bats R — Age 23

YEAR	TEAM	LGE	AB	H	DB	TP	HR	BB	SO	R	RBI	SB	CS	OUT	BA	OBP	SLG	EQA	EQR	DEFENSE	
1998	Wisconsn	Mid	407	89	15	3	12	15	105	33	40	3	1	319	.219	.252	.359	.197	28	70-LF	1
1999	Wisconsn	Mid	539	126	24	2	15	28	135	61	68	2	2	415	.234	.275	.369	.211	42	96-LF	-13
2000	Lancastr	Cal	503	119	11	1	20	36	131	67	79	3	2	386	.237	.292	.382	.223	45	109-LF	-8
2001	Seattle	AL	488	116	15	1	19	37	137	52	65	2	1	373	.238	.291	.389	.234	50		

Juan Silvestre made a lot of postseason All-Star teams after leading the minor leagues in RBI. The voters overlooked that he batted cleanup on one of the best teams in the minors and that his right-center-field stroke fit hand-in-glove with the prevailing breezes at The Hangar. His first-pitch fastball mentality will be severely tested now that he has graduated to Double-A. If he passes, he's a prospect.

Chris Snelling — CF — Bats L — Age 19

YEAR	TEAM	LGE	AB	H	DB	TP	HR	BB	SO	R	RBI	SB	CS	OUT	BA	OBP	SLG	EQA	EQR	DEFENSE	
1999	Everett	Nwn	262	58	8	2	6	19	27	25	26	3	3	207	.221	.280	.336	.202	19	69-CF	2
2000	Wisconsn	Mid	268	67	7	2	8	23	38	32	39	3	2	203	.250	.316	.381	.233	27	66-CF	-6
2001	Seattle	AL	220	55	5	2	5	19	47	25	27	2	2	167	.250	.310	.359	.233	22		

If there is a war to be fought between scouts and statheads, Chris Snelling will be a major battleground. He's no more physically imposing than Joey Ramone but has been one of the best players in both his professional leagues while also being one of the youngest. Though only 5' 10", he generates surprising power and, in spite of average-to-below speed, has the instincts to handle center field. Expect Snelling to keep baffling the hardcore tools goofs, though his power may be down a bit this year as he recovers from a broken bone and strained tendon in his hand.

American League

Ichiro Suzuki — OF — Bats L — Age 27

YEAR	TEAM	LGE	AB	H	DB	TP	HR	BB	SO	R	RBI	SB	CS	OUT	BA	OBP	SLG	EQA	EQR	DEFENSE
1998	ORX	JpP	507	162	33	2	11	31	39	71	61	8	4	349	.320	.366	.458	.275	69	
1999	ORX	JpP	418	129	23	2	18	36	48	73	58	10	6	295	.309	.372	.502	.287	65	
2000	ORX	JpP	396	137	17	1	11	39	39	60	58	18	7	266	.346	.410	.477	.298	65	
2001	Seattle	AL	455	142	21	2	14	40	47	78	79	12	6	319	.312	.368	.459	.287	70	

Ichiro Suzuki will be the first non-pitcher from the Japanese professional leagues to play in the majors. He begins the quest at the peak of his career, following seven consecutive Pacific League batting titles. Mariners' owner Hiroshi Yamauchi made sure that Suzuki would get to play for his team of choice by submitting a $13.1 million bid to the Blue Wave merely for the rights to negotiate with him. Johnny Damon is the player most frequently mentioned when describing Suzuki; it's a fair comparison.

Juan Thomas — DH/1B — Bats R — Age 29

YEAR	TEAM	LGE	AB	H	DB	TP	HR	BB	SO	R	RBI	SB	CS	OUT	BA	OBP	SLG	EQA	EQR	DEFENSE	
1999	New Havn	Eas	270	57	10	0	11	8	104	36	35	0	0	213	.211	.242	.370	.195	18	14-1B	-1
2000	New Havn	Eas	503	116	20	2	19	30	149	48	67	3	0	387	.231	.281	.392	.222	45	27-1B	-3
2001	Seattle	AL	291	63	8	0	13	16	103	25	34	1	0	228	.216	.257	.378	.215	25		

Released by the ChiSox in 1997, "Large Human" bounced around the independent-league boardwalk before signing with New Haven in 1999. Juan Thomas finished among the Eastern League's top five in home runs and slugging average last year but isn't really a prospect because of his age and aversion to all things leather. He is, however, a crowd favorite, launching tape-measure blasts and running the bases as recklessly as a 270-pound man can.

Ramon Vazquez — SS — Bats L — Age 24

YEAR	TEAM	LGE	AB	H	DB	TP	HR	BB	SO	R	RBI	SB	CS	OUT	BA	OBP	SLG	EQA	EQR	DEFENSE			
1998	Lancastr	Cal	471	102	18	2	2	59	68	52	48	6	5	374	.217	.305	.276	.198	33	118-SS	-12		
1999	New Havn	Eas	448	104	24	2	4	46	81	48	36	4	1	345	.232	.308	.321	.214	37	67-SS	-2	40-3B	-2
2000	New Havn	Eas	414	103	23	2	7	40	82	49	45	1	3	314	.249	.317	.365	.228	39	123-SS	0		
2001	Seattle	AL	424	100	22	2	6	49	85	53	46	3	2	326	.236	.315	.340	.232	42				

Meet the new Jose Flores. He has more sock and is better defensively than the old one but doesn't walk as much. Since the Mariners never gave Flores a second thought for a utility infield job, I doubt they will Ramon Vazquez. On a more optimistic note, if somehow his surname became a generic word, it would be worth 141 points in Scrabble were the second "z" to land on a Triple Word Score.

Chris Widger — C — Bats R — Age 30

YEAR	TEAM	LGE	AB	H	DB	TP	HR	BB	SO	R	RBI	SB	CS	OUT	BA	OBP	SLG	EQA	EQR	DEFENSE	
1998	Montreal	NL	421	99	17	1	16	28	80	37	53	6	1	323	.235	.283	.394	.224	39	117-C	1
1999	Montreal	NL	385	99	22	1	14	23	81	40	52	0	4	290	.257	.310	.429	.240	41	101-C	-8
2000	Montreal	NL	284	67	15	2	12	25	57	30	32	1	2	219	.236	.300	.430	.238	30	78-C	-4
2001	Seattle	AL	294	67	13	1	10	26	64	32	37	1	1	228	.228	.291	.381	.231	29		

Oliver's cranky back and Piniella's penchant for veteran receivers brought Chris Widger back to his original organization for the pennant push. He was purely a security blanket, getting only a dozen plate appearances in his eight-week stay. His role this season is just as muddied. Widger's ability to hit southpaws (.291/.351/.532 over the last three seasons) would make for a dandy half of a catching platoon, but Dan Wilson's continued presence on the roster puts the kibosh on that notion.

Dan Wilson — C — Bats R — Age 32

YEAR	TEAM	LGE	AB	H	DB	TP	HR	BB	SO	R	RBI	SB	CS	OUT	BA	OBP	SLG	EQA	EQR	DEFENSE	
1998	Seattle	AL	325	85	17	1	10	23	50	40	45	2	1	241	.262	.319	.412	.244	35	92-C	-2
1999	Seattle	AL	413	112	22	2	8	25	76	45	37	5	0	301	.271	.316	.392	.238	42	114-C	-5
2000	Seattle	AL	269	66	8	0	7	19	46	30	28	1	2	206	.245	.295	.353	.213	22	75-C	3
2001	Seattle	AL	260	63	8	0	7	18	49	26	30	1	0	197	.242	.291	.354	.224	23		

(Dan Wilson *continued*)

My wife insisted that if I couldn't say something nice about Dan Wilson, I shouldn't say anything. Fair enough. Wilson is a genuinely nice guy, an asset to the community who donates as much of his time as any athlete in Seattle. He also has regressed into one of the worst catchers in the league. Gillick would like to deal him but, in one of his first moves as Mariners' GM, extended Wilson's contract through 2002 and included a no-trade clause. The club no longer considers him a starter, so Wilson probably won't see as much playing time as that projection indicates.

PITCHERS (ERA: 4.50, H/9: 9.00, HR/9: 1.00, BB/9: 3.00, K/9: 6.00, KW: 1.00, PERA: 4.50)

Paul Abbott — Throws R — Age 33

YEAR	TEAM	LGE	IP	H	ER	HR	BB	K	ERA	W	L	H/9	HR/9	BB/9	K/9	KW	PERA
1998	Seattle	AL	24.3	23	10	2	9	20	3.70	2	1	8.51	0.74	3.33	7.40	1.11	4.11
1999	Seattle	AL	72.0	47	27	8	26	65	3.38	5	3	5.88	1.00	3.25	8.13	1.25	2.88
2000	Seattle	AL	176.0	153	79	22	67	95	4.04	10	10	7.82	1.13	3.43	4.86	0.71	4.12

Injuries to Jamie Moyer and Freddy Garcia gave him the chance to enter the rotation, an opportunity he seized with both hands, pitching as well as any of the team's other starters. The main concern I have about Paul Abbott is the alarming drop in his strikeout rate, a result of him leaving his change-up at training camp. He needs to find it again because he's a fastball/change-up pitcher trying to survive by spotting a heater that barely grazes 90 mph. The Mariners' surplus of starters means that Abbott is a prime candidate to return to the bullpen.

Ryan Anderson — Throws L — Age 21

YEAR	TEAM	LGE	IP	H	ER	HR	BB	K	ERA	W	L	H/9	HR/9	BB/9	K/9	KW	PERA
1998	Wisconsn	Mid	97.7	98	63	10	84	77	5.81	4	7	9.03	0.92	7.74	7.10	0.46	6.41
1999	New Havn	Eas	122.7	139	91	14	93	103	6.68	4	10	10.20	1.03	6.82	7.56	0.55	6.82
2000	Tacoma	PCL	97.3	86	59	12	58	106	5.46	4	7	7.95	1.11	5.36	9.80	0.91	4.97

Ryan Anderson is the best prospect in baseball. He throws in the high 90s and has been handled carefully. Anderson led all minor-league starters in strikeouts per inning while showing improved control and dominated Pacific Coast League hitters at age 20. The Mariners feel that he is still more a thrower than a pitcher and have the luxury of letting him begin the season at Tacoma. However, as soon as a starter struggles or gets hurt, they'll be stuffing his seven-foot frame into a big-league uniform. I'll be very surprised if that doesn't happen before the All-Star break.

Cha Sueng Baek — Throws R — Age 21

YEAR	TEAM	LGE	IP	H	ER	HR	BB	K	ERA	W	L	H/9	HR/9	BB/9	K/9	KW	PERA
2000	Wisconsn	Mid	114.3	152	97	33	41	53	7.64	3	10	11.97	2.60	3.23	4.17	0.65	8.04

Chu Seung Back was the first player signed out of Korea by Seattle's former Director of Pacific Rim Scouting, Jim Colburn. Baek since has been followed by his prep teammate Shin-Soo Choo, giving the Mariners a solid foothold in that corner of the world. Baek battled elbow tenderness and inconsistency last season but throws in the low 90s and has a well-stocked inventory of pitches. He is part of a nice collection of arms in the organization's low minors, a few of whom should emerge as major-league-caliber hurlers.

Ken Cloude — Throws R — Age 26

YEAR	TEAM	LGE	IP	H	ER	HR	BB	K	ERA	W	L	H/9	HR/9	BB/9	K/9	KW	PERA
1998	Seattle	AL	154.0	176	102	26	69	105	5.96	5	12	10.29	1.52	4.03	6.14	0.76	6.24
1999	Tacoma	PCL	35.7	18	13	4	17	22	3.28	2	2	4.54	1.01	4.29	5.55	0.65	2.57
1999	Seattle	AL	73.0	99	57	8	37	33	7.03	2	6	12.21	0.99	4.56	4.07	0.45	7.03
2000	Tacoma	PCL	69.7	86	62	16	41	42	8.01	2	6	11.11	2.07	5.30	5.43	0.51	7.82

Ken Cloude wasn't right all spring after injuring his elbow in winter ball in Puerto Rico. In June, he finally admitted that he had been pitching through pain and underwent Tommy John surgery. The Mariners have signed him to a minor-league contract, but it will be 2002 before we see if he can resurrect his once-promising career. Cloude's elbow may return stronger than before, but the psychological trauma that he suffered at the hands of Piniella over the years won't heal until he leaves the organization.

Jeff Farnsworth — Throws R — Age 25

YEAR	TEAM	LGE	IP	H	ER	HR	BB	K	ERA	W	L	H/9	HR/9	BB/9	K/9	KW	PERA
1999	Lancastr	Cal	68.0	84	58	11	48	22	7.68	2	6	11.12	1.46	6.35	2.91	0.23	7.62
2000	New Havn	Eas	93.3	93	48	12	30	42	4.63	4	6	8.97	1.16	2.89	4.05	0.70	4.61

The Mariners' second-round draft choice in 1996 is about two years ahead of Cloude in making friends with his new ulnar collateral ligament. Jeff Farnsworth saw his low-90s heat and command of his curveball resurface at New Haven and built on that progress with an outstanding stint in the Arizona Fall League, posting the best strikeout rate in the desert. He could earn a spot as a long reliever in 2002, as he's the type of hard thrower Piniella likes to have tucked away in the bullpen.

Ryan Franklin — Throws R — Age 28

YEAR	TEAM	LGE	IP	H	ER	HR	BB	K	ERA	W	L	H/9	HR/9	BB/9	K/9	KW	PERA
1998	Tacoma	PCL	119.0	143	83	26	39	58	6.28	4	9	10.82	1.97	2.95	4.39	0.74	6.57
1999	Tacoma	PCL	127.0	134	87	23	40	59	6.17	4	10	9.50	1.63	2.83	4.18	0.74	5.38
2000	Tacoma	PCL	150.7	153	110	44	40	96	6.57	5	12	9.14	2.63	2.39	5.73	1.20	6.05

Don't hold it against Ryan Franklin that Tommy Lasorda gushed over him at the Olympics. He could help almost any team in baseball if given half a chance. Franklin has a rubber arm, surprising giddyap on his fastball, and throws as many as six pitches for strikes. His All-Star season at Tacoma and stellar work in Sydney prompted the Mariners to add him to the 40-man roster, but it's likely that he'll join former Rainier teammate Mel Bunch in the Land of the Rising Sun.

Brian Fuentes — Throws L — Age 25

YEAR	TEAM	LGE	IP	H	ER	HR	BB	K	ERA	W	L	H/9	HR/9	BB/9	K/9	KW	PERA
1998	Lancastr	Cal	109.3	126	79	14	89	70	6.50	3	9	10.37	1.15	7.33	5.76	0.39	7.27
1999	New Havn	Eas	54.3	56	44	8	51	41	7.29	1	5	9.28	1.33	8.45	6.79	0.40	7.27
2000	New Havn	Eas	126.3	133	100	14	85	92	7.12	3	11	9.47	1.00	6.06	6.55	0.54	6.05

It doesn't take a degree in Nadi Astrology to forecast Brian Fuentes's ultimate destination. He isn't conservative enough with his pitches to be a starter, and his unorthodox delivery makes him especially tough on left-handed batters (.216/.289/.328), so he's fated to become a lefty specialist. Until Fuentes slices his walk rate, however, Kullaya Swamy sees the color red in his future: Trailways red.

Freddy Garcia — Throws R — Age 24

YEAR	TEAM	LGE	IP	H	ER	HR	BB	K	ERA	W	L	H/9	HR/9	BB/9	K/9	KW	PERA
1998	Jackson	Tex	110.3	93	54	12	67	76	4.40	5	7	7.59	0.98	5.47	6.20	0.57	4.66
1999	Seattle	AL	200.3	192	82	15	72	162	3.68	12	10	8.63	0.67	3.23	7.28	1.13	4.04
2000	Seattle	AL	122.7	105	55	15	54	75	4.04	7	7	7.70	1.10	3.96	5.50	0.69	4.25

Freddy Garcia enjoyed the Venezuelan equivalent of the rubber-chicken circuit a bit too much, reporting to camp overweight and out of shape. He pitched poorly before suffering a hairline fracture of his tibia in his third start, which shelved him until early July. One side benefit of the two-month layoff is that his arm had a chance to further recover from the abuses of 1999. Garcia is a very good starter who could rise to the next level if he stops nibbling around the plates and trusts his overpowering stuff.

John Halama — Throws L — Age 29

YEAR	TEAM	LGE	IP	H	ER	HR	BB	K	ERA	W	L	H/9	HR/9	BB/9	K/9	KW	PERA
1998	New Orln	PCL	113.7	113	52	16	20	55	4.12	6	7	8.95	1.27	1.58	4.35	1.38	4.16
1998	Houston	NL	30.7	36	22	1	12	17	6.46	1	2	10.57	0.29	3.52	4.99	0.71	4.87
1999	Seattle	AL	176.7	178	75	17	45	100	3.82	10	10	9.07	0.87	2.29	5.09	1.11	4.11
2000	Seattle	AL	164.7	190	95	18	47	83	5.19	7	11	10.38	0.98	2.57	4.54	0.88	5.12

A slight loss of command down in the zone can spell doom for a soft tosser, which is what happened to John Halama last season. His pitches found too much of the plate, the league pummeling his feeble assortment at a .308/.361/.473 clip. By August, Piniella had lost all confidence in him and would trot out the hook at the first sniff of trouble. Halama is prime trade bait and will be overvalued by many clubs since good run support helped him to a misleading 14–9 record.

Jeff Heaverlo — Throws R — Age 23

YEAR	TEAM	LGE	IP	H	ER	HR	BB	K	ERA	W	L	H/9	HR/9	BB/9	K/9	KW	PERA
1999	Wisconsn	Mid	16.0	17	8	2	8	13	4.50	1	1	9.56	1.13	4.50	7.31	0.81	5.58
2000	Lancastr	Cal	144.0	181	93	31	50	83	5.81	5	11	11.31	1.94	3.13	5.19	0.83	6.91

The stat line doesn't show how impressive his year was. Heading into the season, Jeff Heaverlo was a slider/fastball pitcher who threw his vicious nickel curve up to 70% of the time. The Mariners asked him to reverse the ratio and add a change-up. Despite reinventing himself and working in one of the best hitters' parks in the minors, he still managed above-average raw numbers in the California League. His ceiling isn't high, but among pitchers in the Mariners' farm system, only Anderson is a better bet to draw a full MLB pension.

Kevin Hodges — Throws R — Age 28

YEAR	TEAM	LGE	IP	H	ER	HR	BB	K	ERA	W	L	H/9	HR/9	BB/9	K/9	KW	PERA
1998	Jackson	Tex	99.0	104	61	13	48	42	5.55	4	7	9.45	1.18	4.36	3.82	0.44	5.53
1999	Jackson	Tex	45.3	44	23	2	21	12	4.57	2	3	8.74	0.40	4.17	2.38	0.29	4.18
1999	New Orln	PCL	25.0	32	26	9	14	10	9.36	0	3	11.52	3.24	5.04	3.60	0.36	9.19
1999	Tacoma	PCL	78.7	78	29	4	33	26	3.32	5	4	8.92	0.46	3.78	2.97	0.39	4.21
2000	Tacoma	PCL	92.3	82	32	5	24	49	3.12	6	4	7.99	0.49	2.34	4.78	1.02	3.17
2000	Seattle	AL	17.3	17	9	4	10	7	4.67	1	1	8.83	2.08	5.19	3.63	0.35	6.48

It was a banner year for the Hodges family. Kevin got his first cuppajoe after nearly ten years in the minors while baby brother Trey was MVP of the College World Series. Hodges flourished under the tutelage of Tacoma pitching coach Jim Slaton, who has a knack for turning anybody with a good work ethic and an open mind into a useful pitcher. No more Joe Table means that Hodges could earn the final seat in the Seattle bullpen, which is the upper limit of his ability.

Justin Kaye — Throws R — Age 25

YEAR	TEAM	LGE	IP	H	ER	HR	BB	K	ERA	W	L	H/9	HR/9	BB/9	K/9	KW	PERA
1998	Wisconsn	Mid	40.3	32	18	5	38	39	4.02	2	2	7.14	1.12	8.48	8.70	0.51	5.76
1998	Lancastr	Cal	28.0	39	27	7	14	17	8.68	1	2	12.54	2.25	4.50	5.46	0.61	8.54
1999	Lancastr	Cal	56.7	67	43	6	45	33	6.83	2	4	10.64	0.95	7.15	5.24	0.37	7.14
2000	New Havn	Eas	76.3	86	40	6	43	66	4.72	3	5	10.14	0.71	5.07	7.78	0.77	5.72

Justin Kaye never really felt comfortable with the delivery the Mariners had him use to reduce the risk of arm troubles, so last year they let him return to his twisting, numbers-to-the-batter windup. Chalk one up in the "if it ain't broke, don't fix it" column. In his first season in Double-A, Kaye's walks dipped by more than two a game while his strikeouts increased—a trend that continued in the Arizona Fall League. Follow-up success at Tacoma should get his foot in the door for a September audition at Safeco Field.

Josue Matos — Throws R — Age 23

YEAR	TEAM	LGE	IP	H	ER	HR	BB	K	ERA	W	L	H/9	HR/9	BB/9	K/9	KW	PERA
1999	Wisconsn	Mid	124.3	159	105	41	48	72	7.60	3	11	11.51	2.97	3.47	5.21	0.75	8.27
2000	Lancastr	Cal	82.0	84	34	14	21	49	3.73	5	4	9.22	1.54	2.30	5.38	1.17	4.90
2000	New Havn	Eas	77.0	82	48	21	26	39	5.61	3	6	9.58	2.45	3.04	4.56	0.75	6.41

Taken in the 27th round of the 1996 draft, Josue Matos has had to prove himself at every level. Thus far, he's done way more than that. His fastball doesn't break the high 80s, but he compensates by mixing four pitches, the best of which is a change-up. This year is the acid test for him to earn the "legitimate prospect" label; even if he passes, it's tough to see him crashing the Mariners' rotation anytime soon.

Gil Meche — Throws R — Age 22

YEAR	TEAM	LGE	IP	H	ER	HR	BB	K	ERA	W	L	H/9	HR/9	BB/9	K/9	KW	PERA
1998	Wisconsn	Mid	132.3	150	103	23	79	85	7.01	4	11	10.20	1.56	5.37	5.78	0.54	6.79
1999	New Havn	Eas	54.7	52	28	5	28	35	4.61	3	3	8.56	0.82	4.61	5.76	0.63	4.72
1999	Tacoma	PCL	29.3	29	13	4	15	16	3.99	2	1	8.90	1.23	4.60	4.91	0.53	5.37
1999	Seattle	AL	85.3	69	41	8	46	45	4.32	4	5	7.28	0.84	4.85	4.75	0.49	4.09
2000	Seattle	AL	84.7	70	33	7	34	57	3.51	5	4	7.44	0.74	3.61	6.06	0.84	3.61

Gil Meche lost 10 mph off his mid-90s fastball last year, sometimes from one inning to the next. Despite being examined at by more doctors than a stripper at an AMA convention, his ailment garnered no more technical description than "a dead arm." That's certainly distressing, but his performance while working at such a disadvantage suggests how dominant he could be when healthy. With no substantive diagnosis, the Mariners enter this season unsure what to expect but certain that Meche's return is crucial to their success.

Jose Mesa — Throws R — Age 35

YEAR	TEAM	LGE	IP	H	ER	HR	BB	K	ERA	W	L	H/9	HR/9	BB/9	K/9	KW	PERA
1998	Clevelnd	AL	53.3	57	31	6	17	32	5.23	2	4	9.62	1.01	2.87	5.40	0.94	4.83
1998	San Fran	NL	29.3	29	14	1	17	23	4.30	1	2	8.90	0.31	5.22	7.06	0.68	4.59
1999	Seattle	AL	69.0	79	36	9	32	40	4.70	3	5	10.30	1.17	4.17	5.22	0.63	5.95
2000	Seattle	AL	80.7	84	42	10	34	80	4.69	4	5	9.37	1.12	3.79	8.93	1.18	5.17

The breeze felt around the Puget Sound region in early November was a collective sigh of relief from Mariner fans when the team bought out the final year of Jose Mesa's contract. Not only is he painful to watch on a performance level, but he is an agonizingly slow worker. The combination tests the limits of human suffering, kind of like self-amputation with an emery board. Mesa signed a two-year deal with the Phillies and goes into camp as the closer.

Jamie Moyer — Throws L — Age 38

YEAR	TEAM	LGE	IP	H	ER	HR	BB	K	ERA	W	L	H/9	HR/9	BB/9	K/9	KW	PERA
1998	Seattle	AL	228.3	217	87	21	36	146	3.43	14	11	8.55	0.83	1.42	5.75	2.03	3.44
1999	Seattle	AL	223.3	216	92	19	39	130	3.71	13	12	8.70	0.77	1.57	5.24	1.67	3.52
2000	Seattle	AL	151.7	160	91	21	44	93	5.40	6	11	9.49	1.25	2.61	5.52	1.06	4.88

The end is near. Jamie Moyer's ERA was 7.41 over the last two months of the season, when his arm angle dropped and he couldn't get a good downward plane on his pitches. Though an injury was suspected, he never admitted to it. There is a school of thought that says pitchers who don't throw hard can pitch forever, but if that were true, Randy Jones would have been on the mound when the Padres shed their mustard uniforms. Piniella is intensely loyal to his veterans, so Moyer will be given every opportunity to find his old form.

Jose Paniagua — Throws L — Age 27

YEAR	TEAM	LGE	IP	H	ER	HR	BB	K	ERA	W	L	H/9	HR/9	BB/9	K/9	KW	PERA
1998	Tacoma	PCL	64.3	62	26	3	26	41	3.64	4	3	8.67	0.42	3.64	5.74	0.79	3.97
1998	Seattle	AL	21.3	14	4	3	4	15	1.69	2	0	5.91	1.27	1.69	6.33	1.88	2.56
1999	Seattle	AL	78.0	71	31	4	42	70	3.58	5	4	8.19	0.46	4.85	8.08	0.83	4.22
2000	Seattle	AL	79.3	64	28	6	32	68	3.18	6	3	7.26	0.68	3.63	7.71	1.06	3.45

Jose Paniagua always had electric stuff but struggled with the base on balls. Roberto Hernandez exorcised that demon, instructing Paniagua to spread his fingers further apart on his fastball for better command. He'll be the team's primary setup man this year, working in tough late-inning situations and occasionally making a fashion statement by sporting red fingernail polish when he pitches. Piniella tends to ride the hot hand, so he needs to be mindful not to overuse Paniagua.

Brandon Parker — Throws R — Age 25

YEAR	TEAM	LGE	IP	H	ER	HR	BB	K	ERA	W	L	H/9	HR/9	BB/9	K/9	KW	PERA
1998	Wisconsn	Mid	110.7	133	108	21	101	75	8.78	2	10	10.82	1.71	8.21	6.10	0.37	8.48
1999	Lancastr	Cal	130.3	163	99	19	75	74	6.84	4	10	11.26	1.31	5.18	5.11	0.49	7.07
2000	Lancastr	Cal	48.0	56	31	6	30	35	5.81	2	3	10.50	1.13	5.63	6.56	0.58	6.61

The move to the bullpen was inevitable because Brandon Parker never has been able to assemble a working off-speed pitch. He returned to Lancaster to serve his apprenticeship and turned the neat trick of being the first Cal League player to appear in two All-Star games. There are a number of hurlers above him on the Mariners' depth chart with similar stuff who find the strike zone more often.

Joel Pineiro   Throws R   Age 22

YEAR	TEAM	LGE	IP	H	ER	HR	BB	K	ERA	W	L	H/9	HR/9	BB/9	K/9	KW	PERA
1998	Wisconsn	Mid	86.0	101	55	21	35	43	5.76	3	7	10.57	2.20	3.66	4.50	0.61	6.98
1998	Lancastr	Cal	41.7	60	43	10	23	25	9.29	1	4	12.96	2.16	4.97	5.40	0.54	8.86
1999	New Havn	Eas	154.0	191	119	29	56	73	6.95	4	13	11.16	1.69	3.27	4.27	0.65	6.62
2000	New Havn	Eas	48.0	46	34	11	13	28	6.38	1	4	8.63	2.06	2.44	5.25	1.08	5.18
2000	Tacoma	PCL	57.7	50	19	4	23	30	2.97	4	2	7.80	0.62	3.59	4.68	0.65	3.67

Joel Pineiro worked on his leg strength over the off-season and was rewarded with an additional 2–3 mph on his fastball. Combined with a full complement of off-speed pitches, the improved heater helped him have a breakthrough campaign. Don't let the baby face fool you—what the Mariners like most about him is that he has the heart of a thief, willing to throw any pitch at any time in the count. Piniella has ruined many similar pitchers, so here's hoping that Pineiro is given more experience in Triple-A and long relief before being thrown to the wolves.

Rob Ramsay   Throws L   Age 27

YEAR	TEAM	LGE	IP	H	ER	HR	BB	K	ERA	W	L	H/9	HR/9	BB/9	K/9	KW	PERA
1998	Trenton	Eas	147.7	145	88	17	61	93	5.36	6	10	8.84	1.04	3.72	5.67	0.76	4.74
1999	Pawtuckt	Int	108.0	112	83	24	37	54	6.92	3	9	9.33	2.00	3.08	4.50	0.73	5.79
1999	Tacoma	PCL	30.7	20	8	3	17	23	2.35	2	1	5.87	0.88	4.99	6.75	0.68	3.42
2000	Seattle	AL	50.3	41	20	3	34	31	3.58	3	3	7.33	0.54	6.08	5.54	0.46	4.33

There is no better illustration of the kinder, gentler Piniella than Rob Ramsay tacking on nearly a full year of major-league service with that walk rate. In previous years, Tony Fossas would have been hauled in to lob grapefruits before the rhododendrons bloomed. All the same, the Mariners know that Ramsay is better suited to starting and plan on returning him to Tacoma to do just that. Ramsay is no pup; he needs to move to an organization more desperate for pitching if he is going to have a career.

Arthur Rhodes   Throws L   Age 31

YEAR	TEAM	LGE	IP	H	ER	HR	BB	K	ERA	W	L	H/9	HR/9	BB/9	K/9	KW	PERA
1998	Baltimor	AL	75.7	62	27	7	30	77	3.21	5	3	7.37	0.83	3.57	9.16	1.28	3.63
1999	Baltimor	AL	53.7	42	32	8	37	56	5.37	2	4	7.04	1.34	6.20	9.39	0.76	5.05
2000	Seattle	AL	68.3	48	30	6	24	73	3.95	4	4	6.32	0.79	3.16	9.61	1.52	2.88

Setting aside the meatball that he served to David Justice in Game 6 of the ALCS, Arthur Rhodes had a pretty good year. However, the effects of a career-high 72 appearances showed, as his ERA was 2.68 before the All-Star break and 6.52 afterwards. Gillick would be wise to go get a true situational left-hander and return Rhodes to the high-leverage, multiple-inning role in which Davey Johnson so splendidly employed him. When Arthur Lee is humming, it doesn't matter on which side of the plate the batter is standing.

Kazuhiro Sasaki   Throws R   Age 33

YEAR	TEAM	LGE	IP	H	ER	HR	BB	K	ERA	W	L	H/9	HR/9	BB/9	K/9	KW	PERA
2000	Seattle	AL	62.3	40	22	9	26	75	3.18	4	3	5.78	1.30	3.75	10.83	1.44	3.29

Closers are overvalued as a species, but "Daimajin" earns bonus points for putting an end to an era of late-inning futility in the Northwest. Everybody knows about his devastating forkball, but the key to his success is effectively spotting the fastball so that he can deploy the forkball. For that reason, I think Sasaki will improve on last year's numbers. He had bone chips removed from his elbow in August of 1999, and it generally takes at least a year to regain full velocity and command following that type of surgery.

Aaron Sele   Throws R   Age 31

YEAR	TEAM	LGE	IP	H	ER	HR	BB	K	ERA	W	L	H/9	HR/9	BB/9	K/9	KW	PERA
1998	Texas	AL	211.3	224	99	11	68	154	4.22	11	12	9.54	0.47	2.90	6.56	1.13	4.22
1999	Texas	AL	205.3	227	96	16	53	177	4.21	11	12	9.95	0.70	2.32	7.76	1.67	4.46
2000	Seattle	AL	208.3	205	97	16	62	131	4.19	11	12	8.86	0.69	2.68	5.66	1.06	3.97

Pat Gillick swooped in and signed Aaron Sele to a two-year deal after noted Baltimore orthopedic surgeon, Dr. Peter Angelos, pronounced him unfit to pitch for the Orioles. Sele responded with his usual above-average innings munching. He also brought his lucky rabbit's foot, receiving the sixth-best run support in the AL after finishing third in that category in 1999 and fourth in 1998. Sele's run of won/loss karma is due to expire unless he is the embodiment of an urban legend: the pitcher who pitches just well enough to win.

Rafael Soriano — Throws R — Age 21

YEAR	TEAM	LGE	IP	H	ER	HR	BB	K	ERA	W	L	H/9	HR/9	BB/9	K/9	KW	PERA
1999	Everett	Nwn	69.3	62	40	14	52	42	5.19	3	5	8.05	1.82	6.75	5.45	0.40	6.37
2000	Wisconsn	Mid	112.0	100	46	8	57	48	3.70	6	6	8.04	0.64	4.58	3.86	0.42	4.21

Rafael Soriano is a converted outfielder so, by definition, his fastball approaches the mid-90s. However, unlike many transformed position players, his heater has plus movement, and he also flashes a respectable slider. In a statement of his potential, the Mariners put him on the 40-man roster even though he has toed the rubber for only two years and has yet to pitch above low-A ball.

Brett Tomko — Throws R — Age 28

YEAR	TEAM	LGE	IP	H	ER	HR	BB	K	ERA	W	L	H/9	HR/9	BB/9	K/9	KW	PERA
1998	Cincnnti	NL	202.0	193	108	22	57	131	4.81	9	13	8.60	0.98	2.54	5.84	1.15	4.06
1999	Cincnnti	NL	168.0	167	92	27	49	111	4.93	8	11	8.95	1.45	2.63	5.95	1.13	4.79
2000	Seattle	AL	91.0	86	47	11	34	56	4.65	4	6	8.51	1.09	3.36	5.54	0.82	4.46

Brett Tomko spent more time in the doghouse in Cincinnati than Schottzie, then earned a spot in Piniella's kennel when he refused to throw at a batter in a spring-training game. As a result of Piniella's pettiness, Tomko opened the season at Tacoma. When Mariner starters began falling like duckpins, he was recalled and proved invaluable as a spot starter and long reliever. Tomko would be a significant upgrade to the rotation, but unless Halama is traded, he'll probably be back in the bullpen.

Enmanuel Ulloa — Throws R — Age 22

YEAR	TEAM	LGE	IP	H	ER	HR	BB	K	ERA	W	L	H/9	HR/9	BB/9	K/9	KW	PERA
1999	Wisconsn	Mid	79.3	99	63	19	41	52	7.15	2	7	11.23	2.16	4.65	5.90	0.63	7.72
2000	Lancastr	Cal	144.0	145	106	34	52	78	6.63	4	12	9.06	2.13	3.25	4.88	0.75	5.83

The Mariners' 21st-round pick in 1997 is another hurler in the team's low minors who has an equal chance of either fattening the club's stockpile of arms or spending the next decade making sure that Tom Bodett left the light on. Enmanuel Ulloa's velocity is just average, but his fastball jumps all over the place and he uses a tailing change-up to great effect against left-handed hitters. His upcoming season with new Double-A affiliate San Antonio will go a long way towards determining whether he needs to learn the finer points of integrated pest management.

Greg Wooten — Throws R — Age 27

YEAR	TEAM	LGE	IP	H	ER	HR	BB	K	ERA	W	L	H/9	HR/9	BB/9	K/9	KW	PERA
1998	Lancastr	Cal	28.7	43	30	10	15	10	9.42	0	3	13.50	3.14	4.71	3.14	0.33	10.14
1999	Lancastr	Cal	107.0	119	67	22	35	34	5.64	4	8	10.01	1.85	2.94	2.86	0.49	5.98
2000	New Havn	Eas	167.0	169	59	19	19	68	3.18	12	7	9.11	1.02	1.02	3.66	1.79	3.79

Greg Wooten had as good a campaign as any pitcher in the minors last year, re-establishing himself as a prospect following Tommy John surgery in August of 1998. After barely making the Ravens' staff, he proceeded to pull a Bret Saberhagen, recording more wins (17) than walks (15). It's almost impossible to work 179 innings in this system given the organization's pitch limits, but Wooten is very economical and uses a power sinker to generate lots of ground balls. The Mariners still aren't all that high on him because of his age, but the way he plowed down Eastern League hitters can't be ignored.

Support-Neutral Statistics				SEATTLE MARINERS						Park Effect: -15.6%		
PITCHER	GS	IP	R	SNW	SNL	SNPCT	W	L	RA	APW	SNVA	SNWAR
Paul Abbott	27	162.7	77	10.0	8.4	.543	9	7	4.26	1.0	0.7	2.2
Freddy Garcia	20	121.3	62	7.0	6.8	.508	9	5	4.60	0.3	0.1	1.2
John Halama	30	166.7	108	7.7	12.0	.392	14	9	5.83	-1.8	-2.0	-0.6
Gil Meche	15	85.7	37	6.0	3.5	.632	4	4	3.89	0.9	1.1	2.0
Jamie Moyer	26	154.0	103	7.3	10.8	.404	13	10	6.02	-1.9	-1.7	-0.4
Joel Pineiro	1	6.0	2	0.6	0.1	.853	1	0	3.00	0.1	0.2	0.3
Rob Ramsay	1	6.0	1	0.5	0.1	.839	0	0	1.50	0.2	0.2	0.2
Aaron Sele	34	211.7	110	12.5	11.4	.523	17	10	4.68	0.4	0.5	2.3
Brett Tomko	8	42.7	26	2.2	2.6	.466	4	2	5.48	-0.3	-0.2	0.2
TOTALS	162	956.7	526	53.8	55.5	.492	71	47	4.95	-1.0	-1.0	7.3

This wasn't a great rotation for a playoff team, but that went largely unnoticed because of the pitcher-friendliness of Safeco Field and a surprisingly effective Seattle bullpen. The Mariners' starting-pitcher difficulties stemmed from a lack of star performances at the top of the rotation. If you rank baseball's aces—defined as the starter on the club with the most Support-Neutral Wins Above Replacement—the Mariners' Aaron Sele rates as the third worst ace in the league behind only the Angels' Jarrod Washburn and the Padres' Woody Williams. But despite getting no great individual performances, and despite collapses from Jamie Moyer and John Halama, Seattle's rotation was passable thanks to good years from surprises at the bottom of the rotation, especially Paul Abbott and Gil Meche.

The Mariner starting staff seems likely to rebound next year. Freddy Garcia and John Halama performed below their previous levels in 2000, and Gil Meche should be more productive in a full season than in a half season. If they do rebound, they'll continue a Saberhagen-style flip-flopping pattern that's been going on since the early 1990s. Here are the Support-Neutral Value Added totals for Mariner rotations since 1992: –7.3, 5.5, –3.1, 0.4, –6.7, 0.9, –2.8, 2.7, –1.0. At least they're consistent in their inconsistency.

For a quick explanation of SN stats, see page 7.

Reliever Evaluation Tools											
PITCHER	G	IP	R	ARA	APR	IRNR/G	EIRS/G	IRP	BRS	RRA	ARP
Paul Abbott	8	16.3	12	7.09	-3.4	0.62	0.28	-0.6	-0.7	6.57	-2.5
Freddy Garcia	1	3.0	0	0.00	1.7	0.00	0.00	0.0	0.0	0.00	1.7
Kevin Hodges	13	17.3	10	5.56	-0.7	0.85	0.38	-1.4	-1.2	5.59	-0.8
John Mabry	1	0.7	2	28.94	-1.8	2.00	0.72	-1.3	0.0	44.68	-2.9
Jose Mesa	66	80.7	48	5.74	-4.9	0.55	0.16	-10.8	-1.1	6.94	-15.6
Jose Paniagua	69	80.3	31	3.72	13.2	0.90	0.26	-5.8	-0.6	4.39	7.2
Joel Pineiro	7	13.3	11	7.96	-4.1	0.86	0.37	-2.9	-0.5	9.66	-6.6
Rob Ramsay	36	44.3	21	4.57	3.1	0.94	0.28	2.9	6.6	5.15	0.2
Arthur Rhodes	72	69.3	34	4.73	3.6	0.76	0.26	3.6	-5.6	3.75	11.2
Frankie Rodriguez	23	47.3	33	6.72	-8.0	0.74	0.29	-0.6	-1.7	6.47	-6.7
Kazuhiro Sasaki	63	62.7	25	3.85	9.4	0.40	0.15	2.8	0.4	3.58	11.3
Brett Tomko	24	49.7	27	5.24	-0.3	0.75	0.26	0.3	1.0	5.39	-1.1
TOTALS	383	485.0	254	5.05	7.8	0.71	0.23			5.28	-4.6

For a quick guide to RET, see page 10.

Tampa Bay Devil Rays

This just isn't a very good baseball franchise right now. The Tampa Bay Devil Rays are entering their fifth year of existence and fourth year of play. Their home is one of the worst parks in the major leagues, even if you give them points for a great new playing field. They generate little to no excitement whether fielding hometown heroes, imported sluggers or a combination of the two.

The D-Rays' biggest problem may be the change in the standards by which expansion teams are measured. It used to be that a new team wasn't expected to be competitive for a long time. The most successful expansion teams, the Royals and Blue Jays, took years to build player-development infrastructures that eventually fed ten-year runs in contention that peaked with World Championships. Some expansion teams, like the Mariners and Padres, took 15 years to even get within shouting distance of success. Other teams, like the Angels, managed a decent season or two in their infancy, but the success was more a fluke than the result of a plan.

The expectations changed in the 1990s. One reason was that the price of a new team increased four-fold compared to the previous expansion, the 1977 debuts of the Toronto Blue Jays and Seattle Mariners. When the Colorado Rockies and Florida Marlins came to life in 1993, their owners had poured a lot more money into their new toys than had the Jays and Mariners owners 16 years earlier. A second reason expectations changes is that MLB altered the expansion-draft rules, making more talent available to new teams. Third, changes in the game's structure, most notably free agency, gave new franchises a fast route to good players. Finally, the realignment and playoff expansion in 1994 made it easier for all teams to reach the postseason.

The 1993 expansion teams blew the doors off of existing expecations for expansion teams. The Colorado Rockies dove into the free-agent market for Larry Walker and Billy Swift, gunning for contention in 1995. They nabbed the NL's wild-card slot that year. Unwilling to be shown up by their expansion brethren, the Florida Marlins, owned by the tremendously wealthy Wayne Huizenga, broke the bank to sign Alex Fernandez, Moises Alou, Kevin Brown, Al Leiter, and Bobby Bonilla, players who would form the core of their 1997 team that won it all.

So when the 1998 expansion came along, things had changed. The D-Rays and the Arizona Diamondbacks wouldn't have the luxury of slow growth—not with expensive new ballparks and $95 million franchise fees. The D'backs spent millions before they played a single game, trading for Matt Williams and giving him a big contract, signing Jay Bell to a five-year, $35 million deal, and snapping up draft-loophole free agent Travis Lee. After their inaugural season they made another splash, signing Randy Johnson, Todd Stottlemyre, and Steve Finley. They would win 103 games and the NL West in 1999, then win 85 more games in 2000.

And the Devil Rays? They signed some veteran free agents before their inaugural season, but instead of building a contender, they focused on getting guys with local connections and long résumés who presumably would draw attention from the rest of the teams, which was lousy. The Devil Rays signed Tampa native Wade Boggs and traded for Tampa native Fred McGriff. Even though these moves failed to hold fans' interest in a 63–99 team, the front office stood pat during the next off-season. That strategy was even less successful, so they shifted gears for 2000, building the team and marketing campaign around an old, expensive lineup core of McGriff, Greg Vaughn, Vinny Castilla, and Jose Canseco. The result of all this maneuvering was a third sub-.500 season and a disappearing fan base.

It's not just the Devil Rays' lack of success that gets your attention. The team has made wrong decisions at just about every turn. For example, they took the best player selected in the Expansion Draft, Bobby Abreu, then immediately traded him to the Phillies for a stopgap at shortstop, Kevin Stocker. Abreu would easily be the Devil Rays' best player, the #3 hitter the team has never really had. Before the Expansion

---

Devil Rays Prospectus

2000 record: 69–93; Fifth place, AL East
Pythagenport W/L: 70–91
Runs Scored: 733 (14th in AL)
Runs Allowed: 842 (8th in AL)
Team EqA: .239 (14th in AL)
2000 Batters' Age: 30.2 (tied for 4th oldest in AL)
2000 Pitchers' Age: 28.7 (tied for 7th oldest in AL)
Ballpark: Tropicana Field; slight hitters' park; Park Factor of 1.019
2000: A bizarre left turn in their planning failed.
2001: There will be improvement without relevance. Relevance comes in 2003.

Draft, blind to the failure rate of high-school pitchers, they had thrown millions of dollars at 1996 draft-loophole free agents Matt White and Bobby Seay.

Then, instead of building the best baseball team they could, they focused on stunts like signing Boggs and McGriff. Playing the local-boy card prevented the Devil Rays from using some of the cheap talent they had on hand for the infield corners, guys like Scott McClain, Steve Cox, and even Bubba Trammell. It also displayed a tortured misunderstanding of their goal. The Devil Rays don't need to worry about drawing cards in an era in which winning—the best drawing card—can be achieved without first going through a long series of losing seasons.

The Devil Rays own a performance profile that looks like that of a traditional expansion team. It's fair to ask if perhaps they are going to be like the Blue Jays or the Royals, suffering for a time before embarking on a long period of winning seasons. Is the organization doing a good job of building its player-development program? Are they in the early stages of establishing a farm system that will yield an exciting, young Devil Rays team? After all, a certain amount of failure is acceptable if the end result is a parade in downtown Tampa Bay.

The problem is that the Devil Rays' system isn't cranking out major leaguers the way the White Sox or A's or Yankees are. The Devil Rays' drafting and development strategy has been focused on athletes rather than players, a preference that originated with their initial draft and can be seen at every level of their system, including the major-league team. It's Chuck LaMar's concept.

Most of the time, we at BP believe that having and executing a plan—even a flawed plan—is better than having no plan and just reacting to needs. The Rockies have taken a big risk this winter in committing $180 million to two pitchers, but that action stems from analysis and thought. The White Sox broke down their contending team from the mid-1990s with one famous trade but from the ashes of that deal grew a division winner in 2000 filled with young talent.

Teams like the Indians have fallen out of favor with us because their operations have shifted from quality planning to flailing away at each problem that emerges. A special brand of derision is saved for teams like the Pirates and Orioles, who seem to have no idea what they're doing beyond lunch, and even that's up in the air depending on what the specials are at Tony's.

The problem with the Devil Rays' plan is that it has a high rate of failure. Drafting athletes and turning them into baseball players occasionally yields a Dave Winfield. More often, the product is Reggie Taylor, a tremendous physical talent who can't do enough things that win baseball games. The Devil Rays love guys like this—Josh Hamilton and Kenny Kelly and Carl Crawford—and their player-acquisition strategy is centered on getting as many of them as possible. Even at the major-league level, the D-Rays have squandered playing time on Randy Winn and Jose Guillen and Jason Tyner, enthralled by their speed. It's been the biggest factor in the team's putrid offense.

The Devil Rays must temper their love of tools players with a recognition that the skills that win games don't always come in the prettiest packages. If their coaching and development staff can make players out of the best of these guys, like Hamilton and Kelly, that's a good thing. But in order to build an offense that wins, the team will also need to sign players who have more than great athleticism.

Such a shift will also help correct a positional imbalance that's becoming a developmental problem: the D-Rays' approach has yielded some good outfield prospects but just about no infield or catching prospects worth a darn. Jorge Cantu is an intriguing 19-year-old shortstop, but no one else in the system who plays on the dirt part of the field projects as a good major leaguer.

It doesn't help that the shopping spree of last winter cost the team three of their top four picks in the 2000 draft, blowing a hole in the player-development program that could take years to repair. Any reasoned analysis would conclude that coughing up cash, playing time, and draft picks was far too high a price to pay for people like Juan Guzman and Greg Vaughn, but the Devil Rays did it anyway.

Are things going to get better? The second half of 2000 was encouraging, as the team played some of its less-athletic, less-well-compensated players and was rewarded with wins. They made some good trades at the July 31 deadline, giving up replaceable talent for a couple of high-upside pitchers in Jesus Colome and Paul Wilson. Wilson could be one of the great stories of 2001, an ex-phenom who has come back from an elbow reconstruction.

Beyond that, there are some signs that reinforcements may be coming from within. The team's franchise player, Josh Hamilton, is as good a tools prospect as you'll find, brutal walk rate and all. He's a young outfielder—center field now, right field later—with excellent power. If he does pan out, he could set this franchise back five years as they chase every all-state quarterback/shooting guard/shortstop in the nation. The D-Rays finally got Kenny Kelly, the University of Miami's starting quarterback before Ken Dorsey, to play baseball full-time. He had an encouraging season at Double-A Orlando.

For the first time, the bonus babies of 1996 had seasons to brag about. Matt White and Bobby Seay look like prospects again, four years after their twin free-agent contracts shook the baseball world. Each now projects to contribute in the major leagues, and both could see time at the TropDome this year. The Devil Rays continued to have success with other

American League

teams' castoffs, building a good rotation with guys like Tanyon Sturtze, Bryan Rekar, and Albie Lopez. Their pitching is not the problem.

Even with these positive developments, it's hard to see the Devil Rays competing with the AL East's powerhouses or even reaching the 87 wins that mark the buy-in for wild-card contention. There has been no indication that the team realizes its offensive problems have less to do with injuries to well-paid old guys and more to do with the presence of as many as six OBP holes in the lineup. It's possible, maybe even probable, that the Devil Rays will have a lineup that includes John Flaherty, Brent Abernathy, Felix Martinez, Vinny Castilla, Jason Tyner, and Gerald Williams. The best projected OBP in that group? Tyner's .335. Four of those players are projected to be below .300 in 2001. If the Devil Rays are trying to bring back the two-hour game, that lineup is a great start.

Picking up Ben Grieve for Roberto Hernandez and Cory Lidle may be the best thing the Devil Rays have ever done. Grieve immediately becomes their best hitter, and he has three years left before free agency. Grieve is exactly the kind of hitter the D-Rays need. The only question is whether they'll suffer his atrocious defense and put him in left field, or give up and make him the full-time DH. Either way, they win the trade.

The Devil Rays aren't a classic expansion team nor one of the new breed. They're not building from within or without. They're simply trundling along, spending some money but not enough, blaming their problems on their fans or the rules or bad luck, failing to see that the plan they're implementing is flawed, and refusing to learn from the success of teams like the White Sox and A's.

HITTERS (BA: .270, OBP: .340, SLG: .440, EqA: .260)

Brent Abernathy   2B   Bats R   Age 23

YEAR	TEAM	LGE	AB	H	DB	TP	HR	BB	SO	R	RBI	SB	CS	OUT	BA	OBP	SLG	EQA	EQR	DEFENSE
1998	Dunedin	Fla	484	128	24	1	3	32	43	55	45	13	7	362	.264	.311	.337	.219	41	118-2B -11
1999	Knoxvill	Sou	576	140	26	1	11	37	50	75	44	17	8	444	.243	.293	.349	.216	48	129-2B -3
2000	Syracuse	Int	358	95	20	1	3	20	33	39	28	9	9	272	.265	.306	.352	.217	30	89-2B -2
2000	Durham	Int	92	23	2	0	2	9	11	12	14	7	2	71	.250	.337	.337	.241	10	24-2B -9
2001	TampaBay	AL	510	133	24	1	7	39	51	70	53	20	9	386	.261	.313	.353	.228	48	

The Devil Rays picked up a decent second-base prospect in Brent Abernathy for two guys to whom they'd given one-year deals the previous winter, Steve Trachsel and Mark Guthrie. That's a nice exchange. Abernathy isn't ready but projects as a better version of Adam Kennedy. If the D-Rays send him to Camp Takeapitch for a couple of summers, he'll eventually have a few All-Star seasons.

Rocco Baldelli   CF   Bats R   Age 19

YEAR	TEAM	LGE	AB	H	DB	TP	HR	BB	SO	R	RBI	SB	CS	OUT	BA	OBP	SLG	EQA	EQR	DEFENSE
2000	Princetn	App	235	45	9	1	2	6	65	21	17	3	1	191	.191	.217	.264	.139	7	60-CF -2

Rocco Baldelli might have made the book even if he hadn't been the Devil Rays' first-round pick in 2000. What a great name! Baldelli is a tools-positive outfielder who some observers considered the best athlete in the draft. He's the quintessential D-Rays' draft pick and has a rough road ahead of him.

Jace Brewer   SS   Bats R   Age 22

YEAR	TEAM	LGE	AB	H	DB	TP	HR	BB	SO	R	RBI	SB	CS	OUT	BA	OBP	SLG	EQA	EQR	DEFENSE
2000	Charl-SC	SAL	139	28	8	1	0	4	30	8	12	1	0	111	.201	.226	.273	.148	5	27-SS -2
2001	TampaBay	AL	69	14	2	0	0	3	32	3	2	0	0	55	.203	.236	.232	.127	2	

Taking Baldelli was only the first questionable move the organization made on draft day. Having coughed up their second-, third-, and fourth-round picks thanks to the previous winter's old-people shopping, they took Jace Brewer in the fifth round then acquiesced to his demands for a major-league contract and a September call-up, making Brewer the first player from last year's draft to reach the majors. He's a shortstop out of Baylor who doesn't come close to meriting the kind of money ($1.5 million) or treatment he's received.

Miguel Cairo — 2B — Bats B — Age 27

YEAR	TEAM	LGE	AB	H	DB	TP	HR	BB	SO	R	RBI	SB	CS	OUT	BA	OBP	SLG	EQA	EQR	DEFENSE	
1998	TampaBay	AL	514	141	26	5	6	23	39	49	46	16	7	380	.274	.312	.379	.233	50	139-2B	13
1999	TampaBay	AL	462	138	15	5	3	20	42	58	34	21	7	331	.299	.336	.372	.243	48	113-2B	8
2000	TampaBay	AL	372	97	17	2	1	25	31	47	31	30	8	283	.261	.311	.325	.226	34	99-2B	-2
2001	Oakland	AL	423	115	16	3	3	29	38	70	43	28	7	315	.272	.319	.345	.239	44		

Never one of our favorites, Miguel Cairo wore out his welcome in Tampa Bay this year, taking criticism for the way he did "the little things." He was released at the end of the season. He's not good enough to be a regular, and he doesn't have a utility infielder's skills, so his career hangs by a thread.

Jorge Cantu — SS — Bats R — Age 19

YEAR	TEAM	LGE	AB	H	DB	TP	HR	BB	SO	R	RBI	SB	CS	OUT	BA	OBP	SLG	EQA	EQR	DEFENSE	
1999	HudsnVal	NYP	288	64	14	1	1	12	63	26	24	1	2	226	.222	.255	.288	.169	13	72-SS	-4
2000	Charl-SC	SAL	189	46	10	1	2	6	42	19	17	1	1	144	.243	.271	.339	.197	12	45-SS	-1
2000	St Pete	Fla	130	33	4	1	1	2	15	14	10	2	1	98	.254	.268	.323	.191	8	32-SS	-9
2001	TampaBay	AL	238	61	10	1	2	9	69	22	22	2	1	178	.256	.283	.332	.203	16		

The Devil Rays don't have the caliber of prospects that some teams do, but the ones they do have are young for their leagues. Jorge Cantu, a slap-hitting shortstop, reached the Florida State League at 18 and didn't embarrass himself. Right now, his only offensive skill is hitting for average, but his age and accomplishments make him the best shortstop prospect in this system.

Vinny Castilla — 3B — Bats R — Age 33

YEAR	TEAM	LGE	AB	H	DB	TP	HR	BB	SO	R	RBI	SB	CS	OUT	BA	OBP	SLG	EQA	EQR	DEFENSE	
1998	Colorado	NL	632	179	23	3	41	37	83	96	122	4	8	461	.283	.328	.524	.271	88	158-3B	-2
1999	Colorado	NL	601	143	18	1	28	44	71	70	82	1	2	460	.238	.291	.411	.230	58	152-3B	-12
2000	TampaBay	AL	331	73	10	1	6	10	37	21	40	1	2	260	.221	.250	.311	.176	17	83-3B	4
2001	TampaBay	AL	460	106	14	1	17	30	59	43	56	1	2	356	.230	.278	.376	.214	38		

Wow, was that a bad idea. We expected Vinny Castilla to be exposed as an altitude-enhanced fraud, but a .176 EqA? In his defense, he played through a back injury for almost the entire season, but even healthy, he wasn't going to be the player the Devil Rays thought they were getting. The effects of altitude on statistics are real, and teams like the D-Rays and Brewers are fooling themselves to think otherwise. If Castilla takes playing time from Aubrey Huff, the Devil Rays are just being stubborn.

Steve Cox — RF/1B — Bats L — Age 26

YEAR	TEAM	LGE	AB	H	DB	TP	HR	BB	SO	R	RBI	SB	CS	OUT	BA	OBP	SLG	EQA	EQR	DEFENSE			
1998	Durham	Int	433	100	20	1	11	45	99	55	55	2	3	336	.231	.306	.358	.222	39	105-1B	11		
1999	Durham	Int	532	160	42	3	19	54	73	86	96	2	2	374	.301	.369	.498	.285	81	122-1B	4		
2000	TampaBay	AL	314	89	16	1	12	42	43	41	33	1	2	227	.283	.375	.455	.277	46	55-RF	-6	19-1B	-3
2001	TampaBay	AL	339	96	22	1	12	46	56	60	62	1	1	244	.283	.369	.460	.279	50				

He's a hitter who got to play when the expensive geezers couldn't. Steve Cox, like a lot of the older hitters we tout, isn't someone who will be a superstar. He is comparable to, even better than, many veterans who get jobs ahead of him, and he costs a tenth or a twentieth what those guys make. If you pay guys like Steve Cox instead of Derek Bell, you get as good or better performance, and you have more money to spend on truly great players. That's how you win.

Carl Crawford — RF — Bats L — Age 19

YEAR	TEAM	LGE	AB	H	DB	TP	HR	BB	SO	R	RBI	SB	CS	OUT	BA	OBP	SLG	EQA	EQR	DEFENSE	
1999	Princetn	App	258	62	9	2	0	5	51	31	14	5	2	198	.240	.256	.291	.174	12	57-RF	-2
2000	Charl-SC	SAL	572	142	18	7	5	21	109	63	40	19	6	436	.248	.276	.330	.203	41	131-RF	-10
2001	TampaBay	AL	369	100	11	5	2	15	90	45	36	14	3	272	.271	.299	.344	.221	31		

Another of the Chuck LaMar All-Stars, Carl Crawford is a young, athletic outfielder and a very raw baseball player. He could have played Division I football or basketball but chose baseball after being the D-Rays' #2 pick in 1999. The improvement he showed in 2000, particularly in power and plate discipline, was impressive for an 18-year-old in the Sally League. He's got a good chance to be a tools pick who becomes a baseball player.

American League

Even if we're right about Crawford, it doesn't change the fact that the Devil Rays are following a misguided draft strategy. Tools guys are easy to like, and if you draft enough of them, one or two eventually have nice careers and make you look good. Overall, though, such a strategy leads to a lot of high-profile flops and a lack of talent coming through your system.

Mike Difelice — C — Bats R — Age 32

YEAR	TEAM	LGE	AB	H	DB	TP	HR	BB	SO	R	RBI	SB	CS	OUT	BA	OBP	SLG	EQA	EQR	DEFENSE	
1998	TampaBay	AL	248	59	14	3	3	14	50	18	23	0	0	189	.238	.281	.355	.209	19	77-C	4
1999	TampaBay	AL	178	56	8	0	7	6	21	20	26	0	0	122	.315	.346	.478	.271	23	51-C	1
2000	TampaBay	AL	203	49	13	1	6	10	36	22	18	0	0	154	.241	.277	.404	.222	18	57-C	-2
2001	TampaBay	AL	189	48	9	1	5	12	34	20	25	0	0	141	.254	.299	.392	.229	18		

Mike Difelice is a catch-and-throw backup with some pop. His occasional power and decent defense make him worth the roster spot, but he's be better off backing up Todd Hundley or someone of that ilk. He doesn't give the D-Rays anything the next guy on the page doesn't.

John Flaherty — C — Bats R — Age 33

YEAR	TEAM	LGE	AB	H	DB	TP	HR	BB	SO	R	RBI	SB	CS	OUT	BA	OBP	SLG	EQA	EQR	DEFENSE	
1998	TampaBay	AL	304	65	6	0	5	21	41	21	25	0	4	243	.214	.267	.283	.172	15	87-C	5
1999	TampaBay	AL	444	125	15	0	16	15	58	51	70	0	2	321	.282	.313	.423	.241	46	113-C	8
2000	TampaBay	AL	392	103	10	0	12	15	52	34	38	0	0	289	.263	.290	.380	.220	33	101-C	-2
2001	TampaBay	AL	365	93	10	0	12	21	52	35	48	0	1	273	.255	.295	.381	.223	32		

Just because a backup catcher plays a lot doesn't mean he's a real starter. John Flaherty isn't much different from Difelice, but he has a better defensive reputation and a couple of .270 BA seasons to his credit, so he plays more.

Jose Guillen — RF — Bats R — Age 25

YEAR	TEAM	LGE	AB	H	DB	TP	HR	BB	SO	R	RBI	SB	CS	OUT	BA	OBP	SLG	EQA	EQR	DEFENSE	
1998	Pittsbrg	NL	578	154	34	2	16	19	94	61	84	3	5	429	.266	.296	.415	.232	55	141-RF	-1
1999	Pittsbrg	NL	120	31	3	0	2	9	20	17	18	1	0	89	.258	.310	.333	.218	10	29-RF	-2
1999	Nashvill	PCL	130	38	4	0	5	6	20	21	18	0	1	93	.292	.330	.438	.252	15	30-RF	-1
1999	TampaBay	AL	167	41	8	0	3	9	33	23	13	0	0	126	.246	.308	.347	.220	14	43-RF	-2
2000	Durham	Int	78	30	6	1	8	7	11	17	25	0	1	49	.385	.440	.795	.368	20	17-RF	-3
2000	TampaBay	AL	315	80	16	5	10	14	59	38	38	3	1	236	.254	.314	.432	.247	36	79-RF	0
2001	TampaBay	AL	432	124	25	2	16	32	82	63	76	2	1	309	.287	.336	.465	.266	56		

It seems like he was a teammate of Willie Stargell, but Jose Guillen is still just 25 years old. His great arm and his ability to drive the ball are his central skills, but he doesn't walk enough to be a real asset. Sometimes a player like this becomes Jermaine Dye, but betting on that is a bad idea. As a platoon partner and defensive replacement for Steve Cox, Guillen can be useful. Think Alex Ochoa's career path.

Ozzie Guillen — IF — Bats L — Age 37

YEAR	TEAM	LGE	AB	H	DB	TP	HR	BB	SO	R	RBI	SB	CS	OUT	BA	OBP	SLG	EQA	EQR	DEFENSE	
1998	Atlanta	NL	268	75	16	1	1	23	23	37	22	1	4	197	.280	.339	.358	.233	26	69-SS	-10
1999	Atlanta	NL	234	56	11	0	3	12	16	20	21	3	2	180	.239	.276	.325	.197	15	47-SS	2
2000	TampaBay	AL	107	26	2	0	3	4	6	20	12	1	0	81	.243	.270	.346	.202	7	18-SS	-1
2001	TampaBay	AL	163	37	2	0	3	12	12	12	14	1	1	127	.227	.280	.294	.188	10		

Watching Ozzie Guillen play for a couple of weeks made the Devil Rays yearn for the terrible Felix Martinez, who held the starting job for the entire second half. Guillen has been a brutal player since his 1992 knee injury but stays in the league because he's supposed to be a good team guy.

Toby Hall — C — Bats R — Age 25

YEAR	TEAM	LGE	AB	H	DB	TP	HR	BB	SO	R	RBI	SB	CS	OUT	BA	OBP	SLG	EQA	EQR	DEFENSE
1998	Charl-SC	SAL	385	97	17	1	4	28	34	42	33	1	3	291	.252	.307	.332	.213	30	95-C -22
1999	St Pete	Fla	214	53	9	0	4	12	10	18	26	0	1	162	.248	.290	.346	.209	16	29-C -3
1999	Orlando	Sou	173	39	5	0	7	2	11	16	25	1	1	135	.225	.237	.376	.193	11	35-C -4
2000	Orlando	Sou	278	82	9	0	8	10	26	31	40	1	1	197	.295	.321	.414	.243	29	55-C -15
2000	Durham	Int	184	52	9	0	7	2	20	18	30	0	0	132	.283	.296	.446	.241	19	41-C -2
2001	TampaBay	AL	437	121	13	0	14	23	40	47	64	0	1	317	.277	.313	.403	.238	44	

Introducing the new John Flaherty. Toby Hall got some attention by hitting .343 in the first half at Orlando. He has some power, will hit anywhere from .220 to .290, and walks about once every ten days. Hall doesn't play the defense that the current Devil Ray catchers do, but he would be cheaper and might become a fan favorite.

Josh Hamilton — CF — Bats L — Age 20

YEAR	TEAM	LGE	AB	H	DB	TP	HR	BB	SO	R	RBI	SB	CS	OUT	BA	OBP	SLG	EQA	EQR	DEFENSE
1999	Princetn	App	233	57	13	2	5	6	47	24	23	5	2	178	.245	.264	.382	.211	18	50-CF -2
1999	HudsnVal	NYP	73	15	3	0	0	0	15	6	6	0	0	58	.205	.210	.247	.111	1	16-CF 6
2000	Charl-SC	SAL	398	97	18	2	9	18	76	44	41	5	3	304	.244	.278	.367	.211	31	81-CF -2
2001	TampaBay	AL	271	72	13	1	6	13	62	30	34	3	1	200	.266	.299	.387	.229	25	

The Franchise is the best of the team's tools prospects, the #1 overall pick in the 1999 draft. He's shown everything but plate discipline so far; since he's just 20 and has only about a year's worth of experience, that's not a significant problem yet. His season was curtailed by a torn knee ligament. The injury was not major, and arthroscopic surgery on the knee was successful.

Josh Hamilton is going to be the Devil Rays' first superstar, so they need to resist the temptation to rush him. Talk of him competing for a job in Tampa Bay this spring is silly, and not just from a performance standpoint. He needs to be told that he is not a complete player and that his selectivity is going to be a factor in his getting to the majors.

We have him as the 14th-best prospect in the game, and if he walks 50 times this year, he'd move up to about second-best. He has that kind of ability, but it's going to take good management by the Devil Rays to turn Hamilton into a superstar, as opposed to another athlete who doesn't put enough runs on the board.

Aubrey Huff — 3B — Bats L — Age 24

YEAR	TEAM	LGE	AB	H	DB	TP	HR	BB	SO	R	RBI	SB	CS	OUT	BA	OBP	SLG	EQA	EQR	DEFENSE
1998	Charl-SC	SAL	270	68	11	1	9	17	42	26	35	1	1	203	.252	.296	.400	.229	25	67-3B 6
1999	Orlando	Sou	496	127	30	2	16	46	82	64	55	1	2	371	.256	.322	.421	.246	56	131-3B 8
2000	Durham	Int	412	119	31	2	17	42	75	63	62	1	2	295	.289	.357	.498	.279	61	89-3B -11
2000	TampaBay	AL	121	35	4	0	5	4	16	11	14	0	0	86	.289	.318	.446	.251	14	31-3B -6
2001	TampaBay	AL	508	153	31	1	24	56	91	90	106	1	1	356	.301	.371	.508	.290	81	

Vinny Castilla's bad back relieved International League pitchers of having to face Aubrey Huff, who has done nothing but hit since being drafted in 1998. He's one of the few players in this organization, minors or majors, with a decent walk rate. Not everyone likes his defense, and a move to first base has been discussed. With Castilla and Fred McGriff still around, Huff will have to fight for a job again this spring.

Russ Johnson — IF — Bats R — Age 28

YEAR	TEAM	LGE	AB	H	DB	TP	HR	BB	SO	R	RBI	SB	CS	OUT	BA	OBP	SLG	EQA	EQR	DEFENSE		
1998	New Orln	PCL	457	124	25	1	5	75	63	76	41	8	8	341	.271	.378	.363	.257	57	100-3B 5		
1999	New Orln	PCL	77	23	3	0	1	13	13	13	9	1	2	56	.299	.404	.377	.268	10	12-2B 0		
1999	Houston	NL	157	43	7	0	6	18	29	22	22	1	3	117	.274	.349	.433	.257	20	24-3B 0		
2000	Houston	NL	45	8	0	0	0	2	9	4	3	1	1	38	.178	.213	.178	.056	0			
2000	TampaBay	AL	183	46	6	0	3	23	27	26	17	4	1	138	.251	.338	.333	.235	18	29-3B 4	14-2B	3
2001	TampaBay	AL	235	60	4	0	5	34	40	36	28	6	4	179	.255	.349	.336	.239	25			

The Astros have a lot of infielders coming through the system, so they used Russ Johnson to get mop-up man Marc Valdes from the D-Rays. Johnson's chance to be a starter is gone, but because he can play three positions and hit with some power, he makes a better backup than most guys. If the Rays somehow dump Vinny Castilla, moving Johnson into a platoon with Huff at third base would be, like the commercial says, cheap and easy.

American League

Kenny Kelly — OF — Bats B — Age 22

YEAR	TEAM	LGE	AB	H	DB	TP	HR	BB	SO	R	RBI	SB	CS	OUT	BA	OBP	SLG	EQA	EQR	DEFENSE	
1998	Charl-SC	SAL	222	51	7	3	2	13	55	29	12	7	2	173	.230	.279	.315	.200	16	54-CF	4
1999	St Pete	Fla	208	48	9	2	3	14	53	27	15	6	3	163	.231	.285	.337	.208	16	51-CF	1
2000	Orlando	Sou	506	117	17	6	3	43	123	61	25	15	11	400	.231	.295	.306	.202	37	124-CF	-2
2001	TampaBay	AL	398	95	14	5	3	36	106	49	36	14	8	311	.239	.302	.322	.213	32		

With Kenny Kelly and Jace Brewer, the Devil Rays led baseball with two unqualified September call-ups. Kelly, who quarterbacked Miami of Florida in all those seasons in which they didn't end up ranked #2 in the nation, finally gave up football to play baseball full-time in 2000. The big jump in walk rate in his first full season is a good sign.

In evaluating Kelly, the player to keep in mind is Kenny Lofton, who didn't commit to playing baseball full-time until he was 24 and had only a handful of at-bats at A-ball at the age of 22. Kelly is ahead of where Lofton was at 22 and is a similar type of player. He's a good bet to become a quality major-league center fielder.

Felix Martinez — SS — Bats B — Age 27

YEAR	TEAM	LGE	AB	H	DB	TP	HR	BB	SO	R	RBI	SB	CS	OUT	BA	OBP	SLG	EQA	EQR	DEFENSE	
1998	KansasCy	AL	85	12	1	1	0	5	19	7	5	3	1	74	.141	.197	.176	.066	0	27-SS	-1
1998	Omaha	PCL	163	36	5	2	2	12	39	20	13	4	2	129	.221	.277	.313	.196	11	42-SS	-2
1999	Wichita	Tex	328	71	16	1	3	26	49	39	26	9	6	263	.216	.278	.299	.191	21	74-SS	0
2000	Durham	Int	150	34	6	1	3	5	30	15	15	2	2	118	.227	.262	.340	.194	10	42-SS	3
2000	TampaBay	AL	297	63	11	4	2	29	62	40	16	9	3	237	.212	.300	.296	.207	23	106-SS	8
2001	TampaBay	AL	320	67	11	2	4	26	68	30	23	10	5	258	.209	.269	.294	.188	20		

Felix Martinez didn't completely suck last season. It was about the worst thing that could have happened for the Devil Rays, because now he'll go into 2001 as the starter. Even at his best, he's a bad player with a decent glove (he led MLB in range factor at shortstop) and a terrible bat. He does, however, appear to have tamed the temper that got him into so much trouble with the Royals.

Quinton McCracken — OF — Bats B — Age 31

YEAR	TEAM	LGE	AB	H	DB	TP	HR	BB	SO	R	RBI	SB	CS	OUT	BA	OBP	SLG	EQA	EQR	DEFENSE	
1998	TampaBay	AL	613	183	38	7	8	40	95	77	59	16	9	439	.299	.344	.423	.257	73	153-CF	10
1999	TampaBay	AL	147	37	6	1	1	13	21	19	17	6	5	115	.252	.316	.327	.217	13	34-LF	2
2000	Durham	Int	338	78	15	1	2	25	64	43	23	8	5	265	.231	.287	.299	.195	22	81-OF	-5
2000	TampaBay	AL	31	5	0	0	0	5	4	4	2	0	1	27	.161	.278	.161	.125	1		
2001	StLouis	NL	262	67	12	2	3	25	48	36	31	6	5	200	.256	.321	.351	.228	25		

He wasn't going to be in the book, but just before press time, the Cardinals signed him to a minor-league contract. Quinton McCracken has the skills to be a decent fourth outfielder and is joining a team with two outfielders, Jim Edmonds and Ray Lankford, from the Major League Crystal Collection. McCracken may be the best bench player on the Cardinals.

Fred McGriff — 1B — Bats L — Age 37

YEAR	TEAM	LGE	AB	H	DB	TP	HR	BB	SO	R	RBI	SB	CS	OUT	BA	OBP	SLG	EQA	EQR	DEFENSE	
1998	TampaBay	AL	562	165	24	1	23	78	105	74	83	6	2	399	.294	.381	.463	.284	86	130-1B	0
1999	TampaBay	AL	522	164	26	1	34	81	97	73	100	1	0	358	.314	.407	.563	.316	101	122-1B	-4
2000	TampaBay	AL	558	155	16	0	28	84	109	77	100	2	0	403	.278	.372	.457	.279	83	143-1B	-9
2001	TampaBay	AL	481	129	14	0	23	84	99	85	92	1	0	352	.268	.377	.441	.279	73		

It's something of a shame to see Fred McGriff playing out his career in obscurity, having been such a great hitter on so many good teams from 1988 to 1997. As much as the Devil Rays love local boys, they'd do themselves good by trading the Crime Dog while he still has some value, thereby picking up talent and freeing at-bats for younger, cheaper players like Cox and Huff. McGriff would be a decent option for the Braves.

Alex Sanchez — CF — Bats L — Age 24

YEAR	TEAM	LGE	AB	H	DB	TP	HR	BB	SO	R	RBI	SB	CS	OUT	BA	OBP	SLG	EQA	EQR	DEFENSE	
1998	St Pete	Fla	547	150	15	6	1	22	79	48	36	24	16	413	.274	.303	.329	.211	42	128-CF	0
1999	Orlando	Sou	503	116	10	3	2	15	94	48	23	24	15	402	.231	.253	.274	.169	24	121-CF	0
2000	Orlando	Sou	87	23	2	1	0	0	13	11	3	1	3	67	.264	.269	.310	.175	4	19-LF	0
2000	Durham	Int	449	122	16	2	2	23	69	62	29	36	16	342	.272	.313	.330	.223	40	107-CF	0
2001	TampaBay	AL	445	112	13	2	1	24	77	51	31	26	13	346	.252	.290	.297	.200	31		

The speedy slap hitter, who was the Devil Rays' best position-player prospect for a time, rebounded from a lousy 1999 to reach Triple-A. Alex Sanchez is a fifth outfielder and pinch runner, comparable to the early versions of Luis Polonia but with better defense. He'll have a career off more than a few benches.

Jared Sandberg — 3B — Bats R — Age 23

YEAR	TEAM	LGE	AB	H	DB	TP	HR	BB	SO	R	RBI	SB	CS	OUT	BA	OBP	SLG	EQA	EQR	DEFENSE	
1998	HudsnVal	NYP	283	66	9	1	9	29	81	31	34	5	2	219	.233	.309	.367	.229	27	67-3B	7
1998	Charl-SC	SAL	197	33	7	0	3	20	80	23	20	2	0	164	.168	.250	.249	.159	8	56-3B	-16
1999	St Pete	Fla	511	118	16	1	17	38	154	54	67	4	1	394	.231	.290	.366	.218	44	129-3B	5
2000	Orlando	Sou	253	59	11	1	5	25	57	26	30	3	2	196	.233	.305	.344	.218	22	59-3B	5
2001	TampaBay	AL	342	81	14	1	10	38	103	43	44	2	1	262	.237	.313	.371	.232	34		

Ryno's nephew reached Double-A and survived, though he's not getting much play as a prospect. Jared Sandberg is neither a stathead favorite nor the kind of athlete that gets the D-Rays excited. He has Aubrey Huff ahead of him at third base, as well. He needs about one more step forward to have a shot at a platoon career. The name helps.

Bobby Smith — 2B — Bats R — Age 27

YEAR	TEAM	LGE	AB	H	DB	TP	HR	BB	SO	R	RBI	SB	CS	OUT	BA	OBP	SLG	EQA	EQR	DEFENSE	
1998	TampaBay	AL	369	104	16	3	12	34	98	45	55	4	3	268	.282	.351	.439	.264	48	84-3B	7
1999	TampaBay	AL	199	36	5	1	3	14	58	18	18	4	4	167	.181	.238	.261	.152	8	44-3B	4
1999	Durham	Int	224	67	12	2	11	22	61	40	35	9	3	160	.299	.369	.518	.292	37	53-3B	3
2000	Durham	Int	263	69	17	1	14	18	65	39	46	10	2	196	.262	.315	.494	.266	36	54-2B	0
2000	TampaBay	AL	174	41	5	0	7	12	54	19	25	2	2	135	.236	.289	.385	.221	16	42-2B	1
2001	TampaBay	AL	369	94	19	1	13	33	109	55	52	11	3	278	.255	.316	.417	.248	43		

It's hard to not feel sorry for the guy. Bobby Smith started the season at Durham playing second base after Vinny Castilla evicted him from third. Brought up in June to supplant Miguel Cairo, he hit .311/.342/.500 for three weeks, then sprained his MCL in a close play at first base on July 5. When he came back in August, the magic was gone: .178/.259/.297. He'll be trying to hold off Brent Abernathy this spring.

Ozzie Timmons — OF — Bats R — Age 30

YEAR	TEAM	LGE	AB	H	DB	TP	HR	BB	SO	R	RBI	SB	CS	OUT	BA	OBP	SLG	EQA	EQR	DEFENSE	
1998	Indianap	Int	329	77	17	2	9	21	68	37	28	1	1	253	.234	.286	.380	.219	28	77-LF	0
1999	Tacoma	PCL	299	67	13	1	14	41	85	39	45	0	1	233	.224	.320	.415	.245	34	53-LF	-1
1999	Seattle	AL	44	5	2	0	1	4	11	4	3	0	1	40	.114	.188	.227	.079	0		
2000	Durham	Int	513	131	22	0	23	56	118	79	79	3	3	385	.255	.335	.433	.255	63	59-RF	-8
2000	TampaBay	AL	41	14	4	0	4	0	6	9	12	0	0	27	.341	.341	.732	.325	8		
2001	TampaBay	AL	464	116	17	0	21	53	118	63	75	1	2	350	.250	.327	.422	.250	55		

You'd like to think that after a season of dealing with the various aches and pains and outs generated by big-money guys like Vinny Castilla and Jose Canseco and Greg Vaughn, the Devil Rays would have learned something from Ozzie Timmons. Timmons hit .300 with some walks and power for Durham, then homered his way through late September for the D-Rays. He's a fantastic cheap solution as part of a DH platoon, comparable to Glenallen Hill, but for just $400,000.

Jason Tyner — OF — Bats L — Age 24

YEAR	TEAM	LGE	AB	H	DB	TP	HR	BB	SO	R	RBI	SB	CS	OUT	BA	OBP	SLG	EQA	EQR	DEFENSE	
1998	St Lucie	Fla	203	51	3	2	0	12	23	20	12	5	5	157	.251	.295	.286	.191	12	43-CF	-5
1999	Binghmtn	Eas	519	138	13	3	1	45	48	63	25	23	9	390	.266	.325	.308	.221	45	121-CF	-2
2000	Norfolk	Int	329	97	6	1	0	24	33	44	24	22	11	242	.295	.346	.319	.233	32	80-CF	0
2000	NY Mets	NL	42	9	2	0	0	0	4	3	5	1	1	34	.214	.230	.262	.142	1	11-LF	0
2000	TampaBay	AL	83	20	2	0	0	3	11	6	7	6	1	64	.241	.276	.265	.191	5	23-LF	4
2001	TampaBay	AL	384	109	7	1	1	29	44	49	38	11	4	279	.284	.334	.315	.226	34		

Not satisfied with having their own Alex Sanchez, the D-Rays picked up the Mets' version at the trade deadline in exchange for Rick White and Bubba Trammell. Tyner is a borderline center fielder defensively, but he'd be an offensive disaster on a corner. Like Sanchez, he could turn into a decent fifth outfielder.

Greg Vaughn — LF — Bats R — Age 35

YEAR	TEAM	LGE	AB	H	DB	TP	HR	BB	SO	R	RBI	SB	CS	OUT	BA	OBP	SLG	EQA	EQR	DEFENSE	
1998	San Dieg	NL	588	166	27	4	54	77	113	119	123	11	4	426	.282	.370	.617	.311	115	150-LF	2
1999	Cincnnti	NL	550	129	19	2	42	77	129	97	106	12	2	423	.235	.332	.505	.274	83	126-LF	7
2000	TampaBay	AL	455	116	23	1	29	74	117	79	69	9	1	340	.255	.362	.501	.286	74	72-LF	3
2001	TampaBay	AL	421	102	16	1	27	79	109	79	85	5	1	320	.242	.362	.477	.282	67		

Greg Vaughn, like Luis Gonzalez and Steve Finley and others, is an argument for taking another look at career paths. He's been a much better player in his thirties than in his late twenties, with just one off-year since 1995. He's always been an underrated defensive player, in part because his bum shoulder keeps him from throwing well. Even with that, he's a bad risk at three years and $21 million left on his deal, especially given the D-Rays' many alternatives.

Gerald Williams — CF — Bats R — Age 34

YEAR	TEAM	LGE	AB	H	DB	TP	HR	BB	SO	R	RBI	SB	CS	OUT	BA	OBP	SLG	EQA	EQR	DEFENSE	
1998	Atlanta	NL	270	81	17	2	11	16	45	46	44	10	5	194	.300	.346	.500	.276	39	76-OF	1
1999	Atlanta	NL	425	114	22	1	17	27	63	70	63	14	10	321	.268	.321	.445	.251	50	100-LF	-1
2000	TampaBay	AL	628	171	28	2	22	27	94	82	84	12	14	471	.272	.306	.428	.238	65	138-CF	0
2001	TampaBay	AL	480	119	20	1	16	32	78	55	62	9	7	368	.248	.295	.394	.228	46		

Small fish, big pond? Big fish, small pond? Last winter, Gerald Williams had to make a decision that many of us have to make in our lives, and he chose the latter. He gained a starting job and made some more money but after Mothers' Day didn't get to play in a single important game. He's overmatched as a regular, an asset as a fourth outfielder, and unwelcome in the Martinez household.

Randy Winn — OF — Bats B — Age 27

YEAR	TEAM	LGE	AB	H	DB	TP	HR	BB	SO	R	RBI	SB	CS	OUT	BA	OBP	SLG	EQA	EQR	DEFENSE	
1998	Durham	Int	123	32	5	1	1	12	24	20	13	6	3	94	.260	.326	.341	.230	12	27-CF	-3
1998	TampaBay	AL	337	96	10	9	1	29	61	49	17	21	11	252	.285	.343	.377	.246	38	85-CF	1
1999	TampaBay	AL	302	81	16	4	2	14	57	42	23	8	9	230	.268	.303	.368	.219	26	77-CF	1
1999	Durham	Int	206	64	19	2	2	12	27	30	23	5	4	146	.311	.351	.451	.264	26	46-CF	1
2000	Durham	Int	307	90	22	3	6	39	56	55	33	12	4	221	.293	.377	.443	.279	45	76-LF	-1
2000	TampaBay	AL	157	39	2	0	2	24	23	25	16	6	8	126	.248	.355	.299	.224	15	43-LF	1
2001	TampaBay	AL	412	113	25	4	6	48	76	71	54	16	12	311	.274	.350	.398	.253	50		

Maybe the Devil Rays know something the rest of the planet doesn't. Maybe they got a tip from aliens who told them that the entire game of baseball is going to change in a way that tremendously increases the value of fast outfielders who can't hit. Maybe Chuck LaMar really is a visionary executive, a Branch Rickey for the 2000s.

Maybe I shouldn't skip my medication.

PITCHERS (ERA: 4.50, H/9: 9.00, HR/9: 1.00, BB/9: 3.00, K/9: 6.00, KW: 1.00, PERA: 4.50)

Wilson Alvarez — Throws L — Age 31

YEAR	TEAM	LGE	IP	H	ER	HR	BB	K	ERA	W	L	H/9	HR/9	BB/9	K/9	KW	PERA
1998	TampaBay	AL	140.7	122	68	16	58	99	4.35	7	9	7.81	1.02	3.71	6.33	0.85	4.12
1999	TampaBay	AL	159.7	149	77	18	63	122	4.34	8	10	8.40	1.01	3.55	6.88	0.97	4.39

Note the lack of a 2000 line. Wilson Alvarez missed the season, at a cost of about $8 million, with a torn rotator cuff. When healthy, he's an effective above-average pitcher; he's just not healthy much anymore. The Devil Rays are counting on a return, but rotator-cuff injuries are about the worst thing that can happen to a pitcher.

Cedrick Bowers — Throws L — Age 23

YEAR	TEAM	LGE	IP	H	ER	HR	BB	K	ERA	W	L	H/9	HR/9	BB/9	K/9	KW	PERA
1998	St Pete	Fla	133.3	152	117	30	102	92	7.90	3	12	10.26	2.03	6.89	6.21	0.45	7.94
1999	Orlando	Sou	114.3	133	112	28	81	87	8.82	2	11	10.47	2.20	6.38	6.85	0.54	8.03
2000	Orlando	Sou	97.0	93	59	15	46	55	5.47	4	7	8.63	1.39	4.27	5.10	0.60	5.21
2000	Durham	Int	18.7	21	14	3	13	15	6.75	1	1	10.13	1.45	6.27	7.23	0.58	6.98

This stealth prospect is a 1996 draftee out of Florida. Cedrick Bowers is still fighting his control, but he's moved through the system fairly steadily, save for a dreadful first half at Orlando in 1999. Because he throws hard and doesn't have a broad repertoire, the assumption is that he'll make the majors as a reliever. He's made it all the way to Triple-A without suffering an injury, and that's half the battle.

Jesus Colome — Throws R — Age 22

YEAR	TEAM	LGE	IP	H	ER	HR	BB	K	ERA	W	L	H/9	HR/9	BB/9	K/9	KW	PERA
1999	Modesto	Cal	120.3	121	66	11	69	69	4.94	5	8	9.05	0.82	5.16	5.16	0.50	5.24
2000	Midland	Tex	104.0	99	64	13	48	59	5.54	4	8	8.57	1.13	4.15	5.11	0.61	4.85
2000	Orlando	Sou	13.3	19	15	4	7	5	10.13	0	1	12.83	2.70	4.73	3.38	0.36	9.25

Jesus Colome, picked up from the A's for Jim Mecir, throws hard. Ricky Vaughn hard. He's started for most of his career, but there is a great temptation to make him a closer, as he possesses a great fastball and slider, but lacks a good change of pace. He's going to be in the majors by September.

Doug Creek — Throws L — Age 32

YEAR	TEAM	LGE	IP	H	ER	HR	BB	K	ERA	W	L	H/9	HR/9	BB/9	K/9	KW	PERA
1999	Iowa	PCL	120.0	115	78	26	74	88	5.85	4	9	8.63	1.95	5.55	6.60	0.59	6.34
2000	Durham	Int	17.0	11	6	1	15	16	3.18	1	1	5.82	0.53	7.94	8.47	0.53	4.22
2000	TampaBay	AL	61.7	47	27	8	30	70	3.94	4	3	6.86	1.17	4.38	10.22	1.17	4.00

Why do we even bother talking about pitchers in this book? Going into May 2000, Doug Creek was a 31-year-old journeyman with a 6.30 ERA in 74 scattered major-league innings. He started out well at Durham, so the D-Rays called him up, and he spent the rest of the season mowing down left-handed batters. They hit .170/.303/.250 against his junk. Has anybody seen Ricky Horton lately?

Dave Eiland — Throws R — Age 34

YEAR	TEAM	LGE	IP	H	ER	HR	BB	K	ERA	W	L	H/9	HR/9	BB/9	K/9	KW	PERA
1998	Durham	Int	163.0	171	71	16	28	76	3.92	9	9	9.44	0.88	1.55	4.20	1.36	4.05
1999	Durham	Int	55.7	59	26	8	9	31	4.20	3	3	9.54	1.29	1.46	5.01	1.72	4.47
1999	TampaBay	AL	79.7	91	51	7	21	50	5.76	3	6	10.28	0.79	2.37	5.65	1.19	4.77
2000	Durham	Int	22.0	30	13	3	3	7	5.32	1	1	12.27	1.23	1.23	2.86	1.17	5.92
2000	TampaBay	AL	54.7	71	38	6	14	16	6.26	2	4	11.69	0.99	2.30	2.63	0.57	5.81

A Yankees fan in the late 1980s, I feel a little silly now when I remember how much my friends and I wanted Dave Eiland promoted and given a rotation job. Eiland and Steve Adkins and Scott Shields and Chuck Cary—they were all products of the Yankee system, and those of us watching Dave LaPoint and Andy Hawkins were convinced that if the team would just use their young guys, they'd win. Well, most of them never amounted to anything. Eiland, who's had the longest career, owns a 12–27 record with a 5.74 ERA. Still, whenever he pitches, I root for him. Fandom is a strange, strange thing.

American League

Trevor Enders — Throws L — Age 26

YEAR	TEAM	LGE	IP	H	ER	HR	BB	K	ERA	W	L	H/9	HR/9	BB/9	K/9	KW	PERA
1998	St Pete	Fla	62.3	52	29	9	21	33	4.19	3	4	7.51	1.30	3.03	4.76	0.79	3.97
1999	Orlando	Sou	88.7	84	40	7	38	37	4.06	5	5	8.53	0.71	3.86	3.76	0.49	4.28
2000	Orlando	Sou	60.3	69	37	14	13	22	5.52	2	5	10.29	2.09	1.94	3.28	0.85	5.99
2000	Durham	Int	25.0	22	9	4	6	11	3.24	2	1	7.92	1.44	2.16	3.96	0.92	3.98

Snapshot: Trevor Enders, age 15, watches a 31-year-old Tony Fossas post a 3.54 ERA for the Brewers in 1989 and immediately knows what he wants to do when he grows up. Now 26 and five years ahead of Fossas and Doug Creek, Enders begins the long, slow march through cities big and small in search of the magical label, "lefty specialist."

Neal Frendling — Throws R — Age 21

YEAR	TEAM	LGE	IP	H	ER	HR	BB	K	ERA	W	L	H/9	HR/9	BB/9	K/9	KW	PERA
1999	Princetn	App	16.7	17	9	2	7	7	4.86	1	1	9.18	1.08	3.78	3.78	0.50	5.07
1999	HudsnVal	NYP	44.7	43	27	5	13	22	5.44	2	3	8.66	1.01	2.62	4.43	0.85	4.15
2000	Charl-SC	SAL	139.3	157	109	32	59	82	7.04	4	11	10.14	2.07	3.81	5.30	0.69	6.64

With a draft that runs 50 rounds (and that used to go until the only players left were Little Leaguers and guys in the Science Club) baseball doesn't leave a lot of room for domestic free agents to make a mark. Neal Frendling, signed in 1999 out of a Chicago suburb, now has two years of good pitching on his résumé and is edging towards prospect status. He throws three pitches for strikes, including a fastball that breaks 90 mph. After all the money the D-Rays spent on Matt White and Bobby Seay, Frendling is closer to a career than either of them.

Juan Guzman — Throws R — Age 34

YEAR	TEAM	LGE	IP	H	ER	HR	BB	K	ERA	W	L	H/9	HR/9	BB/9	K/9	KW	PERA
1998	Toronto	AL	143.0	125	72	17	55	104	4.53	7	9	7.87	1.07	3.46	6.55	0.95	4.10
1998	Baltimor	AL	65.0	57	31	4	29	51	4.29	3	4	7.89	0.55	4.02	7.06	0.88	3.83
1999	Baltimor	AL	122.0	116	54	16	53	90	3.98	7	7	8.56	1.18	3.91	6.64	0.85	4.80
1999	Cincnnti	NL	75.0	67	30	9	17	50	3.60	4	4	8.04	1.08	2.04	6.00	1.47	3.65

The other half of the D-Rays' $13 million folly, Juan Guzman's season lasted 14 batters before he succumbed to a shoulder injury. And he had the *good* year between him and Wilson Alvarez. Like Alvarez, Guzman underwent surgery, and the team is hoping to get more for their money in 2001.

Travis Harper — Throws R — Age 25

YEAR	TEAM	LGE	IP	H	ER	HR	BB	K	ERA	W	L	H/9	HR/9	BB/9	K/9	KW	PERA
1998	HudsnVal	NYP	49.3	46	21	6	27	35	3.83	3	2	8.39	1.09	4.93	6.39	0.65	5.02
1999	St Pete	Fla	73.3	85	46	10	31	44	5.65	3	5	10.43	1.23	3.80	5.40	0.71	5.92
1999	Orlando	Sou	66.0	77	55	16	28	42	7.50	2	5	10.50	2.18	3.82	5.73	0.75	6.97
2000	Orlando	Sou	47.3	50	21	2	13	18	3.99	3	2	9.51	0.38	2.47	3.42	0.69	3.96
2000	Durham	Int	97.3	97	59	20	26	36	5.46	4	7	8.97	1.85	2.40	3.33	0.69	5.13
2000	TampaBay	AL	32.0	28	14	4	12	13	3.94	2	2	7.88	1.13	3.38	3.66	0.54	4.17

They're so certain he's a prospect that they jumped him from Double-A to the majors in one season. It's basically impossible for any pitcher, even one with lots of other positives, to survive with strikeout rates like the ones Travis Harper has posted. He has good control and a history of success, but there's just no way he can be anything more than staff filler, and even that may be a stretch. Talk him up and let someone else have him, rotoheads.

Roberto Hernandez — Throws R — Age 36

YEAR	TEAM	LGE	IP	H	ER	HR	BB	K	ERA	W	L	H/9	HR/9	BB/9	K/9	KW	PERA
1998	TampaBay	AL	70.3	52	28	4	35	51	3.58	4	4	6.65	0.51	4.48	6.53	0.73	3.29
1999	TampaBay	AL	73.0	64	23	1	26	66	2.84	5	3	7.89	0.12	3.21	8.14	1.27	3.11
2000	TampaBay	AL	73.0	70	27	7	18	58	3.33	5	3	8.63	0.86	2.22	7.15	1.61	3.83

(Roberto Hernandez *continued*)

With some decent live arms coming through the system and no hope of contending in 2001, the Devil Rays did well to convert Roberto Hernandez into Ben Grieve. Hernandez is a consistent relief pitcher with a sprinkle of the "closer" fairy dust and no visible scars or contusions. He'll be worth a lot in July when the Royals are 41–46 and looking to purge payroll.

Joe Kennedy — Throws L — Age 22

YEAR	TEAM	LGE	IP	H	ER	HR	BB	K	ERA	W	L	H/9	HR/9	BB/9	K/9	KW	PERA
1998	Princetn	App	61.0	65	43	12	36	19	6.34	2	5	9.59	1.77	5.31	2.80	0.26	6.62
1999	HudsnVal	NYP	86.3	84	39	5	34	45	4.07	5	5	8.76	0.52	3.54	4.69	0.66	4.09
2000	Charl-SC	SAL	124.0	132	76	15	37	67	5.52	5	9	9.58	1.09	2.69	4.86	0.91	4.80

Another left-hander returns from the dead, decades after making his mark as the patriarch of one of America's great political dynasties and the father of a popular presid...oh...not that Joe Kennedy? Sorry. After Doug Creek, I just figured...never mind. This Joe Kennedy is a control-freak left-hander who carved up the Sally League. After hyping the Marlins' Scott Comer in last year's book, we're a little leery of command pitchers who do well in A ball. Kennedy throws three pitches, including a fastball that gets into the low 90s. Check back after Double-A.

Cory Lidle — Throws R — Age 29

YEAR	TEAM	LGE	IP	H	ER	HR	BB	K	ERA	W	L	H/9	HR/9	BB/9	K/9	KW	PERA
2000	Durham	Int	47.0	52	16	4	9	31	3.06	3	2	9.96	0.77	1.72	5.94	1.72	4.29
2000	TampaBay	AL	96.3	105	50	10	22	59	4.67	5	6	9.81	0.93	2.06	5.51	1.34	4.52

Cory Lidle looked like a nasty power/ground-ball pitcher in his rookie season with the Mets in 1997. His elbow had other ideas, and Lidle missed the next two seasons having, and rehabbing from, surgery. He's still a strong ground-ball pitcher, and his second half was highly encouraging. The team needs to pick a role for him and stick with it; high-leverage, multiple-inning outings seem like they will fit him best. He was traded to Oakland in the Grieve deal, and is expected to compete for the A's fifth-starter job.

Albie Lopez — Throws R — Age 29

YEAR	TEAM	LGE	IP	H	ER	HR	BB	K	ERA	W	L	H/9	HR/9	BB/9	K/9	KW	PERA
1998	TampaBay	AL	78.3	68	27	6	27	57	3.10	6	3	7.81	0.69	3.10	6.55	1.06	3.55
1999	TampaBay	AL	63.3	61	34	7	19	35	4.83	3	4	8.67	0.99	2.70	4.97	0.92	4.18
2000	TampaBay	AL	184.3	183	78	19	54	92	3.81	10	10	8.93	0.93	2.64	4.49	0.85	4.24

Six years after he was supposed to be the Indians' ace, Albie Lopez emerged as one of the best pitchers in the American League. Kudos to the Devil Rays for expanding his role after he'd been an effective reliever for them since their inception. Despite Lopez's effectiveness, his strikeout rate was marginal, partly because he tired badly in September; this was his first season above 100 innings since 1996. He should be a reliable mid-rotation starter if not as good as he was last year.

Travis Phelps — Throws R — Age 23

YEAR	TEAM	LGE	IP	H	ER	HR	BB	K	ERA	W	L	H/9	HR/9	BB/9	K/9	KW	PERA
1998	Charl-SC	SAL	82.0	102	61	8	47	45	6.70	2	7	11.20	0.88	5.16	4.94	0.48	6.56
1999	St Pete	Fla	123.3	146	78	14	49	61	5.69	5	9	10.65	1.02	3.58	4.45	0.62	5.74
2000	Orlando	Sou	98.7	93	55	9	48	63	5.02	4	7	8.48	0.82	4.38	5.75	0.66	4.57
2000	Durham	Int	28.0	30	19	8	16	16	6.11	1	2	9.64	2.57	5.14	5.14	0.50	7.47

He is a non-prospect who, like Frendling, signed with the Devil Rays as a non-drafted free agent. Hey, someone has to pitch for the low affiliates of an expansion team. Travis Phelps's primary function is to confuse those people trying to keep the Devil Rays' Travises and Trevors straight.

American League

Bryan Rekar — Throws R — Age 29

YEAR	TEAM	LGE	IP	H	ER	HR	BB	K	ERA	W	L	H/9	HR/9	BB/9	K/9	KW	PERA
1998	TampaBay	AL	85.0	88	49	14	18	51	5.19	3	6	9.32	1.48	1.91	5.40	1.42	4.75
1999	Durham	Int	33.0	28	15	4	8	18	4.09	2	2	7.64	1.09	2.18	4.91	1.13	3.47
1999	TampaBay	AL	94.7	112	58	12	33	52	5.51	4	7	10.65	1.14	3.14	4.94	0.79	5.68
2000	Durham	Int	20.7	16	5	1	4	13	2.18	2	0	6.97	0.44	1.74	5.66	1.63	2.40
2000	TampaBay	AL	171.3	183	77	18	30	91	4.04	9	10	9.61	0.95	1.58	4.78	1.52	4.22

While the Devil Rays have shown no signs of developing hitters or an offense, they've done a pretty good job of building pitching staffs using free talent. Take Bryan Rekar. They diddled around with him at the start of the season, but once they dropped him into the rotation in May, he pitched well. Like Lopez, his peripherals are less-than-outstanding, but the price is right. Let's just say that these two guys won't be outpitched by the Mets' $18 million duo of Kevin Appier and Rick Reed.

Ryan Rupe — Throws R — Age 26

YEAR	TEAM	LGE	IP	H	ER	HR	BB	K	ERA	W	L	H/9	HR/9	BB/9	K/9	KW	PERA
1998	Charl-SC	SAL	50.7	38	28	7	13	27	4.97	2	4	6.75	1.24	2.31	4.80	1.04	3.20
1999	Orlando	Sou	24.3	18	15	2	7	13	5.55	1	2	6.66	0.74	2.59	4.81	0.93	2.79
1999	TampaBay	AL	141.0	126	68	14	45	92	4.34	7	9	8.04	0.89	2.87	5.87	1.02	3.79
2000	TampaBay	AL	91.3	111	61	15	24	58	6.01	3	7	10.94	1.48	2.36	5.72	1.21	5.89
2000	Durham	Int	18.0	24	17	4	7	13	8.50	0	2	12.00	2.00	3.50	6.50	0.93	7.49

He was a bit more wild and homer-prone last year, but the big difference between Ryan Rupe's rookie and sophomore seasons was in the number of hits he allowed. That may not be such a big deal; statheads are doing studies that question the extent to which hit allowed are a function of a pitcher's performance vs. defense and luck. Ryan Rupe pitched better following a brief trip to Durham. We liked him a year ago, we like him now.

Tony Saunders — Throws L — Age 27

YEAR	TEAM	LGE	IP	H	ER	HR	BB	K	ERA	W	L	H/9	HR/9	BB/9	K/9	KW	PERA
1998	TampaBay	AL	191.0	182	84	13	95	159	3.96	11	10	8.58	0.61	4.48	7.49	0.84	4.46
1999	TampaBay	AL	42.7	50	33	5	23	29	6.96	1	4	10.55	1.05	4.85	6.12	0.63	6.25

If you hadn't heard, Tony Saunders re-broke his left humerus during his comeback, then retired and took a front-office position with the Devil Rays. The track records of the four pitchers who have had this horrible injury indicate that it is career-ending: a couple were able to make a handful of post-injury appearances, but both suffered the same injury during their comebacks.

Saunders handled himself admirably throughout his rehabilitation, his comeback, and in the wake of last August's re-injury. Here's hoping he has a lot of success in his new career, and that he's able to play catch with his kids anytime they ask.

Bobby Seay — Throws L — Age 23

YEAR	TEAM	LGE	IP	H	ER	HR	BB	K	ERA	W	L	H/9	HR/9	BB/9	K/9	KW	PERA
1998	Charl-SC	SAL	59.7	67	58	20	39	35	8.75	1	6	10.11	3.02	5.88	5.28	0.45	8.48
1999	St Pete	Fla	52.3	55	28	2	29	27	4.82	2	4	9.46	0.34	4.99	4.64	0.47	4.91
1999	Orlando	Sou	15.7	22	16	3	16	10	9.19	0	2	12.64	1.72	9.19	5.74	0.31	9.96
2000	Orlando	Sou	120.0	142	81	24	56	63	6.07	4	9	10.65	1.80	4.20	4.72	0.56	6.81

For the first time since signing his draft-loophole deal with the Devil Rays, Bobby Seay had a season that produced more hope than frustration. He stayed healthy and was reasonably effective for Orlando, then went to Australia and was a part of the gold-medal-winning Team USA. The organization has a huge investment in him, so he needs only a few good months at Triple-A to reach the majors.

Jason Standridge — Throws R — Age 22

YEAR	TEAM	LGE	IP	H	ER	HR	BB	K	ERA	W	L	H/9	HR/9	BB/9	K/9	KW	PERA
1998	Princetn	App	57.7	78	62	9	39	20	9.68	1	5	12.17	1.40	6.09	3.12	0.26	8.08
1999	Charl-SC	SAL	105.7	82	42	10	42	39	3.58	7	5	6.98	0.85	3.58	3.32	0.46	3.44
1999	St Pete	Fla	44.3	46	22	2	25	16	4.47	2	3	9.34	0.41	5.08	3.25	0.32	4.91
2000	St Pete	Fla	49.7	47	38	10	38	24	6.89	2	4	8.52	1.81	6.89	4.35	0.32	6.67
2000	Orlando	Sou	89.3	86	51	7	45	33	5.14	4	6	8.66	0.71	4.53	3.32	0.37	4.61

(Jason Standridge *continued*)

If you've made it this far into the Devil Rays' chapter, here's your reward: a conventional, pedigreed, live-armed pitching prospect. Jason Standridge, the D-Rays' #1 pick in the 1997 draft, gets into the mid 90s with his fastball and mixes in a nice curve. Command is a problem, so don't look for him to make a contribution in the majors for another year or so. Standridge was recruited to play quarterback by Auburn. I'm not so sure I wouldn't take the Devil Rays over the Arizona Cardinals.

Tanyon Sturtze — Throws R — Age 30

YEAR	TEAM	LGE	IP	H	ER	HR	BB	K	ERA	W	L	H/9	HR/9	BB/9	K/9	KW	PERA
1998	Oklahoma	PCL	32.7	32	15	4	21	20	4.13	2	2	8.82	1.10	5.79	5.51	0.48	5.69
1999	Charlott	Int	99.0	84	53	7	40	73	4.82	4	7	7.64	0.64	3.64	6.64	0.91	3.61
2000	ChiSox	AL	16.3	24	19	3	12	6	10.47	0	2	13.22	1.65	6.61	3.31	0.25	9.25
2000	TampaBay	AL	52.0	43	13	3	11	36	2.25	5	1	7.44	0.52	1.90	6.23	1.64	2.77

Brought over from the White Sox in exchange for Tony Graffanino, Tanyon Sturtze pitched wonderfully for the Devil Rays out of the bullpen, then even better in a late-season audition in the rotation: a 2.76 ERA in six starts with a strikeout-to-walk ratio of 24 to 7. He's not that good but could join Lopez and Rekar to provide a cheap, effective rotation core while the team waits out the injuries to the Six-Million-Dollar Men.

Dan Wheeler — Throws R — Age 23

YEAR	TEAM	LGE	IP	H	ER	HR	BB	K	ERA	W	L	H/9	HR/9	BB/9	K/9	KW	PERA
1998	Charl-SC	SAL	166.3	210	110	32	39	63	5.95	6	12	11.36	1.73	2.11	3.41	0.81	6.30
1999	Orlando	Sou	54.0	59	34	11	9	34	5.67	2	4	9.83	1.83	1.50	5.67	1.89	5.28
1999	Durham	Int	79.0	99	56	18	24	43	6.38	3	6	11.28	2.05	2.73	4.90	0.90	6.84
1999	TampaBay	AL	30.7	33	17	6	10	30	4.99	1	2	9.68	1.76	2.93	8.80	1.50	5.67
2000	TampaBay	AL	23.0	27	12	2	8	16	4.70	1	2	10.57	0.78	3.13	6.26	1.00	5.20
2000	Durham	Int	141.3	183	119	45	42	70	7.58	3	13	11.65	2.87	2.67	4.46	0.83	7.91

After jumping from Double-A to the majors in 1999, Dan Wheeler was expected to be a big part of the 2000 Devil Rays. That plan didn't survive April, as he joined Ryan Rupe in getting battered and demoted. He doesn't have Rupe's stuff or upside and surrendered 35 bombs in 150⅓ innings at Durham last year, so the near-term outlook isn't so great. He should have been given the uniform number 18?

Matt White — Throws R — Age 22

YEAR	TEAM	LGE	IP	H	ER	HR	BB	K	ERA	W	L	H/9	HR/9	BB/9	K/9	KW	PERA
1998	St Pete	Fla	86.7	108	85	21	52	38	8.83	2	8	11.22	2.18	5.40	3.95	0.37	8.06
1999	St Pete	Fla	104.0	125	86	14	41	55	7.44	3	9	10.82	1.21	3.55	4.76	0.67	6.03
2000	Orlando	Sou	109.0	103	74	19	61	59	6.11	4	8	8.50	1.57	5.04	4.87	0.48	5.65
2000	Durham	Int	33.3	35	14	1	16	21	3.78	2	2	9.45	0.27	4.32	5.67	0.66	4.54

Like Seay, with whom he'll forever be linked, Matt White had his best year as a professional. His peripherals are still unimpressive, especially for someone with his fastball, but the Devil Rays are happier with him now than at any point since they wrote the big check. White has more ability than just about every other pitcher in this chapter, so he could force his way into a major-league role as soon as this spring.

Contrast the careers of Seay and White with some of the other guys in this chapter—Frendling, Lopez, Rekar—and you begin to understand why we often say there's no such thing as a pitching prospect. The career paths of pitchers are difficult, perhaps impossible, to forecast with any accuracy.

The Devil Rays, and specifically high-cost pitchers Seay and White, also serve to illustrate another player-development point: making a significant investment in high-school pitchers is a questionable practice.

Paul Wilson Throws R Age 28

YEAR	TEAM	LGE	IP	H	ER	HR	BB	K	ERA	W	L	H/9	HR/9	BB/9	K/9	KW	PERA
1998	St Lucie	Fla	16.7	24	16	4	6	8	8.64	0	2	12.96	2.16	3.24	4.32	0.67	8.22
1998	Norfolk	Int	36.7	41	19	2	9	20	4.66	2	2	10.06	0.49	2.21	4.91	1.11	4.26
2000	St Lucie	Fla	24.0	22	9	0	6	10	3.38	2	1	8.25	0.00	2.25	3.75	0.83	2.88
2000	Norfolk	Int	78.0	84	43	9	26	40	4.96	4	5	9.69	1.04	3.00	4.62	0.77	4.95
2000	TampaBay	AL	50.3	35	17	1	12	38	3.04	4	2	6.26	0.18	2.15	6.79	1.58	2.01

He finally had his elbow rebuilt in the spring of 1999, sat out a year, and you see the results above. Paul Wilson is going to be a major national story by midseason, when Joe Torre names him to the AL All-Star team. It wasn't just his good performance after being traded at the July deadline. It was his effectiveness at every point during his comeback last year. It was the way in which he walked over the AL in August and September, allowing only one home run in 51 innings.

The best part is that now he owns a rebuilt elbow and has basically no mileage on his shoulder. He's entering what should be his prime without any concern about his workload history.

Esteban Yan Throws R Age 27

YEAR	TEAM	LGE	IP	H	ER	HR	BB	K	ERA	W	L	H/9	HR/9	BB/9	K/9	KW	PERA
1998	TampaBay	AL	87.3	73	36	10	35	71	3.71	5	5	7.52	1.03	3.61	7.32	1.01	3.91
1999	TampaBay	AL	61.3	72	35	7	25	44	5.14	3	4	10.57	1.03	3.67	6.46	0.88	5.72
2000	TampaBay	AL	137.3	145	80	21	32	106	5.24	6	9	9.50	1.38	2.10	6.95	1.66	4.81

Somewhere along the line, the Devil Rays have to realize that Esteban Yan isn't a starting pitcher and that they're ruining a good reliever by trying to make him start. His only successful major-league season was the one in which he relieved exclusively. His career ERA as a starter is two runs higher than it is out of the pen, and he's barely been able to go five innings per start. Returned to the pen, he can be a good setup man.

Support-Neutral Statistics — TAMPA BAY DEVIL RAYS — Park Effect: +1.4%

PITCHER	GS	IP	R	SNW	SNL	SNPCT	W	L	RA	APW	SNVA	SNWAR
Dave Eiland	10	40.3	33	2.1	3.6	.373	1	3	7.36	-0.9	-0.7	-0.3
Dwight Gooden	8	36.7	32	1.7	3.7	.318	2	3	7.85	-1.0	-1.0	-0.6
Juan Guzman	1	1.7	8	0.0	0.9	.000	0	1	43.20	-0.6	-0.4	-0.4
Travis Harper	5	28.7	15	2.0	1.5	.565	1	1	4.71	0.2	0.2	0.5
Cory Lidle	11	56.7	41	3.2	4.4	.426	4	4	6.51	-0.7	-0.6	0.0
Albie Lopez	24	157.7	77	10.2	7.3	.584	9	9	4.40	1.5	1.3	2.8
Bryan Rekar	27	165.7	90	9.7	8.6	.531	6	10	4.89	0.7	0.6	1.9
Ryan Rupe	18	91.0	75	4.0	8.0	.333	5	6	7.42	-2.0	-2.1	-1.1
Tanyon Sturtze	5	27.7	8	2.4	0.7	.776	3	0	2.60	0.8	0.8	1.1
Steve Trachsel	23	137.7	76	8.5	8.3	.507	6	10	4.97	0.5	0.1	1.4
Dan Wheeler	2	9.7	10	0.3	1.1	.235	0	1	9.31	-0.4	-0.4	-0.3
Paul Wilson	7	41.0	16	3.5	1.5	.701	1	2	3.51	0.8	0.9	1.4
Esteban Yan	20	107.7	82	4.9	9.2	.348	5	7	6.85	-1.7	-2.0	-1.1
TOTALS	161	902.0	563	52.5	58.6	.473	43	57	5.62	-2.9	-3.2	5.3

It was the best of times and the worst of times for the 2000 Devil Rays starters. Through the end of June, Tampa Bay had by far the worst starting rotation in the majors, costing the team 5.6 wins below average according to Support-Neutral Value Added (SNVA). After June, the D-Rays had the 11th-best rotation in the majors with a 2.4 SNVA. That eight-win improvement represents the biggest midseason turnaround since that of the 1990 Houston Astros, who were also eight wins better in the second half than in the first.

That's mixed news for the Devil Rays. On one hand, several of their second-half standouts figure in the team's immediate plans: Albie Lopez was the 24th-best starter in the majors in the second half with a 8.2–5.4 SN record, former Mets wunderkind Paul Wilson had a terrific seven starts at the tail end of the season, and even Ryan Rupe stunk far less in the second half than he did in the first. On the other hand, a great second-half turnaround does not necessarily predict success for the rotation the next year. In fact, of the 50 best second-half rotation turnarounds of the past 20 years, the rotation's performance in the first half was a better predictor of what they'd do the following year than was their performance in the second half.

For a quick explanation of SN stats, see page 7.

Reliever Evaluation Tools

PITCHER	G	IP	R	ARA	APR	IRNR/G	EIRS/G	IRP	BRS	RRA	ARP
Doug Creek	45	60.7	33	4.80	2.7	0.73	0.29	-0.8	0.8	5.04	1.1
Mike Duvall	2	2.3	2	7.56	-0.6	0.50	0.07	-0.8	0.4	12.24	-1.8
Dave Eiland	7	14.3	13	8.00	-4.5	0.86	0.35	-1.6	0.8	9.45	-6.8
Trevor Enders	9	9.3	13	12.28	-7.4	0.44	0.19	-1.3	0.4	13.97	-9.1
Tony Fiore	11	15.0	16	9.41	-7.0	0.64	0.24	0.8	-1.1	8.27	-5.1
Mark Guthrie	34	32.0	18	4.96	0.8	0.65	0.25	-0.4	0.6	5.32	-0.4
Travis Harper	1	3.3	2	5.29	-0.0	0.00	0.00	0.0	0.0	4.85	0.1
Roberto Hernandez	68	73.3	33	3.97	10.0	0.28	0.11	-0.3	1.4	4.27	7.6
Cory Lidle	20	40.0	20	4.41	3.5	0.90	0.36	-0.6	1.0	4.95	1.1
Albie Lopez	21	27.7	18	5.74	-1.7	0.38	0.16	-0.5	1.7	6.33	-3.5
Jim Mecir	38	49.7	17	3.02	12.0	0.55	0.18	4.8	-1.7	2.02	17.5
Jim Morris	16	10.3	9	7.68	-2.9	0.88	0.39	-1.8	-0.4	8.87	-4.2
Bryan Rekar	3	7.7	2	2.30	2.5	0.00	0.00	0.0	0.0	2.40	2.4
Jeff Sparks	15	20.3	8	3.47	3.9	0.47	0.22	0.3	0.9	3.67	3.4
Tanyon Sturtze	14	25.0	8	2.82	6.6	0.43	0.20	-1.2	0.4	3.53	4.6
Billy Taylor	17	13.7	13	8.39	-4.8	0.41	0.10	0.7	-1.4	7.39	-3.3
Dan Wheeler	9	13.3	4	2.65	3.8	0.33	0.17	0.5	0.0	2.50	4.0
Rick White	44	71.3	30	3.71	11.8	0.66	0.22	6.2	-0.1	3.10	16.6
Paul Wilson	4	10.0	4	3.53	1.9	0.25	0.11	0.4	-1.1	1.99	3.6
Esteban Yan	23	30.0	16	4.70	1.6	0.83	0.33	2.7	-0.1	4.04	3.8
TOTALS	401	529.3	279	4.65	32.2	0.56	0.22			4.66	31.6

For a quick guide to RET, see page 10.

Texas Rangers

There have been some swings of luck in Texas. Hollywood Henderson got to play in the NFL for years, make a bunch of money, and retire wealthy. Then he wins the lottery. On the other end of the spectrum are the folks mistakenly on Texas's prolific death row. Just kidding. I'm sure they're all guilty. Really.

Luck-wise, the Texas Rangers fall somewhere between those extremes. The Rangers were supposed to be a factor in the AL West in 2000, able to fight off the Ken Griffey-less Mariners and the not-quite-ready Athletics. At the end of May, the Rangers were 27-25, keeping pace with the division thanks to the incredible offense and defense of Ivan Rodriguez, who had surprisingly improved an already great offensive game.

Not long after, the luck gods came calling, possibly to even the balance sheet for the travesty of Juan Gonzalez's MVP awards in 1996 and 1999. In June, the Rangers went 10-15, despite being in almost every game. Tim Crabtree alone caused more ulcers in Arlington than a Dubya malaprop, losing four games in relief in the span of a month. The Rangers' offense continued to mash the ball, but the pitching and defense kept finding a way to give up critical runs. For the year, Rangers' pitchers allowed opponents to hit .310/.381/.499 in "close and late" situations. Still, by mid-July, despite the bad breaks and the pitching implosion, the Rangers remained in the running with the A's and Mariners.

Then the 16-ton weight hit. On July 23, Ivan Rodriguez broke the metacarpal bone in his right thumb—he was out for the season. Rodriguez is a player of singular importance; only Pedro Martinez is as integral to the structure and performance of his team. Pudge and Rafael Palmeiro are the crux of the Rangers' offense, and Pudge completely anchors the team's defense. After he went down, the Rangers collapsed, following a .500 start with a 9-21 August. The offense, which had kept the team afloat for the bulk of the season, finally came back to earth, with Royce Clayton (.209/.273/.242), Luis Alicea (.234/.281/.308), Frank Catalanotto (.257/.290/.386), and Mike Lamb (.226/.287/.333) leading the plummet. Oakland and Seattle disappeared on the horizon, and the 2000 season became pretty much a complete loss.

OK, not a *complete loss*. The highlight of the Rangers' 2000 season had actually occurred in late 1999, when they traded one of baseball's most overrated players, Juan Gonzalez, to Randy Smith's Tigers for a package of talented youth. By adding Catalanotto, Gabe Kapler, Francisco Cordero, and Alan Webb, the Rangers imported a bunch of relatively young talent, including a couple of guys who have a chance, albeit slight, to be superstars. The nominal core of the deal, Justin Thompson, predictably went down with another arm injury and is probably finished as a quality starting pitcher. Still, the Rangers shed themselves of serious salary liability and picked up guys who are already contributing and who, unlike Gonzalez, have some upside. Fans should make sure to send thank-you notes to Randy Smith, because that kind of generosity in a general manager is a pretty rare thing.

The swap meet continued into 2000. The Rangers made 126,411 trades during the season, keeping their turnover comparable to that of the marketing department at a CMGi startup. The net effect is that Ricky Ledee and Mike Young are on board, pretty much at no cost (Esteban Loaiza and David Segui).

The Ballpark in Arlington is a pretty severe hitters' park, so it's hard to come down too brutally on the Ranger pitching staff, right? Wrong. The Ranger pitching staff wasn't as bad as John Cerutti on an iron lung, but it was comparable. The Ranger rotation had ERAs that looked like a Boeing inventory list. Rick Helling and Kenny Rogers were healthy and pitched effectively all year, but everyone else who took the mound in Arlington was treated like Ralph Nader at an Al Gore family dinner. Matt Perisho, Darren Oliver, Ryan Glynn, and Doug Davis were dreadful, and Esteban Loaiza was pretty much average before he was moved north of the border. The pitching staff was 42-39 at home with an ERA of 5.26—pretty generic

Rangers Prospectus

2000 record: 71-91; Fourth place, AL West
Pythagenport W/L: 70-92
Runs Scored: 848 (9th in AL)
Runs Allowed: 974 (14th in AL)
Team EqA: .255 (10th in AL)
2000 Batters' Age: 29.6 (6th oldest in AL)
2000 Pitchers' Age: 28.3 (4th youngest in AL)
Ballpark: The Ballpark in Arlington; good hitters' park; Park Factor of 1.062
2000: The offense finally let down the pitching, which went from average to bad.
2001: They could win 75 or 95 depending on the health of a half-dozen guys. The shortstop will be pretty good.

459

considering league offense and ballpark. On the road, they were just south of dismal, allowing a 5.79 ERA and a nifty 29–52 record. This club needs some pitching, to say the least.

Reid Nichols has done an excellent job of rebuilding the Texas farm system over the last couple of years. There's really only one true blue-chip prospect in the system, Kevin Mench, but there are a number of players who have a good chance to be serious contributors. Under the direction of Melvin and Reid Nichols, the Rangers have stockpiled, developed, and flat-out stolen some very good young talent. Jason Romano, Jovanny Cedeno, Mike Young, Hank Blalock, Carlos Pena, Travis Hafner, Spike Lundberg, and Joaquin Benoit all have a shot at pretty decent major-league careers. There are no Rick Ankiels, Alex Rodriguezes, or Andruw Joneses here, but there could be a couple of Rusty Greers. (Instead of devoting more space to Texas minor-league prospects, I'll point you to a tremendous web resource—www.newbergreport.com. Jamey Newberg covers the Rangers' system better than anyone covers any minor-league system.)

The broad development of the Texas organization provides a stark contrast to a system like that of the St. Louis Cardinals. The Cardinals have a few select blue-chip prospects, and the development and investment focus is on picking up guys with very little risk. Once in the system, these players get a disproportionate amount of time and attention. The Rangers have taken a different approach, focusing broadly across a large number of players, each with a higher risk of failure. Both clubs have had some success, but there are reasons to be concerned about the Rangers' approach.

It's important for an organization's different divisions to have their goals aligned. If you're going to develop a broad set of minor-league prospects, you need them to get an opportunity to play. However, Johnny Oates does not have a history of being a player-development guy. If he's given the choice of playing a young guy or a really old veteran, look for Gramps to get every benefit of the doubt.

Player development is a wonderful thing. It provides a team with a source of talent that's inexpensive, if not 100% reliable. Problem is, scheduling profitable innovation just isn't possible. So owner Tom Hicks decided to undertake an acquisition strategy. In line with his behavior in the ownership of other clubs, he executed that strategy with gusto.

On December 1, the Ranger regulars for 2001 looked something like Table 1.

On December 11, they looked something like Table 2.

Getting from Point A to Point B cost a couple of A-ball prospects, about $260 million, and a stunning lack of understanding about the concepts of "aging" and "health." Alex Rodriguez, the best free-agent ever, was signed to a 10-year deal worth $252 million. That's a great move for the Rangers, and it fills a legitimate need. I'm less thrilled about the acquisitions of Randy Velarde, Ken Caminiti, and Andres Galarraga,

Table 1: Ranger Regulars December 1, 2001

C	Ivan Rodriguez	SP	Kenny Rogers
1B	Rafael Palmeiro	SP	Rick Helling
2B	Mike Young/Frank Catalanotto	SP	Darren Oliver
3B	Mike Lamb	SP	J. Fred Muggs
SS	Royce Clayton	SP	YOUR NAME HERE!
OF/DH	Rusty Greer		
OF	Ruben Mateo		
OF	Gabe Kapler		
OF	Ricky Ledee		

Table 2: Ranger Regulars December 11, 2001

C	Ivan Rodriguez	SP	Kenny Rogers
1B	Andres Galarraga	SP	Rick Helling
2B	Randy Velarde	SP	Darren Oliver
3B	Ken Caminiti	SP	Maury Povich
SS	Alex Rodriguez	SP	Gallagher
DH	Rafael Palmeiro		
OF	Ruben Mateo		
OF	Rusty Greer		
OF	Ricky Ledee/Gabe Kapler		

none of whom are exactly the picture of youth or health. Galarraga tailed off badly after May last year, not a good sign in a 39-year-old. Caminiti and Velarde have been productive when healthy—and when young. There's a better than even chance that all three of these acquisitions will come back to bite Melvin and Hicks.

Doug Davis, Ryan Glynn, Matt Perisho and a cast of dozens will audition for the #4 and #5 slots in the rotation, and if Justin Thompson can be patched together with baling wire, he'll be thrown back out there. Darren Oliver's touchdown ERA won't be enough to knock him out of the rotation with the contract he signed; you'll have to wait for his annual injury for that to happen. The acquisition of the new infield means that Romano, Clayton, Young, Lamb, and Catalanotto will be shopped around for a bottom-of-the-rotation starter before spring training, probably knocking J. Fred Muggs out of a job.

Even with the addition of the best player in baseball, the Rangers will be hard-pressed to compete in one of baseball's toughest divisions. The A's and Mariners have a lot of young talent, and most of it is significantly better than the talent coming out of the Texas organization. This team has few championship-caliber players, and it needs Ruben Mateo to come back healthy and productive to have a good future nucleus. Long term, the Rangers are in trouble because they're building a similar but inferior team to their top competition in the division, the A's. Everywhere that Texas has some young talent, Oakland has better young talent. Jason Romano and Mike Young? Jose Ortiz. Hank Blalock? Eric Chavez. Jovanny Cedeno and Joaquin Benoit? Tim Hudson and Barry Zito. Texas realistically has to go out and spend money on some quality if they want to keep pace. They must take advantage of their superior revenue stream.

Signing Rodriguez was an attempt to capitalize on this revenue stream. But what really changed? The offense got about five or six wins better, at most. The team's weaknesses—health, aging, and a lack of starting pitching—are unchanged. Maybe a couple of the displaced players can be packaged for a #4 starter, a la Mark Clark or Ken Hill; still, such a move won't materially change how this team is positioned for the future. In all likelihood, five or six wins aren't going to make the difference in 2001. If that's the case, what's the point in acquiring Caminiti, Galarraga, and Velarde? For the money spent on those three, the Rangers could have invested in the future or at least made a more effective run at the present.

This organization is about to face a major test. In the past, the Rangers have wasted time on moves like getting rid of Dean Palmer to acquire Tom Goodwin, or dumping Fernando Tatis to pick up Todd Stottlemyre and Royce Clayton. At this point, the team finally has a core of young talent that can cover most of the field, and Hicks can spend his money on pressing needs like bullpen help. If the team gives opportunities to guys like Mench, Pena, Young, and Romano, lets them develop around the two Rodriguezes, and spends money wisely, the Rangers will contend with the burgeoning powerhouses in the division.

On a positive note, a lot of the Rangers' problems have been the result of injuries. If Mateo and a couple of the second-line prospects can get healthy, this is a team that could contend. Everything will have to break right for that to happen, and Johnny Oates will have to work some magic in terms of maneuvering around the weaknesses of individual players. That will require a lot of tinkering on a daily basis and the judicious use and development of the young players. If the days of acquiring the likes of Tom Goodwin return, this team is in trouble.

The Rangers' organization needs to focus on drafting reasonable prospects and training great major leaguers. So far, what Texas has mostly done is create a context for the inevitable "Small-Market A's Beat Big-Money Rangers" stories in October. That, too, has value, but I don't think it's what Tom Hicks had in mind. The Alex Rodriguez signing was a tremendous move. The additions of Galarraga, Caminiti, and Velarde are indicators that the tremendous move is an aberration, not the norm.

HITTERS (BA: .270, OBP: .340, SLG: .440, EqA: .260)

Luis Alicea — 2B — Bats B — Age 35

YEAR	TEAM	LGE	AB	H	DB	TP	HR	BB	SO	R	RBI	SB	CS	OUT	BA	OBP	SLG	EQA	EQR	DEFENSE			
1998	Texas	AL	256	70	13	3	7	37	36	50	32	3	3	189	.273	.375	.430	.271	36	40-2B	1	20-3B	-3
1999	Texas	AL	162	32	7	0	4	26	29	31	17	2	1	131	.198	.309	.315	.215	14	30-2B	-3		
2000	Texas	AL	531	154	23	8	6	52	68	78	57	1	3	380	.290	.359	.397	.256	63	119-2B	-9		
2001	Texas	AL	355	92	14	3	6	47	51	52	47	2	3	266	.259	.346	.366	.240	37				

Luis Alicea played exceptionally well in the first half of the season, with solid defense and an OBP near .400. Then he collapsed, hitting approximately like Rey Sanchez after the All-Star break. Alicea rebounded in September and was probably auditioning for a position as a utility man at that point. With Catalanotto, Jason Romano, and Mike Young in this organization, he's not going to be coming back to Arlington.

Hank Blalock — 3B — Bats L — Age 20

YEAR	TEAM	LGE	AB	H	DB	TP	HR	BB	SO	R	RBI	SB	CS	OUT	BA	OBP	SLG	EQA	EQR	DEFENSE	
1999	Savannah	SAL	25	5	0	0	1	1	3	2	2	0	0	20	.200	.243	.320	.177	1		
2000	Savannah	SAL	532	131	23	1	9	44	57	47	56	11	5	406	.246	.306	.344	.220	46	133-3B	2
2001	Texas	AL	279	75	8	0	6	25	47	35	36	3	1	205	.269	.329	.362	.232	27		

He's a good-looking defensive third baseman who held his own at Savannah. Hank Blalock is not likely to arrive in Arlington until at least 2002, but he does have a very bright future. He hits hard line drives; now he needs to develop the ability to get lift and carry on the ball. He has plenty of time.

Frank Catalanotto — 2B/1B — Bats L — Age 27

YEAR	TEAM	LGE	AB	H	DB	TP	HR	BB	SO	R	RBI	SB	CS	OUT	BA	OBP	SLG	EQA	EQR	DEFENSE			
1998	Toledo	Int	105	31	7	2	3	12	21	17	22	0	0	74	.295	.394	.486	.294	17	12-1B	2	11-2B	0
1998	Detroit	AL	212	61	11	2	7	12	35	23	25	2	2	153	.288	.337	.458	.261	27	19-2B	-9	14-1B	1
1999	Detroit	AL	284	79	13	0	13	13	45	39	34	3	4	209	.278	.328	.461	.257	35	25-1B	0	18-2B	-1
2000	Texas	AL	277	79	12	2	10	29	33	51	38	6	2	200	.285	.366	.451	.275	40	39-2B	-6	14-1B	-4
2001	Texas	AL	275	79	12	1	10	23	42	41	47	3	2	198	.287	.342	.447	.259	34				

Frank Catalanotto is one of our favorites here at BP, and it's easy to see why. He plays second base acceptably and seems to do nothing at the plate except hit the ball hard. He still struggles a bit against left-handers but posted a .410 OBP against them in 2000. Catalanotto is at an inflection point in his career; he's certainly good enough to play full time but may now have been typecast as a Dave Hansen type. If some organization finds a way to give him 500 plate appearances, they'll be very pleased with the results.

Royce Clayton — SS — Bats R — Age 31

YEAR	TEAM	LGE	AB	H	DB	TP	HR	BB	SO	R	RBI	SB	CS	OUT	BA	OBP	SLG	EQA	EQR	DEFENSE	
1998	St Louis	NL	360	85	18	1	5	38	48	60	30	18	6	281	.236	.312	.333	.225	34	88-SS	6
1998	Texas	AL	184	51	13	1	5	13	29	30	23	4	4	137	.277	.328	.440	.251	22	52-SS	-1
1999	Texas	AL	459	131	20	5	14	35	91	65	48	7	6	334	.285	.341	.442	.259	57	130-SS	-6
2000	Texas	AL	508	120	20	5	14	36	84	65	50	11	8	396	.236	.291	.378	.221	45	141-SS	0
2001	ChiSox	AL	436	109	19	3	12	43	78	64	61	10	6	333	.250	.317	.390	.239	47		

Ugggg. PAX-TV had a better season than Royce Clayton, behind such fine family fare as *Diagnosis Murder* and *Pablum Theatre*. At the end of 1999, Clayton appeared to have turned an offensive corner, posting career highs in OBP and slugging average. As it turns out, the improvement was short-lived, and his season was effectively a total loss. He had identical extra-base-hit numbers in 1999 and 2000 but lost ten singles and made an extra 50 outs. Barring another run-in with the gentleman below, expect a mild comeback in 2001.

Chad Curtis — LF — Bats R — Age 32

YEAR	TEAM	LGE	AB	H	DB	TP	HR	BB	SO	R	RBI	SB	CS	OUT	BA	OBP	SLG	EQA	EQR	DEFENSE	
1998	NY Yanks	AL	456	117	20	1	12	75	71	80	58	18	5	344	.257	.369	.384	.264	61	125-LF	18
1999	NY Yanks	AL	194	52	4	0	6	41	32	36	24	8	4	146	.268	.402	.381	.276	29	56-LF	-3
2000	Texas	AL	330	88	23	1	8	33	65	44	44	3	3	245	.267	.335	.415	.250	38	71-LF	-9
2001	Texas	AL	238	61	8	0	6	39	47	42	32	6	2	179	.256	.361	.366	.251	28		

There's a thin line between a useful fourth outfielder and a Triple-A favorite. Chad Curtis may have just fallen below that line. He used to be a tweener—not quite enough offense to help you in a corner outfield spot and not quite enough defense to play center field on a regular basis. Now, having lost a step, he's not a great defensive replacement and is really useful only as a platoon player in a limited role. On this club, he's not someone on whom I'd spend any money. He has three good years left in his semi-platoon injury-replacement role.

Tom Evans — 3B — Bats R — Age 26

YEAR	TEAM	LGE	AB	H	DB	TP	HR	BB	SO	R	RBI	SB	CS	OUT	BA	OBP	SLG	EQA	EQR	DEFENSE	
1998	Syracuse	Int	400	107	23	1	13	40	73	46	45	6	5	298	.268	.343	.428	.257	50	108-3B	-6
1999	Oklahoma	PCL	435	105	27	2	9	55	97	64	51	3	3	333	.241	.335	.375	.241	47	119-3B	2
2000	Texas	AL	53	14	4	0	0	9	12	9	4	0	3	42	.264	.381	.340	.238	6	16-3B	1
2001	Detroit	AL	189	48	8	0	5	26	42	28	27	1	2	143	.254	.344	.376	.250	22		

Tom Evans has a Darrell Evans-type skill set. He hits for power and draws some walks but won't knock you out with his glove or batting average. If things go his way, he could end up with a Herbert Perry career, getting a break in his late twenties. There won't be any opportunities for him with Texas, though. Signed with the Tigers, who could use him.

American League

Jason Grabowski — 3B — Bats L — Age 25

YEAR	TEAM	LGE	AB	H	DB	TP	HR	BB	SO	R	RBI	SB	CS	OUT	BA	OBP	SLG	EQA	EQR	DEFENSE			
1998	Savannah	SAL	367	80	10	4	10	41	98	43	35	6	4	291	.218	.297	.349	.217	32	60-C	-10	11-1B	0
1999	Charlott	Fla	443	111	23	3	10	49	76	49	60	6	5	337	.251	.328	.384	.240	47	115-3B	-13		
2000	Tulsa	Tex	499	111	26	3	13	63	114	67	60	4	4	392	.222	.312	.365	.228	49	129-3B	-12		
2001	Texas	AL	427	103	18	2	12	48	100	57	55	5	3	327	.241	.318	.377	.231	42				

He's pretty much a left-handed-hitting version of Evans, but slightly inferior with the glove. There are those in the organization who are very high on Jason Grabowski, but if he has a career in MLB, it will probably be as a Dave Magadan type, playing both infield corners and coming off the bench to try to pop the occasional long ball.

Scarborough Green — CF — Bats B — Age 27

YEAR	TEAM	LGE	AB	H	DB	TP	HR	BB	SO	R	RBI	SB	CS	OUT	BA	OBP	SLG	EQA	EQR	DEFENSE	
1998	Arkansas	Tex	74	22	0	0	2	4	14	10	6	5	1	53	.297	.333	.378	.249	8	18-CF	1
1998	Memphi	PCL	81	15	4	0	0	7	22	10	2	1	3	69	.185	.250	.235	.139	2	22-CF	1
1999	Oklahoma	PCL	356	77	14	4	2	28	83	51	22	18	8	287	.216	.277	.295	.195	24	103-CF	14
2000	Oklahoma	PCL	99	27	4	0	1	18	25	14	8	8	2	74	.273	.388	.343	.267	14	27-CF	0
2001	ChiCubs	NL	258	60	10	1	1	29	62	41	21	17	9	207	.233	.310	.291	.212	21		

Formerly "Bert," Scarborough Green escaped the Cardinals organization only to show pretty poorly in an extended audition made possible by a raft of injuries. He didn't hit at home, on the road, early in the season, or late in the season. Green has very limited skills: he can basically draw a walk and play center field. That might not be enough to fashion a career. He'll probably bounce around and compete with guys like Ernie Young for 25th roster spots from here on out.

Rusty Greer — LF — Bats L — Age 32

YEAR	TEAM	LGE	AB	H	DB	TP	HR	BB	SO	R	RBI	SB	CS	OUT	BA	OBP	SLG	EQA	EQR	DEFENSE	
1998	Texas	AL	591	181	30	5	17	79	83	106	104	1	4	414	.306	.391	.460	.285	90	148-LF	0
1999	Texas	AL	545	162	41	3	20	90	61	102	94	2	2	385	.297	.401	.494	.298	94	145-LF	-1
2000	Texas	AL	386	113	32	3	8	46	56	60	59	4	1	274	.293	.372	.453	.278	56	92-LF	-3
2001	Texas	AL	397	118	27	2	12	56	58	77	74	2	1	280	.297	.384	.466	.283	60		

My God, this team was snakebit during 2000. Rusty Greer plays solid defense, usually plays damn near every game, hits for average, draws some walks, and hits for power. So what happened? He got injured, of course, and missed 50 games. Greer should rebound well in 2001, and I expect him to start picking up his power numbers at the expense of a little bit of average. He was healthy only for about six weeks in 2000, fighting plantar fasciitis and a tweaked shoulder. If healthy, he'll outperform the projection above.

Travis Hafner — 3B/1B — Bats L — Age 24

YEAR	TEAM	LGE	AB	H	DB	TP	HR	BB	SO	R	RBI	SB	CS	OUT	BA	OBP	SLG	EQA	EQR	DEFENSE			
1998	Savannah	SAL	422	84	12	3	11	50	146	45	58	3	1	339	.199	.289	.320	.205	32	64-1B	-6	20-3B	-3
1999	Savannah	SAL	504	119	23	2	19	50	160	69	75	2	2	387	.236	.311	.403	.237	53	99-1B	2		
2000	Charlott	Fla	447	123	19	1	18	50	98	66	75	0	2	326	.275	.360	.443	.268	61	59-1B	-4	18-3B	-4
2001	Texas	AL	481	123	19	1	17	57	138	67	74	1	1	359	.256	.335	.405	.246	54				

I love this guy. Travis Hafner reminds me of a left-handed-hitting Edgar Martinez. He's been old for the leagues in which he's played, so he needs to move quickly, but this guy can hit. He's probably going to be short on opportunities in this organization, but he's definitely off to a great start. Hafner hit an unadjusted .346/.447/.580 in the Florida State League; even at his age, that's nothing to sneeze at. Defensively, he'll never make the majors at third base and will be pressed even at first base.

Bill Haselman — C — Bats R — Age 35

YEAR	TEAM	LGE	AB	H	DB	TP	HR	BB	SO	R	RBI	SB	CS	OUT	BA	OBP	SLG	EQA	EQR	DEFENSE	
1998	Texas	AL	104	33	6	0	6	3	15	11	16	0	0	71	.317	.336	.548	.284	15	27-C	-3
1999	Detroit	AL	142	39	5	0	5	9	24	12	14	2	0	103	.275	.318	.415	.246	15	36-C	0
2000	Texas	AL	191	52	14	0	7	12	33	21	25	0	1	140	.272	.319	.455	.252	22	55-C	0
2001	Texas	AL	139	37	6	0	5	10	25	17	21	0	0	102	.266	.315	.417	.240	14		

(Bill Haselman *continued*)

He's a solid caddy. This is a good gig for Bill Haselman, who has some value off the bench and can spell Ivan Rodriguez on those rare occasions he needs an off day. If Haselman played full time, he could probably rival Ben Grieve for double-play propensity. This is not a fast man, and he hits a lot of ground balls to shortstop.

Gabe Kapler — CF — Bats R — Age 25

YEAR	TEAM	LGE	AB	H	DB	TP	HR	BB	SO	R	RBI	SB	CS	OUT	BA	OBP	SLG	EQA	EQR	DEFENSE	
1998	Jacksnvl	Sou	548	147	35	3	21	41	99	79	96	3	2	403	.268	.323	.458	.256	67	133-RF	2
1999	Toledo	Int	54	15	7	1	2	8	10	9	10	0	1	40	.278	.371	.556	.292	9	14-CF	0
1999	Detroit	AL	413	101	21	4	19	38	67	58	47	10	5	317	.245	.311	.453	.251	50	120-CF	0
2000	Texas	AL	437	130	27	1	15	36	52	54	61	8	5	312	.297	.351	.467	.270	59	116-CF	-4
2001	Texas	AL	505	154	35	2	20	48	78	94	98	9	3	354	.305	.365	.501	.283	76		

The centerpiece of the fleecing of Randy Smith. I wouldn't have traded Gabe Kapler straight up for Juan Gonzalez, much less thrown in several other useful players as well. Kapler is a below-average but acceptable center fielder, and he had a couple of tremendous months in 2000 when he was healthy. Kapler possesses a very powerful stroke and is a good candidate to have a massive offensive breakout in 2001. If someone will give you odds on Kapler outperforming Gonzalez, take Kapler and cut us in on the bet.

Mike Lamb — 3B — Bats L — Age 25

YEAR	TEAM	LGE	AB	H	DB	TP	HR	BB	SO	R	RBI	SB	CS	OUT	BA	OBP	SLG	EQA	EQR	DEFENSE	
1998	Charlott	Fla	541	135	27	2	7	33	71	60	65	7	4	410	.250	.295	.346	.214	43	132-3B	-5
1999	Tulsa	Tex	545	146	38	3	15	40	70	73	70	2	2	401	.268	.323	.431	.249	62	135-3B	-3
2000	Texas	AL	487	133	25	2	6	28	55	60	43	0	2	356	.273	.318	.370	.229	45	128-3B	-14
2000	Oklahoma	PCL	55	13	2	1	2	4	6	6	4	2	1	43	.236	.288	.418	.233	6	12-3B	-5
2001	Texas	AL	546	153	31	2	12	40	70	73	79	3	3	396	.280	.329	.410	.243	58		

Doug Melvin probably didn't want to have Mike Lamb out there all year. In the off-season, the Rangers thought Todd Zeile was pretty much locked up to play third base while Lamb got some more time in Oklahoma City. Zeile, of course, signed with the Mets, and Lamb failed to keep up with AL pitching. He hit well early, then his offense just seemed to evaporate. Lamb is young and has a powerful stroke, but he better get his act together quickly if he wants to have a career as a starting 3B.

Ricky Ledee — RF — Bats L — Age 27

YEAR	TEAM	LGE	AB	H	DB	TP	HR	BB	SO	R	RBI	SB	CS	OUT	BA	OBP	SLG	EQA	EQR	DEFENSE	
1998	Columbus	Int	361	91	16	1	16	44	107	58	33	4	1	271	.252	.338	.435	.259	46	77-RF	-6
1998	NY Yanks	AL	79	20	5	2	1	7	26	13	12	3	1	60	.253	.314	.405	.243	9	20-LF	4
1999	Columbus	Int	116	27	6	1	3	13	29	14	12	3	2	90	.233	.310	.379	.232	12	29-CF	-3
1999	NY Yanks	AL	249	70	13	5	10	26	66	45	40	4	3	182	.281	.349	.494	.275	36	74-LF	-5
2000	NY Yanks	AL	190	47	11	1	7	24	36	22	29	8	4	146	.247	.335	.426	.256	24	45-LF	-2
2000	Clevelnd	AL	62	13	2	1	2	8	8	12	7	0	0	49	.210	.300	.371	.225	6	18-LF	2
2000	Texas	AL	210	48	5	3	4	23	46	21	34	6	3	165	.229	.308	.338	.220	19	53-RF	-1
2001	Texas	AL	399	100	17	3	12	52	97	62	58	7	2	301	.251	.337	.398	.247	46		

Accountability Corner: After Ricky Ledee's 1996 season at Norwich and Columbus, we forecasted him to post about an 840 OPS in 1997 and implied that he should be in the mix for the Yankees' starting job in left-field job and was headed for stardom. Oops. Later in this book, we'll be forecasting stardom for Australian sensation Jacko and 2001 Grammy Awards for Alan O'Day and David Dundas. Ledee has been unbelievably disappointing but is still just 27 years old and is coming into a situation in which he's not likely to receive too many at-bats against tough left-handers. Look for him to greatly outperform that forecast, with the vast majority of his playing time coming against right-handers.

Ruben Mateo — CF — Bats R — Age 23

YEAR	TEAM	LGE	AB	H	DB	TP	HR	BB	SO	R	RBI	SB	CS	OUT	BA	OBP	SLG	EQA	EQR	DEFENSE	
1998	Tulsa	Tex	429	109	24	1	13	21	62	54	51	9	4	324	.254	.303	.406	.235	44	106-CF	1
1999	Oklahoma	PCL	248	72	7	0	14	11	35	39	46	4	2	178	.290	.334	.488	.269	33	59-CF	2
1999	Texas	AL	121	29	9	1	5	3	25	15	17	3	0	92	.240	.263	.455	.235	12	28-CF	0
2000	Texas	AL	204	59	8	0	8	7	31	30	18	7	0	145	.289	.329	.446	.262	26	52-CF	0
2001	Texas	AL	266	79	12	0	14	18	45	45	51	9	1	188	.297	.342	.500	.276	38		

Ouchie. Ruben Mateo's star has fallen dramatically due to injuries, but let's step back a moment. He's just 23 years old and still has tremendous physical ability. He's demonstrated the capacity to adjust as he moves into higher levels of competition. He's held his own defensively in center field, and he's still got a lightning-quick bat. I think he's going to absolutely explode on the league, but probably not until late in the year. Of course, none of that talent matters if he can't stay healthy, and there's some doubt whether Mateo can return from his broken leg. You have to be able to take the field to play on it.

Kevin Mench — LF — Bats R — Age 23

YEAR	TEAM	LGE	AB	H	DB	TP	HR	BB	SO	R	RBI	SB	CS	OUT	BA	OBP	SLG	EQA	EQR	DEFENSE	
1999	Pulaski	App	258	64	11	1	8	15	52	30	28	3	1	195	.248	.291	.391	.226	24	51-LF	4
2000	Charlott	Fla	504	134	26	4	21	59	82	82	80	8	4	374	.266	.347	.458	.267	69	122-LF	-1
2001	Texas	AL	342	103	18	2	15	39	66	63	69	5	2	241	.301	.373	.497	.285	52		

Jamey Newberg, who knows more about the Rangers' minor leaguers than any human being really should, raved about Kevin Mench. It's easy to see why. He already has a tremendously powerful stroke, pretty decent plate discipline, and an uncanny ability to adjust the head of his bat in mid-swing. He reminds me of Troy Glaus offensively. Defensively, he reminds me of Ben Grieve or Greg Luzinski. Mench could hit major-league pitching this season but probably won't reach DeathPenaltyLand until 2003. He's the best prospect in the organization overall.

Rafael Palmeiro — 1B — Bats L — Age 36

YEAR	TEAM	LGE	AB	H	DB	TP	HR	BB	SO	R	RBI	SB	CS	OUT	BA	OBP	SLG	EQA	EQR	DEFENSE	
1998	Baltimor	AL	620	192	31	1	49	78	81	101	126	9	7	434	.310	.392	.600	.315	121	156-1B	10
1999	Texas	AL	553	178	24	1	48	90	63	91	138	2	4	379	.322	.419	.629	.332	120	28-1B	1
2000	Texas	AL	552	156	28	3	38	95	70	94	109	2	1	397	.283	.391	.551	.306	103	105-1B	-9
2001	Texas	AL	497	139	21	1	30	88	65	98	112	2	2	360	.280	.388	.507	.293	84		

He's probably the first baseman on the all-underrated team. Rafael Palmeiro is a truly great player who has never received the recognition that some inferior players, such as Mo Vaughn, have. He has always been a good defensive player, but I don't think he's ever going to recover from that year off in the field. He looked like he had slowed significantly in the field, and the numbers bear that out. I'm rooting for him to make the Hall of Fame.

Carlos Pena — 1B — Bats L — Age 23

YEAR	TEAM	LGE	AB	H	DB	TP	HR	BB	SO	R	RBI	SB	CS	OUT	BA	OBP	SLG	EQA	EQR	DEFENSE	
1998	Savannah	SAL	115	30	8	0	4	6	26	14	13	1	1	86	.261	.309	.435	.244	13	23-1B	1
1999	Charlott	Fla	513	110	23	4	15	55	156	63	72	1	2	405	.214	.300	.363	.221	47	132-1B	-5
2000	Tulsa	Tex	534	132	25	1	21	74	114	84	72	6	0	402	.247	.344	.416	.258	68	136-1B	-15
2001	Texas	AL	458	115	24	1	17	62	120	72	73	3	0	343	.251	.340	.419	.254	56		

Carlos Pena or Kevin Mench will probably take over for Palmeiro. Reid Nichols is very high on Pena, with some justification. Pena hit very well at Double-A, demonstrating phenomenal plate discipline to accompany 66 extra-base hits. He will definitely hit, and his defense is supposedly improving each year. He looks to me like a Fred McGriff-type hitter who should have a very reasonable major-league career.

Juan Piniella — LF — Bats R — Age 23

YEAR	TEAM	LGE	AB	H	DB	TP	HR	BB	SO	R	RBI	SB	CS	OUT	BA	OBP	SLG	EQA	EQR	DEFENSE	
1998	Savannah	SAL	263	71	11	4	2	22	51	32	27	10	5	197	.270	.331	.365	.238	27	67-OF	0
1998	Charlott	Fla	225	58	6	2	2	19	43	24	17	9	3	170	.258	.317	.329	.224	20	53-RF	-1
1999	Tulsa	Tex	463	105	18	1	7	47	130	52	35	8	3	361	.227	.304	.315	.212	37	118-RF	14
2000	Tulsa	Tex	452	98	13	1	4	48	111	49	30	12	5	359	.217	.295	.277	.196	31	121-LF	1
2001	Texas	AL	504	128	16	2	6	57	134	74	52	19	7	383	.254	.330	.329	.227	47		

Speedy. Juan Piniella has a lightning-quick standing start. He can track balls in the gap very well, but his bat simply isn't going to support a career in the majors. If everything breaks his way, he could have Brian L. Hunter's career, but how many GMs are that susceptible to hypnotism?

Bo Porter   OF   Bats R   Age 28

YEAR	TEAM	LGE	AB	H	DB	TP	HR	BB	SO	R	RBI	SB	CS	OUT	BA	OBP	SLG	EQA	EQR	DEFENSE	
1998	WestTenn	Sou	468	108	21	6	7	54	131	56	43	23	10	370	.231	.315	.346	.228	46	120-CF	-5
1999	Iowa	PCL	412	99	18	2	18	53	120	62	44	10	11	324	.240	.334	.425	.250	51	100-CF	2
2000	Sacramen	PCL	484	112	16	2	11	67	126	66	47	22	7	379	.231	.329	.341	.235	51	123-CF	2
2001	Texas	AL	444	107	19	2	11	67	128	80	58	18	10	347	.241	.341	.367	.240	49		

The Rangers profited from the A's having too much good stuff, claiming Bo Porter on waivers after the season. If Mateo's injuries keep him from playing center field, Porter would make a fine fill-in. He also gives the Rangers yet another ex-Athletic on the bench. The Rangers may not use them, but they've got good taste in bench players.

Ivan Rodriguez   C   Bats R   Age 29

YEAR	TEAM	LGE	AB	H	DB	TP	HR	BB	SO	R	RBI	SB	CS	OUT	BA	OBP	SLG	EQA	EQR	DEFENSE
1998	Texas	AL	574	185	38	4	23	30	78	87	89	7	0	389	.322	.359	.523	.289	87	137-C 18
1999	Texas	AL	592	193	25	1	36	18	58	109	106	23	12	410	.326	.347	.554	.288	92	138-C 15
2000	Texas	AL	357	122	26	3	27	14	44	61	76	5	6	240	.342	.368	.658	.316	67	85-C 8
2001	Texas	AL	454	150	27	3	26	27	57	85	105	11	5	309	.330	.368	.575	.300	76	

As everyone knows, Ivan Rodriguez missed a good chunk of 2000 due to injury. Rodriguez has stated that he might be interested in switching to another position over the next few years to cut down on the wear and tear on his body. Can't say I blame him, but he's a pretty darn good catcher. The only thing missing from his offensive game is plate discipline, but it's hard to nitpick a guy hitting .330 or better. Scary thought: if Rodriguez does move to second base or the outfield, it wouldn't surprise me to see him pick up his numbers at the plate a bit. Damn.

Jason Romano   2B   Bats R   Age 22

YEAR	TEAM	LGE	AB	H	DB	TP	HR	BB	SO	R	RBI	SB	CS	OUT	BA	OBP	SLG	EQA	EQR	DEFENSE
1998	Savannah	SAL	536	123	18	2	5	33	99	47	38	14	8	421	.229	.279	.299	.192	34	129-2B -8
1999	Charlott	Fla	463	117	23	7	11	29	83	57	48	15	8	354	.253	.305	.404	.236	48	105-2B -8
2000	Tulsa	Tex	538	126	29	1	6	38	88	63	51	12	6	418	.234	.289	.325	.206	40	123-2B -10
2001	Texas	AL	515	132	22	3	9	42	95	65	59	13	9	392	.256	.312	.363	.223	46	

Jason Romano showed up on a lot of prospect lists last year after hitting nothing but line drives in Charlotte in 1999. Last year, he had trouble with Double-A pitching, but he was only 21 and wasn't totally overmatched. Romano has a comparable skill set to Ray Durham but without the top-flight defense. He's still a couple of years out from the majors but should have a nice career.

Scott Sheldon   UT   Bats R   Age 32

YEAR	TEAM	LGE	AB	H	DB	TP	HR	BB	SO	R	RBI	SB	CS	OUT	BA	OBP	SLG	EQA	EQR	DEFENSE			
1998	Oklahoma	PCL	493	104	23	3	19	47	152	53	65	1	1	390	.211	.282	.385	.220	44	123-SS	-9		
1999	Oklahoma	PCL	448	112	26	2	17	42	117	63	63	7	2	338	.250	.317	.431	.249	52	56-2B	5	31-SS	-2
2000	Texas	AL	122	34	7	0	5	9	34	19	18	0	0	88	.279	.333	.459	.261	15	13-SS	0	12-3B	3
2001	Texas	AL	273	65	10	0	12	27	82	34	40	1	0	208	.238	.307	.407	.234	28				

He finally got a chance to play thanks to some injury problems among the regulars. Scott Sheldon can man any infield position and is a legitimate major-league hitter. He deserves a chance to play on a regular basis. The only difference between Sheldon and a guy like Craig Paquette, who's already pension-eligible, is plain old luck.

Ruben Sierra   OF/DH   Bats B   Age 35

YEAR	TEAM	LGE	AB	H	DB	TP	HR	BB	SO	R	RBI	SB	CS	OUT	BA	OBP	SLG	EQA	EQR	DEFENSE
1998	Norfolk	Int	109	24	2	0	3	10	19	12	15	2	0	85	.220	.286	.321	.206	8	26-RF 0
1998	ChiSox	AL	74	17	4	1	4	3	10	7	11	2	0	57	.230	.260	.473	.239	8	11-RF -1
2000	Oklahoma	PCL	438	117	21	2	12	39	69	50	55	3	1	322	.267	.327	.406	.246	48	80-LF -4
2000	Texas	AL	60	14	0	0	1	3	8	5	7	1	0	46	.233	.270	.283	.182	3	
2001	Texas	AL	232	53	8	1	6	22	65	25	26	2	0	179	.228	.295	.349	.214	19	

Ruben Sierra returned to the site of his glory days and played exactly as one would expect. Once upon a time, Texas fans complained that he was robbed of the 1989 MVP award by Robin Yount. Not all players peak at 27; some peak much earlier, then get chewed up because they never learn to lay off pitches outside of the strike zone.

Pedro Valdes — OF — Bats L — Age 28

YEAR	TEAM	LGE	AB	H	DB	TP	HR	BB	SO	R	RBI	SB	CS	OUT	BA	OBP	SLG	EQA	EQR	DEFENSE			
1998	Iowa	PCL	228	63	9	0	13	22	38	38	30	1	1	166	.276	.340	.487	.270	31	55-RF	-3		
1999	Oklahoma	PCL	388	105	19	1	15	42	60	53	51	1	1	284	.271	.348	.441	.263	50	29-LF	1	11-1B	2
2000	Oklahoma	PCL	351	98	22	1	12	33	44	46	54	1	0	253	.279	.345	.450	.265	46	71-RF	2		
2000	Texas	AL	53	15	4	0	1	5	6	4	4	0	0	38	.283	.345	.415	.255	6				
2001	Texas	AL	417	121	23	1	17	51	62	72	80	1	1	297	.290	.368	.472	.277	60				

He's good enough to play in the majors in a supporting role but won't help a club beyond that. Pedro Valdes toiled for years in Purgatory before jumping to Texas, where his shot came because of injuries. He is the prototypical Quadruple-A player who needs a break to start logging pension time.

B.J. Waszgis — C — Bats R — Age 30

YEAR	TEAM	LGE	AB	H	DB	TP	HR	BB	SO	R	RBI	SB	CS	OUT	BA	OBP	SLG	EQA	EQR	DEFENSE	
1998	Pawtuckt	Int	210	38	8	0	7	20	54	25	32	1	3	175	.181	.252	.319	.181	12	54-C	-6
1999	Columbus	Int	192	45	6	0	5	20	59	26	23	2	1	148	.234	.320	.344	.227	18	53-C	-6
2000	Oklahoma	PCL	262	56	9	2	9	42	75	32	42	1	1	207	.214	.329	.366	.237	28	62-C	-9
2000	Texas	AL	45	10	1	0	0	3	9	5	4	0	0	35	.222	.286	.244	.172	2	11-C	-1
2001	Texas	AL	242	52	8	0	7	33	73	29	27	1	1	191	.215	.309	.335	.215	20		

Catch-and-throw guy. Nothing distinguishes him from a number of receivers who have major-league careers. The signing of Haselman means Waszgis will have to move on to get a chance at get some playing time. A club short on pop could certainly use him as a second catcher and pinch hitter.

Corey Wright — CF — Bats L — Age 21

YEAR	TEAM	LGE	AB	H	DB	TP	HR	BB	SO	R	RBI	SB	CS	OUT	BA	OBP	SLG	EQA	EQR	DEFENSE	
1998	Pulaski	App	139	25	4	2	1	29	27	20	13	4	2	116	.180	.323	.259	.209	12	39-CF	-1
1999	Savannah	SAL	337	72	13	3	1	48	77	46	17	5	5	270	.214	.316	.279	.205	26	88-CF	-3
2000	Charlott	Fla	385	84	14	3	1	60	92	53	19	13	6	307	.218	.332	.278	.217	34	98-CF	2
2000	Tulsa	Tex	70	14	0	0	0	3	21	5	3	1	1	57	.200	.239	.200	.112	1	17-CF	1
2001	Texas	AL	394	92	15	2	2	54	102	54	34	10	7	309	.234	.326	.297	.213	32		

He's a blazing fast center fielder who played tremendous defense this year. Offensively, Corey Wright has Brett Butler's skill set but is still learning how to lay down a bunt. He probably won't hit enough to make the majors, but if he can find an additional 15 singles a year somewhere, he has a chance at a career.

Mike Young — SS/2B — Bats R — Age 24

YEAR	TEAM	LGE	AB	H	DB	TP	HR	BB	SO	R	RBI	SB	CS	OUT	BA	OBP	SLG	EQA	EQR	DEFENSE			
1998	Hagerstn	SAL	529	117	26	3	10	39	101	57	56	5	4	416	.221	.279	.338	.204	39	118-2B	-7	16-SS	-3
1999	Dunedin	Fla	498	124	27	2	4	45	90	58	57	13	3	377	.249	.314	.335	.223	44	66-2B	-3	45-SS	-7
2000	Tennesse	Sou	352	85	22	3	5	25	75	41	37	7	3	270	.241	.293	.364	.219	30	88-2B	0		
2000	Tulsa	Tex	188	51	11	3	1	11	29	21	23	4	2	139	.271	.312	.378	.231	18	41-SS	-1		
2001	Texas	AL	461	122	26	2	7	34	95	61	55	7	1	340	.265	.315	.375	.231	43				

Mike Young would be the top prospect in some organizations. He plays a reasonable shortstop or second base and has already demonstrated every ability you look for in an offensive player. As good as Mench and Jovanny Cedeno are, I think this guy has the best chance of being a productive major leaguer in the near future. He could have a Randy Velarde-type career, hopefully without the nagging injuries that impeded Velarde's development. Most organizations would kill to have even one middle-infield prospect as good as Young or Romano.

PITCHERS (ERA: 4.50, H/9: 9.00, HR/9: 1.00, BB/9: 3.00, K/9: 6.00, KW: 1.00, PERA: 4.50)

Joaquin Benoit — Throws R — Age 21

YEAR	TEAM	LGE	IP	H	ER	HR	BB	K	ERA	W	L	H/9	HR/9	BB/9	K/9	KW	PERA
1998	Savannah	SAL	71.7	84	55	18	25	32	6.91	2	6	10.55	2.26	3.14	4.02	0.64	6.80
1999	Charlott	Fla	95.7	114	74	11	63	50	6.96	3	8	10.72	1.03	5.93	4.70	0.40	6.77
2000	Tulsa	Tex	76.7	73	46	10	32	45	5.40	3	6	8.57	1.17	3.76	5.28	0.70	4.75

Reid Nichols is very pleased with Joaquin Benoit's development during 2000, and it's easy to see why. Benoit improved his control, his velocity and movement were stronger, and he dropped his ERA two runs while making the jump from high-A to Double-A. Successful major-league pitchers usually strike out a few more guys than Benoit does, but he's still young, and his success in the Texas League at the age of 20 is certainly encouraging. If he stays healthy, he looks like a candidate to be moved to the bullpen.

Jovanny Cedeno — Throws R — Age 21

YEAR	TEAM	LGE	IP	H	ER	HR	BB	K	ERA	W	L	H/9	HR/9	BB/9	K/9	KW	PERA
2000	Savannah	SAL	116.7	101	49	3	72	72	3.78	7	6	7.79	0.23	5.55	5.55	0.50	4.06

There's no such thing as a pitching prospect, but if there were, he'd look like Jovanny Cedeno. The Rangers understand that he has to be handled carefully and have shut him down for the most minor of ailments. Cedeno's stuff is extremely nasty. He throws 90–92 mph with ease and knows how to work the ball in and out against both right-handed and left-handed hitters. He doesn't have much of a chance to be an ace, but the fact that he has any chance at all means he's a damn valuable guy. Even in the Sally League, 153 strikeouts in 130 innings is an encouraging sign.

Mark Clark — Throws R — Age 33

YEAR	TEAM	LGE	IP	H	ER	HR	BB	K	ERA	W	L	H/9	HR/9	BB/9	K/9	KW	PERA
1998	ChiCubs	NL	205.0	229	113	23	43	131	4.96	9	14	10.05	1.01	1.89	5.75	1.52	4.68
1999	Texas	AL	75.0	95	59	13	26	42	7.08	2	6	11.40	1.56	3.12	5.04	0.81	6.56
2000	Texas	AL	45.0	61	33	7	18	15	6.60	1	4	12.20	1.40	3.60	3.00	0.42	7.08

His career as anything but a fifth starter/swing man is probably over. Mark Clark was a reliable #3/#4 starter for a period of three years, and that's a pretty good run. He will probably have a little time as a bullpen guy and could polish up that low-and-away junk a bit and start summarily executing right-handed hitters. Clark is a good guy from whom I'll be looking for a comeback and some success. I may or may not get it. He parted ways with the Rangers at his own request in July.

Francisco Cordero — Throws R — Age 23

YEAR	TEAM	LGE	IP	H	ER	HR	BB	K	ERA	W	L	H/9	HR/9	BB/9	K/9	KW	PERA
1998	Jacksnvl	Sou	15.7	19	13	2	9	11	7.47	0	2	10.91	1.15	5.17	6.32	0.61	6.66
1999	Jacksnvl	Sou	48.3	37	11	5	24	37	2.05	4	1	6.89	0.93	4.47	6.89	0.77	3.81
1999	Detroit	AL	19.3	18	6	2	14	18	2.79	1	1	8.38	0.93	6.52	8.38	0.64	5.46
2000	Texas	AL	78.7	81	40	8	36	47	4.58	4	5	9.27	0.92	4.12	5.38	0.65	5.03

Here's the next exhibit in the plundering of Motown. There's actually a lot here not to like, despite the kind of velocity that you don't see very often. Francisco Cordero throws hard, but like a lot of fireballers, he can't always control that velocity within the strike zone. So he walks a few guys, patient hitters work the count on him, and he has to take a little off the fastball to throw a strike. The result can occasionally cause neck strain for Cordero and the fans. If he can improve his control just 10–15%, that could translate into great success as a closer. Of course, you could have said the same for thousands of ex-pitchers who never made the bigs at all.

Tim Crabtree — Throws R — Age 31

YEAR	TEAM	LGE	IP	H	ER	HR	BB	K	ERA	W	L	H/9	HR/9	BB/9	K/9	KW	PERA
1998	Texas	AL	84.3	81	34	2	28	55	3.63	5	4	8.64	0.21	2.99	5.87	0.98	3.51
1999	Texas	AL	64.7	66	22	3	14	52	3.06	4	3	9.19	0.42	1.95	7.24	1.86	3.61
2000	Texas	AL	80.3	80	42	5	23	52	4.71	4	5	8.96	0.56	2.58	5.83	1.13	3.86

He's a reliable reliever who had a great deal of difficulty getting left-handed hitters out in 2000. Tim Crabtree's strikeout rate took a dip after the All-Star break. He's likely been overworked a bit and may not bounce back particularly well in 2001. I wouldn't be surprised to see him play more of a platoon role in the future.

American League

Darwin Cubillan — Throws R — Age 26

YEAR	TEAM	LGE	IP	H	ER	HR	BB	K	ERA	W	L	H/9	HR/9	BB/9	K/9	KW	PERA
1998	Tampa	Fla	58.0	79	52	7	49	38	8.07	1	5	12.26	1.09	7.60	5.90	0.39	8.44
1999	Tampa	Fla	64.7	63	43	15	45	40	5.98	2	5	8.77	2.09	6.26	5.57	0.44	6.85
2000	Syracuse	Int	30.7	16	3	1	13	29	0.88	3	0	4.70	0.29	3.82	8.51	1.12	1.95
2000	Toronto	AL	16.0	19	11	4	8	13	6.19	1	1	10.69	2.25	4.50	7.31	0.81	7.40
2000	Oklahoma	PCL	15.7	8	2	0	4	8	1.15	2	0	4.60	0.00	2.30	4.60	1.00	1.25
2000	Texas	AL	18.7	30	18	3	10	13	8.68	0	2	14.46	1.45	4.82	6.27	0.65	8.95

Darwin Cubillan tore through two separate Triple-A stints like Pedro Martinez through the Minnesota Twins. He has good enough stuff to get people out on a regular basis. If he has a future in the bigs, it's as a setup guy.

Doug Davis — Throws L — Age 25

YEAR	TEAM	LGE	IP	H	ER	HR	BB	K	ERA	W	L	H/9	HR/9	BB/9	K/9	KW	PERA
1998	Charlott	Fla	139.3	135	89	17	96	99	5.75	5	10	8.72	1.10	6.20	6.39	0.52	5.77
1999	Tulsa	Tex	68.0	68	33	14	30	49	4.37	4	4	9.00	1.85	3.97	6.49	0.82	5.80
1999	Oklahoma	PCL	74.3	72	26	5	33	50	3.15	5	3	8.72	0.61	4.00	6.05	0.76	4.32
2000	Oklahoma	PCL	65.3	61	35	11	36	38	4.82	3	4	8.40	1.52	4.96	5.23	0.53	5.52
2000	Texas	AL	100.3	102	48	10	43	63	4.31	5	6	9.15	0.90	3.86	5.65	0.73	4.84

Doug Davis managed to get 13 starts for the Rangers thanks to injuries and ineffectiveness among his staff mates. He doesn't throw real hard and lives and dies by his ability to keep hitters off stride and to move the ball around. There are a lot of pitchers who are very successful doing this. There are a lot more who aren't.

Ryan Glynn — Throws R — Age 26

YEAR	TEAM	LGE	IP	H	ER	HR	BB	K	ERA	W	L	H/9	HR/9	BB/9	K/9	KW	PERA
1998	Tulsa	Tex	146.3	135	72	18	74	71	4.43	7	9	8.30	1.11	4.55	4.37	0.48	4.85
1999	Oklahoma	PCL	85.3	73	44	8	40	36	4.64	4	5	7.70	0.84	4.22	3.80	0.45	4.07
1999	Texas	AL	55.7	66	38	8	27	37	6.14	2	4	10.67	1.29	4.37	5.98	0.69	6.35
2000	Oklahoma	PCL	78.3	69	38	7	37	45	4.37	4	5	7.93	0.80	4.25	5.17	0.61	4.19
2000	Texas	AL	89.3	98	51	11	30	32	5.14	4	6	9.87	1.11	3.02	3.22	0.53	5.13

He's a starter with a broad repertoire. I like Ryan Glynn more than the numbers indicate. Usually, a guy with strikeout rates this low doesn't have a long series of successful years. Sure, he may post a great ERA one season and then hang on for a few years because of it (think Daves Fleming or Johnson), but usually these guys never really have much success. Glynn, however, hadn't posted an ERA above 4.00 in the minors for three seasons, despite iffy strikeout rates. Yes, he's probably a Triple-A Steve Wojciechowski/Jeff Bittiger-type pitcher, but occasionally, someone is the exception to the rule, and Glynn has a chance to be that guy.

Aaron Harang — Throws R — Age 23

YEAR	TEAM	LGE	IP	H	ER	HR	BB	K	ERA	W	L	H/9	HR/9	BB/9	K/9	KW	PERA
1999	Pulaski	App	72.0	70	28	12	22	34	3.50	5	3	8.75	1.50	2.75	4.25	0.77	4.78
2000	Charlott	Fla	141.3	137	94	25	62	78	5.99	5	11	8.72	1.59	3.95	4.97	0.63	5.35

Aaron Harang pitched well at Charlotte but faces an uphill battle to have a major-league career. His stuff is average, with control that's pretty decent but not exactly Bob Tewksbury. Harang is worth keeping an eye on in Double-A. If his strikeout rate jumps, his chance of having a major-league career triples. He was sent to Oakland for Randy Velarde.

Rick Helling — Throws R — Age 30

YEAR	TEAM	LGE	IP	H	ER	HR	BB	K	ERA	W	L	H/9	HR/9	BB/9	K/9	KW	PERA
1998	Texas	AL	214.0	195	90	21	63	152	3.79	13	11	8.20	0.88	2.65	6.39	1.21	3.78
1999	Texas	AL	219.0	209	100	31	65	125	4.11	12	12	8.59	1.27	2.67	5.14	0.96	4.41
2000	Texas	AL	218.0	196	95	21	73	139	3.92	12	12	8.09	0.87	3.01	5.74	0.95	3.84

Ron Coomer is still ducking from one of his curveballs. Rick Helling is a tremendously entertaining and consistent pitcher. He fought some injury troubles earlier in his career, and it's always gratifying to see someone get healthy and pull it together.

(Rick Helling *continued*)

He's an underappreciated starter who is likely to have continued success. I never thought I'd write something like that about a guy who's posted ERAs around 4.50 for three straight years, but considering this offensive era and his home park, Helling has done a tremendous job.

Jonathan Johnson   Throws R   Age 26

YEAR	TEAM	LGE	IP	H	ER	HR	BB	K	ERA	W	L	H/9	HR/9	BB/9	K/9	KW	PERA
1998	Charlott	Fla	10.0	12	9	4	5	6	8.10	0	1	10.80	3.60	4.50	5.40	0.60	8.89
1998	Oklahoma	PCL	106.3	105	68	18	34	65	5.76	4	8	8.89	1.52	2.88	5.50	0.96	4.94
1999	Oklahoma	PCL	65.3	82	49	11	25	25	6.75	2	5	11.30	1.52	3.44	3.44	0.50	6.58
2000	Oklahoma	PCL	52.3	56	45	12	29	42	7.74	1	5	9.63	2.06	4.99	7.22	0.72	6.82
2000	Texas	AL	29.7	32	18	2	14	22	5.46	1	2	9.71	0.61	4.25	6.67	0.79	5.01

Swing man or Quadruple-A starter. Jonathan Johnson will be working to be the 11th or 12th guy on a staff for the next few years. He strikes out enough guys that if he can find his control, he could make a couple million bucks as an effective reliever.

Corey Lee   Throws R   Age 26

YEAR	TEAM	LGE	IP	H	ER	HR	BB	K	ERA	W	L	H/9	HR/9	BB/9	K/9	KW	PERA
1998	Tulsa	Tex	130.3	106	96	23	118	85	6.63	4	10	7.32	1.59	8.15	5.87	0.36	6.26
1999	Tulsa	Tex	117.0	133	90	18	55	72	6.92	3	10	10.23	1.38	4.23	5.54	0.65	6.14
1999	Oklahoma	PCL	25.3	20	6	2	9	17	2.13	2	1	7.11	0.71	3.20	6.04	0.94	3.25
2000	Oklahoma	PCL	105.0	154	129	22	97	57	11.06	1	11	13.20	1.89	8.31	4.89	0.29	10.13

He was pretty much Triple-A's version of Omar Daal. Corey Lee got pounded by righties and lefties, at home and away, day and night. His strikeout rate took a beating, and he posted a 2–12 record for Oklahoma City. That's not real good. It'll take a raft of injuries for Lee to get a legit shot at serious playing time in Arlington.

Colby Lewis   Throws R   Age 21

YEAR	TEAM	LGE	IP	H	ER	HR	BB	K	ERA	W	L	H/9	HR/9	BB/9	K/9	KW	PERA
1999	Pulaski	App	58.3	52	31	7	35	33	4.78	2	4	8.02	1.08	5.40	5.09	0.47	5.01
2000	Charlott	Fla	148.7	178	106	27	55	90	6.42	5	12	10.78	1.63	3.33	5.45	0.82	6.35

Colby Lewis pitched pretty well at Charlotte. He may have been worked a little too hard, throwing 163 innings, but there's a lot here to like. His strikeout rate is fairly reasonable, his control is coming along, and his stuff is above-average across the board. With a little more velocity, which he could well develop, Lewis has a chance at a major-league career.

Spike Lundberg   Throws R   Age 24

YEAR	TEAM	LGE	IP	H	ER	HR	BB	K	ERA	W	L	H/9	HR/9	BB/9	K/9	KW	PERA
2000	Tulsa	Tex	140.7	143	65	15	58	62	4.16	8	8	9.15	0.96	3.71	3.97	0.53	4.83

Reid Nichols and just about everyone in the Texas organization is high on this guy. Spike Lundberg shows a great deal of poise and command of his pitches beyond his years. His strikeout rate isn't tremendous, but he doesn't give the same look to hitters very often. Lundberg will start the season at Triple-A, but don't be surprised to see him in the Texas rotation if someone gets hurt, despite Melvin's conservative development philosophy.

Mike Munoz   Throws L   Age 35

YEAR	TEAM	LGE	IP	H	ER	HR	BB	K	ERA	W	L	H/9	HR/9	BB/9	K/9	KW	PERA
1998	Colorado	NL	40.7	51	27	1	11	19	5.98	2	3	11.29	0.22	2.43	4.20	0.86	4.77
1999	Texas	AL	52.0	48	20	4	14	26	3.46	3	3	8.31	0.69	2.42	4.50	0.93	3.57
2000	Texas	AL	4.3	10	5	1	2	1	10.38	0	0	20.77	2.08	4.15	2.08	0.25	13.03

There's never really been a compelling reason to give Mike Munoz a job except that he's left-handed and ambulatory. His 1999 was superficially good but offered little promise that he'd continue to be successful. He's a lefty specialist who givs up a .307 average to left-handed hitters. Even if you're playing a healthy portion of your games at Coors Field, that's pretty Terry Feltonish. His tidy 13.50 ERA in 2000 may signal the end of the line.

American League

Peter Munro — Throws R — Age 26

YEAR	TEAM	LGE	IP	H	ER	HR	BB	K	ERA	W	L	H/9	HR/9	BB/9	K/9	KW	PERA
1998	Pawtuckt	Int	102.3	107	48	11	33	55	4.22	5	6	9.41	0.97	2.90	4.84	0.83	4.67
1998	Syracuse	Int	43.0	57	42	8	22	31	8.79	1	4	11.93	1.67	4.60	6.49	0.70	7.61
1999	Syracuse	Int	66.7	69	28	6	32	48	3.78	4	3	9.32	0.81	4.32	6.48	0.75	5.03
1999	Toronto	AL	55.3	65	32	5	18	36	5.20	2	4	10.57	0.81	2.93	5.86	1.00	5.20
2000	Syracuse	Int	58.3	51	20	1	25	32	3.09	4	2	7.87	0.15	3.86	4.94	0.64	3.36
2000	Toronto	AL	26.0	36	19	1	12	15	6.58	1	2	12.46	0.35	4.15	5.19	0.63	6.31
2000	Oklahoma	PCL	28.7	26	18	4	15	10	5.65	1	2	8.16	1.26	4.71	3.14	0.33	4.96

Man, how bad would it suck to be designated for assignment so that Mickey Morandini could be added to the roster? Peter Munro has a reasonable arm, but his star's pretty much faded at this point. He will likely be used in relief; the only question is, will it be in the majors or Oklahoma City?

Darren Oliver — Throws L — Age 30

YEAR	TEAM	LGE	IP	H	ER	HR	BB	K	ERA	W	L	H/9	HR/9	BB/9	K/9	KW	PERA
1998	Texas	AL	103.0	130	71	9	35	54	6.20	3	8	11.36	0.79	3.06	4.72	0.77	5.69
1998	St Louis	NL	54.7	61	29	7	21	24	4.77	2	4	10.04	1.15	3.46	3.95	0.57	5.46
1999	St Louis	NL	190.7	187	87	15	62	100	4.11	10	11	8.83	0.71	2.93	4.72	0.81	4.07
2000	Oklahoma	PCL	29.7	22	12	3	15	19	3.64	2	1	6.67	0.91	4.55	5.76	0.63	3.69
2000	Texas	AL	108.7	138	76	12	31	47	6.29	3	9	11.43	0.99	2.57	3.89	0.76	5.74

Some organizations just aren't destined to have good relationships with some players. Darren Oliver was worked harder than he could handle in 1996 and 1997, became ineffective, and was shipped to St. Louis. Tony LaRussa and Dave Duncan promptly milked more than 190 innings out of him. Oliver signed a three-year deal with Texas after the 1999 season and collapsed, wracked by injuries and ineffectiveness. Oliver is fragile and miscast as a guy who can give a team 200 innings. He just can't deliver them without getting hurt. He can still help a club that manages him properly.

Matt Perisho — Throws L — Age 26

YEAR	TEAM	LGE	IP	H	ER	HR	BB	K	ERA	W	L	H/9	HR/9	BB/9	K/9	KW	PERA
1998	Oklahoma	PCL	86.0	84	39	7	44	42	4.08	5	5	8.79	0.73	4.60	4.40	0.48	4.75
1999	Oklahoma	PCL	148.0	151	87	16	86	99	5.29	6	10	9.18	0.97	5.23	6.02	0.58	5.51
2000	Texas	AL	107.7	127	79	15	50	71	6.60	3	9	10.62	1.25	4.18	5.93	0.71	6.21

You'd think there'd be a limit on the number of guys in one organization who post ghastly ERAs in a season. Someone always gets bushwhacked for an 18.00 ERA or something in a couple of innings, but Texas really ran the table on these guys in 2000. Perisho put up his 7.37 ERA in 105 innings. Try to spin that in arbitration. "Often Matt faced batters that neither reached base nor scored!" He has good enough stuff to succeed but has to improve his control 10%. Traded to Detroit.

Andy Pratt — Throws L — Age 21

YEAR	TEAM	LGE	IP	H	ER	HR	BB	K	ERA	W	L	H/9	HR/9	BB/9	K/9	KW	PERA
1999	Savannah	SAL	63.0	77	44	9	23	46	6.29	2	5	11.00	1.29	3.29	6.57	1.00	6.09
2000	Charlott	Fla	83.0	78	58	19	32	56	6.29	3	6	8.46	2.06	3.47	6.07	0.88	5.51
2000	Tulsa	Tex	48.7	66	52	11	35	26	9.62	1	4	12.21	2.03	6.47	4.81	0.37	8.95

Throw out that 7.22 ERA in Tulsa, because Andy Pratt can pitch. He has average-plus stuff across the board and is learning how to make adjustments and get people out with his entire repertoire. Pratt struck out more than 12 batters per nine innings at Savannah and was still striking out more than a batter per inning at Charlotte. Control pitchers are always long shots, but Pratt bears watching. It may take him a year to pull it together, but he'll likely be pitching well in Double-A by July.

Nick Regilio   Throws R   Age 22

YEAR	TEAM	LGE	IP	H	ER	HR	BB	K	ERA	W	L	H/9	HR/9	BB/9	K/9	KW	PERA
1999	Pulaski	App	45.3	33	16	5	21	22	3.18	3	2	6.55	0.99	4.17	4.37	0.52	3.56
2000	Charlott	Fla	77.3	98	68	19	35	37	7.91	2	7	11.41	2.21	4.07	4.31	0.53	7.64

The organization is high on Nick Regilio, but there are some pretty serious warning signs here. Striking out 6.6 batters per nine innings in high-A ball isn't indicative of future success. Regilio doesn't have electric stuff, and his 4.52 ERA masks the fact that he also gave up an additional 11 unearned runs in just 86 innings at Charlotte. He has time to develop, but I don't think he'll have a major-league career.

Kenny Rogers   Throws L   Age 36

YEAR	TEAM	LGE	IP	H	ER	HR	BB	K	ERA	W	L	H/9	HR/9	BB/9	K/9	KW	PERA
1998	Oakland	AL	232.3	200	84	17	58	127	3.25	16	10	7.75	0.66	2.25	4.92	1.09	3.17
1999	Oakland	AL	117.7	125	57	7	33	65	4.36	6	7	9.56	0.54	2.52	4.97	0.98	4.14
1999	NY Mets	NL	73.3	68	33	8	24	49	4.05	4	4	8.35	0.98	2.95	6.01	1.02	4.06
2000	Texas	AL	226.7	237	103	15	58	121	4.09	12	13	9.41	0.60	2.30	4.80	1.04	4.04

Over the years, we've savaged Kenny Rogers. I think the kindest thing we've written about him in six years is "will add stability to the Oakland staff." We've been wrong. Rogers has pitched well, given his clubs a lot of innings, and will likely continue to do so. He had minor elbow surgery immediately after the season; it is not expected to have any effect on him in 2001.

Brian Sikorski   Throws R   Age 26

YEAR	TEAM	LGE	IP	H	ER	HR	BB	K	ERA	W	L	H/9	HR/9	BB/9	K/9	KW	PERA
1998	Jackson	Tex	89.0	84	61	20	52	52	6.17	3	7	8.49	2.02	5.26	5.26	0.50	6.23
1998	New Orln	PCL	79.0	81	60	12	36	44	6.84	2	7	9.23	1.37	4.10	5.01	0.61	5.47
1999	New Orln	PCL	147.0	161	103	35	70	81	6.31	5	11	9.86	2.14	4.29	4.96	0.58	6.75
2000	Oklahoma	PCL	131.3	124	75	13	66	67	5.14	6	9	8.50	0.89	4.52	4.59	0.51	4.71
2000	Texas	AL	38.7	43	24	7	18	30	5.59	1	3	10.01	1.63	4.19	6.98	0.83	6.23

One of the many bodies paraded through the rotation in 2000, Brian Sikorski fared as well as most: he got shellacked. He couldn't throw strikes with his best stuff, and hitters just sat back and waited for a meatball, which Sikorski dutifully delivered to the tune of nine home runs allowed in 37 innings. He's not a serious contender for a major-league job.

Justin Thompson   Throws L   Age 28

YEAR	TEAM	LGE	IP	H	ER	HR	BB	K	ERA	W	L	H/9	HR/9	BB/9	K/9	KW	PERA
1998	Detroit	AL	218.3	212	99	17	67	138	4.08	12	12	8.74	0.70	2.76	5.69	1.03	3.95
1999	Detroit	AL	142.0	140	69	19	46	79	4.37	7	9	8.87	1.20	2.92	5.01	0.86	4.60

I hate to say this, but he's done. Justin Thompson fought elbow problems in the minors, and his shoulder is pretty much blown out. If he does come back in 2001, he won't be effective. Rotator-cuff surgery seems to be considerably more damaging to one's pitching career than Tommy John surgery, and Thompson's cuff is probably in worse shape than Frank Tanana's was. Being a starting pitcher is hard; being a good or great one is that much harder. The human body simply isn't designed to move like that. Here's hoping Thompson bucks the odds.

Mike Venafro   Throws L   Age 27

YEAR	TEAM	LGE	IP	H	ER	HR	BB	K	ERA	W	L	H/9	HR/9	BB/9	K/9	KW	PERA
1998	Tulsa	Tex	47.7	42	26	8	32	28	4.91	2	3	7.93	1.51	6.04	5.29	0.44	5.69
1998	Oklahoma	PCL	16.0	18	13	4	11	10	7.31	0	2	10.13	2.25	6.19	5.63	0.45	7.80
1999	Texas	AL	67.3	58	24	3	17	35	3.21	4	3	7.75	0.40	2.27	4.68	1.03	2.95
2000	Texas	AL	56.0	59	22	1	16	30	3.54	3	3	9.48	0.16	2.57	4.82	0.94	3.75

He's now an official, major-league-approved one-out left-hander. Aside from being left-handed, he has one other very cool thing going for him: he gets people to hit ground balls. Mike Venafro should have a very solid career as a setup guy, coming in to hold runners, get out left-handed hitters, and induce double plays.

Alan Webb   **Throws R**   **Age 21**

YEAR	TEAM	LGE	IP	H	ER	HR	BB	K	ERA	W	L	H/9	HR/9	BB/9	K/9	KW	PERA
1998	W Michgn	Mid	151.3	129	112	26	77	103	6.66	5	12	7.67	1.55	4.58	6.13	0.67	4.94
1999	Jacksnvl	Sou	129.7	140	99	27	69	56	6.87	4	10	9.72	1.87	4.79	3.89	0.41	6.59
2000	Charlott	Fla	76.3	79	38	7	47	23	4.48	4	4	9.31	0.83	5.54	2.71	0.24	5.54
2000	Tulsa	Tex	22.7	37	40	15	25	11	15.88	0	3	14.69	5.96	9.93	4.37	0.22	15.98

Alan Webb regressed in 2000 but is young enough to bounce back. Occasionally, a live arm develops into a pitcher. Hats off to Mr. Melvin for getting Webb as another part of the Juan Gonzalez deal.

John Wetteland   **Throws R**   **Age 34**

YEAR	TEAM	LGE	IP	H	ER	HR	BB	K	ERA	W	L	H/9	HR/9	BB/9	K/9	KW	PERA
1998	Texas	AL	61.0	44	14	5	11	67	2.07	6	1	6.49	0.74	1.62	9.89	3.05	2.38
1999	Texas	AL	65.7	62	25	7	14	57	3.43	4	3	8.50	0.96	1.92	7.81	2.04	3.73
2000	Texas	AL	60.7	62	28	7	18	51	4.15	3	4	9.20	1.04	2.67	7.57	1.42	4.53

At this writing, he's apparently contemplating retirement. John Wetteland is a fine reliever, and there's not a lot to suggest he couldn't continue to be successful. His performance and peripheral numbers show a downward trend, but he's still a better pitcher than the vast majority of the league's hurlers. He does occasionally leave a pitch up.

Jeff Zimmerman   **Throws R**   **Age 28**

YEAR	TEAM	LGE	IP	H	ER	HR	BB	K	ERA	W	L	H/9	HR/9	BB/9	K/9	KW	PERA
1998	Charlott	Fla	13.0	11	3	2	1	7	2.08	1	0	7.62	1.38	0.69	4.85	3.50	3.14
1998	Tulsa	Tex	57.3	40	21	8	25	40	3.30	4	2	6.28	1.26	3.92	6.28	0.80	3.57
1999	Texas	AL	86.0	46	19	7	18	64	1.99	8	2	4.81	0.73	1.88	6.70	1.78	1.72
2000	Texas	AL	71.0	75	36	7	25	71	4.56	3	5	9.51	0.89	3.17	9.00	1.42	4.75

Jeff Zimmerman's last two seasons are a case study in heavy reliever workloads causing problems the following year. Zimmerman was lights out for the first four months of the 1999 season, throwing Bryan Harvey's patented stuff past totally baffled hitters. He started to get tired, became mortal, then looked pretty average this year, with his pitches lacking both velocity and movement. He may bounce back, but the bounce never plays quite like the original.

Support-Neutral Statistics					TEXAS RANGERS					Park Effect: +10.9%	
PITCHER	GS	IP	R	SNW	SNL	SNPCT	W	L	RA	APW	SNVA	SNWAR
Mark Clark	8	36.7	37	1.4	4.0	.255	3	4	9.08	-1.3	-1.2	-0.9
Doug Davis	13	74.7	47	4.5	4.6	.498	4	5	5.67	-0.1	-0.0	0.7
Ryan Glynn	16	88.7	65	4.5	6.8	.399	5	7	6.60	-0.9	-1.0	-0.3
Rick Helling	35	217.0	122	13.4	11.8	.531	16	13	5.06	1.1	0.7	2.7
Esteban Loaiza	17	101.0	67	5.4	6.6	.450	5	6	5.97	-0.4	-0.6	0.3
Darren Oliver	21	108.0	95	4.9	9.0	.355	2	9	7.92	-2.5	-1.9	-1.0
Matt Perisho	13	63.7	62	3.0	5.8	.342	1	7	8.76	-2.0	-1.4	-0.7
Kenny Rogers	34	227.3	126	13.1	11.3	.536	13	13	4.99	1.3	0.8	2.7
Brian Sikorski	5	27.0	22	1.3	2.2	.365	1	3	7.33	-0.5	-0.4	-0.2
TOTALS	162	944.0	643	51.6	62.1	.453	50	67	6.13	-5.4	-5.0	3.2

After losing Juan Gonzalez and Todd Zeile in the off-season, the Rangers entered 2000 hoping to defend their Western Division crown relying largely on an improved starting rotation. Rick Helling was supposed to produce like he had in 1998 and 1999, big-money free agents Kenny Rogers and Darren Oliver were supposed to more than make up for the loss of Aaron Sele, a healthy Mark Clark and a promising Matt Perisho were supposed to provide a solid bottom of the rotation, and newly acquired Justin Thompson was supposed to be ready to return to his outstanding pre-injury level by mid-season.

Whoops.

Rogers and Helling did their parts, providing a decent, if unspectacular, one-two punch. But the rest of the starting rotation was worth greater than two wins below replacement level. If you rank 2000 rotations after removing their top two starters, Texas was second worst in the majors, ahead of only the Expos' dismal rotation.

There is a small silver lining for Rangers fans. The team's best starter over the last two months of the season was not Helling, not Rogers, but rookie Doug Davis, who we called "the most promising Rangers pitching prospect" last year. That he was the best Rangers starter in August and September with an unspectacular 4.2–3.0 record says more about the rest of the Ranger rotation than it does about Davis. Still, he showed some promise of emerging as a solid full-time member of the rotation next year. That silver lining may not sound like much, but beggars can't be choosers.

For a quick explanation of SN stats, see page 7.

Reliever Evaluation Tools											
PITCHER	G	IP	R	ARA	APR	IRNR/G	EIRS/G	IRP	BRS	RRA	ARP
Mark Clark	4	7.3	5	5.74	-0.4	1.75	0.44	-1.4	0.8	8.83	-3.0
Francisco Cordero	56	77.3	51	5.55	-3.0	1.29	0.49	2.6	2.7	5.88	-5.9
Tim Crabtree	68	80.3	52	5.45	-2.2	0.82	0.36	1.8	-4.1	4.81	3.4
Darwin Cubillan	13	17.7	22	10.48	-10.4	0.54	0.17	-1.6	-0.5	10.92	-11.2
Doug Davis	17	24.0	14	4.91	0.8	1.00	0.34	-2.5	0.5	6.88	-4.5
Jonathan Johnson	15	29.0	23	6.67	-4.8	1.00	0.45	-0.4	-2.0	6.36	-3.7
Danny Kolb	1	0.7	5	63.12	-4.3	0.00	0.00	0.0	0.4	63.54	-4.3
Esteban Loaiza	3	6.3	0	0.00	3.7	0.33	0.08	0.2	1.0	1.11	2.9
Mike Munoz	7	4.0	6	12.62	-3.3	0.86	0.47	-0.2	1.1	15.88	-4.7
Matt Perisho	21	41.3	37	7.53	-10.7	0.76	0.27	-1.6	1.0	7.70	-11.5
Scott Sheldon	1	0.3	0	0.00	0.2	0.00	0.00	0.0	0.0	0.22	0.2
Brian Sikorski	5	10.7	9	7.10	-2.3	1.60	0.40	-1.0	0.0	8.56	-4.0
Mike Venafro	77	56.3	27	4.03	7.3	0.97	0.35	2.4	5.6	4.42	4.9
John Wetteland	62	60.0	35	4.91	1.9	0.23	0.09	-0.3	2.3	5.28	-0.6
Jeff Zimmerman	65	69.7	45	5.44	-1.8	1.02	0.39	6.9	-4.2	4.29	7.0
TOTALS	415	485.0	331	5.74	-29.4	0.87	0.33			5.85	-35.0

For a quick guide to RET, see page 10.

Toronto Blue Jays

The Toronto Blue Jays are the worst team in baseball. They should fold the franchise, but since that would create scheduling problems, they'll probably have to play out the year. They'll be lucky to win 35 games, reaching that plateau only because Carlos Delgado and Shannon Stewart are amazing players. It's really a wonder they can get fans to show up at Skydome, though I suppose the chance to see spontaneous sex acts through the hotel windows is a pretty good drawing card.

OK, so the Blue Jays aren't really the worst team in baseball. It's just that the Jays are a team (like the Twins and, more justifiably, the A's) about whom we've gotten a bit too exuberant in our optimism, both in earlier editions of this book and on our website. Whether we're claiming they'll run away with the wild card in 1999 or predicting a division title in 2000 or forecasting the latest of Alex Gonzalez's breakout seasons, BP's enthusiasm for Ontario's Team has been misplaced. So this would be a good year to rip into them, to blast their pitching performances or their putrid play at second base or their refusal to pay more attention to OBP.

Sorry, can't do it.

Despite three straight years of disappointing Toronto baseball, we can't let go of the idea that the Blue Jays are on the brink of something big, a run of success similar to their 1985–1993 stretch that ended with back-to-back championships. There is a tremendous amount of high-quality talent in this system, so much so that the Jays had the luxury of moving some of that talent last year during their failed wild-card run. But unlike, say, the Diamondbacks, the Jays haven't traded their best (or, in the Diamondbacks' case, only) prospects.

For instance, the Blue Jays traded Mike Abernathy and Mike Young last season to garner some pitching for their wild-card push. Both players are decent prospects—Abernathy won a gold medal in Australia last summer, and Young has shown a good glove and a hint of offensive skill—but they pale next to great middle-infield prospects like Cesar Izturis and Felipe Lopez.

Blue Jays Prospectus

2000 record: 83–79; Third place, AL East
Pythagenport W/L: 77–85
Runs Scored: 861 (8th in AL)
Runs Allowed: 908 (11th in AL)
Team EqA: .261 (7th in AL)
2000 Batters' Age: 28.1 (6th youngest in AL)
2000 Pitchers' Age: 28.7 (tied for 7th oldest in AL)
Ballpark: Skydome; slight hitters' park; Park Factor of 1.018
2000: Their good young pitchers didn't perform, and the offense looked better than it was.
2001: They're clearly two steps behind the Yanks and Sox, but only for this year.

The middle infield isn't the only place where the Jays are stacked. Last year, they converted a first-round shortstop, Joe Lawrence, to catcher. He's now part of a solid line of catching prospects that starts with Venezuelan defensive whiz Guillermo Quiroz and runs through power-hitting Josh Phelps. The Jays lack room at the major-league level for corner men and DHs, but they have a number of players at Triple-A Syracuse and Double-A Tennessee who would be playing in the majors for other teams: Andy Thompson, Kevin Witt, and Luis Lopez. The Jays are so deep that they'll never miss Jay Gibbons, a power-hitting first baseman who was lost to the Orioles in the Rule 5 draft.

No doubt about it, the Jays are developing talent. They're developing both quantity and quality, and they're doing so in relative obscurity. The A's have gotten all our accolades for their emphasis on plate discipline and development of college pitchers, and the White Sox were *Baseball America*'s Organization of the Year, but the Jays can go toe-to-toe with those teams or any of the other major talent factories, like the Yankees, Braves, or Expos.

The neat thing about the Jays is that they're picking up talent from many different sources. A look at their best prospects shows a few #1 picks (Vernon Wells, Felipe Lopez, Joe Lawrence), some lower draft picks (Mark Hendrickson, Bob File, and both of the traded second basemen), and some quality non-drafted foreign free agents (Cesar Izturis from Venezuela and Pasqual Coco from the Dominican). They also boast a broad selection of talent; unlike some teams that have a speciality or two, the Jays could assemble a whole team of minor leaguers who are decent prospects. That's impressive.

About the only area in which they've done poorly is high-profile foreign signings. Neither Jose Pett nor Josephang Bernhardt are in the book this year, and for good reason: they combined for about 20 minutes of play in 2000 and are as likely to become major leaguers as Chris Kahrl is to pass up a free bratwurst.

The Blue Jays' future appears even brighter when you consider the impact new ownership might have on the player-acquisition budget. Rogers Communications, a Canadian media and electronics conglomerate, took the Jays off the hands of Interbrew SA last fall. Rogers announced plans to raise the Jays' payroll, but the real impact could come in the draft. The past two seasons, the Jays have made low-cost signability picks in the first round, fumbling away a critical piece of their player-development puzzle.

This kind of penny-pinching damages the Jays perhaps more than any other team, because they've had so much success with their high picks. From 1988 through 1997, every one of their top picks made the majors, as shown in Table 1.

We've added Lopez to the list to show that the streak will continue through 1998. It's really an amazing run, especially when you consider that the Jays didn't draft in the first half of the first round for most of those years. Run down the list and you'll find and an excellent starting outfield, the seeds of a rotation, a couple of quality relievers, and an acceptable infield. Eddie Zosky and Kevin Witt are the worst of the bunch, and each of them nevertheless reached in the majors.

Now compare the players in the list above to the Jays' pinch-penny picks of the past two years. Their 1999 #1 was Alexis Rios, a high-school outfielder from Puerto Rico who didn't play well at either middle-A or low-A last year. He's not on anyone's prospect list. Their 2000 #1, Miguel Negron, has a nearly identical profile and was not considered a first-round talent by most observers. He slugged .258 in rookie ball.

A team that has proven it can maximize the return on its draft picks shouldn't have its hands tied by the money men. Forget the major-league payroll; if Rogers wants to bring back the Jays' glory days, the company will stop forcing the Jays' development staff to make suboptimal selections in the first round and instead let them do what they've done best: get major-league players with high draft picks.

A team with a new owner usually has a glow of optimism surrounding it, but while the Jays have a great future, the immediate outlook isn't quite so rosy. Frankly, a lot of things went right for the Jays in 2000, and even so they still weren't able to capitalize. Carlos Delgado and Darrin Fletcher put up career seasons, while Shannon Stewart has his best year to date. Frank Castillo came back from the dead to be one of the league's best starters. David Wells arrested his decline and pitched well for most of the season.

In order to contend this year, the Jays must solve two basic problems. One is OBP. They have a ton of power: seven players hit at least 20 bombs, and they ranked fourth in the AL with a .469 slugging average. But the team OBP of .341 tied for tenth in the league, and other than Delgado, Fletcher, and Stewart, none of the projected starters is a good bet to post a league-average OBP. Tony Batista is a heck of a power hitter and a good defensive third baseman, but a .307 OBP is unacceptable for a corner infielder. The middle infield could easily shackle the team with 1,000 at-bats of a .300 OBP. With the Jays' lineup all but set—only center field is a question, and that's a two-man battle between Jose Cruz and Vernon Wells—it's not likely that the team is going to improve in this area.

The second problem is the pitching staff. A year ago, one of the reasons we were so optimistic about the Jays was that they had a rotation core that was young and had considerable upside. A year later, following a season in which they were a collective three wins below replacement level, Roy Halladay, Chris Carpenter, and Kelvim Escobar raise more questions than ever before. That the Jays did well last year despite the collapse of their rotation is a tribute to the good performances of Frank Castillo and David Wells.

When it comes to addressing their pitching woes, there's not much the Jays can do. They've brought in Steve Parris to provide bulk innings at the back of the rotation, and they may keep Escobar in the bullpen, but for this team to improve, Carpenter in particular needs to show that he's healthy and capable of staying in a rotation for a complete season. The internal options at the upper levels are plentiful—the Jays have many candidates at Double- and Triple-A for the job of #5 starter/swing man—but the really good starter prospects, the guys who generate excitement, are at least two years away.

Considering the problems the Jays face in both scoring and preventing runs, it's hard to see this team having an impressive 2001 season. In 2002 and beyond, though, the flow of talent from the minors is going to begin. If there's a team in the AL that could have an Indians-style run in its division from 2003–2006, it's the Blue Jays.

Table 1: Toronto's Top Picks Who Have Made the Majors, 1988–1998

Year	Player	Pick
1988:	Ed Sprague	25
1989:	Eddie Zosky	22
1990:	Steve Karsay	22
1991:	Shawn Green	16
1992:	Shannon Stewart	19
1993:	Chris Carpenter	15
1994:	Kevin Witt	28
1995:	Roy Halladay	17
1996:	Billy Koch	4
1997:	Vernon Wells	5
1998:	Felipe Lopez	8

American League

HITTERS (BA: .270, OBP: .340, SLG: .440, EqA: .260)

Tony Batista 3B Bats R Age 27

YEAR	TEAM	LGE	AB	H	DB	TP	HR	BB	SO	R	RBI	SB	CS	OUT	BA	OBP	SLG	EQA	EQR	DEFENSE			
1998	Arizona	NL	295	79	16	1	18	18	49	47	40	1	1	217	.268	.316	.512	.266	40	33-2B	0	29-SS	2
1999	Arizona	NL	144	36	4	0	5	14	16	15	19	2	0	108	.250	.325	.382	.241	15	43-SS	7		
1999	Toronto	AL	373	108	24	1	27	19	72	60	76	2	0	265	.290	.330	.576	.288	59	97-SS	12		
2000	Toronto	AL	617	163	30	2	42	27	110	91	108	5	5	459	.264	.302	.524	.262	81	154-3B	12		
2001	Toronto	AL	512	133	22	1	31	36	97	68	94	3	2	381	.260	.308	.488	.260	65				

While 2000 looks like a great season thanks to the power numbers, the deterioration of Tony Batista's plate discipline and the move to third base suggest that his 1999 campaign might have been better. The signing of Alex Gonzalez means that Tony Batista is going to be a third baseman; he needs to hit .300 or walk 50 times to be valuable.

Homer Bush 2B Bats R Age 28

YEAR	TEAM	LGE	AB	H	DB	TP	HR	BB	SO	R	RBI	SB	CS	OUT	BA	OBP	SLG	EQA	EQR	DEFENSE			
1998	NY Yanks	AL	71	27	1	0	2	5	17	16	5	5	3	47	.380	.421	.479	.299	11	16-2B	-5		
1999	Toronto	AL	482	156	27	4	5	16	75	66	52	30	8	334	.324	.352	.427	.267	61	109-2B	10	17-SS	-3
2000	Toronto	AL	296	63	3	0	3	15	55	36	18	10	5	238	.213	.263	.253	.168	14	75-2B	13		
2001	Toronto	AL	274	77	10	1	4	15	51	38	31	11	4	201	.281	.318	.369	.235	27				

Homer Bush's 1999 and 2000 seasons represent the two ends of the spectrum for a player whose primary skill is hitting for average. The Jays have locked him up for two more years, so they're going to live or die by Bush's ability to slap 150 singles a season. Bush, Batista, and Alex Gonzalez give the Blue Jays a pretty expensive infield that is unlikely to be worth more than a win, maybe two, per season.

Alberto Castillo C Bats R Age 31

YEAR	TEAM	LGE	AB	H	DB	TP	HR	BB	SO	R	RBI	SB	CS	OUT	BA	OBP	SLG	EQA	EQR	DEFENSE	
1998	Norfolk	Int	50	8	1	0	1	9	13	3	5	0	0	42	.160	.288	.240	.180	3	14-C	0
1998	NY Mets	NL	84	18	1	0	3	9	16	13	8	0	2	68	.214	.297	.333	.205	6	26-C	5
1999	St Louis	NL	256	66	5	0	5	20	45	20	30	0	0	190	.258	.316	.336	.220	22	78-C	11
2000	Toronto	AL	184	39	4	0	2	19	33	13	16	0	0	145	.212	.286	.266	.182	10	58-C	3
2001	Toronto	AL	89	18	1	0	1	11	40	7	6	0	0	71	.202	.290	.247	.179	5		

He throws well, hits left-handers a little, and doesn't demand a larger role, so Alberto Castillo is an excellent fit as Darrin Fletcher's backup. This kind of yin and yang in a catching tandem is rare, and it gives a manager a lot of flexibility in maximizing matchups.

Marty Cordova OF Bats R Age 31

YEAR	TEAM	LGE	AB	H	DB	TP	HR	BB	SO	R	RBI	SB	CS	OUT	BA	OBP	SLG	EQA	EQR	DEFENSE	
1998	Minnesot	AL	435	111	18	2	11	49	92	51	67	2	5	329	.255	.337	.382	.241	47	115-LF	2
1999	Minnesot	AL	420	119	26	3	15	43	87	59	67	12	4	305	.283	.361	.467	.277	61	24-RF	-7
2000	Toronto	AL	199	49	4	0	5	15	32	21	17	3	2	152	.246	.309	.342	.219	17	34-LF	-6
2001	Clevelnd	AL	266	71	12	1	8	29	53	41	41	4	2	197	.267	.339	.410	.251	31		

Signing Marty Cordova looked like a good idea for the Blue Jays, who needed a dance partner for Brad Fullmer at DH. Cordova didn't hit, though, and he eventually lost his at-bats to Todd Greene. He's still capable of being an asset, but he's fighting for jobs with a lot of guys who possess the same skill set and more recent records of success.

Jose Cruz CF Bats B Age 27

YEAR	TEAM	LGE	AB	H	DB	TP	HR	BB	SO	R	RBI	SB	CS	OUT	BA	OBP	SLG	EQA	EQR	DEFENSE	
1998	Toronto	AL	351	91	14	3	12	56	88	55	42	9	4	264	.259	.361	.419	.265	48	100-CF	2
1998	Syracuse	Int	142	37	9	1	6	26	32	23	18	5	3	108	.261	.375	.465	.280	22	40-CF	7
1999	Toronto	AL	346	84	18	3	15	60	83	61	44	13	4	266	.243	.355	.442	.270	50	102-CF	10
1999	Syracuse	Int	104	17	4	1	2	24	20	14	11	3	0	87	.163	.320	.279	.219	10	29-LF	4
2000	Toronto	AL	598	145	31	4	32	64	117	87	71	16	6	459	.242	.318	.468	.259	78	159-CF	0
2001	Toronto	AL	511	126	28	2	22	72	115	89	83	13	3	388	.247	.340	.438	.264	69		

(Jose Cruz *continued*)

The Jays finally left Jose Cruz alone—mostly because they had a new center fielder in whom to be disappointed, Vernon Wells—and he was basically a league-average player. The Jays' problem isn't Cruz; it's that a lot of their best hitters are too similar to him: low-OBP, good-power guys like Batista, Brad Fullmer, and Raul Mondesi. Vernon Wells has to play, so Cruz should be elsewhere in 2001.

Carlos Delgado — 1B — Bats L — Age 29

YEAR	TEAM	LGE	AB	H	DB	TP	HR	BB	SO	R	RBI	SB	CS	OUT	BA	OBP	SLG	EQA	EQR	DEFENSE
1998	Toronto	AL	528	159	36	2	42	72	124	96	116	3	0	369	.301	.395	.616	.322	108	136-1B 10
1999	Toronto	AL	568	157	33	1	47	80	128	110	131	1	1	412	.276	.378	.586	.308	108	147-1B 1
2000	Toronto	AL	555	192	44	2	44	115	95	107	129	0	1	364	.346	.470	.670	.363	145	161-1B -11
2001	Toronto	AL	474	146	29	1	37	90	99	112	132	1	0	328	.308	.418	.608	.332	104	

It's interesting to note that in a season in which Carlos Delgado's defensive reputation improved, his Prospectus Fielding Runs score continued its decline. Of course, a .363 EqA means that no one is really talking about Delgado's defense. Delgado is a complete hitter, comparable to what Frank Thomas was throughout the 1990s. The Wilton projection looks pessimistic; another 100 extra-base-hit season is unlikely, but a performance closer to a .360 EqA seems within reach.

Darrin Fletcher — C — Bats L — Age 34

YEAR	TEAM	LGE	AB	H	DB	TP	HR	BB	SO	R	RBI	SB	CS	OUT	BA	OBP	SLG	EQA	EQR	DEFENSE
1998	Toronto	AL	406	118	23	1	10	24	35	38	52	0	0	288	.291	.339	.426	.255	47	116-C -6
1999	Toronto	AL	410	121	20	0	21	22	43	46	79	0	0	289	.295	.339	.498	.273	56	104-C -4
2000	Toronto	AL	412	132	17	1	21	15	41	41	55	1	0	280	.320	.352	.519	.284	60	101-C -6
2001	Toronto	AL	398	115	14	0	16	25	42	51	68	0	0	283	.289	.331	.445	.258	48	

He's been an underrated player for a number of seasons, in part because there are some incredible catchers playing right now. Darrin Fletcher provides left-handed power and a decent OBP without being Todd Hundley defensively.

Ryan Freel — UT — Bats R — Age 25

YEAR	TEAM	LGE	AB	H	DB	TP	HR	BB	SO	R	RBI	SB	CS	OUT	BA	OBP	SLG	EQA	EQR	DEFENSE		
1998	Knoxvill	Sou	250	58	12	2	3	21	34	30	24	9	5	197	.232	.293	.332	.211	20	50-CF -2		
1998	Syracuse	Int	119	25	2	0	2	22	16	15	10	5	3	97	.210	.347	.277	.225	12	24-CF -2		
1999	Knoxvill	Sou	46	10	2	1	1	6	4	6	6	2	1	37	.217	.308	.370	.230	5	11-CF 0		
1999	Syracuse	Int	77	20	3	1	1	6	13	11	8	6	2	59	.260	.337	.364	.246	9	16-CF 0		
2000	Tennesse	Sou	45	10	2	1	0	6	6	9	6	1	1	36	.222	.320	.311	.216	4	11-CF 0		
2000	Syracuse	Int	284	73	10	4	9	28	46	49	25	20	6	217	.257	.338	.415	.259	37	24-2B -1	23-LF 0
2001	Toronto	AL	285	73	12	3	7	32	46	48	37	15	5	217	.256	.331	.393	.250	34			

Ryan Freel is an ex-prospect who has made himself into a good utility player. He can hit for average, take walks, and he runs very well. Freel handled five positions in the minors last season, and a guy who can play anywhere gives a team advantages both in-game and in-season. He deserves a clean shot at a job.

Brad Fullmer — DH — Bats L — Age 26

YEAR	TEAM	LGE	AB	H	DB	TP	HR	BB	SO	R	RBI	SB	CS	OUT	BA	OBP	SLG	EQA	EQR	DEFENSE
1998	Montreal	NL	511	139	39	2	15	37	66	58	73	5	6	378	.272	.323	.444	.251	60	124-1B -9
1999	Montreal	NL	349	94	33	2	9	17	33	36	44	1	3	258	.269	.307	.453	.246	39	85-1B -4
1999	Ottawa	Int	141	40	5	0	9	9	16	23	24	1	2	103	.284	.336	.511	.271	20	23-1B -2
2000	Toronto	AL	478	141	25	1	34	24	62	72	99	3	1	338	.295	.337	.565	.288	75	
2001	Toronto	AL	482	140	29	1	29	35	63	76	102	3	3	345	.290	.338	.535	.282	73	

That's about as good a season as a player can have while walking fewer than 30 times. Brad Fullmer left Felipe Alou's doghouse behind, switched provinces, and had the year hinted at by his 1998 rookie season. Fullmer, a poor first baseman, may have benefited from being locked in at DH all season. Now he just needs to talk to Delgado about being more selective.

American League

Jay Gibbons   1B/LF   Bats L   Age 24

YEAR	TEAM	LGE	AB	H	DB	TP	HR	BB	SO	R	RBI	SB	CS	OUT	BA	OBP	SLG	EQA	EQR	DEFENSE			
1998	Med Hat	Pio	278	76	13	1	10	17	30	31	43	1	0	202	.273	.318	.435	.249	31	35-1B	-1		
1999	Hagerstn	SAL	299	71	14	1	10	23	59	37	44	1	0	228	.237	.293	.391	.227	28	22-1B	-1		
1999	Dunedin	Fla	213	52	8	0	7	19	44	24	26	1	1	161	.244	.306	.380	.229	20	54-1B	1		
2000	Tennesse	Sou	484	130	24	1	17	45	70	69	58	1	1	355	.269	.337	.428	.255	58	95-1B	-12	10-LF	-1
2001	*Baltimor*	*AL*	*440*	*129*	*20*	*1*	*20*	*46*	*74*	*67*	*79*	*2*	*1*	*312*	*.293*	*.360*	*.480*	*.285*	*68*				

The Jays are set at the positions Jay Gibbons can play, so they left him exposed to the Rule 5 draft. The Orioles selected him in the Triple-A phase of the draft, only to block him by signing David Segui. Gibbons will have plenty to discuss with Cal Pickering while he's slapping International League pitchers.

Alex Gonzalez   SS   Bats R   Age 28

YEAR	TEAM	LGE	AB	H	DB	TP	HR	BB	SO	R	RBI	SB	CS	OUT	BA	OBP	SLG	EQA	EQR	DEFENSE	
1998	Toronto	AL	567	139	26	1	15	27	108	70	51	18	5	433	.245	.286	.374	.222	50	158-SS	5
1999	Toronto	AL	153	45	11	0	3	14	21	21	12	4	2	110	.294	.363	.425	.266	20	37-SS	12
2000	Toronto	AL	524	133	29	2	16	36	103	64	66	4	5	396	.254	.307	.408	.235	53	138-SS	-8
2001	*Toronto*	*AL*	*350*	*86*	*13*	*0*	*11*	*25*	*72*	*40*	*43*	*6*	*3*	*267*	*.246*	*.296*	*.377*	*.225*	*32*		

While it's possible that Alex Gonzalez is going to take a significant step forward, he now has 2,600-odd major-league at-bats and a 691 career OPS. Even a "significant step forward" isn't going to do more than make him an average player. The four-year, $24-million deal he signed with the Jays overpays him by half.

Craig Grebeck   IF   Bats R   Age 36

YEAR	TEAM	LGE	AB	H	DB	TP	HR	BB	SO	R	RBI	SB	CS	OUT	BA	OBP	SLG	EQA	EQR	DEFENSE	
1998	Toronto	AL	300	79	18	2	2	29	37	34	27	2	2	223	.263	.336	.357	.235	30	83-2B	5
1999	Toronto	AL	111	41	7	0	0	14	12	17	9	0	0	70	.369	.448	.432	.307	18	16-2B	-4
2000	Toronto	AL	238	70	11	0	6	22	30	35	23	0	0	168	.294	.359	.416	.262	30	53-2B	2
2001	*Toronto*	*AL*	*190*	*50*	*6*	*0*	*4*	*24*	*25*	*27*	*25*	*0*	*0*	*140*	*.263*	*.346*	*.358*	*.243*	*20*		

He's less a utility infielder and more a platoon second baseman now, which is fine because he can handle the job. He just can't play more than two or three times a week. He's not likely to return to the Jays, who have Homer Bush and Jeff Frye under contract, but he'll be a contributor somewhere.

Todd Greene   DH/C   Bats R   Age 30

YEAR	TEAM	LGE	AB	H	DB	TP	HR	BB	SO	R	RBI	SB	CS	OUT	BA	OBP	SLG	EQA	EQR	DEFENSE	
1998	Vancouvr	PCL	109	27	6	0	6	10	18	12	15	1	0	82	.248	.322	.468	.260	14		
1998	Anaheim	AL	71	18	2	0	2	2	18	3	8	0	0	53	.254	.274	.366	.208	5		
1999	Edmonton	PCL	72	15	4	0	3	0	13	7	9	0	0	57	.208	.215	.389	.187	4	12-LF	0
1999	Anaheim	AL	321	79	16	0	16	8	57	35	42	1	4	246	.246	.270	.445	.227	30	11-C	0
2000	Syracuse	Int	91	23	2	0	5	4	18	11	10	1	0	68	.253	.284	.440	.237	9	10-LF	-1
2000	Toronto	AL	85	20	3	0	5	4	16	11	10	0	0	65	.235	.270	.447	.231	8		
2001	*Toronto*	*AL*	*233*	*54*	*8*	*0*	*11*	*12*	*48*	*22*	*31*	*0*	*1*	*180*	*.232*	*.269*	*.408*	*.219*	*20*		

The Blue Jays are making noise about playing him some behind the plate in 2000. Any team trying to employ Todd Greene faces a tough choice: use him as a bat at first base, DH. and left field, while suffering the subpar offense, or use him behind the plate until his shoulder balks. The third choice is to release him and give the job to Tom Wilson, but we've been down that road before.

Cesar Izturis   SS   Bats B   Age 21

YEAR	TEAM	LGE	AB	H	DB	TP	HR	BB	SO	R	RBI	SB	CS	OUT	BA	OBP	SLG	EQA	EQR	DEFENSE			
1998	Hagerstn	SAL	414	93	8	1	1	14	45	37	28	7	5	326	.225	.252	.256	.156	16	121-SS	2		
1999	Dunedin	Fla	532	134	25	6	3	16	67	53	53	14	8	406	.252	.277	.338	.203	38	84-SS	-4	45-2B	3
2000	Syracuse	Int	436	93	12	4	1	14	46	46	25	15	9	352	.213	.239	.266	.157	17	128-SS	18		
2001	*Toronto*	*AL*	*417*	*99*	*14*	*3*	*1*	*20*	*51*	*35*	*29*	*12*	*9*	*327*	*.237*	*.272*	*.293*	*.184*	*24*				

(Cesar Izturis *continued*)

Cesar Izturis is one of the reasons the Jays were able to toss around second-base prospects like so many chads at least year's trade deadline. Izturis fields like a dream and runs well. His performance at Syracuse last season was pretty brutal, but for a 20-year-old making a two-level jump, allowances can be made. He stayed at Triple-A all season, which is the important thing. Izturis has time to develop at the plate; he should force the Blue Jays to move Gonzalez by 2003.

Joe Lawrence   C   Bats R   Age 24

YEAR	TEAM	LGE	AB	H	DB	TP	HR	BB	SO	R	RBI	SB	CS	OUT	BA	OBP	SLG	EQA	EQR	DEFENSE
1998	Dunedin	Fla	463	109	23	3	8	79	100	70	28	5	5	359	.235	.350	.350	.242	52	118-SS -20
1999	Knoxvill	Sou	253	54	12	1	5	42	51	37	16	3	3	202	.213	.329	.328	.227	25	62-3B -3
2000	Dunedin	Fla	384	92	19	1	11	51	84	47	46	9	4	296	.240	.333	.380	.243	43	68-C -16
2000	Tennesse	Sou	138	32	8	0	0	23	28	18	8	3	1	107	.232	.348	.290	.228	13	29-C -3
2001	Toronto	AL	433	103	19	1	11	65	99	68	55	9	3	333	.238	.337	.363	.243	49	

Position-player-to-catcher conversions have a long history of failure, so when the Jays elected to move Joe Lawrence behind the plate from third base, it was easy to be skeptical. Surprisingly, Lawrence took to the change easily, becoming an acceptable catcher (albeit with lousy stats) and retaining his broad offensive skills. Josh Phelps is the Jays' only other catching prospect above low-A ball, so Lawrence is on track to back up Darrin Fletcher in 2003 and be the Jays' starter in 2004.

Felipe Lopez   SS   Bats B   Age 21

YEAR	TEAM	LGE	AB	H	DB	TP	HR	BB	SO	R	RBI	SB	CS	OUT	BA	OBP	SLG	EQA	EQR	DEFENSE
1998	St Cath	NYP	84	24	4	1	1	2	15	9	7	1	1	61	.286	.302	.393	.227	8	17-SS -1
1999	Hagerstn	SAL	551	122	22	2	9	44	166	60	54	7	6	435	.221	.281	.318	.198	38	130-SS -18
2000	Tennesse	Sou	470	108	15	3	8	20	114	45	34	6	5	368	.230	.262	.326	.189	29	122-SS -38
2001	Toronto	AL	402	95	17	1	8	33	114	44	42	6	4	311	.236	.294	.343	.214	33	

Another of the reasons Mike Young and Brent Abernathy are elsewhere, Felipe Lopez jumped from the Sally League to the Southern League in 2000. Like Izturis, he didn't play well, but like Izturis, he was just 20 years old and making a two-level jump. Lopez is the Jays' best tools prospect; with Izturis and Gonzalez ahead of him, he'll get another trip through the South in 2001. Between Lopez and Izturis, Lopez is the one more likely to move to second base.

Luis Lopez   3B   Bats R   Age 27

YEAR	TEAM	LGE	AB	H	DB	TP	HR	BB	SO	R	RBI	SB	CS	OUT	BA	OBP	SLG	EQA	EQR	DEFENSE			
1998	Knoxvill	Sou	444	109	16	1	11	36	60	47	54	0	1	336	.245	.305	.360	.222	39	57-1B	3	28-3B	0
1998	Syracuse	Int	41	8	0	0	1	5	6	5	3	0	0	33	.195	.283	.268	.183	2				
1999	Syracuse	Int	526	150	28	2	3	30	58	61	54	1	0	376	.285	.325	.363	.232	49	80-1B	2	26-3B	1
2000	Syracuse	Int	490	141	20	1	6	37	35	53	64	2	1	350	.288	.340	.369	.241	50	50-3B	-3	31-1B	-2
2001	Toronto	AL	450	119	17	1	7	43	45	56	55	1	0	331	.264	.329	.353	.233	44				

Luis Lopez has gone as far as he's going to go with the Jays, who are loaded at the infield corners. He's become enough of a third baseman that he is a viable option for a team with left-handed power at the corners and a need for a pinch hitter who can rap some doubles. That's a narrow job description, so what he really needs is a manager who likes him.

Dave Martinez   OF   Bats L   Age 36

YEAR	TEAM	LGE	AB	H	DB	TP	HR	BB	SO	R	RBI	SB	CS	OUT	BA	OBP	SLG	EQA	EQR	DEFENSE
1998	TampaBay	AL	308	81	5	0	5	35	46	30	21	7	7	234	.263	.342	.328	.229	29	71-RF 8
1999	TampaBay	AL	510	146	27	5	6	55	69	76	63	12	6	370	.286	.361	.394	.258	63	129-RF -7
2000	TampaBay	AL	103	27	3	2	1	9	15	11	11	1	5	81	.262	.321	.359	.216	9	24-RF 1
2000	ChiCubs	NL	55	10	2	1	0	1	7	5	2	1	0	45	.182	.196	.255	.119	1	
2000	Texas	AL	117	31	3	1	2	13	18	13	11	2	1	87	.265	.344	.359	.241	12	30-RF 4
2000	Toronto	AL	177	55	9	1	2	22	26	27	20	4	2	124	.311	.390	.407	.274	24	47-RF 1
2001	Atlanta	NL	373	93	11	2	5	46	58	52	44	7	6	286	.249	.332	.330	.231	37	

"Dear Diary, today I played baseball. I don't know who I played for. I don't know who I played against. I just know I played baseball. I'm so tired, diary. I've been traded three times in 11 weeks; I've played indoors and outdoors, for good teams and bad, in two leagues and four divisions. I just get up in the morning, go to the nearest stadium, and there's a uniform with my name on it. I can't wait until October, so I can go home to...to...oh, diary...I can't remember where I live!"

American League

Raul Mondesi — RF — Bats R — Age 30

YEAR	TEAM	LGE	AB	H	DB	TP	HR	BB	SO	R	RBI	SB	CS	OUT	BA	OBP	SLG	EQA	EQR	DEFENSE	
1998	LosAngls	NL	591	169	27	5	32	29	105	90	92	15	10	432	.286	.322	.511	.268	80	143-CF	-5
1999	LosAngls	NL	608	154	28	5	33	63	127	93	94	28	9	463	.253	.326	.479	.266	85	154-RF	-1
2000	Toronto	AL	385	104	21	1	25	27	66	74	63	23	7	288	.270	.323	.525	.276	58	94-RF	-6
2001	Toronto	AL	469	122	22	2	25	45	95	79	81	20	6	353	.260	.325	.475	.267	65		

Raul Mondesi is a good player, not a great one, but at $10 million per year, he's being paid like a great one. While the value of his performance has been pretty much the same for the past few years, the shape of that performance has varied. Such players are hard to predict. Mondesi could do all the things in a single season that he's done in separate seasons—hit .300, walk 60 times, rope 80 extra-base hits—and get some MVP votes. He could do none of them and be a disaster.

Mickey Morandini — 2B — Bats L — Age 35

YEAR	TEAM	LGE	AB	H	DB	TP	HR	BB	SO	R	RBI	SB	CS	OUT	BA	OBP	SLG	EQA	EQR	DEFENSE	
1998	ChiCubs	NL	589	173	18	4	9	70	79	94	53	12	1	417	.294	.377	.384	.266	76	146-2B	-2
1999	ChiCubs	NL	457	107	18	4	4	42	58	56	34	4	5	355	.234	.307	.317	.210	36	113-2B	4
2000	Philadel	NL	303	74	11	3	0	25	51	29	20	5	2	231	.244	.309	.300	.208	23	81-2B	-1
2000	Toronto	AL	106	29	2	1	0	6	21	9	7	1	0	77	.274	.313	.311	.211	8	28-2B	6
2001	Toronto	AL	394	94	13	3	3	41	65	45	37	5	3	303	.239	.310	.310	.212	31		

The Blue Jays ensured that they wouldn't miss Homer Bush in the wake of his broken hand by replacing him with a player who was just as bad. Mickey Morandini was a good second baseman for much of the 1990s, but everything we've seen the past two years indicates that he's done.

Josh Phelps — C — Bats R — Age 23

YEAR	TEAM	LGE	AB	H	DB	TP	HR	BB	SO	R	RBI	SB	CS	OUT	BA	OBP	SLG	EQA	EQR	DEFENSE	
1998	Hagerstn	SAL	390	83	15	1	6	29	84	34	30	1	0	307	.213	.274	.303	.190	24	76-C	-13
1999	Dunedin	Fla	405	105	20	2	14	20	120	50	56	3	1	301	.259	.300	.422	.238	42	23-C	-2
2000	Tennesse	Sou	187	39	8	1	7	11	68	20	22	0	0	148	.209	.266	.374	.209	15	38-C	-10
2000	Dunedin	Fla	114	29	4	0	8	9	39	18	21	0	0	85	.254	.312	.500	.262	15	16-C	0
2001	Toronto	AL	330	83	18	1	13	25	112	41	50	1	0	247	.252	.304	.430	.244	36		

He has a very small window of opportunity now that Joe Lawrence has shown he can catch. Josh Phelps has performed best at the plate when he's not above A ball and when he's not catching, two things that will have to change if he's going to have a career. A baseball career, that is. If he wants to go into Web design or something, those traits won't be a problem. Jayson Werth's arrival hurts him.

Shannon Stewart — LF — Bats R — Age 27

YEAR	TEAM	LGE	AB	H	DB	TP	HR	BB	SO	R	RBI	SB	CS	OUT	BA	OBP	SLG	EQA	EQR	DEFENSE	
1998	Toronto	AL	514	146	29	3	13	66	69	86	54	42	16	384	.284	.380	.428	.278	78	127-LF	7
1999	Toronto	AL	603	185	29	2	11	53	76	97	64	34	14	432	.307	.370	.416	.269	81	131-LF	-5
2000	Toronto	AL	589	188	43	5	22	31	72	104	66	21	6	407	.319	.360	.521	.289	91	136-LF	7
2001	Toronto	AL	602	186	33	3	15	53	81	119	93	35	12	428	.309	.365	.449	.277	87		

One of the problems the Jays had down the stretch was the disappearance of their leadoff hitter. Shannon Stewart, who was having his best season through five months, hit only .234/.264/.355 after August 31. That slide skewered the line you see above and kept the Jays from making the Yankees' terrible September mean something. His projection is low; Stewart will be up around a .300 EqA this season.

Andy Thompson — LF — Bats R — Age 25

YEAR	TEAM	LGE	AB	H	DB	TP	HR	BB	SO	R	RBI	SB	CS	OUT	BA	OBP	SLG	EQA	EQR	DEFENSE			
1998	Knoxvill	Sou	477	111	22	1	11	33	73	50	58	4	2	368	.233	.285	.352	.211	38	62-LF	-4	43-3B	-17
1999	Knoxvill	Sou	256	53	11	2	11	24	59	40	36	3	2	205	.207	.287	.395	.225	25	59-RF	-6		
1999	Syracuse	Int	228	59	13	1	13	16	45	32	32	3	0	169	.259	.311	.496	.263	30	42-RF	1		
2000	Syracuse	Int	428	96	22	1	19	41	99	50	53	6	2	334	.224	.302	.414	.238	46	112-LF	-1		
2001	Toronto	AL	428	97	19	1	18	49	99	57	60	5	1	332	.227	.306	.402	.239	46				

(Andy Thompson *continued*)

The Blue Jays have had a few similar guys over the past couple of years, hitters like Andy Thompson, Kevin Witt and Luis Lopez. They're mostly tweeners, unable to make it on their hitting alone and moved from the positions at which they might have had value. Thompson should force his way into a major-league job eventually; the Jays have right-handed hitters at all three of his positions, so it won't happen here.

Vernon Wells — CF — Bats R — Age 22

YEAR	TEAM	LGE	AB	H	DB	TP	HR	BB	SO	R	RBI	SB	CS	OUT	BA	OBP	SLG	EQA	EQR	DEFENSE	
1998	Hagerstn	SAL	514	115	27	1	7	35	88	58	42	4	4	403	.224	.274	.321	.194	34	124-CF	-2
1999	Dunedin	Fla	265	71	12	1	8	19	39	29	28	5	1	195	.268	.318	.411	.245	29	69-CF	-5
1999	Knoxvill	Sou	105	28	6	1	2	9	16	13	11	3	1	78	.267	.325	.400	.245	12	26-CF	1
1999	Syracuse	Int	128	35	7	1	3	8	22	16	16	3	1	94	.273	.320	.414	.246	14	31-CF	0
1999	Toronto	AL	88	23	3	0	2	3	16	8	8	1	1	66	.261	.286	.364	.212	7	21-CF	2
2000	Syracuse	Int	495	111	27	5	14	38	91	64	55	16	3	387	.224	.284	.384	.225	47	119-CF	2
2001	*Toronto*	*AL*	*496*	*128*	*29*	*2*	*16*	*45*	*94*	*73*	*72*	*9*	*2*	*370*	*.258*	*.320*	*.421*	*.250*	*58*		

He didn't repeat his explosive 1999, but Vernon Wells is still the Jays' best prospect. He started badly after losing the Jays' centerfield job to Jose Cruz in the spring but performed better as the season progressed. There's really no difference in Wells from a year ago; don't let his bad year at Syracuse affect your opinion of him.

DeWayne Wise — R5 — Bats L — Age 23

YEAR	TEAM	LGE	AB	H	DB	TP	HR	BB	SO	R	RBI	SB	CS	OUT	BA	OBP	SLG	EQA	EQR	DEFENSE	
1998	Burlingt	Mid	504	101	15	6	2	29	119	44	34	10	8	411	.200	.245	.266	.159	21	121-CF	-3
1999	Rockford	Mid	508	109	18	6	9	25	88	44	54	14	7	406	.215	.256	.327	.191	32	131-CF	7
2000	Toronto	AL	22	3	0	0	0	1	5	3	0	1	0	19	.136	.209	.136	.053	0		
2000	Tennesse	Sou	57	12	3	1	2	5	13	8	6	2	1	46	.211	.274	.404	.223	5	15-CF	-3

The Rule 5 draft is a good idea at its core, but in execution it's problematic. The idea is to give players trapped in organizations an opportunity to play in the major leagues with teams that want them. Those teams must keep Rule 5 picks on their rosters all season, though, so in practice, players selected in the draft often spend the season as glorified bat boys, their skills deteriorating by the day. Forcing a team to keep a player on its roster for the entire season may do more harm than good to the player, so it may be time to modify the rules surrounding the draft.

DeWayne Wise came off seasons of 496 and 502 at-bats and then, after being selected from the Cubs in the 1999 Rule 5 draft, got only 78 at-bats in 2000, appearing mostly as a pinch runner and defensive replacement. There's simply no way that's beneficial to his development or his career. Wise will play center field for Tennessee this summer; he's a pinch runner prospect.

Kevin Witt — 1B — Bats L — Age 25

YEAR	TEAM	LGE	AB	H	DB	TP	HR	BB	SO	R	RBI	SB	CS	OUT	BA	OBP	SLG	EQA	EQR	DEFENSE			
1998	Syracuse	Int	456	112	16	2	19	42	123	59	54	2	2	346	.246	.316	.414	.243	50	96-1B	12	17-LF	1
1999	Syracuse	Int	420	103	20	1	19	52	108	57	53	0	0	317	.245	.331	.433	.255	52	62-1B	8	40-LF	1
1999	Toronto	AL	34	7	1	0	1	2	8	3	5	0	0	27	.206	.250	.324	.182	2				
2000	Syracuse	Int	490	111	19	4	22	36	137	50	58	1	1	380	.227	.284	.416	.229	48	107-1B	-8		
2001	*SanDieg*	*NL*	*462*	*110*	*18*	*2*	*22*	*53*	*137*	*59*	*72*	*1*	*1*	*353*	*.238*	*.317*	*.429*	*.258*	*60*				

After two seasons of trying to bash his way across the U.S./Canada border, Kevin Witt got tired in 2000, having the worst year of his career. In fairness to the Jays, they made a good deal to get Brad Fullmer, who's a better hitter than Witt. They cut him loose, and he's signed a minor league contract with the Padres.

As you near the end of this chapter, keep in mind just how many players in this system have major-league ability, even if their roles would be limited. Some organizations have nothing at the upper levels. The Jays have a half-dozen legitimate prospects and at least a half-dozen other guys who could do a job. That's damn impressive and indicative of a scouting and development program that works.

American League

Chris Woodward — IF — Bats R — Age 25

YEAR	TEAM	LGE	AB	H	DB	TP	HR	BB	SO	R	RBI	SB	CS	OUT	BA	OBP	SLG	EQA	EQR	DEFENSE			
1998	Knoxvill	Sou	253	53	5	0	4	15	50	26	20	2	3	203	.209	.259	.277	.168	12	71-SS	5		
1998	Syracuse	Int	85	16	4	0	2	6	20	8	5	1	1	70	.188	.242	.306	.172	4	20-SS	2		
1999	Syracuse	Int	280	72	16	2	1	31	49	37	16	3	1	209	.257	.333	.339	.231	27	56-SS	3	16-2B	-2
1999	Toronto	AL	26	6	1	0	0	2	5	1	2	0	0	20	.231	.286	.269	.181	1				
2000	Syracuse	Int	143	41	13	1	4	8	31	19	20	1	0	102	.287	.325	.476	.263	18	20-2B	1	10-3B	1
2000	Toronto	AL	104	19	4	0	4	9	26	15	14	1	0	85	.183	.248	.337	.191	7	18-SS	-1		
2001	Toronto	AL	273	65	14	1	7	26	62	34	33	2	1	209	.238	.304	.374	.228	26				

Chris Woodward needs to take a lesson from Clay Bellinger and to take a lot of fly balls. Woodward is a better infielder than Bellinger without the Yankee's bat, but if he can add some value by adding a position or three, he'll give himself a few ways to crack a roster.

PITCHERS (ERA: 4.50, H/9: 9.00, HR/9: 1.00, BB/9: 3.00, K/9: 6.00, KW: 1.00, PERA: 4.50)

Clayton Andrews — Throws L — Age 23

YEAR	TEAM	LGE	IP	H	ER	HR	BB	K	ERA	W	L	H/9	HR/9	BB/9	K/9	KW	PERA
1998	Hagerstn	SAL	147.0	124	74	12	58	90	4.53	7	9	7.59	0.73	3.55	5.51	0.78	3.65
1999	Knoxvill	Sou	125.7	141	85	17	68	59	6.09	4	10	10.10	1.22	4.87	4.23	0.43	6.15
1999	Syracuse	Int	14.3	10	13	5	12	7	8.16	0	2	6.28	3.14	7.53	4.40	0.29	7.02
2000	Syracuse	Int	98.7	110	54	9	39	45	4.93	4	7	10.03	0.82	3.56	4.10	0.58	5.15
2000	Toronto	AL	21.0	31	19	5	7	11	8.14	0	2	13.29	2.14	3.00	4.71	0.79	8.23

He was pitching well at Syracuse when the Jays called him to the majors. However, the move wasn't part of their development plan, but rather a desperate attempt to find someone who could fill the chasm at the back of the rotation. After 20 lousy innings, they threw him back. Clayton Andrews is a decent prospect, effective despite not having a great fastball. Traded to the Reds in the Steve Parris deal, he'll join a cast of thousands with a chance to make the rotation.

John Bale — Throws L — Age 27

YEAR	TEAM	LGE	IP	H	ER	HR	BB	K	ERA	W	L	H/9	HR/9	BB/9	K/9	KW	PERA
1998	Dunedin	Fla	59.0	74	51	10	31	40	7.78	1	6	11.29	1.53	4.73	6.10	0.65	7.15
1999	Knoxvill	Sou	56.3	73	41	10	17	52	6.55	2	4	11.66	1.60	2.72	8.31	1.53	6.58
1999	Syracuse	Int	21.3	15	13	1	10	7	5.48	1	1	6.33	0.42	4.22	2.95	0.35	2.93
2000	Syracuse	Int	74.7	68	37	5	41	50	4.46	4	4	8.20	0.60	4.94	6.03	0.61	4.41
2000	Toronto	AL	4.0	5	6	1	2	6	13.50	0	0	11.25	2.25	4.50	13.50	1.50	7.85

Maybe MLB could do one of those Monster.com commercials, only about left-handed relievers. "When I grow up, I want to work nine minutes a week." "I want my paycheck to depend on getting Ken Griffey out." "I want to live in cities too small for even Red Roof Inn." "I want to be traded for a good catching prospect and have wiseass baseball analysts call it a terrible deal." John Bale might pitch again in the majors, but he's not Werth Jayson.

Pedro Borbon — Throws L — Age 33

YEAR	TEAM	LGE	IP	H	ER	HR	BB	K	ERA	W	L	H/9	HR/9	BB/9	K/9	KW	PERA
1998	Greenvil	Sou	18.0	21	14	3	14	6	7.00	0	2	10.50	1.50	7.00	3.00	0.21	7.62
1998	Richmond	Int	22.7	28	16	1	8	10	6.35	1	2	11.12	0.40	3.18	3.97	0.63	5.20
1999	LosAngls	NL	49.0	38	22	5	26	28	4.04	2	3	6.98	0.92	4.78	5.14	0.54	3.98
2000	Toronto	AL	42.7	43	30	4	29	28	6.33	1	4	9.07	0.84	6.12	5.91	0.48	5.65

He looked like the prize in the box of Cracker Jack, the cherry on the sundae, the chad in the ballot box. Pedro Borbon was going to put the Raul Mondesi/Shawn Green trade over the top for the Jays. Then he started pitching. Pedro Borbon got, by unofficial count, seven right-handed batters out all year. The signing of Dan Plesac means Borbon is fighting for a job this spring. He's still capable of helping a good team.

Toronto Blue Jays

Chris Carpenter — Throws R — Age 26

YEAR	TEAM	LGE	IP	H	ER	HR	BB	K	ERA	W	L	H/9	HR/9	BB/9	K/9	KW	PERA
1998	Toronto	AL	172.3	166	85	16	52	126	4.44	9	10	8.67	0.84	2.72	6.58	1.21	4.03
1999	Toronto	AL	149.0	164	69	13	38	101	4.17	8	9	9.91	0.79	2.30	6.10	1.33	4.52
2000	Toronto	AL	176.0	189	106	24	64	108	5.42	7	13	9.66	1.23	3.27	5.52	0.84	5.24

The positives in Chris Carpenter's season are, 1) it wasn't as bad as it looked—Skydome played like Coors Light last year—and 2) Roy Halladay's tribute to the end of Steve Carlton's career deflected attention from Carpenter. The smart money is on injury: Carpenter had surgery on his right elbow at the end of 1999 and experienced some pain in the spring. He pitched better at the end of the season after spending time in the bullpen, so maybe five months of rest will have an even stronger effect. Rotoheads, he could be a bargain in your league.

Frank Castillo — Throws R — Age 32

YEAR	TEAM	LGE	IP	H	ER	HR	BB	K	ERA	W	L	H/9	HR/9	BB/9	K/9	KW	PERA
1998	Detroit	AL	115.0	140	79	15	37	75	6.18	4	9	10.96	1.17	2.90	5.87	1.01	5.80
1999	Nashvill	PCL	113.0	130	73	19	37	57	5.81	4	9	10.35	1.51	2.95	4.54	0.77	5.82
2000	Toronto	AL	137.0	104	47	14	43	99	3.09	9	6	6.83	0.92	2.82	6.50	1.15	3.14

I don't buy it. Frank Castillo's ratios all were right around where they normally would be, but he allowed about 30% fewer hits. That's not a sudden development spike, that's a fluke. He can be an innings-muncher for the Red Sox, but he's not going to be the #2 starter they desperately need behind Pedro Martinez, and he's not a good bet to make 30 starts.

Pasqual Coco — Throws R — Age 23

YEAR	TEAM	LGE	IP	H	ER	HR	BB	K	ERA	W	L	H/9	HR/9	BB/9	K/9	KW	PERA
1998	St Cath	NYP	72.7	69	72	12	43	38	8.92	1	7	8.55	1.49	5.33	4.71	0.44	5.72
1999	Hagerstn	SAL	89.7	70	34	7	32	38	3.41	6	4	7.03	0.70	3.21	3.81	0.59	3.19
1999	Dunedin	Fla	68.3	82	58	14	42	36	7.64	2	6	10.80	1.84	5.53	4.74	0.43	7.50
2000	Tennesse	Sou	154.7	166	98	25	65	85	5.70	6	11	9.66	1.45	3.78	4.95	0.65	5.69

Pasqual Coco is a fastball/change-up prospect whose name is just begging for him to be successful. After originally being signed by the Jays as an outfielder, Coco becomes the latest converted position player to shine. He made a cameo in Toronto in August, a move which reflected only their desperation. Look for Coco to pitch at Syracuse this year in preparation for a job with the big club in 2002.

Pat Daneker — Throws R — Age 25

YEAR	TEAM	LGE	IP	H	ER	HR	BB	K	ERA	W	L	H/9	HR/9	BB/9	K/9	KW	PERA
1998	Hickory	SAL	106.0	123	66	28	22	43	5.60	4	8	10.44	2.38	1.87	3.65	0.98	6.34
1998	WnstnSlm	Car	48.3	53	15	6	6	22	2.79	3	2	9.87	1.12	1.12	4.10	1.83	4.33
1999	Birmnghm	Sou	101.7	104	50	10	34	44	4.43	5	6	9.21	0.89	3.01	3.90	0.65	4.50
1999	Charlott	Int	48.0	61	31	9	14	26	5.81	2	3	11.44	1.69	2.63	4.88	0.93	6.51
2000	Charlott	Int	137.7	163	100	29	46	52	6.54	4	11	10.66	1.90	3.01	3.40	0.57	6.44
2000	Syracuse	Int	13.0	17	6	2	2	3	4.15	0	1	11.77	1.38	1.38	2.08	0.75	5.85

The White Sox have so many pitching prospects that they can lose one and never miss him—in this case, Pat Daneker, who was waived by the Sox in September and claimed by the Jays. He's part of a bevy of #4 starters with whom the Jays will be filling out their rotation this spring. Despite good breaking stuff and fair command, Daneker's upside is staff filler.

Matt DeWitt — Throws R — Age 23

YEAR	TEAM	LGE	IP	H	ER	HR	BB	K	ERA	W	L	H/9	HR/9	BB/9	K/9	KW	PERA
1998	Pr Willm	Car	133.3	143	91	28	24	61	6.14	4	11	9.65	1.89	1.62	4.12	1.27	5.26
1999	Arkansas	Tex	137.0	153	100	32	68	68	6.57	4	11	10.05	2.10	4.47	4.47	0.50	6.89
2000	Syracuse	Int	62.0	75	40	7	23	31	5.81	2	5	10.89	1.02	3.34	4.50	0.67	5.75
2000	Toronto	AL	14.0	19	11	3	7	6	7.07	0	2	12.21	1.93	4.50	3.86	0.43	8.04

As we suggested in last year's book, Matt DeWitt, a two-pitch pitcher brought over in the Pat Hentgen deal, was moved to the bullpen at Syracuse. He's big and throws hard, so he'll get a number of chances to impress. He broke his leg towards the end of 2000, and his outlook for this year is uncertain. Traded to the White Sox.

Kelvim Escobar — Throws R — Age 25

YEAR	TEAM	LGE	IP	H	ER	HR	BB	K	ERA	W	L	H/9	HR/9	BB/9	K/9	KW	PERA
1998	Syracuse	Int	57.0	52	28	8	23	47	4.42	3	3	8.21	1.26	3.63	7.42	1.02	4.59
1998	Toronto	AL	78.7	68	32	4	30	67	3.66	5	4	7.78	0.46	3.43	7.67	1.12	3.45
1999	Toronto	AL	174.0	190	102	16	65	123	5.28	7	12	9.83	0.83	3.36	6.36	0.95	4.96
2000	Toronto	AL	180.7	173	97	21	66	136	4.83	8	12	8.62	1.05	3.29	6.77	1.03	4.44

Another of the Jays' ineffective starters in 2000, Kelvim Escobar was moved to the bullpen in August to little effect. Correlation isn't causation, but he's been a much different pitcher ever since Tim Johnson rode the hell out of him down the stretch in 1998. He's one of the guys Gary Huckabay likes to describe as being one-walk-per-nine-innings away from very good.

Leo Estrella — Throws R — Age 26

YEAR	TEAM	LGE	IP	H	ER	HR	BB	K	ERA	W	L	H/9	HR/9	BB/9	K/9	KW	PERA
1998	Columbia	SAL	107.7	125	82	21	32	42	6.85	3	9	10.45	1.76	2.67	3.51	0.66	6.01
1998	Hagerstn	SAL	27.0	34	22	2	18	12	7.33	1	2	11.33	0.67	6.00	4.00	0.33	6.79
1999	Dunedin	Fla	152.0	168	92	25	63	62	5.45	6	11	9.95	1.48	3.73	3.67	0.49	5.87
2000	Tennesse	Sou	69.0	74	45	10	32	34	5.87	3	5	9.65	1.30	4.17	4.43	0.53	5.70
2000	Syracuse	Int	84.3	67	44	10	40	34	4.70	4	5	7.15	1.07	4.27	3.63	0.43	4.01

You figure anyone who throws two no-hitters in a season has to be pretty good. Then you remember Tom Drees. Leo Estrella tossed a pair of no-nos last year, one each with Tennessee and Syracuse. The rest of the time, he wasn't very effective, despite a four-pitch repertoire. He'll pitch on both sides of the border this year.

Bob File — Throws R — Age 24

YEAR	TEAM	LGE	IP	H	ER	HR	BB	K	ERA	W	L	H/9	HR/9	BB/9	K/9	KW	PERA
1998	Med Hat	Pio	26.3	24	7	2	5	14	2.39	2	1	8.20	0.68	1.71	4.78	1.40	3.21
1999	Dunedin	Fla	48.7	32	17	4	17	28	3.14	3	2	5.92	0.74	3.14	5.18	0.82	2.65
2000	Tennesse	Sou	32.0	32	24	2	13	23	6.75	1	3	9.00	0.56	3.66	6.47	0.88	4.31
2000	Syracuse	Int	18.3	13	2	1	2	8	0.98	2	0	6.38	0.49	0.98	3.93	2.00	1.93

He's Matt DeWitt with better stuff and a quality performance history. The Jays' bullpen was terrible in 2000, and making it better in 2001 will have more to do with giving hard throwers like Bob File a chance than with signing 38-year-old lefty specialists. His 3.35 ERA in the Arizona Fall League hid an RA of 6.75, so don't get too excited.

John Frascatore — Throws R — Age 31

YEAR	TEAM	LGE	IP	H	ER	HR	BB	K	ERA	W	L	H/9	HR/9	BB/9	K/9	KW	PERA
1998	St Louis	NL	91.7	92	47	11	33	40	4.61	4	6	9.03	1.08	3.24	3.93	0.61	4.72
1999	Arizona	NL	32.0	29	14	5	10	13	3.94	2	2	8.16	1.41	2.81	3.66	0.65	4.35
1999	Toronto	AL	36.3	38	13	4	7	21	3.22	2	2	9.41	0.99	1.73	5.20	1.50	4.18
2000	Toronto	AL	73.0	80	41	11	26	29	5.05	3	5	9.86	1.36	3.21	3.58	0.56	5.48

The DT-ERA of 5.05 understates how bad John Frascatore was in 2000. Michael Wolverton's Adjusted Runs Prevented pegs Frascatore at 10.5 runs worse than a league-average reliever. That's a full win's worth, which spotlights one of the Jays' recent problems: the inability to fill out the roster with the kind of supporting players who get a team into the postseason. Frascatore is an interchangeable part who isn't likely to enjoy job security.

Gary Glover — Throws R — Age 24

YEAR	TEAM	LGE	IP	H	ER	HR	BB	K	ERA	W	L	H/9	HR/9	BB/9	K/9	KW	PERA
1998	Dunedin	Fla	101.7	117	73	15	42	52	6.46	3	8	10.36	1.33	3.72	4.60	0.62	5.95
1998	Knoxvill	Sou	36.3	39	31	3	24	9	7.68	1	3	9.66	0.74	5.94	2.23	0.19	5.81
1999	Knoxvill	Sou	81.0	71	41	7	27	49	4.56	4	5	7.89	0.78	3.00	5.44	0.91	3.64
1999	Syracuse	Int	73.7	89	45	10	33	42	5.50	3	5	10.87	1.22	4.03	5.13	0.64	6.26
2000	Syracuse	Int	159.3	178	104	24	58	91	5.87	6	12	10.05	1.36	3.28	5.14	0.78	5.61

A year ago, Gary Glover looked like a decent prospect, albeit one likely to end up in the bullpen. In 2000, though, he spent the entire year in the Syracuse rotation. He wasn't spectacular, but since the Jays were yanking guys out of Double-A for random starts, Glover's failure to get called up was curious.

All of the Jays' pitching prospects with significant upside, guys like Charles Kegley and Brian Cardwell, are at the low levels of the system. The pitchers at Double-A and Triple-A are capable of competence but not greatness.

Mark Guthrie — Throws L — Age 35

YEAR	TEAM	LGE	IP	H	ER	HR	BB	K	ERA	W	L	H/9	HR/9	BB/9	K/9	KW	PERA
1998	LosAngls	NL	51.3	55	27	4	23	36	4.73	2	4	9.64	0.70	4.03	6.31	0.78	4.98
1999	Boston	AL	46.3	46	26	7	16	34	5.05	2	3	8.94	1.36	3.11	6.60	1.06	4.89
1999	ChiCubs	NL	12.0	7	6	1	3	8	4.50	0	1	5.25	0.75	2.25	6.00	1.33	2.05
2000	ChiCubs	NL	18.3	17	10	1	8	14	4.91	1	1	8.35	0.49	3.93	6.87	0.88	3.98
2000	TampaBay	AL	32.3	31	15	3	14	25	4.18	2	2	8.63	0.84	3.90	6.96	0.89	4.49
2000	Toronto	AL	20.7	19	10	2	7	19	4.35	1	1	8.27	0.87	3.05	8.27	1.36	3.97

One of the more interesting experiments this spring involves Mark Guthrie, who has been signed by the A's and will be given a chance to win a rotation spot. Guthrie, who was a starter when he reached the majors, has never fit the situational left-hander role and has at times been vocal about wanting to start again. It's a low-cost gamble by Billy Beane; if it doesn't work, Guthrie can still contribute as a setup man.

Roy Halladay — Throws R — Age 24

YEAR	TEAM	LGE	IP	H	ER	HR	BB	K	ERA	W	L	H/9	HR/9	BB/9	K/9	KW	PERA
1998	Syracuse	Int	111.3	103	50	12	50	52	4.04	6	6	8.33	0.97	4.04	4.20	0.52	4.50
1998	Toronto	AL	13.7	8	4	2	2	12	2.63	1	1	5.27	1.32	1.32	7.90	3.00	2.18
1999	Toronto	AL	148.7	145	64	16	63	78	3.87	9	8	8.78	0.97	3.81	4.72	0.62	4.67
2000	Toronto	AL	69.3	100	73	11	33	42	9.48	1	7	12.98	1.43	4.28	5.45	0.64	7.85
2000	Syracuse	Int	70.3	82	45	11	20	29	5.76	3	5	10.49	1.41	2.56	3.71	0.73	5.63

Some performances are so bad that conventional explanations are inadequate. Roy Halladay, whose knuckle-curve and cut fastball have had us saying nice things about him for years, provided an excellent illustration of what might happen if the BP staff were allowed to wear major-league uniforms. Halladay was apparently healthy, and he pitched a tiny bit better at Syracuse and after being recalled, so there is hope. The Jays might be well-served to forget 2000 ever happened and start the season with Carpenter, Halladay, and Escobar in the rotation.

Joey Hamilton — Throws R — Age 30

YEAR	TEAM	LGE	IP	H	ER	HR	BB	K	ERA	W	L	H/9	HR/9	BB/9	K/9	KW	PERA
1998	San Dieg	NL	206.7	213	115	18	103	119	5.01	9	14	9.28	0.78	4.49	5.18	0.58	5.04
1999	Toronto	AL	97.3	109	62	11	31	53	5.73	4	7	10.08	1.02	2.87	4.90	0.85	5.09
2000	Syracuse	Int	37.3	39	17	1	12	12	4.10	2	2	9.40	0.24	2.89	2.89	0.50	3.91
2000	Toronto	AL	32.7	26	10	2	9	14	2.76	3	1	7.16	0.55	2.48	3.86	0.78	2.87

While Woody Williams was coming back from an aneurysm and being the Padres' best starter, Joey Hamilton was rehabbing from shoulder surgery and not pitching nearly as often. He threw a good six starts for a team that needed more. Even if he's healthy, he's just another of the Blue Jays' many bulk-starts guys.

Mark Hendrickson — Throws R — Age 27

YEAR	TEAM	LGE	IP	H	ER	HR	BB	K	ERA	W	L	H/9	HR/9	BB/9	K/9	KWH	PERA
1998	Dunedin	Fla	44.3	43	19	4	35	20	3.86	3	2	8.73	0.81	7.11	4.06	0.29	5.86
1999	Knoxvill	Sou	52.3	71	47	6	23	22	8.08	1	5	12.21	1.03	3.96	3.78	0.48	6.82
2000	Dunedin	Fla	44.0	67	46	17	38	20	9.41	1	4	13.70	3.48	7.77	4.09	0.26	11.87
2000	Tennesse	Sou	35.7	35	24	9	13	16	6.06	1	3	8.83	2.27	3.28	4.04	0.62	5.84

He's a late bloomer following an unusual career path. After a great career as a basketball center at Washington State, Mark Hendrickson bounced around the NBA and CBA for a few years. He came back to baseball in 1997 and has pitched fairly well. At 6'9" with a good heater, he makes the scouts drool. He's too old to have a great future, but his back story and size make him stand out in an organization swimming in uninspiring pitching prospects.

American League

Billy Koch — Throws R — Age 26

YEAR	TEAM	LGE	IP	H	ER	HR	BB	K	ERA	W	L	H/9	HR/9	BB/9	K/9	KW	PERA
1998	Dunedin	Fla	114.0	122	78	16	52	59	6.16	4	9	9.63	1.26	4.11	4.66	0.57	5.61
1999	Syracuse	Int	24.7	26	10	3	10	16	3.65	2	1	9.49	1.09	3.65	5.84	0.80	5.16
1999	Toronto	AL	63.3	52	22	4	24	54	3.13	4	3	7.39	0.57	3.41	7.67	1.13	3.33
2000	Toronto	AL	77.7	72	24	5	14	57	2.78	6	3	8.34	0.58	1.62	6.61	2.04	3.18

Billy Koch can be compared to Mariano Rivera, who also throws only one pitch and has a strikeout rate that doesn't seem to fit his stuff or his reputation. Billy Koch pumps a 100-mph fastball to get his saves and is going to need something more to move to the next level.

When you take into account team quality and usage, Koch may be the pitcher with the best chance of breaking Bobby Thigpen's record for saves in a season. Remember, the barrier to that record is opportunity: rarely does a closer get 58 save opportunities. The Jays will be good enough to win but not good enough to blow out a lot of teams. They could have the 60–62 legitimate save situations a pitcher will need to break the record.

Bill James posited that the save record would settle somewhere around 83 games. While he's responsible for much good work, he was off on this one. The theoretical maximum is somewhere between 68 and 72 (yes, it's technically 162) based on the number of save chances even a low-scoring team with a good pitching staff in a pitchers' park might have.

Esteban Loaiza — Throws R — Age 29

YEAR	TEAM	LGE	IP	H	ER	HR	BB	K	ERA	W	L	H/9	HR/9	BB/9	K/9	KW	PERA
1998	Pittsbrg	NL	88.0	93	48	13	27	43	4.91	4	6	9.51	1.33	2.76	4.40	0.80	5.06
1998	Texas	AL	78.7	95	48	12	18	51	5.49	3	6	10.87	1.37	2.06	5.83	1.42	5.61
1999	Texas	AL	119.3	118	54	8	30	73	4.07	6	7	8.90	0.60	2.26	5.51	1.22	3.73
2000	Texas	AL	107.7	121	52	15	23	72	4.35	6	6	10.11	1.25	1.92	6.02	1.57	4.98
2000	Toronto	AL	91.0	87	37	6	20	59	3.66	5	5	8.60	0.59	1.98	5.84	1.48	3.46

He's an underrated pitcher, in part because he keeps getting traded before he can have one good season with one team. Esteban Loaiza's pitching helped keep the rotation together during the chaos of August, when turnover was high. He's a better bet than many more-famous people to be good for the next three seasons.

Lance Painter — Throws L — Age 33

YEAR	TEAM	LGE	IP	H	ER	HR	BB	K	ERA	W	L	H/9	HR/9	BB/9	K/9	KW	PERA
1998	St Louis	NL	45.3	41	23	5	25	32	4.57	2	3	8.14	0.99	4.96	6.35	0.64	4.76
1999	St Louis	NL	61.7	61	35	6	21	47	5.11	3	4	8.90	0.88	3.06	6.86	1.12	4.34
2000	Toronto	AL	66.3	64	31	7	17	51	4.21	3	4	8.68	0.95	2.31	6.92	1.50	3.98

He's a surprisingly effective pitcher, the best of the three players the Blue Jays got for Pat Hentgen. Lance Painter does not have a big platoon split and was properly used for longer outings by Jim Fregosi (about 1⅓ innings per appearance). Like everyone else, he got a couple of starts during the Summer of Doubles. By Labor Day, I half-expected to see those kids from *You Can't Do That on Television* show up on the Skydome mound.

Paul Quantrill — Throws R — Age 32

YEAR	TEAM	LGE	IP	H	ER	HR	BB	K	ERA	W	L	H/9	HR/9	BB/9	K/9	KW	PERA
1998	Toronto	AL	78.7	82	23	4	19	55	2.63	6	3	9.38	0.46	2.17	6.29	1.45	3.84
1999	Toronto	AL	48.0	49	16	4	13	27	3.00	3	2	9.19	0.75	2.44	5.06	1.04	4.10
2000	Toronto	AL	83.0	92	38	6	19	45	4.12	4	5	9.98	0.65	2.06	4.88	1.18	4.31

He was the Jays' second-best reliever in 2000, and that's pretty much been his role ever since 1997. Paul Quantrill strikes out fewer guys and gives up more runs each season, but his ground-ball ways keep him an effective reliever. He has a really weird usage pattern: just 13 holds and three save opportunities in 68 appearances.

Steve Trachsel   **Throws R**   **Age 30**

YEAR	TEAM	LGE	IP	H	ER	HR	BB	K	ERA	W	L	H/9	HR/9	BB/9	K/9	KW	PERA
1998	ChiCubs	NL	200.0	199	104	27	75	121	4.68	9	13	8.96	1.22	3.38	5.45	0.81	4.86
1999	ChiCubs	NL	200.3	215	120	29	52	125	5.39	8	14	9.66	1.30	2.34	5.62	1.20	4.93
2000	TampaBay	AL	137.0	147	63	13	38	74	4.14	7	8	9.66	0.85	2.50	4.86	0.97	4.52
2000	Toronto	AL	62.7	66	32	8	19	30	4.60	3	4	9.48	1.15	2.73	4.31	0.79	4.81

After the season, Steve Trachsel signed with the Mets for two years and less than $10 million. Considering what guys like Andy Ashby and Rick Reed got over the winter, Trachsel won't have to do to all that well to be a bargain. For the first time in his career, he's going to have a home park that forgives fly-ball pitchers. Significant fantasy/roto potential.

David Wells   **Throws L**   **Age 38**

YEAR	TEAM	LGE	IP	H	ER	HR	BB	K	ERA	W	L	H/9	HR/9	BB/9	K/9	KW	PERA
1998	NY Yanks	AL	208.0	181	77	27	25	151	3.33	14	9	7.83	1.17	1.08	6.53	3.02	3.24
1999	Toronto	AL	229.0	227	112	27	49	161	4.40	11	14	8.92	1.06	1.93	6.33	1.64	4.08
2000	Toronto	AL	226.7	243	97	18	24	159	3.85	13	12	9.65	0.71	0.95	6.31	3.31	3.76

David Wells has reached a point where he just doesn't walk people, and that's the kind of skill that makes it possible to lead the league in hits allowed and still have a good year. The idea that he's an ace is the product of a couple of good run-support years recently, mixed in with his ability to munch innings. At age 38 with a waist to match, he's a bad risk. Gord Ash capitalized on his reputation, trading him to the White Sox for Mike Sirotka and various goodies. Talk about resurrecting "winning ugly."

American League

Support-Neutral Statistics — TORONTO BLUE JAYS — Park Effect: +6.0%

PITCHER	GS	IP	R	SNW	SNL	SNPCT	W	L	RA	APW	SNVA	SNWAR
Clayton Andrews	2	5.0	11	0.0	1.5	.029	0	1	19.80	-0.7	-0.7	-0.6
Chris Carpenter	27	156.7	120	8.3	11.6	.418	8	12	6.89	-2.3	-1.6	-0.1
Frank Castillo	24	137.0	58	10.2	5.1	.665	10	5	3.81	2.2	2.4	3.7
Pasqual Coco	1	4.0	4	0.1	0.5	.164	0	0	9.00	-0.1	-0.2	-0.2
Kelvin Escobar	24	152.7	102	8.1	9.3	.466	7	13	6.01	-0.9	-0.6	0.7
Roy Halladay	13	60.7	75	1.6	7.3	.183	4	6	11.13	-3.5	-2.6	-2.2
Joey Hamilton	6	33.0	13	2.7	1.2	.699	2	1	3.55	0.6	0.7	1.1
Esteban Loaiza	14	92.0	45	6.3	4.0	.613	5	7	4.40	1.0	1.1	1.9
Peter Munro	3	15.0	11	1.0	1.2	.470	0	1	6.60	-0.2	-0.1	0.1
Lance Painter	2	9.0	5	0.5	0.5	.496	1	0	5.00	0.0	0.0	0.1
Steve Trachsel	11	63.0	40	3.0	4.1	.418	2	5	5.71	-0.2	-0.5	-0.0
David Wells	35	229.7	115	16.1	10.9	.597	20	8	4.51	2.1	2.5	4.6
TOTALS	162	957.7	599	58.1	57.3	.504	59	59	5.63	-2.0	0.3	9.1

Just how surprising was Frank Castillo's 2000? He entered the year with a mediocre 57–65 career Support-Neutral W/L record after having spent all of 1999 in the minors. He had even received the ultimate confirmation of has-been status: he was omitted from last year's *Baseball Prospectus*. He's just about the last guy you'd have expected to put up the fifth-best Support-Neutral Winning Percentage (SNPct) in the majors in 2000 (minimum: 10 SN decisions).

One way of measuring the extent to which a given season is out of character in the context of a pitcher's career is to divide the pitcher's SNPct in that season by his SNPct outside that season. By that measure, Castillo's 2000 was the third most out-of-character season since 1979, with an SNPct 43% better than in the remainder of his career. That trails only Dwight Gooden's 1985 (48% better than the rest of his career) and Mike Scott's 1986 (45% better). Of course, Gooden's season isn't especially comparable to Castillo's, and Scott's arguably isn't either because of the dramatic impact of his split-fingered fastball. In fact, it's hard to find any season in the past 20 years that looks much like Castillo's. One possibility would be Bob Walk's 1988, in which he came through with an excellent 13.3–9.6 Support-Neutral record after eight years of worse-than-mediocrity. Bad news for Castillo: the following year Walk reverted to his former self, and he never had another above-average season.

For a quick explanation of SN stats, see page 7.

Reliever Evaluation Tools

PITCHER	G	IP	R	ARA	APR	IRNR/G	EIRS/G	IRP	BRS	RRA	ARP
Clayton Andrews	6	15.7	12	6.60	-2.4	0.17	0.15	-0.1	-1.5	5.74	-0.9
John Bale	2	3.7	7	16.45	-4.6	1.50	0.96	-1.1	0.0	19.50	-5.8
Pedro Borbon	59	41.7	37	7.65	-11.4	0.69	0.27	-6.2	-0.5	8.73	-16.4
Chris Carpenter	7	18.7	10	4.62	1.2	0.86	0.25	-0.2	0.7	5.08	0.2
Frank Castillo	1	1.0	0	0.00	0.6	0.00	0.00	0.0	0.0	0.00	0.6
Darwin Cubillan	7	15.7	14	7.70	-4.4	1.00	0.28	-0.2	0.0	8.70	-6.1
Matt DeWitt	8	13.7	13	8.20	-4.6	1.00	0.42	-3.6	0.3	10.94	-8.7
Kelvim Escobar	19	27.3	16	5.04	0.5	0.47	0.20	-1.2	-2.1	4.81	1.2
Leo Estrella	2	4.7	3	5.54	-0.2	0.50	0.16	-0.7	0.0	6.86	-0.9
John Frascatore	60	73.0	51	6.02	-6.7	0.65	0.21	-1.9	0.6	6.50	-10.6
Eric Gunderson	6	6.3	6	8.16	-2.1	0.17	0.04	-0.7	2.8	12.90	-5.4
Mark Guthrie	23	20.7	12	5.00	0.4	0.83	0.29	-0.3	-0.2	4.99	0.5
Roy Halladay	6	7.0	12	14.77	-7.4	1.00	0.31	-4.5	-0.7	20.94	-12.2
Billy Koch	68	78.7	28	3.07	18.6	0.26	0.07	0.5	1.6	3.31	16.5
Peter Munro	6	10.7	11	8.89	-4.4	1.00	0.50	-0.0	-0.9	8.23	-3.6
Lance Painter	40	57.7	32	4.78	2.7	0.85	0.35	-0.8	-2.5	4.66	3.4
Paul Quantrill	68	83.7	45	4.63	5.2	0.85	0.34	-1.2	-1.5	4.71	4.5
TOTALS	388	479.7	309	5.55	-18.9	0.66	0.25			6.02	-43.7

For a quick guide to RET, see page 10.

Re-Thinking Pitcher Abuse

by Rany Jazayerli

PAP is dead. Long live PAP[3].

You encounter many obstacles when a dozen people collaborate to write a single book. Everyone has different viewpoints, unique interests, distinctive writing styles, and opinions all their own—some in utter contradiction to others. It's not easy to meld 12 different stories into a single tale, and it's not easy to join 12 different outlooks on baseball into a cohesive primer like this one.

But there are some undeniable benefits to the process as well, and collaboration is one of them. I could never do what Keith Woolner has done.

The concept of Pitcher Abuse Points (PAP) arose from a simple idea: that while we had the perfect counting metric to measure pitcher workloads—pitch counts—the perfect rate stat *wasn't* achieved simply by dividing the counting stat by opportunity. If you want to calculate batting average, it's easy—hits divided by at-bats. It's easy because the purpose of batting average is to consider all hits as being equal. All hits are *not* created equal, of course, which is why we have slugging average, which weights singles differently from homers.

It doesn't take an advanced degree to figure out that you can calculate pitches per start by simply dividing total pitches by games started. But to assume that pitches per start is the best measure of a pitcher's workload, you have to assume that all pitches are created equal. If you don't believe that, as I didn't, then you have to create a weighted stat, a slugging average of pitch counts.

That was the idea. The details—setting 100 pitches as the threshold, increasing the penalty for each pitch at 10-pitch intervals—were thrown together without extensive testing, without quality assurance, with no greater rationale than 1) they sounded reasonable, and 2) they used round numbers that were easy to digest.

And for over two years, I have tried to use PAP as a framework in which to center the ongoing discussion on pitcher usage. In the process, though, PAP became more than a framework for measurement; it became the *standard* for measurement. Which it was never intended to do. For a device to become the standard for measurement, it must first be proven accurate, demonstrating success in measuring the element it purports to measure.

I had violated one of the fundamental rules of science: I had not presented the evidence. I had not, in fact, *found* any evidence.

Understand, evaluating the effectiveness of PAP is not as simple as identifying the pitchers with the highest PAP scores and then looking to see if they got injured or lost their effectiveness more than the average pitcher. If you look at the pitchers with the highest PAP scores, you're staring at Randy Johnson, Roger Clemens, Pedro Martinez, and others—the best pitchers in baseball, players who have tallied the highest PAP scores because they've earned them. Conversely, the list of the least-abused pitchers in baseball is usually a mishmash of Triple-A lifers and veteran pitchers with three surgical scars on their pitching arms. Pedro Martinez was worked a lot harder than Omar Olivares in 1999; that Olivares was the one who fell apart in 2000 doesn't really tell us anything other than the fact that Omar Olivares is no Pedro Martinez.

Married men live, on average, six to seven years longer than confirmed bachelors. From this, can we deduce that the simple act of tying the knot will add years to your life? Or are we comparing apples to oranges? Married men eat healthier, on the average, than bachelors; they certainly drink less alcohol. They engage in less high-risk behavior and are much less likely to end up on the wrong end of a nine-millimeter. Married men presumably contract fewer venereal diseases than bachelors. Is it marriage that allows men to live longer, or the *tendency* to be a married man? In medical research, they call these "confounding factors."

(One of the great tasks of sabermetrics is exposing the confounding factors that exist in baseball. For example, winning teams tend to have a better clubhouse atmosphere than losing teams, so the media proclaim that chemistry is the key to success, when a more reasonable explanation is that success is the key to chemistry.)

When it came to studying the effect that high PAP scores have on future performance, confounding factors so overwhelmed the process that they threatened to completely obscure the evidence. This was enormously frustrating, because no matter how sound a concept PAP might be in theory, there was no reason for it to gain acceptance without the evidence to back it up. Sabermetrics is defined as "the search for objective knowledge about baseball." The key word there is *objective*. Without evidence, PAP had nothing going for it but conjecture and opinion, two things which are decidedly *not* objective.

So I asked Keith Woolner for help. Keith had the ability to look at PAP with a critical, unbiased eye, and he had the training to do the kind of rigorous analysis that was needed to properly examine the evidence. What he found was that while the basic principles of PAP were right (that pitches are only damaging after a certain threshold, and that they become more damaging with each extra pitch beyond that point), the actual formula was wrong. And thus, PAP³ was born.

Compare the penalties for certain pitch counts, using traditional PAP vs. PAP³, as displayed in Table 1.

Table 1

Pitch Count	PAP	PAP³
100	0	0
105	5	125
110	10	1000
115	20	3375
120	30	8000
125	45	15625
130	60	27000
135	80	42875
140	100	64000

According to traditional PAP, a 120-pitch outing is three times as damaging as a 110-pitch outing. By PAP³, it's eight times as dangerous. Throwing 140 pitches is ten times worse than throwing 110 pitches by traditional PAP; by PAP³, it's 64 times worse.

In other words, the increased slope of PAP³ means that pitch counts between 100 and 110 are less worrisome than we thought, while pitch counts above 120 are much *more* dangerous than we previously believed. Of the 82 starting pitchers with 25 or more starts in 2000, 36 of them had fewer cumulative PAP³ than you would earn with a single 140-pitch outing.

In this year's team capsules, you will see lines that look like Figure 1 (see below).

"NP" refers to the number of pitches thrown, and "NP/GS" is pitches per start. A total of 196 pitchers made at least 10 starts in 2000, and Table 2 shows how they break down in terms of pitches per start.

"MAX" refers to that pitcher's highest pitch count of the year. The nature of PAP³ makes this figure more important than ever. The 133 pitches that Pedro threw in his longest start were more damaging than four 120-pitch outings would have been.

"PAP" refers to traditional PAP. Even though we know

Table 2

NP/GS	Pitchers	Cumulative %
>110	5	2.6%
105-110	29	17.3%
100-105	33	34.2%
95-100	47	58.2%
90-95	37	77.0%
85-90	31	92.9%
<85	14	100%

now that the traditional formula is not the most accurate one, the stat provides a bridge to work in previous books, allowing a rough estimate of how hard a pitcher was worked in previous years compared to 2000. From *Baseball Prospectus 2000*, you can find that Pedro amassed 791 PAP in 29 starts in 1999, an average of 27.3 per start, and even without PAP³ data from 1999, it's safe to say that he was worked a little harder in 1999 than in 2000. In future years, we will eliminate "traditional" PAP entirely and list PAP³ simply as PAP.

"PAP³" refers to the new formulation of PAP that Keith Woolner unveiled, and he showed that "Stress," which is simply PAP³ divided by total pitches thrown, is directly correlated with the long-term risk of a significant arm injury. Table 3 has the distribution.

The inherent nature of pitching means there's no way to completely eliminate injuries, but it's not an unreasonable goal to expect that injury risk be below 20% for all pitchers. Since a Stress level of 30 correlates with a long-term injury risk of 20.4%, it is that quartile of starters with Stress levels above 30 upon whom we should concentrate the bulk of our attention.

Table 3

Stress	Pitchers	Cumulative %
70+	4	2.0%
60-70	6	5.1%
50-60	7	8.7%
40-50	14	15.8%
30-40	18	25.0%
20-30	28	39.3%
10-20	44	61.7%
0-10	75	100%

Figure 1

Pitcher	Team	GS	NP	NP/GS	MAX	PAP	PAP/GS	PAP³	Stress	I	II	III	IV	V
Pedro Martinez	BOS	29	3165	109.1	133	588	20.3	190327	60.1	5	7	11	5	1

The last five Roman numeral columns refer to the number of starts made in each Category. Table 4 has the breakdown.

Table 4

Category	Pitch Range	Risk
I	1-104	Virtually none
II	105-109	Minimal
III	110-121	Moderate
IV	122-132	Significant
V	133+	Severe

There were a total of 40 Category V starts made in 2000, topped off by the 148 pitches Ron Villone threw in his 16-strikeout game against the Cardinals. The distribution of starts in 2000 is listed in Table 5.

Table 5

Category	Starts	%
V	40	0.8%
IV	293	6.0%
III	951	19.6%
II	979	20.2%
I	2595	53.4%
Total	4858	100%

Longtime readers will note that the term "Workload," which referred to PAP levels adjusted for age, has disappeared from the listings. While we have shown that the concept of Pitcher Abuse Points is, in fact, a prognostic indicator of future injury risk, we have not yet shown whether younger pitchers are more susceptible to injury than veterans, and if so, to what degree. This is an area of ongoing research, and we certainly hope that by next year we will be able to include an age modifier. Whereas the original concept of PAP was at least based on certain rational principles (even if the specific numbers were chosen empirically), the age adjustment was essentially pulled out of thin air. The age adjustment worked such that a 26-year-old pitcher would have his PAP score doubled, and a 20-year-old pitcher would have his PAP tripled, relative to pitchers 32 or older. The adjustment was determined by little more than applying common sense to questions like, "Which is worse—Kerry Wood averaging 50 PAP a start, or Randy Johnson averaging 80 PAP a start?" While we said then—and would say now—that the former is probably worse than the latter, we're going to refrain from making numerical adjustments until we have hard evidence. In the meantime, we will still point out a pitcher's age within the team comments when it's relevant.

So who were the hardest-worked pitchers in 2000? See Table 6.

Table 6

Pitcher	GS	PAP^3	NP	Stress
Livan Hernandez	33	422979	3825	110.6
Randy Johnson	35	439098	4021	109.2
Schmidt, Jason	11	101865	1203	84.7
Helling, Rick	35	313875	3791	82.8
Villone, Ron	23	150263	2246	66.9
Leiter, Al	31	229252	3478	65.9
Clemens, Roger	32	218043	3433	63.5
Hitchcock, Sterling	11	70714	1127	62.7
Wolf, Randy	32	217292	3528	61.6
Martinez, Pedro	29	190327	3165	60.1

As an example of just how damaging a single high-pitch outing can be, consider that Villone places fifth on this list despite averaging fewer than 98 pitches per start. If you ignore his 148-pitch outing, Villone wouldn't rank among the top 80 pitchers in Stress level.

The 10 hardest-worked pitchers of 2000 include the defending Cy Young winners in each league and the active career leaders in wins. Clearly, a high workload does not preclude success; on the contrary, success usually leads to a high workload. But the list also contains two pitchers who were being counted on to anchor the Padres' and Pirates' pitching staffs and whose seasons each ended with major arm problems after 11 starts. We might expect pitchers with a Stress level above 60 to have roughly a 40% risk of injury, and 20% of last year's pitchers have already suffered theirs.

And the hardest-worked pitcher of the year? Surviving a big scare from the Big Unit, Livan Hernandez holds on to his crown for the third consecutive season. There may be no doubt that Pedro Martinez is the best pitcher in the majors, but when it comes to quantity instead of quality, there is no more dominant pitcher in baseball than Livan Hernandez.

ANAHEIM	GS	NP	NP/GS	MAX	PAP	PAP/GS	PAP³	STRESS	I	II	III	IV	V
Tim Belcher	9	687	76.3	115	20	2.2	3375	4.9	8	0	1	0	0
Kent Bottenfield	21	2210	105.2	132	225	10.7	63486	28.7	6	10	4	1	0
Brian Cooper	15	1440	96.0	124	81	5.4	18712	13.0	10	2	2	1	0
Jason Dickson	6	453	75.5	103	3	0.5	27	0.1	5	1	0	0	0
Seth Etherton	11	1052	95.6	119	47	4.3	7832	7.4	6	4	1	0	0
Ken Hill	16	1548	96.8	123	96	6.0	19151	12.4	8	5	2	1	0
Al Levine	5	359	71.8	89	0	0.0	0	0.0	5	0	0	0	0
Kent Mercker	7	476	68.0	90	0	0.0	0	0.0	7	0	0	0	0
Ramon Ortiz	18	1733	96.3	123	87	4.8	16717	9.6	11	3	3	1	0
Scott Schoeneweis	27	2570	95.2	117	129	4.8	17487	6.8	13	10	4	0	0
Jarrod Washburn	14	1330	95.0	115	30	2.1	3745	2.8	11	2	1	0	0
Matt Wise	6	577	96.2	118	38	6.3	6120	10.6	2	3	1	0	0
TOTALS	162	14932	92.17	132	768	4.74	157983	10.58	98	40	20	4	0
			12th			13th		13th					

Mike Scioscia doesn't get enough credit for giving direction to a team going nowhere and keeping the Angels in contention far longer than most thought possible. A key to his success was changing his starting rotation from one heavily dependent on old, ineffective starters, to one equally loaded with young, if only marginally more effective hurlers. He did so without overworking his young charges, particularly crucial in light of the fact that most of the Angels' young pitchers were heavily overworked in the minor leagues. Kent Bottenfield was the only pitcher to rack up a Stress level of even 15, and the Angels were the second-most pampered rotation in baseball. Ramon Ortiz, with the most promising (and fragile) arm in the system, was worked harder than sinkerballer Scott Schoeneweis or Jarrod Washburn, but was hardly overworked. Most of the Angels' young pitchers have little star potential, but Scioscia is giving them the best chance to achieve what potential they have.

ARIZONA	GS	NP	NP/GS	MAX	PAP	PAP/GS	PAP³	STRESS	I	II	III	IV	V
Brian Anderson	32	2944	92.0	125	134	4.2	32536	11.1	24	3	3	2	0
Omar Daal	16	1381	86.3	114	25	1.6	2817	2.0	12	3	1	0	0
Geraldo Guzman	10	896	89.6	109	11	1.1	737	0.8	8	2	0	0	0
Randy Johnson	35	4021	114.9	145	1086	31.0	439098	109.2	5	6	9	12	3
Armando Reynoso	30	2649	88.3	128	128	4.3	33993	12.8	21	6	2	1	0
Curt Schilling	13	1343	103.3	120	80	6.2	11625	8.7	3	6	4	0	0
Todd Stottlemyre	18	1496	83.1	101	1	0.1	1	0.0	17	1	0	0	0
TOTALS	162	15337	94.67	145	1465	9.04	520807	33.96	98	27	19	15	3
			11th			6th		3rd					

One of the problems with evaluating pitcher usage patterns on a team-wide scale is that a single pitcher can skew the results. So it is here, where how Randy Johnson was used cast a shadow on the team's PAP numbers almost as large as the Big Unit himself. Johnson's huge Stress level vaulted the Diamondbacks into 3rd place in the NL, despite the fact that Buck Showalter once again handled his other charges well; no other starter had a Stress level over 13. Curt Schilling, only minimally protected by Terry Francona after returning from shoulder surgery, had his Stress level cut by over 80% after the Diamondbacks acquired him. Todd Stottlemyre was of course treated as if his shoulder was held together by a thread—which it is—and Brian Anderson has managed to throw over 200 innings in two of the last three years with impressively low pitch counts. Anderson is probably the most likely left-handed starter in baseball to be the next Jamie Moyer and be more effective in his 30s than he was in his 20s.

ATLANTA	GS	NP	NP/GS	MAX	PAP	PAP/GS	PAP³	STRESS	I	II	III	IV	V
Andy Ashby	15	1339	89.3	136	104	6.9	50031	37.4	13	0	1	0	1
John Burkett	22	2038	92.6	114	41	1.9	4428	2.2	16	4	2	0	0
Tom Glavine	35	3705	105.9	133	408	11.7	96919	26.2	11	9	13	1	1
Greg Maddux	35	3212	91.8	124	130	3.7	24417	7.6	25	5	4	1	0
Kevin Millwood	35	3386	96.7	120	213	6.1	34019	10.0	17	8	10	0	0
Terry Mulholland	20	1785	89.3	115	64	3.2	7651	4.3	14	3	3	0	0
TOTALS	162	15465	95.46	136	960	5.93	217465	14.06	96	29	33	2	2
			11th			15th		16th					

The Braves' season may have ended earlier than in any season since the strike, but it can hardly be blamed on the way Bobby Cox ran his rotation, which was even better than usual. The best rotation in the National League was also the least stressed. That's like winning the World Series with the lowest payroll in baseball: the Braves managed to align two usually contradictary variables. Andy Ashby was the most overused member of the rotation after he was acquired, a hint that the Braves had little interest in re-signing him. Greg Maddux was his usual efficient self, averaging fewer than 92 pitches despite throwing over seven innings per start. (He did throw over 120 pitches in a start for the first time since 1995.) The most reassuring sign for Braves fans was the use of Kevin Millwood, who was worked much harder in 1999. Millwood declined precipitously in 2000, but his lighter workload provides hope that he may bounce back and avoid the Curse of the Braves' Fourth Starter.

BALTIMORE	GS	NP	NP/GS	MAX	PAP	PAP/GS	PAP³	STRESS	I	II	III	IV	V
Scott Erickson	16	1568	98.0	123	137	8.6	29268	18.7	8	2	5	1	0
Jason Johnson	13	1390	106.9	126	187	14.4	43290	31.1	4	2	6	1	0
Jose Mercedes	20	1955	97.8	129	141	7.1	41443	21.2	13	3	2	2	0
Mike Mussina	34	3657	107.6	138	601	17.7	183194	50.1	8	8	12	5	1
John Parrish	8	720	90.0	124	66	8.3	14958	20.8	3	4	0	1	0
Sidney Ponson	32	3433	107.3	129	576	18.0	158887	46.3	7	5	15	5	0
Pat Rapp	30	3096	103.2	137	391	13.0	119439	38.6	15	3	9	2	1
TOTALS	162	16605	102.50	138	2119	13.08	592479	35.68	65	27	51	17	2
			1st			1st		4th					

Whatever reputation Mike Hargrove made for himself in Cleveland had nothing to do with the restraint he showed in handling his rotation, and he continued to work his starters hard in his first year with the Orioles. Mike Mussina's overall workload was not out of line to previous seasons, but Tom Boswell wrote a column suggesting that Mussina's poor start came from high pitch counts straight out of the gate, whereas previous managers had gradually built Mussina's stamina up to 130-pitches by June. My heart bleeds for Sidney Ponson, who may be the most overworked young pitcher in baseball that no one knows about—Livan Hernandez Lite, if you will. Even rookie John Parrish was given an unacceptably high Stress level. At least Matt Riley wasn't promoted into this mess... oh yeah, he tore his Tommy John ligament while in the minor leagues. If you're an Orioles fan looking for a dose of optimism, at least Mussina isn't your problem anymore. That should cheer you up some.

BOSTON	GS	NP	NP/GS	MAX	PAP	PAP/GS	PAP³	STRESS	I	II	III	IV	V
Rolando Arrojo	13	1094	84.2	115	48	3.7	6580	6.0	9	1	3	0	0
Jeff Fassero	23	1883	81.9	105	8	0.3	152	0.1	21	2	0	0	0
Pedro Martinez	29	3165	109.1	133	588	20.3	190327	60.1	5	7	11	5	1
Ramon Martinez	27	2329	86.3	123	77	2.9	15454	6.6	20	5	1	1	0
Tomokazu Ohka	12	1096	91.3	109	13	1.1	793	0.7	10	2	0	0	0
Brian Rose	12	818	68.2	91	0	0.0	0	0.0	12	0	0	0	0
Pete Schourek	21	1731	82.4	105	6	0.3	126	0.1	19	2	0	0	0
Tim Wakefield	17	1606	94.5	121	59	3.5	12690	7.9	13	2	2	0	0
TOTALS	162	14310	88.33	133	801	4.94	226130	15.80	116	22	17	6	1
			14th			11th		8th					

The Red Sox demonstrate how PAP differs from pitch counts. Red Sox starters threw the fewest pitches of any rotation in baseball, but those pitch counts did not hug the mean at all. While Pedro Martinez racked up 17 starts of Category III or higher, the rest of the staff combined for just seven such starts (by comparison, every other team in baseball had at least 22). Without Pedro, there would be no doubt that Jimy Williams and Joe Kerrigan are more protective of their pitchers than anyone in baseball. It seems reasonable to suggest that since Red Sox postseason hopes rest entirely on Pedro's shoulders, he should be worked right up to the limits of reason—and the Red Sox went out of their way to give him more rest than your typical ace starter. Martinez actually made more starts on five or more days of rest (15) than on four days' rest (14). When you consider that the Red Sox finished just two games back in the loss column, you wonder whether they wouldn't be better off letting Pedro consistently start on four days' rest, and pull him after 5 or 6 innings at every reasonable opportunity. 220 innings over 34 starts would be more beneficial to the Red Sox than the same number of innings in 29 starts, thereby reducing the strain on Pedro's arm and letting him to remain in legendary form for the life of his contract.

CHICAGO (NL)	GS	NP	NP/GS	MAX	PAP	PAP/GS	PAP³	STRESS	I	II	III	IV	V
Scott Downs	18	1683	93.5	122	120	6.7	26722	15.9	11	3	3	1	0
Kyle Farnsworth	5	499	99.8	116	41	8.2	5949	11.9	2	1	2	0	0
Daniel Garibay	8	728	91.0	106	10	1.3	280	0.4	6	2	0	0	0
Jon Lieber	35	3668	104.8	124	356	10.2	68957	18.8	12	10	12	1	0
Andrew Lorraine	5	461	92.2	109	9	1.8	729	1.6	4	1	0	0	0
Ruben Quevedo	15	1497	99.8	133	206	13.7	69533	46.4	8	2	3	1	1
Kevin Tapani	30	3151	105.0	135	479	16.0	151277	48.0	10	7	7	5	1
Ismael Valdes	12	1127	93.9	125	63	5.3	17172	15.2	9	1	1	1	0
Kerry Wood	23	2390	103.9	125	248	10.8	50710	21.2	8	4	10	1	0
TOTALS	162	16149	99.69	135	1549	9.56	392372	24.30	77	34	39	10	2
			6th			5th		7th					

CHICAGO (NL) *continued*

All you need to know about Don Baylor is that he not only rushed Kerry Wood into his rotation two months before it was prudent, he forced Wood to make 11 (out of 23) starts of over 120 pitches. Wood, recovering from Tommy John surgery, had a Stress level more than twice as high as Rick Ankiel. Wood's injury frightened Tony LaRussa into going light on Ankiel, but it wasn't enough to frighten Baylor to protect Wood himself! This for a team that finished the season with the worst record in baseball. Ruben Quevedo, who's even younger than Wood, had a Stress level more than twice as high in 15 starts, despite a Boeing ERA (7.47). Ismael Valdes, after years of overuse in LA, was damaged goods and pitched like it, adding his name to the long list of Tommy Lasorda's casualties. On the bright side, Jon Lieber has established himself as one of the most efficient workhorses in baseball, leading the majors in innings (251) with a Stress level under 20.

CHICAGO (AL)	GS	NP	NP/GS	MAX	PAP	PAP/GS	PAP³	STRESS	I	II	III	IV	V
James Baldwin	28	2706	96.6	127	140	5.0	33519	12.4	13	12	1	2	0
Cal Eldred	20	1925	96.3	121	143	7.2	26809	13.9	11	3	6	0	0
Jon Garland	13	1198	92.2	110	21	1.6	1407	1.2	10	2	1	0	0
Sean Lowe	5	412	82.4	92	0	0.0	0	0.0	5	0	0	0	0
Jim Parque	32	3178	99.3	127	269	8.4	61648	19.4	15	8	6	3	0
Mike Sirotka	32	3164	98.9	123	230	7.2	39380	12.4	14	10	7	1	0
Kip Wells	20	1790	89.5	118	38	1.9	6300	3.5	17	2	1	0	0
TOTALS	162	15417	95.17	127	850	5.25	169252	10.98	95	39	22	6	0
			10th			10th		12th					

The benefits of a strong bullpen: the White Sox finished with the AL's best record without a single starting pitcher posting a Stress level over 20. If you want to pick nits, you could claim that anyone with Cal Eldred's injury history should never be allowed to throw more than 100 pitches and that Jon Garland shouldn't have been in the White Sox rotation at all. But all things considered, Jerry Manuel did a fantastic job of spreading out innings among his entire pitching staff. The three mainstays from 1999 were all worked less hard in 2000: James Baldwin (6.2 PAP/S in 1999, 5.0 PAP/S in 2000), Jim Parque (9.1 to 8.4), and Mike Sirotka (12.3 to 7.2). Given that the White Sox are widely considered to have the most minor-league pitching depth in baseball, there is every reason to believe that Manuel's gentle hand will reap benefits for many years to come.

CINCINNATI	GS	NP	NP/GS	MAX	PAP	PAP/GS	PAP³	STRESS	I	II	III	IV	V
Rob Bell	26	2225	85.6	116	63	2.4	7877	3.5	20	3	3	0	0
Elmer Dessens	16	1528	95.5	116	49	3.1	5215	3.4	10	5	1	0	0
Osvaldo Fernandez	14	1108	79.1	113	16	1.1	2197	2.0	13	0	1	0	0
Pete Harnisch	22	1978	89.9	125	117	5.3	32409	16.4	16	3	1	2	0
Denny Neagle	18	1944	108.0	134	277	15.4	82588	42.5	7	2	7	1	1
Steve Parris	33	3296	99.9	133	324	9.8	90963	27.6	19	4	7	2	1
Ron Villone	23	2246	97.7	148	306	13.3	150263	66.9	11	6	3	2	1
Scott Williamson	10	933	93.3	116	51	5.1	7247	7.8	6	2	2	0	0
TOTALS	163	15354	94.20	148	1203	7.38	378759	24.67	103	25	25	7	3
			13th			10th		6th					

One start can make all the difference: Ron Villone's 148-pitch effort (the highest pitch count by any pitcher in 2000) in his last start of the season racked up over 110,000 PAP³, over 29% of the entire season's total. That almost single-handedly explains why the Reds finished in the top half of the NL in PAP³ despite throwing fewer than 95 pitches per start. That doesn't lessen the impact that start had on Villone's arm, but that's no longer the Reds' problem. The other two overworked starters in the rotation, Denny Neagle and Steve Parris, are also ex-Reds. That's a testament either to Jim Bowden's shrewdness or his compulsive need to make deals. Parris has an awful health record and has been abused for two straight years, and I will be stunned if he avoids the DL this season. More important to the Reds' future is that both Rob Bell and Scott Williamson (if he stays in the rotation) were handled very well by Jack McKeon. We'll see if Drill Sergeant Boone treats them as kindly.

CLEVELAND	GS	NP	NP/GS	MAX	PAP	PAP/GS	PAP³	STRESS	I	II	III	IV	V
Jason Bere	11	968	88.0	112	38	3.5	2904	3.0	6	4	1	0	0
Jim Brower	11	984	89.5	122	100	9.1	24248	24.6	6	2	2	1	0
Dave Burba	32	3306	103.3	128	370	11.6	88576	26.8	11	8	10	3	0
Bartolo Colon	30	3239	108.0	129	495	16.5	136831	42.2	11	2	11	6	0
Chuck Finley	34	3645	107.2	135	498	14.6	142964	39.2	11	7	11	4	1
Charles Nagy	11	1001	91.0	129	66	6.0	24902	24.9	8	2	0	1	0
Steve Woodard	11	839	76.3	95	0	0.0	0	0.0	11	0	0	0	0
Jaret Wright	9	865	96.1	125	83	9.2	24137	27.9	6	1	1	1	0
TOTALS	162	15780	97.41	135	1652	10.20	444570	28.17	82	27	36	16	1
			5th			5th		5th					

Charlie Manuel had no experience running a big-league staff before last season, and it showed: he essentially adopted Mike Hargrove's style, as only two of the Indians' starting pitchers (rehab case Jason Bere and control freak Steve Woodard) had Stress levels below 24. Jaret Wright's aggressive workload ended his season after nine starts and made the outlook on his once-limitless future even more cloudy. The same could be said about Charles Nagy, although Nagy's arm had been turned to gristle years ago, and he finally just ran out of fumes. Chuck Finley handled his workload with the aplomb we expect, and Bartolo Colon has yet to wear down after three straight years of high pitch counts. Colon may yet turn out to have a bionic arm that can tolerate these workloads like a Roger Clemens or a David Cone. The Indians can only pray that's the case, because if something snaps, they don't just lose their ace: they lose whatever hope they have of wresting the division back from the White Sox.

COLORADO	GS	NP	NP/GS	MAX	PAP	PAP/GS	PAP^3	STRESS	I	II	III	IV	V
Rolando Arrojo	19	1768	93.1	119	141	7.4	26401	14.9	10	3	6	0	0
Pedro Astacio	32	3182	99.4	130	501	15.7	150985	47.4	15	2	10	5	0
Brian Bohanon	26	2550	98.1	140	310	11.9	104759	41.1	11	5	9	0	1
Kevin Jarvis	19	1637	86.2	115	35	1.8	5104	3.1	16	1	2	0	0
Scott Karl	9	729	81.0	102	2	0.2	8	0.0	8	1	0	0	0
Brian Rose	12	1044	87.0	112	14	1.2	1728	1.7	11	0	1	0	0
Julian Tavarez	12	1073	89.4	126	78	6.5	20501	19.1	8	2	1	1	0
Masato Yoshii	29	2611	90.0	117	68	2.3	6697	2.6	19	8	2	0	0
TOTALS	162	14889	91.91	140	1149	7.09	316183	21.24	102	22	31	6	1
			15th			13th		9th					

In the aftermath of the Jim Leyland disaster of 1999, Buddy Bell came in and restored a semblance of normalcy to the Rockies rotation. Only the Expos starters threw fewer pitches. But the innate qualities of Coors Field is such that starters will get sent to the showers early on a regular basis, so while someone like Scott Karl threw barely 80 pitches per start, the twin towers of Pedro Astacio and Brian Bohanon took more than their share of the workload. Astacio has already proven that not all curveball pitchers wilt at 5280 feet, but he has yet to disprove that curveball pitchers are more vulnerable to a high workload: his ERA jumped more than a run (5.93 vs. 4.87) after the All-Star Break. Overall, Bell's handling of his rotation was neither benign nor malignant, and in any case the Rockies are the only team that needs to worry more about overworking their bullpen than their rotation.

DETROIT	GS	NP	NP/GS	MAX	PAP	PAP/GS	PAP^3	STRESS	I	II	III	IV	V
Willie Blair	17	1545	90.9	110	22	1.3	1342	0.9	13	3	1	0	0
Dave Mlicki	21	1822	86.8	116	34	1.6	4564	2.5	18	2	1	0	0
Brian Moehler	29	2709	93.4	116	55	1.9	5671	2.1	21	6	2	0	0
C.J. Nitkowski	11	985	89.5	114	29	2.6	2995	3.0	7	3	1	0	0
Hideo Nomo	31	3099	100.0	125	246	7.9	53271	17.2	14	9	6	2	0
Steve W. Sparks	15	1552	103.5	131	169	11.3	47991	30.9	7	1	6	1	0
Jeff Weaver	30	3151	105.0	126	345	11.5	76713	24.3	8	9	11	2	0
TOTALS	162	15459	95.43	131	900	5.56	192547	12.46	96	33	28	5	0
			9th			9th		11th					

Phil Garner may have presided over his eighth straight losing season, but as in his final years with the Brewers, he did a fine job of protecting his pitchers. Brian Moehler continues to take a replacement-level fastball and churn out 180 innings of above-average pitching. Although he spent a few weeks on the DL, he has made at least 29 starts every year he's been in the majors. Only two pitchers were used somewhat injudiciously. One of them was Steve Sparks, a 35-year-old knuckleballer called up at mid-season to post a career-best 4.07 ERA. That leaves Jeff Weaver, who has the most potential of any starting pitcher the Tigers have developed in a very long time. Weaver's strict pitch counts during his rookie season was a big story in *BP2K,* and while Phil Garner worked him more aggressively, Weaver had the benefit of an extra year of physical maturity and a season of minimal strain on his arm. As long as Garner doesn't continue to rachet up his workload, Weaver should stay clear of serious injury.

FLORIDA	GS	NP	NP/GS	MAX	PAP	PAP/GS	PAP^3	STRESS	I	II	III	IV	V
A.J. Burnett	13	1346	103.5	115	87	6.7	10070	7.5	4	6	3	0	0
Reid Cornelius	21	1828	87.0	104	12	0.6	126	0.1	17	4	0	0	0
Ryan Dempster	33	3597	109.0	127	491	14.9	117252	32.6	8	8	12	5	0
Alex Fernandez	8	806	100.8	121	54	6.8	10602	13.2	4	2	2	0	0
Vladimir Nunez	12	1047	87.3	110	23	1.9	1757	1.7	8	3	1	0	0
Brad Penny	22	2074	94.3	118	129	5.9	18113	8.7	12	3	7	0	0
Jesus Sanchez	32	2933	91.7	127	260	8.1	53001	18.1	17	4	10	1	0
Chuck Smith	19	1928	101.5	124	143	7.5	28255	14.7	7	8	3	1	0
TOTALS	161	15667	97.31	127	1207	7.50	239688	15.30	77	39	38	7	0
			10th			9th		13th					

FLORIDA continued

While so much attention has been given to the mikes-to-spikes route of Larry Dierker, Bob Brenly, and Buck Martinez, few realize that John Boles is an even rarer bird: you can count on one hand the men who have managed a ballclub without playing the game professionally. That doesn't appear to hurt Boles at all; if anything, from his player development experience, he does a better job than most recognizing the long-term implications of short-term decisions. In particular, he did a good job protecting Burnett and Penny, who give the Marlins two potential aces to lead them back to postseason glory in 2002. The Marlins' current ace, Ryan Dempster, has thrown over 110 pitches in over half of his starts between 1999 and 2000. His workload is a little irresponsible for a team that hasn't been playing for anything, and at 6'1", he's not a terribly big guy. It will be a shame if Dempster isn't there once the Marlins are ready to contend. Finally, while Alex Fernandez probably would have re-injured himself anyway, it's worth noting that he threw over 100 pitches in four of his eight starts, after going over 100 just twice in all of 1999.

HOUSTON	GS	NP	NP/GS	MAX	PAP	PAP/GS	PAP³	STRESS	I	II	III	IV	V
Octavio Dotel	16	1595	99.7	123	155	9.7	36724	23.0	9	1	4	2	0
Scott Elarton	30	3139	104.6	135	539	18.0	188275	60.0	11	5	9	3	2
Chris Holt	32	3264	102.0	138	411	12.8	140425	43.0	13	9	7	2	1
Jose Lima	33	3184	96.5	122	196	5.9	37946	11.9	18	9	5	1	0
Tony McKnight	6	541	90.2	113	20	3.3	2213	4.1	3	2	1	0	0
Wade Miller	16	1724	107.8	132	301	18.8	97914	56.8	4	4	5	3	0
Brian Powell	5	399	79.8	94	0	0.0	0	0.0	5	0	0	0	0
Shane Reynolds	22	2158	98.1	125	219	10.0	48571	22.5	9	6	6	1	0
TOTALS	162	16159	99.75	138	1841	11.36	552068	34.16	74	36	37	12	3
			5th			3rd		2nd					

We've covered the Astros' starting pitcher usage in the team essay, but as you see, Scott Elarton was hardly the only overused starter. Wade Miller averaged nearly 108 pitches per start, which ranks in the top 15 in the majors. While he only made 16 starts in the majors, Miller threw exactly as many innings (105) in 16 games in Triple-A as well. Chris Holt may be disposable, but it's still not fair to him that he had a Stress level over 40, especially after he missed the entire 1998 season with rotator cuff surgery. The irony is that the Astros' two veteran starters were the two least-worked members of the staff, although that can be blamed on Reynolds' back problems and Lima's bad case of the sucks. There's really no silver lining here.

KANSAS CITY	GS	NP	NP/GS	MAX	PAP	PAP/GS	PAP³	STRESS	I	II	III	IV	V
Miguel Batista	9	823	91.4	126	58	6.4	17694	21.5	5	3	0	1	0
Chad Durbin	16	1344	84.0	132	93	5.8	36891	27.4	13	1	1	1	0
Chris Fussell	9	773	85.9	116	36	4.0	5435	7.0	6	1	2	0	0
Brian Meadows	10	945	94.5	120	75	7.5	14553	15.4	6	1	3	0	0
Dan Reichert	18	1806	100.3	123	178	9.9	41011	22.7	9	1	6	2	0
Jose Rosado	5	492	98.4	108	12	2.4	576	1.2	3	2	0	0	0
Blake Stein	17	1850	108.8	128	300	17.6	83021	44.9	4	4	5	4	0
Jeff Suppan	33	3488	105.7	132	565	17.1	181089	51.9	10	8	7	8	0
Mac Suzuki	29	2941	101.4	132	315	10.9	90772	30.9	14	5	8	2	0
Jay Witasick	14	1293	92.4	126	92	6.6	26124	20.2	8	4	1	1	0
TOTALS	162	15892	98.10	132	1724	10.64	497166	31.28	80	30	33	19	0
			4th			4th		4th					

The Royals are the Anti-Braves. Despite the second-worst ERA in the majors, Tony Muser and Brent Strom managed to overwork the youngest rotation in the major leagues: not once all season did a pitcher past his 30th birthday start for the Royals. No one was spared: six different Royal hurlers (min: 10 GS) had a Stress level of 20 or higher, the most in baseball. Strom needs to stop encouraging his pitchers to throw more fastballs and worry about getting them to throw fewer pitches, period. Blake Stein was worked hard for the second straight season, but as in 1999 it was in fewer than 20 starts. If he develops into a dominant pitcher, he may be grateful that he missed half of last season with a broken arm. Jose Rosado has already served his sentence after missing most of the season with shoulder problems, and Mac Suzuki underwent minor shoulder surgery after the season ended. If Jeff Suppan has a hangover from making eight Category IV starts last season (only four pitchers—all older—made more), an already-shaky rotation may fall apart at the seams, eliminating whatever hopes the Royals had of contending this year.

Re-Thinking Pitcher Abuse

Fungoes

LOS ANGELES	GS	NP	NP/GS	MAX	PAP	PAP/GS	PAP^3	STRESS	I	II	III	IV	V
Kevin Brown	33	3454	104.7	124	403	12.2	85500	24.8	7	12	11	3	0
Darren Dreifort	32	3114	97.3	112	66	2.1	4498	1.4	21	9	2	0	0
Eric Gagne	19	1843	97.0	117	59	3.1	7048	3.8	12	5	2	0	0
Orel Hershiser	6	391	65.2	98	0	0.0	0	0.0	6	0	0	0	0
Chan Ho Park	34	3694	108.6	131	515	15.1	136469	36.9	8	8	13	5	0
Carlos Perez	22	1921	87.3	110	31	1.4	1531	0.8	16	5	1	0	0
Ismael Valdes	8	652	81.5	102	2	0.3	8	0.0	7	1	0	0	0
TOTALS	162	15784	97.43 10th	131	1089	6.72 14th	235847	14.94 14th	83	42	29	8	0

In Davey We (still) Trust. Despite getting fired for failing to cover for Kevin Malone's stupidity, Johnson did an admirable job of handling his pitching staff, with one glaring exception. He did get Chan Ho Park to rebound from a terrible 1999 to post career bests in wins and ERA, but if you're going to ride one flamethrowing young veteran starters, why not overwork Darren Dreifort, who was due to become a free agent, instead of Park, who you know is coming back for 2001? That's probably a little callous; Dreifort is a rotator cuff survivor, and if he had been worked harder he probably would have broken down. Then again, that would have spared us from hearing a 39–45 pitcher ask for $11 million a year. Kevin Brown is probably the least-worked ace in the game: 61 pitchers with 10+ starts had higher Stress levels, and 60 of them had higher ERAs as well. Johnson may be gone, but if Eric Gagne develops into a #2 starter, his legacy will live on.

MILWAUKEE	GS	NP	NP/GS	MAX	PAP	PAP/GS	PAP^3	STRESS	I	II	III	IV	V
Jason Bere	20	2024	101.2	127	252	12.6	64978	32.1	9	3	7	1	0
Jeff D'Amico	23	2334	101.5	117	128	5.6	16063	6.9	11	5	7	0	0
Jimmy Haynes	33	3321	100.6	132	256	7.8	64407	19.4	15	12	4	2	0
Jaime Navarro	5	385	77.0	94	0	0.0	0	0.0	5	0	0	0	0
Paul Rigdon	12	1177	98.1	122	86	7.2	17588	14.9	5	4	2	1	0
John Snyder	23	2218	96.4	117	115	5.0	15791	7.1	14	3	6	0	0
Jamey Wright	25	2601	104.0	132	284	11.4	86327	33.2	10	8	4	3	0
Steve Woodard	11	974	88.5	113	40	3.6	4261	4.4	7	1	3	0	0
TOTALS	163	15904	97.57 9th	132	1161	7.12 12th	269415	16.94 12th	87	36	33	7	0

Davey Lopes probably deserves Honorable Mention for Manager of the Year for getting the Brewers to finish in third place. Okay, third place in the NL (Comedy) Central. But he also deserves credit for continuing Phil Garner's soft touch with his rotation. Jamey Wright was handled surprisingly poorly, given that he was coming off shoulder surgery in the offseason and didn't enter the rotation until late May. But Jason Bere was left in ambush for the Indians, and no one else in the rotation reached a Stress level of 20. Jeff D'Amico came back from two lost seasons to finish within a whisker of the NL ERA title. He would have been the most unexpected ERA winner since Steve Ontiveros in 1994, but like Ontiveros, D'Amico's arm is so sensitive that even a workload as light as the one he had last year still puts him at risk of tearing something. Barring a pennant race in September—dream on, Brewer fans—D'Amico's pitch counts should probably never reach triple digits. As a reflection of Lopes's managing style, how everyone was worked bodes well for Ben Sheets this season and Nick Neugebauer in 2002.

MINNESOTA	GS	NP	NP/GS	MAX	PAP	PAP/GS	PAP^3	STRESS	I	II	III	IV	V
Sean Bergman	14	1152	82.3	108	8	0.6	512	0.4	13	1	0	0	0
Matt Kinney	8	756	94.5	110	23	2.9	1469	1.9	4	3	1	0	0
Joe Mays	28	2593	92.6	121	184	6.6	36789	14.2	17	4	7	0	0
Eric Milton	33	3239	98.2	126	266	8.1	58489	18.1	16	9	6	2	0
Brad Radke	34	3522	103.6	130	402	11.8	93354	26.5	9	11	11	3	0
Mark Redman	24	2253	93.9	130	123	5.1	36021	16.0	16	5	2	1	0
J.C. Romero	11	961	87.4	110	13	1.2	1009	1.0	8	2	1	0	0
Johan Santana	5	425	85.0	103	3	0.6	27	0.1	4	1	0	0	0
TOTALS	162	15250	94.14 11th	130	1022	6.31 8th	227670	14.93 9th	92	36	28	6	0

A few years ago, Tom Kelly's reputation at developing young pitchers was in tatters, as guys like Pat Mahomes and Willie Banks and LaTroy Hawkins kept getting bombed after great minor league success. Kelly and embattled pitching coach Dick Such have turned that reputation around, as Eric Milton matched and then surpassed Brad Radke as the team's best pitcher, Joe Mays came out of nowhere to post a good season in 1999, and former #1 draft flop Mark Redman was one of the best rookie starters in baseball. For the most part, Kelly has done a good job of watching his charges' pitch counts. Only Radke, the team's nominal ace, had a Stress level above 20. Matt Kinney was handled well in a late audition, and if he can break out this season, the Twins are a lot closer to having a playoff-caliber rotation than most people realize.

MONTREAL	GS	NP	NP/GS	MAX	PAP	PAP/GS	PAP³	STRESS	I	II	III	IV	V
Tony Armas Jr.	17	1488	87.5	113	33	1.9	3414	2.3	13	2	2	0	0
Dustin Hermanson	30	2943	98.1	128	231	7.7	53528	18.2	16	7	6	1	0
Hideki Irabu	11	853	77.5	103	3	0.3	27	0.0	10	1	0	0	0
Mike Johnson	13	981	75.5	102	2	0.2	8	0.0	12	1	0	0	0
Felipe Lira	7	472	67.4	95	0	0.0	0	0.0	7	0	0	0	0
Trey Moore	8	655	81.9	102	2	0.3	8	0.0	7	1	0	0	0
Carl Pavano	15	1502	100.1	116	77	5.1	11097	7.4	9	2	4	0	0
Mike Thurman	17	1462	86.0	116	51	3.0	6930	4.7	13	2	2	0	0
Javier Vazquez	33	3496	105.9	135	451	13.7	131374	37.6	11	8	10	3	1
TOTALS	162	14703	90.76	135	865	5.34	207744	14.13	107	25	25	4	1
			16th			16th		15th					

If it's Montreal, then that means this entry is contractually obligated to rave about how well Felipe Alou protects his starters, and then bemoan the fact that it doesn't really matter. Alou babied his starters again—the Expos have ranked last or next-to-last in the NL in PAP every year we've run it—with the exception of Javier Vazquez, who was worked harder than any Expo hurler since Pedro Martinez. Despite his experience, Vazquez is only 24 and needs to be protected more carefully this season. Carl Pavano's injury troubles cannot be blamed on his workload; he seems to have been cursed with a balky shoulder, either by genetics or a high school pitching coach. The Expos must hope that Tony Armas Jr. comes from hardier stock, because with Alou's help, Armas has every chance to be the next great Expos pitcher to be traded away in three years. You're right, that's too pessimistic: there's a good chance he won't be traded. After all, the team might be in Northern Virginia by then.

NEW YORK (NL)	GS	NP	NP/GS	MAX	PAP	PAP/GS	PAP³	STRESS	I	II	III	IV	V
Mike Hampton	33	3416	103.5	128	504	15.3	124433	36.4	7	8	14	4	0
Bobby J. Jones	27	2484	92.0	125	197	7.3	45111	18.2	15	4	6	2	0
Al Leiter	31	3478	112.2	136	714	23.0	229252	65.9	5	4	14	6	2
Pat Mahomes	5	493	98.6	107	12	2.4	408	0.8	2	3	0	0	0
Rick Reed	30	2750	91.7	113	69	2.3	6992	2.5	23	4	3	0	0
Glendon Rusch	30	3103	103.4	125	307	10.2	66402	21.4	9	12	7	2	0
TOTALS	162	16199	99.99	136	1813	11.19	473598	29.24	66	35	45	14	2
			4th			4th		5th					

For a team with as much bullpen depth as the Mets, you would have expected Bobby Valentine to be a little more reluctant to use the whip. In particular, his handling of Al Leiter—even before Game 6 of the World Series—leaves a lot to be desired. Leiter spent most of his first six years in the majors on the DL, and his transformation into one of the game's true workhorses is fairly remarkable. But it also means he could return to being a walking injury faster than you can say "Bret Saberhagen." Mike Hampton's Stress level was more reasonable, and given his gentle handling by the Astros in his formative years and the fact that he's an extreme groundball pitcher, he's a decent bet to stay healthy for the life of his new contract. Rick Reed's low workload is testament to his efficiency more than anything else. While Glendon Rusch was given an aggressive workload for a 25-year-old, his short-term prognosis is still very bright.

NEW YORK (AL)	GS	NP	NP/GS	MAX	PAP	PAP/GS	PAP³	STRESS	I	II	III	IV	V
Roger Clemens	32	3433	107.3	129	702	21.9	218043	63.5	10	2	10	10	0
David Cone	29	2781	95.9	137	256	8.8	83260	29.9	17	5	5	1	1
Doc Gooden	5	407	81.4	96	0	0.0	0	0.0	5	0	0	0	0
Orlando Hernandez	29	3067	105.8	134	408	14.1	113068	36.9	10	4	11	3	1
Ramiro Mendoza	9	770	85.6	101	1	0.1	1	0.0	8	1	0	0	0
Denny Neagle	15	1494	99.6	124	217	14.5	50322	33.7	5	3	5	2	0
Andy Pettitte	32	3433	107.3	130	518	16.2	142537	41.5	7	9	10	6	0
TOTALS	161	15994	99.34	137	2102	13.06	607231	37.97	72	24	41	22	2
			3rd			2nd		1st					

The World Champions had the hardest-working rotation in the American League, and who are we to argue with success? Postseason aside, the Yankees had their worst record since 1993 and came within an extra two losses to the Red Sox of sitting out October. To some degree, that workload is a product of their success, not the other way around: of the five primary members of the Yankees' rotation, only Andy Pettite was not 32 or older, and every one of them was an established veteran. David Cone had the lowest Stress level of the five, but Cone's fragility was well documented before the season began, yet Joe Torre continued to ride him hard even after he struggled from the start. Andy Pettite continues to win games, but he hasn't given up less than a hit an inning or had an ERA under 4.20 since 1997. Expect the high Stress levels to continue, as Denny Neagle is being replaced with Mike Mussina. One of these years—maybe this one—Torre's faith in veteran starters will bite the Yankees in the ass.

Re-Thinking Pitcher Abuse

OAKLAND	GS	NP	NP/GS	MAX	PAP	PAP/GS	PAP³	STRESS	I	II	III	IV	V
Kevin Appier	31	3314	106.9	146	533	17.2	194467	58.7	9	7	10	4	1
Gil Heredia	32	3007	94.0	115	81	2.5	8806	2.9	22	7	3	0	0
Tim Hudson	32	3211	100.3	119	237	7.4	31887	9.9	12	10	10	0	0
Mark Mulder	27	2482	91.9	131	156	5.8	46549	18.8	17	6	2	2	0
Omar Olivares	16	1466	91.6	123	64	4.0	13715	9.4	10	4	1	1	0
Ariel Prieto	6	497	82.8	98	0	0.0	0	0.0	6	0	0	0	0
Barry Zito	14	1453	103.8	124	101	7.2	19656	13.5	6	5	2	1	0
TOTALS	161	15646	97.18	146	1172	7.28	315080	20.14	85	39	28	8	1
			6th			7th		7th					

One of these things is not like the others... hint: it's the veteran starter who was in his free-agent year. Kevin Appier recorded over 61% of the team's PUP, including a 146-pitch outing (the longest by an AL starter all year) that accounted for 31% of the team's PUP all by itself. The rest of the rotation was exceptionally well-handled by Art Howe. Tim Hudson and Barry Zito were worked carefully given how successful they were, Mark Mulder only slightly harder. Hudson just might be the first pitcher in the history of baseball to win 20 games without ever throwing 120 pitches in a start. As the A's continue to blaze new trails in building a cost-effective team based on youth, it is reassuring to know that their young pitchers are in good hands with Art Howe and Rick Peterson.

PHILADELPHIA	GS	NP	NP/GS	MAX	PAP	PAP/GS	PAP³	STRESS	I	II	III	IV	V
Andy Ashby	16	1587	99.2	124	127	7.9	27768	17.5	9	2	4	1	0
Kent Bottenfield	8	731	91.4	127	74	9.3	20882	28.6	2	5	0	1	0
Chris Brock	5	506	101.2	108	15	3.0	555	1.1	1	4	0	0	0
Paul Byrd	15	1356	90.4	125	75	5.0	19514	14.4	10	3	1	1	0
Bruce Chen	15	1454	96.9	126	98	6.5	20104	13.8	6	7	1	1	0
Dave Coggin	5	485	97.0	121	35	7.0	9269	19.1	3	1	1	0	0
Omar Daal	12	1172	97.7	115	49	4.1	5508	4.7	7	3	2	0	0
Robert Person	28	3073	109.8	127	456	16.3	115092	37.5	8	3	12	5	0
Cliff Politte	8	817	102.1	119	81	10.1	13707	16.8	1	3	4	0	0
Curt Schilling	16	1724	107.8	135	293	18.3	93294	54.1	4	3	6	2	1
Randy Wolf	32	3528	110.3	135	684	21.4	217292	61.6	5	8	10	8	1
TOTALS	162	16613	102.55	135	1987	12.27	542985	32.68	58	42	41	19	2
			1st			2nd		4th					

It's hard to come up with good reasons for hiring Larry Bowa, but he can't possibly be worse at handling his rotation than Terry Francona was. Curt Schilling was overworked year after year, his shoulder predictably came up lame, he missed the first part of 2000 rehabbing... and when he came back, Francona worked him just as hard as before. Where they once had one of the five best starters in baseball, they now had a pitcher who could only fetch four projects at the trading deadline. Not content with ruining the best of the Phillies' past, Francona did his best to ruin the future as well. Randy Wolf was one of only five pitchers in the majors to average more than 110 pitches per start. His ERA before the Break was 3.68, and 5.22 afterwards. Robert Person was similarly treated, though he was 30 years old. Only Bruce Chen was handled with some sanity after the Braves decided to celebrate Christmas in July. The Phillies have a narrow window to win before Rolen, Lieberthal, and Abreu get fed up, and it's a shame that Francona's heartless treatment of his rotation may have shut that window prematurely.

PITTSBURGH	GS	NP	NP/GS	MAX	PAP	PAP/GS	PAP³	STRESS	I	II	III	IV	V
Jimmy Anderson	26	2254	86.7	129	152	5.8	50089	22.2	20	2	1	3	0
Bronson Arroyo	12	958	79.8	102	2	0.2	8	0.0	11	1	0	0	0
Kris Benson	32	3422	106.9	128	452	14.1	99711	29.1	5	12	12	3	0
Francisco Cordova	17	1504	88.5	123	65	3.8	14137	9.4	13	3	0	1	0
Todd Ritchie	31	2841	91.6	118	121	3.9	21122	7.4	22	4	5	0	0
Jason Schmidt	11	1203	109.4	135	250	22.7	101865	84.7	5	1	1	3	1
Dan Serafini	11	984	89.5	125	65	5.9	17625	17.9	8	0	2	1	0
Jose Silva	19	1631	85.8	115	77	4.1	10916	6.7	13	2	4	0	0
TOTALS	162	14967	92.39	135	1184	7.31	315473	21.08	100	25	25	11	1
			14th			11th		10th					

PITTSBURGH *continued*

For years, we've been generally positive about Gene Lamont's handling of his rotation, and for years, we noted that his handling of Jason Schmidt was the notable exception. For whatever reason, Lamont got it in his head that he could rely on Schmidt to throw more innings and more pitches than the rest of the rotation, despite Schmidt's failing to reach his considerable promise. Last year, Lamont started off riding Schmidt harder than ever, as 4 of Schmidt's 11 starts were Category IV or V. The injury we have been predicting for years finally arrived, and now Schmidt's career is very much in jeopardy. Kris Benson could stand to have the reins loosened a bit, as his ERA after the Break (5.01) was two runs higher than before (3.05). Todd Ritchie, the oldest member of the rotation at 29, was ironically one of its least-worked members. As a general rule of thumb to all you wannabe managers out there: give the highest workloads to your oldest starting pitchers, not simply the most effective ones.

St. LOUIS	GS	NP	NP/GS	MAX	PAP	PAP/GS	PAP^3	STRESS	I	II	III	IV	V
Rick Ankiel	30	3040	101.3	121	174	5.8	27910	9.2	15	6	9	0	0
Andy Benes	27	2770	102.6	123	260	9.6	45261	16.3	10	5	11	1	0
Pat Hentgen	33	3243	98.3	118	174	5.3	22132	6.8	17	9	7	0	0
Darryl Kile	34	3521	103.6	127	404	11.9	99624	28.3	9	14	8	3	0
Britt Reames	7	666	95.1	109	19	2.7	1009	1.5	4	3	0	0	0
Garrett Stephenson	31	3251	104.9	141	433	14.0	144609	44.5	12	9	6	3	1
TOTALS	162	16491	101.80	141	1464	9.04	340545	20.65	67	46	41	7	1
			3rd			7th		11th					

Apparently, you can teach an old dog new tricks. Despite their impressive performance with veteran starters, Tony LaRussa and Dave Duncan hadn't developed a single young starting pitcher during the A's glory years, and after arriving in St. Louis they destroyed the arms of both Alan Benes and Matt Morris. But given a chance for atonement in the person of Rick Ankiel, they showed they were capable of penance, keeping the best young left-hander since Fernando Valenzuela on a firm pitch count. Despite averaging 101 pitches a start, Ankiel never went over 121 pitches, and had a Stress level less than 10. By comparison, Kerry Wood went over 120 pitches eight times in his rookie season. For those of you who consider Scott Boras the embodiment of evil, consider this: before Boras raised a stink about the Cardinals violating an agreement to keep Ankiel's pitch counts under 110, Ankiel's Stress level was 22.5. Afterwards, it was 3.3. As evidence that old habits die hard, we present Garrett Stephenson, who was worked harder than Darryl Kile. Stephenson had a 6.60 ERA in September and will be hard-pressed to prove that he's not a flash in the pan.

SAN DIEGO	GS	NP	NP/GS	MAX	PAP	PAP/GS	PAP^3	STRESS	I	II	III	IV	V
Matt Clement	34	3534	103.9	134	330	9.7	82628	23.4	14	9	9	1	1
Adam Eaton	22	2191	99.6	121	163	7.4	32318	14.8	12	3	7	0	0
Sterling Hitchcock	11	1127	102.5	137	165	15.0	70714	62.7	6	2	1	1	1
Rodrigo Lopez	6	462	77.0	107	11	1.8	407	0.9	4	2	0	0	0
Brian Meadows	22	1896	86.2	120	58	2.6	10665	5.6	18	2	2	0	0
Stan Spencer	8	782	97.8	117	55	6.9	7504	9.6	3	3	2	0	0
Brian Tollberg	19	1724	90.7	121	43	2.3	9451	5.5	15	3	1	0	0
Woody Williams	23	2591	112.7	131	477	20.7	127255	49.1	2	5	12	4	0
Jay Witasick	11	1090	99.1	124	113	10.3	28357	26.0	5	3	1	2	0
TOTALS	162	15923	98.29	137	1415	8.73	369299	23.19	85	32	35	8	2
			7th			8th		8th					

The story of Sterling Hitchcock is eerily similar to that of Jason Schmidt: after starting the season with the highest Stress level of his career, Hitchcock tore his elbow after 11 starts and underwent Tommy John surgery. In fairness to Bruce Bochy, Hitchcock has been handled with significantly more care over the years than Schmidt was. Bochy put Woody Williams' nose to the grindstone last year, and while he rsponded with the best year of his career, he also missed two months after surgery to repair an aneurysm in his right armpit. Matt Clement's bouts of wildness raised his pitch counts more than you'd like, but his Stress level was of minimal concern. Adam Eaton's exceptional debut is even more promising because Bochy handled him well, and the same can be said for Brian Tollberg's surprising performance. If Hitchcock can return this season close to 100%, the Padres' rotation could be one of the best in the National League.

Re-Thinking Pitcher Abuse

SAN FRANCISCO	GS	NP	NP/GS	MAX	PAP	PAP/GS	PAP³	STRESS	I	II	III	IV	V
Shawn Estes	30	3088	102.9	127	282	9.4	65551	21.2	14	7	7	2	0
Mark Gardner	20	1821	91.1	115	31	1.6	3482	1.9	15	4	1	0	0
Livan Hernandez	33	3825	115.9	143	1075	32.6	422979	110.6	4	5	10	10	4
Joe Nathan	15	1451	96.7	123	170	11.3	35668	24.6	5	4	4	2	0
Russ Ortiz	32	3384	105.8	132	453	14.2	115745	34.2	10	6	14	2	0
Kirk Rueter	31	2936	94.7	118	81	2.6	8479	2.9	20	10	1	0	0
TOTALS	162	16592	102.42 / 2nd	143	2092	12.91 / 1st	651904	39.29 / 1st	69	36	37	16	4

Dusty Baker has strong points which make him one of the most well-respected managers in the game, but for the second straight year, the Giants had the most overworked rotation in the NL. Nevertheless, Baker found a way to get the most out of his starting pitchers despite high pitch counts. Livan Hernandez has now stretched his reign as the hardest-worked pitcher in baseball to three straight years, and had his best of the three. He actually picked up steam during the season, going 10–4, 3.19 after the Break. Still, there are signs Hernandez is wearing out: batters hit .390 against Livan after he had thrown 105 pitches, compared to .256 up to that point. Russ Ortiz was worked nearly as much as Hernandez was in 1999, and started the season pitching terribly (4–8, 6.92 ERA at the break), but went 10–4, 3.22 after the break. Hernandez and Ortiz getting hot down the stretch was a large part of why the Giants streaked past Arizona to win the NL West handily. It's not the way we would have done it, but it's unfair to chastise Baker for the means used to achieve his ends. At least until Hernandez quits dragging his feet and finally sets a date for his surgery.

SEATTLE	GS	NP	NP/GS	MAX	PAP	PAP/GS	PAP³	STRESS	I	II	III	IV	V
Paul Abbott	27	2622	97.1	120	172	6.4	28423	10.8	15	4	8	0	0
Freddy Garcia	20	1982	99.1	120	145	7.3	27050	13.6	12	2	6	0	0
John Halama	30	2607	86.9	103	9	0.3	63	0.0	26	4	0	0	0
Gil Meche	15	1455	97.0	114	69	4.6	8381	5.8	9	2	4	0	0
Jamie Moyer	26	2498	96.1	117	106	4.1	11757	4.7	15	8	3	0	0
Aaron Sele	34	3396	99.9	133	239	7.0	57972	17.1	17	8	8	0	1
Brett Tomko	8	740	92.5	106	12	1.5	432	0.6	6	2	0	0	0
TOTALS	162	15501	95.69 / 8th	133	755	4.66 / 14th	134105	8.65 / 14th	101	31	29	0	1

Forget Jason Giambi. The real MVP of the American League last season was Bryan Price, the pitching coach of the least-abused rotation in the major leagues. In 1998 and 1999, Lou Piniella presided over the second-most overworked rotation in the AL. In 2000, Piniella returned, but pitching coach Stan Williams was replaced by Price, and a revolution occurred in Seattle. It's not enough to say that Price convinced Piniella to go to his bullpen earlier; the Mariners actually ranked in the middle of the pack in the AL in terms of average pitches thrown. The Mariners were comfortable letting their pitchers exceed 100 pitches, as their combined total of 60 Category II and III starts were more than seven other teams. But only once all season (Aaron Sele on August 25th) did a Mariner exceed 120 pitches. Every other team in baseball had at least four such starts, and the Yankees had 24. In 1999, the Mariners had 21. Bryan Price had enough faith in pitch counts to install strict limits in his first year on the job, and enough zeal to convince a veteran manager of their merits. Locked in a tight race for both the AL West and the wild card, the Mariners had a 3.61 ERA in September to clinch a playoff spot by one game, then limited the majors' most potent offense to seven runs in three games to advance to the ALCS. For keeping his pitching staff healthy enough to pitch their best when it mattered most, and for watching over the young arms of Freddy Garcia and Gil Meche with care, Bryan Price deserves to be recognized as the *Baseball Prospectus* Coach of the Year.

TAMPA BAY	GS	NP	NP/GS	MAX	PAP	PAP/GS	PAP³	STRESS	I	II	III	IV	V
Dave Eiland	10	667	66.7	99	0	0.0	0	0.0	10	0	0	0	0
Doc Gooden	8	673	84.1	107	7	0.9	343	0.5	7	1	0	0	0
Travis Harper	5	487	97.4	128	63	12.6	22681	46.6	3	1	0	1	0
Cory Lidle	11	919	83.5	112	14	1.3	1728	1.9	10	0	1	0	0
Albie Lopez	24	2402	100.1	136	324	13.5	106472	44.3	10	5	6	2	1
Bryan Rekar	27	2559	94.8	118	86	3.2	10330	4.0	17	7	3	0	0
Ryan Rupe	18	1553	86.3	109	13	0.7	757	0.5	15	3	0	0	0
Tanyon Sturtze	5	464	92.8	118	51	10.2	8919	19.2	2	1	2	0	0
Steve Trachsel	23	2253	98.0	132	194	8.4	57511	25.5	12	6	3	2	0
Paul Wilson	7	622	88.9	98	0	0.0	0	0.0	7	0	0	0	0
Esteban Yan	20	1801	90.1	112	38	1.9	2262	1.3	13	6	1	0	0
TOTALS	161	14619	90.80 / 13th	136	790	4.91 / 12th	211003	14.43 / 10th	109	30	16	5	1

TAMPA BAY continued

The closer you look at the Devil Rays, the more you think they may finally be onto something good. Larry Rothschild seems to have gotten the hint after Tony Saunders shattered his humerus. Despite the loss of Saunders and Wilson Alvarez (who missed the entire season after being given the highest workload on the staff in 1999), Rothschild did his best to repair his rotation with some TLC. Rothschild was fiercely protective of Bryan Rekar, who finally fulfilled some of the promise he'd shown with the Rockies in 1995. Rothschild limited Paul Wilson to less than 100 pitches after Wilson finally completed his four-year journey back to the majors, and Wilson responded by surrendering barely a base runner an inning. Ryan Rupe was afforded similar protection, although old elbow problems that go back to before he was drafted ruined his season. As a team, the Devil Rays' 22 Category III or higher starts were the fewest in baseball. You can forgive Albie Lopez for wondering where all the love went.

TEXAS	GS	NP	NP/GS	MAX	PAP	PAP/GS	PAP^3	STRESS	I	II	III	IV	V
Mark Clark	8	607	75.9	89	0	0.0	0	0.0	8	0	0	0	0
Doug Davis	13	1338	102.9	142	173	13.3	78320	58.5	3	7	2	0	1
Ryan Glynn	16	1456	91.0	109	24	1.5	1512	1.0	12	4	0	0	0
Rick Helling	35	3791	108.3	137	861	24.6	313875	82.8	9	5	10	9	2
Esteban Loaiza	17	1680	98.8	124	150	8.8	27478	16.4	7	4	5	1	0
Darren Oliver	21	1882	89.6	124	103	4.9	20490	10.9	14	3	3	1	0
Matt Perisho	13	1258	96.8	122	99	7.6	21248	16.9	6	4	2	1	0
Kenny Rogers	34	3612	106.2	134	506	14.9	131879	36.5	10	6	15	2	1
Brian Sikorski	5	528	105.6	113	36	7.2	3717	7.0	1	2	2	0	0
TOTALS	162	16152	99.70	142	1952	12.05	598519	37.06	70	35	39	14	4
			2nd			3rd		2nd					

Hmm. So your pitching staff finishes with the worst ERA in the majors, and you manage to simultaneously work your starting rotation harder than all but two teams in baseball. Yeah, I'd say Dick Bosman's firing was deserved. Rick Helling had the highest Stress level in the AL, ahead of two guys named Roger Clemens and Pedro Martinez. Helling has settled in as a dependable innings sponge since he won 20 games in 1998, but he has yet to post an ERA under 4.30 in the majors and was awful in September with a 9.45 ERA. Doug Davis must have hit on Johnny Oates's daughter without realizing it, because a year after he was asked to "take one for the team" and left out there to surrender 10 runs in relief (in his major league debut), Davis was allowed to throw a 142-pitch complete game, the most pitches thrown by a pitcher younger than 25 since Jesus Sanchez tossed 147 for the Marlins in 1998.

TORONTO	GS	NP	NP/GS	MAX	PAP	PAP/GS	PAP^3	STRESS	I	II	III	IV	V
Chris Carpenter	27	2597	96.2	125	221	8.2	51990	20.0	13	8	3	3	0
Frank Castillo	24	2254	93.9	121	176	7.3	32002	14.2	13	3	8	0	0
Kelvim Escobar	24	2527	105.3	130	352	14.7	115250	45.6	8	9	2	5	0
Roy Halladay	13	1208	92.9	110	23	1.8	1253	1.0	9	3	1	0	0
Joey Hamilton	6	510	85.0	104	8	1.3	80	0.2	3	3	0	0	0
Esteban Loaiza	14	1463	104.5	128	170	12.1	46255	31.6	6	3	3	2	0
Steve Trachsel	11	1044	94.9	124	94	8.5	21330	20.4	6	2	2	1	0
David Wells	35	3270	93.4	126	290	8.3	61424	18.8	20	3	11	1	0
TOTALS	162	15512	95.75	130	1335	8.24	329585	21.25	85	35	30	12	0
			7th			6th		6th					

Jim Fregosi may be a kinder, gentler man than he was when he cashed in the futures of Tommy Greene and Ben Rivera for the NL pennant in 1993, but don't tell that to Kelvim Escobar. Escobar had his second straight disappointing season since Tim Johnson took him behind the woodshed in 1998, and with a Stress level of over 45, there's little reason to believe he's going to reverse his downturn. Chris Carpenter was supervised more closely than Escobar, though it didn't prevent him from leading the AL in runs and earned runs allowed. Roy Halladay's record-setting pyrotechnic display had little to do with his workload and more to do with a chronically poor strikeout-to-walk ratio finally catching up to him. Frank Castillo was used judiciously in an impressive comeback, and the same held true for Joey Hamilton, who finally contributed in a Blue Jays uniform for the first time late in the year.

Re-Thinking Pitcher Abuse

Analyzing PAP

by Keith Woolner with Rany Jazayerli

History of PAP

The Pitcher Abuse Point system (PAP) first appeared in the *Baseball Prospectus 1999*. Rany Jazayerli developed PAP as a common-sense quantification of the idea that a pitcher with high pitch counts is at significant risk for injury and/or ineffectiveness. Research dating back to Craig Wright's *The Diamond Appraised* has suggested a 100-pitch limit for developing pitchers.

Abuse Points are awarded to a pitcher after he has thrown 100 pitches in a start. At first, one Abuse Point is awarded for each pitch, but at each successive plateau of 10 pitches, the penalty for each pitch rises by one. Table 1 shows the complete breakdown.

PAP totals are further adjusted by a factor dependent on age, reflecting the relative vulnerability of a young pitcher's arm. These adjusted PAP totals are referred to as Workload.

Since its introduction, PAP has proven to be popular in assessing a team's tendency to overwork its starting rotation. However, to date there has been no solid sabermetric analysis to support any particular pitch count metric, including PAP. Now we're rectifying that situation.

There are two related effects we are interested in studying. The original intent of PAP was to ascertain whether a pitcher is at risk of injury or a permanent reduction in effectiveness due to repeated overwork. And in particular, does PAP (or any similar formula) provide more insight into that risk than simple pitch counts alone?

In addition to the long-term picture, there is an increasing awareness of immediate effects of high-pitch-count outings. Pitchers appear to struggle for several starts after being asked to throw 130 pitches. So a second question is: Do high-pitch-count outings reduce a pitcher's effectiveness for an immediate period of time afterwards?

Table 1: Relationship of Abuse Points Assigned to Start Pitch Count Groups

Pitches 1-100:	no PAP awarded
Pitches 101-110:	1 PAP per pitch
Pitches 111-120:	2 PAP per pitch
Pitches 121-130:	3 PAP per pitch
Pitches 131-140:	4 PAP per pitch
Pitches 141-150:	5 PAP per pitch, and so on

Part 1: The Immediate Impact of High Pitch Counts on Pitcher Effectiveness

Initially, we will focus on the second of these two questions, namely whether high-pitch-count starts have a harmful effect on a pitcher's effectiveness in the days and weeks immediately following the outing. We'll take up the question of long-term injury risk in Part 2.

Using data from The Baseball Workshop/Total Sports, I looked at all starts for which there were reasonably complete pitch-count data during the years 1988-98. For each start, I looked at all other starts by the same pitcher in the preceding 21 days and the following 21 days, and then I tallied the aggregate performance for the before and after periods. Note that the start itself is not part of either group, so the fact that long starts tend to be of higher quality will not affect the results.

Performance Measurements

I looked at four rates of performance to determine whether pitchers were affected by long outings. They are:

Run average (RA)
Hits per inning (H/IP)
Strikeouts per inning (SO/IP)
Inning pitched per game started (IP/GS)

IP/GS indicates whether a pitcher's ability to throw late into a game has been affected. H/IP and SO/IP indicate whether a pitcher's "stuff" has been affected, and RA is, of course, the bottom line—whether or not a pitcher is giving up more runs to the opposition.

Let's look at RA as an example. For every pitcher's start, I computed his total RA for all previous starts both in the three weeks prior and the three weeks following. The ratio of the RA(after) to RA(before) is greater than one if he gave up runs at a higher rate following the start and less than one if he was more effective thereafter. I can compute the ratios for the other starts similarly. I grouped all the starts in a given range, say 100-109 pitches, and aggregated their before and after

Figure 1: RA Ratio—All Pitchers

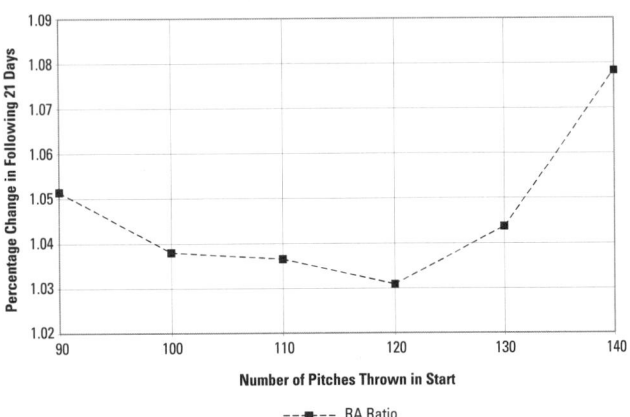

starts and computed the ratios. I then plotted the ratios as a function of the pitch count, as shown on Figure 1.

The interpretation of the data in this chart is that for pitch counts in the range of 100-109 (X axis = 100) pitchers experience about a 3.8% increase in RA during the three weeks following the start than they did in the three weeks immediately prior to it.

The chart shows both promising and surprising results. Perhaps most surprising is that there is a persistent trend for pitchers to do slightly worse in the later time period, regardless of the length of the outing. There are several factors that may account for this. First, it could be something as basic as improvements in the weather in most ballparks between April and August and the resulting boost in offense that accompanies higher temperatures. Or pitchers may simply wear down over the course of a season, making the back end of any period of time appear slightly worse. There is also a survival threshold that comes into play—after a stretch of bad starts, a pitcher may lose his spot in the rotation (or be sent to the minors). In such cases, you can't look for a pitcher to bounce back because there will be few or no starts in the "after" period of this bad stretch to look for a bounce, but the starts preceding the bad stretch will have the bad starts figured into their "after" periods. Regardless of the contributing factors, the important point to note is that the baseline expectation is not a 1.00 ratio, indicating equal performance before and after any given start, but rather a slight decrease in effectiveness across the board in the weeks following an outing of any length.

According to the chart, outings of 130 or more pitches certainly seem to result in worse run prevention in the weeks following. This is consistent with the hypothesis of the negative short-term impact of high pitch counts. However, the rest of the chart seems to indicate the reverse, namely that pitchers are more effective having thrown more pitches, peaking with an outing of around 120 pitches. It even appears that a 90-pitch outing is more harmful to short-term effectiveness than a 130-pitch outing. Is this an indication that pitchers benefit from a heavier regular workload than was previously thought, or is something else going on?

Endurance Differences

One possible explanation is that there are significant qualitative differences between pitchers who throw 90 pitches per start and those who throw 120 pitches per start. Good pitchers are more likely to throw deep into a game, as are those perceived as having more endurance. Pitchers with low pitch counts either get lit up early, are considered fragile or lacking in stamina, or are being carefully nursed back to health following an injury.

To investigate this possibility, I divided the pitchers into two categories based on how many pitches they were typically allowed to throw. For each pitcher, I looked at whether the majority of his starts were above or below the average number of pitches thrown by starters in that season. Based on that ratio, I assigned him to "High Endurance" (>50% of starts above league-average pitch count) or "Low Endurance" (<50% of starts above league-average pitch count).

There are pronounced differences in the quality of pitchers in the two subgroups, as Table 2 shows.

Given the differences in quality, we shouldn't be surprised to find that high-endurance pitchers account for a dramatically larger portion of the starts above 100 pitches. Furthermore, the number of pitches thrown by a pitcher is not a random variable; it derives primarily from a managerial decision based in part on the performance of the pitcher in the particular game. Indeed, high-endurance pitchers account for significantly more of the long outings than the short outings, as you can see in Table 3.

One obvious effect of this is that higher-pitch-count outings should be of better quality, on average. Table 4, which shows ERA and RA for starts of a certain number of pitches, confirms this.

While this data establishes the intuitive point that good pitchers throw more long outings than bad pitchers, this isn't enough to establish that the RA ratio chart above is affected. We must also determine if both low- and high-endurance pitchers share similar proportional declines in performance. Let's examine the pitch-count data for each group in Figure 2.

Table 2: Endurance Subgroups Based on Start Pitch Count

ENDURANCE	PITCHERS	ERA	RA
High	1105	4.06	4.28
Low	1822	4.85	5.10

Table 3: Percentage of High Endurance Pitchers by Start Pitch Count

No. of Pitches	% HIGH
70-79	39.7%
80-89	43.1%
90-99	56.4%
100-109	70.9%
110-119	79.8%
120-129	86.7%
130-139	91.2%
140+	91.2%

Table 4: Pitcher Quality by Start Pitch Count

No. of Pitches	Games Started	No. of Pitchers	ERA	RA
50	563	340	5.25	5.54
55	724	391	5.14	5.39
60	954	443	5.06	5.30
65	1359	504	4.87	5.11
70	1815	549	4.74	4.99
75	2349	588	4.74	4.98
80	2965	607	4.67	4.92
85	3582	620	4.61	4.85
90	4074	608	4.49	4.74
95	4365	596	4.43	4.67
100	4431	573	4.41	4.66
105	4086	531	4.28	4.52
110	3475	474	4.20	4.44
115	2645	418	4.14	4.37
120	2066	371	4.09	4.32
125	1381	299	4.05	4.25
130	817	226	3.96	4.15

Low-endurance pitchers not only throw fewer pitches per start, but they decline significantly more than high-endurance pitchers do from start to start. In fact, the best decline performance by low-endurance pitchers is worse than the worst decline performance from high-endurance pitchers. We may speculate that part of the reason low-endurance pitchers aren't allowed to throw more pitches is their inconsistency from start to start. Any effect from pitch counts is thus being overwhelmed by the pitcher's own inability to maintain a high level of performance. The evidence for this lies in the erratic relationship between pitch counts and short-term decline for low-endurance pitchers.

This study, then, will focus on the short-term effect of high-pitch-count outings among those pitchers regularly counted upon to throw deep into a game. This makes practical sense, as well, since the controversy on pitch counts isn't about whether the Sean Bergmans of the world are being overworked. The argument is about whether the quality pitchers who are relied upon to pitch lots of innings—guys like Kerry Wood, Livan Hernandez, and Rick Helling—are overworked or not.

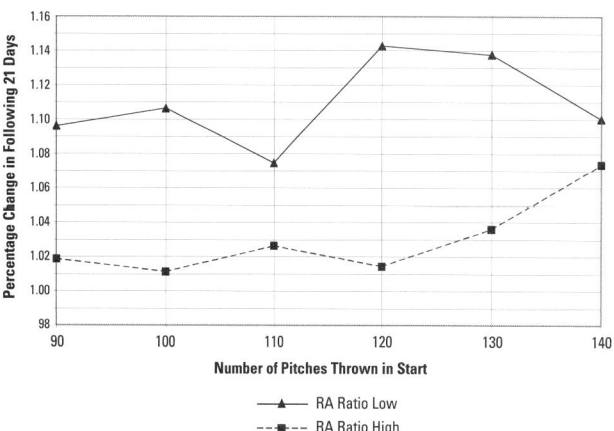

Figure 2: RA Ratio—High vs. Low Endurance Pitchers

Initial results

Let's look again at the change in RA before and after a high-pitch-count start, focusing only on the high-endurance pitchers. For the sake of simplicity, references to pitchers throughout the rest of this discussion refer to our high-endurance subset of pitchers, unless specifically stated otherwise. See Figure 3.

As you can see, there's a strong trend for pitchers to allow more runs following a high-pitch-count outing. A typical high-endurance pitcher gives up 7% more runs per inning in the three weeks following a 140+ pitch outing than

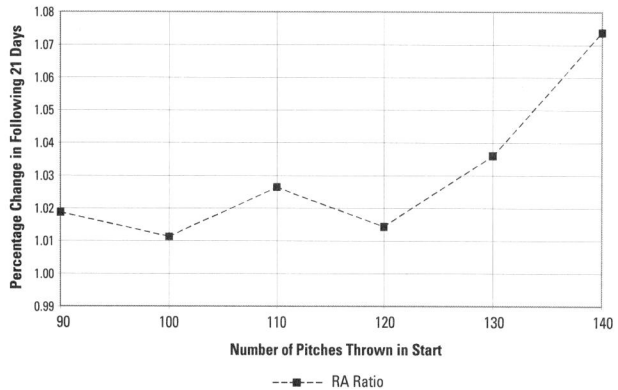

Figure 3: Percentage Change in 21 Days Following Start, High Endurance Pitchers by RA Ratio

Figure 4: Percentage Change in 21 Days Following Start, High Endurance Pitchers by IP/GS, RA Ratio, H Ratio, and SO Ratio

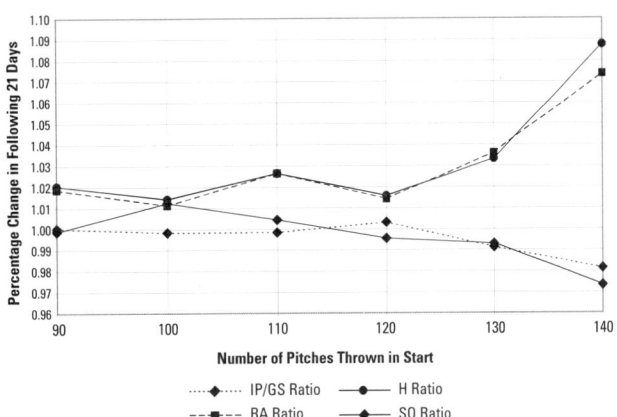

Figure 5: Percentage Change in 21 Days Following Start, High Endurance Pitchers by IP/GS, RA Ratio, H Ratio, and SO Ratio with Performance Index

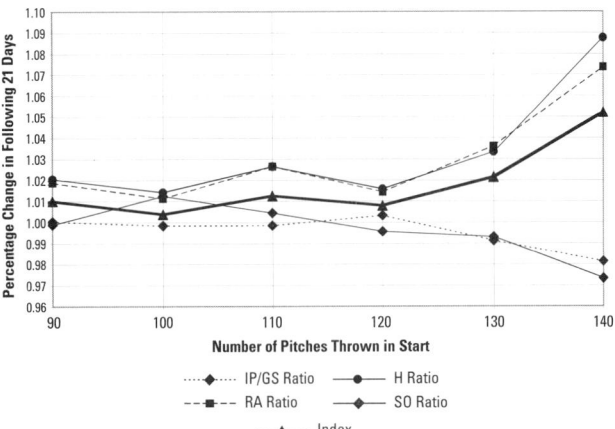

in the three weeks immediately prior. Once again, those measures are:

Run average (RA)
Hits per inning (H/IP)
Strikeouts per inning (SO/IP)
Inning pitched per game started (IP/GS)

Let's plot all four ratios against pitch count in Figure 4.

All four indexes are relatively constant in the 90-100 pitch range, but they show significant declines in effectiveness as pitch counts rise, particularly after 120 pitches. Note that the high IP and SO ratios mean the opposite of high RA and H ratios—a decline in innings pitched or strikeout rate is bad, while a rise in hits or runs allowed means trouble for a pitcher.

The Performance Index

To estimate the overall effect, combining the effect of run prevention and endurance with the leading indicators of pitcher dominance, I averaged the ratios into a single "Performance" index. To get the "good" direction pointing the same way for all of the ratios, I inverted the SO/IP and IP/GS ratios to make high values less desirable. The ratios, along with the average index, are shown in Figure 5.

If we design a metric that is a function of the total number of pitches thrown and that matches the shape of the curve shown above, we would have a reasonably good indicator by which the cost of a long outing on near-term performance could be measured. Notice that the shape of the curve is flatter at the beginning and gets steeper and steeper as the pitch counts increase. This is clearly not a linear trend but a nonlinear function with increasing slope.

As it turns out, PAP was designed to show this same kind of behavior. It is reasonable to wonder, then, how well PAP matches the observed shape of the Performance Index.

PAP vs. Performance Index

For all of the performance metrics we will analyze, there are certain parameters that define the metric maps to the Index curve. I have set all the functions to match the performance index at the NP = 100 and NP = 140 levels, and I observed how the curve matches the shape of the points in between. The NP = 100 level was selected because it matches the first point of continuous decline in any of the indexes, namely strikeout rate. Some of the other metrics may not show substantial decline until higher pitch counts, but strikeout rate appears to be an "early warning system" of trouble ahead.

Let's begin with the original definition of PAP presented in Figure 6.

The classic formulation of PAP shows the right basic shape, but the slope does not curve as sharply as the performance index does. PAP also overestimates the effect of a 120- or 130-pitch outing.

Next, we should consider other functions that share the structure of PAP and that may provide a better match to the empirical data. I parameterized the PAP function so that the threshold at which PAP starts to accumulate (originally 100) and the step at which another Abuse Point accumulates (originally 10) can vary. For example, we could investigate a PAP function that starts accumulating points at 110 pitches, with an increment of 5 pitches. We'll refer to these modified functions as PAP(THRESHOLD,STEP), as in PAP(110,5) in Figure 7, or, for classic PAP, PAP(100,10).

Figure 6: Percentage Change in 21 Days Following Start, High Endurance Pitchers—Performance Index vs. Classic 10-Pitch Step PAP Function

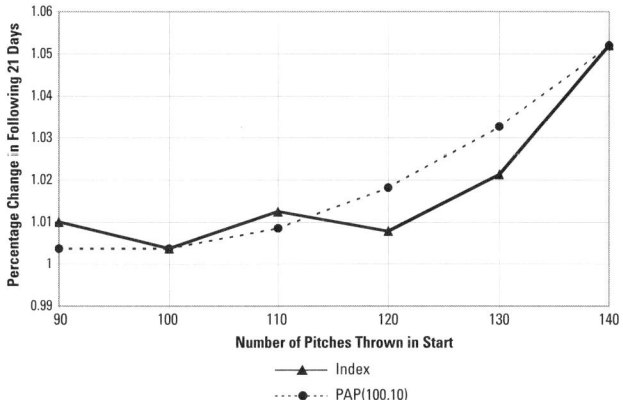

Figure 8: Percentage Change in 21 Days Following Start, High Endurance Pitchers—Performance Index vs. Additive PAP Function

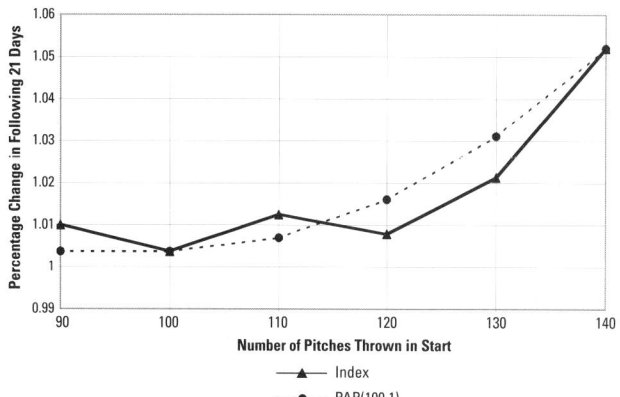

Figure 7: Percentage Change in 21 Days Following Start, High Endurance Pitchers—Performance Index vs. 5-Pitch Step–110-Pitch Threshold PAP Function

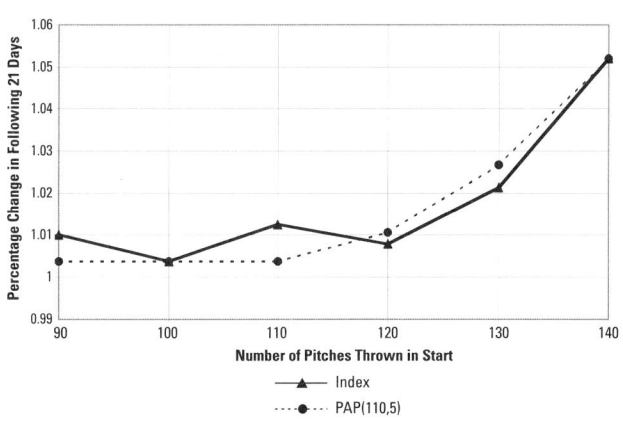

Figure 9: Percentage Change in 21 Days Following Start, High Endurance Pitchers—Performance Index vs. Quadratic PAP Function

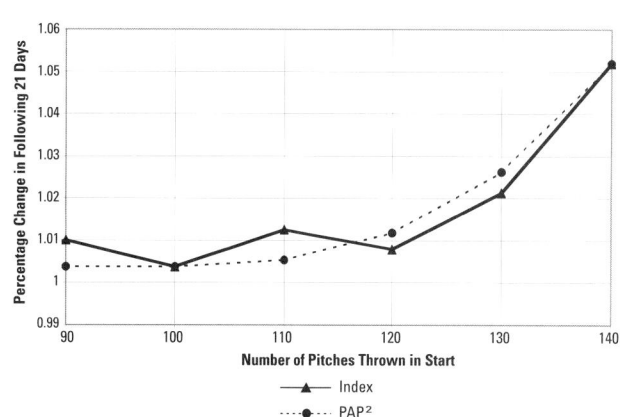

The reduction in the step from ten pitches to five increases the slope, but does so throughout the curve. The change of threshold to 110 pitches mitigates this, as we don't start the curve until later into the outing. Let's look at another PAP function, this time PAP(100,1)—that is, starting at 100 pitches, and adding one abuse point for the first pitch, two for the second pitch, three for the third pitch, and so on for every pitch thereafter. Figure 8 shows those results.

Other PAP Formulae

It's evident that, despite our best efforts, a PAP formulation that relies on the semi-linear increase in abuse points doesn't fully capture the relationship between high pitch counts and reduced effectiveness. Let's look then at other nonlinear functions that show more dramatic curvature. A quadratic relationship (PAP = (NP-100)^2 if NP > 100, 0 otherwise) is shown in Figure 9.

Figure 9's formula shows some improvement, but still not dramatic enough to really match the curve in the critical 120-140 pitch area. Now, let's look at a cubic relationship (PAP = (NP-100)^3 if NP>100, 0 otherwise) in Figure 10.

Voila! The cubic PAP function provides an almost perfect fit with the overall trend in the performance index. In particular, the fit between the value of 120 and 140 is uncanny. We have thus discovered a simple mathematical relationship between the length of a start and the expected impact on a pitcher afterwards.

Figure 10: Percentage Change in 21 Days Following Start, High Endurance Pitchers—Performance Index vs. Cubic PAP Function

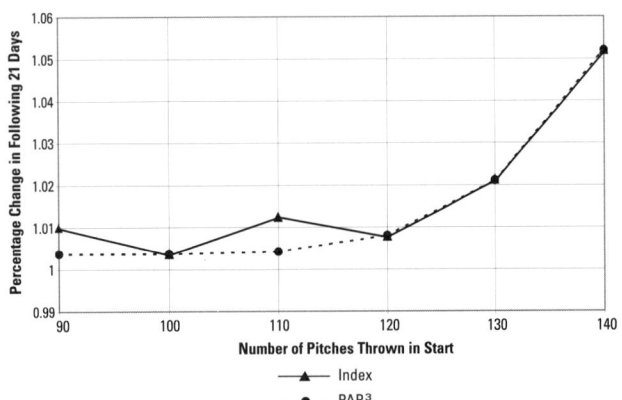

Reformulating PAP

With the empirical data now at hand, Rany and I considered adjusting PAP. In particular, the cubic relationship between pitch count and ineffectiveness needs to be built into the system. We'll designate the system as PAP³, to distinguish it from classic PAP, and define it like this:

PAP³ = [0 if the start has fewer than 100 pitches,
(NP-100)^3 if the start has 100 or more pitches]

One may reasonably wonder how the PAP³ system compares to classic PAP. I've changed the scale of PAP³ to match the range of PAP so that the differences may be seen more easily in Table 5.

Generally speaking, PAP³ is more forgiving on pitch counts between 100 and 135 than was classic PAP, though the penalties for going much above that level are considerably steeper.

One unfortunate side effect of this reformulation is evident in the table above. Though the formula for PAP³ is simple enough, the numbers for PAP³ grow large very quickly. For example, a 129-pitch outing has a PAP³ of 24389—easy to figure with a calculator, though few people would be able to cube 29 in their heads. However, there is a mathematical relationship that can help us out here—logarithms. While logarithms don't change the nature of the underlying relationship, they do allow us to categorize starts with smaller numbers. In Table 6, I've grouped starts by the log of their PAP³ totals. Specifically, I'm using base 10 logs, not natural logs.

Table 6: Relationship of PAP³ (Base 10 Log) to Start Pitch Count

Log(PAP³)	Category	Pitch Range	Risk of Short-Term Decline
—	I	0-100	Virtually none
<=2	II	101-109	Minimal Risk
3	III	110-121	Moderate Risk
4–4.5	IV	122-132	Significant Risk
4.5–5	V	133+	High Risk

For example, a 114-pitch outing has a PAP³ of 2744, and the log(2744) is 3.43, which makes it a Category III start. I used Roman numerals to designate the categories simply to indicate that we are consolidating starts into broad categories rather than precisely measuring a specific effect.

The categories are divided largely by the integer portion of LOG(PAP) except between categories IV and V. Otherwise, the Category IV starts cover too broad a range of expected risk factors (pitch counts of 122–146, or expected declines of about 1% to well over 6%). Still, the categories are ultimately based on empirical analysis and should be easier to discuss sabermetrically (e.g., "Livan Hernandez had 10 Category IV starts and four Category V starts, which is way too high. Dusty Baker needs to lay off").

Sample Results

For the 2000 season, the totals in each category are listed in Table 7.

The individual leaders in each category for 2000 were:
Category I starts: John Halama (26); Greg Maddux (25); Brian Anderson, Brian Meadows (24)
Category II starts: Kent Bottenfield (15); Darryl Kile (14); Kevin Brown, Kris Benson, Jimmy Haynes, James Baldwin (12)

Table 5: Comparison of PAP³ to PAP

No. of Pitches	PAP	PAP3	Scaled PAP3
95	0	0	0
105	5	125	0
115	20	3375	5
125	45	15625	21
135	80	42875	59
145	125	91125	125

Table 7: Pitcher Start Distribution by PAP³ Category

Category	No. of Starts
I	2592
II	977
III	885
IV	346
V	52

Category III starts: Kenny Rogers, Sidney Ponson (15); Mike Hampton, Russ Ortiz, Al Leiter (14)

Category IV starts: Randy Johnson (12); Livan Hernandez, Roger Clemens (10); Rick Helling (9); Randy Wolf, Jeff Suppan (8)

Category V starts: Livan Hernandez (4); Randy Johnson (3); Rick Helling, Scott Elarton, Al Leiter (2)

We can also look at the "average category" of a pitcher's starts. The pitchers with the highest average category (minimum of 10 starts) are listed in Table 8.

Conversely, only one pitcher with 10 or more starts had all of his starts in Category I: Dave Eiland. Others with low category averages include Todd Stottlemyre, Sean Bergman, Mike Johnson, Dwight Gooden, Brian Rose, Bronson Arroyo, Jeff Fassero, Hideki Irabu, and Pete Schourek.

Limitations of the Study

We should sound a few notes of caution here. First is that we haven't yet established what PAP was originally designed to measure—risk of injury from overuse. We've been investigating a related (and easier to assess) phenomenon: short-term ineffectiveness following high-pitch-count outings. PAP³ should not, at this point, be used as a proven indicator of health risks. At best, it should be taken as an early warning indicator that a pitcher is being pushed too hard. It says nothing about whether a pitcher can fully bounce back to his previously established level of performance given enough rest and a more sensible workload. Part 2 addresses the injury risks of heavy workloads.

It's also important to remember that the aggregate performance index curve lumps together pitchers with differing capabilities, physiques, and endurances. Randy Johnson may be able to throw 130 or more pitches without ill effects, while Jason Schmidt may suffer when asked to go more than 90 pitches. However, it is difficult, if not impossible, with present record keeping and medical knowledge to ascertain where a particular pitcher's threshold is. The PAP³ system is an amalgamation of the performance of all pitchers and is a general indication of how pitchers, as a group, respond to different workloads.

Lastly, the PAP^3 formula has been validated only for pitch counts that range up to 140–149. While this is mostly sufficient for recent seasons (starts of 150 or more pitches amount to only 0.14% of all starts since 1988), there's no reason to expect that the cubic relationship holds at the 180–200 pitch level occasionally reached by pitchers in years past. Is a 180-pitch outing eight times worse than a 140-pitch outing, as PAP^3 would suggest? That implies a 38% decline in the pitcher's performance index, a truly gigantic amount, pushing a league-average pitcher (say, 4.50 RA) to below replacement level (about a 6.21 RA). The true estimate of very high pitch counts may have to wait for historical pitch count data or a change in the game which restores the conditions of the dead-ball era or at least the 1960s.

Conclusions

How significant is the effect we've identified? Assuming a fairly abusive usage pattern across a staff, a team's starting rotation could suffer a season-wide decline of about 2%. Considering the effect on both the innings pitched (putting more strain on the bullpen) and extra runs allowed by the starting pitchers, this might amount to perhaps 20–25 runs over the course of a season, worth about 2 to 2.5 games in the standings. It's comparable to the difference in value between Tim Hudson and Kevin Tapani or Todd Ritchie in 2000. That's a trade worth making.

The implications for pitcher usage are rather straightforward; starting pitchers should, in general, be held to 121 or fewer pitches (Categories I, II, and III). There are some circumstances where this need not apply—if winning today's game is significantly more important than the pitcher's next few starts because you're playing a division rival during a pennant race. Also, if a manager believes a pitcher is physically more durable than other pitchers, he may judiciously allow him to throw deeper into games. Naturally, the state of the bullpen and the rest of the starting staff may also figure

Table 8: Pitchers with Highest Average Category (Minimum of 10 Starts)

Pitcher	Game Starts	Average Category
Livan Hernandez	33	3.152
Randy Johnson	35	3.057
Al Leiter	31	2.871
Woody Illiams	23	2.783
Randy Wolf	32	2.750
Rick Helling	35	2.714
Pedro Martinez	29	2.655
Roger Clemens	31	2.613
Sidney Ponson	32	2.563
Blake Stein	17	2.529
Mike Mussina	34	2.500
Robert Person	28	2.500
Andy Pettitte	32	2.469
Jason Schmidt	11	2.455
Mike Hampton	33	2.455
Chan Ho Park	34	2.441
Wade Miller	16	2.438
Ryan Dempster	33	2.424
Kris Benson	32	2.406
Bartolo Colon	30	2.400

into the decision—David Wells after a 5% decline is still a better pitcher than Roy Halladay. However, even though extenuating circumstances may call for pushing a workhorse starter to a Category IV start (up to 132 pitches) or even a low-end Category V start, it should be viewed as nearly inexcusable to let a starting pitcher exceed 140 pitches in any start.

Managers who allow pitchers to throw too many pitches in a start may not only be jeopardizing that pitcher's future but may also be hurting the team's chances at success. For the benefit of another half-inning of work from a tired starter, a manager is gambling with that pitcher's next four or five starts at the very least. The evidence here shows that a season-long strategy to maximize the effectiveness of a pitching staff through managed workloads makes sense, even under an urgent "we need to win now, the future will take care of itself" philosophy.

Part 2: The Long-Term Injury Risk of High Pitch Counts

In Part 1, we derived a new PAP formula (dubbed PAP³) that reflects the typical short-term decline in pitcher performance following a high-pitch-count outing. Now we'll investigate whether PAP³ has any value in predicting which pitchers are liable to get hurt, and if not, whether any PAP-style metric can be derived that has predictive value.

Pitch counts and injuries

Before claiming success for any measure in predicting injury, we need to recognize that all PAP-style metrics are positively correlated with raw pitch counts. Pitchers with high pitch-count totals will tend to have high PAP totals. If a PAP function provides no additional insight into which pitchers will be injured than do pitch count totals alone, there is no reason to bring the added complexity of a PAP system to our sabermetric arsenal. Only if a PAP function provides injury information above and beyond what can be learned from aggregate pitch counts should we consider it successful.

As with the previous study, I looked at starts for all pitchers between 1988-98 for which there were pitch count data in the Baseball Workshop/Total Sports database. The approach I used was to identify starting pitchers who suffered major injuries during that span and to compare them with comparable pitchers who did not suffer major injuries. Pitcher injury data was taken from Neft & Cohen's *The Sports Encyclopedia: Baseball 2000*.

Identifying Injured Pitchers

In the annual season summary section of Neft & Cohen, team rosters are presented and a notation is made if a player was injured for more than 30 days. For the purposes of this study, I selected pitchers who were 1) starting pitchers in the year they were injured, and 2) whose recent history indicated a pattern of starting pitching. Generally speaking, if a pitcher was a full-time or near-full-time reliever in either of the two seasons prior to the injury, he was excluded from consideration. Pitch counts from relief appearances were not included for any pitcher, since relief outings are generally low in total pitch counts and since the hypothesis under consideration is that *high* pitch counts overextend pitchers and lead to injury risk.

Furthermore, I considered only certain types of injuries. A two-letter code in Neft & Cohen indicated the type of injury (if known). Since pitcher overwork would most often be associated with arm injuries, the only injury categories I included were shoulder injury, elbow injury, arm injury, and sore arm. Any injured pitcher with one of these codes was presumed to have injured his pitching arm (the reference does not specify which arm). Note that this categorization considers only the most serious arm injuries, namely those which kept a pitcher out of action for a month or more. Less serious injuries, including missed turns in the rotation and DL stays of fewer than 30 days, are ignored (and in fact, these pitchers are considered "healthy," having not missed 30 or more days due to injury during the season).

Since I wanted to consider pitchers for whom we had pitch-count data for most of their careers, any pitcher who accumulated more than 100 innings in the majors prior to 1988 was excluded.

Note that minor-league pitch counts are not widely available at present. While a more thorough treatment of the impact of career usage and pitch counts on pitcher injury susceptibility would certainly include minor-league numbers, I restricted the investigation to major-league pitch counts only.

Finally, several pitchers appeared on the injured list multiple times during their careers. Physiologically, prior injury makes one prone to future injury. To account for this, only the first season in which a given pitcher suffered a major injury is included in our data.

Using these criteria, a total of 73 injured pitchers were identified.

Defining Comparable Pitchers

In order to identify a set of pitchers with similar workloads who had not been injured, I found matches for each injured pitcher's age and career pitch-count total. For every injured pitcher, then, I would have several pitchers with similar age and usage profiles but who had not been injured. More specifically, for each injured pitcher, I found all pitchers whose career totals through the same age had were within 10% or the injured pitcher's career pitch-count total. That is, if a 25-year-old Jason Bere had about 7800 career pitches in 1995, I matched him with any other 25-year-old pitcher who had between 7020 and 8580 career pitches.

Of course, a further restriction was that any matching pitcher could not be among the 73 injured pitchers, even if he was injured at a different age than the one for which he was being compared. If a single pitcher-season matched more than one injured pitcher, the duplicate entries were removed so that no pitcher-season was counted more than once. A total of 569 healthy comparable seasons were identified, for an average of 7.8 healthy comparable pitchers per injured pitcher.

Note that the term "comparable pitcher" refers only to the aggregate number of pitches thrown in a pitcher's starts, not to his results. Two 27-year-old pitchers with 5000 career pitches would be considered comparable in terms of workload, even if one had a 3.00 ERA and the other a 5.50 ERA. They are comparable in the total amount of work performed (pitches thrown), not in the value of the results.

Career PAP as a Predictor of Injury

Our initial hypothesis is that PAP^3 has predictive power beyond that of raw career pitch-count totals in assessing the likelihood of injury for major league pitchers. To test this hypothesis, I plotted career PAP^3 vs. career pitch counts for all the pitcher-seasons in the sample, shown in figure 11.

Over the course of any pitcher's career, he will invariably pick up PAP^3 in some fraction of his outings. By looking at the usage patterns of many pitchers over the years, you can ascertain the "typical" amount of PAP^3 a major-league pitcher would accumulate given his pitch counts. Linear regression is one technique for mathematically determining what this typical PAP^3 level is. The best-fitting linear regression equation is plotted in the chart above as the solid line.

If pitchers with greater-than-usual PAP^3 are more likely to be injured, we would expect more of the large dots (those indicating injured pitchers) to lie above the trend line in the chart above. It's difficult to tell from visual inspection whether this is the case or not. We can, however, analyze the data itself. Looking at the percentage of each group of pitchers that lies above the trend line, we discover that:

> 31% of all injured pitchers had above-average career PAP^3 totals for their career pitch counts.
>
> 9% of all healthy pitchers had above-average career PAP^3 totals for their career pitch counts.

This analysis suggests that high-PAP^3 pitchers are more than three times as likely to be injured as low-PAP^3 pitchers who've thrown similar numbers of pitches. We have our first piece of evidence that PAP^3 provides predictive information beyond what pitch counts alone can tell us.

As a side note, the careful reader will observe that there are four data points that exceed a career-to-date PAP^3 total of 2,000,000. These four pitcher-seasons are all from the same pitcher and far exceed the workload amassed by any other pitcher. This workhorse is, of course, Randy Johnson, whose career workload looks like a mistake in the chart. Whatever the results of our analysis of PAP^3 and injuries, Johnson is almost certainly an extreme outlier, a remarkable physical specimen for whom comparison to regular major-league pitchers may not apply.

The Workload Stress Metric

Though we now have some indication that high PAP^3 totals are a predictor of injury risk, the results are somewhat buried in the statistics. The key element of the findings above is that more PAP^3 for any given number of pitches indicates higher risk. This leads to the concept of using PAP^3/NP as a measure of how intense or stressful a pitcher's pitches have been. I'll refer to PAP^3/NP as "Workload Stress" or simply "Stress."

I determined career-to-date Stress factors for each pitcher in our sample, with the intention of plotting Stress versus rate of injury. However, since each pitcher in the sample has an injury value of either 0 (healthy) or 1 (injured), a straightforward plot of points would not be particularly revealing.

What I did instead was sort the list of all pitchers by Stress factors and create a moving average or "sliding window" of 50 data points at a time. That is, I took pitchers 1–50 as one data point, pitchers 2–51 for the second data point,

Figure 11: Total PAP vs. Total Pitch Counts

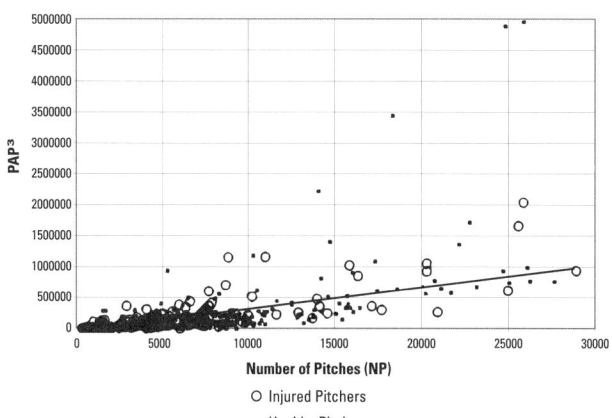

3–52 as the third, and so on, so that with every step I was adding one pitcher with a high Stress factor and dropping the one with the lowest Stress. I averaged the Stress factors for every pitcher in the window and computed the percentage of pitchers in the sample who were injured. This created a sample within the sample for which we can estimate the injury rate for pitchers with Stress factors similar to the sample's average Stress. The results are in Figure 12.

Figure 12: Average Injury Rate as a Function of Stress of Workload (50 Point Forward Averaging)

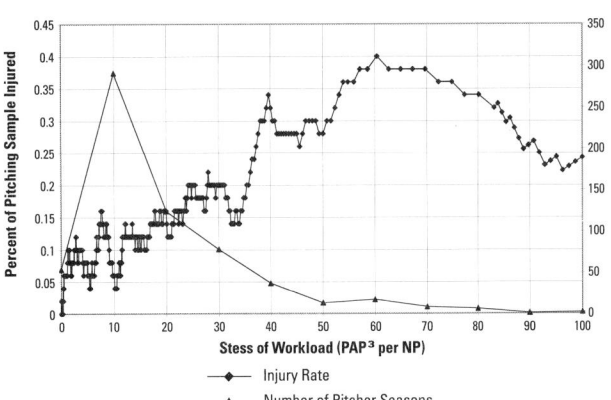

Here we see a more compelling representation of the relationship between PAP³ and injuries. There's a clear trend between Stress and the percentage of pitchers who get injured. There's a relatively constant increase between 0 and 50, with a leveling off thereafter. Over a quarter of pitchers with career Stress factors above 40 have suffered a major injury at some point during the time of the study, compared with less than 15% of those with career Stress factors below 20.

Interestingly, there are indications of a decline as you approach and exceed a Stress factor of 100 (the chart is truncated at Stress = 100 due to lack of sample size above this level). However, the injury rate is still well above that of any Stress factor less than 40. Given the small number of pitchers in the upper end of the chart, it could be a sample-size effect. If we assume, for the sake of argument, that this decline is not simply random fluctuation, I would speculate that it represents a survival effect of sorts. The pitcher who can sustain that high a workload stress is one whose manager has pushed him harder and harder until he got a reputation as a workhorse who can consistently shoulder 130-pitch outings. It takes a while for the pitcher to develop to a point where he can be effective in the late innings (and hence not be pulled for a reliever). Also, a manager may be cautious with a new arm until he's comfortable enough with a pitcher to "know" how far he can go. Thus, the pitchers who end up with the highest levels of stress are the quality arms who've survived the weeding-out process.

The Injury Likelihood Equation

The shape of the line on the chart, with a steeper slope at the beginning and leveling off as you go higher, suggests a logarithmic curve. An example of such a curve is shown in Figure 13.

Figure 13: Average Injury Rate as a Function of Stress of Workload (50 Point Forward Averaging) with Injury Likelihood Trend

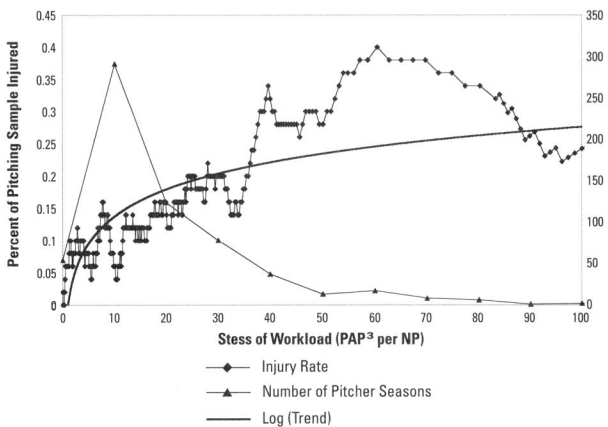

The formula for the trend line shown above (where LN() is the natural log function) is:

$$\text{Prob(Injury)} = 0.06 * \text{LN(Stress)}$$

Or, equivalently:

$$\text{Prob(Injury)} = 0.06 * \text{LN(PAP/NP)}$$

(Technical note: This equation holds for Stress factors greater than or equal to 1. The curve is equal to zero for Stress factors below 1).

What this chart suggests is that a pitcher's career stress factor can help predict the likelihood of that pitcher suffering a major arm injury at some point during his career. For example, a pitcher who's consistently around a Workload Stress of 30 has a 20% chance of missing a month or more due to arm injury at some point in his career.

Statistical Significance of Results

Having derived these apparently impressive results, it's only prudent that we ask whether they are statistically significant or not. One commonly used statistical test is called a Chi-squared test. Though the details of the test will be omitted here, for our purposes, the Chi-squared test determines the likelihood that the results we've seen could result from a random split of a uniform population, given the sample sizes. In other words, Chi-squared will check the possibility that the high and low PAP³ pitchers are actually equally likely to be injured and that the observed differences are due to chance (this is what's called the "null hypothesis"—that PAP³ has no predictive value). If the resulting probability from the Chi-squared test is too high (traditionally around 5%), then we can't reject the possibility that the null hypothesis is true, meaning that the differences could be explained by chance rather than any predictive power of PAP³. Conversely, a very low probability result from the Chi-squared test increases our confidence that the results are not due to chance and that separating pitchers based on PAP³ does provide information about their relative injury risks.

Turning first to the career PAP³ totals, we noted that pitchers with above-average PAP³ totals given their career pitch counts were far more likely to have been injured than pitchers with below-average PAP³ totals. Computing a Chi-squared probability for this sample indicates that the split has only a 0.000018% chance of having occurred by chance. This easily passes the criteria for statistical significance.

Looking next at the Workload Stress factor versus (PAP³/NP), I took a more granular approach, dividing the sample space into quintiles by PAP³/NP, and computed the injury rates in each of the five groups. I then computed the Chi-squared probability of this split occurring by chance. The result were comparable to our previous findings—a relationship like the one observed has a miniscule 0.0000028% chance of happening by chance. Again, the Stress Workload factor clears the bar for statistical significance.

Other PAP Formulae

As with the short-term PAP results, I examined other possible PAP formulae to see if the relationship to injury risk was noticeably stronger. Though I do not present the charts here, I tested classic PAP, other polynomial versions of PAP (e.g. PAP=(NP-100)^2), and I tried varying the baselines (100 pitches, 90 pitches, 110 pitches, etc). There was no dominant winner among the various formulae. In general, they resulted in predictions similar to PAP³. Perhaps it isn't that surprising, since, unlike single starts, usage patterns tend to even out more over the course of a career. Furthermore, even with the results we have, predicting injury is an inexact science, and Workload Stress factors are no guarantee for either health or injury. Therefore, any reasonable metric that gives extra weight to high-pitch-count outings should yield a risk factor that is in the same ballpark as PAP³ (pardon the pun). Because we have a preferred metric for short-term impact that does acceptably well long-term injury risk too, we will stick with simplicity and use a single metric for both purposes. The PAP³ formula will be the basis for our Pitcher Abuse Point work henceforth.

2000 Workload Stress Leaders

We can compute Stress factors for individual pitching seasons (or groups of seasons) to assess whether a pitcher is "on pace" for difficulties. Tables 9 and 10 show the pitchers with the 25 highest and lowest Workload Stress rates for the 2000 season (minimum: 10 games started).

Conclusions and Futures

Injuries to a key pitcher can have a devastating effect on a team's fortunes, not to mention shortening or hindering a pitcher's career. With escalating salaries, proper pitcher usage is increasingly important to maximizing a team's investment in its personnel. As a result, people pay attention to pitch counts, managers and pitching coaches are scrutinized more closely in how they handle a staff, and player-development systems in the minors are increasingly aware of protecting young arms.

Table 9: 25 Highest Pitchers by Workload Stress Rate

Pitcher	GS	PAP	NP	Stress
Livan Hernandez	33	422979	3825	110.58
Randy Johnson	35	439098	4021	109.20
Jason Schmidt	11	101865	1203	84.68
Rick Helling	35	313875	3791	82.79
Ron Villone	23	150263	2246	66.90
Al Leiter	31	229252	3478	65.91
Roger Clemens	32	218043	3433	63.51
Sterling Hitchcock	11	70714	1127	62.75
Randy Wolf	32	217292	3528	61.59
Pedro Martinez	29	190327	3165	60.13
Scott Elarton	30	188275	3139	58.98
Kevin Appier	31	194467	3314	58.68
Doug Davis	13	78320	1338	58.54
Wade Miller	16	97914	1724	56.79
Jeff Suppan	33	181089	3488	51.92
Mike Mussina	34	183194	3657	50.09
Woody Williams	23	127255	2591	49.11
Kevin Tapani	30	151277	3151	48.01
Pedro Astacio	32	150985	3182	47.45
Ruben Quevedo	15	69533	1497	46.45
Sidney Ponson	32	158887	3433	46.28
Kelvim Escobar	24	115250	2527	45.61
Blake Stein	17	83021	1850	44.88
Garrett Stephenson	31	144609	3251	44.48
Albie Lopez	24	106472	2402	44.33

Table 10: 25 Lowest Pitchers by Workload Stress Rate

Pitcher	GS	PAP	NP	Stress
Vladimir Nunez	12	1757	1047	1.68
Darren Dreifort	32	4498	3114	1.44
Scott Karl	13	1339	1037	1.29
Esteban Yan	20	2262	1801	1.26
Jon Garland	13	1407	1198	1.17
J.C. Romero	11	1009	961	1.05
Ryan Glynn	16	1512	1456	1.04
Roy Halladay	13	1253	1208	1.04
Brian Rose	24	1728	1862	0.93
Willie Blair	17	1342	1545	0.87
Geraldo Guzman	10	737	896	0.82
Carlos Perez	22	1531	1921	0.80
Tomokazu Ohka	12	793	1096	0.72
Ryan Rupe	18	757	1553	0.49
Sean Bergman	14	512	1152	0.44
Dwight Gooden	14	343	1161	0.30
Jeff Fassero	23	152	1883	0.08
Pete Schourek	21	126	1731	0.07
Reid Cornelius	21	126	1828	0.07
Hideki Irabu	11	27	853	0.03
John Halama	30	63	2607	0.02
Bronson Arroyo	12	8	958	0.01
Mike Johnson	13	8	981	0.01
Todd Stottlemyre	18	1	1496	0.00
Dave Eiland	10	0	667	0.00

The research presented here has shown, in essence, that not all pitches are created equal. High-pitch-count outings represent the greatest risk for both short-term ineffectiveness and long-term potential for injury. The PAP³ system represents the most comprehensive attempt to date to quantify the impact of starting-pitcher usage over both time horizons, allowing us to estimate, based on empirical evidence, the trade-offs of having a star pitcher throw deep into a game.

However, before we place too much weight on these discoveries, some caveats apply. The results of this study should not be considered final because many active pitchers are included in the study. It will be several years before a large sample of pitch counts for entire pitcher careers becomes available, and such a resource is necessary before we can complete the analysis that has been started here.

It's important to note that the Workload Stress factor is not a prediction of injury risk for a specific season, but rather of injury risk over several years of pitching at that level. Also, PAP³ may underestimate the relationship between high pitch counts and injuries. This study considered only the most major injuries and did not look at minor injuries, missed turns in the rotation, or shifts from starting to relief pitching. We also assumed that the injury effect of high pitch counts would manifest itself in arm problems. It's possible that there would also be effects for other kinds of non-arm injuries (especially back and leg injuries).

The research questions are far from resolved, and there are still many facets to the problem that have yet to be fully addressed. For example, a pitcher's age may be of considerable importance when assessing the risks of specific pitch-count limits, but age was not included in this study. Important data is still missing from the study, such as minor-league, spring-training, and postseason pitch counts. The interactions and spacing between pitcher outings may prove to have a significant effect—does starting on three days' rest vs. four days' rest substantially affect the risk of either injury or ineffectiveness? I did not conduct an exhaustive search for all mathematical representations, favoring the simplicity of a single measure like PAP³. Biomechanical experts may help identify physical characteristics that indicate which pitchers are more or less susceptible or have greater endurance, allowing personalized PAP formulae for individual pitchers.

There also exists the possibility that the relationship between pitch counts and injury risk is not static over time. Improved training methods, changing usage patterns and strategies, new medical technology and techniques and new diagnostics and screening could all impact the negative effects of high pitch counts. Pitch-count data from 1950 may not be terribly informative about the effects on modern pitchers. Similarly, 20 years from now, an entirely different PAP formula may need to be developed to take into account the impact of, say, a yet-to-be-invented machine that rejuvenates muscle tissue instantly. Clearly, we have not learned all we need to know about the effects of pitcher usage.

For now, however, we can confidently say that PAP³ yields information about pitcher performance and durability not provided by pitch counts alone under current playing conditions. Long outings noticeably decrease expected short-term performance, and high-stress workloads over time increase the chances for serious injury. Any strategic analysis of pitcher usage will have to consider the trade-off between winning the current game and the long-term cost. There are clearly times when you will want to ride a workhorse hard, such as a key playoff game (though Al Leiter will attest that there are limits even in the World Series). Finding the right balance between winning now and winning tomorrow remains an interesting challenge, and today we have another tool in our arsenal to assess a team's sustainable pitching strategy.

Acknowledgements

I'd like to thanks Dr. Lutz Mueller of Lumina Decision Systems for his advice and consultation on the design and statistical testing methods in this research.

Park Factors

by Clay Davenport

Last season, the park factor—the amount by which the playing environment increases or decreases run-scoring—was a topic of some controversy. Basically, the usage of park factors by baseball fans can be roughly divided into three camps:

1. Those who do not use park factors at all. To use no park factor is the same as using a 100 park factor all of the time. This is what the majority of baseball fans do, and have done, throughout history; they treat every park the same. For this group, any park factor is controversial; we at BP are regularly assailed by Rockies fans for using park factors to dismiss their team's hitters, for example.

2. Those who use park factors based only on the current year's data. This is the way I have usually done it, along with a few others. There are two powerful arguments for this approach. One is that the single season is the standard for virtually everything we analyze in baseball. Two is that variations in weather and opponent quality cause measurable differences from one season to the next and that these changes have a real effect on players' statistical lines.

3. Those who use three or more years of data for a park factor, averaging the single year's data out over time to reduce the aforementioned variations. The idea here is that those variations were not real changes or effects, but rather random and transient features which have no genuine impact on player statistics. Pete Palmer, after using one-year factors in the first edition of *Total Baseball*, subsequently switched to three-year factors. Some of my BP co-authors do the same: Keith Woolner uses three-year factors to calculate his VORP ratings of players, and Mike Wolverton uses three-year factors for his Support-Neutral pitching data. STATS publishes both one- and three-year averages in its annual Handbooks.

So you can readily see that I have been one of the last holdouts in the sabermetric community who continued using park factors based only on one year of data. I am a meteorologist in my day job, and I do have some familiarity with how small fluctuations in temperature, moisture, and wind can make dramatic differences, so perhaps I wanted to believe in such impacts for baseball.

Two parks caused me special problems in 2000. When I was compiling my daily EqA reports for the BP website, I started calculating park factors based on the year-to-date performance of the park. At times, then, I was using a two-to-six-month park factor. Through May, I found that Skydome had a park factor of over 1400—making it a better hitters' park than Coors Field. I used that figure in my daily EqA reports, much to the annoyance of Carlos Delgado fans, as his ratings took a big hit. I wasn't really worried at the time— I didn't consider the 1400 rating to be any more real, or more likely to continue, than Mike Bordick's .500 slugging average, and I was giving him credit for a .320 EqA. Besides, there were just as many Jays players whose performances, to that date, were better matches for their career records using the 1400 park factor as there were using a more typical 1020 factor. I thought that Skydome's park factor (PF), like Bordick's hitting, would regress to a more normal values as the season wore on. And it did, finishing the year at 1018.

The other oddity was Wrigley Field. Pre-Coors, it was consistently the most hitter-friendly park in the NL; this was true in 1999, when its 1055 PF trailed only Coors. But in the year 2000, Wrigley rated as a 925 park: the second-best pitchers' park in the league, ahead of only Qualcomm Stadium in San Diego. Such changes are fairly common; a couple of parks change by at least 80 points in any two-year period. In fact, Wrigley Field turned in a similar performance in 1992–93, dropping from a 1025 rating to 928—and then coming right back to 1021 in 1994.

Fluctuations like that give us a study possibility, though it is going to be an inferential one and not conclusive. There is no way to know, absotively posilutely fer sher certainly, what the right park factor is for a given park and year, just as there is no way to be certain of the right value for a player's net performance is. We can't know if Wrigley's effects on run scoring really changed so dramatically (because it was cold and the wind blew in a lot?), or if the fluctuation was just random. What we can do is look at how given years for each player fit together and make the assumption that he should perform the same in each. For any given player, that's liable to be a very bad assumption, but if you get enough players, the laws of statistics will start to work in your favor. Like a physicist describing gas molecules, we can make far more accurate statements about the behavior of groups than we can about the behavior of individuals.

The first part of this study involved looking at parks whose PF changed by at least 80 points in two consecutive seasons since 1950. The Cubs made the list three times: for 1969–71, when their PFs went 1056-1196-1099, for 1984–86 (1096-1177-1085), and for 1992–94. Though there were 45 such sequences, all but one were either of the down-then-back-up variety or the up-and-back-down variety. I then looked at the EqAs of players who were on those teams during the entire sequence, using either no park factor, a one-year park factor, or a three-year centered-average park factor (not the same three years as the study; the three-year factor for 1997, for example, averages the 1996, 1997, and 1998 factors.) The method which gave the least variability from one season to the next was considered the best. For example, on the 1984–85 Cubs, take Ron Cey. Using a 1000 park factor all three years, his EqAs were .283 and .269, a 14-point difference. Using one-year park factors, they were .270 and .249, a 21-point difference. Using three-year averages, they were .273 and .256, a 17-point difference. The "no park factor" case, then, would be considered the best. These differences were squared and summed over all players, then I divided by the number of players and took the square root to get what is called the "root-mean-square error," or RMSE. Table 1 shows how it came out for all the teams and players in the sample.

Table 1

PF	RMSE
0	26.5
1	28.4
3	26.4

The one-year park factors were substantially worse than either three-year factors or no factor at all. The evidence strongly suggests that park factors do not change substantially from one year to the next, and that by letting them change that way, we are introducing an extra couple points of error into our analysis. And remember, these are the most extreme cases. If the theories behind the one-year park factor had merit, these are the cases where it would matter.

Just to back up this finding, I broadened the study to include all teams that changed by at least 80 points in a year, not just those that did it two years in a row. I also extended the data to all teams ever, not just 1951–99. I also decided to add a five-year PF. If we do all that, we get pretty much the same results, shown in Table 2:

Table 2

PF	RMSE
0	28.0
1	29.8
3	28.0
5	28.0

Even though "no PF" did as well as other forms of PF, that doesn't mean park factors are unneeded, because these studies included only players who stayed on the same team; any constant park factor would have given the same results. The usefulness of the tool can be seen by looking at all players who changed teams from one year to the next, as Table 3 does.

Table 3

PF	RMSE
0	32.7
1	33.0
3	32.5
5	32.0

Once again, we find that the one-year park factor is the worst possible measure, even for players who changed teams. Most parks were close enough to average that the different park factors didn't matter. Still, factors averaged over a three- or five-year period produced even better results.

So, I am now convinced. One-year park factors are, as Gene Wilder said of Baron von Frankenstein's work in *Young Frankenstein*, "doo-doo." The longer the period of time over which you run the park factors, the better. And that is why this year's *Baseball Prospectus* is using five-year park factors (or as close to a five-year average as we can get), at both the major- and minor-league levels.

Top 40 Prospects

by Rany Jazayerli

2000 was not a good year to be a prospect watcher. Actually, that's an understatement: it was a terrible year to be a prospect watcher. It was a year in which our #15 prospect and favorite sleeper, D'Angelo Jimenez, broke his neck in a car accident before our book hit the stores. Jimenez still managed to play more than teammate Nick Johnson, our #1 prospect, who missed the entire season with a wrist injury so peculiar that no one had a diagnosis for it until after the season ended.

It was a year when Vernon Wells (#5) hit just .243 in Triple-A after hitting .310 or better at three different levels in 1999. It was a year when Ruben Mateo (#7) broke his leg in June and missed the rest of the season. It was a year when Chin-Feng Chen (#17) went from .316 and 31 homers to .277 and 6 homers, a year when Matt Riley (#19) tore his Tommy John ligament, a year when the Twins' trinity of prospects (#10 Michael Cuddyer, #27 Matt LeCroy, #30 Michael Restovich) all stumbled, a year when Chad Hermansen (#23) stopped hitting, Kip Wells (#12) stopped throwing strikes, Dee Brown (#11) and Jack Cust (#13) regressed and Esteban German (#18) had the bat knocked out of his hands, and no one could figure out what happened to Ed Yarnall (#28).

It was a bad year.

While more-heralded prospects struggled or got hurt, a group of unlikely rookies emerged. The AL Rookie of the Year, 32-year-old Japanese veteran Kazuhiro Sasaki, symbolized that group: of the eight players who received votes for the AL ROY, not one made our pre-season Top 40 Prospects list.

There were some bright spots. Three of the top four finishers for NL Rookie of the Year were also three of our top four NL prospects (#2 Rick Ankiel, #3 Pat Burrell, #6 Rafael Furcal). The #5 finisher, Mitch Meluskey, was our #18 prospect in 1999 before missing most of that season with shoulder problems.

And hey, whoever said that projecting prospects was an exact science?

It's a new season, but the hangover from last year's regression *en masse* has made forecasting this season's prospects an even dicier proposition than usual. Johnson and Jimenez symbolize a cadre of players who were top prospects a year ago but whose prospect status for 2001 is very much up in the air. Meanwhile, precious few players emerged in 2000 to take their places, which means that legitimate grade-A prospects are more scarce today than they have been in years. It also means that after the top five or six players, the next 20 or 30 prospects are bunched together so tightly that you might as well pull out a Ouija board to separate them.

That's not to say that a healthy chunk of the players on this list won't develop into quality major leaguers, if not All-Stars. 2000 appears to be a year in which prospects suffered an across-the-board, worrisome decline. Only in retrospect, as those players mature, will many of those declines be washed out and revealed as temporary setbacks in an overall rise in value. (The same could be said about the stock market in 2000, for that matter.)

But determining which of those players is destined to resume his climb upward is tricky, as we rediscover every season. A year ago there were a half-dozen prospects whose ascent seemed assured, any of whom could have been defensible #1 overall prospects, but this year there isn't a single sure-fire bet. Last year, our top prospect was first baseman Nick Johnson, a player at one of the safest positions on the diamond. This season we're going to do the unthinkable and violate our mantra that there's no such thing as a pitching prospect. This year, a pitcher is the *Baseball Prospectus* Prospect of the Year. This year, we're going to put all our stock in Ryan Anderson.

1. Ryan Anderson — LHP — Seattle — Age 21

	H/9	BB/9	K/9	ERA
1999:	9.55	6.27	7.16	5.93
2000:	7.70	4.76	9.52	4.93

Anderson isn't the ideal #1 prospect. He's a pitcher, for one. No matter how appropriately he's handled, no matter how perfect his mechanics, no matter how sturdy his physique, there is simply no way to eliminate the risk that something will snap, crackle, or pop in his golden left arm. Even last season he had to be shut down for "minor" tendinitis and made only 20 starts.

But the most rewarding investments always come with some risk, and the potential is there for Anderson to one day be the successor to his role model, Randy Johnson, as the best left-handed pitcher in baseball. He has the fastball, he has the slider, he has the strikeout rates (146 in just 104 innings last year), he has the just-wild-enough-to-scare-you demeanor on the mound. He's also about three years ahead of where Johnson was on the development curve. Ordinarily, the specter of a 21-year-old pitcher in the hands of Lou

Piniella would frighten us half to death, but the Mariners have a new pitching coach, and Brian Price's work with Gil Meche gives us confidence that the Mariners will not expect too much from Anderson too soon. Anderson still needs another half-season of development in Triple-A, and the Mariners have the pitching depth to afford him that time. Expect him to be in the Mariners rotation by July, and don't be surprised if he turns out to be the best mid-season acquisition made by any playoff contender.

2. Sean Burroughs — 3B — San Diego — Age 20

	AVG	OBP	SLG	EQA
1999:	.279	.353	.363	.247
2000:	.259	.333	.350	.232

After a stellar first pro season in 1999, when he posted a .470 OBP, Burroughs struggled more than expected in Double-A. Despite that, he rises from #4 to #2 in our rankings, which reflects just how weak the minor leagues are in terms of grade-A prospects at the moment. That's not a knock on Burroughs, who played the whole season at age 19 and continues to elicit comparisons to a young George Brett. Brett had more speed and better defense as a youngster, and while his power developed late, that doesn't mean Burroughs's automatically will as well. Burroughs does already have a knack for doubles and walks more than a young Brett did, making comparisons to Wade Boggs more appropriate. When the biggest dilemma becomes which Hall of Fame third baseman is the best comparison, you know you're talking about a special player. Burroughs should be ready by September at the latest, and the Padres are doing their best to accommodate him, moving Xavier Nady to another position and trying to move Phil Nevin to another team.

3. Corey Patterson — CF — Chicago (NL) — Age 21

	AVG	OBP	SLG	EQA
1999:	.247	.271	.417	.225
2000:	.232	.282	.409	.230

After nearly convincing the Cubs to carry him when spring training broke, Patterson headed to Double-A and showed he still had a lot of learning to do as his average dropped 60 points and his extra-base power suffered. The most important development of the season for Patterson, though, was a positive one: his walk rate nearly doubled, a very impressive sign considering he skipped high-A ball and considering that the Cubs are not exactly known for stressing the base on balls. His strikeout rate also jumped, but contrary to conventional wisdom, current research shows that high-strikeout hitters in the minor leagues are actually no less likely to develop than good contact hitters. Patterson got a September call-up that was at least partially on merit, but he absolutely needs another three months in Triple-A. If the Cubs allow him that luxury, they'll soon be able to hold their own in the NL Central(field) against the likes of Griffey, Edmonds, Hidalgo, and Giles. Well, five out of six teams isn't bad.

4. Ben Sheets — RHP — Milwaukee — Age 22

	H/9	BB/9	K/9	ERA
1999:	9.88	5.07	5.61	5.88
2000:	8.82	3.52	5.01	3.52

Would he have ranked this high had he not smoked through the Cuban lineup like a Havana cigar? Or are we doing him an injustice by failing to rank him even higher after he almost single-handedly created the seminal moment in U.S. Olympic baseball history? (Even if that moment was tape-delayed by NBC for 17 hours.) We cannot tell a lie—Sheets ranks where he does because, frankly, he deserves it. Less than 18 months out of college, Sheets had advanced so rapidly through pro ball that the Olympic experience was the only reason he wasn't in the Brewers' rotation in September. Sheets has that rare combination of power stuff, precocious command, and a fearless approach on the mound—everything he'll need to become the ace pitcher the Brewers haven't had since Teddy Higuera was healthy.

5. Roy Oswalt — RHP — Houston — Age 23

	H/9	BB/9	K/9	ERA
1999:	9.73	3.83	4.68	5.72
2000:	8.88	1.92	6.13	3.32

Sheets may not even have been the most impressive pitcher on the U.S. Olympic team. Oswalt started the year as a semi-obscure right-hander out of the Midwest League, but after introducing himself to Double-A with a no walk, 16-K debut in May, Oswalt was obscure no longer. His translated ERA of 3.32 and his relative KW ratio of 1.59 were the best of any minor-league prospect, and while Enron Field may present a unique challenge, keep in mind that Oswalt posted a 1.94 ERA while pitching at the new ballpark in Round Rock, a hitters' haven in its own right. Along with Sheets, who stands 6'1", the 6-foot Oswalt can remind Ryan Anderson that size isn't everything.

6. Vernon Wells — CF — Toronto — Age 22

	AVG	OBP	SLG	EQA
1999:	.268	.314	.403	.241
2000:	.223	.279	.382	.226

After ripping through four levels on his way to the majors in 1999, Wells was unable to unseat Jose Cruz Jr. as the starting center fielder in spring training and was sent to Syracuse where, much like Corey Patterson, he showed that he still had a lot to learn. His falloff was entirely in batting average; his minor-league walk totals the last three years read 49, 48, and 48, while his extra-base hits climbed from 48 to 53 to 54 during his ascent to Triple-A. He's a terrific baserunner and a game-breaker on defense, and his average should bounce back this year. The Jays can afford to start him in Syracuse again, but if they make room for him in center field, he remains a legitimate ROY candidate.

7. Jose Ortiz   2B   Oakland   Age 24

	AVG	OBP	SLG	EQA
1999:	.257	.312	.387	.236
2000:	.307	.353	.485	.278

Hard as it is to believe, there are still sportswriters out there who don't think the A's know what they're doing. Some of them even work in Oakland, where they whined that the A's weren't serious about winning because they traded Randy Velarde. Apparently, giving the job at second to a player who can hit for power and average, walk a little, and steal bases, and play defense doesn't constitute a commitment to excellence if that player is also 23 years old and playing for the major-league minimum. Ortiz adds some speed and athleticism to an A's lineup that has everything else, and his mediocre walk rate should continue to rise as the mantra of plate discipline is beaten into his skull, much as it was for Miguel Tejada.

8. Ichiro Suzuki   RF   Seattle   Age 27

	AVG	OBP	SLG	EQA
1999:	.309	.372	.502	.287
2000:	.346	.410	.477	.298

Is he a prospect? Well, he's still classified as a rookie by the major leagues, and if they aren't going to penalize him for his Japanese League experience, why should we? There's a lot of talk about what Suzuki is not—he's not big, he's not a power hitter, he's not used to facing major-league pitching. We'll tell you what he is: not just the best hitter in Japan, but the best hitter in Japan by acclamation. He may not have the upside of many players on this list, but what prospect possesses the reliability of Suzuki, who has won six straight batting titles? He's a great fit for the Mariners, playing in a park that minimizes his lack of home-run power and accentuates his ability to hit the ball into the gaps. At bat, he resembles Johnny Damon, although the comparison breaks down on the bases or in the field. Expect him to win the Rookie of the Year Award, and then expect a rules change to disqualify Japanese League veterans from future awards.

9. Jimmy Rollins   SS   Philadelphia   Age 22

	AVG	OBP	SLG	EQA
1999:	.231	.279	.333	.203
2000:	.263	.316	.410	.245

Sometimes, you have to go with your gut. Rollins has never hit .280 as a pro, he's never hit more than 12 homers, and his career high in walks is 52. He stands all of 5 feet 8 inches. The promise of Jimmy Rollins cannot be summed up by any one number or any one skill any more than the size of the Great Wall of China can be expressed in any one of its bricks. Rollins has a lot of bricks. He's a switch-hitter, he plays the toughest defensive position well, he hits for extra-base power, he is an exceptional base runner, and he is still very young. Most importantly, he has improved his production across the board while moving up the ladder each of the last two years. Desi Relaford and Marlon Anderson have given Philly middle-infield prospects a bad name, but don't be fooled: Rollins is the real deal and should be one of the three best shortstops in the NL by 2002.

10. Jon Rauch   RHP   Chicago (AL)   Age 22

	H/9	BB/9	K/9	ERA
1999:	11.30	3.52	4.40	8.22
2000:	9.75	3.15	6.13	5.96

Did we say that size isn't everything? Don't tell that to Rauch, who at 6'1" has inched his way past Ryan Anderson and stands to be the tallest player in major league history. Rauch has bounced back from a case of viral meningitis in college to become the crown jewel of the White Sox farm system and Baseball America's Minor League Player of the Year. His mechanics and control are almost unheard of in a pitcher with his height and inexperience, and his ERA has dropped with every promotion since he entered pro ball. The White Sox have the most pitching in the game, but Rauch's talent should force him into the rotation at some point this year.

11. Antonio Perez   SS   Seattle   Age "19"

	AVG	OBP	SLG	EQA
1999:	.231	.291	.318	.203
2000:	.215	.287	.379	.220

It may be small consolation to Mariner fans, but the prize of the Ken Griffey Jr. trade may prove a worthy successor to Alex Rodriguez at shortstop. As an 18-year-old shortstop in high-A ball who had 59 extra-base hits and 58 walks in just 98 games, Perez should really rank in our Top 10, but there are serious concerns that he may be considerably older than his listed age. Whether he's 19 or 22, good defensive shortstops with secondary skills like this are hard to find, something Mariner fans are about to discover this season.

12. Bobby Bradley   RHP   Pittsburgh   Age 20

	H/9	BB/9	K/9	ERA
2000:	9.15	3.24	6.61	6.03

We are normally the epitome of conservatism when it comes to evaluating pitchers in the low minors. Bradley is the only pitcher in our Top 40 who has not yet reached Double-A. He ranks this high because God has seen fit to bless him with The Perfect Curveball. Bradley's deuce has it all: the tightest spin, the latest break, the most perfect arm angle and velocity. You can probably count on one hand the major leaguers today who throw a better one. He also added a foot to his fastball last season, allowing him to completely blow through the South Atlantic League. His DT is astounding when you consider he was four levels from the majors last year. He was shut down for almost half the year with elbow tendinitis, a very bad sign for a curveball pitcher. If he makes it, though, he'll make it big, and his stuff is so electric that he could be in Pittsburgh by this September.

13. Nick Johnson 1B/DL New York (AL) Age 22

	AVG	OBP	SLG	EQA
1999:	.288	.441	.438	.306

No player on this list generated more internal debate among BP authors than Johnson, who missed the entire season with what can best be described as a deep muscle bruise of his wrist that occurred on a checked swing. On one hand, you simply can't ignore such a striking propensity for injury. On the other hand, Johnson posted a .525 OBP in Double-A in 1999. Five twenty-five. Nick the Stick can do some very bad things to pitchers, and while hitters frequently don't rebound from serious wrist injuries until their second year back, Johnson should take over from Tino Martinez by 2002 at the very latest and quickly become one of the most devastating offensive forces in baseball. When he's in the lineup, that is.

14. Josh Hamilton RF Tampa Bay Age 20

	AVG	OBP	SLG	EQA
1999:	.235	.250	.350	.192
2000:	.244	.278	.367	.211

The first pick of the 1999 draft has done nothing to make the Devil Rays regret their selection. Defensively, he has a classic rightfielder's arm—he had comparable potential as a left-handed pitcher—and enough range that the Devil Rays have continued to toy with him in center field. Since entering pro ball, he has hit for high averages and shown considerable power for a teenager. His ceiling is tremendous, but he has a surplus of aggressiveness at the plate, and until the Devil Rays notice and take steps to correct it, he remains one tool short of the perfect player.

15. Chris George LHP Kansas City Age 21

	H/9	BB/9	K/9	ERA
1999:	10.15	3.89	4.91	5.11
2000:	9.47	4.73	4.54	4.99

Nearly a decade after "the next Tom Glavine" became the catchphrase for any promising left-handed starter, the next Tom Glavine has finally arrived. Chris George throws harder than most young lefties not named Ryan Anderson or Rick Ankiel, he is a master at changing speeds, he has exceptional mechanics and tremendous poise on the mound, and he is uncannily articulate and intelligent for someone no older than your typical college senior—without actually attending college. He needs another half-season in Triple-A to work out the kinks in his control but should be the Royals' ace by 2003 at the latest.

16. Carlos Pena 1B Texas Age 23

	AVG	OBP	SLG	EQA
1999:	.214	.300	.363	.221
2000:	.247	.344	.416	.258

The Rangers' first-round pick out of Northeastern University in 1998, Pena has won raves from baseball insiders for his class and poise as well as his talent. (His most notable fan is a certain New England sportswriter who responds to "Peter" and, "Hey, aren't you the guy on the $20 bill?") Pena has a honey-sweet left-handed swing to go with his tremendous plate discipline. The Rangers signed Andres Galarraga for only one year in anticipation of Pena's arrival in 2002. He might not need that long, which is good because Galarraga might not have another good year left in him.

17. Joe Crede 3B Chicago (AL) Age 23

	AVG	OBP	SLG	EQA
1999:	.224	.264	.303	.179
2000:	.276	.324	.426	.252

After making this list two years ago as our #35 prospect, Crede struggled through a painful year in 1999 before finally admitting that a chronic toe injury was not healing. Crede returned after surgery last year looking like his old self, hitting for average and power and playing good defense. The Scott Rolen comparisons are unreasonable and unfair; Rolen had a Rookie of the Year Award on his mantle before he turned 23. But the White Sox, eager to make an impression as the Team of the Future, have anointed Crede as that Team's third baseman. When that future arrives is between Crede and incumbent Herb Perry, a contest unlikely to last the season.

18. C.C. Sabathia LHP Cleveland Age 20

	H/9	BB/9	K/9	ERA
1999:	9.10	6.36	5.34	6.36
2000:	9.41	5.22	6.32	5.54

Sabathia is nearly Anderson's equal as a flame-throwing lefty, with an upper-90s fastball, an intimidating presence on the mound, and the talent to reach Double-A before he turned 20. Most observers feel that Sabathia is a better prospect than Chris George, but there are some concerns about Sabathia's physique—he's 6'7" and at least 260 pounds—and his history of annoying arm injuries. Despite his weight, Sabathia is considered a coach's dream in terms of taking instruction. The Indians are desperate for pitching and may be tempted to start him in their rotation. He needs more developmental time, and the Tribe would be foolish to gamble with his potential by rushing him.

19. Hee Seop Choi   1B   Chicago (NL)   Age 22

	AVG	OBP	SLG	EQA
1999:	.241	.320	.416	.246
2000:	.247	.315	.434	.249

Mark Grace may feel betrayed by a Cubs' organization that has suddenly caught the bug of accountability, but long before he has sucked his last paycheck out of the Diamondbacks, people will be agreeing that the Cubbies didn't make a mistake. The pride of South Korea, Choi possesses every baseball skill that Grace does, and features an extra one that hasn't been seen from a first baseman by the fans at Wrigley since the '80s: power. Lots and lots of power. Choi's tremendous performance at Double-A West Tenn late in the season suggests that the Cubs might not have to dicker around with Julio Zuleta and Todd Hundley at first base for more than a few months.

20. J.R. House   C   Pittsburgh   Age 21

	AVG	OBP	SLG	EQA
1999:	.239	.277	.301	.181
2000:	.267	.322	.421	.246

House can hit. House can catch. What House can't do is decide whether he wants to commit to baseball full-time. House was a two-sport, two-state star in high school, playing baseball in Florida and football in West Virginia, and he dropped to the 5th round in 1999 because teams were unsure whether he would be lured into college football. House abandoned football and has become, without a doubt, the best catching prospect in baseball, but a coaching change at West Virginia has House questioning whether he might suit up as quarterback for the Mountaineers this fall. A more long-term concern is that with Jason Kendall now signed for six years, House may be moved to first base, though third base has not been ruled out either. While these issues cloud his future, they shouldn't obscure this very important fact: House can hit.

21. Alex Escobar   CF   New York (NL)   Age 22

	AVG	OBP	SLG	EQA
2000:	.243	.316	.397	.241

Escobar's return to phenom status last season was a welcome sign here at BP, as we rated him the #3 prospect in the land before the 1999 season, in which he played in a grand total of three games. While his injury history is nothing short of macabre, an ordinary prospect would not be able to shake off the effects of a missed season to have a terrific year in Double-A with essentially no experience above low-A ball. Even with all the missed time, Escobar is still just 22, and he's a legitimate five-tool talent with command of the strike zone. Why the Mets have been so willing to include him in trade offers (including the one that Barry Larkin nixed) is beyond us.

22. Bud Smith   LHP   St. Louis   Age 21

	H/9	BB/9	K/9	ERA
1999:	9.49	3.28	4.80	4.80
2000:	8.38	2.48	5.12	4.11

Lost in the debate over whether George or Sabathia is the better prospect is the fact that Bud Smith had a much better season than either one of them, going 17–2 with a 2.26 ERA. He's also a month younger than George. He ranks below either of them because his stuff is merely very good instead of exceptional, and because, Rick Ankiel aside, Tony La Russa still has little faith in young starters. This is the team that traded Britt Reames for Dustin Hermanson—not a demonstrably better starter—and Steve Kline, whose role as a lefty reliever could have been filled by Smith this season. And then you factor in Fernando Tatis... Smith has already proven he can dominate Triple-A hitters, but the Cardinals have yet to show that they realize he's ready.

23. Kevin Mench   OF   Texas   Age 23

	AVG	OBP	SLG	EQA
1999:	.248	.289	.401	.230
2000:	.266	.347	.458	.267

If only Nietzsche were alive today. "Über" Mench is a masher of the first order, named MVP of the Florida State League (nearly winning the Triple Crown) and then hitting .354/.434/.596 in the AFL. His defense is nothing to write home about, and he isn't the world's fastest player, but along with Carlos Pena, he gives the Rangers two top-notch hitters to enter the lineup in 2002. That both play at the bottom of the defensive spectrum would be an issue for some teams, but I don't think the Rangers are all that concerned, since they already have the two most difficult defensive positions, shortstop and catcher, filled by upper-echelon Hall of Famers.

24. Adam Dunn   OF   Cincinnati   Age 21

	AVG	OBP	SLG	EQA
1999:	.242	.317	.362	.230
2000:	.221	.337	.352	.240

and

25. Austin Kearns   OF   Cincinnati   Age 21

	AVG	OBP	SLG	EQA
1999:	.212	.274	.351	.207
2000:	.240	.328	.406	.247

Dunn and Kearns were the Reds' first two picks in the 1998 draft, they have played in the same outfield for the same minor league teams in both 1999 and 2000, they were both just 20 years old last season, and they are remarkably similar players. Dunn hit .281, 16, 79 with 100 walks and 24 steals; Kearns hit .306, 27, 104 with 90 walks and 18 steals. Dunn is a former Texas A&M quarterback who amazed onlookers with his baseball polish last year. Kearns is a former high school pitcher who projects as a prototypical right fielder. Dunn is considered the better power prospect; Kearns hit for more power last season (including homers in 8 straight games). Most scouts feel that Dunn has the higher upside, but no one is willing to put limitations on what either can do. The Reds' lack of a high-A-ball affiliate allowed both Dunn and Kearns to beat up on low-level pitching last year, so whether they can maintain their stellar performances at Double-A in 2001 will be especially revealing. With Ken Griffey Jr. signed through 2008, the prospect of having him flanked by these two phenoms should warm the hearts of baseball fans in the Queen City.

26. Brad Wilkerson   OF   Montreal   Age 24

	AVG	OBP	SLG	EQA
1999:	.200	.314	.295	.210
2000:	.251	.353	.441	.267

A supplemental first-round draft pick in 1998, Wilkerson was sent directly to Double-A to make his pro debut in 1999 and hit only .235, disappointing a lot of people who failed to notice his 88 walks. (The biggest knock on Wilkerson was that he might have been too patient at the plate, a problem the Expos are expert at correcting.) Returning to Double-A in 2000, Wilkerson hit .336 and doubled in 15.7% of his at-bats (the major league record is 12.2%) before a promotion to Triple-A, where some of his doubles started to turn into homers. A right fielder by trade, he played an admirable center field for the Olympic team, and the presence of The Impaler in Montreal should make Wilkerson one of the strongest-armed left fielders in the majors this season.

27. D'Angelo Jimenez   SS   New York (AL)   Age 23

	AVG	OBP	SLG	EQA
1999:	.292	.353	.426	.261
2000:	.214	.281	.308	.198

It's very easy to look at Jimenez's year as a complete waste, considering he broke a vertebrae in his neck in a car accident before the season and didn't suit up until August. But the fact that Jimenez returned at all is regarded as something of a minor miracle given the degree of his injuries and the fact that he was almost completely immobilized for months. If his quick return has shown Jimenez to be a fast healer—in complete opposition to Nick Johnson—there may be a silver lining to his lost season. He played in the Dominican Winter League to regain his stroke and was doing well at press time, having already drawn 19 walks in 31 games. He will probably return to Triple-A to start the season, but with an offensive cipher at third base and a defensive sieve at second, the Yankees might not wait long to call upon Jimenez to bolster their infield in some capacity.

28. Albert Pujols   3B   St. Louis   Age 21

	AVG	OBP	SLG	EQA
2000:	.260	.300	.423	.238

An unknown 13th-round pick out of junior college in 1999, Pujols streaked through the low minors in his first pro season, getting a late audition in Triple-A to close out the year, popping 67 extra-base hits, and putting on a defensive clinic so impressive that the Cardinals had no qualms sending last year's Third Baseman of the Future, Fernando Tatis, to Montreal. That kind of power from a 20-year-old is rare; that kind of power coupled with an uncanny ability to make contact (just 47 K's vs. 46 walks) is practically unique. While his defensive reputation is considered more potential than present, his fielding numbers in the Midwest League look like Brooks Robinson in the 1970 World Series. A very, very interesting player to watch for in 2001.

29. Keith Ginter   2B/3B   Houston   Age 25

	AVG	OBP	SLG	EQA
1999:	.226	.307	.345	.224
2000:	.270	.352	.443	.272

Ginter just might have had the most impressive minor-league season of any hitter, batting .333/.457/.580 with 26 homers, 82 walks, and even 24 steals for DOUBLE-A Round Rock. (By comparison, NL MVP Jeff Kent hit .334/.424/.596.) Ginter is the oldest player on this list save Suzuki, and second base is not exactly a position the Astros need to fill. But his offensive performance was so impressive that the Astros are rightfully trying to find him a place in their lineup, and he did play an admirable third base in the AFL. The Astros are not the kind of team to promote a player from Double-A straight into their lineup, but if they do so with Ginter, in that ballpark he becomes an excellent candidate for Rookie of the Year.

30. Luke Prokopec   RHP   Los Angeles   Age 23

	H/9	BB/9	K/9	ERA
1999:	10.48	3.11	4.84	7.60
2000:	8.96	1.94	5.45	3.63

Prokopec is an Australian of slender build who received attention last September when the Dodgers called him up only days before he was scheduled to leave for Sydney to lead the Australian Olympic team, just another example of Tommy Lasorda showing that he wouldn't let little things like class and etiquette get in the way of a U.S. victory. Luke has a cool hand on the mound, making up for an average fastball with a superb curveball and the guts of the Crocodile Hunter. He ruined his 1999 season by trying to pitch through tendonitis, but after an outstanding season in 2000 and impressing the Dodgers in that stint in LA to end the season, Prokopec has a chance to win the fifth starter's role this spring.

31. Adrian Hernandez RHP   New York (AL) Age 26

	H/9	BB/9	K/9	ERA
2000:	8.38	4.88	7.50	5.12

Not many minor leaguers come with nicknames already attached, but El Duquecito is the second coming of Orlando (no relation) in many ways: he imitates Orlando's windup and dress style, he asked for Orlando's uniform number after El Duque defected, and he pitched for the same team (the Havana Industriales) before defecting himself last winter. He's not that far from joining his idol in the Yankee rotation, moving through three levels and settling in at Triple-A before tearing a knee ligament on a freak play that ended his season in August. He doesn't throw as hard as Orlando and consequently his upside is more as a #2/#3 starter than as an ace, but his extensive Cuban experience should help him adjust to the major leagues quickly if and when the Yankees promote him this season.

32. Craig Wilson   C/1B   Pittsburgh   Age 24

	AVG	OBP	SLG	EQA
1999:	.238	.312	.424	.243
2000:	.253	.340	.505	.274

It's rare to list a player without a position as one of the top prospects in baseball, but Wilson's bat warrants a mention even if he is squeezed between Jason Kendall ahead of him and J.R. House behind him. Wilson was acquired from the Blue Jays four years ago in the Orlando Merced/Dan Plesac trade but had become largely forgotten despite hitting at every level. In 2000, finally, he posted numbers too impressive to ignore, slugging over .600 in his first crack at Triple-A. His glove is nothing special, and his future is likely at first base, where the Pirates have an inferior player locked up for two more years at $6 million per. Barring a trade, Wilson should become a part of what might be the first bench in history that could out-hit its starting lineup.

33. Luis Rivas   SS/2B   Minnesota   Age 21

	AVG	OBP	SLG	EQA
1999:	.230	.270	.333	.199
2000:	.243	.293	.358	.221

On the surface, Rivas appears to be nothing more than your usual good-field, no-hit middle infielder. But his youth (he was 16 when he entered pro ball and 18 when he spent a full season in high-A ball) gives him an unusual amount of growth potential for someone with five years of minor-league experience. Offensively, he has begun a dramatic transformation from his free-swinging singles approach of two years ago, hitting 41 doubles and 8 triples in 2000 and improving his K/BB ratio from 75/14 to 66/51. He hit his best after a promotion to Triple-A and a late-season call-up to Minnesota, a sign that he won't be overmatched by major-league hurlers. Defensively, he has the skills to be an above-average shortstop, but his lack of polish and the presence of Cristian Guzman convinced the Twins to move Rivas to second base. He embraced the move almost immediately. Rivas has a very good shot at winning the Twins' starting job this spring, and if the Twins are patient with him, he could join the elite of AL second basemen within two or three years.

34. Mike Bynum   LHP   San Diego   Age 23

	H/9	BB/9	K/9	ERA
1999:	8.00	2.33	5.67	3.33
2000:	8.91	4.19	5.00	4.89

So far the Padres' supplemental first-round pick in 1999 has been everything they could have asked for, advancing to Double-A in his first full season while breaking off sliders that some have compared to Steve Carlton's. Any pitcher who can post a 3.00 ERA in the hitters' paradise that is Rancho Cucamonga has major-league ability. Bynum is exactly what the doctor ordered for a team that, sans Sterling Hitchcock, is bereft of left-handed starters. Along with Matt Clement and Adam Eaton, Bynum gives the Padres three potential aces on what could be the most underrated rotation in baseball by year's end.

35. Wilson Betemit   SS/3B   Atlanta   Age 19

	AVG	OBP	SLG	EQA
1999:	.231	.271	.312	.190
2000:	.257	.306	.348	.217

Betemit first attained notoriety in the wake of the Adrian Beltre controversy by accusing the Braves of signing him when he was underage. The Braves got off with just a fine and were able to keep one of the best infield prospects in the low minors. Betemit is still listed as 20 in most publications even though the Braves themselves admit that he is actually more than a year younger than reported. (STATS Inc. still lists Orlando Hernandez as 31 years old, though the entire industry became aware of court documents more than a year ago which show him to be 35.) The controversy swirling around Betemit may have been part of the reason the Braves sent him back to the New York-Penn League, which he dominated for the second straight year. With Rafael Furcal entrenched at shortstop, Betemit's long-term future is likely at third base, where he might be starting for the Braves as soon as 2003.

36. Nick Neugebauer   RHP   Milwaukee   Age 20

	H/9	BB/9	K/9	ERA
1999:	8.31	11.12	8.06	6.96
2000:	7.70	10.55	7.40	6.51

For those of you who fondly remember the glory years of Bobby Witt and not the Mike Morgan end to his career, or if you're just a fan of Nuke LaLoosh in *Bull Durham*, then Nick Neugebauer is for you. On raw stuff alone, you could make a strong case for Neugebauer as the best pitching prospect in baseball, period. He throws four pitches, and every one of them (even his change-up) grades out as well above major-league average. But the man simply cannot throw strikes, allowing more than a walk an inning over his career. In his defense, he's not Bill Bene/Robbie Beckett/Jacob Shumate wild, the kind of pitcher who's a threat to hit the mascot on every pitch. He reached Double-A within days of his 20th birthday, and his control actually improved at that level, if 8.35 walks per 9 innings can be classified as "improvement." He's almost impossible to drive, allowing just two homers all season. To borrow something Darva Conger said to Rick Rockwell on their wedding night, Neugebauer will never be boring. Whether that's a good or a bad thing is something none of us know for sure.

37. Jack Cust   "LF"   Arizona   Age 22

	AVG	OBP	SLG	EQA
1999:	.235	.336	.421	.253
2000:	.221	.350	.375	.250

Cust may have a license plate that reads "BORN2DH," but he remains a top prospect because he's one of the toughest outs in organized baseball. His .440 OBP last season was the *lowest* of his pro career. (He actually posted a .530 OBP in 73 games with Lethbridge in 1998, though his overall season OBP fell below Nick Johnson's 1999 campaign.) But his amazing offensive numbers must be tempered by the fact that he has played in terrific hitters' parks since he entered pro ball. His power fell off considerably last season, and a .526 slugging average is simply not that impressive in El Paso. Still, anyone who can post EqAs of .253 and .250 at ages 20 and 21 has definite Silver Slugger potential. That is, assuming the Diamondbacks can find him a position. He played left field like a pregnant penguin with one of its flippers cut off, and Mark Grace is already an institution in Arizona, so the Diamondbacks must hope that an AL team is willing to make a 22-year-old player a permanent DH.

38. Marcus Giles   2B   Atlanta   Age 23

	AVG	OBP	SLG	EQA
1999:	.281	.333	.424	.252
2000:	.245	.324	.385	.242

This is our third annual Top 40 Prospects list, and Giles is the only player to appear on all three lists. That is a testimony to the Braves' lingering mistrust of his abilities, as he probably would already be in Atlanta were scouts more impressed with his tools. His rise through the minor leagues is utterly atypical, as he has lost power (his slugging average has dropped from .636 to .513 to .472) while gaining speed—he stole nearly as many bases in 2000 (25) as he had in his previous three pro seasons combined (26). He has maintained his plate discipline, drawing more walks than strikeouts for the first time last year, and his defense has improved at least to the point of adequacy. Marcus is a much better player than his brother was at the same age, and Brian has already shown that in this family, short stature is no obstacle to power. Giles the Younger shouldn't have to wait much longer to get his shot at a second-base job, and with the Braves' proven ability to mesh rookies into their lineup, he should contribute from day one.

39. Michael Cuddyer   3B   Minnesota   Age 22

	AVG	OBP	SLG	EQA
1999:	.246	.332	.375	.241
2000:	.236	.303	.346	.218

Luis Rivas aside, 2000 was a terrible year to be a top prospect in the Twins' organization. Cuddyer holds onto his Top 40 ranking by the skin of his teeth, losing 35 points of batting average, 20 walks, and 10 homers in the jump to DOUBLE-A New Britain. His defense at third base has also increasingly come into question. Fortunately, Cuddyer's base of skills was so broad that he could survive the across-the-board hit to his numbers and still turn in an impressive season for a 21-year-old third baseman in Double-A. Corey Koskie continues to be impressive in Minnesota, so the Twins have no need to rush Cuddyer and can spend a year determining whether or not he should be moved to an easier defensive position.

40. Brian Lawrence   RHP   San Diego   Age 25

	H/9	BB/9	K/9	ERA
1999:	9.53	1.95	4.35	4.15
2000:	9.12	2.15	5.47	4.19

Lawrence follows Mike Meyers in our annual token spot that goes to a starting pitcher who bores the scouts but who has simply been too effective to ignore. Lawrence was a 17th-round draft pick as a college senior in 1998, but since he was drafted, he has a career ERA of 2.83 and a K/BB ratio of 431 to 83, or greater than 5 to 1. He had his best year in 2000 and got the sternest test of his career when he was promoted to Triple-A Las Vegas in July. Pitching in a hitters' park in the PCL is the most difficult challenge a pitcher can face in the minor leagues. How did Lawrence respond? He went 4-0 with a 1.93 ERA, 46 strikeouts, and 7 walks in 8 starts. Throw away the radar gun, gang: this guy can pitch. Lawrence could team with Brian Tollberg to give the Padres two tough-as-nails finesse right-handers behind their power pitchers. This could be one terrific rotation in 2001.

Honorable Mention

Josh Beckett, RHP: No doubt, many of you think we're nuts for not including him in our Top 40, and maybe we are. But while everyone else sees a Nolan Ryan clone who was one of the most highly touted high school pitchers ever, we see a 20-year-old who threw only 59 innings and was sent to the DL twice with elbow tendonitis. He's still four levels from the major leagues, so we have plenty of time to correct our mistake next year if he warrants it.

Matt Belisle, RHP: With Jason Marquis headed to the bullpen, Belisle gets to sit in the chair reserved for The Next Great Braves Starter. He's a power pitcher with absurd control, walking just 29 batters in 181 innings at the age of 20. There's only one Maddux, one Glavine, and one Smoltz, but the Braves are hoping they have another Saberhagen. A *healthy* Saberhagen.

Donnie Bridges, RHP: The Expos are touting their #1 draft pick in 1997 as their next top young starter, but while Bridges was very impressive in 2000, he also ranked 2nd in the minors with 201 innings. The Expos were able to spread that out over 30 starts, but there has to be some concern that Bridges was overworked, making him that rare pitcher who might actually benefit by being rushed to the majors so that Felipe Alou can take better care of his arm.

Dee Brown, LF: The best hitting prospect not in our Top 40, Brown has 40-homer potential but struggled in his first exposure to Triple-A as his commitment and hustle were questioned. His ability to hit a baseball 450 feet, however, was not. He has a history of erupting in his second tour through a league, and with Johnny Damon traded, Brown should be in the Royals lineup by mid-season.

Ben Christensen, RHP: We don't like him or what he did to Anthony Molina's face, but we can't deny that he had a terrific first full pro season. Christensen was shut down with shoulder tendonitis after just 17 starts, though, so while he may have avoided jail time, he might not be able to avoid the Curse of Gene Stephenson, which has befallen every Wichita State pitcher drafted in the first round: Tyler Green, Darren Dreifort (who missed a year with a torn rotator cuff), Mike Drumright, and Braden Looper.

Jesus Colome, RHP: Many A's fans would argue that trading Colome for Jim Mecir was the one mistake Billy Beane made last season. (Well, that and surrendering a first-round pick for Mike Magnante.) The A's might not have won the division without Mecir, but Colome can dial it up to 100 and could fit into the Devil Rays' plans as either a top starter or as their closer by 2002.

Jason Hart, 1B: Like Adam Piatt a year ago, Hart is an A's farmhand and disciple of the team's hitting philosophy who exploded at Double-A. He didn't equal Piatt's amazing Triple Crown season and lacks Piatt's defensive versatility, but Hart does have an extra year of development time on his side. The A's would love to keep Jason Giambi around, but you can bet that if the words "$15 million a season" are ever uttered by Giambi's agent, the A's have his replacement at the ready.

Drew Henson, 3B: Henson's chances at major-league stardom have dimmed considerably over the last year. It isn't a problem of talent—not many 20-year-olds playing baseball in their spare time can claim to be above-average players in Double-A—but rather because his performance as the quarterback at the University of Michigan last fall, which was so impressive that he is widely rumored to be a possible #1 overall pick in the 2002 NFL draft. It's going to be a long time before any baseball team offers him a seven-year, $40-million contract with a $10 million signing bonus.

Adam Johnson, RHP: Johnson was widely reported as a signability pick when the Twins selected him #2 overall in last year's draft. But after going straight to the Florida State League and allowing less than a base runner an inning with 92 Ks in 69 innings, Johnson's selection looks pretty strong on merit alone. He's considered a very polished pitcher and could work his way into the Twins' rotation by this fall.

Bobby Kielty, OF: While the Twins' trinity of 1999 prospects all struggled in 2000, Kielty continued his solid progression from undrafted collegian to major-league outfielder. The Twins are hardly a team worth envying, but I can think of a couple dozen teams that wish they had beaten out the Twins for the services of a switch-hitting center fielder who drew 105 walks last season.

Matt Kinney, RHP: Two years after the Twins acquired Kinney in the Greg Swindell trade, he is making Red Sox Nation nervous that they let another good one get away. Kinney doesn't have #1-starter stuff but held his own in the Twins' rotation in eight late-season starts, and with Eric Milton, Brad Radke, and Mark Redman already in Minnesota, he's more than qualified to be one of the better fourth starters in the league this season.

Abraham Nunez, OF: The Diamondbacks are breathing a sigh of relief that Nunez stumbled in 2000 after they foolishly let him go in the Matt Mantei trade, but the Marlins are still optimistic about his future. Before the season, Nunez suffered a shoulder injury that forced him to DH all year and robbed him of his power, but he still advanced to Double-A and showed the on-base ability that, coupled with his speed and the defense and power that should return this year, make him a true five-tool outfielder.

Chris Snelling, OF: The best hitting prospect from Australia since Dave Nilsson, Snelling is not in the Dodger organization and so was not promoted to LA in September. He's a left-handed-hitting outfielder who slugged .483 and had as many walks as strikeouts in the Midwest League, despite playing the entire season at age 18. He is considered to have uncanny baseball instincts for someone from such a fledgling baseball nation, and the Mariners are extremely intrigued by his upside.

Chin-Hui Tsao, RHP: The pride of Taiwan challenged Bobby Bradley for the title of Best Pitcher in the South Atlantic League. While Bradley bested him in that battle, Tsao was able to stay healthy all season. We've never listed a Rockies hurler on our Top 40 list and we won't this year, but Tsao has the ability to dominate Double-A and make the list next season.

Carlos Zambrano, RHP: His listed birthdate is 6/1/1981, but 18-year-old pitchers who make it to Double-A and post a 1.34 ERA in 9 starts don't then get moved to the bullpen, as Zambrano was. Then again, these are the Cubs. Zambrano is one of the jewels of a revamped Cubs' farm system that is a lot stronger than most people realize.

Equivalent Average Leader Boards

MAJOR LEAGUES

First Basemen and Designated Hitters, combined (median EqA: .282)

Rank	Player	Team	EqA
1.	Jason Giambi	OAK	.371
2.	Mark McGwire	STL	.364
3.	Carlos Delgado	TOR	.363
4.	Frank Thomas	CWS	.340
5.	Edgar Martinez	SEA	.338
6.	Todd Helton	COL	.324
7.	Will Clark	B/S	.316
8.	Jeff Bagwell	HOU	.312
9.	Mike Sweeney	KCR	.309
10.	Rafael Palmeiro	TEX	.306
11.	Jim Thome	CLE	.303
12.	Ryan Klesko	SDP	.298
13.	Greg Colbrunn	ARI	.295
14.	David Segui	T/C	.294
15.	John Olerud	SEA	.292
16.	Tony Clark	DET	.288
17.	Brad Fullmer	TOR	.288
18.	Mo Vaughn	ANA	.287
19.	Sean Casey	CIN	.285
20.	Paul Konerko	CWS	.281
21.	Jose Canseco	T/N	.280
22.	Fred McGriff	TBY	.279
23.	Andrew Galarraga	ATL	.278
24.	Derrek Lee	FLA	.278
25.	Kevin Millar	FLA	.278
26.	Chris Richard	S/B	.278
27.	Richie Sexson	C/M	.275
28.	J.T. Snow	SFG	.275
29.	Mark Grace	CHC	.272
30.	David Ortiz	MIN	.269
31.	Todd Zeile	NYM	.266
32.	Scott Spiezio	ANA	.263
33.	Dave McCarty	KCR	.262
34.	Lee Stevens	MON	.261
35.	Pat Burrell	PHI	.261
36.	Mike Stanley	B/O	.260
37.	Harold Baines	B/C	.258
38.	Wally Joyner	ATL	.256
39.	Tino Martinez	NYY	.254
40.	Eric Karros	LAD	.254
41.	Brian Daubach	BOS	.250
42.	Tyler Houston	MIL	.242
43.	Ron Coomer	MIN	.240
44.	Charlie Hayes	MIL	.238
45.	Kevin Young	PIT	.236
46.	Travis Lee	A/P	.235

Second Basemen (median EqA: .252)

Rank	Player	Team	EqA
1.	Jeff Kent	SFG	.322
2.	Edgardo Alfonzo	NYM	.312
3.	Roberto Alomar	CLE	.289
4.	Jose Vidro	MON	.289
5.	Delino DeShields	BAL	.282
6.	Frank Catalanotto	TEX	.275
7.	Luis Castillo	FLA	.275
8.	Quilvio Veras	ATL	.274
9.	Ray Durham	CWS	.269
10.	Damion Easley	DET	.264
11.	Eric Young	CHC	.263
12.	Craig Grebeck	TOR	.262
13.	Randy Velarde	OAK	.261
14.	Chuck Knoblauch	NYY	.260
15.	Craig Biggio	HOU	.258
16.	Luis Alicea	TEX	.256
17.	Jay Bell	ARI	.254
18.	Fernando Vina	STL	.253
19.	Bret Boone	SDP	.250
20.	Jeff Frye	B/C	.247
21.	Todd Walker	M/C	.247
22.	Ron Belliard	MIL	.244
23.	Mark Grudzielanek	LAD	.243
24.	Mark McLemore	SEA	.243
25.	Placido Polanco	STL	.243
26.	Jose Offerman	BOS	.237

Second Basemen (continued)

Rank	Player	Team	EqA
27.	Adam Kennedy	ANA	.235
28.	Pokey Reese	CIN	.234
29.	Jay Canizaro	MIN	.233
30.	Keith Lockhart	ATL	.229
31.	Carlos Febles	KCR	.228
32.	Miguel Cairo	TBY	.226
33.	Warren Morris	PIT	.221
34.	Mickey Morandini	P/T	.210
35.	Jose Vizcaino	L/N	.198
36.	Mike Lansing	C/B	.188
37.	Kevin Jordan	PHI	.176
38.	Homer Bush	TOR	.168

Third Basemen (median EqA: .255)

Rank	Player	Team	EqA
1.	Troy Glaus	ANA	.316
2.	Olmedo Saenz	OAK	.309
3.	Ken Caminiti	HOU	.307
4.	Chipper Jones	ATL	.305
5.	Travis Fryman	CLE	.299
6.	Phil Nevin	SDP	.296
7.	Eric Chavez	OAK	.285
8.	Scott Rolen	PHI	.285
9.	Corey Koskie	MIN	.281
10.	Chris Stynes	CIN	.280
11.	Fernando Tatis	STL	.274
12.	Dean Palmer	DET	.273
13.	Adrian Beltre	LAD	.272
14.	Mike Lowell	FLA	.268
15.	Herb Perry	CWS	.267
16.	Aaron Boone	CIN	.264
17.	Jeff Conine	BAL	.263
18.	Tony Batista	TOR	.262
19.	Joe Randa	KCR	.259
20.	Cal Ripken	BAL	.255
21.	Jeff Cirillo	COL	.255
22.	Robin Ventura	NYM	.252
23.	Bill Spiers	HOU	.251
24.	Enrique Wilson	C/P	.250
25.	Geoff Blum	MON	.248
26.	Carlos Guillen	SEA	.246
27.	Ed Sprague	S/B	.246
28.	Bill Mueller	SFG	.244
29.	Luis Sojo	P/N	.242
30.	David Bell	SEA	.241
31.	Lenny Harris	A/N	.241
32.	Matt Williams	ARI	.235
33.	Chris Truby	HOU	.235
34.	Craig Paquette	STL	.229
35.	Mike Lamb	TEX	.229
36.	Shane Halter	DET	.228
37.	Scott Brosius	NYY	.225
38.	Mike Benjamin	PIT	.222
39.	Aramis Ramirez	PIT	.221
40.	Jose Hernandez	MIL	.217
41.	Russ Johnson	H/T	.215
42.	Willie Greene	CHC	.213
43.	Jose Nieves	CHC	.185
44.	Michael Barrett	MON	.178
45.	Vinny Castilla	TBY	.176

Shortstops (median EqA: .240)

Rank	Player	Team	EqA
1.	Alex Rodriguez	SEA	.343
2.	Nomar Garciaparra	BOS	.337
3.	Derek Jeter	NYY	.310
4.	Miguel Tejada	OAK	.279
5.	Jose Valentin	CWS	.278
6.	Barry Larkin	CIN	.277
7.	Mike Bordick	B/M	.263
8.	Rafael Furcal	ATL	.263
9.	Kevin Elster	LAD	.260
10.	Ricky Gutierrez	CHC	.258
11.	Rich Aurilia	SFG	.258
12.	Omar Vizquel	CLE	.257
13.	Deivi Cruz	DET	.254
14.	Damian Jackson	SDP	.251
15.	Melvin Mora	N/B	.246
16.	Edgar Renteria	STL	.246
17.	Mark Loretta	MIL	.243
18.	Julio Lugo	HOU	.243
19.	Dave Berg	FLA	.236
20.	Alex Gonzalez	TOR	.235
21.	Desi Relaford	P/S	.231
22.	Luis Lopez	MII	.230
23.	Tony Womack	ARI	.229
24.	Benji Gil	ANA	.226
25.	Christian Guzman	MIN	.225
26.	Royce Clayton	TEX	.221
27.	Alex Cora	LAD	.221
28.	Pat Meares	PIT	.220
29.	Kevin Stocker	ANA	.216
30.	Orlando Cabrera	MON	.213
31.	Rey Sanchez	KCR	.210
32.	Andy Fox	A/F	.208
33.	Neifi Perez	COL	.207
34.	Felix Martinez	TBY	.207
35.	Juan Castro	CIN	.199
36.	Tim Bogar	HOU	.191
37.	Alex Gonzalez	FLA	.172

Equivalent Average Leader Boards

Left Fielders and Multi-position Outfielders (median EqA: .268)

Rank	Player	Team	EqA
1.	Barry Bonds	SFG	.348
2.	Gary Sheffield	LAD	.333
3.	Brian Giles	PIT	.322
4.	Darin Erstad	ANA	.315
5.	Bobby Higginson	DET	.305
6.	David Justice	C/N	.305
7.	Cliff Floyd	FLA	.296
8.	Luis Gonzalez	ARI	.293
9.	Alex Ochoa	CIN	.293
10.	Geoff Jenkins	MIL	.292
11.	Glenallen Hill	C/N	.291
12.	Shannon Stewart	TOR	.289
13.	Greg Vaughn	TBY	.286
14.	Ben Grieve	OAK	.285
15.	Benny Agbayani	NYM	.281
16.	Orlando Palmeiro	ANA	.279
17.	Rusty Greer	TEX	.278
18.	Michael Tucker	CIN	.277
19.	Rondell White	M/C	.276
20.	Carlos Lee	CWS	.273
21.	Ray Lankford	STL	.272
22.	Mark Quinn	KCR	.269
23.	Bubba Trammell	T/N	.269
24.	B.J. Surhoff	B/A	.266
25.	Shane Spencer	NYY	.264
26.	Denny Hocking	MIN	.263
27.	Stan Javier	SEA	.262
28.	Dmitri Young	CIN	.260
29.	Henry Rodriguez	C/F	.259
30.	Ron Gant	P/A	.258
31.	Al Martin	S/S	.258
32.	Rickey Henderson	N/S	.255
33.	Richie Sexson	CLE	.252
34.	Wil Cordero	P/C	.250
35.	Chad Curtis	TEX	.250
36.	Roger Cedeno	HOU	.250
37.	Jacque Jones	MIN	.249
38.	Jeff Abbott	CWS	.249
39.	Bobby Bonilla	ATL	.249
40.	Luis Polonia	D/N	.248
41.	Daryle Ward	HOU	.248
42.	Eric Owens	SDP	.244
43.	Troy O'Leary	BOS	.241
44.	Shawon Dunston	STL	.236
45.	Butch Huskey	M/C	.237
46.	Ricky Ledee	N/C/T	.235
47.	Reggie Sanders	ATL	.233
48.	Alex Ramirez	C/P	.231
49.	Terry Shumpert	COL	.227
50.	Wilton Guerrero	MON	.214
51.	Darren Lewis	BOS	.205

Center Fielders (median EqA: .261)

Rank	Player	Team	EqA
1.	Bernie Williams	NYY	.313
2.	Jim Edmonds	STL	.309
3.	Carl Everett	BOS	.305
4.	Richard Hidlago	HOU	.304
5.	Johnny Damon	KCR	.294
6.	Ken Griffey	CIN	.291
7.	Andruw Jones	ATL	.286
8.	Mike Cameron	SEA	.282
9.	Steve Finley	ARI	.281
10.	Brady Anderson	BAL	.274
11.	Kenny Lofton	CLE	.270
12.	Gabe Kapler	TEX	.270
13.	Adrian Brown	PIT	.267
14.	Terrence Long	OAK	.267
15.	Garret Anderson	ANA	.265
16.	Ruben Mateo	TEX	.262
17.	Preston Wilson	FLA	.261
18.	Juan Encarnacion	DET	.260
19.	Jose Cruz	TOR	.259
20.	Marvin Benard	SFG	.250
21.	Jay Payton	NYM	.245
22.	Todd Hollandsworth	L/C	.242
23.	Gerald Williams	TBY	.238
24.	Torii Hunter	MIN	.235
25.	Ruben Rivera	SDP	.232
26.	Carlos Beltran	KCR	.231
27.	Tom Goodwin	C/L	.229
28.	Chris Singleton	CWS	.229
29.	Damon Buford	CHC	.228
30.	Doug Glanville	PHI	.221
31.	Peter Bergeron	MON	.215
32.	Tom Goodwin	LAD	.212
33.	Marquis Grissom	MIL	.205
34.	Brian Hunter	C/C	.205

Right Fielders (median EqA: .276)

Rank	Player	Team	EqA
1.	Manny Ramirez	CLE	.359
2.	Ellis Burks	SFG	.329
3.	Vladimir Guerrero	MON	.320
4.	Sammy Sosa	CHC	.317
5.	Moises Alou	HOU	.314

Right Fielders (continued)

Rank	Player	Team	EqA
6.	Tim Salmon	ANA	.311
7.	John Vander Wal	PIT	.307
8.	Jermaine Dye	KCR	.306
9.	Bob Abreu	PHI	.304
10.	Magglio Ordonez	CWS	.302
11.	Jay Buhner	SEA	.295
12.	Lance Berkman	HOU	.291
13.	Matt Lawton	MIN	.291
14.	Trot Nixon	BOS	.280
15.	J.D. Drew	STL	.279
16.	Shawn Green	LAD	.278
17.	Juan Gonzalez	DET	.278
18.	Steve Cox	TBY	.277
19.	Armando Rios	SFG	.276
20.	Raul Mondesi	TOR	.276
21.	Rich Becker	O/D	.271
22.	Albert Belle	BAL	.271
23.	Eric Davis	STL	.268
24.	Jeffrey Hammonds	COL	.266
25.	Larry Walker	COL	.264
26.	Jeremy Giambi	OAK	.262
27.	Jeromy Burnitz	MIL	.261
28.	Dante Bichette	C/B	.260
29.	Matt Stairs	OAK	.258
30.	Danny Bautista	F/A	.257
31.	Mark Kotsay	FLA	.257
32.	Paul O'Neill	NYY	.256
33.	Derek Bell	NYM	.255
34.	Mike Darr	SDP	.253
35.	Luis Polonia	DET	.249
36.	Jose Guillen	TBY	.247
37.	Brian Jordan	ATL	.242
38.	Dave Martinez	(4)	.240
39.	Midre Cummings	M/B	.235
40.	John Mabry	S/S	.227

Catchers (median EqA: .244)

Rank	Player	Team	EqA
1.	Jorge Posada	NYY	.317
2.	Ivan Rodriguez	TEX	.316
3.	Mike Piazza	NYM	.314
4.	Charles Johnson	B/C	.311
5.	Todd Hundley	LAD	.301
6.	Chad Kreuter	LAD	.286
7.	Darrin Fletcher	TOR	.284
8.	Jason Kendall	PIT	.283
9.	Mitch Meluskey	HOU	.280
10.	Brook Fordyce	C/B	.279
11.	Bobby Estalella	SFG	.274
12.	Gregg Zaun	KCR	.272
13.	Scott Hatteberg	BOS	.269
14.	Joe Oliver	SEA	.266
15.	Javy Lopez	ATL	.261
16.	Mike Lieberthal	PHI	.260
17.	Tony Eusebio	HOU	.257
18.	Brad Ausmus	DET	.253
19.	Damian Miller	ARI	.252
20.	Ben Molina	ANA	.248
21.	Jason Varitek	BOS	.247
22.	Doug Mirabelli	SFG	.241
23.	Ramon Hernandez	OAK	.239
24.	Sandy Alomar	CLE	.238
25.	Raul Casanova	MIL	.236
26.	Brent Mayne	COL	.236
27.	Einar Diaz	CLE	.235
28.	Joe Girardi	CHC	.235
29.	Chris Widger	M/S	.234
30.	Benito Santiago	CIN	.228
31.	Henry Blanco	MIL	.226
32.	Carlos Hernandez	S/S	.226
33.	Eddie Taubensee	CIN	.225
34.	Mike Difelice	TBY	.222
35.	Jeff Reed	CHC	.220
36.	Mike Matheny	STL	.220
37.	John Flaherty	TBY	.220
38.	Wiki Gonzalez	SDP	.219
39.	Mark Johnson	CWS	.215
40.	Dan Wilson	SEA	.213
41.	Mike Redmond	FLA	.208
42.	Paul Bako	H/F/A	.207
43.	Kelly Stinnett	ARI	.202

MINOR LEAGUES

First Basemen

Rank	Player	Team	League	EqA
1.	Alex Cabrera	ELP	TXS	.292
2.	Mario Valdez	SLC	PCL	.291
3.	Chris Donnels	ABQ	PCL	.270
4.	Nate Rolison	CLG	PCL	.269
5.	Travis Hafner	PCH	FSL	.268
6.	Julio Zuleta	IOW	PCL	.265
7.	Todd Sears	CAR	SOU	.261
8.	Jeff Liefer	CHR	INT	.258
9.	Carlos Pena	TUL	TXS	.258
10.	Dan Meier	LYN	CRL	.257
11.	Mark Johnson	NOR	INT	.257
12.	Juan Diaz	TRN	EAS	.256
13.	Buck Jacobsen	HUN	SOU	.255
14.	Jay Gibbons	TEN	SOU	.255
15.	Joe Vitiello	LVG	PCL	.251
16.	Jason Hart	MID	TXS	.251
17.	Damon Minor	FRE	PCL	.250

Equivalent Average Leader Boards

Rank	Player	Team	League	EqA
18.	Chirs Saunders	CHT	SOU	.249
19.	Nate Espy	PIE	SAL	.249
20.	Dernell Stenson	PAW	INT	.248
21.	Morgan Burkhart	PAW	INT	.248
22.	Doug Mientkiewicz	SLC	PCL	.247
23.	Danny Peoples	BUF	INT	.247
24.	Eddie Perez	MEM	PCL	.246
25.	Lyle Overbay	ELP	TXS	.244
26.	Phil Hiatt	CSP	PCL	.242
27.	Brian Lesher	TAC	PCL	.241
28.	Ryan Jackson	DUR	INT	.241
29.	Gene Schall	SWB	INT	.241
30.	Billy Martin	SBN	MDW	.241

Second Basemen

Rank	Player	Team	League	EqA
1.	Jose Ortiz	SAC	PCL	.279
2.	Keith Ginter	ROU	TXS	.272
3.	Bobby Smith	DUR	INT	.266
4.	Ryan Freel	SYR	INT	.259
5.	Jerry Hairston	ROC	INT	.256
6.	Jermaine Clark	NHV	EAS	.254
7.	Kary Bridges	OTT	INT	.252
8.	Hiram Bocachica	ABQ	PCL	.250
9.	Mickey Lopez	HUN	SOU	.247
10.	Richard Paz	FRD	CRL	.247
11.	Marlon Anderson	SWB	INT	.246
12.	Marcus Giles	GRN	SOU	.242
13.	Willie Bloomquist	LNC	CLF	.242
14.	Marcos Scutaro	BUF	INT	.237
15.	Jackie Rexrode	BIR	SOU	.234
16.	Mickey Lopez	IND	INT	.230
17.	Brian Benefield	KIN	CRL	.230
18.	Steve Sisco	RIC	INT	.225
19.	Pedro Santana	JAX	SOU	.225
20.	Mark Burnett	CLN	MDW	.224
21.	Henry Mateo	HAR	EAS	.224
22.	Rob Mackowiak	ALT	EAS	.223
23.	Kevin Connacher	WNS	CRL	.222
24.	Pablo Ozuna	PME	EAS	.221
25.	Ismael Gallo	VRO	FSL	.220
26.	Liu Rodriguez	CHR	INT	.220
27.	Willie Harris	DEL	SAL	.220
28.	Todd Walker	SLC	PCL	.219
29.	Mike Young	TEN	SOU	.219
30.	Amaury Garcia	CLG	PCL	.218

Third Basemen

Rank	Player	Team	League	EqA
1.	Aubrey Huff	DUR	INT	.279
2.	Mark Bellhorn	SAC	PCL	.267
3.	Russ Branyan	BUF	INT	.259
4.	Ryan Minor	ROC	INT	.259
5.	Craig Wilson	CHR	INT	.259
6.	Joe Dillon	WIC	TXS	.253
7.	Joe Crede	BIR	SOU	.252
8.	Morgan Ensberg	ROU	TXS	.249
9.	Daryl Clark	OGD	PIO	.249
10.	Casey Blake	SLC	PCL	.248
11.	Eric Hinske	WTN	SOU	.247
12.	Mike Bell	LOU	INT	.246
13.	Jose Fernandez	IND	INT	.246
14.	Justin Leone	WIS	MDW	.245
15.	Rob Sasser	TOL	INT	.244
16.	Albert Pujols	PEO	MDW	.244
17.	Pedro Feliz	FRE	PCL	.242
18.	Bill Selby	BUF	INT	.242
19.	Simon Pond	KIN	CRL	.241
20.	Luis Lopez	SYR	INT	.241
21.	Ryan Gripp	LNS	MDW	.240
22.	Troy Schader	FTW	MDW	.240
23.	Brian Rust	FRD	CRL	.240
24.	Royce Huffman	KIS	FSL	.240
25.	Brad Seitzer	CHR	INT	.239
26.	Tomas Perez	SWB	INT	.238
27.	Michael Forbes	JAM	NYP	.237
28.	Scott Hodges	JUP	FSL	.236
29.	Mike Edwards	AKR	EAS	.236
30.	Chris Haas	ARK	TXS	.232
31.	Sean Burroughs	MOB	SOU	.232

Shortstops

Rank	Player	Team	League	EqA
1.	Shawn Gilbert	ABQ	PCL	.253
2.	Mike Coolbaugh	COH	INT	.247
3.	Jimmy Rollins	SWB	INT	.245
4.	Elvis Pena	CAR	SOU	.241
5.	Chris Sexton	LOU	INT	.239
6.	Matt Erickson	PME	EAS	.238
7.	Mark Ellis	WIL	CRL	.238
8.	Santiago Perez	IND	INT	.237
9.	Victor Rodriguez	KIN	CRL	.236
10.	Alfonso Soriano	COH	INT	.235
11.	Chris Basak	PTS	NYP	.235
12.	Jorge Velandia	SAC	PCL	.233
13.	Mark DeRosa	RIC	INT	.233
14.	Mendy Lopez	CLG	PCL	.233
15.	Chris Snopek	TAC	PCL	.232
16.	Jose Flores	TAC	PCL	.228
17.	Ramon Vazquez	NHV	EAS	.228
18.	Josh Wilson	UTI	NYP	.227
19.	Dave Post	OTT	INT	.225
20.	Augie Ojeda	IOW	PCL	.225

Shortstops (continued)

Rank	Player	Team	League	EqA
21.	Nate Frese	DAY	FSL	.224
22.	Adam Everett	NWO	PCL	.224
23.	Ralph Milliard	LVG	PCL	.224
24.	J.J. Furmaniak	IDA	PIO	.223
25.	Jeff Patzke	BUF	INT	.222
26.	Giomar Guevara	TOL	INT	.222
27.	Jim Deschaine	LNS	MDW	.222
28.	Jack Wilson	ARK	TXS	.222
29.	Andy Beattie	CLN	MDW	.222
30.	Juan Melo	FRE	PCL	.222

Left Fielders

Rank	Player	Team	League	EqA
1.	Brad Wilkerson	HAR	EAS	.279
2.	Randy Winn	DUR	INT	.279
3.	Dusty Allen	LVG	PCL	.275
4.	Eric Byrnes	SAC	PCL	.274
5.	Billy McMillon	TOL	INT	.273
6.	Kevin Mench	PCH	FSL	.267
7.	Carlos Mendoza	CSP	PCL	.260
8.	John Roskos	LVG	PCL	.258
9.	Ben Broussard	CHT	SOU	.258
10.	Felix Jose	COH	INT	.253
11.	Mike Neill	TAC	PCL	.252
12.	Gary Johnson	LEL	CLF	.251
13.	Jack Cust	ELP	TXS	.250
14.	Cory Harris	PTS	NYP	.248
15.	Adam Hyzdu	ALT	EAS	.247
16.	Ruben Sierra	OKL	PCL	.246
17.	Ryan Thompson	COH	INT	.246
18.	George Lombard	RIC	INT	.245
19.	Brian Cole	SLU	FSL	.244
20.	Andy Bevins	ARK	TXS	.243
21.	Craig Thompson	IDA	PIO	.242
22.	Jody Gerut	CAR	SOU	.242
23.	Ntema Ndungidi	FRD	CRL	.241
24.	John Cotton	CSP	PCL	.241
25.	Adam Dunn	DYT	MDW	.240
26.	Chris Hatcher	IOW	PCL	.239
27.	Rusty Keith	MOD	CLF	.238
28.	Ryan Lane	TUL	TXS	.238
29.	Andy Thompson	SYR	INT	.238

Center Fielders

Rank	Player	Team	League	EqA
1.	Torii Hunter	SLC	PCL	.294
2.	John Barnes	SLC	PCL	.271
3.	Timoniel Perez	NOR	INT	.268
4.	Mike Darr	LVG	PCL	.260
5.	Jeremy Johnson	MED	PIO	.248
6.	Alex Hernandez	ALT	EAS	.244
7.	Bobby Kielty	NBR	EAS	.243
8.	Alex Escobar	BIN	EAS	.241
9.	Chris Prieto	ABQ	PCL	.239
10.	Milton Bradley	OTT	INT	.236
11.	Corey Patterson	WTN	SOU	.235
12.	Lew Ford	AUG	SAL	.235
13.	Bo Porter	SAC	PCL	.235
14.	Mark Little	MEM	PCL	.235
15.	Juan Pierre	CAR	SOU	.234
16.	Kerry Robinson	COH	INT	.234
17.	Chris Snelling	WIS	MDW	.233
18.	Victor Hall	MSO	PIO	.233
19.	Dave Roberts	BUF	INT	.233
20.	Andres Torres	LAK	FSL	.233
21.	Jason Tyner	NOR	INT	.233
22.	Darren Burton	ALT	EAS	.232
23.	Omar Ramirez	NWO	PCL	.231
24.	Mike Curry	WIC	TXS	.230
25.	Jay Sitzman	PIE	SAL	.227
26.	Jamal Strong	EVE	NWN	.226
27.	Jason Conti	TUC	PCL	.226
28.	Reggie Taylor	SWB	INT	.226
29.	Kimera Bartee	LOU	INT	.226
30.	Vernon Wells	SYR	INT	.225

Right Fielders

Rank	Player	Team	League	EqA
1.	Emil Brown	NAS	PCL	.272
2.	Israel Alcantara	PAW	INT	.271
3.	Pedro Valdes	OKL	PCL	.265
4.	Bobby Darula	BLT	MDW	.263
5.	Karim Garcia	ROC	INT	.255
6.	Ozzie Timmons	DUR	INT	.255
7.	Roosevelt Brown	IOW	PCL	.254
8.	Brady Clark	LOU	INT	.254
9.	Ryan McGuire	NOR	INT	.250
10.	Terrmel Sledge	LNC	CLF	.249
11.	Aaron Guiel	OMA	PCL	.248
12.	Austin Kearns	DYT	MDW	.247
13.	Brian Buchanan	SLC	PCL	.245
14.	Chris Wakefield	TOL	INT	.244
15.	Jim Chamblee	PAW	INT	.244
16.	Anthony Sanders	TAC	PCL	.243
17.	Chad Mottola	SYR	INT	.241
18.	Valentino Pascucci	JUP	FSL	.240
19.	Chris Richard	MEM	PCL	.238
20.	Scott Lydy	CHR	INT	.237
21.	Mario Encarnacion	SAC	PCL	.237
22.	Roberto Vaz	SAC	PCL	.235
23.	Ryan Church	MHV	NYP	.234
24.	Gary Johnson	DAY	FSL	.231
25.	Bill Ortega	ARK	TXS	.231

Equivalent Average Leader Boards

Rank	Player	Team	League	EqA
26.	Donovan Ross	CWV	SAL	.231
27.	Reed Johnson	HAG	SAL	.231
28.	Eric Valent	REA	EAS	.230
29.	Craig Monroe	TUL	TXS	.229
30.	Angel Echevarria	CSP	PCL	.228
31.	Pedro Swann	RIC	INT	.228
32.	Scott Krause	IND	INT	.228

Catchers

Rank	Player	Team	League	EqA
1.	Craig Wilson	NAS	PCL	.274
2.	Ramon Castro	CLG	PCL	.262
3.	Shawn Wooten	EDM	PCL	.257
4.	Tom Wilson	COH	INT	.256
5.	Gary Bennett	SWB	INT	.251
6.	Ben Petrick	CSP	PCL	.250
7.	Mike Kinkade	BIN	EAS	.249
8.	Danny Ardoin	SAC	PCL	.247
9.	Matt LeCroy	NBR	EAS	.246
10.	J.R. House	HIC	SAL	.246
11.	Joe Lawrence	DUN	FSL	.243
12.	Toby Hall	ORL	SOU	.243
13.	Dusty Wathan	TAC	PCL	.242
14.	Paul LoDuca	ABQ	PCL	.241
15.	Angel Pena	ABQ	PCL	.241
16.	Mandy Romero	AKR	EAS	.238
17.	B.J. Waszgis	OKL	PCL	.237
18.	Lance Burkhart	BLT	MDW	.237
19.	Javier Cardona	TOL	INT	.236
20.	Tim DeCinces	MOB	SOU	.234
21.	Creighton Gubanich	IND	INT	.231
22.	John Wilson	PTS	NYP	.229
23.	Ben Davis	LVG	PCL	.229
24.	Matt Curtis	KIN	CRL	.228
25.	Giuseppe Chiaramonte	FRE	PCL	.227
26.	Mike Rivera	LAK	FSL	.225
27.	Hector Ortiz	OMA	PCL	.225
28.	A.J. Pierzynski	NBR	EAS	.225
29.	Jason LaRue	LOU	INT	.223
30.	Robert Machado	TAC	PCL	.221

Prospectus Fielding Runs Leader Boards

by Clay Davenport

Here's a brief explanation of how the Prospectus Fielding Runs are calculated, along with rankings by position.*

First Base

First-base defense was evaluated by looking first at three team adjustments:

1. ground-ball/fly-ball ratio: infield assists divided by outfield putouts;
2. balls in play: hits minus home runs plus outfield putouts plus infield assists plus errors;
3. left/right ratio: assists from second base and first base divided by assists from third base and shortstop.

These factors are combined to form an adjustment factor. For example, the 2000 Cardinals had a .95 rating for balls in play, a .87 rating for ground-ball/fly-ball ratio, and a 1.00 left/right split. Because they had fewer balls in play and fewer ground balls than expected, you would expect their infielders to make fewer plays than average. Their first-base position has a .89 rating, meaning that a Cardinal first baseman will be counted as average if he makes 89% as many plays as an average National League first baseman.

The number of putouts a first baseman should make is estimated by looking at how many assists other infielders make, an approach first pointed out by Charles Saeger, a regular on the Orioles mailing list and later a contributor to the *Big Bad Baseball Annual*. I've modified his approach by comparing the results of his formula to Retrosheet data that showed me how many plays first basemen made in the 1980s and 1990s. Assists and errors require no extra adjustments.

For the year 2000, my Gold Glove winners are Todd Helton and John Olerud. Neither is unexpected. Helton had good fielding numbers in the minors and in his rookie season prior to stepping up this year. Olerud has always been among the leaders for his league, and in 1999 he finished in a virtual tie with Rico Brogna.

The genuine awards went to Olerud and, for the sixth year in a row, J.T. Snow. Whatever Snow has done to impress the coaches who vote on the award, it has never translated into statistical terms and didn't this year either.

At the opposite end of the spectrum were Mo Vaughn and Kevin Young. Vaughn has always been awful with the glove, but Young has generally been average or above. He had started to slip in 1999, but the bottom dropped out on him last year.

AL First Basemen

Name	Team	Games	Rating	RAR	RAA
John Olerud	SEA	152	111	29	17
Ron Coomer	MIN	121	105	16	6
Mike Sweeney	KCR	110	105	13	5
Jim Thome	CLE	104	104	12	4
Tino Martinez	NYY	144	101	12	1
David Segui	2 tms	72	107	10	5
Paul Konerko	CWS	120	97	7	-3
Brian Daubach	BOS	77	100	6	0
Will Clark	BAL	70	99	5	-1
Jason Giambi	OAK	123	96	5	-5
Carlos Delgado	TOR	161	94	4	-9
Fred McGriff	TBY	143	93	1	-10
Rafael Palmeiro	TEX	105	91	0	-9
Mo Vaughn	ANA	143	87	-7	-18

NL First Basemen

Name	Team	Games	Rating	RAR	RAA
Todd Helton	COL	152	114	34	22
Eric Karros	LAD	149	111	29	17
Jeff Bagwell	HOU	153	105	20	7
Derrek Lee	FLA	126	105	17	6
Mark Grace	CHC	137	104	16	5
Lee Stevens	MON	118	104	15	5
Todd Zeile	NYM	142	103	15	4
Richie Sexson	MIL	56	116	14	9
J.T. Snow	SFG	143	100	12	0
Ryan Klesko	SDP	123	101	11	1
Sean Casey	CIN	122	98	8	-2
Travis Lee	2 tms	57	104	7	2
Greg Colbrunn	ARI	82	99	6	-1
Mark McGwire	STL	66	95	3	-3
Pat Burrell	PHI	58	91	0	-5
Andres Galarraga	ATL	121	92	0	-10
Kevin Young	PIT	119	83	-10	-20

Top Minor League Performers
(not adjusted for league difficulty)

Name	Team	League	Games	Rating	RAR	RAA
Ryan Jackson	Durha	INT	131	109	22	12
Pete Paciorek	SBern	CLF	117	110	21	12
Eric Sandberg	QuadC	MDW	127	108	21	10
Matt Logan	Duned	FSL	105	110	19	11
Larry Sutton	Memph	PCL	86	113	18	11
Nate Espy	Piedm	SAL	128	107	18	9
Brian Lesher	Tacom	PCL	127	106	18	8
Casey Kelley	Cedar	MDW	73	115	17	11
Eric Battersby	Birmi	SOU	120	107	17	8
Doug Mientkiewicz	SaltL	PCL	81	112	16	10

*These rankings use 55 games at the position as the cutoff; all major leaguers and the top minor leaguers are ranked.
RAR: Runs Above Replacement; **RAA:** Runs Above Average

Second Base

The adjustments for second basemen are similar to those for first basemen, except that the number of putouts they are expected to make depends on the number of assists made by the shortstops and third basemen, as well as the number of men on first base available to be forced at second. Second basemen are also rated for the number of double plays they turn in the field.

My Gold Gloves go to Randy Velarde and Pokey Reese, each of whom was also the winner in 1999. Reese was the actual winner for the second year in a row. In the AL, Roberto Alomar won the real award for the third year in a row and ninth time overall. Alomar is one of those players whose fielding statistics have never measured up to his defensive reputation; while my system has generally rated him better than other systems (rated 76 runs better than average entering the 2000 season, still not as high as his reputation), it showed a sharp dropoff in 2000, from above average to well below.

The Lead Gloves go to Chuck Knoblauch and Mark Lansing. Knoblauch's troubles afield in the last two years are probably familiar to you. Lansing has been extremely inconsistent throughout his career, but there has been a general downward trend that reached its nadir in 2000.

AL Second Basemen

Name	Team	Games	Rating	RAR	RAA
Adam Kennedy	ANA	146	103	35	5
Randy Velarde	OAK	117	109	34	10
Damion Easley	DET	120	108	34	9
Ray Durham	CWS	145	99	29	-1
Homer Bush	TOR	75	117	28	13
Mark MacLemore	SEA	123	101	26	1
Roberto Alomar	CLE	148	96	24	-6
Miguel Cairo	TBY	99	98	19	-2
Luis Alicea	TEX	119	93	16	-8
Carlo Febles	KCR	92	96	14	-4
Delino DeShields	BAL	90	93	13	-6
Jose Offerman	BOS	75	89	7	-8
Jay Canizaro	MIN	78	88	7	-9
Chuck Knoblauch	NYY	78	82	2	-14

NL Second Basemen

Name	Team	Games	Rating	RAR	RAA
Pokey Reese	CIN	129	112	42	16
Fernando Vina	STL	118	112	37	14
Jeff Kent	SFG	141	105	35	7
Ron Belliard	MIL	149	103	33	4
Eric Young	CHC	147	99	28	-1
Jose Vidro	MON	148	99	27	-2
Warren Morris	PIT	130	100	26	0
Jay Bell	ARI	141	99	26	-2
Edgardo Alfonzo	NYM	142	98	25	-3
Craig Biggio	HOU	96	104	23	4
Bret Boone	SDP	123	96	19	-5
Mark Grudzielanek	LAD	146	93	19	-10
Mickey Morandini	PHI	81	100	16	0
Luis Castillo	FLA	134	93	16	-10
Keith Lockhart	ATL	58	100	12	0
Quilvio Veras	ATL	79	92	10	-6
Mike Lansing	COL	86	84	3	-14

Top Minor League Performers
(not adjusted for league difficulty)

Name	Team	League	Games	Rating	RAR	RAA
Glenn Williams	Duned	FSL	97	115	34	15
Pat Manning	Macon	SAL	119	109	34	11
Jay Pecci	Midla	TXS	89	117	33	15
David Eckstein	Pawtu	INT	112	110	33	11
Kevin Hooper	KaneC	MDW	120	108	33	9
Brian Hitchcox	Piedm	SAL	77	121	31	16
Steve Scarborough	Beloi	MDW	121	106	31	7
Sergio Nunez	Clear	FSL	105	110	30	10
Jason Williams	Louis	INT	107	108	30	9
Jermaine Clark	NewHa	EAS	127	104	30	5

Third Base

Third basemen's adjustments are similar to other infielders, except that putouts are largely disregarded; foul territory makes a huge difference in the availability of pop-ups, which is where a typical third baseman gets more than half of his putouts.

My Gold Glove winners for 2000 are a pair of Scotts, Rolen and Brosius. Rolen is the winner for the third time in four years (he lost out last year to Robin Ventura). Brosius picked up his second in a row. Both of them had fairly typical seasons last year.

Rolen was the actual award winner in the NL, but the AL coaches picked Travis Fryman. While Fryman has a fine track record and probably deserved a Gold Glove in the past, he hasn't looked quite as good as before he had knee injuries.

On the Lead Glove side, Dean Palmer is the poster boy for a replacement-level fielder, reliably finishing at the bottom of league rankings. In the NL, the Pirates' Aramis Ramirez played himself off the team with his atrocious play at the hot corner. While he hadn't shown off a great glove in the minors, it didn't look this bad.

Third Base continued

AL Third Basemen

Name	Team	Games	Rating	RAR	RAA
Scott Brosius	NYY	126	113	35	16
Tony Batista	TOR	154	108	35	12
Joe Randa	KCR	155	104	29	6
Travis Fryman	CLE	152	103	27	4
Troy Glaus	ANA	151	103	26	4
Cory Koskie	MIN	135	100	20	0
Cal Ripken Jr.	BAL	73	110	18	7
Herb Perry	2 tms	105	103	18	3
Vinny Castilla	TBY	83	105	16	4
Eric Chavez	OAK	134	97	16	-4
David Bell	SEA	78	103	14	2
Mike Lamb	TEX	128	89	5	-14
Carlos Guillen	SEA	68	90	3	-7
Dean Palmer	DET	107	86	1	-15

NL Third Basemen

Name	Team	Games	Rating	RAR	RAA
Scott Rolen	PHI	125	111	33	14
Robin Ventura	NYM	120	111	31	13
Adrian Beltre	LAD	135	104	26	6
Willie Greene	CHC	75	113	22	10
Bill Mueller	SFG	136	101	21	1
Mike Lowell	FLA	134	101	21	1
Jeff Cirillo	COL	151	99	21	-1
Aaron Boone	CIN	81	110	20	8
Matt Williams	ARI	94	103	17	3
Chipper Jones	ATL	147	97	17	-5
Chris Stynes	CIN	69	103	12	2
Fernando Tatis	STL	75	101	12	1
Jose Hernandez	MIL	91	99	12	-1
Chris Truby	HOU	66	98	9	-1
Phil Nevin	SDP	136	92	9	-11
Craig Paquette	STL	60	92	4	-5
Aramis Ramirez	PIT	56	84	-1	-9

Top Minor League Performers
(not adjusted for league difficulty)

Name	Team	League	Games	Rating	RAR	RAA
Julio Cordido	Baker	CLF	128	120	46	26
Albert Pujols	Peori	MDW	104	119	37	20
Andrew Beinbrink	StPet	FSL	125	113	36	16
Morgan Ensberg	RRock	TXS	136	110	36	14
Hank Blalock	Savan	SAL	133	111	35	14
Scott Hodges	Jupit	FSL	105	112	30	13
Lou Lucca	Memph	PCL	109	112	30	13
Ryan Gripp	Lansi	MDW	122	108	29	10
Luis Figueroa	NewHa	EAS	112	110	28	11
Bo Robinson	Lanca	CLF	130	105	28	6

Shortstop

Shortstop adjustments are almost identical to those given to second basemen, except that their putout rating is dependent on the second baseman's assists.

My Gold Glove awards at shortstop go to Neifi Perez and Rey Sanchez. Sanchez has picked up this award from me three times now, in 1996, 1999, and 2000, despite never having a secure job entering any season; he actually has a higher career rating than Ozzie Smith. Likewise, Perez has captured two titles from me in three seasons (winning in 1998 and 2000, and narrowly losing to Rey Ordonez in 1999). Both are the real deal.

The genuine awards went to Perez and Omar Vizquel. Perez would never have won without Rey Ordonez's injury but is undoubtedly the right choice. Vizquel is another one of those problem players, with a reputation far better than his statistical performance. From the number of plays he makes, he is only a little better than average for his career, and in 2000 was worse than that. There is no denying the style with which he makes them, however.

The Lead Glove awards go to Derek Jeter and Julio Lugo. Jeter's performance has never rated very highly; in five seasons he has never been above average. But last year was the worst yet; he had 41 fewer assists and 10 more errors in 10 fewer games than the year before. Lugo, a rookie who had only rated as an average shortstop in the Florida and Texas Leagues in 1998 and 1999, was simply overmatched at the major league level.

AL Shortstops

Name	Team	Games	Rating	RAR	RAA
Rey Sanchez	KCR	133	119	53	25
Alex Rodriguez	SEA	146	110	45	15
Deivi Cruz	DET	150	105	39	8
Felix Martinez	TBY	106	108	30	8
Royce Clayton	TEX	141	99	29	-1
Jose Valentin	CWS	139	100	28	0
Omar Vizquel	CLE	151	97	27	-4
Miguel Tejada	OAK	157	97	27	-5
Kevin Stocker	2 tms	93	104	23	4
Nomar Garciaparra	BOS	133	95	22	-6
Alex Gonzalez	TOR	138	94	21	-8
Cristian Guzman	MIN	148	94	21	-9
Benji Gil	ANA	81	98	15	-2
Mike Bordick	BAL	96	94	14	-6
Derek Jeter	NYY	146	84	7	-23

NL Shortstops

Name	Team	Games	Rating	RAR	RAA
Neifi Perez	COL	158	117	59	27
Rich Aurilia	SFG	136	107	37	10
Orlando Cabrera	MON	107	111	33	12
Mark Loretta	MIL	81	115	28	12
Edgar Renteria	STL	142	99	27	-2
Pat Meares	PIT	119	101	25	1
Tim Bogar	HOU	79	111	24	9
Damian Jackson	SDP	83	106	21	5
Tony Womack	ARI	143	93	19	-10
Ricky Gutierrez	CHC	116	95	17	-6
Desi Relaford	2 tms	119	93	16	-8
Walt Weiss	ATL	58	107	15	4
Alex Gonzalez	FLA	97	95	15	-5
Alex Cora	LAD	97	93	12	-7
Barry Larkin	CIN	97	91	11	-9
Rafael Furcal	ATL	97	91	10	-9
Julio Lugo	HOU	57	84	2	-9

Top Minor League Performers
(not adjusted for league difficulty)

Name	Team	League	Games	Rating	RAR	RAA
Cesar Izturis	Syrac	INT	128	119	50	24
Nate Frese	Dayto	FSL	108	122	47	24
Donaldo Mendez	Michi	MDW	100	120	41	20
Nick Ortiz	Wichi	TXS	108	116	39	17
Mike Moriarty	SaltL	PCL	120	112	39	14
Carlos Mendoza	SJose	CLF	103	116	38	16
Mark Ellis	Wilmi	CRL	127	109	38	12
Kelly Dransfeldt	OklaC	PCL	114	111	36	12
Josh Reding	Harri	EAS	127	109	36	11
Derek Mitchell	Jacks	SOU	105	113	35	14

Fungoes

Left Field

Outfield ratings were derived separately for each of the outfield positions, although these were based only on total outfield statistics and the number of games played at each of the outfield positions.

The top-rated left fielders in 2000 were Darin Erstad and Eric Owens. Erstad, as it turns out, won one of the outfield Gold Glove spots in the AL, so his selection is uncontroversial. Owens spent a lot of time in center so it isn't surprising he leads left fielders. At the low end of the scale, perennial cellar-dwellers Al Martin and Wil Cordero battled to a dead heat for the NL title, while Chad Curtis embarrassed himself in the AL.

AL Left Fielders

Name	Team	Games	Rating	RAR	RAA
Darin Erstad	ANA	136	112	31	16
Bob Higginson	DET	145	107	25	10
Jacque Jones	MIN	137	105	23	7
Shannon Stewart	TOR	136	105	21	7
Carlos Lee	CWS	138	103	18	4
B.J. Surhoff	BAL	102	104	15	4
Troy O'Leary	BOS	129	101	14	1
Greg Vaughn	TBY	72	104	11	3
Mark Quinn	KCR	81	101	10	1
Rickey Henderson	SEA	83	101	10	1
Ben Grieve	OAK	129	97	10	-4
David Justice	2 tms	107	96	8	-4
Rusty Greer	TEX	92	97	6	-3
Chad Curtis	TEX	71	87	-1	-9

NL Left Fielders

Name	Team	Games	Rating	RAR	RAA
Eric Owens	SDP	144	104	22	6
Geoff Jenkins	MIL	130	103	18	4
Rondell White	2 tms	91	106	16	7
Barry Bonds	SFG	125	103	16	4
Luis Gonzalez	ARI	152	99	13	-2
Ron Gant	PHI	83	100	9	0
Henry Rodriguez	2 tms	80	100	8	0
Michael Tucker	CIN	70	100	8	0
Benny Agbayani	NYM	83	98	7	-2
Dmitri Young	CIN	90	97	6	-3
Reggie Sanders	ATL	83	96	6	-3
Ray Lankford	STL	97	95	5	-5
Gary Sheffield	LAD	119	94	5	-7
Cliff Floyd	FLA	92	95	4	-5
Al Martin	SDP	74	90	0	-7
Wil Cordero	PIT	73	90	0	-7

Top Minor League Performers
(not adjusted for league difficulty)

Name	Team	League	Games	Rating	RAR	RAA
Byron Gettis	ChaWV	SAL	94	114	21	13
Juan Piniella	Tulsa	TXS	121	106	19	7
Chin-Feng Chen	SanAn	TXS	127	105	18	6
Marlon Byrd	Piedm	SAL	103	108	17	8
B.J. Barns	Lynch	CRL	115	105	16	6
Tony Peters	Duned	FSL	107	105	16	5
Kevin Mench	Charl	FSL	122	103	16	4
Wayne Kirby	Roche	INT	103	104	15	4
Nathan Janowicz	MahoV	NYP	68	112	14	8
Tony Alvarez	Hicko	SAL	101	106	14	6

Center Field

Center field is the glamour position in the outfield, and it isn't uncommon for all three Gold Glove winners to be center fielders. Last year, though, the AL only named one, Bernie Williams. The NL named three: Steve Finley, Jim Edmonds, and Andruw Jones.

From my perspective, Jones is an excellent choice, Edmonds an OK one, and Finley a poor one, coasting on a once-deserved reputation. Jones's numbers compare well with the greatest outfielders in history, such as Tris Speaker, Willie Mays, and Richie Ashburn, even though 2000 was his worst season to date. I also don't care much for the choice of Bernie Williams; Chris Singleton was probably the best of the group, although no one in the AL can be regarded as dominating.

AL Center Fielders

Name	Team	Games	Rating	RAR	RAA
Chris Singleton	CWS	145	106	28	9
Johnny Damon	KCR	133	106	24	8
Mike Cameron	SEA	148	103	24	4
Kenny Lofton	CLE	135	104	23	5
Torii Hunter	MIN	96	109	22	9
Jose Cruz Jr.	TOR	159	101	22	1
Garret Anderson	ANA	140	101	20	2
Juan Encarnacion	DET	138	101	19	1
Gerald Williams	TBY	138	101	19	1
Bernie Williams	NYY	134	100	18	0
Luis Matos	BAL	57	112	15	7
Carlos Beltran	KCR	88	101	13	1
Carl Everett	BOS	121	98	13	-3
Brady Anderson	BAL	122	98	12	-3
Gabe Kapler	TEX	116	97	11	-4
Terrence Long	OAK	137	93	10	-9

NL Center Fielders

Name	Team	Games	Rating	RAR	RAA
Andruw Jones	ATL	161	112	40	20
Richard Hidalgo	HOU	150	113	38	20
Ken Griffey Jr.	CIN	141	106	27	9
Tom Goodwin	2 tms	140	105	25	7
Preston Wilson	FLA	156	103	24	4
Doug Glanville	PHI	149	102	22	3
Ruben Rivera	SDP	121	104	21	5
Jim Edmonds	STL	141	103	21	4
Peter Bergeron	MON	129	103	20	4
Marquis Grissom	MIL	139	101	20	2
Jay Payton	NYM	128	102	18	2
Marvin Benard	SFG	141	101	18	1
Steve Finley	ARI	144	100	18	0
Damon Buford	CHC	136	100	17	0
Todd Hollandsworth	2 tms	106	102	15	2
Brian L. Hunter	2 tms	61	103	9	2
Adrian Brown	PIT	75	97	7	-2

Top Minor League Performers
(not adjusted for league difficulty)

Name	Team	League	Games	Rating	RAR	RAA
Jeremy Owens	RaCuc	CLF	138	118	40	25
Lew Ford	Augus	SAL	124	118	35	22
Luis Saturria	Arkan	TXS	127	114	32	18
Junior Brignac	MyrtB	CRL	128	113	30	16
Mike Byas	Fresn	PCL	132	110	29	13
Ryan Ludwick	Modes	CLF	118	113	28	15
Alejandro Diaz	Chatt	SOU	122	111	28	14
Andres Torres	Lakel	FSL	104	114	27	15
Ron Calloway	Jupit	FSL	117	111	27	13
Rontrez Johnson	Trent	EAS	133	108	27	11

Prospectus Fielding Runs Leader Boards

Right Field

No, I don't think Paul O'Neill was anywhere this close to being the best right fielder in the AL, even though he did lead the league in chances and was third in chances per game. The Yankees have a large bias in their defensive stats towards right field that the outfield rating system did not pick up. Jermaine Dye won the Gold Glove award he should have gotten in 1999, but his numbers were way down this year.

In the NL, Mark Kotsay, Bobby Abreu, and Brian Jordan are at the top of a tight field. Looking only at time spent in right field, J.D. Drew was better than all of them, but the rating below does include his sub-par performance as a center fielder and drags him down. Houston, with Moises Alou and Lance Berkman, had real problems in the outfield last year, which didn't help Jose Lima any.

AL Right Fielders

Name	Team	Games	Rating	RAR	RAA
Dave Martinez	4 tms	107	106	19	6
Paul O'Neill	NYY	124	102	17	2
Tim Salmon	ANA	119	101	14	1
Ricky Ledee	3 tms	116	99	12	-1
Trot Nixon	BOS	105	99	12	-1
Magglio Ordonez	CWS	140	96	11	-5
Jose Guillen	TBY	79	101	10	1
Jermaine Dye	KCR	135	95	8	-7
Jay Buhner	SEA	85	96	7	-3
Albert Belle	BAL	101	94	6	-6
Raul Mondesi	TOR	94	94	5	-6
Matt Lawton	MIN	134	93	5	-10
Matt Stairs	OAK	96	93	4	-7
Juan Gonzalez	DET	59	91	2	-5
Rich Becker	DET	60	90	1	-6
Manny Ramirez	CLE	80	89	0	-9

NL Right Fielders

Name	Team	Games	Rating	RAR	RAA
Mark Kotsay	FLA	130	105	22	7
Bob Abreu	PHI	151	103	21	4
Brian Jordan	ATL	130	104	20	5
Jeromy Burnitz	MIL	149	99	16	-1
Vladimir Guerrero	MON	138	99	14	-2
Larry Walker	COL	82	105	13	4
Ellis Burks	SFG	92	103	13	3
Danny Bautista	ARI	87	101	12	1
J.D. Drew	STL	109	100	12	0
Dante Bichette	CIN	108	100	12	0
Jeffrey Hammonds	COL	106	99	11	-1
Shawn Green	LAD	151	96	11	-6
Derek Bell	NYM	127	97	10	-4
Sammy Sosa	CHC	150	95	9	-8
Armando Rios	SFG	58	103	8	2
Lance Berkman	HOU	83	98	7	-2
Moises Alou	HOU	97	94	5	-6
John VanderWal	PIT	70	94	4	-4
Eric Davis	STL	58	93	2	-4

Top Minor League Performers
(not adjusted for league difficulty)

Name	Team	League	Games	Rating	RAR	RAA
Aaron Rowand	Birmi	SOU	138	109	27	13
Ken Woods	ScWiB	INT	128	109	27	12
Nate Murphy	Edmon	PCL	114	111	24	12
Cody Ross	WMich	MDW	120	109	22	11
Scott Neuberger	Orlan	SOU	117	109	22	10
Eric Johnson	ColuG	SAL	64	123	21	15
Pete Tucci	Mobil	SOU	128	105	21	7
Miguel Diaz	Potom	CRL	90	112	20	11
Spencer Oborn	Burli	MDW	124	107	20	9
Brett Casper	Baker	CLF	123	107	20	8

Catcher

Catchers' ratings are fundamentally different from the ratings for other positions, in that only one of the traditional statistics—errors—has any impact. Most of their rating is determined by looking at how many stolen bases a "replacement level" catcher—a catcher whose caught-stealing rate is 25% below the league average against whom opposing runners attempt to run 25% more often—would allow. Passed balls and errors also figure in.

The top catchers in the majors last year were Mike Matheny and Brad Ausmus. Matheny won the genuine Gold Glove, but Ausmus was passed over in favor of the injured Ivan Rodriguez. Ausmus's numbers were the equal of Rodriguez's this year, but Rodriguez was thoroughly dominating in each of the past two years. His continuing selection is no shock.

Prospectus Fielding Runs Leader Boards

AL Catchers

Name	Team	Games	Rating	RAR	RAA
Brad Ausmus	DET	142	109	35	13
Ben Molina	ANA	125	105	25	6
Jorge Posada	NYY	135	101	23	2
Ivan Rodriguez	TEX	85	109	21	8
Charles Johnson	2 tms	113	101	19	2
Ramon Hernandez	OAK	122	98	17	-2
Mark Johnson	CWS	69	107	16	5
Dan Wilson	SEA	75	104	15	3
Einar Diaz	CLE	74	104	14	3
John Flaherty	TBY	101	98	13	-2
Alberto Castillo	TOR	58	105	12	3
Darrin Fletcher	TOR	101	95	11	-5
Brook Fordyce	2 tms	85	98	10	-4
Jason Varitek	BOS	119	93	10	-8
Bill Haselman	TEX	55	100	8	0
Joe Oliver	SEA	55	98	8	-1
Sandy Alomar Jr.	CLE	88	93	8	-6
Mike Difelice	TBY	57	97	7	-2
Greg Zaun	KCR	65	91	4	-6

NL Catchers

Name	Team	Games	Rating	RAR	RAA
Mike Matheny	STL	115	114	35	16
Henry Blanco	MIL	81	117	27	14
Mike Lieberthal	PHI	102	106	23	6
Jason Kendall	PIT	145	99	23	-1
Joe Girardi	CHC	96	106	22	6
Damian Miller	ARI	89	107	21	6
Chad Kreuter	LAD	67	108	16	5
Bobby Estalella	SFG	95	100	16	0
Javy Lopez	ATL	122	97	16	-4
Benito Santiago	CIN	67	104	14	3
Wiki Gonzalez	SDP	76	103	14	2
Jeff Reed	CHC	64	102	12	1
Mike Redmond	FLA	66	102	12	1
Paul Bako	3 tms	65	102	12	1
Brent Mayne	COL	91	97	12	-3
Mike Piazza	NYM	119	93	12	-8
Kelly Stinnett	ARI	70	100	11	0
Doug Mirabelli	SFG	65	100	10	0
Chris Widger	MON	78	96	10	-3
Carlos Hernandez	2 tms	64	97	9	-2
Mitch Meluskey	HOU	91	93	9	-6
Raul Casanova	MIL	58	95	6	-3
Tony Eusebio	HOU	59	93	6	-4
Eddie Taubensee	CIN	67	92	6	-5
Todd Hundley	LAD	79	89	4	-9

Top Minor League Performers
(not adjusted for league difficulty)

Name	Team	League	Games	Rating	RAR	RAA
Guillermo Rodriguez	Baker	CLF	115	106	49	7
Jean Boscan	Macon	SAL	86	122	47	19
Brandon Marsters	FtMye	FSL	105	117	47	18
Brian Moon	Hunts	SOU	95	121	45	20
John Hernandez	SBern	CLF	78	119	44	15
John Buck	Michi	MDW	100	113	42	13
Scott Maynard	Lanca	CLF	90	109	42	8
Ryan Christianson	Wisco	MDW	94	112	38	11
Corky Miller	Chatt	SOU	101	111	37	11
Aaron Nieckula	Visal	CLF	61	120	35	12

Prospectus Fielding Runs Leader Boards

Parks and Park Factors

"Park" is the park factor used to compile the ratings for the 2000 season. When possible, it is the average of the 2000, 1999, and 1998 single-season park factors.

Leagues:

AL = American League,	Eas = Eastern League	NL = National League	Pio = Pioneer League
App = Appalachian League	FSL = Florida State League	Nwn = Northwest League	SAL = South Atlantic League
Car = Carolina League	Int = International League	NYP = New York-Penn League	Sou = Southern League
Cal = California League	Mid = Midwest League	PCL = Pacific Coast League	Tex = Texas League

Team	League	Level	Park	Team	League	Level	Park	Team	League	Level	Park
Akron	Eas	AA	1001	Chattang	Sou	AA	1019	Helena	Pio	Rookie	957
Albuquer	PCL	AAA	1075	ChiCubs	NL	Major	997	Hickory	SAL	Mid A	1021
Altoona	Eas	AA	940	ChiSox	AL	Major	1012	High Des	Cal	High A	1139
Anaheim	AL	Major	997	Cincnnti	NL	Major	1022	Houston	NL	Major	1072
Arizona	NL	Major	999	Clearwtr	FSL	High A	1054	HudsnVal	NYP	Low A	1002
Arkansas	Tex	AA	981	Clevelnd	AL	Major	1046	Huntsvil	Sou	AA	982
Ashevlle	SAL	Mid A	1105	Clinton	Mid	Mid A	1002	IdahoFls	Pio	Rookie	970
Atlanta	NL	Major	979	ColSprin	PCL	AAA	1111	Indianap	Int	AAA	994
Auburn	NYP	Low A	1038	Colorado	NL	Major	1288	Iowa	PCL	AAA	945
Augusta	SAL	Mid A	951	Columbia	SAL	Mid A	1015	Jacksnvl	Sou	AA	979
Bakrsfld	Cal	High A	1012	Columbus	Int	AAA	1000	Jamestwn	NYP	Low A	1048
Baltimor	AL	Major	969	Columbus	SAL	Mid A	1066	JohnsnCy	App	Rookie	1098
Batavia	NYP	Low A	988	Danville	App	Rookie	992	Jupiter	FSL	High A	964
Beloit	Mid	Mid A	1005	Dayton	Mid	Mid A	1056	KaneCnty	Mid	Mid A	1012
Billings	Pio	Rookie	999	Daytona	FSL	High A	1040	KansasCy	AL	Major	1042
Binghmtn	Eas	AA	1068	Delmarva	SAL	Mid A	968	Kingsprt	App	Rookie	1009
Birmnghm	Sou	AA	955	Detroit	AL	Major	973	Kinston	Car	High A	981
BlngtnNC	App	Rookie	941	Dunedin	FSL	High A	1049	Kissimme	FSL	High A	979
Bluefld	App	Rookie	1088	Durham	Int	AAA	987	Lakeland	FSL	High A	1041
Boise	Nwn	Low A	1020	Edmonton	PCL	AAA	1030	Lancastr	Cal	High A	1103
Boston	AL	Major	1021	El Paso	Tex	AA	1114	Lansing	Mid	Mid A	1087
Bowie	Eas	AA	1006	Elizbthn	App	Rookie	950	LasVegas	PCL	AAA	1052
Brevard	FSL	High A	963	Erie	Eas	AA	1084	Lk Elsin	Cal	High A	950
Bristol	App	Rookie	1022	Eugene	Nwn	Low A	1001	LosAngls	NL	Major	940
Buffalo	Int	AAA	982	Everett	Nwn	Low A	1068	Louisvil	Int	AAA	1037
Burlingt	Mid	Mid A	1057	Florida	NL	Major	955	Lowell	NYP	Low A	974
Butte	Pio	Rookie	1130	Frederck	Car	High A	992	Lynchbrg	Car	High A	1036
Calgary	PCL	AAA	1114	Fresno	PCL	AAA	1062	Macon	SAL	Mid A	1023
CapeFear	SAL	Mid A	989	Ft Myers	FSL	High A	957	MahngVal	NYP	Low A	960
Carolina	Sou	AA	1017	Ft Wayne	Mid	Mid A	982	Martnsvl	App	Rookie	942
CedarRpd	Mid	Mid A	1010	GreatFls	Pio	Rookie	954	Med Hat	Pio	Rookie	988
Charl-SC	SAL	Mid A	1005	Greensbr	SAL	Mid A	989	Memphis	PCL	AAA	958
Charl-WV	SAL	Mid A	980	Greenvil	Sou	AA	1095	Michigan	Mid	Mid A	1049
Charlott	FSL	High A	995	Hagerstn	SAL	Mid A	1072	Midland	Tex	AA	1074
Charlott	Int	AAA	1075	Harrisbg	Eas	AA	1040	Milwauke	NL	Major	999

Fungoes

Team	League	Level	Park
Minnesot	AL	Major	1053
Missoula	Pio	Rookie	967
Mobile	Sou	AA	979
Modesto	Cal	High A	1001
Montreal	NL	Major	976
Mudville	Cal	High A	855
Myrtle B	SAL	Mid A	901
NY Mets	NL	Major	952
NY Yanks	AL	Major	975
Nashvill	PCL	AAA	944
New Brit	Eas	AA	974
New Havn	Eas	AA	970
New Jrsy	NYP	Low A	963
New Orln	PCL	AAA	888
Norfolk	Int	AAA	998
Norwich	Eas	AA	970
Oakland	AL	Major	968
Ogden	Pio	Rookie	1030
Oklahoma	PCL	AAA	945
Omaha	PCL	AAA	961
Oneonta	NYP	Low A	988
Orlando	Sou	AA	998
Ottawa	Int	AAA	1020
Pawtuckt	Int	AAA	1006
Peoria	Mid	Mid A	967
Philadel	NL	Major	1028
Piedmont	SAL	Mid A	999
Pittsbrg	NL	Major	1002
Pittsfld	NYP	Low A	946
Portland	Eas	AA	1040
Portland	Nwn	Low A	948
Potomac	Car	High A	1041
Pr Willm	Car	High A	980
Princetn	App	Rookie	989
Pulaski	App	Rookie	1009
Quad Cit	Mid	Mid A	970
Queens	NYP	Low A	1021
R Cucmng	Cal	High A	980
Reading	Eas	AA	1022
Richmond	Int	AAA	1035
Rochestr	Int	AAA	955
Rockford	Mid	Mid A	993
Round Rock	Tex	AA	950
Sacramen	PCL	AAA	951
Salem OR	Nwn	Low A	1023
Salem VA	Car	High A	1036
SaltLake	PCL	AAA	1103
SanAnton	Tex	AA	903
San Bern	Cal	High A	976
San Dieg	NL	Major	918
San Fran	NL	Major	925
San Jose	Cal	High A	951
Sarasota	FSL	High A	1011
Savannah	SAL	Mid A	947
Scran-WB	Int	AAA	965
Seattle	AL	Major	940
Shrevprt	Tex	AA	953
Spokane	Nwn	Low A	979
St Cath	NYP	Low A	973
St Louis	NL	Major	1007
St Lucie	FSL	High A	992
St Pete	FSL	High A	992
StatenIs	NYP	Low A	1114
Sth Bend	Mid	Mid A	988
Syracuse	Int	AAA	1049
Tacoma	PCL	AAA	916
TampaBay	AL	Major	1019
Tampa	FSL	High A	980
Tennesse	Sou	AA	1093
Texas	AL	Major	1062
Toledo	Int	AAA	994
Toronto	AL	Major	1018
Trenton	Eas	AA	974
Tucson	PCL	AAA	1082
Tulsa	Tex	AA	978
Utica	NYP	Low A	1010
Vancouvr	Nwn	Low A	886
Vermont	NYP	Low A	1029
Vero Bch	FSL	High A	1059
Visalia	Cal	High A	994
W Michgn	Mid	Mid A	919
Watertwn	NYP	Low A	970
WestTenn	Sou	AA	977
Wichita	Tex	AA	1042
Willmspt	NYP	Low A	1022
Wilmngtn	Car	High A	957
Wisconsn	Mid	Mid A	982
WnstnSlm	Car	High A	1041
Yakima	Nwn	Low A	969

Parks and Park Factors

Biographies

Jeff Bower is a senior engineer for a manufacturing company, and the president of NW SABR. He lives in Seattle with his family of four. When not watching, playing, or coaching baseball, he can be found restoring the family's century-old house and imploring the dog to return the balls that she fetches.

Clay Davenport is a meteorologist, dancer, and NTN player (HRBAKR) in Washington, D.C. In 2000, he made it through an entire softball season without getting hit in the head for the first time in three years.

Jeff Hildebrand is currently a visiting assistant professor of mathematics at Allegheny College. His past outlets for causing trouble have included writing for and performing in a radio comedy show, and helping negotiate a union contract.

Gary Huckabay is a Director of Marketing for a subsidiary of Vivendi/Universal, and the guy who made the original fateful phone call to Clay Davenport five years ago. Gary has also been in management consulting at KPMG, and earned his MBA at UC Davis.

Rany Jazayerli is a Dermatology resident at Henry Ford Hospital in Detroit, on Year 10 of a 12-year regimen of higher education, where he's learning how to stomp out skin disease and despise managed care.

Chris Kahrl is one of the founders of *Baseball Prospectus*. He's moved to Maryland, where he's cultivating a Ditka moustache in tribute to the Da Coach and the 15 years he loved living in Chicago. He's still trying to come to terms with the shock of living in a single-team market, having always believed two-team markets were his birthright. Well, at least there are a bunch of Civil War battlefields nearby to keep him happy.

Keith Law writes on fantasy baseball for ESPN.com and *Fantasy Baseball Index*, and has been a member of *Baseball Prospectus* since 1996. He works in business development for a Boston-area software firm and holds a Master's of Science in Industrial Administration from Carnegie Mellon University.

Mat Olkin is a writer and copy editor for *Baseball Weekly*. He contributes to the STATS *Major League Scouting Notebook* and the *Fantasy Baseball Index*, and pens his own annual book, the *Baseball Examiner*. His father is a Red Sox fan; Mat thus learned at an early age the hazards of rooting for the Red Sox, and decided to pull for the Brewers instead.

Dave Pease works for a wireless communications company in sunny San Diego. His hobbies include baseball, maintaining *Baseball Prospectus Online*, watching his portfolio crash and burn, and wondering if he'll ever finish school.

Joseph S. Sheehan is the managing editor of *Baseball Prospectus Online*. In 2001, he'll try to spend less time playing Strat-O-Matic and more time learning the piano.

Michael Wolverton has been writing about baseball since age 7, when he wrote a fan letter to Tony Oliva. He is still waiting for a reply. He works as a research scientist in the San Francisco Bay Area, where he lives with his wife Cindy and sons Scott, 4, and Mark, 1.

Keith Woolner lives in Silicon Valley and works for Lumina, which develops software to analyze complex mathematical decision problems. He maintains the Stathead.com baseball website, runs the Red Sox mailing list, and moderates the Usenet newsgroup rec.sport.baseball.analysis. He holds undergraduate degrees in Mathematics, Computer Science, and Management from M.I.T., and a Master's degree in Decision Analysis from Stanford University. Jim "Catfish" Hunter threw a perfect game on his birthday.

Derek Zumsteg lives and drinks on Seattle's east side, and during the daytime is a fiery project manager for a wireless service provider. Anyone with a decent softball team that needs an on-base machine and a fast outfielder/catcher can recruit him.

Dedications

Jeff Bower: To my wife, Vivian Little, who understands and tolerates my obsession with baseball because she has a similar love of ballet. However, unlike me, she is so talented that she was able to convert her passion into a professional career.

Clay Davenport: To Susan, for everything.

Jeff Hildebrand: To Jennifer Ziebarth and Rowan Littell for their valued friendship and support. Also to my co-authors for bringing me on board with this project. It's been a lot of fun.

Gary Huckabay: My efforts on this work are dedicated to my wife and partner of 10 years, Kathy Schofield. Except for her taste in men, she's pretty much perfect. This book is not dedicated to CalTrans at all.

Rany Jazayerli: To the brave men, women, and, especially, children of Palestine, for helping me to remember how inconsequential the game of baseball is in the great scheme of things. And to those rare journalists who cover the Middle East in a fair and impartial manner, for sticking to the truth no matter how unpopular it might be.

Chris Kahrl: To all of the people who have given me free tickets over the years, starting with Charlie Davis, my supervisor at the University of Chicago Physical Plant, and a guy with great seats near home plate in Old Comiskey, but also to the Murphys, the McGuires, Tim Ells, Heidi Reich-Aguilar, my brother Ben, Mat Olkin, and probably others during my Teamster days. There is no better gift, and I am grateful.

Keith Law: To my wife, Christa; my parents, in-laws, and families; and to the BP team, who continue to amaze me by improving the quality of our work.

Mat Olkin: To any and all persons who feel that baseball's labor and management ought to be less concerned with pursuing pyrrhic victories against each and more concerned with preserving the sport's relationship with its fans; persons in positions of power in baseball who work to foster dialogue and understanding between labor and management; and persons who work to ensure that a labor stoppage never again will deprive fans of the sport they support so devotedly.

Dave Pease: To Debbbbbb, with looooooove...

Joseph S. Sheehan: My work on our sixth edition is dedicated to the 170-odd people who bought *Baseball Prospectus 1996*. It's all your fault.

Michael Wolverton: As usual, my family—my sons Scott and Mark and my lovely wife Cindy—were exceptionally tolerant and supportive of a dad and husband who goes MIA every year at book writing time. I'd tell them it'll get better next year, but they've heard that one before.

Keith Woolner: I'd like to dedicate my work to all of the pitchers whose careers were cut short due to overwork, and to the hope that there will be fewer of them in the future. Thanks to Craig Wright, a pioneer in the area of pitcher-abuse research. Thanks also to Dr. Lutz Mueller for technical and statistical advice. And of course thanks to Kathy, for reasons too numerous to mention.

Derek Zumsteg: To Jill, who tolerates me working all hours of the night and scooting off to minor-league games, and to Will Clark, for a time the best player in baseball and my favorite player for much longer, and my dad for taking me to Mariners games when we were two of two thousand.

Index

The following is an alphabetical index of the 1,644 players in Baseball Prospectus 2001. Davenport Translations for players not listed here can be found at http://www.baseballprospectus.com.

A

Abbott, Jeff	313
Abbott, Kurt	175
Abbott, Paul	436
Abernathy, Brent	445
Abreu, Bobby	189
Acevedo, Juan	150
Adams, Terry	132
Agamennone, Brandon	166
Agbayani, Benny	175
Aguilera, Rick	56
Ah Yat, Paul	211
Ainsworth, Kurt	254
Alcantara, Israel	296
Alexander, Manny	296
Alfonseca, Antonio	102
Alfonzo, Edgardo	175
Alfonzo, Eliezer	142
Alicea, Luis	461
Allen, Chad	379
Allen, Luke	127
Almanza, Armando	102
Almanzar, Carlos	238
Almonte, Erick	396
Alomar Jr., Sandy	330
Alomar, Roberto	330
Alou, Moises	111
Alvarez, Gabe	233
Alvarez, Tony	203
Alvarez, Wilson	452
Ambres, Chip	95
Amezaga, Alfredo	263
Anderson, Brady	279
Anderson, Brian	24
Anderson, Garret	263
Anderson, Jimmy	211
Anderson, Luke	254
Anderson, Marlon	189
Anderson, Matt	353
Anderson, Ryan	436
Anderson, Wes	102
Andrews, Clayton	483
Andrews, Shane	48
Ankiel, Rick	225
Appier, Kevin	419
Aramboles, Ricardo	403
Ardoin, Danny	379
Arias, Alex	189
Armas Jr., Tony	166
Arrojo, Rolando	303
Arroyo, Bronson	211
Arteaga, J.D.	180
Ashby, Andy	39
Astacio, Pedro	86
Atchley, Justin	71
Aurilia, Rich	248
Ausmus, Brad	347
Austin, Jeff	369
Aven, Bruce	127
Averette, Robert	86
Avery, Steve	39
Aybar, Manny	102

B

Bacsik, Mike	337
Baek, Cha Sueng	436
Baerlocher, Ryan	369
Baez, Danny	337
Bagwell, Jeff	111
Bailey, Jeff	95
Baines, Harold	313
Baisley, Brad	194
Baker, Brad	303
Bako, Paul	33
Baldelli, Rocco	445
Baldwin, James	320
Bale, John	483
Balfour, Grant	387
Barajas, Rod	17
Barcelo, Lorenzo	320
Barker, Glen	112
Barker, Kevin	142
Barnes, John	380
Barnes, Larry	263
Barrett, Michael	159
Bartee, Kimera	65
Basak, Chris	175
Batista, Tony	477
Baughman, Justin	264
Bautista, Danny	17
Baxter, Gerik	239
Beck, Rod	303
Becker, Rich	347
Beckett, Josh	103
Beirne, Kevin	321
Belcher, Jason	142
Belcher, Tim	270
Belinda, Stan	39
Belisle, Matt	39
Belitz, Todd	419
Bell, David	429
Bell, Derek	175
Bell, Jay	18
Bell, Mike	65
Bell, Rob	71
Belle, Albert	279
Bellhorn, Mark	411
Belliard, Ron	142
Bellinger, Clay	396
Beltran, Carlos	362
Beltre, Adrian	127
Benard, Marvin	248
Benes, Alan	225
Benes, Andy	225
Benitez, Armando	180
Benjamin, Mike	203
Bennett, Gary	189
Benoit, Joaquin	468
Benson, Kris	211
Bere, Jason	337
Berg, Dave	95
Bergeron, Peter	159
Berkman, Lance	112
Bernero, Adam	353
Berroa, Angel	411
Betemit, Wilson	33
Betts, Todd	95
Bichette, Dante	296
Biddle, Rocky	321
Bierbrodt, Nick	24
Bigbie, Larry	279
Biggio, Craig	112
Blair, Willie	354
Blake, Casey	380
Blalock, Hank	461
Blanco, Henry	143
Blanco, Tony	296
Blank, Matt	166
Bloomquist, Willie	429
Blum, Geoff	159
Bocachica, Hiram	127
Boehringer, Brian	239
Bogar, Tim	112
Bohanon, Brian	86
Bonds, Barry	248
Bones, Ricky	103
Bonifay, Josh	203
Bonilla, Bobby	34
Boone, Aaron	66
Boone, Bret	233
Borbon, Pedro	483
Borchard, Joe	314
Bordick, Mike	176
Borkowski, David	354
Bottalico, Ricky	369
Bottenfield, Kent	194
Bowen, Rob	380
Bowers, Cedrick	452
Bowie, Micah	56
Boyd, Jason	194
Bradford, Chad	321
Bradley, Bobby	211
Bradley, Milton	160
Bradley, Ryan	403
Brantley, Jeff	194
Branyan, Russ	330
Brea, Lesli	287
Brester, Jason	194
Brewer, Jace	445
Brewington, Jamie	337
Bridges, Donnie	166
Brignac, Junior	34
Brocail, Doug	354
Brock, Chris	195
Brogna, Rico	297
Brooks, Jeff	18
Brosius, Scott	397
Broussard, Ben	66
Brower, Jim	338
Brown, Adrian	203
Brown, Brant	48
Brown, Dee	362
Brown, Emil	204
Brown, Jamie	338
Brown, Kevin (LA)	132
Brown, Kevin (MIL)	143
Brown, Roosevelt	49
Brunette, Justin	226
Buchanan, Brian	380
Buck, John	113
Buddie, Mike	150
Buehrle, Mark	321
Buford, Damon	49
Buhner, Jay	429
Bump, Nate	103
Burba, Dave	338
Burford, Kevin	79
Burkett, John	39
Burkhart, Morgan	297
Burks, Ellis	249
Burnett, A.J.	103
Burnitz, Jeromy	143
Burns, Kevin	113
Burnside, Adrian	133
Burrell, Pat	190
Burroughs, Sean	233
Bush, Homer	477
Butler, Brent	79

Index

Butler, Matt	40	Cintron, Alex	18	Cruz, Deivi	348	Dunn, Adam	67
Bynum, Mike	239	Cirillo, Jeff	79	Cruz, Jacob	331	Dunston, Shawon	221
Byrd, Paul	195	Clapp, Stubby	220	Cruz, Juan	56	Dunwoody, Todd	364
Byrnes, Eric	411	Clark, Daryl	144	Cruz, Nelson	355	Durazo, Erubiel	20
		Clark, Howie	280	Cubillan, Darwin	469	Durbin, Chad	370
C		Clark, Jermaine	430	Cuddyer, Mike	381	Durham, Ray	315
Cabrera, Alex	18	Clark, Mark	468	Cummings, Midre	298	Dye, Jermaine	364
Cabrera, Jolbert	331	Clark, Tony	348	Cunnane, Will	240		
Cabrera, Jose	118	Clark, Will	220	Curry, Mike	363	**E**	
Cabrera, Orlando	160	Clayton, Royce	462	Curtis, Chad	462	Easley, Damion	348
Caceres, Wilmy	66	Clemens, Roger	403	Cust, Jack	20	Eaton, Adam	240
Cairo, Miguel	446	Clement, Matt	239			Ebert, Derrin	40
Calero, Kiko	370	Cline, Pat	144	**D**		Eberwein, Kevin	234
Cameron, Mike	429	Closser, J.D.	19	D'Amico, Jeff (MIL)	150	Echevarria, Angel	144
Cameron, Troy	34	Cloude, Ken	436	D'Amico, Jeff (KC)	370	Eckstein, David	265
Caminiti, Ken	113	Coco, Pasqual	484	Daal, Omar	196	Edmonds, Jim	221
Cammack, Eric	181	Coffie, Ivanon	280	Damon, Johnny	363	Edwards, Mike	332
Camp, Jared	370	Coggin, Dave	195	Daneker, Pat	484	Eiland, Dave	452
Canizaro, Jay	380	Colangelo, Mike	264	Darensbourg, Vic	104	Elarton, Scott	118
Canseco, Jose	397	Colbrunn, Greg	19	Darr, Mike	233	Eldred, Cal	322
Cantu, Jorge	446	Cole, Brian	176	Daubach, Brian	298	Ellis, Mark	365
Capuano, Chris	25	Cole, Eric	114	Davey, Tom	240	Elster, Kevin	128
Cardona, Javier	347	Coleman, Michael	297	Davis, Allen	133	Embree, Alan	255
Carlyle, Buddy	239	Collier, Lou	144	Davis, Ben	233	Encarnacion, Juan	348
Carpenter, Chris	484	Colome, Jesus	452	Davis, Doug	469	Encarnacion, Mario	412
Carrara, Giovanni	86	Colon, Bartolo	338	Davis, Eric	220	Enders, Trevor	453
Carrasco, Hector	304	Comer, Scott	103	Davis, J.J.	204	Ensberg, Morgan	114
Caruso, Joe	363	Cone, David	403	Davis, Kane	150	Erickson, Matt	96
Caruso, Mike	314	Conine, Jeff	280	Davis, Lance	71	Erickson, Scott	287
Casanova, Raul	143	Conti, Jason	19	Davis, Russ	249	Ernster, Mark	144
Casey, Sean	66	Cook, Aaron	87	Dawkins, Gookie	67	Erstad, Darin	265
Casimiro, Carlos	280	Cook, Dennis	181	Day, Zach	338	Escobar, Alex	176
Castilla, Vinny	446	Coomer, Ron	381	De la Rosa, Tomas	160	Escobar, Kelvim	485
Castillo, Alberto	477	Cooper, Brian	270	De los Santos, Valerio	150	Espinosa, David	67
Castillo, Frank	484	Cora, Alex	128	Decker, Steve	264	Espy, Nate	190
Castillo, Jose	204	Cordero, Francisco	468	DeHaan, Kory	234	Estalella, Bobby	250
Castillo, Luis	96	Cordero, Wil	331	DeJean, Mike	87	Estes, Shawn	255
Castro, Juan	66	Cordido, Julio	249	del Toro, Miguel	254	Estrada, Horacio	151
Castro, Ramon	96	Cordova, Francisco	212	Delgado, Carlos	478	Estrella, Leo	485
Catalanotto, Frank	462	Cordova, Marty	477	Delgado, Wilson	364	Etherton, Seth	270
Cedeno, Jovanny	468	Cormier, Rheal	304	Dellaero, Jason	315	Eusebio, Tony	114
Cedeno, Roger	113	Cornejo, Nate	354	Dellucci, David	20	Evans, Tom	462
Cepicky, Matt	160	Cornelius, Reid	104	Dempster, Ryan	104	Everett, Adam	114
Cervantes, Chris	25	Coste, Chris	331	DePaula, Sean	339	Everett, Carl	298
Chacon, Shawn	86	Cota, Humberto	204	DeRosa, Mark	34	Eyre, Scott	322
Chamblee, Jim	297	Cotton, John	80	DeShields, Delino	281		
Chantres, Carlos	321	Cotton, Joseph	196	Dessens, Elmer	72	**F**	
Chavez, Eric	411	Counsell, Craig	19	DeWitt, Matt	484	Fabregas, Jorge	365
Chavez, Raul	113	Cox, Mike	181	Diaz, Alejandro	67	Faison, Vince	234
Checo, Robinson	133	Cox, Ryan	254	Diaz, Einar	332	Farnsworth, Jeff	437
Chen, Bruce	195	Cox, Steve	446	Diaz, Juan	298	Farnsworth, Kyle	57
Chen, Chin-Feng	128	Crabtree, Robbie	254	DiFelice, Mark	88	Fasano, Sal	412
Chiaramonte, Giuseppe	249	Crabtree, Tim	468	Difelice, Mike	447	Fassero, Jeff	305
Chiasson, Scott	419	Crawford, Carl	446	Dillon, Joe	364	Febles, Carlos	365
Chiperfield, Calvin	354	Crawford, Paxton	304	DiPoto, Jerry	88	Feliz, Pedro	250
Cho, Jin Ho	304	Crede, Joe	314	DiSarcina, Gary	264	Fernandez, Alex	104
Choate, Randy	403	Creek, Doug	452	Dorame, Randey	88	Fernandez, Jose	145
Choi, Hee Seop	49	Crespo, Cesar	96	Dotel, Octavio	118	Fernandez, Osvaldo	72
Chouinard, Bobby	87	Crespo, Felipe	249	Downs, Scott	167	Fetters, Mike	134
Christensen, Ben	56	Cresse, Brad	20	Dreifort, Darren	133	Fick, Robert	349
Christensen, McKay	314	Cressend, Jack	387	Drew, J.D.	220	Figgins, Chone	80
Christenson, Ryan	412	Crosby, Bubba	128	Drew, Tim	339	Figueroa, Juan	287
Christiansen, Jason	226	Croushore, Rich	304	Ducey, Rob	190	Figueroa, Nelson	196
Christianson, Ryan	430	Crowder, Chuck	87	Duckworth, Brandon	196	File, Bob	485
Christman, Tim	87	Cruz Jr., Jose	477	Duncan, Courtney	56	Finley, Chuck	339

Name	Page	Name	Page	Name	Page	Name	Page
Finley, Steve	21	Girardi, Joe	50	Guthrie, Mark	486	Hernandez, Carlos (STL)	221
Fisher, Peter	387	Girdley, Josh	167	Gutierrez, Ricky	51	Hernandez, Fernando	119
Flaherty, John	447	Glanville, Doug	190	Guttormson, Rickey	240	Hernandez, Jose	146
Fletcher, Darrin	478	Glaser, Eric	306	Guzman, Cristian	382	Hernandez, Livan	256
Flores, Randy	404	Glauber, Keith	72	Guzman, Elpidio	266	Hernandez, Orlando	405
Florie, Bryce	305	Glaus, Troy	265	Guzman, Geraldo	25	Hernandez, Ramon	414
Floyd, Cliff	97	Glavine, Tom	40	Guzman, Juan (BAL)	288	Hernandez, Roberto	453
Fogg, Josh	322	Glendenning, Mike	250	Guzman, Juan (TB)	453	Herndon, Junior	240
Ford, Lew	381	Gload, Ross	50	Guzman, Wilson	212	Hershiser, Orel	134
Fordyce, Brook	281	Glover, Gary	485	Gwynn, Tony	235	Hiatt, Phil	81
Forster, Scott	167	Glynn, Ryan	469	**H**		Hidalgo, Richard	115
Fossum, Casey	305	Gobble, Jimmy	371	Haas, Chris	221	Higginson, Bobby	350
Foulke, Keith	322	Goetz, Geoff	105	Hackman, Luther	226	Hiljus, Erik	355
Fox, Andy	97	Gold, J.M.	151	Hafner, Travis	463	Hill, Bobby	51
Franco, John	181	Goldbach, Jeff	50	Hairston, Jerry	281	Hill, Glenallen	397
Franco, Matt	176	Gomes, Wayne	196	Halama, John	437	Hinch, A.J.	414
Franklin, Ryan	437	Gomez, Alexis	365	Hall, Toby	448	Hinske, Eric	51
Franklin, Wayne	118	Gomez, Chris	234	Hall, Victor	22	Hitchcock, Sterling	241
Frascatore, John	485	Gomez, Richard	349	Halladay, Roy	486	Hochgesang, Josh	414
Freel, Ryan	478	Gonzalez, Alex (FLA)	97	Hallmark, Pat	365	Hocking, Denny	382
Freeman, Choo	80	Gonzalez, Alex (TOR)	479	Halter, Shane	350	Hodges, Kevin	438
Freire, Alejandro	349	Gonzalez, Dicky	181	Hamilton, Darryl	177	Hodges, Scott	161
Frendling, Neal	453	Gonzalez, Jeremi	57	Hamilton, Joey	486	Hoffman, Trevor	241
Frese, Nate	49	Gonzalez, Juan	349	Hamilton, Jon	332	Hollandsworth, Todd	81
Frias, Hanley	21	Gonzalez, Luis	21	Hamilton, Josh	448	Holliday, Matt	82
Frye, Jeff	80	Gonzalez, Wiki	234	Hammonds, Jeffrey	81	Hollins, Damon	146
Fryman, Travis	332	Gooden, Dwight	404	Hampton, Mike	182	Holmes, Darren	25
Fuentes, Brian	437	Goodwin, Tom	129	Haney, Chris	339	Holt, Chris	119
Fullmer, Brad	478	Gordon, Brian	21	Hansen, Dave	129	Holt, Daylan	414
Fultz, Aaron	255	Gordon, Tom	306	Harang, Aaron	469	Holtz, Mike	271
Furcal, Rafael	34	Grabowski, Jason	463	Harnisch, Pete	72	House, Craig	88
Furniss, Eddy	204	Grace, Mark	50	Harper, Travis	453	House, J.R.	206
Fussell, Chris	370	Graffanino, Tony	315	Harris, Lenny	177	Houston, Tyler	146
Fyhrie, Mike	270	Graman, Alex	404	Hart, Jason	413	Howard, Thomas	221
G		Graves, Danny	72	Harvey, Ken	366	Howington, Ty	73
Gagne, Eric	134	Grebeck, Craig	479	Harville, Chad	419	Howry, Bobby	323
Galarraga, Andres	35	Green, Chad	145	Hasegawa, Shigetoshi	270	Hudson, Tim	420
Gamble, Jerome	305	Green, Jason	118	Haselman, Bill	463	Huff, Aubrey	448
Gant, Ron	265	Green, Scarborough	463	Hatteberg, Scott	299	Huffman, Royce	115
Garbe, B.J.	381	Green, Shawn	129	Haverbusch, Kevin	205	Huisman, Rick	119
Garces, Rich	305	Greene, Todd	479	Hawkins, LaTroy	388	Hummel, Tim	315
Garcia, Amaury	97	Greene, Willie	51	Haynes, Jimmy	151	Hundley, Todd	129
Garcia, Carlos	134	Greer, Rusty	463	Haynes, Nathan	266	Hunter, Brian L.	68
Garcia, Freddy	437	Grieve, Ben	413	Hazlett, Andy	306	Hunter, Brian R.	190
Garcia, Jose	151	Griffey Jr., Ken	67	Heams, Shane	355	Hunter, Torii	382
Garcia, Karim	281	Griffiths, Jeremy	182	Heaverlo, Jeff	438	Huskey, Butch	82
Garciaparra, Nomar	298	Grilli, Jason	105	Hebson, Bryan	167	Huson, Jeff	52
Gardner, Mark	255	Grimsley, Jason	404	Helling, Rick	469	Hutchinson, Chad	226
Garibay, Daniel	57	Grindell, Nate	332	Helms, Wes	35	Hyzdu, Adam	206
Garland, Jon	322	Gripp, Ryan	51	Helton, Todd	81	**I**	
Garza, Chris	387	Grissom, Marquis	145	Hemphill, Bret	266	Ibanez, Raul	431
George, Chris	371	Groom, Buddy	288	Henderson, Rickey	430	Infante, Omar	350
German, Esteban	412	Grudzielanek, Mark	129	Hendrickson, Mark	486	Inge, Brandon	350
Gerut, Jody	81	Guardado, Eddie	388	Henry, Doug	255	Inglin, Jeff	315
Giambi, Jason	413	Gubanich, Creighton	145	Henson, Drew	68	Irabu, Hideki	168
Giambi, Jeremy	413	Guerrero, Cristian	146	Hentgen, Pat	226	Ireland, Eric	119
Gibbons, Jay	479	Guerrero, Julio	299	Heredia, Felix	57	Isringhausen, Jason	420
Gil, Benji	265	Guerrero, Junior	371	Heredia, Gil	420	Izturis, Cesar	479
Gil, Geronimo	128	Guerrero, Vladimir	161	Herges, Matt	134	**J**	
Giles, Brian	205	Guerrero, Wilton	161	Hermansen, Chad	205		
Giles, Marcus	35	Guerrier, Matt	323	Hermanson, Dustin	167	Jackson, Damian	235
Gilkey, Bernard	299	Guillen, Carlos	430	Hernandez, Adrian	404	Jacobsen, Buck	147
Ginter, Keith	115	Guillen, Jose	447	Hernandez, Alex	205	Jacquez, Thomas	197
Ginter, Matt	323	Guillen, Ozzie	447	Hernandez, Carlos (HOU)	119	Jaha, John	414
		Gulan, Mike	98				

Index

James, Mike	227
Jarvis, Kevin	88
Javier, Stan	431
Jefferies, Gregg	350
Jenkins, Geoff	147
Jenkins, Neil	351
Jennings, Jason	89
Jensen, Marcus	382
Jensen, Ryan	256
Jester, Joe	250
Jeter, Derek	397
Jimenez, D'Angelo	397
Jimenez, Jose	89
Johnson, Adam	388
Johnson, Ben	235
Johnson, Brian	398
Johnson, Charles	316
Johnson, Eric	333
Johnson, Gary	266
Johnson, Jason	288
Johnson, Jonathan	470
Johnson, Mark	316
Johnson, Mike	168
Johnson, Nick	398
Johnson, Randy	25
Johnson, Russ	448
Johnston, Clint	212
Johnstone, John	256
Jones, Andruw	35
Jones, Bobby J.	182
Jones, Bobby M.	182
Jones, Chipper	35
Jones, Doug	420
Jones, Jacque	383
Jones, Marcus	421
Jones, Terry	161
Jones, Todd	355
Jordan, Brian	36
Jordan, Kevin	191
Joyner, Wally	36
Judd, Mike	135
Justice, David	398

K

Kalinowski, Josh	89
Kamieniecki, Scott	40
Kapler, Gabe	464
Karros, Eric	130
Karsay, Steve	340
Kaye, Justin	438
Kearns, Austin	68
Keisler, Randy	405
Keith, Rusty	415
Keller, Kris	356
Kelly, Kenny	449
Kelly, Roberto	398
Kelton, Dave	52
Kendall, Jason	206
Kennedy, Adam	267
Kennedy, Joe	454
Kent, Jeff	250
Kershner, Jason	197
Kielty, Bobby	383
Kile, Darryl	227
Kim, Byung-Hyun	26
Kim, Sun Woo	306
King, Ray	152
Kingsale, Eugene	282
Kinkade, Mike	282
Kinney, Matt	388
Kirby, Scott	147
Klassen, Danny	22
Klesko, Ryan	235
Kline, Steve	168
Knight, Brandon	405
Knoblauch, Chuck	399
Knotts, Gary	105
Koch, Billy	487
Kohlmeier, Ryan	288
Konerko, Paul	316
Koplove, Mike	26
Koskie, Corey	383
Kotsay, Mark	98
Krawczyk, Jack	152
Kreuter, Chad	130
Krynzel, David	147
Kuzmic, Craig	431

L

Lackey, John	271
Lamb, Mike	464
Lampkin, Tom	431
Landestoy, Gilbert	271
Langerhans, Ryan	36
Lankford, Ray	222
Lansing, Mike	299
Lara, Mauricio	306
Larkin, Andy	371
Larkin, Barry	68
LaRocca, Greg	235
Larson, Brandon	69
LaRue, Jason	69
Lawrence, Brian	241
Lawrence, Joe	480
Lawton, Matt	383
Laxton, Brett	371
Leach, Bryan	306
LeCroy, Matt	384
Ledee, Ricky	464
Ledesma, Aaron	82
Lee, Carlos	316
Lee, Corey	470
Lee, David	89
Lee, Derek	152
Lee, Derrek	98
Lee, Sang-Hoon	307
Lee, Travis	191
Leese, Brandon	105
Lehr, Justin	421
Leiter, Al	182
Lemon, Tim	222
Leon, Donny	399
Leon, Jose	282
Leone, Justin	432
Leskanic, Curtis	152
Levine, Al	271
Levrault, Allen	153
Lewis, Colby	470
Lewis, Darren	300
Lewis, Derrick	40
Lewis, Mark	282
Leyritz, Jim	130
Lidge, Brad	120
Lidle, Cory	454
Lieber, Jon	57
Lieberthal, Mike	191
Liefer, Jeff	317
Ligtenberg, Kerry	40
Lima, Jose	120
Lincoln, Mike	388
Lindsey, Rodney	351
Liniak, Cole	52
Lira, Felipe	168
Lloyd, Graeme	168
Loaiza, Esteban	487
Lockhart, Keith	36
Lockwood, Mike	415
LoDuca, Paul	130
Loewer, Carlton	241
Lofton, Kenny	333
Lohse, Kyle	389
Loiselle, Rich	212
Lomasney, Steve	300
Lombard, George	36
Long, Garrett	206
Long, Terrence	415
Looper, Braden	105
Lopez, Albie	454
Lopez, Felipe	480
Lopez, Javy	37
Lopez, Jose	212
Lopez, Luis (MIL)	147
Lopez, Luis (TOR)	480
Lopez, Mickey	148
Lopez, Rodrigo	241
Loretta, Mark	148
Lorraine, Andrew	340
Loux, Shane	356
Lowe, Derek	307
Lowe, Sean	323
Lowell, Mike	98
Lowery, Terrell	251
Lubozynski, Matt	271
Ludwick, Ryan	415
Luebbers, Larry	73
Lugo, Julio	115
Lukasiewicz, Mark	271
Lunar, Fernando	283
Lundberg, Spike	470
Luuloa, Keith	267

M

Mabry, John	236
MacDougal, Mike	372
Machado, Albenis	162
Machado, Anderson	191
Machado, Robert	432
Mackowiak, Rob	206
Maddux, Greg	41
Magadan, Dave	236
Magee, Wendell	351
Magnante, Mike	421
Mahomes, Pat	183
Mairena, Oswaldo	58
Majewski, Gary	323
Maldonado, Carlos	116
Mantei, Matt	26
Manto, Jeff	333
Manwiller, Tim	421
Manzanillo, Josias	213
Marquis, Jason	41
Marrero, Eli	222
Marsonek, Sam	405
Martin, Al	432
Martin, Tom	340
Martines, Jason	26
Martinez, Dave	480
Martinez, Edgar	432
Martinez, Felix	449
Martinez, Pedro	307
Martinez, Ramon (SF)	251
Martinez, Ramon (BOS)	307
Martinez, Tino	399
Martinez, Willie	340
Marx, Tommy	356
Masaoka, Onan	135
Mateo, Henry	162
Mateo, Ruben	464
Matheny, Mike	222
Mathews, T.J.	421
Matos, Josue	438
Matos, Luis	283
Mattes, Troy	169
Matthews Jr., Gary	52
Matthews, Lamont	131
Maurer, Dave	242
Maxwell, Jason	384
Mayne, Brent	82
Mays, Joe	389
McCarty, Dave	366
McClain, Scott	82
McClendon, Matt	41
McConnell, Sam	213
McCracken, Quinton	449
McCutcheon, Mike	26
McDonald, Darnell	283
McDonald, John	333
McElroy, Chuck	288
McEwing, Joe	177
McGlinchy, Kevin	41
McGriff, Fred	449
McGwire, Mark	223
McKay, Cody	416
McKinley, Josh	162
McKnight, Tony	120
McLemore, Mark	432
McMillon, Billy	351
McNamara, Rusty	191
McNeal, Aaron	116
Meadows, Brian	372
Meadows, Tydus	53
Meares, Pat	207
Meche, Gil	438
Mecir, Jim	422
Meier, Dan	207
Melhuse, Adam	83
Melian, Jackson	69
Melo, Juan	251
Meluskey, Mitch	116
Mench, Kevin	465

Name	Page	Name	Page	Name	Page	Name	Page
Mendoza, Carlos	83	Myers, Greg	284	Osting, Jimmy	197	Petrick, Ben	84
Mendoza, Ramiro	405	Myers, Mike	90	Osuna, Antonio	135	Pettitte, Andy	406
Menechino, Frank	416	Myers, Randy	242	Oswalt, Roy	121	Pettyjohn, Adam	357
Mercado, Hector	73	Myers, Rodney	242	Overbay, Lyle	22	Phelps, Josh	481
Mercedes, Jose	289	Myette, Aaron	324	Owens, Eric	237	Phelps, Travis	454
Mercker, Kent	272	**N**		Owens, Jeremy	237	Phillips, Brandon	163
Merloni, Lou	300			Owens, Ryan	22	Phillips, Paul	367
Merriman, Terrell	317	Nady, Xavier	236	Ozias, Todd	257	Piatt, Adam	417
Mesa, Jose	439	Nagy, Charles	340	Ozuna, Pablo	99	Piazza, Mike	178
Meyers, Chad	53	Nannini, Mike	121	**P**		Pichardo, Hipolito	308
Meyers, Mike	58	Nathan, Joe	256			Pickering, Calvin	285
Miceli, Danny	106	Nation, Joey	58	Padilla, Roy	341	Pickler, Jeff	149
Middlebrook, Jason	242	Ndungidi, Ntema	284	Padilla, Vicente	198	Piedra, Jorge	54
Mientkiewicz, Doug	384	Neagle, Denny	406	Painter, Lance	487	Pierre, Juan	84
Mieses, Jose	153	Neill, Mike	433	Palmeiro, Orlando	268	Pierzynski, A.J.	385
Millar, Kevin	98	Nelson, Jeff	406	Palmeiro, Rafael	465	Pineiro, Joel	440
Miller, Damian	22	Nen, Robb	257	Palmer, Dean	352	Piniella, Juan	465
Miller, Greg	120	Neugebauer, Nick	153	Paniagua, Jose	439	Plesac, Dan	27
Miller, Justin	422	Nevin, Phil	236	Paquette, Craig	223	Poe, Ryan	154
Miller, Matt	356	Nicholson, Kevin	236	Paradis, Mike	290	Polanco, Placido	223
Miller, Travis	389	Nichting, Chris	341	Park, Chan Ho	136	Politte, Cliff	198
Miller, Trever	135	Nickle, Doug	197	Parker, Brandon	439	Polonia, Luis	400
Miller, Wade	121	Niekro, Lance	252	Parker, Christian	406	Ponson, Sidney	290
Mills, Alan	289	Nieves, Jose	53	Parque, Jim	324	Porter, Bo	466
Mills, Ryan	389	Nina, Elvin	272	Parra, Christian	42	Posada, Jorge	400
Millwood, Kevin	41	Nitkowski, C.J.	357	Parris, Steve	73	Pose, Scott	367
Milton, Eric	390	Nixon, Trot	300	Parrish, David	399	Pote, Lou	273
Minor, Ryan	283	Noel, Todd	406	Parrish, John	290	Powell, Brian	121
Mirabelli, Doug	251	Nomo, Hideo	357	Pascucci, Valentino	163	Powell, Jay	121
Mlicki, Dave	356	Norris, Ben	27	Patterson, Corey	54	Powell, Jeremy	169
Moehler, Brian	357	Norton, Greg	317	Patterson, Danny	357	Pratt, Andy	471
Moeller, Chad	384	Norton, Phil	58	Patterson, Jarrod	163	Pratt, Scott	334
Molina, Ben	267	Nunez, Abraham (FLA)	99	Patterson, John	27	Pratt, Todd	178
Molina, Gabe	42	Nunez, Abraham (PIT)	207	Paul, Josh	318	Pride, Curtis	301
Mondesi, Raul	481	Nunez, Jorge	131	Pavano, Carl	169	Priest, Eddie	73
Montgomery, Steve	242	Nunez, Jose	183	Payton, Jay	178	Prieto, Ariel	423
Moore, Trey	169	Nunez, Vladimir	106	Paz, Richard	285	Prince, Tom	192
Mora, Melvin	284	Nunnari, Talmadge	162	Pearce, Josh	227	Prinz, Bret	28
Moraga, David	89	Nussbeck, Mark	289	Peavy, Jacob	243	Prokopec, Luke	136
Morales, Willie	284	**O**		Pellow, Kit	367	Pujols, Albert	223
Morandini, Mickey	481			Pena, Angel	131	Punto, Nick	192
Mordecai, Mike	162	Ochoa, Alex	69	Pena, Carlos	465	Purvis, Rob	324
Morgan, Mike	27	O'Connor, Brian	213	Pena, Elvis	83	**Q**	
Morgan, Scott	267	Offerman, Jose	301	Pena, Jesus	308		
Morris, Matt	227	Ohka, Tomokazu	307	Pena, Juan (BOS)	308	Quantrill, Paul	487
Morris, Warren	207	Ohman, Will	59	Pena, Juan (OAK)	422	Quevedo, Ruben	59
Morrison, Robbie	372	Ojeda, Augie	53	Pena, Wily Mo	400	Quinn, Mark	367
Moss, Damian	42	O'Leary, Troy	301	Penny, Brad	106	**R**	
Mota, Danny	390	Olerud, John	433	Peoples, Danny	334		
Mota, Guillermo	169	Olivares, Omar	422	Percival, Troy	272	Radinsky, Scott	228
Mota, Tony	131	Oliver, Darren	471	Perez, Antonio	433	Radke, Brad	390
Mouton, James	148	Oliver, Joe	433	Perez, Carlos	136	Rain, Steve	59
Mouton, Lyle	148	Olivo, Miguel	416	Perez, Eddie	37	Raines Jr., Tim	285
Moyer, Jamie	439	Olson, Gregg	135	Perez, Eduardo	223	Ramirez, Alex	208
Mueller, Bill	252	O'Neill, Paul	399	Perez, Jhonny	116	Ramirez, Aramis	208
Mulder, Mark	422	Ordaz, Luis	366	Perez, Neifi	83	Ramirez, Horacio	43
Mulholland, Terry	42	Ordonez, Magglio	317	Perez, Odalis	42	Ramirez, Julio	99
Mullen, Scott	372	Ordonez, Rey	177	Perez, Santiago	148	Ramirez, Manny	334
Munoz, Billy	334	Oropeza, Asdrubal	37	Perez, Timoniel	178	Ramos, Mario	423
Munoz, Mike	470	Orosco, Jesse	227	Perez, Tomas	192	Ramsay, Rob	440
Munro, Peter	471	Ortiz, David	385	Perisho, Matt	471	Randa, Joe	368
Munson, Eric	351	Ortiz, Hector	366	Perry, Herb	318	Rapp, Pat	290
Murray, Calvin	252	Ortiz, Jose	416	Person, Robert	198	Ratliff, Jon	423
Murray, Dan	373	Ortiz, Ramon	272	Peters, Chris	213	Rauch, Jon	324
Mussina, Mike	289	Ortiz, Russ	257	Peterson, Kyle	153	Reames, Britt	228
Myers, Brett	197	Osik, Keith	208	Petkovsek, Mark	272	Reboulet, Jeff	368

Name	Page	Name	Page	Name	Page	Name	Page
Redding, Tim	122	Rolen, Scott	192	Seanez, Rudy	43	Spradlin, Jerry	59
Reding, Josh	163	Rolison, Nate	100	Sears, Todd	386	Sprague, Ed	238
Redman, Julian	208	Rollins, Jimmy	192	Seay, Bobby	455	Springer, Russ	29
Redman, Mark	390	Romano, Jason	466	Sefcik, Kevin	193	Spurgeon, Jay	291
Redmond, Mike	99	Romero, J.C.	391	Segui, David	335	Stahl, Rich	291
Reed, Jeff	54	Roneberg, Brett	100	Seguignol, Fernando	164	Stairs, Matt	417
Reed, Keith	285	Roque, Rafael	154	Selby, Bill	335	Standridge, Jason	455
Reed, Rick	183	Rosado, Jose	373	Sele, Aaron	440	Stanford, Jason	342
Reed, Steve	341	Rose, Brian	90	Serafini, Dan	214	Stanifer, Rob	309
Reese, Pokey	69	Rose, Mike	23	Serrano, James	170	Stanley, Mike	417
Regalado, Maximo	136	Roskos, John	237	Serrano, Wascar	243	Stanton, Mike	407
Regilio, Nick	472	Rowand, Aaron	318	Servais, Scott	253	Stechschulte, Gene	229
Reichert, Dan	373	Ruan, Wilken	164	Service, Scott	423	Stein, Blake	374
Reid, Justin	214	Rueter, Kirk	258	Sessions, Doug	122	Stenson, Dernell	302
Reith, Brian	74	Ruffin, Johnny	28	Sexson, Richie	149	Stentz, Brent	392
Reitsma, Chris	74	Rupe, Ryan	455	Shaw, Jeff	137	Stephens, John	292
Rekar, Bryan	455	Rusch, Glendon	184	Shearn, Tom	122	Stephenson, Garrett	229
Relaford, Desi	237	Ryan, B.J.	291	Sheets, Ben	154	Stevens, Lee	165
Remlinger, Mike	43	Ryan, Jason	391	Sheffield, Gary	132	Stewart, Shannon	481
Renteria, Edgar	224	Ryan, Mike	386	Sheldon, Scott	466	Stinnett, Kelly	23
Requena, Alex	334	Ryan, Rob	23	Shields, Scot	273	Stocker, Kevin	268
Restovich, Mike	385	**S**		Shinjo, Tsuyoshi	179	Stottlemyre, Todd	29
Rexrode, Jackie	318	Sabathia, C.C.	342	Shuey, Paul	342	Strange, Pat	184
Reyes, Al	136	Saberhagen, Bret	308	Shumate, Jacob	43	Strickland, Scott	170
Reyes, Dennys	74	Sadler, Donnie	301	Shumpert, Terry	84	Strong, Joe	107
Reynolds, Shane	122	Saenz, Olmedo	417	Sierra, Ruben	466	Stull, Everett	155
Reynoso, Armando	28	Salazar, Oscar	417	Sikorski, Brian	472	Sturtze, Tanyon	456
Rhodes, Arthur	440	Salazar, Ruben	386	Silva, Jose	215	Stynes, Chris	70
Richard, Chris	286	Salmon, Tim	268	Silvestre, Juan	434	Sullivan, Scott	74
Riedling, John	74	Sanches, Brian	373	Simas, Bill	325	Suppan, Jeff	374
Rigdon, Paul	154	Sanchez, Alex	450	Simmons, Brian	319	Surhoff, B.J.	37
Riggan, Jerrod	183	Sanchez, Freddy	302	Singleton, Chris	319	Surkont, Keith	424
Riley, Matt	290	Sanchez, Jesus	107	Sirotka, Mike	325	Suzuki, Ichiro	435
Riley, Mike	257	Sanchez, Rey	368	Skrmetta, Matt	215	Suzuki, Mac	375
Rincon, Juan	390	Sandberg, Eric	386	Sledge, Terrmel	164	Sweeney, Mark	149
Rincon, Ricardo	341	Sandberg, Jared	450	Slocumb, Heathcliff	243	Sweeney, Mike	368
Rios, Armando	252	Sanders, Anthony	434	Slusarski, Joe	123	Swindell, Greg	29
Ripken, Cal	286	Sanders, Reggie	37	Smith, Bobby	450	**T**	
Riske, David	341	Santana, Johan	391	Smith, Brian	215	Taglienti, Jeff	90
Ritchie, Todd	214	Santana, Julio	170	Smith, Bud	228	Tam, Jeff	424
Rivas, Luis	385	Santana, Osmany	335	Smith, Chuck	107	Tankersley, Dennis	243
Rivera, Juan	400	Santana, Pedro	352	Smith, Jason	54	Tapani, Kevin	60
Rivera, Luis	291	Santangelo, F.P.	131	Smith, Mark	101	Tatis, Fernando	224
Rivera, Mariano	407	Santiago, Benito	70	Smoltz, John	44	Taubensee, Eddie	70
Rivera, Mike	352	Santiago, Jose	374	Smyth, Steve	59	Tavarez, Julian	90
Rivera, Ruben	237	Santiago, Ramon	352	Sneed, John	198	Taylor, Reggie	193
Rivera, Saul	391	Santos, Angel	302	Snelling, Chris	434	Tejada, Miguel	418
Roach, Jason	183	Santos, Jose	100	Snow, Bert	423	Telemaco, Amaury	198
Roberts, Brian	286	Santos, Victor	358	Snow, J.T.	253	Telford, Anthony	170
Roberts, Dave	335	Sasaki, Kazuhiro	440	Snyder, John	155	Tessmer, Jay	407
Roberts, Grant	184	Sasser, Rob	352	Sojo, Luis	401	Teut, Nathan	60
Roberts, Mark	324	Sauerbeck, Scott	214	Song, Seung	309	t'Hoen, E.J.	268
Robinson, Bo	434	Saunders, Tony	455	Sonnier, Shawn	374	Thomas, Brad	392
Rocker, John	43	Scanlan, Bob	154	Sorensen, Zach	336	Thomas, Evan	199
Rodgers, Bobby	106	Schader, Troy	238	Soriano, Alfonso	401	Thomas, Frank	319
Rodriguez, Alex	434	Schilling, Curt	28	Soriano, Rafael	441	Thomas, Juan	435
Rodriguez, Felix	257	Schmack, Brian	325	Sosa, Juan	84	Thome, Jim	336
Rodriguez, Francisco	273	Schmidt, Jason	214	Sosa, Sammy	54	Thompson, Andy	481
Rodriguez, Henry	100	Schneider, Brian	164	Sparks, Steve	358	Thompson, Eric	424
Rodriguez, Ivan	466	Schoeneweis, Scott	273	Speier, Justin	342	Thompson, Justin	472
Rodriguez, Jose	228	Schoening, Brent	392	Spencer, Shane	401	Thompson, Travis	75
Rodriguez, Liu	318	Schourek, Pete	308	Spencer, Stan	243	Thomson, John	91
Rodriguez, Rich	184	Scutaro, Marcos	149	Spiers, Bill	116	Thurman, Corey	375
Rodriguez, Wilfredo	122	Seabol, Scott	400	Spiezio, Scott	268	Thurman, Mike	170
Rogers, Ed	286	Seale, Marvin	178	Spoljaric, Paul	374	Thurston, Joe	132
Rogers, Kenny	472			Spooneybarger, Tim	44		

Name	Page	Name	Page	Name	Page	Name	Page
Timlin, Mike	229	Vazquez, Ramon	435	Weibl, Clint	229	Winn, Randy	451
Timmons, Ozzie	450	Velandia, Jorge	179	Weichard, Paul	209	Wise, DeWayne	482
Toca, Jorge	179	Velarde, Randy	418	Weiss, Walt	38	Wise, Matt	274
Tollberg, Brian	244	Venafro, Mike	472	Wells, Bob	392	Witasick, Jay	244
Tomko, Brett	441	Ventura, Robin	179	Wells, David	488	Witt, Kevin	482
Torcato, Tony	253	Veras, Quilvio	38	Wells, Kip	325	Wohlers, Mark	75
Torres, Andres	353	Veras, Wilton	303	Wells, Vernon	482	Wolf, Randy	199
Towers, Josh	292	Veres, Dave	229	Wendell, Turk	185	Womack, Tony	24
Trachsel, Steve	488	Vidro, Jose	165	Weong Seo, Jay	185	Wood, Kerry	60
Tracy, Andy	165	Villone, Ron	75	Werth, Jayson	286	Woodard, Steve	343
Trammell, Bubba	179	Vina, Fernando	224	West, Brian	326	Woodward, Chris	483
Trombley, Mike	292	Vining, Ken	325	Westbrook, Jake	343	Wooten, Greg	441
Truby, Chris	117	Vitiello, Joe	238	Weston, Aron	209	Wooten, Shawn	269
Tsao, Chin-Hui	91	Vizcaino, Jose	402	Wetteland, John	473	Worrell, Tim	61
Tucker, Michael	70	Vizcaino, Luis	424	Wheeler, Dan	456	Wright, Corey	467
Tucker, T.J.	171	Vizquel, Omar	336	White, Devon	132	Wright, Danny	326
Turnbow, Derrick	273	Vogelsong, Ryan	258	White, Gabe	91	Wright, Jamey	155
Turner, Chris	401			White, Matt	456	Wright, Jaret	343
Tyner, Jason	451	**W**		White, Rick	185	Wright, Ron	70
		Wade, Travis	123	White, Rondell	55	Wuertz, Michael	61
U		Wagner, Billy	123	Whiten, Mark	336	Wunsch, Kelly	326
Ulloa, Enmanuel	441	Wagner, Denny	425	Wickman, Bob	343		
Urbina, Ugueth	171	Wainwright, Adam	44	Widger, Chris	435	**Y**	
Uribe, Juan	85	Wakefield, Tim	309	Wigginton, Ty	180	Yan, Esteban	457
Urquiola, Carlos	23	Wakeland, Chris	353	Wilkerson, Brad	165	Yarnall, Ed	75
Utley, Chase	193	Walbeck, Matt	269	Wilkins, Marc	215	Yennaco, Jay	61
		Walker, Kevin	244	Williams, Bernie	402	Yoshii, Masato	91
V		Walker, Larry	85	Williams, Dave	216	Young, Dmitri	71
Valdes, Ismael	137	Walker, Todd	85	Williams, Gerald	451	Young, Eric	55
Valdes, Marc	123	Walker, Tyler	184	Williams, Jeff	137	Young, Ernie	225
Valdes, Pedro	467	Wall, Donne	244	Williams, Jerome	258	Young, Kevin	210
Valdez, Mario	418	Wallace, Jeff	215	Williams, Matt	24	Young, Mike	467
Valent, Eric	193	Ward, Daryle	117	Williams, Mike	216	Young, Tim	309
Valentin, Javier	386	Ward, Jeremy	29	Williams, Woody	244		
Valentin, John	302	Wasdin, John	91	Williamson, Scott	75	**Z**	
Valentin, Jose	319	Washburn, Jarrod	274	Wilson, Craig (PIT)	210	Zambrano, Carlos	61
Valenzuela, Mario	320	Washington, Rico	209	Wilson, Craig (CHW)	320	Zapp, A.J.	38
Van Hekken, Andy	358	Waszgis, B.J.	467	Wilson, Dan	435	Zaun, Gregg	369
Van Poppel, Todd	60	Wathan, Derek	101	Wilson, Enrique	210	Zeile, Todd	180
Vander Wal, John	208	Wayne, Justin	171	Wilson, Jack	210	Zimmerman, Jeff	473
Vargas, Claudio	107	Weathers, Dave	155	Wilson, Kris	375	Zito, Barry	425
Varitek, Jason	302	Weaver, Jeff	358	Wilson, Paul	457	Zuleta, Julio	55
Vaughn, Greg	451	Webb, Alan	473	Wilson, Preston	101		
Vaughn, Mo	269	Weber, Ben	274	Wilson, Tom	402		
Vazquez, Javier	171	Wehner, John	209	Winchester, Jeff	85		